Ford Sierra Owners Workshop Manual

Steve Rendle

Models covered
Saloon (Sapphire and Hatchback), Estate and P100 Pick-up models, including special/limited editions, with four-cylinder sohc, dohc & CVH petrol engines and two-wheel-drive

Does not cover V6 or Diesel engines, four-wheel-drive models, RS Cosworth or 1992 model 1.8 litre CVH engine with single point fuel injection

(903-6U4) ABCD

Haynes Publishing Group
Sparkford Nr Yeovil
Somerset BA22 7JJ England

Haynes Publications, Inc
861 Lawrence Drive
Newbury Park
California 91320 USA

Acknowledgements
Thanks are due to Champion Spark Plug who supplied the illustrations showing spark plug conditions, to Holt Lloyd Limited who supplied the illustrations showing bodywork repair, and to Duckhams Oils who provided lubrication data. Certain other illustrations are the copyright of the Ford Motor Company Limited and are used with their permission. Thanks are also due to Sykes-Pickavant Limited, who supplied some of the workshop tools, and all those people at Sparkford who assisted in the production of this manual.

A book in the **Haynes Owners Workshop Manual Series**

Printed by J. H. Haynes & Co. Ltd., Sparkford, Nr Yeovil, Somerset BA22 7JJ, England

ISBN 1 85010 808 0

British Library Cataloguing in Publication Data
A catalogue record for this book is available from the British Library

We take great pride in the accuracy of information given in this manual, but vehicle manufacturers make alterations and design changes during the production run of a particular vehicle of which they do not inform us. No liability can be accepted by the authors or publishers for loss, damage or injury caused by any errors in, or omissions from, the information given.

Restoring and Preserving our Motoring Heritage

Few people can have had the luck to realise their dreams to quite the same extent and in such a remarkable fashion as John Haynes, Founder and Chairman of the Haynes Publishing Group.

Since 1965 his unique approach to workshop manual publishing has proved so successful that millions of Haynes Manuals are now sold every year throughout the world, covering literally thousands of different makes and models of cars, vans and motorcycles.

A continuing passion for cars and motoring led to the founding in 1985 of a Charitable Trust dedicated to the restoration and preservation of our motoring heritage. To inaugurate the new Museum, John Haynes donated virtually his entire private collection of 52 cars.

Now with an unrivalled international collection of over 210 veteran, vintage and classic cars and motorcycles, the Haynes Motor Museum in Somerset is well on the way to becoming one of the most interesting Motor Museums in the world.

A 70 seat video cinema, a cafe and an extensive motoring bookshop, together with a specially constructed one kilometre motor circuit, make a visit to the Haynes Motor Museum a truly unforgettable experience.

Every vehicle in the museum is preserved in as near as possible mint condition and each car is run every six months on the motor circuit.

Enjoy the picnic area set amongst the rolling Somerset hills. Peer through the William Morris workshop windows at cars being restored, and browse through the extensive displays of fascinating motoring memorabilia.

From the 1903 Oldsmobile through such classics as an MG Midget to the mighty 'E' Type Jaguar, Lamborghini, Ferrari Berlinetta Boxer, and Graham Hill's Lola Cosworth, there is something for everyone, young and old alike, at this Somerset Museum.

Haynes Motor Museum

Situated mid-way between London and Penzance, the Haynes Motor Museum is located just off the A303 at Sparkford, Somerset (home of the Haynes Manual) and is open to the public 7 days a week all year round, except Christmas Day and Boxing Day.

Contents

Ford Sierra L

Ford Sierra Sapphire GLS

Ford Sierra Chausseur Estate

About this manual

Its aim

The aim of this manual is to help you get the best value from your vehicle. It can do so in several ways. It can help you decide what work must be done (even should you choose to get it done by a garage), provide information on routine maintenance and servicing, and give a logical course of action and diagnosis when random faults occur. However, it is hoped that you will use the manual by tackling the work yourself. On simpler jobs it may even be quicker than booking the car into a garage and going there twice, to leave and collect it. Perhaps most important, a lot of money can be saved by avoiding the costs a garage must charge to cover its labour and overheads.

The manual has drawings and descriptions to show the function of the various components so that their layout can be understood. Then the tasks are described and photographed in a step-by-step sequence so that even a novice can do the work.

Its arrangement

The manual is divided into fourteen Chapters, each covering a logical sub-division of the vehicle. The Chapters are each divided into Sections, numbered with single figures, eg 5; and the Sections into paragraphs (or sub-sections), with decimal numbers following on from the Section they are in, eg 5.1, 5.2, 5.3 etc.

It is freely illustrated, especially in those parts where there is a detailed sequence of operations to be carried out. There are two forms of illustration: figures and photographs. The figures are numbered in sequence with decimal numbers, according to their position in the Chapter – eg Fig. 6.4 is the fourth drawing/illustration in Chapter 6. Photographs carry the same number (either individually or in related groups) as the Section or sub-section to which they relate.

There is an alphabetical index at the back of the manual as well as a contents list at the front. Each Chapter is also preceded by its own individual contents list.

References to the 'left' or 'right' of the vehicle are in the sense of a person in the driver's seat facing forwards.

Unless otherwise stated, nuts and bolts are removed by turning anti-clockwise, and tightened by turning clockwise.

Vehicle manufacturers continually make changes to specifications and recommendations, and these, when notified, are incorporated into our manuals at the earliest opportunity.

We take great pride in the accuracy of information given in this manual, but vehicle manufacturers make alterarations and design changes during the production run of a particular vehicle of which they do not inform us. No liability can be accepted by the authors or publishers for loss, damage or injury caused by any errors in, or omissions from, the information given.

Project vehicles

The vehicles used in the preparation of this manual, and which appear in many of the photographic sequences, were; a 1983 2.0 litre carburettor Hatchback model, a 1985 1.8 litre Hatchback model, a 1985 2.0iS model, a 1987 1.8 litre Saloon model, a 1989 1.8 LX Hatchback model, a 1989 2.0 litre carburettor Estate model, and a 1989 P100 model.

Introduction to the Ford Sierra

The Ford Sierra was first introduced in late 1982 with the option of seven different engines and four different trim levels. This manual covers the four cylinder in-line petrol engines, but other models in the range are fitted with V6 or diesel engines.

The Sierra was introduced by Ford as the successor to the Cortina, and initially received a mixed reception, as it was one of the first vehicles to make use of the 'aeroback' body style designed to reduce the air drag coefficient to a minimum in the interests of fuel economy. Mechanically the Sierra is similar to the Cortina, with the exception of all-round independent suspension.

Initially, 1.3, 1.6 and 2.0 litre carburettor engines were available, with Hatchback and Estate body styles. In late 1984, a 1.8 litre engine became available, and in 1985, a performance orientated 2.0 litre fuel injection engine was introduced. Towards the end of 1986, the 1.3 litre engine was phased out. In order to fill a gap in the range, a Saloon body style, designated the Sapphire, was introduced in early 1987, and shortly afterwards, the 1.8 litre CVH engine replaced the previously used 1.8 litre OHC engine throughout the model range. In early 1988, a Sierra-based P100 pick-up model became available to replace the previous Cortina-based design. The P100 consists of a Sierra-type 'cab' and front suspension, and a Ford Transit-type rear suspension and 2.0 litre engine.

A wide range of standard and optional equipment is available within the Sierra range to suit most tastes, including an anti-lock braking system.

For the home mechanic, the Sierra is a straightforward vehicle to maintain and repair since design features have been incorporated to reduce the actual cost of ownership to a minimum, and most of the items requiring frequent attention are easily accessible.

General dimensions, weights and capacities

For modifications, and information applicable to later models, see Supplement at end of manual

Dimensions

Overall length:	
Saloon	4467.0 mm (176.0 in)
Hatchback:	
All models up to 1987 except GLS, 2.0iS and Ghia	4407.0 mm (173.6 in)
GLS and 2.0iS models up to 1987	4460.0 mm (175.7 in)
Ghia models up to 1987	4425.0 mm (174.3 in)
All models from 1987	4425.0 mm (174.3 in)
Estate:	
All models up to 1987 except Ghia	4506.0 mm (177.5 in)
Ghia models up to 1987	4522.0 mm (178.2 in)
All models from 1987	4511.0 mm (177.7 in)
P100	4900.0 mm (193.1 in)
Overall width:	
All models up to 1987 except Base, GLS, 2.0iS and Ghia	1867.0 mm (73.6 in)
Base models up to 1987	1821.0 mm (71.7 in)
GLS, 2.0iS and Ghia models up to 1987	1920.0 mm (75.6 in)
All models from 1987 except P100*	1694.0 mm (66.7 in)
P100	1920.0 mm (75.6 in)
Overall height:	
Saloon:	
All models except GLS	1359.0 mm (53.5 in)
GLS models	1352.0 mm (53.3 in)
Hatchback:	
All models up to 1987 except GLS and 2.0iS	1420.0 mm (55.9 in)
GLS and 2.0iS models up to 1987	1392.0 mm (54.8 in)
All models from 1987 except GLS	1359.0 mm (53.5 in)
GLS models from 1987	1352.0 mm (53.3 in)
Estate:	
All models up to 1987 except Base and Ghia	1443.0 mm (56.9 in)
Base models up to 1987	1417.0 mm (55.8 in)
Ghia models up to 1987	1506.0 mm (59.3 in)
All models from 1987	1386.0 mm (54.6 in)
P100	1520.0 mm (59.9 in)
Wheelbase:	
All models except P100	2608.0 mm (102.8 in)
P100 models	2910.0 mm (114.7 in)
Track:	
Front:	
All models except P100	1453.0 mm (57.2 in)
P100 models	1449.0 mm (57.1 in)
Rear:	
All models except P100	1468.0 mm (57.8 in)
P100 models	1414.0 mm (55.7 in)

**Excluding exterior rear view mirrors*

Weights

Kerb weight†:	
Saloon	1025 to 1135 kg (2260 to 2503 lbs)
Hatchback	1010 to 1145 kg (2227 to 2525 lbs)
Estate	1065 to 1185 kg (2348 to 2613 lbs)
P100	1370 kg (3021 lbs)
Maximum gross vehicle weight	Refer to VIN plate
Maximum roof rack load	75 kg (165 lbs)
Minimum towing hitch downward load	25 kg (55 lbs)
Maximum towing hitch downward load	50 kg (110 lbs)

†Exact kerb weights depend upon model and specification

Capacities

Engine oil:	
OHC engines:	
With filter	3.75 litres (6.6 pints)
Without filter	3.25 litres (5.7 pints)
1.8 CVH engine:	
With filter	4.0 litres (7.0 pints)
Without filter	3.5 litres (6.2 pints)
Cooling system (including heater):	
OHC models	8.0 litres (14.1 pints)
CVH models	9.5 litres (16.7 pints)
Fuel tank:	
All models except P100	60.0 litres (13.2 gals)
P100 models	66.0 litres (14.5 gals)
Manual gearbox:	
A1 and A2 types	0.98 litre (1.72 pints)
B type	1.46 litres (2.57 pints)
C type	1.25 litres (2.20 pints)
N type up to 1987	1.90 litres (3.34 pints)
N type from 1987	1.25 litres (2.20 pints)
Automatic transmission:	
C3 type	6.3 litres (11.1 pints)
A4LD type	8.5 litres (15.0 pints)
Final drive (from dry):	
All models except 1.3 and 1.6 litre Hatchback and P100	0.9 litre (1.6 pints)
1.3 and 1.6 litre Hatchback models	0.8 litre (1.4 pints)
P100 models (rear axle)	1.14 litres (2.0 pints)
Power steering	0.65 litre (1.14 pints)

Jacking, towing and wheel changing

Jacking, towing and wheel changing

The jack supplied with the vehicle tool kit should only be used for changing roadwheels. When carrying out any other kind of work, raise the vehicle using a trolley jack, and always supplement the jack with axle stands positioned under the vehicle jacking points.

To change a roadwheel, first remove the spare wheel and jack from their stowage positions. On Saloon, Hatchback and Estate models, the jack and spare wheel are located in the luggage compartment. On P100 models, the jack is located behind the passenger seat, and the spare wheel is located under the rear of the cargo area. Firmly apply the handbrake and engage first gear on manual gearbox models or 'P' on automatic transmission models. Place chocks at the front and rear of the

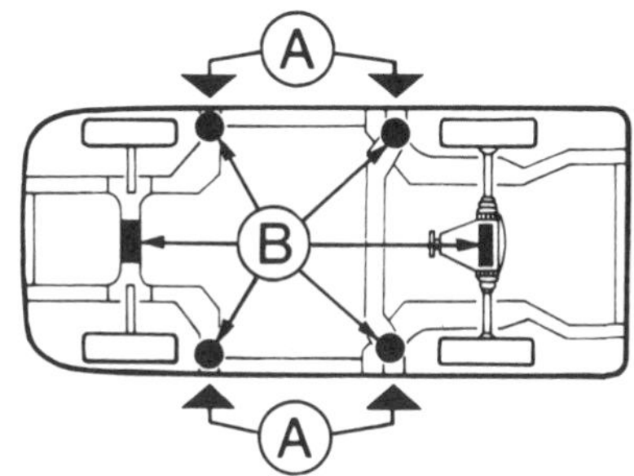

Location of jacking points – Saloon, Hatchback and Estate models

A Jacking points for use with vehicle jack
B Jacking points for use with trolley jack or axle stands

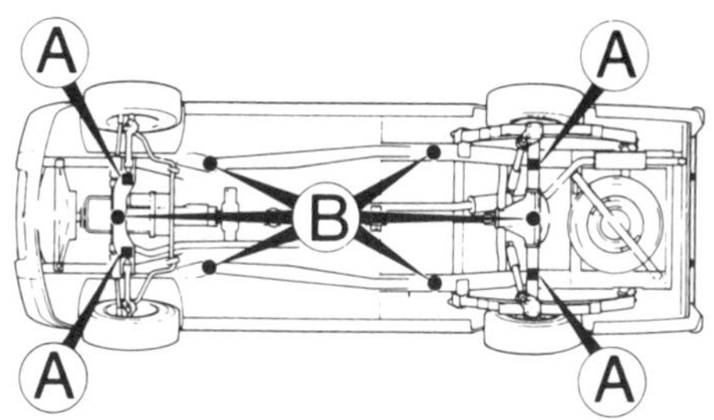

Location of jacking points – P100 models

A Jacking points for use with vehicle jack
B Jacking points for use with trolley jack or axle stands

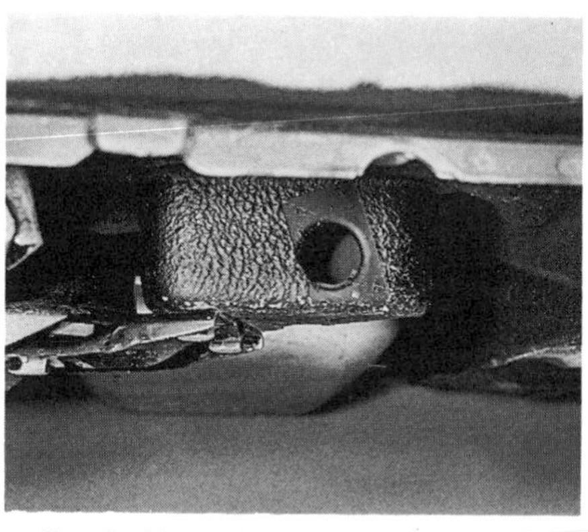

Rear jacking point – Hatchback model

Jack location by front wheel – Hatchback model

Axle stand correctly positioned under front jacking point – Hatchback model

Front towing eye – Hatchback model

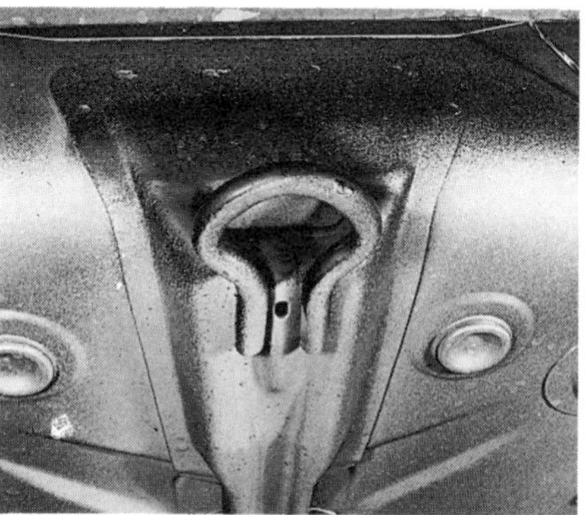

Rear towing eye – Hatchback model

wheel diagonally opposite the one to be changed.

Where applicable remove the wheel trim and slacken the wheel nuts using the wheel brace provided in the tool kit. Position the jack head under the jacking point nearest the wheel to be changed. Raise the jack until the wheel is clear of the ground, then remove the wheel nuts and the wheel. Fit the spare wheel and secure it with the wheel nuts. Lower the jack until the tyre is just touching the ground, and tighten the wheel nuts moderately tight. Now lower the jack fully and tighten the wheel nuts securely in a diagonal sequence. Where applicable, refit the wheel trim then withdraw the jack and stow the wheel and the jack in their respective locations.

When jacking up the vehicle with a trolley jack, position the jack head under one of the relevant jacking points (note that on P100 models, the jacking points for use with a trolley jack are different to those for use with the vehicle jack). Do not jack the vehicle under the sump or any of the steering or suspension components. Supplement the jack using axle stands. The jacking points and axle stand positions are shown in the accompanying illustrations. **Never** *work under, around, or near a raised vehicle, unless it is adequately supported in at least two places.*

Towing

Towing eyes are fitted to the front and rear of the vehicle for attachment of a tow rope. Always turn the ignition key to position 'II' when the vehicle is being towed, so that the steering lock is released and the direction indicator and brake lamps are operational.

Before being towed, release the handbrake and place the gear lever in neutral. On automatic transmission models, the towing speed must not exceed 25 mph (40 kph), and the towing distance must not exceed 12 miles (20 km). For longer distances, or if transmission damage is suspected, the propeller shaft should be removed, or the rear of the vehicle should be lifted clear of the ground.

Push or tow starting is not possible on vehicles fitted with automatic transmission.

Buying spare parts and vehicle identification numbers

For modifications, and information applicable to later models, see Supplement at end of manual

Buying spare parts

Spare parts are available from many sources, for example: Ford dealers, other garages and accessory shops, and motor factors. Our advice regarding spare parts sources is as follows:

Officially appointed Ford dealers – This is the best source for parts which are peculiar to your car and are not generally available (eg complete cylinder heads, internal gearbox components, badges, interior trim etc). It is also the only place at which you should buy parts if your vehicles is still under warranty. To be sure of obtaining the correct parts it will always be necessary to give the storeman your car's vehicle identification number, and if possible, to take the 'old' part along for positive identification. Remember that many parts are available on a factory exchange scheme – any parts returned should always be clean! It obviously makes good sense to go straight to the specialists on your car for this type of part for they are best equipped to supply you.

Other garages and accessory shops – These are often very good places to buy materials and components needed for the maintenance of your car (eg oil filters, spark plugs, bulbs, drivebelts, oils and greases, touch-up paint, filler paste, etc). They also sell general accessories, usually have convenient opening hours, charge lower prices and can often be found not far from home.

Motor factors – Good factors will stock all of the more important components which wear out relatively quickly (eg clutch components, pistons, valves, exhaust systems, brake cylinders/pipes/hoses/ seals/shoes and pads etc). Motor factors will often provide new or reconditioned components on a part exchange basis – this can save considerable amount of money.

Vehicle identification numbers

Modifications are a continuing and unpublished process in vehicle manufacture quite apart from major model changes. Spare parts manuals and lists are compiled upon a numerical basis, the individual vehicle numbers being essential to correct identification of the component required.

When ordering spare parts, always give as much information as possible. Quote the car model, year of manufacture, body and engine numbers as appropriate.

The vehicle identification plate is mounted on the right-hand side of the front body panel and may be seen once the bonnet is open.

The engine number is located on the right-hand side of the cylinder block in front of the engine mounting bracket on OHC engines, or on the front upper right-hand side of the cylinder block on CVH engines.

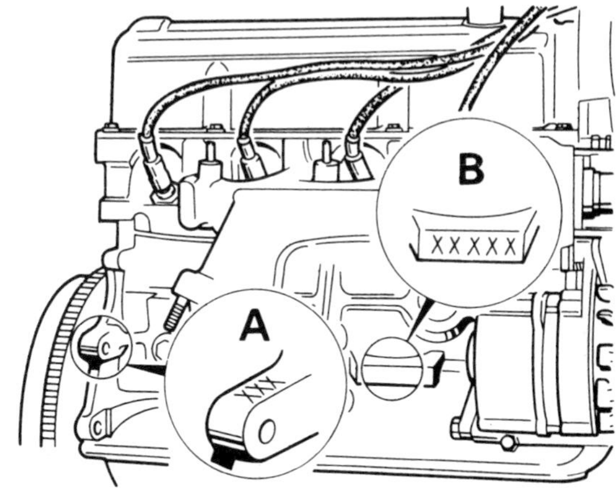

Engine code (A) and engine number (B) locations – OHC engines

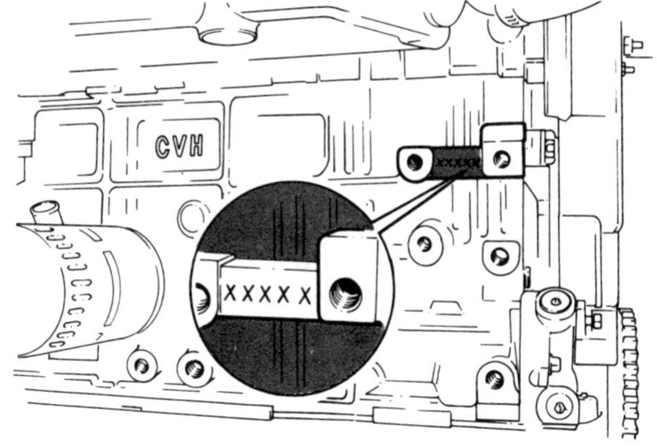

Engine number location – CVH engine

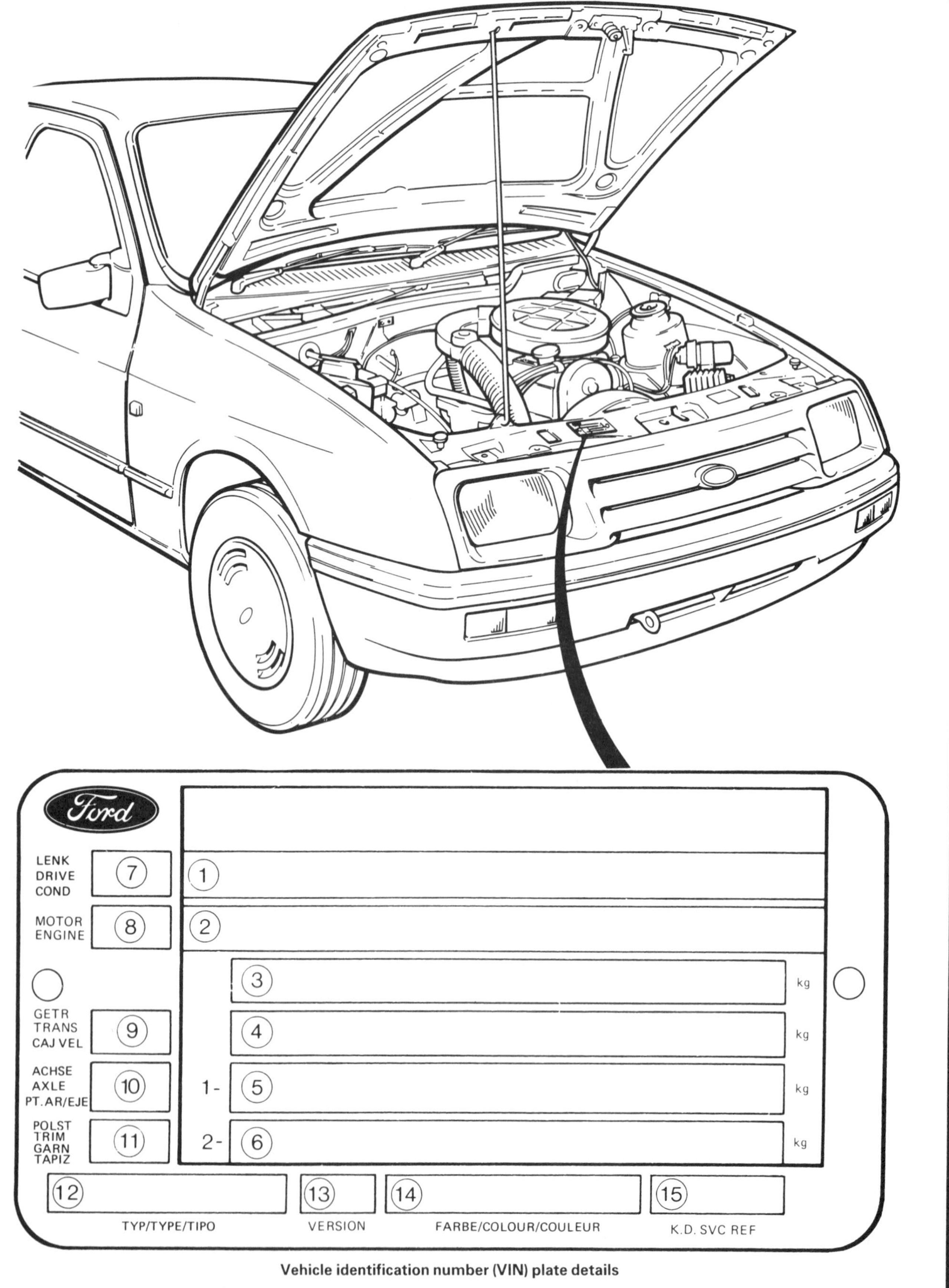

Vehicle identification number (VIN) plate details

1 Type approval number
2 Vehicle identification number (VIN)
3 Gross vehicle weight
4 Gross train weight
5 Permitted front axle loading
6 Permitted rear axle loading
7 LHD or RHD
8 Engine code
9 Transmission code
10 Final drive code
11 Interior trim code
12 Vehicle type number
13 Blank
14 Paint code
15 Blank

General repair procedures

Whenever servicing, repair or overhaul work is carried out on the car or its components, it is necessary to observe the following procedures and instructions. This will assist in carrying out the operation efficiently and to a professional standard of workmanship.

Joint mating faces and gaskets

Where a gasket is used between the mating faces of two components, ensure that it is renewed on reassembly, and fit it dry unless otherwise stated in the repair procedure. Make sure that the mating faces are clean and dry with all traces of old gasket removed. When cleaning a joint face, use a tool which is not likely to score or damage the face, and remove any burrs or nicks with an oilstone or fine file.

Make sure that tapped holes are cleaned with a pipe cleaner, and keep them free of jointing compound if this is being used unless specifically instructed otherwise.

Ensure that all orifices, channels or pipes are clear and blow through them, preferably using compressed air.

Oil seals

Whenever an oil seal is removed from its working location, either individually or as part of an assembly, it should be renewed.

The very fine sealing lip of the seal is easily damaged and will not seal if the surface it contacts is not completely clean and free from scratches, nicks or grooves. If the original sealing surface of the component cannot be restored, the component should be renewed.

Protect the lips of the seal from any surface which may damage them in the course of fitting. Use tape or a conical sleeve where possible. Lubricate the seal lips with oil before fitting and, on dual lipped seals, fill the space between the lips with grease.

Unless otherwise stated, oil seals must be fitted with their sealing lips toward the lubricant to be sealed.

Use a tubular drift or block of wood of the appropriate size to install the seal and, if the seal housing is shouldered, drive the seal down to the shoulder. If the seal housing is unshouldered, the seal should be fitted with its face flush with the housing top face.

Screw threads and fastenings

Always ensure that a blind tapped hole is completely free from oil, grease, water or other fluid before installing the bolt or stud. Failure to do this could cause the housing to crack due to the hydraulic action of the bolt or stud as it is screwed in.

When tightening a castellated nut to accept a split pin, tighten the nut to the specified torque, where applicable, and then tighten further to the next split pin hole. Never slacken the nut to align a split pin hole unless stated in the repair procedure.

When checking or retightening a nut or bolt to a specified torque setting, slacken the nut or bolt by a quarter of a turn, and then retighten to the specified setting.

Locknuts, locktabs and washers

Any fastening which will rotate against a component or housing in the course of tightening should always have a washer between it and the relevant component or housing.

Spring or split washers should always be renewed when they are used to lock a critical component such as a big-end bearing retaining nut or bolt.

Locktabs which are folded over to retain a nut or bolt should always be renewed.

Self-locking nuts can be reused in non-critical areas, providing resistance can be felt when the locking portion passes over the bolt or stud thread.

Split pins must always be replaced with new ones of the correct size for the hole.

Special tools

Some repair procedures in this manual entail the use of special tools such as a press, two or three-legged pullers, spring compressors etc. Wherever possible, suitable readily available alternatives to the manufacturer's special tools are described, and are shown in use. In some instances, where no alternative is possible, it has been necessary to resort to the use of a manufacturer's tool and this has been done for reasons of safety as well as the efficient completion of the repair operation. Unless you are highly skilled and have a thorough understanding of the procedure described, never attempt to bypass the use of any special tool when the procedure described specifies its use. Not only is there a very great risk of personal injury, but expensive damage could be caused to the components involved.

Tools and working facilities

Introduction

A selection of good tools is a fundamental requirement for anyone contemplating the maintenance and repair of a motor vehicle. For the owner who does not possess any, their purchase will prove a considerable expense, offsetting some of the savings made by doing-it-yourself. However, provided that the tools purchased meet the relevant national safety standards and are of good quality, they will last for many years and prove an extremely worthwhile investment.

To help the average owner to decide which tools are needed to carry out the various tasks detailed in this manual, we have compiled three lists of tools under the following headings: *Maintenance and minor repair, Repair and overhaul,* and *Special.* The newcomer to practical mechanics should start off with the *Maintenance and minor repair* tool kit and confine himself to the simpler jobs around the vehicle. Then, as his confidence and experience grow, he can undertake more difficult tasks, buying extra tools as, and when, they are needed. In this way, a *Maintenance and minor repair* tool kit can be built-up into a *Repair and overhaul* tool kit over a considerable period of time without any major cash outlays. The experienced do-it-yourselfer will have a tool kit good enough for most repair and overhaul procedures and will add tools from the *Special* category when he feels the expense is justified by the amount of use to which these tools will be put.

It is obviously not possible to cover the subject of tools fully here. For those who wish to learn more about tools and their use there is a book entitled *How to Choose and Use Car Tools* available from the publishers of this manual.

Maintenance and minor repair tool kit

The tools given in this list should be considered as a minimum requirement if routine maintenance, servicing and minor repair operations are to be undertaken. We recommend the purchase of combination spanners (ring one end, open-ended the other); although more expensive than open-ended ones, they do give the advantages of both types of spanner.

Combination spanners - 10, 11, 12, 13, 14 & 17 mm
Adjustable spanner - 9 inch
Gearbox/rear axle drain plug key
Spark plug spanner (with rubber insert)
Spark plug gap adjustment tool
Set of feeler gauges
Brake bleed nipple spanner
Screwdriver - 4 in long x $\frac{1}{4}$ in dia (flat blade)
Screwdriver - 4 in long x $\frac{1}{4}$ in dia (cross blade)
Combination pliers - 6 inch
Hacksaw (junior)
Tyre pump
Tyre pressure gauge
Oil can
Fine emery cloth (1 sheet)
Wire brush (small)
Funnel (medium size)

Repair and overhaul tool kit

These tools are virtually essential for anyone undertaking any major repairs to a motor vehicle, and are additional to those given in the *Maintenance and minor repair* list. Included in this list is a comprehensive set of sockets. Although these are expensive they will be found invaluable as they are so versatile - particularly if various drives are included in the set. We recommend the $\frac{1}{2}$ in square-drive type, as this can be used with most proprietary torque wrenches. If you cannot afford a socket set, even bought piecemeal, then inexpensive tubular box spanners are a useful alternative.

The tools in this list will occasionally need to be supplemented by tools from the *Special* list.

Sockets (or box spanners) to cover range in previous list
Reversible ratchet drive (for use with sockets)
Extension piece, 10 inch (for use with sockets)
Universal joint (for use with sockets)
Torque wrench (for use with sockets)
'Mole' wrench - 8 inch
Ball pein hammer
Soft-faced hammer, plastic or rubber
Screwdriver - 6 in long x $\frac{5}{16}$in dia (flat blade)
Screwdriver - 2 in long x $\frac{5}{16}$in square (flat blade)
Screwdriver - $1\frac{1}{2}$ in long x $\frac{1}{4}$ in dia (cross blade)
Screwdriver - 3 in long x $\frac{1}{8}$ in dia (electrician's)
Pliers - electrician's side cutters
Pliers - needle nosed
Pliers - circlip (internal and external)
Cold chisel - $\frac{1}{2}$ inch
Scriber
Scraper
Centre punch
Pin punch
Hacksaw
Steel rule/straight-edge
Allen keys (inc. splined/Torx type if necessary)
Selection of files
Wire brush (large)
Axle-stands
Jack (strong trolley or hydraulic type)

Special tools

The tools in this list are those which are not used regularly, are expensive to buy, or which need to be used in accordance with their manufacturers' instructions. Unless relatively difficult mechanical jobs are undertaken frequently, it will not be economic to buy many of these tools. Where this is the case, you could consider clubbing together with friends (or joining a motorists' club) to make a joint purchase, or borrowing the tools against a deposit from a local garage or tool hire specialist.

The following list contains only those tools and instruments freely available to the public, and not those special tools produced by the vehicle manufacturer specifically for its dealer network. You will find occasional references to these manufacturers' special tools in the text of this manual. Generally, an alternative method of doing the job without the vehicle manufacturers' special tool is given. However, sometimes, there is no alternative to using them. Where this is the case and the relevant tool cannot be bought or borrowed, you will have to entrust the work to a franchised garage.

Valve spring compressor
Piston ring compressor
Balljoint separator
Universal hub/bearing puller
Impact screwdriver
Micrometer and/or vernier gauge
Dial gauge
Stroboscopic timing light
Dwell angle meter/tachometer
Universal electrical multi-meter
Cylinder compression gauge
Lifting tackle
Trolley jack
Light with extension lead
Splined sockets (see Chapter 1)
Torx sockets (see Chapter 1)

Buying tools

For practically all tools, a tool factor is the best source since he will have a very comprehensive range compared with the average garage or accessory shop. Having said that, accessory shops often offer excellent quality tools at discount prices, so it pays to shop around.

There are plenty of good tools around at reasonable prices, but always aim to purchase items which meet the relevant national safety standards. If in doubt, ask the proprietor or manager of the shop for advice before making a purchase.

Care and maintenance of tools

Having purchased a reasonable tool kit, it is necessary to keep the tools in a clean serviceable condition. After use, always wipe off any dirt, grease and metal particles using a clean, dry cloth, before putting the tools away. Never leave them lying around after they have been used. A simple tool rack on the garage or workshop wall, for items such as screwdrivers and pliers is a good idea. Store all normal wrenches and sockets in a metal box. Any measuring instruments, gauges, meters, etc, must be carefully stored where they cannot be damaged or become rusty.

Take a little care when tools are used. Hammer heads inevitably become marked and screwdrivers lose the keen edge on their blades from time to time. A little timely attention with emery cloth or a file will soon restore items like this to a good serviceable finish.

Working facilities

Not to be forgotten when discussing tools, is the workshop itself. If anything more than routine maintenance is to be carried out, some form of suitable working area becomes essential.

It is appreciated that many an owner mechanic is forced by circumstances to remove an engine or similar item, without the benefit of a garage or workshop. Having done this, any repairs should always be done under the cover of a roof.

Wherever possible, any dismantling should be done on a clean, flat workbench or table at a suitable working height.

Any workbench needs a vice: one with a jaw opening of 4 in (100 mm) is suitable for most jobs. As mentioned previously, some clean dry storage space is also required for tools, as well as for lubricants, cleaning fluids, touch-up paints and so on, which become necessary.

Another item which may be required, and which has a much more general usage, is an electric drill with a chuck capacity of at least $\frac{5}{16}$ in (8 mm). This, together with a good range of twist drills, is virtually essential for fitting accessories such as mirrors and reversing lights.

Last, but not least, always keep a supply of old newspapers and clean, lint-free rags available, and try to keep any working area as clean as possible.

Spanner jaw gap comparison table

Jaw gap (in)	Spanner size
0.250	$\frac{1}{4}$ in AF
0.276	7 mm
0.313	$\frac{5}{16}$ in AF
0.315	8 mm
0.344	$\frac{11}{32}$ in AF; $\frac{1}{8}$ in Whitworth
0.354	9 mm
0.375	$\frac{3}{8}$ in AF
0.394	10 mm
0.433	11 mm
0.438	$\frac{7}{16}$ in AF
0.445	$\frac{3}{16}$ in Whitworth; $\frac{1}{4}$ in BSF
0.472	12 mm
0.500	$\frac{1}{2}$ in AF
0.512	13 mm
0.525	$\frac{1}{4}$ in Whitworth; $\frac{5}{16}$ in BSF
0.551	14 mm
0.563	$\frac{9}{16}$ in AF
0.591	15 mm
0.600	$\frac{5}{16}$ in Whitworth; $\frac{3}{8}$ in BSF
0.625	$\frac{5}{8}$ in AF
0.630	16 mm
0.669	17 mm
0.686	$\frac{11}{16}$ in AF
0.709	18 mm
0.710	$\frac{3}{8}$ in Whitworth; $\frac{7}{16}$ in BSF
0.748	19 mm
0.750	$\frac{3}{4}$ in AF
0.813	$\frac{13}{16}$ in AF
0.820	$\frac{7}{16}$ in Whitworth; $\frac{1}{2}$ in BSF
0.866	22 mm
0.875	$\frac{7}{8}$ in AF
0.920	$\frac{1}{2}$ in Whitworth; $\frac{9}{16}$ in BSF
0.938	$\frac{15}{16}$ in AF
0.945	24 mm
1.000	1 in AF
1.010	$\frac{9}{16}$ in Whitworth; $\frac{5}{8}$ in BSF
1.024	26 mm
1.063	$1\frac{1}{16}$ in AF; 27 mm
1.100	$\frac{5}{8}$ in Whitworth; $\frac{11}{16}$ in BSF
1.125	$1\frac{1}{8}$ in AF
1.181	30 mm
1.200	$\frac{11}{16}$ in Whitworth; $\frac{3}{4}$ in BSF
1.250	$1\frac{1}{4}$ in AF
1.260	32 mm
1.300	$\frac{3}{4}$ in Whitworth; $\frac{7}{8}$ in BSF
1.313	$1\frac{5}{16}$ in AF
1.390	$\frac{13}{16}$ in Whitworth; $\frac{15}{16}$ in BSF
1.417	36 mm
1.438	$1\frac{7}{16}$ in AF
1.480	$\frac{7}{8}$ in Whitworth; 1 in BSF
1.500	$1\frac{1}{2}$ in AF
1.575	40 mm; $\frac{15}{16}$ in Whitworth
1.614	41 mm
1.625	$1\frac{5}{8}$ in AF
1.670	1 in Whitworth; $1\frac{1}{8}$ in BSF
1.688	$1\frac{11}{16}$ in AF
1.811	46 mm
1.813	$1\frac{13}{16}$ in AF
1.860	$1\frac{1}{8}$ in Whitworth; $1\frac{1}{4}$ in BSF
1.875	$1\frac{7}{8}$ in AF
1.969	50 mm
2.000	2 in AF
2.050	$1\frac{1}{4}$ in Whitworth; $1\frac{3}{8}$ in BSF
2.165	55 mm
2.362	60 mm

Conversion factors

Length (distance)						
Inches (in)	X	25.4	= Millimetres (mm)	X	0.0394	= Inches (in)
Feet (ft)	X	0.305	= Metres (m)	X	3.281	= Feet (ft)
Miles	X	1.609	= Kilometres (km)	X	0.621	= Miles
Volume (capacity)						
Cubic inches (cu in; in³)	X	16.387	= Cubic centimetres (cc; cm³)	X	0.061	= Cubic inches (cu in; in³)
Imperial pints (Imp pt)	X	0.568	= Litres (l)	X	1.76	= Imperial pints (Imp pt)
Imperial quarts (Imp qt)	X	1.137	= Litres (l)	X	0.88	= Imperial quarts (Imp qt)
Imperial quarts (Imp qt)	X	1.201	= US quarts (US qt)	X	0.833	= Imperial quarts (Imp qt)
US quarts (US qt)	X	0.946	= Litres (l)	X	1.057	= US quarts (US qt)
Imperial gallons (Imp gal)	X	4.546	= Litres (l)	X	0.22	= Imperial gallons (Imp gal)
Imperial gallons (Imp gal)	X	1.201	= US gallons (US gal)	X	0.833	= Imperial gallons (Imp gal)
US gallons (US gal)	X	3.785	= Litres (l)	X	0.264	= US gallons (US gal)
Mass (weight)						
Ounces (oz)	X	28.35	= Grams (g)	X	0.035	= Ounces (oz)
Pounds (lb)	X	0.454	= Kilograms (kg)	X	2.205	= Pounds (lb)
Force						
Ounces-force (ozf; oz)	X	0.278	= Newtons (N)	X	3.6	= Ounces-force (ozf; oz)
Pounds-force (lbf; lb)	X	4.448	= Newtons (N)	X	0.225	= Pounds-force (lbf; lb)
Newtons (N)	X	0.1	= Kilograms-force (kgf; kg)	X	9.81	= Newtons (N)
Pressure						
Pounds-force per square inch (psi; lbf/in²; lb/in²)	X	0.070	= Kilograms-force per square centimetre (kgf/cm²; kg/cm²)	X	14.223	= Pounds-force per square inch (psi; lbf/in²; lb/in²)
Pounds-force per square inch (psi; lbf/in²; lb/in²)	X	0.068	= Atmospheres (atm)	X	14.696	= Pounds-force per square inch (psi; lbf/in²; lb/in²)
Pounds-force per square inch (psi; lbf/in²; lb/in²)	X	0.069	= Bars	X	14.5	= Pounds-force per square inch (psi; lbf/in²; lb/in²)
Pounds-force per square inch (psi; lbf/in²; lb/in²)	X	6.895	= Kilopascals (kPa)	X	0.145	= Pounds-force per square inch (psi; lbf/in²; lb/in²)
Kilopascals (kPa)	X	0.01	= Kilograms-force per square centimetre (kgf/cm²; kg/cm²)	X	98.1	= Kilopascals (kPa)
Millibar (mbar)	X	100	= Pascals (Pa)	X	0.01	= Millibar (mbar)
Millibar (mbar)	X	0.0145	= Pounds-force per square inch (psi; lbf/in²; lb/in²)	X	68.947	= Millibar (mbar)
Millibar (mbar)	X	0.75	= Millimetres of mercury (mmHg)	X	1.333	= Millibar (mbar)
Millibar (mbar)	X	0.401	= Inches of water (inH_2O)	X	2.491	= Millibar (mbar)
Millimetres of mercury (mmHg)	X	0.535	= Inches of water (inH_2O)	X	1.868	= Millimetres of mercury (mmHg)
Inches of water (inH_2O)	X	0.036	= Pounds-force per square inch (psi; lbf/in²; lb/in²)	X	27.68	= Inches of water (inH_2O)
Torque (moment of force)						
Pounds-force inches (lbf in; lb in)	X	1.152	= Kilograms-force centimetre (kgf cm; kg cm)	X	0.868	= Pounds-force inches (lbf in; lb in)
Pounds-force inches (lbf in; lb in)	X	0.113	= Newton metres (Nm)	X	8.85	= Pounds-force inches (lbf in; lb in)
Pounds-force inches (lbf in; lb in)	X	0.083	= Pounds-force feet (lbf ft; lb ft)	X	12	= Pounds-force inches (lbf in; lb in)
Pounds-force feet (lbf ft; lb ft)	X	0.138	= Kilograms-force metres (kgf m; kg m)	X	7.233	= Pounds-force feet (lbf ft; lb ft)
Pounds-force feet (lbf ft; lb ft)	X	1.356	= Newton metres (Nm)	X	0.738	= Pounds-force feet (lbf ft; lb ft)
Newton metres (Nm)	X	0.102	= Kilograms-force metres (kgf m; kg m)	X	9.804	= Newton metres (Nm)
Power						
Horsepower (hp)	X	745.7	= Watts (W)	X	0.0013	= Horsepower (hp)
Velocity (speed)						
Miles per hour (miles/hr; mph)	X	1.609	= Kilometres per hour (km/hr; kph)	X	0.621	= Miles per hour (miles/hr; mph)
*Fuel consumption**						
Miles per gallon, Imperial (mpg)	X	0.354	= Kilometres per litre (km/l)	X	2.825	= Miles per gallon, Imperial (mpg)
Miles per gallon, US (mpg)	X	0.425	= Kilometres per litre (km/l)	X	2.352	= Miles per gallon, US (mpg)

Temperature

Degrees Fahrenheit = (°C x 1.8) + 32

Degrees Celsius (Degrees Centigrade; °C) = (°F - 32) x 0.56

**It is common practice to convert from miles per gallon (mpg) to litres/100 kilometres (l/100km), where mpg (Imperial) x l/100 km = 282 and mpg (US) x l/100 km = 235*

Safety first!

Professional motor mechanics are trained in safe working procedures. However enthusiastic you may be about getting on with the job in hand, do take the time to ensure that your safety is not put at risk. A moment's lack of attention can result in an accident, as can failure to observe certain elementary precautions.

There will always be new ways of having accidents, and the following points do not pretend to be a comprehensive list of all dangers; they are intended rather to make you aware of the risks and to encourage a safety-conscious approach to all work you carry out on your vehicle.

Essential DOs and DON'Ts

DON'T rely on a single jack when working underneath the vehicle. Always use reliable additional means of support, such as axle stands, securely placed under a part of the vehicle that you know will not give way.

DON'T attempt to loosen or tighten high-torque nuts (e.g. wheel hub nuts) while the vehicle is on a jack; it may be pulled off.

DON'T start the engine without first ascertaining that the transmission is in neutral (or 'Park' where applicable) and the parking brake applied.

DON'T suddenly remove the filler cap from a hot cooling system – cover it with a cloth and release the pressure gradually first, or you may get scalded by escaping coolant.

DON'T attempt to drain oil until you are sure it has cooled sufficiently to avoid scalding you.

DON'T grasp any part of the engine, exhaust or catalytic converter without first ascertaining that it is sufficiently cool to avoid burning you.

DON'T allow brake fluid or antifreeze to contact vehicle paintwork.

DON'T syphon toxic liquids such as fuel, brake fluid or antifreeze by mouth, or allow them to remain on your skin.

DON'T inhale dust – it may be injurious to health (see *Asbestos* below).

DON'T allow any spilt oil or grease to remain on the floor – wipe it up straight away, before someone slips on it.

DON'T use ill-fitting spanners or other tools which may slip and cause injury.

DON'T attempt to lift a heavy component which may be beyond your capability – get assistance.

DON'T rush to finish a job, or take unverified short cuts.

DON'T allow children or animals in or around an unattended vehicle.

DO wear eye protection when using power tools such as drill, sander, bench grinder etc, and when working under the vehicle.

DO use a barrier cream on your hands prior to undertaking dirty jobs – it will protect your skin from infection as well as making the dirt easier to remove afterwards; but make sure your hands aren't left slippery. Note that long-term contact with used engine oil can be a health hazard.

DO keep loose clothing (cuffs, tie etc) and long hair well out of the way of moving mechanical parts.

DO remove rings, wristwatch etc, before working on the vehicle – especially the electrical system.

DO ensure that any lifting tackle used has a safe working load rating adequate for the job.

DO keep your work area tidy – it is only too easy to fall over articles left lying around.

DO get someone to check periodically that all is well, when working alone on the vehicle.

DO carry out work in a logical sequence and check that everything is correctly assembled and tightened afterwards.

DO remember that your vehicle's safety affects that of yourself and others. If in doubt on any point, get specialist advice.

IF, in spite of following these precautions, you are unfortunate enough to injure yourself, seek medical attention as soon as possible.

Asbestos

Certain friction, insulating, sealing, and other products – such as brake linings, brake bands, clutch linings, torque converters, gaskets, etc – contain asbestos. *Extreme care must be taken to avoid inhalation of dust from such products since it is hazardous to health.* If in doubt, assume that they *do* contain asbestos.

Fire

Remember at all times that petrol (gasoline) is highly flammable. Never smoke, or have any kind of naked flame around, when working on the vehicle. But the risk does not end there – a spark caused by an electrical short-circuit, by two metal surfaces contacting each other, by careless use of tools, or even by static electricity built up in your body under certain conditions, can ignite petrol vapour, which in a confined space is highly explosive.

Always disconnect the battery earth (ground) terminal before working on any part of the fuel or electrical system, and never risk spilling fuel on to a hot engine or exhaust.

It is recommended that a fire extinguisher of a type suitable for fuel and electrical fires is kept handy in the garage or workplace at all times. Never try to extinguish a fuel or electrical fire with water.

Note: *Any reference to a 'torch' appearing in this manual should always be taken to mean a hand-held battery-operated electric lamp or flashlight. It does NOT mean a welding/gas torch or blowlamp.*

Fumes

Certain fumes are highly toxic and can quickly cause unconsciousness and even death if inhaled to any extent. Petrol (gasoline) vapour comes into this category, as do the vapours from certain solvents such as trichloroethylene. Any draining or pouring of such volatile fluids should be done in a well ventilated area.

When using cleaning fluids and solvents, read the instructions carefully. Never use materials from unmarked containers – they may give off poisonous vapours.

Never run the engine of a motor vehicle in an enclosed space such as a garage. Exhaust fumes contain carbon monoxide which is extremely poisonous; if you need to run the engine, always do so in the open air or at least have the rear of the vehicle outside the workplace.

If you are fortunate enough to have the use of an inspection pit, never drain or pour petrol, and never run the engine, while the vehicle is standing over it; the fumes, being heavier than air, will concentrate in the pit with possibly lethal results.

The battery

Never cause a spark, or allow a naked light, near the vehicle's battery. It will normally be giving off a certain amount of hydrogen gas, which is highly explosive.

Always disconnect the battery earth (ground) terminal before working on the fuel or electrical systems.

If possible, loosen the filler plugs or cover when charging the battery from an external source. Do not charge at an excessive rate or the battery may burst.

Take care when topping up and when carrying the battery. The acid electrolyte, even when diluted, is very corrosive and should not be allowed to contact the eyes or skin.

If you ever need to prepare electrolyte yourself, always add the acid slowly to the water, and never the other way round. Protect against splashes by wearing rubber gloves and goggles.

When jump starting a car using a booster battery, for negative earth (ground) vehicles, connect the jump leads in the following sequence: First connect one jump lead between the positive (+) terminals of the two batteries. Then connect the other jump lead first to the negative (–) terminal of the booster battery, and then to a good earthing (ground) point on the vehicle to be started, at least 18 in (45 cm) from the battery if possible. Ensure that hands and jump leads are clear of any moving parts, and that the two vehicles do not touch. Disconnect the leads in the reverse order.

Mains electricity and electrical equipment

When using an electric power tool, inspection light etc, always ensure that the appliance is correctly connected to its plug and that, where necessary, it is properly earthed (grounded). Do not use such appliances in damp conditions and, again, beware of creating a spark or applying excessive heat in the vicinity of fuel or fuel vapour. Also ensure that the appliances meet the relevant national safety standards.

Ignition HT voltage

A severe electric shock can result from touching certain parts of the ignition system, such as the HT leads, when the engine is running or being cranked, particularly if components are damp or the insulation is defective. Where an electronic ignition system is fitted, the HT voltage is much higher and could prove fatal.

Routine maintenance

Maintenance is essential for ensuring safety and desirable for the purpose of getting the best in terms of performance and economy from your vehicle. Over the years the need for periodic lubrication – oiling, greasing, and so on – has been drastically reduced if not totally eliminated. This has unfortunately tended to lead some owners to think that because no such action is required, components either no longer exist, or will last for ever. This is certainly not the case; it is essential to carry out regular visual examination as comprehensively as possible in order to spot any possible defects at an early stage before they develop into major expensive repairs.

The following service schedules are a list of the maintenance requirements, and the intervals at which they should be carried out, as recommended by the manufacturers. Where applicable, these procedures are covered in greater detail near the beginning of each relevant Chapter.

Every 250 miles (400 km) or weekly – whichever comes first

Engine, cooling system, brakes and steering

Check the engine oil level and top up if necessary (Chapter 1)
Check the coolant level and top up if necessary (Chapter 2)
Check the brake fluid level and top up if necessary (Chapter 10)
Check the power steering fluid level and top up if necessary (where applicable) (Chapter 11)

Lamps and wipers

Check the operation of all interior and exterior lamps, and the wiper and washers (Chapter 13)
Check the washer fluid level(s) and top up if necessary (Chapter 13), adding a screen wash such as Turtle Wax High Tech Screen Wash

Tyres

Check the tyre pressures (Chapter 11)
Visually examine the tyres for wear or damage (Chapter 11)

Every 6000 miles (10 000 km) or 6 months – whichever occurs first

Engine (Chapter 1)

Change the engine oil and renew the oil filter
Clean the oil filler cap and inspect for damage
Check for oil leaks and rectify as necessary

Cooling system (Chapter 2)

Check the coolant level and top up if necessary
Check for coolant leaks and rectify as necessary
Inspect the radiator matrix for blockage (eg dead insects) and clean as necessary

Fuel and exhaust systems (Chapter 3)

Check for fuel leaks and rectify as necessary
Check and if necessary adjust the idle speed (where applicable) and mixture
Check the operation of the throttle linkage and lubricate if necessary
Check the exhaust system for corrosion, leaks and security
Check all vacuum hoses for condition and security

Ignition and engine management systems (Chapter 4)

Check all wiring and vacuum hoses for condition and security

Braking system (Chapter 10)

Check brake pad and shoe friction material for wear and renew if necessary
Check for brake fluid leaks and rectify as necessary
Check brake fluid level warning lamp operation

Suspension and steering (Chapter 11)

Check power steering fluid level and top up if necessary (where applicable)
Check for power steering fluid leaks and rectify as necessary (where applicable)
Check tightness of roadwheel nuts

Electrical system (Chapter 13)

Check the operation of all interior and exterior lamps and all electrical systems
Check all exposed wiring for condition and security
Check the washer fluid level(s) and top up if necessary

Every 12 000 miles (20 000 km) or 12 months – whichever occurs first

In addition to the items in the 6-monthly service, carry out the following:

Engine (Chapter 1)

Check and if necessary adjust the valve clearances (OHC engines only)
Inspect the crankcase ventilation system for condition and security

Cooling system (Chapter 2)

Check the condition and tension of the coolant pump drivebelt (OHC models only)

Ignition system (Chapter 4)

Renew the spark plugs

Manual gearbox (Chapter 6)

Check for oil leaks and rectify as necessary
Check oil level and top up if necessary

Automatic transmission (Chapter 7)

Check for fluid leaks and rectify as necessary
Check fluid level and top up if necessary
Check condition of gear selector and kickdown linkages and lubricate if necessary

Final drive and driveshafts (Chapter 9)

Check for oil leaks and rectify as necessary
Check final drive oil level and top up if necessary
Check the driveshaft gaiters for condition and security

Braking system (Chapter 10)

Check the handbrake mechanism for operation and security

Suspension and steering (Chapter 11)

Check all components for wear and damage

Bodywork (Chapter 12)

Check all panels and structural members for corrosion and damage
Lubricate all locks and hinges
Clean air conditioning condenser and check refrigerant charge (where applicable)

Electrical system (Chapter 13)

Check the condition and tension of the alternator drivebelt

Every 24 000 miles (40 000 km) or 24 months – whichever occurs first

In addition to the items in the 6 and 12-monthly services, carry out the following:

Engine (Chapter 1)

Renew the crankcase vent valve (OHC models only)

Fuel system (Chapter 3)

Renew the air cleaner element
Check the operation of the air cleaner air intake temperature control (carburettor models only)
Renew the fuel filter (fuel injection models only)
Renew the pulse air filter element – Chapter 14 (1.6 CVH models only)

Ignition system (Chapter 4)

Inspect and clean the distributor cap and HT leads

Automatic transmission (Chapter 7)

Check brake band adjustment

Every 36 000 miles (60 000 km) or 24 months – whichever occurs first

In addition to the items in the 6, 12 and 24-monthly services, carry out the following:

Cooling system (Chapter 2)

Renew the coolant

Every 36 000 miles (60 000 km) or 36 months – whichever occurs first

In addition to the items in the 6, 12 and 24-monthly services, carry out the following:

Braking system (Chapter 10)

Renew the brake fluid

Every 36 000 miles

In addition to the other service requirements, carry out the following:

Engine (Chapter 1)

Renew the timing belt (optional on OHC engines, compulsory on CVH engines)

Underbonnet view of a 1983 2.0 litre OHC carburettor model (air cleaner removed)

1 Brake fluid reservoir
2 Windscreen wiper motor
3 Battery
4 Ignition coil
5 Carburettor
6 Distributor
7 Fuel pressure regulator
8 Thermostat housing
9 Radiator top hose
10 Upper fan shroud
11 Alternator
12 Windscreen washer reservoir
13 Oil filler cap
14 Coolant expansion tank
15 Suspension strut top
16 VIN plate
17 Fusebox

Underbonnet view of a 1985 2.0iS model

1 Battery
2 Brake servo non-return valve
3 Ignition coil
4 Suspension strut top
5 Fuel filter
6 Air cleaner
7 Airflow meter
8 Fuel pressure regulator
9 Air intake hose
10 Throttle body
11 Alternator
12 VIN plate
13 Windscreen washer reservoir
14 Coolant expansion tank
15 Oil filler cap
16 Idle speed control valve
17 Inlet manifold
18 Brake fluid reservoir
19 Fusebox
20 Windscreen wiper motor
21 Engine oil level dipstick

Underbonnet view of a 1989 1.8 LX model (air cleaner removed)

1 Battery
2 Suspension strut top
3 Ignition coil
4 Coolant expansion tank
5 Alternator
6 Distributor cap shroud
7 VIN plate
8 Electric cooling fan
9 Radiator top hose
10 Windscreen washer reservoir
11 Fuel vapour separator
12 Thermostat housing
13 Oil filler cap
14 Carburettor
15 Brake fluid reservoir
16 Engine oil level dipstick
17 Windscreen wiper motor
18 Fusebox

Front underside view of a 1989 1.8 LX model

1 Disc brake calliper
2 Tie-rod end
3 Tie-rod
4 Gaiters
5 Steering rack
6 Crossmember
7 Suspension lower arm
8 Anti-roll bar
9 Starter motor
10 Engine sump
11 Clutch release cable
12 Gearbox
13 Windscreen washer reservoir
14 Horn
15 Alternator

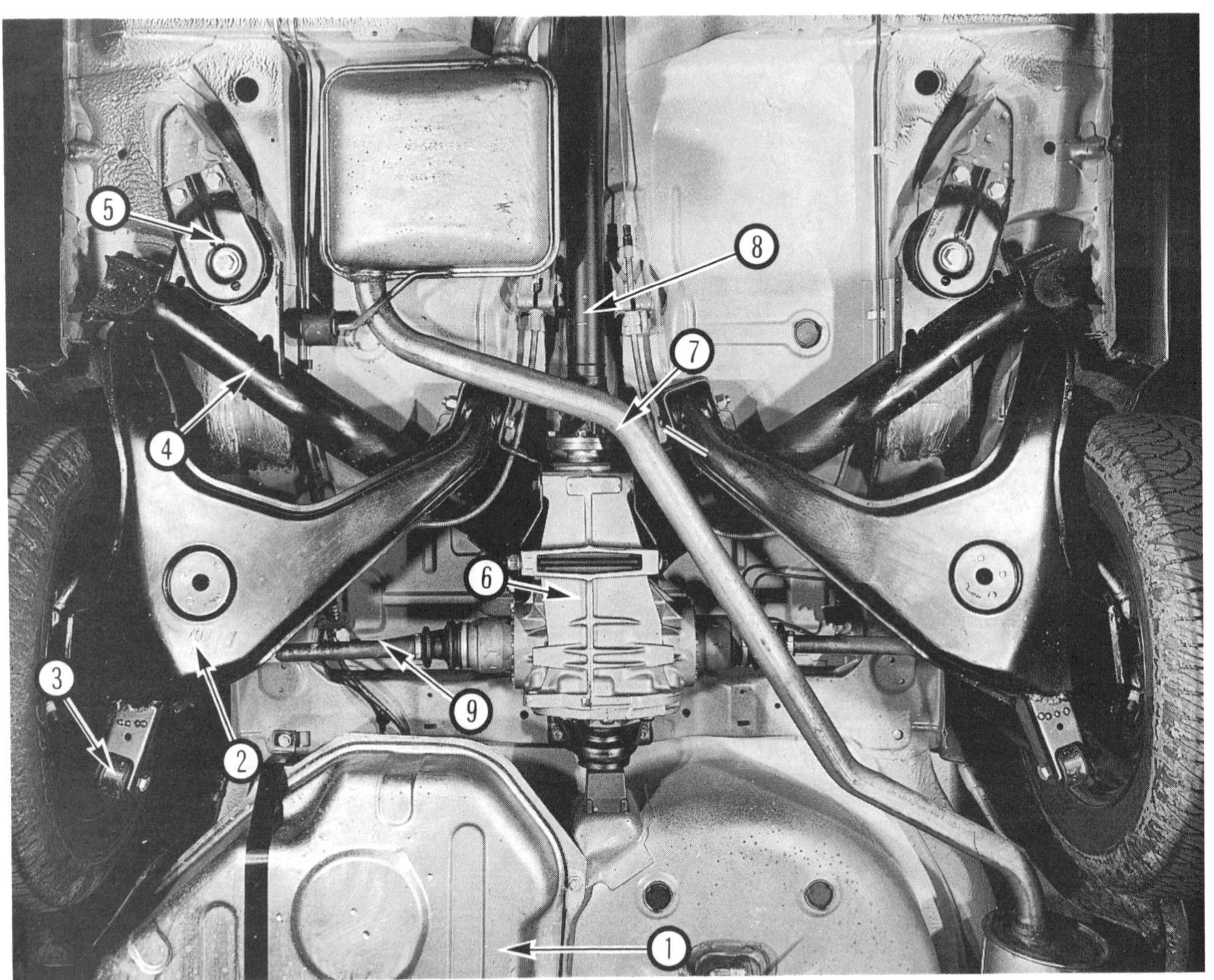

Rear underside view of a Hatchback model

1. *Fuel tank*
2. *Suspension lower arm*
3. *Lower shock absorber mounting*
4. *Suspension crossmember*
5. *Suspension guide plate*
6. *Final drive unit*
7. *Exhaust system*
8. *Propeller shaft*
9. *Driveshaft*

Rear underside view of a P100 model

1 Suspension leaf spring
2 Rear axle
3 Shock absorber
4 Propeller shaft
5 Exhaust system
6 Handbrake cable adjuster
7 Brake load apportioning valve

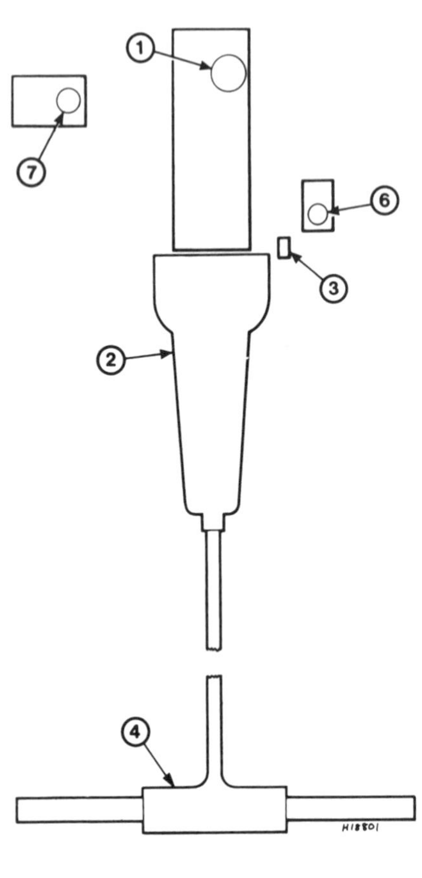

CVH engines

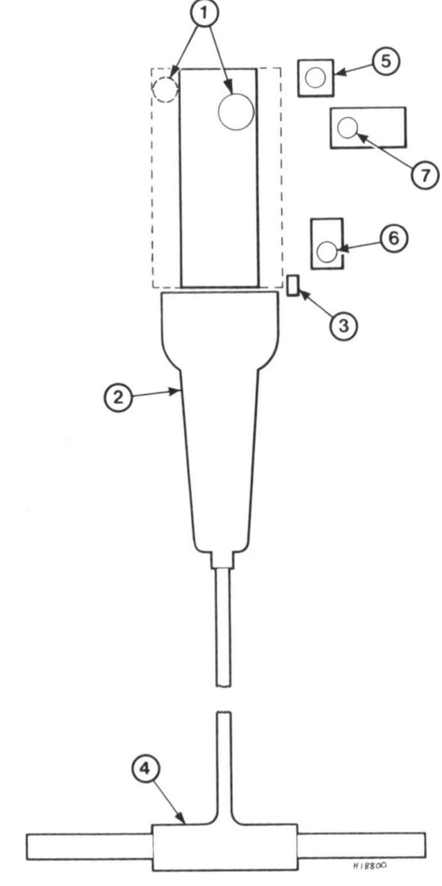

OHC and DOHC engines

Recommended lubricants and fluids

Component or system	Lubricant type/specification	Duckhams recommendation
1 Engine	Multigrade engine oil, viscosity range SAE 10W/30 to 20W/50, to API SG/CD or better	Duckhams QXR, Hypergrade, or 10W/40 Motor Oil
2 Manual gearbox		
4-speed	Gear oil, viscosity SAE 80EP, to Ford spec SQM-2C 9008-A	Duckhams Hypoid 80
5-speed (except MT75 type)	Gear oil, viscosity SAE 80EP, to Ford spec ESD-M2C 175-A	Duckhams Hypoid 75W/90S
5-speed MT75 type	Gear oil to Ford spec ESD-M2C 186-A	Duckhams Uni-Matic
3 Automatic transmission	ATF to Ford spec SQM-2C 9010-A	Duckhams Uni-Matic or D-Matic
4 Final drive	Hypoid gear oil, viscosity SAE 90EP to Ford spec SQM-2C 9002-AA or 9003-AA	Duckhams Hypoid 90S
5 Power steering	ATF to Ford spec SQM-2C 9010-A	Duckhams Uni-Matic or D-Matic
6 Brake hydraulic system	Brake fluid to Ford spec Amber SAM-1C 9103-A	Duckhams Universal Brake and Clutch Fluid
7 Cooling system	Soft water and antifreeze to Ford spec SSM-97B 9103-A or SDM-M97B49-A (see Chapter 14)	Duckhams Universal Antifreeze and Summer Coolant

Fault diagnosis

Introduction

The vehicle owner who does his or her own maintenance according to the recommended schedules should not have to use this section of the manual very often. Modern component reliability is such that, provided those items subject to wear or deterioration are inspected or renewed at the specified intervals, sudden failure is comparatively rare. Faults do not usually just happen as a result of sudden failure, but develop over a period of time. Major mechanical failures in particular are usually preceded by characteristic symptoms over hundreds or even thousands of miles. Those components which do occasionally fail without warning are often small and easily carried in the vehicle.

With any fault finding, the first step is to decide where to begin investigations. Sometimes this is obvious, but on other occasions a little detective work will be necessary. The owner who makes half a dozen haphazard adjustments or replacements may be successful in curing a fault (or its symptoms), but he will be none the wiser if the fault recurs and he may well have spent more time and money than was necessary. A calm and logical approach will be found to be more satisfactory in the long run. Always take into account any warning signs or abnormalities that may have been noticed in the period preceding the fault – power loss, high or low gauge readings, unusual noises or smells, etc – and remember that failure of components such as fuses or spark plugs may only be pointers to some underlying fault.

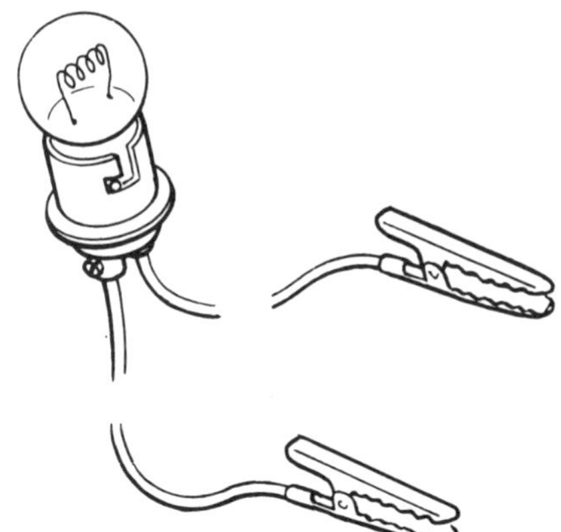

A simple test lamp is useful for tracing electrical faults

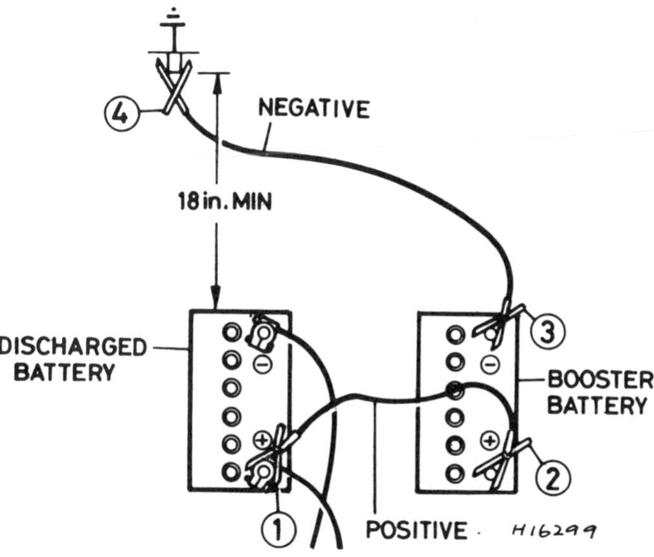

Jump start lead connections for negative earth – connect leads in order shown

The pages which follow here are intended to help in cases of failure to start or breakdown on the road. There is also a Fault Diagnosis Section at the end of each Chapter which should be consulted if the preliminary checks prove unfruitful. Whatever the fault, certain basic principles apply. These are as follows:

Verify the fault. This is simply a matter of being sure that you know what the symptoms are before starting work. This is particularly important if you are investigating a fault for someone else who may not have described it very accurately.

Don't overlook the obvious. For example, if the vehicle won't start, is there petrol in the tank? (Don't take anyone else's word on this particular point, and don't trust the fuel gauge either!) If an electrical fault is indicated, look for loose or broken wires before digging out the test gear.

Cure the disease, not the symptom. Substituting a flat battery with a fully charged one will get you off the hard shoulder, but if the underlying cause is not attended to, the new battery will go the same way. Similarly, changing oil-fouled spark plugs for a new set will get you moving again, but remember that the reason for the fouling (if it wasn't simply an incorrect grade of plug) will have to be established and corrected.

Don't take anything for granted. Particularly, don't forget that a 'new' component may itself be defective (especially if it's been rattling round in the boot for months), and don't leave components out of a fault diagnosis sequence just because they are new or recently fitted. When you do finally diagnose a difficult fault, you'll probably realise that all the evidence was there from the start.

Electrical faults

Electrical faults can be more puzzling than straightforward mechanical failures, but they are no less susceptible to logical analysis if the basic principles of operation are understood. Vehicle electrical wiring exists in extremely unfavourable conditions – heat, vibration and chemical attack – and the first things to look for are loose or corroded connections and broken or chafed wires, especially where the wires pass through holes in the bodywork or are subject to vibration.

All metal-bodied vehicles in current production have one pole of the battery 'earthed', ie connected to the vehicle bodywork, and in nearly all modern vehicles it is the negative (–) terminal. The various electrical components – motors, bulb holders etc – are also connected to earth, either by means of a lead or directly by their mountings. Electric current flows through the component and then back to the battery via the bodywork. If the component mounting is loose or corroded, or if a good path back to the battery is not available, the circuit will be incomplete and malfunction will result. The engine and/or gearbox are also earthed by means of flexible metal straps to the body or subframe; if these straps are loose or missing, starter motor, generator and ignition trouble may result.

Assuming the earth return to be satisfactory, electrical faults will be due either to component malfunction or to defects in the current supply. Individual components are dealt with in Chapter 13. If supply wires are

Carrying a few spares can save you a long walk!

broken or cracked internally this results in an open-circuit, and the easiest way to check for this is to bypass the suspect wire temporarily with a length of wire having a crocodile clip or suitable connector at each end. Alternatively, a 12V test lamp can be used to verify the presence of supply voltage at various points along the wire and the break can be thus isolated.

If a bare portion of a live wire touches the bodywork or other earthed metal part, the electricity will take the low-resistance path thus formed back to the battery: this is known as a short-circuit. Hopefully a short-circuit will blow a fuse, but otherwise it may cause burning of the insulation (and possibly further short-circuits) or even a fire. This is why it is inadvisable to bypass persistently blowing fuses with silver foil or wire.

Spares and tool kit

Most vehicles are supplied only with sufficient tools for wheel changing; the *Maintenance and minor repair* tool kit detailed in *Tools and working facilities,* with the addition of a hammer, is probably sufficient for those repairs that most motorists would consider attempting at the roadside. In addition a few items which can be fitted without too much trouble in the event of a breakdown should be carried. Experience and available space will modify the list below, but the following may save having to call on professional assistance:

Spark plugs, clean and correctly gapped
HT lead and plug cap – long enough to reach the plug furthest from the distributor
Distributor rotor
Drivebelt(s) – emergency type may suffice
Spare fuses
Set of principal light bulbs
Tin of radiator sealer and hose bandage
Exhaust bandage
Roll of insulating tape
Length of soft iron wire
Length of electrical flex
Torch or inspection lamp (can double as test lamp)
Battery jump leads
Tow-rope
Ignition water dispersant aerosol
Litre of engine oil
Sealed can of hydraulic fluid
Emergency windscreen
Worm drive clips

If spare fuel is carried, a can designed for the purpose should be used to minimise risks of leakage and collision damage. A first aid kit and a warning triangle, whilst not at present compulsory in the UK, are obviously sensible items to carry in addition to the above.

When touring abroad it may be advisable to carry additional spares which, even if you cannot fit them yourself, could save having to wait while parts are obtained. The items below may be worth considering:

Clutch and throttle cables
Cylinder head gasket
Alternator brushes
Tyre valve core

One of the motoring organisations will be able to advise on availability of fuel etc in foreign countries.

1 Engine will not start

Engine fails to turn when starter operated

Flat battery (recharge, use jump leads, or push start)
Battery terminals loose or corroded
Battery earth to body defective
Engine earth strap loose or broken
Starter motor (or solenoid) wiring loose or broken
Automatic transmission selector in wrong position, or inhibitor switch faulty (where applicable)
Ignition/starter switch faulty
Major mechanical failure (seizure)
Starter or solenoid internal fault (see Chapter 13)

Starter motor turns engine slowly

Partially discharged battery (recharge, use jump leads, or push start)
Battery terminals loose or corroded
Battery earth to body defective
Engine earth strap loose
Starter motor (or solenoid) wiring loose
Starter motor internal fault (see Chapter 13)

Starter motor spins without turning engine

Flat battery
Flywheel gear teeth damaged or worn
Starter motor mounting bolts loose

Engine turns normally but fails to start
Damp or dirty HT leads and distributor cap (crank engine and check for spark) – try moisture dispersant such as Holts Wet Start
No fuel in tank
Faulty automatic choke (carburettor models)
Fouled or incorrectly gapped spark plugs (remove, clean and regap)
Other ignition system fault (see Chapter 4)
Other fuel system fault (see Chapter 3)
Poor compression (see Chapter 1)
Major mechanical failure (eg camshaft drive)

Engine fires but will not run
Air leaks at carburettor/throttle body or inlet manifold
Fuel starvation (see Chapter 3)
Other ignition fault (see Chapter 4)

2 Engine cuts out and will not restart

Engine cuts out suddenly – ignition fault
Loose or disconnected LT wires
Wet HT leads or distributor cap (after traversing water splash)
Coil failure (check for spark)
Other ignition fault (see Chapter 4)

Engine misfires before cutting out – fuel fault
Fuel tank empty
Fuel pump defective or filter blocked (check for delivery)
Fuel tank filler vent blocked (suction will be evident on releasing cap)
Carburettor needle valve sticking (where applicable)
Blockage due to fuel contamination
Other fuel system fault (see Chapter 3)

Engine cuts out – other causes
Serious overheating
Major mechanical failure (eg camshaft drive)

3 Engine overheats

Ignition (no-charge) warning light illuminated
Slack or broken drivebelt – retension or renew (Chapter 2)

Ignition warning light not illuminated
Coolant loss due to internal or external leakage (see Chapter 2)
Thermostat defective
Low oil level
Brakes binding
Radiator clogged externally or internally
Cooling fan not operating correctly
Engine waterways clogged
Ignition timing incorrect or automatic advance malfunctioning
Mixture too weak

Note: *Do not add cold water to an overheated engine or damage may result*

4 Low engine oil pressure

Gauge reads low or warning light illuminated with engine running
Oil level low or incorrect grade
Defective gauge or sender unit
Wire to sender unit earthed
Engine overheating
Oil filter clogged or bypass valve defective
Oil pressure relief valve defective
Oil pick-up strainer clogged
Oil pump worn or mountings loose
Worn main or big-end bearings

Note: *Low oil pressure in a high-mileage engine at tickover is not necessarily a cause for concern. Sudden pressure loss at speed is far more significant. In any event, check the gauge or warning light sender before condemning the engine.*

5 Engine noises

Pre-ignition (pinking) on acceleration
Incorrect grade of fuel
Ignition timing incorrect
Distributor faulty or worn (where applicable)
Worn or maladjusted carburettor (where applicable)
Excessive carbon build-up in engine
Engine management system fault (Chapter 4)

Whistling or wheezing noises
Leaking vacuum hose
Leaking carburettor/throttle body or manifold gasket
Blowing head gasket

Tapping or rattling
Incorrect valve clearances (OHC engines)
Worn valve gear
Broken piston ring (ticking noise)

Knocking or thumping
Unintentional mechanical contact (eg fan blades)
Worn drivebelt
Peripheral component fault (alternator, water pump etc)
Worn big-end bearings (regular heavy knocking, perhaps less under load)
Worn main bearings (rumbling and knocking, perhaps worsening under load)
Piston slap (most noticeable when cold)

Chapter 1 Engine

For modifications, and information applicable to later models, see Supplement at end of manual

Contents

Specifications

PART A: OHC ENGINES

1.3 litre engine

General

Engine type	Four-cylinder, in-line, single overhead camshaft
Firing order	1-3-4-2

Engine code	JCT
Bore	79.02 mm
Stroke	66.00 mm
Cubic capacity	1294 cc
Compression ratio	9.0:1
Compression pressure at starter motor speed	11 to 13 bar
Maximum continuous engine speed	5800 rpm
Maximum engine power (DIN)	44 kW at 5700 rpm
Maximum engine torque (DIN)	98 Nm at 3100 rpm

Cylinder block

Bore diameter:	
Standard class 1	79.000 to 79.010 mm
Standard class 2	79.010 to 79.020 mm
Standard class 3	79.020 to 79.030 mm
Standard class 4	79.030 to 79.040 mm
Oversize class A	79.510 to 79.520 mm
Oversize class B	79.520 to 79.530 mm
Oversize class C	79.530 to 79.540 mm
Standard service	79.030 to 79.040 mm
Oversize 0.5	79.530 to 79.540 mm
Oversize 1.0	80.030 to 80.040 mm

Crankshaft

Endfloat	0.08 to 0.28 mm (0.003 to 0.011 in)
Main bearing running clearance	0.010 to 0.064 mm
Main bearing journal diameter:	
Standard	56.970 to 56.990 mm
Undersize 0.25	56.720 to 56.740 mm
Undersize 0.50	56.470 to 56.490 mm
Undersize 0.75	56.220 to 56.240 mm
Undersize 1.00	55.970 to 55.990 mm
Main bearing thrustwasher thickness:	
Standard	2.30 to 2.35 mm
Oversize	2.50 to 2.55 mm
Big-end bearing running clearance	0.006 to 0.060 mm
Big-end bearing journal diameter:	
Standard	51.980 to 52.000 mm
Undersize 0.25	51.730 to 51.750 mm
Undersize 0.50	51.480 to 51.500 mm
Undersize 0.75	51.230 to 51.250 mm
Undersize 1.00	50.980 to 51.000 mm

Pistons and piston rings

Piston diameter:	
Standard class 1	78.965 to 78.975 mm
Standard class 2	78.975 to 78.985 mm
Standard class 3	78.985 to 78.995 mm
Standard class 4	78.995 to 79.005 mm
Standard service	78.990 to 79.015 mm
Service oversize 0.5	79.490 to 79.515 mm
Service oversize 1.0	79.990 to 80.015 mm
Piston ring end gap:	
Top	0.300 to 0.500 mm
Centre	0.300 to 0.500 mm
Bottom	0.400 to 1.400 mm

Auxiliary shaft

Endfloat	0.050 to 0.204 mm (0.002 to 0.008 in)

Cylinder head

Valve seat angle	44° 30′ to 45° 00′
Service correction cutter*:	
Upper correction angle	30°
Lower correction angle:	
Inlet	75°
Exhaust	62.5°
Valve seat width	1.5 to 2.0 mm
Valve guide bore:	
Standard	8.063 to 8.088 mm
Oversize 0.2	8.263 to 8.288 mm
Oversize 0.4	8.463 to 8.488 mm

**Not for use with hardened valve seats*

Camshaft

Endfloat	0.104 to 0.204 mm (0.004 to 0.008 in)
Thrustplate thickness	3.98 to 4.01 mm (0.156 to 0.158 in)
Bearing journal diameter:	
Front	41.987 to 42.013 mm
Centre	44.607 to 44.633 mm
Rear	44.987 to 45.013 mm

Valves – general

Valve clearance (cold engine):	
Inlet	0.20 ± 0.03 mm (0.008 ± 0.001 in)
Exhaust	0.25 ± 0.03 mm (0.010 ± 0.001 in)
Valve timing:	
Inlet opens	22° BTDC
Inlet closes	54° ABDC
Exhaust opens	64° BBDC
Exhaust closes	12° ATDC
Valve spring free length	47.00 mm (1.85 in)

Inlet valves

Stem diameter:	
Standard	8.025 to 8.043 mm
Oversize 0.2	8.225 to 8.243 mm
Oversize 0.4	8.425 to 8.443 mm
Oversize 0.6	8.625 to 8.643 mm
Oversize 0.8	8.825 to 8.843 mm

Exhaust valves

Stem diameter:	
Standard	7.999 to 8.017 mm
Oversize 0.2	8.199 to 8.217 mm
Oversize 0.4	8.399 to 8.417 mm
Oversize 0.6	8.599 to 8.617 mm
Oversize 0.8	8.799 to 8.817 mm

Lubrication system

Oil type/specification	Multigrade engine oil, viscosity range SAE 10W/30 to 20W/50, to API SG/CD or better (Duckhams QXR, Hypergrade, or 10W/40 Motor Oil)
Oil capacity:	
With filter	3.75 litres (6.6 pints)
Without filter	3.25 litres (5.7 pints)
Oil filter	Champion C102
Oil pump clearances:	
Outer rotor to body	0.153 to 0.304 mm (0.006 to 0.012 in)
Inner rotor to outer rotor	0.050 to 0.200 mm (0.002 to 0.008 in)
Rotor endfloat	0.039 to 0.104 mm (0.002 to 0.004 in)

Torque wrench settings

	Nm	lbf ft
Main bearing cap bolts	88 to 102	65 to 75
Big-end bearing cap nuts	40 to 47	30 to 35
Crankshaft pulley bolt:		
Strength class 8.8	55 to 60	41 to 44
Strength class 10.9	100 to 115	74 to 85
Camshaft sprocket bolt	45 to 50	33 to 37
Auxiliary shaft sprocket bolt	45 to 50	33 to 37
Flywheel bolts	64 to 70	47 to 52
Oil pump bolts	17 to 21	13 to 15
Oil pump cover bolts	9 to 13	7 to 10
Sump bolts:		
Stage 1	1 to 2	0.7 to 1.5
Stage 2	6 to 8	4 to 6
Stage 3 (after running engine for 20 minutes)	8 to 10	6 to 7
Sump drain plug	21 to 28	15 to 21
Oil pressure warning lamp switch	12 to 15	9 to 11
Valve adjustment ball-pin locknuts:		
7 mm thick nuts	45 to 50	33 to 37
8 mm thick nuts	50 to 55	37 to 41
Cylinder head bolts:		
Splined type bolts:		
Stage 1	40 to 55	30 to 41
Stage 2	50 to 70	37 to 52
Stage 3 (after 20 minutes)	73 to 83	54 to 61
Stage 4 (after running engine for 15 minutes at 1000 rpm)	95 to 115	70 to 85

Are your plugs trying to tell you something?

Normal.
Grey-brown deposits, lightly coated core nose. Plugs ideally suited to engine, and engine in good condition.

Heavy Deposits.
A build up of crusty deposits, light-grey sandy colour in appearance.
Fault: Often caused by worn valve guides, excessive use of upper cylinder lubricant, or idling for long periods.

Lead Glazing.
Plug insulator firing tip appears yellow or green/yellow and shiny in appearance.
Fault: Often caused by incorrect carburation, excessive idling followed by sharp acceleration. Also check ignition timing.

Carbon fouling.
Dry, black, sooty deposits.
Fault: over-rich fuel mixture.
Check: carburettor mixture settings, float level, choke operation, air filter.

Oil fouling.
Wet, oily deposits. Fault: worn bores/piston rings or valve guides; sometimes occurs (temporarily) during running-in period.

Overheating.
Electrodes have glazed appearance, core nose very white – few deposits. Fault: plug overheating. Check: plug value, ignition timing, fuel octane rating (too low) and fuel mixture (too weak).

Electrode damage.
Electrodes burned away; core nose has burned, glazed appearance. Fault: pre-ignition. Check: for correct heat range and as for 'overheating'.

Split core nose.
(May appear initially as a crack). Fault: detonation or wrong gap-setting technique. Check: ignition timing, cooling system, fuel mixture (too weak).

WHY DOUBLE COPPER IS BETTER FOR YOUR ENGINE.

Champion Double Copper plugs are the first in the world to have copper core in both centre and earth electrode. This innovative design means that they run cooler by up to 100°C – giving greater efficiency and longer life. These double copper cores transfer heat away from the tip of the plug faster and more efficiently. Therefore, Double Copper runs at cooler temperatures than conventional plugs giving improved acceleration response and high speed performance with no fear of pre-ignition.

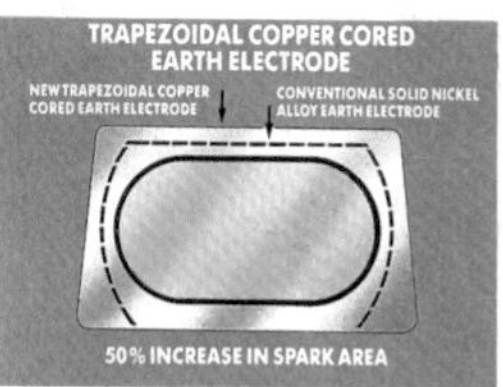

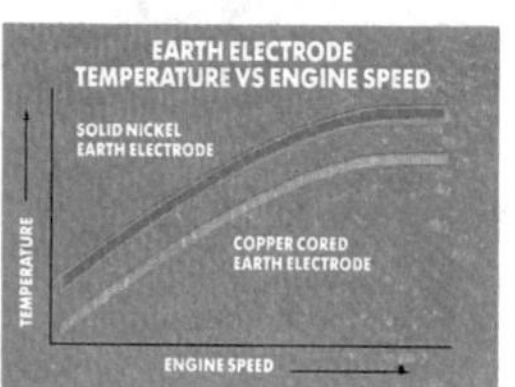

Champion Double Copper plugs also feature a unique trapezoidal earth electrode giving a 50% increase in spark area. This, together with the double copper cores, offers greatly reduced electrode wear, so the spark stays stronger for longer.

FASTER COLD STARTING

FOR UNLEADED OR LEADED FUEL

ELECTRODES UP TO 100°C COOLER

BETTER ACCELERATION RESPONSE

LOWER EMISSIONS

50% BIGGER SPARK AREA

THE LONGER LIFE PLUG

Plug Tips/Hot and Cold.
Spark plugs must operate within well-defined temperature limits to avoid cold fouling at one extreme and overheating at the other.
Champion and the car manufacturers work out the best plugs for an engine to give optimum performance under all conditions, from freezing cold starts to sustained high speed motorway cruising.
Plugs are often referred to as hot or cold. With Champion, the higher the number on its body, the hotter the plug, and the lower the number the cooler the plug.

Plug Cleaning
Modern plug design and materials mean that Champion no longer recommends periodic plug cleaning. Certainly don't clean your plugs with a wire brush as this can cause metal conductive paths across the nose of the insulator so impairing its performance and resulting in loss of acceleration and reduced m.p.g.
However, if plugs are removed, always carefully clean the area where the plug seats in the cylinder head as grit and dirt can sometimes cause gas leakage.
Also wipe any traces of oil or grease from plug leads as this may lead to arcing.

This photographic sequence shows the steps taken to repair the dent and paintwork damage shown above. In general, the procedure for repairing a hole will be similar; where there are substantial differences, the procedure is clearly described and shown in a separate photograph.

First remove any trim around the dent, then hammer out the dent where access is possible. This will minimise filling. Here, after the large dent has been hammered out, the damaged area is being made slightly concave.

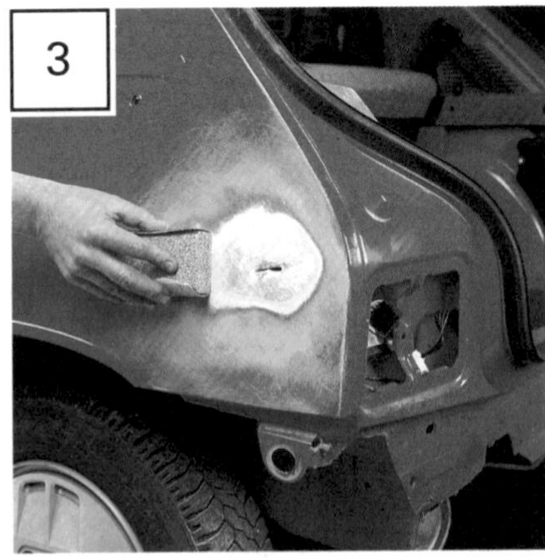

Next, remove all paint from the damaged area by rubbing with coarse abrasive paper or using a power drill fitted with a wire brush or abrasive pad. 'Feather' the edge of the boundary with good paintwork using a finer grade of abrasive paper.

Where there are holes or other damage, the sheet metal should be cut away before proceeding further. The damaged area and any signs of rust should be treated with Turtle Wax Hi-Tech Rust Eater, which will also inhibit further rust formation.

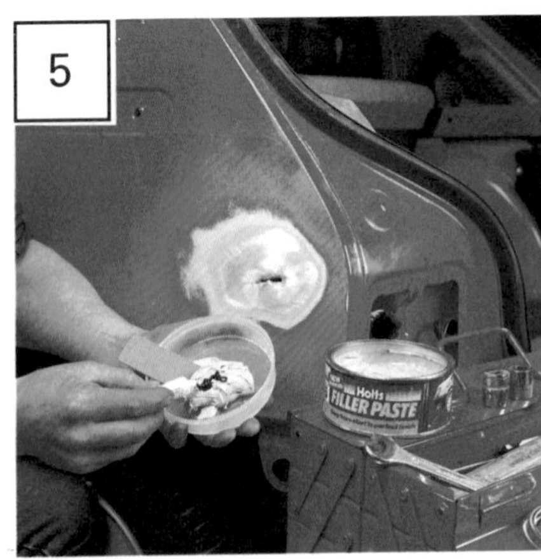

For a large dent or hole mix Holts Body Plus Resin and Hardener according to the manufacturer's instructions and apply around the edge of the repair. Press Glass Fibre Matting over the repair area and leave for 20-30 minutes to harden. Then ...

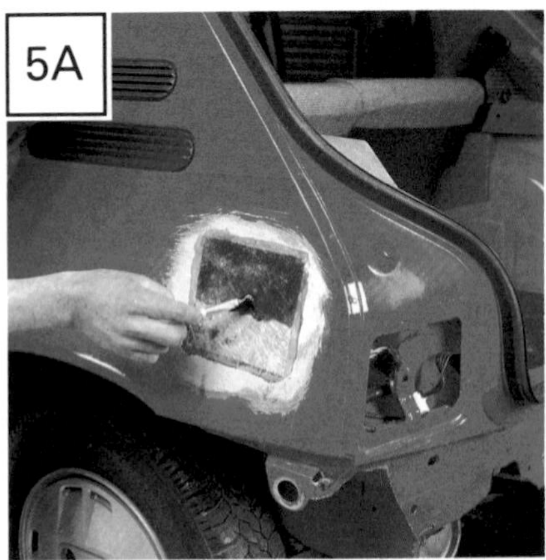

... brush more Holts Body Plus Resin and Hardener onto the matting and leave to harden. Repeat the sequence with two or three layers of matting, checking that the final layer is lower than the surrounding area. Apply Holts Body Plus Filler Paste as shown in Step 5B.

For a medium dent, mix Holts Body Plus Filler Paste and Hardener according to the manufacturer's instructions and apply it with a flexible applicator. Apply thin layers of filler at 20-minute intervals, until the filler surface is slightly proud of the surrounding bodywork.

For small dents and scratches use Holts No Mix Filler Paste straight from the tube. Apply it according to the instructions in thin layers, using the spatula provided. It will harden in minutes if applied outdoors and may then be used as its own knifing putty.

Use a plane or file for initial shaping. Then, using progressively finer grades of wet-and-dry paper, wrapped round a sanding block, and copious amounts of clean water, rub down the filler until glass smooth. 'Feather' the edges of adjoining paintwork.

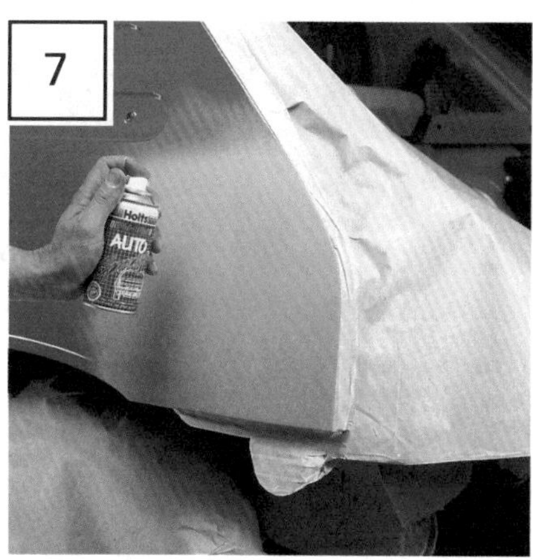

Protect adjoining areas before spraying the whole repair area and at least one inch of the surrounding sound paintwork with Holts Dupli-Color primer.

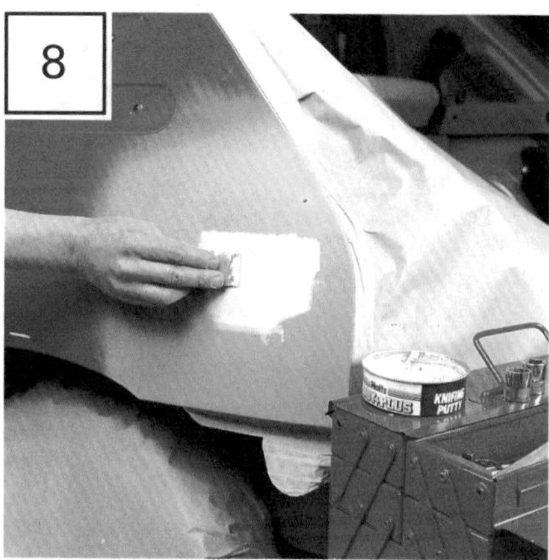

Fill any imperfections in the filler surface with a small amount of Holts Body Plus Knifing Putty. Using plenty of clean water, rub down the surface with a fine grade wet-and-dry paper – 400 grade is recommended – until it is really smooth.

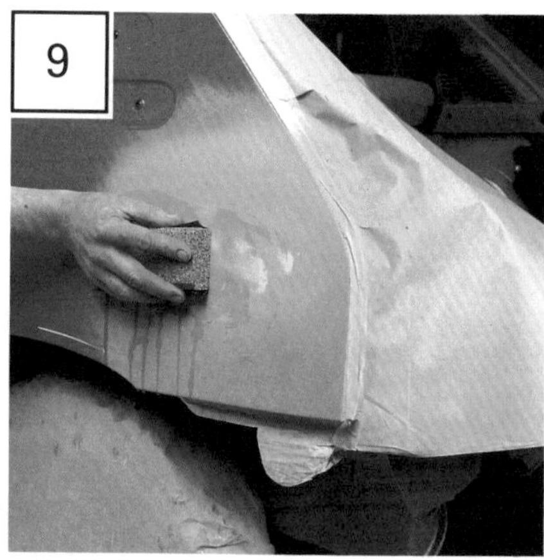

Carefully fill any remaining imperfections with knifing putty before applying the last coat of primer. Then rub down the surface with Holts Body Plus Rubbing Compound to ensure a really smooth surface.

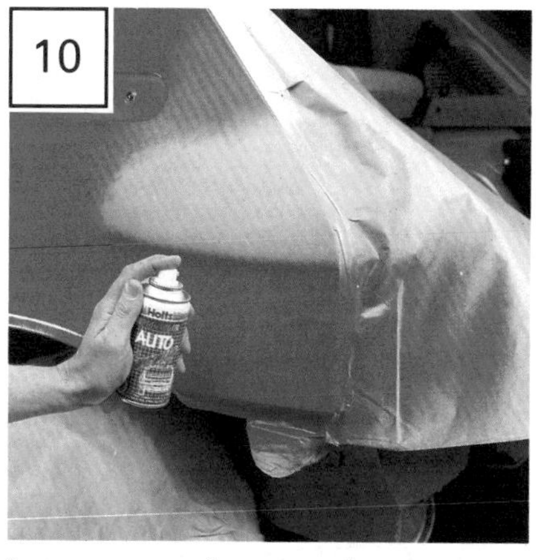

Protect surrounding areas from overspray before applying the topcoat in several thin layers. Agitate Holts Dupli-Color aerosol thoroughly. Start at the repair centre, spraying outwards with a side-to-side motion.

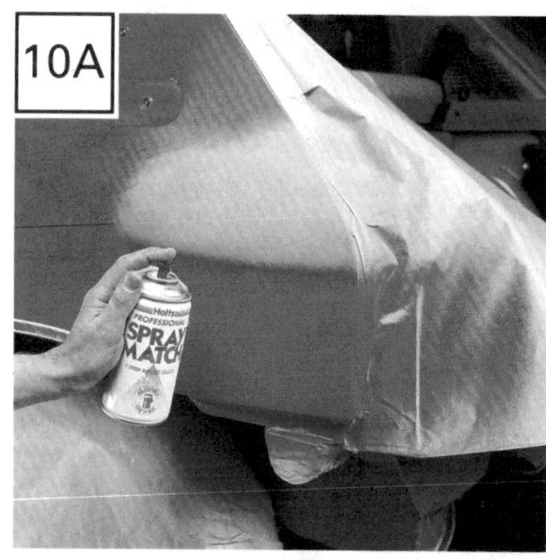

If the exact colour is not available off the shelf, local Holts Professional Spraymatch Centres will custom fill an aerosol to match perfectly.

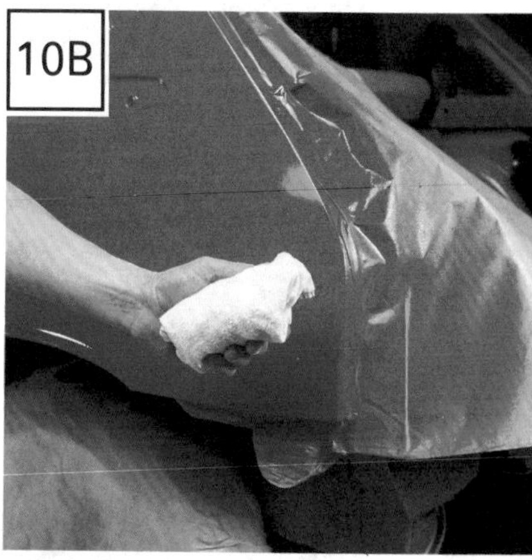

To identify whether a lacquer finish is required, rub a painted unrepaired part of the body with wax and a clean cloth.

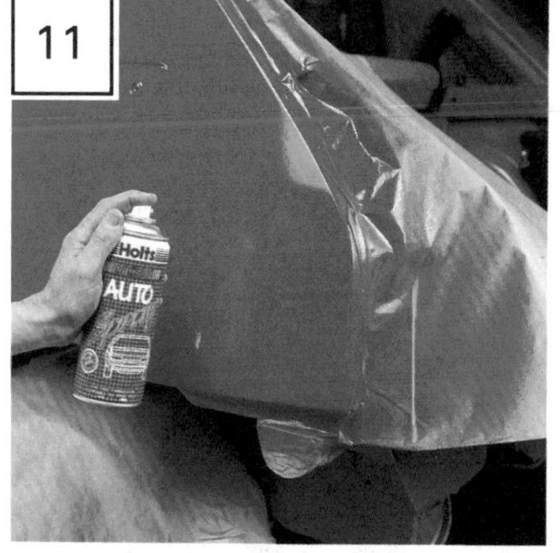

If *no* traces of paint appear on the cloth, spray Holts Dupli-Color clear lacquer over the repaired area to achieve the correct gloss level.

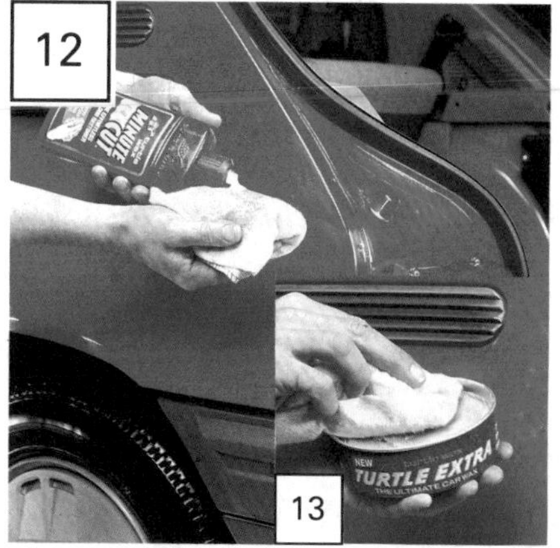

The paint will take about two weeks to harden fully. After this time it can be 'cut' with a mild cutting compound such as Turtle Wax Minute Cut prior to polishing with a final coating of Turtle Wax Extra.

When carrying out bodywork repairs, remember that the quality of the finished job is proportional to the time and effort expended.

THE ICE IN-CAR ENTERTAINMENT MANUAL
Choosing Installing Improving
AUTOMOBILE ELECTRICAL & ELECTRONIC SYSTEMS
The Car BODYWORK REPAIR Manual
NEW EDITION
The WASHING MACHINE Manual
AUTOMOTIVE FUEL INJECTION SYSTEMS
A Technical Guide
WEBER CARBURETTOR
FORD VEHICLE CARBURETTOR
Repair & Service
JAGUAR E-TYPE
GUIDE TO PURCHASE & D.I.Y. RESTORATION
MG MIDGET & AUSTIN-HEALEY SPRITE
MINI
CAPRI
MORRIS MINOR
Improve & Modify
ESCORT & ORION
Lindsay Porter & Dave Pollard

Torque wrench settings (continued)

	Nm	lbf ft
Cylinder head bolts:		
Torx type bolts:		
Stage 1	35 to 40	26 to 30
Stage 2	70 to 75	52 to 55
Stage 3 (after 5 minutes)	Tighten through a further 90°	Tighten through a further 90°
Camshaft cover bolts (see Fig. 1.6):		
Stage 1	6 to 8	4 to 6
Stage 2	2 to 3	1.5 to 2
Stage 3	6 to 8	4 to 6
Stage 4	6 to 8	4 to 6
Timing cover bolts	13 to 17	10 to 13
Timing belt tensioner bolts:		
Models with tensioner spring:		
Spring bolt	17 to 21	13 to 15
Pivot bolt	20 to 25	15 to 18
Models without tensioner spring	20 to 25	15 to 18
Oil pick-up tube/strainer-to-oil pump bolts	11 to 14	8 to 10
Oil pick-up tube/strainer-to-cylinder block bolts	17 to 21	13 to 15

1.6 litre engine

General

Engine type	Four-cylinder, in-line, single overhead camshaft	
Firing order	1-3-4-2	
Engine codes	LCS, LCT, LSD and LSE	
	LCS and LCT	**LSD and LSE**
Bore	87.67 mm	81.32 mm
Stroke	66.00 mm	76.95 mm
Cubic capacity	1593 cc	1597 cc
Compression ratio	9.2:1	9.5:1
Compression pressure at starter motor speed	11 to 13 bar	11 to 13 bar
Maximum continuous engine speed	5800 rpm	5950 rpm
Maximum engine power (DIN)	55 kW at 5300 rpm	55 kW at 4900 rpm
Maximum engine torque (DIN)	120 Nm at 2900 rpm	123 Nm at 2900 rpm

Cylinder block

	LCS and LCT	**LSD and LSE**
Bore diameter:		
Standard class 1	87.650 to 87.660 mm	81.300 to 81.310 mm
Standard class 2	87.660 to 87.670 mm	81.310 to 81.320 mm
Standard class 3	87.670 to 87.680 mm	81.320 to 81.330 mm
Standard class 4	87.680 to 87.690 mm	81.330 to 81.340 mm
Oversize class A	88.160 to 88.170 mm	81.810 to 81.820 mm
Oversize class B	88.170 to 88.180 mm	81.820 to 81.830 mm
Oversize class C	88.180 to 88.190 mm	81.830 to 81.840 mm
Standard service	87.680 to 87.690 mm	81.330 to 81.340 mm
Oversize 0.5	88.180 to 88.190 mm	81.830 to 81.840 mm
Oversize 1.0	88.680 to 88.690 mm	82.330 to 82.340 mm

Crankshaft

Specifications as for 1.3 litre engine except for the following:

Main bearing thrustwasher thickness from 1987:	
Standard	2.28 to 2.33 mm
Oversize	2.48 to 2.53 mm

Pistons and piston rings

	LCS and LCT	**LSD and LSE**
Piston diameter:		
Standard class 1	87.615 to 87.625 mm	81.265 to 81.275 mm
Standard class 2	87.625 to 87.635 mm	81.275 to 81.285 mm
Standard class 3	87.635 to 87.645 mm	81.285 to 81.295 mm
Standard class 4	87.645 to 87.655 mm	81.295 to 81.305 mm
Standard service	87.640 to 87.665 mm	81.290 to 81.315 mm
Service oversize 0.5	88.140 to 88.165 mm	81.790 to 81.815 mm
Service oversize 1.0	88.640 to 88.665 mm	82.290 to 82.315 mm
Piston ring end gap:		
Top	0.300 to 0.500 mm	0.300 to 0.500 mm
Centre	0.300 to 0.500 mm	0.300 to 0.500 mm
Bottom	0.400 to 1.400 mm	0.400 to 1.400 mm

Auxiliary shaft

Endfloat	0.050 to 0.204 mm (0.002 to 0.008 in)

Cylinder head

Specifications as for 1.3 litre engine

Camshaft

Specifications as for 1.3 litre engine except for the following:

Endfloat:	
Engine codes LCS, LCT and LSE	0.104 to 0.204 mm (0.004 to 0.008 in)
Engine code LSD	0.090 to 0.170 mm (0.003 to 0.007 in)

Valves – general

Specification as for 1.3 litre engine

Inlet valves

Specifications as for 1.3 litre engine

Exhaust valves

Specifications as for 1.3 litre engine

Lubrication system

Specifications as for 1.3 litre engine

Torque wrench settings

Specification as for 1.3 litre engine

1.8 litre engine

General

Engine type	Four-cylinder, in line, single overhead camshaft
Firing order	1-3-4-2
Engine codes	REB and RED
Bore	86.20 mm
Stroke	76.95 mm
Cubic capacity	1796 cc
Compression ratio	9.5:1
Compression pressure at starter motor speed	11 to 13 bar
Maximum continuous engine speed	5850 rpm
Maximum engine power (DIN)	66kW at 5400 rpm
Maximum engine torque (DIN)	140 Nm at 3500 rpm

Cylinder block

Bore diameter:	
Standard class 1	86.180 to 86.190 mm
Standard class 2	86.190 to 86.200 mm
Standard class 3	86.200 to 86.210 mm
Standard class 4	86.210 to 86.220 mm
Oversize class A	86.690 to 86.700 mm
Oversize class B	86.700 to 86.710 mm
Oversize class C	86.710 to 86.720 mm
Standard service	86.210 to 86.220 mm
Oversize 0.5	86.710 to 86.720 mm
Oversize 1.0	87.210 to 87.220 mm

Crankshaft

Specifications as for 1.3 litre engine except for the following:

Main bearing thrustwasher thickness from 1987:	
Standard	2.28 to 2.33 mm
Oversize	2.48 to 2.53 mm

Pistons and piston rings

Piston diameter:	
Standard class 1	86.145 to 86.155 mm
Standard class 2	86.155 to 86.165 mm
Standard class 3	86.165 to 86.175 mm
Standard class 4	86.175 to 86.185 mm
Standard service	86.170 to 86.195 mm
Service oversize 0.5	86.670 to 86.695 mm
Service oversize 1.0	86.170 to 86.195 mm
Piston ring end gap:	
Top	0.300 to 0.500 mm
Centre	0.300 to 0.500 mm
Bottom	0.400 to 1.400 mm

Auxiliary shaft

Endfloat	0.050 to 0.204 mm (0.002 to 0.008 in)

Cylinder head

Specifications as for 1.3 litre engine

Camshaft
Specifications as for 1.3 litre engine

Valves – general
Specifications as for 1.3 litre engine except for the following:

Valve clearance (cold engine):	
Inlet	0.20 ± 0.03 mm (0.008 ± 0.001 in)
Exhaust	0.25 ± 0.03 mm (0.010 ± 0.001 in)
Valve timing:	
Inlet opens	24° BTDC
Inlet closes	64° ABDC
Exhaust opens	70° BBDC
Exhaust closes	18° ATDC

Inlet valves
Specifications as for 1.3 litre engine

Exhaust valves
Specifications as for 1.3 litre engine

Lubrication system
Specifications as for 1.3 litre engine

Torque wrench settings
Specifications as for 1.3 litre engine

2.0 litre engine

General

Engine type	Four-cylinder, in-line, single overhead camshaft
Firing order	1-3-4-2
Engine codes	NES and NET (carburettor, except P100), NRB and N4A (fuel injection), and NAE (P100)
Bore	90.82 mm
Stroke	76.95 mm
Cubic capacity	1993 cc
Compression ratio:	
All except engine code NAE	9.2:1
Engine code NAE	8.2:1
Compression pressure at starter motor speed:	
All except engine code NAE	11 to 13 bar
Engine code NAE	10 to 12 bar
Maximum continuous engine speed:	
Engine code NES	5850 rpm
Engine codes NET and NAE	5800 rpm
Engine codes NRB and N4A	6050 rpm
Maximum engine power (DIN):	
Engine codes NES and NET	77kW at 5200 rpm
Engine codes NRB and N4A	85kW at 5500 rpm
Engine code NAE	57kW at 4500 rpm
Maximum engine torque (DIN):	
Engine codes NES and NET	157 Nm at 4000 rpm
Engine codes NRB and N4A	160 Nm at 4000 rpm
Engine code NAE	143 Nm at 2800 rpm

Cylinder block

Bore diameter:	
Standard class 1	90.800 to 90.810 mm
Standard class 2	90.810 to 90.820 mm
Standard class 3	90.820 to 90.830 mm
Standard class 4	90.830 to 90.840 mm
Oversize class A	91.310 to 91.320 mm
Oversize class B	91.320 to 91.330 mm
Oversize class C	91.330 to 91.340 mm
Standard service	90.830 to 90.840 mm
Oversize 0.5	91.330 to 91.340 mm
Oversize 1.0	91.830 to 91.840 mm

Crankshaft
Specifications as for 1.3 litre engine except for the following:

Main bearing thrustwasher thickness:	
All except engine codes NES, NET, NRB and N4A from 1987:	
Standard	2.30 to 2.35 mm
Oversize	2.50 to 2.55 mm
Engine codes NES, NET, NRB and N4A from 1987:	
Standard	2.28 to 2.33 mm
Oversize	2.48 to 2.53 mm

Pistons and piston rings

Piston diameter:	
Standard class 1	90.765 to 90.775 mm
Standard class 2	90.775 to 90.785 mm
Standard class 3	90.785 to 90.795 mm
Standard class 4	90.795 to 90.805 mm
Standard service:	
Up to 1985	90.780 to 90.805 mm
From 1985	90.790 to 90.815 mm
Service oversize 0.5:	
Up to 1985	91.280 to 91.305 mm
From 1985	91.290 to 91.315 mm
Service oversize 1.0:	
Up to 1985	91.780 to 91.805 mm
From 1985	91.790 to 91.815 mm
Piston ring end gap:	
Top:	
Up to 1985	0.038 to 0.048 mm
From 1985	0.400 to 0.600 mm
Centre:	
Up to 1985	0.038 to 0.048 mm
From 1985	0.400 to 0.600 mm
Bottom	0.400 to 1.400 mm

Auxiliary shaft

Endfloat	0.050 to 0.204 mm (0.002 to 0.008 in)

Cylinder head

Specifications as for 1.3 litre engine

Valves – general

Specifications as for 1.3 litre engine except for the following:

Valve clearance (cold engine):		
Inlet	0.20 ± 0.03 mm (0.008 ± 0.001 in)	
Exhaust	0.25 ± 0.003 mm (0.010 ± 0.001 in)	
Valve timing:	**All except engine code NAE**	**Engine code NAE**
Inlet opens	24° BTDC	18° BTDC
Inlet closes	64° ABDC	58° ABDC
Exhaust opens	70° BBDC	70° BBDC
Exhaust closes	18° ATDC	6° ATDC

Inlet valves

Specifications as for 1.3 litre engine

Exhaust valves

Specifications as for 1.3 litre engine

Lubrication system

Specifications as for 1.3 litre engine

Torque wrench settings

Specifications as for 1.3 litre engine except for the following:

	Nm	lbf ft
Crankshaft pulley bolt:		
Fuel injection models up to 1987	115 to 130	85 to 96
Fuel injection models from 1987	100 to 115	74 to 85

PART B: CVH ENGINE

General

Engine type	Four-cylinder, in-line, single overhead camshaft
Firing order	1-3-4-2
Engine code	R2A
Bore	80.00 mm
Stroke	88.00 mm
Cubic capacity	1769 cc
Compression ratio	9.3:1
Compression pressure at starter motor speed	11 to 13 bar
Maximum continuous engine speed	5850 rpm
Maximum engine power (DIN)	66 kW at 5250 rpm
Maximum engine torque (DIN)	147 Nm at 3000 rpm

Cylinder block

Bore diameter:	
Standard class 1	79.940 to 79.950 mm
Standard class 2	79.950 to 79.960 mm
Standard class 3	79.960 to 79.970 mm
Standard class 4	79.970 to 79.980 mm
Standard class 5	79.980 to 79.990 mm
Standard class 6	79.990 to 80.000 mm
Oversize class A	80.000 to 80.010 mm
Oversize class B	80.010 to 80.020 mm
Oversize class C	80.020 to 80.030 mm

Crankshaft

Endfloat	0.10 to 0.20 mm (0.004 to 0.008 in)
Main bearing running clearance	0.028 to 0.067 mm
Main bearing journal diameter:	
Standard	53.980 to 54.000 mm
Undersize 0.25	53.730 to 54.750 mm
Undersize 0.50	53.480 to 53.500 mm
Undersize 0.75	53.230 to 53.250 mm
Centre main thrust bearing shell width:	
Standard	28.825 to 28.875 mm
Undersize 0.15	28.675 to 28.725 mm
Big-end bearing running clearance	0.020 to 0.065 mm
Big-end bearing journal diameter:	
Standard	43.890 to 43.910 mm
Undersize 0.25	43.640 to 43.660 mm
Undersize 0.50	43.390 to 43.410 mm
Undersize 0.75	43.140 to 43.160 mm
Undersize 1.00	42.890 to 42.910 mm

Pistons and piston rings

Piston diameter:	
Standard class 1	79.910 to 79.920 mm
Standard class 2	79.920 to 79.930 mm
Standard class 3	79.930 to 79.940 mm
Standard class 4	79.940 to 79.950 mm
Standard class 5	79.950 to 79.960 mm
Standard class 6	79.960 to 79.970 mm
Oversize class A	79.970 to 79.980 mm
Oversize class B	79.980 to 79.990 mm
Oversize class C	79.990 to 80.000 mm
Piston ring end gap	Not available at time of writing

Camshaft

Endfloat	0.15 to 0.20 mm (0.006 to 0.008 in)
Thrustplate thickness	4.99 to 5.01 mm (0.1966 to 0.1974 in)
Bearing journal diameter	45.7625 to 45.7375 mm

Valves and valve springs – general

Valve clearance	Not applicable (hydraulic cam followers)
Valve timing:	
Inlet opens	22° BTDC
Inlet closes	54° ABDC
Exhaust opens	64° BBDC
Exhaust closes	12° ATDC
Valve spring free length	47.20 mm (1.86 in)

Inlet valves

Stem diameter:	
Standard	8.025 to 8.043 mm
Oversize 0.38	8.405 to 8.423 mm
Oversize 0.76	8.825 to 8.843 mm

Exhaust valves

Stem diameter (standard)	7.996 to 8.017 mm

Lubrication system

Oil type/specification	Multigrade engine oil, viscosity range SAE 10W/30 to 20W/50, to API SG/CD or better (Duckhams QXR, Hypergrade, or 10W/40 Motor Oil)
Oil capacity:	
With filter	4.0 litres (7.0 pints)
Without filter	3.5 litres (6.2 pints)

Oil filter	Champion C104
Oil pump clearances:	
Outer rotor to body	0.074 to 0.161 mm (0.003 to 0.006 in)
Inner rotor to outer rotor	0.050 to 0.180 mm (0.002 to 0.007 in)
Rotor endfloat	0.013 to 0.070 mm (0.0005 to 0.0028 in)

Torque wrench settings	Nm	lbf ft
Main bearing cap bolts	90 to 108	66 to 80
Big-end bearing cap nuts	26 to 34	19 to 25
Crankshaft pulley bolt	110 to 130	81 to 96
Camshaft sprocket bolt	95 to 115	70 to 85
Flywheel bolts	73 to 91	54 to 67
Oil pump bolts	11 to 16	8 to 12
Oil pump cover bolts	9 to 12	7 to 9
Sump bolts:		
M6 bolts	8 to 11	6 to 8
M8 bolts	20 to 30	15 to 22
Sump drain plug	20 to 30	15 to 22
Rocker arm bolts	23 to 30	17 to 22
Cylinder head bolts:		
Stage 1	40 to 60	30 to 44
Stage 2	Slacken bolts by half a turn	Slacken bolts by half a turn
Stage 3	40 to 60	30 to 44
Stage 4	Tighten through a further 90°	Tighten through a further 90°
Stage 5	Tighten through a further 90°	Tighten through a further 90°
Camshaft cover bolts	8 to 11	6 to 8
Timing cover bolts	8 to 11	6 to 8
Timing cover nuts	5 to 7	4 to 5
Timing belt tensioner bolts	23 to 30	17 to 22
Oil pick-up tube/strainer-to-oil pump bolts	10 to 13	7 to 9
Camshaft thrustplate bolts	9 to 13	6 to 9
Crankshaft rear oil seal housing bolts	8 to 11	6 to 8

PART A: OHC ENGINES

1 General description

The engine is of four-cylinder, in-line overhead camshaft type, mounted at the front of the vehicle and available in 1.3, 1.6, 1.8 and 2.0 litre versions.

The crankshaft incorporates five main bearings. Thrustwashers are fitted to the centre main bearing in order to control crankshaft endfloat.

The camshaft is driven by a toothed belt and operates the slightly angled valves via cam followers which pivot on ball-pins.

The auxiliary shaft which is also driven by the toothed belt, drives the distributor, oil pump and fuel pump.

The cylinder head is of crossflow design with the inlet manifold mounted on the left-hand side and the exhaust manifold mounted on the right-hand side.

Lubrication is by means of a bi-rotor pump which draws oil through a strainer located inside the sump, and forces it through a full-flow filter into the engine oil galleries where it is distributed to the crankshaft, camshaft and auxiliary shaft. The big-end bearings are supplied with oil via internal drillings in the crankshaft. The undersides of the pistons are supplied with oil from drillings in the big-ends. The distributor shaft is intermittently supplied with oil from the drilled auxiliary shaft. The camshaft followers are supplied with oil via a drilled spray tube from the centre camshaft bearing.

A semi-closed crankcase ventilation system is employed whereby piston blow-by gases are drawn into the inlet manifold via an oil separator and control valve.

2 Maintenance and inspection

1 At the intervals specified in the *'Routine maintenance'* Section at the beginning of this manual, carry out the following tasks.

2 Check the engine oil level as follows. With the vehicle parked on level ground, and with the engine having been stopped for a few minutes, withdraw the oil level dipstick, wipe it on a clean rag, and re-insert it fully. Withdraw the dipstick again and read off the oil level relative to the 'MAX' and 'MIN' marks. The oil level should be between the marks. If the level is at or below the 'MIN' mark, top up through the filler on the camshaft cover without delay (photo). The quantity of oil required to raise the level from 'MIN' to 'MAX' on the dipstick is approximately 1.0 litre (1.76 pints). Do not overfill.

3 Renew the engine oil and oil filter as described in Section 3.

4 Check and if necessary adjust the valve clearances as described in Section 4.

5 Clean the oil filler cap with paraffin, and inspect for signs of damage or deterioration. Renew if necessary.

6 Inspect the engine for evidence of oil, coolant, or fuel leaks and rectify as necessary.

7 Inspect the crankcase ventilation hose for blockage or damage. Clean or renew as necessary.

8 Renew the crankcase vent valve with reference to Section 5.

9 Although not specified by the manufacturers, consideration should be given to renewing the timing belt as a precautionary measure every 36 000 miles (60 000km) or so. If the belt breaks or slips in service, piston and valve damage may result.

3 Engine oil and filter – renewal

1 The oil should be drained when the engine is warm, immediately after a run.

2 Park the vehicle on level ground, position a container of suitable capacity under the sump, and unscrew the drain plug using a suitable socket or spanner (photo). Oil will be released before the drain plug is withdrawn, so take precautions to avoid scalding, as the oil may be hot. Allow the oil to drain for at least 15 minutes.

3 When the oil has finished draining, clean the drain plug washer, the plug threads and the mating face of the sump, then refit and tighten the drain plug.

4 Place a suitable container under the oil filter, and remove the filter, if necessary using a chain or strap wrench to slacken it and then unscrewing it by hand (photo). If a suitable wrench is not available, drive a large screwdriver through the filter and use the screwdriver as a lever to unscrew the filter. Be prepared for the spillage of hot oil.

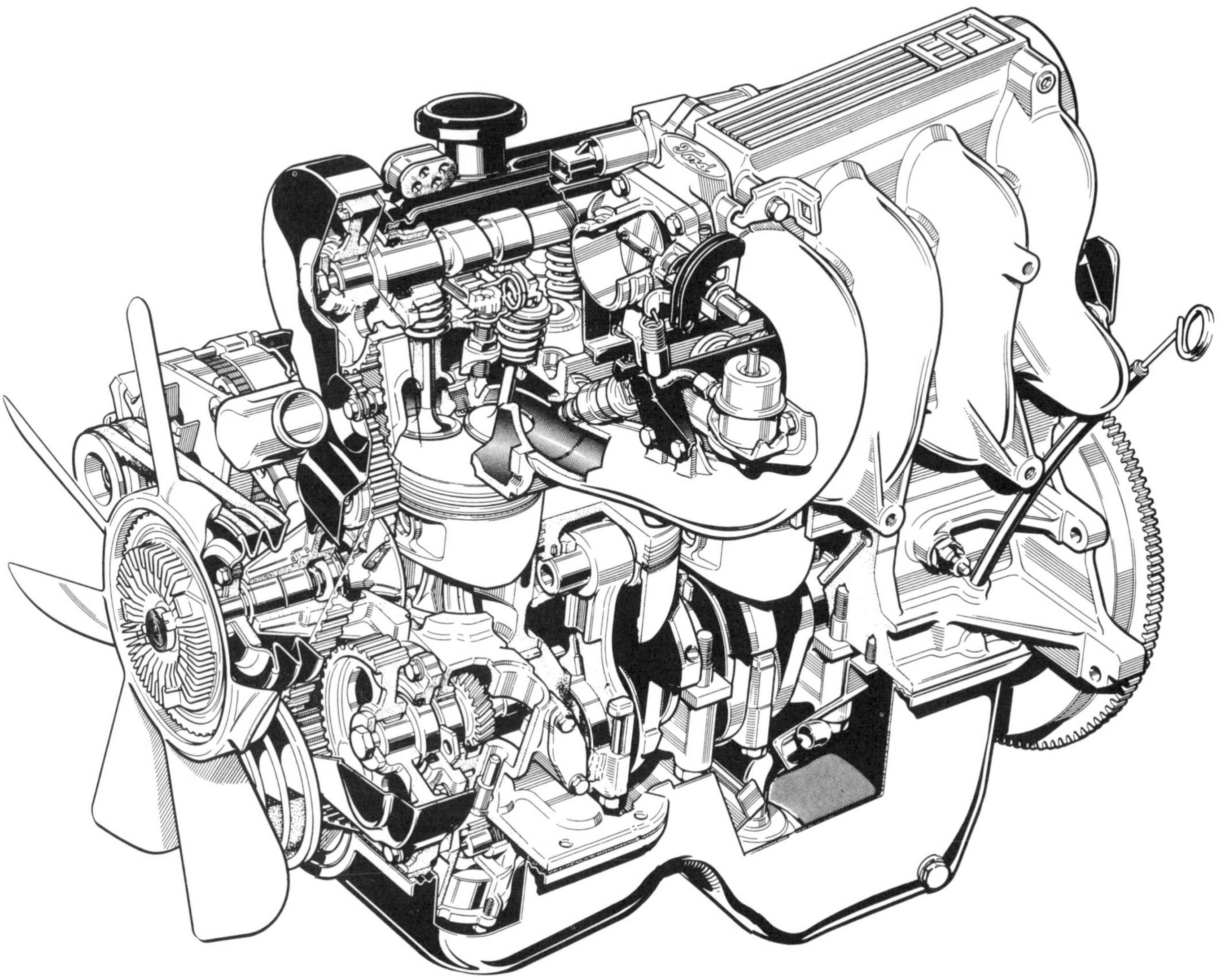

Fig 1.1 Cutaway view of 2.0 litre fuel injected OHC engine (Sec 1)

2.2 Topping-up the engine oil level

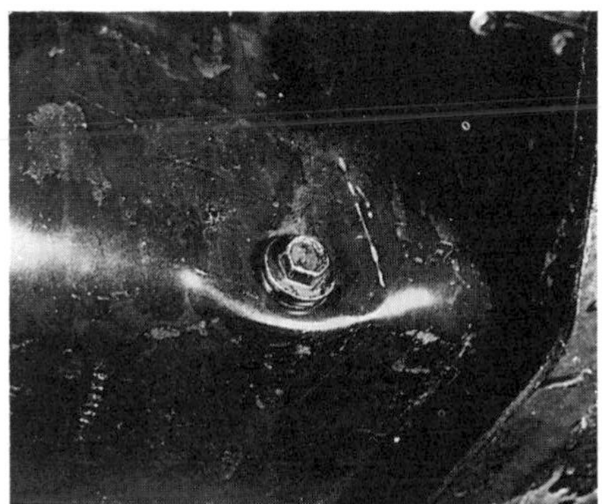
3.2 Sump drain plug location

3.4 Unscrewing the oil filter

5 Wipe clean the filter mounting face on the cylinder block.
6 Smear a little clean engine oil on the sealing ring of the new filter, then screw the filter onto the threaded tube and tighten it *by hand only*. If there are no specific instructions included with the filter, tighten it until the sealing ring contacts the mounting face on the cylinder block, then tighten a further three-quarters of a turn.
7 Fill the engine with the correct quantity and grade of oil through the oil filler on the camshaft cover. Ensure that the oil filler cap is refitted on completion.
8 When the engine is started, there may be a delay in the extinguishing of the oil pressure warning lamp while the new filter fills with oil. Run the engine and check for leaks from the filter and drain plug, then stop

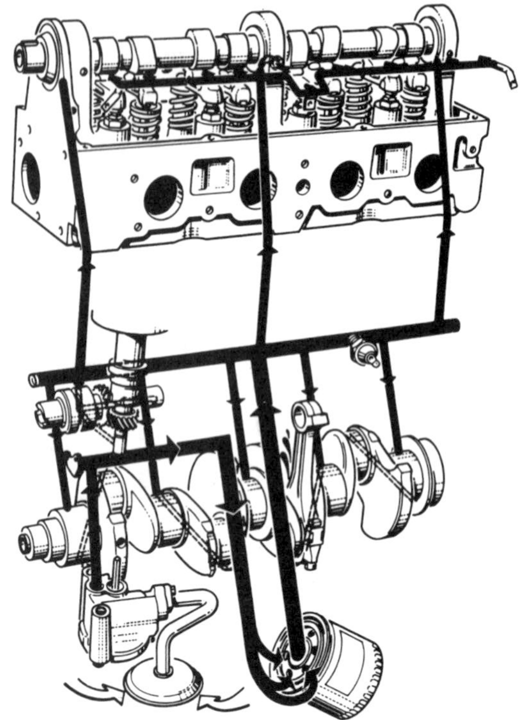
Fig 1.2 Engine lubrication circuit (Sec 1)

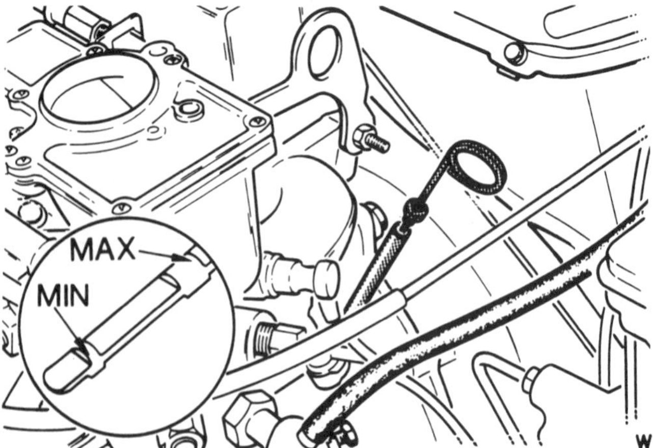

Fig 1.3 Oil level dipstick location and markings on models without oil level sensor (Sec 2)

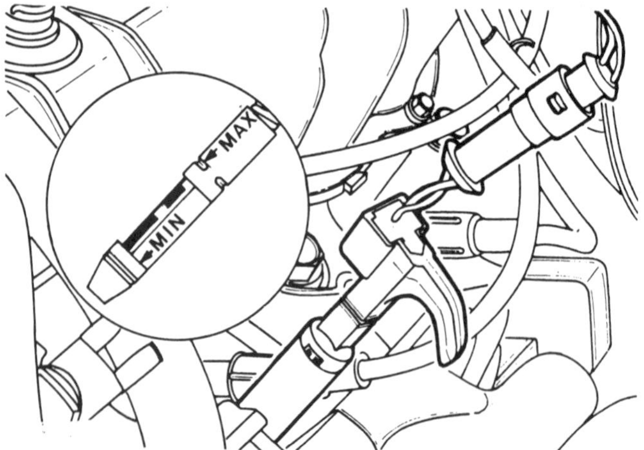

Fig 1.4 Oil level dipstick location and markings on models with oil level sensor (Sec 2)

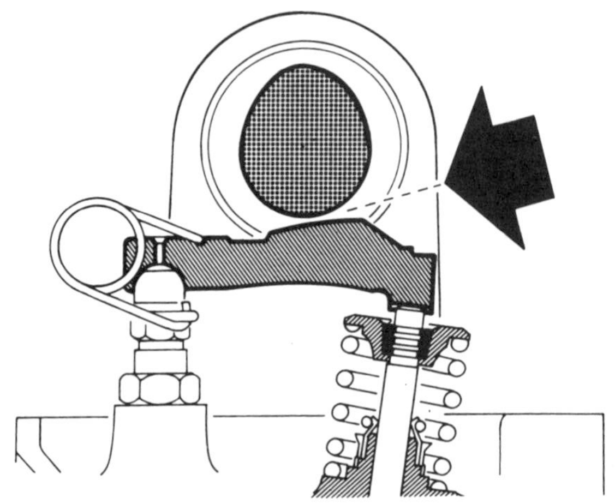
Fig 1.5 Cam lobe correctly positioned for checking valve clearance. Insert feeler gauge as shown by arrow (Sec 4)

the engine and check the oil level, with reference to Section 2, paragraph 2 if necessary.

9 Dispose of the old engine oil safely. **Do not** pour it down a drain – this is illegal and causes pollution.

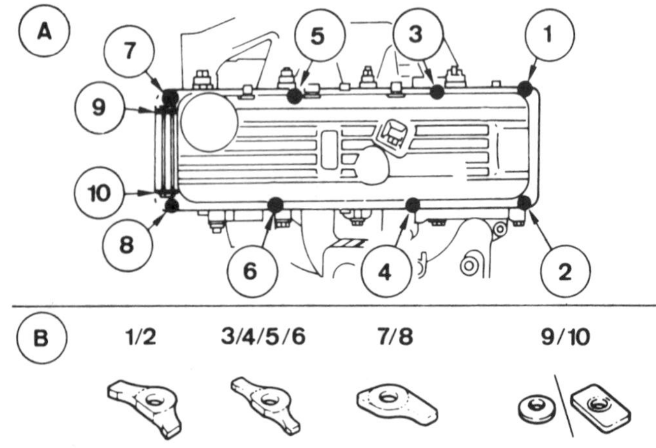

Fig 1.6 Camshaft cover bolts (A) and spacer plates (B) (Sec 4)

Tighten bolts in following stages:
Stage 1 Bolts 1 to 6
Stage 2 Bolts 7 and 8
Stage 3 Bolts 9 and 10
Stage 4 Bolts 7 and 8 (again)

4 Valve clearances – checking and adjustment

1 The valve clearances must be checked with the engine cold. On carburettor models remove the air cleaner as described in Chapter 3.

2 Disconnect the HT leads from the spark plugs and release them from the clips on the camshaft cover.

3 On fuel injection models, unbolt and remove the bracing strut securing the inlet manifold to the right-hand side of the cylinder head.

4 Where applicable, unclip any hoses and wires from the camshaft cover, then unscrew the ten securing bolts and remove the camshaft cover and gaskets. Take care not to lose the spacer plates which fit under the bolt heads, where applicable.

5 Numbering from the front (camshaft sprocket) end of the engine, the exhaust valves are 1, 3, 5 and 7, and the inlet valves are 2, 4, 6 and 8.

6 Turn the engine clockwise using a suitable socket on the crankshaft pulley bolt, until the exhaust valve of No 1 cylinder (valve No 1) is fully

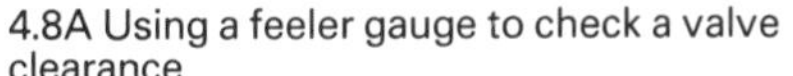

4.8A Using a feeler gauge to check a valve clearance

4.8B Adjusting a valve clearance

4.9 Camshaft cover gasket dovetails

closed; ie the cam lobe is pointing vertically upwards. It will be easier to turn the engine if the spark plugs are removed, but if this is done, take care not to allow dirt or other foreign matter to enter the spark plug holes.

7 Insert a feeler gauge of the correct thickness between the cam follower and the heel of the No 1 valve cam lobe. The feeler gauge should be a firm sliding fit. If not, loosen the locknut and adjust the ball-pin position accordingly by turning the adjuster nut, then tighten the locknut. Allowance must be made for tightening the locknut, as this tends to decrease the valve clearance. Recheck the adjustment after tightening the locknut.

8 Repeat the procedure given in paragraphs 6 and 7 for the remaining valves (photos). With the carburettor/inlet manifold fitted, some difficulty may be experienced when adjusting the exhaust valve clearances, and a suitable open-ended spanner bent to 90° will be found helpful.

9 Check the condition of the camshaft cover gasket, and renew if necessary. Fit the gasket to the camshaft cover ensuring that the locating tabs and dovetails are correctly located (photo), then refit the camshaft cover and tighten the securing bolts in the order shown in Fig. 1.6, ensuring the spacer plates are in position under the bolt heads, where applicable.

10 On fuel injection models, refit the inlet manifold bracing strut.

11 Where applicable refit the spark plugs. Reconnect the HT leads and locate them in the clips on the camshaft cover.

12 Where applicable, refit any wires and hoses to the clips on the camshaft cover, and on carburettor models refit the air cleaner as described in Chapter 3.

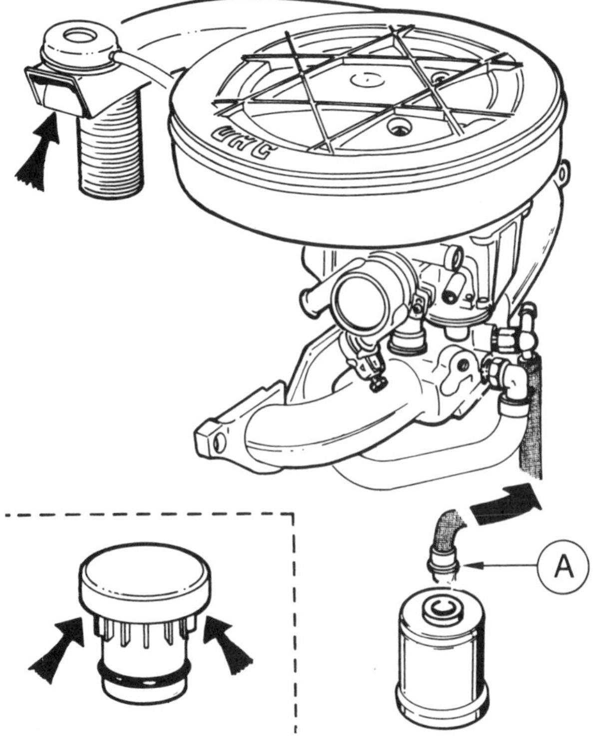

Fig 1.7 Crankcase ventilation system – carburettor models (Sec 5)

A Vent valve

5 Crankcase ventilation system – description and maintenance

Carburettor models

1 The crankcase ventilation system consists of the special oil filler cap, containing a steel wool filter, and an oil separator and vent valve on the left-hand side of the engine. This is connected by hose to the inlet manifold. The system operates according to the vacuum in the inlet manifold. Air is drawn through the filler cap, through the crankcase, and then together with piston blow-by gases through the oil separator and vent valve to the inlet manifold. The blow-by gases are then drawn into the engine together with the fuel/air mixture.

2 Regularly inspect the hose for blockage or damage; clean or renew as necessary. A blocked hose can cause a build-up of crankcase pressure, which in turn can cause oil leaks.

3 At the intervals specified in the *'Routine maintenance'* Section at the beginning of this manual, carry out the following tasks.

4 Clean the oil filler cap with paraffin.

5 Renew the vent valve by pulling it from the oil separator and loosening the hose clip (photo). Fit the new valve, tighten the clip, and insert it into the oil separator grommet.

Fuel injection models

6 The system is closed, consisting of an oil separator on the left-hand side of the engine and a hose connecting it to the inlet air trunking.

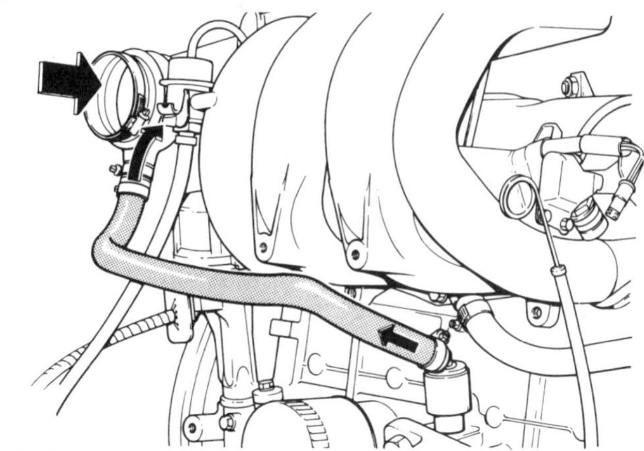

Fig 1.8 Crankcase ventilation system – fuel injection models (Sec 5)

Because the trunking is not subject to manifold vacuum, no vent valve is needed.

7 Check the condition of the hose occasionally (see paragraph 2).

6 Compression test – description and interpretation

1 When engine performance is poor, or if misfiring occurs which cannot be attributed to the ignition or fuel system, a compression test can provide diagnostic clues. If the test is performed regularly it can give warning of trouble before any other symptoms become apparent.

2 The engine must be at operating temperature, the battery must be fully charged and the spark plugs must be removed. The services of an assistant will also be required.

3 Disable the ignition system by disconnecting the coil LT feed. Fit the compression tester to No 1 spark plug hole. (The type of tester which screws into the spark plug hole is to be preferred.)

4 Have the assistant hold the throttle wide open and crank the engine on the starter. Record the highest reading obtained on the compression tester.

5 Repeat the test on the remaining cylinders, recording the pressure developed in each.

6 Desired pressures are given in the Specifications. If the pressure in any cylinder is low, introduce a teaspoonful of clean engine oil into the spark plug hole and repeat the test.

7 If the addition of oil temporarily improves the compression pressure, this indicates that bore, piston or piston ring wear was responsible for the pressure loss. No improvement suggests that leaking or burnt valves, or a blown head gasket, may be to blame.

8 A low reading from the two adjacent cylinders is almost certainly due to the head gasket between them having blown.

9 On completion of the test, refit the spark plugs and reconnect the coil LT feed.

7 Major operations possible with the engine in the vehicle

1 The following operations can be carried out without removing the engine from the vehicle:

(a) *Removal and servicing of the cylinder head*
(b) *Removal of the camshaft after removal of the cylinder head*
(c) *Removal of the timing belt and sprockets*
(d) *Removal of the sump*
(e) *Removal of the oil pump*
(f) *Removal of the pistons and connecting rods*
(g) *Removal of the big-end bearings*
(h) *Removal of the engine mountings*
(i) *Removal of the clutch and flywheel*
(j) *Removal of crankshaft front and rear oil seals*
(k) *Removal of the auxiliary shaft*

8 Major operations requiring engine removal

The following operations can only be carried out after removing the engine from the vehicle:

(a) *Removal of the crankshaft main bearings*
(b) *Removal of the crankshaft*

9 Method of engine removal

The engine may be lifted out either on its own, or together with the manual gearbox/automatic transmission. Unless work is to be carried out on the manual gearbox/automatic transmission, it is recommended that the engine is removed on its own. Where automatic transmission is fitted, the engine should where possible be removed on its own due to the additional weight of the transmission.

Warning: *Vehicles equipped with air conditioning:*

Components of the air conditioning system may obstruct work being undertaken on the engine, and it is not always possible to unbolt and move them aside sufficiently, within the limits of their flexible connecting pipes. In such a case, the system should be discharged by a Ford dealer or air conditioning specialist.

The refrigerant is harmless under normal conditions, but in the presence of a naked flame (or a lighted cigarette) it forms a highly toxic gas. Liquid refrigerant spilled on the skin will cause frostbite. If refrigerant enters the eyes, rinse them with a diluted solution of boric acid and seek medical advice immediately.

10 Engine – removal leaving manual gearbox in vehicle

Note: *Refer to the warning at the end of Section 9 before proceeding. A suitable hoist and lifting tackle will be required for this operation*

1 Disconnect the battery negative lead.

2 Remove the bonnet as described in Chapter 12.

3 On carburettor models remove the air cleaner as described in Chapter 3.

4 On fuel injection models, disconnect the crankcase ventilation hose from the air intake hose, then disconnect the air intake hose from the throttle body. Depress the locking clip on the airflow meter wiring plug and disconnect the plug (pulling on the plug, not the wiring) then release the four securing clips and lift off the air cleaner lid with the airflow meter and air intake hose.

5 Remove the four retaining clips and unscrew the two retaining screws, then withdraw the upper section of the cooling fan shroud from the radiator. Unclip and remove the lower section of the shroud.

6 Remove the thermo-viscous cooling fan as described in Chapter 2.

7 Drain the cooling system as described in Chapter 2.

8 Disconnect the upper radiator hose and where applicable, the expansion tank hose from the thermostat housing.

9 Disconnect the coolant hoses from the coolant pump, and where applicable from the inlet manifold and automatic choke. Unclip the coolant hose from the bracket on the exhaust manifold hot air shroud/heat shield, or the camshaft cover, as applicable.

10 On carburettor models, where applicable disconnect the vacuum pipe from the engine management module.

11 Disconnect the brake servo vacuum from the inlet manifold.

12 On carburettor models, disconnect the fuel hoses from the carburettor and where applicable the mechanical fuel pump and plug the ends of the hoses to minimise petrol spillage. Remember to take adequate fire precautions.

13 On fuel injection models, disconnect the fuel feed line from the fuel pressure regulator, then disconnect the fuel supply hose from the fuel rail. Position a suitable container beneath the pressure regulator, then slowly loosen the fuel feed union to relieve the pressure in the fuel lines before disconnecting the union. Take adequate fire precautions. Plug the ends of the hoses to minimise petrol spillage.

14 Disconnect the throttle cable, and where applicable remove the bracket, as described in Chapter 3.

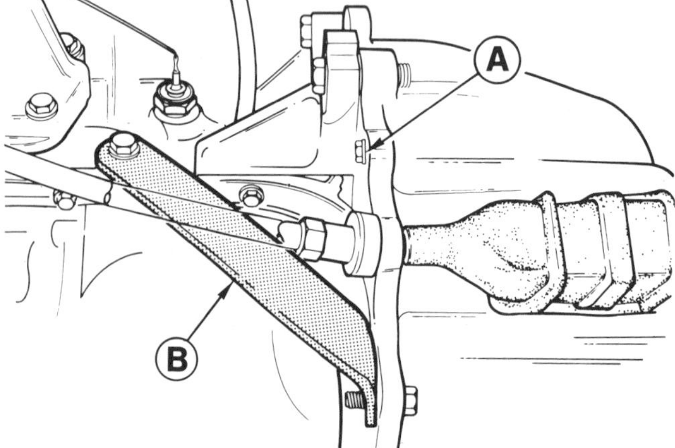

Fig 1.9 Engine adapter plate bolt (A) and engine-to-gearbox brace (B) (Sec 10)

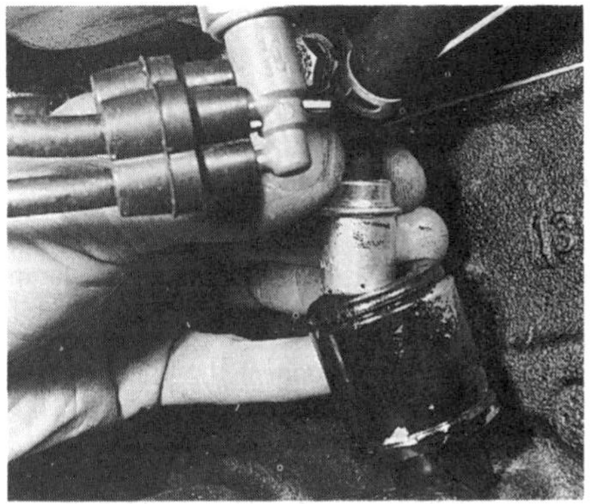

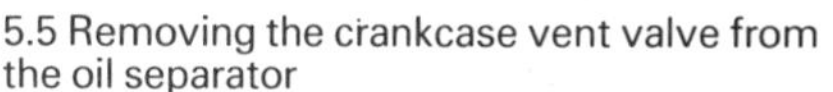

5.5 Removing the crankcase vent valve from the oil separator

10.33 Lifting the engine from the vehicle

12.20 Lifting the engine/gearbox assembly from the vehicle

15 Disconnect the HT lead from the ignition coil.
16 Disconnect the wiring from the following components as applicable depending on model:

Alternator
Starter motor
Distributor
Oil pressure warning lamp switch
Temperature gauge sender
Engine coolant temperature sensor
Automatic choke
Automatic choke pull-down solenoid
Carburettor anti-dieselling valve
Inlet manifold heater
Carburettor stepper motor
Fuel injection harness
Dipstick

17 Where applicable, detach the power steering pump from the cylinder block and move it to one side, with reference to Chapter 11.
18 Unscrew and remove the top engine-to-gearbox bolts which are accessible from the engine compartment. Note the location of the earth strap on one of the bolts.
19 Note the location of the earth strap on the rear inlet manifold stud, then remove the nut and disconnect the strap.
20 Apply the handbrake, jack up the front of the vehicle and support on axle stands.
21 Drain the engine oil into a suitable container.
22 Remove the starter motor as described in Chapter 13.
23 Remove the exhaust downpipe as described in Chapter 3.
24 Unscrew the nuts or bolts, as applicable, securing the engine mountings to the crossmember. Recover the washers.
25 Unscrew and remove the remaining engine-to-gearbox bolts, and remove the bolt from the engine adaptor plate – see Fig. 1.9.
26 Remove the two securing bolts and disconnect the engine-to-gearbox brace from the engine and gearbox.
27 Working inside the vehicle, place a wooden block under the clutch pedal to raise it fully against its stop which will hold the automatic adjuster pawl clear of the toothed quadrant.
28 Disconnect the clutch cable from the clutch release arm, and pass the cable through the bellhousing with reference to Chapter 5 if necessary. Where applicable, remove the clip securing the clutch cable to the right-hand engine mounting bracket. Note the cable routing for use when refitting.
29 Lower the vehicle to the ground, and support the gearbox with a trolley jack, using a block of wood between the jack and the gearbox to spread the load.
30 Make a final check to ensure that all relevant wires, pipes and hoses have been disconnected to facilitate engine removal.
31 Attach a suitable hoist to the engine lifting brackets located at the front and rear of the cylinder head, and carefully take the weight of the engine. The engine should be supported horizontally, ie do not allow it to tilt front to rear.
32 Raise the engine until the engine mountings are clear of the crossmember then pull the engine forwards to disconnect it from the gearbox. Ensure that the gearbox is adequately supported, and take care not to strain the gearbox input shaft. It may be necessary to rock the engine a little to release it from the gearbox.
33 Once clear of the gearbox, lift the engine from the vehicle, taking care not to damage the radiator fins (photo).

11 Engine – removal leaving automatic transmission in vehicle

Note: *Refer to the warning at the end of Section 9 before proceeding. A suitable hoist and lifting tackle will be required for this operation.*
1 Proceed as described in Section 10, paragraphs 1 to 17 inclusive, but additionally, where applicable, disconnect the kickdown cable from the carburettor/inlet manifold with reference to Chapter 7 if necessary.
2 Unscrew and remove the top engine-to-transmission bolts which are accessible from the engine compartment. Note the location of the earth strap, vacuum pipe bracket, and transmission dipstick tube bracket.
3 Proceed as described in Section 10, paragraphs 20 to 24 inclusive.
4 Working through the starter motor aperture, unscrew the four torque converter-to-driveplate nuts. It will be necessary to turn the crankshaft, using a suitable spanner on the crankshaft pulley bolt, in order to gain access to each nut in turn through the aperture.
5 Unscrew and remove the remaining engine-to-transmission bolts, and remove the bolt from the engine adaptor plate. Where applicable pull the blanking plug from the adaptor plate.
6 Remove the two securing bolts and disconnect the engine-to-transmission brace from the engine and transmission.
7 Lower the vehicle to the ground, and support the transmission with a trolley jack, using a block of wood between the jack and the transmission to spread the load.
8 Proceed as described in Section 10, paragraphs 30 and 31.
9 Raise the engine until the engine mountings are clear of the crossmember, then pull the engine forwards to disconnect it from the transmission. Ensure that the torque converter is held firmly in place in the transmission housing, otherwise it could fall out resulting in fluid spillage and possible damage. It may be necessary to rock the engine a little to release it from the transmission.
10 Once clear of the transmission lift the engine from the vehicle, taking care not to damage the radiator fins.

12 Engine/manual gearbox assembly – removal and separation

Note: *Refer to the warning at the end of Section 9 before proceeding. A suitable hoist and lifting tackle will be required for this operation*
1 Proceed as described in Section 10, paragraphs 1 to 17 inclusive.
2 Note the location of the earth strap on the rear inlet manifold stud, then remove the nut and disconnect the strap.
3 Working inside the vehicle, unscrew the gear lever knob and remove the centre console as described in Chapter 12. Where a full length console is fitted, it is only necessary to remove the front tray.
4 Detach the outer gaiter from the retaining frame and withdraw it over the gear lever.
5 Unscrew the securing screws on early models, or release the clips on later models, and remove the gaiter retaining frame and inner gaiter.
6 Using a suitable Torx key, remove the screws securing the gear lever to the gearbox extension housing, and withdraw the gear lever. Note how the base of the gear lever locates over the selector shaft.

7 Jack up the vehicle and support on axle stands. Ensure that there is sufficient working room beneath the vehicle.
8 To improve access, disconnect the exhaust downpipe from the manifold and remove the exhaust system as described in Chapter 3.
9 Remove the propeller shaft as described in Chapter 8.
10 Where applicable bend back the locktabs, then unscrew the two bolts in each case securing the two anti-roll bar U-clamps to the vehicle underbody. Lower the anti-roll bar as far as possible.
11 Proceed as described in Section 10, paragraphs 27 and 28.
12 Drain the engine oil into a suitable container.
13 Unscrew the nuts or bolts, as applicable, securing the engine mountings to the crossmember. Recover the washers.
14 Disconnect the wiring from the reversing lamp switch.
15 Remove the retaining circlip, and withdraw the speedometer cable from the gearbox extension housing.
16 Support the gearbox with a trolley jack, using a block of wood between the jack and the gearbox to spread the load.
17 Unscrew the four bolts securing the gearbox crossmember to the vehicle underbody. Unscrew the central bolt securing the crossmember to the gearbox and remove the crossmember. Note the position of the earth strap, where applicable. Recover the mounting cup and where applicable the exhaust mounting bracket and heat shield.
18 Make a final check to ensure that all relevant wires, pipes and hoses have been disconnected to facilitate removal of the engine/gearbox assembly.
19 Attach a suitable hoist to the engine lifting brackets located at the front and rear of the cylinder head. Arrange the lifting tackle so that the engine/gearbox assembly will assume a steep angle of approximately 40° to 45° as it is being removed.
20 Raise the engine/gearbox so that the engine mountings are clear of the crossmember, then ease the assembly forwards, at the same time lowering the trolley jack which is supporting the gearbox. Lift the assembly from the vehicle, taking care not to damage surrounding components (photo).
21 With the engine/gearbox assembly removed, temporarily reconnect the anti-roll bar to the underbody if the vehicle is to be moved.
22 To separate the engine from the gearbox, proceed as follows.
23 Remove the starter motor.
24 Support the engine and gearbox horizontally on blocks of wood.
25 Unscrew the two securing bolts and disconnect the engine-to-gearbox brace from the engine and gearbox.
26 Unscrew and remove the engine-to-gearbox bolts, noting the location of the earth strap, and remove the bolt from the engine adaptor plate – see Fig. 1.9.
27 Pull the engine and gearbox apart, taking care not to strain the gearbox input shaft. It may be necessary to rock the units slightly to separate them.

13 Engine/automatic transmission assembly – removal and separation

Note: *Refer to the warning at the end of Section 9 before proceeding. A suitable hoist and lifting tackle will be required for this operation. Any suspected faults in the automatic transmission should be referred to a Ford dealer or automatic transmission specialist before removal of the unit, as the specialist fault diagnosis equipment is designed to operate with the transmission in the vehicle.*
1 Proceed as described in Section 10, paragraphs 1 to 17 inclusive, but additionally, where applicable disconnect the kickdown cable from the carburettor/inlet manifold with reference to Chapter 7 if necessary.
2 Note the location of the earth strap on the rear inlet manifold stud, then remove the nut and disconnect the strap.
3 Jack up the vehicle and support on axle stands. Ensure that there is sufficient working room beneath the vehicle.
4 To improve access, disconnect the exhaust downpipe from the manifold and remove the exhaust system as described in Chapter 3.
5 Remove the propeller shaft as described in Chapter 8.
6 Where applicable bend back the locktabs, then unscrew the two bolts, in each case securing the two anti-roll bar U-clamps to the vehicle underbody. Lower the anti-roll bar as far as possible.
7 Unscrew the unions and disconnect the fluid cooler pipes from the transmission. Plug the open ends of the pipes and the transmission to prevent dirt ingress and fluid leakage. Remove the fluid cooler pipe bracket from the engine mounting bracket, and place it to one side.
8 Remove the two clips securing the selector rod, and detach the selector rod from the manual selector lever, and the selector lever on the transmission.
9 Disconnect the kickdown cable from the lever on the transmission, and where applicable, detach the cable from the bracket on the transmission. On C3 type transmissions it will be necessary to unscrew the locknut in order to remove the cable from the bracket. Withdraw the cable from the vehicle.
10 Disconnect the wiring from the starter inhibitor/reversing lamp switch and where applicable, on A4LD type transmissions, the kickdown solenoid and the lock-up clutch.
11 Remove the securing screw, and disconnect the speedometer cable from the transmission extension housing. Plug the opening in the transmission to prevent dirt ingress.
12 Disconnect the vacuum pipe from the vacuum diaphragm unit, and unclip the pipe from its securing bracket on the transmission housing where applicable.
13 Drain the engine oil into a suitable container.
14 Unscrew the nuts or bolts, as applicable, securing the engine mountings to the crossmember. Recover the washers.
15 Support the transmission with a trolley jack, using a block of wood to spread the load.
16 Unscrew the four bolts securing the transmission crossmember to the vehicle underbody. Note the position of the earth strap, where applicable. Unscrew the central bolt securing the crossmember to the transmission and remove the crossmember. Recover the mounting cup and where applicable the exhaust mounting bracket.
17 Make a final check to ensure that all relevant wires, pipes and hoses have been disconnected to facilitate removal of the engine/transmission assembly.
18 Attach a suitable hoist to the engine lifting brackets located at the front and rear of the cylinder head. Arrange the lifting tackle so that the engine/transmission assembly will assume a steep angle of approximately 40° to 45° as it is being removed.
19 Raise the engine/transmission so that the engine mountings are clear of the crossmember, then ease the assembly forwards, at the same time lowering the trolley jack which is supporting the transmission. Lift the assembly from the vehicle, taking care not to damage surrounding components.
20 With the engine/transmission assembly removed, temporarily reconnect the anti-roll bar to the underbody if the vehicle is to be moved.
21 To separate the engine from the transmission, proceed as follows.
22 Remove the starter motor.
23 Support the engine and transmission horizontally on blocks of wood.
24 Working through the starter motor aperture, unscrew the four torque converter-to-driveplate nuts. It will be necessary to turn the crankshaft using a suitable spanner on the crankshaft pulley bolt in order to gain access to each nut in turn through the aperture.
25 Unscrew the two securing bolts and disconnect the engine-to-transmission brace from the engine and transmission.
26 Unscrew and remove the engine-to-transmission bolts, noting the locations of the earth strap, vacuum pipe bracket, and transmission dipstick tube bracket. Remove the bolt from the engine adaptor plate, and where applicable pull the blanking plug from the adaptor plate.
27 Pull the engine and transmission apart, ensuring that the torque converter is held firmly in place in the transmission housing, otherwise it could fall out resulting in fluid spillage and possible damage. It may be necessary to rock the units slightly to separate them.

14 Engine – refitting (manual gearbox in vehicle)

1 Reverse the procedure described in Section 10, noting the following points.
2 Before attempting to refit the engine, check that the clutch friction disc is centralised as described in Chapter 5, Section 7. This is necessary to ensure that the gearbox input shaft splines will pass through the splines in the centre of the friction disc.
3 Check that the clutch release arm and bearing are correctly fitted and lightly grease the input shaft splines.
4 Check that the engine adaptor plate is correctly positioned on its locating dowels.
5 Refit the exhaust downpipe as described in Chapter 3.

6 Reconnect the clutch cable to the release arm with reference to Chapter 5, Section 3, ensuring that it is routed as noted during removal.
7 Fill the engine with the correct grade and quantity of oil.
8 Fill the cooling system as described in Chapter 2.
9 Check and if necessary adjust the tension of the alternator and where applicable the power steering pump drivebelt(s) as described in Chapter 2.
10 Adjust the throttle cable as described in Chapter 3.

15 Engine – refitting (automatic transmission in vehicle)

1 Reverse the procedure described in Section 11, noting the following points.
2 Check that the engine adaptor plate is correctly positioned on its locating dowels.
3 As the torque converter is only loosely engaged in the transmission, care must be taken to prevent the torque converter from falling out forwards. When the torque converter hub is fully engaged with the fluid pump drivegear in the transmission, distance 'A' in Fig. 7.8 (Chapter 7) must be as specified. Incorrect installation of the torque converter will result in damage to the transmission.
4 As the engine is installed, guide the torque converter studs through the holes in the driveplate, noting that on the C3 type transmission, the torque converter fluid drain plug must line up with the opening in the driveplate (see Fig. 7.9 in Chapter 7). When the engine is positioned flush with the engine adaptor plate and the transmission housing, check that the torque converter is free to move axially a small amount before refitting and tightening the engine-to-transmission bolts.
5 Do not tighten the torque converter-to-driveplate nuts until the lower engine-to-transmission bolts have been fitted and tightened.
6 Refit the exhaust downpipe as described in Chapter 3.
7 Fill the engine with the correct grade and quantity of oil.
8 Fill the cooling system as described in Chapter 2.
9 Check and if necessary adjust the tension of the alternator and where applicable the power steering pump drivebelt(s) as described in Chapter 2.
10 Adjust the throttle cable as described in Chapter 3.
11 Where applicable, adjust the kickdown cable as described in Chapter 7.

16 Engine/manual gearbox assembly – reconnection and refitting

1 Reverse the procedure described in Section 12, noting the following points.
2 Before attempting to reconnect the engine to the gearbox, check that the clutch friction disc is centralised as described in Chapter 5, Section 7. This is necessary to ensure that the gearbox input shaft splines will pass through the splines in the centre of the friction disc.
3 Check that the clutch release arm and bearing are correctly fitted, and lightly grease the input shaft splines.
4 Check that the engine adaptor plate is correctly positioned on its locating dowels.
5 Refit the propeller shaft as described in Chapter 8.
6 Refit the exhaust system as described in Chapter 3.
7 Reconnect the clutch cable to the release arm with reference to Chapter 5, Section 3, ensuring that it is routed as noted during removal.
8 Fill the engine with the correct grade and quantity of oil.
9 Fill the cooling system as described in Chapter 2.
10 Check and if necessary top up the gearbox oil level as described in Chapter 6.
11 Check and if necessary adjust the tension of the alternator and where applicable the power steering pump drivebelt(s) as described in Chapter 2.
12 Adjust the throttle cable as described in Chapter 3.

17 Engine/automatic transmission assembly – reconnection and refitting

1 Reverse the procedure described in Section 13, noting the following points.
2 Check that the engine adaptor plate is correctly positioned on its locating dowels.
3 As the torque converter is only loosely engaged in the transmission, care must be taken to prevent the torque converter from falling out forwards. When the torque converter hub is fully engaged with the fluid pump drivegear in the transmission, distance 'A' in Fig. 7.8 (Chapter 7) must be as specified. Incorrect installation of the torque converter will result in damage to the transmission.
4 As the engine and transmission are reconnected, guide the torque converter studs through the holes in the driveplate, noting that on the C3 type transmission, the torque converter fluid drain plug must line up with the opening in the driveplate (see Fig. 7.9 in Chapter 7). When the engine is positioned flush with the engine adaptor plate and the transmission housing, check that the torque converter is free to move axially a small amount before refitting and tightening the engine-to-transmission bolts.
5 Do not tighten the torque converter-to-driveplate nuts until the lower engine-to-transmission bolts have been fitted and tightened.
6 Reconnect the selector rod and adjust as described in Chapter 7, Section 7.
7 Refit the propeller shaft as described in Chapter 8.
8 Refit the exhaust system as described in Chapter 3.
9 Fill the engine with the correct grade and quantity of oil.
10 Fill the cooling system as described in Chapter 2.
11 Check and if necessary top up the transmission fluid level as described in Chapter 7.
12 Check and if necessary adjust the tension of the alternator and where applicable the power steering pump drivebelt(s) as described in Chapter 2.
13 Adjust the throttle cable as described in Chapter 3.
14 Where applicable, adjust the kickdown cable as described in Chapter 7.

18 Engine mountings – renewal

1 The engine mountings incorporate hydraulic dampers and must be renewed if excessive engine movement is evident.

18.3 Removing an engine mounting securing bolt

18.4 Withdrawing an engine mounting

2 Working in the engine compartment, unscrew the central nuts securing the engine mounting brackets to the tops of the mountings. Recover the washers where applicable.
3 Remove the two bolts or the central nut and washer (as applicable) in each case securing the mountings to the crossmember (photo).
4 Raise the engine using a suitable hoist and lifting tackle attached to the engine lifting brackets on the cylinder head, or a jack with an interposed block of wood under the sump, until the mountings can be withdrawn (photo).
5 Fit the new mountings, then lower the engine onto them.
6 Fit the bolts or the nuts and washers (as applicable) securing the mountings to the crossmember, and tighten them.
7 Fit and tighten the central nuts, and washers where applicable, securing the engine mounting brackets to the tops of the mountings.

19 Engine dismantling – general

1 It is best to mount the engine on a dismantling stand, but if this is not available, stand the engine on a strong bench at a comfortable working height. Failing this, it will have to be stripped down on the floor.
2 Cleanliness is most important, and if the engine is dirty, it should be cleaned with paraffin while keeping it in an upright position.
3 Avoid working with the engine directly on a concrete floor, as grit presents a real source of trouble.
4 As parts are removed, clean them in a paraffin bath. However, do not immerse parts with internal oilways in paraffin as it is difficult to remove, usually requiring a high pressure hose. Clean oilways with nylon pipe cleaners.

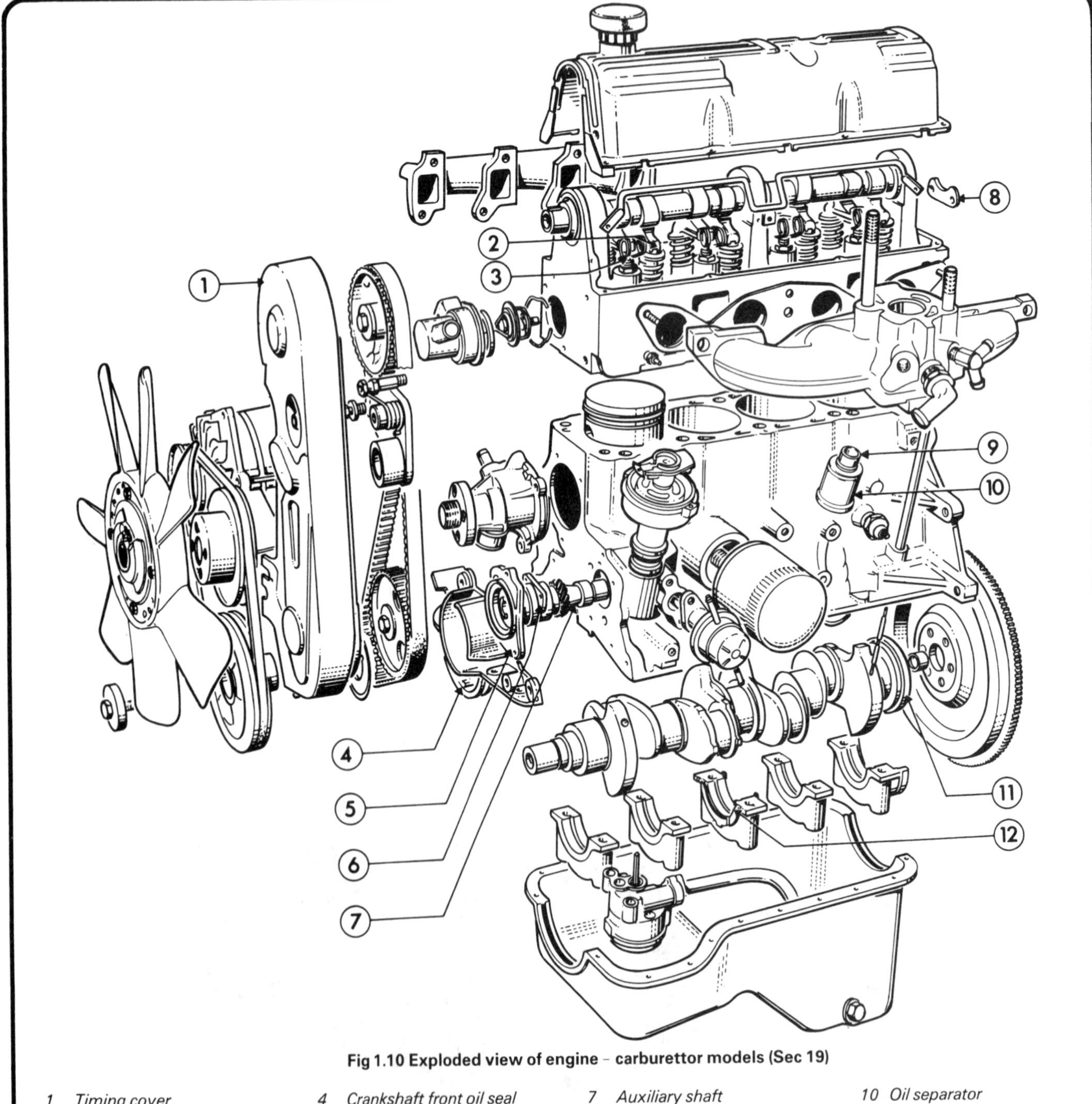

Fig 1.10 Exploded view of engine – carburettor models (Sec 19)

1 Timing cover
2 Cam follower
3 Cam follower retaining spring
4 Crankshaft front oil seal
5 Auxiliary shaft cover
6 Auxiliary shaft thrustplate
7 Auxiliary shaft
8 Camshaft thrustplate
9 Vent valve
10 Oil separator
11 Crankshaft rear oil seal
12 Crankshaft thrustwasher

19.6 Engine gasket set

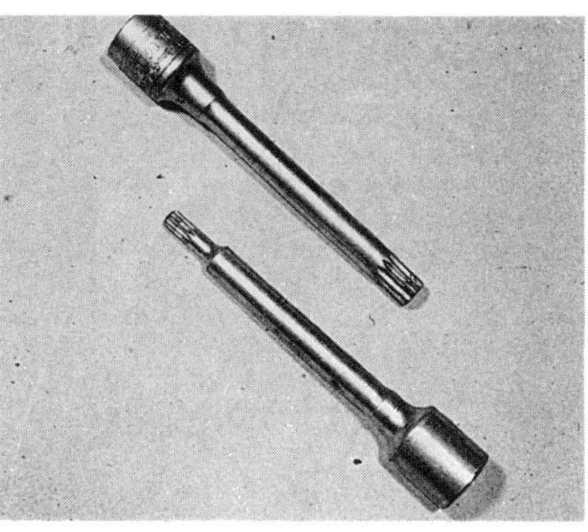
19.9 Splined sockets required for removal of certain bolts

19.10A Removing the right-hand engine mounting bracket

19.10B Removing the left-hand engine mounting bracket

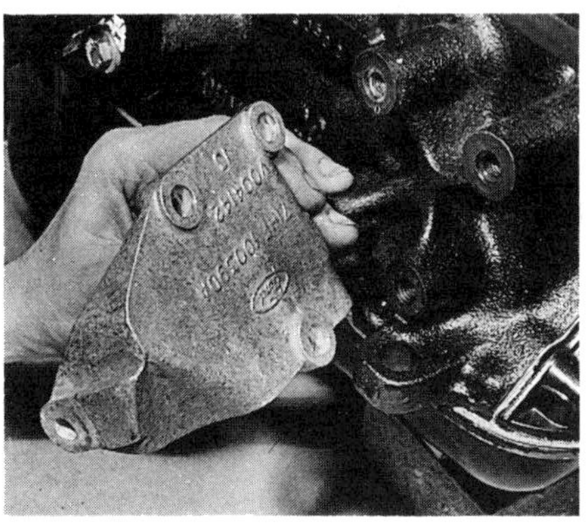
19.10C Removing the alternator mounting bracket

5 It is advisable to have suitable containers available to hold small items according to their use, as this will help when reassembling the engine and also prevent possible losses.

6 Always obtain a complete set of new gaskets for use during engine reassembly, but retain the old gaskets with a view to using them as a pattern to make a replacement if a new one is not available (photo).

7 Where possible, refit securing nuts, bolts and washers to their locations after removing the relevant components. This will help to protect the threads and will also prevent possible losses.

8 Retain unserviceable components in order to compare them with the new parts supplied.

9 Suitable splined sockets will be required for removal of the oil pump bolts, the timing belt tensioner bolts on early models (up to mid-1985), and the cylinder head bolts on early models (up to early 1984) (photo), and a size T55 Torx socket will be required to remove the cylinder head bolts on later models (from early 1984).

10 Before dismantling the main engine components, the following externally mounted ancillary components can be removed, with reference to the relevant Chapters, where applicable:

Inlet manifold (and carburettor, where applicable) – see Chapter 3
Exhaust manifold – see Chapter 3
Fuel pump and operating pushrod (where applicable) – see Chapter 3
Alternator – see Chapter 13
Distributor, HT leads and spark plugs – see Chapter 4
Coolant pump, thermostat and housing – see Chapter 2
Temperature gauge sender and oil pressure warning lamp switch – see Chapters 2 and 13 respectively
Oil filter – see Section 3 of this Chapter
Dipstick
Engine mounting brackets (photos)
Crankcase ventilation valve and oil separator – see Section 5 of this Chapter
Clutch – see Chapter 5
Alternator mounting bracket (photo)

20 Timing belt and sprockets – removal and refitting

Note: *Refer to the warning at the end of Section 9 before proceeding. On models from mid-1985 (without a timing belt tensioner spring) the belt tension should be checked using Ford special tool No 21-113 after refitting. On models up to mid-1985 (with a tensioner spring), a suitable splined socket will be required for the tensioner spring bolt. A suitable puller may be required to remove the sprockets*

1 If the engine is in the vehicle, carry out the following operations:

(a) *Disconnect the battery negative lead*
(b) *Remove the thermo-viscous cooling fan – see Chapter 2*
(c) *Remove the coolant pump/alternator/power-steering pump drivebelt(s) – see Chapter 2*
(d) *For improved access, remove the radiator and disconnect the radiator top hose from the thermostat housing – see Chapter 2*

2 Unscrew the three securing bolts and washers and withdraw the timing cover. Note the position of the fourth bolt above the crankshaft pulley which can be left in place.

3 Using a socket on the crankshaft pulley bolt, turn the engine clockwise until the TDC (top dead centre) mark on the crankshaft pulley is aligned with the pointer on the crankshaft front oil seal housing (see Fig. 4.8 in Chapter 4) and the pointer on the camshaft sprocket backplate is aligned with the indentation on the cylinder head (photo).

4 On models up to mid-1985 (with a tensioner spring), loosen the timing belt tensioner spring bolt using the special splined socket, then loosen the tensioner pivot bolt (photo). If necessary for improved access, remove the thermostat housing with reference to Chapter 2. Press the tensioner against the spring tension and tighten the pivot bolt to retain the tensioner in the released position.

5 On models from mid-1985 (without a tensioner spring), loosen the timing belt tensioner bolts, and move the tensioner away from the belt (photo). If necessary for improved access, remove the thermostat housing with reference to Chapter 2.

6 Mark the running direction of the belt if it is to be re-used, then slip it off the camshaft sprocket.

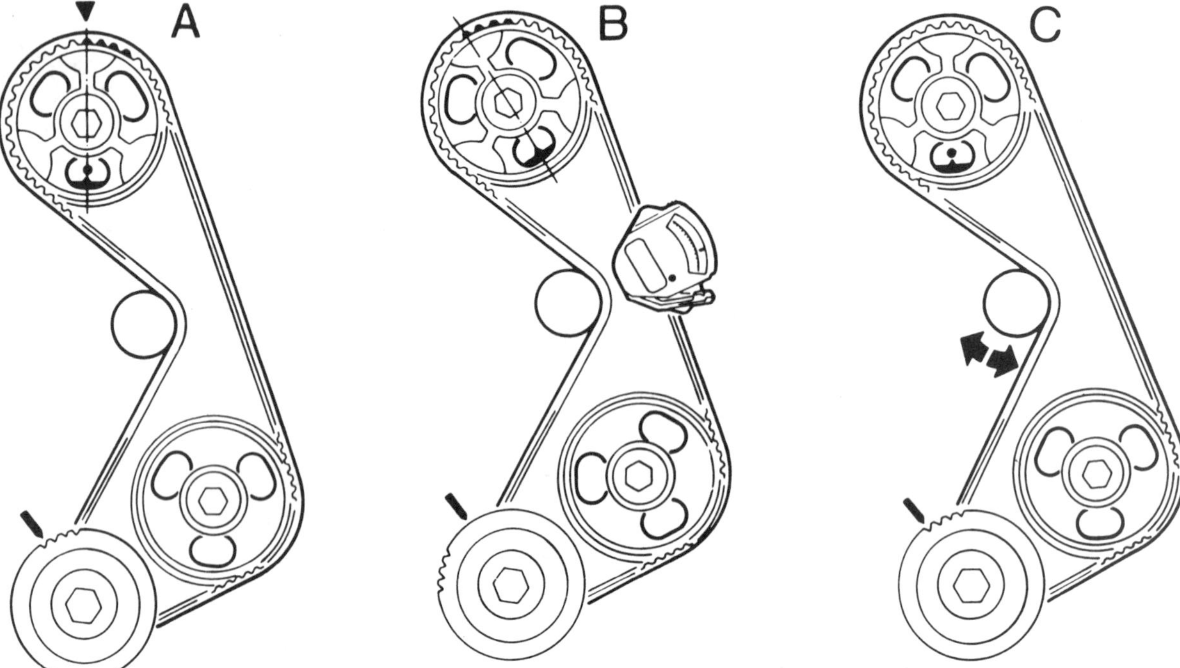

Fig 1.11 Timing belt tension checking sequence – models from mid-1985 (Sec 20)

A No 1 cylinder at TDC
B No 1 cylinder at 60° BTDC for checking
C Return No 1 cylinder to TDC for adjustment

7 Slacken the crankshaft pulley bolt. Prevent the crankshaft from turning by engaging top gear (manual gearbox only) and having an assistant apply the brake pedal hard, or by removing the starter motor and jamming the ring gear teeth with a lever. Alternatively, if the pulley has peripheral bolt holes, screw in a couple of bolts and use a lever between them to jam it. Do not allow the crankshaft to turn very far, or piston/valve contact may occur.
8 Remove the bolt and washer and withdraw the pulley. If the pulley will not come off easily, refit the bolt part way and use a puller (photos). A puller will almost certainly be required on fuel-injection models.
9 Remove the guide washer from in front of the crankshaft sprocket, then remove the timing belt (photo). Do not kink it or get oil on it if it is to be re-used.
10 If desired, the sprocket can be removed as follows, otherwise proceed to paragraph 21.
11 Remove the crankshaft sprocket, refitting the bolt part way and using a puller if necessary (photo).
12 Unscrew the auxiliary shaft sprocket bolt while holding the sprocket stationary with a screwdriver inserted through one of the holes.
13 Remove the auxiliary shaft sprocket, refitting the bolt part way and using a puller if necessary (photo).
14 Hold the camshaft sprocket stationary using a home-made tool similar to that shown in photo 59.17 in Part B of this Chapter, with two bolts engaged in the sprocket holes, and unscrew the bolt and washer. Alternatively, remove the camshaft cover and hold the camshaft using a spanner on the boss behind the No 6 valve cam.
15 Remove the camshaft sprocket, refitting the bolt part way and using a puller if necessary, then remove the backplate, noting which way round it is fitted (photos).
16 If desired, the camshaft oil seal can be removed using self-tapping screws and a pair of grips. A new seal can be fitted using a suitable tube drift to press it into place. Lubricate the seal lips with clean engine oil before installation.
17 Refit the sprockets as follows.
18 Fit the camshaft sprocket backplate, as noted during removal, then fit the sprocket. Insert the bolt, hold the camshaft or sprocket as during removal, and tighten the bolt to the specified torque (photo). Where applicable, refit the camshaft cover.
19 Fit the auxiliary shaft sprocket with the ribs towards the engine. Fit the sprocket bolt and tighten it to the specified torque, counterholding the sprocket with a bar through one of the holes.
20 Fit the crankshaft sprocket, chamfered side inwards.
21 Fit the timing belt over the crankshaft sprocket, but do not engage

20.3 TDC pointer on camshaft sprocket backplate aligned with indentation on cylinder head

20.4 Loosening the timing belt tensioner spring bolt using a splined socket – models up to mid-1985

20.5 Timing belt tensioner bolts (arrowed) – models from mid-1985

20.8A Removing a cast type crankshaft pulley

20.8B Using a puller to remove a pressed type crankshaft pulley

20.9 Removing the guide washer from the crankshaft

20.11 Removing the crankshaft sprocket

20.13 Removing the auxiliary shaft sprocket

20.15A Removing the camshaft sprocket ...

20.15B ... and backplate

20.18 Tightening the camshaft sprocket bolt while holding the camshaft stationary using a spanner on the camshaft boss

20.21 Fitting the timing belt over the crankshaft sprocket

it with the other sprockets yet (photo). Be careful not to kink the belt. If the old belt is being refitted, observe the previously noted running direction.

22 Refit the guide washer and the crankshaft pulley. Fit the bolt and washer and tighten just enough to seat the pulley, being careful not to turn the crankshaft.

23 Make sure that the TDC pointer on the camshaft sprocket backplate is still aligned with the indentation on the cylinder head.

24 Make sure that the TDC mark on the crankshaft pulley is still aligned with the pointer on the oil seal housing. If necessary, turn the crankshaft by the shortest possible route to align the marks.

25 If the distributor is fitted, turn the auxiliary shaft sprocket so that the rotor arm points to the No 1 HT segment position in the distributor cap.

26 Fit the timing belt over the sprockets and round the tensioner.

27 On models up to mid-1985 (with a tensioner spring), slacken the pivot bolt, and allow the tensioner roller to rest against the belt. Using a socket on the crankshaft pulley bolt, turn the crankshaft through two complete revolutions in a clockwise direction, to bring No 1 cylinder back to TDC. Tighten the tensioner pivot bolt and then the spring bolt to the specified torque. Do not turn the crankshaft anti-clockwise with the belt tensioner released. Proceed to paragraph 33.

28 On models from mid-1985 (without a tensioner spring), move the tensioner to tension the belt roughly and nip up the tensioner bolts. Using a socket on the crankshaft pulley bolt, turn the crankshaft through two complete revolutions in a clockwise direction (to bring No 1 cylinder back to TDC), then turn the crankshaft 60° anti-clockwise (No 1 cylinder at 60° BTDC).

29 The belt tension should now be checked by applying Ford tension gauge, tool No 21-113 to the longest belt run. Desired gauge readings are:

Used belt – 4 to 5
New belt – 10 to 11

If the tension gauge is not available, a rough guide is that the belt tension is correct when the belt can be twisted 90° in the middle of the longest run with the fingers, using moderate pressure (photo). In this case, the vehicle should be taken to a Ford dealer so that the belt tension can be checked using the special gauge at the earliest opportunity.
30 If adjustment of belt tension is necessary, turn the crankshaft clockwise to bring No 1 cylinder to TDC, then slacken the tensioner bolts and move the tensioner to increase or decrease the belt tension. Tighten the tensioner bolts to the specified torque.
31 Turn the crankshaft 90° clockwise past TDC, then anti-clockwise back to the 60° BTDC position (No 1 cylinder at 60° BTDC). Check the belt tension again.
32 Repeat the procedure given in paragraphs 30 and 31 until the belt tension is correct.
33 Tighten the crankshaft pulley bolt to the specified torque, preventing the crankshaft from turning as described in paragraph 7 (photo).
34 Refit the timing cover and tighten its bolts.
35 If the engine is in the vehicle, reverse the operations described in paragraph 1.
36 When the engine is next started, check the ignition timing as described in Chapter 4.

21 Cylinder head – removal and refitting (engine in vehicle)

Note: *Refer to the warning at the end of Section 9, and the note at the beginning of Section 22 before proceeding*
1 Disconnect the battery negative lead.
2 Drain the cooling system as described in Chapter 2.
3 Disconnect the coolant hose from the thermostat housing.
4 Disconnect the wiring from the temperature gauge sender.
5 Disconnect the HT leads from the spark plugs and from the clips on the camshaft cover and remove the spark plugs.
6 On carburettor models, remove the air cleaner as described in Chapter 3.
7 The cylinder head can be removed either with or without the manifolds. If desired, the inlet manifold can be unbolted and moved to one side, leaving the wires, hoses, pipes and cables connected, but care must be taken not to strain any of the wires, hoses, pipes or cables.
8 Unscrew the three securing nuts and disconnect the exhaust downpipe from the manifold flange. Recover the gasket.
9 Disconnect the coolant hose from the clip on the exhaust manifold hot air shroud, and if desired, remove the exhaust manifold as described in Chapter 3.
10 If the inlet manifold is to be removed with the cylinder head, disconnect all relevant wires, hoses, pipes and cables, otherwise, unbolt the manifold and move it to one side, ensuring that it is adequately supported. Refer to Chapter 3, Section 42 or 65 as applicable.
11 If not already done, unclip any wires and hoses from the camshaft cover, noting their locations for use when refitting, and on fuel injection models unbolt the bracing strut securing the inlet manifold to the right-hand side of the cylinder head.
12 If desired, remove the thermostat and housing, and the temperature gauge sender with reference to Chapter 2.
13 Proceed as described in Section 22.
14 With the cylinder head refitted as described in Section 22, proceed as follows.
15 Where applicable, refit the temperature gauge sender and the thermostat and housing as described in Chapter 2.
16 Refit the manifolds and/or reconnect all wires, hoses, pipes and cables, as applicable, with reference to Chapter 3.
17 Reconnect the exhaust downpipe to the manifold, using a new gasket.
18 Refit the coolant hose to the clip on the exhaust manifold hot air shroud.
19 Refit the spark plugs and reconnect the HT leads.
20 Reconnect the temperature gauge sender wiring.
21 Reconnect the coolant hoses to the thermostat housing.
22 Fill the cooling system as described in Chapter 2.
23 If not already done, refit any hoses and wires to the camshaft cover, as noted during removal, and on fuel injection models refit the inlet manifold bracing strut. If splined type cylinder head bolts have been used, leave these operations until the bolts have been finally tightened after running the engine.
24 Refit the air cleaner on carburettor models.
25 Reconnect the battery negative lead.
26 If splined type cylinder head bolts have been used, start the engine and run it at 1000 rpm for 15 minutes, then stop the engine, remove the air cleaner and the camshaft cover as described previously, and finally tighten the cylinder head bolts to the fourth stage (see Specifications). Refit the camshaft cover on completion, then refit any hoses and wires, and on fuel injection models the inlet manifold bracing strut. Refit the air cleaner.

22 Cylinder head – removal and refitting (engine removed)

Note: *Up to early 1984, splined type cylinder head bolts were used, and from early 1984, size TSS Torx bolts were used. Torx type bolts must always be renewed after slackening. The two types of bolts are interchangeable, but only in complete sets – the two types must not be mixed on the same engine. A suitable special socket will be required for removal of the bolts, and a new cylinder head gasket must be used when refitting.*
1 With the manifolds removed, proceed as follows.
2 Remove the timing belt as described in Section 20.
3 Where applicable, disconnect the breather hose from the camshaft cover.
4 Unscrew the ten securing bolts and remove the camshaft cover and gasket. Take care not to lose the spacer plates which fit under the bolt heads, where applicable.
5 Using the relevant special socket, unscrew the ten cylinder head bolts half a turn at a time in the reverse order to that shown in Fig. 1.12.
6 With the bolts removed, lift the cylinder head from the block (photo). If the cylinder head is stuck, tap it free with a wooden mallet. *Do not insert a lever into the joint between the cylinder head and block, as this may result in damage to the mating faces.* Place the cylinder head on blocks of wood to prevent damage to the valves.
7 Recover the gasket.
8 Commence refitting as follows.
9 With the cylinder head supported on blocks of wood, check and if necessary adjust the valve clearances with reference to Section 4. This work is easier to carry out on the bench rather than in the vehicle.
10 Turn the crankshaft so that No 1 piston is approximately 20.00 mm (0.8 in) before TDC. This precaution will prevent any damage to open valves.
11 Make sure that the mating faces of the cylinder block and cylinder head are perfectly clean, then locate the new gasket on the block making sure that all the internal holes are aligned (photo). *Do not use jointing compound.*
12 Turn the camshaft so that the TDC pointer on the camshaft sprocket backplate is aligned with the indentation on the front of the cylinder head.

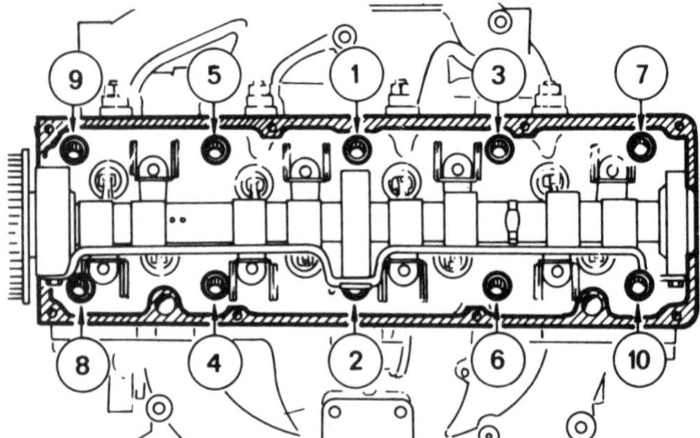

Fig 1.12 Cylinder head bolt tightening sequence (Sec 22)

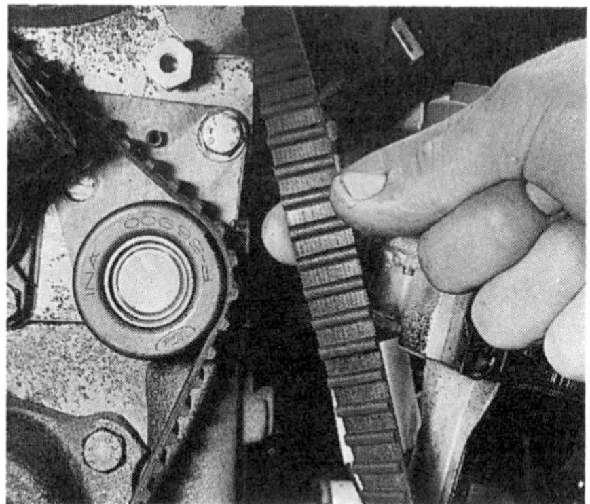
20.29 Twisting the timing belt to assess its tension

20.33 Holding a pressed type crankshaft pulley with two bolts and a lever while tightening the bolt

22.6 Lifting the cylinder head from the block

22.11 Fitting a new cylinder head gasket

23.2A Compressing a valve spring

23.2B Removing a valve spring and cap

13 Lower the cylinder head onto the gasket. The help of an assistant will ensure that the gasket is not dislodged.
14 Lightly oil the cylinder head bolt threads and heads, then insert the bolts into their locations in the cylinder head. Note that if the original bolts were of the Torx type, new bolts must be used when refitting.
15 Using the relevant special socket, tighten the bolts in the order shown in Fig. 1.12 to the stages given in the Specifications. *Note that the bolt tightening stages are different for splined and Torx type bolts.* If splined type bolts are used, they must be finally tightened to the fourth stage after the engine has been run for 15 minutes (see Specifications).
16 Check the condition of the camshaft cover gasket and renew if necessary. Fit the gasket to the camshaft cover, ensuring that the locating tabs and dovetails are correctly located, then refit the camshaft cover and tighten the securing bolts in the order shown in Fig. 1.6, ensuring that the spacer plates are in position under the bolt heads, where applicable.
17 Where applicable, reconnect the breather hose to the camshaft cover.
18 Refit the timing belt as described in Section 20.

23 Cylinder head – dismantling and reassembly

Note: *A valve spring compressor will be required during this procedure. New valve stem oil seals should be used on reassembly.*
1 With the cylinder head removed, remove the camshaft as described in Section 25.
2 Using a valve spring compressor, compress one of the valve springs until the split collets can be removed from the groove in the valve stem. Release the compressor and remove the cap and spring, identifying them for location. If the cap is difficult to release, do not continue to tighten the compressor, but gently tap the top of the tool with a hammer. Always make sure that the compressor is firmly located on the valve head and the cap. Withdraw the valve (photos).
3 Repeat the procedure given in paragraph 2 for the remaining valves, keeping all components identified for location so that they can be refitted in their original positions.
4 Prise the valve stem oil seals from the tops of the valve guides (photo).
5 Unscrew the cam follower ball-pins from the cylinder head, keeping them identified for location.
6 If desired, the cylinder head can be inspected and if necessary renovated as described in Section 24.
7 Commence reassembly by refitting the cam follower ball-pins to their original locations, where applicable.
8 Lubricate the valve stems and guides with SAE 80/90 hypoid oil, then insert the valves into their original guides.
9 Wrap a thin layer of adhesive tape over the collet groove of each valve, then smear the new oil seals with a little SAE 80/90 hypoid oil and slide them down the valve stems onto the guides. If necessary use a suitable metal tube to press the oil seals into the guides. Remove the adhesive tape.
10 Working on each valve in turn, fit the valve spring and cap, then compress the spring using the valve spring compressor and fit the split collets to the groove in the valve stem. Release the compressor and tap the end of the valve stem with a soft-faced mallet to settle the components. If the original components are being refitted, ensure that they are refitted in their original locations.
11 Refit the camshaft as described in Section 25.

24 Cylinder head – inspection and renovation

Note: *On engines fitted with hardened valve seats for use with unleaded petrol (see Chapter 4, Section 11), valve and valve seat grinding and recutting cannot be carried out without the use of specialist equipment. Consult a Ford dealer for further advice.*
1 This operation will normally only be required at comparatively high

23.2C Removing a valve

23.4 Removing a valve stem oil seal

25.4A Unscrewing a camshaft oil supply tube securing bolt

25.4B Withdrawing the camshaft oil supply tube

25.5 Note how the cam follower retaining springs are fitted

25.6 Removing a cam follower

mileages. However, if persistent pre-ignition ('pinking') occurs and performance has deteriorated even though the engine adjustments are correct, de-carbonizing and valve grinding may be required.

2 With the cylinder head removed, use a scraper to remove the carbon from the combustion chambers and ports. Remove all traces of gasket from the cylinder head surface, then wash it thoroughly with paraffin.

3 Use a straight edge and feeler blade to check that the cylinder head surface is not distorted. If it is, it must be resurfaced by a suitably equipped engineering works.

4 If the engine is still in the vehicle, clean the piston crowns and cylinder bore upper edges, but make sure that no carbon drops between the pistons and bores. To do this, locate two of the pistons at the top of their bores and seal off the remaining bores with paper and masking tape. Press a little grease between the two pistons and their bores to collect any carbon dust; this can be wiped away when the piston is lowered. To prevent carbon build-up, polish the piston crown with metal polish, but remove all traces of the polish afterwards.

5 Examine the heads of the valves for pitting and burning, especially the exhaust valve heads. Renew any valve which is badly burnt. Examine the valve seats at the same time. If the pitting is very slight, it can be removed by grinding the valve heads and seats together with coarse, then fine, grinding paste.

6 Where excessive pitting has occurred, the valve seats must be recut or renewed by a suitably equipped engineering works.

7 Valve grinding is carried out as follows. Place the cylinder head upside down on a bench on blocks of wood.

8 Smear a trace of coarse carborundum paste on the valve seat face and press a suction grinding tool onto the valve head. With a semi-rotary action, grind the valve head to its seat, lifting the valve occasionally to redistribute the grinding paste. When a dull matt even surface is produced on the mating surface of both the valve seat and the valve, wipe off the paste and repeat the process with fine carborundum paste as before. A light spring placed under the valve head will greatly ease this operation. When a smooth unbroken ring of light grey matt finish is produced on the mating surface of both the valve and seat, the grinding operation is complete.

9 Scrape away all carbon from the valve head and stem, and clean away all traces of grinding compound. Clean the valves and seats with a paraffin soaked rag, then wipe with a clean rag.

10 If the guides are worn they will need reboring for oversize valves or for fitting guide inserts. The valve seats will also need recutting to ensure they are concentric with the stems. This work should be entrusted to a Ford dealer or local engineering works.

11 Check that the free length of the valve springs is as specified, and renew if necessary. Do not renew individual springs; if any springs are excessively worn, renew all the springs as a set.

25 Camshaft and cam followers – removal, inspection and refitting

Note: *A new camshaft oil seal should be used when refitting the camshaft*

1 Remove the cylinder head as described in Section 21 or 22 as applicable.

2 Hold the camshaft stationary using a suitable spanner on the cast boss behind the No 6 valve cam, and unscrew the camshaft sprocket bolt and washer.

3 Remove the camshaft sprocket, using a suitable puller if necessary, and withdraw the sprocket backplate, noting which way round it is fitted.

4 Remove the three securing bolts and withdraw the camshaft oil supply tube (photos).

5 Note how the cam follower retaining springs are fitted, then unhook them from the cam followers (photo).

6 Loosen the locknuts and back off the ball-pin adjuster nuts until the cam followers can be removed (photo). Note their locations for use when refitting. It will be necessary to rotate the camshaft during this operation.

7 Unscrew the two bolts and remove the camshaft thrustplate from the rear bearing housing (photos).

8 Carefully withdraw the camshaft from the rear of the cylinder head, taking care not to damage the bearings (photo).

25.7A Unscrew the securing bolts ...

25.7B ... and remove the camshaft thrustplate

25.8 Withdrawing the camshaft

25.9 Prising out the camshaft oil seal

25.13 Fitting a new camshaft oil seal using a socket

25.14 Lubricating a camshaft bearing

9 Prise the oil seal from the front bearing in the cylinder head (photo).
10 Examine the surfaces of the camshaft journals and lobes, and the cam followers for wear. If wear is excessive, considerable noise would have been noticed from the top of the engine when running, and a new camshaft and followers must be fitted.
11 Check the camshaft bearings for wear, and if necessary have them renewed by a Ford dealer.
12 Check the camshaft oil supply tube for obstructions, making sure that the jet holes are clear.
13 Commence refitting by driving a new oil seal into the cylinder head front bearing, using a suitable tube drift or socket (photo). Smear the seal lip with clean engine oil.
14 Lubricate the camshaft, bearings and thrustplate with SAE 80/90 hypoid oil, then carefully insert the camshaft from the rear of the cylinder head, taking care not to damage the bearings (photo).
15 Locate the thrustplate in the camshaft groove, then insert and tighten the bolts.
16 Using a dial test indicator if available, or feeler gauges, check that the camshaft endfloat is within the limits given in the Specifications. If not, renew the thrustplate and re-check. If this does not bring the endfloat within limits, the camshaft must be renewed.
17 Lubricate the ball-pins with SAE 80/90 hypoid oil, then refit the cam followers to their original locations, and refit the retaining springs as noted during removal. It will be necessary to rotate the camshaft during this operation.
18 Fit the oil supply tube and tighten the bolts.
19 Fit the camshaft sprocket backplate, as noted during removal.
20 Fit the camshaft sprocket, then insert and tighten the bolt (with washer in place) to the specified torque, holding the camshaft stationary as described in paragraph 2.
21 With the cylinder head supported on blocks of wood, adjust the valve clearances with reference to Section 4. This work is easier to carry out on the bench rather than in the vehicle.
22 Refit the cylinder head as described in Section 21 or 22 as applicable.

26 Auxiliary shaft – removal, inspection and refitting

Note: *A new gasket should be used when refitting the auxiliary shaft cover (see text)*

1 Remove the timing belt and the auxiliary shaft sprocket as described in Section 20.
2 Remove the distributor as described in Chapter 4.
3 Remove the mechanical fuel pump and operating pushrod (where applicable) as described in Chapter 3.
4 Unscrew the three securing bolts and remove the auxiliary shaft cover (photos).
5 Unscrew the cross-head screws, using an impact screwdriver if necessary, remove the thrustplate and withdraw the auxiliary shaft from the cylinder block (photos).
6 Cut the cover gasket along the top of the crankshaft front oil seal housing and scrape off the gasket.
7 Examine the shaft for wear and damage, and renew it if necessary.
8 If desired, the oil seal in the cover can be renewed as follows.
9 Support the cover on blocks of wood and drive out the old oil seal. Drive the new seal into place using a suitable metal tube or socket. The sealing lip must face towards the cylinder block. Smear the sealing lip with clean engine oil before installation (photos).
10 Commence refitting by lubricating the auxiliary shaft journals with clean engine oil, then insert the shaft into the cylinder block.
11 Locate the thrustplate in the shaft groove, then insert the cross-head screws and tighten them with an impact screwdriver.
12 Using a dial test indicator (if available), or feeler gauges, check that the auxiliary shaft endfloat is within the limits given in the Specifications. If not, renew the thrustplate and re-check. If this does not bring the endfloat within limits, the auxiliary shaft must be renewed.
13 Cut out the relevant section of a new gasket, and locate it on the cylinder block, then refit the auxiliary shaft cover and tighten the securing bolts.
14 Where applicable, refit the fuel pump as described in Chapter 3.

26.4A Unscrew the auxiliary shaft cover securing bolts (arrowed) ...

26.4B ... and remove the cover

26.5A Unscrew the auxiliary shaft thrust plate securing screws (arrowed) ...

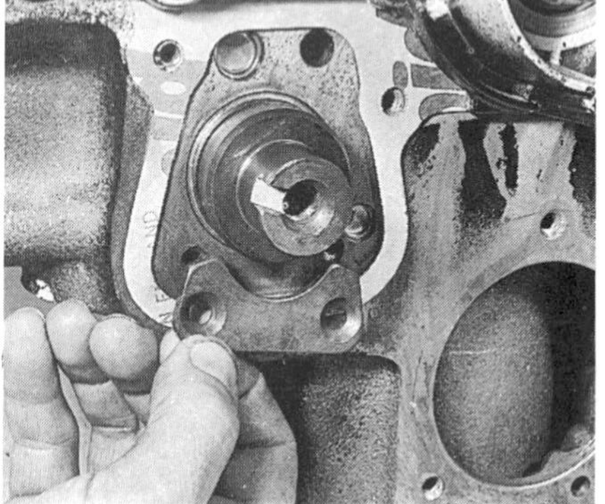
26.5B ... remove the thrustplate ...

26.5C ... and withdraw the auxiliary shaft

26.9A Driving out the auxiliary shaft cover oil seal

26.9B Using a socket to fit a new auxiliary shaft cover oil seal

27.5 Withdrawing the engine adaptor plate

27.10 Flywheel located on crankshaft

15 Refit the distributor as described in Chapter 4.

16 Refit the auxiliary shaft sprocket and the timing belt as described in Section 20.

27 Flywheel/driveplate - removal, inspection and refitting

Note: *The manufacturers recommend that the flywheel/driveplate securing bolts are renewed after slackening. Suitable thread-locking agent will be required to coat the bolt threads.*

1 If the engine is in the vehicle, remove the clutch as described in Chapter 5, or the automatic transmission as described in Chapter 7, as applicable.

2 Prevent the flywheel/driveplate from turning by jamming the ring gear teeth or by bolting a strap between the flywheel/driveplate and the cylinder block.

3 Make alignment marks on the flywheel/driveplate and the end of the crankshaft, so that the flywheel/driveplate can be refitted in its original position.

4 Unscrew the securing bolts and withdraw the flywheel/driveplate. *Do not drop it, it is very heavy.* Note that on models with A4LD type automatic transmission, the driveplate may be secured with one or two reinforcing plates depending on model.

5 The engine adaptor plate may now be withdrawn from the dowels if required (photo).

6 With the flywheel/driveplate removed, the ring gear can be examined for wear and damage.

7 If the ring gear is badly worn or has missing teeth it should be renewed. The old ring can be removed from the flywheel/driveplate by cutting a notch between two teeth with a hacksaw and then splitting it with a cold chisel. Wear eye protection when doing this.

8 Fitting of a new ring gear requires heating the ring to 400°F (204°C). This can be done by polishing four equally spaced sections of the gear, laying it on a suitable heat resistant surface (such as fire bricks) and heating it evenly with a blow lamp or torch until the polished areas turn a light yellow tinge. Do not overheat, or the hard wearing properties will be lost. The gear has a chamfered inner edge which should fit against the shoulder on the flywheel. When hot enough, place the gear in position quickly, tapping it home if necessary, and let it cool naturally

27.11 Coat the flywheel securing bolts with thread-locking agent

27.12A Using a strap to prevent the flywheel from turning ...

27.12B ... as the securing bolts are tightened

28.3A Removing the crankshaft front oil seal housing

28.3B Driving the crankshaft front oil seal from the housing

28.4 Using a socket to fit a new crankshaft front oil seal

28.5A Crankshaft front oil seal housing/auxiliary shaft cover located on front of cylinder block

28.5B Checking the alignment of the crankshaft front oil seal housing

29.2 Crankshaft rear oil seal location (arrowed)

without quenching in any way.

9 Commence refitting of the flywheel/driveplate by refitting the engine adaptor plate to the dowels on the rear of the cylinder block, where applicable.

10 Ensure that the mating faces are clean, then locate the flywheel/driveplate on the rear of the crankshaft, aligning the previously made marks (photo).

11 Coat the threads of the securing bolts with a liquid thread-locking agent, then insert the bolts (photo). Note that the manufacturers recommend the use of new bolts. Where applicable refit the reinforcing plate(s) on models with A4LD type automatic transmission.

12 Prevent the flywheel/driveplate from turning as described in paragraph 2, then tighten the securing bolts to the specified torque in a diagonal sequence (photos).

13 If the engine is in the vehicle, refit the clutch as described in Chapter 5, or the automatic transmission as described in Chapter 7, as applicable.

28 Crankshaft front oil seal - renewal

Note: *A new gasket will be required for refitting if the oil seal housing is removed during this procedure*

1 Remove the timing belt and the crankshaft sprocket as described in Section 20.

2 If an oil seal removal tool is available, the oil seal can be removed at this stage. It may also be possible to remove the oil seal by drilling the outer face and using self-tapping screws and a pair of grips.

3 If the oil seal cannot be removed as described in paragraph 2, remove the sump as described in Section 30, and the auxiliary shaft sprocket (see Section 20), then unbolt the oil seal housing and the auxiliary shaft front cover. Recover the gasket. The oil seal can then be driven out from the inside of the housing (photos).

4 Clean the oil seal housing, then drive in a new seal using a suitable metal tube or socket. Make sure that the seal lip faces into the engine

and lightly smear the lip with clean engine oil (photo).

5 Where applicable, refit the oil seal housing and the auxiliary shaft front cover, using a new gasket, and tighten the bolts. Using a straight edge, ensure that the bottom face of the oil seal housing is aligned with the bottom face of the cylinder block before finally tightening the bolts (photos). Refit the auxiliary shaft sprocket (see Section 20), and refit the sump as described in Section 30.

6 Refit the crankshaft sprocket and timing belt as described in Section 20.

29 Crankshaft rear oil seal – renewal

1 Remove the flywheel/driveplate and the engine adaptor plate as described in Section 27.

2 Extract the oil seal using an oil seal removal tool if available. It may also be possible to remove the oil seal by drilling the outer face and using self-tapping screws and a pair of grips (photo).

3 Clean the oil seal housing, then drive in a new seal using a suitable metal tube or socket. Make sure that the seal lip faces into the engine and lightly smear the lip with clean engine oil.

4 Refit the engine adaptor plate and the flywheel/driveplate as described in Section 27.

30 Sump – removal and refitting

Note: *New gaskets and sealing strips will be required for refitting, and suitable sealing compound will be required to coat the gasket faces.*

1 If the engine is in the vehicle, proceed as follows, otherwise proceed to paragraph 12.

2 Disconnect the battery negative lead.

3 Apply the handbrake, jack up the front of the vehicle and support on axle stands.

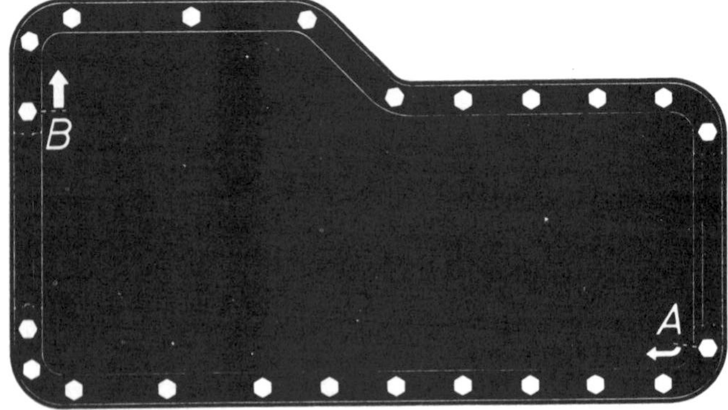

Fig 1.13 Sump bolt tightening sequence – refer to text (Sec 30)

4 Drain the engine oil into a suitable container.

5 Remove the starter motor, with reference to Chapter 13 if necessary.

6 Unscrew the nuts or bolts, as applicable, securing the engine mountings to the crossmember.

7 Working in the engine compartment, unscrew the bolt securing the intermediate shaft to the steering column, swivel the clamp plate to one side, and disconnect the intermediate shaft.

8 Where applicable, detach the brake lines from the crossmember, with reference to Chapter 10 if necessary.

9 Support the engine using a hoist, or a bar and blocks of wood resting on the suspension turrets. Attach the lifting tackle to the engine lifting brackets on the cylinder head. If using a support bar, the engine may be lifted slightly by using the bar as a lever before resting it on the wooden blocks (photos).

10 Support the front crossmember with a trolley jack, then unscrew

30.9A Make up wooden blocks ...

30.9B ... to fit the front suspension turrets ...

30.9C ... to support a metal bar ...

30.9D ... and support the engine

30.10 Unscrew the front crossmember securing bolts

30.11A Lower the suspension ...

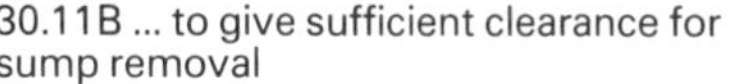
30.11B ... to give sufficient clearance for sump removal

30.12A Unscrew the securing bolts ...

30.12B ... and withdraw the sump

the bolts securing the crossmember to the underbody (photo).

11 Lower the crossmember just enough to give sufficient clearance to remove the sump (photos).

12 Unscrew the twenty-three securing bolts and withdraw the sump (photos). If the sump is stuck, carefully tap it sideways to free it. Do not prise between the mating faces. Note that if the engine has been removed, it is preferable to keep the engine upright until the sump has been removed to prevent sludge from entering the engine internals.

13 Recover the gaskets and sealing strips.

14 Thoroughly clean the mating faces of the cylinder block and sump.

15 Commence refitting by applying sealing compound (available from a Ford dealer) to the corners of the front and rear rubber sealing strip locations in the cylinder block, then press the sealing strips into the grooves in the rear main bearing cap and the crankshaft front oil seal housing (photos).

16 Apply a little sealing compound to the mating face of the cylinder block, then place the sump gaskets in position, ensuring that the end tabs locate correctly beneath the rubber sealing strips (photo).

17 Locate the sump on the gaskets and loosely fit the securing bolts.

18 Tighten the bolts in the two stages given in the Specifications, with reference to Fig. 1.13. Tighten to the first stage in a clockwise sequence starting at point 'A', then tighten to the second stage in a clockwise sequence starting at point 'B'. Tighten to the third stage after the engine has been running for twenty minutes.

19 If the engine is in the vehicle proceed as follows.

20 Carefully lift the crossmember with the jack, then refit the securing bolts and tighten to the specified torque.

21 Withdraw the jack, then lower the engine and remove the lifting tackle.

22 Where applicable, refit the brake lines to the crossmember, with reference to Chapter 10 if necessary.

23 Ensure that the front wheels are pointing straight ahead and that the steering wheel is centred, then reconnect the intermediate shaft to the steering column. Secure the clamp plate with the bolt.

24 Refit the engine mounting bolts and tighten to the specified torque.

25 Refit the starter motor, with reference to Chapter 13 if necessary.

26 Lower the vehicle to the ground.

27 Ensure that the sump drain plug is fitted, then fill the engine with the correct quantity and grade of oil. If necessary, renew the oil filter before filling the engine with oil, as described in Section 3.

28 Reconnect the battery negative lead.

29 Start the engine and check for leaks around the sump, and where applicable the oil filter. When the engine is started, there may be a delay in the extinguishing of the oil pressure warning lamp while the system pressurises.

30 Run the engine for twenty minutes then stop the engine and tighten the sump bolts to the third stage given in the Specifications, starting at point 'A' in Fig. 1.13, and working clockwise.

31 Check the oil level.

32 Dispose of any old engine oil safely. **Do not** pour it down a drain – this is illegal and causes pollution.

31 Oil pump – removal and refitting

1 Remove the sump as described in Section 30.

2 Unscrew the bolt securing the pick-up tube and strainer to the cylinder block (photo).

3 Using a suitable splined socket, unscrew the two securing bolts and withdraw the oil pump and strainer (photo).

4 If desired, the hexagon-shaped driveshaft can be withdrawn, but note which way round it is fitted (photo). The driveshaft engages with the lower end of the distributor driveshaft.

5 Thoroughly clean the mating faces of the oil pump and cylinder block. If desired the pump can be dismantled and inspected as described in Section 32.

6 Commence refitting by inserting the oil pump driveshaft into the cylinder block in its previously noted position.

7 Prime the pump by injecting oil into it and turning it by hand (photo).

8 Fit the pump, insert the securing bolts, and tighten them to the specified torque.

9 Fit the pick-up tube securing bolt and tighten it.

10 Refit the sump as described in Section 30.

32 Oil pump – dismantling, inspection and reassembly

Note: *A new pressure relief valve plug and pick-up tube gasket will be required for reassembly*

1 If oil pump wear is suspected, check the cost and availability of new parts and the cost of a new pump. Examine the pump as described in this Section and then decide whether renewal or repair is the best course of action.

2 Unbolt the pick-up tube and strainer. Recover the gasket.

3 Unscrew the three securing bolts and remove the oil pump cover (photo).

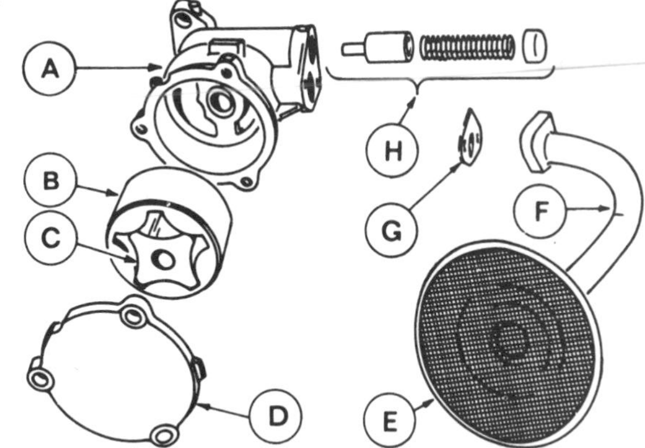

Fig 1.14 Exploded view of the oil pump (Sec 32)

A Body
B Outer rotor
C Inner rotor
D Cover
E Strainer
F Pick-up tube
G Gasket
H Pressure relief valve

30.15A Apply sealing compound ...

30.15B ... then fit the rubber sealing strips

30.16 Locate the sump gasket end tabs beneath the rubber sealing strips

31.2 Unscrewing the oil pick-up tube securing bolt

31.3 Unscrewing an oil pump securing bolt

31.4 Withdrawing the oil pump driveshaft

31.7 Priming the oil pump

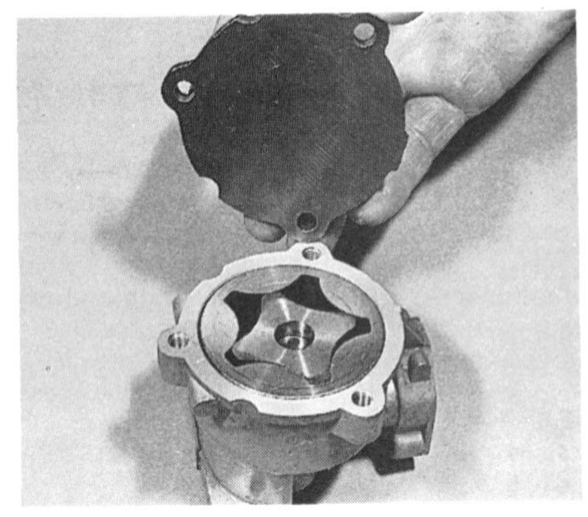

32.3 Removing the oil pump cover

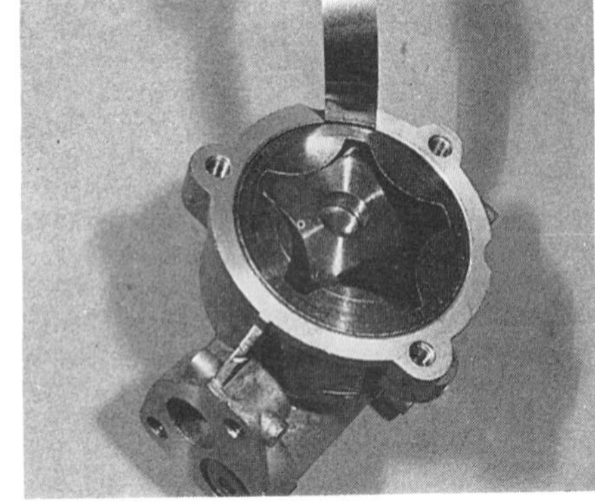

32.10A Checking the oil pump outer rotor-to-body clearance

4 Mark the rotor faces so that the rotors can be refitted in their original positions, then lift the rotors from the pump body.

5 Remove the pressure relief valve plug by piercing it with a punch and levering it out, then withdraw the spring and plunger.

6 Thoroughly clean all parts in petrol or paraffin and wipe dry using a non-fluffy rag.

7 Commence reassembly by lubricating the relief valve plunger. Fit the plunger and spring.

8 Fit a new relief valve plug, flat side outwards and seat it with a drift until it is flush with the pick-up mating face.

9 Lubricate the rotors and fit them, observing the marks made when dismantling, if applicable.

10 The necessary clearances may now be checked using a machined straight edge (a good steel rule) and a set of feeler gauges. The critical clearances are between the lobes of the centre rotor and convex faces of the outer rotor; between the outer and pump body; and between both rotors and the end cover plate (endfloat). The desired clearances are given in the Specifications (photos).

11 Endfloat can be measured by placing a straight edge across the pump body and measuring the clearance between the two rotors and the straight edge using feeler gauges (photo).

12 New rotors are only available as a pair. If the rotor-to-body clearance is excessive, a complete new pump should be fitted.

13 Refit the pump cover and tighten the securing bolts.

14 Fit the pick-up tube and strainer, using a new gasket.

15 Temporarily insert the driveshaft into the pump and make sure that the rotors turn freely.

16 Prime the pump before refitting, as described in Section 31.

33 Pistons and connecting rods – removal and refitting

1 Remove the sump as described in Section 30, and the cylinder head as described in Section 21 or 22 as applicable.

2 Check the big-end bearing caps for identification marks and if necessary use a centre-punch to identify the caps and corresponding connecting rods (photo).

3 Turn the crankshaft so that No 1 crankpin is at its lowest point, then unscrew the nuts and tap off the bearing cap. Keep the bearing shells in the cap and connecting rod.

32.10B Checking the oil pump inner-to-outer rotor clearance

32.11 Checking the oil pump rotor endfloat

33.2 Big-end cap and connecting rod identification numbers

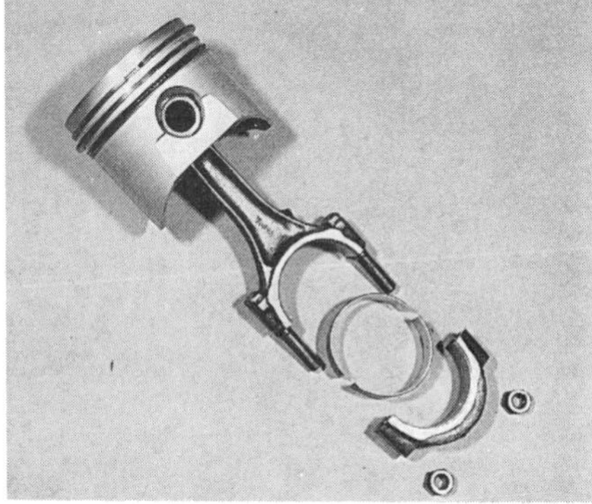
33.4 Piston, connecting rod and big-end bearing components

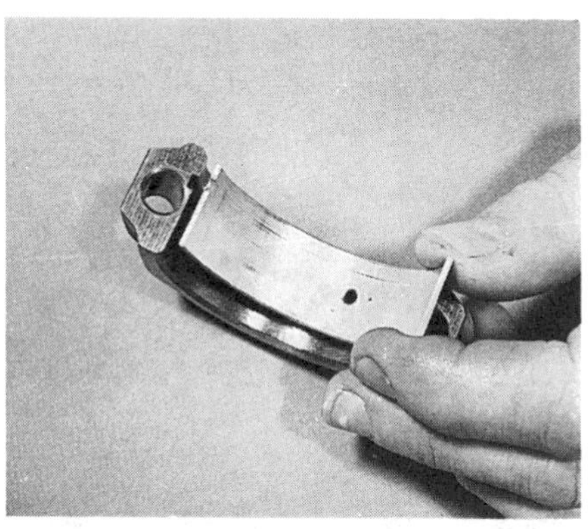
33.9A Fitting a bearing shell to a big-end bearing cap

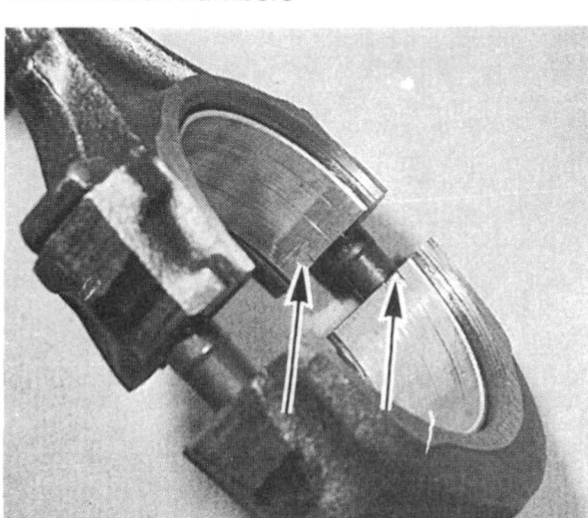
33.9B The bearing shell lugs (arrowed) must be adjacent to each other

33.10 Lubricating a cylinder bore

33.11A Fitting a piston ring compressor

33.11B Arrow on piston crown must face front of engine

4 Using the handle of a hammer, push the piston and connecting rod up the bore and withdraw from the top of the cylinder block. Loosely refit the cap to the connecting rod (photo).

5 Repeat the procedure in paragraphs 3 and 4 on No 4 piston and connecting rod, then turn the crankshaft through half a turn and repeat the procedure on Nos 2 and 3 pistons and connecting rods.

6 The pistons and connecting rods, and the big-end bearings can be examined and if necessary renovated as described in Sections 34 and 36 respectively.

7 Commence refitting as follows.

8 Clean the backs of the bearing shells and the recesses in the connecting rods and big-end caps.

9 Press the bearing shells into the connecting rods and caps in their correct positions and oil them liberally. Note that the lugs in corresponding shells must be adjacent to each other (photos).

10 Lubricate the cylinder bores with clean engine oil (photo).

11 Fit a piston ring compressor to No 1 piston, then insert the piston and connecting rod into No 1 cylinder. With No 1 crankpin at its lowest point, drive the piston carefully into the cylinder with the wooden handle of a hammer, and at the same time guide the connecting rod onto the crankpin. Make sure that the arrow on the piston crown is facing the front of the engine (photos).

12 Oil the crankpin, then fit the big-end bearing cap in its previously noted position, and tighten the nuts to the specified torque (photos).

13 Check that the crankshaft turns freely.

14 Repeat the procedure given in paragraphs 11 to 13 inclusive on the remaining pistons.

15 Refit the cylinder head as described in Section 21 or 22 as applicable and the sump as described in Section 30.

34 Pistons and connecting rods – examination and renovation

1 Examine the pistons for ovality, scoring, and scratches. Check the connecting rods for wear and damage. The connecting rods carry a letter indicating their weight class; all the rods fitted to one engine must be of the same class.

2 The gudgeon pins are an interference fit in the connecting rods, and if new pistons are to be fitted to the existing connecting rods, the work

33.12A Lubricating a crankpin

33.12B Tightening a big-end bearing cap nut

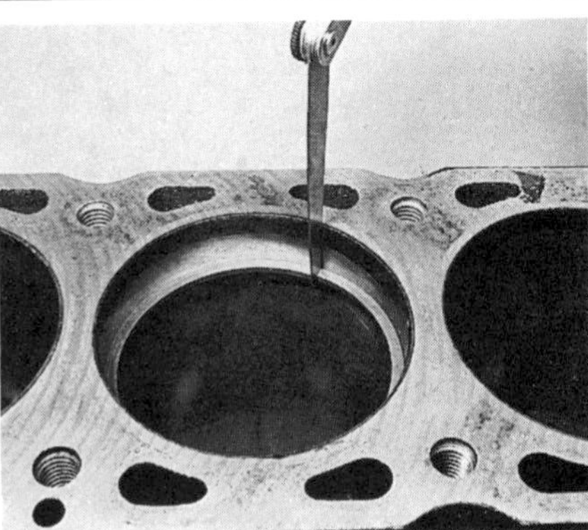
34.4A Checking a piston ring gap at the top of the cylinder bore ...

34.4B ... and the bottom of the cylinder bore

35.5 Main bearing cap identification marks. The arrow points to the front of the engine

35.6 Checking crankshaft endfloat

should be carried out by a Ford dealer who will have the necessary tooling. Note that the oil splash hole in the connecting rod must be located on the right-hand side of the piston (the arrow on the piston crown faces forwards).

3 If new rings are to be fitted to the existing pistons, expand the old rings over the top of the pistons. The use of two or three old feeler gauges will be helpful in preventing the rings dropping into empty grooves. Note that the oil control ring is in three sections.

4 Before fitting the new rings to the pistons, insert them into the cylinder bore and use a feeler gauge to check that the end gaps are within the specified limits (photos).

5 Clean out the piston ring groove using a piece of old piston ring as a scraper. Be careful not to scratch the aluminium surface of the pistons. Protect your fingers – piston ring edges are sharp. Also probe the groove oil return holes.

6 Fit the oil control ring sections with the spreader ends abutted opposite the front of the piston. The side ring gaps should be 25 mm (1.0 in) either side of the spreader gap. Fit the tapered lower compression ring with the 'TOP' mark towards the top of the piston and the gap 150° from the spreader gap, then fit the upper compression ring with the gap 150° on the other side of the spreader gap. Note that the compression rings are coated with a molybdenum skin which must not be damaged. Note also that the compression rings are made of cast iron, and will snap if expanded too far.

35 Crankshaft and main bearings – removal and refitting

1 With the engine removed from the vehicle, remove the timing belt, crankshaft sprocket and auxiliary shaft sprocket as described in Section 20, and the flywheel/driveplate as described in Section 27.

2 Remove the pistons and connecting rods as described in Section 33. If no work is to be done on the pistons and connecting rods, there is no need to push the pistons out of the cylinder bores.

3 Unbolt the crankshaft front oil seal housing and the auxiliary shaft front cover and remove the gasket.

4 Remove the oil pump and pick-up tube as described in Section 31.

5 Check the main bearing caps for identification marks and if necessary use a centre-punch to identify them (photo).

6 Before removing the crankshaft, check that the endfloat is within the specified limits by inserting a feeler blade between the centre crankshaft web and the thrustwashers (photo). This will indicate whether or not new thrustwashers are required.

7 Unscrew the bolts and tap off the main bearing caps complete with bearing shells (photos). If the thrustwashers are to be re-used identify them for location. Recover the sealing wedges from either side of the rear bearing cap.

8 Lift the crankshaft from the crankcase and remove the rear oil seal. Recover the remaining thrustwashers (photos).

9 Extract the bearing shells, keeping them identified for location (photo).

10 The crankshaft and bearings can be examined and if necessary renovated as described in Section 36.

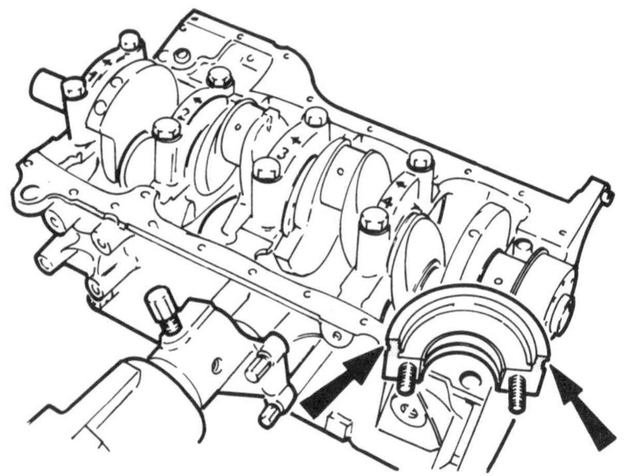
Fig 1.15 Coat the arrowed areas of the rear main bearing cap with sealant (Sec 35)

35.7A Removing the centre main bearing cap ...

35.7B ... and the rear main bearing cap

35.8A Lifting the crankshaft from the crankcase

35.8B Removing a thrustwasher from the centre main bearing

35.9 Centre main bearing shell

35.20 Lubricating a main bearing shell

11 Commence refitting as follows.
12 Wipe the bearing shell locations in the crankcase with a soft, non-fluffy rag.
13 Wipe the crankshaft journals with a soft, non-fluffy rag.
14 If the old main bearing shells are to be renewed (not to do so is a false economy, unless they are virtually new) fit the five upper halves of the main bearing shells to their location in the crankcase.
15 Identify each main bearing cap and place in order. The number is cast on to the cap and on intermediate caps an arrow is also marked which should point towards the front of the engine.
16 Wipe each cap bearing shell location with a soft non-fluffy rag.
17 Fit the bearing half shell onto each main bearing cap.
18 Apply a little grease to each side of the centre main bearing so as to retain the thrustwashers.
19 Fit the upper halves of the thrustwashers into their grooves either side of the main bearing. The slots must face outwards.
20 Lubricate the crankshaft journals and the upper and lower main bearing shells with clean engine oil (photo) and locate the rear oil seal (with lip lubricated) on the rear of the crankshaft.
21 Carefully lower the crankshaft into the crankcase.
22 Lubricate the crankshaft main bearing journals again, and then fit No 1 bearing cap. Fit the two securing bolts but do not tighten yet.
23 Make sure that the mating faces are clean, then apply sealant (Loctite 518 or equivalent) to the areas on the rear main bearing cap shown in Fig. 1.15.
24 Fit the rear main bearing cap. Fit the two securing bolts but as before do not tighten yet.
25 Apply a little grease to either side of the centre main bearing cap so as to retain the thrustwashers. Fit the thrustwashers with the tag located in the groove and the slots facing outwards (photo).
26 Fit the centre main bearing cap and the two securing bolts, then refit the intermediate main bearing caps. Make sure that the arrows point towards the front of the engine.
27 Lightly tighten all main bearing cap securing bolts and then fully tighten in a progressive manner to the specified torque wrench setting.
28 Check that the crankshaft rotates freely. Some stiffness is to be expected with new components, but there must be no tight spots or binding.
29 Check that the crankshaft endfloat is within the specified limits by inserting a feeler gauge between the centre crankshaft web and the thrustwashers.
30 Make sure that the rear oil seal is fully located onto its seating. Coat the rear main bearing cap sealing wedges with sealing compound, then press them into position using a blunt screwdriver with the rounded red face towards the cap (photo).
31 Refit the oil pump and pick-up tube as described in Section 31.
32 Refit the crankshaft front oil seal housing and the auxiliary shaft front cover using a new gasket, and tighten the securing bolts. Smear the lip of the oil seal with clean engine oil before fitting; and using a straight edge, ensure that the bottom face of the oil seal housing is aligned with the bottom face of the cylinder block before finally tightening the bolts.
33 Refit the pistons and connecting rods as described in Section 33.
34 Refit the flywheel/driveplate as described in Section 27, and the auxiliary shaft sprocket, crankshaft sprocket, and timing belt as described in Section 20.

36 Crankshaft and bearings – examination and renovation

1 Examine the bearing surfaces of the crankshaft for scratches or scoring and, using a micrometer, check each journal and crankpin for ovality. Where this is found to be in excess of 0.0254 mm (0.001 in) the crankshaft will have to be reground and undersize bearings fitted.
2 Crankshaft regrinding should be carried out by a suitable engineering works, who will normally supply the matching undersize main and big-end shell bearings.
3 Note that undersize bearings may already have been fitted, either in production or by a previous repairer. Check the markings on the backs of the old bearing shells, and if in doubt take them along when buying new

ones. Production undersizes are also indicated by paint marks as follows:

White line on main bearing cap – parent bore 0.40 mm oversize
Green line on crankshaft front counterweight – main bearing journals 0.25 mm undersize
Green spot on counterweight – big-end bearing journals 0.25 mm undersize

4 If the crankshaft endfloat is more than the maximum specified amount, new thrustwashers should be fitted to the centre main bearings. These are usually supplied together with the main and big-end bearings on a reground crankshaft.
5 An accurate method of determining bearing wear is by the use of Plastigage. The crankshaft is located in the main bearings (and big-end bearings if necessary) and the Plastigage filament located across the journal which must be dry. The cap is then fitted and the bolts/nuts tightened to the specified torque. On removal of the cap the width of the filaments is checked against a scale which shows the bearing running clearance. This clearance is then compared with that given in the Specifications (photos).
6 If the spigot bearing in the rear of the crankshaft requires renewal, extract it with a suitable puller. Alternatively fill it with heavy grease and use a close fitting metal dowel driven into the centre of the bearing. Drive the new bearing into the crankshaft with a soft metal drift.

37 Cylinder block and bores – examination and renovation

1 The cylinder bores must be examined for taper, ovality, scoring and scratches. Start by examining the top of the bores; if these are worn, a slight ridge will be found which marks the top of the piston ring travel. If the wear is excessive, the engine will have had a high oil consumption rate accompanied by blue smoke from the exhaust.
2 If available, use an inside dial gauge to measure the bore diameter just below the ridge and compare it with the diameter at the bottom of the bore, which is not subject to wear. If the difference is more than 0.152 mm (0.006 in), the cylinders will normally require reboring with new oversize pistons fitted.
3 Proprietary oil control rings can be obtained for fitting to the existing pistons if it is felt that the degree of wear does not justify a rebore. However, any improvement brought about by such rings may be short-lived.
4 If new pistons or piston rings are to be fitted to old bores, deglaze the bores with abrasive paper or a 'glaze buster' tool. The object is to produce a light cross-hatch pattern to assist the new rings to bed in.
5 If there is a ridge at the top of the bore and new piston rings are being fitted, either the top piston ring must be stepped ('ridge dodger' pattern) or the ridge must be removed with a ridge reamer. If the ridge is left, the piston ring may hit it and break.
6 Thoroughly examine the crankcase and cylinder block for cracks and damage and use a piece of wire to probe all oilways and waterways to ensure they are unobstructed.

38 Examination and renovation – general

1 With the engine completely stripped, clean all the components and examine them for wear. Each part should be checked, and where necessary renewed or renovated as described in the relevant Sections. Renew main and big end shell bearings as a matter of course, unless it is known that they have had little wear and are in perfect condition.
2 If in doubt as to whether to renew a component which is still just serviceable, consider the time and effort which will be incurred should it fail at an early date. Obviously the age and expected lift of the vehicle must influence the standards applied.
3 Gaskets, oil seals and O-rings must all be renewed as a matter of routine. Flywheel and Torx type cylinder head bolts must be renewed because of the high stresses to which they are subjected.
4 Take the opportunity to renew the engine core plugs while they are easily accessible. Knock out the old plugs with a hammer and chisel or punch. Clean the plug seats, smear the new plugs with sealant and tap them squarely into position.

39 Engine reassembly – general

1 To ensure maximum life with minimum trouble from a rebuilt engine, not only must everything be correctly assembled, but it must also be spotlessly clean. All oilways must be clear, and locking washers and spring washers must be fitted where indicated. Oil all bearings and other working surfaces thoroughly with clean engine oil during assembly.
2 Before assembly begins, renew any bolts or studs with damaged threads.
3 Gather together a torque wrench, oil can, clean rag, and a set of engine gaskets and oil seals, together with a new oil filter.
4 If they have been removed, new Torx type cylinder head bolts and new flywheel bolts will be required.
5 After reassembling the main engine components, refer to Section 19 and refit the ancillary components listed, referring to the Chapters indicated where necessary. Delicate items such as the alternator and distributor may be left until after the engine has been refitted if preferred.
6 If the crankcase ventilation oil separator was removed, apply a liquid sealing agent to its tube before pressing it into the cylinder block.

40 Initial start-up after overhaul or major repair

1 Make a final check to ensure that everything has been reconnected to the engine and that no rags or tools have been left in the engine bay.
2 Check that oil and coolant levels are correct.
3 Start the engine. This may take a little longer than usual as fuel is pumped up to the engine.
4 Check that the oil pressure light goes out when the engine starts.
5 Run the engine at a fast tickover and check for leaks of oil, fuel or coolant. Also check power steering and transmission fluid cooler

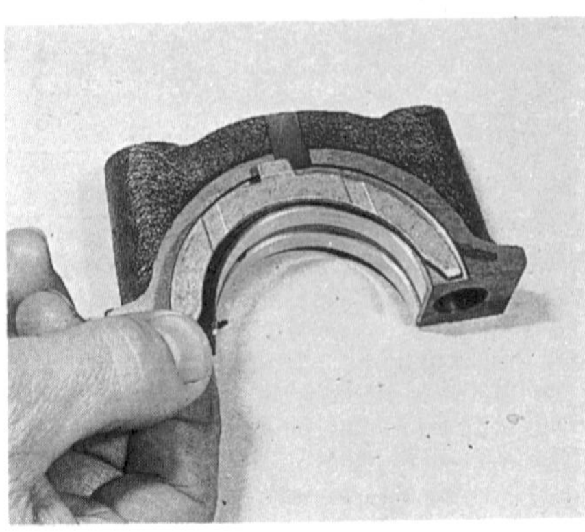

35.25 Fitting a thrustwasher to the centre main bearing cap

35.30 Fitting a sealing wedge to the rear main bearing cap

36.5A Flattened Plastigage filament (arrowed)

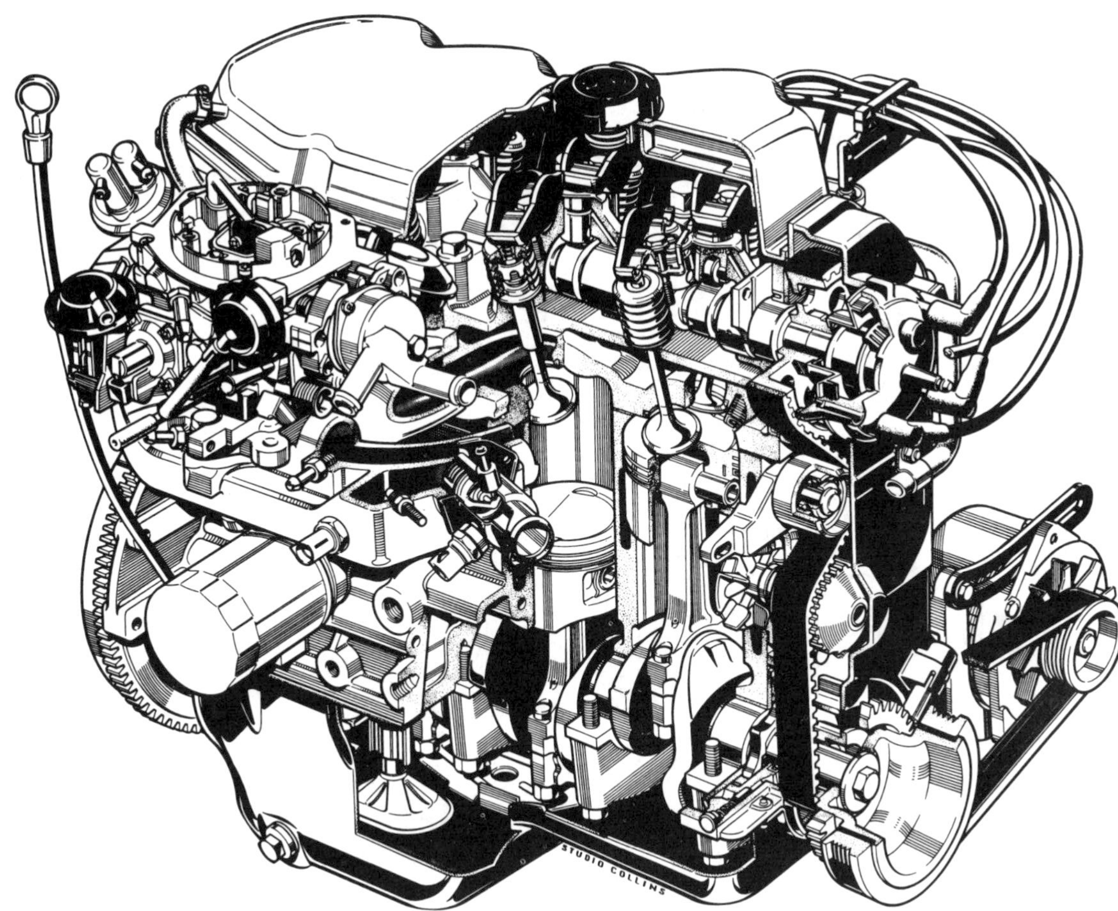

Fig 1.16 Cutaway view of CVH engine (Sec 41)

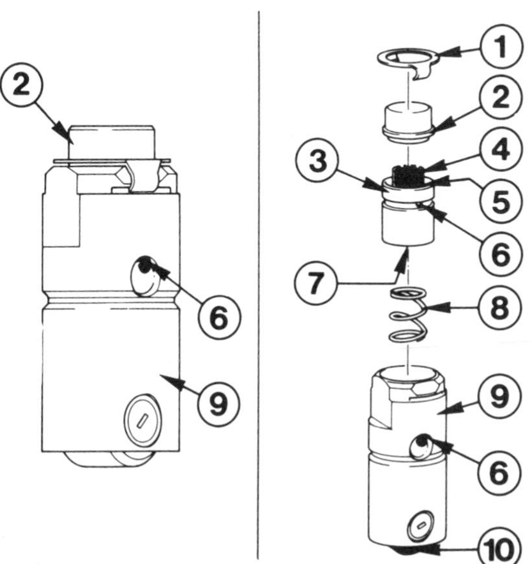

Fig 1.17 Hydraulic cam follower components (Sec 41)

1 Circlip
2 Plunger cap
3 Plunger
4 Stand pipe
5 Oil held back when engine is stopped
6 Oil feed from engine lubrication circuit
7 Non-return valve location
8 Plunger spring
9 Housing with pressure chamber
10 Roller

unions, where applicable. Some smoke and odd smells may be experienced as assembly lubricant burns off the exhaust manifold and other components.

6 Bring the engine to normal operating temperature, then check the ignition timing as described in Chapter 4, and the idle speed (where applicable) and mixture as described in Chapter 3.

7 If splined type cylinder head bolts have been used, stop the engine after it has been running for 15 minutes, then remove the crankshaft cover and tighten the cylinder head bolts to the fourth stage given in the Specifications, in the order shown in Fig. 1.12.

8 When the engine has completely cooled, re-check the oil and coolant levels, and check, and if necessary adjust, the valve clearances as described in Section 4.

9 If new bearings, pistons etc have been fitted, the engine should be run-in at reduced speeds and loads for the first 500 miles (800 km) or so. It is beneficial to change the engine oil and filter after this mileage.

PART B: CVH ENGINE

41 General description

The CVH (Compound Valve angle, Hemispherical combustion chambers) engine is of four-cylinder, in-line overhead camshaft type, mounted at the front of the vehicle. The engine is only available in 1.8 litre form, and was introduced to replace the 1.8 OHC engine previously used in the Sierra range.

The crankshaft incorporates five main bearings. The centre main bearing has a flanged bearing shell (thrust bearing) fitted to the cylinder block to control crankshaft endfloat

The camshaft is driven by a toothed belt and operates the compound angled valves via roller type hydraulic cam followers, which eliminates the need for valve clearance adjustment. The cam followers operate in the following way. When the valve is closed, pressurised

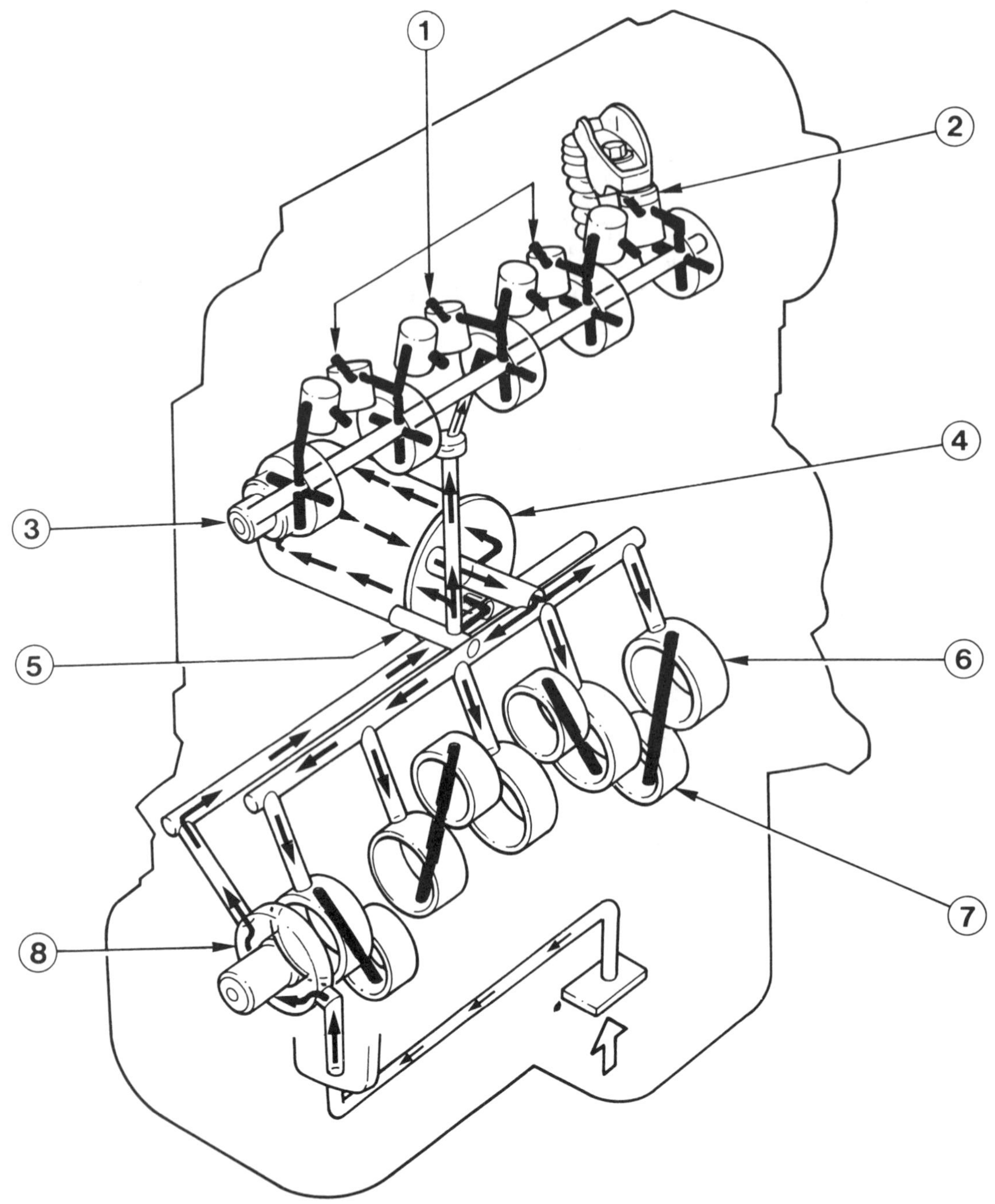

Fig 1.18 Engine lubrication circuit (Sec 41)

1 Oil feed to rocker arms
2 Hydraulic cam followers
3 Camshaft
4 Oil filter
5 Oil feed to oil pressure warning lamp switch
6 Crankshaft main bearings
7 Big-end bearings
8 Oil pump

engine oil passes through ports in the body of the cam follower and the plunger into the cylinder feed chamber. From this chamber, oil flows through a ball type non-return valve into the pressure chamber. The tension of the coil spring causes the plunger to press the rocker arm against the valve and to eliminate any free play.

As the cam lifts the cam follower, the oil pressure in the pressure chamber increases and causes the non-return valve to close the port to the feed chamber. As oil cannot be compressed, it forms a rigid link between the body of the cam follower, the cylinder and the plunger which then rise as one component to open the valve.

The clearance between the body of the cam follower and the cylinder is accurately designed to meter a specific quantity of oil as it escapes from the pressure chamber. Oil will only pass along the cylinder bore when pressure is high during the moment of valve opening. Once the valve has closed, the escape of oil will produce a small amount of free play and no pressure will exist in the pressure chamber. Oil from the feed chamber can then flow through the non-return valve into the pressure chamber so that the cam follower cylinder can be raised by the pressure of the coil spring, thus eliminating any play in the arrangement until the valve is operated again.

As wear occurs between rocker arm and valve stem, the quantity of oil which flows into the pressure chamber will be slightly more than the quantity lost during the expansion cycle of the cam follower. Conversely, when the cam follower is compressed by the expansion of the valve, a slightly smaller quantity of oil will flow into the pressure chamber than was lost.

To reduce valve clatter when the engine is started, a small plastic stand pipe retains oil inside the plunger. When the engine is started, the

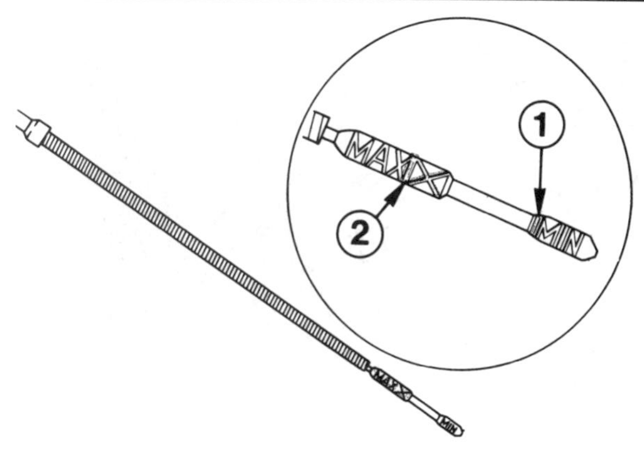

Fig 1.19 Oil level dipstick markings (Sec 42)

1 MIN *2 MAX*

reservoir in the plunger (and via the non-return valve, the pressure chamber) are immediately filled with oil. This reduces the noise often associated with hydraulic cam followers as they pressurise with oil after engine start-up.

The cam follower rollers run in needle bearings, which greatly reduces friction as the rollers follow the cam profile.

The distributor and fuel pump are driven directly from the camshaft, and the oil pump is driven directly from the front of the crankshaft.

The cylinder head is of crossflow design, with the inlet manifold mounted on the right-hand side and the exhaust manifold mounted on the left-hand side.

Lubrication is by means of a bi-rotor pump which draws oil through a strainer located inside the sump, and forces it through a full-flow filter into the oil galleries where it is distributed to the crankshaft and camshaft. The big-end bearings are supplied with oil via internal drillings in the crankshaft. The undersides of the pistons are supplied with oil from drillings in the big-ends. The hydraulic cam followers are supplied with oil from the camshaft bearings via short passages in the cylinder head.

A semi-closed crankcase ventilation system is employed whereby piston blow-by gases are drawn from the crankcase, through the

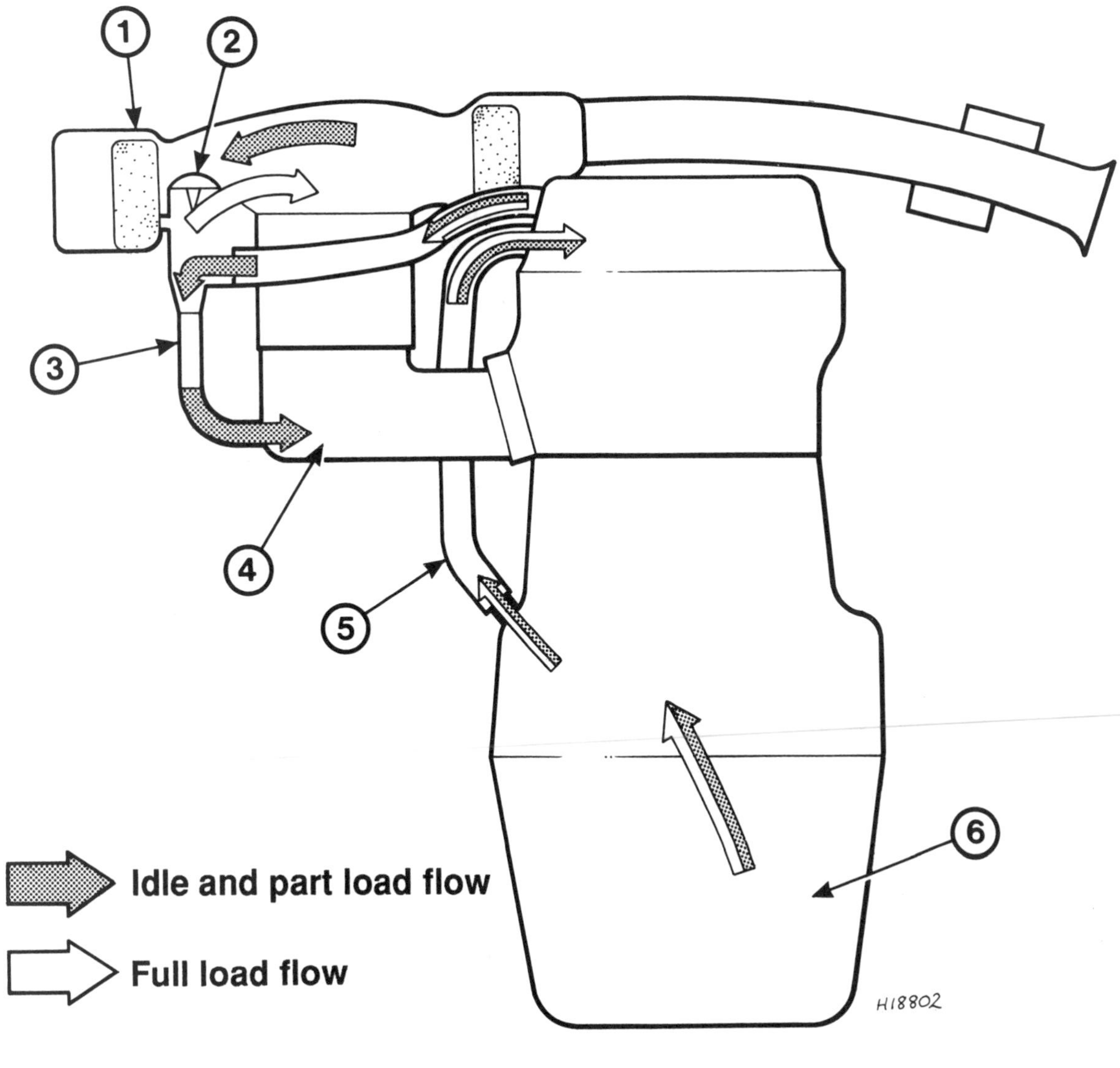

Idle and part load flow

Full load flow

H18802

Fig 1.20 Crankcase ventilation system (Sec 44)

1 Air cleaner
2 Mushroom valve
3 Orifice
4 Inlet manifold
5 Ventilation hose
6 Crankcase

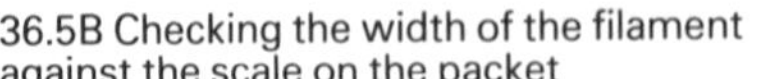
36.5B Checking the width of the filament against the scale on the packet

42.2 Topping-up the engine oil

44.5 Loosening the crankcase ventilation hose clip

camshaft cover via an external vent hose, out to an oil separator built into the base of the air cleaner.

42 Maintenance and inspection

1 At the intervals specified in the *Routine maintenance* Section at the beginning of this manual, carry out the following tasks.
2 Check the engine oil level as follows. With the vehicle parked on level ground, and with the engine having been stopped for a few minutes, withdraw the oil level dipstick, wipe it on a clean rag, and re-insert it fully. Withdraw the dipstick again and read off the oil level relative to the 'MAX' and 'MIN' marks. The oil level should be between the marks. If the level is at or below the 'MIN' mark, top up through the filler on the camshaft cover without delay (photo). The quantity of oil required to raise the level from 'MIN' to 'MAX' on the dipstick is approximately 0.75 litre (1.32 pints). Do not overfill.
3 Renew the engine oil and filter as described in Section 3 in Part A of this Chapter.
4 Inspect the oil filler cap for signs of damage or deterioration. Renew if necessary.
5 Inspect the engine for evidence of oil, coolant or fuel leaks and rectify as necessary.
6 Inspect the crankcase ventilation hose for blockage or damage. Clean or renew as necessary.
7 Inspect the oil separator and mushroom valve in the air cleaner for blockage, and clean if necessary.
8 Renew the timing belt as described in Section 59.

43 Engine oil and filter – renewal

Refer to Section 3 in Part A of this Chapter.

44 Crankcase ventilation system – description and maintenance

1 The crankcase ventilation system consists of a ventilation hose running from the crankcase to the camshaft cover, and an oil separator and mushroom valve built into the air cleaner.
2 Under all engine conditions, the piston blow-by gases flow from the crankcase up the external ventilation hose, through the camshaft cover to the oil separator in the air cleaner.
3 Under idle and part-load conditions, the flow from the oil separator is into the inlet manifold through an orifice. This flow is supplemented by clean air from the air cleaner.
4 Under full-load conditions, the mushroom valve at the top of the oil separator lifts, and the blow-by gases are fed into the engine via the carburettor.
5 Regularly inspect the hose for blockage or damage; clean or renew as necessary (photo). A blocked hose can cause a build-up of crankcase pressure, which in turn can cause oil leaks.
6 At the same time, check that the oil separator and mushroom valve are not blocked, and clean if necessary.

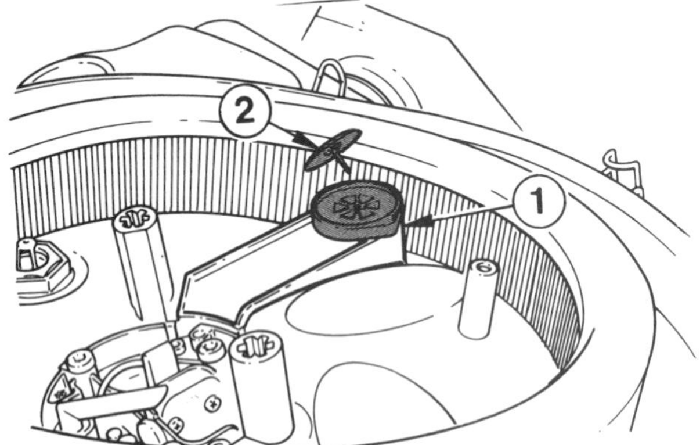

Fig 1.21 Oil separator (1) and mushroom valve (2) locations in air cleaner (Sec 44)

45 Compression test – description and interpretation

Refer to Section 6 in Part A of this Chapter.

46 Major operations possible with the engine in the vehicle

The following operations can be carried out without removing the engine from the vehicle:

(a) *Removal and servicing of the cylinder head*
(b) *Removal of the camshaft after removal of the cylinder head*
(c) *Removal of the timing belt and sprockets*
(d) *Removal of the engine mountings*
(e) *Removal of the clutch and flywheel*
(f) *Removal of the crankshaft front and rear oil seals*

47 Major operations requiring engine removal

The following operations can only be carried out after removing the engine from the vehicle:

(a) *Removal of the sump*
(b) *Removal of the oil pump*
(c) *Removal of the pistons and connecting rods*
(d) *Removal of the big-end bearings*
(e) *Removal of the crankshaft main bearings*
(f) *Removal of the crankshaft*

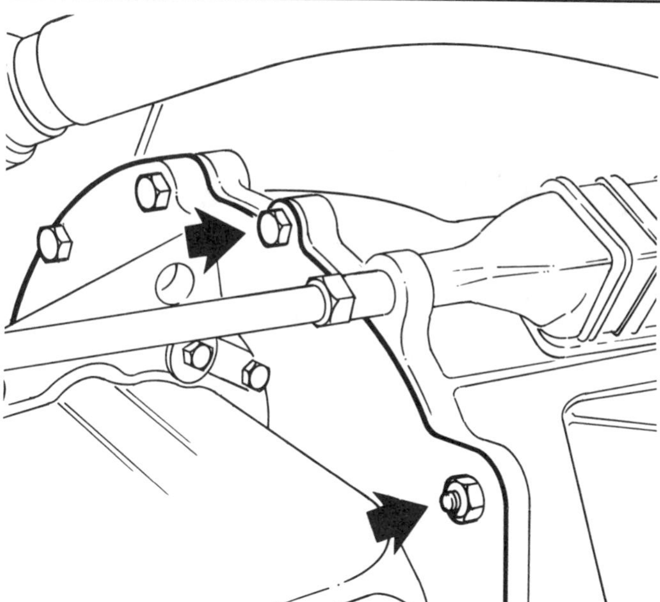

Fig 1.22 Remove the two bolts (arrowed) from the engine adapter plate (Sec 49)

48 Method of engine removal

Refer to Section 9 in Part A of this Chapter.

49 Engine – removal leaving manual gearbox in vehicle

Note: *A suitable hoist and lifting tackle will be required for this operation*

1 Disconnect the battery negative lead.
2 Remove the bonnet as described in Chapter 12.
3 Remove the air cleaner as described in Chapter 3.
4 Disconnect the cooling fan wiring plug, then unscrew the retaining nuts and washers and withdraw the fan shroud and cooling fan assembly.
5 Drain the cooling system as described in Chapter 2.
6 Disconnect the coolant hoses from the coolant pump elbow, and detach the heater hose from the clip on the front of the timing cover.
7 Disconnect the upper radiator hose and the expansion tank hose from the thermostat housing (photo).
8 Disconnect the heater hose from the automatic choke.
9 Disconnect the brake servo vacuum hose from the inlet manifold (photo).
10 Disconnect the throttle damper solenoid vacuum pipes from the throttle damper and the carburettor 'T'-piece connector.
11 Disconnect the engine management module vacuum pipe from the inlet manifold.
12 Disconnect the fuel hoses from the carburettor and fuel pump, and plug the ends of the hoses to minimise petrol spillage. Take adequate fire precautions.
13 Disconnect the throttle cable as described in Chapter 3.
14 Disconnect the HT leads from the coil and spark plugs, unclip the leads from the camshaft cover, and remove the distributor cap, rotor arm and housing, with reference to Chapter 4.
15 Disconnect the wiring from the following components:

Alternator
Starter motor
Oil pressure warning lamp switch
Temperature gauge sender
Engine coolant temperature sensor
Automatic choke
Cooling fan switch
Crankshaft speed/position sensor
Engine earth strap to battery tray (photo)

16 Unscrew and remove the top engine-to-gearbox bolts which are accessible from the engine compartment.
17 Apply the handbrake, jack up the front of the vehicle and support on axle stands.
18 Drain the engine oil into a suitable container.
19 Remove the starter motor as described in Chapter 13.
20 Remove the exhaust downpipe as described in Chapter 3.
21 Unscrew the two nuts securing the engine mountings to the crossmember. Recover the washers.
22 Unscrew and remove the remaining engine-to-gearbox bolts, noting the location of the earth strap (photo), and remove the two bolts from the engine adaptor plate – see Fig. 1.22.
23 Working inside the vehicle, place a wooden block under the clutch pedal to raise it fully against its stop which will hold the automatic adjuster pawl clear of the toothed quadrant.
24 Disconnect the clutch cable from the release arm, and pass the cable through the bellhousing, with reference to Chapter 5 if necessary. Remove the clip securing the clutch cable to the right-hand engine mounting bracket. Note the cable routing for use when refitting.
25 Lower the vehicle to the ground, and support the gearbox with a trolley jack using a block of wood between the jack and the gearbox to spread the load.
26 Make a final check to ensure that all relevant wires, pipes and hoses have been disconnected to facilitate engine removal.
27 Attach a suitable hoist to the engine lifting brackets located at the front and rear of the cylinder head, and carefully take the weight of the engine. The engine should be supported horizontally, ie do not allow it to tilt front to rear.
28 Raise the engine until the engine mounting studs are clear of the crossmember, then pull the engine forwards to disconnect it from the gearbox. Ensure that the gearbox is adequately supported, and take care not to strain the gearbox input shaft. It may be necessary to rock the engine a little to release it from the gearbox.
29 Once clear of the gearbox, lift the engine from the vehicle, taking care not to damage the radiator fins (photo).

50 Engine – removal leaving automatic transmission in vehicle

Note: *A suitable hoist and lifting tackle will be required for this operation*

1 Proceed as described in Section 49, paragraphs 1 to 15 inclusive, but additionally, where applicable disconnect the kickdown cable from the carburettor, with reference to Chapter 7 if necessary.
2 Unscrew and remove the top engine-to-transmission bolts which are accessible from the engine compartment. Note the location of the vacuum pipe bracket and transmission dipstick tube bracket.
3 Proceed as described in Section 49, paragraphs 17 to 21 inclusive.
4 Working through the starter motor aperture, unscrew the four torque converter-to-driveplate nuts. It will be necessary to turn the crankshaft using a suitable spanner on the crankshaft pulley bolt in order to gain access to each nut in turn through the aperture.
5 Unscrew and remove the remaining engine-to-transmission bolts, noting the location of the earth strap, and remove the two bolts from the engine adaptor plate. Where applicable pull the blanking plug from the adaptor plate.
6 Lower the vehicle to the ground and support the transmission with a trolley jack, using a block of wood between the jack and the transmission to spread the load.
7 Make a final check to ensure that all relevant wires, pipes and hoses have been disconnected to facilitate engine removal.
8 Attach a suitable hoist to the engine lifting brackets located at the front and rear of the cylinder head, and carefully take the weight of the engine. The engine should be supported horizontally, ie do not allow it to tilt front to rear.
9 Raise the engine until the engine mounting studs are clear of the crossmember, then pull the engine forwards to disconnect it from the transmission. Ensure that the torque converter is held firmly in place in the transmission housing, otherwise it could fall out resulting in fluid spillage and possible damage. It may be necessary to rock the engine a little to release it from the transmission.
10 Once clear of the transmission, lift the engine from the vehicle, taking care not to damage the radiator fins.

49.7 Disconnect the upper radiator hose (1) and the expansion tank hose (2) from the thermostat housing

49.9 Disconnecting the brake servo vacuum hose from the inlet manifold

49.15 Engine earth strap securing screw (arrowed) on battery tray

49.22 Earth strap location under engine-to-gearbox bolt

49.29 Lifting the engine from the vehicle

51 Engine/manual gearbox assembly – removal and separation

Note: *A suitable hoist and lifting tackle will be required for this operation*

1 Proceed as described in Section 49, paragraphs 1 to 15 inclusive.

2 Working inside the vehicle, unscrew the gear lever knob and remove the centre console as described in Chapter 12. Where a full-length console is fitted, it is only necessary to remove the front tray.

3 Detach the outer gaiter from the retaining frame and withdraw it over the gear lever.

4 Release the clips and remove the gaiter retaining frame and inner gaiter.

5 Using a suitable Torx key, remove the screws securing the gear lever to the gearbox extension housing, and withdraw the gear lever. Note how the base of the gear lever locates over the selector shaft.

6 Jack up the vehicle and support on axle stands. Ensure that there is sufficient working room beneath the vehicle.

7 To improve access, disconnect the exhaust downpipe from the manifold and remove the exhaust system as described in Chapter 3.

8 Remove the propeller shaft as described in Chapter 8.

9 Where applicable bend back the locktabs, then unscrew the two bolts securing each of the two anti-roll bar U-clamps to the vehicle underbody. Lower the anti-roll bar as far as possible.

10 Proceed as described in Section 49, paragraphs 23 and 24.

11 Drain the engine oil into a suitable container.

12 Unscrew the two nuts securing the engine mountings to the crossmember. Recover the washers.

13 Disconnect the wiring from the reversing lamp switch.

14 Remove the retaining circlip, and withdraw the speedometer cable from the gearbox extension housing.

15 Support the gearbox with a trolley jack, using a block of wood between the jack and the gearbox to spread the load.

16 Unscrew the four bolts securing the gearbox crossmember to the vehicle underbody. Unscrew the central bolt securing the crossmember to the gearbox and remove the crossmember. Note the position of the earth strap, where applicable. Recover the mounting cup and where applicable the exhaust mounting bracket and heat shield.

17 Make a final check to ensure that all relevant wires, pipes and hoses have been disconnected to facilitate removal of the engine/gearbox assembly.

18 Attach a suitable hoist to the engine lifting brackets located at the front and rear of the cylinder head. Arrange the lifting tackle so that the engine/gearbox assembly will assume a steep angle of approximately 40° to 45° as it is being removed.

19 Raise the engine/gearbox so that the engine mounting studs are clear of the crossmember, then ease the assembly forwards, at the same time lowering the trolley jack which is supporting the gearbox. Lift the assembly from the vehicle, taking care not to damage the surrounding components.

20 With the engine/gearbox assembly removed, temporarily reconnect the anti-roll bar to the underbody if the vehicle is to be moved.

21 To separate the engine from the gearbox, proceed as follows.

22 Remove the starter motor.

23 Support the engine and gearbox horizontally on blocks of wood.

24 Unscrew and remove the engine-to-gearbox bolts, noting the location of the earth strap, and remove the two bolts from the engine adaptor plate – see Fig. 1.22.

25 Pull the engine and gearbox apart, taking care not to strain the gearbox input shaft. It may be necessary to rock the units slightly to separate them.

52 Engine/automatic transmission assembly – removal and separation

Note: *A suitable hoist and lifting tackle will be required for this operation. Any suspected faults in the automatic transmission should be referred to a Ford dealer or automatic transmission specialist before removal of the unit, as the specialist fault diagnosis equipment is designed to operate with the transmission in the vehicle.*

1 Proceed as described in Section 49, paragraphs 1 to 15 inclusive,

but additionally, where applicable disconnect the kickdown cable from the carburettor, with reference to Chapter 7 if necessary.
2 Jack up the vehicle and support on axle stands. Ensure that there is sufficient working room beneath the vehicle.
3 To improve access, disconnect the exhaust downpipe from the manifold and remove the exhaust system as described in Chapter 3.
4 Remove the propeller shaft as described in Chapter 8.
5 Where applicable bend back the locktabs, then unscrew the two bolts securing each of the two anti-roll bar U-clamps to the vehicle underbody. Lower the anti-roll bar as far as possible.
6 Unscrew the unions and disconnect the fluid cooler pipes from the transmission. Plug the open ends of the pipes and the transmission to prevent dirt ingress and fluid leakage. Remove the fluid cooler pipe bracket from the engine mounting bracket and place it to one side.
7 Remove the two clips securing the selector rod, and detach the selector rod from the manual selector lever, and the selector lever on the transmission.
8 Where applicable, disconnect the kickdown cable from the transmission and withdraw the cable from the vehicle.
9 Disconnect the wiring from the starter inhibitor/reversing lamp switch, the lock-up clutch and where applicable the kickdown solenoid.
10 Remove the securing screw, and disconnect the speedometer cable from the transmission extension housing. Plug the opening in the transmission to prevent dirt ingress.
11 Disconnect the vacuum pipe from the vacuum diaphragm unit, and unclip the pipe from its securing bracket on the transmission housing.
12 Drain the engine oil into a suitable container.
13 Unscrew the two nuts securing the engine mountings to the crossmember. Recover the washers.
14 Support the transmission with a trolley jack using a block of wood between the jack and the transmission to spread the load.
15 Unscrew the four bolts securing the transmission crossmember to the vehicle underbody. Note the position of the earth strap, where applicable. Unscrew the central bolt securing the crossmember to the transmission and remove the crossmember. Recover the mounting cup and the exhaust mounting bracket.
16 Make a final check to ensure that all relevant wires, pipes and hoses have been disconnected to facilitate removal of the engine/transmission assembly.
17 Attach a suitable hoist to the engine lifting brackets located at the front and rear of the cylinder head. Arrange the lifting tackle so that the engine/transmission assembly will assume a steep angle of approximately 40° to 45° as it is being removed.
18 Raise the engine/transmission so that the engine mounting studs are clear of the crossmember, then ease the assembly forwards, at the same time lowering the trolley jack which is supporting the transmission. Lift the assembly from the vehicle, taking care not to damage surrounding components.
19 With the engine/transmission assembly removed, temporarily reconnect the anti-roll bar to the underbody if the vehicle is to be moved.
20 To separate the engine from the transmission, proceed as follows.
21 Remove the starter motor.
22 Support the engine and transmission horizontally on blocks of wood.
23 Working through the starter motor aperture, unscrew the four torque converter-to-driveplate nuts. It will be necessary to turn the crankshaft using a suitable spanner on the crankshaft pulley bolt in order to gain access to each nut in turn through the aperture.
24 Unscrew and remove the engine-to-transmission bolts, noting the locations of the earth strap, vacuum pipe bracket, and transmission dipstick tube bracket. Remove the two bolts from the engine adaptor plate, and where applicable pull the blanking plug from the adaptor plate.
25 Pull the engine and transmission apart, ensuring that the torque converter is held firmly in place in the transmission housing, otherwise it could fall out resulting in fluid spillage and possible damage. It may be necessary to rock the units slightly to separate them.

53 Engine – refitting (manual gearbox in vehicle)

1 Reverse the procedure described in Section 49, noting the following points.
2 Before attempting to refit the engine, check that the clutch friction disc is centralised as described in Chapter 5, Section 7. This is necessary to ensure that the gearbox input shaft splines will pass through the splines in the centre of the friction disc.
3 Check that the clutch release arm and bearing are correctly fitted, and lightly grease the input shaft splines.
4 Check that the engine adaptor plate is correctly positioned on its locating dowels.
5 Refit the exhaust downpipe as described in Chapter 3.
6 Reconnect the clutch cable to the release arm with reference to Chapter 5, Section 3, ensuring that it is routed as noted during removal.
7 Fill the engine with the correct grade and quantity of oil.
8 Fill the cooling system as described in Chapter 2.
9 Check and if necessary adjust the tension of the alternator drivebelt as described in Chapter 2.
10 Adjust the throttle cable as described in Chapter 3.

54 Engine – refitting (automatic transmission in vehicle)

1 Reverse the procedure described in Section 50, noting the following points.
2 Check that the engine adaptor plate is correctly positioned on its locating dowels.
3 As the torque converter is only loosely engaged in the transmission, care must be taken to prevent the torque converter from falling out forwards. When the torque converter hub is fully engaged with the fluid pump drivegear in the transmission, distance 'A' in Fig. 7.8 (Chapter 7) must be as specified. Incorrect installation of the torque converter will result in damage to the transmission.
4 As the engine is installed, guide the torque converter studs through the holes in the driveplate. When the engine is positioned flush with the engine adaptor plate and the transmission housing, check that the torque converter is free to move axially a small amount before refitting and tightening the engine-to-transmission bolts.
5 Do not tighten the torque converter-to-driveplate nuts until the lower engine-to-transmission bolts have been fitted and tightened.
6 Refit the exhaust downpipe as described in Chapter 3.
7 Fill the engine with the correct grade and quantity of oil.
8 Fill the cooling system as described in Chapter 2.
9 Check and if necessary adjust the tension of the alternator drivebelt as described in Chapter 2.
10 Adjust the throttle cable as described in Chapter 3.
11 Where applicable, adjust the kickdown cable as described in Chapter 7.

55 Engine/manual gearbox assembly – reconnection and refitting

1 Reverse the procedure described in Section 51, noting the following points.
2 Before attempting to reconnect the engine to the gearbox, check that the clutch friction disc is centralised as described in Chapter 5, Section 7. This is necessary to ensure that the gearbox input shaft splines will pass through the splines in the centre of the friction disc.
3 Check that the clutch release arm and bearing are correctly fitted, and lightly grease the input shaft splines.
4 Check that the engine adaptor plate is correctly positioned on its locating dowels.
5 Refit the propeller shaft as described in Chapter 8.
6 Refit the exhaust system as described in Chapter 3.
7 Reconnect the clutch cable to the release arm with reference to Chapter 5, Section 3, ensuring that it is routed as noted during removal.
8 Fill the engine with the correct grade and quantity of oil.
9 Fill the cooling system as described in Chapter 2.
10 Check and if necessary top up the gearbox oil level as described in Chapter 6.
11 Check and if necessary adjust the tension of the alternator drivebelt as described in Chapter 2.
12 Adjust the throttle cable as described in Chapter 3.

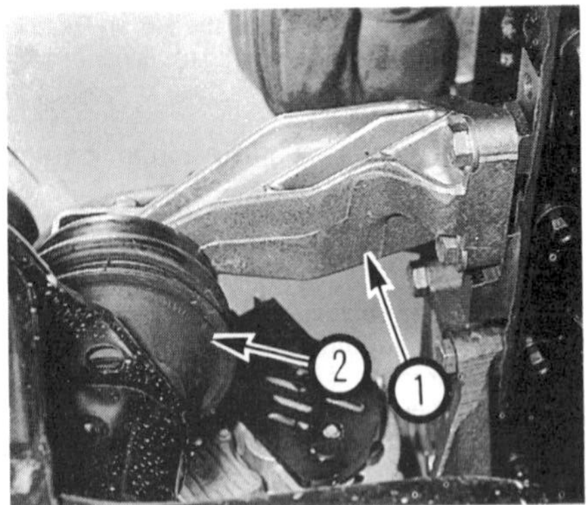

57.1 Engine mounting bracket (1) and mounting (2)

57.6 Locating pin on mounting must engage with hole (arrowed) in engine mounting bracket

58.10 Removing the oil pressure warning lamp switch

56 Engine/automatic transmission assembly - reconnection and refitting

1 Reverse the procedure described in Section 52, noting the following points.
2 Check that the engine adaptor plate is correctly positioned on its locating dowels.
3 As the torque converter is only loosely engaged in the transmission, care must be taken to prevent the torque converter from falling out forwards. When the torque converter hub is fully engaged with the fluid pump drivegear in the transmission, distance 'A' in Fig. 7.8 (Chapter 7) must be as specified. Incorrect installation of the torque converter will result in damage to the transmission.
4 As the engine and transmission are reconnected, guide the torque converter studs through the holes in the driveplate. When the engine is positioned flush with the engine adaptor plate and the transmission housing, check that the torque converter is free to move axially a small amount before refitting and tightening the engine-to-transmission bolts.
5 Do not tighten the torque converter-to-driveplate nuts until the lower engine-to-transmission bolts have been fitted and tightened.
6 Reconnect the selector rod and adjust as described in Chapter 7, Section 7.
7 Refit the propeller shaft as described in Chapter 8.
8 Refit the exhaust system as described in Chapter 3.
9 Fill the engine with the correct grade and quantity of oil.
10 Fill the cooling system as described in Chapter 2.
11 Check and if necessary top up the transmission fluid level as described in Chapter 7.
12 Check and if necessary adjust the tension of the alternator drivebelt as described in Chapter 2.
13 Adjust the throttle cable as described in Chapter 3.
14 Where applicable, adjust the kickdown cable as described in Chapter 7.

57 Engine mountings - renewal

1 The engine mountings incorporate hydraulic dampers and must be renewed if excessive engine movement is evident (photo).
2 Working in the engine compartment, unscrew the central nuts securing the engine mounting brackets to the tops of the mountings. Recover the washers.
3 Apply the handbrake, jack up the front of the vehicle and support on axle stands.
4 Working underneath the vehicle, remove the central nuts securing the mountings to the crossmember. Recover the washers.
5 Raise the engine using a suitable hoist and lifting tackle attached to the engine lifting brackets on the cylinder head, or a jack and interposed block of wood under the sump, until the mountings can be withdrawn.
6 Fit the new mountings, then lower the engine onto them. Note that the locating pins on the mountings must engage with the corresponding holes in the engine mounting brackets (photo).
7 Fit the nuts and washers securing the mountings to the crossmember and tighten the nuts.
8 Lower the vehicle to the ground and fit the nuts and washers securing the engine mounting brackets to the mountings. Tighten the nuts.

58 Engine dismantling - general

1 It is best to mount the engine on a dismantling stand, but if this is not available, stand the engine on a strong bench at a comfortable working height. Failing this, it will have to stripped down on the floor.
2 Cleanliness is most important, and if the engine is dirty, it should be cleaned with paraffin while keeping it in an upright position.
3 Avoid working with the engine directly on a concrete floor, as grit presents a real source of trouble.
4 As parts are removed, clean them in a paraffin bath. However, do not immerse parts with internal oilways in paraffin as it is difficult to remove, usually requiring a high pressure hose. Clean oilways with nylon pipe cleaners.
5 It is advisable to have suitable containers available to hold small items according to their use, as this will help when reassembling the engine and also prevent possible losses.
6 Always obtain a complete set of new gaskets for use during engine reassembly, but retain the old gaskets with a view to using them as a pattern to make a replacement if a new one is not available.
7 Where possible, refit securing nuts, bolts and washers to their locations after removing the relevant components. This will help to protect the threads and will also prevent possible losses.
8 Retain unserviceable components in order to compare them with the new components supplied.
9 A suitable Torx socket will be required to remove the oil pump cover securing screws.
10 Before dismantling the main engine components, the following externally mounted ancillary components can be removed, with reference to the relevant Chapters, where applicable.

Inlet manifold and carburettor - see Chapter 3
Exhaust manifold - see Chapter 3
Fuel pump and operating pushrod - see Chapter 3
Alternator - see Chapter 13
Spark plugs - see Chapter 4
Oil pressure warning lamp switch (photo)
Oil filter - see Section 3 in Part A of this Chapter
Dipstick
Engine mounting brackets
Clutch - see Chapter 5
Alternator mounting bracket
Crankshaft speed/position sensor - see Chapter 4
Engine lifting brackets

59.3 Withdrawing the crankshaft pulley

59.5A Timing cover securing bolt location (arrowed)

59.5B Withdrawing the timing cover

59 Timing belt and sprockets – removal and refitting

Note: *The belt tension should be checked using Ford special tool No 21-113 after refitting. A suitable puller may be required to remove the sprockets. If the camshaft sprocket is removed, a new retaining bolt must be used on refitting, and suitable sealant (Loctite 74 or 274, or Omnifit 30M blue) will be required to coat the bolt threads*

1 If the engine is in the vehicle, carry out the following operations:

- *(a) Disconnect the battery negative lead*
- *(b) Remove the alternator drivebelt – see Chapter 2*
- *(c) Remove the distributor cap, rotor arm and housing – see Chapter 4*
- *(d) Disconnect the wiring plug from the crankshaft speed/position sensor – see Chapter 4*
- *(e) Unclip the coolant hoses from the timing cover, and position them across the top of the camshaft cover out of the way.*
- *(f) If desired for improved access, remove the fan shroud and cooling fan assembly, although this is not essential – see Chapter 2*

2 Slacken the crankshaft pulley bolt. Prevent the crankshaft from turning by engaging top gear (manual gearbox only) and having an assistant apply the brake pedal hard, or by removing the starter motor and jamming the ring gear teeth with a lever.

3 Remove the bolt and washer and withdraw the pulley (photo). If the pulley will not come off easily, refit the bolt part way and use a puller, but take care not to damage the sensor toothed disc.

4 Unscrew the two timing cover securing nuts, and recover the earth tag and the coolant hose clip.

5 Unscrew the two securing bolts and withdraw the timing cover (photos).

6 Refit the crankshaft pulley bolt, and using a socket on the bolt, turn the engine clockwise until the TDC (top dead centre) lug on the crankshaft sprocket is uppermost, and in line with the notch in the oil pump flange, and the pointer on the camshaft sprocket is aligned with the dot on the cylinder head front face (photos).

7 Loosen the two timing belt tensioner bolts, press the tensioner to the left against the spring tension, and tighten the two bolts to retain the tensioner in the released position.

8 Mark the running direction of the belt if it is to be re-used, then slip it off the sprockets, and withdraw the belt (photo).

9 If desired, the camshaft and crankshaft sprockets can be removed as follows, otherwise proceed to paragraph 19. The coolant pump sprocket is integral with the pump and cannot be removed separately.

10 Unscrew the crankshaft pulley bolt, preventing the crankshaft from turning as before if necessary, then remove the crankshaft sprocket. Refit the bolt part way and use a puller if necessary. Recover the Woodruff key from the end of the crankshaft and remove the thrustwasher (photos).

11 Unscrew the camshaft sprocket bolt while holding the sprocket stationary with a 41 mm ring spanner. Alternatively, make up a tool similar to that shown in use in photo 59.17 and hold the sprocket using two bolts engaged in the sprockets holes. Recover the distributor rotor shaft which is held in place by the camshaft sprocket bolt (photo).

12 Remove the camshaft sprocket, refitting the bolt part way and using a puller if necessary (photos).

13 If desired, the timing belt backplate can be removed by lifting it from the studs (photo) and the timing belt tensioner and coolant pump can be removed with reference to Chapter 2.

14 If required, the camshaft oil seal can be removed using self-tapping screws and a pair of grips. A new seal can be fitted using a suitable tube drift to press it into place. Lubricate the seal lips with clean engine oil before installation.

15 Refit the sprockets as follows.

16 Where applicable, refit the timing belt tensioner and coolant pump, locate the timing belt backplate over the studs, then fit the camshaft sprocket and the distributor rotor shaft.

17 The camshaft sprocket bolt must be coated with sealant before installation. The manufacturers recommend Loctite 74 or 274, or Omnifit 30M blue. With the sealant applied, insert the bolt, hold the camshaft sprocket stationary as during removal, and tighten the bolt to the specified torque (photo).

18 Refit the thrustwasher with the convex side facing forwards, and refit the Woodruff key, then refit the crankshaft sprocket with the 'FRONT' mark facing forwards.

19 Fit the timing belt over the crankshaft sprocket, but do not engage it with the other sprockets yet. Be careful not to kink the belt, and if the old belt is being refitting, observe the previously noted running direction.

20 Make sure that the TDC pointer on the camshaft sprocket is still

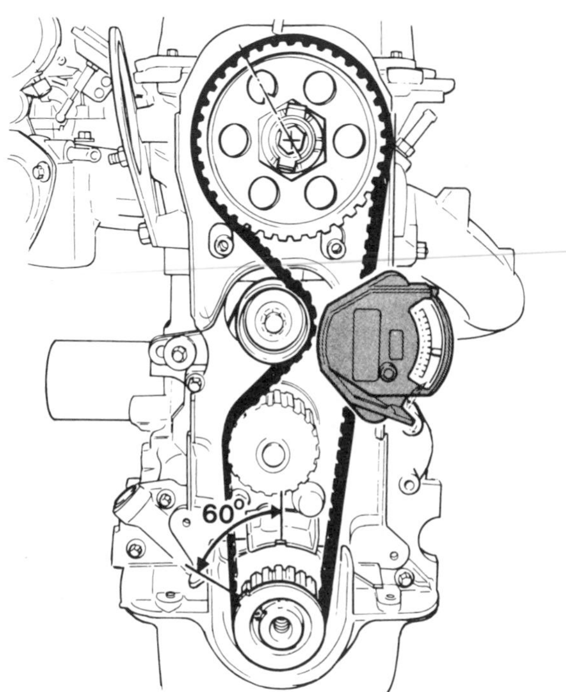

Fig 1.23 No 1 cylinder at 60° BTDC for checking of timing belt tension (Sec 59)

59.6A TDC lug on crankshaft sprocket aligned with notch in oil pump flange

59.6B TDC pointer on camshaft sprocket aligned with dot on cylinder head

59.8 Withdrawing the timing belt

59.10A Remove the crankshaft sprocket ...

59.10B ... the Woodruff key ...

59.10C ... and the thrustwasher

59.11 Removing the camshaft sprocket bolt and distributor rotor shaft

59.12A Using a puller ...

59.12B ... to remove the camshaft sprocket

59.13 Removing the timing belt backplate

59.17 Tightening the camshaft sprocket bolt while holding the sprocket stationary using an improvised tool with two bolts engaged in the sprocket holes

59.25 Twisting the timing belt to assess its tension

59.29 Earth tag (1) and coolant hose clip (2) locations on timing cover

60.3A Disconnecting the heater coolant hose from the coolant pump elbow

60.3B Coolant bypass hose connection at cylinder head

60.10A Withdraw the inlet manifold ...

60.10B ... and move it to one side

aligned with the dot on the cylinder head front face.

21 Check that the TDC lug on the crankshaft sprocket is still in line with the notch in the oil pump flange. If necessary, refit the crankshaft pulley bolt, if not already done, and using a socket on the bolt, turn the crankshaft by the shortest possible route to align the lug and notch.

22 Starting at the crankshaft and working in an anti-clockwise direction, fit the timing belt over the camshaft sprocket, round the tensioner roller, and over the coolant pump sprocket.

23 Slacken the tensioner bolts, allow the tensioner roller to rest against the belt, then tighten the tensioner bolts.

24 Refit the crankshaft pulley bolt, if not already done, and using a socket on the bolt, turn the engine through two revolutions in a clockwise direction (to bring No 1 cylinder back to TDC), then turn the crankshaft 60° anti-clockwise (No 1 cylinder at 60° BTDC).

25 The belt tension should now be checked by applying Ford tension gauge, tool No 21-113 to the longest belt run. Desired gauge readings are:

Used belt - 4 to 6
New belt - 10 to 11

If the tension gauge is not available, a rough guide is that the belt tension is correct when the belt can be twisted 90° in the middle of the longest run with the fingers using moderate pressure (photo). In this case, the vehicle should be taken to a Ford dealer so that the belt tension can be checked using the special gauge at the earliest opportunity.

26 If adjustment of belt tension is necessary, turn the crankshaft clockwise to bring No 1 cylinder to TDC, then slacken the tensioner bolts and move the tensioner to increase or decrease the belt tension. Tighten the tensioner bolts to the specified torque.

27 Turn the crankshaft 90° clockwise past TDC, then anti-clockwise back to the 60° BTDC position (No 1 cylinder at 60° BTDC). Check the belt tension again.

28 Repeat the procedure given in paragraphs 26 and 27 until the belt tension is correct.

29 Refit the timing cover and secure with the two bolts and nuts. Ensure that the earth tag and the coolant hose clip are fitted under the relevant nuts (photo).

30 Unscrew the crankshaft pulley bolt, then refit the crankshaft pulley and the bolt and washer. Tighten the crankshaft pulley bolt to the specified torque, preventing the crankshaft from turning as described in paragraph 2.

31 If the engine is in the vehicle, reverse the operations described in paragraph 1.

60 Cylinder head - removal and refitting (engine in vehicle)

Note: *Refer to the note at the beginning of Section 61 before proceeding*

1 Disconnect the battery negative lead.

2 Drain the cooling system as described in Chapter 2.

3 Disconnect the heater coolant hose from the coolant pump elbow, and the coolant bypass hose from the left-hand side of the cylinder head, then unclip the hoses from the timing cover and move them to one side out of the way (photos).

4 Remove the air cleaner as described in Chapter 3.

5 Disconnect the HT leads from the spark plugs and coil, identifying them for position if necessary, unclip the leads from the camshaft cover, then remove the distributor cap, rotor arm and housing as described in Chapter 4. Remove the spark plugs.

6 Disconnect the cylinder head earth lead from the battery tray.

7 The cylinder head can be removed either with or without the manifolds. If desired, the inlet manifold can be unbolted and moved to one side, leaving the wires, hoses, pipes and cables connected, but care must be taken not to strain any of the wires, hoses, pipes or cables.

8 Unscrew the three securing nuts and disconnect the exhaust downpipe from the manifold flange. Recover the gasket.

9 If desired, remove the exhaust manifold as described in Chapter 3.

10 If the inlet manifold is to be removed with the cylinder head, disconnect all relevant wires, hoses, pipes and cables, otherwise unbolt the manifold and move it to one side, ensuring that it is adequately supported. Refer to Chapter 3, Section 42 (photos).

11 If desired, remove the fuel pump and operating pushrod as described in Chapter 3.

12 Proceed as described in Section 61.

13 With the cylinder head refitted as described in Section 61, proceed as follows.

61.4A Remove the camshaft cover ...

61.4B ... and the gasket

61.6A Withdraw the cylinder head bolts ...

61.6B ... and lift the cylinder head from the block

61.7 Recover the cylinder head gasket

61.10A Fit the locating dowels (arrowed) to the block ...

14 Where applicable, refit the fuel pump and operating pushrod as described in Chapter 3.
15 Refit the manifolds and/or reconnect all wires, hoses, pipes and cables, as applicable, with reference to Chapter 3.
16 Reconnect the exhaust downpipe to the manifold, using a new gasket.
17 Reconnect the earth lead to the battery tray.
18 Refit the spark plugs, then refit the distributor cap, rotor arm and housing, and reconnect the HT leads.
19 Refit the air cleaner as described in Chapter 3.
20 Reconnect the coolant hoses to the coolant pump elbow and the cylinder head, and locate them in the clip on the timing cover.
21 Fill the cooling system as described in Chapter 2.
22 Reconnect the battery negative lead.

61 Cylinder head – removal and refitting (engine removed)

Note: *The cylinder head bolts must always be renewed after slackening, and a new cylinder head gasket and camshaft cover gasket must be used on refitting. If the engine has recently run, the cylinder head must be allowed to cool to room temperature before it is removed*
1 With the manifolds removed, proceed as follows.
2 Remove the timing belt, camshaft sprocket, and timing belt backplate as described in Section 59.
3 Disconnect the crankcase ventilation hose from the camshaft cover.
4 Unscrew the nine securing bolts and remove the camshaft cover and gasket (photos).
5 Unscrew the ten cylinder head bolts half a turn at a time in the reverse order to that shown in Fig. 1.24.
6 With the bolts removed, lift the cylinder head from the block (photos). If the cylinder head is stuck, tap it free with a wooden mallet. Do not insert a lever into the joint between the cylinder head and block as this may result in damage to the mating faces. Place the cylinder head on blocks of wood to prevent damage to the valves.
7 Recover the gasket, and the locating dowels if they are loose (photo).

Fig 1.24 Cylinder head bolt tightening sequence (Sec 61)

8 Commence refitting as follows.
9 Turn the crankshaft so that No 1 piston is approximately 20.0 mm (0.8 in) before TDC. This precaution will prevent any damage to open valves.
10 Make sure that the mating faces of the cylinder block and cylinder head are perfectly clean, then refit the locating dowels to the block, where applicable, and locate a new gasket over the dowels with the red sealing bead and the '1.8' mark uppermost (photos). *Do not use jointing compound.*
11 Turn the camshaft so that the TDC pointer on the camshaft sprocket is aligned with the dot on the cylinder head front face.
12 Lower the cylinder head onto the gasket, making sure that the locating dowels engage (photo).
13 Insert the new cylinder head bolts into their locations in the cylinder head, then tighten the bolts in the order shown in Fig. 1.24 to the five stages given in the Specifications (photos).
14 Fit a new camshaft cover gasket to the cylinder head, ensuring that the gasket locates correctly over the edges of the cylinder head (photo).

61.10B ... then locate a new gasket ...

61.10C ... with the red sealing bead and '1.8' mark uppermost

61.12 Lowering the cylinder head onto the gasket

61.13A Tighten the cylinder head bolts using a torque wrench ...

61.13B ... then an angle gauge

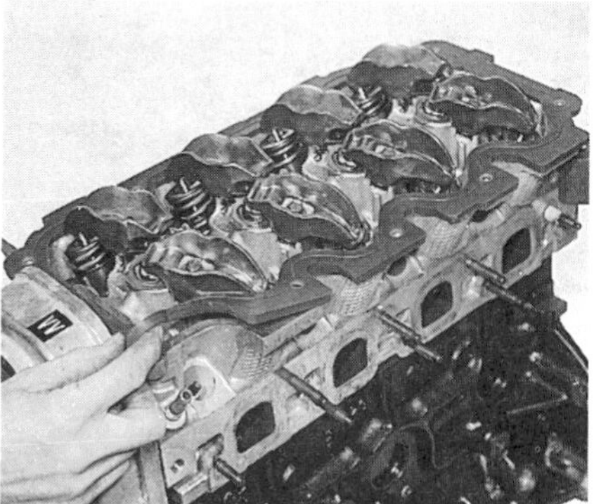
61.14 Ensure that the gasket locates over the edges of the cylinder head

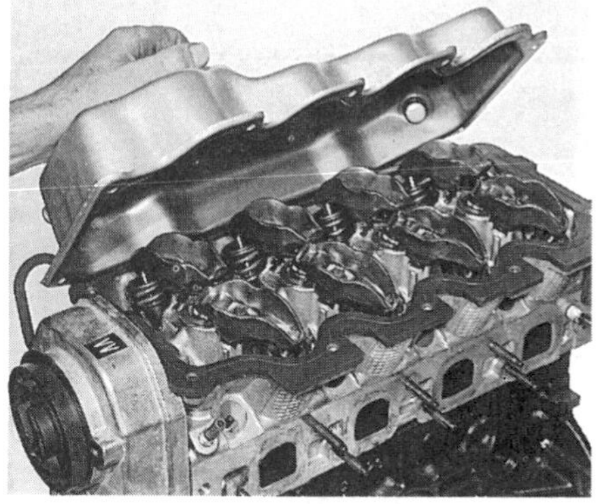
61.15A Fit the camshaft cover ...

61.15B ... ensuring that the studded bolts (arrowed) are correctly located

62.2A Compress the valve spring ...

15 Refit the camshaft cover and tighten the bolts evenly, ensuring that the studded bolts which retain the HT lead clips are refitted to their correct positions (photos).

16 Reconnect the crankcase ventilation hose to the camshaft cover.

17 Refit the timing belt backplate, camshaft sprocket and timing belt as described in Section 59.

62 Cylinder head - dismantling and reassembly

Note: *A valve spring compressor will be required during this procedure. New valve stem oil seals should be used on reassembly.*

1 With the cylinder head removed, remove the camshaft as described in Section 64.

2 Using a valve spring compressor, compress one of the valve springs until the split collets can be removed from the grooves in the valve stem. Release the compressor and remove the cap and spring, identifying them for location. If the cap is difficult to release, do not continue to tighten the compressor, but gently tap the top of the tool with a hammer. Always make sure that the compressor is firmly located on the valve head and the cap (photos).

3 Prise the oil seal from the valve stem, and remove the spring seat, then withdraw the valve (photos).

4 Repeat the procedure given in paragraphs 2 and 3 for the remaining valves, keeping all components identified for location so that they can be refitted in their original positions. Note that the inlet valve springs are fitted with metal dampers. The damper is an integral part of the spring and cannot be removed (photo).

5 If desired, the cylinder head can be inspected and if necessary renovated as described in Section 63.

6 Commence reassembly by lubricating the valve stems and guides with SAE 80/90 hypoid oil, then insert the valves into their original guides.

7 Refit the spring seats over the valve stems.

8 Wrap a thin layer of adhesive tape over the collet grooves of each valve, then smear the new oil seals with a little hypoid oil and slide them down the valve stems onto the spring seats. Use a suitable metal tube to

62.2B ... to free the split collets ...

62.2C ... then remove the cap and spring

62.3A Remove the spring seat ...

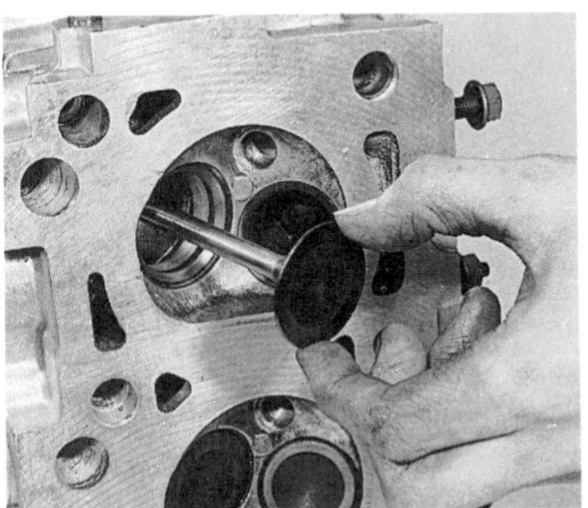
62.3B ... and valve

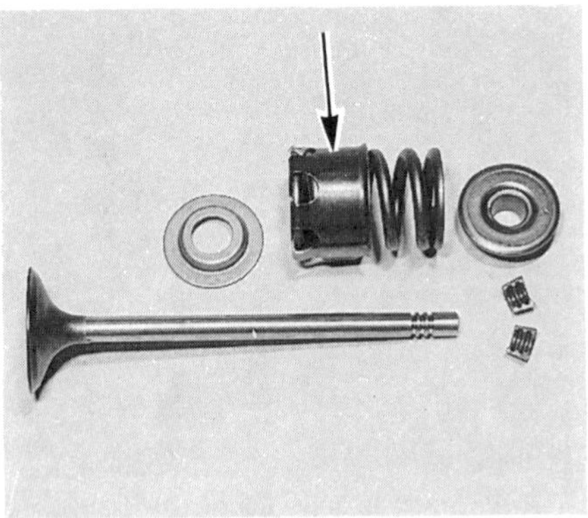
62.4 Inlet valve components. Spring damper arrowed

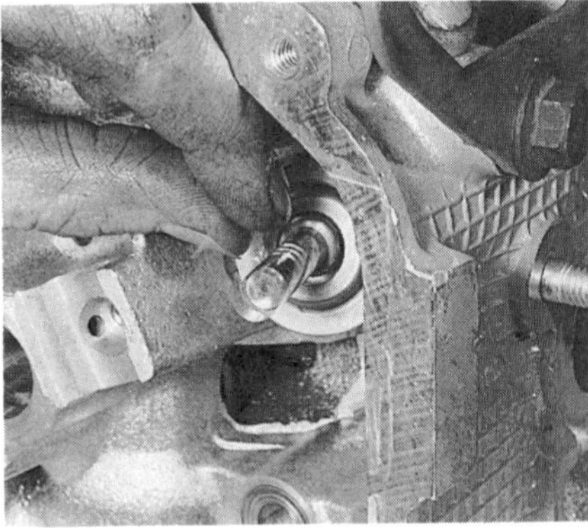
62.8A Wrap adhesive tape round the collet grooves ...

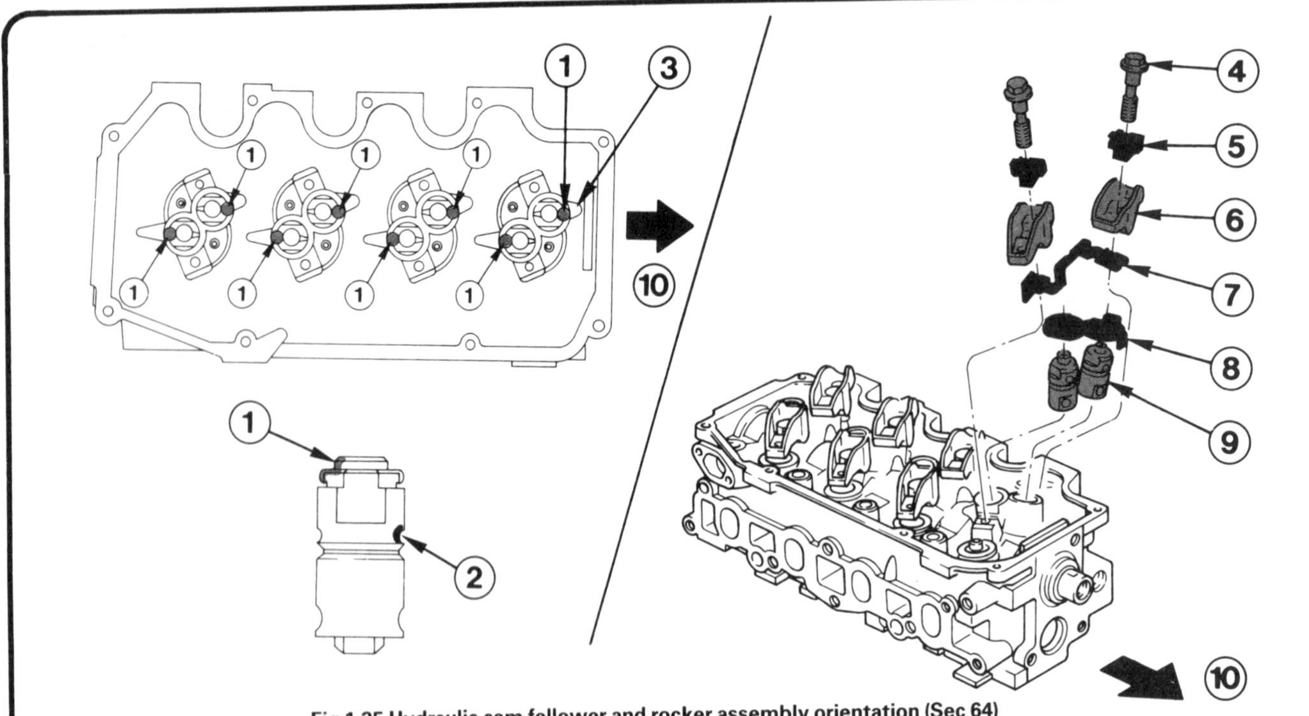

Fig 1.25 Hydraulic cam follower and rocker assembly orientation (Sec 64)

1 *Cam follower colour markings*
2 *Oil port in cam follower*
3 *Oil supply hole in cylinder head*
4 *Securing bolt*
5 *Rocker arm guide*
6 *Rocker arm*
7 *Cam follower guide retainer – stepped end to inlet side*
8 *Cam follower guide – stepped end to exhaust side*
9 *Cam follower*
10 *Front of engine*

62.8B ... then fit the oil seal ...

62.8C ... and seat the seal using a metal tube

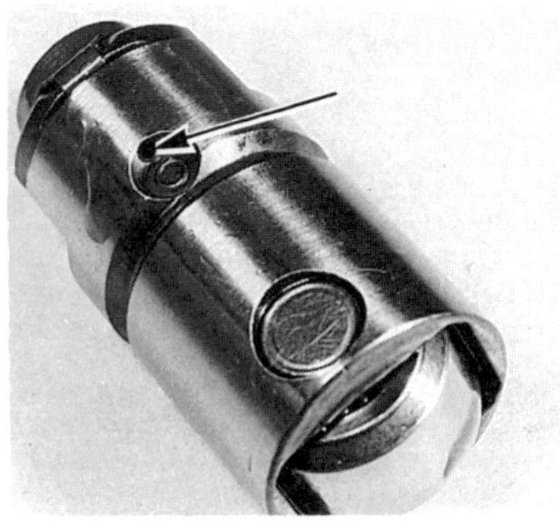

64.9A Hydraulic cam follower oil port (arrowed)

seat the seals, then remove the adhesive tape from the valves (photos).

9 Working on each valve in turn, fit the valve spring and cap, then compress the spring using the valve spring compressor and fit the split collets to the groove in the valve stem. Release the compressor and tap the end of the valve stem with a soft-faced mallet to settle the components. If the original components are being refitted, ensure that they are refitted in their original locations.

10 Refit the camshaft as described in Section 64.

63 Cylinder head – inspection and renovation

Refer to Section 24 in Part A of this Chapter, but pay particular attention to the note at the beginning of the Section, as all CVH engines are fitted with hardened valve seats.

64 Camshaft and cam followers – removal, inspection and refitting

Note: *A new camshaft oil seal should be used when refitting*

1 Remove the cylinder head as described in Section 60 or 61 as applicable.

2 Unscrew the securing bolts and remove the rocker arm guides, rocker arms, and cam follower guide retainers, then lift out the cam follower guides and the cam followers. Keep all components in the correct order so that each component can be refitted in the original position if it is to be re-used. It is advisable to store the cam followers upright in an oil bath until they are to be refitted. Ensure that the depth of oil is sufficient to fully cover the cam followers.

3 Prise out the camshaft oil seal, taking care not to damage the surface of the camshaft. If necessary use self-tapping screws and a suitable pair of grips to withdraw the seal.

4 Unscrew the two securing bolts and withdraw the camshaft thrustplate from the front of the cylinder head.

5 Carefully withdraw the camshaft from the front of the cylinder head, taking care not to damage the bearings. If necessary, loosely refit the camshaft sprocket and bolt to aid removal.

6 Examine the surfaces of the camshaft journals and lobes, and the cam follower rollers for wear. If wear is excessive, considerable noise would have been noticed from the top of the engine when running, and a new camshaft and followers must be fitted. It is unlikely that this level of wear will occur unless a considerable mileage has been covered. Note that the cam followers cannot be dismantled for renewal of individual components.

7 Check the camshaft bearings in the cylinder head for wear. If excessive wear is evident, it may be possible to have the head machined by a suitably equipped engineering workshop to enable a camshaft with oversize bearing journals to be fitted. The only other course of action available is renewal of the cylinder head.

8 Check the cam follower bores in the cylinder head for wear. If excessive wear is evident, the cylinder head must be renewed.

9 Check the cam follower oil ports and the oil holes in the cylinder head for obstructions (photo).

10 Commence refitting by lubricating the camshaft, bearings and thrustplate with hypoid oil, then carefully insert the camshaft from the front of the cylinder head, taking care not to damage the bearings (photo).

11 Locate the thrustplate in the camshaft groove, then refit the bolts and tighten them. Note that the stamped number on the thrustplate should face forwards (photos).

12 Using a dial test indicator if available, or feeler gauges, check that the camshaft endfloat is within the limits given in the Specifications. If not, renew the thrustplate and re-check. If this does not bring the endfloat within limits, the camshaft must be renewed.

13 Remove the thrustplate bolts, coat the threads with sealing compound, then refit and tighten the bolts.

14 Smear the lip of the new camshaft oil seal with clean engine oil, then fit the seal using the camshaft sprocket bolt and a suitable tool similar to that shown (photo). The tool can be improvised using a metal tube of suitable diameter and a large washer or metal disc. Draw the seal into position so that it rests on the shoulder.

15 Lubricate the cam followers with hypoid oil, refit them to their original locations, with the colour marking pointing to the oil feed hole in the cylinder head (photo). The oil feed port in the cam follower should be **opposite** the oil feed hole in the cylinder head – see Fig. 1.25.

16 Lubricate the tops of the cam followers, then refit the four cam follower guides to their original locations with their 'stepped' ends pointing towards the exhaust side of the cylinder head (photo).

17 Refit the four cam follower guide retainers to their original locations with their 'stepped' ends pointing towards the inlet side of the cylinder head (photo).

18 Temporarily refit the camshaft sprocket, and turn the camshaft so that the TDC pointer on the sprocket is aligned with the dot on the cylinder head front face (ie the pointer is at the 12 o'clock position).

19 Refit rocker arms Nos 1, 2, 4 and 5 together with their rocker arm guides and securing bolts, to their original locations – see Fig. 1.26. Lubricate the contact faces of the rocker arms and guides and the valve stems with hypoid oil, and ensure that the guides seat correctly in their locations in the cylinder head (photo). Tighten the securing bolts to the specified torque.

20 Turn the camshaft through 180° so that the camshaft sprocket keyway is aligned with the dot on the cylinder head front face (ie the

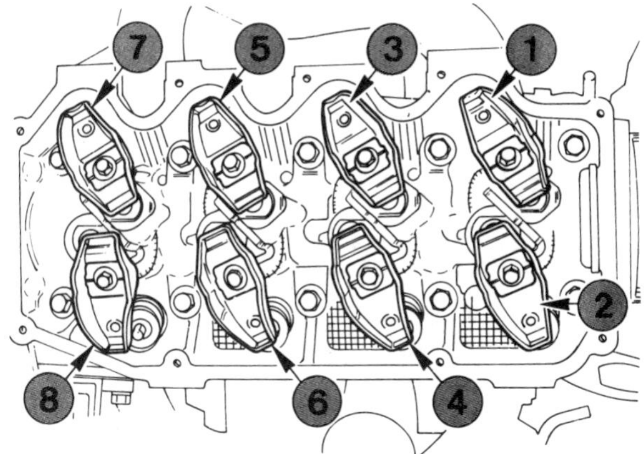

Fig 1.26 Rocker arm numbering sequence (Sec 64)

64.9B Cam follower oil supply hole (arrowed) in cylinder head

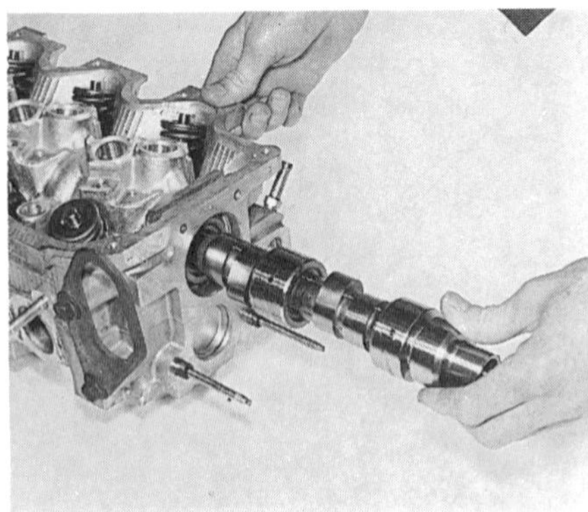
64.10 Refitting the camshaft

64.11A Refit the camshaft thrustplate ...

64.11B ... and tighten the securing bolts

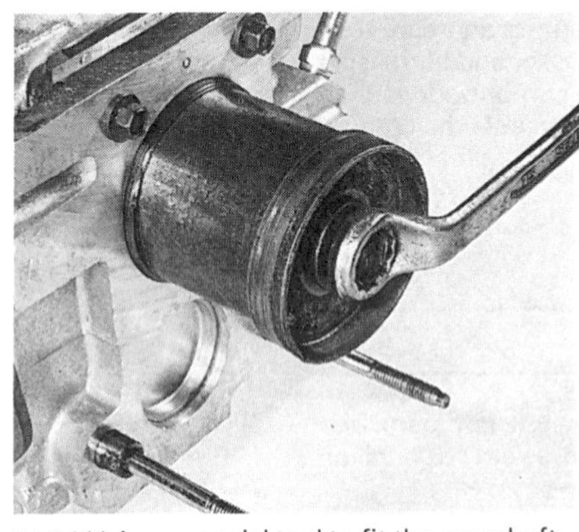
64.14 Using a special tool to fit the camshaft oil seal

64.15 Refit the cam followers ...

64.16 ... guides ...

64.17 ... and retainers

64.19 Lubricate the valve stem contact faces and refit the rocker arms and guides

64.20 Camshaft sprocket keyway aligned with dot on cylinder head

64.21 Tightening a rocker arm securing bolt

65.2A New flywheel bolts are supplied ready-coated with thread-locking compound

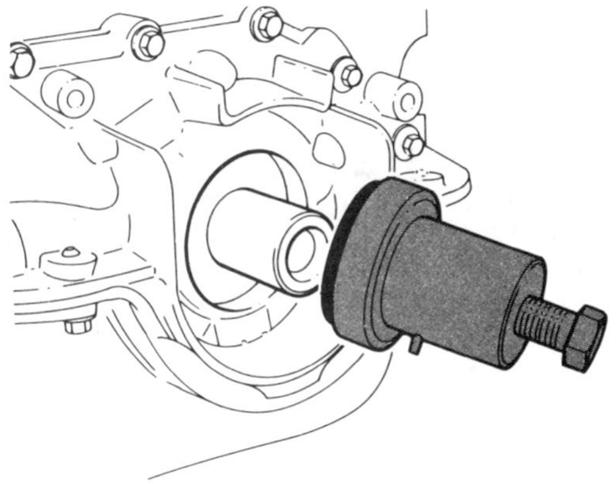
Fig 1.27 Using a special tool to fit the crankshaft front oil seal (Sec 66)

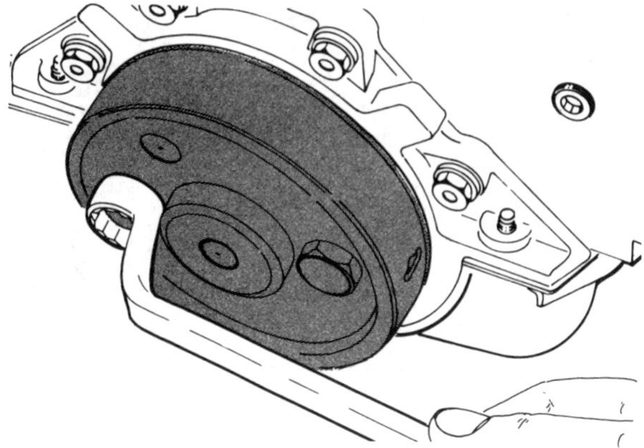
Fig 1.28 Using a special tool to fit the crankshaft rear oil seal (Sec 67)

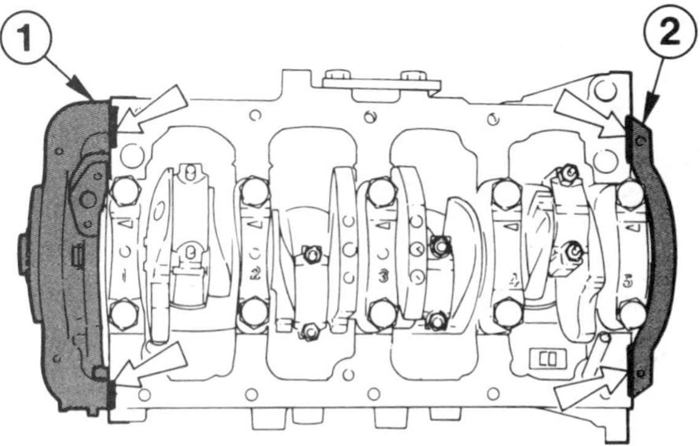

Fig 1.29 Apply sealing compound to the areas shown before fitting the sump gasket (Sec 68)

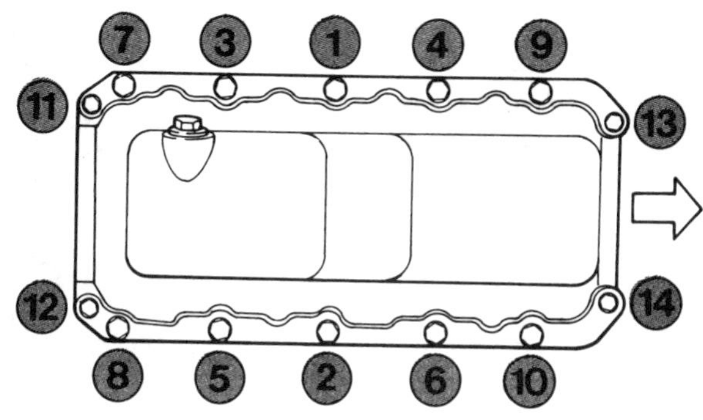

Fig 1.30 Sump bolt tightening sequence (Sec 68)

TDC pointer on the sprocket is at the 6 o'clock position) (photo).

21 Repeat the procedure given in paragraph 19 for rocker arms Nos 3, 6, 7 and 8 (photo).

22 Remove the camshaft sprocket and refit the cylinder head as described in Section 60 or 61 as applicable.

65 Flywheel/driveplate - removal, inspection and refitting

1 Refer to Section 27 in Part A of this Chapter, but also note the following points.

2 The flywheel/driveplate securing bolts must be renewed when refitting, and the new bolts are supplied ready-coated with thread-locking compound (photos).

3 The ring gear cannot be renewed independently of the flywheel/driveplate. If the ring gear is badly worn or has missing teeth, a new flywheel/driveplate must be fitted.

66 Crankshaft front oil seal - renewal

1 Remove the timing belt and the crankshaft sprocket and thrust-washer as described in Section 59.

2 Withdraw the oil seal using an oil seal removal tool or by drilling the oil seal outer face and using self-tapping screws and a pair of grips.

3 Clean the oil seal housing, then smear the lip of a new oil seal with clean engine oil.

4 Fit the oil seal using the crankshaft pulley bolt and a suitable tool similar to that shown in Fig. 1.27. The tool can be improvised using a metal tube of suitable diameter and a large washer or metal disc. Draw the seal into position so that it rests on the shoulder (photo). **Do not** drive the seal into position using a tube drift.

5 Refit the thrustwasher, crankshaft sprocket and timing belt as described in Section 59.

67 Crankshaft rear oil seal - renewal

1 Remove the flywheel/driveplate as described in Section 65.

2 Prise out the oil seal. If necessary, drill the outer face of the oil seal and use self-tapping screws and a pair of grips to withdraw the seal (photo).

3 Clean the oil seal housing, then fit the new oil seal using two flywheel/driveplate securing bolts and a tool similar to that shown in Fig. 1.28. A suitable tool can be improvised using a narrow strip of metal sheet bent to form a circle of the correct diameter, and a large metal disc with appropriate holes drilled to allow the flywheel/driveplate securing bolts to pass through. Make sure that the seal lip faces into the engine and lightly smear the lip with clean engine oil.

4 Refit the flywheel/driveplate as described in Section 65.

68 Sump - removal and refitting

Note: *A new gasket and new sump bolts must be used when refitting, and suitable sealant will be required (available from a Ford dealer). Note that it is preferable to keep the engine upright until the sump has been removed to prevent sludge from entering the engine internals.*

1 With the engine removed, proceed as follows.

2 Remove the flywheel/driveplate and the engine adaptor plate as described in Section 65.

3 Unscrew the fourteen securing bolts and withdraw the two re-inforcing strips and the sump (photos). If the sump is stuck, carefully tap

65.2B Using an improvised tool to hold the flywheel stationary while tightening the securing bolts

66.4 Crankshaft front oil seal (arrowed) located in oil pump housing

67.2 Crankshaft rear oil seal location (arrowed)

68.3A Unscrew the securing bolts ...

68.3B ... and withdraw the sump

68.6 Applying sealing compound to the cylinder block and oil pump housing mating faces

68.7 Ensure that the gasket locates correctly on the oil pump housing

69.4 Oil strainer/pick-up tube securing nut (arrowed) on No 4 main bearing cap

69.5 Removing the oil pick-up tube from the oil pump

it sideways to free it. Do not prise between the mating faces.

4 Recover the gasket.

5 Thoroughly clean the mating faces of the cylinder block and sump.

6 Commence refitting by applying sealing compound (available from a Ford dealer) to the cylinder block, oil pump housing and crankshaft rear oil seal housing mating faces at the points shown in Fig. 1.29 (photo). Note that the sump must be fitted within ten minutes of applying the sealing compound.

7 Fit a new gasket, ensuring that it engages correctly in the grooves in the crankshaft rear oil seal carrier and the oil pump housing (photo).

8 Locate the sump on the gasket and loosely fit the securing bolts.

9 Tighten all the bolts slightly to obtain a light and even gasket preload.

10 Tighten the bolts to the specified torque in the sequence shown in Fig. 1.30. Note that the ten M8 bolts and the four M6 bolts are tightened to different torques.

11 Refit the engine adaptor plate and the flywheel/driveplate as described in Section 65.

69 Oil pump – removal and refitting

Note: *New oil pump and oil pick-up tube gaskets should be used when refitting*

1 With the engine removed, proceed as follows.

2 Remove the timing belt, crankshaft sprocket and thrustwasher as described in Section 59.

3 Remove the sump as described in Section 68.

4 Unscrew and remove the nut securing the oil strainer/pick-up tube to No 4 main bearing cap (photo).

5 Using a suitable Allen key, unscrew the two bolts securing the oil pick-up tube to the oil pump, and withdraw the oil strainer/pick-up tube. Recover the washers and gasket (photo).

6 Unscrew and remove the six securing bolts, and withdraw the oil pump over the front of the crankshaft. Recover the gasket.

7 If desired, the pump can be dismantled and inspected as described in Section 70.

69.10 Refitting the oil pump

70.2A Remove the oil pump cover ...

70.2B ... for access to the rotors

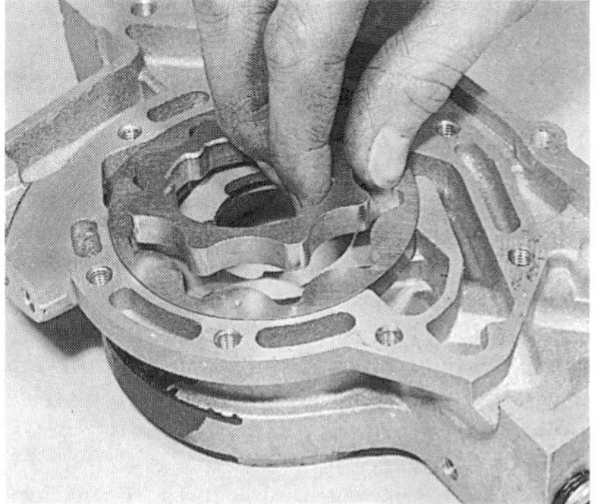
70.3 Lifting out the oil pump inner rotor

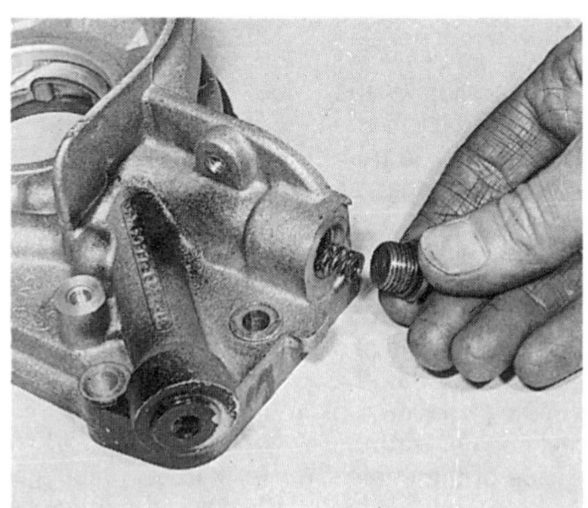
70.4A Unscrew the pressure relief valve plug ...

70.4B ... and withdraw the spring and plunger

8 Commence refitting by prising the crankshaft front oil seal from the pump housing.
9 Prime the pump by injecting clean engine oil into it and turning it by hand.
10 Using a new gasket, fit the oil pump over the front of the crankshaft, ensuring that the central rotor engages with the flats on the crankshaft (photo). Fit the securing bolts, and using a straight-edge, ensure that the bottom face of the oil pump is aligned with the bottom face of the cylinder block before finally tightening the bolts.
11 Using a new gasket, fit the oil pick-up tube to the oil pump and secure with the two bolts.
12 Refit the oil strainer/pick-up tube securing nut to No 4 main bearing cap.
13 Refit the sump as described in Section 68.
14 Fit the crankshaft front oil seal using a suitable tool as described in Section 66.
15 Refit the thrustwasher, crankshaft sprocket and timing belt as described in Section 59.

70 Oil pump – dismantling, inspection and reassembly

1 If oil pump wear is suspected, check the cost and availability of new parts and the cost of a new pump. Examine the pump as described in this Section and then decide whether renewal or repair is the best course of action.
2 Using a suitable Torx socket, unscrew the seven securing bolts and remove the oil pump cover (photos).
3 Mark the rotor faces so that the rotors can be refitted in their original positions, then lift the rotors from the pump housing (photo).
4 Unscrew the pressure relief valve plug and withdraw the spring and plunger (photos).
5 Thoroughly clean all parts in petrol or paraffin and wipe dry using a non-fluffy rag.
6 Commence reassembly by lubricating the relief valve plunger. Fit the plunger and spring, and screw the plug into place.
7 Lubricate the rotors and fit them, observing the marks made when dismantling, if applicable.
8 The necessary clearances may now be checked using a machined straight- edge (such as a good steel rule) and a set of feeler gauges. The critical clearances are between the lobes of the centre rotor and convex faces of the outer rotor; between the outer rotor and pump body; and between both rotors and the cover plate (endfloat). The serviceable clearances are given in the Specifications.
9 Endfloat can be measured by placing a straight-edge across the pump body and measuring the clearance between the two rotors and the straight-edge using feeler gauges.
10 Refit the pump cover and tighten the securing bolts.
11 Prime the pump before refitting, as described in Section 69.

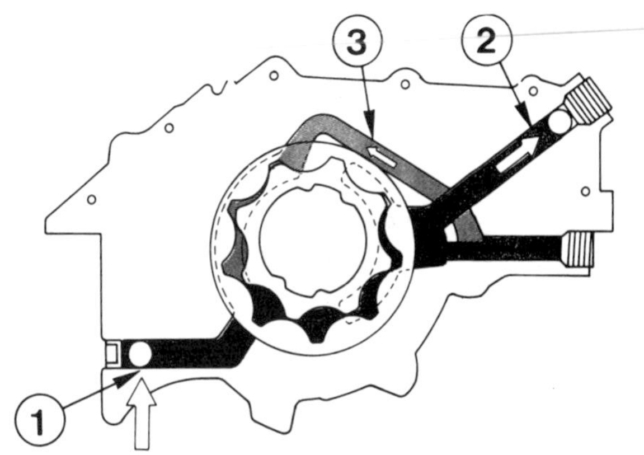

Fig 1.31 Oil pump flow (Sec 70)

1 Oil supply from sump
2 Pressurised oil to engine lubrication circuit
3 Oil feed from pressure relief valve to suction side of oil pump

71 Pistons and connecting rods – removal and refitting

1 With the engine removed from the vehicle, remove the sump as described in Section 68 and the cylinder head as described in Section 61.

2 Check the big-end caps for identification marks and if necessary use a centre-punch to identify the caps and connecting rods (photo).

3 Turn the crankshaft so that No 1 crankpin is at its lowest point, then unscrew the nuts and tap off the cap. Keep the bearing shells in the cap and connecting rod.

4 Using the handle of a hammer, push the piston and connecting rod up the bore and withdraw from the top of the cylinder block. Loosely refit the cap to the connecting rod.

5 Repeat the procedure in paragraphs 3 and 4 on No 4 piston and connecting rod, then turn the crankshaft through half a turn and repeat the procedure on Nos 2 and 3 pistons and connecting rods.

6 The pistons and connecting rods, and the big-end bearings can be examined and if necessary renovated as described in Sections 72 and 74 respectively.

7 Commence refitting as follows.

8 Clean the backs of the bearing shells and the recesses in the connecting rods and big-end caps.

9 Press the bearing shells into the connecting rods and caps in their correct positions and oil them liberally. Note that the lugs must be adjacent to each other (photo).

10 Lubricate the cylinder bores with engine oil.

11 Fit a ring compressor to No 1 piston then insert the piston and connecting rod into No 1 cylinder. With No 1 crankpin at its lowest point, drive the piston carefully into the cylinder with the wooden handle of a hammer, and at the same time guide the connecting rod onto the crankpin. The piston must be fitted with the cut-out in the piston crown (and the lug on the piston skirt), facing the front of the engine, with the oil hole in the connecting rod on the inlet manifold side of the engine (photos).

12 Oil the crankpin, then fit the big-end bearing cap in its previously noted position, and tighten the nuts to the specified torque (photos).

13 Check that the crankshaft turns freely.

14 Repeat the procedure given in paragraphs 11 to 13 inclusive on the remaining pistons.

15 Refit the cylinder head as described in Section 61 and the sump as described in Section 68.

72 Pistons and connecting rods – examination and renovation

1 Examine the pistons for ovality, scoring, and scratches. Check the connecting rods for wear or damage.

2 The gudgeon pins are an interference fit in the connecting rods, and if new pistons are to be fitted to the existing connecting rods the work should be carried out by a Ford dealer who will have the necessary tooling. Note that the oil hole in the connecting rod must be located on the right-hand side of the piston (the cut-out in the piston crown and the lug on the piston skirt face forwards).

3 If new rings are to be fitted to the existing pistons, expand the old rings over the top of the pistons. The use of two or three old feeler gauges will be helpful in preventing the rings dropping into empty grooves (photo). Note that the oil control ring is in three sections.

4 Before fitting the piston rings, clean out the piston ring grooves using a piece of old piston ring as a scraper. Be careful not to scratch the aluminium surface of the pistons. Protect your fingers – piston ring edges are sharp. Also probe the groove oil return holes.

5 Fit the oil control ring sections with the spreader ends abutted opposite the front of the piston. The side ring gaps should be 25 mm (1.0 in) either side of the spreader gap. Fit the tapered lower compression ring with the 'TOP' mark towards the top of the piston and the gap 150° from the spreader gap, then fit the upper compression ring with the gap 150° on the other side of the spreader gap. Note that the compression rings are coated with a molybdenum skin which must not be damaged.

71.2 Big-end cap and connecting rod identification marks (arrowed)

71.9 Bearing shell lug (arrowed) must engage with groove in big-end cap

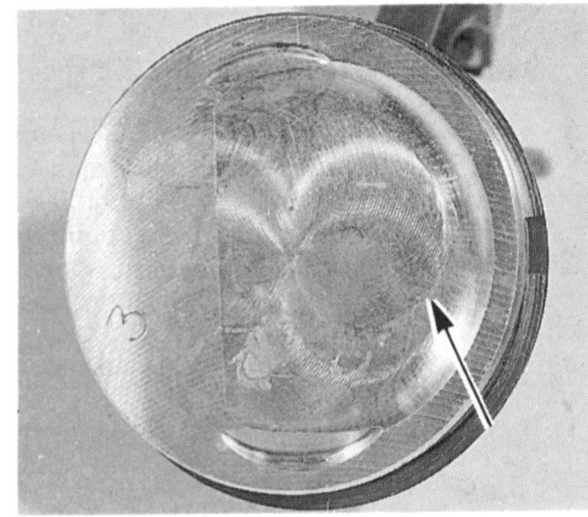

71.11A Cut-out (arrowed) in piston crown ...

71.11B ... and lug (arrowed) on piston skirt must face the front of the engine

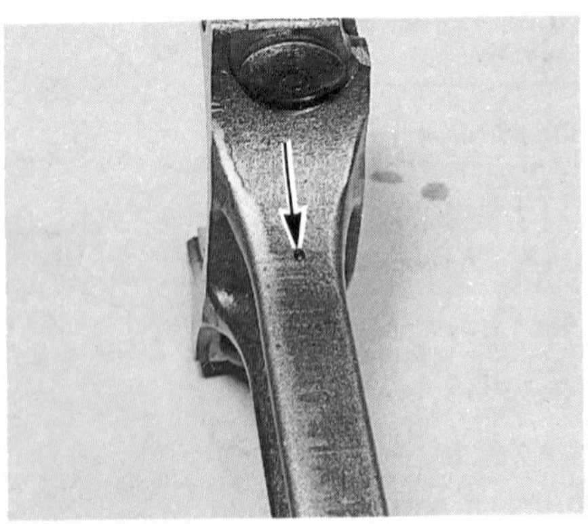

71.11C Connecting rod oil hole (arrowed) must face inlet manifold side of engine

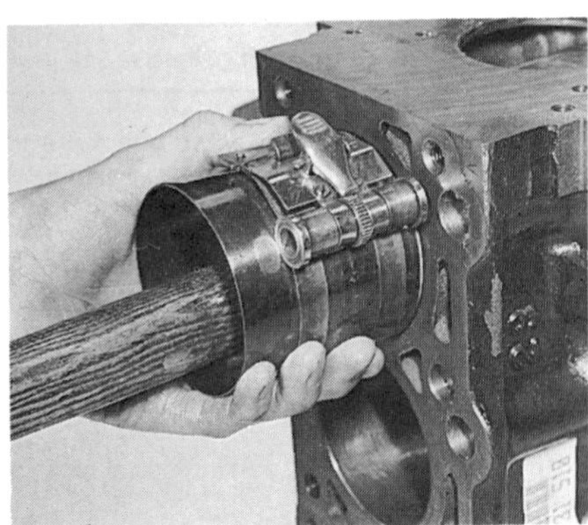

71.11D Fitting a piston and connecting rod into the cylinder bore

71.12A Fit the big-end bearing cap ...

71.12B ... and tighten the securing nuts

72.3 Using an old feeler gauge to aid the fitting of a piston ring

73.6 Checking crankshaft endfloat

73.14A Rear main bearing shell in cylinder block

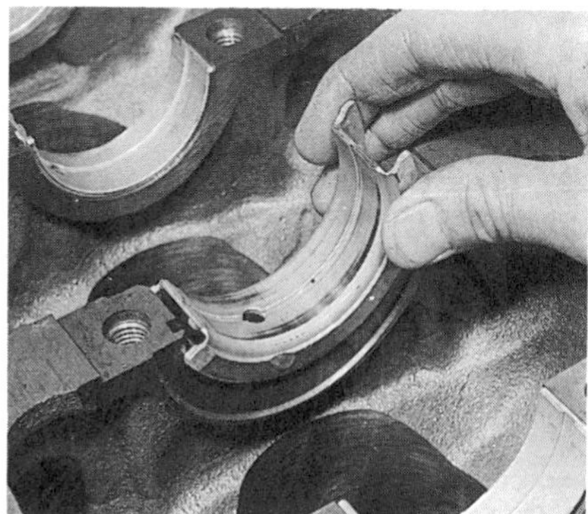
73.14B Centre main thrust bearing shell in cylinder block

73.19 Lowering the crankshaft into the crankcase

73.21 Fitting the centre main bearing cap

73.23A The arrows on the bearing caps must point towards the front of the engine

73 Crankshaft and main bearings - removal and refitting

1 With the engine removed from the vehicle, remove the timing belt, crankshaft sprocket and thrustwasher as described in Section 59.
2 Remove the pistons and connecting rods as described in Section 71. If no work is to be done on the pistons and connecting rods, there is no need to push the pistons out of the cylinder bores.
3 Remove the oil pump and pick-up tube as described in Section 69.
4 Unscrew the four securing bolts and remove the crankshaft rear oil seal housing.
5 Check the main bearing caps for identification marks and if necessary use a centre-punch to identify them.
6 Before removing the crankshaft, check that the endfloat is within the specified limits by inserting a feeler gauge between the centre crankshaft web and the thrustbearing shell (photo). This will indicate whether a new thrustbearing shell is required.
7 Unscrew the bolts and tap off the main bearing caps complete with bearing shells.
8 Lift the crankshaft from the crankcase.
9 Extract the bearing shells, keeping them identified for location.
10 The crankshaft and bearings can be examined and if necessary renovated as described in Section 74.
11 Commence refitting as follows.
12 Wipe the bearing shell locations in the crankcase with a soft, non-fluffy rag.
13 Wipe the crankshaft journals with a soft, non-fluffy rag.
14 If the old main bearing shells are to be renewed (not to do so is a false economy, unless they are virtually new) fit the five upper halves of the main bearing shells to their location in the crankcase. Note the flanged thrustbearing shell should be fitted to the centre bearing location (photos).
15 Identify each main bearing cap and place in order. The number is cast on to the cap and an arrow is also marked which should point towards the front of the engine.
16 Wipe the cap bearing shell location with a soft non-fluffy rag.
17 Fit the bearing half shell onto each main bearing cap.
18 Lubricate the crankshaft journals and the upper and lower main bearing shells with clean engine oil.
19 Carefully lower the crankshaft into the crankcase (photo).

73.23B Tightening a main bearing cap bolt. Note studded bolt location (arrowed) on No 4 bearing cap

73.26A Fit the crankshaft rear oil seal housing ...

73.26B ... and tighten the securing bolts

20 Lubricate the crankshaft main bearing journals again, then fit No 1 bearing cap. Fit the two securing bolts but do not tighten yet.
21 Fit the rear bearing cap, then the centre bearing cap, but as before do not tighten the bolts yet (photo).
22 Fit the intermediate bearing caps and securing bolts, noting that the studded bolt which retains the oil strainer/pick-up tube fits on the inlet manifold side of No 4 bearing cap. Again, do not tighten the bolts yet.
23 Check that the arrows on the bearing caps all point towards the front of the engine, and lightly tighten all the bearing cap bolts, then finally tighten the bolts in a progressive manner to the specified torque (photos).
24 Check that the crankshaft rotates freely. Some stiffness is to be expected with new components, but there must be no tight spots or binding.
25 Check that the crankshaft endfloat is within the specified limits by inserting a feeler gauge between the centre crankshaft web and the thrustbearing cap.
26 Lubricate the oil seal lip with clean engine oil, then carefully fit the crankshaft rear oil seal housing. Using a straight-edge, ensure that the bottom face of the oil seal housing is aligned with the bottom face of the cylinder block before finally tightening the securing bolts (photos).
27 Carefully prise the crankshaft front oil seal from the oil pump housing, then refit the oil pump, oil strainer/pick-up tube and crankshaft front oil seal as described in Section 69.
28 Refit the pistons and connecting rods as described in Section 71.
29 Refit the thrustwasher, crankshaft sprocket and timing belt as described in Section 59.

74 Crankshaft and bearings - examination and renovation

1 Examine the bearing surfaces of the crankshaft for scratches or scoring and, using a micrometer, check each journal and crankpin for ovality. Where this is found to be in excess of 0.0254 mm (0.001 in) the crankshaft will have to be reground and undersize bearings fitted.
2 Crankshaft regrinding should be carried out by a suitable engineering works, who will normally supply the matching undersize main and big-end shell bearings.
3 Note that undersize bearings may already have been fitted, either in production or by a previous repairer. Check the markings on the backs of the old bearing shells, and if in doubt take them along when buying new ones.
4 If the crankshaft endfloat is more than the maximum specified amount, a new thrustbearing shell should be fitted to the centre main bearing.
5 An accurate method of determining bearing wear is by the use of Plastigage. The crankshaft is located in the main bearings (and big-end bearings if necessary) and the Plastigage filament located across the journal which must be dry. The cap is then fitted and the bolts/nuts tightened to the specified torque. On removal of the cap the width of the filament is checked with a plastic gauge and the running clearance compared with that given in the Specifications.
6 If the spigot bearing in the rear of the crankshaft requires renewal extract it with a suitable puller. Alternatively fill it with heavy grease and use a close fitting metal dowel driven into the centre of the bearing. Drive the new bearing into the crankshaft with a soft metal drift.

75 Cylinder block and bores - examination and renovation

Refer to Section 37 in Part A of this Chapter, but note that the crankcase ventilation baffle should be removed from its location at the rear of the cylinder block and cleaned if necessary (photo).

76 Initial start-up after overhaul or major repair

1 Make a final check to ensure that everything has been reconnected to the engine and that no rags or tools have been left in the engine bay.
2 Check that oil and coolant levels are correct.
3 Start the engine. This may take a little longer than usual as fuel is pumped up to the engine.
4 Check that the oil pressure light goes out when the engine starts.
5 Run the engine at a fast tickover and check for leaks of oil, fuel and coolant. Also check transmission fluid cooler unions where applicable. Some smoke and odd smells may be experienced as assembly lubricant burns off the exhaust manifold and other components.
6 Bring the engine to normal operating temperature, then check the idle speed and mixture as described in Chapter 3.
7 When the engine has completely cooled, re-check the oil and coolant levels.

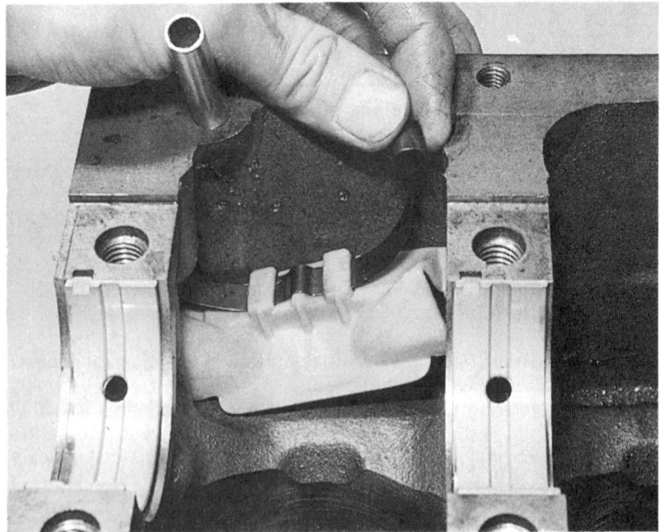

75.1 Removing the crankcase ventilation baffle

8 If new bearings, pistons etc have been fitted, the engine should be run-in at reduced speeds and loads for the first 500 miles (800 km) or so. It is beneficial to change the engine oil and filter after this mileage.

77 Examination and renovation – general

Refer to Section 38 in Part A of this Chapter.

78 Engine reassembly – general

1 To ensure maximum life with minimum trouble from a rebuilt engine, not only must everything be correctly assembled, but it must also be spotlessly clean. All oilways must be clear, and locking washers and spring washers must be fitted where indicated. Oil all bearings and other working surfaces thoroughly with engine oil during assembly.
2 Before assembly begins, renew any bolts or studs with damaged threads.
3 Gather together a torque wrench, oil can, clean rag, and a set of engine gaskets and oil seals, together with a new oil filter.
4 If they have been removed, new cylinder head bolts and new flywheel bolts will be required.
5 After reassembling the main engine components, refer to Section 58 and refit the ancillary components listed, referring to the Chapters indicated where necessary. Delicate items such as the alternator may be left until after the engine has been refitted.

PART C: FAULT DIAGNOSIS

79 Fault diagnosis – engine

Symptom	Reason(s)
Engine fails to turn over when starter operated	Discharged or defective battery Dirty or loose battery leads Defective starter solenoid or switch Engine earth strap disconnected Defective starter motor
Engine turns over but will not start	Ignition system components damp or wet HT leads loose or disconnected Shorted or disconnected LT leads Coil LT leads connected wrong way round Defective ignition switch Faulty coil No fuel in fuel tank Vapour lock in fuel line (in hot conditions or at high altitude) Blocked carburettor float chamber needle valve (where applicable) Faulty fuel pump Fuel filter blocked Blocked carburettor jets (where applicable)
Engine stalls and will not start	Ignition failure – in severe rain or after traversing water splash No petrol in petrol tank Petrol tank breather choked Sudden obstruction in carburettor (where applicable) Water in fuel system
Engine misfires or idles unevenly	Ignition leads loose Battery leads loose on terminals Battery earth strap loose on body attachment point Engine earth lead loose Low tension lead to terminals on coil loose Low tension lead from distributor loose Dirty, or incorrectly gapped spark plugs Tracking across distributor cap (oily or cracked cap) Ignition too retarded Faulty coil Mixture too weak Sticking engine valve Incorrect valve clearance (OHC engines only) Air leak at carburettor/throttle body (as applicable) Air leak at inlet manifold-to-cylinder head or inlet manifold-to-carburettor/throttle body joint (as applicable) Weak or broken valve springs Worn valve guides or stems Worn pistons and piston rings

Symptom	Reason(s)
Lack of power and poor compression	Burnt out exhaust valves Sticking or leaking valves Worn valve guides and stems Weak or broken valve springs Blown cylinder head gasket (accompanied by increase in noise) Worn pistons and piston rings Worn or scored cylinder bores Ignition timing wrongly set Incorrect valve clearances (OHC engines only) Incorrectly set spark plugs Mixture too rich or too weak Fuel filter blocked causing top end fuel starvation Distributor automatic advance weights or vacuum advance and retard mechanism not functioning correctly (where applicable) Faulty fuel pump giving top end fuel starvation
Excessive oil consumption	Badly worn, perished or missing valve stem oil seals Excessively worn valve stems and valve guides Worn piston rings Worn pistons and cylinder bores Excessive piston ring gap allowing blow-by Piston oil return holes choked
Oil being lost due to leaks	Leaking oil filter gasket Leaking rocker cover gasket Leaking crankshaft oil seal Leaking sump gasket
Unusual noises from engine	Worn valve gear (noisy tapping from camshaft cover) Worn big-end bearings (regular heavy knocking) Worn main bearings (rumbling and vibration) Worn crankshaft (knocking, rumbling and vibration)
Engine runs on after switching off	Faulty carburettor anti-dieselling valve (where applicable) Excessive carbon build-up in combustion chambers

Note: *This Section is not intended as an exhaustive guide to fault diagnosis, but summarises the more common faults which may be encountered during a vehicle's life. Consult a dealer for more detailed advice.*

Chapter 2 Cooling system

For modifications, and information applicable to later models, see Supplement at end of manual

Contents

Specifications

System type

OHC models ... Pressurised, with belt-driven coolant pump, crossflow radiator, thermo-viscous fan, thermostat, and expansion tank
CVH models ... Pressurised, with timing belt driven coolant pump, crossflow radiator, electric fan, thermostat, and expansion tank

Thermostat

Nominal temperature rating (fully open):
- OHC models ... 88°C (190°F)
- CVH models ... 100°C (212°F)

Opening temperature:
- OHC models ... 85 to 89°C (185 to 192°F)
- CVH models ... 88°C (190°F)

Expansion tank cap opening pressure

OHC models:
- Up to 1987 ... 0.85 to 1.1 bar (12 to 16 lbf/in^2)
- From 1987 ... 1.0 to 1.25 bar (15 to 18 lbf/in^2)

CVH models ... 1.0 to 1.25 bar (15 to 18 lbf/in^2)

Coolant pump/alternator drivebelt tension

OHC models ... 10.0 mm (0.4 in) deflection midway between coolant pump and alternator (or power steering pump) pulleys under firm thumb pressure

Coolant mixture

Type/specification ... Soft water and antifreeze to Ford spec SSM-97B-9103-A (Duckhams Universal Antifreeze and Summer Coolant)

System capacity:

OHC models ... 8.0 litres (14.1 pints)
CVH models ... 9.5 litres (16.7 pints)

Torque wrench settings

	Nm	lbf ft
Radiator upper mounting nuts	21 to 25	15 to 18
Radiator lower mounting bolts	8 to 12	6 to 9
Coolant pump bolts:		
OHC models:		
M8 bolts	17 to 21	13 to 15
M10 bolts	35 to 42	26 to 31
CVH models	8 to 11	6 to 8

Torque wrench settings (continued)

	Nm	lbf ft
Thermostat housing bolts:		
OHC models	17 to 20	13 to 15
CVH models	8 to 11	6 to 8
Cooling fan shroud-to-radiator nuts/bolts	8 to 11	6 to 8
Coolant pump pulley bolts (OHC models)	21 to 28	15 to 21
Cooling fan blades-to-fan hub bolts (OHC models)	8 to 10	6 to 7

1 General description

The cooling system is of pressurised type, and consists of a front-mounted radiator, coolant pump, cooling fan, wax type thermostat, and an expansion tank.

The radiator matrix is manufactured from honeycombed metal, and the end tanks are made of plastic. On automatic transmission models, the right-hand end tank incorporates the transmission fluid cooler.

The coolant pump is located on the front face of the engine block, and is driven by the alternator drivebelt(s) on OHC models, or by the timing belt in the case of CVH models. The pump is of the impeller type.

The cooling fan draws cold air over the radiator matrix to assist the cooling process when the forward speed of the vehicle is too low to provide sufficient cooling airflow, or the ambient temperature is unusually high. OHC models have a thermo-viscous fan, whereas CVH models have an electrically-operated fan.

The thermo-viscous fan is controlled by the temperature of the air behind the radiator. When the air temperature reaches a predetermined level, a bi-metallic coil commences to open a valve within the unit, and silicon fluid is fed through a system of vanes. Half the vanes are driven directly by the coolant pump, and the remaining half are connected to the fan blades. The vanes are arranged so that drive is transmitted to the fan blades in relation to the viscosity of the silicon fluid, and this in turn depends on ambient temperature and engine speed. The fan is therefore only operating when required, and compared with direct-drive type fans represents a considerable improvement in fuel economy, drivebelt wear and fan noise.

The electrically-operated fan is switched on by a temperature sensor mounted in the thermostat housing when the temperature reaches a

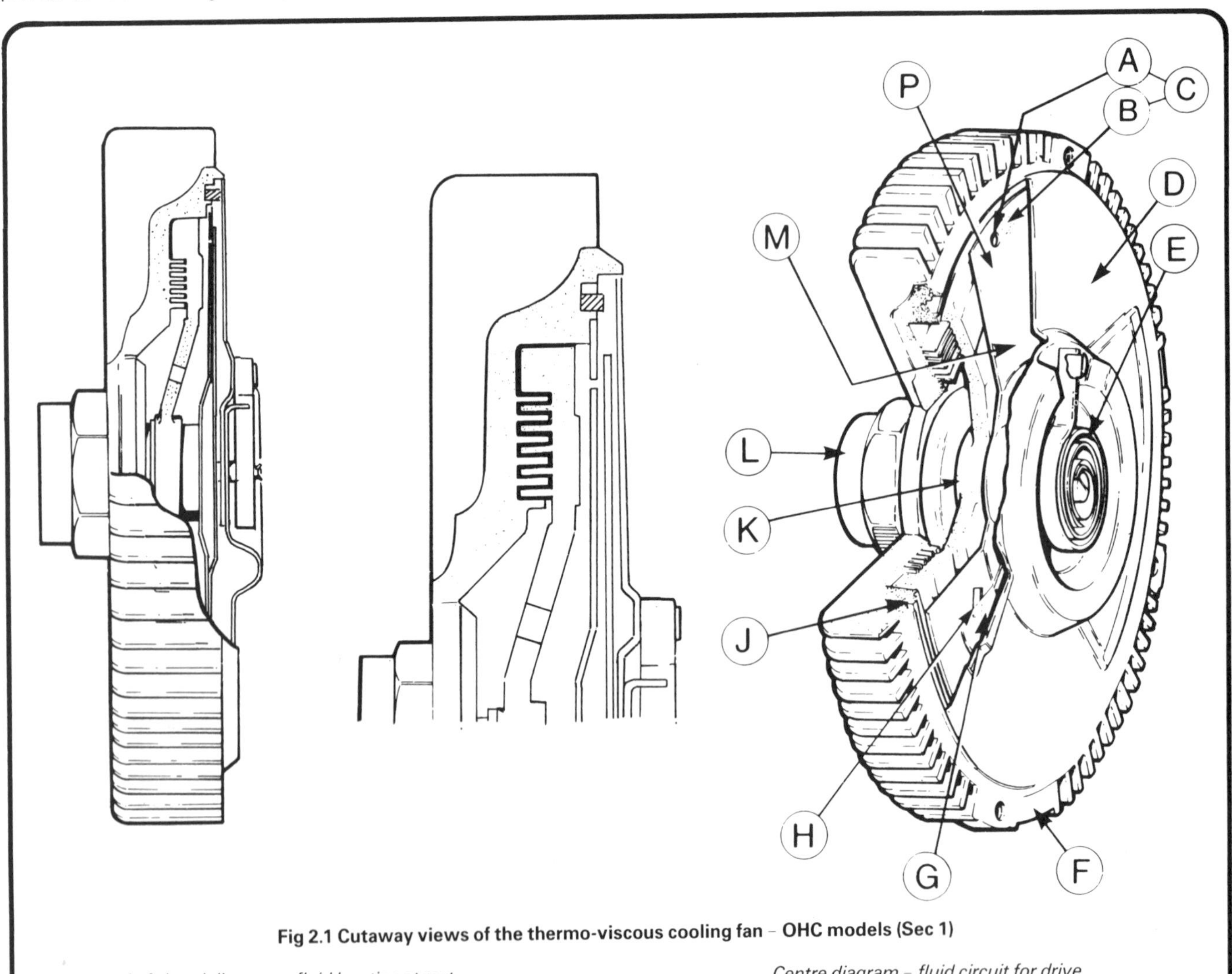

Fig 2.1 Cutaway views of the thermo-viscous cooling fan – OHC models (Sec 1)

Left-hand diagram – fluid location at rest

Centre diagram – fluid circuit for drive

A Discharge port
B Weir
C Ram pump
D Front casing
E Bi-metallic coil
F Main casing
G Control valve
H Intake port
J Seal
K Rotor
L Driveshaft
M Fluid reservoir
P Pump plate

predetermined level. The fan is therefore only operating when required, and like the thermo-viscous fan, offers a considerable advantage over direct-drive type fans.

The thermostat is located in a housing on the cylinder head on OHC models, or on the front of the inlet manifold on CVH models, and its purpose is to ensure rapid engine warm-up by restricting the flow of coolant to the engine when cold, and also to assist in regulating the normal operating temperature of the engine.

The expansion tank incorporates a pressure cap which effectively pressurises the cooling system as the coolant temperature rises, thereby increasing the boiling point of the coolant. The tank also has a further degas function. Any accumulation of air bubbles in the coolant is returned to the tank and released in the air space, thus maintaining the efficiency of the coolant. The pressure cap also incorporates a vacuum relief valve which prevents a vacuum forming in the system as it cools.

The system functions as follows. Cold coolant in the bottom of the radiator circulates through the bottom hose to the coolant pump where the pump impeller pushes the coolant through the passages within the cylinder block, cylinder head and inlet manifold. After cooling the cylinder bores, combustion chambers and valve seats, the coolant reaches the underside of the thermostat which is initially closed. A small proportion of the coolant passes from the thermostat housing to the expansion tank, but the main circulation is through the inlet manifold, automatic choke (where applicable), and heater matrix, finally returning to the coolant pump. When the coolant reaches a predetermined temperature, the thermostat opens and hot water passes through the top hose to the top of the radiator. As the coolant circulates through the radiator, it is cooled by the flow of air to the vehicle's forward motion, supplemented by the action of the cooling fan where necessary. By the time it reaches the bottom of the radiator the coolant is cooled, and the cycle is repeated. Circulation of coolant continues through the expansion tank, inlet manifold, automatic choke (where applicable) and heater at all times, the heater temperature being controlled by an air flap.

2 Maintenance and inspection

1 At the intervals specified in the '*Routine maintenance*' Section at the beginning of this manual, carry out the following tasks.

2 Check the coolant level as follows.

3 Observe the level of coolant through the translucent walls of the expansion tank. The level should be up to the 'MAX' mark when the engine is cold, and may be slightly above this mark when the engine is hot.

4 If topping-up is necessary, wait for the system to cool down if it is hot. There is a risk of scalding if the cap is removed whilst the system is hot. Place a thick rag over the expansion tank cap and slacken the cap a little to release any pressure. When all pressure has been released, carry on unscrewing the cap and remove it.

5 Top up the 'MAX' mark with the specified coolant – see Section 6 (photo). In an emergency, plain water can be used, but remember that it is diluting the proper coolant. Do not add cold water to an overheated engine which is still hot.

6 Refit the expansion tank cap securely when the level is correct. Check for leaks if there is a frequent need for topping-up.

7 On OHC models, inspect the coolant pump drivebelt(s) for wear or damage, and check the belt tension. Re-tension or renew the belt(s) as necessary – see Section 12.

8 Renew the coolant, as described in Sections 3 to 6. At the same time inspect all the coolant hoses and hose clips for deterioration. It is worth renewing the hoses as a precautionary measure, rather than risk a burst hose on the road.

9 Occasionally, clean insects and road debris from the radiator matrix using an air jet or soft brush.

3 Cooling system – draining

1 Disconnect the battery negative lead.

2 It is preferable to drain the cooling system with the engine cold. If this is not possible, take precautions against scalding when removing the expansion tank cap. Place a thick rag over the cap and slacken the cap a little to release any pressure. When all pressure has been released, carry on unscrewing the cap and remove it.

3 Early models have no radiator drain plug, so the radiator must be drained by detaching the bottom coolant hose from the outlet on the right-hand side of the radiator. Later OHC models have a drain plug

2.5 Topping-up the coolant level – OHC model

3.4 Unscrew the clip and remove the rubber cap from the bleed spigot – OHC models

3.6A Disconnect the bottom hose from the radiator – OHC models

3.6B Radiator drain plug (arrowed) – CVH models

3.7 Cylinder block drain plug (arrowed) – OHC models (engine removed)

located in the base of the left-hand radiator end tank, while all CVH models have a drain plug in the right-hand radiator end tank.
4 Certain OHC models have a bleed spigot on the thermostat housing, which is covered by a rubber cap. The cap should be removed from the spigot before commencing draining (photo).
5 With the expansion tank cap removed, place a suitable container beneath the radiator bottom hose or drain plug as applicable.
6 On early models, loosen the clip and ease the bottom hose away from the radiator outlet. On later models, unscrew the drain plug (photos). Allow the coolant to drain into the container.
7 On OHC models, place a second container beneath the drain plug on the right-hand side of the cylinder block (photo). Unscrew the drain plug and allow the coolant to drain into the container. No cylinder block drain plug is fitted on CVH models.
8 Dispose of the drained coolant safely, or keep it in a covered container if it is to be re-used.

4 Cooling system – flushing

1 After some time the radiator and engine waterways may become restricted or even blocked with scale or sediment, which reduces the efficiency of the cooling system. When this occurs, the coolant will appear rusty and dark in colour and the system should then be flushed. Begin by draining the cooling system as described in Section 3.
2 Disconnect the top hose from the radiator, then insert a garden hose and allow water to circulate through the radiator until it runs clear from the outlet.
3 Insert the hose in the expansion tank filler neck and allow water to run out of the bottom hose, and cylinder block on OHC models, until clear. If, after a reasonable period the water still does not run clear, the radiator can be flushed with a good proprietary cleaning agent such as Holts Radflush or Holts Speedflush.
4 Disconnect the inlet hose from the inlet manifold, connect the garden hose, and allow water to circulate through the manifold, automatic choke (where applicable), heater and out through the bottom hose until clear.
5 In severe cases of contamination the system should be reverse flushed. To do this, remove the radiator as described in Section 7, invert it, and insert a hose in the outlet. Continue flushing until clear water runs from the inlet.
6 The engine should also be reverse flushed. To do this, remove the thermostat and insert the hose into the cylinder head on OHC models, or into the inlet manifold on CVH models. Continue flushing until clear water runs from the bottom hose, and cylinder block on OHC models.
7 The regular renewal of antifreeze/corrosion inhibitor is recommended to prevent contamination of the system.

5 Cooling system – filling

1 Where applicable, refit the radiator and the thermostat.
2 Reconnect any disturbed hoses and refit and tighten the cylinder block drain plug and/or radiator drain plug, as applicable.
3 On OHC models fitted with a bleed spigot on the thermostat housing, ensure that the rubber cap is removed.
4 Pour coolant in through the expansion tank filler hole until the level is up to the 'MAX' mark.
5 Where applicable, refit the rubber cap to the bleed spigot when coolant starts to emerge from the spigot. Tighten the clip.
6 Squeeze the coolant hoses to help disperse air locks. Top up the coolant further if necessary, then refit and tighten the expansion tank cap.
7 Run the engine up to operating temperature, checking for coolant leaks. Stop the engine and allow it to cool, then re-check the coolant level. Top up the level as necessary, taking care to avoid scalding as the expansion tank cap is removed.

6 Coolant mixture – general

Note: *The antifreeze/corrosion inhibitor mixture is toxic and must not be allowed to contact the skin. Precautions must also be taken to prevent the mixture contacting the vehicle bodywork and clothing*
1 The antifreeze/corrosion inhibitor should be renewed every two years or 36 000 miles (60 000 km) whichever comes first. This is necessary not only to maintain the antifreeze properties (although the antifreeze content does not deteriorate), but mostly to prevent corrosion which would otherwise occur as the properties of the inhibitors become progressively less effective.
2 Always use the specified type of antifreeze, and never use an antifreeze containing methanol, as the methanol evaporates.
3 Before filling the cooling system, the system should be completely drained and flushed, and all hoses should be checked for security.
4 The specified coolant mixture is 45 to 50% antifreeze and 50 to 55% clean soft water (by volume). Mix the required quantity in a clean container and then fill the system as described in Section 5. Save any surplus mixture for topping-up.

7 Radiator – removal and refitting

1 Disconnect the battery negative lead.
2 Drain the cooling system as described in Section 3.
3 If not already done, disconnect the bottom hose from the radiator.
4 Disconnect the top hose and the expansion tank hose from the radiator (photos).
5 On automatic transmission models, place a suitable container beneath the fluid cooler pipe connections at the radiator. Unscrew the union and plug the upper pipe, then repeat the procedure on the lower pipe.
6 Apply the handbrake, jack up the front of the vehicle and support on axle stands.
7 To improve access, remove the cooling fan shroud as follows, according to model.
8 On OHC models, remove the four retaining clips and unscrew the two retaining screws, then withdraw the upper section of the fan shroud. Unclip and remove the lower section of the shroud.
9 On CVH models, unclip the wiring connector from the fan motor, then unscrew the retaining nuts and washers, and withdraw the fan shroud and cooling fan assembly (photo).
10 On OHC models, unscrew and remove the upper radiator mounting nuts and washers (photo).
11 Unscrew and remove the lower mounting bolts and washers, and withdraw the radiator from under the vehicle (photo).
12 If desired, the radiator can be inspected and cleaned as described in Section 8.

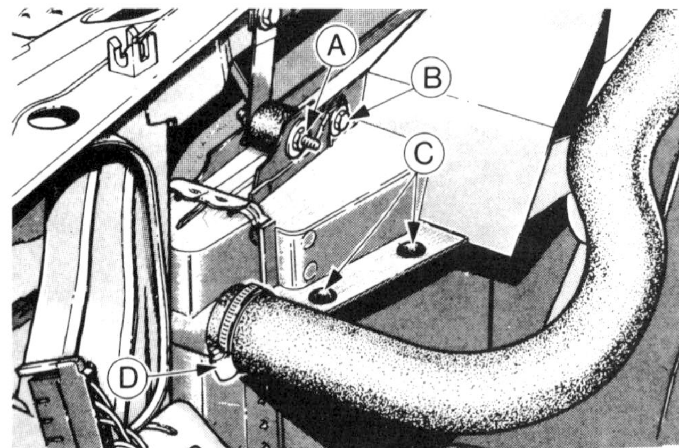

Fig 2.2 Radiator and cooling fan shroud upper mountings – OHC models (Sec 7)

A Radiator mounting nut
B Shroud securing screw
C Shroud securing clips
D Radiator top hose clip

7.4A Disconnect the expansion tank hose from the radiator – OHC models

7.4B Disconnect the expansion tank hose from the radiator – CVH models

7.9 Unscrew the fan shroud/radiator retaining nuts – CVH models

7.10 Unscrew the upper radiator mounting nuts – OHC models

7.11 Lower radiator mounting bolt

13 Refitting is a reversal of removal, bearing in mind the following points.
14 Refill the cooling system as described in Section 5.
15 On automatic transmission models, check and if necessary top up the transmission fluid level as described in Chapter 7.

8 Radiator – inspection and cleaning

1 If the radiator has been removed because of suspected blockage, reverse-flush it as described in Section 4.
2 Clean dirt and debris from the radiator fins, using an air jet or water and a soft brush. Be careful not to damage the fins, or cut your fingers.
3 A radiator specialist can perform a 'flow test' on the radiator to establish whether an internal blockage exists.
4 A leaking radiator must be referred to a specialist for permanent repair. Do not attempt to weld or solder a leaking radiator, as damage to the plastic parts may result.
5 In an emergency, minor leaks from the radiator can be cured by using a radiator sealant such as Holts Radweld with the radiator *in situ.*

9 Thermostat – removal and refitting

Note: *A new thermostat housing gasket must be used on refitting*
1 Disconnect the battery negative lead.
2 Drain the cooling system as described in Section 3.
3 Proceed as follows according to model.

OHC models

4 Disconnect the radiator top hose and expansion tank hose from the thermostat housing situated at the front of the cylinder head (photos).
5 Unscrew the two securing bolts and remove the housing and gasket.
6 Using a screwdriver, prise the retaining clip from the housing, and extract the thermostat and sealing ring (photos).

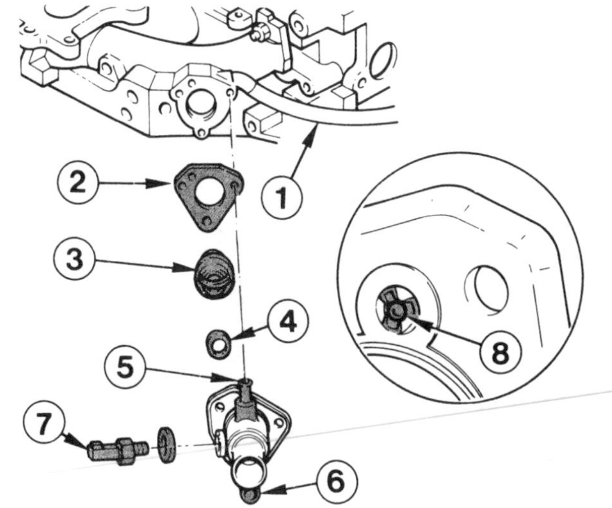

Fig 2.3 Thermostat and associated components – CVH models (Sec 9)

1 Bypass hose to cylinder head
2 Gasket
3 Thermostat
4 Sealing ring
5 To expansion tank
6 To automatic choke
7 Cooling fan switch
8 Pressure relief valve

7 If desired, the thermostat can be tested as described in Section 10.
8 Refitting is a reversal of removal, bearing in mind the following points.
9 Clean the housing and the mating face of the cylinder head. Check the thermostat sealing ring for condition and renew it if necessary. Use a new gasket when refitting the housing.
10 Note that the thermostat wax capsule must face into the cylinder

9.4A Radiator top hose connection at thermostat housing – OHC models

9.4B Disconnect the expansion tank hose from the thermostat housing – OHC models

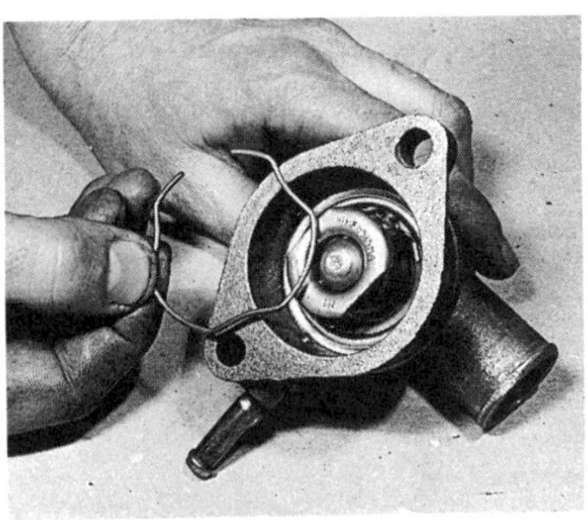
9.6A Prise out the retaining clip ...

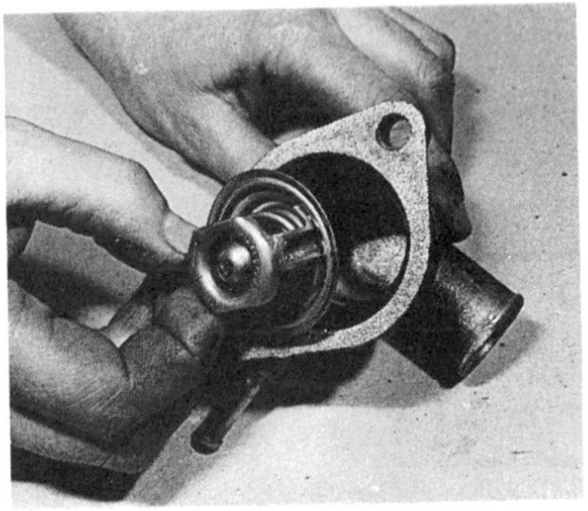
9.6B ... and extract the thermostat ...

9.6C ... and sealing ring – OHC models

9.10 Thermostat flow direction markings (arrowed)

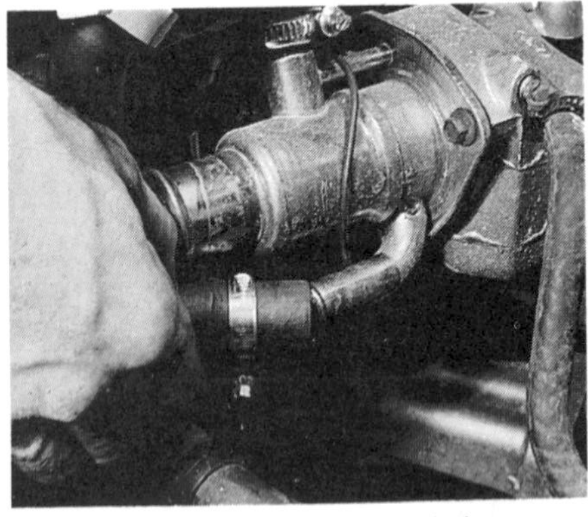
9.13A Disconnect the automatic choke hose, ...

9.13B ... the radiator top hose ...

9.13C ... and the expansion tank hose – CVH models

head with the flow direction arrow facing forward (photo).
11 Refill the cooling system as described in Section 5.

CVH models

12 Disconnect the wiring plug from the cooling fan switch on the thermostat housing situated at the front of the inlet manifold.
13 Disconnect the automatic choke hose, radiator top hose and expansion tank hose from the thermostat housing. Where applicable, take care not to strain the wiring which is routed around the housing. If necessary, disconnect the wiring connector (photos).
14 Unscrew the three securing bolts and remove the housing and gasket (photo).
15 Lift the thermostat from the housing, and carefully prise out the sealing ring.
16 If desired, the thermostat can be tested as described in Section 10.
17 Refitting is a reversal of removal, bearing in mind the following points.
18 Clean the housing and the mating face of the inlet manifold. Check the thermostat sealing ring for condition and renew it if necessary. Use a new gasket when refitting the housing.
19 Note that the thermostat wax capsule must face into the inlet manifold, with the flow direction arrow pointing forward, in line with the pressure relief valve in the housing (photo).
20 Refill the cooling system as described in Section 5.

10 Thermostat – testing

1 To test the thermostat, suspend it by a piece of string in a container of water.
2 Gradually heat the water, and using a thermometer with a range of at least 100°C, note the temperature at which the thermostat starts to open.
3 Remove the thermostat from the water and check that it is fully closed when cold.

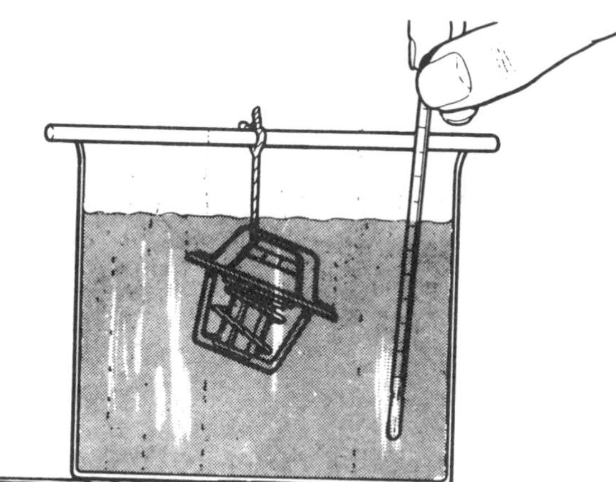

Fig 2.4 Testing the thermostat opening temperature (Sec 10)

4 Renew the thermostat if the opening temperature is not as given in the Specifications, or if the unit does not fully close when cold.

11 Coolant pump – removal and refitting

Note: *A new coolant pump gasket must be used on refitting*

1 Disconnect the battery negative lead.
2 Drain the cooling system as described in Section 3.

OHC models

3 Disconnect the heater and radiator bottom hoses from the coolant pump.
4 Remove the thermo-viscous fan as described in Section 13.
5 If not already done, remove the coolant pump drivebelt as described in Section 12, then unscrew the four retaining bolts and remove the coolant pump pulley. If necessary, the pulley can be prevented from turning using a strap wrench. This can be improvised using an old drivebelt, and a suitable socket and wrench.
6 Unbolt and remove the timing belt cover, with reference to Chapter 1 if necessary.
7 Unscrew the three retaining bolts, and remove the coolant pump and gasket from the front of the cylinder block. Note that on certain models, the alternator adjusting link is secured by the right-hand retaining bolt (photos).
8 If the coolant pump is faulty, it must be renewed, as it is not possible to obtain individual components.
9 Before refitting, clean the mating faces of the coolant pump and cylinder block.
10 Refitting is a reversal of removal, bearing in mind the following points.
11 Use a new gasket, and tighten the retaining bolts to the specified torque.
12 Before fitting the coolant pump pulley, ensure that the timing belt cover support bolt is located in its hole in the pump.
13 Refit the thermo-viscous fan as described in Section 13.
14 Refill the cooling system as described in Section 5.

CVH models

Note: *A suitable puller will be required to remove the camshaft sprocket, and suitable sealer (see text) will be required for the camshaft sprocket bolt threads*

15 Unscrew the two securing nuts, and disconnect the coolant elbow from the left-hand side of the coolant pump (photo).
16 Remove the timing belt as described in Chapter 1.
17 Unscrew the camshaft sprocket bolt, and withdraw the distributor drive sleeve.
18 Screw the camshaft sprocket bolt part way back into the end of the camshaft, and using a suitable puller, pull the sprocket from the camshaft.
19 Remove the plastic rear timing belt cover.
20 Unscrew the two retaining bolts, and remove the timing belt tensioner (photo).

9.14 Removing the thermostat housing and gasket – CVH models

9.19 Correct orientation of thermostat with flow direction arrow pointing towards pressure relief valve – CVH models

11.7A Unscrew the coolant pump retaining bolts – OHC models

11.7B Note the location of the alternator adjusting link under the right-hand retaining bolt

11.15 Disconnect the coolant elbow from the coolant pump– CVH models

11.20 Remove the timing belt tensioner – CVH models

11.21 Withdraw the coolant pump – CVH models

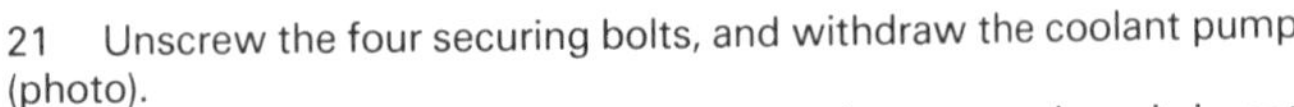

21 Unscrew the four securing bolts, and withdraw the coolant pump (photo).
22 If the coolant pump is faulty, it must be renewed, as it is not possible to obtain individual components.
23 Before refitting, clean the mating faces of the coolant pump and cylinder block.
24 Refitting is a reversal of removal, bearing in mind the following points.
25 Use a new gasket, and tighten the securing bolts to the specified torque.
26 Before refitting the camshaft sprocket bolt, the threads must be coated with sealer (Loctite 74 or 274, or Omnifit 30M blue), as the bolt acts as an oil seal for the hollow camshaft. Do not forget to fit the distributor drive sleeve.
27 Refit and tension the timing belt as described in Chapter 1.
28 Refill the cooling system as described in Section 5.

12 Coolant pump/alternator drivebelt(s) (OHC models) – checking, renewal and tensioning

1 At the intervals specified in the '*Routine maintenance*' Section at the beginning of this manual, the drivebelt(s) should be checked and if necessary re-tensioned. Check the full length of the drivebelt(s) for cracks and deterioration. It will be necessary to turn the engine in order to check that portion of the drivebelt(s) in contact with the pulleys. If a drivebelt is unserviceable, renew it as follows. Note that two drivebelts are fitted to models equipped with power steering, and both should be renewed if either one is unserviceable. Where fitted, the air conditioning compressor is driven by a separate belt.
2 Disconnect the battery negative lead.
3 Where applicable, remove the air conditioning compressor drivebelt as described in Chapter 12.
4 Loosen the alternator mounting and adjustment nuts and bolts, and pivot the alternator towards the cylinder block.
5 Slip the drivebelt(s) from the alternator, water pump, crankshaft and (where applicable) the power steering pump pulleys, and ease the belt(s) over the fan blades.
6 Fit the new drivebelt(s) over the pulleys, then lever the alternator away from the cylinder block until the specified belt tension is achieved. Lever the alternator using a wooden or plastic lever at the pulley end to prevent damage and straining the brackets. It is helpful to partially tighten the adjustment link bolt before tensioning the drivebelt(s).
7 Tighten the alternator mounting and adjustment nuts and bolts in the order shown in Fig. 2.6.
8 Where applicable, refit and tension the air conditioning compressor drivebelt as described in Chapter 12.
9 Reconnect the battery negative lead.
10 The drivebelt(s) tension should be rechecked and if necessary adjusted after the engine has been run for a minimum of ten minutes.

13 Thermo-viscous cooling fan (OHC models) – removal and refitting

1 Disconnect the battery negative lead.
2 Remove the four retaining clips and unscrew the two retaining

Fig 2.5 Drivebelt tension checking point – model without power steering (Sec 12)

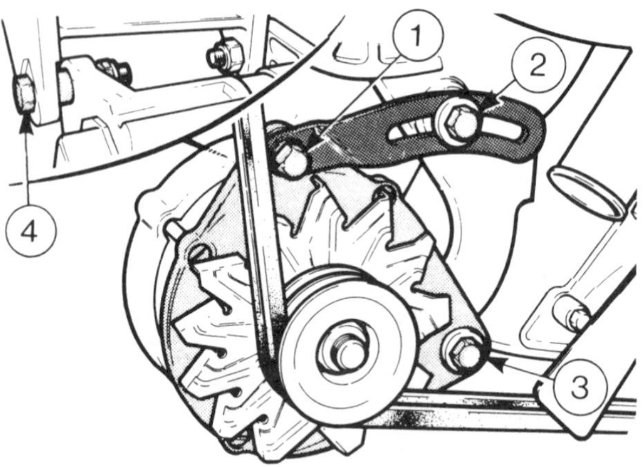

Fig 2.6 Alternator mounting tightening sequence (Sec 12)

Note twin belt layout shown as fitted to models with power steering

13.2A Remove the retaining clips ...

13.2B ... and screws ...

13.2C ... and withdraw the upper section of the fan shroud – OHC models

screws, then withdraw the upper section of the fan shroud (photos).

3 The cooling fan hub nut must now be unscrewed from the coolant pump drive flange. A thin cranked 32.0 mm (1.25 in AF) spanner with a jaw thickness not exceeding 5.0 mm (0.2 in) will be required – see Fig. 2.7. Alternatively, if two of the coolant pump pulley bolts are removed, a normal thickness spanner can be used. **Note that the fan hub nut has a left-hand thread**, (ie it is undone in a clockwise direction.) If the pulley turns as the nut is undone, remove the drivebelt, and clamp an old drivebelt round the pulley to restrain it, using self-locking pliers. Tap the spanner with a mallet if required to remove the nut.

4 If required, the fan blades can be separated from the fan hub by unscrewing the four securing bolts.

5 Refitting is a reversal of removal, but where applicable, take care not to overtighten the bolts securing the fan blades to the fan hub, as thread damage may require the whole unit to be renewed. Where applicable, refit and tension the drivebelt as described in Section 12.

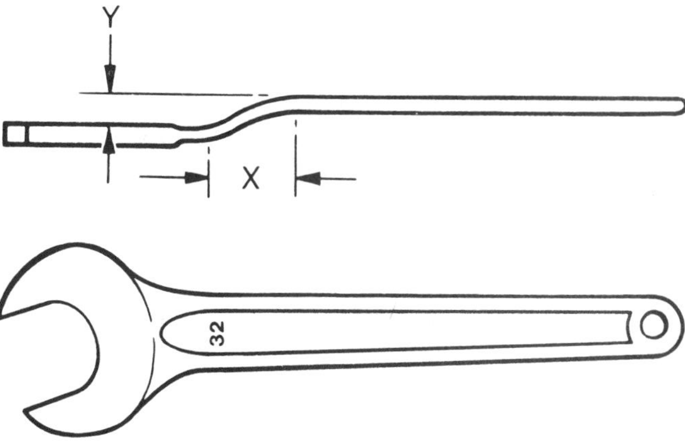

Fig 2.7 Modified spanner required for removing the thermo-viscous cooling fan (Sec 13)

X = 25.0 mm (1.0 in) *Y = 12.0 mm (0.5 in)*

14 Electric cooling fan (CVH models) – removal and refitting

1 Unclip the wiring connector from the fan motor, then unscrew the retaining nuts and washers, and withdraw the fan shroud and cooling fan assembly (photo).

2 To remove the fan blades, prise the securing clip from the end of the motor shaft (photo).

3 The motor can be separated from the fan shroud by unscrewing the three securing nuts and bolts.

4 Note that on models with automatic transmission, two cooling fans are fitted. Both fans are secured to the fan shroud in the same manner.

5 Refitting is a reversal of removal, but when refitting the fan blades, ensure that the direction of rotation arrow faces away from the motor, towards the radiator.

15 Expansion tank and coolant level sensor – removal and refitting

1 With the engine cold, slowly unscrew the expansion tank cap to release any remaining pressure from the cooling system. Remove the cap (photo).

14.1 Withdrawing the fan shroud and cooling fan assembly – CVH models

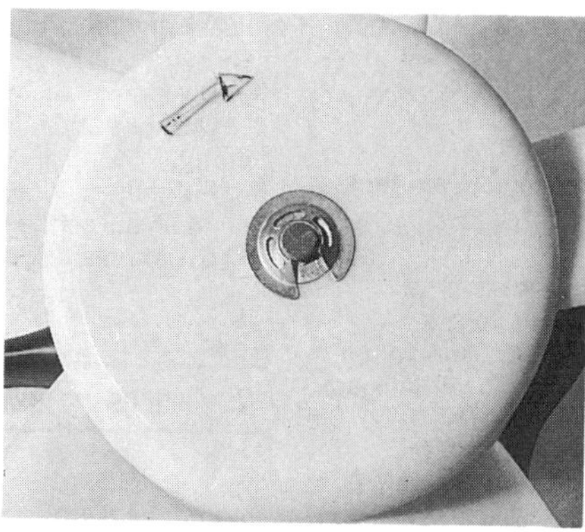
14.2 Fan blade securing clip and direction of rotation arrow – CVH models

15.1 Expansion tank mounting and hose connections – CVH models

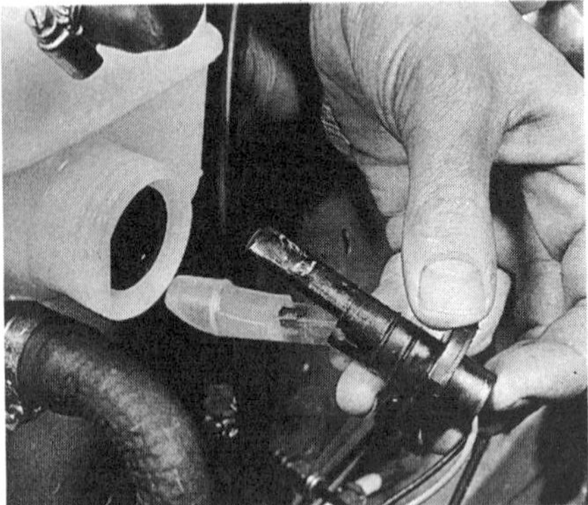

15.8 Removing the coolant level sensor – OHC models

16.3A Disconnect the temperature gauge sender wiring – OHC models

16.3B Disconnect the temperature gauge sender wiring – CVH model

16.4 Remove the sender from the cylinder head – OHC model

17.1 Disconnecting the wiring plug from the cooling fan switch – CVH models

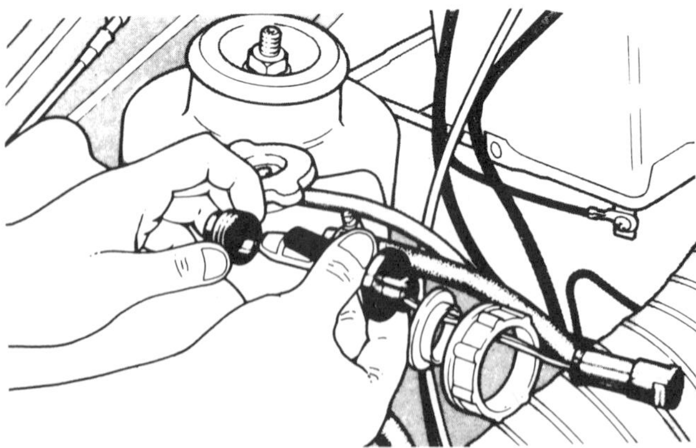

Fig 2.8 Removing the coolant level sensor from the expansion tank (Sec 15)

2 Place a suitable container beneath the expansion tank.
3 Disconnect and plug the upper hose.
4 Where applicable, disconnect the coolant level sensor wiring plug.
5 Unscrew the expansion tank securing screws, and tilt the tank so that the coolant runs to the sealed end.
6 Disconnect and plug the lower hose.
7 Drain the expansion tank into the container and remove the tank.
8 Where applicable, the coolant level sensor can be removed from the tank by unscrewing the collar from the sensor, then withdrawing the spacer, sensor and seal. Renew the seal if necessary. Note that the sensor can only be fitted in one position (photo).
9 Refitting is a reversal of removal.
10 On completion, top up the coolant level to the maximum mark, then refit the expansion tank cap and run the engine at a fast idling speed for several minutes. Check the expansion tank for leaks, then stop the engine and if necessary top up the coolant level.

16 Temperature gauge sender – removal and refitting

1 The temperature gauge sender is located on the front left-hand side of the cylinder head, just in front of the inlet manifold on OHC models, or on the front face of the inlet manifold, next to the thermostat housing, on CVH models.
2 With the engine cold, slowly unscrew the expansion tank cap to release any remaining pressure from the cooling system, then refit the cap.
3 Disconnect the wiring from the sender terminal (photos).
4 Unscrew and remove the sender, and temporarily plug the aperture (photo).
5 Refitting is a reversal of removal, but smear a little sealing compound on the sender unit threads before fitting.
6 On completion, check and if necessary top up the coolant level.

17 Cooling fan switch (CVH models) – removal and refitting

1 The cooling fan switch is located on the right-hand side of the thermostat housing (photo).
2 Removal and refitting of the switch is as described for the temperature gauge sender in paragraph 2 onwards of Section 16.

18 Fault diagnosis – cooling system

Symptom	Reason(s)
Overheating	Coolant level low Coolant pump drivebelt slipping or broken (OHC models) Radiator blocked or radiator grille restricted Collapsed or blocked coolant hose Thermostat not opening properly Cooling fan not working Ignition timing incorrect (accompanied by loss of power and possibly misfiring) Fuel mixture too weak Exhaust system restricted Engine oil level low Blown cylinder head gasket (water/steam being forced down expansion tank overflow pipe under pressure) Brakes binding Engine not yet run-in
Overcooling/slow warm up	Thermostat missing, jammed open or of incorrect rating Cooling fan operating too early
Coolant loss	Damaged or deteriorated hose Leaking water pump or thermostat housing gasket Blown cylinder head gasket Leaking radiator Cracked cylinder head Leaking engine core plug
Oil in expansion tank (may be ignored if slight oil deposit present initially after major overhaul or decarbonising)	Blown cylinder head gasket Cracked cylinder head or engine block

Note: *This Section is not intended as an exhaustive guide to fault diagnosis, but summarises the more common faults which may be encountered during a vehicle's life. Consult a dealer for more detailed advice.*

Chapter 3 Fuel and exhaust systems

For modifications, and information applicable to later models, see Supplement at end of manual

Contents

Specifications

Part A: Carburettor fuel system

General

Fuel tank capacity:	
All models except P100	60.0 litres (13.2 gals)
P100 models	66.0 litres (14.5 gals)

Fuel octane rating:		
Leaded	97 RON (4-star)	
Unleaded (see Chapter 4, Section 11)	95 RON (Premium)	
Carburettor application and type:		
1.3 litre models	Ford VV	
1.6 litre models (engine codes LCS and LCT)	Ford VV	
1.6 litre models (engine codes LSD and LSE)	Weber 2V (28/30 DFTH)	
1.8 litre models	Pierburg 2V (2E3)	
2.0 litre models up to 1985	Weber 2V (32/36 DGAV)	
2.0 litre models from 1985 (except P100)	Weber 2V (30/34 DFTH)	
P100 models	Ford VV	

Air filter element

Application:	
1.3 litre and 1.6 litre (Ford carburettor)	Champion W110
1.6 litre (Weber carburettor) and 1.8 litre (OHC engine)	Champion W118
1.6 litre (1984-on) and 2.0 litre carburettor engine	Champion W152
1.8 litre CVH engine	Champion W219

Ford VV carburettor

Idle speed:	
1.3 and 1.6 litre models	800 ± 25 rpm
P100 models	800 ± 50 rpm
Idle mixture (CO content):	
1.3 and 1.6 litre models	1.5 ± 0.5%
P100 models	1.0 ± 0.5%

Weber 2V (28/30 DFTH) carburettor

Idle speed	775 to 825 rpm	
Idle mixture (CO content)	0.75 to 1.25%	
Fast idle speed	1600 to 1800 rpm	
Float level (with gasket)	5.5 to 6.5 mm (0.22 to 0.26 in)	
Automatic choke vacuum pull-down	6.0 to 6.5 mm (0.24 to 0.26 in)	
	Primary	**Secondary**
Throttle barrel diameter	28.0 mm	30.0 mm
Venturi diameter	21.0 mm	23.0 mm
Idle jet	50	40 (70*)
Main jet	97 (95*)	110 (115*)
Air correction jet	185 (195*)	190 (170*)
Emulsion tube	F59	F22

**Re-jetting sizes for improved economy*

Weber 2V (32/36 DGAV) carburettor

Idle speed	800 ± 25 rpm	
Idle mixture (CO content)	1.5 ± 0.2%	
Fast idle speed	2900 ± 100 rpm	
Float level (without gasket):		
Brass float	41.0 mm (1.61 in)	
Plastic float	35.3 mm (1.39 in)	
Automatic choke vacuum pull-down	6.5 ± 0.25 mm (0.26 ± 0.01 in)	
Automatic choke phasing dimension	1.5 ± 0.25 mm (0.06 ± 0.01 in)	
	Primary	**Secondary**
Throttle barrel diameter	32.0 mm	36.0 mm
Venturi diameter	26.0 mm	27.0 mm
Idle jet	45	45
Main jet:		
Manual gearbox	130	130
Automatic transmission	130	132
Air correction jet:		
Manual gearbox	165	120
Automatic transmission	170	120
Emulsion tube:		
Manual gearbox	F66	F66
Automatic transmission	F50	F66

Weber 2V (30/34 DFTH) carburettor (Part Nos 85HF 9510 CA and DA)

Idle speed	800 rpm (electronically controlled)
Idle mixture (CO content)	0.75 to 1.25%
Float level (with gasket)	7.5 to 8.5 mm (0.30 to 0.33 in)
Automatic choke vacuum pull-down:	
Manual gearbox	9.0 mm (0.35 in)
Automatic transmission	8.0 mm (0.32 in)

Weber 2V (30/34 DFTH) carburettor (continued)

	Primary	Secondary
Throttle barrel diameter	30.0 mm	34.0 mm
Venturi diameter	25.0 mm	27.0 mm
Idle jet	45	45
Main jet:		
Manual gearbox	112	135
Automatic transmission	110	135
Air correction jet:		
Manual gearbox	165	150
Automatic transmission	160	150
Emulsion tube	F22	F22

Weber 2V (30/34 DFTH) carburettor (Part Nos 85HF 9510 CB and DB)

Idle speed	875 rpm (electronically controlled)	
Idle mixture (CO content)	1.0 ± 0.25%	
Float level (with gasket)	8.0 ± 0.5 mm (0.32 ± 0.02 in)	
Automatic choke vacuum pull-down	6.0 mm (0.24 in)	
	Primary	**Secondary**
Throttle barrel diameter	30.0 mm	34.0 mm
Venturi diameter	25.0 mm	27.0 mm
Idle jet	42	45
Main jet	110	130
Air correction jet:		
Manual gearbox	160	160
Automatic transmission	170	160
Emulsion tube	F22	F22

Pierburg 2V (2E3) carburettor – OHC models (Part No 85HF 9510 AB)

Idle speed	800 ± 20 rpm	
Idle mixture (CO content)	1.3%	
Fast idle speed	830 ± 30 rpm	
Automatic choke vacuum pull-down	3.0 mm (0.12 in)	
Idle fuel jet	45	
Idle air bleed	115	
	Primary	**Secondary**
Venturi diameter	23.0 mm	26.0 mm
Main jet	107.5	130

Pierburg 2V (2E3) carburettor – OHC models (Part Nos 85HF 9510 JB and KC)

Idle speed:		
Manual gearbox	850 to 900 rpm	
Automatic transmission	775 to 825 rpm	
Idle mixture (CO content)	1.0 to 1.5%	
Fast idle speed	Not available at time of writing	
Automatic choke vacuum pull-down:		
Manual gearbox	4.0 mm (0.16 in)	
Automatic transmission	3.7 mm (0.15 in)	
Idle fuel jet	45	
Idle air bleed:		
Manual gearbox	120	
Automatic transmission	115	
	Primary	**Secondary**
Venturi diameter	23.0 mm	26.0 mm
Main jet	102.5	130

Pierburg 2V (2E3) carburettor – CVH models

Idle speed:		
Manual gearbox	850 to 900 rpm	
Automatic transmission	775 to 825 rpm	
Idle mixture (CO content)	0.75 to 1.25%	
Fast idle speed	2000 rpm	
Automatic choke vacuum pull-down:		
Manual gearbox	2.3 mm (0.09 in)	
Automatic transmission	2.5 mm (0.10 in)	
Idle fuel jet	47.5	
Idle air bleed	135	
	Primary	**Secondary**
Venturi diameter	22.0 mm	23.0 mm
Main jet:		
Manual gearbox	100	105
Automatic transmission	97.5	105

Torque wrench settings

	Nm	lbf ft
Fuel pump bolts (mechanical pump)	14 to 18	10 to 13
Inlet manifold	16 to 20	12 to 15
Exhaust manifold	35 to 40	26 to 30
Exhaust manifold-to-downpipe nuts	35 to 40	26 to 30
Exhaust downpipe-to-main system nuts	35 to 40	26 to 30
Exhaust U-bolt clamp nuts	38 to 45	28 to 33

Part B: Fuel injection system

General

System type	Bosch L-Jetronic
Fuel tank capacity (all models)	60.0 litres (13.1 gallons)
Fuel octane rating:	
Leaded	97 RON (4-star)
Unleaded (see Chapter 4, Section 11)	95 RON (Premium)
System control pressure	2.5 bar
Air filter	Champion U507
Fuel filter	Champion L204

Idle adjustments

Idle speed (dependent on idle speed adjustment wire – see Section 59):	
Manual gearbox	875 rpm
Automatic transmission	800 rpm
Idle mixture (CO content)	0.5 to 1.0%

Torque wrench settings

Refer to Part A Specifications for items not listed here

	Nm	lbf ft
Fuel pressure regulator fuel feed union nut	15 to 20	11 to 15
Fuel pressure regulator securing nut	20 to 25	15 to 18
Fuel rail securing bolts	8 to 10	6 to 7
Idle speed control valve nuts	8 to 10	6 to 7

PART A: CARBURETTOR FUEL SYSTEM

1 General description

The fuel system on all carburettor models comprises a fuel tank, a fuel pump, a fuel pressure regulator and/or vapour separator, a downdraught carburettor and a thermostatically-controlled air cleaner.

On Saloon, Hatchback and Estate models, the fuel tank is mounted under the rear of the vehicle, on the right-hand side. On P100 models, the fuel tank is mounted behind the cab, between the chassis frame and the load area. The tank is ventilated, and has a simple filler pipe and a fuel gauge sender unit.

On all models except those with air conditioning, the fuel pump is a mechanical diaphragm type, actuated by a pushrod bearing on an eccentric cam on the auxiliary shaft on OHC models, or on the camshaft on CVH models. Models with air conditioning have an electric fuel pump mounted under the rear of the vehicle, next to the fuel tank.

The fuel pressure regulator and/or vapour separator is used to stabilise the fuel supply to the carburettor. The pressure regulator provides a constant fuel pressure, and hence maintains a constant float level in the carburettor which reduces exhaust emission levels. The vapour separator purges vapour from the carburettor fuel supply, thus improving hot starting qualities. All models up to 1985 are fitted with a fuel pressure regulator. All models from 1985 except 2.0 litre models and CVH models are fitted with a combined fuel pressure regulator/vapour separator. 2.0 litre models from 1985 and CVH models are fitted with a vapour separator only.

The carburettor may be either a Ford variable venturi (VV) type, a Weber twin venturi (2V) type, or a Pierburg twin venturi (2V) type, depending on model. Each type of carburettor is available in several versions to suit particular engine and equipment combinations. Fuller descriptions of each carburettor type are given in the relevant Sections of this Chapter.

The air cleaner has a vacuum or waxstat controlled air intake supplying a blend of hot and cold air to suit the prevailing engine operating conditions. A fuller description is given in Section 6.

Refer to Chapter 4 for details of the conditions required to operate engines on unleaded petrol.

2 Fuel system – precautions

Warning: *Many of the procedures given in this Chapter involve the disconnection of fuel pipes and system components which may result in some fuel spillage. Before carrying out any operation on the fuel system, refer to the precautions given in the 'Safety first!' Section at the beginning of this manual and follow them implicitly. Petrol is a highly dangerous and volatile substance, and the precautions necessary when handling it cannot be overstressed.*

Certain adjustment points in the fuel system are protected by tamperproof caps, plugs or seals. In some territories, it is an offence to drive a vehicle with broken or missing tamperproof seals. Before disturbing a tamperproof seal, check that no local or national laws will be broken by doing so, and fit a new tamperproof seal after adjustment is complete, where required by law. Do not break tamperproof seals on a vehicle which is still under warranty.

When working on fuel system components, scrupulous cleanliness must be observed, and care must be taken not to introduce any foreign matter into fuel lines or components. Carburettors in particular are delicate instruments, and care should be taken not to disturb any components unnecessarily. Before attempting work on a carburettor, ensure that the relevant spares are available. Full overhaul procedures for carburettors have not been given in this Chapter, as complete strip-down of a carburettor is unlikely to cure a fault which is not immediately obvious, without introducing new problems. If persistent problems are encountered, it is recommended that the advice of a Ford dealer or carburettor specialist is sought. Most dealers will be able to provide carburettor re-jetting and servicing facilities, and if necessary it should be possible to purchase a reconditioned carburettor of the relevant type.

Refer to Chapter 4, Section 2 for precautions to be observed when working on vehicles fitted with an engine management system.

3 Maintenance and inspection

Note: *Refer to Section 2 before proceeding.*

1 At the intervals specified in the *'Routine maintenance'* Section at the

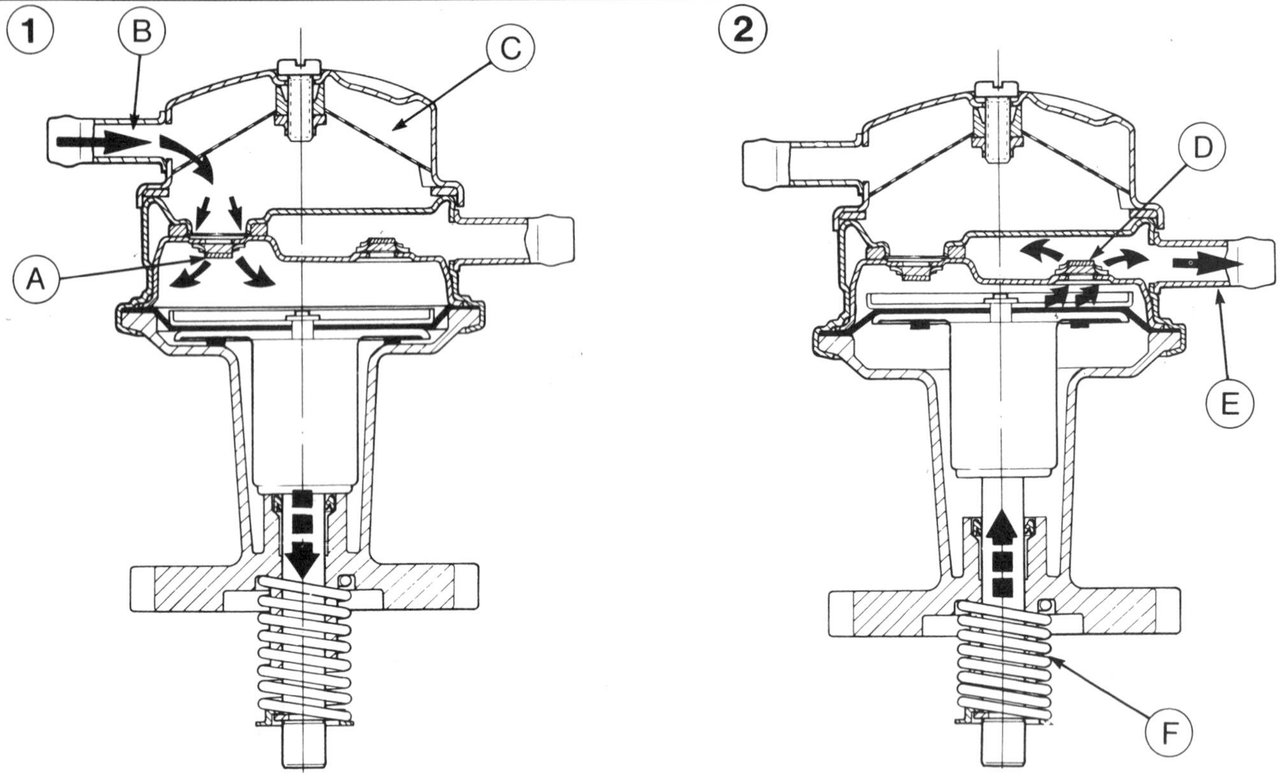

Fig 3.1 Schematic view of mechanical fuel pump operation – early OHC models (Sec 1)

1 Fuel being drawn into pump
2 Fuel being discharged by pump
A Fuel inlet one-way valve
B Fuel inlet
C Fuel filter
D Fuel outlet one-way valve
E Fuel outlet
F Pushrod return spring

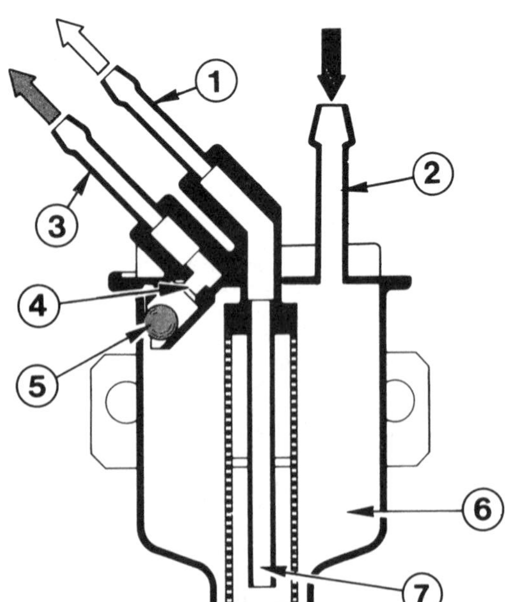

Fig 3.2 Schematic view of fuel vapour separator – CVH models (Sec 1)

1 Carburettor fuel feed
2 Fuel supply
3 Fuel return
4 Bypass in return connection
5 Ball check valve
6 Vapour separator and reservoir
7 Riser tube with filter

beginning of this manual, carry out the following tasks.

2 Examine the rigid and flexible fuel pipes and hoses for leaks and damage. Pay particular attention to the plastic coating on the rigid pipes which protects them against corrosion. Bend the flexible hoses sharply with the fingers and examine the surface of the hoses for signs of cracking or perishing of the rubber. Renew if evident.

3 Examine the fuel tank for leaks and for signs of corrosion or damage.

4 Check and if necessary adjust the engine idle speed (where applicable) and idle mixture settings as described in Section 17, 24, or 34, as applicable.

5 Check the operation of the throttle linkage and lubricate the linkage, cable, and pedal pivot with a few drops of engine oil.

6 Renew the air cleaner element as described in Section 4.

7 Check the operation of the air cleaner intake air temperature control as described in Section 6.

8 Examine the exhaust system for leaks, damage and security, as described in Section 44.

4 Air cleaner element – renewal

1 Remove the screws from the top of the air cleaner cover (photo).

2 Where applicable release the spring clips around the edge of the cover, then lift or prise off the cover (photos).

3 Lift out the air cleaner element (photo). Wipe the inside of the air cleaner body clean, taking care not to allow dirt to enter the carburettor throat. Also clean the inside of the cover.

4 Place a new element in position, then refit the air cleaner cover by reversing the removal operations.

5 Air cleaner – removal and refitting

1 On CVH models, disconnect the battery negative lead.

2 Remove the screws from the top of the air cleaner cover.

4.1 Remove the air cleaner cover screws ...

4.2A ... release the spring clips ...

4.2B ... and lift off the cover ...

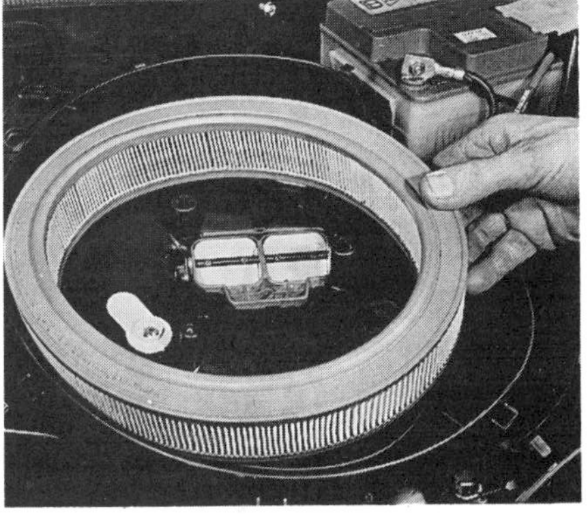

4.3 ... for access to the element

5.3 Disconnecting the cold air intake hose from the air cleaner spout

5.4 Hot air intake hose on hot air shroud

3 Disconnect the cold air intake hose from the air cleaner spout or the intake on the front body panel. The hose is secured by toggle clips (photo).

4 Disconnect the hot air intake hose from the air cleaner spout or the hot air shroud on the exhaust manifold (photo).

5 Disconnect the vacuum hose from the inlet manifold (photo).

6 Where applicable, on OHC models remove the screw securing the air cleaner body to the camshaft cover.

7 Withdraw the air cleaner, and on CVH models, disconnect the wiring plug from the air charge temperature sensor mounted in the base of the air cleaner body, and disconnect the breather hose from the camshaft cover.

8 Refitting is a reversal of removal, ensuring that the vacuum hose is securely connected.

6 Air cleaner intake air temperature control – description and testing

OHC models

Note: *A vacuum pump will be required to test the control components.*

1 The air cleaner is thermostatically-controlled by a vacuum-operated system to provide air at the most suitable temperature for combustion with minimum exhaust emission levels.

2 The optimum air temperature is achieved by drawing in cold air from an intake at the front of the vehicle, and blending it with hot air drawn from a shroud on the exhaust manifold. The proportion of hot and cold air is varied by the position of a flap valve in the air cleaner intake spout, which is controlled by a vacuum diaphragm unit. The vacuum is regulated by a heat sensor located within the air cleaner body, to ensure that the appropriate degree of inlet manifold vacuum is applied to the flap valve, thus maintaining the air temperature within preset limits (photos).

3 To check the operation of the air temperature control, the engine must be cold. First observe the position of the flap valve which should be fully closed prior to starting the engine – see Fig. 3.4. The position of the flap can be observed by disconnecting the cold air intake hose from the air cleaner spout and looking into the spout.

4 Start the engine and allow it to idle. Check that the flap is now fully open to admit hot air from the exhaust manifold shroud. If the flap does not fully open, stop the engine and check the vacuum diaphragm unit and heat sensor as follows.

5 Working under the base of the air cleaner body, disconnect the diaphragm unit-to-heat sensor vacuum pipe at the sensor end, and connect a vacuum pump to the diaphragm unit. Apply a vacuum of 100.0 mm (4.0 in) of mercury.

6 If the flap opens, then the heat sensor is faulty and should be renewed. If the flap remains closed, then the diaphragm unit is faulty, and a new air cleaner body will have to be obtained, as the diaphragm unit is not available separately.

7 On completion of the checks, disconnect the vacuum pump, and reconnect the vacuum pipe and cold air intake hose.

Fig 3.3 Air cleaner securing screws (arrowed) – OHC models (Sec 5)

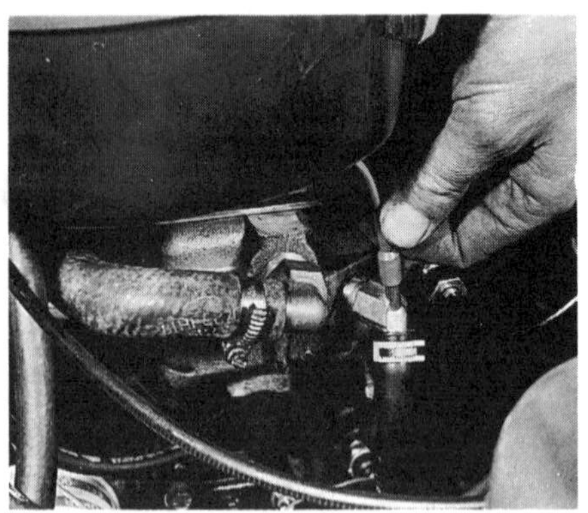

5.5 Disconnecting the air cleaner vacuum hose from the inlet manifold

6.2A Air cleaner vacuum diaphragm unit

6.2B Air cleaner heat sensor viewed from inside air cleaner

CVH models

8 The waxstat-controlled air cleaner performs the same hot and cold air blending operation using a flap valve, as described in paragraph 2, but the flap valve is controlled by a wax capsule and is not dependent on inlet manifold vacuum.
9 When the engine is cold, the wax in the capsule contracts and the flap is pulled back to shut off the cold air intake. As the under-bonnet temperature rises, the wax expands and the flap is opened to admit only cold air.
10 To test the unit the engine must initially be cold.
11 Disconnect the hot air intake hose from the air cleaner spout and observe the position of the flap which should be fully open to allow only hot air to enter.
12 Refit the hose and warm up the engine to normal operating temperature.
13 Disconnect the hot air intake hose again, and observe the position of the flap which should be fully closed to admit only cold air.
14 If the flap positions are not as described, the waxstat is defective and the complete air cleaner must be renewed as the waxstat is not available separately.
15 On completion of the checks, stop the engine and reconnect the hot air intake hose.

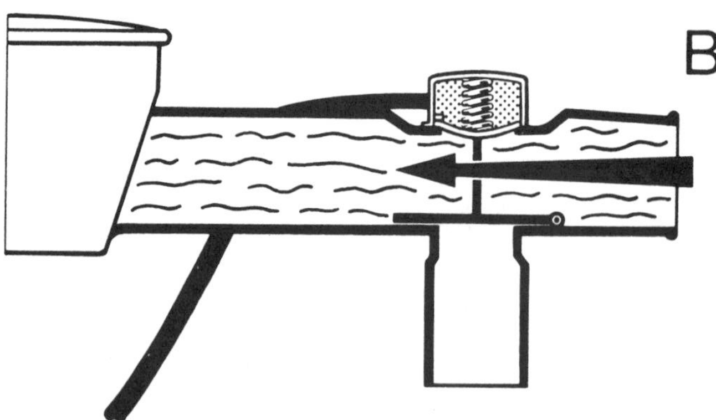

Fig 3.4 Air cleaner flap valve operation – OHC models (Sec 6)

A Flap fully open to admit hot air
B Flap fully closed to admit cold air

7 Fuel pressure regulator (models up to 1985) – removal and refitting

Note: *Refer to Section 2 before proceeding.*
1 The fuel pressure regulator is located on the left-hand side of the engine compartment (photo).
2 Disconnect the battery negative lead.
3 Identify the fuel hose locations, as an aid to refitting. Note that there are three hose connections on models without a fuel flow sensor unit, and two hose connections on models with a fuel flow sensor unit.
4 Disconnect and plug the fuel hoses.
5 Remove the two securing screws and withdraw the regulator.
6 Refitting is a reversal of removal, ensuring that the fuel hoses are correctly connected. If the hoses were originally secured with crimped type clips, discard them and use new worm drive clips.

8 Fuel vapour separator (models from 1985) – removal and refitting

Note: *Refer to Section 2 before proceeding.*
1 On OHC models, the vapour separator is located on the left- hand side of the engine compartment. On CVH models, the vapour separator is located on the right-hand side of the engine compartment (photos).
2 Disconnect the battery negative lead.
3 Identify the fuel hose locations as an aid to refitting, then disconnect and plug the hoses.
4 Remove the two securing screws and withdraw the vapour separator.
5 Refitting is a reversal of removal, ensuring that the fuel hoses are correctly connected. If the hoses were originally secured with crimped type clips, discard them and use new worm drive clips.

9 Fuel pump – testing

Note: *Refer to Section 2 before proceeding.*

Mechanical fuel pump

1 On OHC engines, the fuel pump is located on the left-hand side of

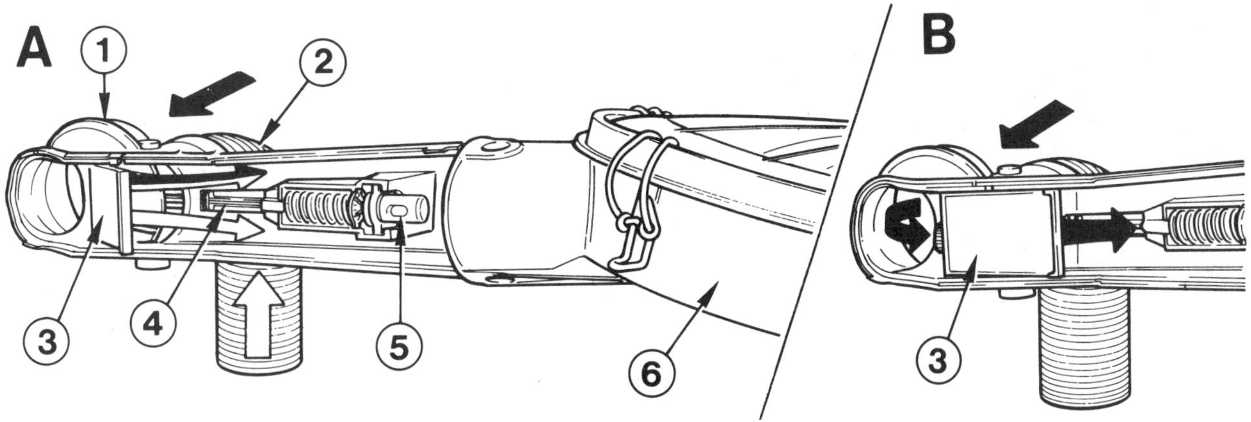

Fig 3.5 Air cleaner flap valve operation – CVH models (Sec 6)

A Flap fully open to admit hot air
B Flap fully closed to admit cold air
1 Air intake spout
2 Hot air intake hose
3 Flap valve
4 Link arm
5 Waxstat
6 Air cleaner body

7.1 Fuel pressure regulator location – models up to 1985

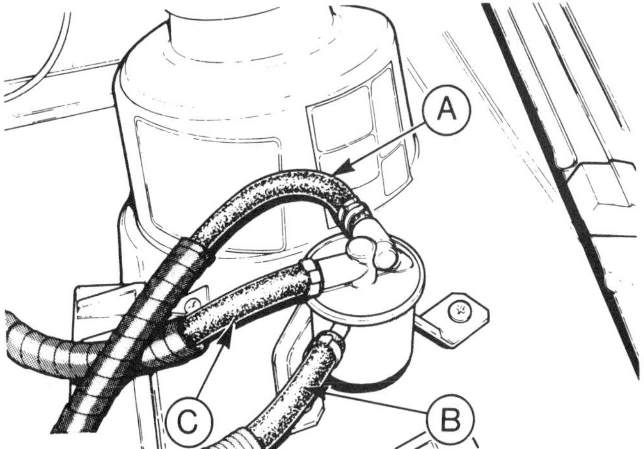

Fig 3.6 Fuel vapour separator location – 2.0 litre models from 1985 (Sec 8)

A Fuel return hose
B Fuel supply hose
C Carburettor fuel feed hose

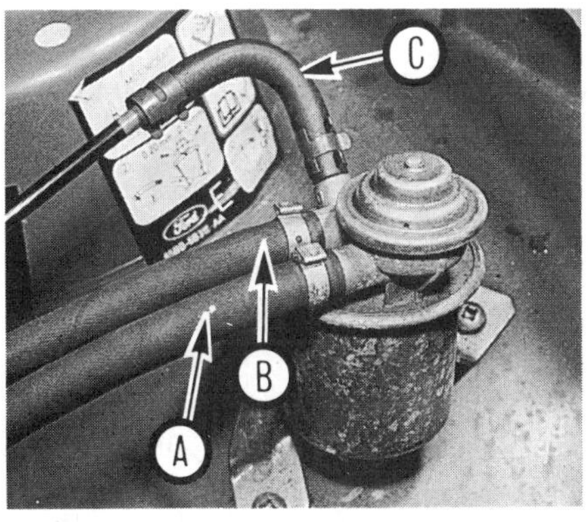

8.1A Fuel pressure regulator/vapour separator location – models from 1985
A Fuel supply hose
B Carburettor fuel feed hose
C Fuel return hose

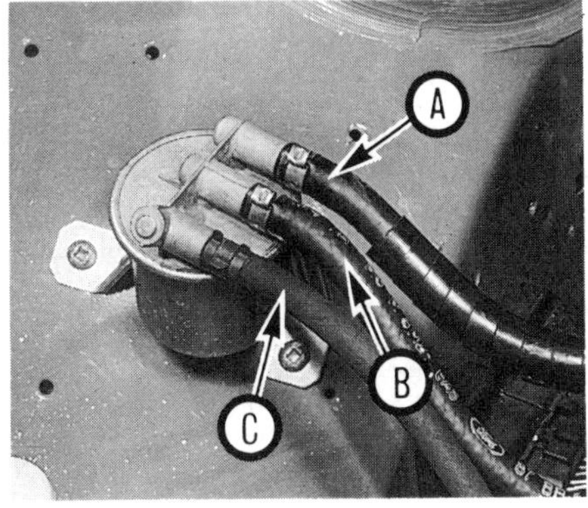

8.1B Fuel vapour separator location – CVH models
A Fuel supply hose
B Carburettor fuel feed hose
C Fuel return hose

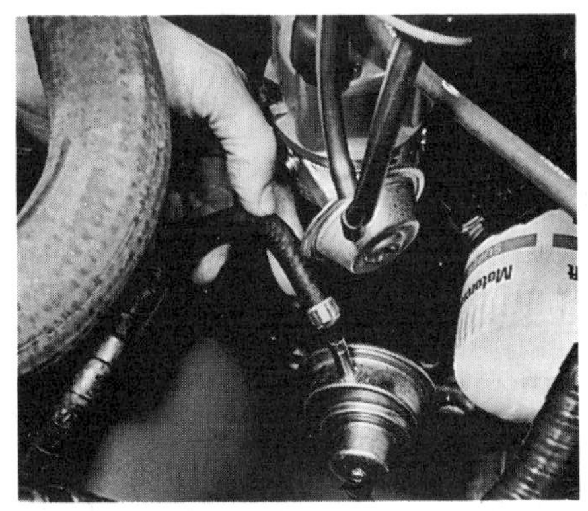

9.3 Disconnecting outlet hose from fuel pump – OHC model

the cylinder block, next to the oil filter. On CVH engines the fuel pump is located on the rear right-hand corner of the cylinder head.
2 To test the pump, disconnect the ignition coil LT '–/1' lead to prevent the engine from firing.
3 Disconnect the outlet hose from the pump, and place a wad of rag next to the pump outlet (photo). Take appropriate fire precautions.
4 Have an assistant crank the engine on the starter motor, and check that well-defined spurts of petrol are ejected from the fuel pump outlet. If not, the pump is faulty. Dispose of the petrol-soaked rag safely.
5 On some early pumps, the top cover can be removed for access to the filter. Removing the pump and cleaning the filter as described in Section 10 may cure the problem. On models with a sealed pump, or where cleaning the interior of the pump and filter does not solve the problem, the pump should be renewed, as no spares are available. (Check that there is petrol in the fuel tank before condemning the pump!)
6 On completion of the test, reconnect the outlet hose to the pump. If the hose was originally secured with a crimped type clip, discard this and use a new worm drive clip. Reconnect the coil LT lead.

Electric fuel pump

7 The fuel pump is located under the rear of the vehicle, next to the fuel tank.
8 If the pump is functioning, it should be possible to hear it 'buzzing' by listening under the rear of the vehicle when the ignition is switched on.
9 If the pump appears to have failed completely, check the appropriate fuse and relay.
10 To test the pump, disconnect the fuel supply hose from the pressure regulator or vapour separator (as applicable) in the engine compartment. Lead the hose into a measuring cylinder.
11 Take appropriate fire precautions, then switch on the ignition for 30 seconds (do not start the engine), and measure the quantity of petrol delivered: it should be at least 400 ml (0.7 pint). If not, the pump is faulty and should be renewed, as no spares are available.
12 On completion of the test, reconnect the hose to the pressure regulator or vapour separator, as applicable, and if the hose was originally secured with a crimped type clip, discard this and fit a new worm drive clip.

10 Fuel pump – removal and refitting

Note: *Refer to Section 2 before proceeding.*

Mechanical fuel pump

Note: *A new gasket must be used when refitting the pump.*
1 Refer to Section 9, paragraph 1 for details of fuel pump location.
2 Disconnect the battery negative lead.
3 For improved access on CVH models, remove the air cleaner as described in Section 5.
4 Identify the hose locations as an aid to refitting, then disconnect the hoses from the pump and plug them.
5 Remove the two securing bolts and withdraw the pump from the cylinder block or cylinder head, as applicable (photo).
6 Recover the gasket, and if desired remove the operating pushrod (photo).
7 Clean the exterior of the pump with paraffin and wipe dry. Clean all traces of gasket from the pump flange and the cylinder block or cylinder head, as applicable.
8 On early pumps with a removable top cover, remove the securing screw and withdraw the cover and the nylon mesh filter with seal. Clean the filter, the cover and the pump with petrol. Locate the filter in the cover and fit the cover to the pump, so that the indentations on the cover and pump are aligned. Tighten the cover securing screw (photos).
9 Refitting is a reversal of removal, but fit a new gasket, and tighten the securing bolts to the specified torque. Ensure that the hoses are correctly connected, and if the hoses were originally secured with crimped type clips, discard these and use new worm drive clips.

Electric fuel pump

10 The fuel pump is located under the rear of the vehicle, next to the fuel tank.
11 Disconnect the battery negative lead.
12 Chock the front wheels, then jack up the rear of the vehicle and support on axle stands.

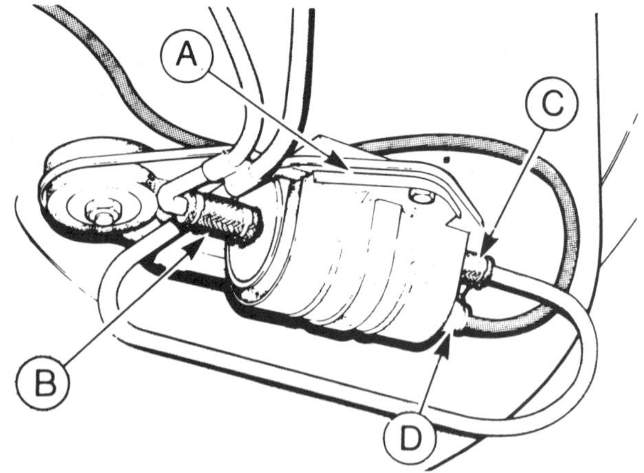

Fig 3.7 Electric fuel pump – models with air conditioning (Sec 10)

A Clamping bracket
B Fuel inlet
C Fuel outlet
D Wiring plug

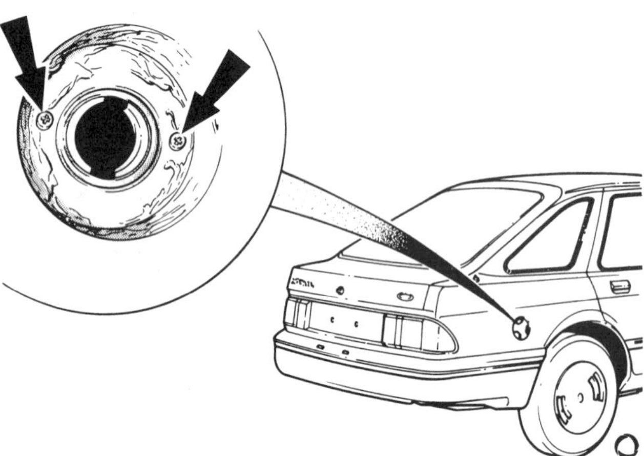

Fig 3.8 Fuel filler pipe-to-body panel securing screws (arrowed) – Saloon, Hatchback and Estate models up to 1987 (Sec 11)

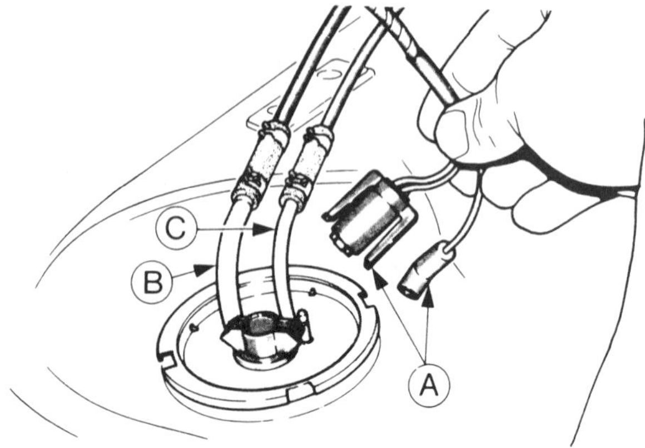

Fig 3.9 Fuel level sender unit connections – Saloon, Hatchback and Estate models (Sec 11)

A Wiring plugs
B Fuel outlet pipe
C Fuel inlet pipe

13 Clean the area around the pump mounting, and position a suitable container under the pump.
14 Using a hose clamping tool or self-locking pliers, clamp the fuel tank-to-pump hose to prevent excessive petrol spillage, or alternatively make arrangements to collect the contents of the fuel tank which will otherwise be released. Disconnect the hose from the pump.
15 Disconnect the fuel outlet hose from the pump and plug the hose

10.5 Withdrawing the fuel pump from the cylinder head - CVH model

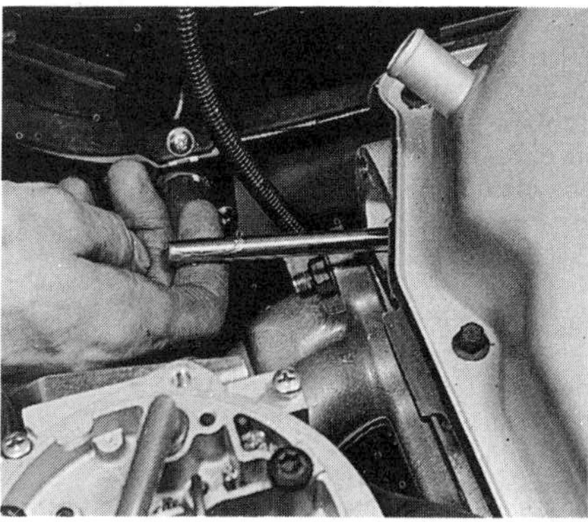
10.6 Withdrawing the fuel pump operating pushrod - CVH model

10.8A Removing the top cover from an early type fuel pump ...

10.8B ... for access to the mesh filter

11.7 Fuel tank securing strap - retaining bolt arrowed

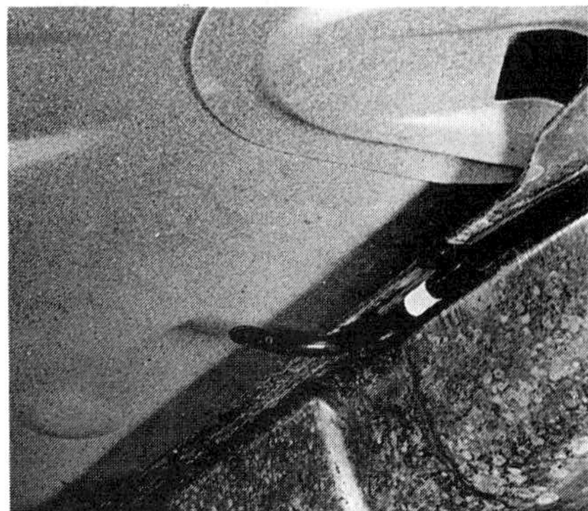
11.14 Fuel tank ventilation pipe correctly positioned on fuel tank

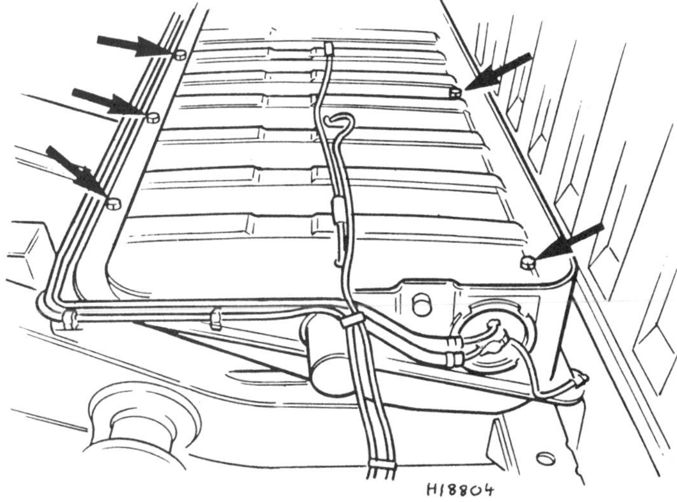

Fig 3.10 Fuel tank securing bolts (arrowed) - P100 models (Sec 11)

to prevent petrol spillage. **Caution:** *Petrol under pressure may spray out of the outlet as the hose is disconnected.*
16 Disconnect the wiring plug from the pump.
17 Slacken the clamping bolt, and slide the pump from the bracket assembly.
18 Refitting is a reversal of removal, but make sure that the rubber sleeve is correctly located around the pump body in the bracket, and ensure that the fuel hoses are securely connected. If the hoses were originally secured with crimped type clips, discard these and use new worm drive clips.

11 Fuel tank - removal and refitting

Note: *Refer to Section 2 before proceeding.*
1 Run the fuel level as low as possible before removing the tank.
2 Disconnect the battery negative lead.
3 Remove the tank filler cap, then syphon or pump out the tank contents (there is no drain plug). It may be necessary to disconnect the fuel tank-to-fuel pump hose in order to fully drain the tank. Store the petrol in a suitable sealed container.

Saloon, Hatchback and Estate models

4 Working in the fuel filler recess, remove the two screws on models up to 1987, or the single screw on models from 1987, securing the upper end of the fuel filler pipe to the body panel.
5 Chock the front wheels, then jack up the rear of the vehicle and support on axle stands.
6 Unscrew the two securing bolts from the left-hand tank flange, and on models from 1987, the single bolt from the right-hand tank flange.
7 Support the tank, then remove the bolt from the securing strap (photo). Unhook the remaining end of the strap from the underbody.
8 Lower the tank sufficiently to disconnect the two wiring plugs from the fuel level sender unit.
9 Identify the fuel hose locations for use when refitting, then disconnect the hoses from the sender unit and plug them.
10 Withdraw the fuel tank from under the vehicle.
11 If desired, the fuel level sender unit can be removed as described in Section 12.
12 The fuel filler and ventilation pipes can be removed from the tank by loosening the securing clips.
13 If the tank is contaminated with sediment or water, swill it out with clean petrol. If the tank has a leak, or is damaged, it should be repaired by a specialist, or alternatively renewed. Do not under any circumstances

attempt to solder or weld a fuel tank.
14 Refitting is a reversal of removal, but ensure that the ventilation pipe is correctly positioned in its groove in the tank, and is not trapped between the tank and the vehicle underbody (photo). Ensure that the fuel hoses and the fuel filler and ventilation pipes are correctly connected, and if the hoses or pipes were originally secured with crimped type clips, discard these and use new worm drive clips.

P100 models

15 Remove the cargo area as described in Chapter 12, Section 21.
16 Disconnect the wiring plug from the fuel level sender unit, and release the wiring from the clip on the fuel tank flange.
17 Identify the fuel hose locations for use when refitting, then disconnect the hoses from the sender unit and plug them.
18 Detach the fuel pipes from their clips on the tank.
19 Remove the five tank securing bolts, and lift the tank from the chassis frame.
20 Proceed as described in paragraphs 11 to 13 inclusive.
21 Commence refitting by loosening the bolts securing the front tank mounting brackets to the chassis frame.
22 Lower the tank into position and loosely refit the securing bolts. Tighten the three rear securing bolts.
23 Pull down on the front of the tank and tighten the bolts securing the front tank mounting brackets to the chassis frame when the brackets contact the insulating pads, then tighten the front tank securing bolts.
24 Further refitting is a reversal of removal, but ensure that all hoses and pipes are correctly connected, and if the hoses or pipes were originally secured with crimped type clips, discard these and use new worm drive clips. Refit the cargo area as described in Chapter 12, Section 21.

12 Fuel level sender unit – removal and refitting

Note: *Refer to Section 2 before proceeding. A new seal must be used when refitting the sender unit.*

Saloon, Hatchback and Estate models

1 Remove the fuel tank as described in Section 11.
2 Unscrew the sender unit from the tank by engaging two crossed screwdrivers in the slots on either side of the sender unit mounting flange. Recover the seal.
3 Refitting is a reversal of removal, but fit a new seal, and refit the fuel tank as described in Section 11.

P100 models

4 Remove the cargo area as described in Chapter 12, Section 21.
5 Disconnect the wiring plug from the sender unit.
6 Identify the fuel hose locations, as an aid to refitting, then disconnect the hoses from the sender unit and plug them.
7 Proceed as described in paragraph 2.
8 Refitting is a reversal of removal, but fit a new seal, and ensure that the fuel hoses are correctly connected. If the hoses were originally secured with crimped type clips, discard these and use new worm drive clips. Refit the cargo area as described in Chapter 12, Section 21.

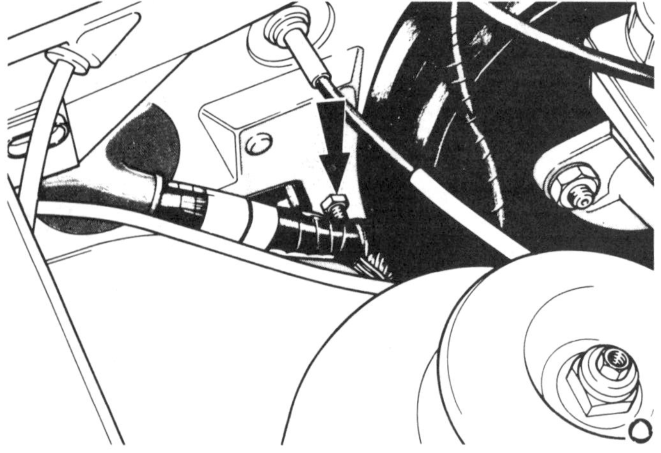

Fig 3.11 Throttle pedal securing nut (arrowed) in engine compartment (Sec 13)

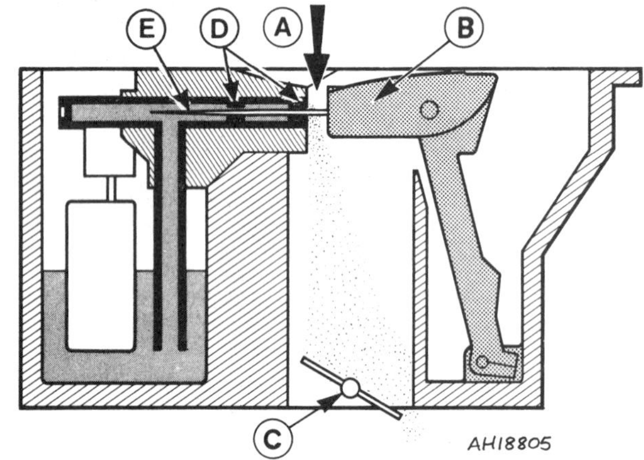

Fig 3.12 Schematic view of Ford VV type carburettor (Sec 15)

A Air intake
B Air valve (almost closed)
C Throttle plate
D Main and secondary jets
E Metering rod

13 Throttle pedal – removal and refitting

1 Disconnect the battery negative lead.
2 Remove the lower facia panel from the driver's side as described in Chapter 12.
3 Prise off the securing clip and disconnect the end of the throttle

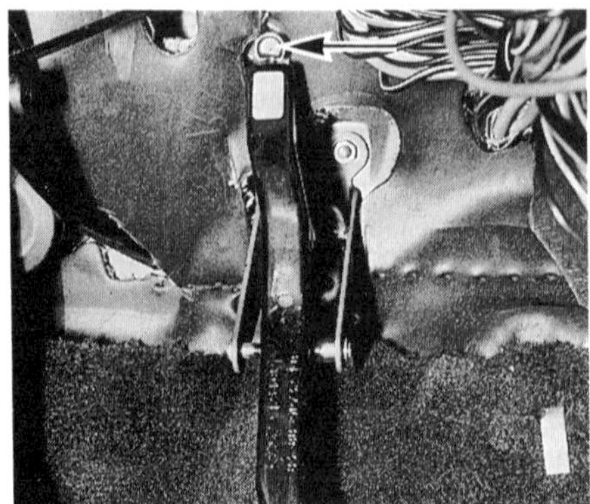

13.3 Throttle pedal assembly – cable connection arrowed

14.6 Disconnecting the throttle cable end from the throttle lever – Weber 2V type carburettor

14.7 Removing the throttle cable sheath retainer securing clip – CVH model

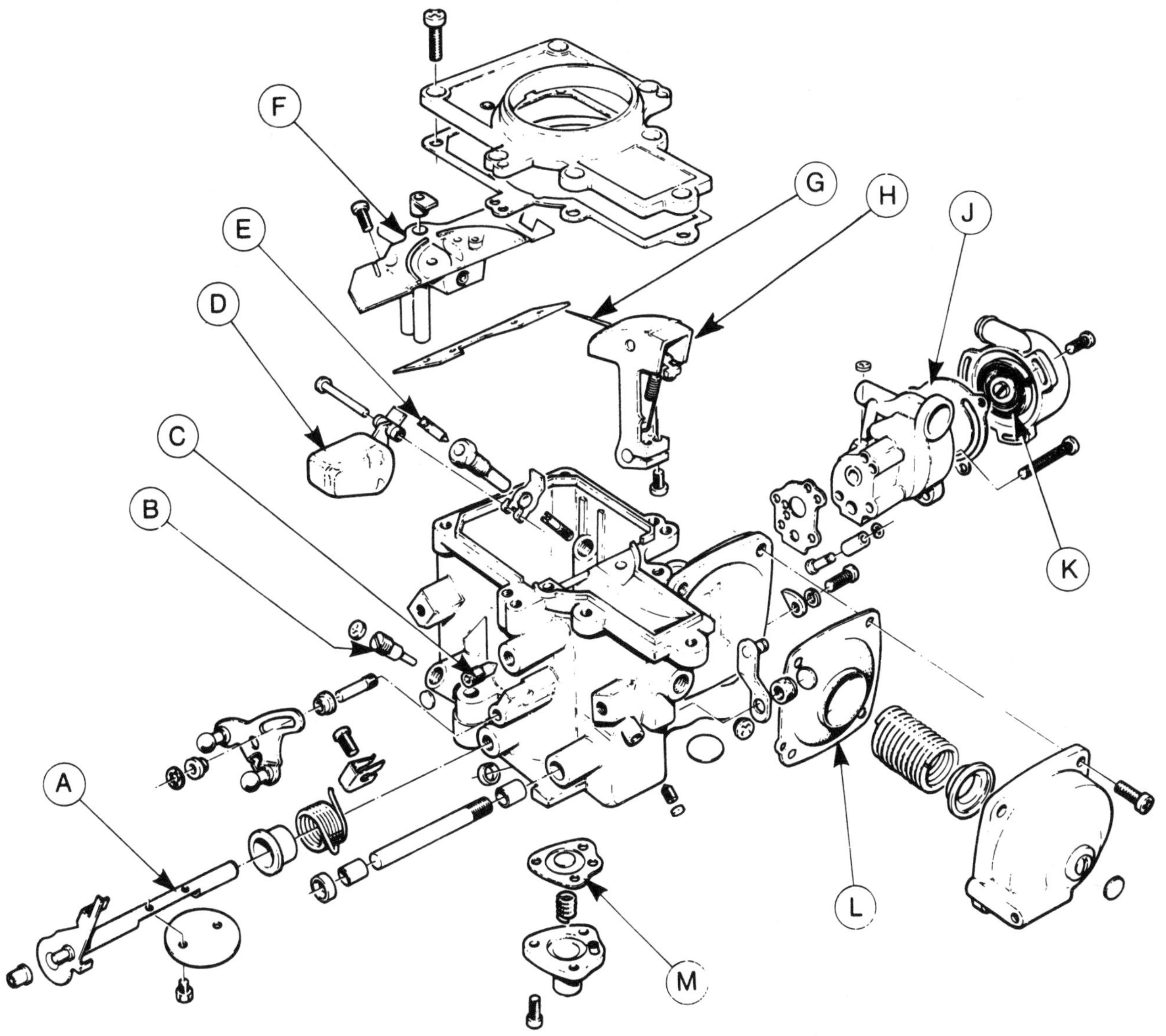

Fig 3.13 Exploded view of Ford VV type carburettor (Sec 15)

A *Throttle spindle*
B *Mixture screw*
C *By-pass leak adjuster*
D *Float*
E *Needle valve*
F *Main jet body*
G *Metering rod*
H *Air valve*
J *Automatic choke unit*
K *Bi-metal coil*
L *Carburettor control diaphragm*
M *Accelerator pump diaphragm*

cable from the top of the pedal (photo).

4 Remove the two securing nuts, one accessible from the driver's footwell, the other from the engine compartment, and withdraw the pedal and bracket assembly.

5 Refitting is a reversal of removal, but on completion check the throttle cable adjustment as described in Section 14, paragraph 9.

14 Throttle cable - removal, refitting and adjustment

1 Disconnect the battery negative lead.

2 Working inside the vehicle, remove the lower facia panel from the driver's side as described in Chapter 12.

3 Prise off the securing clip and disconnect the end of the throttle cable from the top of the pedal.

4 Working in the engine compartment, free the cable sheath from the bulkhead, and pull the cable through into the engine compartment. It will probably be necessary to pull the cable grommet from the bulkhead in order to free the cable sheath.

5 For improved access, remove the air cleaner as described in Section 5.

6 Disconnect the cable end from the throttle linkage. The cable end may be attached to the linkage with a balljoint and spring clip, a spring clip only, or the cable end may simply locate in a slot in the throttle lever (photo).

7 Prise off the spring clip securing the cable sheath to the cable bracket at the carburettor inlet manifold. Depress the four lugs on the plastic cable retainer simultaneously so that the retainer can be slid from the bracket, or remove the retainer securing clip, as applicable (photo). Take care not to damage the cable sheath.

8 Refitting is a reversal of removal, but before refitting the air cleaner, adjust the cable as follows.

9 Have an assistant fully depress the throttle pedal and hold it in this position. On models with automatic transmission, where applicable ensure that the kickdown cable does not restrict the pedal movement.

Turn the adjusting sleeve at the carburettor inlet manifold cable bracket until the throttle is just fully open. Have the assistant release and then fully depress the throttle pedal, and check that the throttle is again fully open. Adjust if necessary, then refit the air cleaner. On models with automatic transmission, where applicable check the operation of the kickdown cable, and adjust if necessary.

15 Carburettor (Ford VV type) – description

The Ford VV (variable venturi) carburettor is theoretically more efficient than fixed jet types due mainly to improved fuel atomisation, especially at low engine speeds and loads. It also overcomes the need for mixture correction devices. The carburettor operates as follows.

Fuel is supplied to the carburettor via a needle valve which is actuated by the float. When the fuel level is low in the float chamber in the carburettor, the float drops and opens the needle valve. When the correct fuel level is reached the float will close the valve and shut off the fuel supply.

The float level on this type of carburettor is not adjustable, since minor variations in the fuel level do not affect the performance of the carburettor. The valve needle is prevented from vibrating by means of a ball and light spring, and to further ensure that the needle seals correctly it is coated in a rubber-like coating of Viton.

The float chamber is vented internally via the main jet body and carburettor air inlet, thus avoiding the possibility of petrol vapour escaping into the atmosphere.

The air/fuel mixture intake is controlled by the air valve which is moved according to the operating demands of the engine. The valve is actuated by a diaphragm which moves according to the vacuum supplied through the venturi between the air valve and the throttle plate. As the air valve and diaphragm are connected they move correspondingly.

When the engine is idling the air intake requirement is low and therefore the valve moves towards the closed position, causing a high air speed over the main jet exit. However as the throttle plate is opened, the control vacuum (depression within the venturi) increases and is channelled to the diaphragm which then opens the air valve to balance the control spring and control vacuum.

When the throttle is opened further this equality of balance is maintained as the air valve is progressively opened to equalise the control spring and control vacuum forces throughout the speed range.

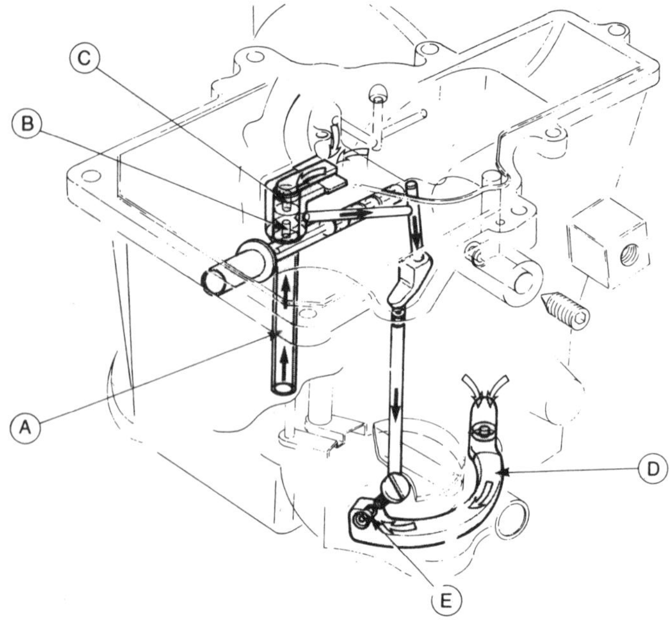

Fig 3.14 Schematic diagram of idle system – Ford VV type carburettor (Sec 15)

A Main pick-up tube
B Idle fuel jet
C Idle air jet
D Idle air bypass gallery
E Idle discharge tube

Fuel from the float chamber is drawn up the pick-up tube and then regulated by two jets and the tapered metering needle on the air valve, before being drawn into the main venturi by the vacuum – see Fig. 3.12. At low engine speeds the metering needle taper moves further into the main jet to restrict the fuel supply. On acceleration and at high engine speeds the needle is moved out of the main jet by the action of the air valve. As the needle is tapered, the amount by which it is moved regulates the amount of fuel passing through the main jet.

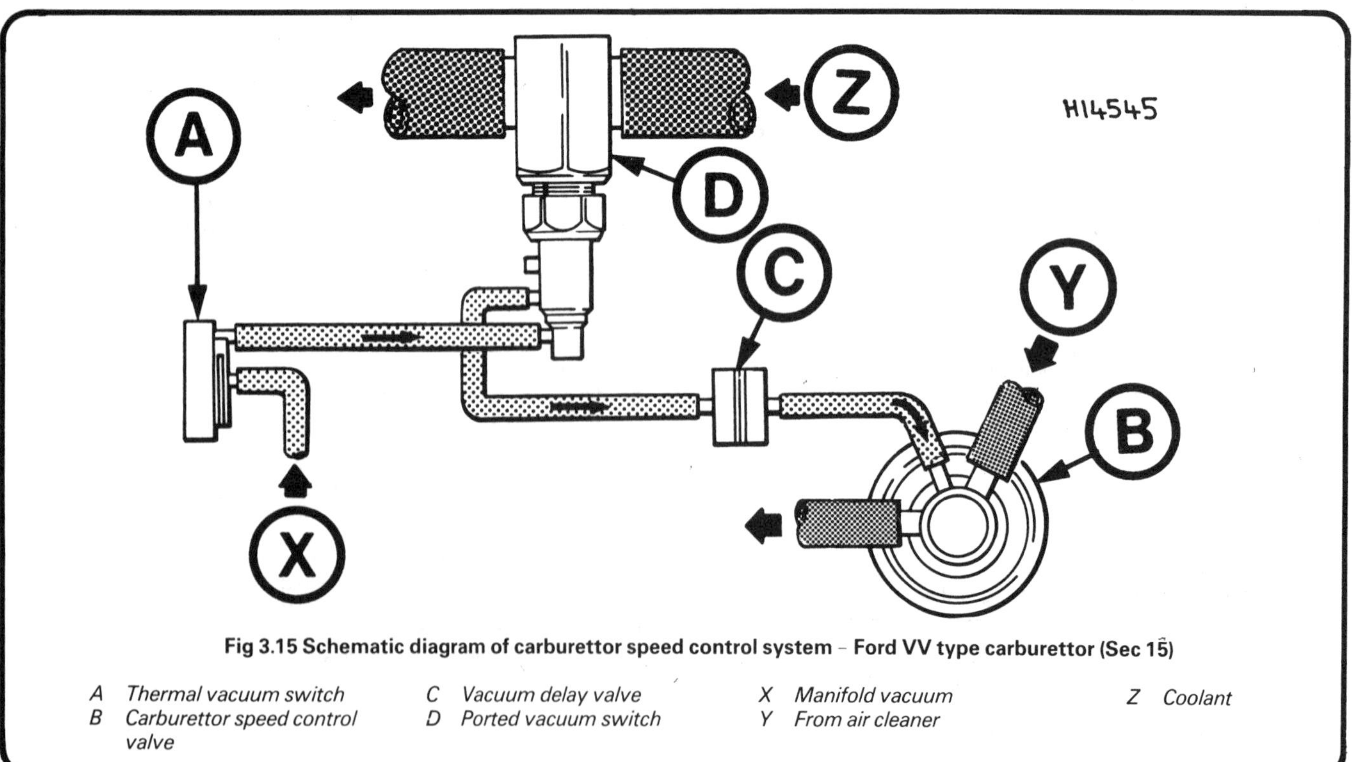

Fig 3.15 Schematic diagram of carburettor speed control system – Ford VV type carburettor (Sec 15)

A Thermal vacuum switch
B Carburettor speed control valve
C Vacuum delay valve
D Ported vacuum switch
X Manifold vacuum
Y From air cleaner
Z Coolant

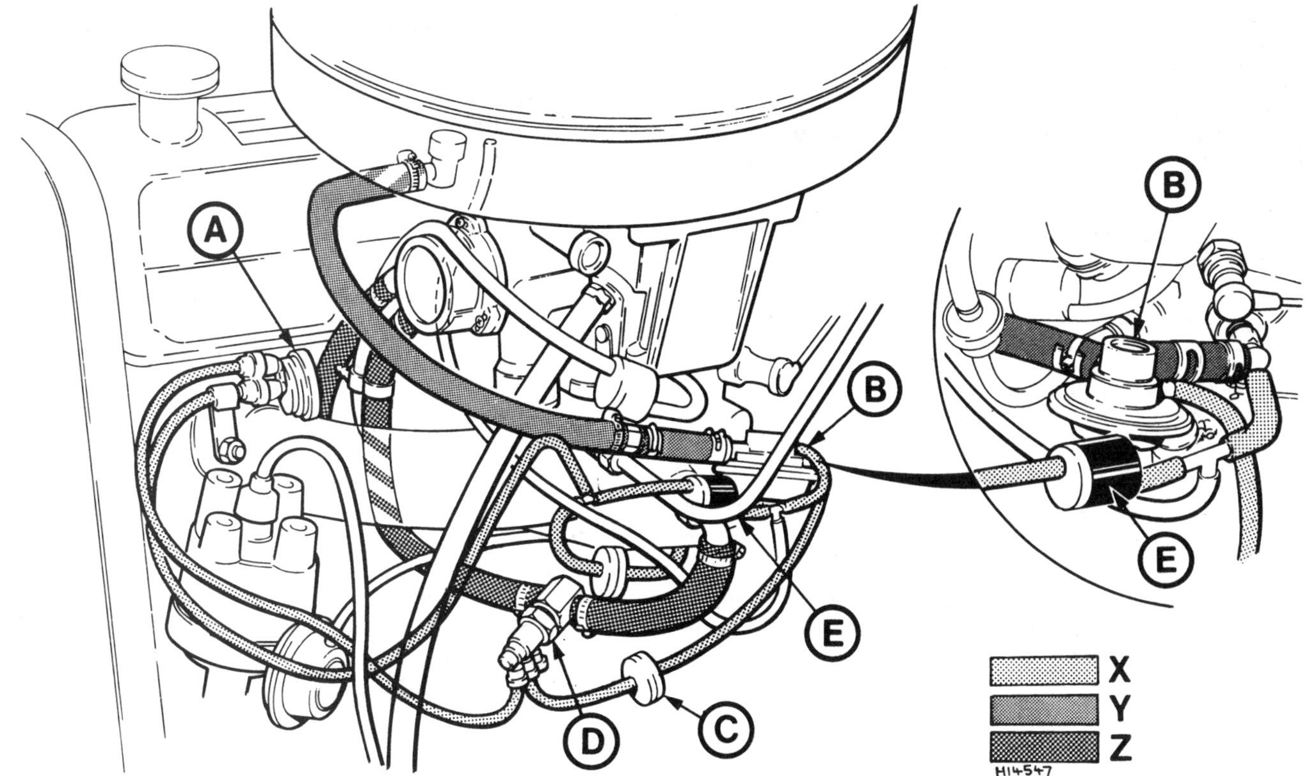

Fig 3.16 Location of carburettor speed control system components – Ford VV type carburettor (Sec 15)

A Thermal vacuum switch
B Carburettor speed control valve
C Vacuum delay valve
D Ported vacuum switch
E Fuel trap (not fitted to all models)
X Manifold vacuum
Y From air cleaner
Z Coolant

An idling system is used, with 70% of the idle air/fuel mixture supplied by the idling system and 30% by the main system. At idle, fuel is drawn through the main pick-up tube, passes through the idle fuel jet, and then mixes with the air supplied by the idle air jet. The air/fuel mixture then passes on through the inner galleries to the mixture control screw which regulates the fuel supply at idle. This mixture then combines with air drawn through the idle air bypass gallery from the main venturi, and finally enters the main venturi below the throttle valve at an accelerated rate of flow, via the idle discharge tube.

Throttle actuation is via a progressive linkage which has a cam and roller mechanism. The advantage of this system is that a large initial throttle pedal movement allows only a small throttle plate opening. As the throttle pedal approaches its maximum travel, the throttle plate movement accelerates accordingly. This system aids economy, gives good engine response throughout the load range on smaller engines, and enables the same size of carburettor to be employed on models across the range.

To counterbalance the sudden decrease in vacuum when initially accelerating, a restrictor is fitted into the air passage between the main venturi and the diaphragm. The restrictor causes the air valve to open slowly when an increase in air flow occurs, which in turn causes a higher vacuum in the main venturi for a brief moment, caused by the increase in air velocity. The increase in vacuum increases the fuel flow into the main venturi, thus preventing a 'flat spot'. The large amounts of fuel required under heavy acceleration are supplied by the accelerator pump.

The accelerator pump injects fuel directly into the main venturi when acceleration causes a drop in vacuum. This richening of the mixture prevents engine hesitation under heavy acceleration. The accelerator pump is a diaphragm type and is operated by vacuum drawn from beneath the throttle plate in the main venturi. During acceleration the vacuum under the throttle plate decreases, the diaphragm return spring pushes the diaphragm, and the fuel in the accelerator pump is fed via the inner galleries through a one-way valve into the main venturi. The system incorporates a back-bleeder and a vacuum break air hole. The back-bleeder allows excess fuel vapour to return to the float chamber when prolonged idling causes the carburettor temperature to rise and thus the fuel in the accelerator pump to vaporise. The vacuum break air hole allows air into the pump outlet tube which reduces the vacuum at the accelerator pump jet at high engine speeds, thus preventing fuel being drawn out of the accelerator pump system.

A fully automatic choke system is fitted incorporating a coolant-heated bi-metallic spring. According to the temperature of the coolant, the spring in the choke unit expands or contracts. This in turn actuates the choke mechanism, which consists of a variable needle jet and a variable air supply. Fuel to the choke jet is drawn from the main pick-up tube via internal galleries. When the bi-metallic spring is contracted (engine cold), it pulls the tapered choke needle from the jet to increase the fuel supply. The spring expands as the engine warms up and the needle reduces the fuel supply as it re-enters the jet. The choke air supply is drawn from the main venturi, just above the throttle plate. The fuel mixes with the air in the choke air valve and is then delivered to the main venturi.

A choke pull-down system is used, whereby if the engine is under choke but is only cruising, ie not under heavy load, the choke is released. The system is operated by a vacuum-operated piston which is connected to the spindle in the choke unit by levers.

An anti-dieselling (anti-run-on) valve is fitted to the carburettor body. The valve shuts off the fuel supply to the idling system when the ignition is switched off and so prevents the engine running-on or 'dieselling'. The valve is a solenoid type and is actuated electrically. When the ignition is switched off, the valve allows a plunger to enter the idle discharge tube, thus stopping the fuel supply. When the ignition is switched on, the solenoid is actuated and the plunger is withdrawn from the idle discharge tube.

Certain later models are fitted with a carburettor speed control system which improves driveability during the warm-up period in cold ambient conditions.

The main component of the system is the carburettor speed control valve (CSCV). Under the influence of manifold vacuum the CSCV admits extra air to the inlet manifold, so weakening what would otherwise be an excessively rich mixture.

Vacuum is applied to the CSCV via a delay valve, a ported vacuum switch (PVS) and a thermal vacuum switch (TVS). The delay valve prevents premature operation of the CSCV during start-up, and damps out the effect of sudden changes in throttle position. The PVS responds to coolant temperature, only allowing vacuum to pass to the CSCV when coolant temperature is below 35°C (95°F). The TVS responds to air temperature, only allowing vacuum to pass when air temperature is below 10°C (50°F). Thus the CSCV is only activated when both coolant and ambient air temperatures are low.

16 Carburettor (Ford VV type) – removal and refitting

Note: *Refer to Section 2 before proceeding. A new gasket must be used when refitting the carburettor. A tachometer and an exhaust gas analyser will be required to check the idle speed and mixture on completion.*

1 Disconnect the battery negative lead.
2 Remove the air cleaner as described in Section 5.
3 Relieve the pressure in the cooling system by unscrewing the expansion tank cap. If the engine is warm, place a thick rag over the cap and unscrew the cap slowly as a precaution against scalding. Refit the cap after relieving the pressure.
4 Identify the automatic choke coolant hose locations, as an aid to refitting, then disconnect the hoses (being prepared for coolant spillage.) Either plug the hoses or secure them with their ends facing upwards to prevent loss of coolant.
5 Disconnect the wiring from the anti-dieselling (anti-run-on) valve.
6 Disconnect the fuel hose and vacuum pipe (photo). Plug the end of the fuel hose to minimise petrol spillage.
7 Disconnect the throttle cable from the carburettor throttle lever with reference to Section 14 if necessary (photo).
8 Remove the two securing nuts and washers, and lift the carburettor from the inlet manifold studs (photos). Recover the gasket.
9 Refitting is a reversal of removal, bearing in mind the following points.
10 Ensure that the mating faces of the inlet manifold and carburettor are clean, and use a new gasket.
11 Ensure that the coolant hoses, fuel hose, and vacuum pipe are correctly routed and free from restrictions. If any of the hoses were originally secured with crimped type clips, discard these and use new worm drive clips on refitting.
12 On completion, check and if necessary top up the coolant level as described in Chapter 2, and check and if necessary adjust the idle speed and mixture as described in Section 17.

17 Carburettor (Ford VV type) – idle speed and mixture adjustment

Note: *Refer to Section 2 before proceeding. Before carrying out any carburettor adjustments, ensure that the ignition timing and spark plug gaps are set as specified. To carry out the adjustments an accurate tachometer and an exhaust gas analyser (CO meter) will be required.*

1 Ensure that the air cleaner is correctly fitted, and that all vacuum hoses and pipes are securely connected and free from restrictions, then run the engine until it is at normal operating temperature.
2 Stop the engine, and connect a tachometer and an exhaust gas analyser in accordance with the manufacturer's instructions.
3 Start the engine and run it at 3000 rpm for 30 seconds, ensuring that all electrical loads are switched off (headlamps, heater blower etc), then allow the engine to idle and check the idle speed and CO content. Note that the CO reading will initially rise, then fall and finally stabilise after between 5 and 25 seconds.
4 If necessary, adjust the idle speed screw to give the specified idle speed – see Fig. 3.17.
5 Checking and adjustment should be completed within 30 seconds of the meter readings stabilising. If this has not been possible, repeat paragraphs 3 and 4, ignoring the reference to starting the engine.
6 Adjustment of the mixture (CO content) is not normally required during routine maintenance, but if the reading noted in paragraph 3 is not as specified, proceed as follows.

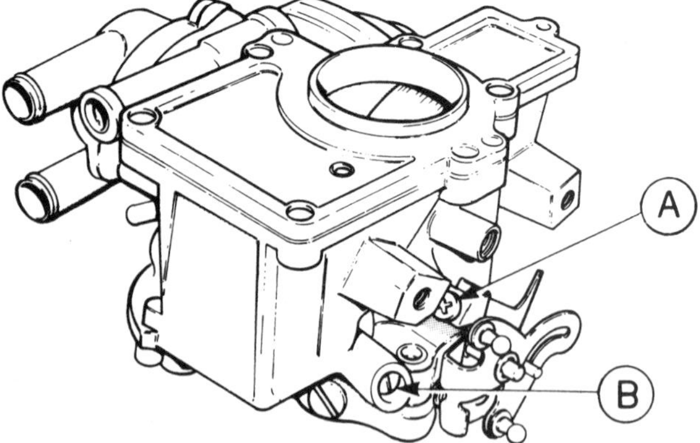

Fig 3.17 Ford VV type carburettor adjustment screw locations (Sec 17)

A Idle speed screw *B Idle mixture screw*

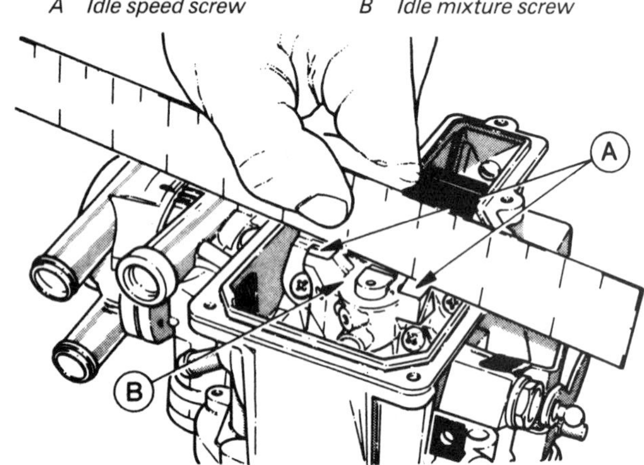

Fig 3.18 Using a straight edge to check the alignment of the main jet body – Ford VV type carburettor (Sec 18)

A Alignment flanges *B Main jet body*

7 Using a thin screwdriver, remove the tamperproof seal from the mixture screw – see Fig. 3.17.
8 Run the engine at 3000 rpm for 30 seconds, then allow the engine to idle, and using a small screwdriver or a 4.0 mm Allen key, as applicable, adjust the mixture screw to give the specified CO content.
9 Checking and adjustment should be completed within 30 seconds of the meter readings stabilising. If this has not been possible, repeat paragraph 8.
10 If necessary adjust the idle speed, then recheck the CO content.
11 On completion of the adjustments, stop the engine and disconnect the tachometer and exhaust gas analyser. Fit a new tamperproof seal to the mixture screw.

18 Needle valve and float (Ford VV type carburettor) – removal and refitting

Note: *Refer to Section 2 before proceeding. A new carburettor top cover gasket must be used on reassembly, and if the float is removed, a new main jet body gasket will be required. A tachometer and an exhaust gas analyser will be required to check the idle speed and mixture on completion.*

1 Disconnect the battery negative lead.
2 Remove the air cleaner as described in Section 5.
3 Thoroughly clean all external dirt from the carburettor.
4 Remove the seven securing screws and lift off the carburettor top cover (photo). Recover the gasket.

16.6 Disconnecting the fuel hose – Ford VV type carburettor

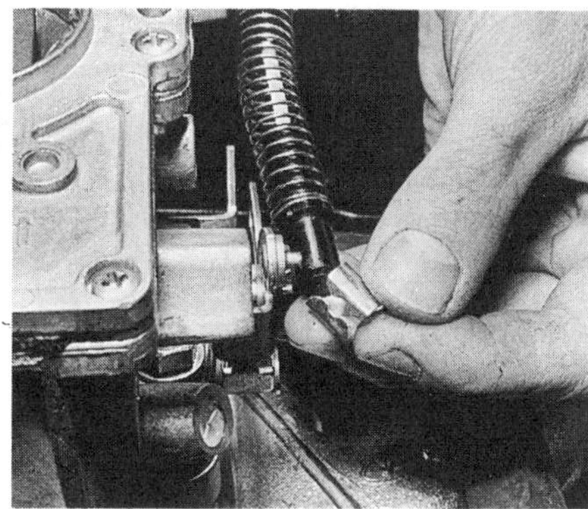

16.7 Disconnecting the throttle cable from the throttle lever – Ford VV type carburettor

16.8A Remove the securing nuts and washers ...

16.8B ... and lift the carburettor from the inlet manifold – Ford VV type carburettor

18.4 Lifting off the carburettor top cover (carburettor removed) – Ford VV type carburettor

18.8A Main jet body securing screws (arrowed) – Ford VV type carburettor

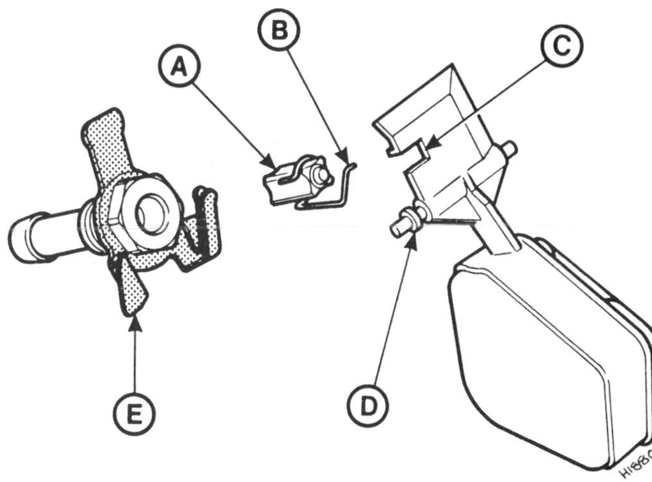

Fig 3.19 Needle valve and float components – Ford VV type carburettor (Sec 18)

A Needle valve
B Clip
C Float cut-out
D Spacer washer
E Float pivot pin bracket

5 Unclip the float pivot pin from its bracket and unhook the needle valve clip from the float cut-out. Position the float clear of the needle valve.

6 Using a pair of pointed pliers, lift out the needle valve, taking care not to allow it to drop into the float chamber. Remove the clip from the needle valve if desired.

7 To remove the float, it is necessary to remove the main jet body.

8 Remove the four securing screws, hold the air valve fully open, and carefully lift the main jet body from the carburettor, pulling it clear of the metering rod on the air valve (photos). Great care must be taken not to bend or distort the metering rod in any way. Recover the gasket.

9 The float can now be lifted from the carburettor body.

10 Inspect the components for damage and renew as necessary. Check the needle valve for wear, and check the float for leaks by shaking it to see if it contains petrol.

11 If the float has been removed, commence refitting as follows, otherwise proceed to paragraph 16.

12 Position the float in the carburettor body.

13 Ensure that the mating faces of the carburettor and main jet body are clean, and position a new gasket on the carburettor face (photo).

14 Hold the air valve fully open, and carefully refit the main jet body to the carburettor, guiding the metering rod into the jet body. Great care must be taken not to bend or distort the metering rod in any way. Refit the main jet body securing screws, but do not fully tighten them at this stage.

15 Using a straight edge, adjust the main jet body until the two alignment flanges, 'A' in Fig. 3.18, are flush with the top face of the carburettor body, then fully tighten the securing screws.

16 Ensure that the needle valve clip is correctly positioned in its groove in the needle valve, then position the clip in the float cut-out.

17 Refit the float pivot pin to its bracket, ensuring that the spacer washer is positioned between the bracket and the float – see Fig. 3.19.

18 Operate the float several times to check for free movement.

19 Fit a new top cover gasket, then refit the top cover and tighten the securing screws.

20 Refit the air cleaner as described in Section 5, and reconnect the battery negative lead.
21 Check and if necessary adjust the idle speed and mixture as described in Section 17.

19 Carburettor control diaphragm (Ford VV type carburettor) – renewal

Note: *Early carburettors were fitted with a black-coloured diaphragm, whereas later carburettors have a blue- coloured diaphragm. If renewal is necessary, a blue-coloured diaphragm should be used regardless of the type originally fitted.*
1 Disconnect the battery negative lead.
2 For improved access, remove the air cleaner as described in Section 5.
3 Thoroughly clean all external dirt from the area around the diaphragm housing.
4 Remove the four securing screws and lift off the diaphragm cover. Recover the diaphragm return spring and seat.
5 Fold back the diaphragm rubber from the housing flange, then using a small screwdriver prise free the circlip to release the diaphragm from the air valve operating lever (photo). Take care not to lose the circlip.
6 Commence refitting by reconnecting the diaphragm to the air valve operating lever, noting that the diaphragm should be orientated with the small vacuum hole at the bottom left-hand corner. Ensure that the circlip is correctly fitted.
7 Hold the air valve fully open, and retain it in this position until the diaphragm cover has been fitted. This will ensure that the diaphragm is not trapped.
8 Ensure that the mating faces of the housing flange and diaphragm cover are clean, then locate the diaphragm on the housing flange, ensuring that the vacuum hole in the diaphragm is aligned with the corresponding holes in the housing flange and the diaphragm cover (photo).
9 Locate the return spring and seat on the diaphragm, then carefully refit the diaphragm cover. Tighten the securing screws progressively to avoid distorting the diaphragm.
10 Release the air valve, then refit the air cleaner and reconnect the battery negative lead.

20 Accelerator pump diaphragm (Ford VV type carburettor) – renewal

1 Remove the carburettor as described in Section 16.
2 Invert the carburettor, taking precautions to catch the petrol which will drain out, and thoroughly clean all external dirt from the area around the accelerator pump housing.
3 Remove the three securing screws and lift off the accelerator pump cover. Recover the diaphragm return spring and seat.
4 Lift the diaphragm from the housing flange.
5 Clean the mating faces of the housing flange and the accelerator pump cover, and ensure that the coloured spacer is in position in the housing – see Fig. 3.20.
6 Commence refitting by locating the diaphragm on the housing flange, with the gasket side uppermost. Ensure that the vacuum hole in the diaphragm is aligned with the corresponding holes in the housing flange and the accelerator pump cover.
7 Locate the seat and return spring on the diaphragm, then carefully refit the accelerator pump cover. Ensure that the spring locates correctly, and tighten the cover securing screws progressively to avoid distorting the diaphragm.
8 Refit the carburettor as described in Section 16.

21 Automatic choke unit (Ford VV type carburettor) – removal, checking and refitting

Note: *Refer to Section 2 before proceeding. New bi-metal housing and choke unit gaskets must be used when refitting. A tachometer and an exhaust gas analyser will be required to check the idle speed and mixture on completion.*
1 Disconnect the battery negative lead.

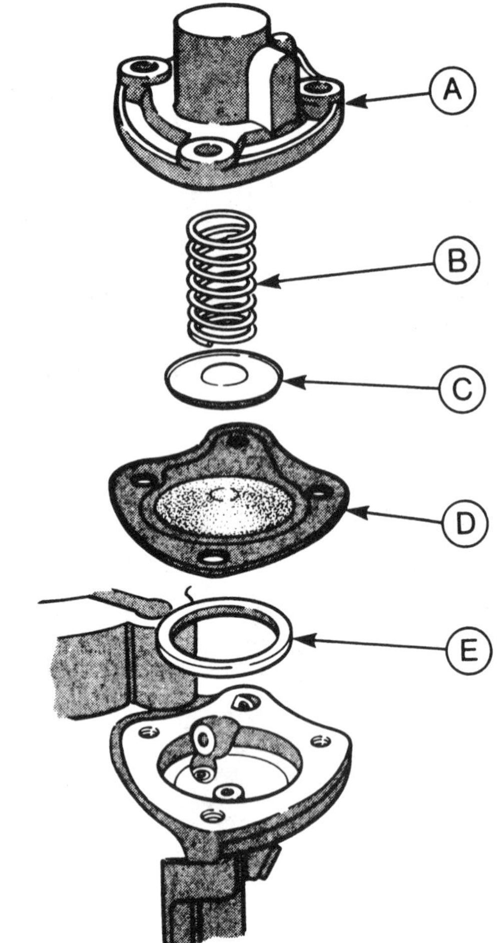

Fig 3.20 Accelerator pump components – Ford VV type carburettor (Sec 20)

A Pump cover
B Return spring
C Spring seat
D Diaphragm
E Coloured spacer

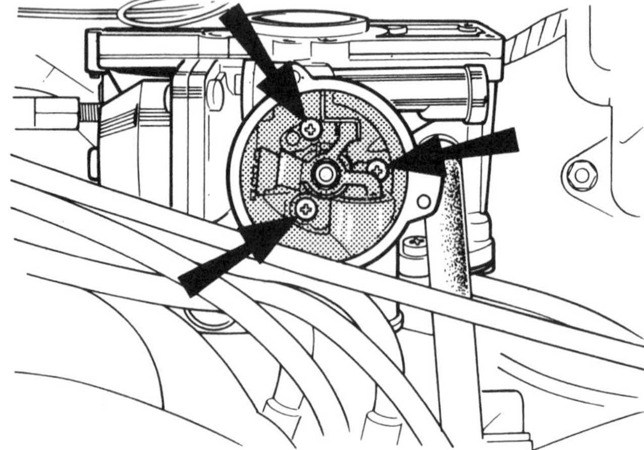

Fig 3.21 Automatic choke unit securing screws (arrowed) – Ford VV type carburettor (Sec 21)

2 Remove the air cleaner as described in Section 5.
3 Note the position of the bi-metal housing alignment marks for use when refitting, then remove the three securing screws and lift off the bi-metal housing (photo). If necessary make additional alignment marks for clarity. Place the housing to one side, taking care not to strain the coolant hoses. Recover the gasket.

18.8B Lifting the main jet body from the carburettor (carburettor removed) – Ford VV type carburettor

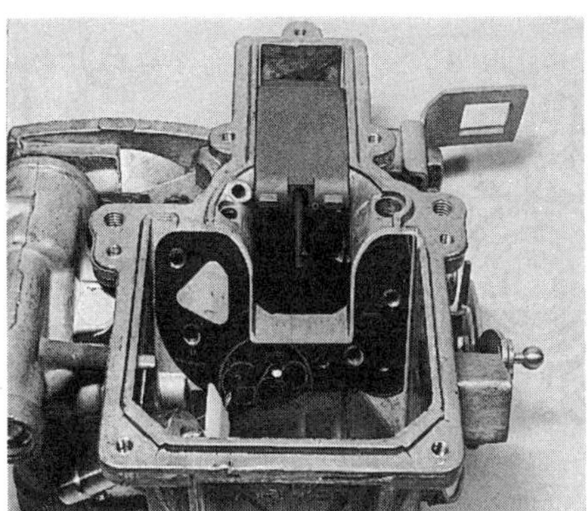

18.13 Main jet body gasket in position (carburettor removed) – Ford VV type carburettor

19.5 Carburettor control diaphragm securing circlip (arrowed) – Ford VV type carburettor

19.8 Carburettor control diaphragm vacuum hole correctly positioned (arrowed) – Ford VV type carburettor

21.3 Automatic choke bi-metal housing alignment marks – Ford VV type carburettor

21.16 Ensure that the bi-metal coil engages with the linkage lever centre slot (arrowed) – Ford VV type carburettor

4 Remove the three securing screws and lift the choke unit from the carburettor. Recover the gasket.

5 The choke mechanism can be checked for correct operation as follows.

6 Clean the unit by gently blowing out any dust or dirt with an air line or foot pump.

7 Using a small screwdriver or thin rod, raise the pull-down piston (Fig. 3.22) and allow it to drop under its own weight, checking that it falls smoothly to the lower limit of its travel.

8 Repeat this check, but with the choke linkage lever held in various positions. If the piston binds in any position throughout its total travel, try cleaning the unit once more with an air line, nothing else, then repeat the checks. Under no circumstances attempt to ease a sticking piston with lubrication of any kind, otherwise the calibration of the piston will be affected and its operating characteristics radically altered. Check also that the choke control spring leg is seated in its slot in the choke lever (Fig. 3.23). If not, carefully slip it back into place. Check the operation of the piston once more and if it still sticks, renew the choke unit and bi-metal housing as an assembly.

9 Check the choke metering rod by carefully moving the needle bracket (Fig. 3.24) through its full range of travel using a small screwdriver. As with the pull-down piston, the check should be made with the linkage lever held in various positions. Ensure that the rod does not bind in any position throughout its total travel. If binding does occur it may be lightly lubricated with 'Ballistol Spray' which should be available from main Ford dealers. Do not use any other lubricant otherwise a sludge build-up may occur, and do not allow overspray to contact the pull-down piston or linkage. If the metering rod is partially or completely seized, lubrication will not help and the choke unit and bi-metal housing should be renewed as an assembly.

10 If both the metering rod and the pull-down piston are satisfactory, but binding was noticed when moving the linkage lever, then the central shaft should be lightly lubricated from the rear of the choke unit using the 'Ballistol Spray'.

11 If it is necessary to remove the bi-metal housing for renewal, proceed as follows, otherwise proceed to paragraph 14.

12 Relieve the pressure in the cooling system by unscrewing the expansion tank cap. If the engine is warm, place a thick rag over the cap and unscrew the cap slowly as a precaution against scalding. Refit the cap after relieving the pressure.

13 Identify the automatic choke coolant hose locations for use when refitting, then disconnect the hoses (being prepared for coolant spillage.) Either plug the hoses or secure them with their ends facing upwards to prevent loss of coolant. Withdraw the bi-metal housing. Drain the coolant from the housing into a suitable container.

14 If a new choke unit is to be fitted, it will first be necessary to tap out the bi-metal housing securing screw holes. The threads can be tapped out using the securing screws which are self-tapping. **Do not** cut the threads with a standard tap.

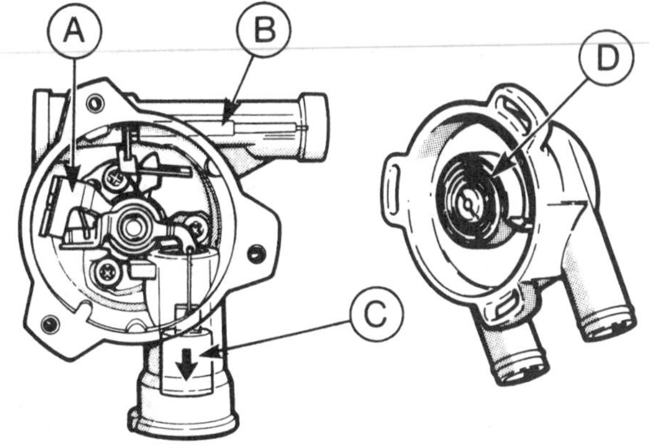

Fig 3.22 Automatic choke components – Ford VV type carburettor (Sec 21)

A Choke linkage
B Metering rod
C Pull-down piston
D Bi-metal coil

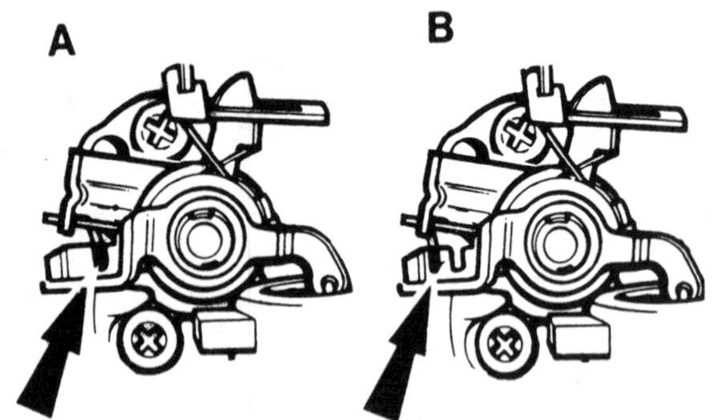

Fig 3.23 Correct position of choke control spring leg – Ford VV type carburettor (Sec 21)

A Correctly located *B Incorrectly located*

15 Refit the choke unit using a new gasket and tighten the securing screws.

16 Refit the bi-metal housing, using a new gasket, and ensuring that the bi-metal coil engages with the linkage lever centre slot (photo). Loosely refit the securing screws starting with the lower one.

17 Align the marks on the choke unit and the bi-metal housing as noted during removal, then tighten the bi-metal housing securing screws.

18 Where applicable, reconnect the coolant hoses to the bi-metal housing.

19 Refit the air cleaner as described in Section 5, and reconnect the battery negative lead.

20 If the coolant hoses have been disconnected, check the coolant level as described in Chapter 2.

21 Check and if necessary adjust the idle speed and mixture as described in Section 17.

22 Carburettor (Weber 2V type) – description

The Weber 2V (twin venturi) carburettor is of fixed jet, sequential throttle type. The primary throttle valve operates alone except at high engine speeds and loads when the secondary throttle valve is operated, until at full throttle both are fully open. This arrangement allows good fuel economy during light acceleration and cruising, but also gives maximum power at full throttle. On 2.0 litre models up to 1985, the secondary throttle valve is activated mechanically, whereas on all other models it is vacuum-operated according to the vacuum produced in the primary venturi. The primary throttle barrel and venturi diameters are smaller than their secondary counterparts. The carburettor is a complicated instrument with various refinements and sub-systems added, according to model and equipment, to achieve improved driveability, economy and exhaust emission levels.

A separate idle system operates independently from the main jet system, supplying fuel via the mixture control screw, and on certain models an anti-dieselling (anti-run-on) valve is incorporated in the idle circuit to shut of the fuel supply when the ignition is switched off.

The main jets are calibrated to suit engine requirements at mid-range throttle openings. To provide the necessary fuel enrichment at full throttle, a vacuum-operated power valve is used. The valve provides extra fuel under the low vacuum conditions associated with wide throttle openings.

To provide an enrichened mixture during acceleration, an accelerator pump delivers extra fuel to the primary main venturi. The accelerator pump is operated mechanically by a cam on the throttle linkage.

To prevent the engine from stalling when idling from a cold start, on certain models the carburettor incorporates a low vacuum enrichment device. This device only operates when the engine is cold, and a ported vacuum switch which is sensitive to engine coolant temperature shuts off the vacuum supply when the engine reaches normal operating temperature. This device senses the low vacuum associated with engine stalling and supplies extra fuel to enrich the mixture, thus preventing stalling.

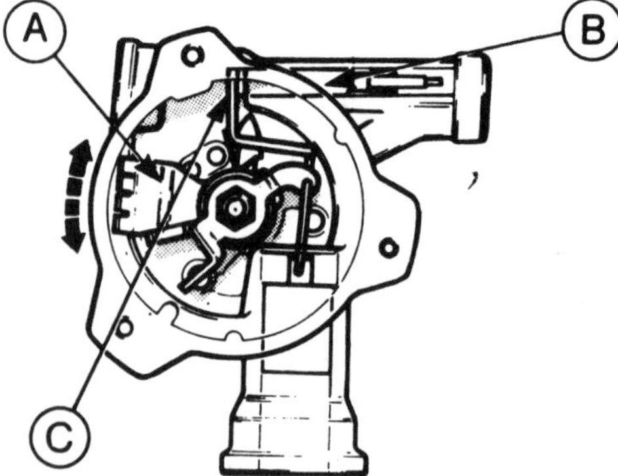

Fig 3.24 Checking choke operation – Ford VV type carburettor (Sec 21)

A Linkage lever
B Metering rod
C Needle bracket

A fully automatic choke is fitted, operated by a coolant or electrically-heated bi-metal coil depending on model. When the engine is cold, the bi-metal coil is fully wound up, holding the choke plate(s) closed. As the engine warms up the bi-metal coil is heated and therefore unwinds, progressively opening the choke plate(s). A vacuum-operated pull-down system is employed whereby, if the engine is under choke, but is only cruising (ie not under heavy load) the choke plate(s) is/are opened against the action of the bi-metal coil. Similarly a mechanical pull-down system is operated by a cam on the throttle linkage to open the choke plate(s) if full throttle is used (which is to be avoided wherever possible). The pull-down systems prevent an over-rich mixture which reduces fuel economy and may cause unnecessary engine wear when the engine is cold. On models with a vacuum-operated secondary throttle valve, only the primary barrel is fitted with a choke plate, as the secondary throttle valve only operates under conditions where choke is not required.

On models with a vacuum-operated secondary throttle valve and automatic transmission, the secondary throttle valve is prevented from opening when the engine is cold by a ported vacuum switch. The switch is sensitive to engine coolant temperature, and bleeds off the vacuum supply to the secondary throttle valve until the engine reaches normal operating temperature.

2.0 litre models from 1985 are fitted with a carburettor stepper motor which operates in conjunction with the ESC II engine management system to control the engine idle speed, and the throttle plate position during deceleration, engine shut-off and start-up. Further details are given in Chapter 4.

23 Carburettor (Weber 2V type) – removal and refitting

1 Proceed as described in Section 16, but note the following.

2 On models with an electrically-heated automatic choke, ignore all references to the cooling system and coolant hoses.

3 Not all Weber carburettors are fitted with an anti-dieselling valve.

4 Disconnect all relevant wiring plugs and vacuum pipes, if necessary noting their locations for use when refitting.

5 Disconnect the link arm from the throttle linkage instead of disconnecting the throttle cable.

6 The carburettor is secured to the inlet manifold by four nuts and washers.

24 Carburettor (Weber 2V type) – idle speed and mixture adjustment

Models without stepper motor

1 Proceed as described in Section 17, but note the following.

2 To remove the mixture screw tamperproof seal, it will be necessary

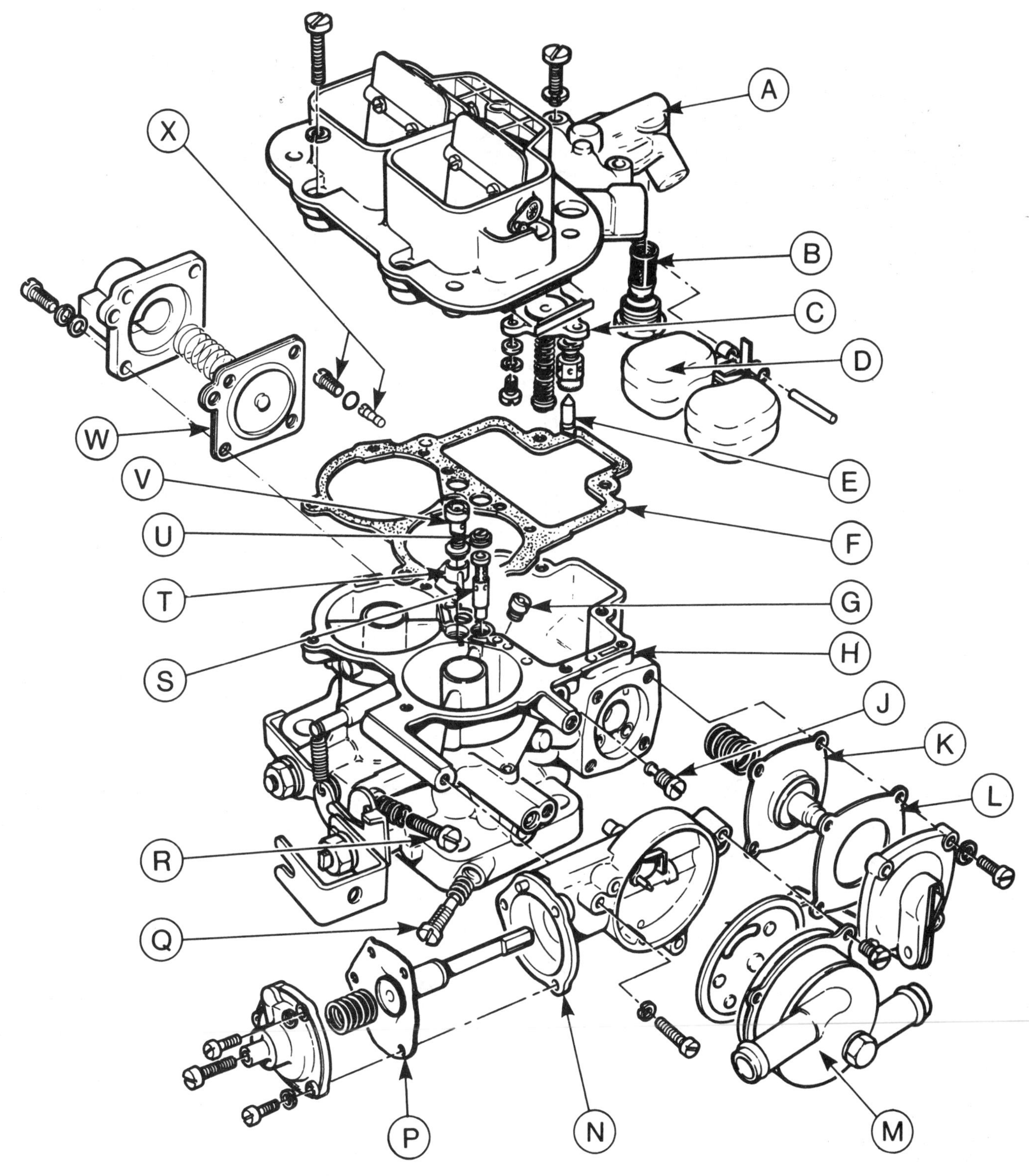

Fig 3.25 Exploded view of Weber 2V type carburettor – 2.0 litre models up to 1985 (Sec 22)

A Top cover assembly
B Fuel filter
C Power valve assembly
D Float
E Needle valve
F Gasket
G Main jet
H Main body assembly
J Primary idle jet assembly
K Accelerator pump diaphragm
L Accelerator pump gasket
M Automatic choke bi-metal housing assembly
N Automatic choke assembly
P Vacuum pull-down diaphragm assembly
Q Idle mixture screw
R Idle speed screw
S Emulsion tube
T Accelerator pump jet
U Air correction jet
V Accelerator pump outlet check ball valve assembly
W Low vacuum enrichment diaphragm
X Secondary idle jet and holder

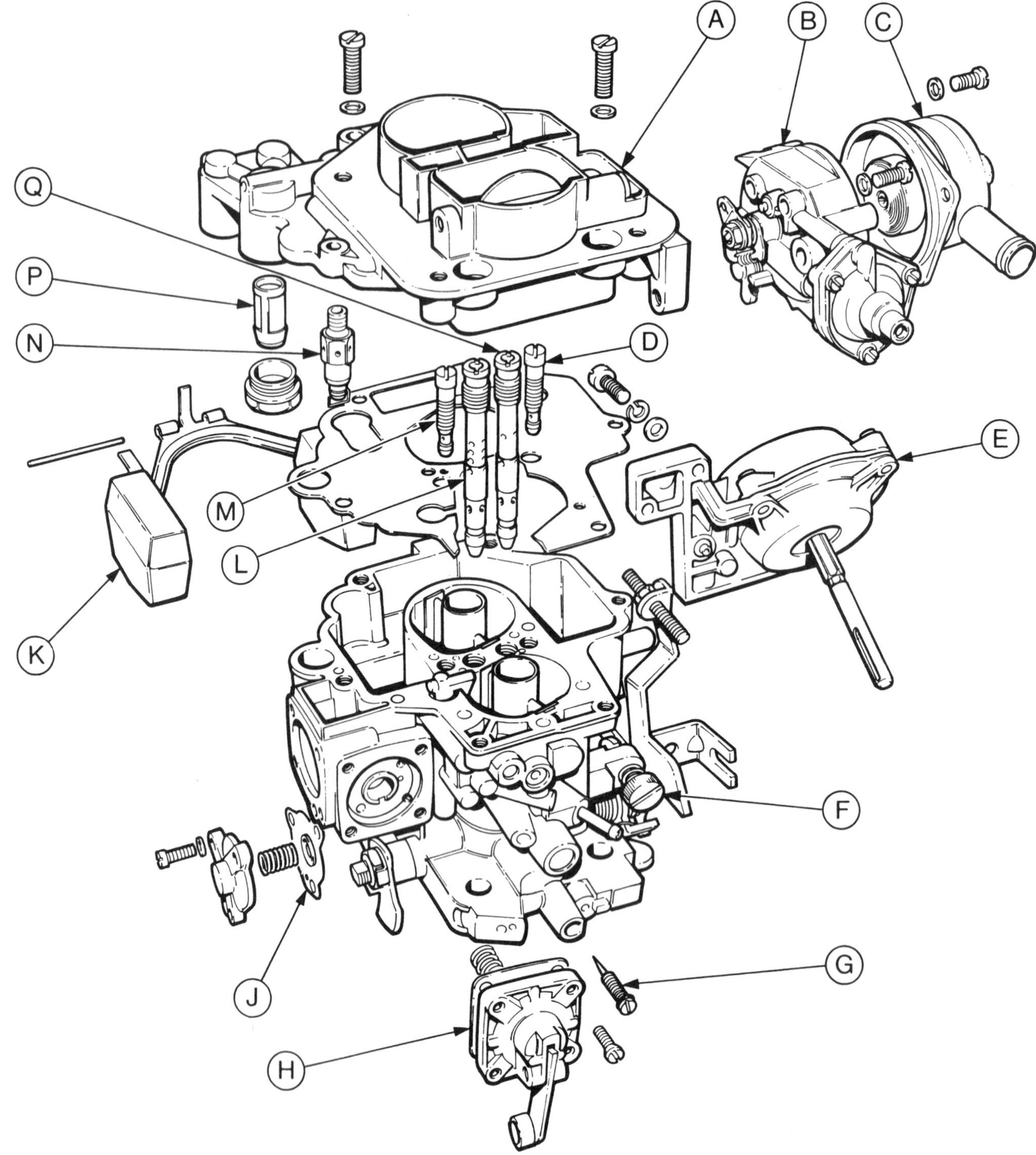

Fig 3.26 Exploded view of Weber 2V type carburettor – 1.6 litre models (Sec 22)

A Top cover assembly
B Automatic choke assembly
C Automatic choke bi-metal housing assembly
D Secondary idle jet
E Secondary throttle valve vacuum unit
F Idle speed screw
G Idle mixture screw
H Accelerator pump assembly
J Power valve diaphragm
K Float
L Primary emulsion tube
M Primary idle jet
N Needle valve
P Fuel filter
Q Secondary emulsion tube

to drill the seal in order to prise it from the mixture screw housing. Alternatively a self-tapping screw can be used to draw out the seal. If the tamperproof seal is to be renewed, ensure that a blue-coloured replacement seal is fitted.

3 It is permissible to loosen the air cleaner securing screws to allow easier access to the carburettor adjustment screws, but ensure that all vacuum hoses and pipes are securely connected. Refer to Figs. 3.28 and 3.29 for adjustment screw locations.

Models with stepper motor (ESC II system)

4 The idle speed is controlled by the ESC II module via the stepper motor. The only idle speed adjustment possible is provided by the 'idle

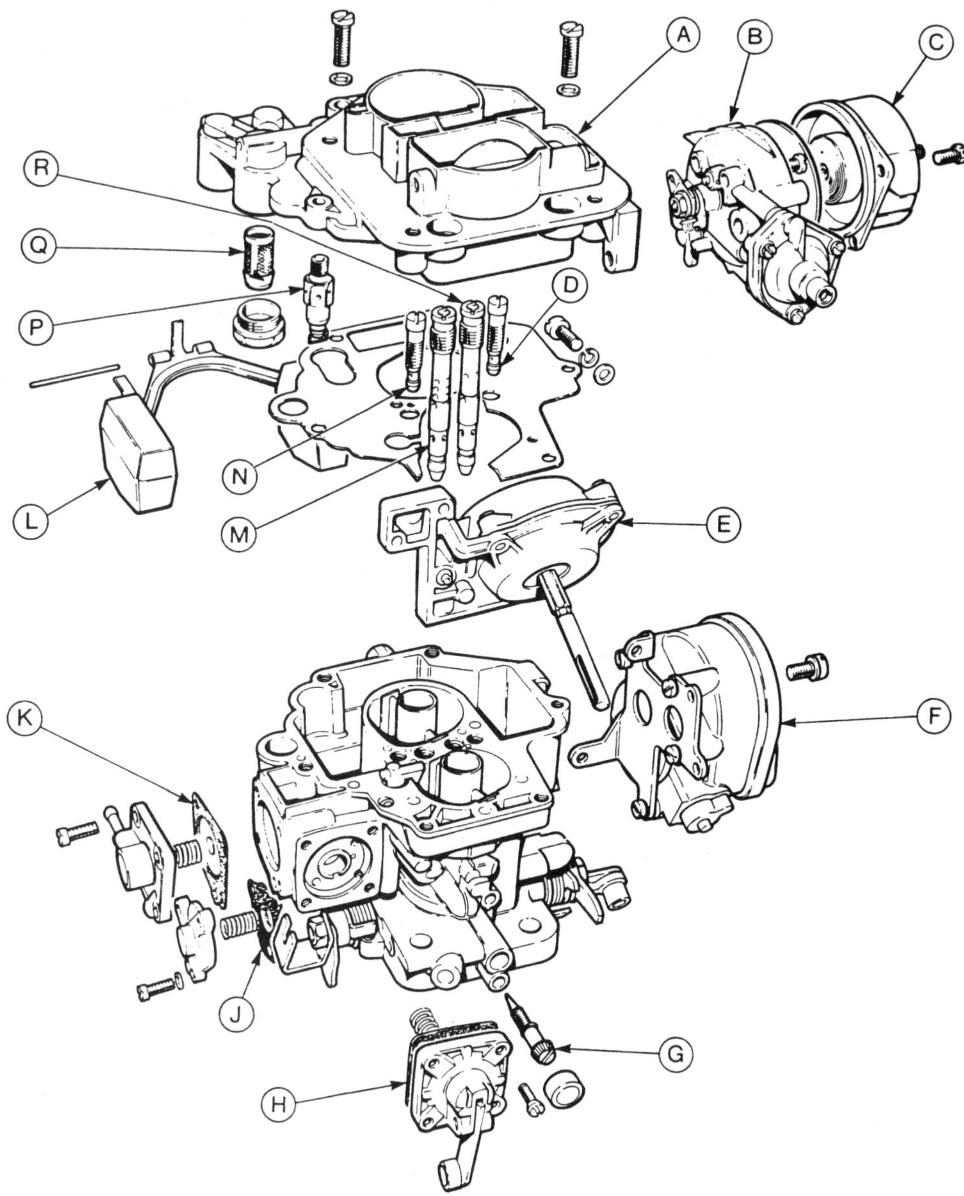

Fig 3.27 Exploded view of Weber 2V type carburettor – 2.0 litre models from 1985 (Sec 22)

A Top cover assembly
B Automatic choke assembly
C Automatic choke bi-metal housing
D Secondary idle jet
E Secondary throttle valve vacuum unit
F Stepper motor
G Idle mixture screw
H Accelerator pump assembly
J Power valve diaphragm
K Low vacuum enrichment diaphragm
L Float
M Primary emulsion tube
N Primary idle jet
P Needle valve
Q Fuel filter
R Secondary emulsion tube

speed adjustment' wire, which can be earthed to raise the idle speed by 75 rpm – see Chapter 4, Section 11. No other method of idle speed adjustment should be attempted. If the idle speed is incorrect, the problem should be referred to a Ford dealer, as the problem probably lies in the ESC II module for which special diagnostic equipment is required.

5 If necessary, the mixture can be adjusted as described in Section 17, paragraph 6 onwards, with reference to paragraphs 2 and 3 of this Section. **Do not** attempt to adjust the idle speed on completion of mixture adjustment. Refer to Fig. 3.30 for adjustment screw location.

25 Needle valve and float (Weber 2V type carburettor) – removal, refitting and adjustment

Note: *Refer to Section 2 before proceeding. A new carburettor top cover gasket must be used on reassembly. A tachometer and an exhaust gas analyser will be required to check the idle speed (where applicable) and mixture on completion.*

Removal and refitting

1 Disconnect the battery negative lead.

2 Remove the air cleaner as described in Section 5.

3 Thoroughly clean all external dirt from the carburettor.

4 Disconnect the fuel supply hose at the carburettor and plug the end to minimise petrol spillage.

5 Remove the six securing screws and lift off the carburettor top cover. Recover the gasket.

6 Tap out the float retaining pin from the top cover, then lift out the float assembly and the needle valve.

7 Inspect the components for damage and renew as necessary. Check the needle valve for wear, and check the float assembly for leaks by shaking it to see if it contains petrol.

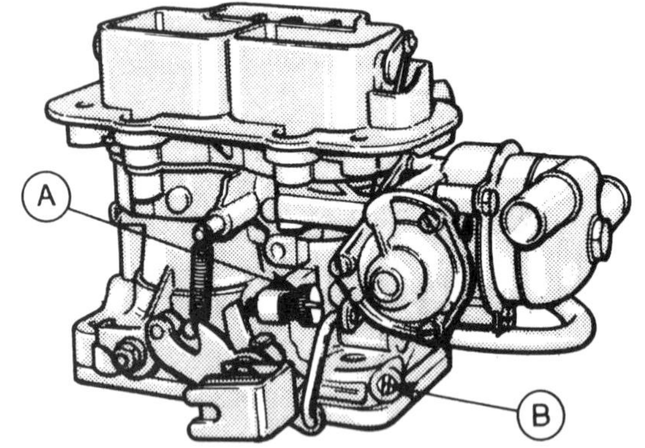

Fig 3.28 Weber 2V type carburettor adjustment screw locations – 2.0 litre models up to 1985 (Sec 24)

A Idle speed screw *B Idle mixture screw*

Fig 3.30 Weber 2V type carburettor idle mixture adjustment screw location (arrowed) – 2.0 litre models from 1985 (Sec 24)

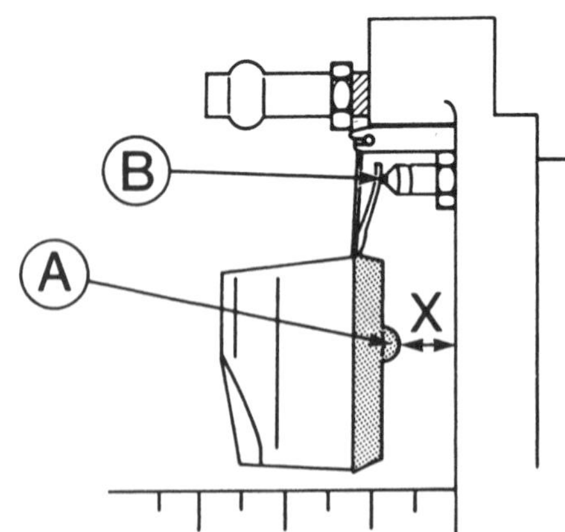

Fig 3.32 Float level adjustment – later Weber 2V type carburettors (Sec 25)

A Raised portion of float
B Adjustment tang
X Float level (see Specifications)

8 Clean the mating faces of the carburettor body and top cover.

9 Refitting is a reversal of removal, bearing in mind the following points.

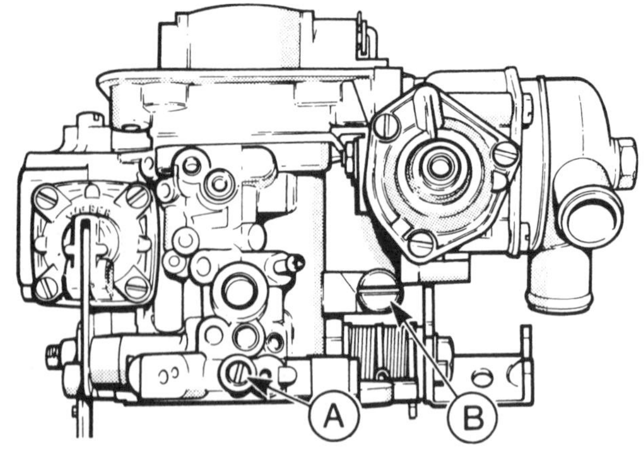

Fig 3.29 Carburettor adjustment screw locations – 1.6 litre models (Sec 24)

A Idle mixture screw *B Idle speed screw*

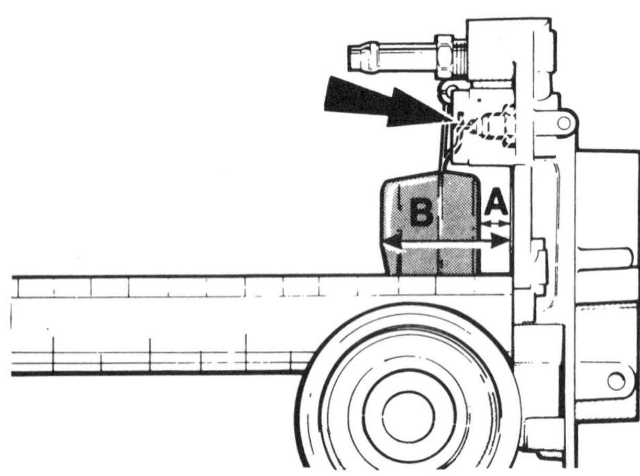

Fig 3.31 Float level adjustment – early Weber 2V type carburettors (Sec 25)

A Measurement for all models except 2.0 litre models up to 1985
B Measurement for 2.0 litre models up to 1985
For float level values see Specifications
Adjusting tang arrowed

10 If a new needle valve is being fitted, transfer the spring clip from the old valve.

11 Before refitting the carburettor top cover, check and if necessary adjust the float level as described in paragraph 14 onwards. Check the float and needle valve for full and free movement.

12 If the fuel supply hose was originally secured with a crimped type clip, discard this and use a new worm drive clip on refitting.

13 On completion, check and if necessary adjust the idle speed (where applicable) and mixture as described in Section 24.

Float level adjustment

14 With the carburettor top cover removed as described in paragraphs 1 to 5 inclusive, proceed as follows.

15 On all vehicles except 2.0 litre models up to 1985, fit a new gasket to the top cover, then hold the top cover in a vertical position and measure the distance between the face of the gasket and the top of the float – see Figs. 3.31 and 3.32. On 2.0 litre models up to 1985, make sure that a gasket is **not** fitted to the top cover, then hold the top cover in a vertical position and measure the distance between the face of the top cover and the base of the float – see Fig. 3.31.

16 If the distance is not as specified, adjust by bending the tag on the float assembly.

17 Refit the carburettor top cover by reversing the removal operations, with reference to paragraphs 12 and 13, using a new gasket.

26 Secondary throttle valve vacuum diaphragm (Weber 2V type carburettor) – renewal

Note: *Refer to Section 2 before proceeding.*
1 Disconnect the battery negative lead.
2 Remove the air cleaner as described in Section 5.
3 Disconnect the diaphragm operating rod from the throttle linkage.
4 Remove the four securing screws and lift off the diaphragm cover. Recover the spring.
5 Carefully withdraw the diaphragm and operating rod assembly from the housing.
6 If desired, the housing can be removed from the carburettor by unscrewing the two securing bolts.
7 Clean the mating faces of the housing and diaphragm cover.
8 Commence refitting by inserting the diaphragm and operating rod assembly into the housing. Locate the diaphragm on the vacuum port dowel.
9 Refit the spring and the cover, ensuring that the spring is correctly located, and tighten the cover securing screws progressively to avoid distorting the diaphragm.
10 Where applicable, refit the housing to the carburettor.
11 Reconnect the diaphragm operating rod to the throttle linkage.
12 Refit the air cleaner as described in Section 5, and reconnect the battery negative lead.

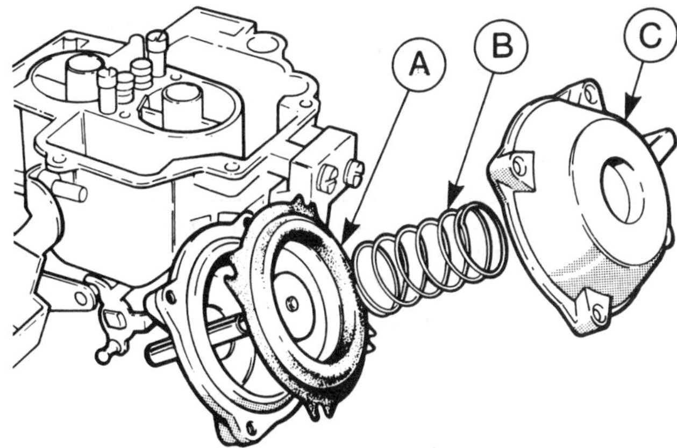

Fig 3.33 Secondary throttle valve vacuum unit components – Weber 2V type carburettor (Sec 26)

A Diaphragm *B Spring* *C Cover*

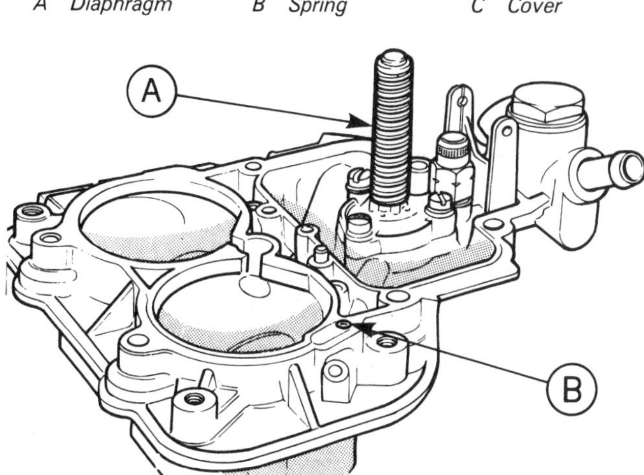

Fig 3.34 Power valve (A) and air bleed hole (B) – Weber 2V type carburettor (2.0 litre models up to 1985) (Sec 27)

27 Power valve diaphragm (Weber 2V type carburettor) – renewal

Note: *Refer to Section 2 before proceeding.*
1 Disconnect the battery negative lead.

1.6 litre models and 2.0 litre models from 1985

2 For improved access remove the air cleaner as described in Section 5.
3 Thoroughly clean all external dirt from the area around the power valve housing.
4 Remove the three securing screws and lift off the power valve cover. Recover the diaphragm return spring.
5 Lift the diaphragm from the housing flange.
6 Clean the mating faces of the housing flange and the power valve cover.
7 Commence refitting by locating the diaphragm on the housing flange, ensuring that the vacuum hole in the diaphragm is aligned with the corresponding holes in the housing flange and the power valve cover.
8 Locate the return spring on the diaphragm, then carefully refit the power valve cover. Ensure that the spring locates correctly, and tighten the cover securing screws progressively to avoid distorting the diaphragm.
9 Refit the air cleaner as described in Section 5, and reconnect the battery negative lead.

2.0 litre models up to 1985

10 Remove the carburettor top cover and the float as described in Section 25.
11 To check the operation of the diaphragm, hold the diaphragm down, block the air bleed hole with a finger and release the diaphragm – see Fig. 3.34. The diaphragm should stay down – if not, renew it as follows.
12 Remove the three securing screws and withdraw the diaphragm assembly from the carburettor top cover.
13 Commence refitting by placing the diaphragm assembly in position on the carburettor top cover and loosely refitting the securing screws.
14 Compress the diaphragm return spring to ensure that the diaphragm is not distorted, and hold the spring in this position while the securing screws are fully tightened.
15 Check the operation of the diaphragm as described in paragraph 11.
16 Refit the float and carburettor top cover as described in Section 25.

28 Low vacuum enrichment diaphragm (Weber 2V type carburettor) – renewal

1 The procedure is as described in Section 27, paragraphs 1 to 9 inclusive, but note the following.
2 If necessary disconnect the vacuum pipe from the diaphragm cover, and ensure that it is securely reconnected on completion.
3 The diaphragm cover is secured by four screws (photo).

29 Accelerator pump diaphragm (Weber 2V type carburettor) – renewal

1 The procedure is as described in Section 27, paragraphs 1 to 9 inclusive, but note the following.

2 The accelerator pump cover is secured by four screws (photo).
3 The diaphragm return spring is fitted between the pump housing and the diaphragm, not between the diaphragm and the cover.
4 There is no vacuum hole in the diaphragm.

30 Automatic choke unit (Weber 2V type carburettor) – removal, overhaul, refitting and adjustment

Removal, overhaul and refitting

Note: *Refer to Section 2 before proceeding. A tachometer and an exhaust gas analyser will be required to check the idle speed and mixture on completion. If the coolant housing is to be removed (where applicable), a new gasket will be required for refitting.*

1 Disconnect the battery negative lead.
2 Remove the air cleaner as described in Section 5.
3 On models with an electrically-heated choke, disconnect the wiring from the bi-metal housing, then proceed to paragraph 7.
4 On models with a coolant-heated choke, relieve the pressure in the cooling system by unscrewing the expansion tank cap. If the engine is warm, place a thick rag over the cap and unscrew the cap slowly as a precaution against scalding. Refit the cap after relieving the pressure.
5 Identify the automatic choke coolant hose locations for use when refitting, then disconnect the hoses (being prepared for coolant spillage.) Either plug the hoses or secure them with their ends facing upwards to prevent loss of coolant.
6 Unscrew the central securing bolt and remove the choke coolant housing. Recover the gasket. Drain the coolant from the housing into a suitable container.
7 Note the position of the alignment marks on the choke housing and bi-metal housing, and if necessary make additional marks to aid refitting, then remove the three securing screws and lift off the clamp ring and bi-metal housing (photo). Detach the internal heat shield.
8 Remove the three choke housing securing screws (where applicable, disconnect the fast idle cam return spring for access to one of the screws), then disconnect the choke link from the operating lever and withdraw the choke assembly. Recover the O-ring from the rear of the choke housing.

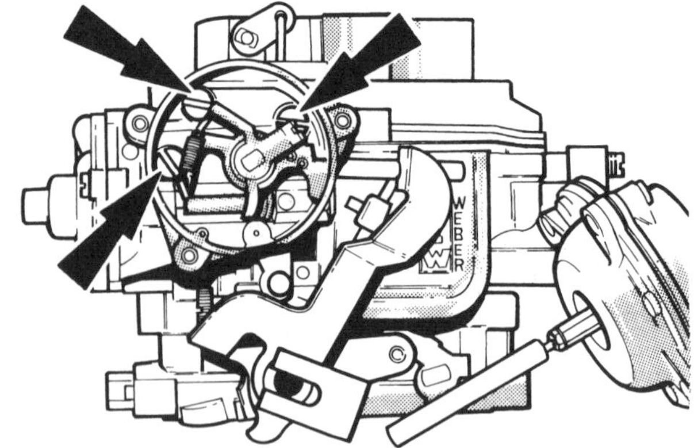

Fig 3.35 Automatic choke housing securing screws (arrowed) – Weber 2V type carburettor (Sec 30)

9 Remove the three securing screws and lift off the vacuum pull-down diaphragm cover, then withdraw the spring and diaphragm from the housing.
10 Dismantle the remaining components if necessary, with reference to Fig. 3.36.
11 Clean all components and examine them for wear and damage. Check the pull-down diaphragm for splits. Do not use any lubricants during the reassembly procedure.
12 Reassemble the components to the main choke housing as applicable.
13 Refit the vacuum pull-down diaphragm, spring and cover. Ensure that the spring is correctly located, and tighten the cover securing screws progressively to avoid distorting the diaphragm.
14 Ensure that the O-ring is correctly located on the rear of the housing, then reconnect the choke link to the operating lever, and refit the choke assembly to the carburettor. Where applicable, reconnect the

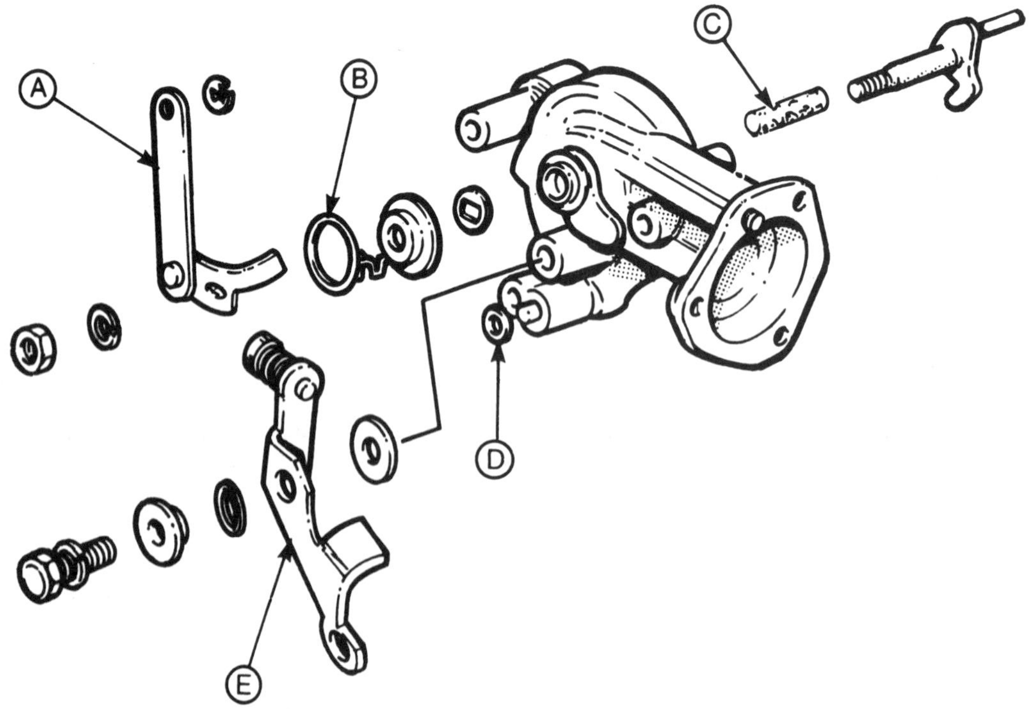

A B C D E

Fig 3.36 Automatic choke components – Weber 2V type carburettor (Sec 30)

A Choke operating lever
B Fast idle cam return spring
C Spindle sleeve
D O-ring
E Choke link

28.3 Low vacuum enrichment diaphragm location (arrowed) – Weber 2V type carburettor

29.2 Accelerator pump location (arrowed) – Weber 2V type carburettor

30.7 Automatic choke unit – Weber 2V type carburettor

1 Coolant housing
2 Bi-metal housing
3 Vacuum pull-down unit

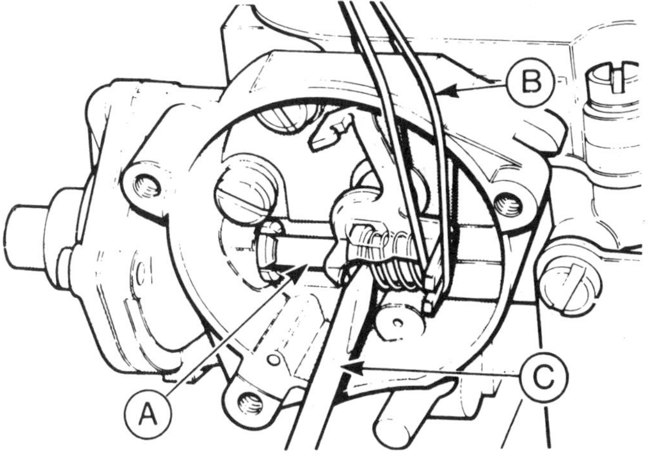

Fig 3.37 Automatic choke vacuum pull-down adjustment – Weber 2V type carburettor (Sec 30)

A Diaphragm rod
B Rubber band
C Small screwdriver

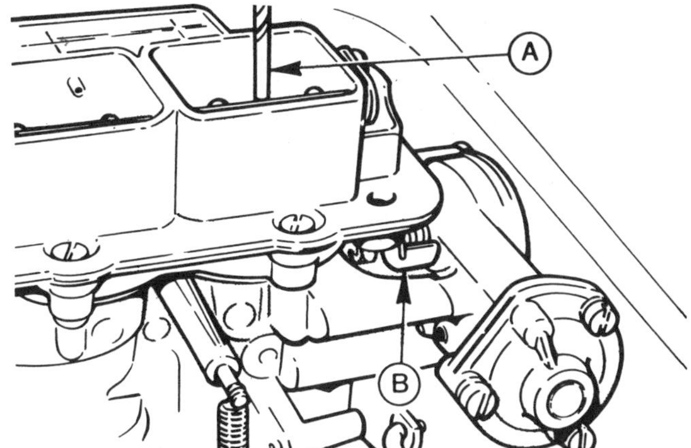

Fig 3.38 Automatic choke phasing adjustment – Weber 2V type carburettor (2.0 litre models up to 1985) (Sec 30)

A Twist drill
B Adjustment tag

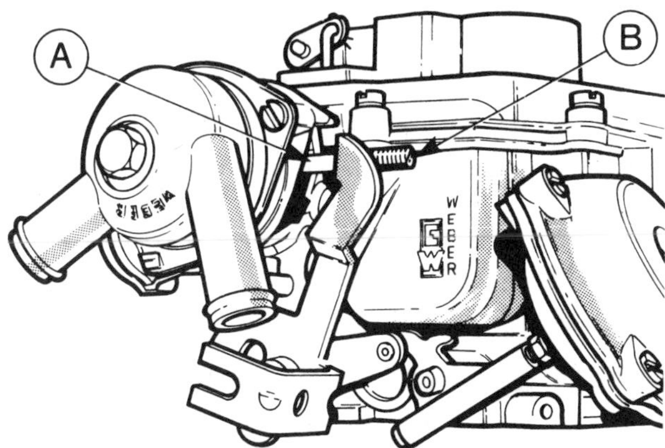

Fig 3.39 Fast idle speed adjustment – Weber 2V type carburettor (1.6 litre models) (Sec 30)

A Screw on third (middle) step of cam
B Fast idle screw

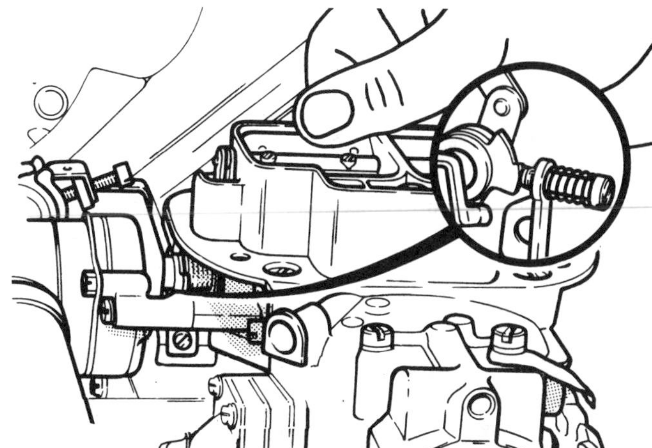

Fig 3.40 Fast idle speed adjustment – Weber 2V type carburettor (2.0 litre models) (Sec 30)

fast idle cam return spring after tightening the choke housing securing screws.

15 Check and if necessary adjust the vacuum pull-down as described later in this Section.

16 On 2.0 litre models up to 1985, check and if necessary adjust the choke phasing as described later in this Section.

17 Refit the internal heat shield, ensuring that the hole in the heat shield locates on the peg cast in the choke housing.

18 Connect the bi-metal spring to the choke lever, position the bi-metal housing and the clamp ring on the choke housing and loosely fit the securing screws. Align the marks on the choke housing and bi-metal housing as noted during removal, then tighten the securing screws.

19 On models with a coolant-headed choke, refit the coolant housing using a new gasket, and reconnect the coolant hoses. Check and if necessary top up the coolant level as described in Chapter 2.
20 On models with an electrically-heated choke, reconnect the wiring to the bi-metal housing.
21 Refit the air cleaner as described in Section 5, and reconnect the battery negative lead.
22 On all models except those fitted with a stepper motor, check and if necessary adjust the fast idle speed as described later in this Section.

Vacuum pull-down adjustment

23 With the choke bi-metal housing removed as described in paragraphs 1 to 7, proceed as follows.
24 Fit a rubber band over the choke plate operating lever, and tension the rubber band to hold the choke plate(s) fully closed.
25 Open and then release the throttle to ensure that the choke plate(s) is/are fully closed.
26 Using a small screwdriver inside the choke housing, push the diaphragm rod against the spring tension onto its stop. Hold the rod in this position.
27 Using a drill shank of appropriate diameter, or a similar item, measure the clearance between the choke plate and the wall of the primary barrel. Measure the clearance on the lower side of the choke plate (photo). Check that the clearance is as given in the Specifications.
28 If adjustment is necessary, remove the plug from the centre of the pull-down diaphragm cover, and turn the adjustment screw located under the plug until the clearance is correct. Refit the plug on completion of adjustment.
29 Remove the drill and the rubber band, and refit the bi-metal housing as described in paragraphs 17 to 22.

Choke phasing adjustment

30 This procedure only applies to 2.0 litre models up to 1985.
31 If not already done, remove the air cleaner as described in Section 5.
32 Hold the throttle partly open and position the fast idle cam so that the fast idle adjustment screw rests on the upper section of the cam (photo).
33 Release the throttle to hold the cam in position, then push the choke plates down until the step on the cam rests against the adjustment screw.
34 Proceed as described in paragraph 27.
35 If adjustment is necessary, bend the adjustment tag to achieve the desired clearance – see Fig. 3.38.
36 Remove the drill, and where applicable refit the air cleaner as described in Section 5.

Fast idle speed adjustment

37 This procedure does not apply to models fitted with a carburettor stepper motor, for which no adjustment is possible.
38 Check the idle speed and mixture as described in Section 24. The idle speed **must** be correct before attempting to check or adjust the fast idle speed.
39 With the engine at normal operating temperature, and a tachometer connected in accordance with the manufacturer's instructions, proceed as follows.
40 Remove the air cleaner as described in Section 5.
41 Partially open the throttle, hold the choke plate(s) fully closed, then release the throttle so that on 1.6 litre models the fast idle adjustment screw rests on the third (middle) step of the fast idle cam, and on 2.0 litre models the fast idle adjustment screw rests on the highest step of the fast idle cam.
42 Release the choke plate(s), checking that it/they remain(s) fully open; if not, the automatic choke mechanism is faulty, or the engine is not at normal operating temperature.
43 Without touching the throttle pedal, start the engine and check that the fast idle speed is as specified. If adjustment is necessary, turn the fast idle adjustment screw until the correct speed is obtained.
44 On completion of adjustment, stop the engine and disconnect the tachometer, then refit the air cleaner as described in Section 5.

31 Stepper motor (Weber 2V type carburettor) – removal and refitting

Refer to Chapter 4, Section 13.

32 Carburettor (Pierburg 2V type) – description

The Pierburg 2V (twin venturi) carburettor is of fixed jet, sequential throttle type. The primary throttle valve operates alone except at high engine speeds and loads when the secondary throttle valve is operated, until at full throttle both are fully open. This arrangement allows good fuel economy during light acceleration and cruising, but also gives maximum power at full throttle. The secondary throttle valve is vacuum-operated according to the vacuum produced in the primary venturi. The primary throttle barrel and venturi diameters are smaller than their secondary counterparts. The carburettor is a complicated instrument with various refinements and sub-systems added, according to model and equipment, to achieve improved driveability, economy and exhaust emission levels.

A separate idle system operates independently from the main jet system, supplying fuel via the mixture control screw.

The main jets are calibrated to suit engine requirements at midrange throttle openings. To provide the necessary fuel enrichment at full throttle, a vacuum-operated power valve is used. The valve provides extra fuel under the low vacuum conditions associated with wide throttle openings.

To provide an enrichment mixture during acceleration, an accelerator pump delivers extra fuel to the primary main venturi. The accelerator pump is operated mechanically by a cam on the throttle linkage.

A fully automatic choke is fitted, operated by a coolant and electrically-heated bi-metal coil. When the engine is cold, the bi-metal coil is fully wound up, holding the choke plate (fitted to the primary barrel) closed. As the engine warms up the bi- metal coil is heated and therefore unwinds, progressively opening the choke plate. On OHC models the power supply to the choke electrical heater is controlled by a thermo-time switch, which cuts the power supply when the engine reaches a pre-set temperature, at which point the engine coolant becomes the main heat source. On CVH models, the power supply to

30.27 Using a twist drill to check the vacuum pull-down adjustment – Weber 2V type carburettor

30.32 Position the fast idle adjustment screw on the upper section of the cam (arrowed) – Weber 2V type carburettor

33.4 Throttle arm retaining clip (arrowed) – Pierburg 2V type carburettor

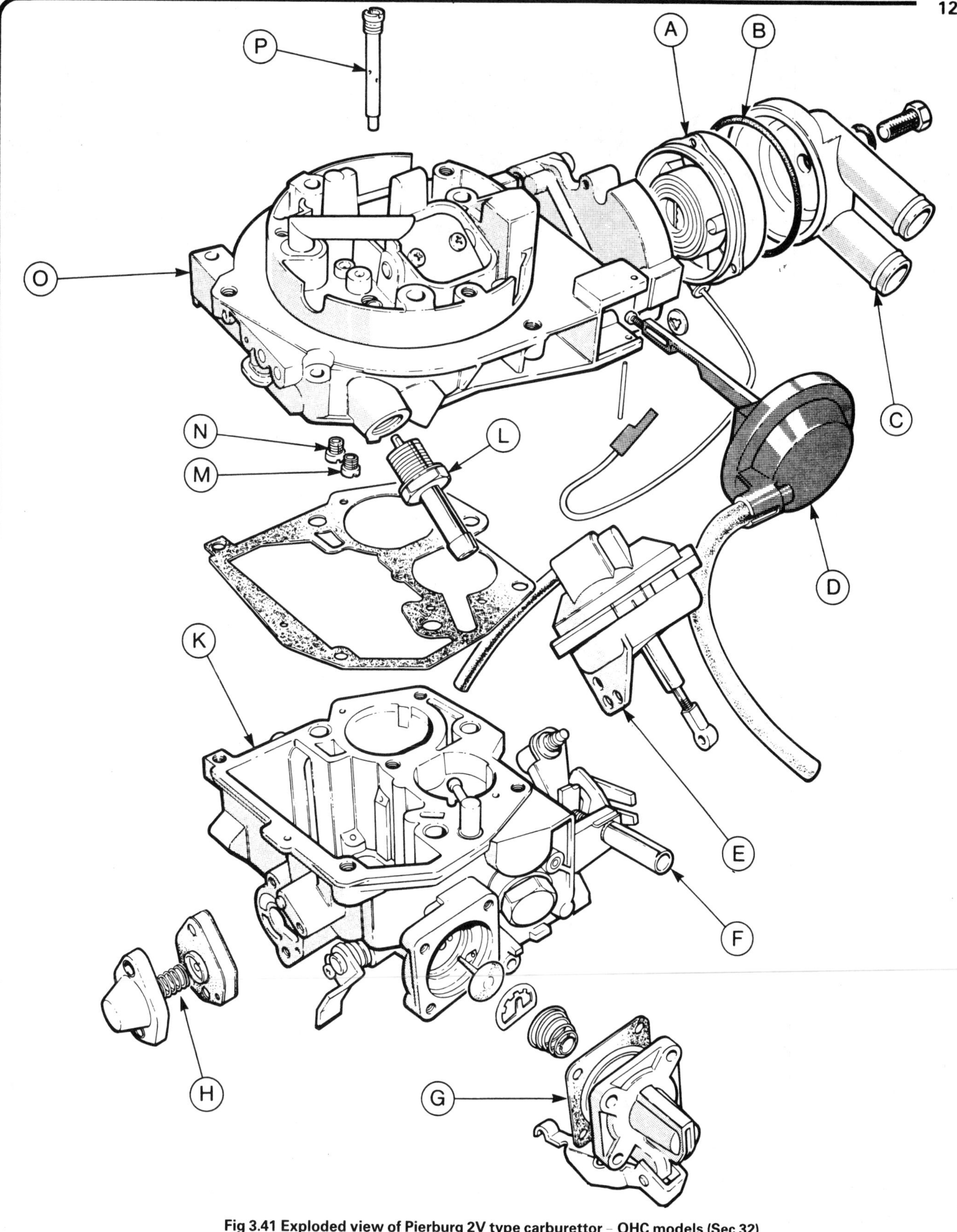

Fig 3.41 Exploded view of Pierburg 2V type carburettor – OHC models (Sec 32)

A *Automatic choke bi-metal housing*
B *O-ring*
C *Automatic choke coolant housing*
D *Automatic choke vacuum pull-down unit*
E *Secondary throttle valve vacuum unit*
F *Idle speed screw*
G *Accelerator pump diaphragm*
H *Power valve assembly*
K *Carburettor body*
L *Fuel inlet pipe and filter*
M *Primary main jet*
N *Secondary main jet*
O *Top cover assembly*
P *Idle jet*

33.5 Removing the carburettor securing screws (arrowed) – Pierburg 2V type carburettor

35.8 Carburettor top cover securing screws (arrowed) – early Pierburg 2V type carburettor

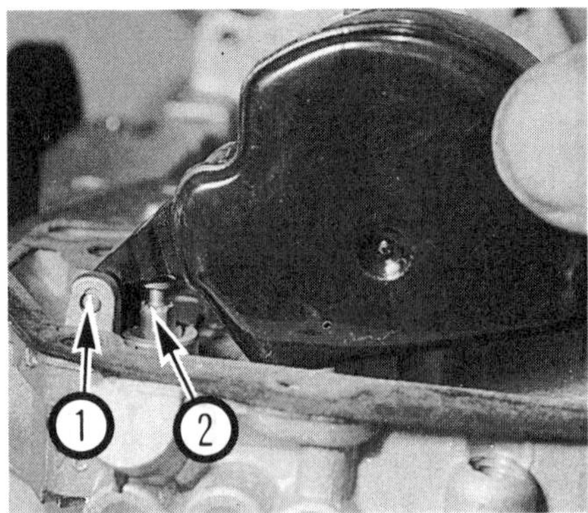

35.9 Needle valve and float assembly – Pierburg 2V type carburettor
1 Float retaining pin
2 Needle valve

the electrical heater is controlled by the ESC Hybrid module, via a relay, which pulses the power supply, thus slowing down the rate at which the choke plate opens, improving driveability and overall fuel consumption when the engine is cold. A vacuum-operated pull-down system is employed whereby, if the engine is under choke, but is only cruising (ie not under heavy load) the choke plate is opened against the action of the bi-metal coil. The pull-down system prevents an over-rich mixture which reduces fuel economy and may cause unnecessary engine wear when the engine is cold. Certain later OHC models are fitted with a secondary pull-down solenoid which operates in conjunction with the main diaphragm unit to modify the pull-down characteristics, improving fuel economy.

CVH models are fitted with a vacuum-operated throttle damper, which is controlled by the ESC Hybrid module via a solenoid valve. The throttle damper prevents sudden closing of the throttle during deceleration, thus maintaining combustion of the air/fuel mixture which reduces harmful exhaust gas emissions. Refer to Chapter 4 for further details.

An unusual feature of the Pierburg carburettor is that the float level cannot be adjusted.

33 Carburettor (Pierburg 2V type) – removal and refitting

1 Proceed as described in Section 16, but note the following.
2 The Pierburg carburettor is not fitted with an anti-dieselling valve.
3 Disconnect all relevant wiring plugs and vacuum pipes, if necessary noting their locations as an aid to refitting.
4 Disconnect the throttle arm from the throttle lever by removing the retaining clip instead of disconnecting the throttle cable (photo).
5 The carburettor is secured to the inlet manifold by three Torx type screws (photo).

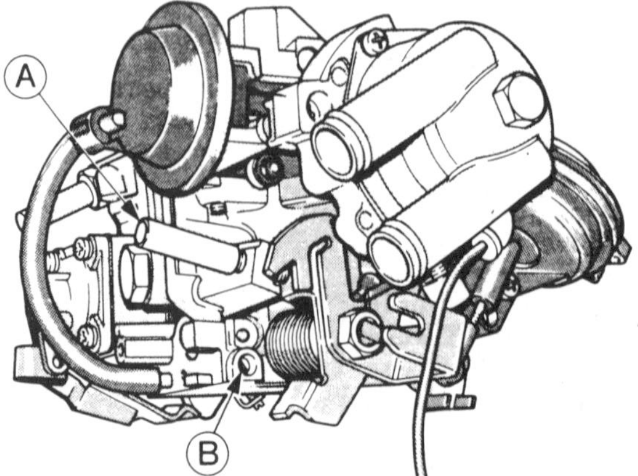

Fig 3.42 Pierburg 2V type carburettor adjustment screw locations (Sec 34)

A Idle speed screw *B Idle mixture screw*

6 On CVH models an insulator block is fitted between the carburettor and the inlet manifold in place of a gasket. There is no need to renew the insulator block on refitting.

34 Carburettor (Pierburg 2V type) – idle speed and mixture adjustment

Proceed as described in Section 17. Refer to Fig. 3.42 for adjustment screw locations.

35 Needle valve and float (Pierburg 2V type carburettor) – removal and refitting

Note: *Refer to Section 2 before proceeding. A new carburettor top cover gasket must be used on reassembly. A tachometer and an exhaust gas analyser will be required to check the idle speed and mixture on completion.*

1 Disconnect the battery negative lead.
2 Remove the air cleaner as described in Section 5.
3 Thoroughly clean all external dirt from the carburettor.
4 Disconnect the fuel supply hose at the carburettor and plug the end to minimise petrol spillage.
5 Relieve the pressure in the cooling system by unscrewing the expansion tank cap. If the engine is warm, place a thick rag over the cap and unscrew the cap slowly as a precaution against scalding. Refit the cap after relieving the pressure.
6 Identify the automatic choke coolant hose locations as an aid to refitting, then disconnect the hoses (being prepared for coolant spillage.) Either plug the hoses or secure them with their ends facing upwards to prevent loss of coolant.
7 Disconnect the wiring from the choke electrical heater, and disconnect the vacuum pipe from the choke pull-down unit.
8 Remove the carburettor top cover securing screws (five on early models, four on later models) and lift off the top cover (photo). Recover the gasket.
9 Using a suitable pin punch, tap the float retaining pin from the base of the top cover and lift out the float and needle valve (photo).
10 Inspect the components for damage and renew as necessary. Check the needle valve for wear, and check the float for leaks by shaking it to see if it contains petrol.
11 Clean the mating faces of the carburettor body and top cover.
12 Refitting is a reversal of removal, bearing in mind the following points.
13 After refitting, check the float and needle valve for full and free movement. Note that no adjustment of the float level is possible.
14 Ensure that all hoses, pipes and wires are correctly reconnected.
15 If the fuel supply hose was originally secured with a crimped type clip, discard this and use a new worm drive clip on refitting.
16 On completion, check and if necessary top up the coolant level as described in Chapter 2, and check and if necessary adjust the idle speed and mixture as described in Section 17.

36 Secondary throttle valve vacuum diaphragm (Pierburg 2V type carburettor) – renewal

Note: *The diaphragm unit must be renewed in its entirety, as no spares are available.*

1 Disconnect the battery negative lead.
2 Remove the air cleaner as described in Section 5.
3 Disconnect the vacuum pipe from the diaphragm unit.
4 Prise the diaphragm operating rod balljoint from the secondary throttle valve linkage.
5 Remove the two securing screws and withdraw the diaphragm unit from the carburettor body (photo).
6 Refitting is a reversal of removal.

37 Power valve diaphragm (Pierburg 2V type carburettor) – renewal

Note: *Refer to Section 2 before proceeding.*

1 Disconnect the battery negative lead.
2 For improved access remove the air cleaner as described in Section 5.
3 Thoroughly clean all external dirt from the area around the power valve housing.
4 Remove the two securing screws and lift off the power valve cover, spring, and diaphragm assembly.
5 Using a small screwdriver, release the diaphragm assembly from the nylon clips fitted to the cover bolt holes, and separate the diaphragm assembly from the cover. Recover the spring (photo).
6 Clean the mating faces of the cover and housing.
7 Locate the spring on the cover and diaphragm assembly, ensuring that it is correctly seated, then press the diaphragm assembly and cover together until the clips lock into the diaphragm assembly. Note that the vacuum hole in the diaphragm must align with the corresponding hole in the housing flange and cover.
8 Refit the assembly to the carburettor and secure with the two screws.
9 Refit the air cleaner as described in Section 5, and reconnect the battery negative lead.

38 Accelerator pump diaphragm (Pierburg 2V type carburettor) – renewal

Note: *Refer to Section 2 before proceeding.*

1 Disconnect the battery negative lead.
2 For improved access remove the air cleaner as described in Section 5.
3 Thoroughly clean all external dirt from the area around the accelerator pump housing.
4 Remove the four securing screws and lift off the accelerator pump cover. Recover the diaphragm, spring, seal retainer, and seal. Note the orientation of the seal retainer (photos).
5 Clean the mating faces of the cover and housing.
6 Check the condition of the seal and renew if necessary.
7 Commence refitting by locating the seal, seal retainer, and spring in the housing. Note that the seal retainer can only be fitted in one position. The larger diameter of the spring should rest against the seal retainer.
8 Locate the diaphragm on the housing, ensuring that the spring is correctly seated, and refit the cover. Tighten the cover securing screws progressively to avoid distorting the diaphragm.
9 Refit the air cleaner as described in Section 5, and reconnect the battery negative lead.

39 Throttle damper (Pierburg 2V type carburettor) – removal, refitting and adjustment.

Refer to Chapter 4, Section 14.

40 Automatic choke unit (Pierburg 2V type carburettor) – removal, refitting and adjustment

Removal and refitting

Note: *Refer to Section 2 before proceeding. A tachometer and an exhaust gas analyser will be required to check the idle speed and mixture on completion. If the coolant housing is removed, new O-rings will be required for refitting.*

1 Disconnect the battery negative lead.
2 Remove the air cleaner as described in Section 5.
3 Note the position of the bi-metal housing alignment marks, as an aid to refitting, if necessary making additional marks for clarity. Then remove the three securing screws and lift off the bi-metal housing (photo). Place the housing to one side, taking care not to strain the coolant hoses or electric choke heater wire.
4 Remove the three screws securing the choke housing to the carburettor body, and withdraw the choke assembly, taking care not to bend the choke operating rod (photo).
5 If it is necessary to remove the bi-metal housing for renewal, proceed as follows, otherwise proceed to paragraph 10.
6 Relieve the pressure in the cooling system by unscrewing the expansion tank cap. If the engine is warm, place a thick rag over the cap and unscrew the cap slowly as a precaution against scalding. Refit the cap after relieving the pressure.
7 Identify the automatic choke coolant hose locations for use when refitting, then disconnect the hoses (being prepared for coolant spillage). Either plug the hoses or secure them with their ends facing upwards to prevent loss of coolant.
8 Disconnect the wiring from the electric choke heater and withdraw

36.5 Removing the secondary throttle valve vacuum diaphragm unit securing screws (carburettor removed) – Pierburg 2V type carburettor

37.5 Power valve components – Pierburg 2V type carburettor

38.4A Removing the accelerator pump diaphragm – Pierburg 2V type carburettor

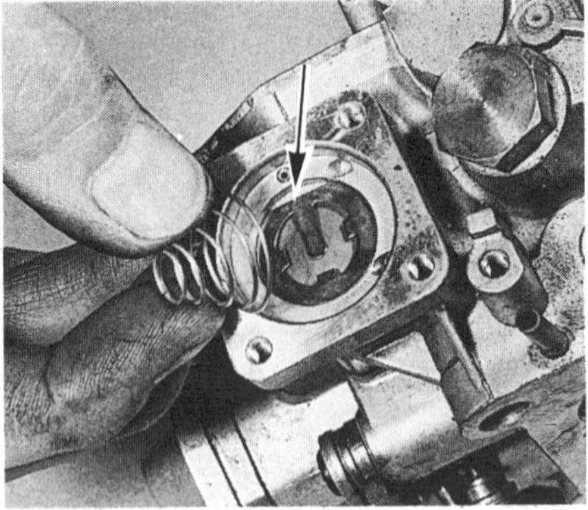
38.4B Removing the accelerator pump diaphragm spring. Note the position of the seal retainer flat (arrowed) – Pierburg 2V type carburettor

38.4C Removing the accelerator pump seal – Pierburg 2V type carburettor

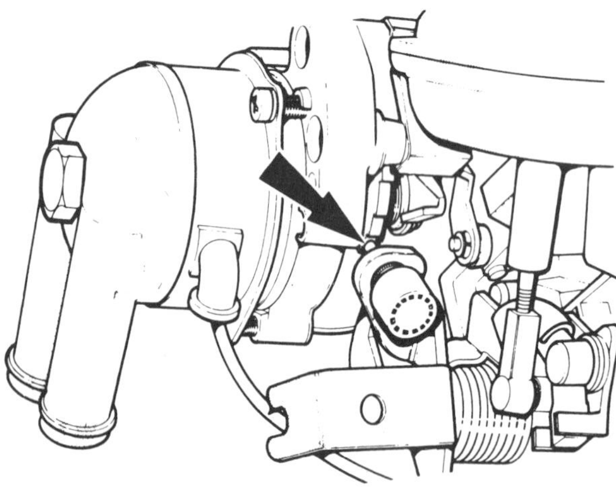
Fig 3.43 Fast idle speed adjustment – Pierburg 2V type carburettor (Sec 40)

Screw (arrowed) should rest on lowest (6th) step of cam

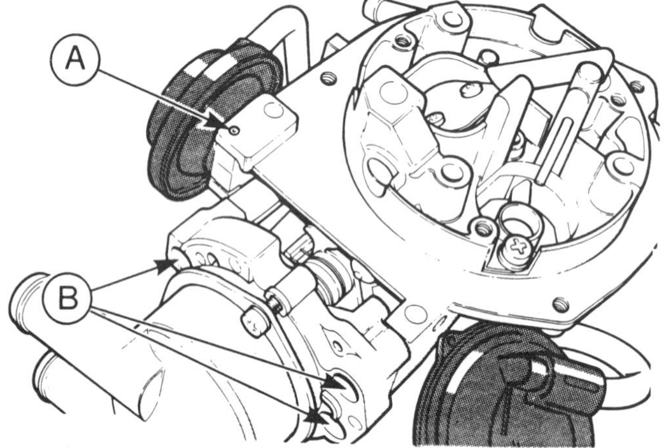

Fig 3.44 Automatic choke vacuum pull-down unit removal – Pierburg 2V type carburettor (Sec 41)

A Roll pin *B Choke assembly securing screws*

the bi-metal housing.

9 The coolant housing can be separated from the bi-metal housing by unscrewing the central securing bolt. Recover the O-rings from under the bolt head, and from the rim of the coolant housing.

10 Commence refitting by locating the choke assembly on the carburettor body, ensuring that the lever on the choke assembly engages with the choke operating rod. Tighten the three securing screws.

11 Connect the bi-metal spring to the choke lever, position the bi-metal housing on the choke housing and loosely fit the securing screws (photo). Align the marks on the bi-metal housing and the choke housing as noted during removal, then tighten the securing screws.

12 Where applicable, refit the coolant housing to the bi-metal housing, using new O-rings if necessary, and reconnect the coolant hoses and electric choke heater wiring.

13 Refit the air cleaner as described in Section 5, and reconnect the battery negative lead.

14 If the coolant hoses have been disconnected, check the coolant level as described in Chapter 2.

15 Check and if necessary adjust the fast idle speed as follows.

Fast idle speed adjustment

16 Check the idle speed and mixture as described in Section 17. The idle speed **must** be correct before attempting to check or adjust the fast idle speed.

17 With the engine at normal operating temperature, and a tachometer connected in accordance with the manufacturer's instructions, proceed as follows.

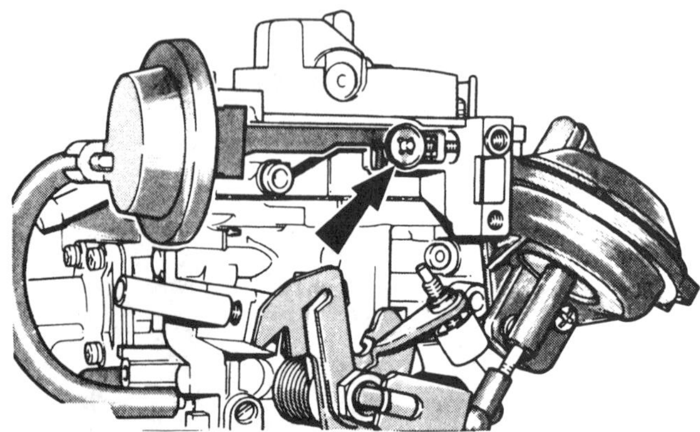
Fig 3.45 Automatic choke vacuum pull-down unit removal – Pierburg 2V type carburettor (Sec 41)

Star clip (arrowed) must be prised off

18 Remove the air cleaner as described in Section 5.

19 Position the fast idle speed adjustment screw on the lowest (6th) step of the fast idle cam.

20 Check that the fast idle speed is as specified. If adjustment is

40.3 Automatic choke bi-metal housing alignment marks – Pierburg 2V type carburettor

40.4 Withdrawing the choke assembly from the carburettor (carburettor removed) – Pierburg 2V type carburettor

40.11 Ensure that the sleeve on the bi-metal spring (1) engages with the choke lever (2) – Pierburg 2V type carburettor

required, stop the engine and proceed as follows.

21 Remove the tamperproof cap from the fast idle speed adjustment screw.

22 Ensure that the adjustment screw is still resting on the lowest step of the fast idle cam, then open the throttle so that a small screwdriver can be used to adjust the screw from below the carburettor.

23 Start the engine and recheck the fast idle speed.

24 If necessary, repeat the procedure given in paragraphs 22 and 23 until the correct fast idle speed is obtained.

25 On completion of adjustment, stop the engine and disconnect the tachometer, then refit the tamperproof cap to the adjustment screw, and refit the air cleaner as described in Section 5.

41 Automatic choke vacuum pull-down unit(s) (Pierburg 2V type carburettor) – removal, refitting and adjustment

Main diaphragm unit – removal and refitting

Note: *Refer to Section 2 before proceeding. A new star clip must be used when refitting the diaphragm unit.*

1 Disconnect the battery negative lead.

2 Remove the air cleaner as described in Section 5.

3 Disconnect the diaphragm unit vacuum pipe(s).

4 Using a suitable pin punch, tap out the roll pin securing the diaphragm unit to the carburettor top cover – see Fig. 3.44.

5 Remove the three screws securing the choke assembly to the carburettor. Allow the choke assembly to drop down, but do not disconnect the choke linkage.

6 Remove the star clip which secures the diaphragm unit to the carburettor top cover, and withdraw the diaphragm unit.

7 Refitting is a reversal of removal, but use a new star clip to secure the diaphragm unit to the carburettor top cover, and before refitting the air cleaner, check and if necessary adjust the choke pull-down as follows.

Vacuum pull-down adjustment

8 With the air cleaner removed, proceed as follows.

9 Position the fast idle speed adjustment screw on the highest step of the fast idle cam.

10 Move the pull-down arm fully towards the diaphragm unit by pushing on the adjustment screw. Hold the arm in this position.

11 Using a drill shank of appropriate diameter, or a similar item, measure the clearance between the lower side of the choke plate and the wall of the primary barrel (photo). Check that the clearance is as given in the Specifications.

12 If adjustment is necessary, turn the adjustment screw in the appropriate direction, using a 2 mm Allen key, until the clearance is correct.

13 Refit the air cleaner as described in Section 5.

Secondary pull-down solenoid – removal and refitting

14 This unit is fitted to certain later OHC models, and operates in conjunction with the main diaphragm unit.

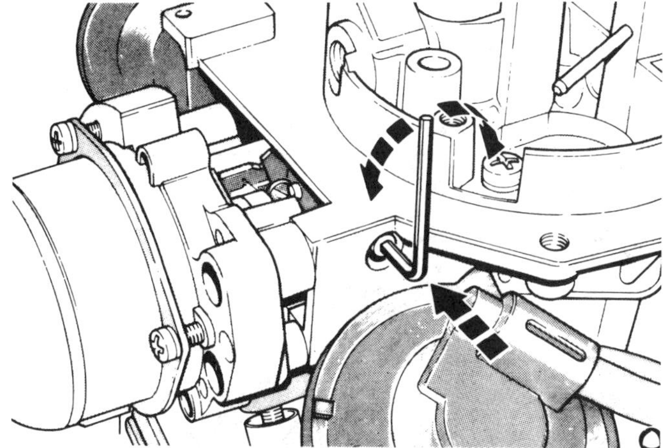

Fig 3.46 Automatic choke vacuum pull-down adjustment – Pierburg 2V type carburettor (Sec 41)

Turn adjustment screw as shown to give specified clearance

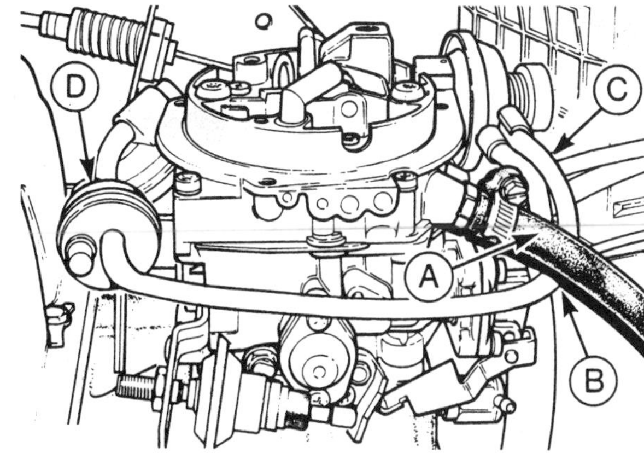

Fig 3.47 Secondary choke pull-down solenoid location and vacuum hose routing – Pierburg 2V type carburettor (Sec 41)

A Fuel supply hose
B Hose clip location
C Vacuum pipe
D Solenoid unit

15 To remove the solenoid unit, first proceed as described in paragraphs 1 to 3 inclusive.

16 Disconnect the wiring plug, then unscrew the securing bolt and withdraw the solenoid unit and its mounting bracket from the carburettor.

41.11 Using a twist drill to check the vacuum pull-down adjustment - Pierburg 2V type carburettor

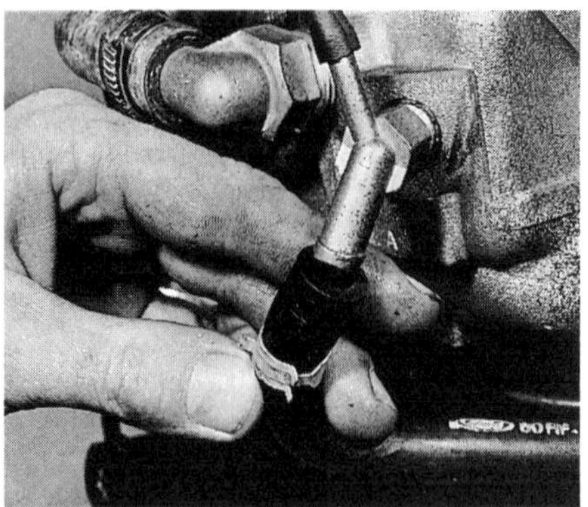

42.8A Disconnecting the crankcase ventilation ...

42.8B ... and brake servo vacuum hoses from the inlet manifold - OHC models

17 Refitting is a reversal of removal, but ensure that the vacuum hose is correctly routed through its clip on the carburettor fuel supply - see Fig. 3.47.

42 Inlet manifold - removal and refitting

OHC models

1 Disconnect the battery negative lead.
2 Partially drain the cooling system as described in Chapter 2.
3 Remove the air cleaner as described in Section 5.
4 Disconnect the coolant hoses from the automatic choke (where applicable), and the inlet manifold. Identify the hose locations for use when refitting.
5 Disconnect the fuel supply hose at the carburettor and plug the end to minimise petrol spillage.
6 Disconnect all relevant wiring and vacuum pipes from the carburettor, if necessary noting the locations for use when refitting.
7 Disconnect the throttle cable from the throttle linkage, with reference to Section 14 if necessary.
8 Disconnect the crankcase ventilation and brake servo vacuum hoses from the inlet manifold. The brake servo vacuum hose is secured with a union nut (photos).
9 Disconnect any remaining wiring and vacuum pipes from the inlet manifold, if necessary noting the locations as an aid to refitting.
10 Where necessary, unbolt the throttle cable bracket from the top of the inlet manifold for improved access, and unbolt the dipstick tube bracket.
11 Unscrew the two nuts and four bolts securing the manifold to the cylinder head, noting the location of the rear engine lifting bracket (photo).
12 Lift the inlet manifold from the cylinder head, and recover the gasket (photo).
13 If desired, the carburettor can be removed from the inlet manifold by unscrewing the securing nuts or screws. Refer to the relevant Section describing carburettor removal and refitting if necessary. Recover the gasket.
14 Refitting is a reversal of removal bearing in mind the following points.
15 Ensure that all mating faces are clean.
16 Renew the gasket(s), and apply a bead of sealant at least 5.0 mm (0.2 in) wide around the central coolant aperture on both sides of the manifold-to-cylinder head gasket.
17 Tighten the manifold securing nuts and bolts progressively to the specified torque, ensuring that the engine lifting bracket is in place.
18 Make sure that all hoses, pipes and wires are correctly reconnected, and if the fuel supply hose was originally secured with a crimped type clip, discard this and use a new worm drive clip on refitting.
19 On completion, refill the cooling system as described in Chapter 2, adjust the throttle cable as described in Section 14, and check and if necessary adjust the idle speed and mixture as described in Section 17, 24, or 34 as applicable.

CVH models

20 Proceed as described in paragraphs 1 to 3 inclusive.
21 Disconnect the coolant hoses from the automatic choke, thermostat housing and inlet manifold, noting their locations for use when refitting.
22 Disconnect the fuel supply hose at the carburettor and plug the end to minimise petrol spillage.
23 Disconnect all relevant wiring and vacuum pipes from the carburettor, thermostat housing and inlet manifold, noting the locations as an aid to refitting.
24 Disconnect the throttle cable from the throttle linkage, with reference to Section 14 if necessary.
25 Unbolt the dipstick tube from the inlet manifold and withdraw the dipstick and dipstick tube from the cylinder block.
26 Unscrew the seven nuts securing the manifold to the cylinder head, then lift the manifold from the cylinder head, and recover the gasket.
27 If desired, the carburettor can be removed from the manifold by removing the securing screws. Refer to Section 33 if necessary. Recover the insulator block (photos).
28 The carburettor intermediate plate can be removed from the manifold by unscrewing the three securing screws. Recover the gasket.
29 If necessary, the thermostat and housing can be removed from the manifold as described in Chapter 2.
30 Refitting is a reversal of removal, bearing in mind the following points.
31 Ensure that all mating faces are clean and renew the gasket(s).
32 Tighten the manifold securing nuts progressively to the specified torque.
33 Make sure that all hoses, pipes and wires are correctly reconnected, and if the fuel supply hose was originally secured with a crimped type clip, discard this and use a new worm drive clip on refitting.
34 On completion, refill the cooling system as described in Chapter 2, adjust the throttle cable as described in Section 14, and check and if necessary adjust the idle speed and mixture as described in Section 17.

43 Exhaust manifold - removal and refitting

1 Disconnect the battery negative lead.
2 Remove the air cleaner as described in Section 5, and pull the hot air pick-up pipe from the exhaust manifold hot air shroud.
3 Remove the securing screws (2 screws on OHC models, 3 screws on CVH models) and lift the hot air shroud from the manifold. Note the position of the coolant hose bracket which is secured by the front hot air shroud securing screw on OHC models (photo).
4 Unscrew the securing nuts, and disconnect the exhaust downpipe from the manifold (photo). Recover the gasket. Support the exhaust downpipe from underneath the vehicle, with an axle stand for example, to avoid placing unnecessary strain on the exhaust system.
5 Disconnect the HT leads from the spark plugs, if necessary identifying them for locations, and place them to one side out of the way.
6 Unscrew the eight securing nuts, noting the location of the front engine lifting bracket secured by the front two nuts on OHC models, and lift the manifold from the cylinder head. Recover the gasket(s) where applicable (photos).

42.11 Rear engine lifting bracket location – OHC models

42.12 Lifting the inlet manifold from the cylinder head – OHC models

42.27A Removing the carburettor ...

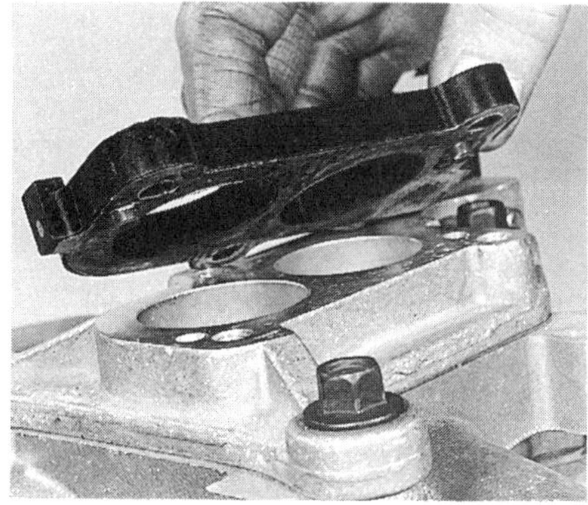
42.27B ... and the insulator block from the inlet manifold – CVH models

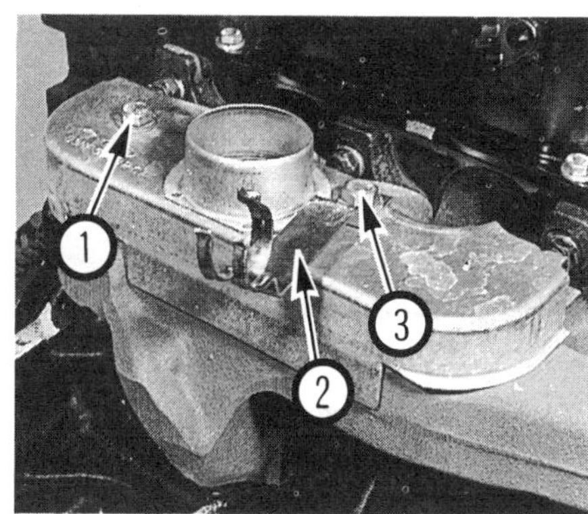

43.3 Exhaust manifold hot air shroud showing securing screws (1 and 3) and coolant hose clip (2) – OHC models

43.4 Unscrewing an exhaust downpipe securing nut

43.6A Unscrew the exhaust manifold securing nuts ...

43.6B ... noting the location of the front engine lifting bracket, ...

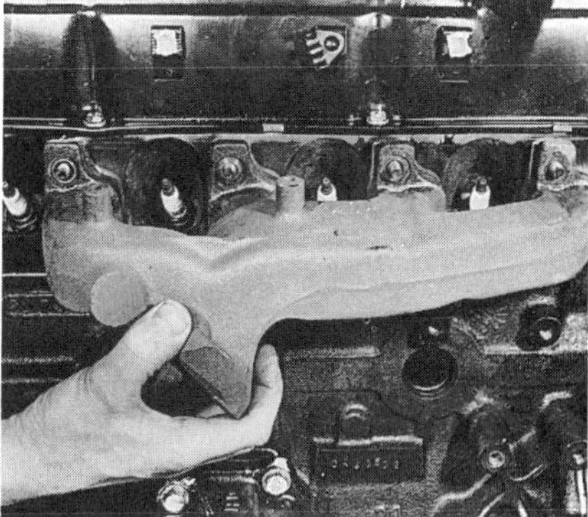
43.6C ... and lift off the exhaust manifold – OHC models

43.6D OHC models have a separate exhaust manifold gasket for each exhaust port

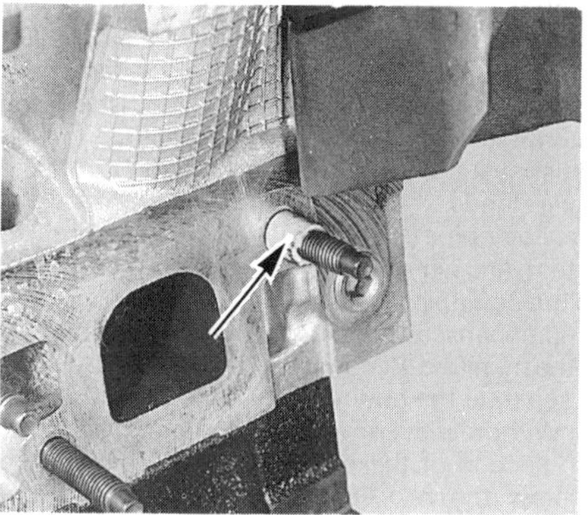
43.8 Remove the plastic spacer (arrowed) before fitting exhaust manifold gasket to CVH models

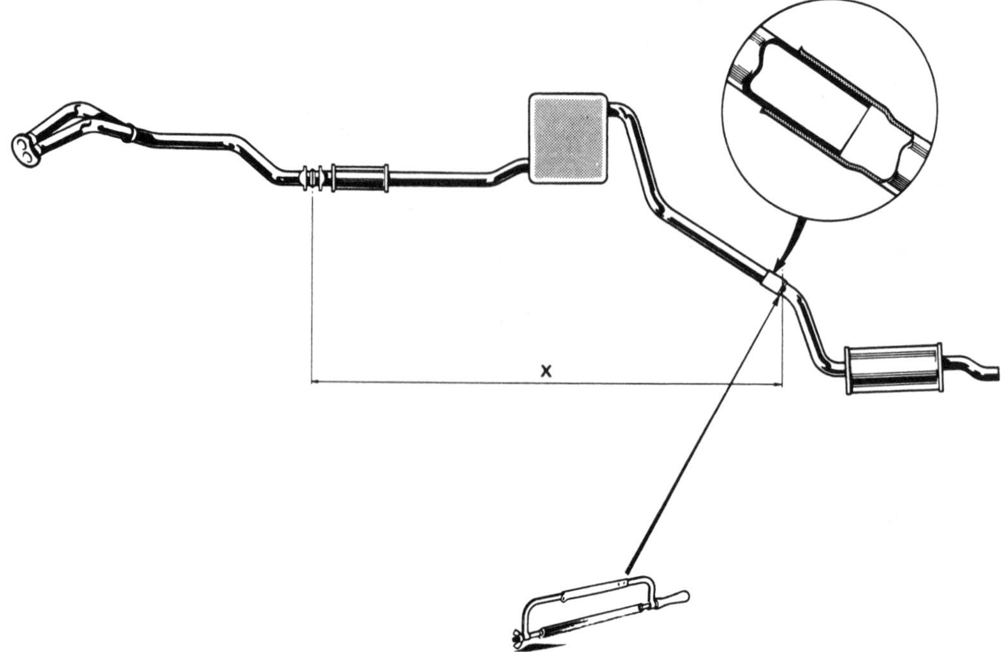

Fig 3.48 Cutting point when fitting a service replacement exhaust system section – Saloon, Hatchback and Estate models (Sec 44)

X = 1639 mm for all models up to 1987 except 1.3 and 1.6 litre Hatchback
X = 1681 mm for 1.3 and 1.6 litre Hatchback models up to 1987
X = 2063 mm for all models from 1987

7 Refitting is a reversal of removal, bearing in mind the following.
8 Ensure that all mating faces are clean, and renew all gaskets. Note that on CVH models, no gasket is fitted between the manifold and cylinder head in production, but a gasket must be used when refitting. Where applicable, remove the plastic spacer from the rear manifold stud before fitting the gasket (photo).
9 Tighten the manifold securing nuts progressively to the specified torque, and similarly tighten the exhaust downpipe securing nuts. Do not forget to fit the engine lifting bracket on OHC models.
10 Ensure that the HT leads are reconnected to their correct cylinders.

44 Exhaust system – checking, removal and refitting

1 The exhaust system should be examined for leaks, damage, and security at the intervals specified in the *'Routine maintenance'* Section at the beginning of this manual. To do this, apply the handbrake, then start the engine and allow it to idle. Lie down on each side of the vehicle in turn and check the full length of the exhaust system for leaks, while an assistant temporarily places a wad of cloth over the tailpipe. If a leak is evident, stop the engine and use a proprietary repair kit such as Holts Flexiwrap and Holts Gun Gum to seal it. Holts Flexiwrap is an MOT approved permanent exhaust repair. If an excessive leak or damage is evident, renew the relevant section of the exhaust system. Check the rubber mountings for deterioration and renew if necessary.
2 To remove the exhaust system, jack up the front and rear of the vehicle and support on axle stands.
3 If desired, the exhaust downpipe can be removed independently of the remainder of the system, and similarly the main part of the system can be removed, leaving the downpipe in place.
4 To remove the downpipe, unscrew the securing nuts and disconnect the downpipe from the manifold. Recover the gasket. Unscrew the two nuts and bolts, and separate the downpipe flanged joint from the remainder of the system. Withdraw the downpipe (photos).
5 To remove the main section of the exhaust system leaving the downpipe in place, unscrew the two securing nuts and bolts and separate the flanged joint from the downpipe. Unhook the rubber mountings and withdraw the system from underneath the vehicle. The number and type of rubber mountings varies according to model (photos). If necessary to avoid confusion, note how the mountings are fitted to enable correct refitting. Note that on P100 models the system must be manipulated to pass over the rear axle.
6 Refitting is a reversal of removal, but ensure that all mating faces are clean, and fit a new gasket between the downpipe and manifold (photo). Do not fully tighten the joint fittings until the system is in position and correctly aligned in its mountings under the vehicle. Ensure that no part of the exhaust system is closer than 25.0 mm (1.0 in) to the underbody.
7 Service replacement exhaust systems are available in three sections; downpipe, centre section and rear section. The service replacement sections fit together using socket joints, therefore the centre section of a production exhaust system cannot be renewed without also renewing the rear section.
8 To renew the centre and/or rear section(s) of the exhaust system, first remove the main system as described in paragraph 5.
9 To fit a service replacement rear section to a production system, use a hacksaw to cut through the pipe at the point shown in Fig. 3.48 or 3.49 as applicable. Apply exhaust sealant to the mating surfaces of the two

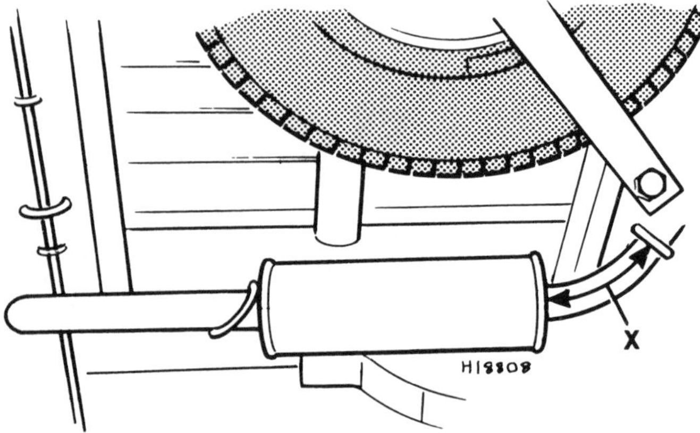

Fig 3.49 Cutting point when fitting a service replacement exhaust system section – P100 models (Sec 44)

X = 226mm

44.4A Exhaust downpipe-to-manifold flanged joint viewed from underneath vehicle

44.4B Exhaust downpipe-to-main system flanged joint

44.5A Rear exhaust section mounting – Hatchback model

44.5B Rear exhaust mounting – P100 model

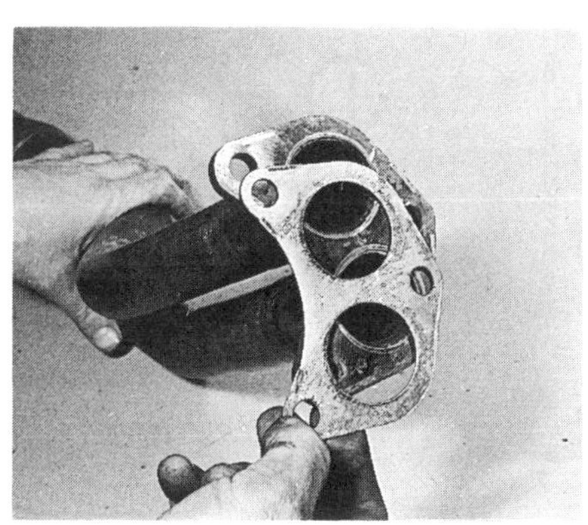
44.6 Fit a new downpipe-to-manifold gasket

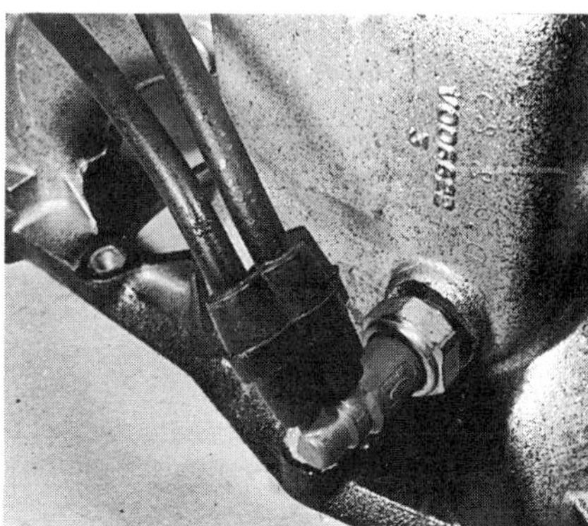
45.1 Low vacuum enrichment ported vacuum switch location in inlet manifold – model with Weber 2V type carburettor

sections, then push the two sections together and fit a U-bolt clamp to the centre of the joint. Do not fully tighten the U-bolt clamp nuts until the system is in position and correctly aligned in its mountings under the vehicle.

10 To renew a service replacement section, unscrew the nuts and remove the U-bolt clamp from the joint. Tap around the joint to break the seal, and separate the centre and rear sections. Ensure that the joint mating surfaces are clean, then apply exhaust sealant, push the new section onto the remaining section, and fit the U-bolt clamp to the centre of the joint. Do not fully tighten the U-bolt clamp nuts until the system is in position and correctly aligned in its mountings under the vehicle.

45 Vacuum valves, ported vacuum switches and fuel traps removal and refitting

Refer to Chapter 4, Section 17 (photo).

PART B: FUEL INJECTION SYSTEM

46 General description

The fuel injection system is of the Bosch L-Jetronic type. The system is under the overall control of the EEC IV engine management system (see Chapter 4), which also controls the ignition timing.

Fuel is supplied from the rear-mounted fuel tank by an electric fuel pump mounted next to the tank, via a pressure regulator, to the fuel rail. The fuel rail acts as a reservoir for the four fuel injectors, which inject fuel into the cylinder inlet tracts, upstream of the inlet valves. The fuel injectors receive an electrical pulse once per crankshaft revolution, which operates all four injectors simultaneously. The duration of the electrical pulse determines the quantity of fuel injected, and pulse duration is computed by the EEC IV module on the basis of information received from the various sensors.

Inducted air passes from the air cleaner through a vane type airflow meter before passing to the cylinder inlet tracts via the throttle valve. A flap in the vane airflow meter is deflected in proportion to the airflow; this deflection is converted into an electrical signal and passed to the EEC IV module. An adjustable air bypass channel provides the means of idle mixture adjustment.

A throttle position sensor enables the EEC IV module to compute not only throttle position, but also its rate of change. Extra fuel can thus be provided for acceleration when the throttle is opened suddenly. Information from the throttle position sensor is also used to cut off fuel on the overrun, thus improving fuel economy and reducing exhaust gas emissions.

Idle speed is controlled by a variable orifice solenoid valve which regulates the amount of air bypassing the throttle valve. The valve is controlled by the EEC IV module; there is no provision for direct adjustment of the idle speed.

Additional sensors inform the EEC IV module of engine coolant and air temperature. On models fitted with automatic transmission, a sensor registers the change from 'P' or 'N' to a drive position, and causes the idle speed to be adjusted accordingly to compensate for the additional load. Similarly on models fitted with air conditioning, a sensor registers when the compressor clutch is in operation.

A 'limited operation strategy' (LOS) means that the vehicle is still driveable, albeit at reduced power and efficiency, in the event of a failure in the EEC IV module or its sensors.

A fuel filter is incorporated in the fuel supply line to ensure that the fuel supplied to the injectors is clean.

On models produced from mid-1986 onwards, a fuel pump inertia cut-off switch is fitted. This switch breaks the electrical circuit to the fuel pump in the event of an accident or similar impact, cutting off the fuel supply to the engine.

Refer to Chapter 4 for details of the conditions required to operate engines on unleaded petrol.

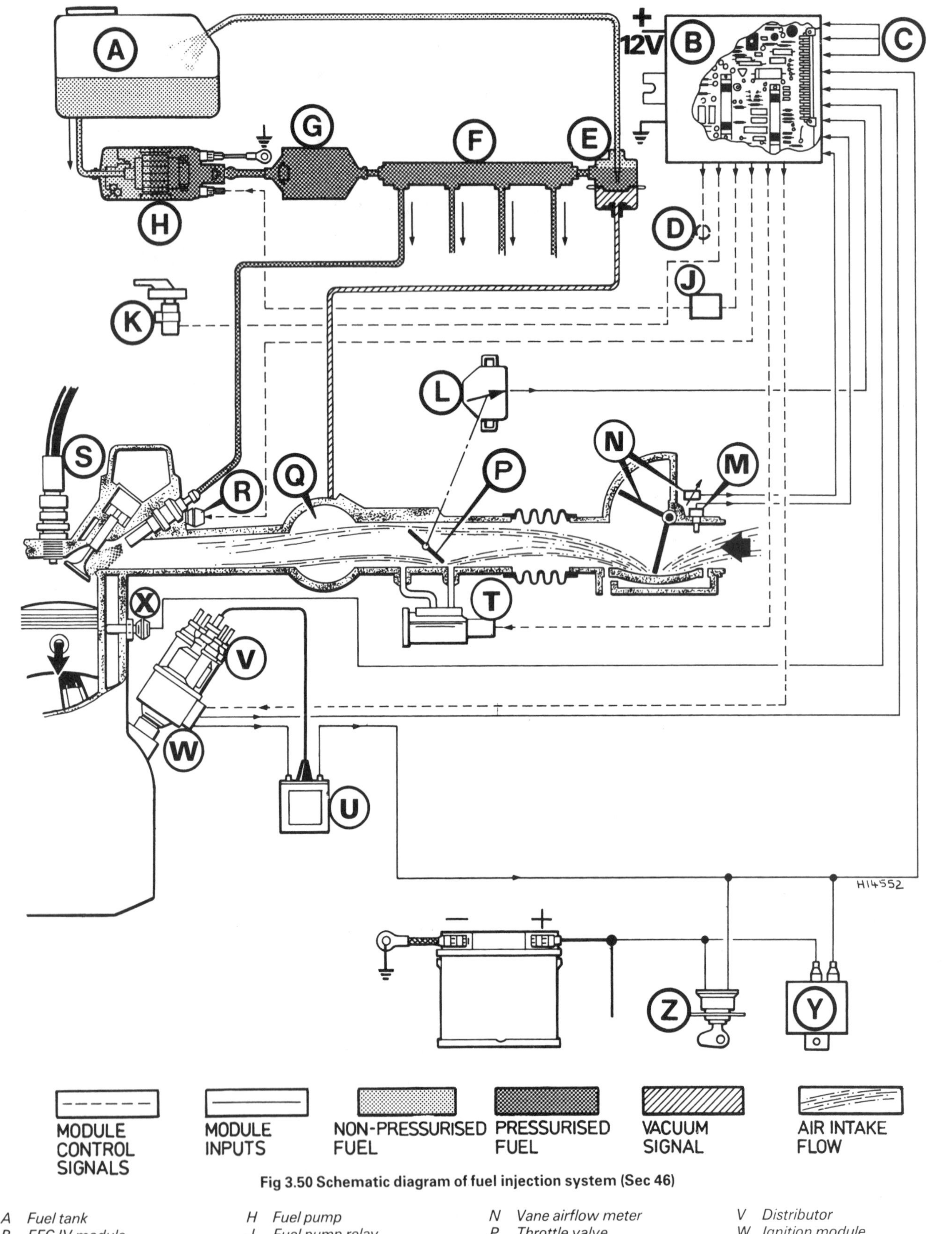

Fig 3.50 Schematic diagram of fuel injection system (Sec 46)

A Fuel tank
B EEC IV module
C Module inputs
D Self-test output
E Fuel pressure regulator
F Fuel rail
G Fuel filter
H Fuel pump
J Fuel pump relay
K CVT transducer (not UK models)
L Throttle position sensor
M Vane air temperature sensor
N Vane airflow meter
P Throttle valve
Q Inlet manifold
R Fuel injector
S Spark plug
T Idle speed control valve
U Ignition coil
V Distributor
W Ignition module
X Engine coolant temperature sensor
Y Power relay
Z Ignition switch

47 Fuel injection system – precautions

Refer to Section 2, but note that the fuel injection system is pressurised, therefore extra care must be taken when disconnecting fuel lines. When disconnecting a fuel line union, loosen the union slowly to avoid a sudden release of pressure which may cause fuel spray.

48 Maintenance and inspection

1 Refer to Section 3, noting the following points.
2 The only means of idle speed adjustment provided is by the yellow 'idle speed adjustment' wire (see Chapter 4, Section 11) which allows the idle speed to be raised by 75 rpm.
3 Ignore the reference to the air cleaner intake air temperature control.
4 Additionally, renew the fuel filter at the specified intervals.
5 Check the idle mixture as described in Section 59, and renew the air cleaner element as described in Section 49.

49 Air cleaner element – renewal

1 Disconnect the battery negative lead.
2 Depress the locking clip on the airflow meter wiring plug and disconnect the plug. Pull on the plug, not the wiring (photo).
3 Loosen the securing clip and disconnect the air intake hose from the airflow meter.
4 Release the four securing clips and lift off the air cleaner lid with the airflow meter (photo).
5 Lift out the old air cleaner element, then wipe the inside of the air cleaner casing and lid clean (photo).
6 Fit the new element with the sealing lip uppermost.
7 Refit the air cleaner lid and secure with the four clips.
8 Reconnect the air intake hose to the airflow meter, ensuring that the securing clip is correctly aligned – see Fig. 3.51. Reconnect the wiring plug.
9 Reconnect the battery negative lead.

50 Air cleaner – removal and refitting

1 Proceed as described in Section 49, paragraphs 1 to 4 inclusive.
2 Remove the left-hand front wheel arch liner, as described in Chapter 12.
3 Working under the wheel arch, unscrew the three air cleaner securing nuts and washers.
4 Disconnect the air intake tube, and withdraw the air cleaner from the engine compartment.
5 Refitting is a reversal of removal.

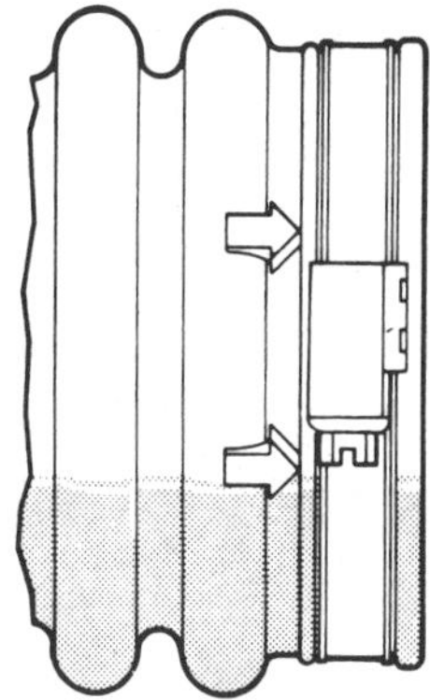

Fig 3.51 Air intake hose clip correctly aligned (Sec 49)

51 Fuel filter – renewal

Note: *Refer to Section 47 before proceeding.*
1 The fuel filter is located on the left-hand side of the engine compartment (photo).
2 Disconnect the battery negative lead.
3 Position a suitable container beneath the filter, then slowly loosen the fuel inlet union to relieve the pressure in the fuel lines.
4 Disconnect the fuel inlet and outlet unions. Be prepared for petrol spillage. If necessary, identify the fuel line unions for use when refitting.
5 Loosen the filter clamp screw, and withdraw the filter from the clamp. Drain the petrol from the filter into the container. Dispose of the filter carefully.
6 Fit the new filter, ensuring that the arrows on the filter body point in the direction of fuel flow.
7 Tighten the clamp screw, and reconnect the fuel inlet and outlet unions. Ensure that the unions are correctly connected.
8 Reconnect the battery negative lead, and check the fuel line unions for leaks, pressurising the system by switching the ignition on and off several times.

52 Fuel pressure regulator – removal and refitting

Note: *Refer to Section 47 before proceeding.*
1 Disconnect the battery negative lead.
2 Position a suitable container beneath the pressure regulator, then slowly loosen the fuel feed union to relieve the pressure in the fuel lines.
3 Disconnect the fuel feed and return lines. Be prepared for petrol spillage.
4 Disconnect the vacuum pipe from the top of the pressure regulator.
5 Unscrew the securing nut from the base of the pressure regulator and withdraw the unit (photo).
6 Refitting is a reversal of removal, but if the fuel return line was

49.2 Disconnecting the airflow meter wiring plug

49.4 Air cleaner lid securing clip

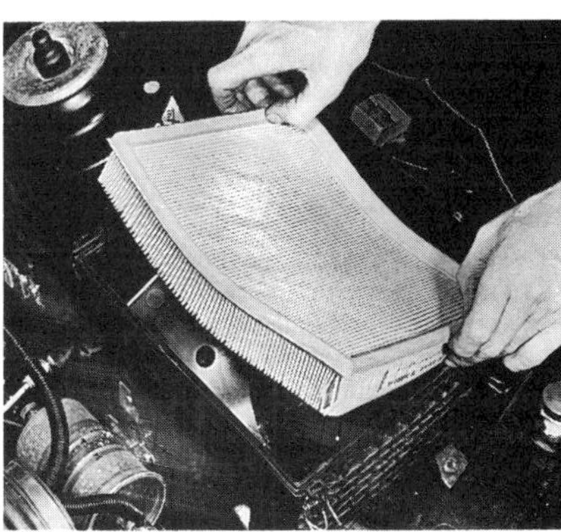

49.5 Lifting out the air cleaner element

51.1 Fuel filter location – outlet union arrowed

52.5 Withdrawing the fuel pressure regulator

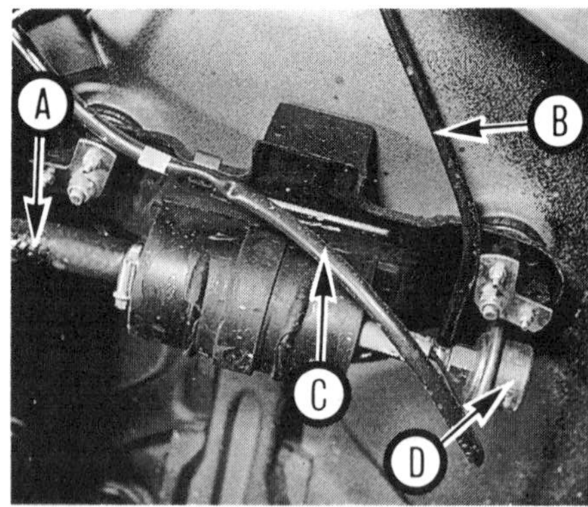

54.1 Fuel pump location
A Inlet hose
B Outlet hose
C Electrical feed
D Flow damper

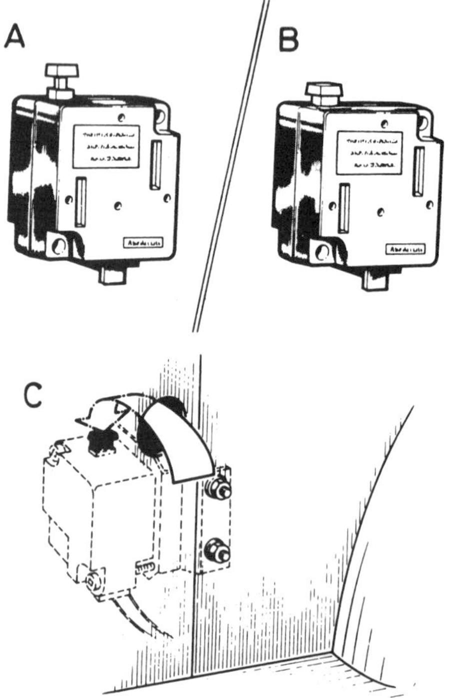

Fig 3.52 Fuel pump inertia cut-off switch – Hatchback and Estate models (Sec 53)

A Activated mode (fuel cut-off)
B Normal mode (fuel flowing)
C Trim panel access hole

originally secured with a crimped type clip, discard this and use a new worm drive clip.

7 On completion check the fuel line connections for leaks, pressurising the system by switching the ignition on and off several times.

53 Fuel pump – testing

1 If the fuel pump is functioning, it should be possible to hear it 'buzzing' by listening under the rear of the vehicle when the ignition is switched on. Unless the engine is started, the fuel pump should switch off after approximately one second. If the noise produced is excessive, this may be due to a faulty fuel flow damper. The damper can be renewed by unscrewing it from the pump outlet union with reference to Section 54.

2 If the pump appears to have failed completely, check the appropriate fuse and relay, and where applicable check the state of the fuel pump inertia cut-off switch as follows.

3 The inertia cut-off switch is fitted to models produced from mid-1986 onwards, and is located behind the passenger compartment left-hand side trim panel on Hatchback and Estate models, or in the spare wheel well on Saloon models. The switch incorporates a reset button which should normally be in the depressed position. Check the position of the reset button before assuming that a fault exists in the fuel pump.

4 To test the fuel pump, special equipment is required, and it is recommended that any suspected faults are referred to a Ford dealer.

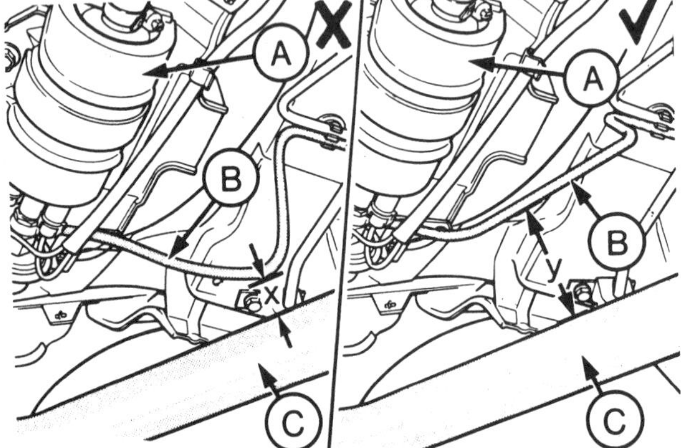

Fig 3.53 Correct and incorrect routing of fuel pump outlet pipe (Sec 54)

A Fuel pump
B Outlet pipe
C Exhaust pipe
X = 30.0 mm (1.2 in) approx
Y = 100.0 mm (3.9 in) approx

54 Fuel pump – removal and refitting

Note: *Refer to Section 47 before proceeding.*

1 The fuel pump is located under the rear of the vehicle next to the fuel tank (photo).

2 Disconnect the battery negative lead.

3 Chock the front wheels, then jack up the rear of the vehicle and support on axle stands.

4 Clean the area around the pump mounting, and position a suitable container under the pump.

5 Using a hose clamping tool or self-locking pliers, clamp the fuel tank-to-pump hose to prevent excessive petrol spillage, or alternatively make arrangements to collect the contents of the fuel tank which will otherwise be released. Disconnect the hose from the pump.

6 Slowly loosen the fuel flow damper fitted to the pump outlet union, to relieve the pressure in the fuel line, then remove the damper and disconnect the outlet pipe from the pump. Plug the end of the pipe to prevent excessive petrol spillage.

7 Disconnect the wiring plug(s), then slacken the clamp bolt and slide the pump from the bracket assembly.

8 Refitting is a reversal of removal, noting the follows.
9 When refitting the flow damper to the pump ensure that the pump outlet pipe is correctly routed – see Fig. 3.53. It is possible to inadvertently rotate the banjo union through 180°, which routes the outlet pipe too close to the exhaust.
10 After refitting and securing the pump, but before lowering the vehicle, reconnect the battery and switch the ignition on and off several times to pressurise the fuel system. Check for leaks around the pump; if all is satisfactory, switch off the ignition and lower the vehicle.

55 Fuel tank – removal and refitting

Refer to Section 11.

56 Fuel level sender unit – removal and refitting

Refer to Section 12.

57 Throttle pedal – removal and refitting

Refer to Section 13.

58 Throttle cable – removal, refitting and adjustment

Refer to Section 14.

59 Idle speed and mixture – adjustment

Note: *Refer to Section 47 before proceeding. Before carrying out any adjustments ensure that the ignition timing and spark plug gaps are set as specified. To carry out the adjustments an accurate tachometer and an exhaust gas analyser (CO meter) will be required.*
1 Idle speed is controlled by the EEC IV module, and the only means of adjustment provided is by the yellow 'idle speed adjustment' wire (see Chapter 4, Section 11) which allows the idle speed to be raised by 75 rpm. The idle mixture can be checked and if necessary adjusted as follows, although adjustment of the mixture is not normally required during routine maintenance.
2 Run the engine until it is at normal operating temperature.
3 Stop the engine and connect a tachometer and an exhaust gas analyser in accordance with the manufacturer's instructions.
4 Start the engine and run it at 3000 rpm for 15 seconds, ensuring that all electrical loads (headlamps, heater blower etc) are switched off, then allow the engine to idle and check the CO content. Note that the CO reading will initially rise, then fall and finally stabilise.
5 If adjustment is necessary, remove the tamperproof cap from the base of the airflow meter, and turn the mixture screw using a suitable Allen key to give the specified CO content (photo).
6 Checking and adjustment should be completed within 30 seconds of the meter readings stabilising. If this has not been possible, run the engine at 3000 rpm, for 15 seconds, then allow the engine to idle. Re-check the CO content and carry out further adjustment if necessary.
7 On completion of adjustment, stop the engine and disconnect the tachometer and exhaust gas analyser. Fit a new tamperproof cap to the mixture screw.

60 Throttle position sensor – removal and refitting

Note: *During this procedure ensure that the sensor wiper is not rotated beyond its normal operating arc.*
1 Disconnect the battery negative lead.
2 Free the throttle position sensor wiring plug from the retaining clip located on the underside of the throttle body. Disconnect the wiring plug halves by releasing the locktabs and pulling on the plug halves, not the wiring – see Fig. 3.55.
3 Bend back the locktabs and unscrew the two sensor retaining bolts

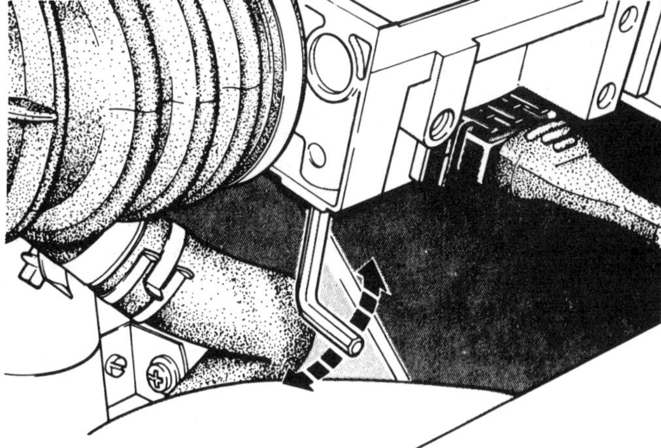

Fig 3.54 Adjusting the idle mixture (Sec 59)

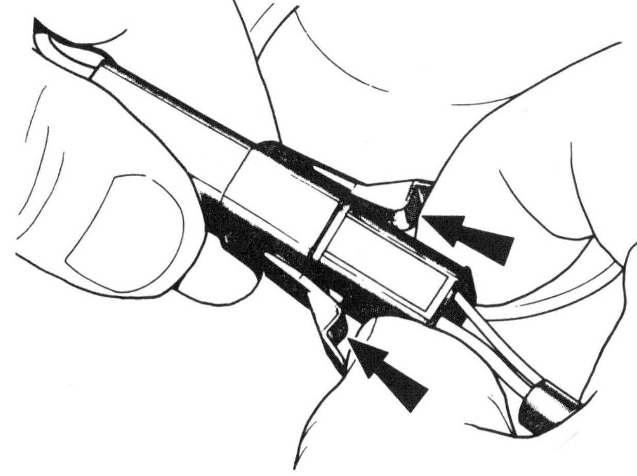

Fig 3.55 Releasing locktabs to disconnect throttle position sensor wiring plug halves (Sec 60)

(photo). Withdraw the locking plate and sensor from the throttle shaft.
4 Refitting is a reversal of removal, ensuring that the moulded side of the sensor faces towards the inlet manifold, and that the flat on the sensor wiper engages with the flat on the throttle shaft.

61 Idle speed control valve – removal and refitting

Note: *A new gasket must be used when refitting the valve.*
1 Disconnect the battery negative lead.
2 Disconnect the idle speed control valve wiring plug by releasing the retaining clip and pulling on the plug, not the wiring (photo).
3 Unscrew the two retaining nuts and withdraw the valve from the inlet manifold (photo). Recover the gasket.
4 Clean the valve and manifold mating faces before refitting, taking care not to allow dirt to enter the manifold.
5 Refitting is a reversal of removal, using a new gasket.
6 On completion, start the engine and check that the idle speed is stable – if not, check for air leaks around the valve. Switch on all available electrical loads and check that the idle speed is maintained – if not, suspect a faulty valve.

62 Airflow meter – removal and refitting

Note: *A tachometer and an exhaust gas analyser will be required to check the idle mixture on completion.*
1 Disconnect the battery negative lead.
2 Depress the locking clip on the airflow meter wiring plug and disconnect the plug. Pull on the plug, not the wiring.

59.5 Airflow meter removed and inverted to show mixture screw location (arrowed)

60.3 Unscrewing the throttle position sensor retaining bolts (arrowed)

61.2 Disconnecting the idle speed control valve wiring plug

61.3 Unscrewing an idle speed control valve retaining nut

62.5 Airflow meter-to-air cleaner lid bolts (arrowed)

3 Loosen the securing clip and disconnect the air intake hose from the airflow meter.
4 Release the four securing clips and lift off the air cleaner lid with the airflow meter.
5 Remove the four securing bolts and separate the airflow meter from the air cleaner lid (photo). Recover the seal.
6 Refitting is a reversal of removal, ensuring that the seal is correctly located on the air cleaner lid, and that the air intake hose clip is correctly aligned - see Fig. 3.51.
7 On completion, check and if necessary adjust the idle mixture as described in Section 59.

63 Fuel injectors - removal and refitting

Note: *Refer to Section 47 before proceeding. A tachometer and an exhaust gas analyser will be required to check the idle mixture on completion. New seals and retaining clips must be used when refitting the injectors, and special grease will be required - see paragraph 12.*
1 Disconnect the battery negative lead.
2 Disconnect the crankcase ventilation hose from the air intake hose, then disconnect the air intake hose from the inlet manifold and the airflow meter.
3 Disconnect the HT lead from the coil, then remove the distributor cap, with reference to Chapter 4, Section 7, and position the cap and HT leads clear of the fuel rail assembly.
4 Disconnect the wiring plugs from the idle speed control valve, the throttle position sensor and the engine coolant temperature sensor.
5 Remove the fuel pressure regulator as described in Section 52.
6 Unscrew the securing bolt and remove the throttle return spring bracket. Disconnect the throttle return spring.
7 Disconnect the fuel supply hose from the fuel rail. Be prepared for petrol spillage.
8 Disconnect the wiring plugs from the fuel injectors, noting their locations for use when refitting.
9 Remove the three securing bolts and withdraw the fuel rail and fuel injectors from the inlet manifold as an assembly (photos).

Fig 3.56 Fuel injector retaining clip (A) (Sec 63)

10 To remove a fuel injector from the fuel rail, remove the retaining clip and withdraw the injector.
11 Overhaul of the fuel injectors is not possible, as no spares are available. If faulty, an injector must be renewed.
12 Commence refitting by fitting new seals to both ends of each fuel injector. Even if only one injector has been removed, new seals must be fitted to all four injectors (photo). Coat the seals with silicone grease to Ford specification ESEM - ICI71A. Similarly, renew all four fuel injector retaining clips.
13 Further refitting is a reversal of removal, ensuring that all hoses, wiring plugs and leads are correctly connected. When reconnecting the air intake hose, make sure that the hose clips are correctly aligned - see Fig. 3.51.
14 On completion, check and if necessary adjust the idle mixture as described in Section 59.

63.9A Fuel rail front securing bolt (arrowed) ...

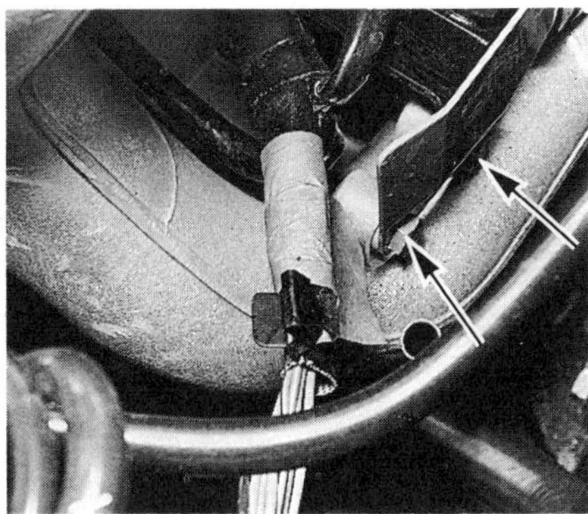
63.9B ... and rear securing bolts

63.12 Fuel injector with seals removed

65.5 Unscrew the securing bolts and remove the throttle cable bracket

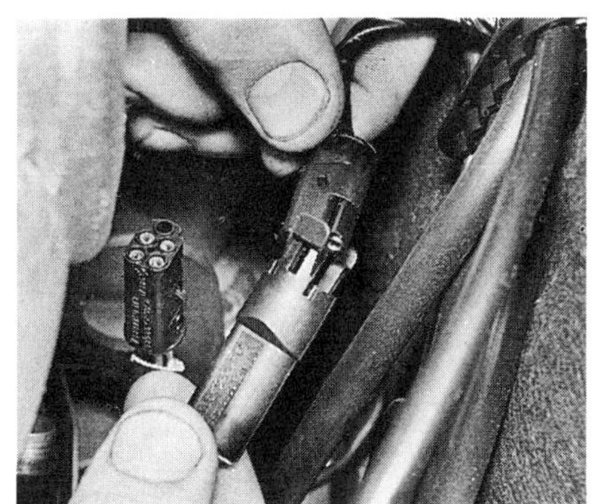
65.6 Disconnecting a fuel injection harness wiring plug

65.11 Unscrew the two securing nuts (arrowed) and remove the inlet manifold bracing strut

64 Throttle body - removal and refitting

Note: *A tachometer and an exhaust gas analyser will be required to check the idle mixture on completion. A new gasket must be used when refitting the throttle body.*

1 Disconnect the battery negative lead.

2 Free the throttle position sensor wiring plug from the retaining clip on the underside of the throttle body. Disconnect the wiring plug halves by releasing the locktabs and pulling on the plug halves, not the wiring.

3 Disconnect the throttle cable from the throttle lever, with reference to Section 14 if necessary.

4 Disconnect the crankcase ventilation hose from the air intake hose, then disconnect the air intake hose from the throttle body and the airflow meter.

5 Remove the four securing bolts and withdraw the throttle body from the inlet manifold. Recover the gasket.

6 Refitting is a reversal of removal, bearing in mind the following points.

7 Ensure that all mating faces are clean, and fit a new gasket.

8 When reconnecting the air intake hose, make sure that the hose clips are correctly aligned - see Fig. 3.51.

9 On completion, adjust the throttle cable as described in Section 14, and check and if necessary adjust the idle mixture as described in Section 59.

65 Inlet manifold - removal and refitting

Note: *Refer to Section 47 before proceeding. A tachometer and an exhaust gas analyser will be required to check the idle mixture on completion. A new gasket must be used when refitting the manifold.*

1 Disconnect the battery negative lead.

2 Partially drain the cooling system as described in Chapter 2.

3 Disconnect the crankcase ventilation hose from the air intake hose, then disconnect the air intake hose from the inlet manifold and the airflow meter.

4 Disconnect the HT lead from the coil, then remove the distributor cap, with reference to Chapter 4, Section 7, and position the cap and HT leads clear of the inlet manifold assembly.

5 Unscrew the two securing bolts and remove the throttle cable bracket (photo). Disconnect the cable end from the throttle lever, and move the bracket to one side.

6 Disconnect the fuel injection harness wiring plugs at the bulkhead end of the manifold (photo).

7 Disconnect the oil pressure warning lamp switch wire from below the manifold.

8 Disconnect the fuel supply hose from the fuel rail. Loosen the union nut slowly to relieve the pressure in the fuel system, and be prepared for petrol spillage.

9 Disconnect the fuel return hose from the fuel pressure regulator. Be prepared for petrol spillage.

10 Disconnect the coolant hose and the brake servo vacuum hose from the inlet manifold.

11 Unscrew the two securing nuts and remove the bracing strut which runs from the manifold to the right-hand side of the cylinder head (photo).

12 Unscrew the two bolts securing the lower manifold bracket to the left-hand side of the cylinder block (photo).

13 Remove the four bolts and two nuts securing the inlet manifold to the cylinder head, and carefully withdraw the manifold. If the distributor obstructs removal, extract the front manifold stud by locking two nuts together and using them to unscrew the stud (photo). Alternatively, the distributor can be removed, although this is not recommended unless absolutely essential. Recover the gasket. Note that an earth strap may be located on one of the manifold securing bolts or studs; where applicable, note its location as an aid to refitting.

14 With the manifold removed, the various fuel injection system

65.12 Lower inlet manifold bracket (arrowed)

65.13 Where necessary use two nuts locked together (arrowed) to remove the front inlet manifold stud

components can be separated from the manifold with reference to the relevant Sections of this Chapter.

15 Refitting is a reversal of removal, bearing in mind the following points.

16 Renew the gasket, and apply a bead of sealant at least 5.0 mm (0.2 in) wide around the central coolant aperture on both sides of the gasket. Ensure that all mating faces are clean.

17 Tighten the manifold securing nuts and bolts progressively to the specified torque, where applicable ensuring that the earth strap is in position.

18 Make sure that all hoses, cables, wires and leads are correctly reconnected. When reconnecting the air intake hose, make sure that the hose clips are correctly aligned – see Fig. 3.51.

19 On completion, refill the cooling system as described in Chapter 2, adjust the throttle cable as described in Section 14, and check and if necessary adjust the idle mixture as described in Section 59.

66 Exhaust manifold – removal and refitting

1 Refer to Section 43, but note the following points.

2 Ignore the references to removal and refitting of the air cleaner and hot air pick-up pipe, and note that a heat shield is fitted in place of the hot air shroud.

3 Note the location of the inlet manifold bracing strut which is secured to one of the manifold studs by an extra nut.

67 Exhaust system – checking, removal and refitting

Refer to Section 44.

PART C: FAULT DIAGNOSIS

68 Fault diagnosis – carburettor fuel system

Note: *High fuel consumption and poor performance are not necessarily due to carburettor faults. Make sure that the ignition system is properly adjusted, and that the engine itself is in good mechanical condition. Items such as binding brakes or under-inflated tyres should not be overlooked.*

Symptom	Reason(s)
Engine will not start	Fuel tank empty Fault in fuel line Faulty fuel pressure regulator (where applicable) Fuel pump faulty Faulty fuel pump relay or blown fuse (models with air conditioning) Faulty or maladjusted automatic choke Air leak at inlet manifold Engine management system fault (where applicable) Ignition system fault
Fuel consumption excessive	Leak in fuel system Air cleaner element choked, giving rich mixture Faulty fuel pressure regulator (where applicable) Carburettor worn Carburettor float chamber flooding due to incorrect level or worn needle valve Carburettor idle adjustments incorrect Faulty or maladjusted automatic choke Engine management system fault (where applicable) Unsympathetic driving style

Symptom	Reason(s)
Lack of power	Fault in fuel line Faulty fuel pressure regulator (where applicable) Fuel pump faulty Air leak at inlet manifold Faulty or maladjusted automatic choke Engine management system fault (where applicable) Ignition system fault
Poor or erratic idling	Carburettor idle adjustments incorrect Air leak at inlet manifold Faulty fuel pressure regulator (where applicable) Leak in ignition advance vacuum hose Leak in brake servo vacuum hose Engine management system fault (where applicable) Ignition system fault
Backfiring in exhaust	Air leak in exhaust system Ignition timing incorrect Mixture grossly incorrect Exhaust valve(s) burnt or sticking, or valve clearance(s) too small
Spitting back in inlet manifold or carburettor	Mixture very weak Ignition timing incorrect Inlet valve(s) burnt or sticking, or valve clearance(s) too small

Note: *This Section is not intended as an exhaustive guide to fault diagnosis, but summarises the more common faults which may be encountered during a vehicle's life. Consult a dealer for more detailed advice, particularly where an engine management system fault is suspected.*

69 Fault diagnosis – fuel injection system

Note: *High fuel consumption and poor performance are not necessarily due to fuel injection system faults. Make sure that the ignition system is properly adjusted, and that the engine itself is in good mechanical condition. Items such as binding brakes or under-inflated tyres should not be overlooked.*

Symptom	Reason(s)
Engine will not start	Fuel tank empty Fault in fuel line Fuel pump faulty Faulty fuel pump relay or blown fuse Fuel pump inertia cut-off switch tripped (where applicable) Air leak at inlet manifold Fuel filter blocked Faulty fuel pressure regulator Faulty idle speed control valve Faulty fuel injector(s) Engine management system fault Ignition system fault
Fuel consumption excessive	Leak in fuel system Faulty fuel pressure regulator Mixture adjustment incorrect Air cleaner element choked Faulty airflow meter Faulty throttle position sensor Faulty idle speed control valve Engine management system fault Unsympathetic driving style
Lack of power	Fault in fuel line Faulty fuel pressure regulator Faulty fuel injector(s) Fuel pump faulty Air leak at inlet manifold Air cleaner element choked Engine management system fault Ignition system fault

Symptom	Reason(s)
Poor or erratic idling	Faulty idle speed control valve Air leak at inlet manifold Faulty fuel pressure regulator Faulty airflow meter Leak in brake servo vacuum hose Engine management system fault Ignition system fault
Backfiring in exhaust	Air leak in exhaust system Ignition timing incorrect Mixture grossly incorrect Exhaust valve(s) burnt or sticking, or valve clearance(s) too small
Spitting back in inlet manifold or throttle body	Mixture very weak Ignition timing incorrect Inlet valve(s) burnt or sticking, or valve clearance(s) too small

Note: *This Section is not intended as an exhaustive guide to fault diagnosis, but summarises the more common faults which may be encountered during a vehicle's life. In depth fault diagnosis of the fuel injection and engine management systems requires the use of specialist dedicated test equipment. Consult a dealer for more detailed advice.*

Chapter 4 Ignition and engine management systems

For modifications, and information applicable to later models, see Supplement at end of manual

Contents

Specifications

System type

1.3 litre models	Bosch inductive discharge system
1.6 litre models (except Economy)	Bosch inductive discharge system
1.6 litre Economy models	ESC system with Lucas 'Hall effect' distributor
1.8 litre OHC models	ESC II system with Bosch 'Hall effect' distributor
1.8 litre CVH models	ESC Hybrid system
2.0 litre carburettor models up to 1985	Bosch inductive discharge system
2.0 litre carburettor models from 1985 (except P100)	ESC II system with Bosch 'Hall effect' distributor
P100 models	Bosch inductive discharge system
2.0 litre fuel injection models up to 1987	EEC IV system with Motorcraft 'Hall effect' distributor
2.0 litre fuel injection models from 1987	EEC IV system with Bosch 'Hall effect' distributor

Coil

Output (minimum)	25.0 kilovolts
Primary winding resistance	0.72 to 0.88 ohm
Secondary winding resistance	4500 to 7000 ohms

Distributor

Direction of rotor arm rotation	Clockwise
Firing order	1 – 3 – 4 – 2 (No 1 cylinder nearest timing cover)
Dwell angle	Automatically controlled by electronic module (not adjustable)

Ignition timing (at idle with vacuum pipe disconnected)

	Leaded petrol (4-star, 97 RON)	**Unleaded petrol (Premium, 95 RON)**
1.3 litre models	12° BTDC	8° BTDC*
1.6 litre models with VV carburettor	12° BTDC	8° BTDC*
1.6 litre models with 2V carburettor	10° BTDC	6° BTDC†
1.8 litre OHC models	10° BTDC	6° BTDC†
1.8 litre cvh models	ESC Hybrid controlled, no adjustment possible	
2.0 litre carburettor models up to 1985	8° BTDC	4° BTDC*
2.0 litre carburettor models from 1985 (except P100)	10° BTDC	6° BTDC†
P100 models	6° BTDC	2° BTDC†
2.0 litre fuel injection models	12° BTDC	8° BTDC†

**Fill with leaded petrol (4-star, 97 RON) every 4th tankful*

†Not all vehicles are suitable for continuous operation on unleaded petrol. Refer to Section 11

Spark plugs

Make and type:	
All models except 1.8 CVH and P100	Champion F7YCC or RF7YC
1.8 CVH engine	Champion RC7YCC or RC7YC
P100 model	Champion RF7YC or F7YC
Electrode gap:	
Champion F7YCC or RC7YCC	0.8 mm (0.032 in)
Champion RF7YC, F7YC or RC7YC	0.7 mm (0.028 in)

HT leads

Application:	
All OHC models	Champion LS-09 boxed set
1.8 CVH	Champion LS-14 boxed set
Maximum resistance per lead	30 000 ohms

Torque wrench settings

	Nm	lbf ft
Spark plugs:		
OHC models	20 to 28	15 to 21
CVH models	18 to 33	13 to 24
Crankshaft speed/position sensor clamp bolt (ESC Hybrid system)	4 to 7	3 to 5
Camshaft sprocket bolt (CVH models)	50 to 62	37 to 46

1 General description

The ignition system is responsible for igniting the air/fuel mixture in each cylinder at the correct moment in relation to engine speed and load. A number of different ignition systems are fitted to models within the Sierra/P100 range, ranging from a basic breakerless electronic system to a fully integrated engine management system controlling ignition and fuel injection systems. Each system is described in further detail later in this Section.

The ignition system is based on feeding low tension voltage from the battery to the coil where it is converted to high tension voltage. The high tension voltage is powerful enough to jump the spark plug gap in the cylinders many times a second under high compression pressures, providing that the system is in good condition. The low tension (or primary) circuit consists of the battery, the lead to the ignition switch, the lead from the ignition switch to the low tension coil windings (terminal +/15) and also to the supply terminal on the electronic module, and the lead from the low tension coil windings (terminal –/1) to the control terminal on the electronic module. The high tension (or secondary) circuit consists of the high tension coil windings, the HT (high tension) lead from the coil to the distributor cap, the rotor arm, the HT leads to the spark plugs, and the spark plugs.

The system functions in the following manner. Current flowing through the low tension coil windings produces a magnetic field around the high tension windings. As the engine rotates, a sensor produces an electrical impulse which is amplified in the electronic module and used to switch off the low tension circuit.

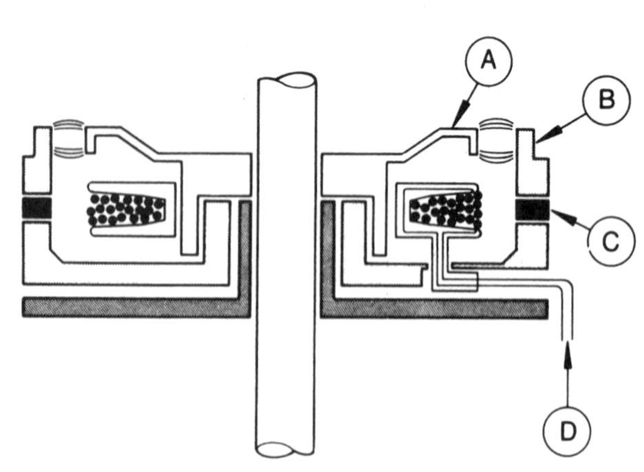

Fig 4.1 Cross section of Bosch inductive discharge distributor trigger components (Sec 1)

A Trigger wheel
B Stator arm
C Permanent magnet
D Wires from trigger coil

Fig 4.2 Lucas 'Hall effect' distributor trigger components (Sec 1)

A Trigger vane
B Permanent magnet
C Sensor
D Wires from sensor

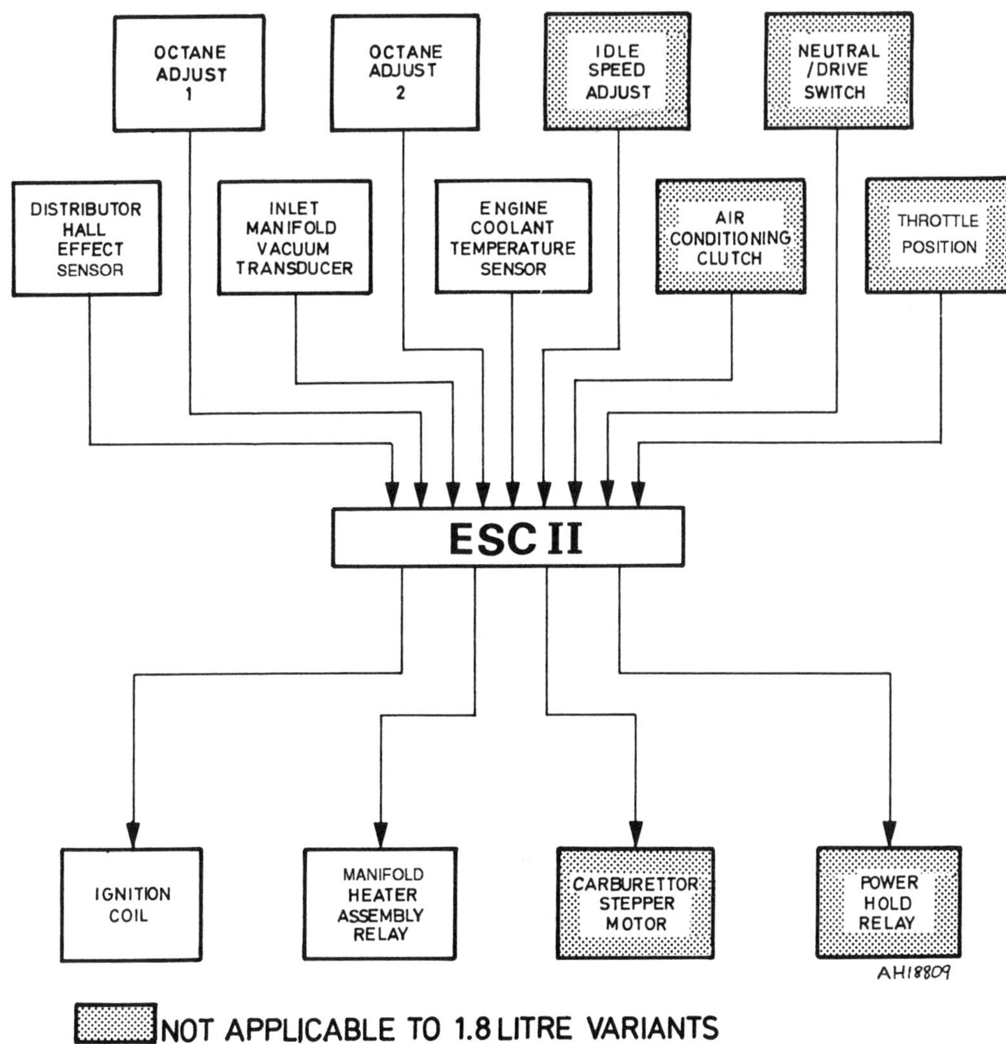

Fig 4.3 Schematic diagram of ESC II system operation (Sec 1)

The subsequent collapse of the magnetic field over the high tension windings produces high tension voltage which is then fed to the relevant spark plug via the distributor cap and rotor arm. The low tension circuit is automatically switched on again by the electronic module, to allow the magnetic field to build up again before the firing of the next spark plug. The ignition is advanced and retarded automatically to ensure that the spark occurs at the correct instant in relation to the engine speed and load.

To improve driveability during warm-up conditions and to reduce exhaust emission levels, a vacuum-operated, temperature-sensitive spark control system is fitted to certain vehicles. Refer to Sections 16 and 17 for further details.

Inductive discharge system

This is the least sophisticated system fitted to the Sierra/P100 range, and comprises a breakerless distributor and an electronic switching/amplifier module in addition to the coil and spark plugs.

The electrical impulse which is required to switch off the low tension circuit is generated by a magnetic trigger coil in the distributor. A trigger wheel rotates within a magnetic stator, the magnetic field being provided by a permanent magnet. The magnetic field across the two poles (stator arm and trigger wheel) is dependent on the air gap between the two poles. When the air gap is at its minimum, the trigger wheel arm is directly opposite the stator arm, and this is the trigger point. As the magnetic flux between the stator arm and trigger wheel varies, a voltage is induced in the trigger coil mounted below the trigger wheel, and this voltage is sensed and then amplified by the electronic module and used to switch off the low tension circuit. There is one trigger wheel arm and one stator arm for each cylinder (4).

The ignition advance is a function of the distributor and is controlled both mechanically and by a vacuum operated system. The mechanical governor mechanism consists of two weights which move out from the distributor shaft as the engine speed rises due to centrifugal force. As they move outwards, they rotate the trigger wheel relative to the distributor shaft and so advance the spark. The weights are held in position by two light springs and it is the tension of the springs which is largely responsible for correct spark advancement.

The vacuum control consists of a diaphragm, one side of which is connected via a small bore hose to the carburettor or inlet manifold and the other side to the distributor. Depression in the inlet manifold and/or carburettor, which varies with engine speed and throttle position, causes the diaphragm to move, so moving the baseplate and advancing or retarding the spark. A fine degree of control is achieved by a spring in the diaphragm assembly.

ESC (Electronic Spark Control) system

This system is only fitted to early 'Economy' models, and comprises a 'Hall effect' distributor, and an ESC module, in addition to the coil and spark plugs.

The electrical impulse which is required to switch off the low tension circuit is generated by a sensor in the distributor. A trigger vane rotates in the gap between a permanent magnet and the sensor. The trigger vane has four cut-outs, one for each cylinder. When one of the trigger vane cut-outs is in line with the sensor, magnetic flux can pass between

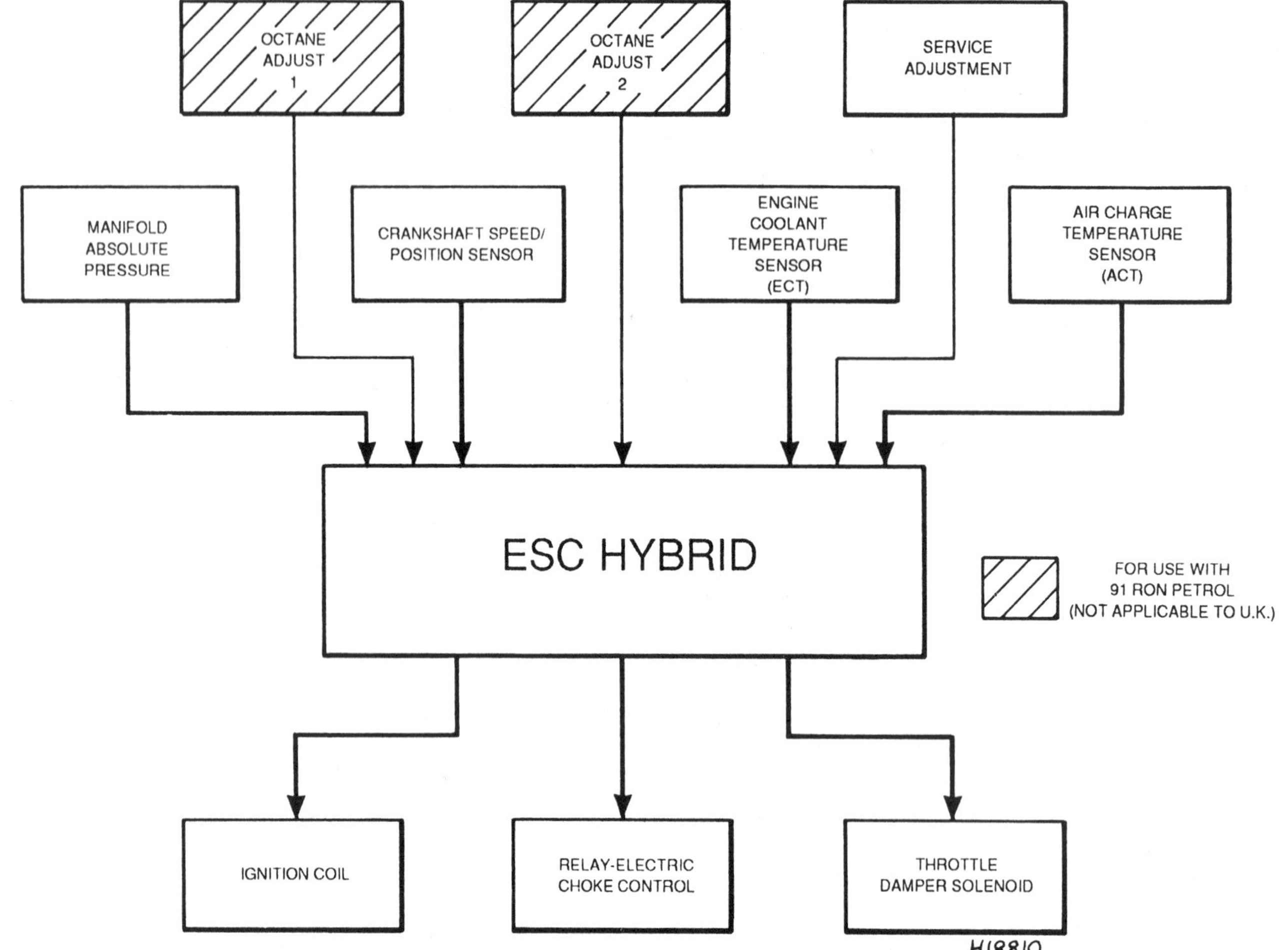

Fig 4.4 Schematic diagram of ESC Hybrid system operation (Sec 1)

the magnet and the sensor. When a trigger vane segment is in line with the sensor, the magnetic flux is diverted through the trigger vane away from the sensor. The sensor senses the change in magnetic flux and sends an impulse to the ESC module, which switches off the low tension circuit.

The ignition advance is a function of the ESC module and is controlled by vacuum. The module is connected to the inlet manifold by a vacuum pipe, and a transducer in the module translates the vacuum signal into electrical voltage. From the vacuum signal, the ESC module determines engine load, and engine speed is determined from the interval between impulses supplied by the distributor sensor. The module has a range of spark advance settings stored in its memory, and a suitable setting is selected for the relevant engine speed and load. The degree of advance can thus be constantly varied to suit the prevailing engine speed and load conditions.

ESC II (Electronic Spark Control II) system

This system is a development of the ESC system described previously in this Section, but it enables more accurate control of engine operation due to the inclusion of additional monitoring features and control outputs.

Vehicles fitted with the ESC II system have an electric inlet manifold heater which warms the air/fuel mixture when the engine is cold, thus reducing the amount of fuel enrichment required, lowering fuel consumption and improving driveability when the engine is cold. The heater is operated by the ESC II module which receives information on the engine temperature from an engine coolant temperature sensor mounted in the inlet manifold.

On 2.0 litre models, the ESC II module operates a carburettor stepper motor to control the engine idle speed. Using information on engine speed, load, temperature and throttle position (supplied by a switch on the carburettor), the module operates the stepper motor to maintain a constant idle speed. On models equipped with automatic transmission and/or air conditioning, additional inputs are supplied to the module to allow it to operate the stepper motor to compensate for the additional engine load imposed by the automatic transmission/air conditioning. The ESC II module also operates a 'power hold' relay which allows the stepper motor to function briefly after the ignition has been switched off in order to perform an anti-run-on and manifold ventilation cycle.

ESC Hybrid (Electronic Spark Control Hybrid) system

This system is fitted to 1.8 CVH models, and comprises various sensors and an ESC Hybrid module, in addition to the coil and spark plugs. The distributor serves purely to distribute the HT voltage to the spark plugs and consists simply of a rotor arm mounted directly on the end of the camshaft, and a distributor cap.

The electrical impulse which is required to switch off the low tension circuit is generated by a crankshaft speed/position sensor which is activated by a toothed wheel on the crankshaft. The toothed wheel has 35 equally spaced teeth with a gap in the 36th position. The gap is used by the sensor to determine the crankshaft position relative to TDC (top dead centre) of No 1 piston.

Engine load information is supplied to the ESC Hybrid module by a vacuum transducer within the module which is connected to the inlet manifold by a vacuum pipe. Additional inputs are supplied by an inlet manifold-mounted engine coolant temperature sensor, and an air charge temperature sensor mounted in the base of the air cleaner. The module selects the optimum ignition advance setting based on the information received from the various sensors. The degree of advance can thus be constantly varied to suit the prevailing engine conditions.

In addition to the ignition circuit, the module also controls an electric choke heater, and a solenoid valve which in turn controls a throttle

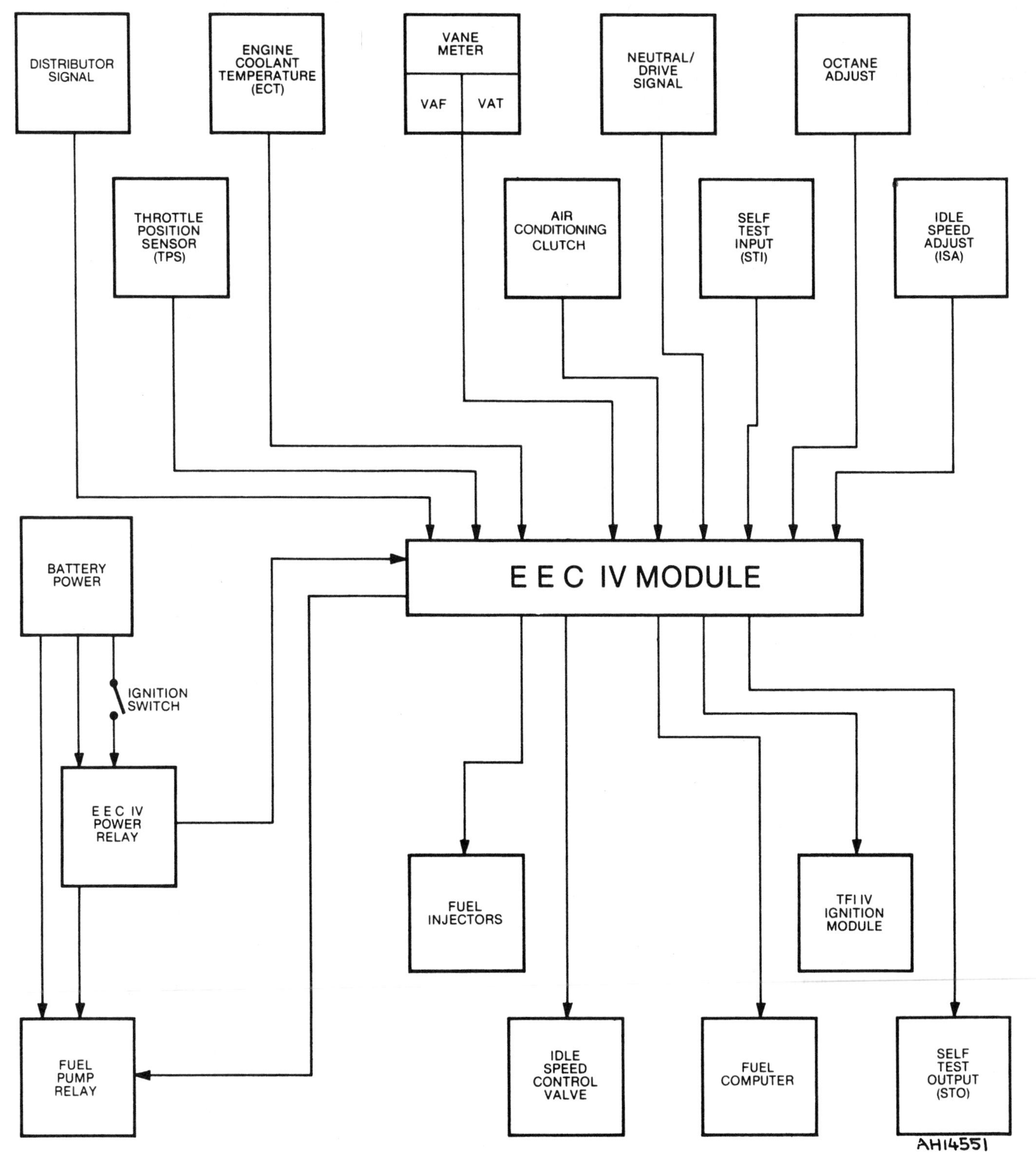

Fig 4.5 Schematic diagram of EEC IV system operation (Sec 1)

damper on the carburettor. The electric choke heater is operated by the module using information supplied by the engine coolant temperature sensor. The heater is used to slow down the rate at which the choke comes off, thereby improving driveability and overall fuel consumption when the engine is cold. The solenoid valve controls the vacuum supply to the carburettor throttle damper. The throttle damper prevents sudden closing of the throttle during deceleration, thus maintaining combustion of the air/fuel mixture which reduces harmful exhaust gas emissions.

Note that there is no provision for adjustment of ignition timing with the ESC Hybrid system.

EEC IV (Electronic Engine Control IV) system

This system is only fitted to 2.0 litre fuel injection models, and controls both the ignition and fuel injection systems.

The EEC IV module receives information from a 'Hall effect' distributor sensor (similar to that described previously in this Section for the ESC system), an engine coolant temperature sensor mounted in the inlet manifold, a throttle position sensor, and an air flow meter.

Additionally, on models equipped with automatic transmission and/or air conditioning, additional inputs are supplied to the module to allow it to raise the idle speed to compensate for the additional engine load imposed by the automatic transmission/air conditioning. The module provides outputs to control the fuel pump, fuel injectors, idle speed, and ignition circuit. Using the inputs from the various sensors, the EEC IV module computes the optimum ignition advance, and fuel injector pulse duration to suit the prevailing engine conditions. This system gives very accurate control of the engine under all conditions, improving fuel consumption and driveability, and reducing exhaust gas emissions. A 'limited operation strategy' (LOS) means that the vehicle is still driveable, albeit at reduced power and efficiency, in the event of a failure in the module or its sensors.

Further details of the fuel injection system components are given in Chapter 3.

2 Ignition and engine management systems – precautions

Warning: *The HT voltage generated by an electronic ignition system is extremely high, and in certain circumstances could prove fatal. Take care to avoid receiving electric shocks from the HT side of the ignition system. Do not handle HT leads, or touch the distributor or coil when the engine is running. If tracing faults in the HT circuit, use well insulated tools to manipulate live leads.*

Engine management modules are very sensitive components, and certain precautions must be taken to avoid damage to the module when working on a vehicle equipped with an engine management system as follows.

When carrying out welding operations on the vehicle using electric welding equipment, the battery and alternator should be disconnected.

Although underbonnet-mounted modules (all except EEC IV) will tolerate normal underbonnet conditions, they can be adversely affected by excess heat or moisture. If using welding equipment or pressure washing equipment in the vicinity of the module, take care not to direct heat, or jets of water or steam at the module. If this cannot be avoided, remove the module from the vehicle, and protect its wiring plug with a plastic bag.

Before disconnecting any wiring, or removing components, always ensure that the ignition is switched off.

On models with underbonnet-mounted modules, do not run the engine with the module detached from the body panel, as the body acts as an effective heat sink, and the module may be damaged due to internal overheating.

Do not attempt to improvise fault diagnosis procedures using a test lamp or multimeter, as irreparable damage could be caused to the module.

After working on ignition/engine management system components, ensure that all wiring is correctly reconnected before reconnecting the battery or switching on the ignition.

On some early Bosch distributors it is possible that with the distributor cap removed, if the engine is cranked, the cap securing clips may fall inward and jam the trigger wheel/vane, knocking it out of alignment. If this happens, the distributor will have to be renewed as the trigger wheel/vane cannot be repositioned. Care should therefore be taken not to crank the engine with the distributor cap removed. Later distributors have redesigned clips which eliminate the problem.

3 Maintenance and inspection

1 At the intervals specified in the *'Routine maintenance'* Section at the beginning of this manual, the following tasks should be carried out.
2 Renew the spark plugs as described in Section 4.
3 Remove the distributor cap and HT leads and wipe them clean. Also wipe clean the coil tower and make sure that the plastic safety cover is securely fitted where applicable. Remove the rotor arm, then visually check the distributor cap, rotor arm, and HT leads for hairline cracks and signs of arcing. Where applicable, apply two or three drops of engine oil to the recess in the top of the distributor spindle. When refitting the distributor cap, check that the ends of the HT leads are fitted securely to the cap, plugs, and coil. Also make sure that the spring-tensioned carbon brush in the centre of the distributor cap moves freely, and that the HT segments are not worn excessively (photo).
4 Inspect the electrical and vacuum connections of the ignition/engine management systems, and make sure that they are clean and secure.

4 Spark plugs and HT leads – inspection and renewal

1 The correct functioning of the spark plugs is vital for the correct running and efficiency of the engine. It is essential that the plugs fitted are appropriate for the engine, and the suitable type is specified at the beginning of this chapter. If this type is used and the engine is in good condition, the spark plugs should not need attention between scheduled replacement intervals. Spark plug cleaning is rarely necessary and should not be attempted unless specialised equipment is available as damage can easily be caused to the firing ends.
2 Where necessary, for improved access remove the air cleaner and/or the inlet hose as described in Chapter 3.
3 If necessary, identify each HT lead for position, so that the leads can be refitted to their correct cylinders, then disconnect the leads from the plugs by pulling on the connectors, not the leads. Note that the position of No 1 cylinder HT lead in the distributor cap is marked with either a pip, or a number '1'.
4 Clean the area around each spark plug using a small brush, then using a plug spanner (preferably with a rubber insert), unscrew and remove the plugs (photo). Cover the spark plug holes with a clean rag to prevent the ingress of any foreign matter.
5 The condition of the spark plugs will tell much about the overall condition of the engine.
6 If the insulator nose of the spark plug is clean and white, with no deposits, this is indicative of a weak air/fuel mixture, or too hot a plug. (A hot plug transfers heat away from the electrode slowly – a cold plug transfers it away quickly).
7 If the tip and insulator nose is covered with hard black-looking deposits, then this is indicative that the mixture is too rich. Should the plug be black and oily, then it is likely that the engine is fairly worn, as well as the mixture being too rich.
8 If the insulator nose is covered with light tan to greyish brown

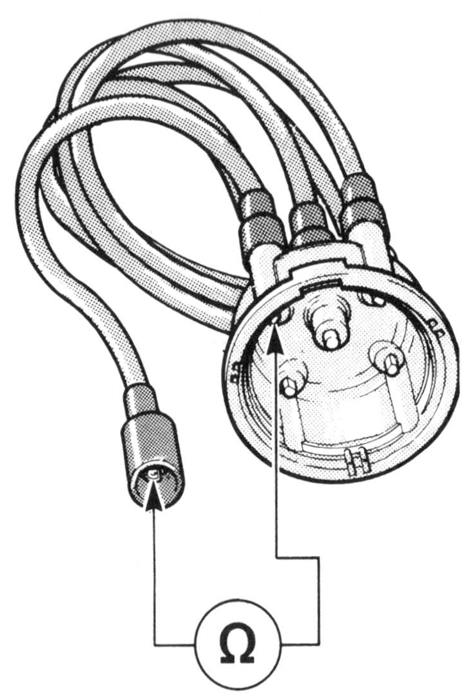

Fig 4.6 Method of testing an HT lead with an ohmmeter (Sec 4)

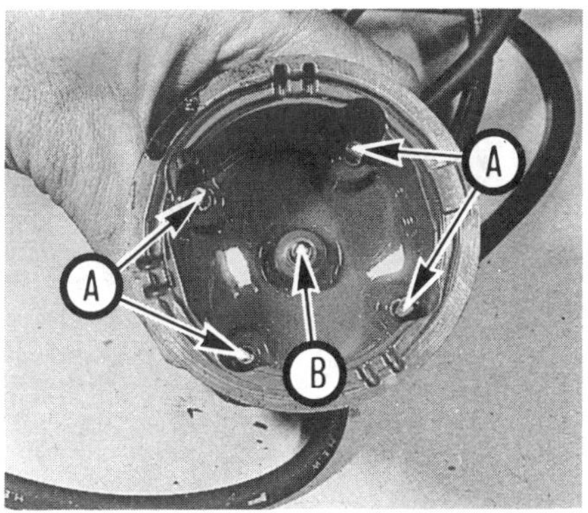

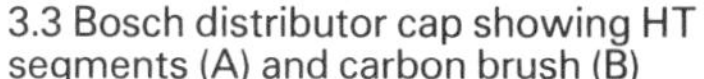
3.3 Bosch distributor cap showing HT segments (A) and carbon brush (B)

4.4 Removing a spark plug – CVH model

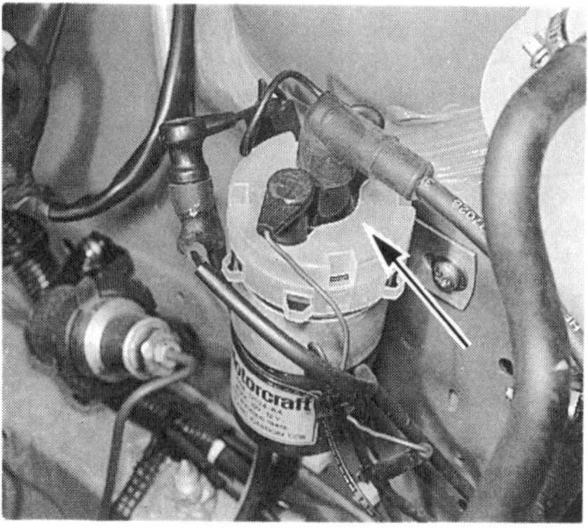
5.1 Ignition coil – CVH model. Plastic cover arrowed

deposits, then the mixture is correct and it is likely that the engine is in good condition.

9 The spark plug gap is of considerable importance, as, if it is too large or too small, the size of the spark and its efficiency will be seriously impaired. The spark plug gap should be set to the figure given in the Specifications at the beginning of this Chapter. To set it, measure the gap with a feeler gauge, and then bend open, or close the *outer* plug electrode until the correct gap is achieved. The centre electrode should *never* be bent as this may crack the insulation and cause plug failure, if nothing worse.

10 Before fitting the spark plugs, check that the threaded connector sleeves are tight and that the plug exterior surfaces are clean. As the plugs incorporate taper seats also make sure that the threads and seats are clean.

11 Screw in the spark plugs by hand, then tighten them to the specified torque. *Do not exceed the torque figure.*

12 Push the HT leads firmly onto the spark plugs, and where applicable refit the air cleaner and/or inlet hose.

13 The HT leads and distributor cap should be cleaned and checked at the intervals given in the *'Routine maintenance'* Section at the beginning of this manual. To test the HT leads, remove them together with the distributor cap as described in Section 7 or 8 as applicable, then connect an ohmmeter to the end of each lead and its appropriate terminal within the cap in turn. If the resistance of any lead is greater than the maximum given in the Specifications, check that the lead connection in the cap is good before renewing the lead.

5 Coil – description and testing

1 The coil is located on the left-hand side of the engine compartment and is retained by a metal strap (photo). It is of high output type and the HT tower should be kept clean at all times to prevent possible arcing. Bosch and Femsa coils are fitted with protective plastic covers and Polmot coils are fitted with an internal fusible link.

2 To ensure the correct HT polarity at the spark plugs, the LT coil leads must always be connected correctly. The black lead must always be connected to the terminal marked +/15, and the green lead to the terminal marked –/1. Incorrect connections can cause poor starting, misfiring, and short spark plug life.

3 To test the coil first disconnect the LT and HT leads. Connect an ohmmeter between both LT terminals and check that the primary winding resistance is as given in the Specifications. Connect the ohmmeter between the HT terminal and either LT terminal and check that the secondary winding resistance is as given in the Specifications. If either winding resistance is not as specified, the coil should be renewed. Reconnect the LT and HT leads on completion.

6 Coil – removal and refitting

1 Disconnect the battery negative lead.

2 Disconnect the LT and HT leads from the coil (photo).

3 Remove the securing screw(s) and detach the coil and strap assembly from the body panel. Note that on models with the ESC system, the coil strap is secured by the top ESC module securing screw. On certain models with the ESC II or EEC IV systems, an 'octane adjustment' service lead may be connected to one of the coil securing screws (see Section 11).

4 Refitting is a reversal of removal, but ensure that all leads are securely connected.

7 Distributor cap and rotor arm (OHC models) – removal and refitting

1 Disconnect the battery negative lead.

2 Where applicable, unclip the screening can from the top of the distributor and disconnect the earth strap (photo).

3 If necessary, identify each HT lead for position, so that the leads can be refitted to their correct cylinders, then disconnect the leads from the

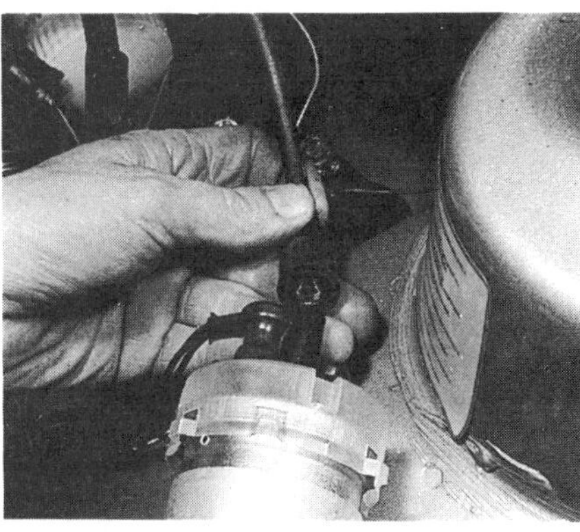
6.2 Disconnecting the HT lead from the coil – OHC model

7.2 Unclipping the distributor screening can – Motorcraft distributor

7.3 HT lead holder on camshaft cover – OHC model

7.7 Securing distributor cap with spring clip – Bosch distributor

7.10 Removing a distributor cap securing screw – Motorcraft distributor

7.11 Removing a rotor arm (disc) securing screw – Motorcraft distributor

spark plugs by pulling on the connectors, not the leads. Similarly, disconnect the HT lead from the coil. Where applicable, slide the HT lead holder from the clip on the camshaft cover (photo).

Lucas distributors

4 Remove the two securing screws and lift off the distributor cap.
5 The rotor arm is a push-fit on the end of the distributor shaft.
6 Refitting is a reversal of removal, noting that the rotor arm can only be fitted in one position. Ensure that the HT leads are correctly connected.

Bosch distributors

7 Prise away the spring clips with a screwdriver and lift off the distributor cap. On fuel injection models, disconnect the crankcase ventilation hose from the air intake hose, then disconnect the air intake hose from the inlet manifold and the airflow meter for improved access.
8 Refitting is a reversal of removal, noting that the rotor arm can only be fitted in one position. Ensure that the HT leads are correctly connected, and on fuel injection models ensure that the air intake hose clips are correctly aligned – refer to Fig. 3.51.

Motorcraft distributors

9 For improved access, disconnect the crankcase ventilation hose from the air intake hose, then disconnect the air intake hose from the inlet manifold and the airflow meter for improved access.
10 Remove the two securing screws and lift off the distributor cap (photo).
11 Remove the two securing screws and withdraw the rotor arm (disc) (photo). Note that on some vehicles, the rotor arm tip may be coated with silicone grease to assist radio interference suppression. Do not attempt to clean the grease off if it is present. If radio interference problems are experienced, consult a Ford dealer or an in-car entertainment specialist.
12 Proceed as described in paragraph 6, but additionally ensure that the air intake hose clips are correctly aligned – refer to Fig. 3.51.

8 Distributor components (CVH models) – removal and refitting

1 The distributor fitted to the CVH engine is unlike any conventional distributor, in that it has no main body and no adjustments are possible. The distributor is used purely to distribute HT voltage to the spark plugs. To remove the distributor components, proceed as follows.
2 Disconnect the battery negative lead.

Distributor cap

3 Pull the two halves of the distributor cap shroud apart and remove the shroud. Disconnect the earth strap from the tag on the timing cover (photo).
4 If necessary, identify each HT lead for position, so that the leads can be refitted to their correct cylinders, then disconnect the leads from the spark plugs by pulling on the connectors, not the leads. Unclip the HT lead holders from their studs on the camshaft cover (photo).
5 Depress the two securing screws and turn them anti-clockwise through 90°, then lift off the distributor cap.
6 Disconnect the HT lead from the coil by pulling on the connector, not the lead, and remove the distributor cap.
7 Refitting is a reversal of removal, but ensure that the HT leads are fitted to their correct cylinders.

Rotor arm and housing

8 With the distributor cap removed as described previously, compress the two lugs on the rotor shaft and withdraw the rotor arm (photo).
9 The rotor housing can now be removed by pulling it from the timing cover (photo).
10 Refitting is a reversal of removal, but note that the rotor arm can only be fitted in one position.

Rotor shaft

11 The rotor shaft is retained by the camshaft sprocket bolt.
12 To remove and refit the rotor shaft, refer to Chapter 1, Section 59, and remove the timing cover and the camshaft sprocket bolt. Note that there is no need to remove the timing belt or the sprockets.

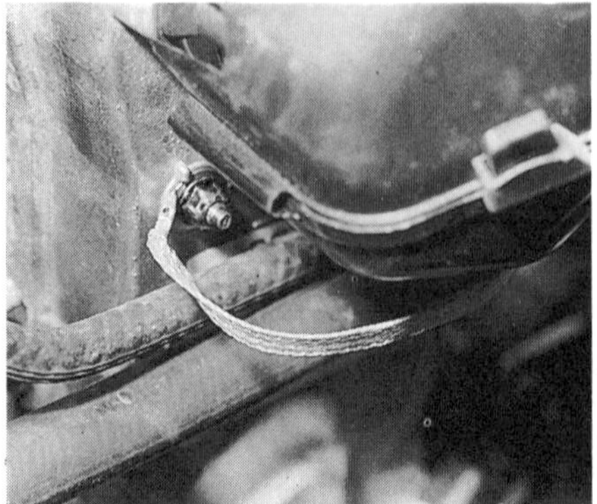
8.3 Distributor cap shroud earth strap connection – CVH model

8.4 HT lead holders (arrowed) on camshaft cover – CVH model

8.8 Removing the rotor arm – CVH model

8.9 Removing the rotor housing – CVH model

9.6 Disconnecting vacuum pipe from vacuum advance unit – Bosch distributor

9.7A Rotor arm tip aligned with scribed line on distributor body – Bosch distributor

9.7B Trigger vane segment leading edge aligned with sensor rib – Motorcraft distributor

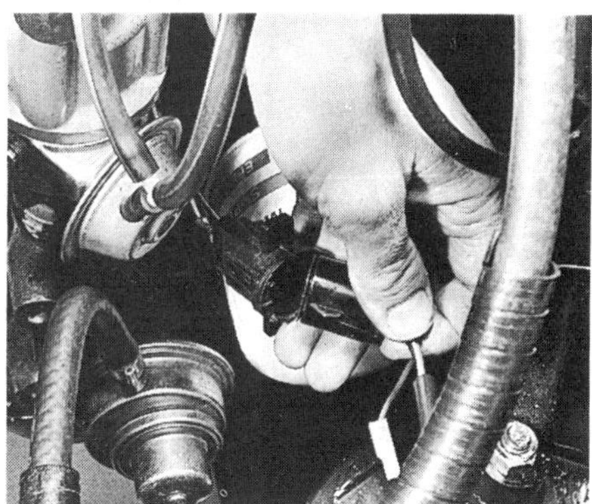

9.8 Disconnecting distributor wiring plug – Bosch distributor

9.10 Unscrewing distributor clamp bolt – Bosch distributor

9 Distributor (OHC models) – removal and refitting

Note: *During production the engine ignition timing is accurately set using a microwave process, and sealant is applied to the distributor clamp bolt. Removal of the distributor should be avoided except where excessive bearing wear has occurred due to high mileage or during major engine overhaul. A timing light will be required to check the ignition timing after refitting the distributor.*

1 Disconnect the battery negative lead.

2 If necessary, identify each HT lead for position, so that the leads can be refitted to their correct cylinders, then disconnect the leads from the spark plugs by pulling on the connectors, not the leads.

3 Where applicable, unclip the screening can from the top of the distributor and disconnect the earth strap. On fuel injection models, disconnect the crankcase ventilation hose from the air intake hose, then disconnect the air intake hose from the inlet manifold and the airflow meter for improved access.

4 Prise away the spring clips with a screwdriver, or remove the two securing screws, as applicable, and lift off the distributor cap.

5 Disconnect the HT lead from the coil by pulling on the connector, not the lead, then slide the HT lead holder from the clip on the camshaft cover, and withdraw the distributor cap.

6 Where applicable, disconnect the vacuum pipe from the vacuum advance unit on the side of the distributor (photo).

7 Using a suitable socket or spanner on the crankshaft pulley bolt, turn the crankshaft to bring No 1 cylinder to the firing point. If the distributor cap is secured by clips, make sure that the clips stay clear of the distributor moving parts. No 1 cylinder is at the firing point when:

(a) *The relevant timing marks are in alignment – see Section 10*

(b) *The tip of the rotor arm is pointing to the position occupied by the No 1 cylinder HT lead terminal in the distributor cap. Note that the position of No 1 HT lead terminal is identified by a pip or a number '1'*

(c) *On Lucas distributors, the cut-out in the trigger vane is aligned with the sensor – see Fig. 4.7*

(d) *On Bosch distributors, the tip of the rotor arm is aligned with the scribed line on the distributor body (where applicable, remove rotor arm and dust cover, then refit rotor arm to check alignment with scribed line) (photo)*

(e) *On Motorcraft distributors, the tip of the rotor arm is aligned with a notch in the distributor body. Mark the relevant notch (there may be several) for reference when refitting. Also, the leading edge of one of the trigger vane segments is aligned with the rib on the sensor (remove the two securing screws and lift off the rotor arm to view the trigger vane and sensor) (photo).*

8 Disconnect the distributor wiring plug, where applicable depressing

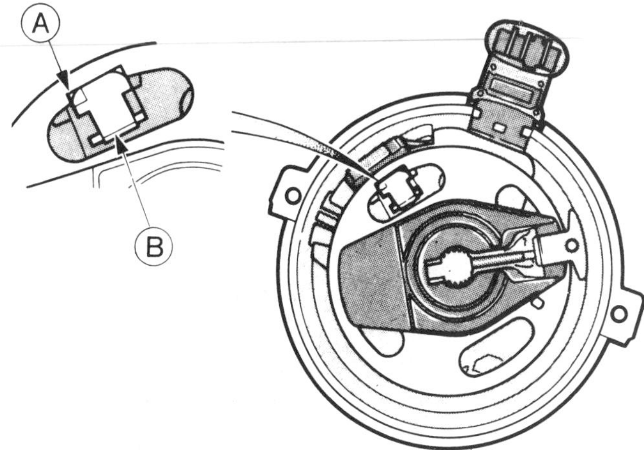

Fig 4.7 Lucas distributor showing trigger vane position with No 1 cylinder at firing point (Sec 9)

A Trigger vane cut-out *B Sensor*

the locking tab(s). Pull on the plug, not the wiring (photo).

9 Make alignment marks between the distributor body and the cylinder block.

10 Scrape the sealant from the distributor clamp bolt, then unscrew and remove the bolt and clamp (photo).

11 Withdraw the distributor from the cylinder block. As the distributor is removed, the rotor arm will turn clockwise due to the skew gear drive. Note the new position of the rotor arm relative to the distributor body, if necessary making an alignment mark (some distributors already have an alignment mark).

12 Check the distributor spindle for excessive side-to-side movement. If evident, the distributor must be renewed, as the only spares available are the cap, rotor arm, module (where applicable), and driveshaft O-ring (photo).

13 Commence refitting by checking that No 1 cylinder is still at the firing point. The relevant timing marks should be aligned. If the engine has been turned whilst the distributor has been removed, check that No 1 cylinder is on its firing stroke by removing the No 1 cylinder spark plug and placing a finger over the plug hole. Turn the crankshaft until compression can be felt, which indicates that No 1 piston is rising on its firing stroke. Continue turning the crankshaft until the relevant timing marks are in alignment.

14 Turn the rotor arm to the position noted in paragraph 11. If a new distributor is being fitted, and no alignment marks are present, transfer the marks from the old distributor to the new distributor.

15 Hold the distributor directly over the aperture in the cylinder block with the previously made marks on the distributor body and cylinder block aligned, then lower the distributor into position. Again, if a new distributor is being fitted, transfer the alignment mark from the old distributor body to the new distributor body. As the skew gear drive meshes, the rotor arm will turn anti-clockwise.

16 With the distributor fitted and the marks on the distributor body and cylinder block aligned, check that the rotor arm is positioned as described in paragraph 7 – if not, withdraw the distributor, re-position the driveshaft and try again.

17 Refit the clamp, then insert and tighten the bolt. Do not fully tighten the bolt at this stage.

18 Refit the distributor wiring plug, and where applicable reconnect the vacuum pipe, and refit the dust cover and/or rotor arm.

19 Refit the distributor cap, and reconnect the HT leads to the spark plugs and coil. Ensure that the leads are refitted to their correct cylinders.

20 Where applicable, refit the screening can to the top of the distributor and reconnect the earth strap. On fuel injection models, reconnect the air intake hose, ensuring that the clips are correctly aligned – refer to Fig. 3.51.

21 Reconnect the battery negative lead.

22 Check and if necessary adjust the ignition timing as described in Section 10.

10 Ignition timing (OHC models) – adjustment

Note: *During production the ignition timing is accurately set using a microwave process, and sealant is applied to the distributor clamp bolt. Because the electronic components require no maintenance, checking the ignition timing does not constitute part of the routine maintenance schedule, and the procedure is therefore only necessary after removal and refitting of the distributor. A timing light will be required for this procedure. For details of ignition timing adjustment in order to operate vehicles on unleaded petrol, refer to Section 11.*

1 Before checking the ignition timing, the following conditions must be met:

- *(a) The engine must be at normal operating temperature*
- *(b) Where applicable, the vacuum pipe to the distributor vacuum unit or electronic module (as applicable) must be disconnected from the vacuum unit or electronic module and plugged*
- *(c) The idle speed must be below 900 rpm (isolate 'idle speed adjustment' wire if necessary – see Section 11)*
- *(d) Any earthed 'octane adjustment' wires must be temporarily isolated (see Section 11)*

2 Wipe clean the crankshaft pulley timing marks and the pointer on the crankshaft front oil seal housing. Note that two alternative types of pulley may be fitted – see Fig. 4.8. The desired timing values are given in the Specifications. If necessary, use white paint or chalk to highlight the relevant timing mark(s) (photo).

3 Connect a stroboscope timing light to the No 1 cylinder HT lead, following the manufacturer's instructions.

4 With the engine idling at normal operating temperature, point the timing light at the marks on the crankshaft pulley, and check that the appropriate timing mark appears stationary in line with the timing cover pointer. Take care not to get the timing light leads, clothing etc tangled in the cooling fan blades or other moving parts of the engine.

5 If adjustment is necessary, stop the engine, slacken the distributor clamp bolt, and turn the distributor body slightly. Turn the distributor body clockwise to retard the ignition timing (move the timing closer to TDC) and anti-clockwise to advance the timing. Note that the required distributor body movement will be half of the required crankshaft movement (ie an adjustment of 5° in ignition timing will require the

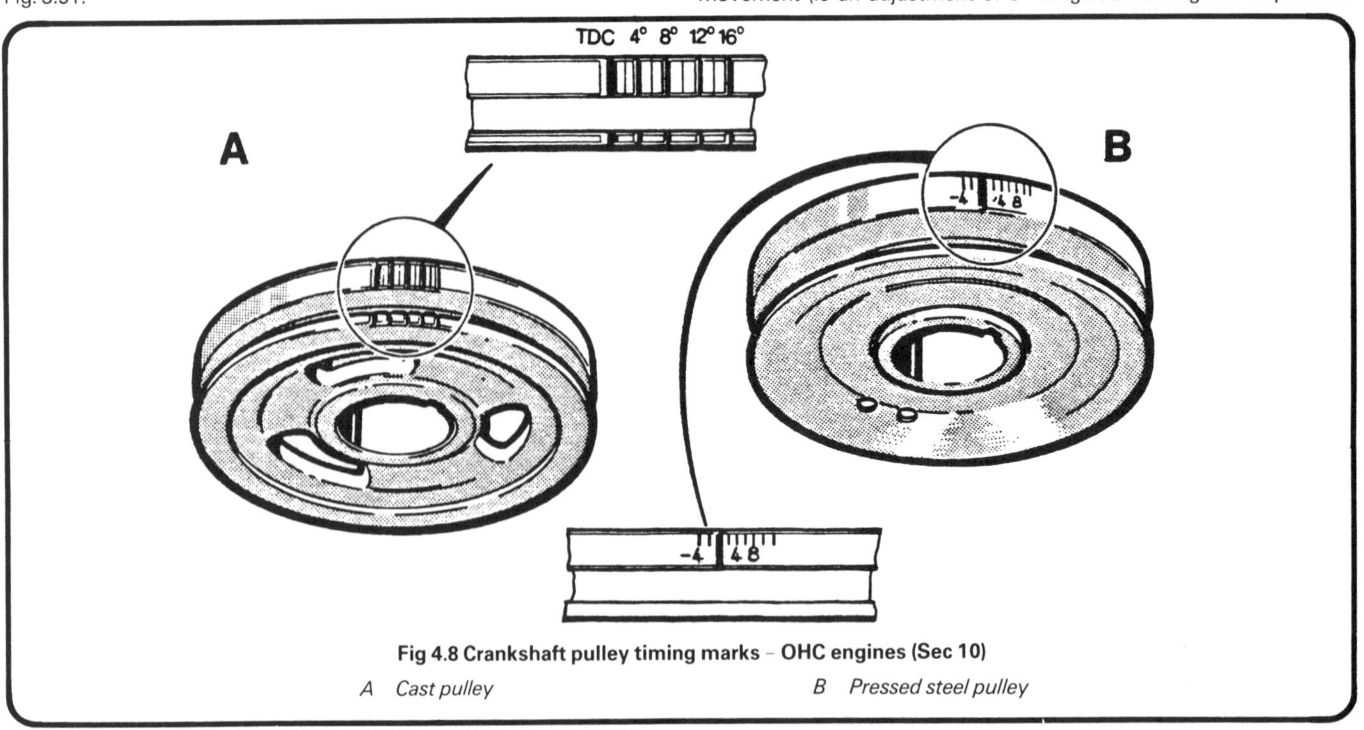

Fig 4.8 Crankshaft pulley timing marks – OHC engines (Sec 10)

A Cast pulley *B Pressed steel pulley*

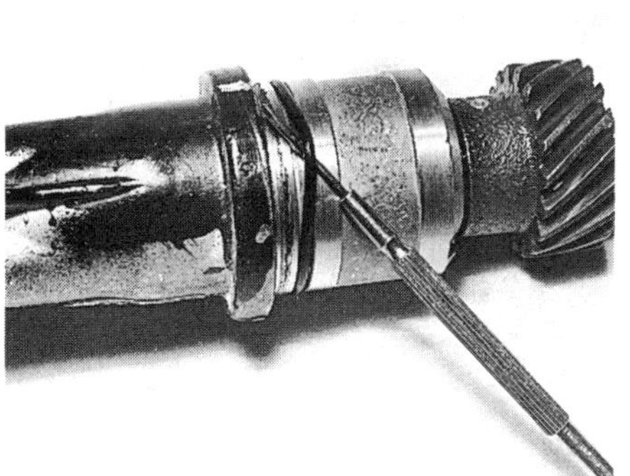

9.12 Removing distributor driveshaft O-ring – Motorcraft distributor

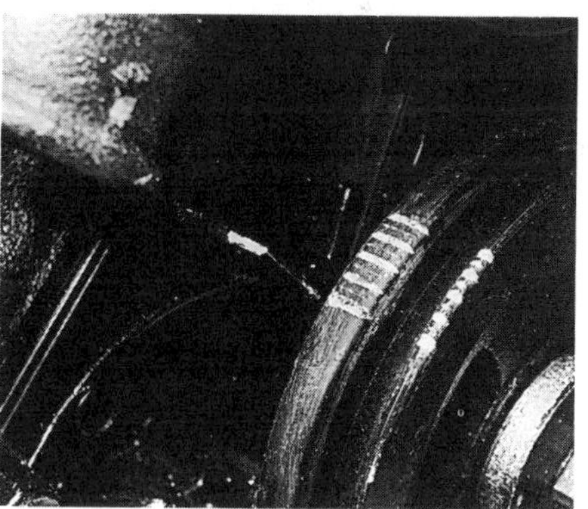

10.2 Highlighted timing marks – OHC engine with cast crankshaft pulley

12.3A Disconnecting ESC II module wiring plug

distributor body to be turned 2.5°). Tighten the clamp bolt and re-check the timing.

6 On models with inductive discharge ignition systems, the mechanical and vacuum advance mechanisms can be checked as follows. On all other models, proceed to paragraph 10.

7 With the engine idling, timing light connected, and vacuum pipe disconnected as described in the preceding paragraphs, increase the engine speed to approximately 2000 rpm (if desired, connect a tachometer to the engine in accordance with the manufacturer's instructions). Note the approximate distance which the relevant pulley mark moves out of alignment with the pointer.

8 Reconnect the vacuum pipe to the distributor or electronic module, as applicable, and repeat the procedure given in the previous paragraph, when for the same increase in engine speed, the alignment differential between the pulley mark and pointer should be greater than previously observed.

9 If the pulley mark does not appear to move during the first part of the check, a fault in the distributor mechanical advance mechanism is indicated. No increased movement of the mark during the second part of the check indicates a punctured diaphragm in the distributor vacuum unit, or a leak in the vacuum line.

10 On completion of the adjustments and checks, stop the engine and disconnect the timing light. Where applicable, reconnect the vacuum pipe, if not already done, and reconnect any 'octane adjustment' and 'idle speed adjustment' wires. Make a final check to ensure that the distributor clamp bolt is tight.

11 Finally, the idle speed and mixture should be checked and adjusted as necessary as described in Chapter 3.

11 Ignition timing – adjustment for use with unleaded petrol

Note: *Refer to the Specifications Section at the beginning of this Chapter for ignition timing values for use with unleaded petrol*

1 To run an engine on unleaded petrol, certain criteria must be met, and it may be helpful to first describe the various terms used for the different types of petrol.

2 **Normal leaded petrol (4-star, 97 RON):** Petrol which has a low amount of lead added during manufacture (0.15 g/litre), in addition to the natural lead found in crude oil.

3 **Unleaded petrol (Premium, 95 RON):** Has no lead added during manufacture, but still has the natural lead content of crude oil.

4 **Lead free petrol:** Contains no lead. It has no lead added during manufacture, and the natural lead content is refined out. This type of petrol is not currently available for general use in the UK and should not be confused with unleaded petrol.

5 To run an engine continuously on unleaded petrol, suitable hardened valve seat inserts must be fitted to the cylinder head.

6 The OHC engines fitted to the Sierra/P100 range which have suitable valve seat inserts fitted at manufacture can be identified by letters stamped on the cylinder head next to No 4 spark plug as follows:

1.6 litre engines	*M, MM, N, or NN*
1.8 litre engines	*S or SS*
2.0 litre engines	*L, P, PP, R, or RR*

7 All CVH engines have suitable valve seat inserts fitted.

8 Vehicles which have no identification letter stamped on the cylinder head, and are not fitted with suitable valve seat inserts, may still be run

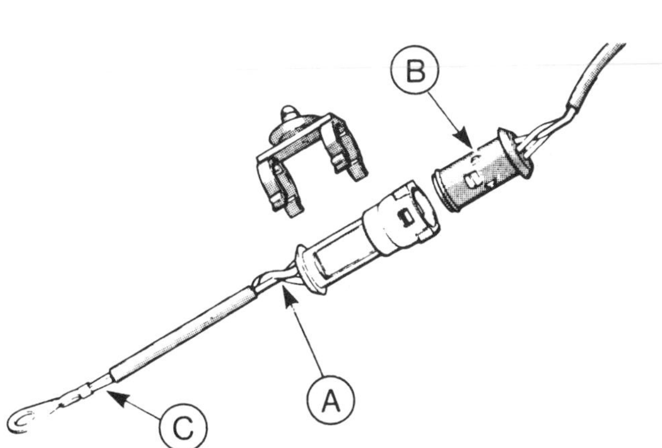

Fig 4.9 Service adjustment lead and plug – ESC II and EEC IV systems (Sec 11)

A Red, blue and yellow wires
B Plug
C Wire cutting point

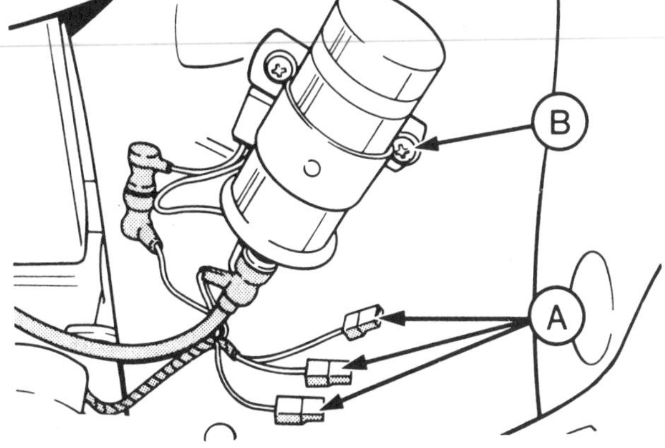

Fig 4.10 Lucar type 'octane adjustment' connectors – early models with ESC II and EEC IV systems (Sec 11)

A Red, blue and yellow connectors
B Coil securing screw (earthing point)

on unleaded petrol (although continuous use is not recommended), provided that every fourth tank filling is of normal leaded petrol, ie – three tanks of unleaded petrol followed by one tank of normal leaded petrol.

9 When running an OHC engine on unleaded petrol (Premium, 95 RON), the ignition timing **must** be retarded as described in the following sub-Sections. There is no requirement for ignition timing adjustment when running CVH engines on unleaded petrol.

Inductive discharge ignition system and ESC system

10 On vehicles fitted with an inductive discharge ignition system, or the ESC system, the ignition timing should be retarded as specified, using the procedure given in Section 10.

ESC II and EEC IV systems

11 On vehicles fitted with the ESC II or EEC IV systems, there is a facility for retarding the ignition timing without physically disturbing the distributor.

12 Adjustment is made by earthing one or two wires ('octane adjustment' wires) which terminate in a wiring plug next to the ignition coil. Ideally a service adjustment lead, available from a Ford dealer should be used. One end of the lead plugs into the 'octane adjustment' wiring plug, and the other end should be earthed by fixing to one of the ignition coil securing screws.

13 Cut and insulate the wires in the service lead which are **not** to be earthed.

14 The amount of ignition retardation provided by earthing the wire(s) is as follows:

System	Degrees of retardation		
	Blue wire	Red wire	Blue and red wires
ESC II (except 1.8 litre) models from February 1987)	*2*	*4*	*6*
ESC II (1.8 litre models from February 1987)	*4*	*2*	*6*
EEC IV	*4*	*2*	*6*

15 Once the ignition timing has been retarded, the vehicle can be operated on either leaded or unleaded petrol.

16 On 2.0 litre models, if the yellow wire ('idle speed adjustment' wire) in the service lead is earthed, the idle speed will be raised by 75 rpm. If the vehicle already has a single yellow fly lead connected prior to connecting the service lead, ensure that the yellow wire in the service lead is earthed.

17 Note that some early models have coloured 'Lucar' connectors fitted in place of the 'octane adjustment' wiring plug. The principle for ignition timing adjustment on these vehicles is as described previously for vehicles with the 'octane adjustment' wiring plug.

18 On completion of ignition timing adjustment, the idle speed and mixture should be checked and adjusted as necessary, as described in Chapter 3.

12 Electronic modules – removal and refitting

Note: *Refer to Section 2 for precautions to be observed when working with electronic modules*

1 Disconnect the battery negative lead.

All models except EEC IV

2 All modules except the ESC Hybrid module are mounted on the left-hand side of the engine compartment. The ESC Hybrid module is mounted on the right-hand side of the engine compartment.

3 Disconnect the module wiring plug by pulling on the plug, not the wiring. On ESC II modules, except those fitted to 1.8 litre models from February 1987, a locking tab at the lower end of the wiring plug must be depressed before unhooking the upper end of the plug from the module. On ESC II modules fitted to 1.8 litre models from February 1987, and ESC Hybrid modules, the wiring plug is secured by a screw which is integral with the plug (photos).

4 Where applicable, disconnect the vacuum pipe from the module (photo).

5 Remove the two or three securing screws, as applicable, and withdraw the module from the engine compartment. Note that the top

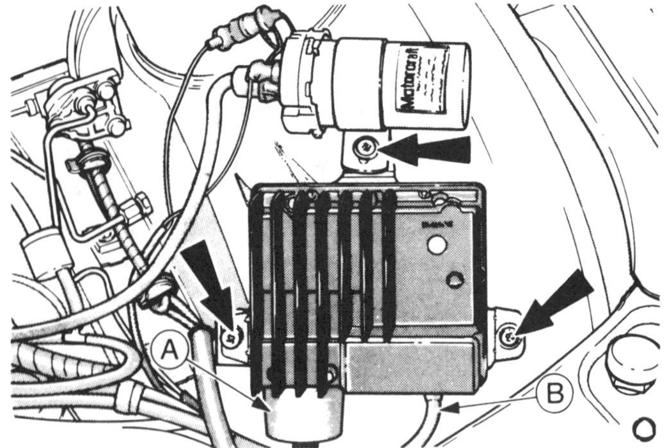

Fig 4.11 ESC module securing screws (arrowed) (Sec 12)

A Wiring plug *B Vacuum pipe*

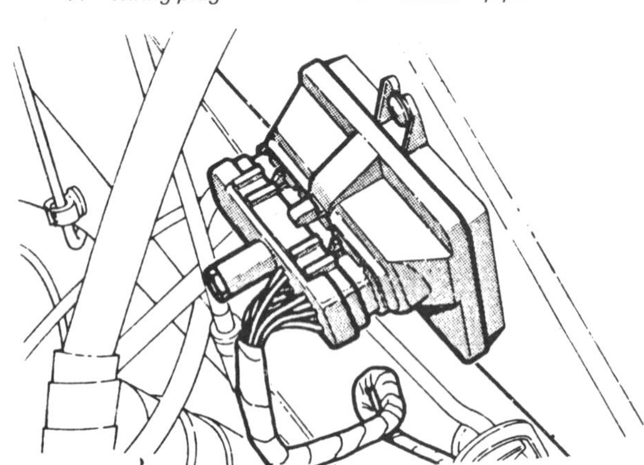

Fig 4.12 ESC II module – 1.8 litre models from February 1987 (Sec 12)

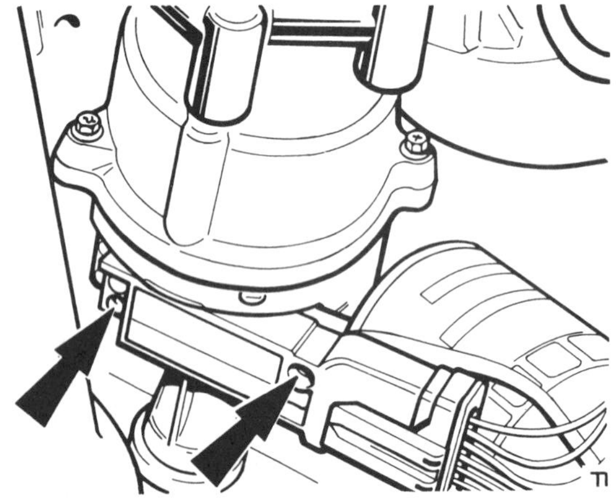

Fig 4.13 EEC IV ignition module securing screws (arrowed) – models up to 1987 (Sec 12)

securing screw of the ESC module also secures the ignition coil strap.

6 Refitting is a reversal of removal, but ensure that the underside of the module and the corresponding area of the body panel are clean.

EEC IV modules

Ignition module – models up to 1987

Note: *When refitting, the rear face of the module must be coated with heat sink compound. Refer to a Ford dealer for advice if necessary.*

7 The module is mounted on the distributor body.

8 Disconnect the distributor wiring plug by depressing the locking

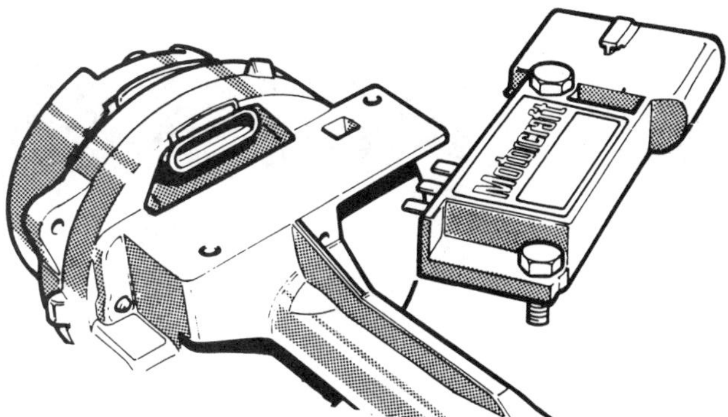

Fig 4.14 EEC IV ignition module removed – models up to 1987 (Sec 12)

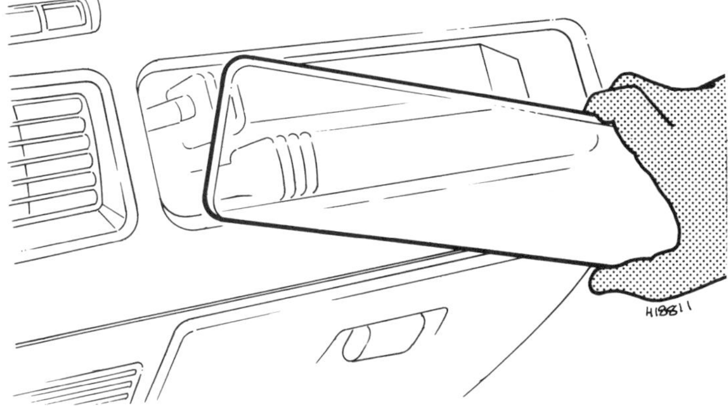

Fig 4.16 Unclip the trim panel from above the glovebox for access to the EEC IV engine management module – models from 1987 (Sec 12)

tabs. Pull on the plug, not the wiring.

9 Remove the two securing screws from the module, then slide the module downwards and withdraw it.

10 Refitting is a reversal of removal, but the rear face of the module must be coated with heat sink compound. Do not force the module into position, as damage to the electrical contacts may result.

Ignition module – models from 1987

11 The module is mounted on the left-hand side of the engine compartment.

12 Disconnect the module wiring plug by depressing the locking tabs. Pull on the plug, not the wiring.

13 Remove the two securing screws and withdraw the module from the engine compartment.

14 Refitting is a reversal of removal, but ensure that the underside of the module and the corresponding area of the body panel are clean.

Engine management module

15 The module is located inside the passenger compartment behind the passenger side facia.

16 Unclip the trim panel from below the glovebox on models up to 1987, or from above the glovebox on models from 1987.

17 Unclip the module retainer and withdraw the module.

18 The wiring plug is secured by a screw which is integral with the plug. Disconnect the wiring plug and remove the module.

19 Refitting is a reversal of removal, noting that the wiring plug will only fit in one position.

13 ESC II system components – removal and refitting

Note: *Procedures for removal and refitting of the ignition system components and electronic module are given elsewhere in the relevant Sections of this Chapter.*

1 Disconnect the battery negative lead.

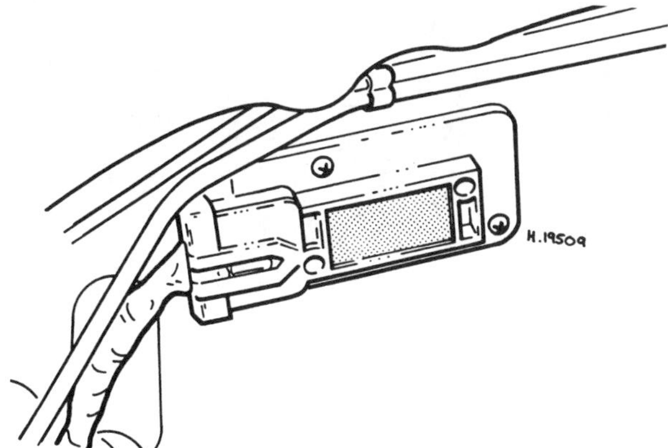

Fig 4.15 EEC IV ignition module – models from 1987 (Sec 12)

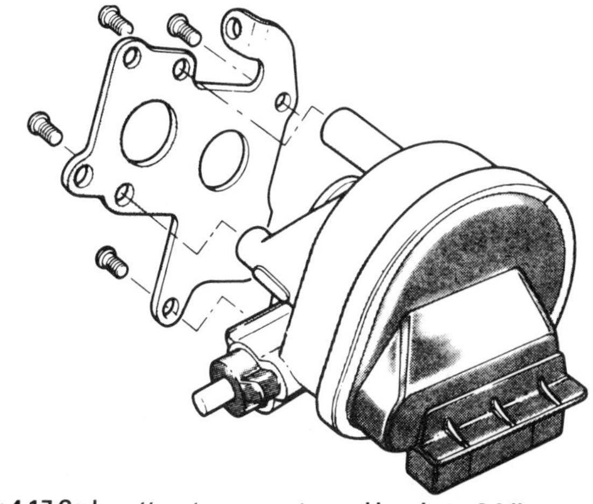

Fig 4.17 Carburettor stepper motor and bracket – 2.0 litre models with ESC II system (Sec 13)

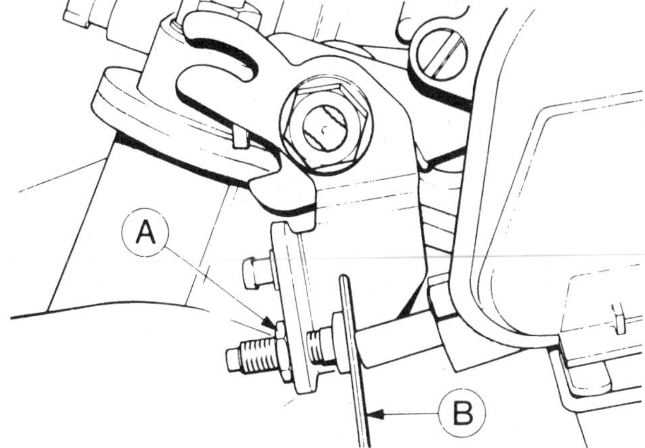

Fig 4.18 Carburettor stepper motor adjustment – 2.0 litre models with ESC II system (Sec 13)

A Locknut *B Feeler blade*

Engine coolant temperature sensor

2 The sensor is located in the underside of the inlet manifold.

3 Partially drain the cooling system as described in Chapter 2. Note that there is no need to remove the cylinder block drain plug.

4 Disconnect the sensor wiring plug by pulling on the plug, not the wiring (photo).

5 Unscrew the sensor from the inlet manifold and remove it.

6 Refitting is a reversal of removal. Fill the cooling system as described in Chapter 2.

12.3B Disconnecting ESC Hybrid module wiring plug

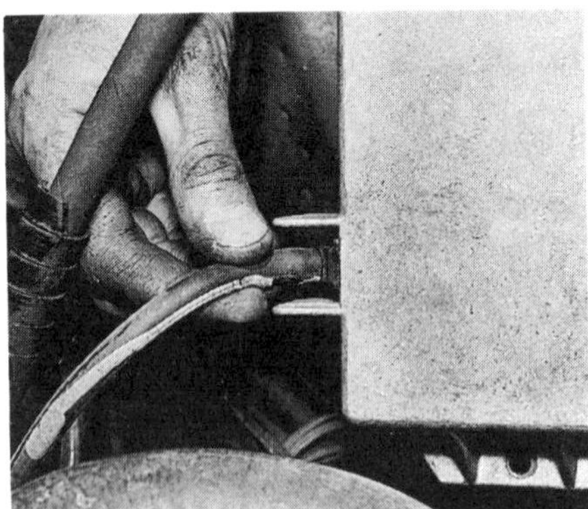
12.4 Disconnecting ESC II module vacuum pipe

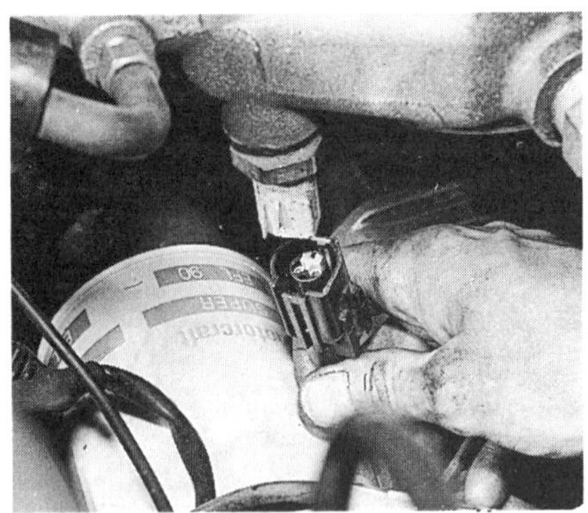
13.4 Disconnecting engine coolant temperature sensor wiring plug – ESC II system

Inlet manifold heater

Note: *When refitting the heater, a new gasket and O-ring must be used.*

7 Do not attempt to remove the heater while it is hot.

8 For improved access, remove the air cleaner as described in Chapter 3.

9 Disconnect the wiring from the heater.

10 Unscrew the three securing bolts and remove the heater. Recover the gasket and O-ring (photo).

11 Refitting is a reversal of removal, using a new gasket and O-ring, but be careful to tighten the securing bolts evenly, otherwise the heater may tilt and jam in its recess.

Carburettor stepper motor (2.0 litre models)

Note: *Irregular idle is not necessarily caused by a faulty or badly adjusted stepper motor. Good electrical contact between the stepper motor plunger and the adjusting screw (which from the throttle position switch) is essential. Before attempting adjustment or renewal of the motor, try the effect of cleaning the plunger and adjusting screw contact faces with abrasive paper followed by switch cleaning fluid. Switch cleaning fluid is available from electronic component shops. Refer to Chapter 3, Section 2 before proceeding.*

12 Remove the air cleaner as described in Chapter 3.

13 Depress the locking tab and disconnect the stepper motor wiring plug. Pull on the plug, not the wiring.

14 Remove the four securing screws and withdraw the stepper motor and bracket from the carburettor.

15 If desired, the stepper motor can be separated from the bracket by removing the four securing screws.

16 Commence refitting by securing the stepper motor to the bracket, where applicable.

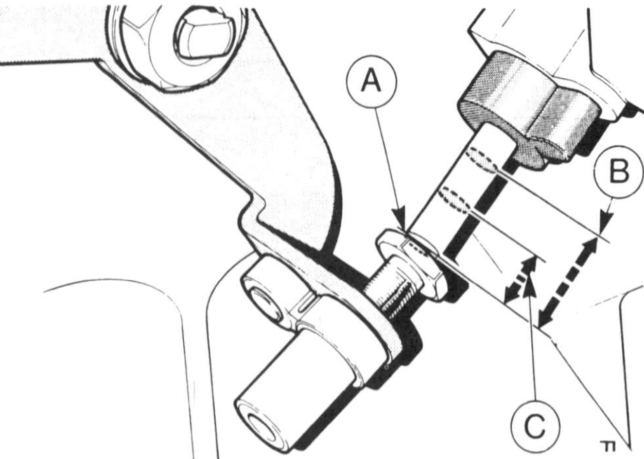

Fig 4.19 Carburettor stepper motor plunger positions – 2.0 litre models with ESC II system (Sec 13)

A Vent manifold/start
B Anti-dieselling
C Normal idle

17 Refit the stepper motor and bracket to the carburettor and secure with the four screws.

18 Reconnect the wiring plug.

19 Reconnect the air cleaner vacuum hose to the inlet manifold, and position the air cleaner to one side to allow access to the carburettor and stepper motor.

20 Reconnect the battery negative lead.

21 Connect a tachometer to the engine in accordance with the manufacturer's instructions.

22 Start the engine, then check and if necessary adjust the idle mixture as described in Chapter 3, Section 24.

23 Ensure that all electrical loads are switched off (headlamps, heater blower etc). If the 'idle speed adjustment' wire is earthed, temporarily isolate it – see Section 11. Where applicable, ensure that the automatic transmission gear selector lever is in the 'N' or 'P' position.

24 Accelerate the engine to a speed greater than 2500 rpm, allow it to return to idle, then repeat. Insert a feeler blade of 1.0 mm (0.04 in) thickness between the stepper motor plunger and the adjusting screw – see Fig. 4.18. With the feeler blade in place the engine speed should be 875 ± 25 rpm.

25 If adjustment is necessary, remove the tamperproof cap from the adjusting screw locknut. Slacken the locknut, then turn the adjusting screw to achieve the correct engine speed and tighten the locknut.

26 Repeat the procedure given in paragraph 24 and check that the engine speed is still correct. Readjust if necessary.

27 Stop the engine, remove the feeler blade, and disconnect the tachometer.

28 Refit the air cleaner as described in Chapter 3, ensuring that the vacuum hose is securely connected. If the 'idle speed adjustment' wire was previously earthed, reconnect it.

29 Re-start and then stop the engine, observing the movement of the stepper motor plunger. Immediately after stopping the engine, the plunger should move to the 'anti-dieselling' position, and after a few seconds it should extend to the 'vent manifold/start' position – see Fig. 4.19.

30 Re-check and if necessary adjust the idle mixture as described in Chapter 3, Section 24.

31 If necessary, refit the tamperproof caps to the mixture adjustment screw and the stepper motor adjustment screw locknut.

14 ESC Hybrid system components – removal and refitting

Note: *Procedures for removal and refitting of the ignition system components and electronic module are given elsewhere in the relevant Sections of this Chapter*

1 Disconnect the battery negative lead.

Crankshaft speed/position sensor

2 The sensor is mounted in a bracket on the timing cover.

3 Disconnect the sensor wiring plug by pulling on the plug, not the wiring (photo).

4 Slacken the sensor clamping screw and slide the sensor from its bracket.

13.10 Removing inlet manifold heater – ESC II system

14.3 Disconnecting crankshaft speed/position sensor wiring plug – ESC Hybrid system

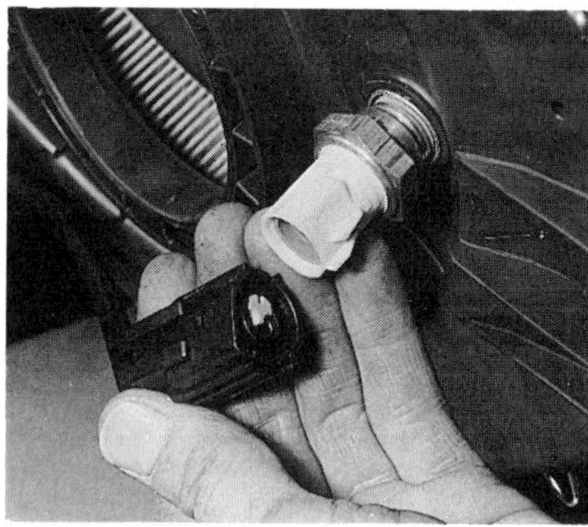
14.13 Disconnecting air charge temperature sensor wiring plug – ESC Hybrid system

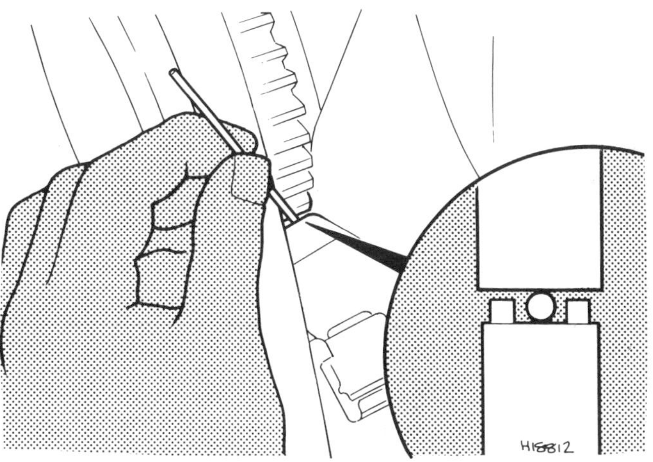

Fig 4.20 Setting the gap between the crankshaft speed/position sensor and the crankshaft toothed wheel – ESC Hybrid system (Sec 14)

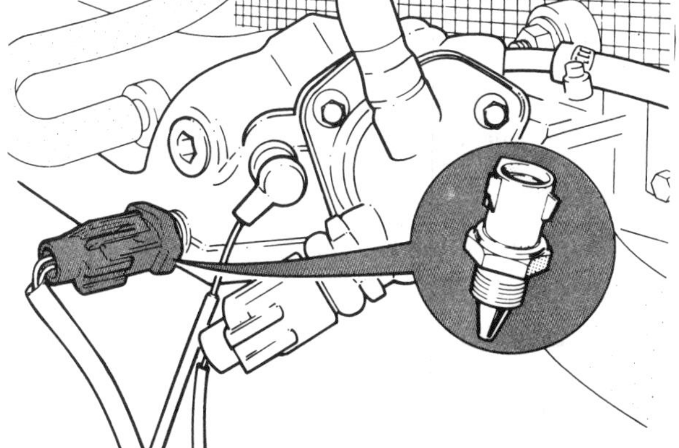
Fig 4.21 Engine coolant temperature sensor location – ESC Hybrid system (Sec 14)

5 Refitting is a reversal of removal, but the clearance between the sensor and the toothed wheel on the crankshaft must be set at 1.0 mm (0.04 in). This can be achieved by inserting a suitable length of wire or rod with a diameter of 1.0 mm (0.04 in) between the sensor and the toothed wheel – see Fig. 4.20. Do not overtighten the clamping screw, as damage to the sensor may result.

Engine coolant temperature sensor

6 The sensor is located in the side of the inlet manifold.
7 Partially drain the cooling system as described in Chapter 2.
8 Disconnect the sensor wiring plug by pulling on the plug, not the wiring.
9 Unscrew the sensor from the inlet manifold and remove it.
10 Refitting is a reversal of removal. Fill the cooling system as described in Chapter 2.

Air change temperature sensor

11 The sensor is located in the base of the air cleaner.
12 Remove the air cleaner as described in Chapter 3.
13 Disconnect the sensor wiring plug by pulling on the plug, not the wiring (photo).
14 Unscrew the sensor from the air cleaner using a suitable spanner.
15 Refitting is a reversal of removal. Refit the air cleaner as described in Chapter 3. Ensure that the vacuum hose is securely connected.

Electric choke heater

16 The electric choke heater is an integral part of the automatic choke housing on the carburettor. Removal and refitting of the automatic choke housing is covered in Chapter 3, Section 40.
17 The operation of the electric choke heater relay can be checked by starting the engine from cold, and placing a finger on the relay – see Fig. 4.22. It should be possible to feel the relay switching on and off. If this is not the case, renew the relay.

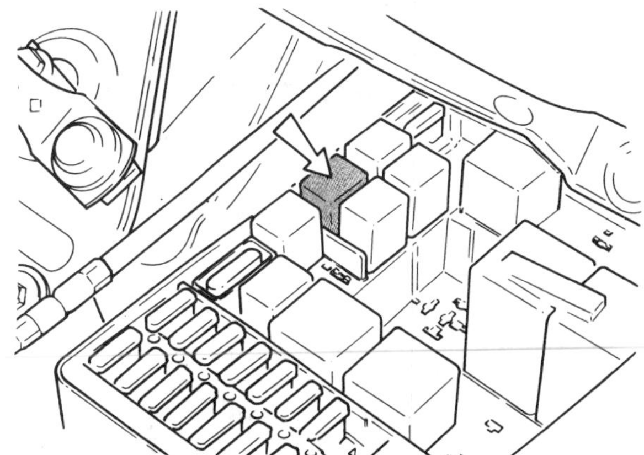
Fig 4.22 Electric choke heater relay location (arrowed) in main fusebox – ESC Hybrid system (Sec 14)

Throttle damper control solenoid

18 The solenoid is located on the right-hand side of the engine compartment (photo).
19 Disconnect the solenoid wiring plug by pulling on the plug, not the wiring.
20 Disconnect the two vacuum pipes from the solenoid, noting their locations for use when refitting.
21 Remove the securing screw and withdraw the solenoid from the body panel.
22 Refitting is a reversal of removal, but note that the locating lug on

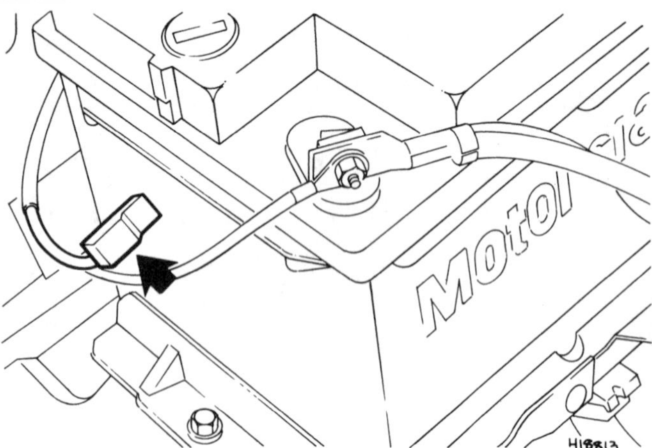

Fig 4.23 Service adjustment lead location (arrowed) – ESC Hybrid system (Sec 14)

the solenoid bracket should engage with the body panel, and make sure that the vacuum pipes are correctly connected.

Throttle damper

23 Remove the air cleaner as described in Chapter 3.
24 Disconnect the vacuum pipe from the throttle damper.
25 Remove the two securing screws and detach the throttle damper and bracket assembly from the carburettor (photo).
26 Commence refitting by securing the throttle damper and bracket assembly to the carburettor with the two screws. Ensure that the throttle lever is correctly positioned in the slot in the throttle damper actuating arm.
27 Reconnect the vacuum pipe to the throttle damper.
28 Reconnect the air cleaner vacuum hose to the inlet manifold, and reconnect the air change temperature sensor wiring plug, then place the air cleaner to one side to allow access to the throttle damper.
29 Reconnect the battery negative lead.
30 Connect a tachometer to the engine in accordance with the manufacturer's instructions.
31 Start the engine, then check and if necessary adjust the idle speed and mixture as described in Chapter 3, Section 34.
32 Earth the 'service adjustment' lead, located in the battery negative wiring loom – see Fig. 4.23, for a minimum of 10 seconds. The throttle damper actuating arm should move to the fully retracted position, raising the engine speed.
33 The engine speed should stabilise at 1700 ± 100 rpm. If adjustment is necessary, turn the adjusting screw on the end of the throttle damper actuating arm to give the correct speed. Turn the screw clockwise to increase the engine speed, or anti-clockwise to reduce the engine speed.
34 On completion of adjustment, stop the engine and disconnect the tachometer.
35 Where necessary, ensure that any tamperproof seals are refitted, then refit the air cleaner as described in Chapter 3, ensuring that the vacuum hose is securely connected. Isolate the 'service adjustment' lead.
36 Start the engine and check that normal idle speed is resumed, then stop the engine.

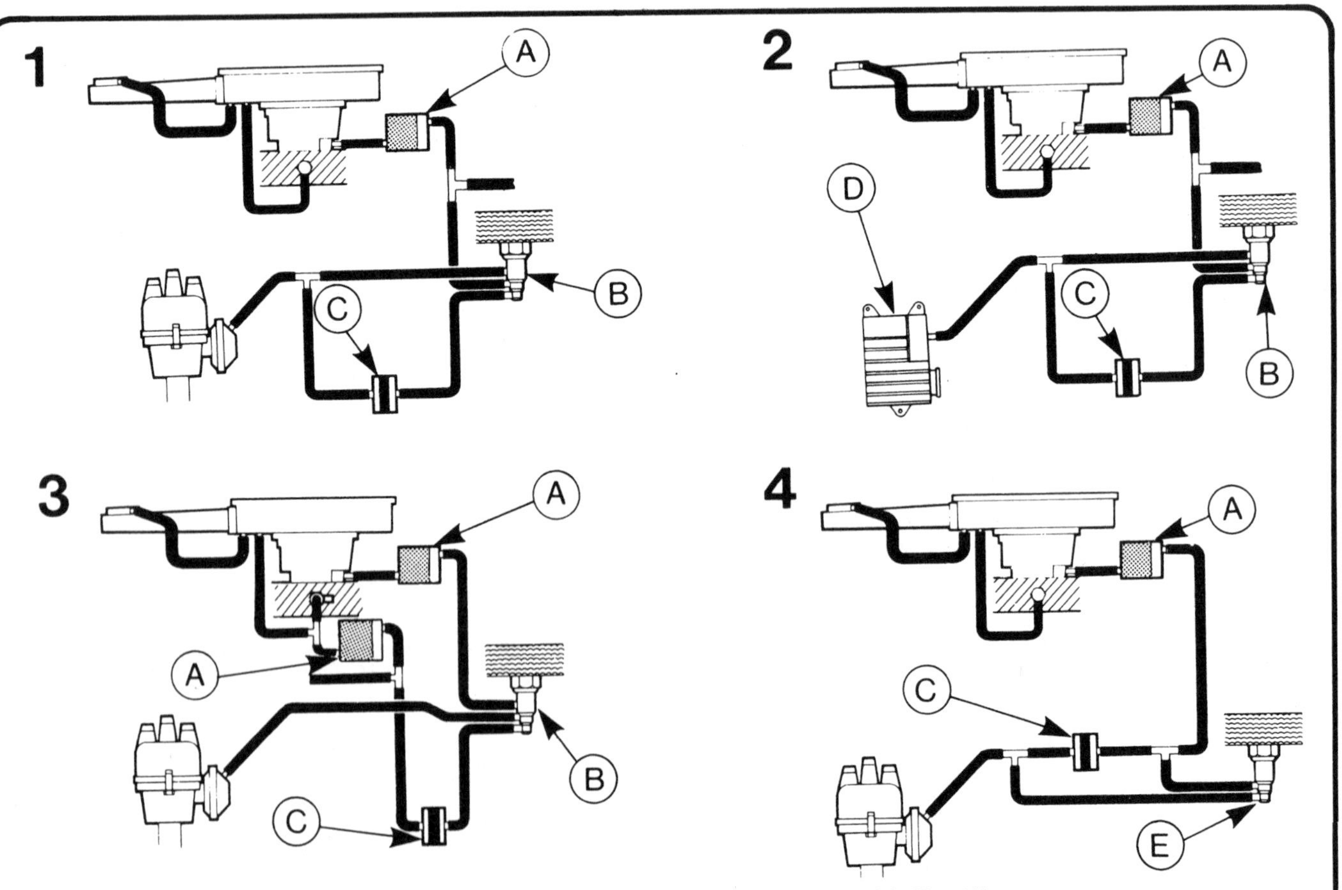

Fig 4.24 Typical spark control system layouts – early models (Sec 16)

1 1.3 and 1.6 litre models (except Economy) with manual gearbox
2 1.6 litre Economy models
3 1.6 litre models with automatic transmission
4 2.0 litre models
A Fuel trap
B Ported vacuum switch (3-port)
C Vacuum sustain valve
D ESC module
E Ported vacuum switch (2-port)

14.18 Throttle damper control solenoid – ESC Hybrid system

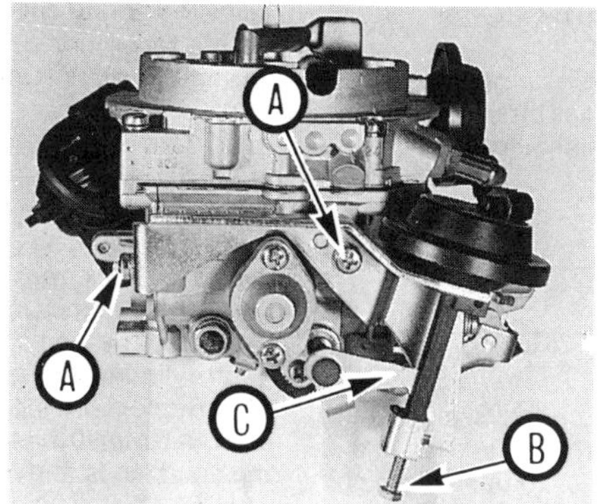

14.25 Throttle damper assembly – ESC Hybrid system (carburettor removed for clarity)
A Securing screws
B Adjusting screw
C Throttle lever

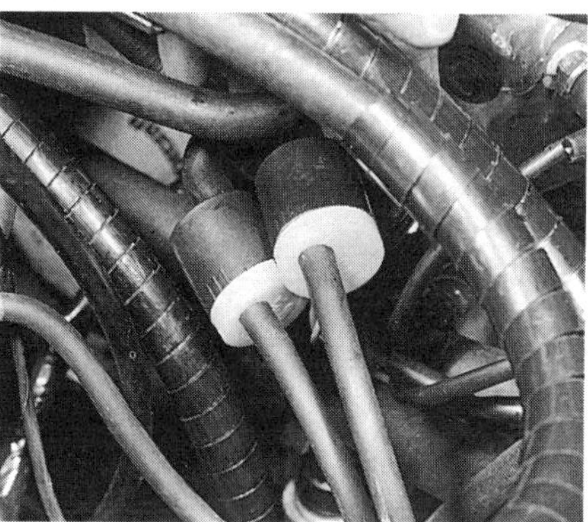

16.2 Spark control system valves – CVH model

15 EEC IV system components – removal and refitting

Note: *Procedures for removal and refitting of the ignition system components and electronic module are given elsewhere in the relevant Sections of this Chapter*

1 For details of engine coolant temperature sensor removal and refitting, refer to Section 13, paragraphs 2 to 6 inclusive. Removal and refitting procedures for all fuel injection system components are given in Chapter 3.

16 Spark control system – general description

The system is designed to ensure that the rate of ignition vacuum advance is compatible with the change in air/fuel mixture flow under all throttle conditions, thus resulting in more complete combustion and reduced exhaust emission levels. The system is not fitted to fuel injection models.

Under part throttle cruising conditions, ignition vacuum advance is required to allow time for the air/fuel mixture in the cylinders to burn. When returning to a part throttle opening after accelerating or decelerating, the ignition vacuum advance increases before the air/fuel mixture has stabilised. On certain engines this can lead to short periods of incomplete combustion and increased exhaust emission levels. To overcome this condition a spark delay valve is incorporated in the vacuum line between the carburettor and the distributor or electronic module (as applicable) to reduce the rate at which the ignition is advanced. Under certain conditions, particularly during the period of engine warm-up, some engines may suffer from poor throttle response. This problem can be overcome by the incorporation of a spark sustain valve either individually or in conjunction with the spark delay valve. The spark sustain valve is used to maintain vacuum under changing throttle conditions, thus stabilising the combustion process (photo).

On certain models, the operation of the valves is controlled by a ported vacuum switch to which the vacuum lines are connected. The valve operates in a similar manner to that of the cooling system thermostat. A wax filled sensor is attached to a plunger which operates a valve. The switch is actuated by the change in engine coolant temperature. As the engine warms up and coolant temperature increases, the wax expands, causing the plunger to move within the switch to open or close the vacuum ports accordingly. In this way the vacuum supply to the valves can be controlled according to engine temperature.

The actual arrangement and number of valves and switches varies considerably according to model, equipment fitted and operating territory. Additionally, one or more fuel traps and one-way valves may be included to prevent fuel vapour from being drawn into the vacuum lines, and to further control the vacuum supply.

17 Spark control system components – removal and refitting

Spark delay and sustain valves

1 Disconnect the vacuum pipes at the valve and withdraw the valve.
2 When refitting a spark delay valve, the valve must be positioned with the black end (marked 'CARB') towards the carburettor and the coloured end (marked 'DIST') towards the distributor or electronic module (as applicable).
3 When refitting a spark sustain valve, the valve must be positioned with the end marked 'VAC' towards the carburettor and the side marked 'DIST' towards the distributor or electronic module (as applicable).

Ported vacuum switch

4 Where fitted, the switch(es) may be located in the inlet manifold and/or in an adaptor fitted in one of the coolant hoses.
5 To remove a switch, partially drain the cooling system as described in Chapter 2. Note that there is no need to remove the cylinder block drain plug.
6 Mark the vacuum pipes for location so that they can be refitted in their correct positions, then disconnect the pipes from the switch.
7 Unscrew the valve from its location.
8 Refitting is a reversal of removal, ensuring that the vacuum pipes are correctly connected. Refill the cooling system as described in Chapter 2.

Fuel trap

9 Disconnect the vacuum pipes at the fuel trap and withdraw the fuel trap.
10 When refitting, the fuel trap must be positioned with the black end (marked 'CARB') towards the carburettor, and the white side (marked 'DIST') towards the distributor, electronic module, or ported vacuum switch (as applicable).

Spark control system additional components

11 According to model, engine and equipment, additional compo-

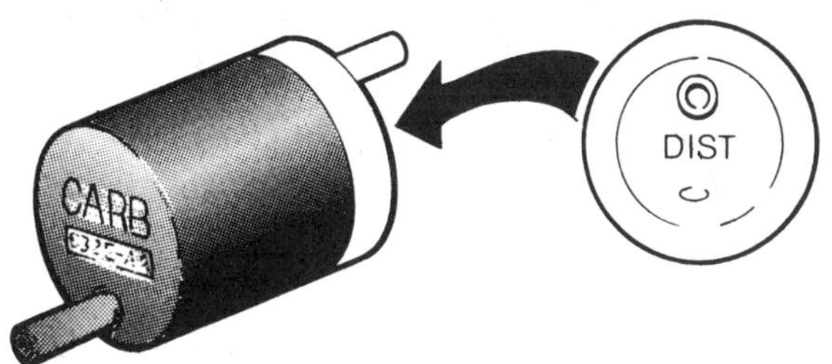

Fig 4.25 Fuel trap vacuum connection markings (Sec 17)

nents such as one-way valves or solenoids may also be fitted as part of the spark control system.

12 The removal and refitting procedures for these components are basically as described previously, and provided that all attachments are marked for position prior to removal, no problems should be encountered.

18 Fault diagnosis – ignition system

Note: *Refer to Section 2 before proceeding.*

1 There are two main symptoms indicating ignition faults, either the engine will not start or fire, or the engine is difficult to start and misfires. If a regular misfire is present, the fault is almost sure to be in the high tension (secondary) circuit.

Engine fails to start

2 If the motor fails to turn the engine, check the battery and starter motor with reference to Chapter 13.

3 Disconnect an HT lead from any spark plug and hold the end of the cable approximately 5 mm (0.2 in) away from the cylinder head using *well insulated pliers.* While an assistant spins the engine on the starter motor, check that a regular blue spark occurs. If so, remove, clean, and re-gap the spark plugs as described in Section 4.

4 If no spark occurs, disconnect the coil HT lead from the distributor cap and check for a spark as in paragraph 3. If sparks now occur, check the distributor cap, rotor arm, and HT leads as described in Sections 3 and 4, and renew them as necessary.

5 If no sparks occur, check the resistance of the coil HT lead as described in Section 4 and renew as necessary. Should the lead be serviceable check that all wiring and multi-plugs are secure on the distributor and/or electronic module (as applicable).

6 Check the coil as described in Section 5.

7 If the engine fails to start due to either damp HT leads or distributor cap, a moisture dispersant, such as Holts Wet Start, can be very effective. To prevent the problem recurring, Holts Damp Start can be used to provide a sealing coat, so excluding any further moisture from the ignition system. In extreme difficulty, Holts Cold Start will help to start a car when only a very poor spark occurs.

8 If the above checks reveal no faults but there is still no spark, the distributor or the electronic module must be suspect. Consult a Ford dealer for further testing, or test by substitution of a known good unit.

Engine misfires

9 If the engine misfires regularly, run it at a fast idling speed. Pull off each of the plug HT leads in turn and listen to the note of the engine. *Hold the plug leads with a well insulated pair of pliers as protection against a shock from the HT supply.*

10 No difference in engine running will be noticed when the lead from the defective circuit is removed. Removing the lead from one of the good cylinders will accentuate the misfire.

11 Remove the plug lead from the end of the defective plug and hold it about 5 mm (0.2 in) away from the cylinder head. Restart the engine. If the sparking is fairly strong and regular, the fault must lie in the spark plug.

12 The plug may be loose, the insulation may be cracked, or the electrodes may have burnt away, giving too wide a gap for the spark to jump. Worse still, one of the electrodes may have broken off. Either renew the plug, or clean it, reset the gap, and then test it.

19 Fault diagnosis – engine management system

Note: *Refer to Section 2 before proceeding*

1 If no fault has been found in the ignition system (see Section 18), then a fault in the engine management system must be suspected.

2 Do not immediately assume that a fault is caused by a faulty electronic module. First check that all the wiring is in good condition and that all wiring plugs are securely connected. Similarly check any vacuum pipes, where applicable.

3 Unless components are freely available for testing by substitution, further investigation should be left to a Ford dealer or other competent specialist.

4 Note that relays, modules and similar components cannot necessarily be substituted from another vehicle. The control modules in particular are dedicated to particular engine, transmission and territory combinations.

Chapter 5 Clutch

For modifications, and information applicable to later models, see Supplement at end of manual

Contents

Specifications

Clutch type	Single dry plate operated by self- adjusting cable	
Friction disc diameter		
1.3 models	190.0 mm (7.5 in)	
1.6 litre models:		
Early models	190.0 mm (7.5 in)	
Later models	215.0 mm (8.5 in)	
1.8 and 2.0 litre models	215.0 mm (8.5 in)	
Torque wrench setting	**Nm**	**lbf ft**
Clutch cover to flywheel	20 to 25	15 to 18

1 General description

The clutch is of single dry plate type, and consists of five main components: friction disc, pressure plate, diaphragm spring, cover and release bearing.

The friction disc is free to slide along the splines of the gearbox input shaft, and is held in position between the flywheel and the pressure plate due to the pressure exerted on the pressure plate by the diaphragm spring. Friction lining material is riveted to both sides of the friction disc, and spring cushioning between the friction linings and the hub absorbs transmission shocks and helps to ensure a smooth take up of power as the clutch is engaged.

The diaphragm spring is mounted on pins and is held in place in the cover by annular fulcrum rings.

The release bearing is located on a guide sleeve at the front of the gearbox, and the bearing is free to slide on the sleeve under the action of the release arm which pivots inside the clutch bellhousing.

The release arm is operated by the clutch pedal via a cable. A self-adjusting mechanism on the clutch pedal automatically adjusts the cable free play to compensate for wear in the clutch components. The self-adjusting mechanism consists of a pawl, toothed quadrant and tension spring. When the pedal is released the tension spring pulls the quadrant through the teeth of the pawl until all free play of the clutch cable is taken up. When the pedal is depressed the pawl teeth engage with the quadrant teeth thus locking the quadrant.

Depressing the clutch pedal actuates the release arm by means of the cable. The release arm pushes the release bearing forwards to bear against the centre of the diaphragm spring, thus pushing the centre of the diaphragm spring inwards. The diaphragm spring is sandwiched between two fulcrum rings in the cover, and so as the centre of the spring is pushed in, the outside of the spring is pushed out, so allowing the pressure plate to move backwards away from the friction disc.

When the clutch pedal is released, the diaphragm spring forces the pressure plate into contact with the friction linings on the friction disc, and simultaneously pushes the friction disc forwards on its splines, forcing it against the flywheel. The friction disc is now firmly sandwiched between the pressure plate and the flywheel, and drive is taken up.

2 Maintenance

1 The clutch mechanism is maintenance free, as the operating cable is self-adjusting. However, should the self-adjusting mechanism malfunction, the cable may become over-tensioned, resulting in clutch slip and rapid wear of components. The cable adjustment can be checked as follows.

2 With the aid of an assistant, or using a wooden block, lift the clutch pedal to the top of its travel and hold it firmly against the pedal stop. Grasp the cable sheath at the bulkhead and check that it can be pulled away from the bulkhead by hand. If so, adjustment is correct.

3 If the cable sheath does not move easily by hand, try to free the adjuster pawl from the quadrant by jerking the inner cable sharply away from the bulkhead. If the cable then frees, reposition the cable sheath so that it seats against the bulkhead, and re-check the adjustment as described previously.

4 If the cable cannot be freed, a new cable will be required. Proceed as follows.

5 **Wear safety glasses and gloves during the following operation as the cable may be under considerable tension.** Remove the rubber boot from the clutch release arm on the bellhousing. Hold the cable sheath at the bulkhead and cut the inner cable as near as possible to the release arm. Remove and renew the cable as described in Section 3.

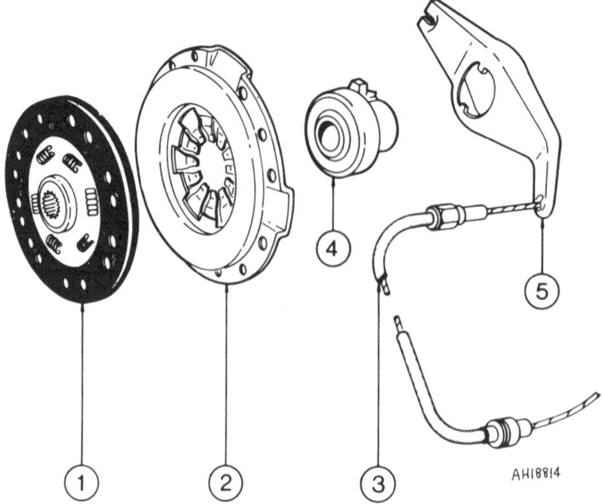

Fig 5.1 Clutch components (Sec 1)

1 Friction disc
2 Pressure plate/diaphragm spring/cover assembly
3 Cable
4 Release bearing
5 Release arm

3 Clutch cable – removal and refitting

1 Apply the handbrake, jack up the front of the vehicle and support on axle stands.
2 Place a wooden block under the clutch pedal to raise it fully against its stop which will hold the automatic adjuster pawl clear of the toothed quadrant.
3 Working beneath the vehicle, remove the rubber boot from the clutch release arm on the bellhousing (photos). On some models the boot is secured with a clip.
4 To disconnect the end of the inner cable from the release arm, pull the cable end towards the rear of the vehicle and either slide the cable so that it passes through the larger hole in the release arm, or remove the cable retainer as applicable (photos).
5 Remove the rubber boot from the cable.
6 Working inside the vehicle, remove the lower facia panel from the driver's side as described in Chapter 12.
7 Unhook and remove the inner cable from the toothed quadrant on the pedal.
8 Withdraw the cable through the bulkhead into the engine compartment, taking careful note of its routing (photo).
9 Pull the clutch end of the cable through the hole in the bellhousing, and remove the rubber bush from the cable where applicable.
10 Refitting is a reversal of removal, bearing in mind the following points.
11 Ensure that the cable is routed as noted during removal.
12 Ensure that the clutch pedal is held firmly against its stop, as described in paragraph 2, until the inner cable is secured to the release arm.
13 On completion, release the clutch pedal and operate the clutch normally to ensure that the adjuster pawl is engaged with the toothed quadrant.
14 Check the operation of the clutch mechanism. The pedal should move by hand 10 to 15 mm (0.39 to 0.59 in) from its rest position upwards to the pedal stop position and should return the same distance when released.

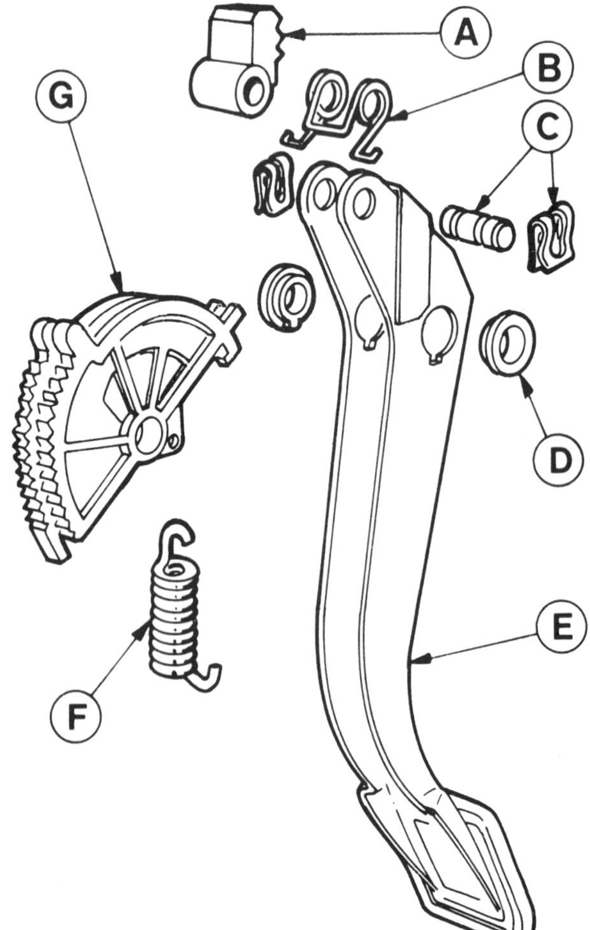

Fig 5.2 Clutch pedal and automatic adjuster components (Sec 4)

A Adjuster pawl
B Spring
C Pawl pivot shaft and clip
D Nylon bush
E Pedal
F Toothed quadrant tension spring
G Adjuster toothed quadrant

4 Clutch pedal – removal, overhaul and refitting

1 Apply the handbrake, jack up the front of the vehicle and support on axle stands. Disconnect the battery negative lead.
2 Proceed as described in Section 3, paragraphs 2 to 4 inclusive.
3 Working inside the vehicle, remove the lower facia panel from the driver's side as described in Chapter 12.
4 Unhook and remove the inner cable from the toothed quadrant on

3.3A Rubber boot on bellhousing covering clutch release arm

3.3B Rubber boot removed to expose release arm and cable end

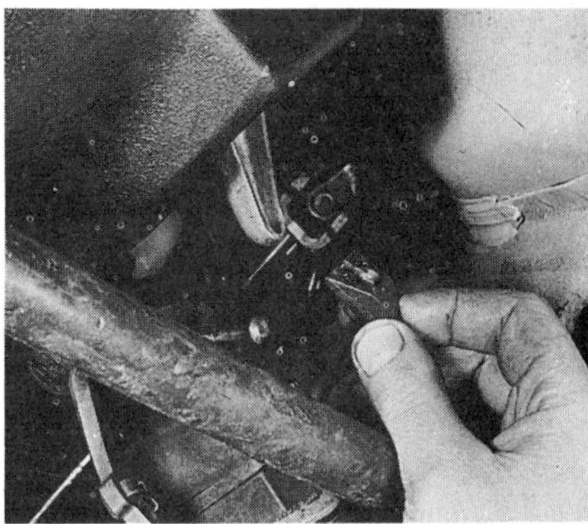
3.4A Removing the cable retainer to release the cable end

3.4B Alternative type of cable-to-release arm fitting

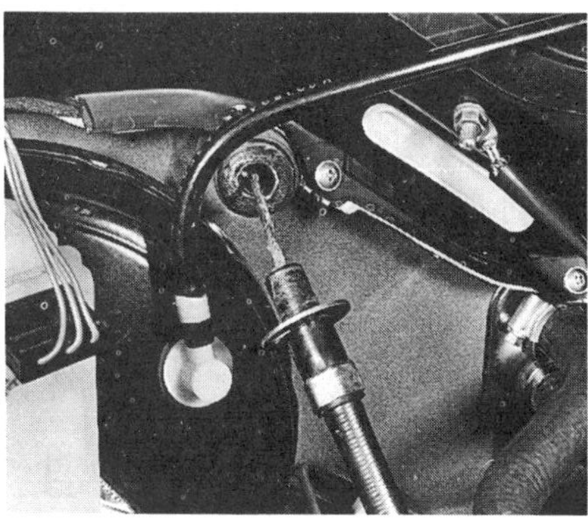
3.8 Withdrawing the cable through the bulkhead

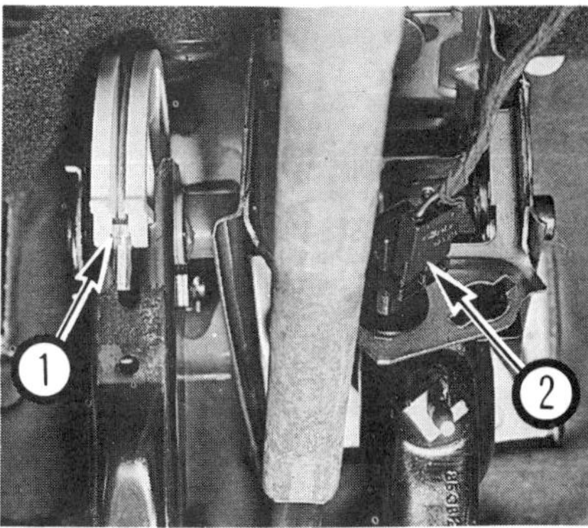

4.4 Unhook the cable from the toothed quadrant (1) and disconnect the brake light switch (2)

4.6A Pedal bracket/brake servo right-hand securing nut (arrowed)

4.6B Unscrewing the pedal bracket top securing bolt

4.8 Pivot shaft outboard circlip

4.9A Cable bracket self-locking nuts (arrowed)

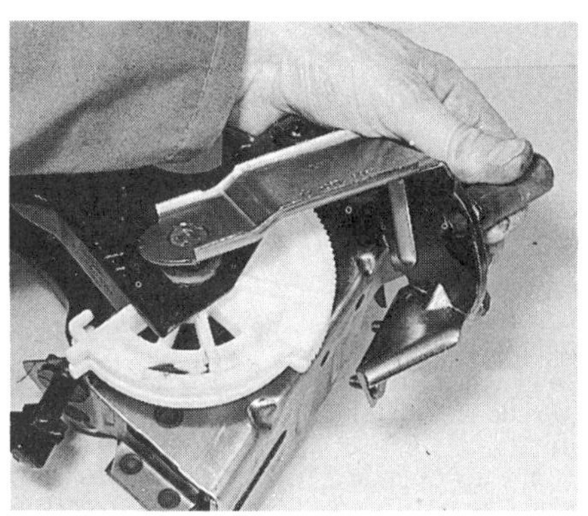
4.9B Removing the cable bracket

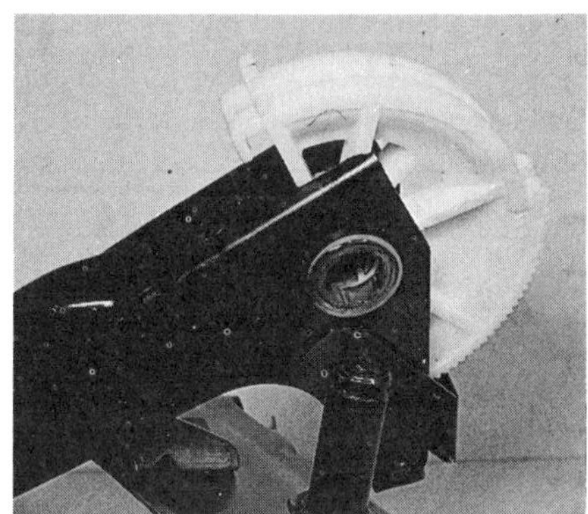
4.10 Removing the clutch pedal from the pivot shaft

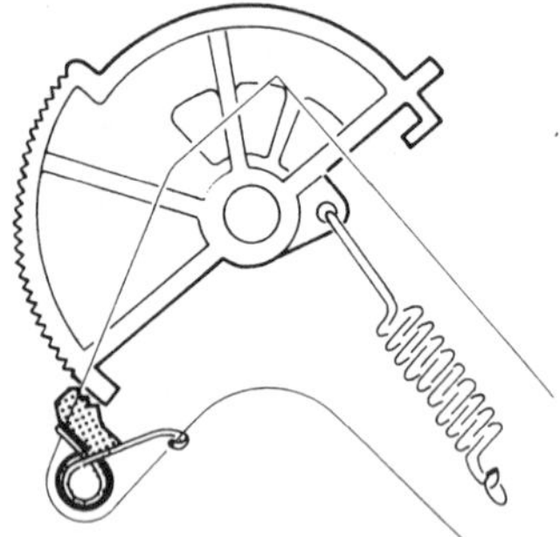

Fig 5.3 Adjuster pawl and toothed segment at initial setting (Sec 4)

the clutch pedal and disconnect the leads from the brake lamp switch (photo).
5 Remove the clip from the brake servo/ABS hydraulic unit pushrod on the brake pedal.
6 Unscrew the two nuts and single bolt which hold the pedal bracket to the bulkhead. Note that the two nuts are screwed onto the brake servo/ABS hydraulic unit studs (photos).
7 Carefully withdraw the pedal bracket from around the steering column.
8 With the pedal assembly on the bench, extract the outboard circlip from the clutch pedal end of the pivot shaft (photo).
9 Unscrew the two small self-locking nuts, and remove the clutch cable bracket (photos).
10 The clutch pedal can now be slid from the pivot shaft, noting the position of any washers, spacers and springs which may be fitted (photo).
11 To dismantle the clutch pedal and adjuster mechanism, proceed as follows.
12 Prise the nylon bushes from each side of the pedal and remove the toothed quadrant. Unhook the spring.
13 Prise one of the clips from the adjuster pawl pivot shaft, withdraw the shaft and remove the pawl and spring.
14 Clean all the components and examine them for wear and damage, renewing as necessary.
15 Lubricate the bores of the adjuster pawl and toothed quadrant with graphite grease.
16 Assemble the adjuster pawl, spring and pivot shaft to the pedal, and refit the clip removed when dismantling.
17 Attach the spring to the toothed quadrant, then insert the quadrant into the pedal and press in the two nylon bushes.
18 Lift the adjuster pawl and turn the toothed quadrant so that the pawl rests on the smooth curved surface at the end of the teeth - see Fig. 5.3.
19 Attach the toothed quadrant spring to the pedal.
20 Lubricate the pedal pivot shaft with a molybdenum disulphide based grease, then refit the pedal assembly to the shaft. Refit any washers, spacers and springs in their original positions.
21 Refit the clutch cable bracket, and tighten the two self-locking nuts.
22 Refit the circlip to the clutch pedal end of the pivot shaft.
23 Refitting of the pedal assembly is a reversal of removal, but refer to Section 3, paragraphs 11 to 14 inclusive when reconnecting the clutch cable.

5 Clutch - removal

1 In order to remove the clutch it will be necessary to remove either the engine (Chapter 1) or the gearbox (Chapter 6). Unless the engine requires a major overhaul, it is easier and quicker to remove the gearbox.
2 If the original clutch is to be refitted, mark the clutch cover and flywheel for alignment which will ensure identical positioning on refitting. This is not necessary if a new clutch is to be fitted.
3 Progressively unscrew, in a diagonal sequence, the six bolts and spring washers which secure the clutch cover to the flywheel. This will prevent distortion of the cover and will also prevent the cover from suddenly flying off due to binding on the dowels.
4 With all the bolts removed, lift off the clutch assembly, pulling it from the dowels if necessary. Be prepared to catch the friction disc as the cover assembly is lifted from the flywheel, and note which way round the friction disc is fitted (photo). The side nearest the flywheel is normally marked 'FLYWHEEL SIDE' or 'SHWUNGRADSEITE'.

6 Clutch - inspection

1 With the clutch assembly removed, clean off all traces of dust using a dry cloth. Although most friction discs now have asbestos-free linings, some do not, and it is wise to take suitable precautions; *asbestos dust is harmful, and must not be inhaled.*
2 Examine the linings of the friction disc for wear and loose rivets, distortion, cracks, broken torsion springs and worn splines. The surface of the friction linings may be highly glazed, but, as long as the friction material pattern can be clearly seen, this is satisfactory. If there is any sign of oil contamination, indicated by a continuous, or patchy, shiny black discolouration, the plate must be renewed and the source of the contamination traced and rectified. This will be either a leaking crankshaft oil seal or gearbox input shaft oil seal - or both. Renewal procedures are given in Chapter 1 and Chapter 6 respectively. The friction disc must also be renewed if the lining thickness has worn down to, or just above, the level of the rivet heads.
3 Check the machined faces of the flywheel and pressure plate. If either is grooved, or heavily scored, renewal is necessary. The pressure plate must also be renewed if any cracks are apparent, or if the diaphragm spring is damaged or its pressure suspect.
4 With the gearbox removed it is advisable to check the condition of the release bearing, as described in Section 8.

7 Clutch - refitting

1 It is important to ensure that no oil or grease gets on the friction disc linings, or the pressure plate and flywheel faces. It is advisable to refit the clutch assembly with clean hands, and to wipe down the pressure plate and flywheel faces with a clean rag before assembly begins.
2 Place the friction disc against the flywheel, ensuring that it is fitted the correct way round. The projecting torsion spring hub should be farthest from the flywheel, and the 'FLYWHEEL SIDE' or 'SHWUNGRADSEITE' mark should face towards the flywheel (photos).
3 Fit the clutch cover assembly, fitting it over the locating dowels, and aligning the previously made marks on the clutch cover and flywheel. Insert the six bolts and spring washers and tighten them finger-tight so that the friction disc is gripped, but can still be moved.
4 The friction disc must now be centralised so that when the engine and gearbox are mated, the gearbox input shaft splines will pass through the splines in the centre of the friction disc.
5 Centralisation can be carried out by inserting a round bar or a long screwdriver through the hole in the centre of the friction disc, so that the end of the bar rests in the spigot bearing in the centre of the crankshaft. Where possible use a blunt instrument, and if a screwdriver is used, wrap tape around the blade to prevent damage to the bearing surface. Moving the bar sideways or up and down will move the friction disc in whichever direction is necessary to achieve centralisation. With the bar removed, view the friction disc hub in relation to the hole in the end of the crankshaft and the circle created by the ends of the diaphragm spring fingers. When the hub appears exactly in the centre, all is correct. Alternatively, if a clutch aligning tool can be obtained, this will eliminate all the guesswork obviating the need for visual alignment (photo).
6 Tighten the cover retaining bolts gradually, in a diagonal sequence, to the specified torque wrench setting (photos).
7 Refit the gearbox (Chapter 6) or engine (Chapter 1) as applicable.

8 Clutch release bearing and arm - removal, inspection and refitting

Note: *The release bearing is secured to the release arm with spring clips. If the bearing is to be removed but not renewed, check to ensure that new spring clips can be obtained, as the old clips cannot be re-used. New clips will be supplied with a new bearing.*
1 With the gearbox and engine separated to provide access to the

5.4 Removing the clutch cover assembly and friction disc

7.2A Fitting friction disc and cover assembly. Note orientation of friction disc

7.2B Alternative friction disc orientation marking

7.5 Centralising the friction disc using a clutch aligning tool

7.6A Tightening a clutch cover retaining bolt

7.6B Clutch fitted to flywheel ready for fitting of the gearbox

8.3A Withdrawing the release bearing from the guide sleeve

8.3B Release bearing retaining clip with tag arrowed

8.4 Release arm and fulcrum pin (arrowed)

clutch, attention can be given to the release bearing located in the clutch bellhousing over the gearbox input shaft.

2 If not already done, remove the rubber boot from the release arm and disconnect the clutch cable with reference to Section 3.

3 The release bearing must now be freed from the release arm. The bearing is secured by spring clips which can only be freed by reaching behind the release arm. Access is extremely limited, and a small angled tool such as an Allen key will be required to depress the tags at top and bottom of the bearing. It is likely that the clips will be broken during the removal process, and in any case they should be renewed when the bearing is refitted. When the bearing is free, withdraw it from the guide sleeve (photos).

4 Pull the release arm from the fulcrum pin, then withdraw the arm over the input shaft, guiding the end through the bellhousing aperture (photo).

5 Spin the release bearing and check it for roughness. Hold the outer race and attempt to move it laterally against the inner race. If any excessive movement or roughness is evident, renew the bearing. If a new clutch has been fitted, it is wise to renew the release bearing as a matter of course.

6 Refitting is a reversal of removal, but use new bearing retaining clips, and reconnect the cable to the release arm with reference to Section 3.

9 Fault diagnosis – clutch

Symptom	Reason(s)
Judder when taking up drive	Loose or worn engine/gearbox mountings Friction disc linings worn or contaminated with oil Clutch cable sticking or defective Friction disc hub sticking on input shaft splines
Clutch fails to disengage	Clutch cable sticking or defective Excessive cable free play – self-adjusting mechanism inoperative Friction disc linings contaminated with oil Friction disc hub sticking on input shaft splines
Clutch slips	Clutch cable sticking or defective Self-adjusting mechanism inoperative Faulty pressure plate or weak or broken diaphragm spring Friction disc linings contaminated with oil
Noise when depressing clutch pedal	Worn release bearing Defective release mechanism Faulty pressure plate or diaphragm spring
Noise when releasing clutch pedal	Faulty pressure plate or diaphragm spring Broken friction disc torsion spring(s) Gearbox internal wear

Note: *This Section is not intended as an exhaustive guide to fault diagnosis, but summarises the more common faults which may be encountered during a vehicle's life. Consult a dealer for more detailed advice.*

Chapter 6 Manual gearbox

For modifications, and information applicable to later models, see Supplement at end of manual

Contents

Specifications

Type

Four forward speeds (A, B and C type gearboxes) or five forward speeds (N type gearbox) and reverse. Synchromesh on all forward speeds

Application

1.3 litre models	A1 and C types
1.6 litre models with Ford VV carburettor	A2, B, C and N types
1.6 litre models with Weber 2V carburettor	B, C and N types
1.8 litre models	B and N types
2.0 litre models	B and N types

Ratios

4-speed gearbox:	**A1**	**A2**	**B**	**C**
1st	3.66:1	3.34:1	3.65:1	3.58:1
2nd	2.18:1	1.99:1	1.97:1	2.01:1
3rd	1.43:1	1.42:1	1.37:1	1.40:1
4th	1.00:1	1.00:1	1.00:1	1.00:1
Reverse	4.24:1	3.87:1	3.66:1	3.32:1

5-speed gearbox (N type):	**All models except P100**	**P100 models**
1st	3.65:1	3.91:1
2nd	1.97:1	2.29:1
3rd	1.37:1	1.38:1
4th	1.00:1	1.00:1
5th	0.82:1	0.82:1
Reverse	3.66:1	3.66:1

Lubrication

Oil type/specification:	
4-speed gearbox	Gear oil, viscosity SAE 80EP, to Ford spec SQM-2C 9008-A (Duckhams Hypoid 80)
5-speed gearbox	Gear oil, viscosity SAE 80EP, to Ford spec ESD-M2C 175-A (Duckhams Hypoid 75W/90S)

Oil capacity

A1 and A2 types	0.98 litre (1.72 pints)
B type	1.46 litres (2.57 pints)
C type	1.25 litres (2.20 pints)
N type up to 1987	1.90 litres (3.34 pints)
N type from 1987	1.25 litres (2.20 pints)

Torque wrench settings

	Nm	lbf ft
Clutch housing-to-gearbox casing bolts	70 to 90	52 to 66
Clutch housing-to-engine bolts	40 to 50	30 to 37
Clutch release bearing guide sleeve bolts:		
All except C type	9 to 11	7 to 8
C type	21 to 25	15 to 18
Extension housing-to-gearbox casing bolts	45 to 49	33 to 36
Top cover bolts:		
All except C type	10 to 13	7 to 10
C type	21 to 25	15 to 18
Gearbox crossmember-to-underbody bolts	20 to 25	14 to 18
Gearbox crossmember-to-gearbox bolt	50 to 57	37 to 42
Reversing light switch	1 to 2	0.8 to 1.5
Oil filler/level plug	33 to 41	24 to 30
5th driving gear retaining nut (N type)	120 to 150	89 to 111
5th gear locking plate bolts (N type)	21 to 26	15 to 19
Gear lever-to-extension housing screws	21 to 26	15 to 19

1 General description

The manual gearbox may be of four or five-speed type, depending on model. Three different types of four-speed gearbox have been fitted to Sierra models, these being the A, B and C types. The A and B type gearboxes are similar, but all A type gearboxes have an integral clutch housing, whereas B type gearboxes may have either an integral or bolt-on clutch housing. The C type gearbox is substantially different to the A and B types, and procedures differ in detail. A five-speed N type gearbox is also available, with the fifth gear installed in the tailshaft housing of the gearbox on an extended gear cluster.

All gearboxes follow conventional rear-wheel-drive practice. Drive from the clutch is picked up by the input shaft, which runs in line with the mainshaft. The input shaft gear and mainshaft gears are in constant mesh with the countershaft gear cluster. Selection of gears is by sliding synchromesh hubs, which lock the appropriate mainshaft gear to the mainshaft.

Gear selection is by means of a floor-mounted lever which fits directly into the gearbox extension housing and operates the selector shaft. The selector shaft operates the selector forks which act on the synchroniser units.

When contemplating overhaul of a gearbox, due consideration should be given to the costs involved, since it is often more economical to obtain a service exchange or good secondhand gearbox rather than fit new parts to the existing unit.

2 Maintenance and inspection

1 Maintenance is limited to checking the oil level periodically, and checking for leaks if the level is low. Proceed as follows.
2 For improved access, jack up the vehicle and support on axle stands. Note that the vehicle must be level in order to carry out an accurate check.
3 If the transmission is hot due to the vehicle having been driven recently, allow it to cool for a few minutes. This is necessary because the oil can foam when hot, leading to a false level reading.
4 Wipe clean around the filler/level plug, which is located on the left-hand side of the gearbox. Unscrew the plug and remove it (photo).
5 Using a suitably marked piece of bent wire as a dipstick, check that the oil level is as follows, according to gearbox type:

Gearbox type	Oil level
All four-speed gearboxes	*0 to 5.0 mm (0 to 0.2 in) below lower edge of filler/level hole*
All five-speed gearboxes up to April 1984 (build code E6) except those subsequently fitted with a modified extension housing	*Level with bottom edge of filler/level hole*
All five-speed gearboxes from May 1984 (build code EC) to end of April 1985 (build code FP) and all vehicles built up to April 1984 (build code E6) subsequently fitted with a modified gearbox extension housing	*20.0 to 25.0 mm (0.79 to 0.99 in) below lower edge of filler/level hole*
All five-speed gearboxes from May 1985 (build code FB)	*0 to 5.0 mm (0 to 0.2 in) below lower edge of filler/level hole*

Note that the vehicle build code appears as the twelfth and thirteenth characters of the VIN number on the plate in the engine compartment
6 Top up the level if necessary, using clean oil of the specified type. Do not overfill, as this can lead to leakage and difficult gear changing. Allow excess oil to drip out of the filler/level hole if necessary. Refit and tighten the filler/level plug on completion.
7 The frequent need for topping-up can only be due to leaks, which should be rectified. The most likely sources of leaks are the rear extension housing and input shaft oil seals. Oil seal renewal is described in Section 5 for all gearbox types.
8 No periodic oil changing is specified, and no drain plug is fitted.

3 Gearbox – removal and refitting (leaving engine in vehicle)

1 Removal of the engine and manual gearbox as an assembly is described in Chapter 1, Section 12.
2 Disconnect the battery negative lead.
3 Working in the engine compartment, unscrew and remove the four upper engine-to-gearbox bolts, noting the location of the earth lead.
4 Working inside the vehicle, unscrew the gear lever knob and remove the centre console as described in Chapter 12. Where a full length console is fitted, it is only necessary to remove the front tray.
5 Detach the outer gaiter from the retaining frame and withdraw it over the gear lever (photo).
6 Undo the securing screws on early models, or release the clips on later models, and remove the gaiter retaining frame and inner gaiter (photos).
7 Using a suitable Torx key, remove the screws securing the gear lever to the gearbox extension housing, and withdraw the gear lever. Note how the base of the gear lever locates over the selector shaft (photos).
8 Jack up the vehicle and support on axle stands. Ensure that there is sufficient working room beneath the vehicle.
9 To improve access, disconnect the exhaust downpipe from the manifold and remove the exhaust system as described in Chapter 3.
10 Remove the propeller shaft as described in Chapter 8.
11 Where applicable, bend back the locktabs, then unscrew the two bolts securing each of the two anti-roll bar U-clamps to the vehicle underbody. Lower the anti-roll bar as far as possible.
12 Disconnect the wiring from the starter motor and remove the starter motor with reference to Chapter 13 if necessary.

2.4 Gearbox filler/level plug location (arrowed) – N type gearbox

3.5 Detach the gear lever outer gaiter from the retaining frame

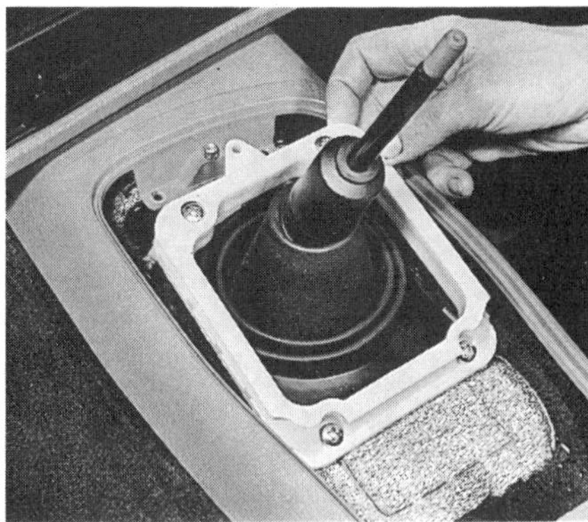

3.6A Remove the gaiter retaining frame ...

3.6B ... and the inner gaiter

3.7A Remove the gear lever securing screws ...

3.7B ... and withdraw the gear lever

3.13 Disconnect the wiring from the reversing lamp switch

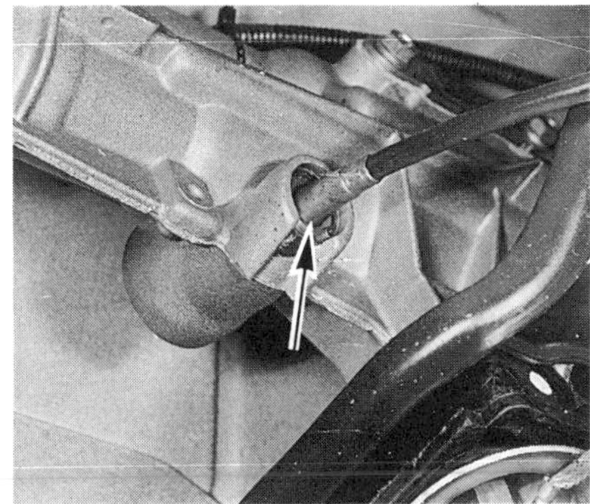

3.14 Remove the circlip (arrowed) and withdraw the speedometer cable – N type gearbox

3.17A Unscrew the gearbox crossmember securing bolts (arrowed) ...

13 Disconnect the wiring from the reversing lamp switch (photo).

14 Remove the retaining circlip, and withdraw the speedometer cable from the gearbox extension housing (photo).

15 Disconnect the clutch cable from the release arm with reference to Chapter 5, Section 3.

16 Support the gearbox with a trolley jack, and an interposed block of wood to spread the load.

17 Unscrew the four bolts securing the gearbox crossmember to the vehicle underbody. Unscrew the central bolt securing the crossmember to the gearbox and remove the crossmember. Note the position of the earth strap, where applicable. Recover the mounting cup and where applicable the exhaust mounting bracket and heat shield (photos).

18 Unscrew and remove the remaining engine-to-gearbox bolts, noting the location of the engine/gearbox brace on the right-hand side of the gearbox on OHC models (photo).

19 With the help of an assistant, lift the gearbox from the engine, using the trolley jack to take the weight. Do not allow the weight of the gearbox to hang on the input shaft. It may be necessary to rock the transmission a little to release it from the engine.

20 With the gearbox removed, temporarily reconnect the anti-roll bar to the underbody if the vehicle is to be moved.

21 Refitting is a reversal of removal, taking note of the following points.

22 Before attempting to refit the gearbox, check that the clutch friction disc is centralised as described in Chapter 5, Section 7. This is necessary to ensure that the gearbox input shaft splines will pass through the splines in the centre of the friction disc.

23 Check that the clutch release arm and bearing are correctly fitted, and lightly grease the input shaft splines.

24 Check that the engine adapter plate is correctly positioned on its locating dowels.

25 Refit the propeller shaft as described in Chapter 8.

3.17B ... and recover the mounting cup

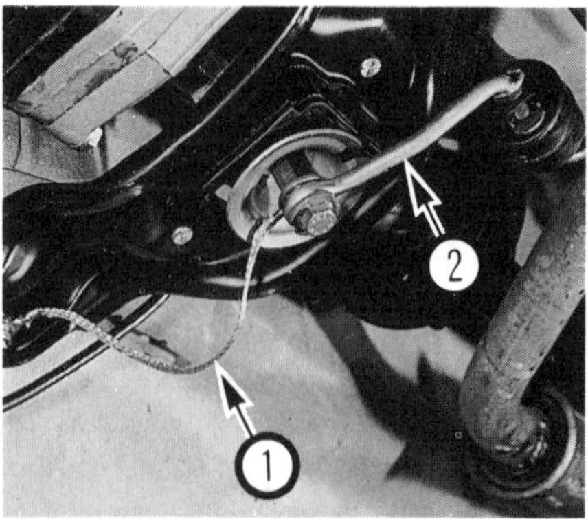

3.17C Gearbox crossmember earth strap (1) and exhaust mounting bracket (2) – 1.8 litre CVH model

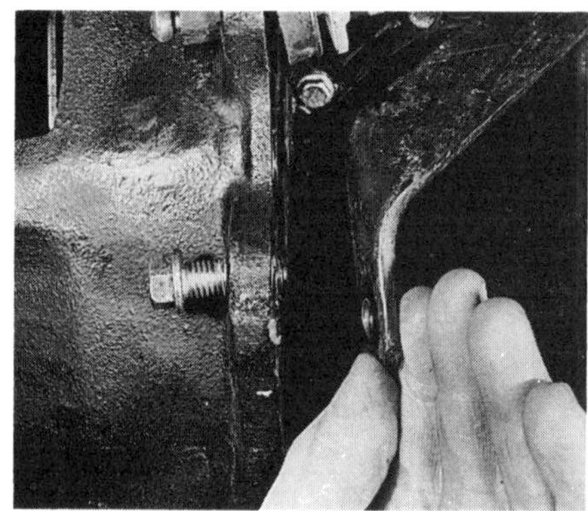
3.18 Unscrew the engine/gearbox brace – OHC models

26 Refit the exhaust system as described in Chapter 3.

27 Reconnect the clutch cable to the release arm with reference to Chapter 5, Section 3.

28 On completion, check and if necessary top up the gearbox oil level as described in Section 2.

4 Gearbox (A, B and C types) – dismantling into major assemblies

1 Clean the exterior of the gearbox with paraffin and wipe dry.

2 Remove the clutch release bearing and arm with reference to Chapter 5.

3 Where applicable, unbolt the clutch housing from the front of the gearbox.

4 Working through the gear lever aperture, use a screwdriver or small drift to tap out the extension housing rear cover (photo).

5 Proceed as follows according to gearbox type.

A and B gearboxes

6 Unscrew the securing bolts and remove the top cover and gasket.

7 Invert the gearbox and allow the oil to drain, then turn it upright again.

8 Using a screwdriver, unscrew the selector locking mechanism plug, then extract the spring and locking pin. A pen magnet can be used to assist removal of the spring and locking pin (photo).

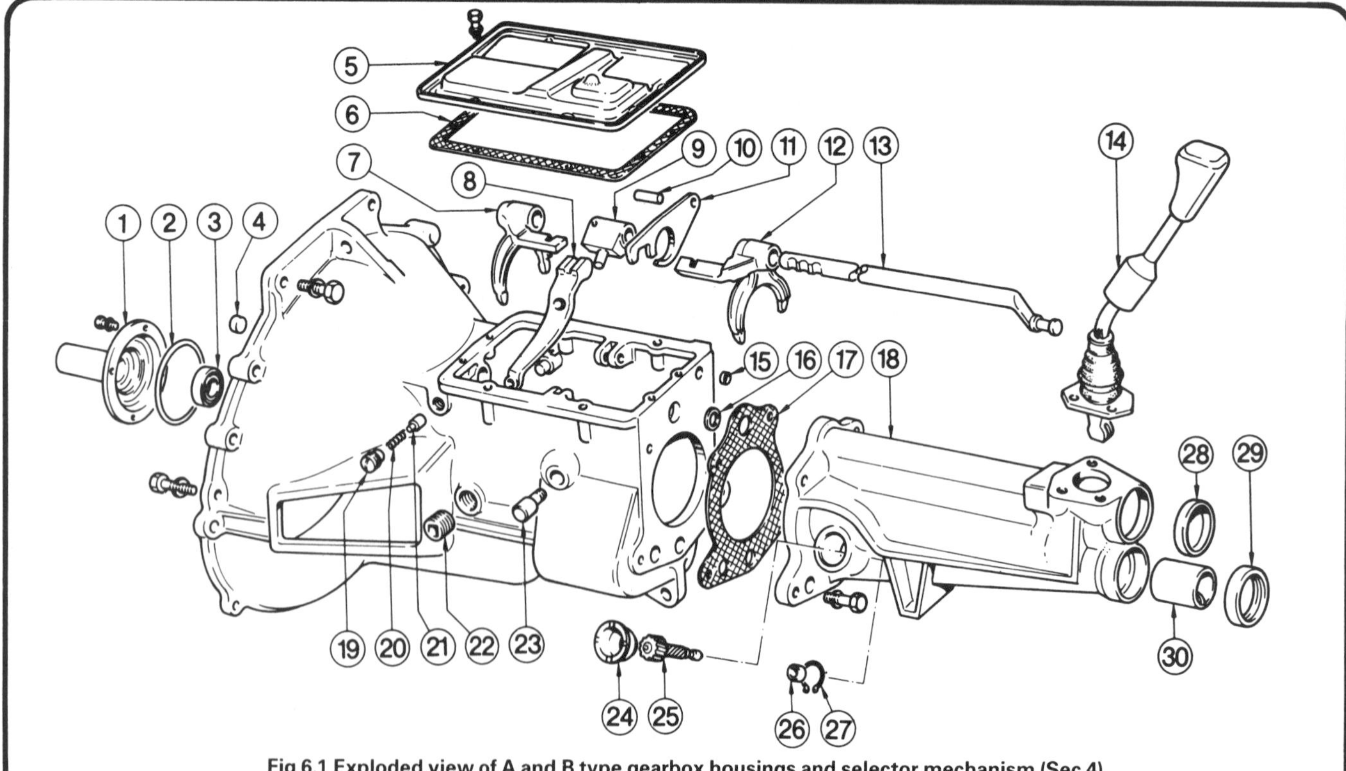

Fig 6.1 Exploded view of A and B type gearbox housings and selector mechanism (Sec 4)

1 Guide sleeve
2 O-ring
3 Oil seal
4 Plug
5 Cover
6 Gasket
7 3rd/4th gear selector fork
8 Reverse gear relay lever
9 Selector boss
10 Roll pin
11 Selector locking plate
12 1st/2nd gear selector fork
13 Selector shaft
14 Gear lever assembly
15 Plug
16 Oil seal
17 Gasket
18 Extension housing
19 Threaded plug
20 Spring
21 Locking pin
22 Oil filler plug
23 Plug
24 Cap
25 Speedometer drive pinion
26 Oil seal
27 Circlip
28 Cover
29 Oil seal
30 Bush

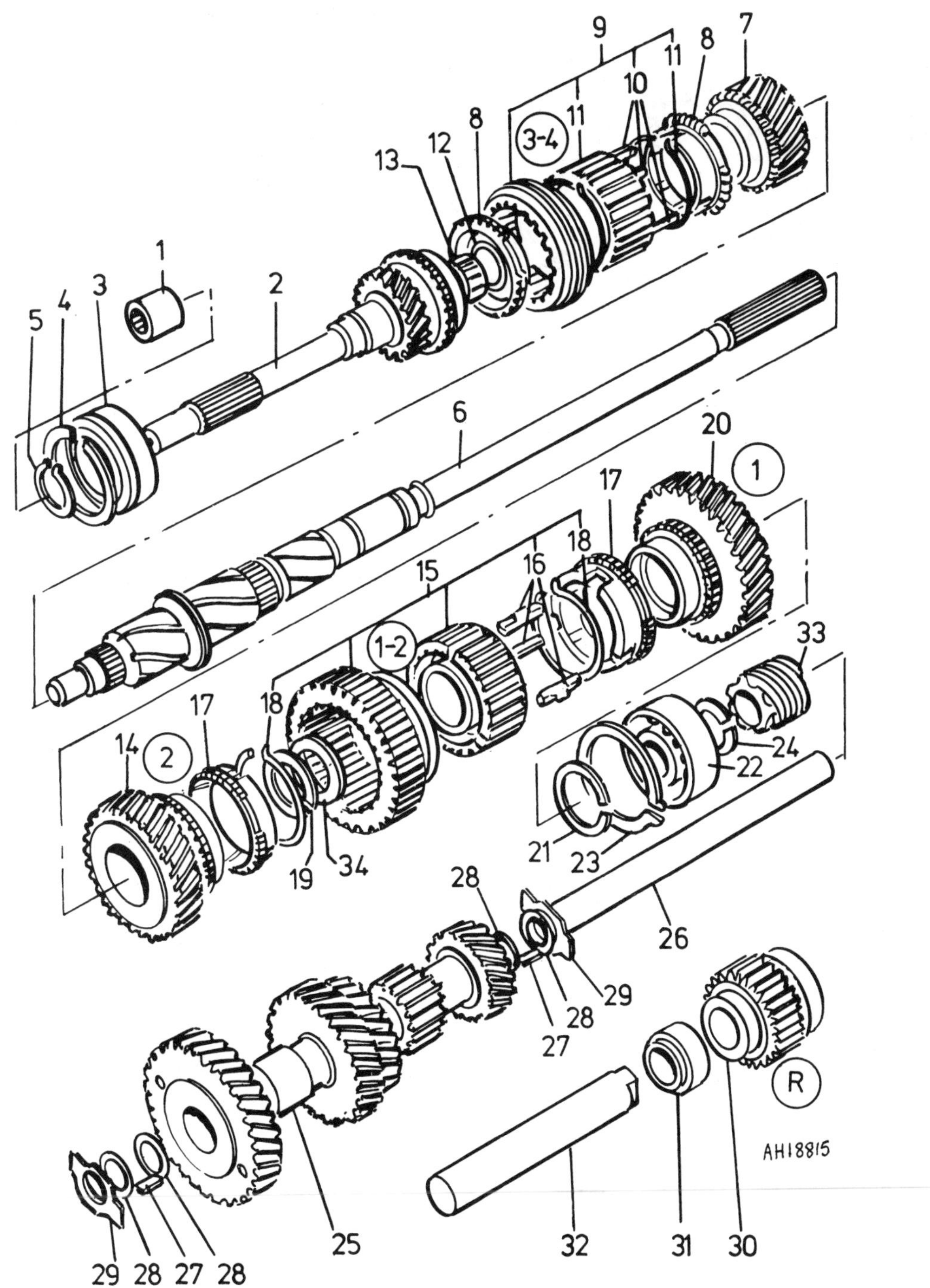

Fig 6.2 Exploded view of A type gearbox gear assemblies (Sec 4)

1 *Spigot bearing*
2 *Input shaft*
3 *Bearing*
4 *Large circlip*
5 *Small circlip*
6 *Mainshaft*
7 *3rd gear*
8 *3rd and 4th gear synchroniser rings*
9 *3rd/4th gear synchroniser unit*
10 *Blocker bars*
11 *Blocker bar springs*
12 *Circlip*
13 *Needle roller bearing*
14 *2nd gear*
15 *1st/2nd gear synchroniser unit*
16 *Blocker bars*
17 *1st and 2nd gear synchroniser rings*
18 *Blocker bar springs*
19 *Circlip*
20 *1st gear*
21 *Circlip*
22 *Mainshaft bearing*
23 *Circlip*
24 *Circlip*
25 *Countershaft gear cluster*
26 *Countershaft*
27 *Needle rollers*
28 *Spacers*
29 *Thrustplates*
30 *Reverse idler gear*
31 *Spacer*
32 *Reverse idler shaft*
33 *Speedometer drivegear*
34 *Thrustwasher*

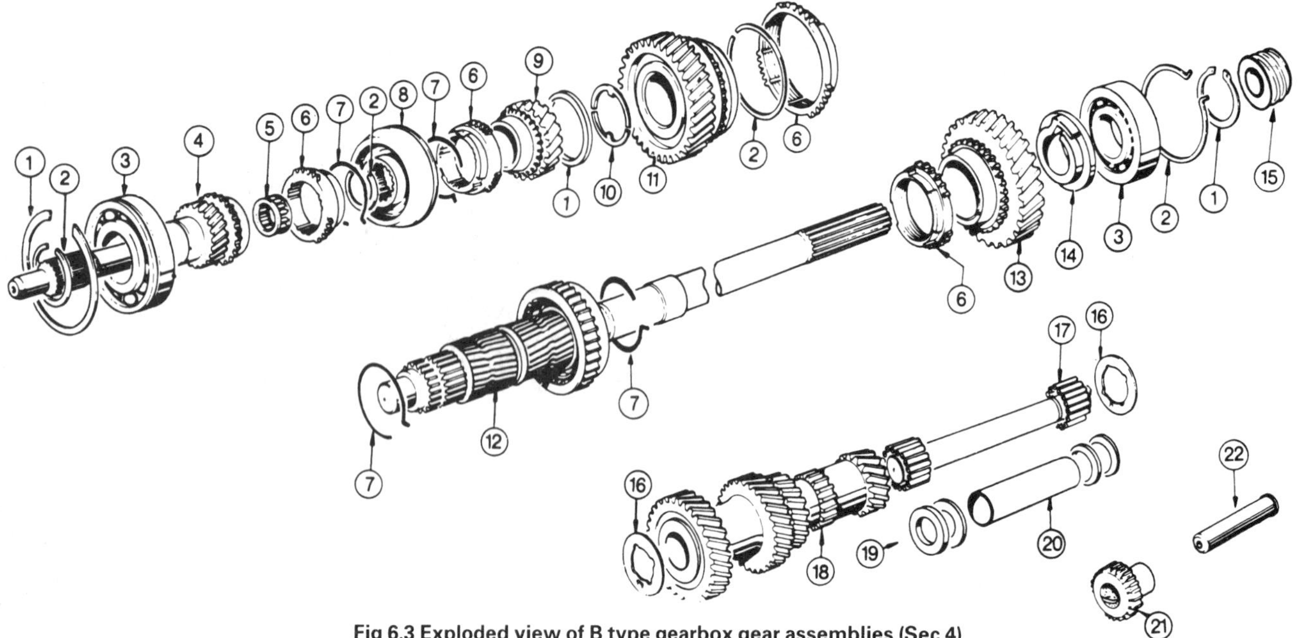

Fig 6.3 Exploded view of B type gearbox gear assemblies (Sec 4)

1 *Circlip*
2 *Circlip*
3 *Grooved ball bearing*
4 *Input shaft*
5 *Needle roller bearing*
6 *Synchroniser rings*
7 *Blocker bar springs*
8 *Synchroniser hub*
9 *3rd gear*
10 *Thrust half washers*
11 *2nd gear*
12 *Mainshaft with synchroniser unit*
13 *1st gear*
14 *Oil scoop ring*
15 *Speedometer drivegear*
16 *Thrustwasher*
17 *Needle rollers*
18 *Countershaft gear cluster*
19 *Spacers*
20 *Spacer tube*
21 *Reverse gear idler*
22 *Idler shaft*

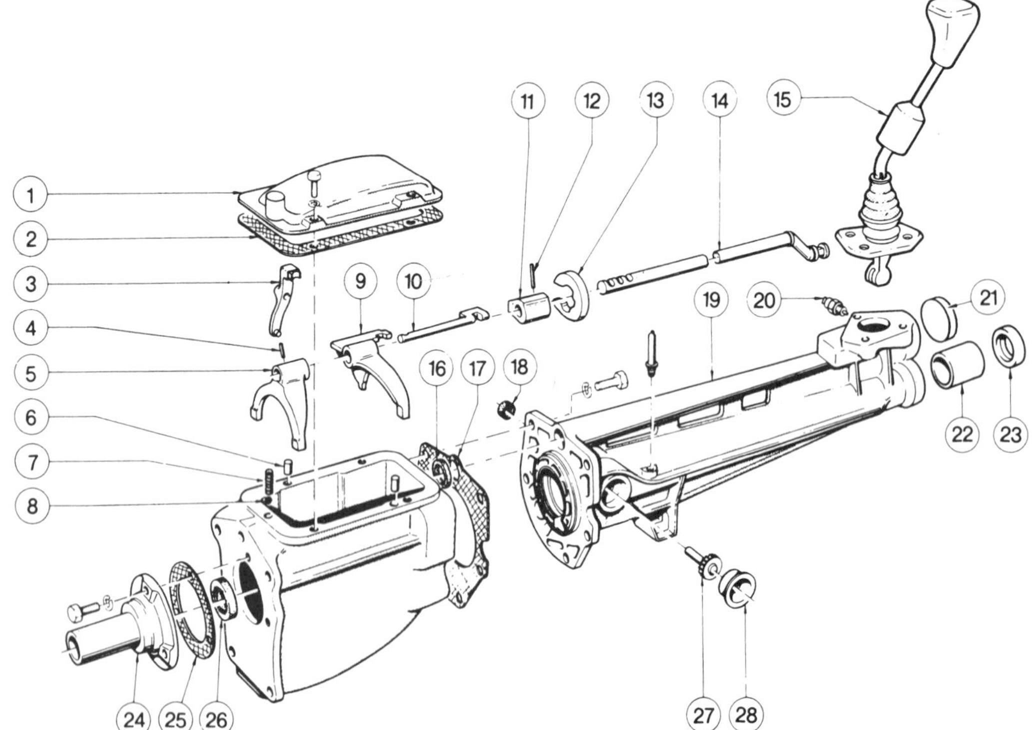

Fig 6.4 Exploded view of C type gearbox housings and selector mechanism (Sec 4)

1 *Cover*
2 *Gasket*
3 *Reverse gear relay lever*
4 *Roll pin*
5 *3rd/4th gear selector fork*
6 *Centring pin*
7 *Spring*
8 *Locking ball*
9 *1st/2nd gear selector fork*
10 *Selector fork connecting shaft*
11 *Selector boss*
12 *Roll pin*
13 *Selector locking plate*
14 *Selector shaft*
15 *Gear lever assembly*
16 *Oil seal*
17 *Gasket*
18 *Oil seal*
19 *Extension housing*
20 *Reversing light switch*
21 *Cover*
22 *Bush*
23 *Oil seal*
24 *Guide sleeve*
25 *Gasket*
26 *Oil seal*
27 *Speedometer drive pinion*
28 *Cover*

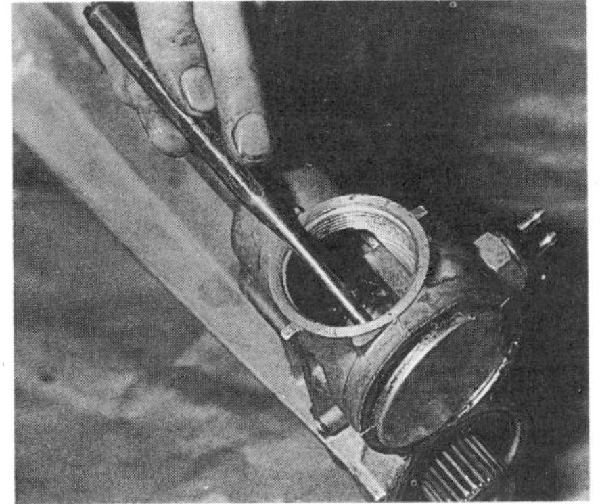

4.4 Tap out the extension housing rear cover

4.8 Extract the selector locking pin and spring

4.9 Extract the blanking plug from the rear of the gearbox casing

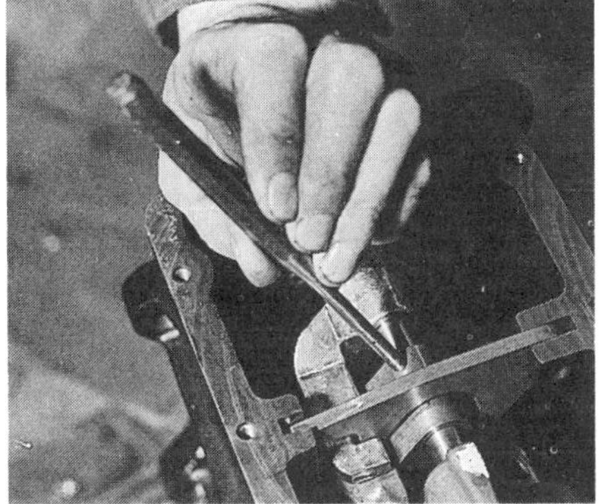

4.10A Drive the roll pin from the selector boss ...

4.10B ... and withdraw the selector shaft

4.11A Withdraw the selector locking plate and selector boss ...

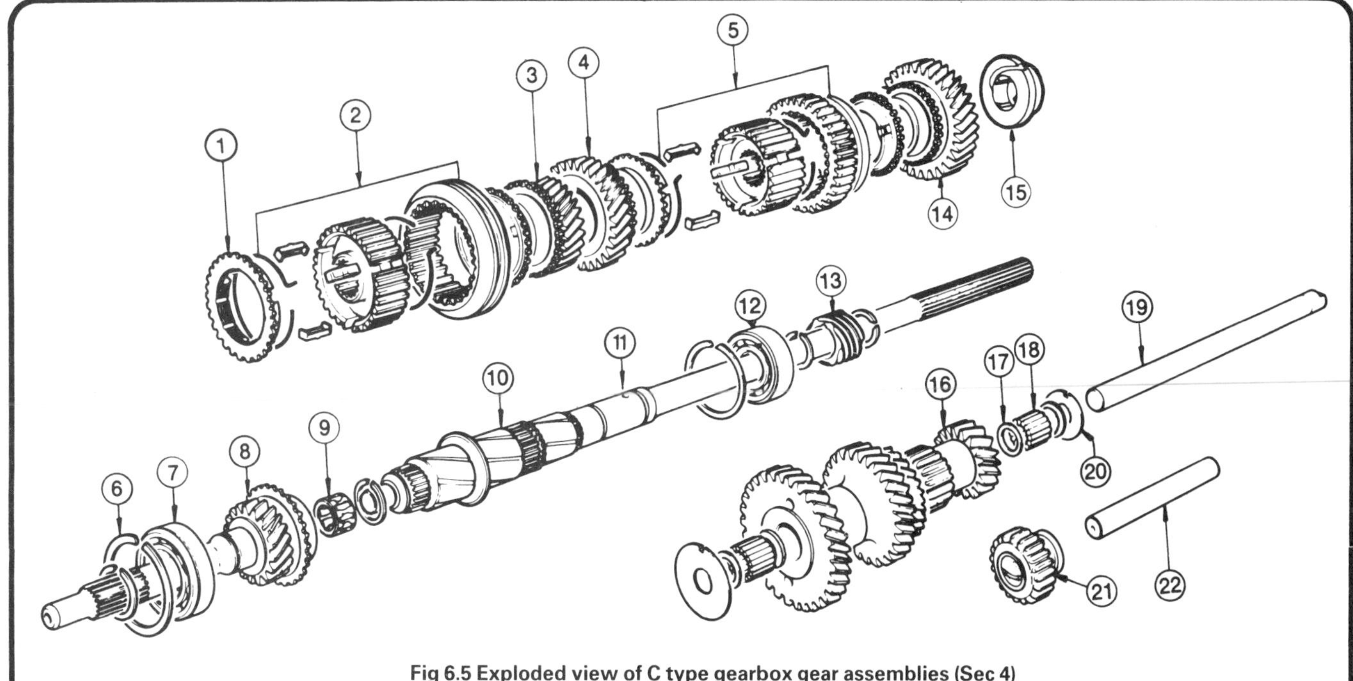

Fig 6.5 Exploded view of C type gearbox gear assemblies (Sec 4)

1 *Synchroniser ring*
2 *3rd/4th gear synchroniser unit*
3 *3rd gear*
4 *2nd gear*
5 *1st/2nd gear synchroniser unit*
6 *Circlip*
7 *Ball bearing*
8 *Input shaft*
9 *Needle roller bearing*
10 *Mainshaft*
11 *Locking ball*
12 *Ball bearing*
13 *Speedometer drivegear*
14 *1st gear*
15 *Oil scoop ring*
16 *Countershaft gear cluster*
17 *Spacer*
18 *Needle rollers*
19 *Countershaft*
20 *Thrustwasher*
21 *Reverse idler gear*
22 *Idler shaft*

4.11B ... and the selector forks

4.23 Remove the countershaft from the rear of the main casing

4.25 Withdraw the extension housing and mainshaft

4.27A Unscrew the bolts ...

4.27B ... and withdraw the clutch release bearing guide sleeve ...

4.27C ... and O-ring – B type gearbox

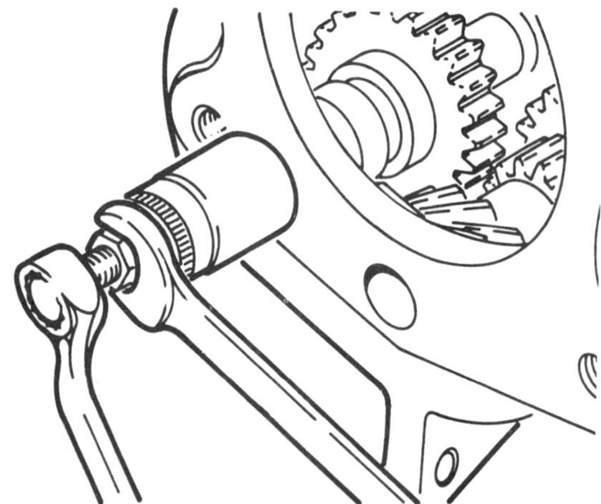
Fig 6.6 Method of removing the reverse gear idler shaft (Sec 4)

9 Extract the blanking plug from the rear of the gearbox casing and using a suitable drift through the hole, drive out the selector locking plate roll pin (photo).

10 Drive the roll pin from the selector boss then withdraw the selector shaft through the selector forks and out of the rear extension housing (photos).

11 Note the location of the components, then withdraw the selector locking plate and selector boss, and selector forks (photos).

12 Proceed to paragraph 21.

C type gearbox

13 Unscrew the bolts and remove the top cover and gasket, taking care not to lose the selector locking spring located in the front of the cover.

14 Extract the selector locking ball with a pen magnet or greased screwdriver.

15 Invert the gearbox and allow the oil to drain, then turn it upright again.

16 Using a suitable drift, drive the roll pin from the selector boss, but first move the selector shaft forward to prevent damage to 1st gear.

17 Withdraw the selector shaft from the rear extension housing, and remove the selector boss and locking plate.

18 Engage 2nd gear and press the reverse gear relay lever to the rear.

19 Note the location of the selector forks, then remove them together with the connecting shaft.

20 Drive out the roll pin and remove the forks from the connecting shaft.

All gearbox types

21 Unscrew the bolts securing the extension housing to the main gearbox casing.

22 Release the extension housing complete with mainshaft from the main casing, then turn the extension housing so that the cut-away reveals the countershaft.

23 Invert the gearbox and use a soft metal drift to tap the countershaft rearwards until it can be removed from the rear of the main casing (photo). Take care not to lose the needle roller bearings and spacers from inside the gear cluster, and the thrust washers at each end of the gear cluster.

24 Turn the gearbox upright and allow the countershaft gear cluster to move to the bottom of the main casing.

25 Withdraw the extension housing complete with mainshaft from the main casing (photo).

26 Remove the input shaft needle roller bearing from the end of the mainshaft or from the centre of the input shaft.

27 Unscrew the bolts and withdraw the clutch release bearing guide sleeve from the front of the main casing. Note that the cut-out on the sleeve faces to the bottom of the casing. Remove the O-ring (A and B type gearboxes) or gasket (type C gearbox) (photos).

28 Using a soft metal drift drive the input shaft and bearing from the casing. On A and B type gearboxes, drive the shaft forwards using the drift inside the casing. On the C type gearbox, extract the large circlip, then drive the assembly rearwards using the drift on the bearing outer race.

4.29 Remove the countershaft gear cluster

4.33 Withdraw the mainshaft from the extension housing

6.1 Extract the small circlip from the input shaft

29 Remove the countershaft gear cluster together with the thrust washers, keeping them identified for location (photo). Take care not to lose the needle roller bearings and spacers from inside the gear cluster.
30 Screw a suitable bolt into the end of the reverse gear idler shaft, and using a nut, washer and socket, pull out the idler shaft. Note the fitted position of the reverse idler gear, then remove it.
31 Extract the circlip, where applicable, and withdraw the reverse relay lever from the pivot pin. On the B type gearbox, also disengage the return spring.
32 Prise out the speedometer drivegear cover from the extension housing and withdraw the drive pinion.
33 Squeeze the ends of the mainshaft bearing circlip together and extract it from the extension housing. Using a soft-faced mallet, drive the mainshaft from the extension housing (photo).

5 Gearbox components (A, B and C types) – inspection

1 Thoroughly clean the interior of the gearbox, and check for dropped needle rollers and roll pins.
2 Carefully clean and then examine all the component parts for general wear, distortion, slackness of fit, and damage to machined faces and threads.
3 Examine the gears for excessive wear and chipping of the teeth. Renew them as necessary.
4 Examine the countershaft for signs of wear, where the needle rollers bear. If a small ridge can be felt at either end of the shaft, it will be necessary to renew it. Renew the thrustwashers at each end.
5 The four synchroniser rings should be renewed as a matter of course.
6 The needle roller bearing and cage, located between the nose of the mainshaft and the annulus in the rear of the input shaft, is also liable to wear, and should be renewed as a matter of course.
7 Examine the condition of the two ball bearing assemblies, one on the input shaft and one on the mainshaft. Check them for noisy operation, looseness between the inner and outer races, and for general wear. Normally they should be renewed on a gearbox that is being rebuilt.
8 If either of the synchroniser units is worn it will be necessary to buy a complete assembly, as the parts are not sold individually. Also check the blocker bars for wear.
9 Examine the ends of the selector forks where they rub against the channels in the periphery of the synchroniser units. If possible compare the selector forks with new units to help determine the wear that has occurred. Renew them if worn.
10 If the bearing bush in the extension housing is badly worn it is best to take the extension housing to your local Ford dealer to have the bearing pulled out and a new one fitted.
11 The oil seals in the extension housing and clutch release bearing guide sleeve should be renewed as a matter of course. Drive out the old seal with the aid of a drift or screwdriver. It will be found that the seal comes out quite easily. With a piece of wood or suitably sized tube to spread the load evenly, carefully tap a new seal into place, ensuring that it enters the bore squarely.

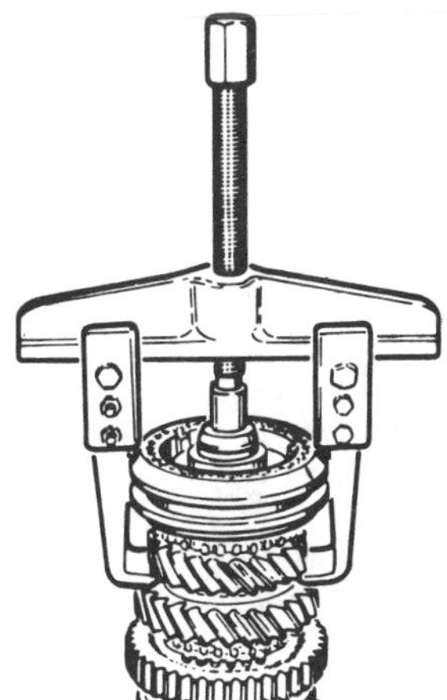
Fig 6.7 Using a two-legged puller to remove the 3rd gear and 3rd/4th gear synchroniser unit from the mainshaft (Sec 7)

6 Gearbox input shaft (A, B and C types) – dismantling and reassembly

1 Extract the small circlip from the input shaft (photo).
2 Locate the bearing outer track on top of an open vice, then using a soft-faced mallet, drive the input shaft down through the bearing.
3 Remove the bearing from the input shaft, noting that the circlip groove in the outer track is towards the front splined end of the shaft.
4 Place the input shaft on a block of wood and lightly grease the bearing location shoulder.
5 Locate the new bearing on the input shaft with the circlip groove facing the correct way, then using a metal tube on the inner track, drive the bearing fully home.
6 Refit the small circlip.

7 Gearbox mainshaft (A, B and C types) – dismantling and reassembly

Note: *A suitable puller will be required to pull the gears from the mainshaft*
1 Remove the 4th gear synchroniser ring from the 3rd/4th gear synchroniser unit.
2 Extract the circlip and slide the 3rd/4th gear synchroniser unit together with the 3rd gear from the front of the mainshaft, using a two-legged puller if necessary. Remove the 3rd gear synchroniser ring (photos).
3 Proceed as follows according to gearbox type.

A type gearbox

4 Extract the circlip retaining the mainshaft bearing, then using a suitable puller, remove the 1st gear complete with the mainshaft bearing and speedometer drivegear. Alternatively, support the 1st gear and press the mainshaft downwards.
5 Remove the 1st gear synchroniser ring from the 1st/2nd gear synchroniser unit.

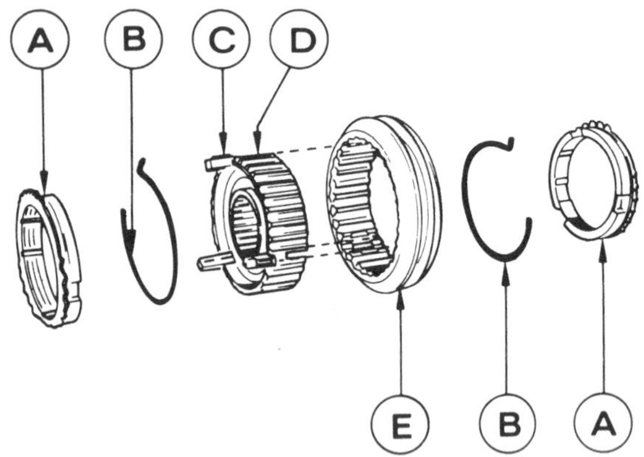

Fig 6.8 Exploded view of a synchroniser unit (Sec 7)

A Synchroniser ring
B Blocker bar springs
C Blocker bars
D Hub
E Sleeve

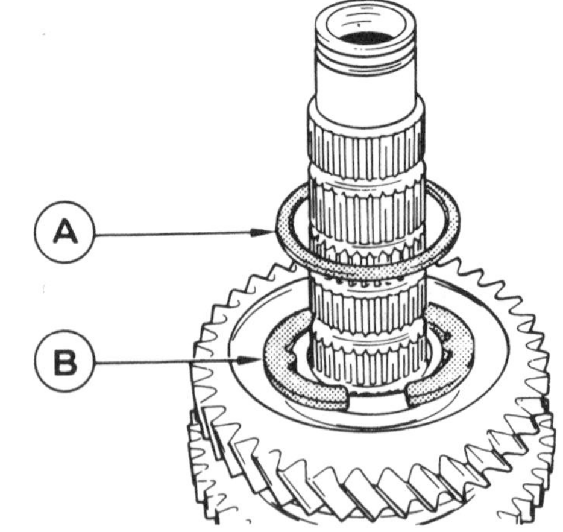

Fig 6.9 Thrustwasher retaining circlip (A) and thrustwasher halves (B) – B type gearbox (Sec 7)

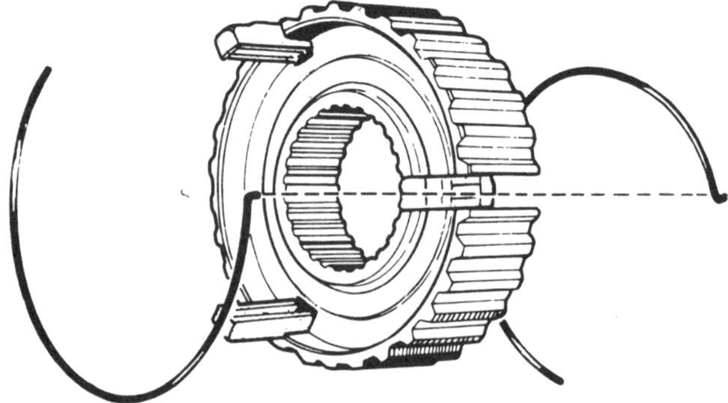
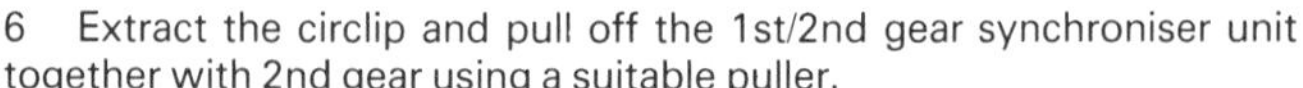

Fig 6.10 Correct orientation of synchroniser blocker bar springs (Sec 7)

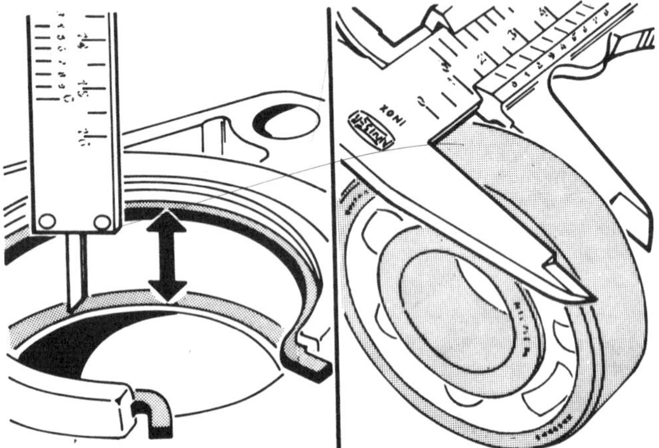

Fig 6.11 Measurements required to establish required thickness of mainshaft bearing retaining circlip (Sec 7)

6 Extract the circlip and pull off the 1st/2nd gear synchroniser unit together with 2nd gear using a suitable puller.

7 Separate the 2nd gear from the 1st/2nd gear synchroniser unit and remove the 2nd gear synchroniser ring.

8 If necessary the synchroniser units may be dismantled, but first mark each hub and sleeve in relation to each other. Slide the sleeve from the hub and remove the blocker bars and springs.

9 Proceed to paragraph 23.

B type gearbox

10 Extract the circlip retaining the 2nd gear, then extract the thrust-washer halves.

11 Slide the 2nd gear from the front of the mainshaft and remove the 2nd gear synchroniser ring and thrust ring where applicable (photo).

12 Mark the 1st/2nd gear synchroniser unit hub and sleeve in relation to each other and note the location of the selector fork groove. Slide the sleeve forward from the hub and remove the blocker bars and springs.

13 Extract the circlip retaining the mainshaft bearing, then using a suitable puller, remove 1st gear complete with the oil scoop ring, mainshaft bearing and speedometer drivegear (photo). Alternatively, support the 1st gear and press the mainshaft downwards.

14 Remove the 1st gear synchroniser ring.

15 If necessary the 3rd/4th gear synchroniser unit may be dismantled,

7.2A Extract the circlip ...

7.2B ... and remove the 3rd/4th gear synchroniser unit, 3rd gear synchroniser ring, and 3rd gear

7.11 Remove the 2nd gear and synchroniser ring

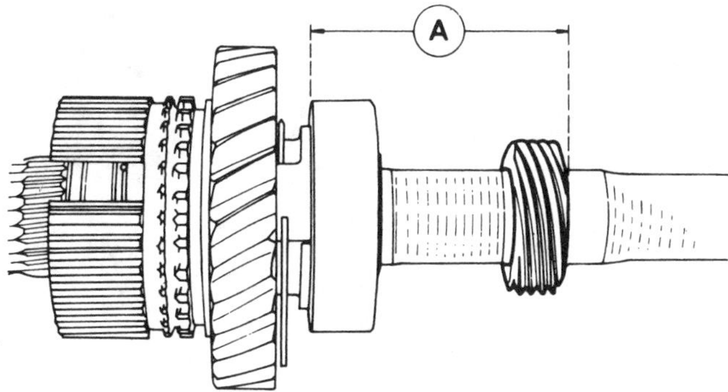

Fig 6.12 Speedometer drivegear fitting position (Sec 7)

A = 51.20 mm (2.02 in) for A type gearbox
A = 49.25 mm (1.94 in) for B type gearbox

but first mark the hub and sleeve in relation to each other. Slide the sleeve from the hub and remove the blocker bars and springs. Note that the 1st/2nd gear synchroniser hub cannot be removed from the mainshaft.
16 Proceed to paragraph 23.

C type gearbox

17 Extract the circlip and remove the speedometer drivegear and locking ball from the rear of the mainshaft.
18 Extract the circlip retaining the mainshaft bearing, then using a suitable puller remove the 1st gear complete with the oil scoop ring and mainshaft bearing. Alternatively, support the 1st gear and press the mainshaft downwards.
19 Remove the 1st gear synchroniser ring from the 1st/2nd gear synchroniser unit.
20 Extract the circlip and pull off the 1st/2nd gear synchroniser unit together with 2nd gear using a suitable puller.
21 Separate the 2nd gear from the 1st/2nd gear synchroniser unit and remove the 2nd gear synchroniser ring.
22 If necessary the synchroniser units may be dismantled, but first mark each hub and sleeve in relation to each other. Slide the sleeve from the hub and remove the blocker bars and springs.

All gearbox types

23 Clean all the components in paraffin, wipe dry and examine them for wear and damage. Obtain new components as necessary. During reassembly lubricate the components with the specified type of gearbox oil, and where new parts are being fitted, lightly grease the contact surfaces.
24 Commence reassembly by assembling the synchroniser units. Slide the sleeves on the hubs in their previously noted positions, then insert the blocker bars and fit the springs as shown in Fig. 6.10.
25 Continue reassembly as follows according to gearbox type.

A type gearbox

26 Slide the 2nd gear onto the rear of the mainshaft and locate the synchroniser ring on the gear cone. Fit the circlip and thrustwasher if applicable.
27 Locate the 1st/2nd gear synchroniser unit on the mainshaft splines with the selector fork groove to the rear. Tap the unit fully home using a metal tube, then fit the circlip if applicable.
28 Fit the 1st gear synchroniser ring to the 1st/2nd gear synchroniser unit with the blocker bars located in the slots.
29 Slide the 1st gear onto the mainshaft.
30 If a new mainshaft bearing or extension housing is being fitted, the required thickness of the bearing retaining circlip in the extension housing must be determined at this stage. Using vernier calipers, measure the width of the bearing outer track (B), then measure the total width of the bearing location in the extension housing (A) – the difference (ie A minus B) represents the required thickness of the retaining circlip. Dimension A can be obtained by fitting the existing circlip, and pushing it until it is flush with the upper shoulder of its groove in the extension housing. Measure the distance between the bottom shoulder of the bearing recess, and the upper face of the circlip – see Fig. 6.11. Obtain a circlip of the correct thickness from your local Ford dealer.
31 Fit the small circlip if applicable, then loosely locate the bearing retaining circlip as determined from paragraph 30 on the mainshaft.
32 Smear a little grease on the mainshaft, then fit the bearing and drive it fully home using a metal tube on the inner track. Fit the circlip.
33 Locate the speedometer drivegear on the mainshaft and use a metal tube to tap it into the position shown in Fig. 6.12.
34 Proceed to paragraph 49.

B type gearbox

35 Fit the 1st gear synchroniser ring to the 1st/2nd gear synchroniser unit with the blocker bars located in the slots.
36 Slide the 1st gear and oil scoop ring (with the oil groove towards 1st gear) onto the mainshaft.
37 If a new mainshaft bearing or extension housing is being fitted, determine the required thickness of the bearing retaining circlip, as described in paragraph 30, then locate it loosely on the mainshaft.
38 Smear a little grease on the mainshaft, then fit the bearing and drive it fully home using a metal tube on the inner track. Fit the circlip.
39 Locate the speedometer drivegear on the mainshaft and use a metal tube to tap it into the position shown in Fig. 6.12.
40 Fit the 2nd gear synchroniser ring to the 1st/2nd gear synchroniser unit with the blocker bars located in the slots. Fit the thrust ring where applicable.
41 Slide the 2nd gear onto the front of the mainshaft and retain with the thrustwasher halves and circlip.
42 Proceed to paragraph 49.

C type gearbox

43 Slide the 2nd gear onto the rear of the mainshaft and locate the synchroniser ring on the gear cone.
44 Locate the 1st/2nd gear synchroniser unit on the mainshaft splines with the selector fork groove to the rear. Tap the unit fully home using a metal tube, then fit the circlip.
45 Fit the 1st gear synchroniser ring to the 1st/2nd gear synchroniser unit with the blocker bars located in the slots.
46 Slide the 1st gear and oil scoop ring (with the oil groove towards 1st gear) onto the mainshaft.
47 If a new mainshaft bearing or extension housing is being fitted, determine the required thickness of the bearing retaining circlip, as described in paragraph 30, then locate it loosely on the mainshaft.
48 Smear a little grease on the mainshaft, then fit the bearing and drive it fully home using a metal tube on the inner track. Fit the circlip.
49 Insert the locking ball in the mainshaft detent, then slide on the speedometer drivegear and secure with the circlip.

All gearbox types

50 Slide the 3rd gear onto the front of the mainshaft, then locate the synchroniser ring on the gear cone.
51 Locate the 3rd/4th gear synchroniser unit on the mainshaft splines with the long side of the hub facing the front. Tap the unit fully home using a metal tube, then fit the circlip. Make sure that the slots in the 3rd gear synchroniser ring are aligned with the blocker bars as the synchroniser unit is being fitted.
52 Fit the 4th gear synchroniser ring to the 3rd/4th gear synchroniser unit with the blocker bars located in the slots.

8 Gearbox (A, B and C types) – reassembly

1 Immerse the extension housing in hot water for several minutes, then remove it, quickly insert the mainshaft, and push the bearing fully home. If necessary place the extension housing on the edge of the bench and use a soft-faced mallet to drive the mainshaft home (photo).
2 Using long nose pliers and a screwdriver, refit the bearing circlip (photo).
3 Apply a little grease to the extension housing mating face and fit a new gasket (photo).
4 Insert the speedometer drive pinion in the extension housing, smear a little sealer on the cover, then tap the cover into the housing.
5 Fit the reverse relay lever (and return spring on the B type gearbox) onto the pivot pin in the main casing, and, where applicable, fit the circlip.
6 Position the reverse idler gear in the main casing with the long shoulder facing the rear and engaged with the relay lever. Slide in the idler shaft and tap fully home with a soft-faced mallet.

7.13 Extract the circlip retaining the mainshaft bearing

8.1 Drive the mainshaft home with a soft-faced mallet

8.2 Fit the bearing circlip using long nose pliers and a screwdriver

8.3 Fit a new gasket to the extension housing

8.7 Fit the outer spacer to the countershaft gear cluster needle rollers

7 Smear grease inside the ends of the countershaft gear cluster, then fit the spacers and needle roller bearings (photo). If the needle rollers are being renewed, make sure that all the rollers at any one end of the gear cluster come from the same pack. Do not mix old and new needle rollers, or rollers from different packs. On the type A gearbox there are 21 needle rollers at each end with identical spacers either side of the rollers. On the type B gearbox there is a central spacer tube with thin spacers either side followed by 19 needle rollers and thick spacers on each side. Note that the long needle rollers must be fitted to the rear of the gear cluster. On the type C gearbox there are 20 needle rollers at each end with identical spacers either side of the rollers. Make sure that there is sufficient grease to hold the needle rollers in position during the subsequent operation, and if available, fit a dummy shaft of a length slightly less than the gear cluster.

8 Stick the thrustwashers on the inner faces of the main casing with the location tabs correctly positioned.

9 Lower the gear cluster to the bottom of the main casing, keeping the thrustwashers in position.

10 Insert the input shaft fully into the main casing, using a soft metal drift if necessary. On the C type gearbox, refit the large circlip.

11 Fit the clutch release bearing guide sleeve together with a new O-ring (A and B type gearboxes) or gasket (C type gearbox). Check that the cut-out on the sleeve faces the bottom of the casing, then apply sealer to the bolt threads. Insert the bolts, and tighten to the specified torque in diagonal sequence.

12 Oil the needle roller bearing and locate it in the centre of the input shaft.

13 Insert the mainshaft together with the extension housing into the main casing, so that the front of the mainshaft enters the needle roller bearing in the centre of the input shaft. Turn the extension housing so that the cut-away reveals the countershaft bore.

14 While keeping the thrustwashers in place, invert the gearbox so that the countershaft gear cluster meshes with the mainshaft and input shaft.

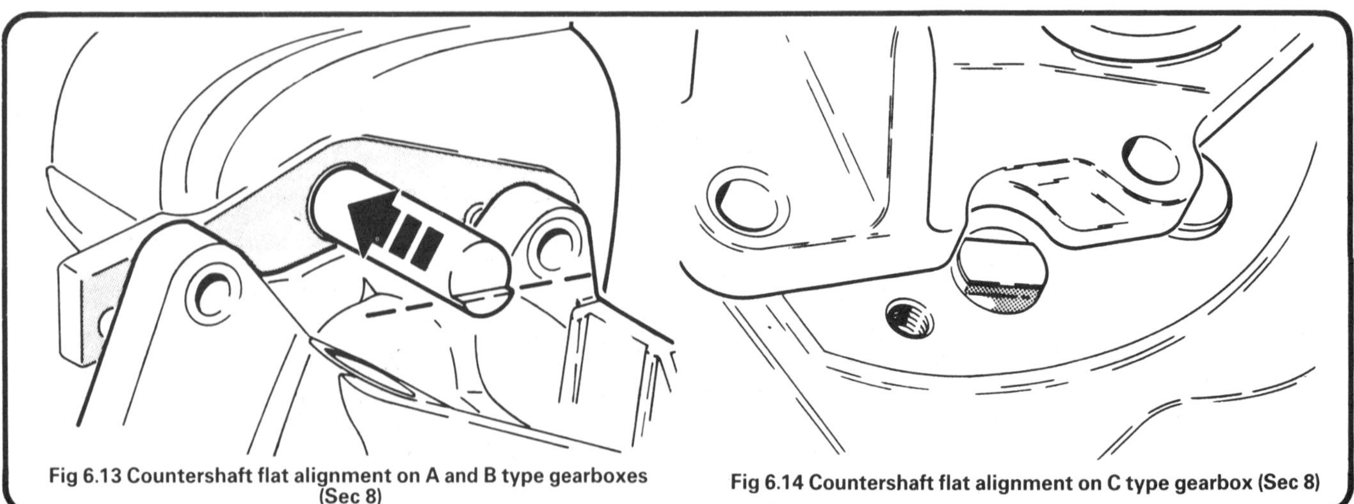

Fig 6.13 Countershaft flat alignment on A and B type gearboxes (Sec 8)

Fig 6.14 Countershaft flat alignment on C type gearbox (Sec 8)

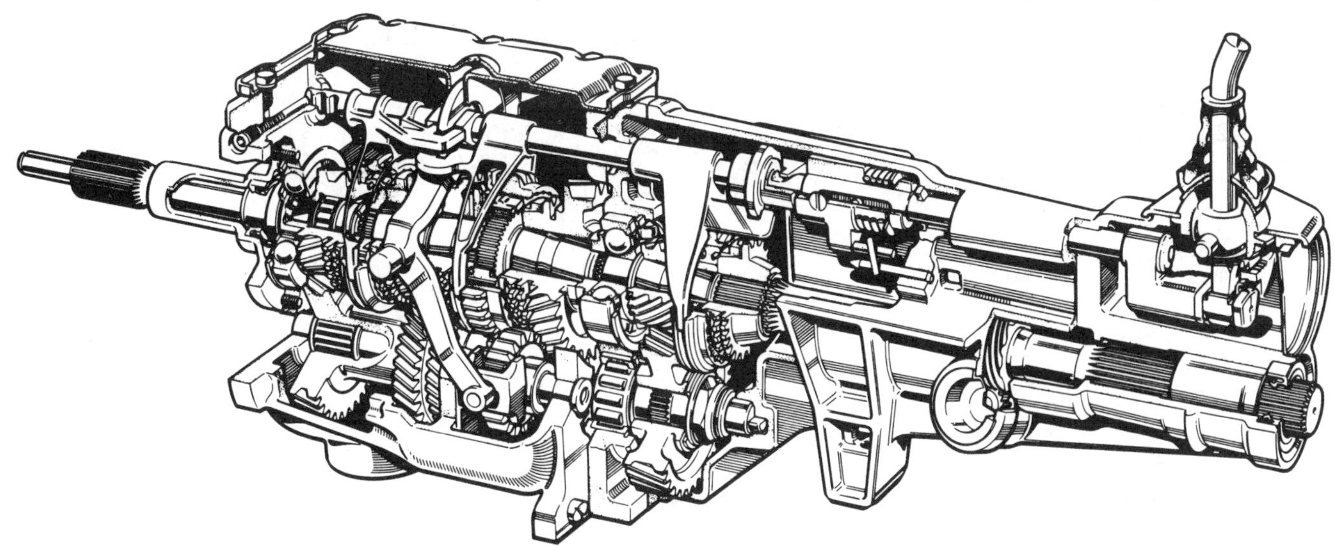

Fig 6.15 Cutaway view of N type gearbox (Sec 9)

15 Line up the thrustwashers and insert the countershaft from the rear of the main casing. Using a soft metal drift, drive the countershaft into the main casing until flush. The flat on the rear end of the countershaft must be horizontal (Figs. 6.13 and 6.14).
16 Fully insert the extension housing and make sure that the 4th gear synchroniser ring is correctly aligned with the synchroniser unit.
17 Apply sealer to the bolt threads, then insert the bolts and tighten to the specified torque in diagonal sequence.
18 Proceed as follows according to gearbox type.

A and B type gearboxes

19 Locate the selector locking plate in the main casing and retain with the roll pin.
20 Coat a new blanking plug with sealer and tap it into the rear of the casing.
21 Fit the selector forks and selector boss, then insert the selector shaft from the rear and guide it through the selector components.
22 Align the holes, then drive the roll pin into the selector boss and selector shaft.
23 Insert the selector locking pin and spring, apply sealer to the plug threads, then insert and tighten the plug.
24 Fit the gearbox top cover together with a new gasket, and tighten the bolts to the specified torque in diagonal sequence.
25 Proceed to paragraph 34.

C type gearbox

26 Assemble the selector forks to the connecting shaft, then align the holes and drive the roll pin into the 3rd/4th gear selector fork and shaft.
27 Engage 2nd gear and press the reverse gear relay lever to the rear.
28 Fit the selector forks to their respective synchroniser units.
29 Lightly grease the selector shaft, then insert it into the rear extension housing. Hold the selector boss and locking plate in position, and guide the selector shaft through the selector components. Note that the roll pin hole in the selector boss must face to the rear.
30 Align the holes, then drive the roll pin into the selector boss and selector shaft until it is about 1.0 mm (0.04 in) below the surface.
31 Insert the selector locking ball in the main casing.
32 Grease the selector locking spring and locate it in the top cover.
33 Fit the gearbox top cover together with a new gasket, and tighten the bolts to the specified torque in diagonal sequence.

All gearbox types

34 Fit the extension housing rear cover using a little sealer, and stake it in several places to secure.
35 Where applicable fit the clutch housing to the front of the gearbox, apply sealer to the bolt threads, then insert the bolts and tighten them to the specified torque in diagonal sequence.
36 Fit the clutch release bearing and arm with reference to Chapter 5.

9 Gearbox (N type) – dismantling into major assemblies

Note: *A suitable puller and socket will be required to pull the 5th driving gear from the countershaft gear cluster*

1 Clean the exterior of the gearbox with paraffin and wipe dry.
2 Remove the clutch release bearing and arm with reference to Chapter 5.
3 Unscrew and remove the reversing lamp switch (photo).
4 Unbolt the clutch housing from the front of the gearbox. Remove the gasket (photos).
5 Unscrew the bolts and withdraw the clutch release bearing guide sleeve and gasket from the front of the gearbox (photos).

9.3 Remove the reversing lamp switch

9.4A Unscrew the securing bolts (arrowed) ...

9.4B ... and remove the clutch bellhousing

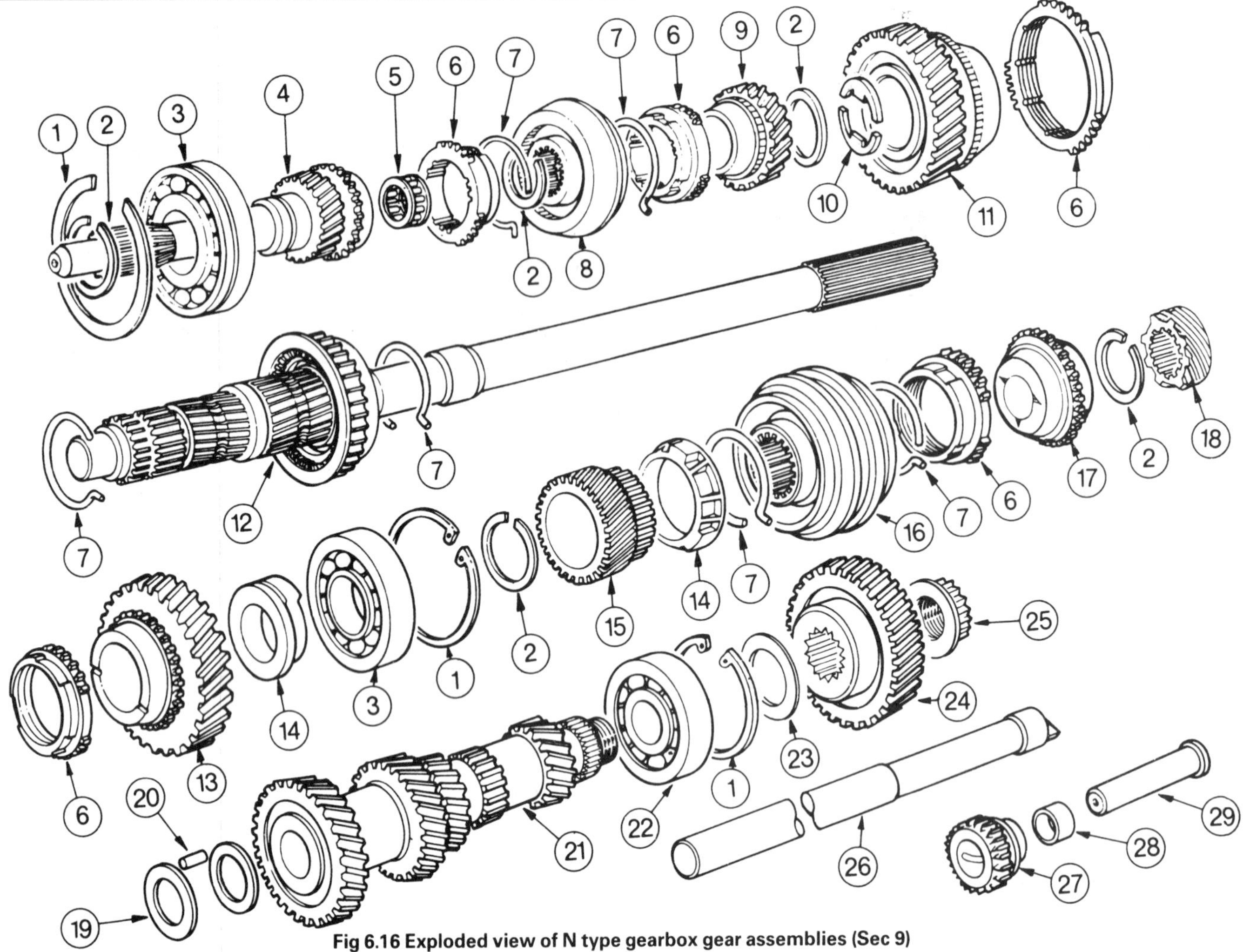

Fig 6.16 Exploded view of N type gearbox gear assemblies (Sec 9)

1 *Circlip*
2 *Circlip*
3 *Ball bearing*
4 *Input shaft*
5 *Needle roller bearing*
6 *Synchroniser rings*
7 *Blocker bar springs*
8 *3rd/4th gear synchroniser unit*
9 *3rd gear*
10 *Thrust half washer*
11 *2nd gear*
12 *Mainshaft with synchroniser unit*
13 *1st gear*
14 *Oil scoop ring*
15 *5th driven gear*
16 *5th gear synchroniser unit*
17 *5th gear synchroniser hub*
18 *Speedometer drivegear*
19 *Spacer*
20 *Needle rollers*
21 *Countershaft gear cluster*
22 *Roller bearing*
23 *Washer*
24 *5th driving gear*
25 *12 sided nut*
26 *Countershaft*
27 *Reverse idler gear*
28 *Bush*
29 *Idler shaft*

6 Unscrew the bolts and remove the top cover and gasket (photos).
7 Invert the gearbox and allow the oil to drain, then turn it upright again.
8 Unscrew the bolts and lift the 5th gear locking plate from the extension housing (photo).
9 Extract the 5th gear locking spring and pin from the extension housing, using a pen magnet if necessary (photos).
10 Working through the gear lever aperture, use a screwdriver or small drift to tap out the extension housing rear cover (photo).
11 Select reverse gear and pull the selector shaft fully to the rear. Support the shaft with a piece of wood, then drive out the roll pin and withdraw the connector from the rear of the shaft (photos).
12 Unbolt and remove the extension housing from the rear of the gearbox. If necessary, tap the housing with a soft-faced mallet to release it from the dowels. Remove the gasket (photos).
13 Prise the cover from the extension housing and withdraw the speedometer drivegear (photo).
14 Select neutral, then using an Allen key, unscrew the selector locking mechanism plug from the side of the main casing. Extract the spring and locking pin, if necessary using a pen magnet (photos).
15 Drive the roll pin from the selector boss and selector shaft.
16 If necessary, the selector shaft centralising spring and 5th gear locking control may be removed. Using a small screwdriver, push out the plug and pin and slide the control from the selector shaft (photos).
17 Note the location of the selector components, then withdraw the selector shaft from the rear of the gearbox and remove the selector boss and locking plate, 1st/2nd gear and 3rd/4th gear selector forks, and 5th gear interlock sleeve and selector fork. Note that the roll pin hole in the selector boss is towards the front (photos).
18 Extract the circlip and pull the 5th gear synchroniser unit from the main casing, leaving it loose on the mainshaft (photos).
19 Slide the 5th driven gear from the synchroniser unit hub (photo).
20 Select 3rd gear and either 1st or 2nd gear by pushing the respective synchroniser sleeves – this will lock the mainshaft and countershaft gear cluster.
21 Unscrew and remove the 5th driving gear retaining nut while an assistant holds the gearbox stationary (photo). The nut is tightened to a high torque setting, and an additional extension bar may be required.
22 Remove the washer and pull the 5th driving gear from the countershaft gear cluster using a two-legged puller and socket in contact with the cluster. Remove the spacer ring (photos). Select neutral.
23 Extract the circlip retaining the countershaft gear cluster bearing in the intermediate housing (photo).
24 Using a soft-faced mallet, tap the intermediate housing free of the

9.5A Withdraw the clutch release bearing guide sleeve ...

9.5B ... and gasket

9.6A Unscrew the securing bolts ...

9.6B ... and remove the top cover ...

9.6C ... and gasket

9.8 Lift the 5th gear locking plate from the extension housing

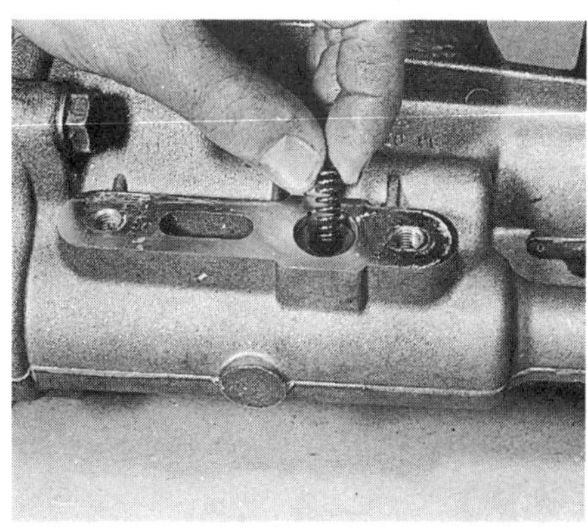
9.9A Extract the 5th gear locking spring ...

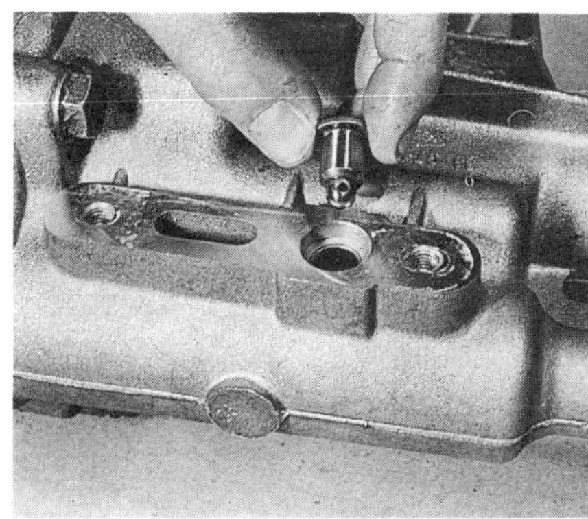
9.9B ... and pin

9.10 Tap out the extension housing rear cover

9.11A Drive out the roll pin ...

9.11B ... and withdraw the selector shaft connector

9.12A Remove the extension housing ...

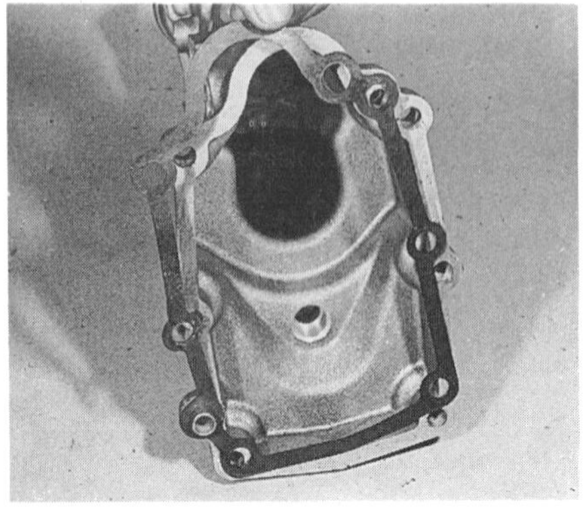
9.12B ... and gasket

9.13 Withdraw the speedometer drivegear

9.14A Unscrew the plug ...

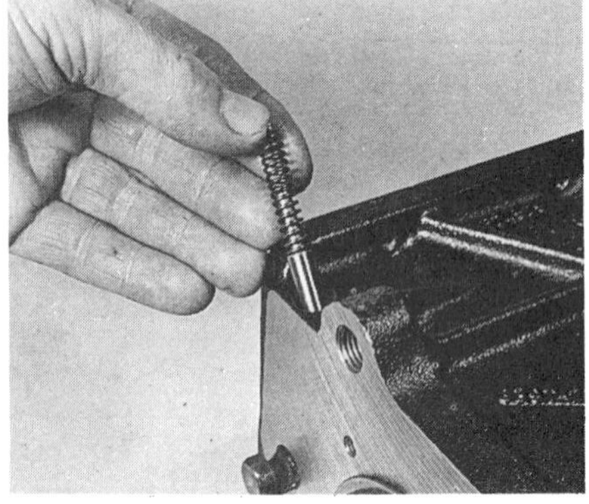
9.14B ... and extract the selector locking spring and pin

9.16A Use a screwdriver ...

9.16B ... to push out the plug ...

9.16C ... and pin

9.17A Remove the selector boss and locking plate ...

9.17B ... 1st/2nd gear selector fork ...

9.17C ... 3rd/4th gear selector fork ...

9.17D ... 5th gear interlock sleeve ...

9.17E ... and 5th gear selector fork

9.18A Extract the circlip ...

9.18B ... and remove the 5th gear synchroniser dog hub ...

9.18C ... and 5th gear synchroniser unit

9.19 Slide the 5th driven gear from the synchroniser unit hub

9.21 Remove the 5th driving gear retaining nut

9.22A Remove the washer ...

9.22B ... and pull the 5th driving gear from the countershaft gear cluster

9.22C Remove the 5th driving gear ...

9.22D ... and the spacer ring

main casing, and pull the intermediate housing rearwards as far as possible. Using a screwdriver inserted between the intermediate housing and main casing, prise the bearing from the shoulder on the countershaft gear cluster and remove it from the intermediate housing (photo).

25 Using a soft metal drift from the front of the main casing, drive the countershaft rearwards sufficiently to allow the gear cluster to be lowered to the bottom of the casing. Take care not to lose the needle roller bearings and spacers from inside the gear cluster.

26 Ease the input shaft from the front of the casing, if necessary using a small drift inside the gearbox to move the bearing slightly forwards, then using levers beneath the large bearing circlip (photo).

27 Remove the 4th gear synchroniser ring. Remove the input shaft needle roller bearing from the end of the mainshaft, or from the centre of the input shaft (photos).

28 Remove the mainshaft and intermediate housing from the main casing. Remove the gasket (photos).

29 Withdraw the countershaft and gear cluster from the main casing (photo).

30 Insert a suitable bolt into the reverse gear idler shaft, and using a nut, washer and socket, pull out the idler shaft. Note the fitted position of the reverse idler gear, then remove it (photos).

31 Remove the guide from the reverse relay lever, then extract the circlip and remove the relay lever from the pivot (photo).

32 Remove the magnetic disc from the bottom of the main casing. Also remove any needle rollers which may have been displaced from the countershaft gear cluster (photo).

10 Gearbox components (N type) – inspection

The procedure is basically as given in Section 5, however there are five synchroniser rings, no countershaft gear cluster thrustwashers, two ball bearings and one roller bearing.

9.23 Extract the countershaft gear cluster retaining circlip

9.24 Prise the bearing from the shoulder on the countershaft gear cluster

9.26 Remove the input shaft

9.27A Remove the 4th gear synchroniser ring

9.27B Remove the input shaft needle roller bearing

9.28A Remove the mainshaft and intermediate housing ...

9.28B ... and the gasket

9.29 Withdraw the countershaft and gear cluster

9.30A Use a bolt, nut, washer and socket to pull out the reverse gear idler shaft

9.30B Remove the reverse idler gear

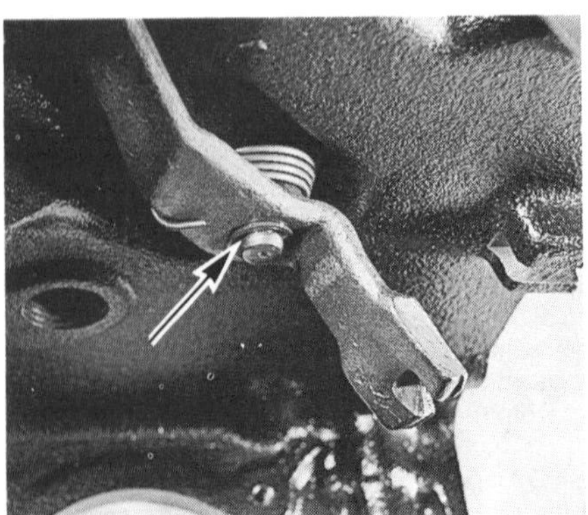
9.31 Extract the circlip (arrowed) and remove the reverse relay lever

9.32 Magnetic disc location in bottom of main casing

12.1A Extract the circlip ...

12.1B ... and remove the 3rd/4th synchroniser unit and ring ...

12.1C ... and 3rd gear

11 Gearbox input shaft (N type) – dismantling and reassembly

The procedure is identical to that described in Section 6.

12 Gearbox mainshaft (N type) – dismantling and reassembly

Note: *A suitable puller will be required to pull the speedometer drivegear from the mainshaft*

1 Extract the circlip and slide the 3rd/4th gear synchroniser unit together with the 3rd gear from the front of the mainshaft, using a two-legged puller if necessary. Separate the gear and unit and remove the 3rd gear synchroniser ring (photos).

2 Remove the outer circlip from the 2nd gear, then extract the thrustwasher halves (photos).

3 Slide the 2nd gear from the front of the mainshaft and remove the 2nd gear synchroniser ring (photos).

4 Mark the 1st/2nd gear synchroniser unit hub and sleeve in relation to each other, and note the location of the selector fork groove, then slide the sleeve forward from the hub and remove the blocker bars and springs. Note that the synchroniser hub cannot be removed from the mainshaft (photos).

5 Using a suitable puller, pull the speedometer drivegear off the rear of the mainshaft (photo).

6 Extract the circlip, then remove the 5th gear synchroniser unit and 5th driven gear from the mainshaft.

7 Extract the small circlip retaining the mainshaft bearing, then support the intermediate housing on blocks of wood and drive the mainshaft through the bearing with a soft-faced mallet (photos).

8 Remove the oil scoop ring, 1st gear, and 1st gear synchroniser ring (photo).

9 If required, extract the large retaining circlip and drive the ball bearing from the intermediate housing using a metal tube on the bearing outer track (photo). The synchroniser units may be dismantled,

12.2A Remove the outer circlip ...

12.2B ... and extract the thrustwasher halves

12.3A Remove the 2nd gear ...

12.3B ... and synchroniser ring

12.4A Remove the 1st/2nd gear synchroniser sleeve ...

12.4B ... and blocker bars

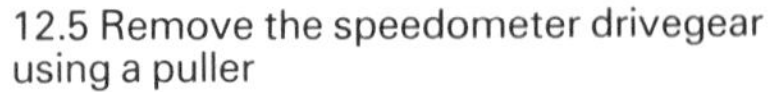

12.5 Remove the speedometer drivegear using a puller

12.7A Extract the small circlip ...

12.7B ... then drive the mainshaft through the bearing

but first mark each hub and sleeve in relation to one another. Slide the sleeve from the hub and remove the blocker bars and springs.

10 Clean all the components in paraffin, wipe dry and examine them for wear and damage. Obtain new components as necessary. During reassembly lubricate the components with the specified type of gearbox oil and where new parts are being fitted lightly grease the contact surfaces.

11 Commence reassembly by assembling the synchroniser units. Slide the sleeves on the hubs in their previously noted positions, then insert the blocker bars and fit the springs as shown in Fig. 6.10.

12 Where applicable, support the intermediate housing, then, using a metal tube on the outer track, drive in the new bearing and fit the large retaining circlip.

13 Fit the blocker bar spring to the rear of the 1st/2nd gear synchroniser hub, followed by the 1st gear synchroniser ring (photo).

14 Slide the 1st gear and oil scoop ring (with the oil groove towards 1st gear) onto the mainshaft.

15 Using a metal tube on the mainshaft bearing inner track, drive the intermediate housing onto the mainshaft and fit the small circlip. Make sure that the large bearing retaining circlip is towards the rear of the mainshaft.

16 Locate the 5th driven gear and 5th gear synchroniser with circlip, loose on the mainshaft. Tap the speedometer drivegear lightly onto its shoulder – its final position will be determined later.

17 Fit the 1st/2nd gear synchroniser sleeve to the hub in its previously noted position, with the selector groove facing forward, then insert the blocker bars and fit the springs as shown in Fig. 6.10.

18 Fit the 2nd gear synchroniser ring to the 1st/2nd synchroniser unit with the blocker bars located in the slots.

19 Slide the 2nd gear onto the front of the mainshaft and retain with the thrustwasher halves and outer circlip (photo).

20 Slide the 3rd gear onto the front of the mainshaft, then locate the synchroniser ring on the gear cone.

21 Locate the 3rd/4th gear synchroniser unit on the mainshaft splines with the long side of the hub facing the front (photo). Tap the unit fully home using a metal tube, then fit the circlip. Make sure that the slots in the 3rd gear synchroniser ring are aligned with the blocker bars as the synchroniser unit is being fitted.

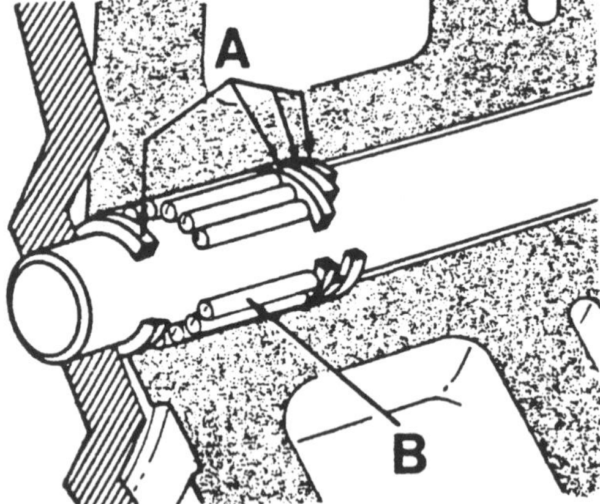

Fig 6.17 Needle roller (B) and spacer (A) arrangement when reassembling early N type gearbox (Sec 13)

13 Gearbox (N type) – reassembly

1 Locate the magnetic disc in the bottom of the main casing.

2 Fit the reverse relay lever onto the pivot and retain with the circlip. Fit the guide to the lever.

3 Position the reverse idler gear in the main casing with the long shoulder facing the rear and engaged with the relay lever. Slide in the idler shaft and tap fully home with a soft-faced mallet.

4 Smear grease inside the end of the countershaft gear cluster, then fit the spacers and needle roller bearings – there are 21 needle rollers. If the needle rollers are being renewed, make sure that all the rollers at any one end of the gear cluster come from the same pack. Do not mix old and new needle rollers, or rollers from different packs. On early models, the countershaft bearing bore was 33.0 mm long; on later models it is 27.75 mm long, and the needle rollers are correspondingly shorter. When rebuilding an early gearbox, use the newer shorter rollers, and insert two extra spacers behind them – see Fig. 6.17. Make sure that

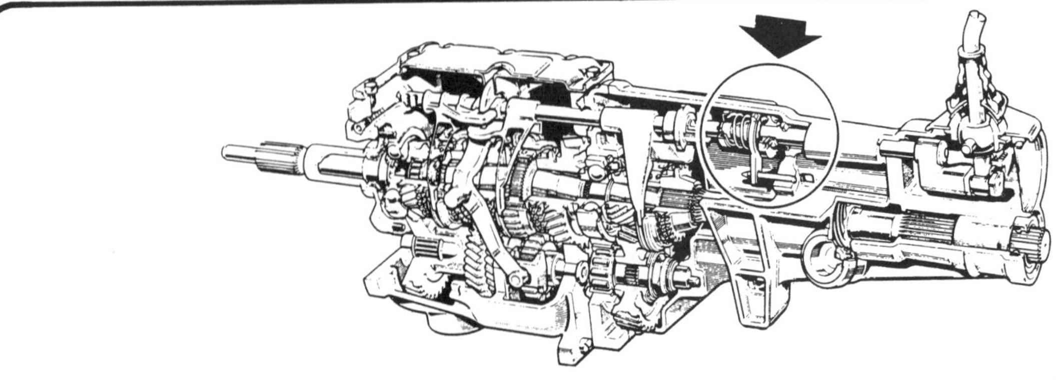

Fig 6.18 Modified selector locking control components (arrowed) – later N type gearbox (Sec 13)

12.8 Remove the oil scoop ring

12.9 Extract the large bearing retaining circlip

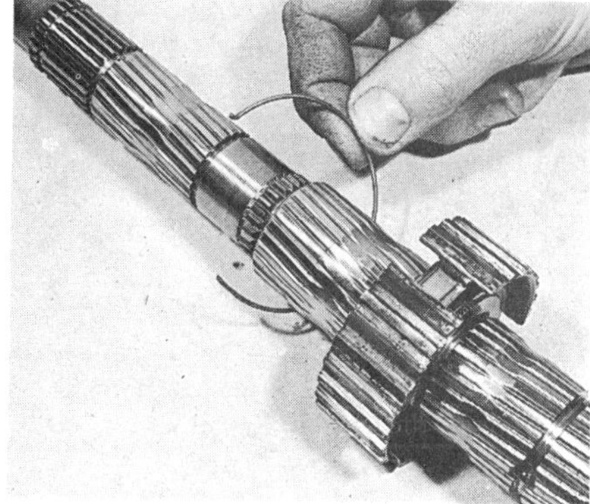
12.13 Fit the blocker bar spring to the rear of the 1st/2nd gear synchroniser hub

12.19 Locating hole (arrowed) for 2nd gear thrustwasher halves

12.21 Locate the 3rd/4th gear synchroniser unit on the mainshaft splines

13.4A Insert the rear spacers in the countershaft gear cluster ...

13.4B ... followed by the needle rollers ...

13.4C ... and the front spacers

13.8 Fit the input shaft needle roller bearing

there is sufficient grease to hold the needle rollers in position during the subsequent operation (photos).

5 Insert the countershaft in the gear cluster until the front end is flush with the front gear on the cluster.

6 Locate the countershaft and gear cluster in the bottom of the main casing.

7 Position a new gasket on the main casing, then fit the mainshaft and intermediate housing, and temporarily secure with two bolts.

8 Fit the input shaft needle roller bearing to the end of the mainshaft, or in the centre of the input shaft (photo).

9 Fit the 4th gear synchroniser ring to the 3rd/4th gear synchroniser unit with the cut-outs over the blocker bars, then fit the input shaft assembly and tap the bearing fully into the casing up to the retaining circlip (photo).

10 Invert the gearbox so that the countershaft gear cluster meshes with the input shaft and mainshaft gears.

11 Using a soft metal drift, drive the countershaft into the main casing until flush at the front face – the flat on the rear end of the countershaft must be horizontal (photo).

12 Using a metal tube, tap the countershaft gear cluster bearing into the intermediate housing and secure with the circlip (photo).

13 Fit the spacer ring then, using a metal tube, tap the 5th driving gear onto the splines of the countershaft gear cluster.

14 Fit the thrustwasher and retaining nut. Select 3rd gear and either 1st or 2nd gear by pushing the respective synchroniser sleeves. While an assistant holds the gearbox stationary, tighten the nut to the specified torque, then lock it by peening the collar on the nut into the slot in the gear cluster (photos).

15 Select neutral, then slide the 5th driven gear into mesh with the driving gear.

16 Slide the 5th gear synchroniser unit complete with spacer onto the 5th driven gear. Using a metal tube, drive the dog hub and 5th gear synchroniser ring onto the mainshaft splines while guiding the synchroniser ring onto the blocker bars. Fit the circlip (photos).

17 Tap the speedometer drivegear into its correct position on the mainshaft – the distance between the gear and the 5th gear dog hub circlip should be 123.0 to 124.0 mm (4.8 to 4.9 in) (photo).

18 Locate the 5th gear selector fork in its synchroniser sleeve and locate the interlock sleeve in the groove (short shoulder to front), then insert the selector shaft through the sleeve and selector fork into the main casing.

19 Locate the 1st/2nd gear and 3rd/4th gear selector forks in their

13.9 Fit the input shaft

13.11 Flat on rear end of countershaft must be horizontal before driving into main casing

13.12 Fit the countershaft gear cluster bearing

13.14A Tighten the 5th driving gear nut ...

13.14B ... then peen the collar on the nut into the slot in the gear cluster

13.16A Fit the spacer to the 5th gear synchroniser unit

13.16B Fit the 5th gear synchroniser unit ...

13.16C ... followed by the synchroniser ring and dog hub ...

13.16D ... and the circlip

13.17 Check the distance between the circlip and the speedometer drivegear

13.21 Drive the roll pin into the selector boss and selector shaft

13.23 Fit the speedometer drivegear cover

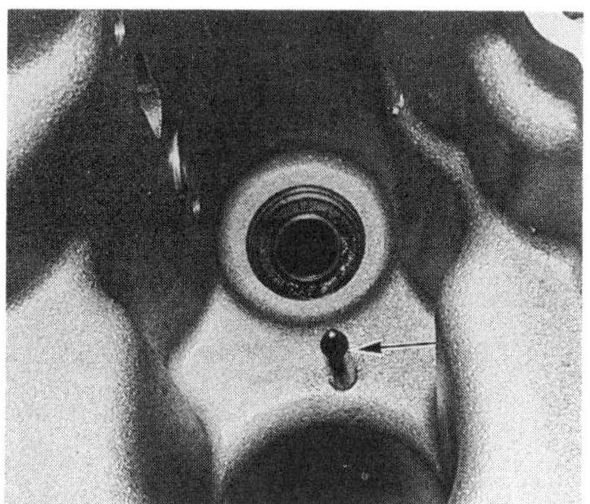

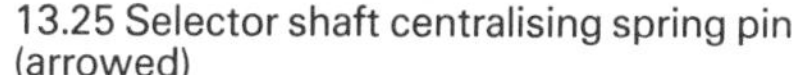

13.25 Selector shaft centralising spring pin (arrowed)

13.26 Tighten the extension housing bolts

13.30 Apply sealer to the 5th gear locking plate location

respective synchroniser sleeves, position the selector boss and locking plate, and insert the selector shaft through the components into the front of the main casing. The roll pin hole in the selector boss must be towards the front.

20 If removed, refit the selector shaft centralising spring and 5th gear locking control by inserting the pin and plug. Note that during 1987, modifications were made to the locking control components, and the later components are not interchangeable with the earlier ones.

21 Align the holes, then drive the roll pin into the selector boss and selector shaft (photo).

22 Insert the selector locking pin and spring, apply sealer to the plug threads, then insert and tighten the plug using an Allen key.

23 Fit the speedometer drivegear to the rear extension housing. Apply a little sealer to the cover, then press it into the housing (photo).

24 Remove the temporarily fitted bolts from the intermediate housing, then select 4th gear.

25 Stick a new gasket to the extension housing with grease, and fit the housing to the intermediate housing. Take care not to damage the rear oil seal, and make sure that the selector shaft centralising spring locates on the pin (photo).

26 Insert the bolts and tighten them to the specified torque in diagonal sequence (photo). Before inserting the three bolts which go right through the main casing, apply sealer to their threads.

27 Select reverse gear and locate the connector on the rear of the selector shaft. Support the shaft with a piece of wood, then drive in the roll pin. Select neutral.

28 Press the rear cover into the extension housing.

29 Check that the 5th gear interlock sleeve is correctly aligned, then insert the 5th gear locking pin and spring.

30 Apply sealer to the 5th gear locking plate location on the extension housing, fit the locking plate, and insert and tighten the bolts to the specified torque (photo). When refitting the locking plate on later gearboxes with the modified locking control components (see paragraph 20), only tighten the bolts finger-tight at first. Check the engagement of all gears, changing the position of the plate slightly if necessary. Fully tighten the bolts when satisfied.

31 Fit the gearbox top cover, together with a new gasket, and tighten the bolts to the specified torque in diagonal sequence.

32 Fit the clutch release bearing guide sleeve (oil slot downwards), together with a new gasket, and tighten the bolts to the specified torque in diagonal sequence. If there is evidence of sealer on the bolt threads, re-coat them with fresh sealer before refitting.

33 Fit the clutch housing to the front of the gearbox together with a new gasket. Apply sealer to the bolt threads, then insert the bolts and tighten them to the specified torque in diagonal sequence.

34 Insert and tighten the reversing lamp switch in the extension housing.

35 Fit the clutch release bearing and arm with reference to Chapter 5.

36 After the gearbox has been refitted to the vehicle, fill it with the specified quantity and type of gear oil, and check the oil level as described in Section 2.

14 Fault diagnosis – manual gearbox

Symptom	Reason(s)
Gearbox noisy in neutral	Input shaft bearing worn Oil level low, or incorrect grade
Gearbox noisy when moving (in all gears)	Mainshaft bearing worn Oil level low, or incorrect grade
Gearbox noisy in only one gear	Worn, damaged or chipped gear teeth
Gearbox jumps out of gear	Worn synchroniser units Worn gears Worn selector components
Ineffective synchromesh	Worn synchroniser unit or ring
Difficulty in engaging gears	Worn selector components Seized input shaft pilot bearing (in flywheel) Clutch fault (see Chapter 5)

Note: *This Section is not intended as an exhaustive guide to fault diagnosis, but summarises the more common faults which may be encountered during a vehicle's life. Consult a dealer for more detailed advice.*

Chapter 7 Automatic transmission

For modifications, and information applicable to later models, see Supplement at end of manual

Contents

Specifications

Type

Models up to 1985	Ford C3 type with three forward speeds and one reverse, epicyclic gear train with hydraulic control and torque converter
Models from 1985	Ford A4LD type with four forward speeds and one reverse, epicyclic gear train with hydraulic control and torque converter. Torque converter lock-up in third and fourth gears

Ratios

1st	2.47 : 1
2nd	1.47 : 1
3rd	1.00 : 1
4th (A4LD type only)	0.75 : 1
Reverse	2.11 : 1

Transmission fluid

Type	Automatic transmission fluid (ATF) to Ford spec SQM-2C 9010-A (Duckhams Uni-Matic or D-Matic)

Capacity

C3 type	6.3 litres (11.1 pints)
A4LD type	8.5 litres (15.0 pints)

Torque wrench settings

	Nm	lbf ft
Engine-to-transmission bolts	30 to 37	22 to 27
Transmission crossmember-to-underbody bolts	20 to 25	15 to 19
Transmission crossmember-to-transmission bolt	50 to 57	37 to 42
Fluid cooler pipe connector to transmission housing	24 to 30	18 to 22
Fluid cooler pipe to connector	22 to 24	16 to 18
Torque converter-to-driveplate nuts:		
C3 transmission	30 to 40	22 to 30
A4LD transmission	32 to 38	24 to 28
Torque converter fluid drain plug	27 to 40	20 to 29
Kickdown solenoid mounting bracket bolts (A4LD type transmission)	29 to 41	21 to 30
Brake band adjuster screw	13	10
Brake band adjuster screw locknut	50 to 58	37 to 43
Vacuum diaphragm unit bracket bolt	1 to 2	0.7 to 1.5
Starter inhibitor/reversing light switch	10 to 14	7 to 10
Sump bolts:		
C3 type transmission	13 to 20	10 to 15
A4LD type transmission:		
Plastic gasket	8 to 11	6 to 8
Cork gasket	15 to 18	11 to 13

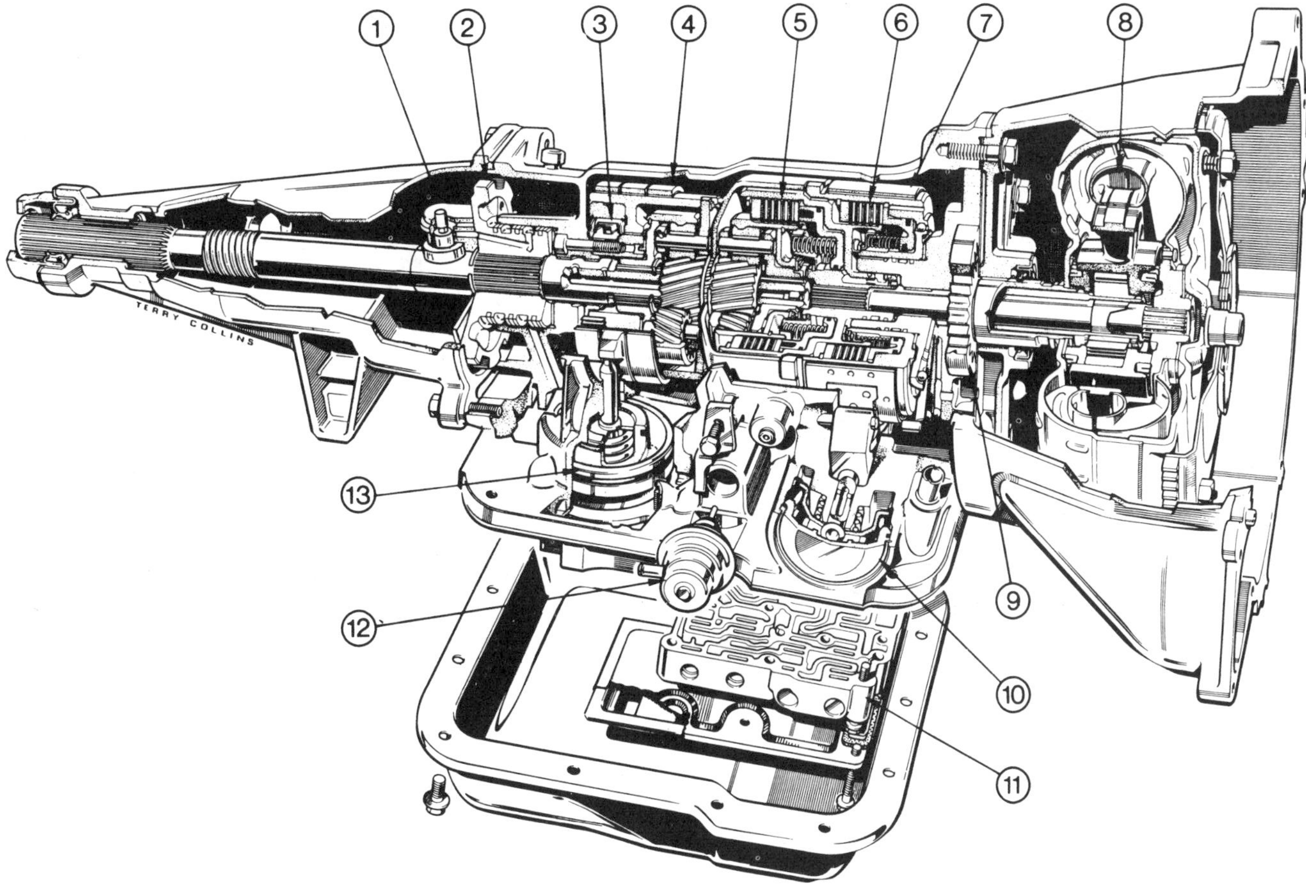

Fig 7.1 Cutaway view of C3 type automatic transmission (Sec 1)

1 *Centrifugal governor*
2 *Parking gear*
3 *One way clutch*
4 *Rear brake band*
5 *Forward clutch*
6 *Reverse and top gear clutch*
7 *Front brake band*
8 *Torque converter*
9 *Hydraulic pump*
10 *Front servo*
11 *Valve body*
12 *Vacuum diaphragm unit*
13 *Rear servo*

1 General description

The automatic transmission takes the place of the clutch and manual gearbox. Early models were fitted with a C3 type 3-speed transmission whilst later models use the more advanced A4LD type 4-speed unit.

The transmission consists of two main components. A hydraulic torque converter, capable of torque multiplication, transmits power from the engine to a hydraulically-operated epicyclic gearbox.

In the case of the C3 type transmission, the gearbox comprises two planetary gearsets providing three forward ratios and one reverse ratio. The A4LD type transmission comprises three planetary gearsets providing four forward ratios and one reverse ratio, and the torque converter locks up in 3rd and 4th gears, so avoiding power losses due to converter slip. 4th gear on the A4LD type transmission is an overdrive, maximum speed being obtained in 3rd.

The planetary geartrains provide the desired gear ratio according to which of their components are held stationary or allowed to turn. The geartrain components are held or released by friction clutches and brake bands which are actuated by hydraulic valves. The C3 type transmission has three friction clutches and two brake bands, whereas the A4LD type transmission has three friction clutches, three brake bands, and additionally two one-way clutches. An oil pump within the transmission provides the necessary hydraulic pressure to operate the various clutches and brakes.

Driver control of the transmission is by a selector lever which allows fully automatic operation with a hold facility on 1st and 2nd gear in the case of the C3 type transmission, and 1st, 2nd and 3rd gears in the case of the A4LD type transmission. The transmission will change automatically through all forward gears according to speed, load and throttle position. If gears are selected manually, the transmission will not change down until speed has reduced sufficiently to avoid damage.

A 'kickdown' facility causes the transmission to change down a gear (subject to speed) if the accelerator pedal is depressed fully and held down. This is useful when rapid acceleration is required, for example when overtaking. Kickdown is controlled by a cable linked to the transmission and the throttle cable, or on later models with the A4LD type transmission, by a throttle-operated switch and a solenoid actuator on the transmission.

Due to the complexity of the automatic transmission, any repair or overhaul work must be referred to a Ford dealer or automatic transmission specialist with the necessary equipment for fault diagnosis and repair. The contents of this Chapter are therefore confined to supplying any service information and instructions which can be used by the home mechanic.

2 Maintenance and inspection

1 At the intervals specified in the *'Routine maintenance'* Section at the beginning of this manual, carry out the following tasks.
2 Check the hydraulic fluid level as described in Section 3.
3 Check the brake band adjustment as described in Section 6.
4 Lubricate the selector and kickdown linkages.
5 Inspect the transmission and the fluid cooler unions for leaks. The fluid cooler is mounted at the front of the vehicle with the radiator. If necessary the rear extension housing oil seal can be renewed as described in Section 9.
6 Periodic fluid renewal is not specified, and no drain plug is fitted. If it

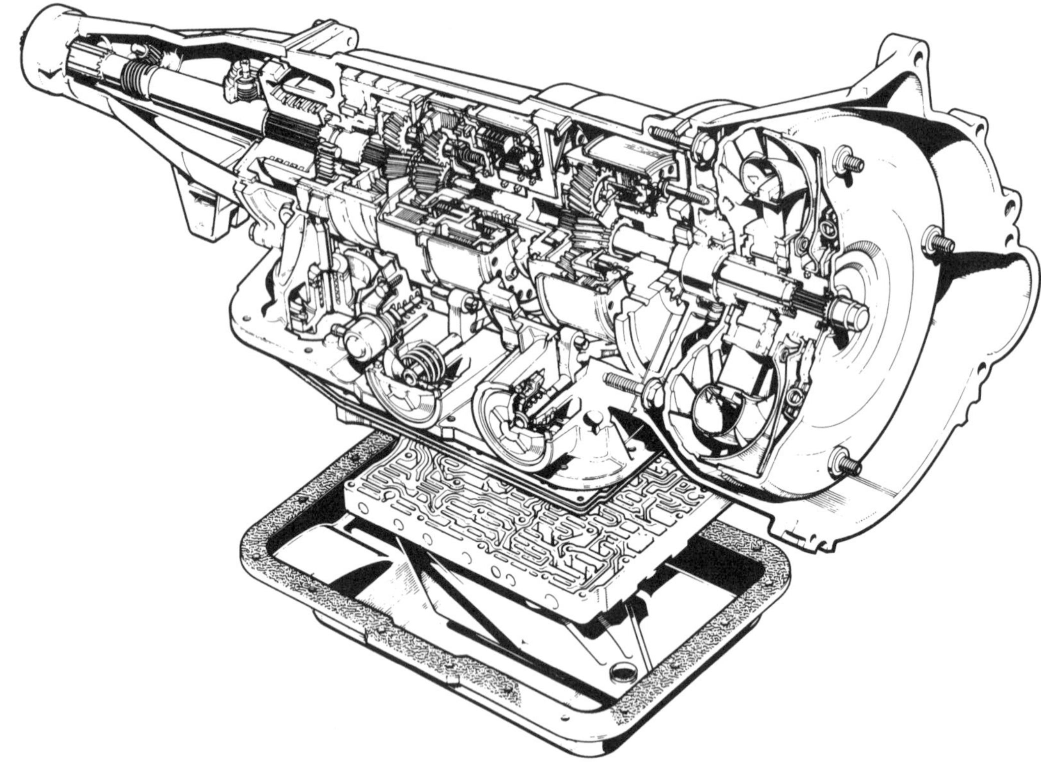

Fig 7.2 Cut-away view of A4LD type automatic transmission (Sec 1)

is wished to renew the fluid, it will be necessary to remove the transmission sump for draining.

3 Fluid level – checking

1 The vehicle must be positioned on level ground. Apply the handbrake.
2 Start the engine and allow it to idle, then fully depress the brake pedal and move the selector lever through all its positions three times, finishing in position 'P'.
3 Wait for approximately one minute, then with the engine still idling withdraw the transmission fluid level dipstick, wipe it clean with a non-fluffy rag, re-insert it and withdraw it again. The fluid level should be between the 'MIN' and 'MAX' marks. If necessary top up the level with the specified type of fluid through the dipstick tube, then re-check the level.
4 Refit the dipstick and switch off the engine on completion.

4 Transmission – removal and refitting (leaving engine in vehicle)

Note: *Any suspected faults must be referred to a Ford dealer or automatic transmission specialist before removal of the unit, as the specialist fault diagnosis equipment is designed to operate with the transmission in the vehicle*
1 Removal of the engine and automatic transmission as an assembly is described in Chapter 1, Section 13.
2 Disconnect the battery negative lead.
3 Working in the engine compartment, unscrew and remove the four upper engine-to-transmission bolts, noting the location of the earth lead, vacuum pipe bracket, and the transmission dipstick tube bracket.
4 Jack up the vehicle and support on axle stands. Ensure that there is sufficient working room beneath the vehicle.
5 To improve access, disconnect the exhaust downpipe from the manifold and remove the exhaust system as described in Chapter 3.
6 Remove the propeller shaft as described in Chapter 8.
7 Where applicable bend back the locktabs, then unscrew the two bolts securing each of the two anti-roll bar U-clamps to the vehicle underbody. Lower the anti-roll bar as far as possible.
8 Withdraw the dipstick and remove the dipstick tube from the right-hand side of the transmission. Plug the opening in the transmission to prevent dirt ingress.
9 Disconnect the wiring from the starter motor and remove the starter motor with reference to Chapter 13 if necessary.
10 Where applicable, pull the blanking plug from the engine adaptor plate.
11 Unscrew the unions and disconnect the fluid cooler pipes from the transmission. Plug the open ends of the pipes and the transmission to prevent dirt ingress and fluid leakage. If necessary, remove the fluid cooler pipe bracket from the engine mounting and place it to one side.
12 Remove the two clips securing the selector rod, and detach the selector rod from the manual selector lever, and the selector lever on the transmission.

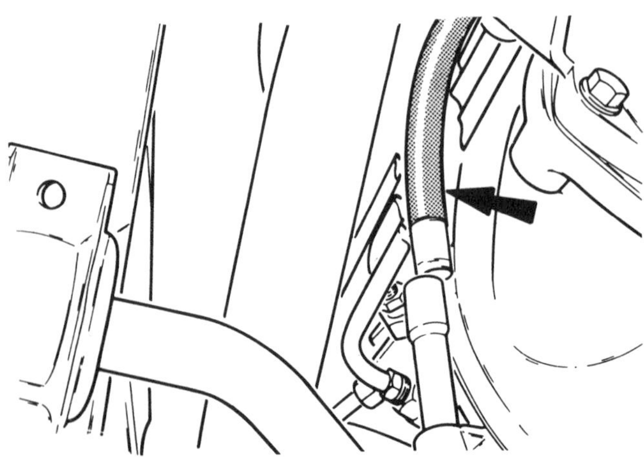

Fig 7.3 Transmission fluid dipstick tube (arrowed) (Sec 4)

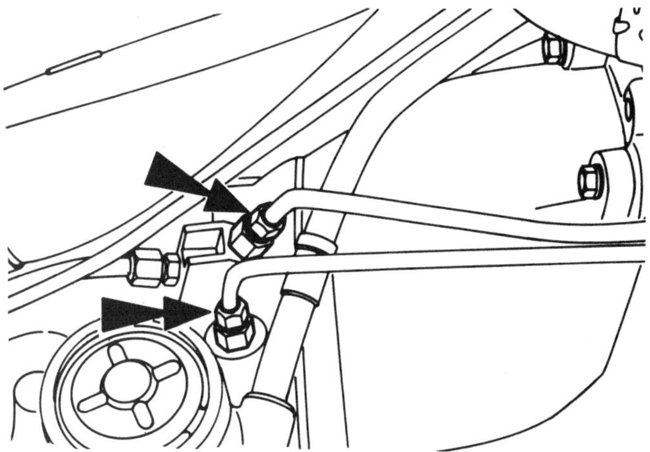
Fig 7.4 Transmission fluid cooler pipes (arrowed) (Sec 4)

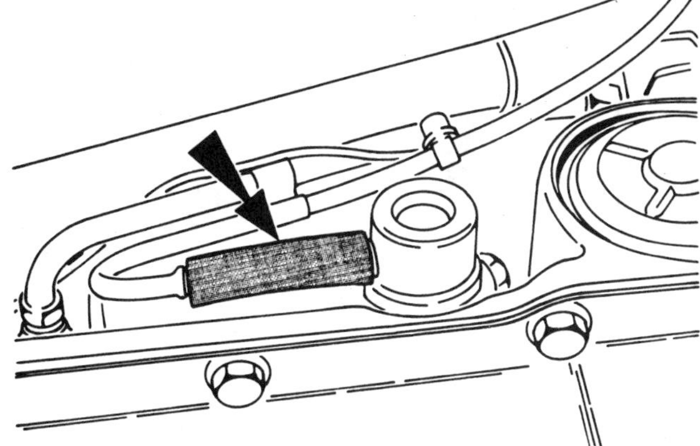
Fig 7.5 Vacuum diaphragm unit pipe (arrowed) (Sec 4)

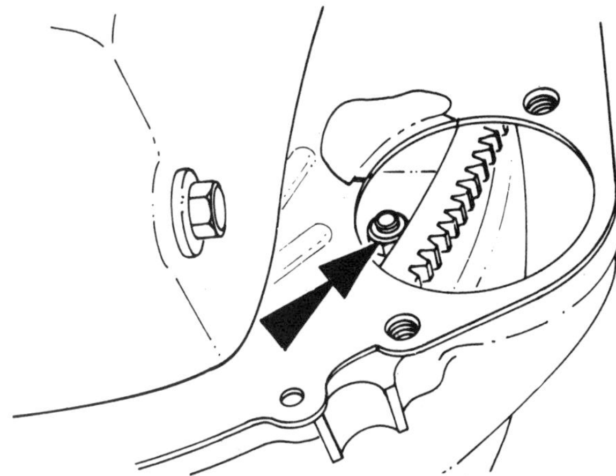
Fig 7.6 Torque converter-to-driveplate nut (arrowed) positioned in starter motor aperture (Sec 4)

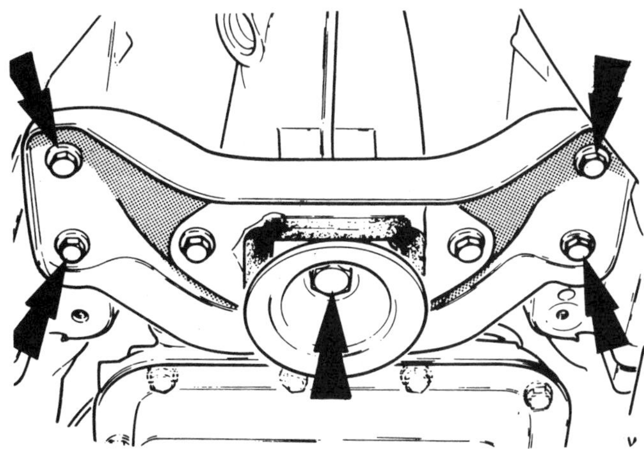
Fig 7.7 Transmission crossmember securing bolts (arrowed) (Sec 4)

13 Disconnect the kickdown cable from the lever on the transmission, and where applicable, detach the cable from the bracket on the transmission housing. On C3 type transmissions it will be necessary to unscrew the locknut in order to remove the cable from the bracket.
14 Disconnect the wiring from the starter inhibitor/reversing lamp switch and where applicable, on A4LD type transmissions, the kickdown solenoid and the lock-up clutch.
15 Remove the securing screw, and disconnect the speedometer cable from the transmission extension housing. Plug the opening in the transmission to prevent dirt ingress.
16 Disconnect the vacuum pipe from the vacuum diaphragm unit, and unclip the pipe from its securing bracket on the transmission housing where applicable.
17 Working through the starter motor aperture, unscrew the four torque converter-to-driveplate nuts. It will be necessary to turn the crankshaft using a suitable spanner on the crankshaft pulley bolt in order to gain access to each nut in turn through the aperture.
18 Support the transmission with a trolley jack, using an interposed block of wood to spread the load.
19 Unscrew the four bolts securing the transmission crossmember to the vehicle underbody. Note the position of the earth strap, where applicable. Unscrew the central bolt securing the crossmember to the transmission and remove the crossmember. Recover the mounting cup and where applicable the exhaust mounting bracket.
20 Unscrew and remove the remaining engine-to-transmission bolts, noting the location of the engine/transmission brace on the right-hand side of the transmission on OHC models.
21 With the help of an assistant, lift the transmission from the engine, using the trolley jack to take the weight. Ensure that the torque converter is held firmly in place in the transmission housing during removal, otherwise it could fall out resulting in fluid spillage and possible damage.

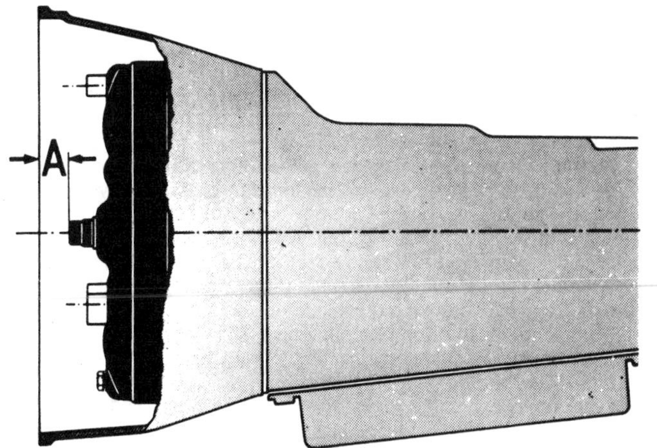

Fig 7.8 Torque converter correctly installed (Sec 4)

A = 10.0 mm (0.39 in) minimum for C3 type transmission
A = 9.0 mm (0.35 in) minimum for A4LD type transmission

It may be necessary to rock the transmission a little to release it from the engine.
22 With the transmission removed, temporarily reconnect the anti-roll bar to the underbody if the vehicle is to be moved.
23 Refitting is a reversal of removal, taking note of the following points.
24 As the torque converter is only loosely engaged in the transmission, the transmission must be kept inclined during installation to prevent the torque converter from falling out forwards. When the

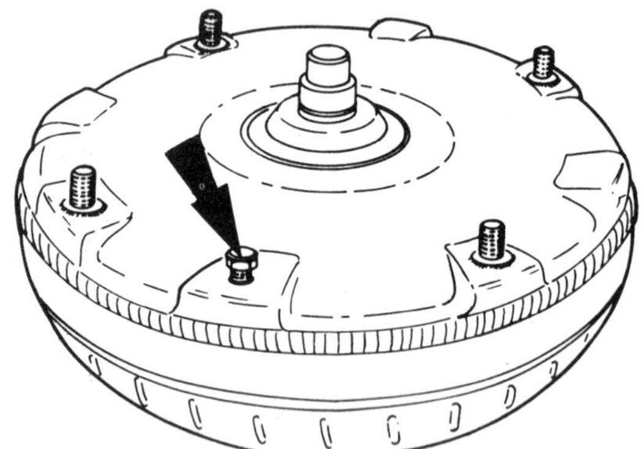

Fig 7.9 Torque converter drain plug (arrowed) must line up with opening in driveplate – C3 type transmission (Sec 4)

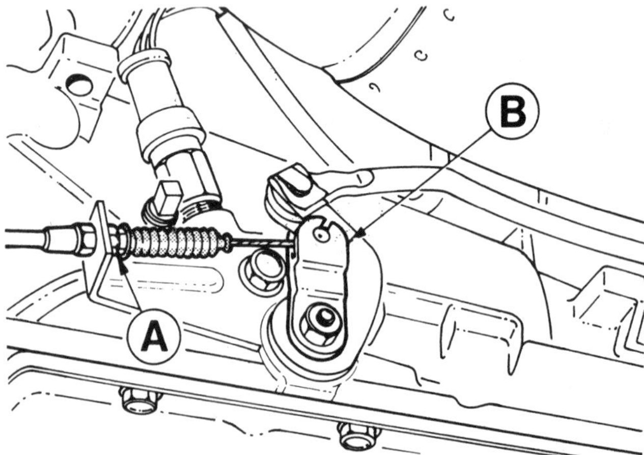

Fig 7.11 Kickdown cable linkage at transmission – C3 type transmission (Sec 5)

A Locknut *B Kickdown lever*

torque converter hub is fully engaged with the fluid pump drivegear in the transmission, distance 'A' in Fig. 7.8 must be as specified. Incorrect installation of the torque converter will result in damage to the transmission.

25 As the transmission is installed, guide the torque converter studs through the holes in the driveplate, noting that on the C3 type transmission, the torque converter fluid drain plug must line up with the opening in the driveplate (see Fig. 7.9). When the transmission housing is positioned flush with the engine adaptor plate and the engine block, check that the torque converter is free to move axially a small amount before refitting and tightening the engine-to-transmission bolts.

26 Do not tighten the torque converter-to-driveplate nuts until the lower engine-to-transmission bolts and the transmission crossmember have been fitted and tightened.

27 Where applicable, reconnect the kickdown cable, and adjust as described in Section 5.

28 Reconnect the selector rod and adjust as described in Section 7.

29 Refit the propeller shaft as described in Chapter 8.

30 Refit the exhaust system as described in Chapter 3.

31 On completion, with the vehicle standing on level ground, check and if necessary top up the hydraulic fluid level as described in Section 3.

5 Kickdown cable – removal, refitting and adjustment

C3 type transmission

1 Disconnect the cable from the lever on the carburettor/inlet manifold by removing the pin and spring clip.

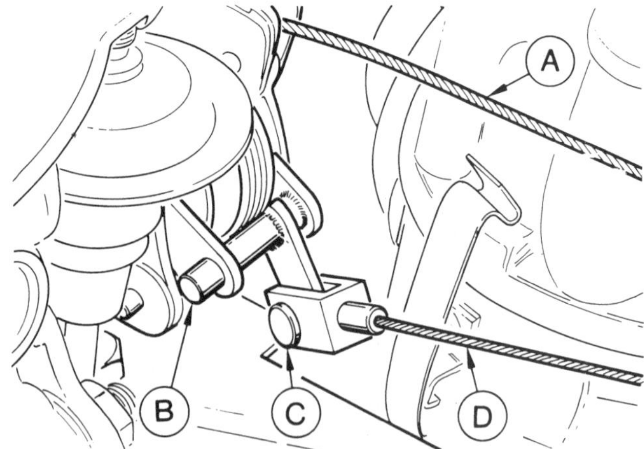

Fig 7.10 Kickdown cable linkage at carburettor – C3 type transmission (Sec 5)

A Throttle cable *C Pin and spring clip*
B Lever *D Kickdown cable*

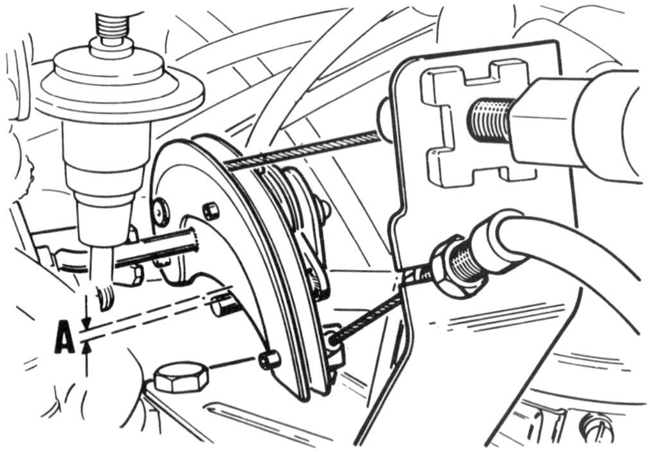

Fig 7.12 Kickdown cable adjustment dimension (Sec 5)

A = 0.8 to 1.0 mm (0.03 to 0.04 in)

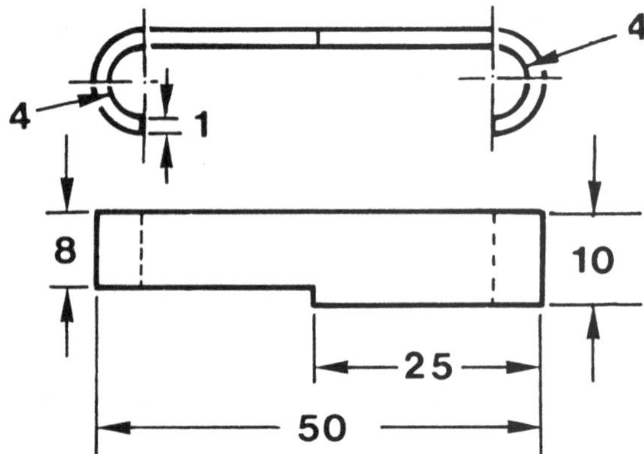

Fig 7.13 Kickdown cable setting gauge – A4LD type transmission (mechanically-operated kickdown) (Sec 5)

All dimensions in mm

2 Unscrew the locknut, and release the cable from the bracket on the carburettor/inlet manifold by sliding the cable through the slotted opening in the bracket.

3 To improve access, apply the handbrake, jack up the front of the vehicle and support on axle stands.

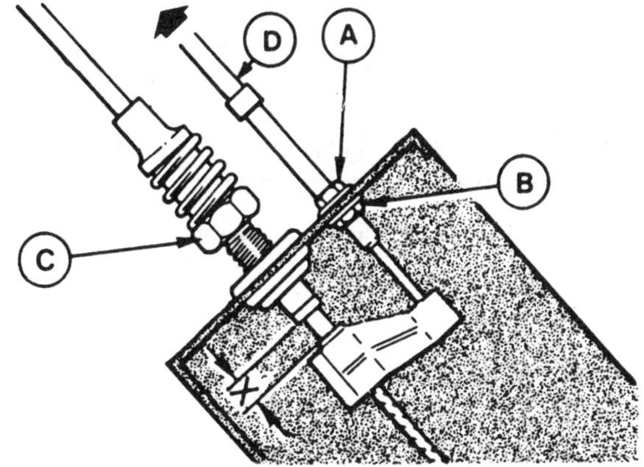

Fig 7.14 Kickdown cable adjustment – A4LD type transmission (mechanically-operated kickdown) (Sec 5)

A Kickdown cable adjuster nut
B Locknut
C Throttle cable adjuster nut
D Kickdown cable
X See text

4 Repeat the procedure given in paragraph 2 at the cable bracket on the transmission.
5 Unhook the cable from the kickdown lever on the transmission, and withdraw the cable from the vehicle.
6 Refitting is a reversal of removal, but on completion check the cable adjustment as follows.
7 Before adjusting the cable, check that the carburettor throttle valve(s) is/are fully open when the throttle pedal is fully depressed. Refer to Chapter 3 if necessary.
8 Have an assistant depress the throttle pedal sufficiently to open the throttle valve(s) fully, then pivot the kickdown lever on the transmission as far as the stop, and lock it in this position.
9 Adjust the cable by means of the locknuts until the gap 'A' in Fig. 7.12 between the throttle quadrant and the kickdown lever is as specified. Tighten the locknuts.
10 Re-check the adjustment on completion by releasing then fully depressing the throttle pedal, and re-adjust the cable if necessary.

A4LD type transmission (mechanically-operated kickdown)

11 Cable removal and refitting is as described in paragraphs 1 to 6, but cable adjustment should be carried out as follows.
12 Make up a sheet metal setting gauge to the dimensions shown in Fig. 7.13.
13 Slacken the adjuster nut 'A' and the locknut 'B' in Fig. 7.14, and unscrew the nuts to the ends of the thread on the cable sheath.
14 Have an assistant depress the throttle pedal to its stop and hold it in this position. Ensure that the pedal travel is not restricted by mats or carpets.
15 Working in the engine compartment, turn the throttle cable adjuster nut 'C' to achieve a dimension 'X' (see Fig. 7.14) of 10.0 mm (0.39 in). Use the appropriate end of the setting gauge to check the gap. Ensure that the spring and spring cup at the end of the cable sheath do not turn as the adjuster nut is turned, as this may result in the dimension 'X' altering when the vehicle is in use.
16 Remove the setting gauge and re-insert it with the 8.0 mm (0.32 in) end in gap 'X'. Have the assistant release the throttle pedal, which will clamp the gauge in position.
17 Pull the kickdown cable sheath in the direction of the arrow in Fig. 7.14 as far as the stop. Hold the sheath in this position, ensuring that the locknut 'B' is not touching the cable bracket, and secure the sheath by tightening adjuster nut 'A' and locknut 'B'. When tightening locknut 'B' ensure that the cable sheath and adjuster nut 'A' do not turn. Adjustment is now complete.
18 On completion, check that the kickdown mechanism operates correctly.

A4LD type transmission (solenoid-operated kickdown)

19 From mid-1986, the A4LD transmission kickdown cable was replaced by a solenoid unit.
20 The solenoid is bolted to the transmission housing and is connected to the kickdown lever by a cable.

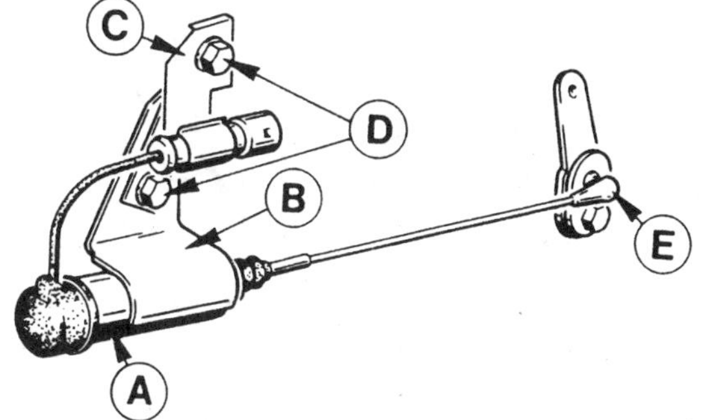

Fig 7.15 Kickdown solenoid assembly – A4LD transmission (solenoid operated kickdown) (Sec 5)

A Solenoid
B Mounting bracket
C Wiring connector bracket
D Bolts
E Cable end ball-stud

21 To remove the solenoid and cable, for improved access, apply the handbrake, then jack up the front of the vehicle and support on axle stands.
22 Prise the cable end from the ball-stud on the kickdown lever.
23 Pull the wiring connector from its bracket, and separate the two halves of the connector.
24 Loosen the solenoid mounting bracket bolts, and withdraw the solenoid from the bracket.
25 Refitting is a reversal of removal, but before tightening the mounting bracket bolts, adjust the cable as follows.
26 Have an assistant switch on the ignition, with the selector lever in any position. **Under no circumstances start the engine.**
27 Have the assistant depress the throttle pedal to its stop, actuating the kickdown, and hold the pedal in this position.
28 Turn the kickdown lever on the transmission anti-clockwise against its stop, then slide the solenoid towards the front of the vehicle to put the cable under slight tension.
29 Tighten the lower solenoid mounting bracket bolt, then the upper bolt to the specified torque.
30 Have the assistant release the throttle pedal, when the kickdown cable should return to its normal position, then depress and release the pedal several times. Check that with the throttle pedal fully depressed, there is a clearance of between 0.3 and 0.8 mm (0.01 to 0.03 in) between the kickdown lever and its stop. This clearance must exist, as if the cable is over-tensioned the kickdown lever may return to its normal position inadvertently during operation.
31 Switch off the ignition and lower the vehicle.

6 Brake band(s) – adjustment

Note: *A brake band torque wrench – Ford tool No 17-005, or a conventional torque wrench and a splined socket of suitable size to fit the square section head of the adjuster screw(s) will be required for this operation.*

1 For improved access, apply the handbrake, then jack up the front of the vehicle and support on axle stands.
2 The brake band adjuster screw(s) is/are situated on the left-hand side of the transmission housing, forward of the kickdown lever. Note that the C3 type transmission has a single adjuster screw for adjustment of the front brake band, whereas the A4LD type transmission has two adjuster screws for adjustment of the front and intermediate brake bands.
3 Disconnect the kickdown cable from the kickdown lever on the transmission housing.
4 Loosen the locknut on the front brake band adjuster screw, and back off the adjuster screw several turns.
5 Using the Ford special tool or a suitable equivalent, tighten the adjuster screw to the specified torque, then back off the screw two complete turns, and tighten the locknut. Ensure that the adjuster screw

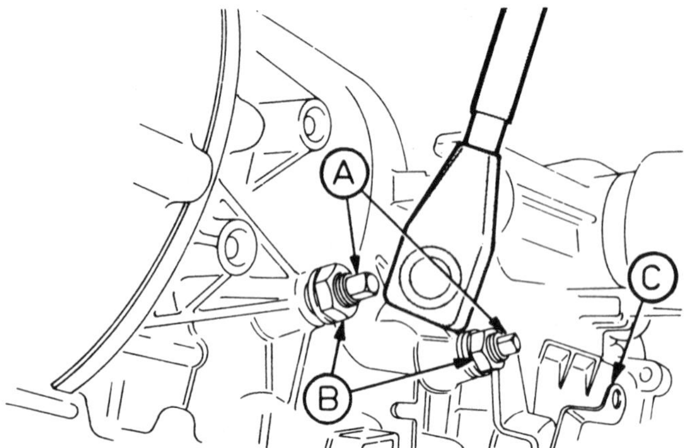

Fig 7.16 Brake band adjustment – A4LD type transmission (Sec 6)

A Adjuster screws
B Locknuts
C Kickdown lever

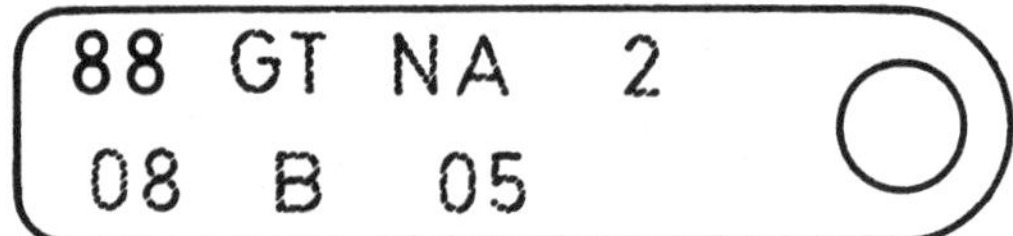

Fig 7.17 Transmission identification tag with part number starting with '88' (Sec 6)

does not turn as the locknut is tightened.
6 Repeat the procedure given in paragraphs 4 and 5 for the remaining adjuster screw on A4LD type transmissions, but on all models where the part number on the transmission identification tag starts with '88' (see Fig. 7.17) and additionally on all 1.8 CVH engine models, the adjuster screw should be backed off two and a half turns after tightening to the specified torque. On all other models, the adjuster screw should be backed off two turns.
7 Reconnect the kickdown cable, and lower the vehicle to the ground on completion.

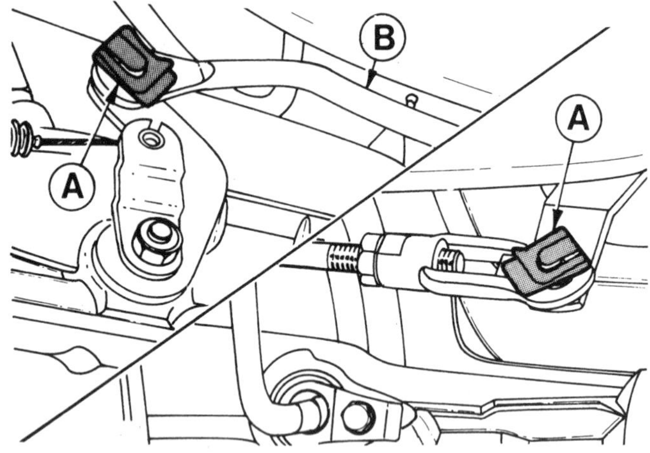

Fig 7.18 Selector rod end fittings (Sec 7)

A Securing clips
B Selector rod

7 Selector rod – removal, refitting and adjustment

Note: *The vehicle must be standing on its wheels when adjusting the selector rod*

1 Remove the securing clips from each end of the selector rod, and withdraw the rod. Check the condition of the guide bushes at each end of the rod and renew as necessary.
2 Engage the manual selector lever in the following position according to transmission type:

C3 type transmission – 'D'
A4LD type transmission up to 1987 – 'DE'
A4LD type transmission from 1987 – 'D'

3 Move the selector lever on the transmission housing to the corresponding position.
4 Fit the selector rod to the selector lever on the transmission housing, and secure it with the clip.
5 Offer the remaining end of the selector rod to the manual selector lever. If it will fit without strain, and without disturbing the selector lever on the transmission, or the manual selector lever, adjustment is correct.
6 If adjustment is necessary, slacken the selector rod locknut, then rotate the rod end-piece to lengthen or shorten the rod until it is a comfortable fit on the manual selector lever. Tighten the locknut when adjustment is complete.
7 Check that the manual selector lever accurately engages each function, and check the operation of the starter inhibitor/reversing light switch. It should only be possible to start the engine with the manual selector lever in positions 'N' or 'P', and the reversing lights should operate with the selector lever in position 'R' when the ignition is switched on. Also check that the parking pawl engages correctly with the selector lever in position 'P' – the selector lever must be pressed down before it can be moved from position 'P' to another position, and also before it can be moved from position 'N' to 'R'. Re-adjust the selector rod if necessary.

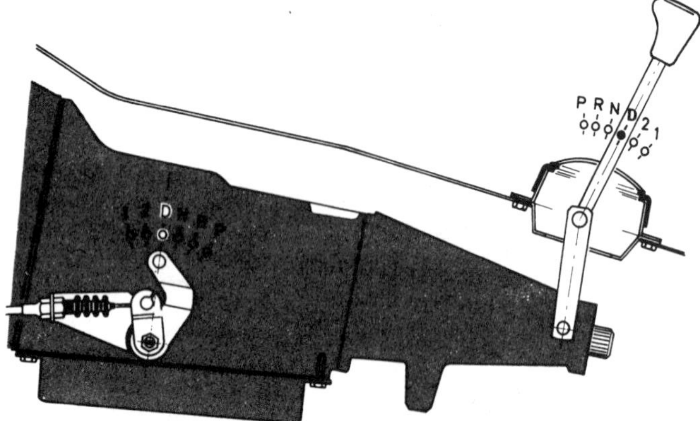

Fig 7.19 Manual selector lever and transmission selector lever in 'D' position – C3 type transmission (Sec 7)

8 Gear selector mechanism – removal, overhaul and refitting

1 Remove the securing clip and disconnect the selector rod from the manual selector lever underneath the vehicle.
2 Working inside the vehicle, unscrew the selector lever handle from the threaded end of the lever, then remove the three retaining screws and withdraw the centre console front upper panel.
3 Pull the selector gate cover and the bulbholder from the selector housing.
4 Unscrew the four securing bolts and withdraw the selector housing and selector gate from the floorpan.
5 To dismantle the gear selector mechanism, proceed as follows.
6 Detach the manual selector lever from the lower selector shaft, by removing the clip from the end of the link pin, and withdrawing the pin – see Fig. 7.21. Recover the two bushes and the spring.
7 Remove the clip from the end of the lower selector shaft, and withdraw the selector lever arm and the shaft from the selector housing. Lift out the complete upper selector lever assembly.

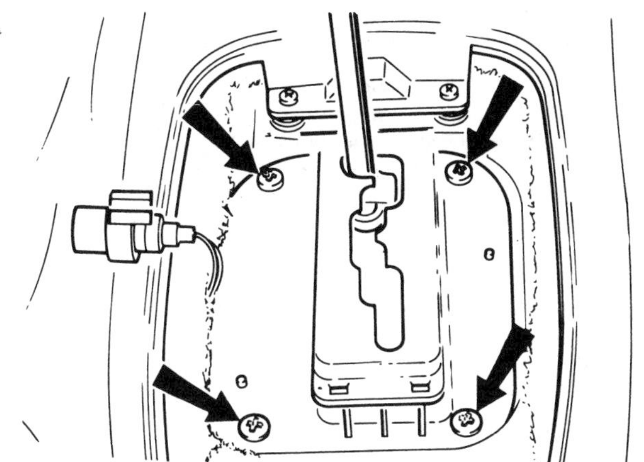
Fig 7.20 Selector housing and selector gate securing bolts (arrowed) (Sec 8)

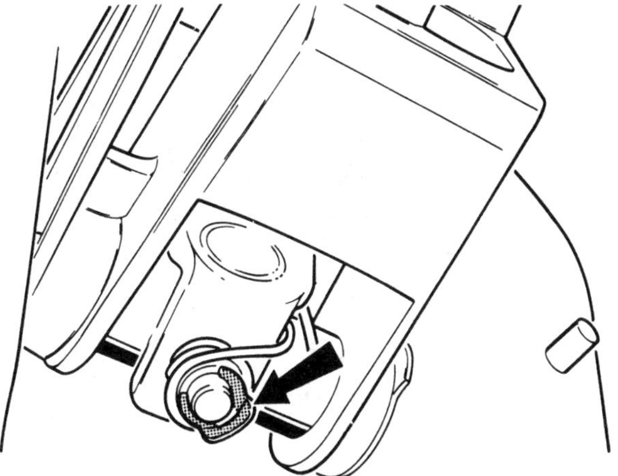
Fig 7.21 Selector shaft link pin clip (arrowed) (Sec 8)

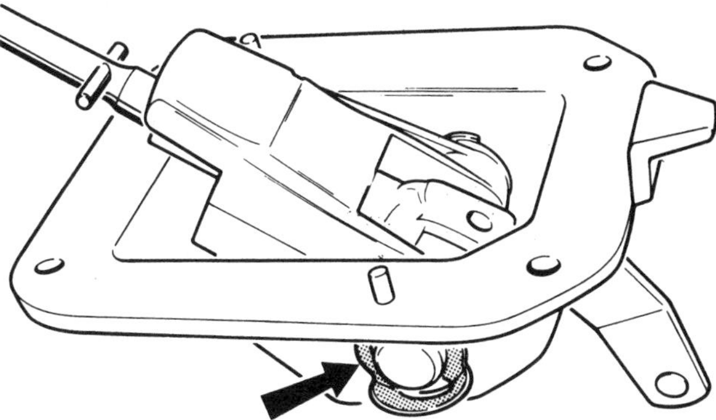
Fig 7.22 Lower selector shaft end clip (arrowed) (Sec 8)

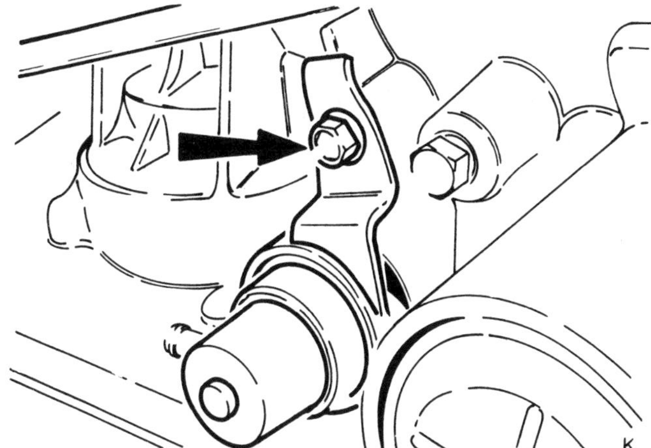

Fig 7.23 Vacuum diaphragm unit bracket bolt (arrowed) – C3 type transmission (Sec 10)

8 Withdraw the upper selector lever and spring from the selector lever guide.
9 Examine all components for wear and damage, and renew as necessary.
10 Reassembly and refitting is a reversal of dismantling and removal, but on completion, check the selector rod adjustment as described in Section 7.

9 Transmission extension housing oil seal – renewal

1 Remove the propeller shaft as described in Chapter 8.
2 Using a suitable thin-bladed tool, prise the oil seal from the end of the extension housing. Be prepared for fluid spillage.
3 Fit the new oil seal carefully using a suitable tube drift.
4 Refit the propeller shaft as described in Chapter 8.
5 Check and if necessary top up the transmission fluid level as described in Section 3.

10 Vacuum diaphragm unit – removal and refitting

Note: *A new O-ring must be used when refitting the vacuum diaphragm unit*
1 Apply the handbrake, jack up the front of the vehicle and support on axle stands.
2 Detach the propeller shaft centre bearing from the underbody by unscrewing the two securing bolts. Note the position and number of the slotted shims between the centre bearing bracket and the underbody.
3 Support the weight of the transmission with a trolley jack.
4 Where applicable, unhook the exhaust mounting from the bracket on the transmission crossmember, then unbolt the crossmember from the underbody and the transmission.
5 Carefully lower the transmission.
6 Disconnect the vacuum hose from the diaphragm unit, on the right-hand side of the transmission housing.
7 Unscrew the diaphragm unit bracket bolt, and detach the bracket.
8 Remove the diaphragm unit and actuating pin. Be prepared for fluid spillage.
9 Before refitting the diaphragm unit, check that the throttle valve moves freely.
10 Refitting is a reversal of removal, bearing in mind the following points.
11 Use a new O-ring when refitting the diaphragm unit to the transmission.
12 Refit the slotted shims between the propeller shaft centre bearing bracket and the underbody in their original noted positions.
13 On completion, check and if necessary top up the transmission fluid level as described in Section 3.

11 Starter inhibitor/reversing lamp switch – removal and refitting

Note: *A new O-ring must be used when refitting the switch.*
1 For improved access, apply the handbrake, jack up the front of the vehicle and support on axle stands.
2 Disconnect the battery negative lead.
3 Disconnect the wiring plug from the switch on the left-hand side of the transmission housing.

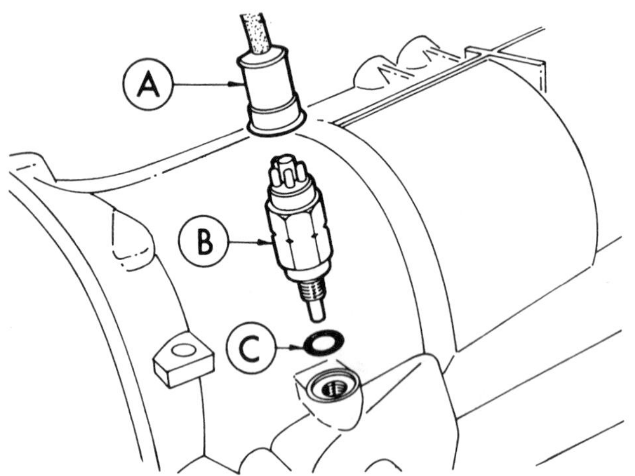

Fig 7.24 Starter inhibitor/reversing light switch – C3 type transmission (Sec 11)

A Wiring plug
B Switch
C O-ring

4 Unscrew the switch and remove the O-ring.
5 Refitting is a reversal of removal, but use a new O-ring.
6 On completion, check the operation of the switch. It should only be possible to start the engine with the manual selector lever in positions 'N' or 'P', and the reversing lamps should operate with the selector lever in position 'R' when the ignition is switched on.

12 Fault diagnosis – automatic transmission

Faults with automatic transmissions are nearly always the result of low fluid level or incorrect adjustment of the selector linkage or kick-down cable. Fluid leaks will normally be clearly visible, but note that it is possible for fluid loss to occur due to a faulty vacuum diaphragm unit, in which case fluid may be drawn into the inlet manifold possibly resulting in engine 'pinking'.

Detailed fault diagnosis is beyond the scope of the home mechanic, and any internal transmission faults should be referred to a Ford dealer or automatic transmission specialist who has the necessary special equipment to carry out the work.

Chapter 8 Propeller shaft

For modifications, and information applicable to later models, see Supplement at end of manual

Contents

Specifications

Type ..... Two-piece tubular steel with rubber mounted centre bearing. Hardy-Spicer universal joints with front rubber coupling on most models

Torque wrench settings

	Nm	lbf ft
Propeller shaft-to-final drive unit bolts	57 to 67	42 to 49
Centre bearing bracket to underbody	18 to 23	13 to 17

1 General description

1 Drive is transmitted from the gearbox/automatic transmission at the front of the vehicle to the final drive unit at the rear of the vehicle by means of a two-piece propeller shaft.

2 To allow for relative movement of the gearbox/automatic transmission and final drive unit, the propeller shaft has a flexible joint at each end, and the two sections of the shaft are joined by a central flexible joint. Standard universal joints are used at the rear and centre of the shaft, and on some models at the front. On later models, a rubber coupling is used at the front of the shaft which reduces noise and vibration levels. Some models have a vibration damper fitted to the forward end of the coupling (photo). A propeller shaft with a front rubber coupling may be fitted to early models in place of the universal joint type if desired. The front end of the propeller shaft is splined, allowing it to

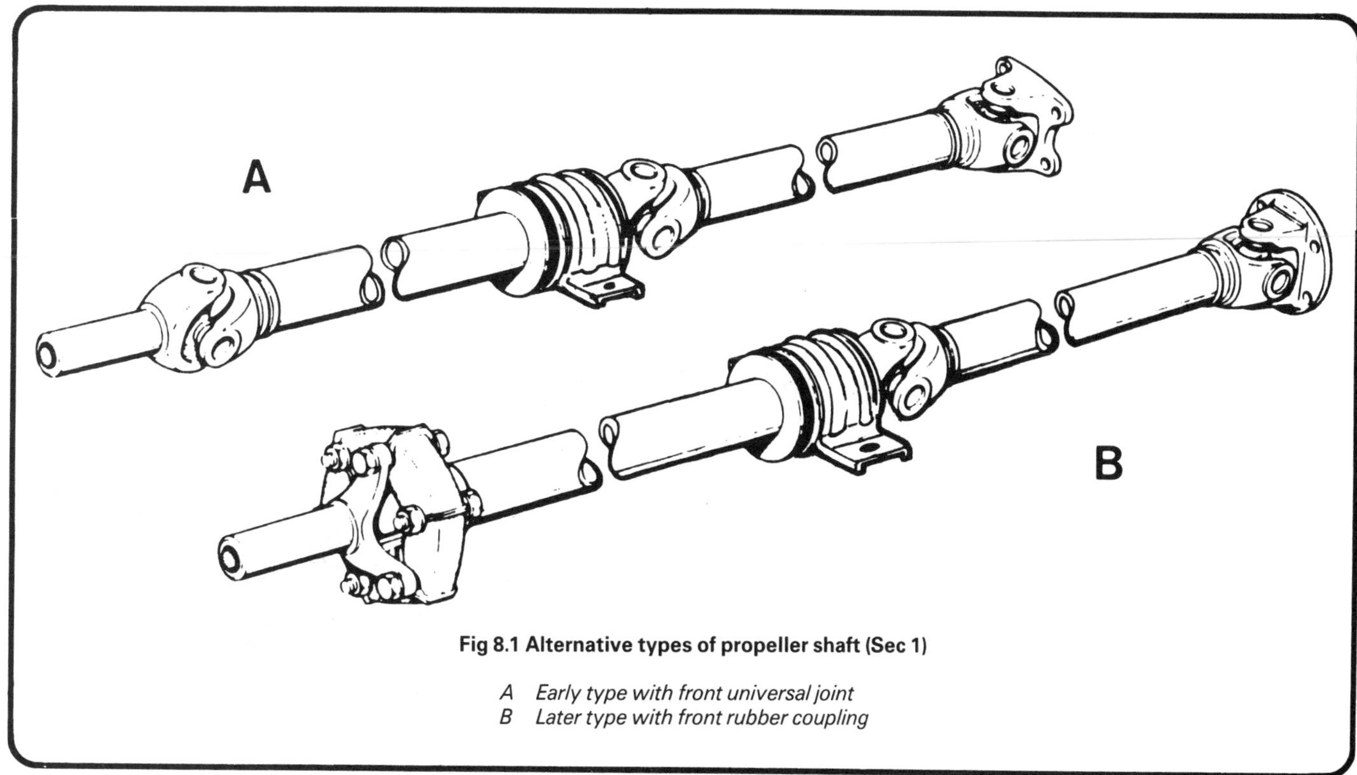

Fig 8.1 Alternative types of propeller shaft (Sec 1)

A Early type with front universal joint
B Later type with front rubber coupling

1.2 Vibration damper fitted to front rubber coupling on some models

1.3 Centre bearing and centre universal joint

slide in the gearbox/automatic transmission in order to take up fore and aft movement of the gearbox/automatic transmission relative to the final drive unit.

3 The propeller shaft is supported at its centre, forward of the central universal joint, by a bearing secured to the vehicle underbody (photo).

4 On Saloon, Hatchback and Estate models, the position of the final drive unit ensures that the working angles of the joints do not exceed one degree, and therefore wear in the joints is likely to be minimal unless very high mileages have been covered. The universal joints cannot be serviced, although it is possible to renew the centre bearing and the front rubber coupling where applicable.

2 Maintenance

1 No periodic maintenance is specified for the propeller shaft, but checks of the various components can be made as follows.

2 Wear in the universal joints is characterised by vibration in the transmission, or a knocking on changing from drive to overrun or vice versa.

3 To test a universal joint, jack up the vehicle and support it on axle stands. It is only strictly necessary to jack up the rear of the vehicle, but this provides only limited access. Attempt to turn the propeller shaft either side of the joint in alternate opposite directions. Also attempt to lift each side of the joint. Any movement within the universal joint is indicative of considerable wear, and if evident the complete propeller shaft must be renewed.

4 Wear in the centre bearing is characterised by noise in the transmission.

5 The centre bearing is more difficult to test for wear. If bearing movement (as distinct from universal joint or rubber insulator movement) can be felt when lifting the propeller shaft front section next to the bearing bracket, the bearing should be removed as described in Section 4 and checked for roughness while spinning the outer race by hand. If excessive wear is evident, renew the bearing.

6 Deterioration of the rubber coupling will be self-evident on inspection. Look particularly for cracks around the bolt holes. A new coupling can be fitted if necessary with reference to Section 5.

3 Propeller shaft – removal and refitting

Note: *New spring washers must be fitted to the propeller shaft-to-final drive unit bolts on refitting.*

1 Jack up the vehicle and support on axle stands. It is only strictly necessary to jack up the rear of the vehicle, but this provides only limited access.

2 For improved access the rear section of the exhaust system (ie from the joint) can be removed as described in Chapter 3, but this is not essential.

3 Mark the rear universal joint flange and final drive flange in relation to each other if the original propeller shaft is to be refitted. This is not necessary if a new propeller shaft is to be fitted.

4 Unscrew and remove the four bolts and spring washers securing the propeller shaft to the final drive unit (photo). In order to hold the shaft stationary as the bolts are unscrewed, apply the handbrake, or alternatively, insert a suitable bar or screwdriver through the universal joint yoke.

5 Unscrew the two bolts securing the centre bearing bracket to the underbody, and lower the bracket and shaft, noting the location and number of slotted shims between the bracket and underbody (photos).

3.4 Three of the propeller shaft-to-final drive securing bolts (arrowed)

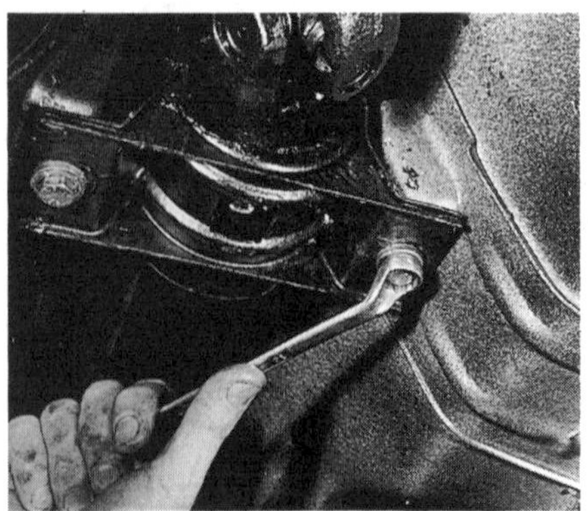
3.5A Unscrewing a centre bearing bracket securing bolt

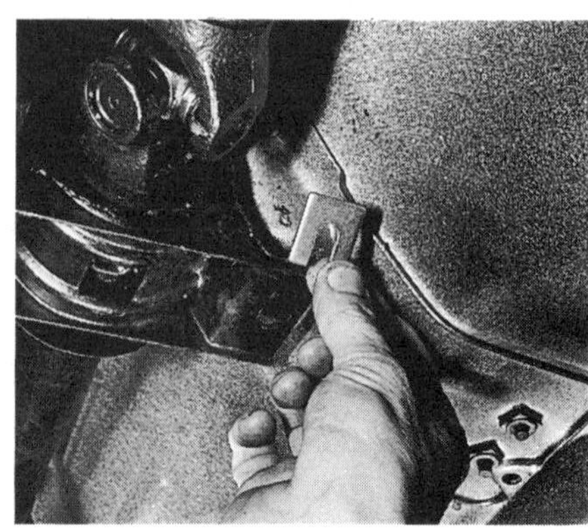
3.5B Removing a slotted shim from the centre bearing bracket

6 The front of the propeller shaft must now be disconnected from the gearbox/transmission by pulling the shaft rearwards. To prevent any loss of oil/fluid from the gearbox/automatic transmission, a suitable plug should be inserted into the oil seal. Alternatively a plastic bag can be positioned over the opening and retained with an elastic band.
7 Withdraw the propeller shaft from under the vehicle.
8 Remove the plug or plastic bag, as applicable, from the gearbox/automatic transmission and wipe clean the oil seal and the propeller shaft splined spigot. If there is evidence that the oil seal has been leaking, or if it is damaged, now is an opportune time to renew it. To renew the oil seal, prise out the old seal using a suitable screwdriver, and drive in the new seal carefully, using a suitable tube drift.
9 Insert the propeller shaft splined spigot into the gearbox/automatic transmission, taking care to avoid damage to the oil seal.
10 Locate the rear of the propeller shaft on the final drive unit, aligning any previously made marks. Fit new spring washers and tighten the securing bolts to the specified torque. Hold the shaft stationary as during the removal procedure.
11 Loosely attach the axle bearing bracket to the underbody with the two bolts.
12 Insert the slotted shims between the centre bearing bracket and the underbody in their original noted locations. Hand-tighten the two securing bolts.
13 On Saloon, Hatchback and Estate models, using a straight edge of suitable length, check that the two sections of the propeller shaft are accurately aligned. The joint angles should not exceed one degree, although this is impossible to measure in practice, and it is sufficient to ensure that the shaft runs straight in the horizontal plane from front to rear. If necessary adjust the shim thickness to give accurate alignment. Tighten the centre bearing bracket bolts to the specified torque on completion.
14 Refit the rear section of the exhaust system, if removed, with reference to Chapter 3, then lower the vehicle to the ground.
15 With the vehicle level, check and if necessary top up the oil/fluid level in the gearbox/automatic transmission with reference to Chapter 6 or Chapter 7 as applicable.

4 Propeller shaft centre bearing – renewal

Note: *A suitable bearing puller will be required to pull the centre bearing from the propeller shaft.*
1 Remove the propeller shaft as described in Section 3.
2 Mark the front and rear sections of the propeller shaft in relation to each other, and also mark the exact position of the U-shaped washer located beneath the bolt head in the central universal joint (photo).
3 Bend back the tab on the lock washer and loosen the bolt in the central universal joint so that the U-shaped washer can be removed.
4 With the U-shaped washer removed, slide the rear section of the propeller shaft from the front section.
5 Pull the mounting bracket and insulator rubber from the centre bearing.
6 Remove the outer protective dust cap, then using a suitable puller, pull the centre bearing and inner dust cap from the front section of the propeller shaft.
7 Wipe clean the centre bearing components, and fit the inner dust cap to the new bearing. Pack the cavity between the cap and the bearing with molybdenum disulphide based grease.
8 Push the centre bearing and inner dust cap onto the front section of the propeller shaft, using a metal tube of suitable diameter on the bearing inner race. Note that the red seal end of the bearing must face towards the splined end of the shaft.
9 Fit the outer dust cap, and pack the cavity between the cap and bearing with molybdenum disulphide grease.
10 If necessary a new insulator rubber can be fitted to the bearing bracket by bending back the retaining tongues on the bracket. Make sure that the flange of the new insulator is located on its seat before bending the retaining tongues back.
11 Ease the bearing bracket together with the insulator rubber over the centre bearing.

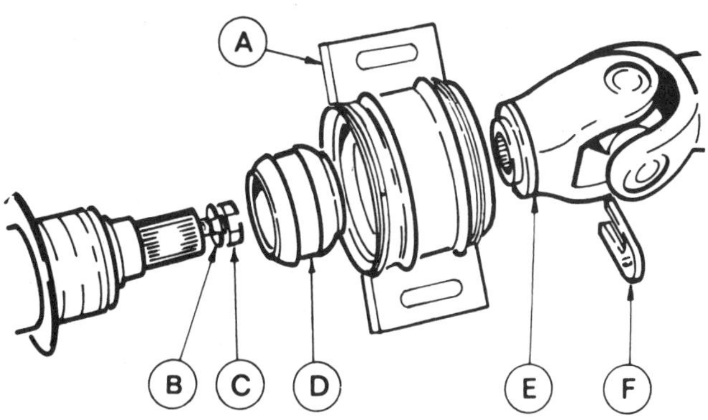

Fig 8.2 Exploded view of the centre bearing (Sec 4)

A Mounting bracket with rubber insulator
B Lock washer
C Bolt
D Bearing and dust caps
E Splined universal joint yoke
F U-shaped washer

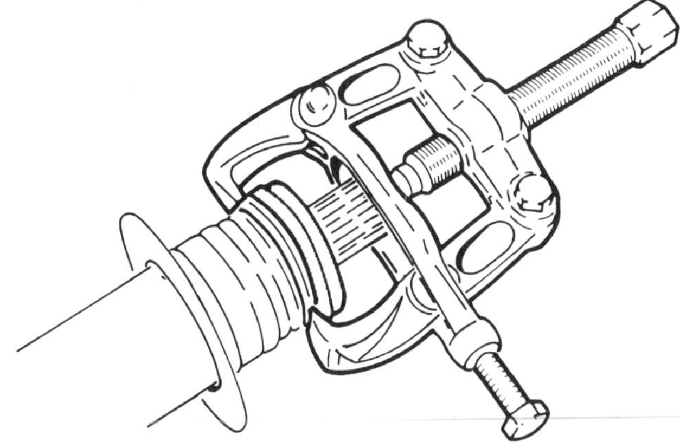

Fig 8.3 Using a puller to remove the centre bearing (Sec 4)

4.2 U-shaped washer (arrowed) located beneath bolt head

5.3 Note the fitted direction of the rubber coupling bolts

12 Slide the rear section of the propeller shaft onto the front section, ensuring that the previously made marks are aligned.
13 Refit the U-shaped washer in its previously noted position, with the peg facing towards the bearing bracket – see Fig. 8.4.
14 Tighten the bolt and bend over the tab on the lock washer to secure.
15 Refit the propeller shaft as described in Section 3.

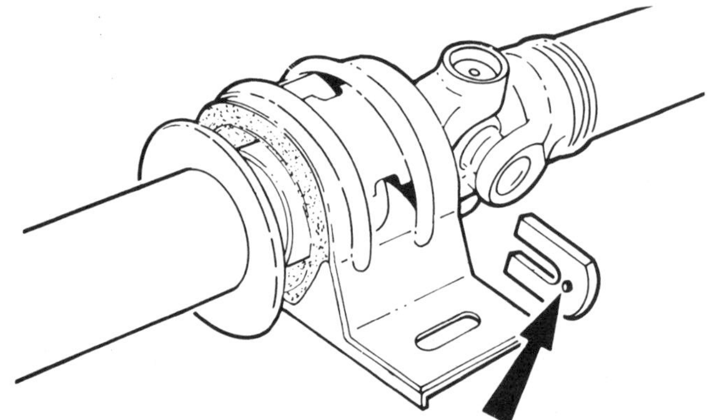

Fig 8.4 Correct position of peg (arrowed) when fitting U-shaped washer (Sec 4)

5 Propeller shaft front rubber coupling – renewal

1 Remove the propeller shaft as described in Section 3.
2 Fit a compressor around the circumference of the rubber coupling and tighten it until it just begins to compress the coupling. If a compressor is not available, two large worm drive hose clips joined end to end will serve the same purpose.
3 Mark the relative positions of the propeller shaft sections on either side of the coupling, and then progressively slacken and remove the six nuts, spring washers and bolts. Note which way round each bolt is fitted (photo).
4 Remove the coupling from the propeller shaft. If the original coupling is to be refitted, leave the compressor in position. A new coupling is normally supplied with a compressor already fitted, but if this is not the case, fit the compressor to the new coupling.
5 Refitting is a reversal of removal, ensuring that the previously made marks on the shaft sections are aligned, and that the bolts are fitted as noted during removal.
6 Remove the compressor on completion, and refit the propeller shaft as described in Section 3.

6 Fault diagnosis – propeller shaft

Symptom	Reason(s)
Vibration	Propeller shaft distorted Propeller shaft out of balance Deteriorated rubber insulator on centre bearing Worn splines at front of propeller shaft Worn propeller shaft joints or centre bearing
Knock or clunk when taking up drive	Worn propeller shaft joints Loose propeller shaft-to-final drive unit bolts Worn final drive pinion splines Excessive backlash in final drive gears
Rumble, increasing with road speed	Worn centre bearing

Note: *This Section is not intended as an exhaustive guide to fault diagnosis, but summarises the more common faults which may be encountered during a vehicle's life. Consult a dealer for more detailed advice.*

Chapter 9 Final drive and driveshafts

Contents

Specifications

Final drive type

Saloon, Hatchback and Estate models	Light alloy housing, bolted to rear suspension crossmember and underbody.
P100 models	Cast iron housing. Live beam axle, bolted to rear leaf springs.

Driveshaft type

Saloon, Hatchback and Estate models:	
Models with rear drum brakes	Open, fully floating with double tripode joints. Splined fit in final drive unit and rear hubs
Models with rear disc brakes	Open, fully floating with double Lobro joints. Bolted to final drive unit and rear hubs
P100 models	Enclosed, one-piece shafts running in rear axle housing. Splined fit in differential and bolted to rear hubs

Final drive ratio

1.3 litre models	3.77:1
1.6 litre models (except Economy):	
Saloon and Hatchback models	3.62:1
Estate models	3.92:1
1.6 litre Economy models	3.38:1
1.8 litre models	
4-speed and Automatic models	3.62:1
5-speed models	3.92:1
2.0 litre carburettor models (except P100):	
Manual	3.62:1
Automatic	3.38:1
2.0 litre fuel injection models:	
Manual	3.92:1
Automatic	3.62:1
P100 models	4.625:1

Lubrication

Final drive unit oil capacity (from dry):	
All models except 1.3 and 1.6 litre Hatchback and P100	0.9 litre (1.6 pints)
1.3 and 1.6 litre Hatchback models	0.8 litre (1.4 pints)
P100 models (rear axle)	1.14 litres (2.0 pints)
Final drive unit oil level (distance below filler plug hole):	
All models except P100	10.0 mm (0.4 in)
P100 models	25.0 mm (1.0 in)
Final drive unit oil type/specification (all models)	Hypoid gear oil, viscosity SAE 90EP to Ford spec SQM-2C 9002-AA or 9003-AA (Duckhams Hypoid 90S)
Driveshaft joint grease type/specification	Lithium based molybdenum disulphide grease to Ford spec SQM-1C 9004-A (Duckhams LBM10)

Torque wrench settings

	Nm	lbf ft
Saloon, Hatchback and Estate models		
Final drive unit rear cover bolts	45 to 60	33 to 44
Oil filler plug	35 to 45	26 to 33
Final drive pinion drive flange nut	100 to 120	74 to 89
Final drive unit-to-suspension crossmember bolts	70 to 90	52 to 66
Final drive unit-to-underbody bolts (gold coloured	60	44
Rear hub nut	250 to 290	185 to 214
Lobro type driveshaft-to-final drive bolts	38 to 43	28 to 32
Lobro type driveshaft-to-rear hub bolts	38 to 43	28 to 32
Rear hub carrier/brake backplate-to-lower suspension arm bolts*:		
Type X	52 to 64	38 to 47
Type Y	80 to 100	60 to 74
**See Chapter 11, Section 15*		
P100 models		
Brake backplate-to-axle nuts	45 to 54	33 to 40
Driveshaft-to-hub bolts	60 to 78	44 to 58
Rear hub nut	280 to 300	207 to 221
Axle-to-leaf spring U-bolt nuts	39 to 58	29 to 43

1 General description

The purpose of the final drive unit is to transmit drive from the propeller shaft to the rear wheels, whilst allowing for the difference in rotational speed between the inside and outside roadwheels when cornering. This difference in speed is allowed for by the use of a differential gear assembly. When travelling in a straight line, both wheels will rotate at the same speed, but when cornering, the inside wheel is allowed to rotate at a slower speed than the outside wheel, thus providing improved handling characteristics and greatly reduced tyre wear.

On P100 models, the final drive unit and driveshafts are incorporated in a solid rear axle assembly, whereas on Saloon, Hatchback and Estate models, the independent rear suspension allows the use of a separate final drive unit and fully floating driveshafts. The two final drive arrangements are described in more detail as follows.

Saloon, Hatchback and Estate models

The final drive unit is bolted directly to the rear underbody and the rear suspension crossmember. The final drive housing is made from light alloy. Oil seals are fitted to the final drive housing to retain oil at the drive pinion, and the two differential side bearings.

A conventional crownwheel and pinion arrangement is used, with both the differential and the drive pinion housing in taper roller bearings.

Drive from the differential is taken to the roadwheels by two open driveshafts with a constant velocity joint at each end. Two types of driveshaft are used depending on model. Models with rear drum brakes use tripode joint type driveshafts which are splined at both ends. The

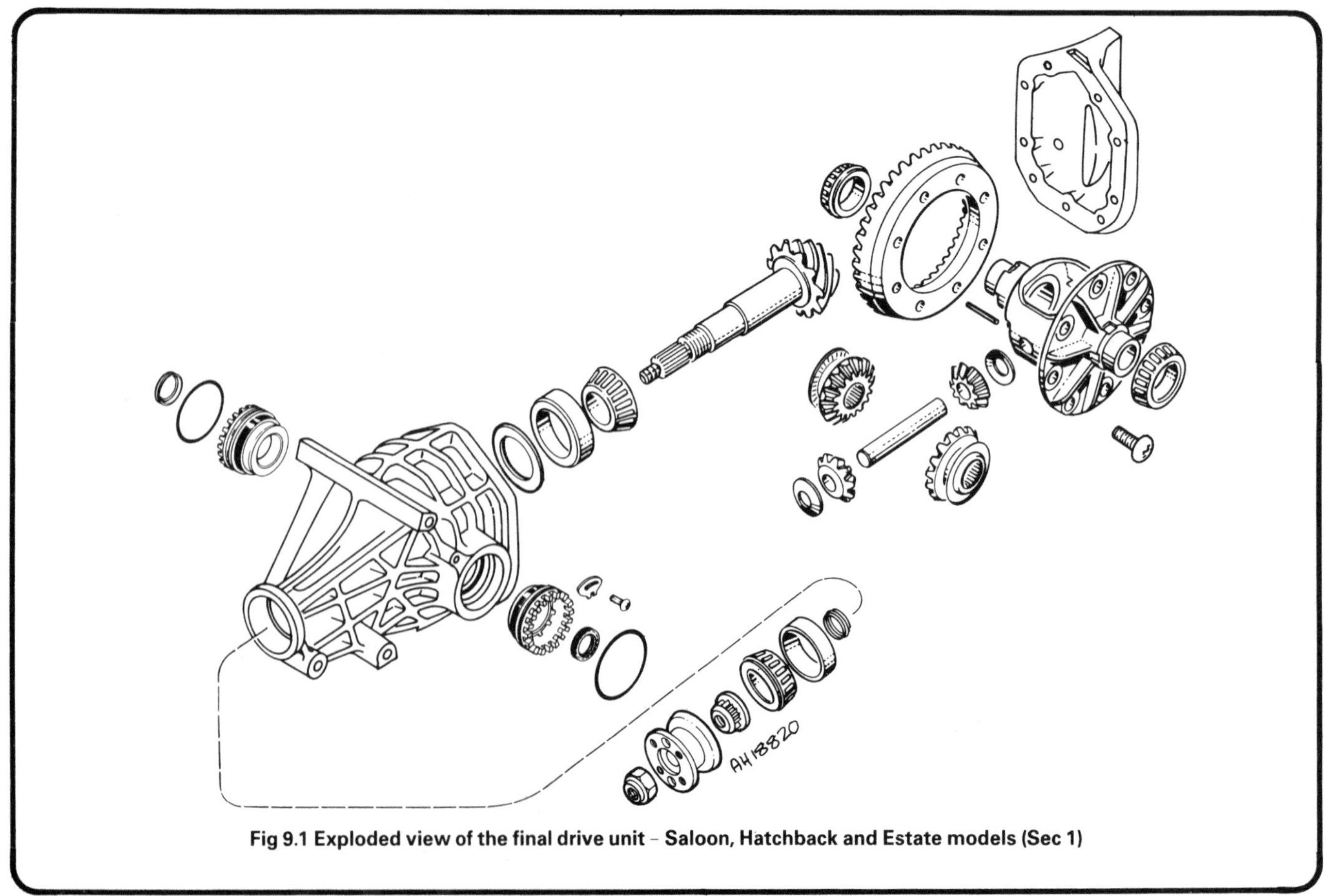

Fig 9.1 Exploded view of the final drive unit – Saloon, Hatchback and Estate models (Sec 1)

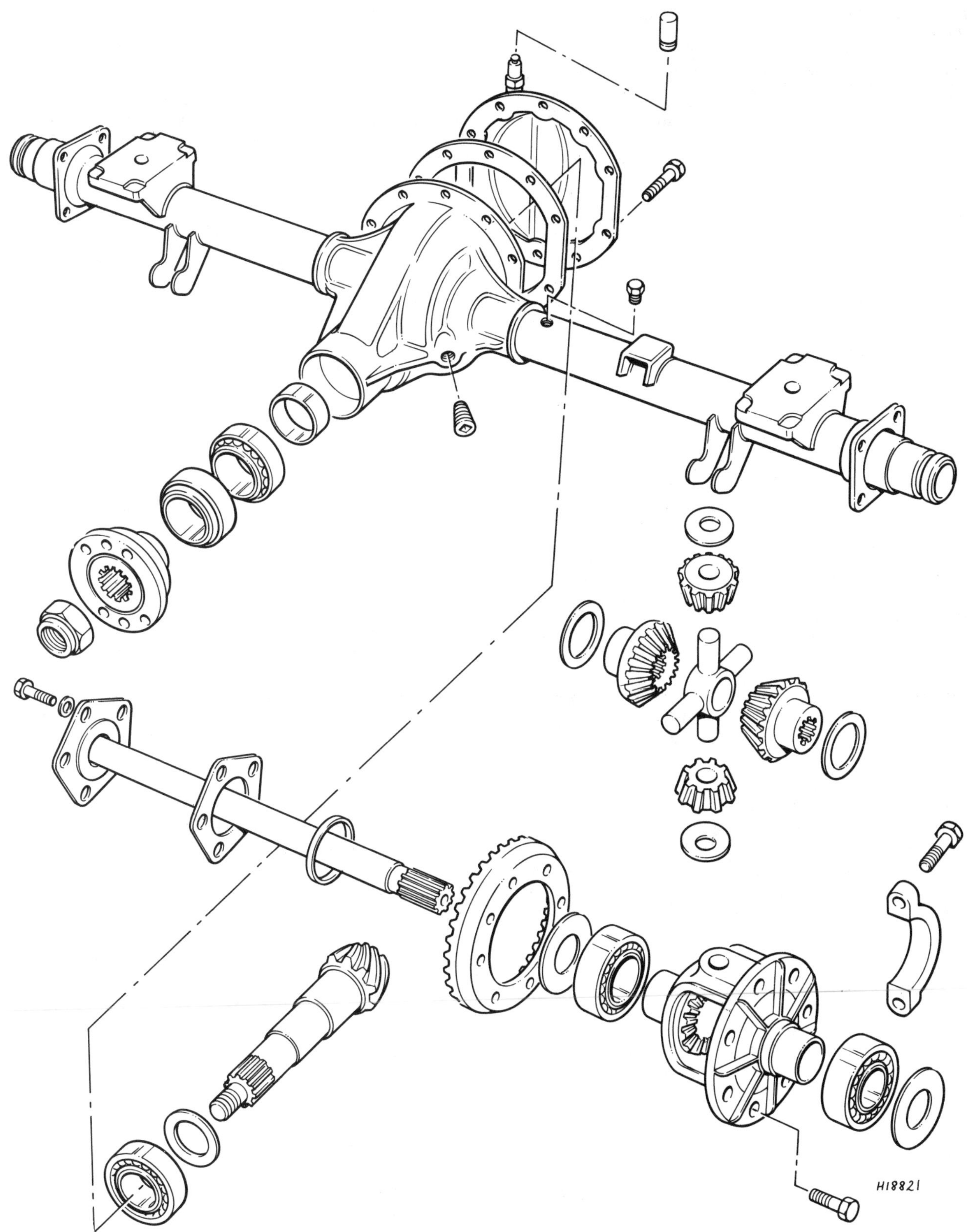

Fig 9.2 Exploded view of the rear axle assembly – P100 models (Sec 1)

inner ends fit into the differential, and the outer ends fit into the rear hubs and are retained by the rear hub nuts. Models with rear disc brakes use Lobro joint type driveshafts which are simply bolted by flanges to the final drive unit and the rear hubs.

P100 models

The rear axle assembly is bolted rigidly to the rear suspension leaf springs. The rear axle casing is made from cast iron.

A conventional crownwheel and pinion arrangement is used, with

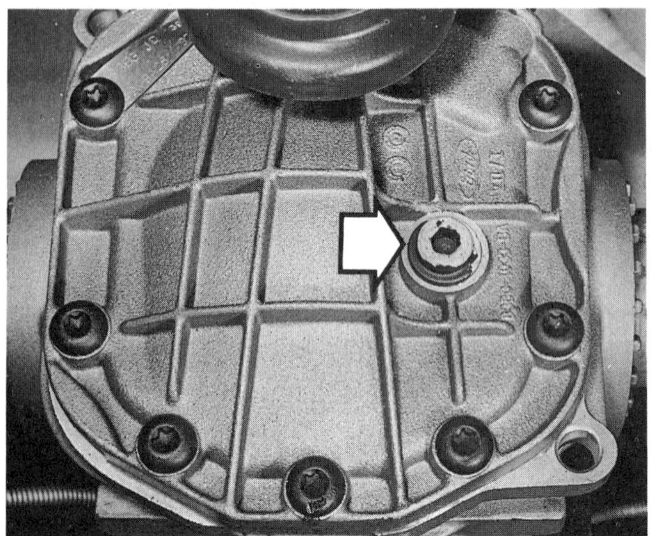

2.2A Final drive unit filler plug location (arrowed) – Saloon, Hatchback and Estate models

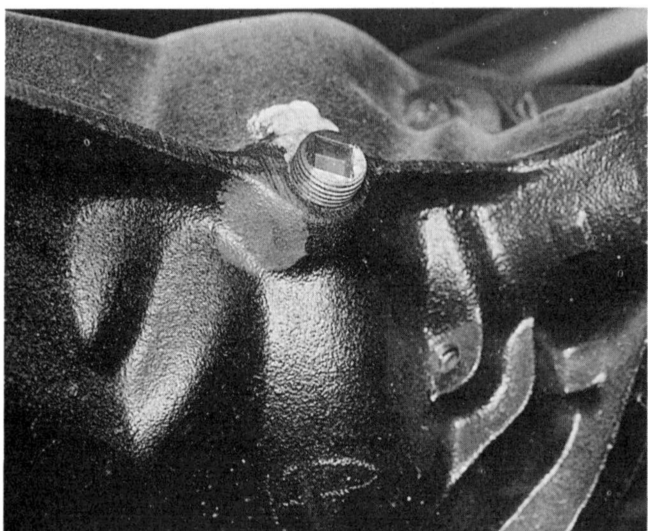

2.2B Rear axle filler plug location – P100 models

both the differential and the drive pinion running in taper roller bearings.

Drive from the differential is taken to the roadwheels by two rigid driveshafts enclosed in the rear axle casing. The inner ends of the driveshafts are splined and fit into the differential, and the outer ends are bolted to the rear hubs.

2 Routine maintenance

1 At the intervals specified in the *'Routine maintenance'* Section at the beginning of this manual, the final drive unit oil level should be checked and if necessary topped up. To do this, jack up the front and rear of the vehicle and support on axle stands. The vehicle must be level.

2 Using a suitable tool (the type of plug used varies according to model), unscrew and remove the filler plug (photos). It is advisable to wipe clean the area around the plug before removal, to prevent dirt ingress.

3 Using a piece of bent wire as a dipstick, check that the oil level is no more than the specified distance below the filler plug hole. If necessary top up with the specified type of oil. Do not overfill.

4 Refit and tighten the filler plug. On some models thread-locking compound may have been used on the filler plug in production. Do not use thread-locking compound when the plug is refitted.

5 There is no requirement for periodic oil changing, and no drain plug is provided.

6 Whilst the vehicle is raised, examine the driveshaft joint rubber gaiters where applicable. Damaged or leaking gaiters must be renewed without delay to avoid damage to the joint itself through dirt or water ingress.

3 Final drive unit (Saloon, Hatchback and Estate models) – removal and refitting

Note: *From May 1986, revised final drive unit rear mounting bolts have been used in production. Whenever the earlier type of bolts are removed, they should be discarded and the later type fitted. The earlier bolts are coloured blue, and the later type bolts are coloured gold.*

1 Loosen the rear roadwheel nuts, jack up the vehicle and support on axle stands. It is only strictly necessary to jack up the rear of the vehicle, but this provides only limited access.

2 Remove the rear roadwheels.

3 If required, for improved access the rear section of the exhaust system (ie from the joint) can be removed with reference to Chapter 3, but this is not essential. The same applies to the rear anti-roll bar where applicable – refer to Chapter 11.

4 Remove the propeller shaft as described in Chapter 8.

5 On models fitted with rear drum brakes, disconnect the driveshafts at their outboard ends and withdraw the inboard ends of the driveshafts from the final drive unit, as described in Section 7. Once withdrawn from the final drive unit, the driveshafts can be left in place, but support the centre and inboard sections of the shafts so that the deflection of each tripode joint does not exceed 13°

6 On models fitted with rear disc brakes, unbolt the inboard ends of the driveshafts from the final drive unit. The driveshafts can be left in place, but they should be supported to avoid straining the joints.

7 Support the final drive unit with a trolley jack, using an interposed block of wood between the jack and the final drive to spread the load.

8 Unscrew the four bolts from the final drive unit rear mounting on the underbody (photo). Note the location and number of any shims which may be fitted.

9 Remove the final drive unit vent pipe from the hole in the underbody (photo).

10 Unscrew the single front bolt on each side securing the final drive unit to the rear suspension crossmember (photo).

11 Lower the final drive unit slightly, and unscrew the two through-bolts and nuts securing the final drive unit to the rear suspension crossmember. Note the location and number of any shims which may be fitted to the top through-bolt between the final drive unit and the

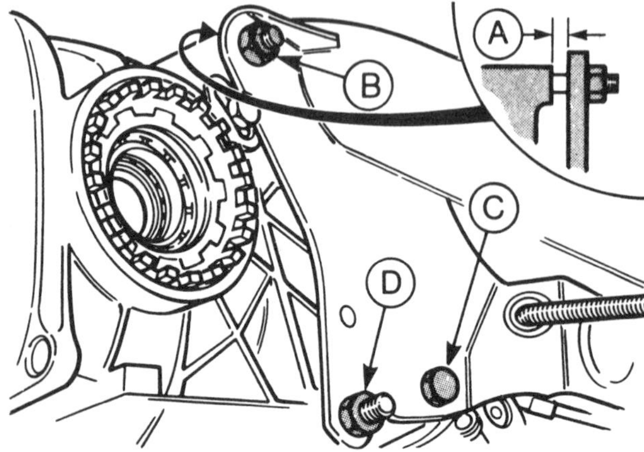

Fig 9.3 Final drive unit mounting details (Sec 3)

A Gap to be shimmed
B Top through-bolt
C Front bolt
D Bottom through-bolt

3.8 Final drive unit rear mounting

3.9 Removing the final drive unit vent pipe

3.10 Final drive unit-to-rear crossmember front securing bolt (1) and through-bolts (2)

crossmember mating flanges. Be prepared to catch these shims as the through-bolt is removed.

12 Lower the final drive unit and remove it from under the vehicle.

13 When refitting the final drive unit, the following procedure must be observed.

14 Refit the final drive unit to the rear suspension crossmember, and loosely fit the securing bolts. Insert the top through-bolt with any shims noted during removal.

15 Refit the final drive unit rear mounting to the vehicle underbody, with reference to the note at the beginning of this Section. Position any shims noted during removal in their original positions and tighten the securing bolts to the specified torque.

16 Tighten the single front bolt on each side, and the bottom through-bolt securing the final drive unit to the rear suspension crossmember, to the specified torque. A spanner will be required to hold the nut on the through-bolt as the bolt is tightened.

17 If shims were not fitted to the top through-bolt during removal, they should have been located in their original positions, and the through-bolt can be tightened to the specified torque, holding the nut with a spanner. If no shims were fitted, proceed as follows.

18 Using feeler gauges, measure the gap ('A' in Fig. 9.3) on each side between the final drive unit and the rear suspension crossmember mating flanges.

19 Select and insert appropriate shims at each end of the through-bolt so that with the shims in position they just contact both the final drive unit and the rear suspension crossmember. If no gap was measured, then no shims will be required. Shims are available from a Ford dealer in thicknesses of 0.5, 1.0 and 1.5 mm (0.03, 0.04 and 0.05 in).

20 With the appropriate shims located where necessary, tighten the through-bolt to the specified torque, holding the nut with a spanner.

21 The remainder of the refitting procedure is a reversal of removal, bearing in mind the following.

22 On models with rear drum brakes, reconnect the driveshafts as described in Section 7.

23 Refit the propeller shaft as described in Chapter 8.

24 Where applicable, refit the rear section of the exhaust system and/or the rear anti-roll bar with reference to Chapters 3 and 11 respectively.

25 On completion, check and if necessary top up the final drive unit oil level as described in Section 2.

4 Final drive unit pinion oil seal (Saloon, Hatchback and Estate models) - renewal

Note: *A suitable puller will be required to remove the final drive flange from the pinion.*

1 The pinion oil seal can be renewed without removing the final drive unit, as follows.

2 Remove the propeller shaft as described in Chapter 8.

3 Hold the final drive flange stationary by applying the handbrake. Alternatively bolt a long bar to the flange, or screw two bolts into adjacent holes and insert a long bar between them.

4 Unscrew the self-locking drive flange nut (photo).

5 Place a suitable container beneath the final drive unit to catch any oil which may be lost as the drive flange is removed.

6 Using a suitable puller, pull the drive flange from the pinion (photos).

7 Using a screwdriver, lever the oil seal from the final drive unit (photo).

8 Clean the area of the final drive housing where the oil seal seats, and clean the drive flange and the end of the pinion.

9 The new oil seal will be supplied ready packed with grease, and the grease must be left in place when the seal is fitted. Drive the new seal squarely into the final drive housing until flush using a suitable tube drift.

10 Slide the drive flange onto the pinion splines, taking care not to damage the oil seal.

11 Fit the self-locking nut and tighten it to the specified torque while holding the drive flange stationary using one of the methods described in paragraph 3 (photo). Ideally a new self- locking nut should be used, but if the old nut is re-used, it should not be unscrewed and tightened more than three times otherwise it will lose its self-locking characteristic.

4.4 Removing the self-locking drive flange nut

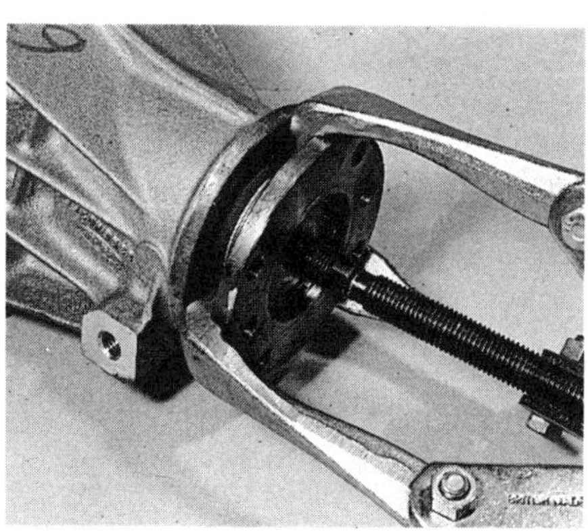

4.6A Using a puller to remove the drive flange

4.6B Drive flange removed showing splines on flange and pinion

Fig 9.4 Installing the final drive unit pinion oil seal (Sec 4)

12 Refit the propeller shaft as described in Chapter 8.
13 Check and if necessary top up the final drive unit oil level as described in Section 2.

5 Final drive unit differential bearing oil seal (Saloon, Hatchback and Estate models) – renewal

Models with rear drum brakes

1 The differential bearing oil seals can be renewed without removing the final drive unit, as follows.
2 Remove the relevant driveshaft as described in Section 7.
3 Using a depth gauge, or a narrow steel rule, measure the fitted depth of the oil seal. This should be approximately 11.0 mm (0.4 in) measured from the outer face of the bearing retaining ring (photo).
4 Using a screwdriver, lever the oil seal from the differential bearing housing.
5 Clean the oil seal seating area in the bearing housing.
6 Smear the lips of the new oil seal with a little molybdenum disulphide grease, then using a suitable tube drift, press the seal squarely into the bearing housing to the previously noted depth.
7 Refit the driveshaft as described in Section 7.

Models with rear disc brakes

8 Remove the final drive unit as described in Section 3.
9 Remove the final drive unit rear cover. Place a suitable container under the final drive unit, as the oil will drain out when the rear cover is removed. The cover is secured by nine Torx bolts.
10 Clean the old sealant from the cover and final drive unit mating faces, taking care to keep it out of the interior of the unit.
11 Remove the circlip securing the relevant output flange inside the final drive unit. If both oil seals are being renewed, **do not get the circlips mixed up,** as their thickness is selected and may differ from side to side.
12 Withdraw the output flange, and clean the seal seating area.
13 Proceed as described in paragraphs 3 to 6 inclusive.
14 Refit the output flange, being careful not to damage the oil seal. Refit the original securing clip.
15 Apply liquid sealant (to Ford spec SQM-46 9523-A) to the mating faces of the rear cover and final drive unit.
16 Fit the rear cover, and tighten the securing bolts in a diagonal sequence to the specified torque.
17 Refit the final drive unit as described in Section 3.

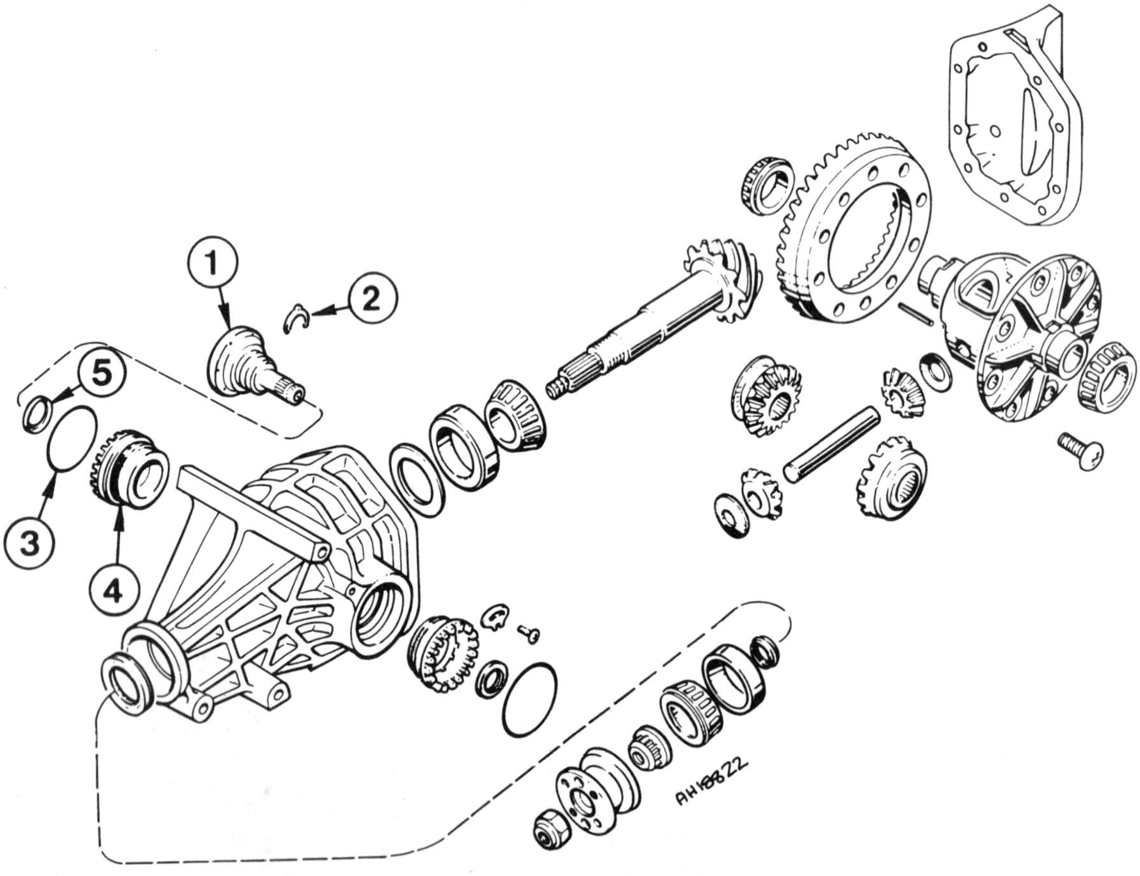

Fig 9.5 Exploded view of final drive unit – models with rear disc brakes (Sec 5)

1 Output flange
2 Circlip
3 O-ring
4 Bearing housing
5 Oil seal

4.7 Pinion oil seal location in final drive unit

4.11 Tightening the pinion drive flange nut

5.3 Differential bearing oil seal location in final drive unit (arrowed)

6 Final drive unit (Saloon, Hatchback and Estate models) – overhaul

Overhaul of the final drive unit is a complex task, and requires the use of several special tools and fixtures not normally available to the home mechanic. The pinion and differential bearing oil seals can be renewed as described in Sections 4 and 5 respectively, but it is recommended that any further overhaul work is referred to a Ford dealer.

7 Driveshaft (Saloon, Hatchback and Estate models) – removal and refitting

Models with rear drum brakes

1 If a driveshaft is being removed for dismantling or renewal, loosen the relevant rear hub nut with the vehicle resting on its wheels. If the driveshaft is being removed for access, this is not necessary. On early models, relieve the staking before loosening the nut. Later models use self-locking nuts, and it is important to note that where this type of nut is fitted, the left-hand nut has a left-hand thread, ie it is undone in a clockwise direction. Before loosening the nut, ensure that the handbrake is applied, and check the relevant rear wheel. A suitable extension bar will be required, as the nut is extremely tight.

2 Loosen the rear roadwheel nuts on the side concerned, chock the front wheels, and jack up the rear of the vehicle and support on axle stands.

3 Remove the rear roadwheel.

4 Remove the brake drum retaining spire washer(s) from the wheel stud(s) and remove the brake drum (photos). Ensure that the handbrake is released before removing the brake drum, otherwise the drum will be held in place by the clamping action of the brake shoes.

5 Remove the two nylon fasteners, and remove the plastic shield from the rear of the brake backplate (photo).

6 Using a socket inserted through one of the holes in the drive flange, unscrew the four bolts securing the hub carrier and brake backplate to the lower suspension arm (photo). The drive flange can be rotated to gain access to all four bolts.

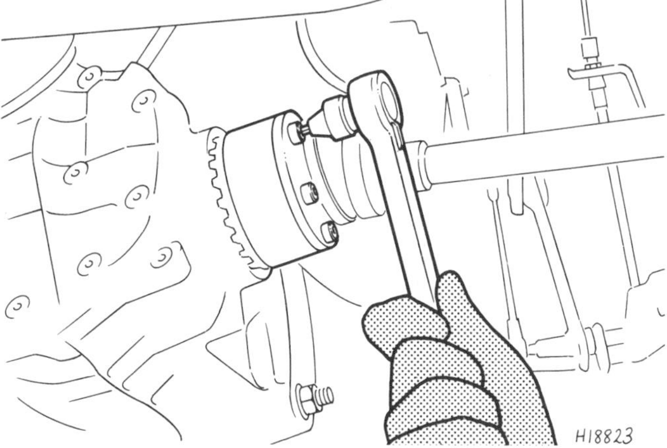

Fig 9.6 Unscrewing the driveshaft-to-final drive unit bolts – models with rear disc brakes (Sec 7)

7 Place a suitable container beneath the final drive unit to catch any oil which may be released as the driveshaft is withdrawn.

8 The complete driveshaft and hub assembly can now be withdrawn, passing it through the hole in the brake backplate (photo). Note that the driveshaft joints should not be allowed to deflect through an angle exceeding 13°.

9 When the driveshaft and hub assembly has been withdrawn, refit the brake backplate with the four securing bolts to avoid straining the brake pipe.

10 If the driveshaft has been removed for dismantling or renewal, proceed as described in Section 8.

11 Refitting is a reversal of removal, bearing in mind the following.

7.4A Brake drum retaining spire washers (arrowed)

7.4B Removing the brake drum

7.5 Removing the plastic shield from the brake backplate

7.6 Unscrewing a hub/brake backplate-to-lower suspension arm securing bolt

7.8 Withdrawing the driveshaft and hub assembly

7.13 Tightening the rear hub nut

12 When refitting the bolts securing the hub carrier and brake backplate to the lower suspension arm, refer to the note in Section 15 of Chapter 11.
13 Where applicable, tighten the rear hub nut to the specified torque with the vehicle resting on its roadwheels (photo). Apply the handbrake and chock the relevant rear wheel. If a staked type nut is used, lock the nut by staking its outer ring into the groove in the driveshaft.
14 On completion, check and if necessary top up the final drive unit oil level as described in Section 2.

Models with rear disc brakes

15 Chock the front wheels, jack up the rear of the vehicle and support on axle stands.
16 Apply the handbrake to prevent the driveshaft from turning, then unscrew the six Torx bolts securing the inboard end of the driveshaft to the final drive unit. Recover the lockwashers. Support the driveshaft.
17 Similarly remove the six bolts which secure the outboard end of the driveshaft to the rear hub. Remove the driveshaft.
18 At all times, avoid bending the driveshaft joints to excessive angles, and do not allow the shaft to hang down from one end.
19 Refitting is a reversal of removal. Tighten the securing bolts to the specified torque.

8 Driveshaft (Saloon, Hatchback and Estate models) – dismantling, overhaul and reassembly

Models with rear drum brakes

Note: *Before contemplating overhaul of a driveshaft, cneck to ensure that suitable replacement parts can be obtained. Suitable pullers will be required to remove the drive flange and joint spiders, and to refit the joint cover. A new rear hub nut of the correct type must be used on reassembly.*
1 With the driveshaft removed as described in Section 7, unscrew and discard the rear hub nut.
2 Using a suitable puller, pull the drive flange from the end of the stub shaft.
3 The hub carrier complete with bearings can now be removed by sliding it from the end of the stub shaft (photo). For details of rear wheel bearing renewal, refer to Chapter 11.
4 If the complete driveshaft is being renewed, refit the hub carrier and drive flange to the new driveshaft as described in paragraph 25 onwards. If the driveshaft is to be dismantled for overhaul, proceed as follows, bearing in mind the note at the beginning of this Section.
5 Remove the clips from the rubber gaiter on the outboard joint.
6 Using a hacksaw, cut the metal joint cover around part of its circumference, then cut the cover along the driveshaft axis, and using a pair of pliers, peel back the cover from the joint until the swaged end is

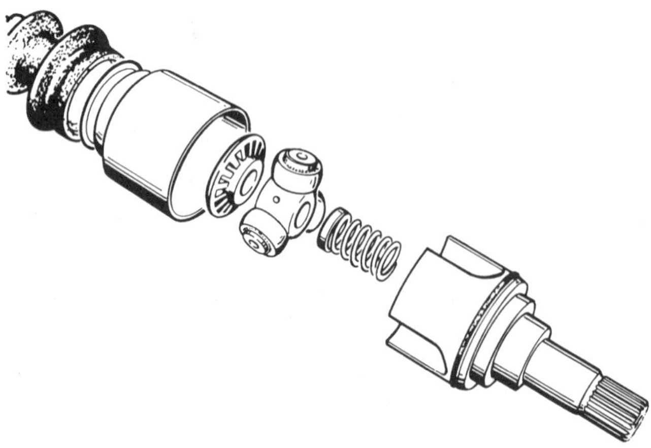
Fig 9.7 Exploded view of driveshaft joint – models with rear drum brakes (Sec 8)

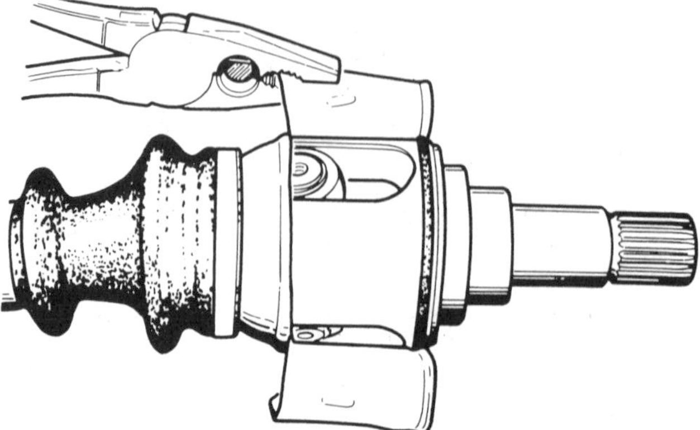
Fig 9.8 Removing a driveshaft joint cover – models with rear drum brakes (Sec 8)

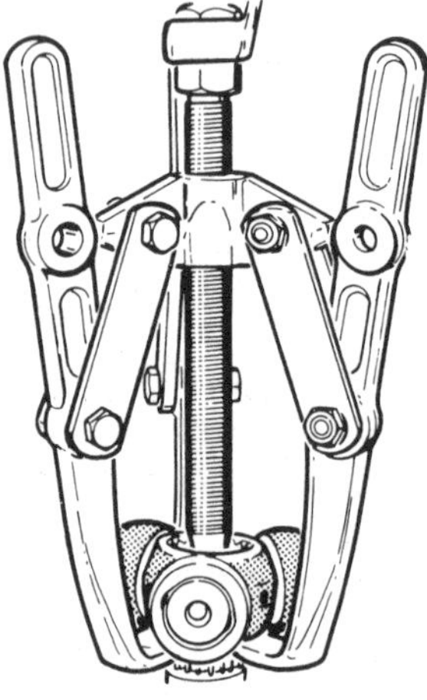
Fig 9.9 Removing a driveshaft joint spider using a three-legged puller – models with rear drum brakes (Sec 8)

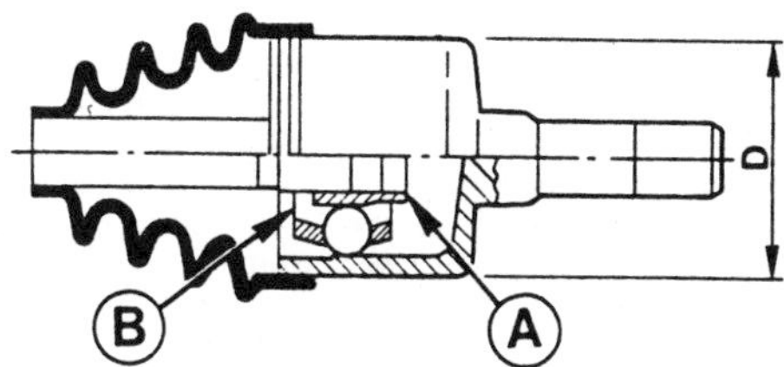

Fig 9.10 Driveshaft joint grease application areas and quantities (Sec 8)

Model with rear drum brakes		
Gaiter type	**Grease at A**	**Grease at B**
Gaiter with 2 beads	*15g*	*65 to 70g*
Gaiter with 3 beads	*15g*	*85g*
Models with rear disc brakes		
Diameter D	**Grease at A**	**Grease at B**
100 mm	*60g*	*10g*
108 mm	*80g*	*15g*

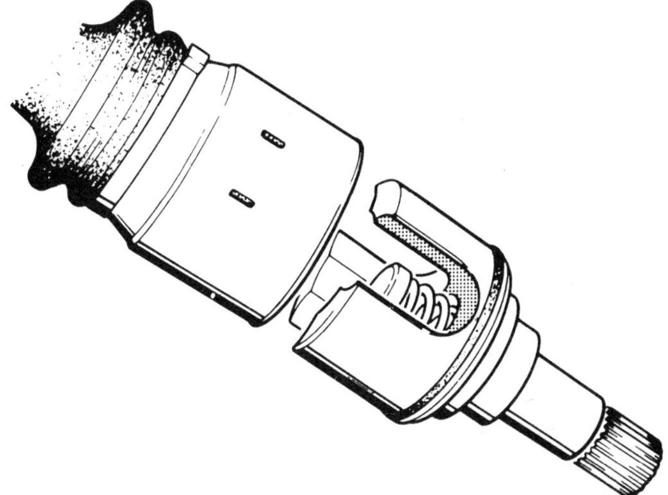

Fig 9.11 The six notches in the joint cover must engage with the cut-outs in the stub shaft – models with rear drum brakes (Sec 8)

released. As the cover is removed, the end stub shaft will be pushed from the driveshaft under the action of the spring in the joint. The spring will drop out as the stub shaft is removed.

7 Mark the joint spider in relation to the driveshaft centre section, then extract the retaining circlip.

8 Push the rubber gaiter and the remains of the joint cover along the driveshaft away from the joint.

9 Using a suitable puller, pull the joint spider from the splined end of the driveshaft.

10 Remove the plastic washer, the remains of the joint cover and the rubber gaiter from the driveshaft.

11 Remove the rubber O-ring from the groove in the stub shaft.

12 Wash all the components in paraffin and wipe them dry, then examine them for wear and damage. Check the joint spider roller bearings for rough operation and excessive wear. Renew the components as necessary, and obtain a new joint cover gaiter, and rubber O-ring.

13 Locate the rubber gaiter followed by the joint cover and plastic washer (convex side first) onto the driveshaft centre section.

14 Locate the joint spider on the driveshaft splines, aligning the previously made marks, and drive it onto the shaft using a suitable tube drift.

15 Fit the joint spider retaining circlip to the end of the driveshaft.

16 Fit the rubber O-ring into the groove in the stub shaft, and locate the spring in the hole inside the stub shaft.

17 Mount the driveshaft centre section in a vice, and fit the stub shaft over the joint spider. Pack the joint with approximately 15 grammes of the specified grease at point 'A' in Fig. 9.10, and smear a little grease on the rubber O-ring.

18 Push the stub shaft onto the driveshaft centre section so that the internal spring is compressed, then using a suitable puller, pull the joint cover over the stub shaft, making sure that the six notches in the cover engage with the cut-outs in the stub shaft. Take care not to damage the O-ring.

19 Swage the joint cover onto the stub shaft at three equally spaced points, then remove the puller.

20 Swage the remainder of the joint cover around its complete circumference.

21 From the inner end of the joint cover, pack the joint at point 'B' in Fig. 9.10 with the specified type and quantity of grease.

22 Locate the rubber gaiter on the joint cover and driveshaft, ensuring that it is not twisted or stretched, then fit and tighten the retaining clips.

23 Repeat the procedure given in paragraphs 5 to 22 on the inboard joint.

24 When overhaul of the driveshaft assembly is complete, the hub carrier and drive flange can be refitted as follows.

25 Fit the drive flange to the hub carrier in order to centralise the bearings, then using a soft-faced mallet, drive the drive flange/hub carrier assembly onto the stub shaft (photo).

26 Fit a new rear hub nut of the correct type, but leave tightening the

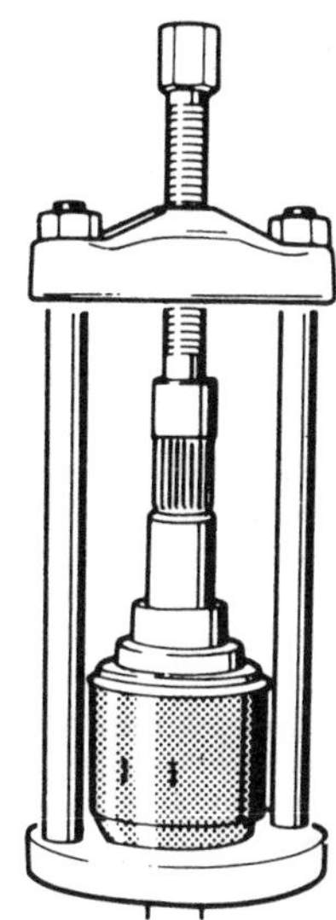

Fig 9.12 Using a puller to fit the joint cover – models with rear drum brakes (Sec 8)

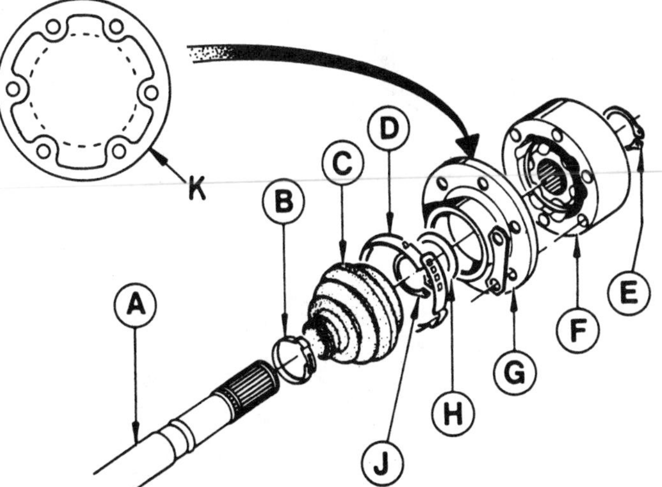

Fig 9.13 Exploded view of driveshaft joint – models with rear disc brakes (Sec 8)

A Shaft
B Gaiter securing clip
C Gaiter
D Gaiter securing clip
E Outer circlip
F Joint
G Joint inner cover
H Dished washer (if fitted)
J Inner circlip
K Sealant application area

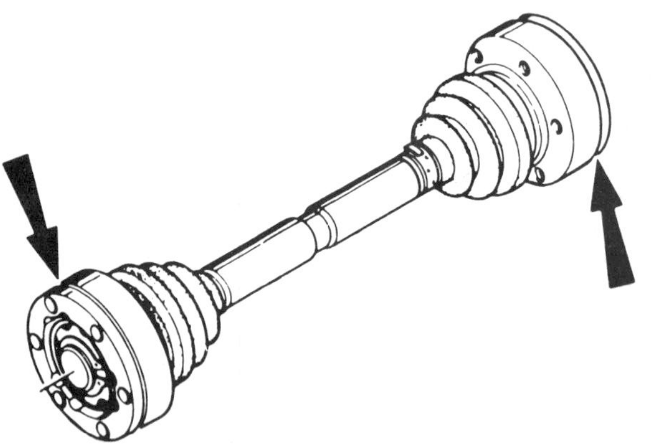

Fig 9.14 Correct fitting of joints to driveshaft with grooves (arrowed) outermost – models with rear disc brakes (Sec 8)

nut until the driveshaft has been refitted, and the vehicle is resting on its wheels, as described in Section 7.

Models with rear disc brakes

27 The driveshafts cannot be dismantled for overhaul, but the joints and rubber gaiters can be renewed as follows.
28 With the driveshaft removed as described in Section 7, undo or cut the clips which secure the relevant gaiter to the driveshaft. Pull the gaiter back from the joint.
29 Remove the outer circlip which secures the joint to the driveshaft.
30 Pull the joint from the driveshaft and remove the dished washer (where fitted) and the inner circlip from the shaft.
31 The gaiter can now be removed from the driveshaft.
32 Renew the components as necessary, the gaiter clips must be renewed in any case.
33 Pack the joint with the specified type and quantity of grease – see Fig. 9.10.
34 Fit the gaiter and the joint inner cover to the driveshaft, then fit the inner circlip and the dished washer (where applicable).
35 Apply sealant (to Ford specification ESK-M46275-A – available from a Ford dealer) to the joint inner cover face where it mates with the joint – inset in Fig. 9.13. Clean any grease from the corresponding face of the joint.
36 Fit the joint, grooves outermost, and secure with the outer circlip.
37 Secure the gaiter with new clips.
38 Repeat the procedure for the remaining joint as necessary.
39 Refit the driveshaft as described in Section 7.

9 Rear axle (P100 models) – removal and refitting

Note: *When refitting the rear axle, new rear hub nuts and driveshaft O-rings must be used, and all self-locking nuts and spring washers must be renewed.*

1 Loosen the rear roadwheel nuts, chock the front wheels, and jack up the rear of the vehicle and support on axle stands placed under the side members. Note that a loaded vehicle must not be jacked under the differential casing.
2 Mark the position of one of the roadwheels in relation to the brake drum, then remove the roadwheel.
3 Mark the position of the brake drum in relation to one of the wheel studs, then remove the brake drum retaining spire washer(s) from the wheel stud(s) and remove the brake drum. Ensure that the handbrake is released before removing the brake drum, otherwise the drum will be held in place by the clamping action of the brake shoes.
4 Mark the position of the driveshaft flange in relation to the hub, unscrew the five retaining bolts, and remove the driveshaft from the

8.3 Removing the hub from the stub shaft

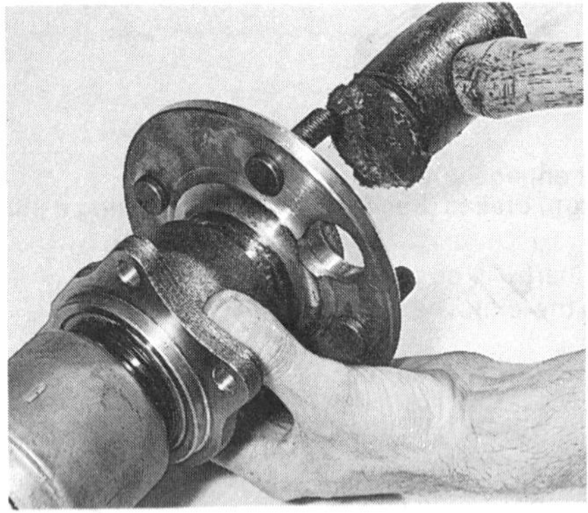

8.25 Driving the drive flange/hub assembly onto the driveshaft

9.11 View of right-hand axle tube showing brake load apportioning valve spring bracket (1) and brake pipe junction (2) – P100 models

9.13 Brake pipe securing clips (arrowed) on rear axle – P100 models

9.15 Rear axle-to-leaf spring U-bolts and counterplate

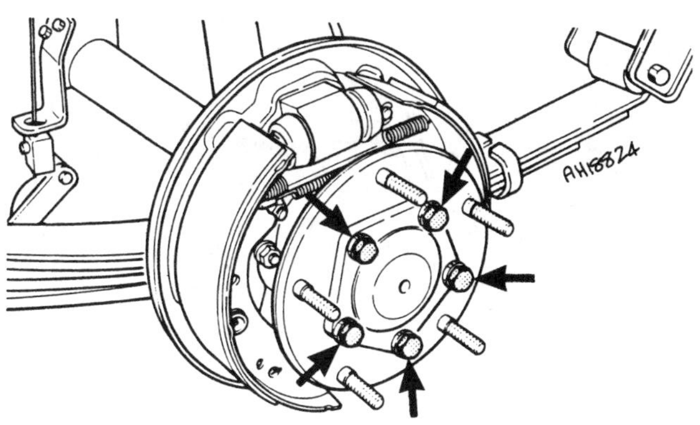

Fig 9.15 Brake drum removed showing driveshaft retaining bolts (arrowed) – P100 models (Sec 9)

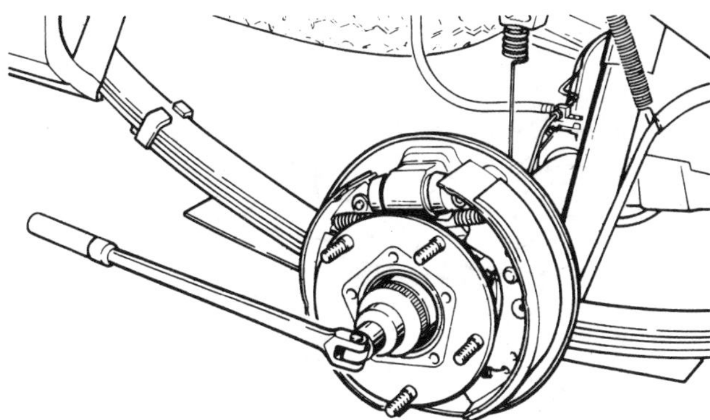

Fig 9.16 Unscrewing a rear hub nut – P100 models (Sec 9)

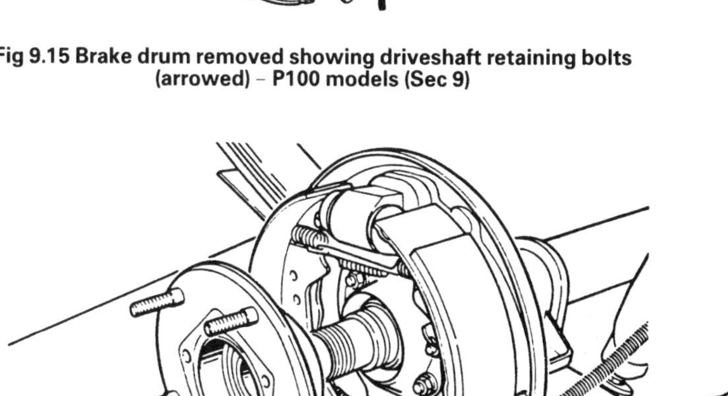

Fig 9.17 Removing a rear hub – P100 models (Sec 9)

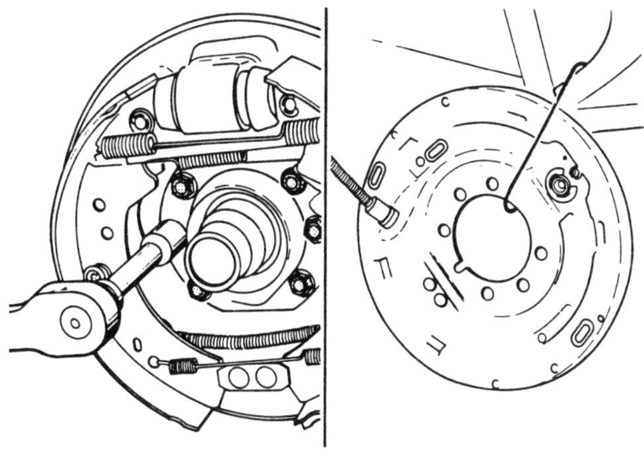

Fig 9.18 Unscrewing the brake backplate and oil baffle retaining bolts – P100 models (Sec 9)

axle tube. Be prepared for oil spillage. Note the gasket fitted between the driveshaft flange and the hub.

5 Relieve the staking on the rear hub nut, and using a 50 mm socket and a suitable extension bar, unscrew the nut. Note that the nut is extremely tight.

6 Pull off the hub, and remove the O-ring and spacer sleeve from the recess in the hub.

7 Unscrew the brake pipe from the wheel cylinder on the brake backplate. Plug the end of the pipe and the wheel cylinder to prevent leakage and dirt ingress.

8 Unscrew the six retaining nuts, and remove the brake backplate and the oil baffle. Tie the backplate to the vehicle underbody, away from the axle tube.

9 Repeat the operations described in paragraphs 2 to 8 inclusive on the remaining side of the vehicle.

10 Unscrew the brake pipe from the brake hose on the right-hand side of the chassis crossmember. Plug the ends of the pipe and hose to prevent leakage and dirt ingress, then detach the hose from the cross-member by removing the U-shaped retaining clip – see Fig. 9.19.

11 Unscrew the two bolts securing the brake load apportioning valve spring bracket to the right-hand axle tube, and allow the bracket to hang freely from the spring (photo).

12 Unscrew the bolt securing the brake pipe junction to the right-hand axle tube.

13 Unclip the brake pipe from the axle, and place to one side to avoid damage (photo).

14 Disconnect the propeller shaft from the final drive unit as described in Chapter 8. Support the propeller shaft by suspending it from one of the chassis crossmembers with string.

15 Unscrew the nuts, and remove the two U-bolts on each side of the vehicle which secure the axle to the leaf springs. Note that there is no need to disconnect the shock absorbers from the U-bolt counterplates (photo).

16 The axle can now be removed from the vehicle with the aid of an assistant, by sliding it to one side until it can be withdrawn under the leaf spring on the opposite side.

17 To refit the axle proceed as follows, with reference to the note at the beginning of this Section.

18 Slide the axle under the vehicle, and with the aid of an assistant, lift one end and slide it over the leaf spring. Slide the axle fully to one side, so that the remaining end can be slid over its leaf spring.

19 Align the axle on the left springs so that the locating pins on the springs engage with the corresponding holes in the axle.

20 Fit the U-bolts over the axle tubes and into the U-bolt counter-plates (with shock absorbers still attached). Screw on the nuts and tighten them to the specified torque. Note that the U- bolt counterplates must be engaged with the locating pins on the leaf springs.

21 Reconnect the propeller shaft to the final drive unit as described in Chapter 8, but note that the propeller shaft centre bearing may have to be unbolted from the underbody and refitted after the propeller shaft has been connected to the final drive unit, in order to ensure that the propeller shaft is fitted without any undue stress.

22 Refit the brake pipe to its clips on the axle.

23 Refit the brake pipe junction to the right-hand axle tube and tighten its securing bolt.

24 Refit the brake load apportioning valve spring bracket to the right-hand axle tube and tighten its two retaining bolts.

25 Refit the brake hose to the pipe on the chassis crossmember. Refit the retaining clip and tighten the union.

26 The brake, hub and driveshaft assemblies can now be refitted to each side of the axle as follows.

27 Coat the area of the oil baffle shown in Fig. 9.20 with sealant (to Ford spec SPM-46-9112-F), then refit the baffle and the backplate to the axle, tightening the six securing nuts to the specified torque. Ensure that the drain hole in the brake backplate is free from blockage.

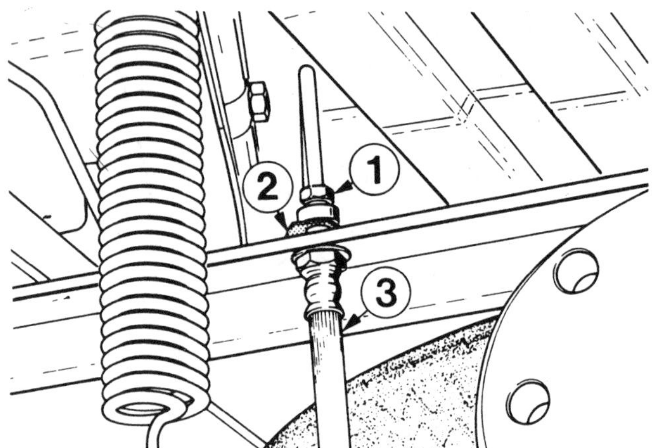

Fig 9.19 Brake pipe connection on chassis crossmember – P100 models (Sec 9)

1 Union nut
2 U-shaped clip
3 Brake hose

Fig 9.20 Fitting the oil baffle to the brake backplate – P100 models (Sec 9)

A Oil baffle
B Drain hole
C Sealant application area

28 Refit the brake pipe to the cylinder on the brake backplate, and tighten the union.
29 Lightly grease the hub oil seal, and fit the wheel hub. (Renewal of the oil is described in Chapter 11.)
30 Screw on a new rear hub nut, and tighten to the specified torque. Stake the nut into the groove in the axle tube after tightening.
31 Refit the spacer sleeve to the recess in the hub, bevelled side facing outwards, and fit a new O-ring.
32 Slide the driveshaft into the axle tube, with a new gasket, and tighten the five retaining bolts to the specified torque. Ensure that the previously made marks on the driveshaft flange and the hub are aligned.
33 Refit the brake drum and retaining spire washer(s), ensuring that the previously made marks on the drum and wheel stud are aligned.
34 Repeat the procedure given in paragraphs 27 to 33 inclusive on the remaining side of the vehicle.
35 Bleed the rear brake circuit as described in Chapter 10.
36 Check the handbrake operation and adjust if necessary as described in Chapter 10.
37 Check the axle oil level and top up if necessary as described in Section 2. Note that the vehicle must be level.
38 Refit the roadwheels, ensuring that the previously made marks on wheels and brake drums are aligned, then lower the vehicle to the ground.
39 Tighten the roadwheel nuts with the vehicle resting on its wheels.
40 Check the brake load apportioning adjustment as described in Chapter 10.

10 Rear axle (P100 models) – overhaul

Overhaul of the rear axle is a complex task, and requires the use of several special tools and fixtures not normally available to the home mechanic. The driveshafts and their O-rings can be renewed as described in Section 11, but it is recommended that any further overhaul work is referred to a Ford dealer.

11 Driveshaft and driveshaft O-ring (P100 models) – removal, renewal and refitting

1 Loosen the rear roadwheel nuts on the relevant side of the vehicle, chock the front wheels, and jack up the rear of the vehicle and support on axle stands.
2 Mark the position of the roadwheel in relation to the brake drum, then remove the roadwheel.
3 Mark the position of the brake drum in relation to one of the wheel studs, then remove the brake drum retaining spire washer(s) from the wheel stud(s) and remove the brake drum. Ensure that the handbrake is released before removing the brake drum, otherwise the drum will be held in place by the clamping action of the brake shoes.
4 If the original driveshaft is to be refitted, mark the position of the driveshaft flange in relation to the hub. If a new driveshaft is to be fitted, this is not necessary. Unscrew the five retaining bolts and remove the driveshaft from the axle tube. Be prepared for oil spillage. Note the gasket fitted between the driveshaft flange and the hub.
5 The O-ring can now be prised from the spacer sleeve in the hub recess.
6 Refitting is a reversal of removal, bearing in mind the following points.
7 Always renew the O-ring when a driveshaft is removed, and use a new gasket between the driveshaft flange and the hub.
8 If the original driveshaft is being refitted, align the previously made marks on the driveshaft flange and hub. Align the marks on the brake drum and wheel stud, and on the roadwheel and brake drum.
9 On completion, check and if necessary top up the axle oil level as described in Section 2. Note that the vehicle must be level.

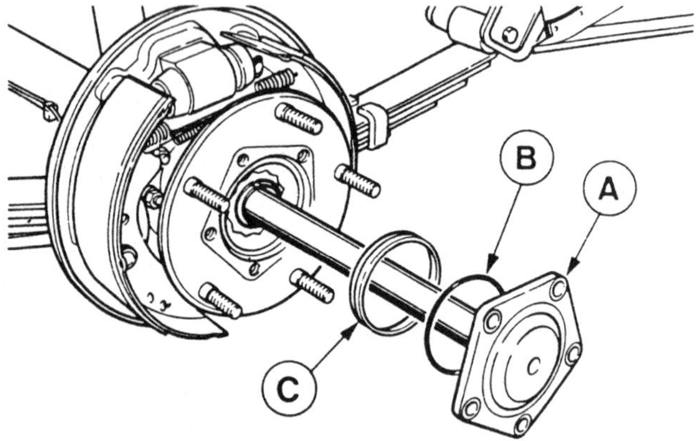

Fig 9.21 Withdrawing a driveshaft – P100 models (Sec 11)

A Driveshaft flange
B O-ring
C Spacer sleeve

12 Fault diagnosis – final drive and driveshafts

Symptom	Reason(s)
Excessive final drive unit noise	Oil level low or incorrect grade Worn bearings Worn or badly adjusted crownwheel and pinion Loose or deteriorated final drive mountings
Oil leakage from final drive unit	Pinion oil seal and/or differential bearing oil seals worn (as applicable) Rear cover leaking Rear cover or housing cracked
Grating, knocking or vibration from driveshafts	Worn joints (where applicable) Bent driveshaft Securing bolts loose (where applicable)

Note: *This Section is not intended as an exhaustive guide to fault diagnosis, but summarises the more common faults which may be encountered during a vehicle's life. Consult a dealer for more detailed advice.*

Chapter 10 Braking system

For modifications, and information applicable to later models, see Supplement at end of manual

Contents

Specifications

System type

Conventional braking system (except P100 models)	Front discs and rear drums with vacuum servo assistance, dual hydraulic circuit split front/rear, deceleration sensitive pressure relief valve in rear hydraulic circuit. Cable-operated handbrake on rear wheels.
ABS	Front and rear discs operated via electrically-driven hydraulic pump, dual hydraulic circuit split front/rear, pressure regulating valve in rear hydraulic circuit. Cable-operated handbrake on rear wheels
P100 models	Front discs and rear drums with vacuum servo assistance, dual hydraulic circuit split front/rear, load apportioning valve in rear hydraulic circuit. Cable-operated handbrake on rear wheels

Front discs

Type:	
1.3 and 1.6 litre models	Solid
1.8 and 2.0 litre models	Ventilated
Diameter	240.0 mm (9.46 in)
Maximum disc run-out	0.15 mm (0.006 in)
Minimum pad friction material thickness	1.5 mm (0.06 in)

Rear discs (ABS)

Type	Solid
Diameter	252.7 mm (9.96 in)
Maximum disc run-out	0.15 mm (0.006 in)
Minimum pad friction material thickness	1.5 mm (0.06 in)

Rear drums

Internal diameter:	
1.3 and 1.6 litre Saloon and Hatchback models	203.2 mm (8.0 in)
1.8 and 2.0 litre Saloon and Hatchback models and all Estate models	228.6 mm (9.0 in)
P100 models	256.0 mm (10.1 in)
Minimum shoe friction material thickness	1.0 mm (0.04 in)

Brake fluid type/specification

Brake fluid to Ford spec Amber SAM-1C-9103-A (Duckhams Universal Brake and Clutch Fluid)

Torque wrench settings

	Nm	lbf ft
Calliper carrier bracket-to-hub carrier bolts	51 to 61	38 to 45
Front calliper guide bolts	20 to 25	15 to 18
Rear calliper guide bolts (ABS)	31 to 35	23 to 26
Rear brake backplate nuts – P100 models	45 to 54	33 to 40
Servo-to-bulkhead nuts (conventional braking system)	35 to 45	26 to 33
Master cylinder-to-servo nuts	20 to 25	15 to 18
Hydraulic unit-to-bulkhead nuts (ABS)	41 to 51	30 to 38
Hydraulic unit accumulator (ABS)	34 to 46	25 to 34
Pump mounting bolt (ABS)	7 to 9	5 to 7
High pressure hose-to-pump union (ABS)	7 to 12	5 to 9
Wheel sensor mounting bolts (ABS)	8 to 11	6 to 8

1 General description

The braking system is of the dual circuit hydraulic type. The front and rear circuits are operated independently from a tandem master cylinder, so that in the event of a hydraulic failure in one circuit, full braking force will still be available to two wheels through the remaining circuit.

A deceleration sensitive valve on Saloon, Hatchback and Estate models not fitted with an Anti-lock Braking System (ABS), and a load apportioning valve on P100 models, is incorporated in the rear brake hydraulic circuit. The valve regulates the pressure applied to the rear brakes and reduces the possibility of the rear wheels locking under heavy braking.

All models are fitted with front disc brakes, with solid or ventilated discs depending on model. The callipers are of single piston sliding type, which ensures that equal pressure is applied to each disc pad.

Non-ABS models are fitted with rear drum brakes, incorporating leading and trailing shoes operated by double-acting wheel cylinders. A self-adjuster mechanism is fitted which consists of a toothed quadrant which is kept in contact with a toothed pin attached to the shoe strut by means of a spring. The quadrant incorporates an arm which locates in a slot in the leading shoe. As the shoe linings wear the quadrant is pulled from the pin when the footbrake is operated, and automatically repositioned to effectively lengthen the shoe strut.

ABS is available as an option for all models except the P100. The system comprises an electronic control unit, roadwheel sensors, hydraulic actuator with electrically-driven hydraulic pump, and the necessary valves and switches. Disc brakes are fitted to all four wheels. The front disc brakes are similar to those fitted to non-ABS models, but the rear brakes incorporate a self- adjusting mechanism, and a mechanical handbrake mechanism. The purpose of the system is to prevent wheel(s) locking during heavy brake applications. This is achieved by automatic release of the brake on the locked wheel, followed by reapplication of the brake. This procedure is carried out four times per second by the control valves in the valve block. The valves are controlled by the electronic control unit which itself receives signals from the wheel sensors, which monitor the locked or unlocked state of the wheels. A pressure regulating valve is incorporated in the rear hydraulic circuit to maintain the desired pressure ratio between the front and rear circuits.

Note: *The photographs depicting the ABS components were taken using a Ford Granada. The system fitted to the Sierra differs slightly in having the valve block mounted remotely from the hydraulic unit.*

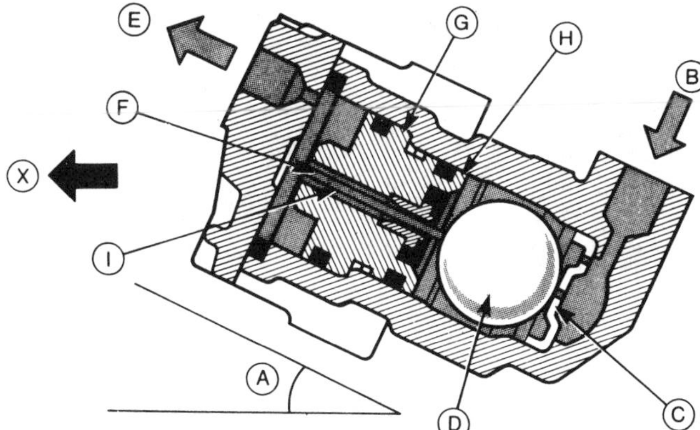

Fig 10.1 Cross-section of deceleration sensitive valve fitted to Saloon, Hatchback and Estate models – early type shown (Sec 1)

A Installation angle
B Fluid inlet
C Diffuser
D Ball
E Fluid outlet
F Piston bore
G Large piston
H Small piston
I Hollow pin
Arrow X indicates front of vehicle

2 Routine maintenance

1 At the intervals specified in the *'Routine maintenance'* Section at the beginning of this manual, the following tasks should be carried out.

2 Check the brake fluid level in the reservoir. Note that the level will drop slightly as the friction material wears, but any sudden drop in level, or the need for frequent topping-up should be investigated immediately. Always top up with the specified type of hydraulic fluid which has been stored in an airtight container (photo). Hydraulic fluid is hygroscopic (it absorbs moisture from the atmosphere) and must not be stored in an open container; for the same reason, do not shake the container before topping-up.

3 Inspect the thickness of the friction material on the disc pads and the brake shoes, as applicable, as described in the relevant Sections of this Chapter. Renew as necessary. At the same time inspect the condition of the discs and drums as applicable.

4 Examine the rigid and flexible hydraulic pipes and hoses for leaks and damage. Pay particular attention to the plastic coating on the rigid pipes which protects them against corrosion. Bend the flexible hoses sharply with the fingers and examine the surface of the hoses for signs

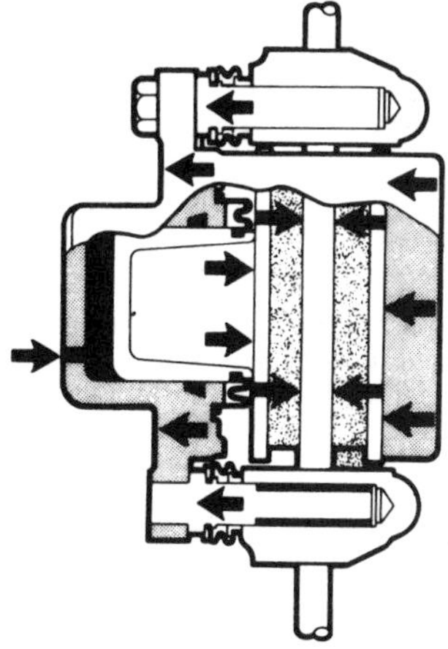

Fig 10.2 Cross-section of front disc calliper showing force direction when brakes are applied (Sec 1)

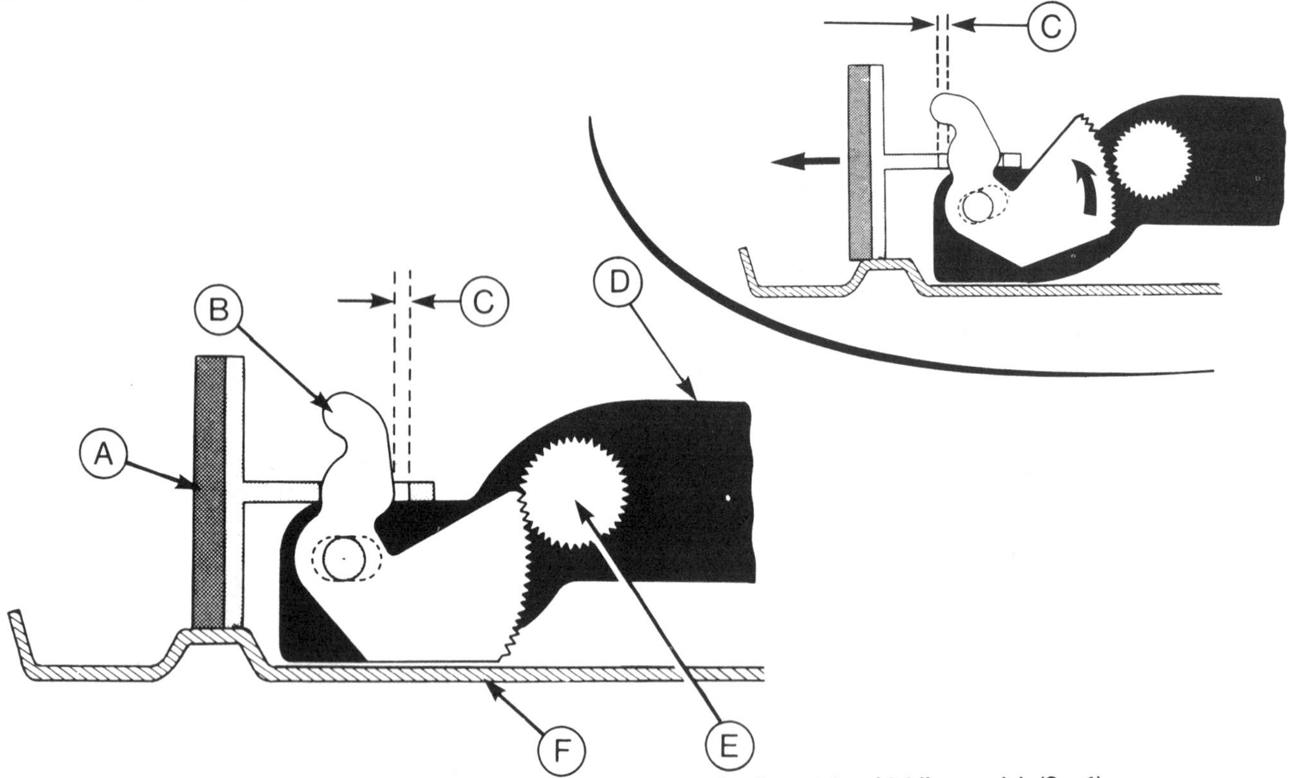

Fig 10.3 Operation of rear drum brake self-adjuster mechanism – 1.8 and 2.0 litre models (Sec 1)

A Leading brake shoe
B Toothed quadrant lever
C Shoe return gap
D Adjuster strut
E Toothed pin
F Brake backplate
Inset shoes adjuster position as brakes are applied

2.2 Topping-up brake fluid level – 1.8 litre model

3.5 Removing the dust cap from a wheel cylinder bleed screw

of cracking or perishing of the rubber. Renew if evident.

5 Check the operation of the hydraulic fluid level warning system. Unscrew the filler cap from the fluid reservoir and allow the float to hang downwards. With the ignition switched on the warning light should be illuminated.

6 Inspect the handbrake cable and linkage and lubricate the exposed parts. Adjustment should only be necessary to compensate for cable stretch or after fitting a new cable – see Section 30.

7 Renew the hydraulic fluid at the specified intervals as described in Section 3 or 4, as applicable. At the same time, consider renewing the flexible hoses and rubber seals as a precautionary measure.

3 Brake hydraulic system (conventional braking system) – bleeding

Note: *If brake fluid is spilt on the paintwork, the affected area must be washed down with cold water immediately – brake fluid is an effective paint stripper!*

1 If any of the hydraulic components in the braking system have been removed or disconnected, or if the fluid level in the reservoir has been allowed to fall appreciably, it is inevitable that air will have been introduced into the system. The removal of all this air from the hydraulic

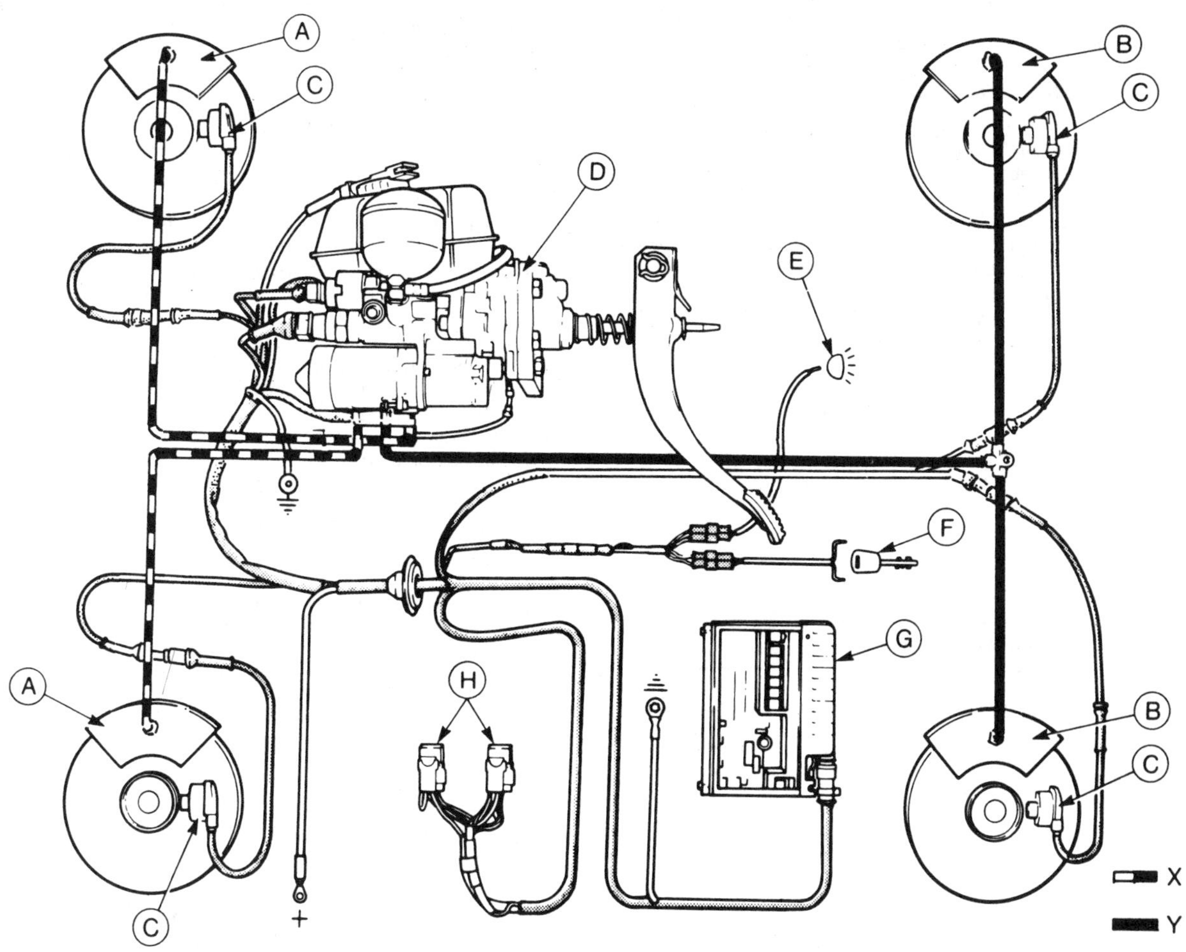

Fig 10.4 Components of anti-lock braking system (ABS) (Sec 1)

A Front disc callipers
B Rear disc callipers
C Wheel sensors
D Hydraulic unit
E Dashboard-mounted warning light
F Ignition switch
G Computer module
H Relays and diodes
X Front hydraulic circuit
Y Rear hydraulic circuit

system is essential if the brakes are to function correctly, and the process of removing it is known as bleeding.

2 Where an operation has only affected one circuit (front or rear) of the hydraulic system, then it will only be necessary to bleed the relevant circuit. If the master cylinder has been disconnected and reconnected, or the fluid level has been allowed to fall appreciably, then the complete system must be bled.

3 One of three methods can be used to bleed the system.

Bleeding – two-man method

4 Gather together a clean jar and a length of rubber or plastic bleed tubing which will fit the bleed screws tightly. The help of an assistant will be required.

5 Remove the dust cap where fitted, and clean around the bleed screw on the relevant calliper or wheel cylinder, then attach the bleed tube to the screw (photo). If the complete system is being bled, start at the front left-hand calliper.

6 Check that the fluid reservoir is topped up and then destroy the vacuum in the brake servo by giving several applications of the brake pedal.

7 Immerse the open end of the bleed tube in the jar which should contain two or three inches of hydraulic fluid. The jar should be positioned about 300 mm (12.0 in) above the bleed screw to prevent any possibility of air entering the system down the threads of the bleed screw when it is slackened.

8 Open the bleed screw half a turn and have your assistant depress the brake pedal slowly to the floor and then, after the bleed screw is retightened, quickly remove his foot to allow the pedal to return unimpeded. Repeat the procedure.

9 Observe the submerged end of the tube in the jar. When air bubbles cease to appear, tighten the bleed screw when the pedal is being held fully down by your assistant.

10 Top up the fluid reservoir. It must be kept topped up throughout the bleeding operations. If the connecting holes to the master cylinder are exposed at any time due to low fluid level, then air will be drawn into the system and work will have to start all over again.

11 Assuming that the complete system is being bled, the procedure described in the preceding paragraphs should be repeated on the front right-hand calliper followed by the rear right-hand and left-hand wheel cylinders.

12 On completion, remove the bleed tube, and discard the fluid which has been bled from the system unless it is required for bleed jar purposes. Never re-use old fluid.

13 On completion of bleeding, top up the fluid level in the reservoir. Check the action of the brake pedal, which should be firm and free from any 'sponginess' which would indicate that air is still present in the system.

Bleeding – with one-way valve

14 There are a number of one-man brake bleeding kits currently available from motor accessory shops. It is recommended that one of these kits should be used whenever possible, as they greatly simplify the bleeding operation and also reduce the risk of expelled air or fluid being drawn back into the system.

15 Proceed as described in paragraphs 5 and 6.

16 Open the bleed screw half a turn, then depress the brake pedal to the floor and slowly release it. The one-way valve in the bleeder device will prevent expelled air from returning to the system at the completion

of each stroke. Repeat this operation until clear hydraulic fluid, free from air bubbles, can be seen coming through the tube. Tighten the bleed screw.
17 Proceed as described in paragraphs 11 to 13.

Bleeding – with pressure bleeding kit

18 These too are available from motor accessory shops and are usually operated by air pressure from the spare tyre.
19 By connecting a pressurised container to the master cylinder fluid reservoir, bleeding is then carried out by simply opening each bleed screw in turn and allowing the fluid to run out, rather like turning on a tap, until no air bubbles are visible in the fluid being expelled.
20 Using this system, the large reserve of fluid provides a safeguard against air being drawn into the master cylinder during the bleeding operations.
21 This method is particularly effective when bleeding 'difficult' systems or when bleeding the entire system at time of routine fluid renewal.
22 Begin bleeding with reference to paragraphs 5 and 6 and proceed as described in paragraphs 11 to 13.

4 Brake hydraulic system (ABS) – bleeding

Caution: *Remember that brake fluid is poisonous and that the rear brake hydraulic circuit may be under considerable pressure. Take care not to allow hydraulic fluid to spray into the face or eyes. Refer to the note at the beginning of Section 3.*
1 Keep the fluid reservoir replenished throughout the bleeding operations.
2 Remove the dust cap where fitted, and clean around the bleed screw on the left-hand front calliper. Fit a bleed tube to the screw and immerse the open end in a jar containing clean hydraulic fluid.
3 Open the bleed valve one full turn and have an assistant depress the brake pedal fully and hold it down.
4 Close the bleed valve and release the brake pedal. Repeat the procedure until fluid ejected from the end of the tube is free from air bubbles.
5 Repeat the operations on the right-hand front calliper.
6 Fit the bleed tube to the left-hand rear calliper and open the bleed valve one full turn.
7 Have an assistant depress the brake pedal fully and hold it down.
8 Switch on the ignition to position II.
9 Allow the fluid to bleed from the tube for at least 15 seconds, when the fluid should be free from air bubbles.
10 Close the bleed valve.
11 Release the brake pedal and wait for the hydraulic pump to stop.
12 Fit the bleed tube to the right-hand rear calliper and open the bleed valve one full turn.
13 Have your assistant depress the brake pedal through half its travel and hold it there. Allow the fluid to bleed from the tube for at least 15 seconds, when the fluid should be free from air bubbles.
14 Close the bleed valve.
15 Release the brake pedal and wait for the hydraulic pump to stop then switch off the ignition.
16 Top up the reservoir with clean fluid.
17 When the hydraulic system is being bled for the purpose of renewing the fluid at the specified interval, as each calliper is bled, operate the brake pedal continuously until clean fluid is seen to enter the jar.
18 When the hydraulic pump is running its note will be heard to change once fluid has purged through it. Do not allow the pump to run continuously for more than two minutes. If it does run for a longer period, switch off the ignition and allow the motor to cool for ten minutes.
19 On completion, discard the fluid which has been bled from the system unless it is required for bleed jar purposes. Never re-use old fluid.
20 Check the action of the brake pedal, which should be firm and free from any 'sponginess', which would indicate that air is still present in the system.

5 Disc pads – inspection and renewal

Note: *When working on the brake components, take care not to disperse brake dust into the air, or to inhale it, since it may contain asbestos which is injurious to health.*

Front disc pads

1 The disc pad friction material can be inspected for wear without removing the roadwheels. Working beneath the vehicle, insert a mirror between the calliper and the roadwheel and check that the friction material thickness is not less than the minimum given in the Specifications (photo).
2 If any one of the pads has worn below the specified limit, the front pads must be renewed as an axle set (4 pads).
3 To renew the pads, slacken the front roadwheel nuts, apply the handbrake, then jack up the front of the vehicle and support on axle stands. Remove the roadwheels. On P100 models, mark the position of the roadwheels in relation to the wheel studs before removal.
4 Proceed as follows according to model.

Girling calliper (1.3 and early 1.6 litre models)
5 Where applicable, disconnect the wiring to the disc pad wear sensor.
6 Unscrew and remove the bolt from the upper calliper guide pin, while holding the pin stationary with a spanner – see Fig. 10.6.
7 Swing the calliper downwards and lift out the disc pads. If the outboard pad is stuck to the calliper, free it using a screwdriver with the guide pin bolt fitted, as shown in Fig. 10.7. Do not use a screwdriver to free the inboard pad, as this may damage the piston dust seal. The inboard pad can be freed by hand after lowering the calliper.

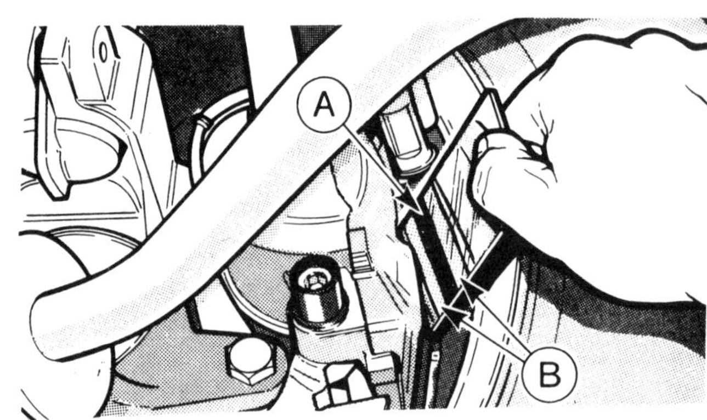

Fig 10.5 Using a mirror to inspect the disc pad friction material for wear (Sec 5)

A Brake disc *B Brake disc pads*

Fig 10.6 Unscrewing the bolt from the upper calliper guide pin – Girling calliper (Sec 5)

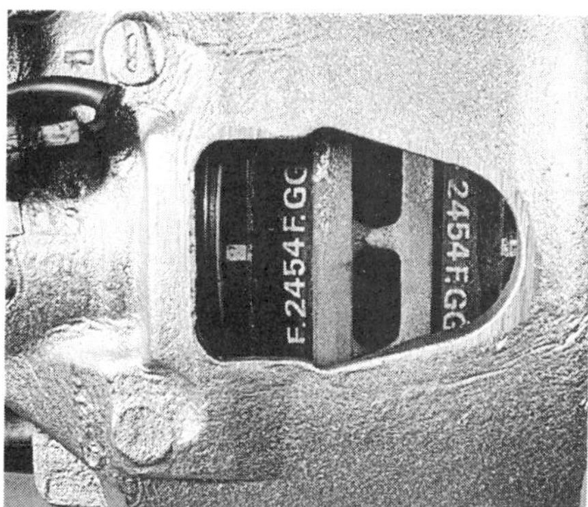
5.1 Disc pads viewed through calliper inspection hole (roadwheel removed)

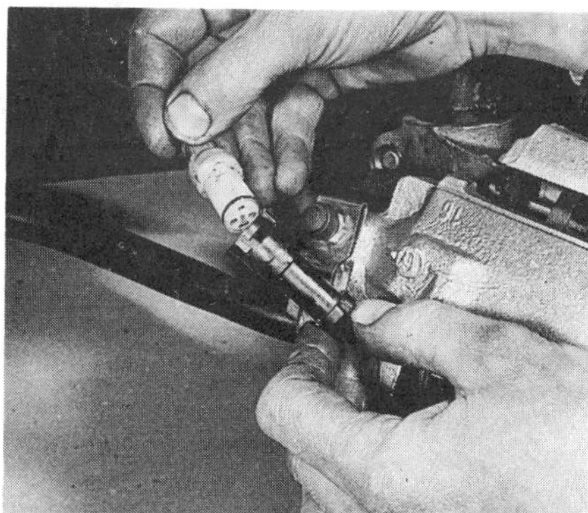
5.17 Disconnect the pad wear sensor wiring plug – Teves calliper

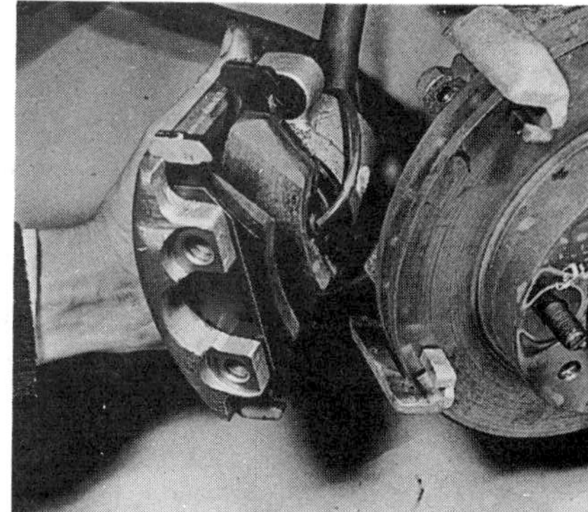
5.18 Withdrawing a calliper from its carrier bracket – Teves calliper

5.19 Withdraw the disc pads from the calliper – Teves calliper

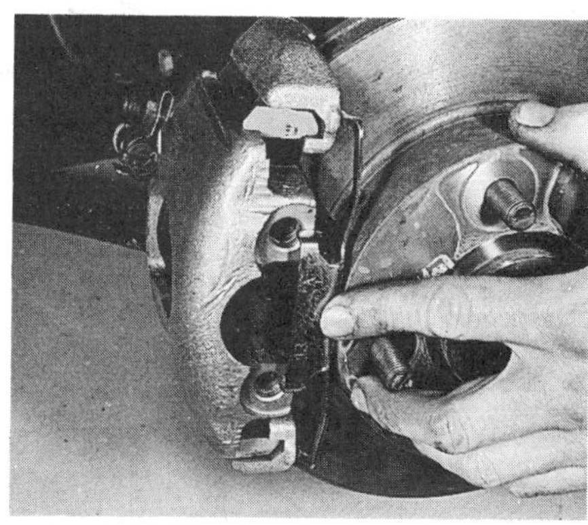
5.20 Refitting the calliper retaining clip – Teves calliper

5.26 Rear disc pad wear sensor wiring clip (arrowed) – ABS

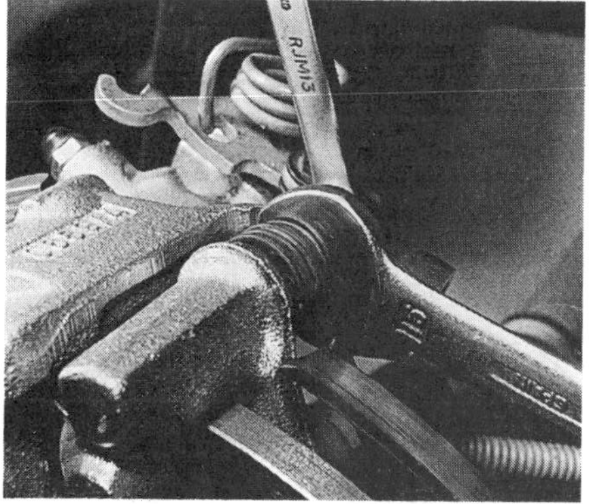
5.27 Unscrewing the forward calliper guide pin bolt – ABS

5.28 Lift out the disc pads – ABS

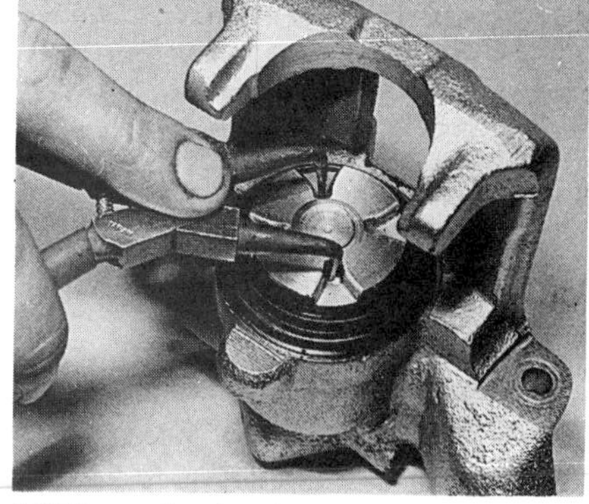
5.30 Retracting the piston using circlip pliers

8 Brush all dust and dirt from the calliper, pads and disc, but do not inhale it as it may be injurious to health. Scrape any corrosion from the disc.

9 As the new pads will be thicker than the old ones, the piston must be pushed squarely into its bore to accommodate the new thicker pads. Depressing the piston will cause the fluid level in the reservoir to rise, so to avoid spillage, syphon out some fluid using an old hydrometer or a teat pipette. Refer to the note at the beginning of Section 3. Do not lever between the piston and disc to depress the piston – ideally a spreader tool, applying equal force to both sides of the calliper, should be used.

10 Further refitting is a reversal of removal bearing in mind the following points.

11 If disc pads with wear sensors are fitted, the pad with the sensor wire should be fitted inboard.

12 Ensure that the anti-rattle clips are correctly located on the calliper.

13 Repeat the procedure on the opposite front brake.

14 On completion, apply the footbrake hard several times to settle the pads, then check and if necessary top up the fluid level in the reservoir.

15 Avoid heavy braking, if possible, for the first hundred miles or so after fitting new pads. This will allow the pads to bed in and reach full efficiency.

Teves calliper (Later 1.6, 1.8 and 2.0 litre models)

16 Prise the retaining clip from the calliper. Hold it with a pair of pliers to avoid it causing personal injury.

17 Unclip the pad wear sensor from the calliper, and disconnect the wiring plug (photo).

18 Using a 7 mm Allen key, unscrew and remove the two guide bolts securing the calliper to the carrier bracket, and withdraw the calliper (photo). Support the calliper on an axle stand to avoid straining the hydraulic hose.

19 Withdraw the disc pads from the calliper (photo). It may be necessary to prise the outboard pad with a screwdriver to release it from the calliper. Do not use a screwdriver to free the inboard pad, as this may damage the piston dust seal.

20 Proceed as described in paragraphs 8 to 15 inclusive, but in addition ensure that the clip on the back of the inboard pad fits into the piston recess, refit the calliper retaining clip, and ignore the reference to

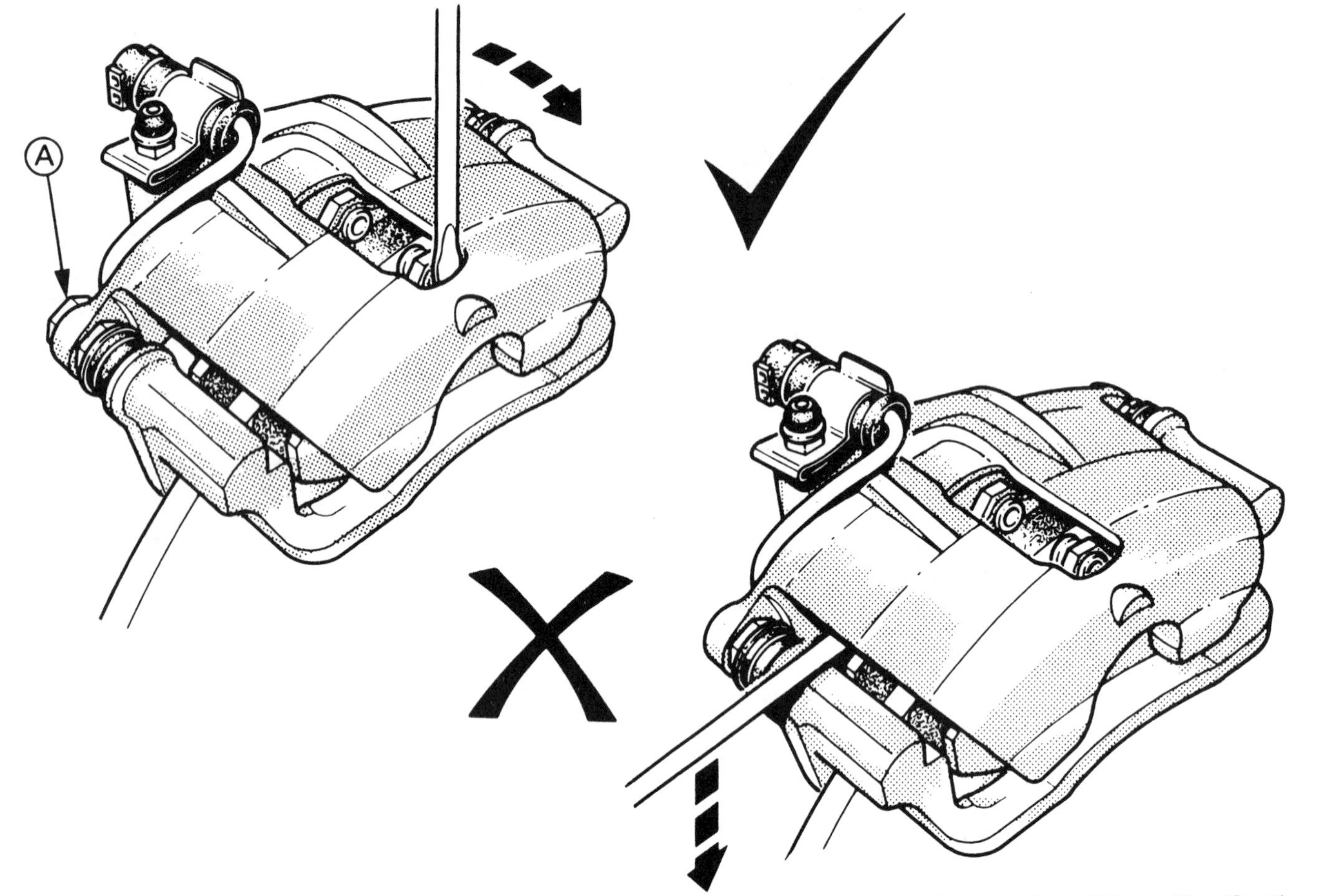

Fig 10.7 Correct and incorrect methods of freeing stuck outboard disc pad. Guide pin bolt (A) must be in position – Girling calliper (Sec 5)

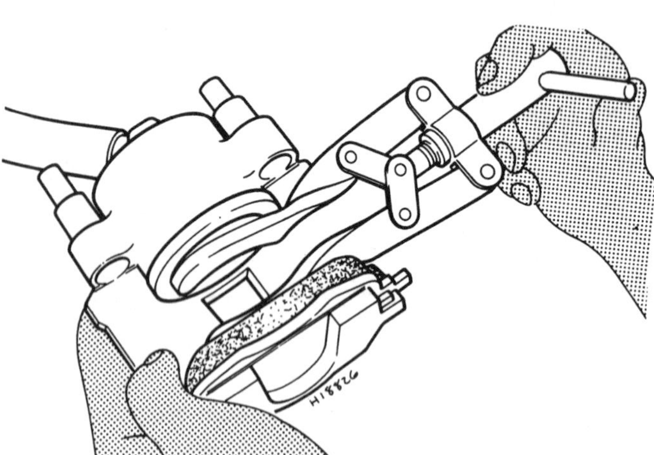

Fig 10.8 Using a spreader tool to depress the calliper piston into its bore – Teves calliper (Sec 5)

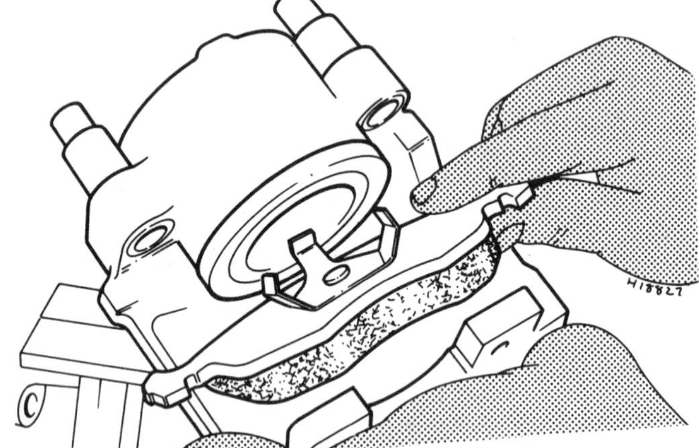

Fig 10.9 The clip on the back of the inboard disc pad fits into the piston recess – Teves calliper (Sec 5)

the anti-rattle clips (photo). On P100 models align the previously made marks on the roadwheels and wheel studs.

Rear disc pads (ABS)

21 Slacken the rear roadwheel nuts, chock the front wheels, then jack up the rear of the vehicle and support on axle stands. Remove the roadwheel.

22 The disc pads can be inspected through the top of the calliper after removal of the blanking spring clip. Check that the friction material thickness is not less than the minimum given in the Specifications.

23 If any one of the pads has worn below the specified limit, the rear pads must be renewed as an axle set (4 pads).

24 To renew the pads, proceed as follows.

25 Release the handbrake, and free the handbrake cable from the suspension lower arm by bending back the tangs.

26 Where applicable, disconnect the wiring to the disc pad wear sensor (photo).

27 Unscrew and remove the bolt from the forward calliper guide pin, while holding the pin stationary with a spanner (photo).

28 Swing the calliper rearwards and lift out the disc pads (photo). **Do not** depress the brake pedal with the calliper removed.

29 Brush all dirt and dust from the calliper, pads and disc, but do not inhale it as it may be injurious to health. Scrape any corrosion from the disc.

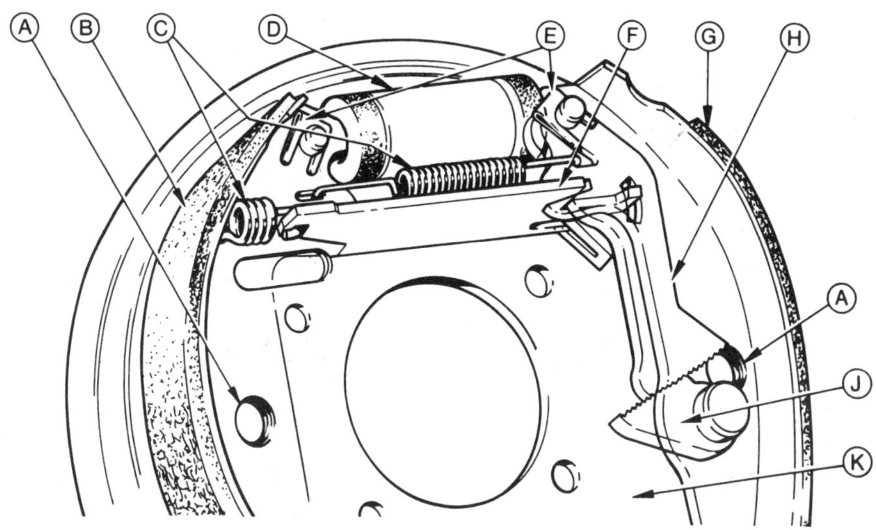

Fig 10.10 Rear drum brake self-adjuster assembly – 1.3 and 1.6 litre models (Sec 6)

A Shoe hold-down points
B Trailing brake shoe
C Self-adjuster strut and top return springs
D Wheel cylinder
E Spring clips
F Self-adjuster strut
G Leading brake shoe
H Large ratchet segment
J Small ratchet segment
K Brake backplate

30 As the new pads will be thicker than the old ones, the piston must be retracted into its bore to accommodate the new thicker pads. Retracting the piston will cause the fluid level in the reservoir to rise, so to avoid spillage, syphon out some fluid using an old hydrometer or a teat pipette. Refer to the note at the beginning of Section 3. Retract the calliper piston by turning it clockwise. Ford tool No 12-006 is designed for this purpose, but a pair of circlip pliers or any similar tool can be used instead (photo).
31 Remove the backing paper from the new pads, and fit them to the calliper.
32 Further refitting is a reversal of removal, bearing in mind the following points.
33 If disc pads with wear sensors are fitted, the pad with the sensor wire should be fitted inboard.
34 Repeat the procedure on the opposite rear brake.
35 On completion, switch on the ignition and apply the footbrake hard several times to settle the pads. Switch off the ignition, then check and if necessary top up the fluid level in the reservoir. Check the operation of the handbrake.
36 Avoid heavy braking, if possible, for the first hundred miles or so after fitting new pads. This will allow the pads to bed in and reach full efficiency.

6 Rear brake shoes (drum brakes) – inspection and renewal

Note: *Refer to the note at the beginning of Section 5.*

1 The shoe friction material can be inspected for wear without removing the roadwheels. Working beneath the vehicle, prise the plug from the brake backplate, and using an inspection lamp or torch, check that the friction material thickness is not less than the minimum given in the Specifications (photo).
2 If any one of the shoes has worn below the specified limit, the shoes must be renewed as an axle set (4 shoes).
3 To renew the shoes, slacken the rear roadwheel nuts, chock the front wheels, then jack up the rear of the vehicle and support on axle stands. Remove the rear roadwheels, and release the handbrake. On P100 models, mark the position of the roadwheels in relation to the brake drums before removal.
4 Proceed as follows according to model.

1.3 and 1.6 litre models

5 Remove the brake drum retaining spire washer(s) from the wheel stud(s) and remove the brake drum. If the drum will not pass over the

Fig 10.11 Lubrication points on brake backplate (Sec 6)

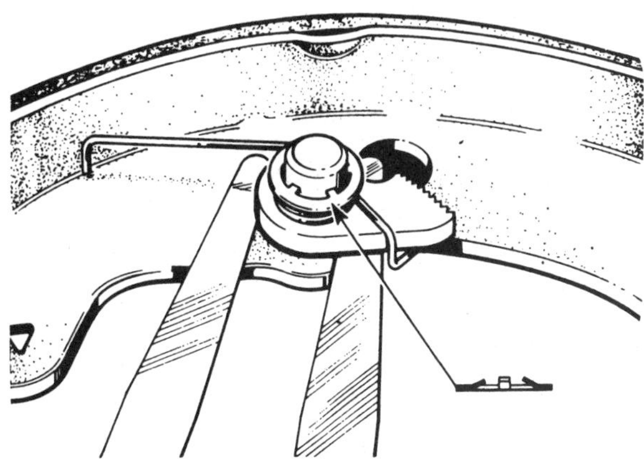

Fig 10.12 Using feeler blades to set clearance between smaller ratchet segment and brake shoe web. Spring clip arrowed – 1.3 and 1.6 litre models (Sec 6)

6.1 Rear brake shoe inspection hole plug (arrowed)

6.5A Brake drum retaining spire washer (arrowed) – 1.6 litre model

6.5B Releasing the automatic adjuster using a screwdriver – 1.6 litre model

6.5C Drum removed showing screwdriver pressing on adjuster ratchet – 1.6 litre model

6.6A Top shoe return spring (arrowed) – 1.6 litre model

6.6B Bottom shoe return spring – 1.6 litre model

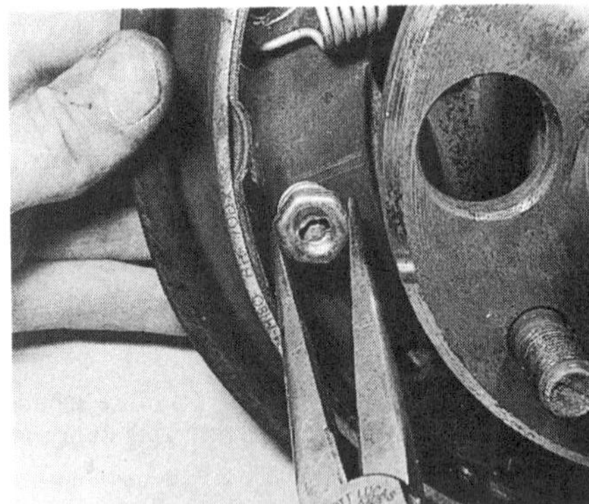
6.7 Using pliers to remove a shoe hold-down cup – 1.6 litre model

6.9 Disconnecting the handbrake cable from the trailing shoe lever – 1.6 litre model

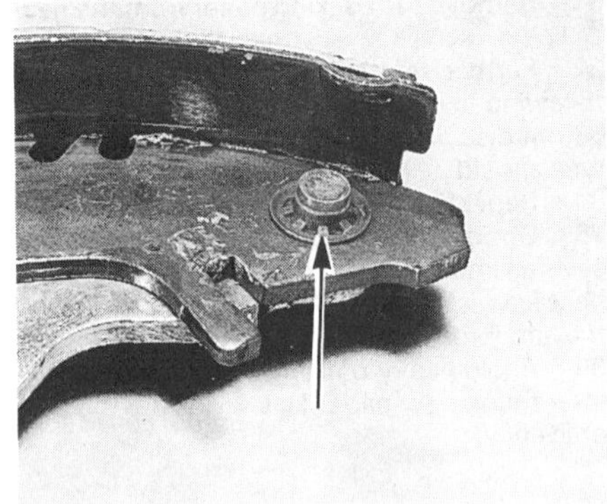
6.11 Handbrake lever-to-trailing shoe securing clip (arrowed) – 1.6 litre model

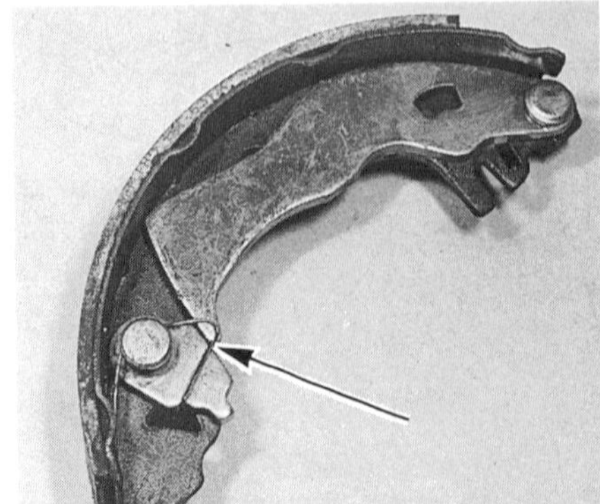
6.13 Fully retract the self-adjuster ratchet (arrowed) before refitting the trailing shoe – 1.6 litre model

6.14 Strut and spring fitted to top of trailing shoe – 1.6 litre model

6.15 Engage the hole in the adjuster with the hook on the strut (arrowed) – 1.6 litre model

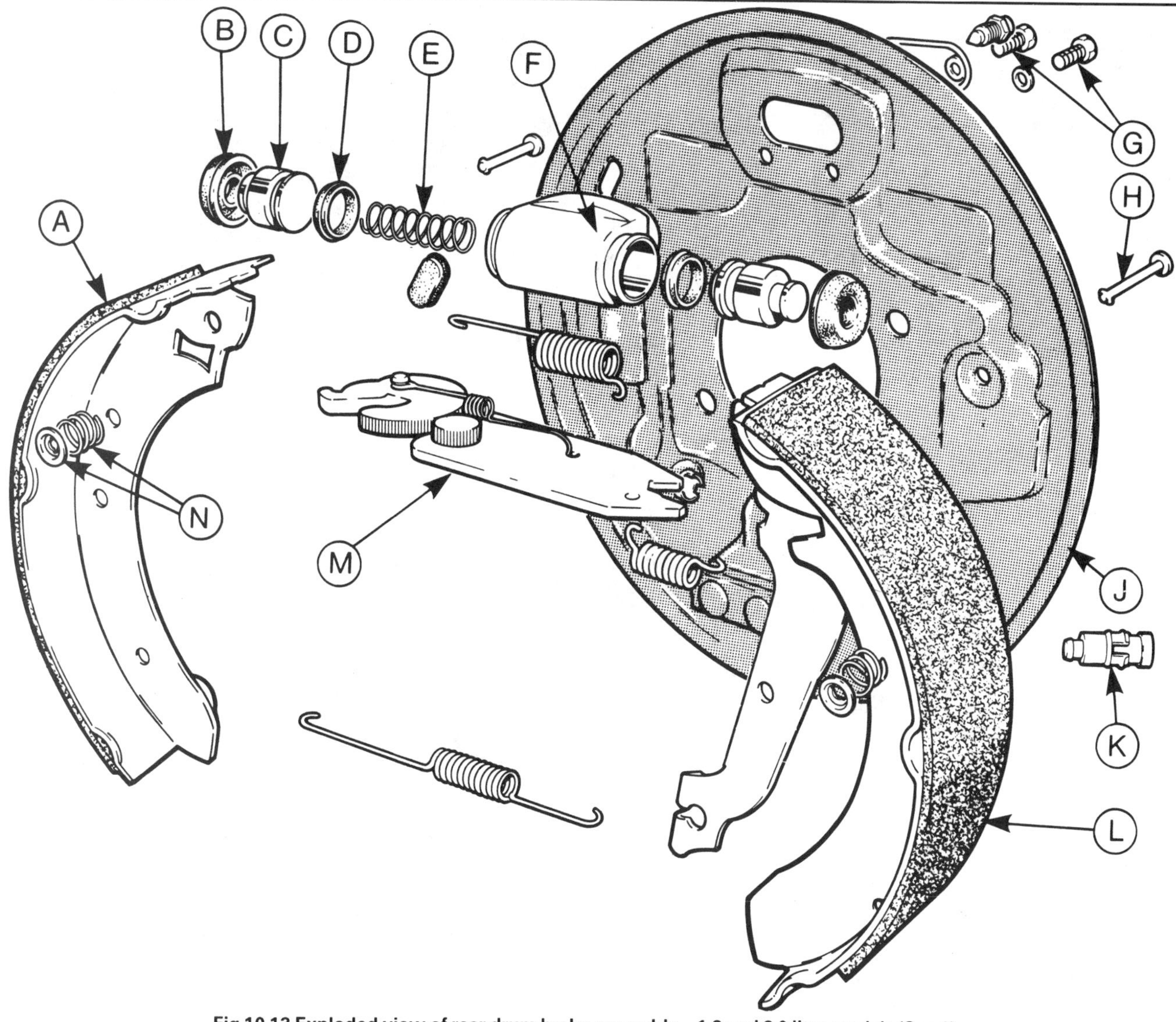

Fig 10.13 Exploded view of rear drum brake assembly – 1.8 and 2.0 litre models (Sec 6)

A Leading brake shoe
B Dust-excluding seal
C Piston
D Piston seal
E Spring
F Wheel cylinder housing
G Bolts
H Hold-down pin
J Brake backplate
K Adjuster plunger
L Trailing brake shoe
M Self-adjuster strut
N Hold-down spring and cup

shoes, it is possible to release the automatic adjuster mechanism by inserting a screwdriver through the small hole in the drum and pressing down on the ratchet (photos).

6 Using a wire hook or a pair of long-nosed pliers, remove the top and bottom shoe return springs. Note the fitted positions of the springs for reference when refitting (photos).

7 Remove the hold-down cup, spring and pin from each shoe by depressing the cup and turning it through 90° (photo).

8 Pull the bottom of the leading (front) shoe towards the front of the vehicle so that the self-adjuster ratchets separate, then disengage the shoe from the strut by twisting it. Remove the shoe and adjuster mechanism.

9 Pull the trailing (rear) shoe away from the backplate far enough to gain access to the handbrake cable. Disconnect the handbrake cable from the lever and remove the shoe with strut and lever (photo).

10 Clean and inspect all components, and lubricate the shoe contact points on the backplate – see Fig. 10.11. Take care not to inhale any dust, as it may be injurious to health.

11 Remove the strut from the trailing shoe by unhooking it from its spring. If a handbrake lever is not attached to the new shoe, remove the old lever by prising off the clip and driving out the pin. Use a new clip on reassembly (photo).

12 Similarly transfer the self-adjuster components to the new leading shoe. Note that a small clearance (0.2 mm/0.008 in) must exist between the underside of the smaller ratchet segment and the brake shoe web. Insert feeler blades of the correct thickness beneath the ratchet when fitting the spring clip, then withdraw the blades. The larger segment should be fitted without any clearance.

13 Commence reassembly by engaging the self-adjuster ratchet teeth as shown (photo).

14 Offer the trailing shoe to the backplate, fitting the handbrake cable to the handbrake lever and (if not already done) the strut and spring to the top of the shoe (photo).

15 Fit the leading shoe and adjuster mechanism, engaging the hole in the adjuster with the hook on the strut (photo).

16 Fit the top and bottom return springs: this is most easily done by allowing the ends of the shoe to pass in front of the wheel cylinder and the bottom pivot point, then engaging the shoes in their correct positions after the springs have been fitted. Be careful not to damage the wheel cylinder rubber boots.

17 Fit and secure the hold-down pins, springs and cups.

18 Back off the self-adjuster mechanism, by depressing the lower (small) ratchet segment, to enable the brake drum to pass over the shoes. Centre the shoes relative to the backplate.

6.24 Rear brake assembly (drum removed) – 1.8 litre model

6.25 Leading shoe hold-down cup (arrowed) – 2.0 litre model

6.26A Wheel cylinder, self-adjuster strut and springs – 2.0 litre model

6.26B Shoe lower anchor bracket and return spring – 2.0 litre model

8.5 Withdrawing a rear calliper from its carrier bracket – ABS

19 Refit the drum, making sure that the small hole is in line with one of the two large holes in the drive flange. Secure the drum by pushing the spire washer(s) over the wheel stud(s).
20 Have an assistant operate the footbrake several times: a series of clicks should be heard from the drum as the self- adjuster mechanism operates. When the clicking no longer occurs, adjustment is complete.
21 Renew the brake shoes on the other side of the vehicle, then check the handbrake adjustment as described in Section 30.
22 Refit the roadwheels, lower the car and tighten the wheel nuts.

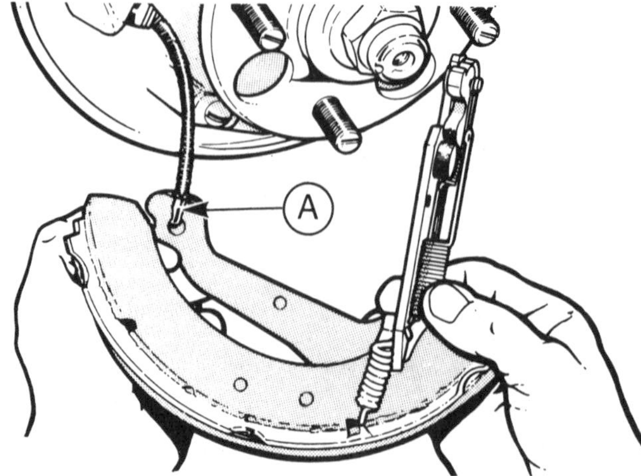

Fig 10.14 Removing the trailing brake shoe – 1.8 and 2.0 litre models (Sec 6)

A Handbrake cable and slot

23 Avoid harsh braking if possible for the first hundred miles or so until the new linings have bedded in.

1.8 and 2.0 litre models

24 Proceed as described in paragraph 5, but on P100 models mark the position of the brake drum in relation to one of the wheel studs (photo).
25 Remove the hold-down cup, spring and pin from the leading (front) shoe by depressing the cup and turning it through 90° (photo).
26 Note the fitted positions of the shoe return springs for reference when refitting, then release the leading shoes from the wheel cylinder and the anchor bracket using a screwdriver as a lever (photo).
27 Unhook the return springs and remove the leading shoe. Note the direction of wheel rotation arrows on the shoes.
28 Remove the hold-down cup, spring and pin from the trailing (rear) shoe by depressing the cup and turning it through 90°.
29 Withdraw the trailing shoe and disconnect the handbrake cable from the lever.
30 Unhook the springs from the trailing shoe and remove the self-adjuster strut.
31 Clean and inspect all components and lubricate the shoe contact points on the backplate – see Fig. 10.11. Take care not to inhale any dust, as it may be injurious to health.
32 Commence reassembly by fitting the springs to the trailing shoe and attaching the self-adjuster strut.
33 Attach the handbrake cable to the lever and position the trailing shoe on the wheel cylinder and anchor bracket. Ensure that the upper return spring is located on the self-adjuster strut.
34 Refit the hold-down pin, spring and cup to the trailing shoe.
35 Connect the return springs to the leading shoe, then locate the lower end in the anchor bracket and lever the upper end onto the toothed quadrant lever and wheel cylinder. Be careful not to damage the wheel cylinder rubber boot.
36 Refit the hold-down pin, spring and cup to the leading shoe.
37 Using a screwdriver, push the self-adjuster toothed quadrant fully towards the backplate to its initial setting.
38 Proceed as described in paragraphs 19 to 23 inclusive, but on P100 models, align the previously made marks on the brake drums and wheel studs, and on the roadwheels and brake drums.

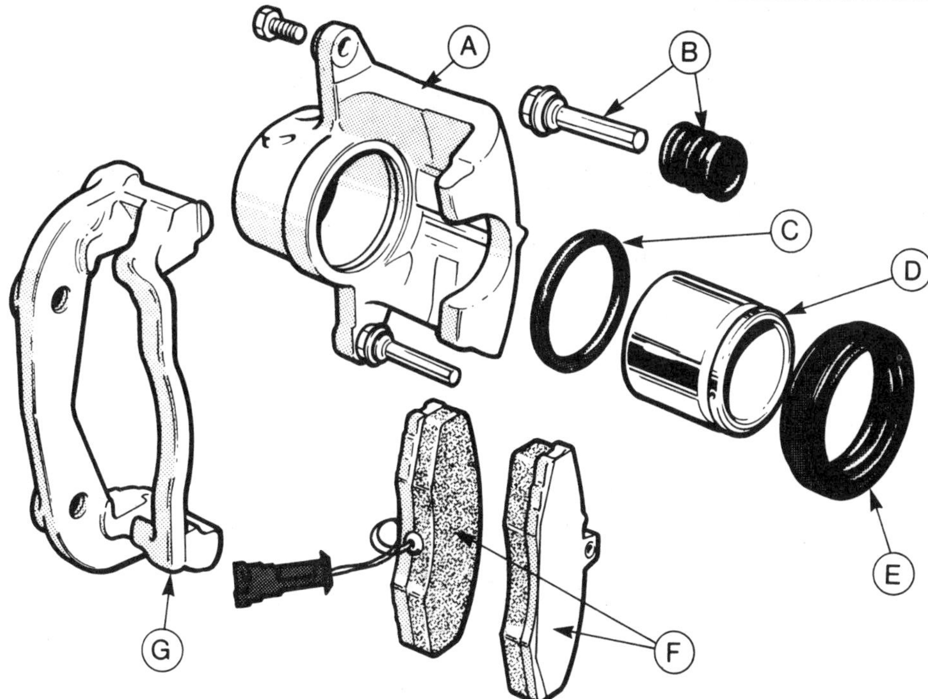

Fig 10.15 Exploded view of Girling front disc calliper (Sec 7)

A Calliper
B Guide pin and dust boot
C Piston seal
D Piston
E Dust-excluding seal
F Disc pads
G Calliper carrier bracket

7 Front disc calliper – removal, overhaul and refitting

1 Apply the handbrake, loosen the relevant roadwheel nuts, then jack up the front of the vehicle and support on axle stands. Remove the roadwheel. On P100 models, mark the position of the roadwheel in relation to one of the wheel studs before removal.
2 Remove the brake fluid reservoir cap and secure a piece of polythene over the filler neck with a rubber band, or by refitting the cap. This will reduce the loss of fluid during the following procedure.
3 Disconnect the flexible fluid hose from the rigid brake pipe under the wing of the vehicle, or alternatively unscrew the flexible hose from the union on the calliper. Take care not to twist the hose, and plug the open ends to prevent fluid loss and dirt ingress.
4 Remove the disc pads as described in Section 5.
5 On models fitted with Girling callipers (1.3 and early 1.6 litre models), unscrew and remove the bolt from the lower calliper guide pin, while holding the pin stationary with a spanner, then remove the calliper.
6 On models fitted with Teves callipers (later 1.6, 1.8 and 2.0 litre models), remove the calliper from the vehicle.
7 If required, the calliper carrier bracket can be unbolted and removed from the hub carrier.
8 Brush away all external dirt and dust, but take care not to inhale any dust as it may be injurious to health.
9 Pull the dust-excluding rubber seal from the end of the piston.
10 Apply air pressure to the fluid inlet union, and eject the piston. Only low air pressure is required for this, such as is produced by a foot-operated tyre pump. Position a thin piece of wood between the piston and calliper body to prevent damage to the end face of the piston in the event of its being ejected suddenly.
11 Using a suitable pointed instrument, prise the piston seal from the groove in the cylinder bore. Take care not to scratch the surface of the bore.
12 Clean the piston and calliper body with methylated spirit and allow to dry. Examine the surfaces of the piston and cylinder bore for wear, damage and corrosion. If the piston surface alone is unserviceable, a new piston must be obtained, along with seals. If the cylinder bore is unserviceable, the complete calliper must be renewed. The seals must be renewed regardless of the condition of the other components.
13 Coat the piston and seals with clean brake fluid, then manipulate the piston seal into the groove in the cylinder bore.
14 Push the piston squarely into its bore.
15 Fit the dust-excluding rubber seal between the piston and calliper, then depress the piston fully.
16 Refit the calliper and where applicable the carrier bracket by reversing the removal operations. Tighten the mounting bolts to the specified torque.
17 On P100 models, when refitting the roadwheel align the previously made marks on the roadwheel and wheel stud.
18 On completion, bleed the front brake circuit as described in Section 3 or 4, as applicable.

8 Rear disc calliper (ABS) – removal and refitting

1 With the ignition switched off, pump the brake pedal at least 20 times, or until it becomes hard, to depressurise the system.
2 Chock the front wheels, slacken the relevant roadwheel nuts, then jack up the rear of the vehicle and support on axle stands. Remove the roadwheel and release the handbrake.
3 Where applicable, disconnect the wiring to the disc pad wear sensor.
4 Proceed as described in Section 7, paragraphs 2 and 3, but note that the rigid brake pipe is clipped to the suspension lower arm.
5 Unscrew and remove the two guide bolts securing the calliper to the carrier bracket, while holding the pins with a spanner. Unhook the handbrake cable from the lever, and withdraw the calliper (photo). Alternatively, the two carrier bracket-to-hub carrier bolts can be unscrewed, and the calliper and carrier can be separated on the bench, but in this case the handbrake cable must be disconnected from the carrier bracket by removing the retaining circlip.
6 If desired, the calliper can be overhauled as described in Section 9, but pay particular attention to the note at the beginning of that Section.
7 Refitting is a reversal of removal, but on completion bleed the rear brake circuit as described in Section 4, and check the operation of the handbrake.

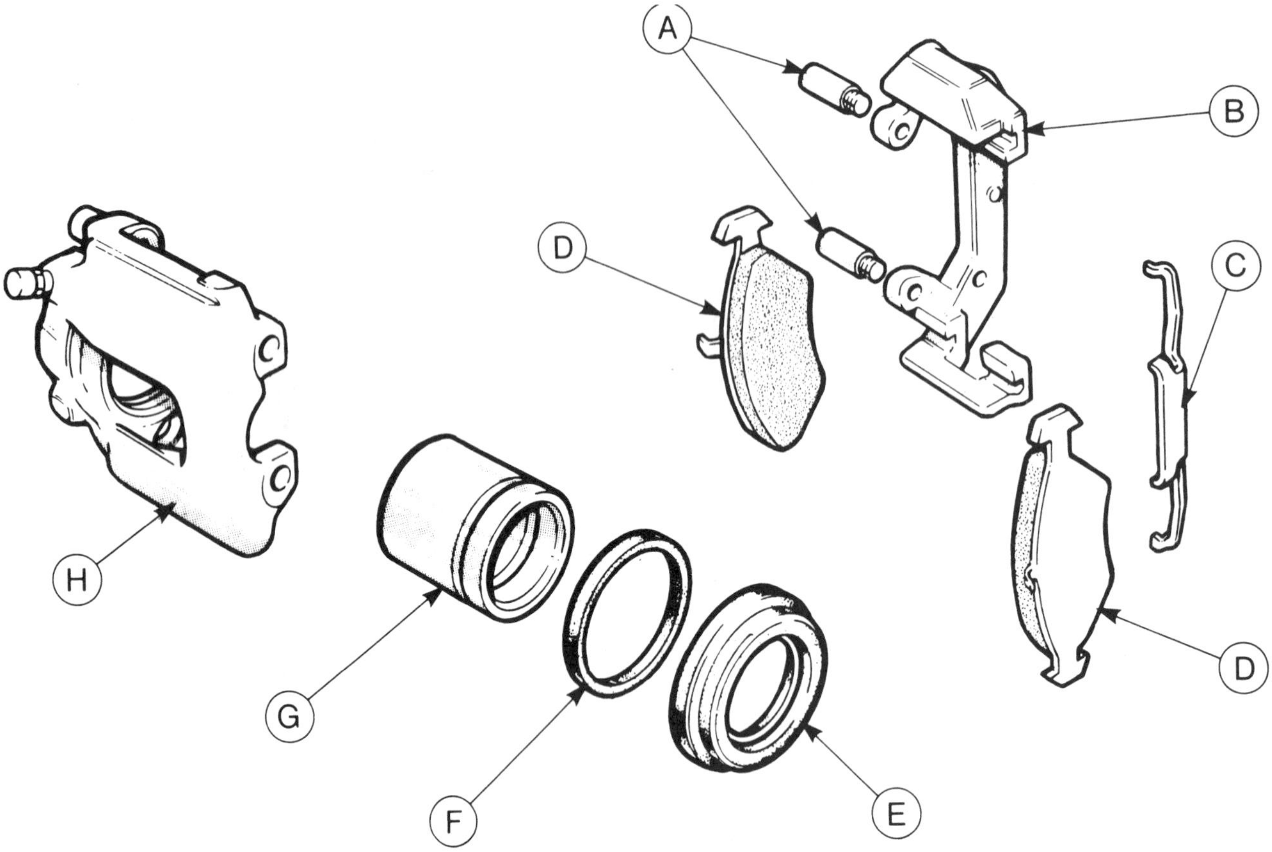

Fig 10.16 Exploded view of Teves front disc calliper (Sec 7)

A Guide bolts
B Calliper carrier bracket
C Calliper retaining clip
D Disc pads
E Dust-excluding seal
F Piston seal
G Piston
H Calliper

9 Rear disc calliper (ABS) – overhaul

Note: *Complete dismantling of the rear calliper should not be attempted unless Ford spring compressor (tool No 12-007) is available, or unless the problems likely to arise in the absence of the tool are understood. Renewal of the piston seal, dust-excluding seal and piston adjuster nut seal requires no special tools.*

1 Clean the calliper, taking care not to inhale any dust which may be injurious to health, and mount it in a soft-jawed vice.

2 Rotate the piston anti-clockwise, using Ford tool No 12-006, or a pair of circlip pliers or similar tool, until it protrudes from the calliper bore by approximately 20.0 mm (0.8 in). Free the dust-excluding seal from the groove in the piston, then continue unscrewing the piston and remove it. Remove and discard the dust-excluding seal.

3 The piston and bore may now be cleaned and examined as described in Section 7, paragraph 12.

4 The piston adjuster nut seal should be renewed as follows.

5 Remove the circlip from the piston, then extract the thrustwashers, wave washer and thrust bearing. Note the fitted sequence of these components. Finally remove the nut (photos).

6 Remove the seal from the nut, noting which way round it is fitted. Clean the nut with methylated spirit. Lubricate the new seal with clean hydraulic fluid and fit it to the nut.

7 If no further dismantling is required, proceed to paragraph 20.

8 For further dismantling it is virtually essential to have Ford tool 12-007 in order to compress the adjuster spring. This tool appears to be a cut-down adjuster nut with a handle for turning it. In the workshop it was found that the actual piston adjuster nut could be used to compress the spring if it were turned with circlip pliers (photo). This works well enough for dismantling, but reassembly proved extremely difficult because of the limited clearance between the skirt of the nut and the calliper bore.

9 Having compressed the adjuster spring just enough to take the load off the circlip, release the circlip inside the calliper bore. Remove the spring compressor, then extract the circlip, spring cover, spring and washer (photo).

10 A long thin pair of circlip pliers will now be required to release the key plate retaining circlip from the calliper bore (photo). With the circlip removed, the pushrod and key plate can be pulled out.

11 Remove the handbrake strut from the calliper bore.

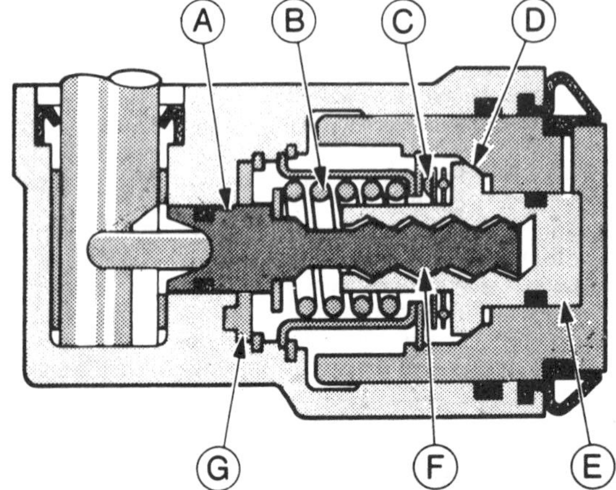

Fig 10.17 Sectional view of rear disc calliper showing self-adjuster mechanism (brakes released) – ABS (Sec 9)

A Handbrake pushrod
B Adjuster spring
C Washer
D Adjuster nut-to-piston contact face
E Adjuster nut
F Pushrod thread
G Key plate

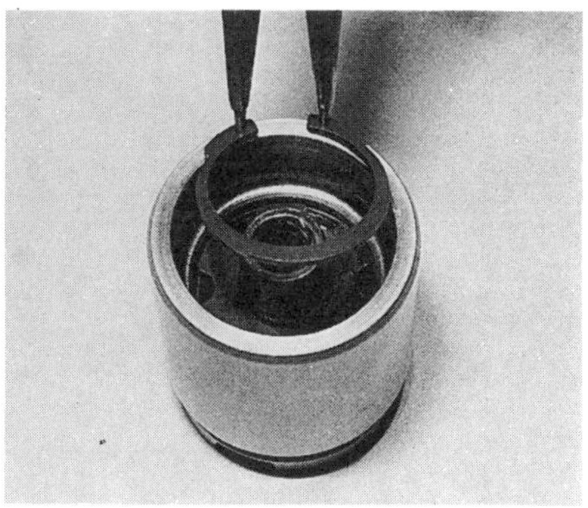
9.5A Remove the circlip from the rear calliper piston – ABS...

9.5B ... followed by the thrustwasher...

9.5C ... a wave washer and (not shown) another thrustwasher...

9.5D ... then the thrust bearing...

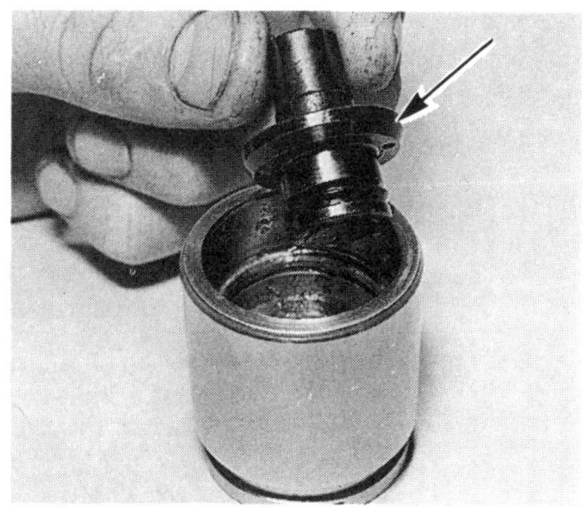
9.5E ... and finally the adjuster nut itself. Note the seal (arrowed) on the nut

9.8 Using the piston adjuster nut to compress the adjuster spring – ABS

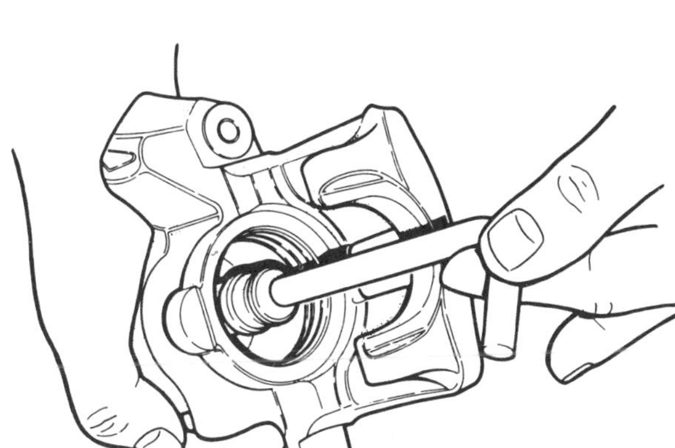
Fig 10.18 Ford tool 12-007 for compressing rear disc calliper adjuster spring – ABS (Sec 9)

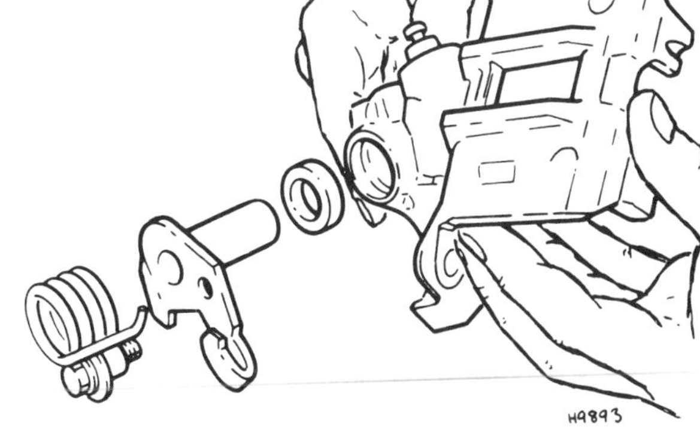

Fig 10.19 Handbrake shaft and associated components – ABS (Sec 9)

12 Remove the handbrake lever return spring and stop bolt. Pull the lever and shaft nut out of the calliper. Prise out the shaft seal.

13 Clean the handbrake shaft using wire wool; renew the shaft if it is badly corroded. The shaft bush in the calliper can also be renewed if necessary. Pull out the old bush with an internal puller or slide hammer, and press in the new bush to 7.5 mm (0.30 in) below the shaft seal lip – see Fig. 10.20. The slot in the side of the bush must line up with the pushrod bore in the calliper.

14 Having renewed components as necessary, commence re-assembly by smearing a little brake grease or anti-seize compound on the handbrake shaft and bush.

15 Fit a new handbrake shaft seal to the calliper. Pass the shaft

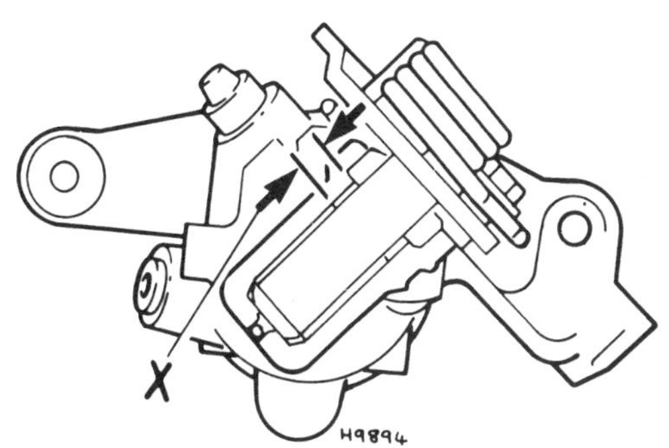

Fig 10.20 Handbrake shaft bush correctly fitted – ABS (Sec 9)

X = 7.5 mm (0.30 in)

9.9A Extract the circlip from the calliper bore – ABS...

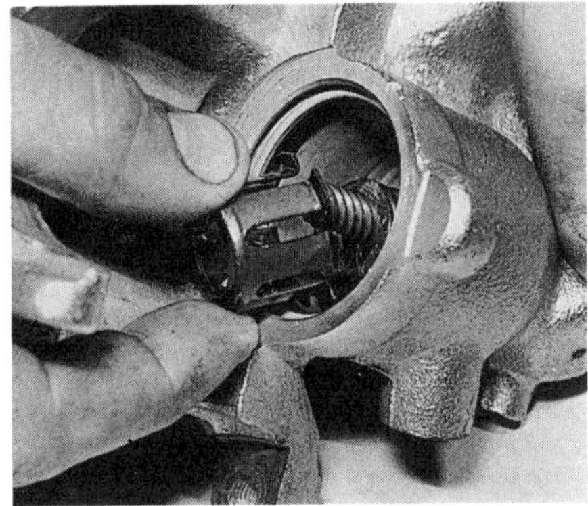
9.9B ... then the spring cover...

9.9C ... the spring itself...

9.9D ... and the washer

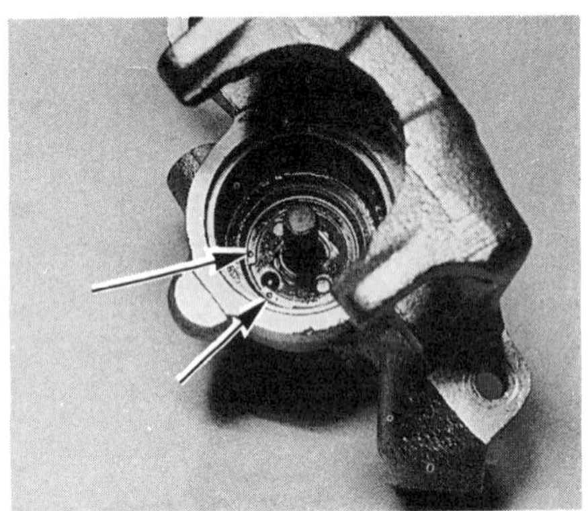
9.10 Remove the circlip (ends arrowed) to release the pushrod and key plate – ABS

9.22 Dust-excluding seal fitted to piston and calliper bore – ABS

through the seal and into the calliper, taking care not to damage the seal lips.

16 Refit the handbrake lever stop bolt and return spring.

17 Refit the handbrake strut, lubricating it with brake grease.

18 Fit a new O-ring to the base of the pushrod. Refit the pushrod and the key plate, engaging the pip on the key plate with the recess in the calliper. Secure the key plate with the circlip.

19 Refit the washer, spring and spring cover. Compress the spring and refit the circlip, then release the spring compressor.

20 Lubricate the calliper bore with clean hydraulic fluid and fit a new piston seal.

21 Reassemble the piston components. Lubricate the contact face of the adjuster nut with a little brake grease, then fit the adjuster nut (with new seal), thrust bearing, thrustwasher, wave washer and the second thrustwasher. Secure with the circlip.

22 Fit a new dust-excluding seal to the grooves in the piston and calliper bore as the piston is refitted (photo). Screw the piston into the calliper bore with the tool used during removal.

23 Renew the guide pin gaiters and apply a little brake grease or anti-seize compound to the guide pins when refitting the calliper to its carrier bracket.

10 Brake disc – examination, removal and refitting

Note: *From 1987, thicker brake discs were fitted. If the later discs are fitted to earlier models, longer wheel studs must be fitted to accommodate the increased thickness. Consult a dealer for further advice.*

Front disc

1 Apply the handbrake, loosen the relevant roadwheel nuts, then jack up the front of the vehicle and support on axle stands. Remove the roadwheel.

2 Remove the disc calliper and carrier bracket with reference to Section 7, but do not disconnect the flexible hose. Support the calliper on an axle stand to avoid straining the flexible hose.

3 Rotate the disc and examine it for deep scoring or grooving. Light scoring is normal, but if excessive, the disc should be removed and either renewed or reground by a suitable specialist. Scrape any corrosion from the disc.

4 Using a dial gauge or a flat metal block and feeler gauges, check that the disc run-out does not exceed the limit given in the Specifications. To do this, fix the measuring equipment, and rotate the disc, noting the variation in measurement as the disc is rotated. The difference between the minimum and maximum measurements recorded is known as disc run-out.

5 Mark the position of the brake disc in relation to the drive flange and on Saloon, Hatchback and Estate models, remove the retaining screw or spire washer(s), as applicable, and remove the disc. On P100 models, also mark the position of the wheel adaptor plate in relation to the disc and drive flange, then unscrew the five retaining nuts and remove the wheel adaptor plate and disc.

6 Refitting is a reversal of removal, but when refitting ensure that the mating faces of the disc, drive flange and on P100 models the wheel adaptor plate, are clean. Align the marks made on the disc, drive flange, and where applicable the wheel adaptor plate, during removal, and refit the disc calliper and carrier bracket with reference to Section 7.

Rear disc (ABS)

7 Chock the front wheels, loosen the relevant roadwheel nuts, then jack up the rear of the vehicle and support on axle stands. Remove the roadwheel and release the handbrake.

8 Detach the handbrake cable from the retaining clip on the lower arm.

9 Unscrew the two calliper carrier bracket-to-hub carrier bolts and remove the calliper assembly. Support the calliper on an axle stand to avoid straining the flexible hose.

10 Proceed as described in paragraphs 3 and 4.

11 Mark the position of the brake disc in relation to the drive flange, remove the retaining spire washer(s), and withdraw the disc.

12 Refitting is a reversal of removal, but ensure that the mating faces of the disc and drive flanges are clean, and align the marks made on the disc and drive flange during removal.

11 Brake drum – inspection and renewal

1 Whenever a brake drum is removed, brush out the dust, taking care not to inhale any, as it may be injurious to health.
2 Examine the internal friction surface of the drum. If deeply scored, or so worn that the drum has become ridged to the width of the shoes, then both drums must be renewed.
3 Regrinding is not recommended as the internal diameter of the drum will no longer be compatible with the shoe friction material contact diameter.

12 Rear wheel cylinder (drum brakes) – removal, overhaul and refitting

Saloon, Hatchback and Estate models

1 Chock the front wheels, loosen the relevant roadwheel nuts, then jack up the rear of the vehicle and support on axle stands. Remove the roadwheel and release the handbrake.
2 Remove the retaining spire washer(s) from the wheel stud(s) and pull off the brake drum. If the drum will not pass over the shoes, it is possible to release the automatic adjuster mechanism by inserting a screwdriver through the small hole in the drum and pressing down on the ratchet.
3 Remove the brake fluid reservoir cap and secure a piece of polythene over the filler neck with a rubber band, or by refitting the cap. This will reduce the loss of fluid during the following procedure.
4 Unscrew the union nut and disconnect the fluid pipe from the wheel cylinder (photo). Plug the open ends of the pipe and wheel cylinder to prevent fluid loss and dirt ingress.
5 Pull the tops of the brake shoes apart so that the self-adjuster mechanism holds them clear of the wheel cylinder.
6 Unscrew the two retaining bolts from the rear of the brake backplate, and withdraw the wheel cylinder and sealing ring.
7 The wheel cylinder can now be dismantled as follows.
8 Prise the dust-excluding rubber seals from the ends of the wheel cylinder, and withdraw the pistons and central spring, identifying the pistons so that they can be refitted in their original positions.
9 Prise the seals from the pistons.
10 Clean all the components in methylated spirit and allow to dry. Examine the surfaces of the pistons and cylinder bore for wear, scoring and corrosion. If evident, the complete wheel cylinder must be renewed, but if the components are in good condition, discard the seals and obtain a repair kit.
11 Dip the new seals in clean brake fluid and fit them to the piston grooves, using fingers only to manipulate them. Ensure that the seal lips face into the wheel cylinder as shown in Fig. 10.13.
12 Carefully insert the pistons and central spring into the cylinder, and fit the dust-excluding rubber seals. Ensure that the pistons are fitted in their original positions.
13 Wipe the brake backplate clean, then fit the wheel cylinder together with a new sealing ring, and tighten the securing bolts.
14 Reconnect the fluid pipe to the wheel cylinder and tighten the union nut.
15 Using a screwdriver, push the self-adjuster toothed quadrant fully towards the backplate to its initial setting.
16 Further refitting is a reversal of removal, but on completion apply the footbrake several times in order to set the brake shoes in their normal positions, and bleed the rear brake circuit as described in Section 3.

P100 models

17 The procedure is as described in paragraphs 1 to 16 inclusive, but with the following differences.
18 Before removing the roadwheel, mark its position in relation to the brake drum. Similarly, mark the position of the brake drum in relation to one of the wheel studs. Align the marks when refitting.
19 The wheel cylinder is secured to the brake backplate by a circlip instead of the two bolts used on other models – see Fig. 10.21.

13 Rear brake backplate (drum brakes) – removal and refitting

Saloon, Hatchback and Estate models

1 Remove the rear brake shoes as described in Section 6.
2 Disconnect the handbrake cable from the backplate by extracting the U-clip.
3 Remove the wheel cylinder as described in Section 12.
4 Remove the driveshaft as described in Chapter 9, Section 7, but do not refit the securing bolts to the backplate.
5 Remove the backplate.
6 If required, prise out the handbrake stop button.
7 Refitting is a reversal of removal, with reference to Sections 12 and 6 respectively when refitting the wheel cylinder and brake shoes. Refit the driveshaft as described in Chapter 9, Section 7.

P100 models

Note: *When refitting the backplate, a new rear hub nut and driveshaft O-ring must be used.*

8 Proceed as described in paragraphs 1 to 3 inclusive.
9 Remove the driveshaft as described in Chapter 9, Section 11.
10 Relieve the staking on the rear hub nut, and using a 50 mm socket and a suitable extension bar, unscrew the nut. Note that the nut is extremely tight.
11 Pull off the hub.
12 Unscrew the six retaining nuts and remove the backplate and the oil baffle.
13 If required, prise out the handbrake stop button.
14 Refitting is a reversal of removal, bearing in mind the following points.
15 When refitting the backplate and the oil baffle, coat the area of the oil baffle shown in Fig. 9.20 (see Chapter 9) with sealant to Ford spec

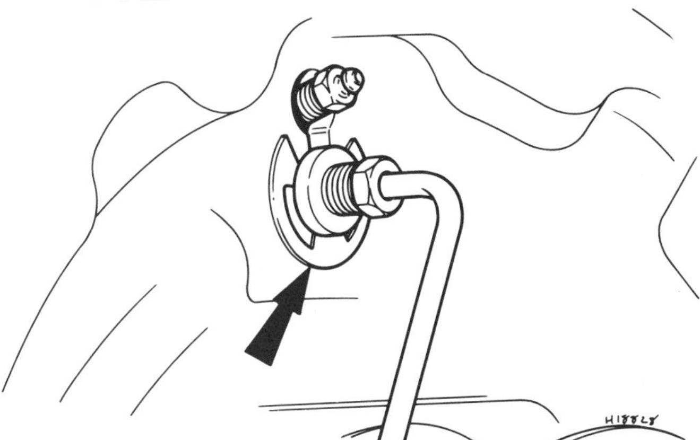

Fig 10.21 Wheel cylinder securing circlip (arrowed) – P100 models (Sec 12)

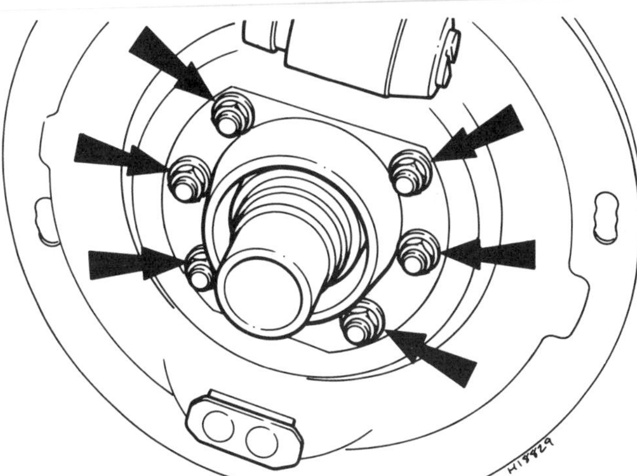

Fig 10.22 Brake backplate and oil baffle retaining nuts – P100 models (Sec 13)

12.4 Fluid pipe union (1) and wheel cylinder retaining bolts (2) – Hatchback model

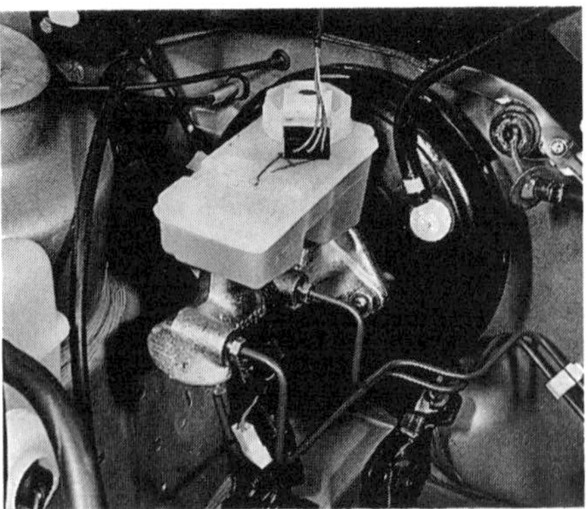

15.2 Disconnect the wiring plug from the low fluid level switch – Hatchback model

16.5 Remove the clip (arrowed) from the servo pushrod

SPM-4G-9112-F, then refit the baffle and the backplate to the axle, tightening the six securing nuts to the specified torque.
16 Use a new rear hub nut, and tighten to the specified torque. Stake the nut into the groove in the axle tube after tightening.
17 Refit the driveshaft, using a new O-ring, as described in Chapter 9, Section 11. Refer to Sections 12 and 6 respectively when refitting the wheel cylinder and brake shoes.

14 Rear disc splash shield (ABS) – removal and refitting

Note: *A suitable puller will be required to remove the drive flange, and a new rear hub nut must be used on reassembly.*
1 Loosen the rear hub nut with the vehicle resting on its wheels. Note that the left-hand nut has a left-hand thread, ie it is undone in a clockwise direction. Before loosening the nut, ensure that the handbrake is applied, and chock the relevant rear wheel. A suitable extension bar will be required, as the nut is extremely tight.
2 Loosen the relevant rear roadwheel nuts, chock the front wheels, then jack up the rear of the vehicle and support on axle stands. Remove the roadwheel and release the handbrake.
3 Free the handbrake cable from its clip on the suspension lower arm.
4 Unscrew the two calliper carrier bracket-to-hub carrier bolts, and remove the calliper, supporting it on an axle stand to avoid straining the flexible hose.
5 Mark the position of the brake disc in relation to the drive flange, remove the retaining spire washer(s), and remove the disc.
6 Unscrew and remove the rear hub nut, and using a suitable puller, pull off the drive flange.
7 Unscrew the four bolts securing the hub carrier and splash shield to the lower arm. Remove the hub carrier and splash shield, whilst supporting the driveshaft. Support the driveshaft by placing axle stands underneath it, or by securing with string to the underbody. Avoid bending the driveshaft joints to excessive angles, and do not allow the shaft to hang down from one end.
8 Refitting is a reversal of removal, bearing in mind the following points.
9 When reassembling the drive flange and the hub carrier, fit the drive flange to the hub carrier in order to centralise the bearings, then using a soft-faced mallet, drive the drive flange/hub carrier assembly onto the end of the stub axle.
10 Refit the hub carrier/splash shield-to-lower arm securing bolts with reference to the note at the beginning of Section 15 in Chapter 11.
11 When refitting the brake disc, align the previously made marks on disc and drive flange.
12 Fit a new rear hub nut of the correct type, and tighten it with the vehicle resting on its roadwheels. Apply the handbrake and chock the relevant rear wheel when finally tightening the hub nut.

15 Master cylinder (conventional braking system) – removal, overhaul and refitting

Note: *Before commencing overhaul, obtain a repair kit containing new pistons and seals.*
1 Depress the brake pedal several times to dissipate the vacuum in the servo.
2 Disconnect the wiring plug from the low fluid level switch on the fluid reservoir cap (photo).
3 Place a suitable container beneath the master cylinder, then unscrew the union nuts and disconnect the two fluid pipes. Plug the ends of the pipes to prevent dirt ingress.
4 Unscrew the two mounting nuts and spring washers, and withdraw the master cylinder from the servo. Cover the master cylinder with rag

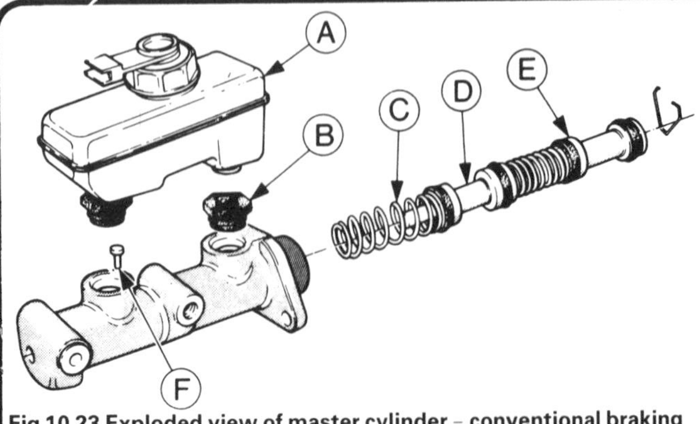

Fig 10.23 Exploded view of master cylinder – conventional braking system (Sec 15)

A Fluid reservoir
B Sealing rubber
C Spring
D Secondary piston
E Primary piston
F Stop pin

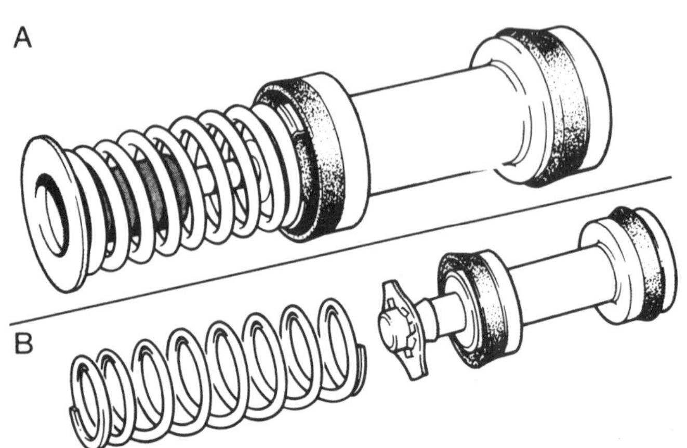

Fig 10.24 Master cylinder primary piston (A) and secondary piston (B) – conventional braking system (Sec 15)

or a plastic bag to prevent spillage of hydraulic fluid on the vehicle paintwork. If fluid is accidentally spilt on the paintwork, wash off immediately with cold water – brake fluid is an effective paint stripper!
5 Drain the remaining fluid from the master cylinder, and clean the exterior surfaces with methylated spirit.
6 Pull the fluid reservoir from the top of the master cylinder and prise out the sealing rubbers.
7 Mount the master cylinder in a vice, then depress the primary piston slightly and extract the circlip and washer. Withdraw the primary piston assembly.
8 Depress the secondary piston and remove the stop pin from the fluid aperture.
9 Remove the master cylinder from the vice and tap it on the bench to remove the secondary piston assembly.
10 Prise the seals from the secondary piston. Do not attempt to dismantle the primary piston.
11 Clean all the components in methylated spirit and examine them for wear and damage. In particular check the surfaces of the pistons and cylinder bore for scoring and corrosion. If the cylinder bore is worn, renew the complete master cylinder, otherwise obtain a repair kit including pistons and seals.
12 Check that the fluid inlet and outlet ports are free and unobstructed. Dip the new pistons and seals in clean brake fluid.
13 Fit the seals to the secondary piston using the fingers only to manipulate them into the grooves. Note that the sealing lips must face away from each other.
14 Insert the secondary piston and spring into the cylinder. Turn the piston slowly as the first seal enters to avoid trapping the sealing lip. Similarly insert the primary piston and spring, then fit the washer and circlip.
15 Depress the primary and secondary pistons and refit the secondary piston stop pin.
16 Fit the fluid reservoir sealing rubbers and press the reservoir into them. If the rubbers are worn or perished, or if leakage has been evident, fit the new rubbers.
17 Refitting is a reversal of removal, but tighten the mounting nuts and pipe union nuts to the specified torque, and finally bleed the hydraulic system as described in Section 3.

16 Vacuum servo (conventional braking system) – description, removal and refitting

1 The vacuum servo is fitted between the brake pedal and the master cylinder and provides assistance to the driver when the pedal is depressed, reducing the effort required to operate the brakes. The unit is operated by vacuum from the inlet manifold. With the brake pedal released, vacuum is channelled to both sides of the internal diaphragm, however when the pedal is depressed, one side of the diaphragm is opened to the atmosphere, resulting in assistance to the pedal effort. Should the vacuum servo develop a fault, the hydraulic system is not affected, however greater effort will be required at the pedal.
2 To remove the servo, first remove the master cylinder as described in Section 15.
3 Disconnect the vacuum hose from the servo.
4 Working inside the vehicle, remove the lower facia panel from the driver's side as described in Chapter 12.
5 Remove the clip from the servo pushrod on the brake pedal (photo).
6 Unscrew the two mounting nuts and washers securing the servo to the bulkhead, and lift the servo from the bulkhead. Note that the two mounting nuts also secure the pedal bracket to the bulkhead.
7 If required, the vacuum hose can be disconnected from the inlet manifold, and the non-return valve can be checked for correct operation by ensuring that it is only possible to blow through it in one direction.
8 No overhaul of the servo is possible, and if faulty, it must be renewed as a complete unit.
9 Refitting is a reversal of removal, but when refitting the servo to the bulkhead, ensure that the pushrod is correctly located in the pedal and that the clip is secure. Refit the master cylinder with reference to Section 15.

17 Fluid reservoir (ABS) – removal and refitting

Note: *New seals must be used between the reservoir and the hydraulic unit on reassembly*
1 Disconnect the battery negative lead.
2 Depressurise the hydraulic system by pumping the brake pedal at least 20 times, or until it becomes hard.
3 Disconnect the wiring multi-plugs from the reservoir cap and remove the cap.
4 Unscrew the reservoir securing screw, and remove the securing clip, noting that the clip also supports the clutch cable.
5 Prepare a suitable container to collect the fluid as the hydraulic unit is drained, then remove the securing spring clip and disconnect the low pressure fluid hose from the pump (photos). Allow the fluid to drain out of the hose into the container. If fluid is accidentally spilt on the paintwork, wash off immediately with cold water – brake fluid is an effective paint stripper!
6 Pull the reservoir out of the seals on the hydraulic unit and remove it (photo).
7 Note the spigot locating bush on the rear hydraulic unit inlet, which may stay in the hydraulic unit or may come out with the reservoir (photo).
8 Refitting is a reversal of removal, but use new seals between the reservoir and the hydraulic unit.
9 On completion, bleed the complete hydraulic system as described in Section 4, and check for leaks around all disturbed components.

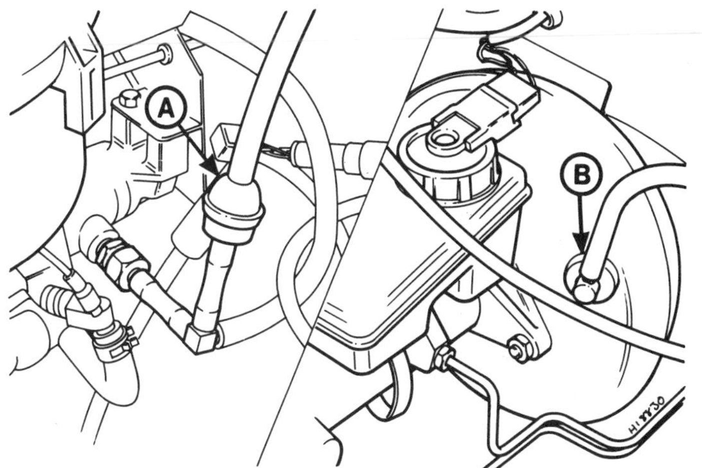

Fig 10.25 Servo vacuum hose non-return valve (A) and servo connection (B) – conventional braking system (Sec 16)

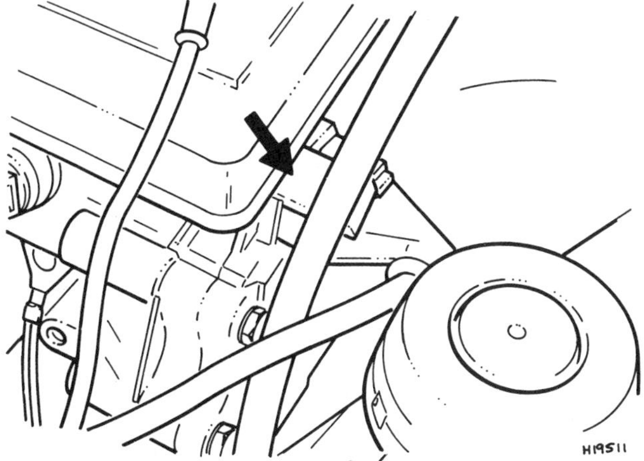

Fig 10.26 Reservoir securing clip (arrowed) also supports clutch cable – ABS (Sec 17)

17.5A Remove the securing spring clip...

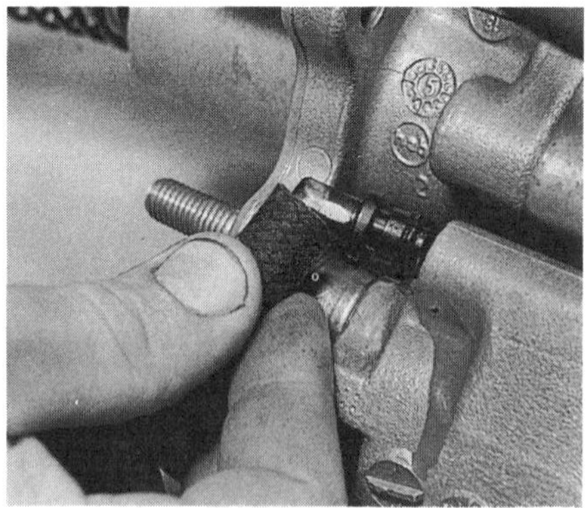
17.5B ... and disconnect the low pressure fluid hose

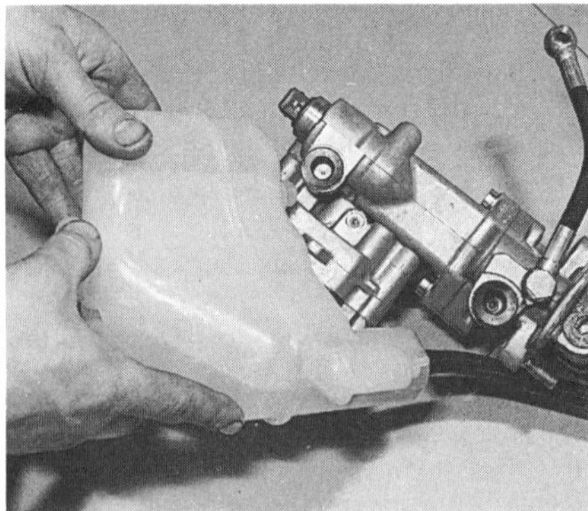
17.6 Removing the fluid reservoir from the hydraulic unit

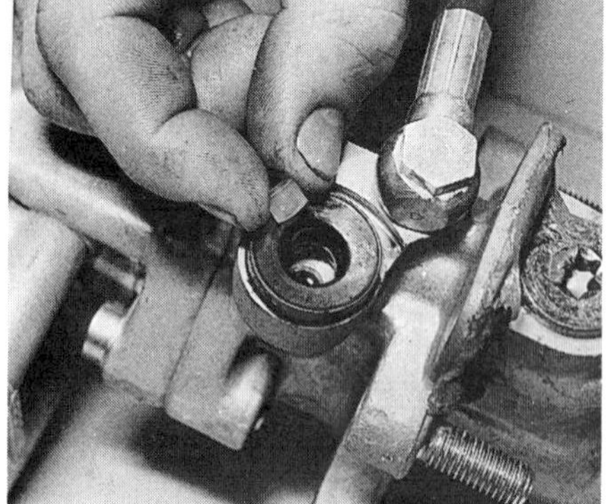
17.7 Removing the spigot locating bush from the rear hydraulic unit inlet

18.3A Disconnecting the low fluid level switch multi-plug...

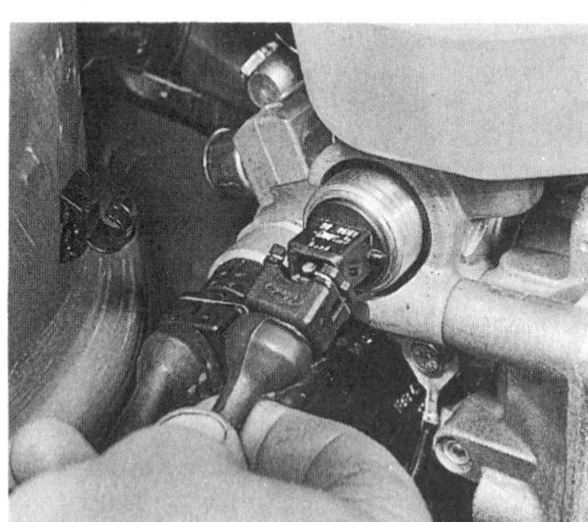
18.3B ... the main valve multi-plug...

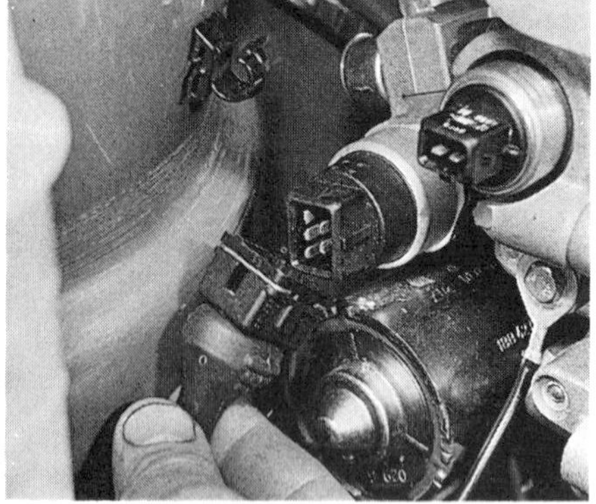
18.3C ... and the pressure switch multi-plug

18.8 Hydraulic unit-to-bulkhead securing nuts (arrowed)

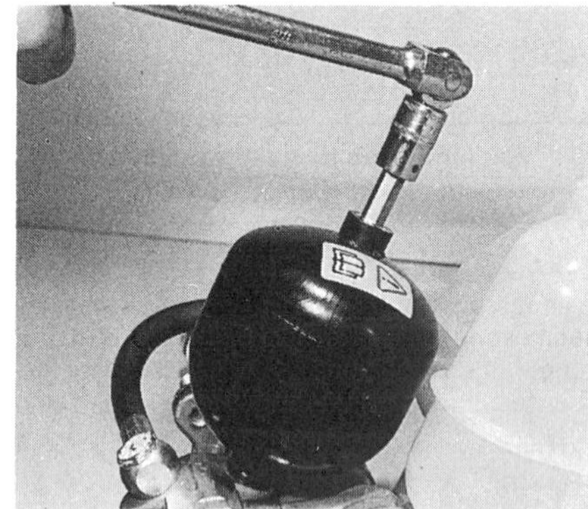
19.4A Unscrew the accumulator...

18 Hydraulic unit (ABS) – removal and refitting

Note: *A new gasket must be used between the hydraulic unit and the bulkhead on refitting*

1 Disconnect the battery negative lead.

2 Depressurise the hydraulic system by pumping the brake pedal at least 20 times, or until it becomes hard.

3 Disconnect the six multi-plugs from the hydraulic unit. They are all different, so there is no need to label them. When a plug has a spring clip retainer, lift the clip before pulling out the plug. To release the pump plug, pull back the rubber boot and the plug sleeve (photos).

4 Unbolt the earth strap from the unit.

5 Prepare a suitable container to catch spilt fluid. Mark the hydraulic pipes so that they can be refitted in their original positions, then disconnect them from the base of the unit. Plug the open ends of the pipes and hydraulic unit to prevent fluid leakage and dirt ingress. If fluid is accidentally spilt on the paintwork, wash off immediately with cold water – brake fluid is an effective paint stripper!

6 Working inside the vehicle, remove the lower facia panel from the driver's side as described in Chapter 12.

7 Remove the clip from the hydraulic unit pushrod on the brake pedal.

8 With an assistant supporting the hydraulic unit, unscrew the four nuts which secure the unit to the bulkhead (photo). Withdraw the unit from under the bonnet.

9 Recover the gasket fitted between the unit and the bulkhead.

10 Drain the fluid from the reservoir. **Do not** actuate the pushrod with the unit removed.

11 Dismantling of the hydraulic unit should be limited to the operations described in the following Sections.

12 Refitting is a reversal of removal, bearing in mind the following points.

13 Do not refill the fluid reservoir until reassembly and refitting is complete.

14 Use a new gasket between the hydraulic unit and the bulkhead.

15 Ensure that the hydraulic pipes are reconnected to the correct unions.

16 On completion, bleed the complete hydraulic system as described in Section 4, and check for leaks around all disturbed components.

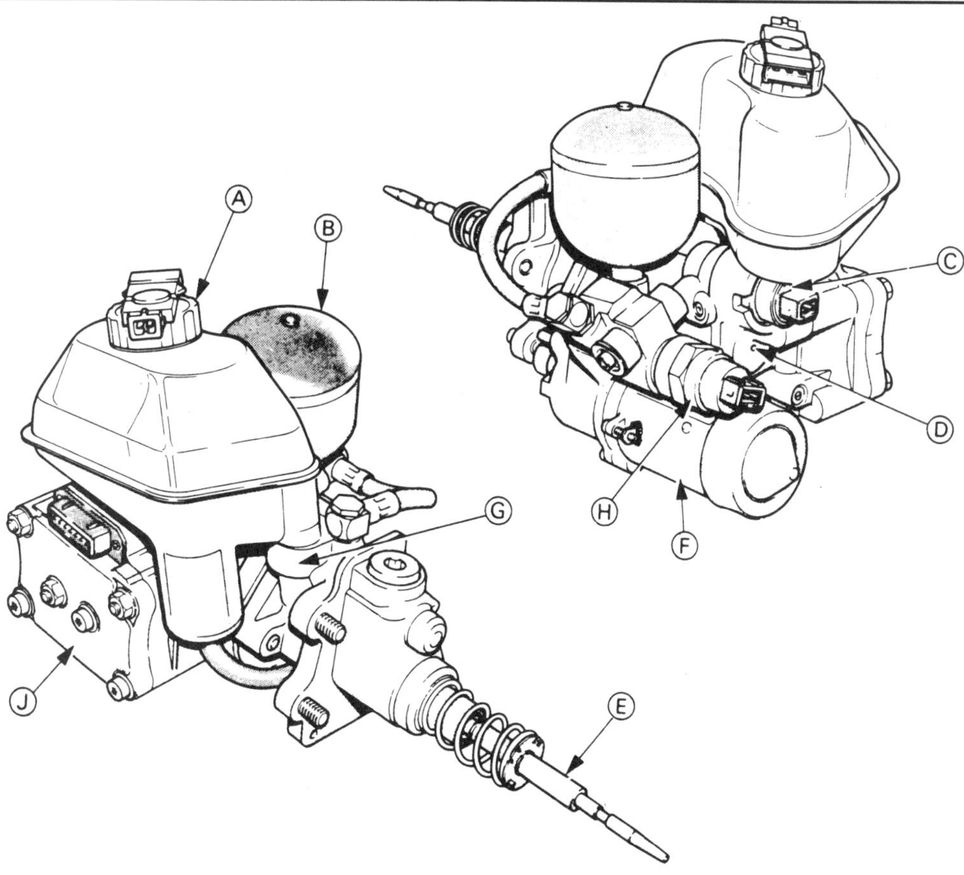

Fig 10.27 Hydraulic unit components – ABS (Sec 18)

A Fluid reservoir
B Accumulator
C Main valve
D Master cylinder
E Pushrod
F Pump and motor
G Pressure switch
H Booster
J Valve block

19 Hydraulic unit accumulator (ABS) – removal and refitting

Note: *A new O-ring must be used between the accumulator and the hydraulic unit on refitting*

1 Disconnect the battery negative lead.

2 Depressurise the hydraulic system by pumping the brake pedal at least 20 times, or until it becomes hard.

3 Wrap a clean rag round the base of the accumulator to catch any spilt fluid.

4 Unscrew the accumulator using a hexagon key. Remove the accumulator, being prepared for fluid spillage (photos). If fluid is accidentally spilt on the paintwork, wash off immediately with cold water – brake fluid is an effective paint stripper!

5 Fit a new O-ring to the base of the accumulator, fit the accumulator and tighten it.

6 Reconnect the battery. Switch on the ignition and check that the hydraulic unit pump stops within 60 seconds; if not, the accumulator is likely to be faulty.

7 On completion, bleed the complete hydraulic system as described in Section 4, and check for leaks around all disturbed components.

20 Hydraulic unit pump and motor (ABS) – removal and refitting

Note: *New sealing washers must be used on the high pressure fluid hose banjo union, and a new O-ring must be used between the accumulator and the hydraulic unit on refitting*

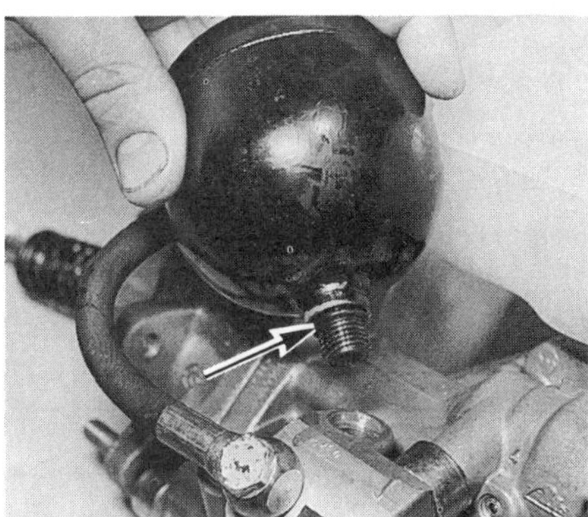

19.4B ... and remove it, noting the O-ring (arrowed)

20.5 Hydraulic unit pump mounting bolt

21.3 Unscrewing the hydraulic unit pressure switch

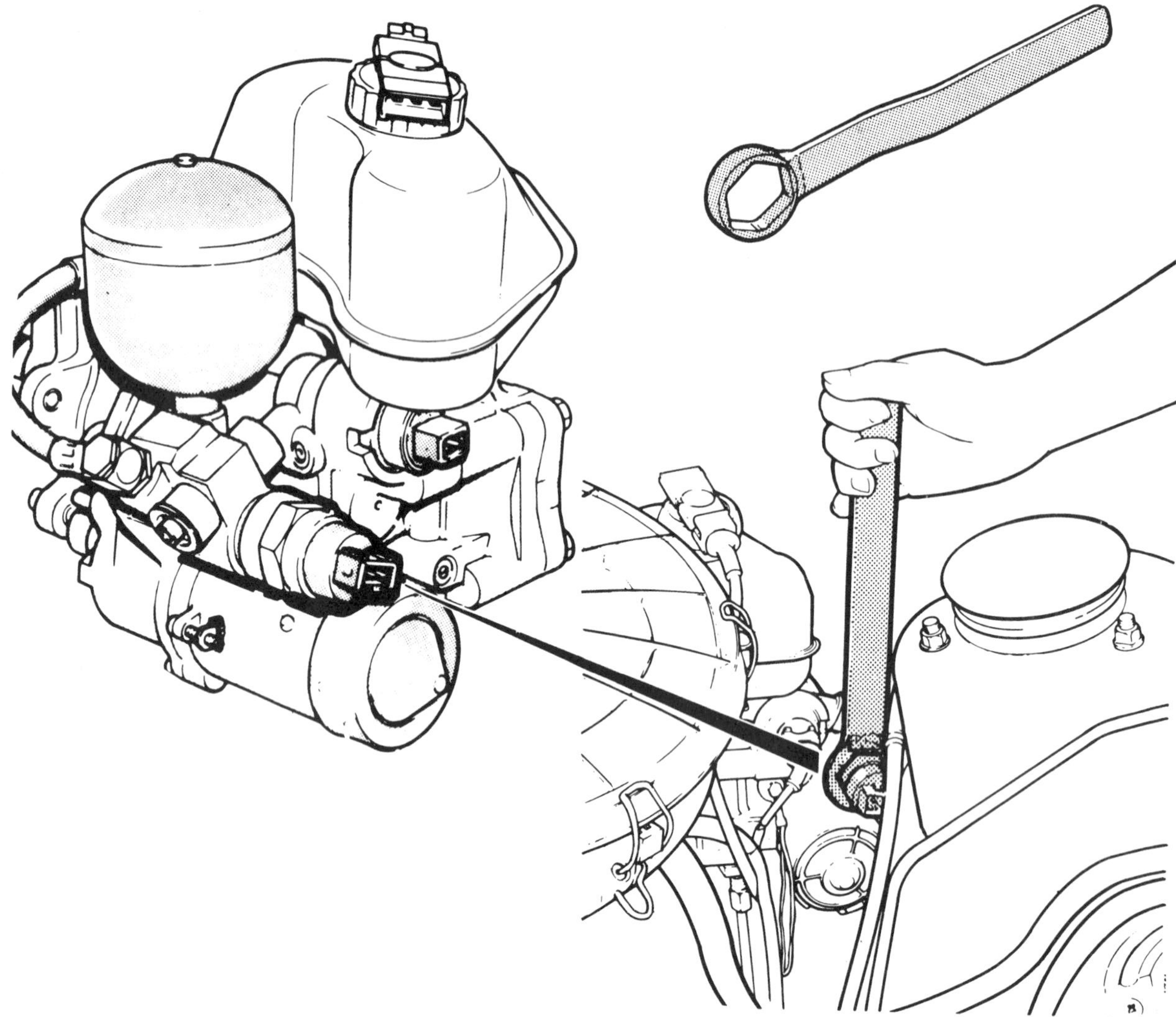

Fig 10.28 Ford tool No 12-008 for removing hydraulic unit pressure switch – ABS. Left-hand drive shown, right-hand drive similar (Sec 21)

1 Remove the accumulator as described in Section 19.
2 Prepare a suitable container to catch spilt fluid, and disconnect the high pressure fluid hose from the pump.
3 Remove the securing spring clip and disconnect the low pressure fluid hose from the pump. Allow the fluid to drain out of the hose into the container. If fluid is accidentally spilt on the paintwork, wash off immediately with cold water – brake fluid is an effective paint stripper!
4 Disconnect the multi-plugs from the pressure switch and the pump motor.
5 Remove the pump mounting bolt (photo).
6 Pull the pump and motor assembly off the mounting spigot and remove it.
7 Recover the mounting bushes and renew them if necessary.
8 If a new pump is to be fitted, transfer the pressure switch to it, using a new O-ring.
9 Commence refitting by offering the pump to the mounting spigot, then reconnecting the low pressure fluid hose.
10 Refit and tighten the pump mounting bolt.
11 Reconnect the high pressure fluid hose, using new sealing washers on the banjo union.
12 Refit the accumulator, using a new O-ring.
13 Reconnect the multi-plugs and the battery.
14 Refill the fluid reservoir, then switch on the ignition and allow the pump to prime itself. Allow the pump to run for a maximum of two minutes at a time then leave it for ten minutes to cool down.
15 On completion, bleed the complete hydraulic system as described in Section 4, and check for leaks around all disturbed components.

21 Hydraulic unit pressure switch (ABS) – removal and refitting

Note: *To remove the pressure switch from the hydraulic unit in situ, Ford tool No 12-008 or a locally made equivalent will be required – see Fig. 10.28. The switch may be removed without special tools after removing the hydraulic unit complete or the pump above. A new O-ring must be used when refitting the switch.*

1 Disconnect the battery negative lead.
2 Depressurise the hydraulic system by pumping the brake pedal at least 20 times, or until it becomes hard.
3 Disconnect the multi-plug from the switch, then unscrew and remove the switch (photo).
4 Refit the switch using a new O-ring. Position the plastic sleeve so that the drain hole faces the pump motor, then tighten the switch (photo).
5 Reconnect the multi-plug and the battery.
6 On completion, bleed the complete hydraulic system as described in Section 4, and check for leaks around all disturbed components.

22 Valve block (ABS) – removal and refitting

1 Disconnect the battery negative lead.
2 Depressurise the hydraulic system by pumping the brake pedal at

21.4 Refit the pressure switch with the drain hole (arrowed) in the plastic sleeve facing the pump motor

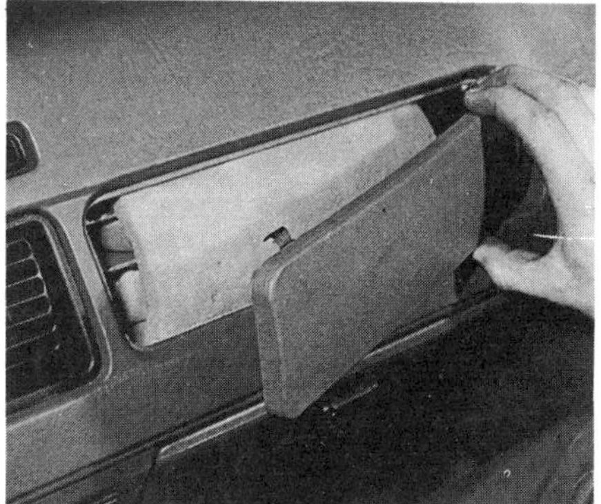
23.2 Remove the facia trim panel

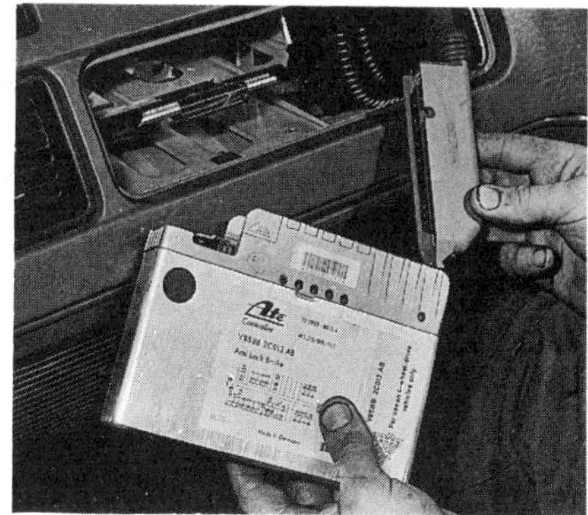
23.4 Withdraw the module and disconnect the multi-plug

Fig 10.29 Unscrewing the valve block mounting bracket nuts (arrowed) – ABS (Sec 22)

least 20 times, or until it becomes hard.

3 Apply the handbrake, and slacken the left-hand front wheel nuts. Jack up the front of the vehicle and support on axle stands. Remove the left-hand front wheel.

4 Remove the plastic liner from under the wheel arch – see Chapter 12.

5 Prepare a suitable container to catch spilt fluid, clean around the unions on the valve block, then unscrew and disconnect the fluid pipes. Plug the open ends of the pipes and valve block to prevent fluid leakage and dirt ingress. If fluid is accidentally spilt on the paintwork, wash off immediately with cold water – brake fluid is an effective paint stripper!

6 Disconnect the multi-plug and the earth strap from the valve block.

7 Working through the wheel arch, unscrew the three nuts which secure the valve block mounting bracket.

8 Remove the valve block and mounting bracket, taking care not to spill brake fluid on the paintwork.

9 No further dismantling of the valve block is possible, but the pressure regulating valve in the rear brake pipe union can be renewed if desired.

10 Refitting is a reversal of removal.

11 On completion, bleed the complete hydraulic system as described in Section 4, and check for leaks around all disturbed components.

23 Computer module (ABS) – removal and refitting

1 Disconnect the battery.

2 Working inside the vehicle, prise out the facia trim panel from the passenger's side (photo). Remove the insulation.

3 To remove the now exposed module, push it as necessary to release the retaining catch.

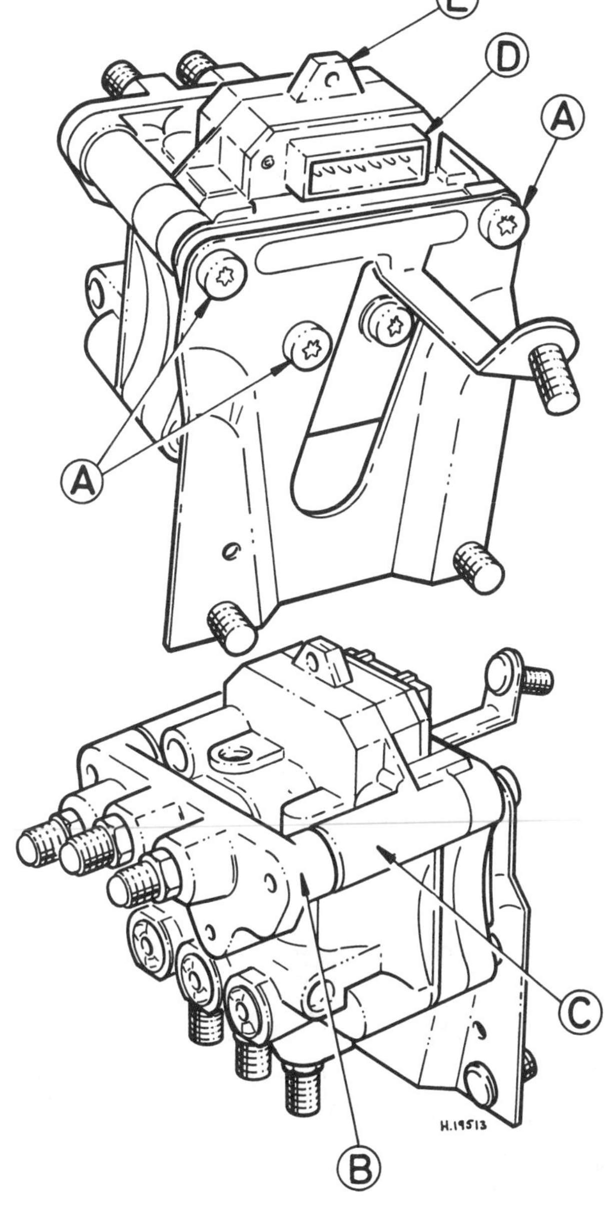

Fig 10.30 Valve block and associated components – ABS (Sec 22)

A Bracket screws
B Adaptor plate
C Valve block
D Multi-plug
E Earth strap anchor point

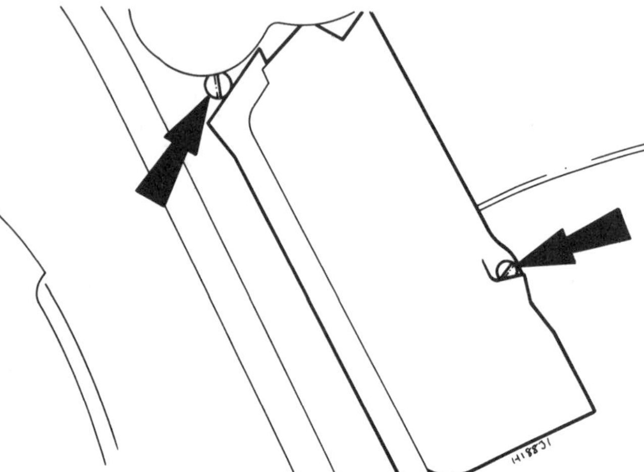

Fig 10.31 Remove the side kick panel (securing screws arrowed) for access to the rear wheel sensor wiring plug – ABS (Sec 24)

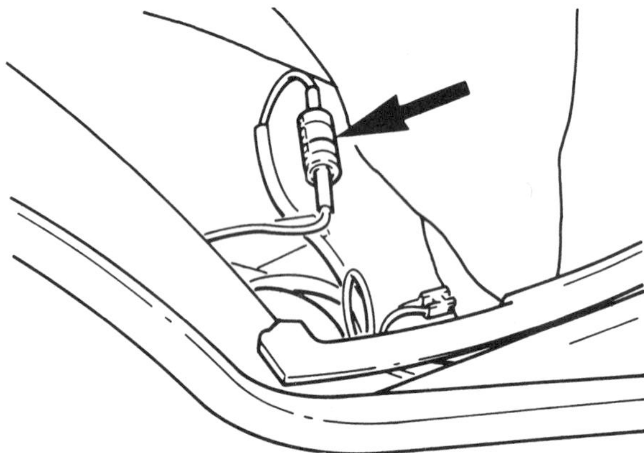

Fig 10.32 Rear wheel sensor wiring plug (arrowed) – ABS (Sec 24)

4 Withdraw the module, and disconnect the multi-plug (photo).
5 Refitting is a reversal of removal, but on completion check the operation of the ABS warning lamp as described in the manufacturer's handbook.

24 Wheel sensor (ABS) – removal and refitting

Note: *A new O-ring must be used when refitting a sensor.*

Front wheel sensor

1 Apply the handbrake, loosen the relevant front roadwheel nuts, then jack up the front of the vehicle and support on axle stands. Remove the roadwheel.
2 Working under the bonnet, unclip the ABS wiring loom from the chassis side member, and disconnect the wheel sensor wiring plug.
3 Unscrew the mounting bolt and withdraw the sensor (photos).
4 Refitting is a reversal of removal, bearing in mind the following points.
5 Clean the bore in the hub carrier, and smear the bore and the sensor with lithium based grease.
6 Use a new O-ring seal when refitting the sensor.

Rear wheel sensor

7 Chock the front wheels, loosen the relevant rear roadwheel nuts, then jack up the rear of the vehicle and support on axle stands. Release the handbrake and remove the roadwheel.
8 Working inside the vehicle, lift up the rear seat cushion, then remove the side kick panel and fold the carpet forwards to gain access to the wheel sensor wiring plug.
9 Remove the wiring plug from its clip, and disconnect it.
10 Prise out the floor panel grommet, then feed the sensor wiring through the floor panel.
11 Free the handbrake cable from its clip on the suspension lower arm.
12 Where applicable, disconnect the wiring to the disc pad wear sensor.
13 Unscrew and remove the bolt from the forward calliper guide pin, while holding the pin stationary with a spanner.
14 Swing the calliper rearwards to gain access to the wheel sensor.
15 Unscrew the bolt securing the sensor to its mounting bracket.
16 Refitting is a reversal of removal, bearing in mind the following points.
17 Clean the bore in the sensor mounting bracket, and smear the bore and the sensor with lithium based grease.
18 Use a new O-ring seal when refitting the sensor.

25 Deceleration sensitive valve (Saloon, Hatchback and Estate models with conventional braking system) – removal and refitting

1 The deceleration sensitive valve is located on the left-hand side of the engine compartment (photo).
2 Place a suitable container beneath the valve to catch spilled fluid, then unscrew the union nuts and disconnect the fluid pipes. Plug the open ends of the pipes and valve to prevent fluid leakage and dirt ingress. If fluid is accidentally spilt on the paintwork, wash off immediately with cold water – brake fluid is an effective paint stripper!
3 On early models, the valve is secured to the mounting bracket on the inner wing by a single bolt. Unscrew the bolt and remove the valve.
4 On later models, the valve is secured to the mounting bracket by a clip as shown in Fig. 10.33. Remove the clip and slide out the valve.
5 Refitting is a reversal of removal, but note that the early type of valve must be fitted with the cover bolts facing forwards, and the later type of valve must be fitted with the smaller diameter stepped end facing forwards.
6 On completion, bleed the rear hydraulic circuit as described in Section 3.

24.3A Unscrew the mounting bolt...

24.3B ... and withdraw the wheel sensor (front wheel sensor)

25.1A Early type deceleration sensitive valve – Hatchback model

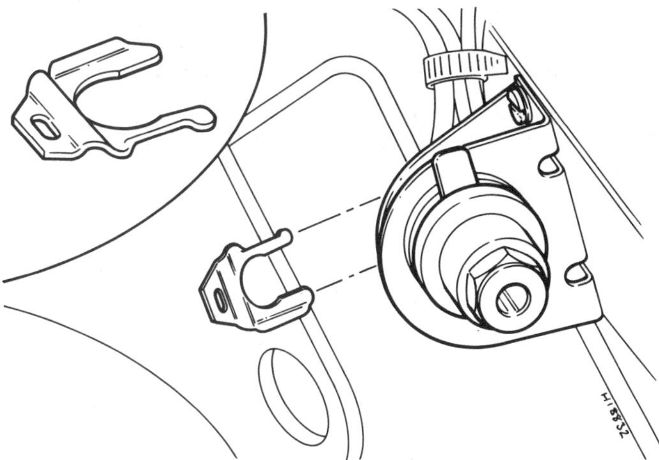

Fig 10.33 Later type deceleration sensitive valve and securing clip – Saloon, Hatchback and Estate models with conventional braking system (Sec 25)

26 Load apportioning valve (P100 models) – removal and refitting

1 Chock the front wheels, jack up the rear of the vehicle and support on axle stands.
2 The load apportioning valve is located on the right-hand side of the vehicle underbody above the axle.
3 Remove the spring clip and clevis pin, and detach the spring from the valve operating lever (photo).
4 Place a suitable container beneath the valve to catch spilled fluid, then unscrew the union nuts and disconnect the fluid pipes. Plug the open ends of the pipes and valve to prevent fluid leakage and dirt ingress.
5 Unscrew the three securing nuts and bolts from the valve mounting bracket, and remove the valve assembly.
6 Refitting is a reversal of removal, but note that the fluid inlet pipe from the master cylinder must be connected to the lower valve port, and the fluid outlet pipe to the rear brakes must be connected to the upper valve port.
7 On completion, bleed the rear hydraulic circuit as described in Section 3, and check the valve adjustment as described in Section 27.

27 Load apportioning valve (P100 models) – adjustment

1 The vehicle must be unladen, at normal kerb weight (a full tank of petrol, but no driver or load).
2 With the vehicle standing on its roadwheels, remove the spring clip and clevis pin, and detach the spring from the valve operating lever.
3 Loosen the locknut on the abutment block at the bottom of the spring (photo).
4 Slide the spring through the grommet in the bracket on the axle, until the correct 'X' dimension is obtained between the centre of the spring eye and the centre of the valve operating lever eye – see Fig. 10.35.
5 Hold the spring in position, slide the abutment block against the underside of the grommet, and tighten the locknut.
6 Attach the free end of the spring to the valve operating lever, and refit the clevis pin and spring clip.

28 Brake fluid pipes and hoses – removal and refitting

1 To remove a flexible hose, always free it from any mounting bracket(s) first by prising out the U-shaped retaining clip, and then using two close-fitting spanners to disconnect the hose-to-rigid pipe union (photo).
2 Once disconnected from the rigid pipe, the flexible hose may be unscrewed from the calliper or wheel cylinder union, as applicable.
3 When reconnecting pipe or hose fittings, note that the seal is made at the swaged end of the pipe, so do not continue to tighten a union if it is tight, yet still stands proud of the surface into which it is screwed.
4 A flexible hose must never be installed twisted, but a slight 'set' is permissible to give it clearance from adjacent components. This can be achieved by turning the hose slightly before fitting the U-shaped retaining clip to the mounting bracket.
5 Rigid pipelines can be made to pattern by motor factors supplying brake components.

29 Handbrake cable – removal and refitting

1 Chock the front wheels, loosen the rear roadwheel nuts, then jack up the rear of the vehicle and support on axle stands. Release the handbrake and remove the roadwheels.
2 Slacken the handbrake cable adjuster with reference to Section 30 if necessary.
3 Extract the securing circlip and pivot pin, and detach the handbrake equaliser from the linkage on the underbody (photo).
4 On models with a conventional braking system, remove the brake

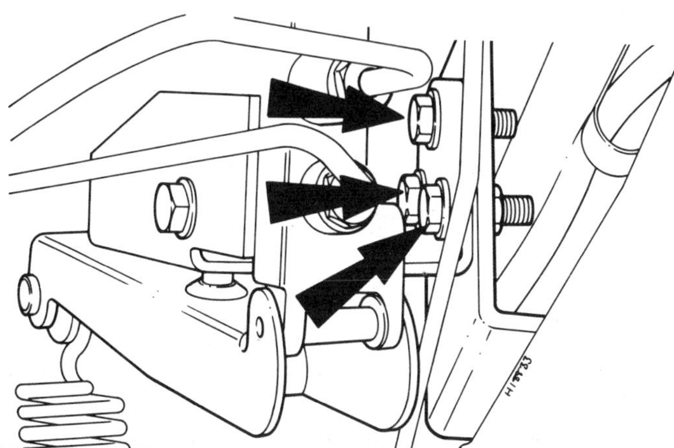

Fig 10.34 Load apportioning valve securing bolts (arrowed) – P100 models (Sec 26)

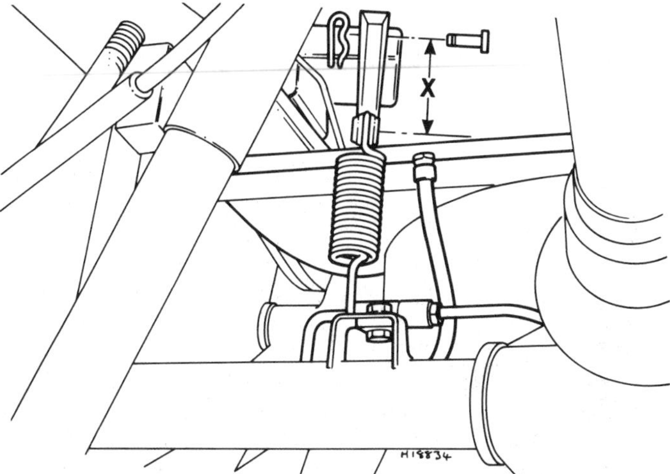

Fig 10.35 Load apportioning valve adjustment – P100 models (Sec 27)

X = 77.0 mm (3.0 in) with vehicle unladen at normal kerb weight

25.1B Later type deceleration sensitive valve – Hatchback model

26.3 Remove the spring clip (arrowed) and clevis pin from the valve operating lever – P100 model

27.3 Loosen the locknut (arrowed) on the abutment block – P100 model

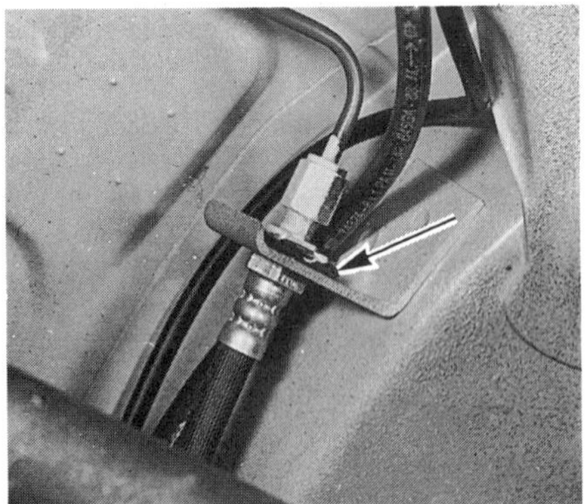
28.1 Flexible hose-to-rigid pipe union. U-shaped retaining clip arrowed

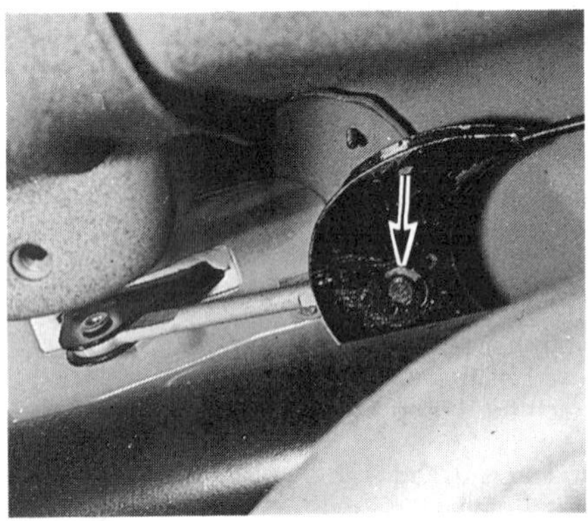
29.3 Handbrake equaliser securing circlip (arrowed) and pivot pin – P100 model

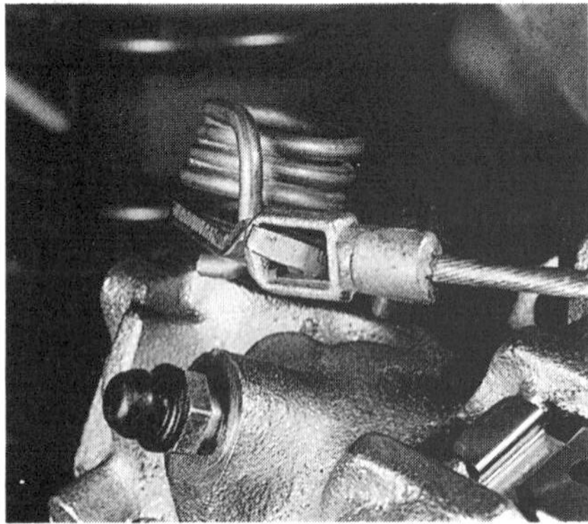
29.5A Handbrake cable-to-operating lever attachment – ABS

29.5B Handbrake cable-to-calliper carrier bracket attachment – ABS

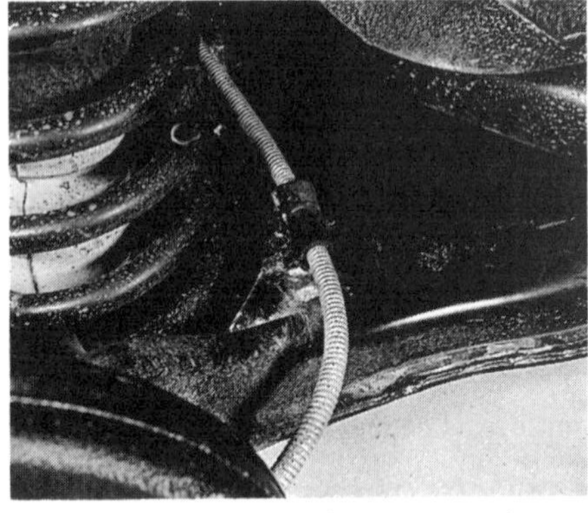
29.6 Handbrake cable-to-lower suspension arm attachment – Hatchback model

shoes and disconnect the handbrake cables from the operating levers as described in Section 6, then disconnect the cables from the brake backplates by extracting the U-clips.

5 On models with ABS, unhook the handbrake cables from the operating levers on the callipers, then disconnect the cables from the calliper carrier brackets by removing the retaining circlips (photos).

6 On Saloon, Hatchback and Estate models bend back the tangs and release the cables from the lower suspension arms, then feed the cables through the holes in the suspension crossmember and release them from the brackets on the underbody, noting that the right-hand cable is retained by a circlip (photo). Withdraw the cable assembly from the vehicle.

7 On P100 models, release the cables from the brackets on the chassis crossmember, noting that the left-hand cable is retained by a circlip, then unhook the cable support springs and withdraw the cable assembly from the vehicle (photo).

8 Refitting is a reversal of removal, but on models with a conventional braking system, refit the brake shoes with reference to Section 6.

9 On completion, adjust the cable as described in Section 30.

30 Handbrake cable – adjustment

Note: *Where fitted, the adjuster locking pin must be renewed on completion of adjustment.*

Conventional braking system (except P100 models)

1 The handbrake cable is normally self-adjusting in use, however adjustment may be required to compensate for cable switch over a long period, and is also necessary after fitting a new cable.

29.7 Handbrake cable support spring (arrowed) – P100 model

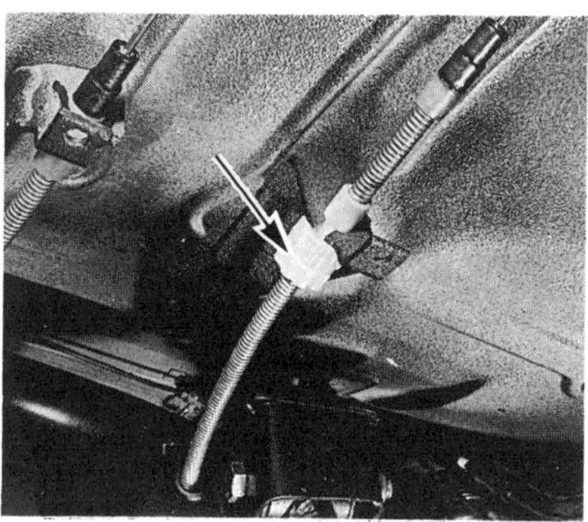
30.3 Handbrake cable adjuster on left-hand underbody bracket (arrowed) – Hatchback model

30.5 Plastic plunger (arrowed) in brake backplate – Hatchback model

30.11 Make alignment marks between each handbrake operating lever and calliper body – ABS

30.17 Handbrake cable adjuster on right-hand side of chassis crossmember – P100 model

31.3 Handbrake equaliser and linkage on underbody – Hatchback model

2 Chock the front wheels, jack up the rear of the vehicle and support on axle stands. Release the handbrake.
3 Unscrew the locknut from the adjuster located on the left-hand underbody bracket (photo). On later models, a locking pin is fitted to the bracket to lock the adjuster nuts in position. Where applicable, remove the locking pin before unscrewing the locknut.
4 Apply the footbrake vigorously several times to set the self-adjuster mechanism.
5 Turn the adjuster until the plastic plungers located in the brake lockplates are free to turn, and the total movement of both plungers added together is between 0.5 and 1.0 mm (0.02 and 0.04 in) (photo).
6 Tighten the adjuster locknut against the adjuster nut by hand (two clicks), then tighten further by a minimum of two and a maximum of four clicks, using a suitable spanner or pliers.
7 Where applicable, fit a new adjuster locking pin. The old pin should not be re-used.
8 Check that with the handbrake released, the rear wheels are free to rotate and no brake 'bind' is evident. The handbrake lever travel should be between two and four clicks of the ratchet. If brake 'bind' or excessive lever travel is evident, check the handbrake cable routing, and check the self-adjuster mechanism for wear or damage.

ABS

9 Proceed as described in paragraphs 1 to 3 inclusive.
10 Bend back the tangs and release the cables from the lower suspension arms.
11 Ensure that both handbrake operating levers are returned to their stops on the callipers, then make alignment marks between the levers and the calliper bodies (photo).
12 Turn the adjuster until either lever just starts to move, as indicated by the alignment marks.
13 Apply the handbrake and release it several times to equalise the cable runs.
14 With the handbrake released, proceed as described in paragraphs 6 and 7.
15 Refit the cables to the lower suspension arms, and secure by bending over the tangs.
16 Check that with the handbrake released, the rear wheels are free to rotate and no brake 'bind' is evident. The handbrake lever travel should be between two and four clicks of the ratchet. If brake 'bind' or excessive lever travel is evident, check the handbrake cable routing, and check the calliper mechanism for wear or damage.

P100 models

17 Proceed as described in paragraphs 1 to 4 inclusive, but note that the adjuster is located on the right-hand side of the chassis crossmember (photo).
18 Apply the handbrake, pulling the lever upwards three clicks.
19 Turn the adjuster until both rear wheels are locked and cannot be turned by hand.
20 Proceed as described in paragraphs 6 and 7.
21 Check that with the handbrake released, the rear wheels are free to rotate and no brake 'bind' is evident. The handbrake lever travel should be between three and five clicks of the ratchet. If brake 'bind' or excessive lever travel is evident, check the handbrake cable routing, and check the self-adjuster mechanism for wear or damage.

31 Handbrake lever – removal and refitting

1 Chock the rear wheels, jack up the front of the vehicle and support on axle stands. Release the handbrake. Disconnect the battery negative lead.

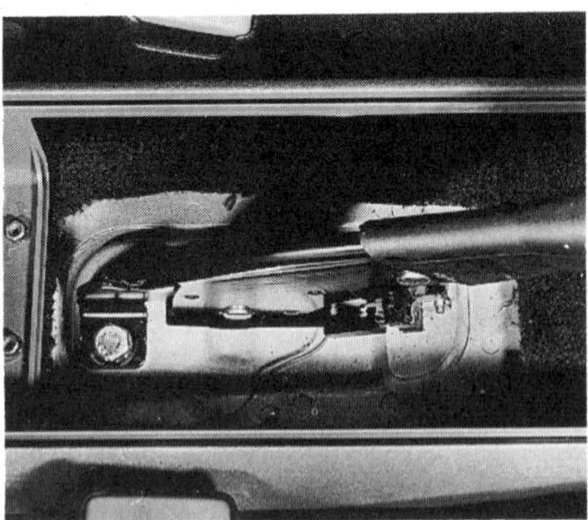

31.4 Centre console removed to reveal handbrake assembly – Hatchback model

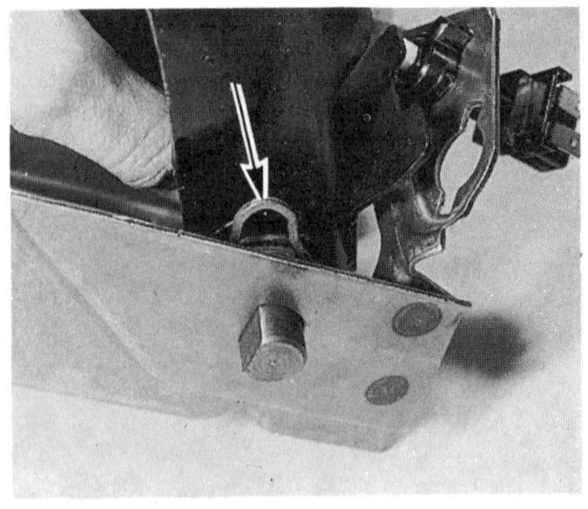

32.2 Extract the inboard circlip (arrowed) to remove the pedal pivot shaft

2 Slacken the handbrake cable adjuster with reference to Section 30 if necessary.
3 Extract the securing circlip and pivot pin, and detach the handbrake equaliser from the linkage on the underbody (photo).
4 Working inside the vehicle, remove the handbrake lever rubber gaiter and/or the centre console, as necessary, as described in Chapter 12 (photo).
5 Disconnect the wiring connector from the handbrake 'on' warning switch.
6 Unscrew the two handbrake lever mounting bolts, and carefully lift the lever through the underfloor gaiter.
7 If required, the handbrake 'on' warning switch can be removed with reference to Chapter 13, Section 27.
8 Refitting is a reversal of removal, but on completion, adjust the handbrake cable as described in Section 30.

32 Brake pedal – removal and refitting

1 Remove the clutch pedal as described in Chapter 5, Section 4.
2 Extract the inboard circlip from the brake pedal end of the pivot shaft (photo).
3 The brake pedal can now be removed from the pedal bracket by sliding out the pivot shaft, noting the position of any washers and spacers which may be fitted.
4 If desired, the nylon bushes can be prised from each side of the pedal for renewal, and the brake lamp switch can be removed with reference to Chapter 13, Section 28.
5 Refitting is a reversal of removal, fitting any washers and spacers in their original positions. Refit the clutch pedal as described in Chapter 5, Section 4.

33 Fault diagnosis – braking system

Symptom	Reason(s)
Excessive pedal travel	Low fluid level Air in hydraulic system Fluid leak Faulty rear brake self-adjuster mechanism (where applicable) Faulty master cylinder (where applicable) Faulty vacuum servo (where applicable) Excessive disc run-out Poor ABS pump earth connection (where applicable)
Brake pedal feels spongy	Air in hydraulic system Fluid leak Faulty master cylinder (where applicable) Faulty vacuum servo (where applicable)
Excessive pedal pressure required to stop vehicle	Air in hydraulic system Fluid leak Faulty vacuum servo (where applicable) Calliper or wheel cylinder piston seized Pad or shoe friction material worn or contaminated Incorrect grade of pads fitted New pads or shoes fitted – not yet bedded-in Faulty ABS pump (where applicable) Poor ABS pump earth connection (where applicable)
Brakes pull to one side	Pad or shoe friction material worn or contaminated Calliper or wheel cylinder piston seized Faulty rear brake self-adjuster mechanism (where applicable) Pads or shoes renewed on one side only Disc or drum badly worn or distorted Tyre, steering or suspension defect – see Chapter 10

Symptom	Reason(s)
Brakes binding	Air in hydraulic system Calliper or wheel cylinder piston seized Faulty master cylinder Faulty rear brake self-adjuster mechanism (where applicable) Incorrectly adjusted handbrake cable
Judder felt through brake pedal or steering wheel when braking	Excessive disc run-out or thickness variation Pads or shoe friction material badly worn or contaminated Calliper mountings loose or worn Wear in suspension or steering components – see Chapter 10
Pedal pulsates when braking hard – models with ABS	Normal feature of ABS – no fault

Note: *This Section is not intended as an exhaustive guide to fault diagnosis, but summarises the more common faults which may be encountered during a vehicle's life. Consult a dealer for more detailed advice, particularly regarding faults with ABS.*

Chapter 11 Suspension and steering

For modifications, and information applicable to later models, see Supplement at end of manual

Contents

Specifications

Front suspension

Type ... Independent by MacPherson struts with coil springs and integral telescopic shock absorbers. Anti-roll bar fitted to all models

Rear suspension

Type:
- Saloon, Hatchback and Estate models ... Independent by semi-trailing arms and coil springs with telescopic shock absorbers mounted behind coil springs on Saloon and Hatchback models, but concentric with coil springs on Estate models. Self-levelling rear shock absorbers on certain Estate models. Anti-roll bar fitted to certain models
- P100 models ... Live beam axle with leaf springs and telescopic shock absorbers

Steering

Type ... Rack-and-pinion steering gear linked to collapsible steering column by flexible coupling and universal joint. Power steering available on certain models

Steering gear lubricant type ... Semi-fluid grease (Duckhams Adgear 00)

Power steering fluid type ... ATF to Ford spec SQM-2C-9010-A (Duckhams Uni-Matic or D-Matic)

Power steering fluid capacity ... 0.65 litre (1.14 pints)

Front wheel alignment*

Production toe-setting:
- Saloon, Hatchback and Estate models ... 2.0 mm (0.08 in) ± 1.0 mm (0.04 in) toe-in
- P100 models ... 2.0 mm (0.08 in) ± 2.0 mm (0.08 in) toe-in

Service tolerance before adjustment is required ... 0.5 mm (0.02 in) toe-out to 4.5 mm (0.18 in) toe-in

**Toe-setting figures are quoted for vehicle at kerb weight with 3.0 litres (0.66 gallons) of fuel in tank*

Wheels

Type ... Pressed steel or alloy

Size:
- Saloon, Hatchback and Estate models:
  - Steel ... 13 x 4.50 in, 13 x 5.50 in, or 14 x 5.50 in
  - Alloy ... 14 x 5.50 in
- P100 models ... 14 x 5.50 in

Tyres

Note: *Manufacturers often modify tyre sizes and pressure recommendations. The following is intended as a guide only. Refer to your vehicle handbook or a Ford dealer for the latest recommendations*

Size:		
Saloon and Hatchback models	165 R 13H, 165 R 135, 165 R 13T, 185/70 R 13H, 185/70 R 135, 185/70 R 13T, 195/60 R 14H, 195/60 VR 14 or 195/65 R 14T	
Estate models	175 R 13H, 175 R 135, 175 R 13T, 195/70 R 13H, 195/65 R 14T, 195/60 R 14H or 195/60 VR 14	
P100 models	185 R 14 8PR	
Pressures (cold) in lbf/in² (bar):	**Front**	**Rear**
All Saloon, Hatchback and Estate models with normal load*	26 (1.8)	26 (1.8)
All Saloon and Hatchback models with full load	29 (2.0)	36 (2.5)
Estate models with full load:		
175 R 13H, 175 R 135, 175 R 13T 195/70 R 13H and 195/65 R 14T tyres	29 (2.0)	48 (2.8)
195/60 R 14H and 195/60 VR 14 tyres	29 (2.0)	36 (2.5)
P100 models with light load†	26 (1.8)	36 (2.5)
P100 models with full load	50 (3.5)	65 (4.5)

**Normal load is defined as up to three passengers (or equivalent). For sustained high speeds add 1.5 lbf/in² (0.1 bar) for every 6 mph (10 km/h) over 100 mph (160 km/h)*

†A light load is defined as one passenger plus up to 100 kg (220 lb) payload

Torque wrench settings

	Nm	lbf ft
Front suspension		
Roadwheel nuts:		
Saloon, Hatchback and Estate models (steel and alloy wheels)	70 to 100	52 to 74
P100 models	85 to 90	63 to 66
Hub nut:		
Saloon, Hatchback and Estate models	310 to 350	229 to 258
P100 models	390 to 450	288 to 332
Strut upper mounting nut	40 to 52	30 to 38
Hub carrier-to-strut pinch-bolt	77 to 92	57 to 68
Crossmember-to-underbody bolts	70 to 90	52 to 66
Engine mounting-to-crossmember nut:		
Saloon, Hatchback and Estate models	50 to 70	37 to 52
P100 models	41 to 58	30 to 43
Anti-roll bar-to-lower arm nut	70 to 110	52 to 81
Anti-roll bar U-clamp-to-underbody bolts	55 to 70	41 to 52
Lower arm-to-hub carrier balljoint nut	65 to 85	48 to 63
Lower arm inner pivot bolt:		
Stage 1 ('clamping' torque)	45	33
Loosen fully, then Stage 2 ('snug' torque)	15	11
Stage 3	Tighten through a further 90°	Tighten through a further 90°
Rear suspension		
Saloon, Hatchback and Estate models:		
Lower arm-to-crossmember pivot bolts	80 to 95	59 to 70
Front guide plate-to-underbody bolts	41 to 51	30 to 38
Front guide plate-to-crossmember bolt	100	74
Suspension/final drive unit rear mounting-to- underbody bolts (gold coloured)	60	44
Suspension/final drive unit rear mounting-to-final drive unit rear cover bolts	40 to 50	30 to 37
Anti-roll bar-to-underbody bracket bolts	20 to 25	15 to 18
Hub carrier/brake backplate-to-lower arm bolts*:		
Type X	52 to 64	38 to 47
Type Y	80 to 100	59 to 74
Hub nut	250 to 290	185 to 214
**See Section 15*		
P100 models:		
Shock absorber-to-chassis crossmember bolt	60 to 70	44 to 52
Leaf spring-to-front bracket bolt	157 to 196	116 to 145
Leaf spring-to-spring shackle bolt	157 to 196	116 to 145
Spring shackle-to-underbody bolt	80 to 85	59 to 63
Axle-to-leaf spring U-bolt nuts	39 to 58	29 to 43
Manual steering		
Steering gear-to-crossmember bolts:		
Stage 1 ('clamping' torque)	45	33
Loosen fully, then Stage 2 ('snug' torque)	15	11
Stage 3	Tighten through a further 90°	Tighten through a further 90°

Torque wrench settings (continued)

	Nm	lbf ft
Tie-rod end locknut	57 to 68	42 to 50
Tie-rod end-to-hub carrier nut*	20 to 32	15 to 24
Tie-rod-to-steering rack balljoint	72 to 88	53 to 65
Steering wheel nut	45 to 55	33 to 41
Intermediate shaft-to-inner column clamp bolt	20 to 25	15 to 18
Flexible coupling-to-steering gear clamp nut	24 to 26	17 to 19
Column mounting pinch-bolt	45 to 55	33 to 41
Pinion retaining nut	70 to 100	52 to 74
Slipper plug†	4 to 5	3 to 4

**Tighten nut to specified torque and then tighten to next available split pin hole*
†Tighten nut to specified torque and then loosen off 60° to 70°

Power steering (where different to manual steering)		
Tie-rod to steering rack balljoint	70 to 77	52 to 57
Flexible coupling-to-steering gear clamp bolt	16 to 20	12 to 15
Intermediate shaft-to-inner column clamp bolt	16 to 20	12 to 15
Pinion locknut	37 to 47	27 to 35
Slipper plug	3 to 4	2 to 3
Pump rear support bar nut and bolt	41 to 51	30 to 38
Pump mounting bracket-to-engine bolts	52 to 64	38 to 47
Pump pulley bolt	10 to 12	7 to 9
Fluid hose-to-pinion housing bolt	21 to 26	15 to 19
Fluid pressure hose-to-pump union	26 to 31	19 to 23
Fluid return hose-to-pump union	16 to 20	12 to 15

1 General description

The front suspension is of independent MacPherson strut type incorporating coil springs and integral telescopic shock absorbers. The lower end of each strut is attached to a hub carrier, which carries the wheel hub and bearings, and the brake assembly. The lower end of each hub carrier is attached to a suspension lower arm by a sealed balljoint. The inboard ends of the lower arms are attached to the front suspension crossmember and the lower arms thus provide lateral location for the strut assemblies. The upper end of each strut is bolted to a suspension turret on the vehicle body. An anti-roll bar is mounted to the rear of the lower arms, and resists the roll tendency of the front suspension.

On Saloon, Hatchback and Estate models, the rear suspension is also of independent type, incorporating semi-trailing arms, coil springs and telescopic shock absorbers. The semi-trailing arms are attached to the suspension crossmember at their forward ends, and to the hub carriers at the rear. The coil springs are located between the semi-trailing arms and the vehicle underbody. On Saloon and Hatchback models, the shock absorbers are mounted behind the coil springs, but on Estate models they are concentric with the coil springs. On some Estate models the shock absorbers are of the self-levelling type. The suspension crossmember is attached to the vehicle underbody, and to the final drive unit. Certain models are fitted with an anti-roll bar which is mounted to the rear of the final drive unit, and is attached to the semi-trailing arms by connecting links.

The rear suspension on P100 models consists of a beam axle located and supported by a leaf spring on each side, and utilizing telescopic

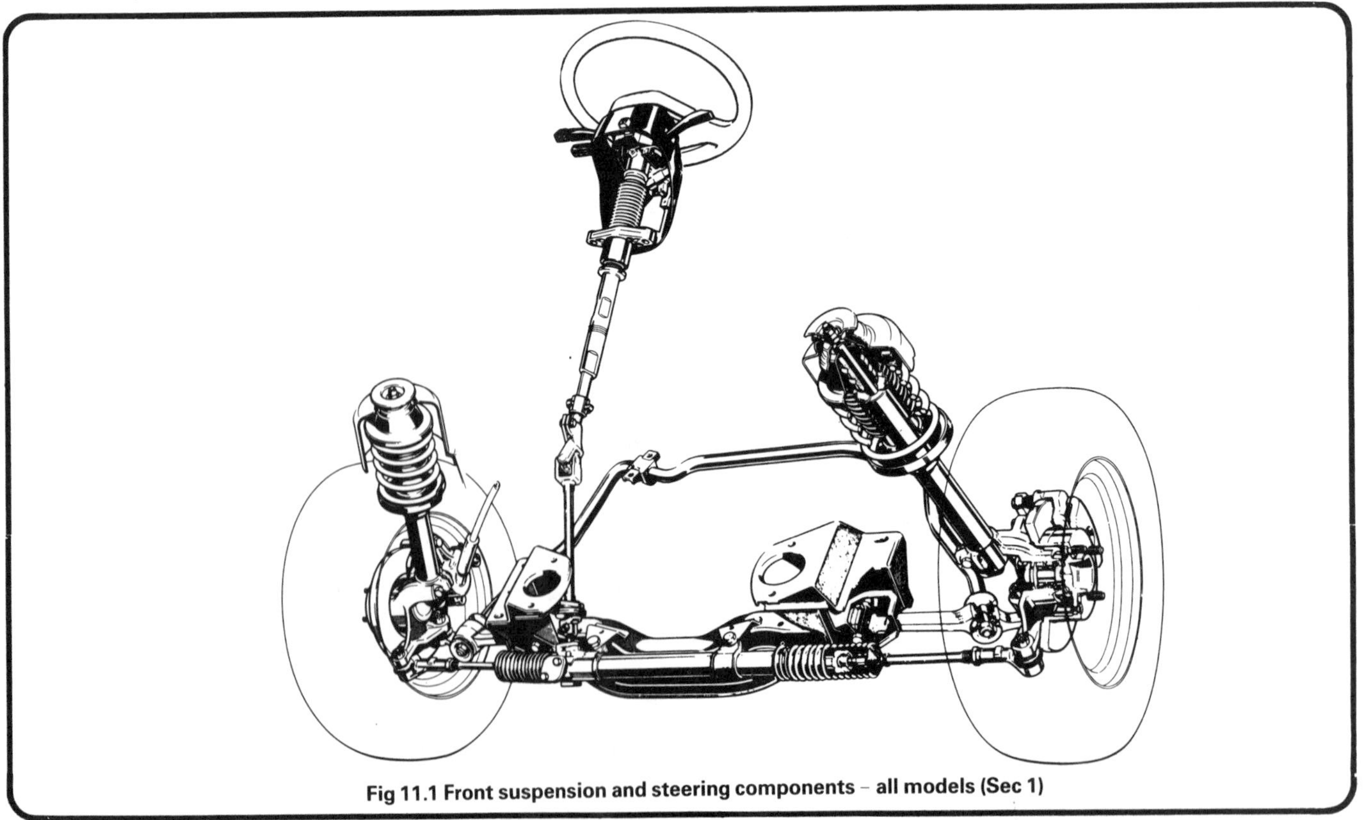

Fig 11.1 Front suspension and steering components – all models (Sec 1)

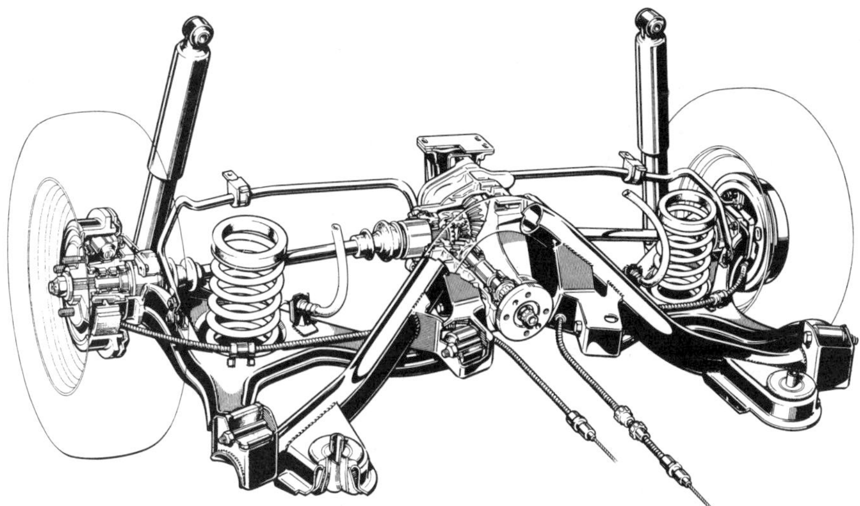

Fig 11.2 Rear suspension and final drive components – Saloon and Hatchback models (Sec 1)

shock absorbers to control vertical movement. The hub and brake assemblies are attached directly to each side of the axle. The axle is bolted to the leaf springs using U-bolts and counterplates, and the shock absorbers are attached to the counterplates at their lower ends and the vehicle underbody at their upper ends.

The steering gear is of the conventional rack and pinion type located ahead of the front wheels. Movement of the steering wheel is transmitted to the steering gear by means of a shaft containing a universal joint. The front hub carriers are connected to the steering gear by tie-rods, each having an inner and outer balljoint. Power-assisted steering is available on some models, assistance being provided hydraulically by an engine-driven pump.

2 Routine maintenance

1 At the intervals specified in the '*Routine maintenance*' Section at the beginning of this manual, the following checks should be carried out.
2 Check the tyre pressures and adjust if necessary. The pressures should be checked with the tyres cold. At the same time, inspect the tyres for wear and damage – see Section 38, and check the tightness of the roadwheel nuts.
3 Check the steering and suspension components for wear and damage. Ensure that all dust covers are secure and intact. Check all rubber bushes and mountings for wear and splits, and wipe away any oil or grease contamination. Examine the steering gear rubber gaiters for splits and leakage and renew if necessary.
4 Check the front suspension lower balljoints for wear by levering up the suspension lower arms (see Fig. 11.3) – there should be negligible free play. If a balljoint is worn, the complete lower arm must be renewed. The tie-rod end balljoints can be checked in a similar manner, or by observing them whilst an assistant rocks the steering wheel back and forth. Tie-rod end renewal is described in Section 36.
5 Check the shock absorbers by bouncing the vehicle up and down at each corner in turn. When released, the corner concerned should come to rest within one complete oscillation. Continued movement or squeaking and groaning noises from the shock absorber indicate that renewal is required.
6 On models with power steering, check the fluid level in the reservoir. The reservoir is mounted on the front right-hand side of the engine block. If topping-up is necessary, inspect the steering gear, hydraulic hoses and pump for leaks and rectify as necessary. At the same time, check the tension and condition of the power steering pump drivebelt.
7 The wheel bearings can be checked for wear by raising the vehicle on a jack or axle stands and spinning the relevant roadwheel. Any roughness or excessive noise indicates worn bearings, which must be renewed, as no adjustment is possible. It is unlikely that any wear will be evident unless the vehicle has covered a very high mileage, and it should be noted that it is normal for the bearings to exhibit slight endfloat, which is perceptible as wheel rock at the wheel rim.

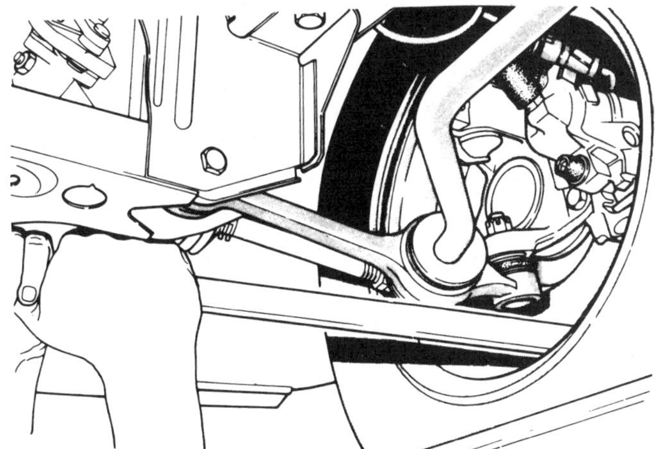

Fig 11.3 Levering up lower arm to check balljoint for wear (Sec 2)

3 Front suspension crossmember – removal and refitting

1 Remove the steering gear as described in Section 27 or 29, as applicable.
2 Support the engine with a jack and interposed block of wood under the sump.
3 Unscrew and remove the engine mounting nuts from the top of the mountings in the engine bay – see Fig. 11.4
4 Raise the engine slightly with the jack, and ensure that it is safely supported, and just clear of the engine mounting rubbers.
5 Unscrew and remove the nuts, washers and pivot bolts securing the lower arms to the crossmember, and pull the arms from the crossmember. Note that the pivot bolt heads face to the rear of the vehicle.
6 Where applicable, remove the brake pipes from the clips on the crossmember, taking care not to strain them, and detach any cables or electrical leads which may be secured with clips or cable ties, noting their positions.
7 Support the crossmember with a jack, then unscrew and remove the four mounting bolts.
8 Lower the crossmember and withdraw it from under the vehicle.

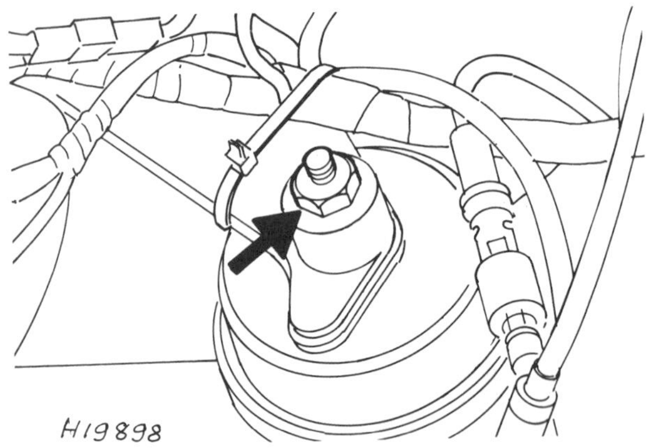

Fig 11.4 Engine mounting nut (arrowed) (Sec 3)

Fig 11.5 Front suspension crossmember mounting bolts (arrowed) (Sec 3)

9 If desired, the engine mountings can now be unbolted from the crossmember.
10 Refitting is a reversal of removal, but bear in mind the following points.
11 Do not tighten the lower arm pivot bolts until the weight of the vehicle is resting on its wheels. This is to prevent 'wind up' of the rubber bushes which will occur when the vehicle is lowered if the bolts have been tightened with no load on the suspension. The following procedure must be used when tightening the pivot bolts. Tighten the bolt to the specified 'clamping' torque, then loosen the bolt fully. Re-tighten to the specified 'snug' torque and then further tighten the bolt through the specified angle.
12 Refit any cables or electrical leads in their original positions, where applicable.
13 When lowering the engine onto its mountings, ensure that the locating pegs on the mountings engage with the holes in the mounting brackets.
14 Refit the steering gear with reference to Section 27 or 29, as applicable.

4 Front suspension lower arm – removal and refitting

Note: *A balljoint separator tool will be required for this operation.*
1 To improve access, raise the front of the vehicle on ramps. Do not jack the vehicle up at this stage. Apply the handbrake.
2 Unscrew and remove the nut, washer and pivot bolt securing the relevant lower arm to the crossmember (photo).
3 Remove the anti-roll bar-to-lower arm securing nut and recover the dished washer and plastic cover (where applicable) – see Fig. 11.6.
4 Ensure that the handbrake is applied, jack up the front of the vehicle and support on axle stands.
5 Remove the split pin and unscrew the castellated nut from the lower arm balljoint. Using a balljoint separator tool, disconnect the lower arm from the hub carrier. The lower arm can now be withdrawn from the vehicle. Recover the remaining dished washer and plastic cover (where applicable) from the end of the anti-roll bar.
6 If the lower arm has been removed due to a worn balljoint, the complete arm must be renewed.
7 The anti-roll bar compliance bushes can be renewed as described in Section 9, paragraphs 2 to 4, but note that the bushes on both sides of the vehicle must be renewed at the same time. The lower arm inner pivot bush can be renewed as described in Section 10, paragraphs 6 and 7.
8 To refit the lower arm, proceed as follows.
9 Fit the shallow dished washer (colour coded black or green) and the plastic cover (where applicable) to the end of the anti-roll bar, then refit the lower arm to the anti-roll bar. Fit the remaining plastic cover (where applicable) and the deep dished washer (colour coded yellow or black) and refit the securing nut. Do not tighten the nut at this stage. Note that the convex faces of the dished washers must face the lower arm.
10 Reconnect the balljoint to the hub carrier, refit the castellated nut and tighten to the specified torque. Fit a new split pin.
11 Locate the end of the lower arm in the crossmember, and refit the pivot bolt, washer and nut. If necessary, push the outer rim of the

4.2 Front suspension lower arm-to-crossmember pivot bolt and nut

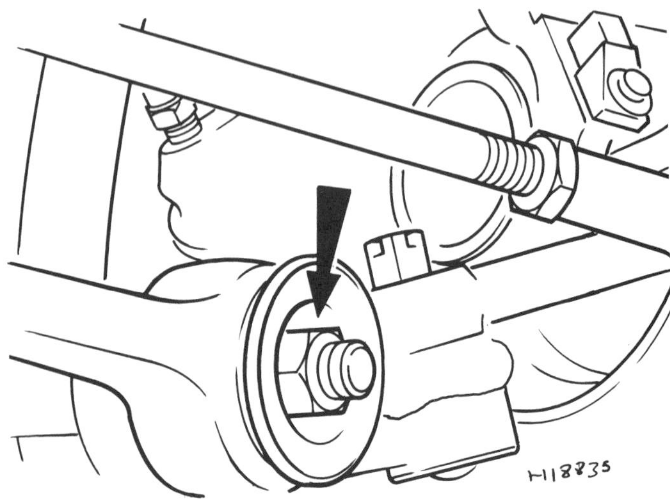

Fig 11.6 Front anti-roll bar-to-lower arm securing nut (arrowed) (Sec 4)

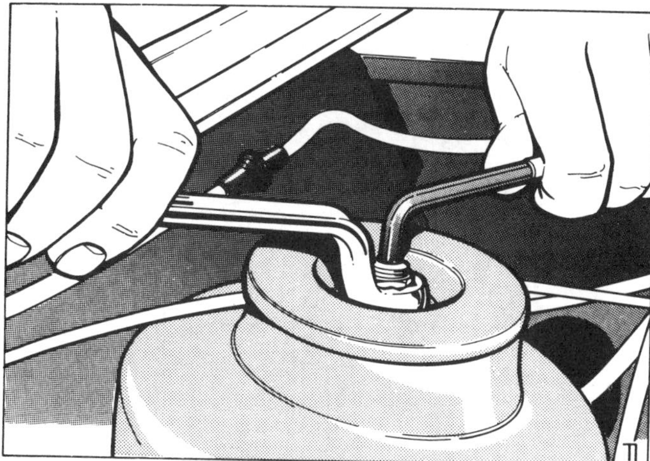
Fig 11.7 Hold the strut piston rod with a 6 mm Allen key when unscrewing the upper mounting nut (Sec 5)

roadwheel in order to line up the holes in the lower arm bush and the crossmember. Note that the pivot bolt head should face to the rear of the vehicle. Do not tighten the bolt at this stage.
12 Lower the vehicle so that its weight is resting on the roadwheels, and bounce the vehicle to settle the suspension.
13 Tighten the lower arm pivot bolt, following the procedure given in Section 3, paragraph 11.
14 Tighten the anti-roll bar-to-lower arm securing nut to the specified torque.
15 Lower the vehicle from the ramps, if not already done.

5 Front suspension strut – removal, overhaul and refitting

Note: *A spring compressor tool will be required if the strut is to be dismantled.*
1 Loosen the relevant front roadwheel nuts, apply the handbrake, jack up the front of the vehicle and support on axle stands.
2 Remove the roadwheel. On P100 models mark the position of the roadwheel in relation to one of the wheel studs before removal.
3 Remove the front brake calliper with reference to Chapter 10, but do not disconnect the hydraulic hose. Support the calliper on an axle stand to avoid straining the hose.
4 Where applicable, unbolt the ABS wheel sensor from the hub carrier and detach the wire from the clip on the strut. Unplug the connector and place the sensor to one side.
5 Unscrew and remove the pinch-bolt which secures the hub carrier to the strut. Using a suitable lever, such as a cold chisel, lever the hub carrier clamp legs and wedge them apart.
6 Lever the suspension lower arm downwards to separate the hub carrier from the bottom of the strut.

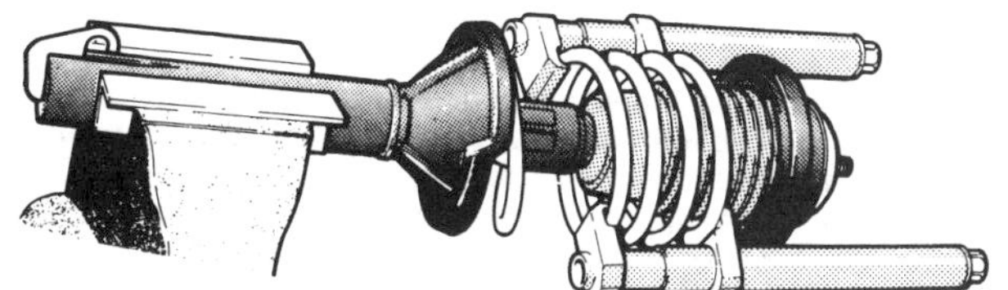
Fig 11.8 Suspension strut fitted with spring compressors (Sec 5)

7 Working in the engine compartment, unscrew the strut upper mounting nut, at the same time supporting the strut from below. Use a 6 mm Allen key inserted in the end of the strut piston rod to prevent the rod from turning as the upper mounting nut is unscrewed. On some models, the upper mounting nut may be fitted with a plastic cover. Note the upper mounting cup under the nut.
8 Withdraw the strut from under the wing of the vehicle.
9 To dismantle the strut, proceed as follows.
10 Using spring compressors, compress the coil spring. Do not attempt to compress the spring without using purpose-made spring compressors, as the spring is under considerable tension, and personal injury may occur if it is suddenly released.
11 Hold the piston rod as described in paragraph 7, unscrew the nut from the piston rod and remove the lower cup, bearing, spring seat, gaiter, coil spring and bump stop (photo).
12 Working in the engine compartment, remove the upper cup and nylon spacer, and if required prise out the rubber insulator (photo).
13 Clean all the components and examine them for wear and damage.

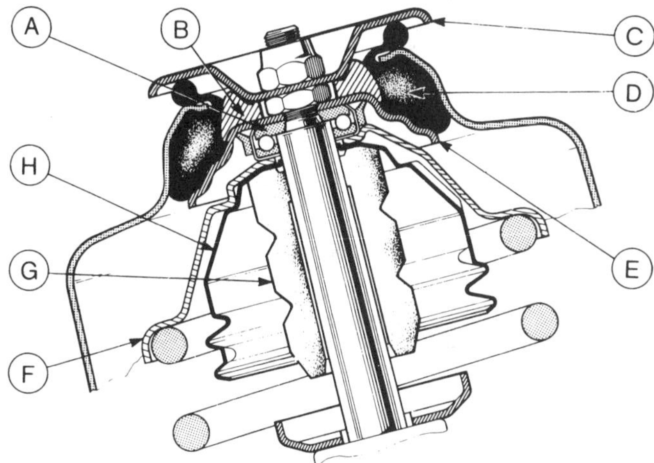

Fig 11.9 Cross-section of the front strut upper mounting (Sec 5)

A Bearing
B Nylon spacer
C Upper cup
D Rubber insulator
E Lower cup
F Spring seat
G Bump stop
H Gaiter

5.11 Front strut piston rod nut (arrowed)

5.12 Front strut rubber insulator and nylon spacer viewed from underneath

6.8 Unscrewing the hub carrier-to-strut pinch-bolt

Check the action of the shock absorber by mounting it vertically in a vice and operating the piston rod several times through its full stroke. If any uneven resistance is evident, the shock absorber must be renewed. Renew any worn or damaged components as applicable.
14 Reassembly and refitting is a reversal of dismantling and removal, bearing in mind the following points.
15 When reassembling, ensure that the gaiter is fitted over the bump stop, and that the ends of the coil spring are correctly located on the spring seats. Also ensure that the bearing is correctly located on the upper spring seat.
16 Fit the nylon spacer over the piston rod before fitting the strut to the top mounting.
17 Tighten all fixings to the specified torque, and refit the brake calliper with reference to Chapter 10.
18 On P100 models align the previously made marks on the roadwheel and wheel stud.

6 Front hub carrier – removal and refitting

Note: *A balljoint separator tool will be required for this operation.*
1 Loosen the relevant front roadwheel nuts, apply the handbrake, jack up the front of the vehicle and support on axle stands.
2 Remove the roadwheel. On P100 models mark the position of the roadwheel in relation to one of the wheel studs before removal.
3 Remove the front brake calliper with reference to Chapter 10, but do not disconnect the hydraulic hose. Support the calliper on an axle stand, or suspend it with wire from the coil spring to avoid straining the hose.
4 Mark the position of the brake disc in relation to the drive flange, and on Saloon, Hatchback and Estate models, remove the retaining screw or spire washer(s), as applicable, and remove the disc. On P100 models, unscrew the five retaining nuts and remove the wheel adaptor plate and disc.
5 Where applicable, unbolt the ABS wheel sensor from the hub carrier and unplug the wiring connector. Place the sensor to one side.
6 Remove the split pin and unscrew the castellated nut securing the tie-rod end to the hub carrier. Using a balljoint separator tool, disconnect the tie-rod end from the hub carrier.
7 Repeat the procedure given in the previous paragraph for the lower arm-to-hub carrier balljoint.
8 Unscrew and remove the pinch-bolt which secures the hub carrier to the strut (photo). Using a suitable lever, such as a cold chisel, lever the hub carrier clamp legs and wedge them apart. Withdraw the hub carrier from the strut.
9 Refitting is a reversal of removal, but use new split pins on the castellated nuts, and align the previously made marks on the brake disc and hub. Tighten all fixings to the specified torque, and refit the brake calliper with reference to Chapter 10.
10 On P100 models align the previously made marks on the roadwheel and wheel stud.

7 Front wheel bearings – renewal

1 Remove the hub carrier as described in Section 6.
2 Reverse the roadwheel nuts and screw them fully onto the studs to protect the threads, then mount the hub carrier assembly in a vice as shown in Fig. 11.11.
3 Prise the dust cap from the rear of the hub carrier, and unscrew the hub nut with a suitable socket. Note that on all models manufactured before late December 1982, both left and right-hand nuts have a right-hand thread, but as from this date, left-hand thread assemblies were progressively fitted to the right-hand hub carrier. The modified right-hand hub can be identified by the letter 'R' stamped on its outer face (see Fig. 11.12), or by the colour of the hub nut nylon insert; blue indicates a normal right-hand thread, and yellow indicates a left-hand thread.
4 Remove the splined washer, and tap the hub carrier from the drive flange. Recover the bearing inner race and rollers from the inner end of the hub carrier.
5 Prise the oil seal from the outer end of the hub carrier and remove the remaining bearing inner race and rollers.
6 Using a soft metal drift, drive the bearing outer races from the hub carrier, taking care not to damage the inner surface of the carrier.
7 Clean the hub carrier and drive flange with paraffin, wipe dry and examine for damage and wear. Note that the components are machined to very close tolerances, and the bearings are supplied in matched pairs,

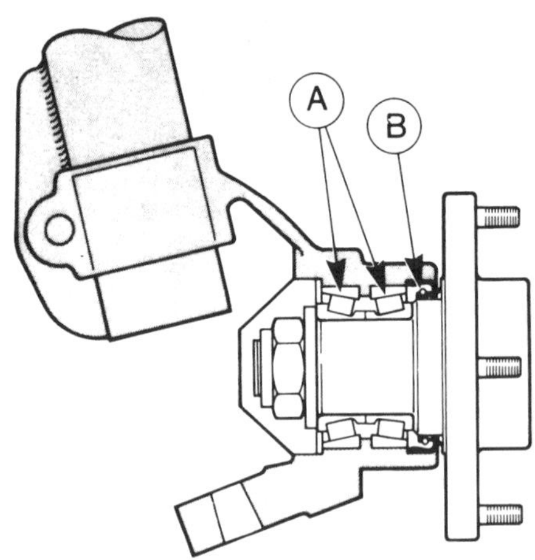

Fig 11.10 Cross-section of front hub carrier showing wheel bearings (Sec 7)

A Matched taper roller bearings *B Oil seal*

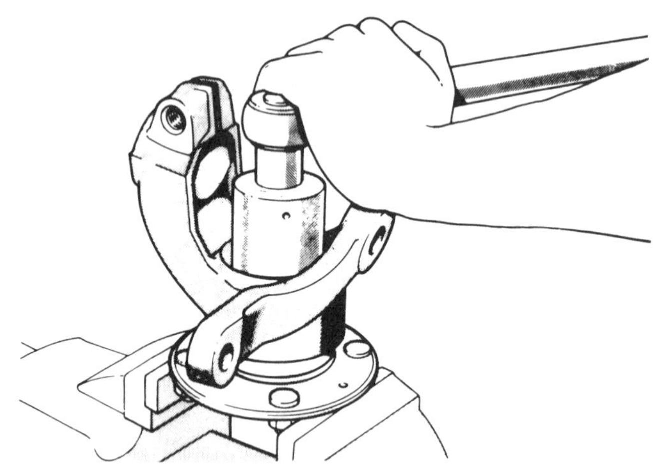

Fig 11.11 Front hub carrier mounted in vice to unscrew hub nut (Sec 7)

Fig 11.12 Identification of right-hand front hub incorporating a left-hand thread (Sec 7)

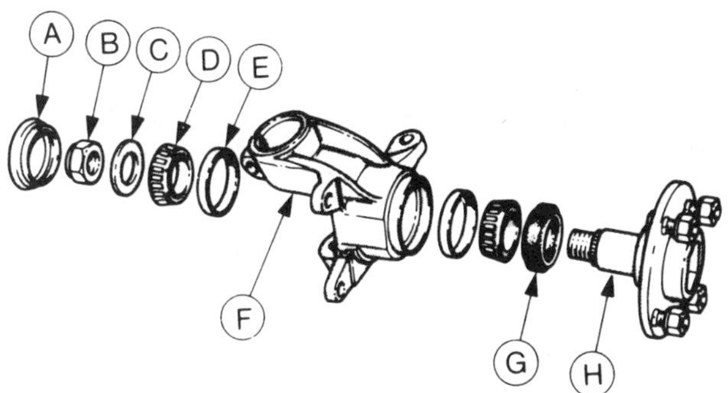

Fig 11.13 Front hub components (Sec 7)

A Dust cap
B Hub nut
C Splined washer
D Taper roller bearing
E Bearing outer race
F Hub carrier
G Oil seal
H Drive flange

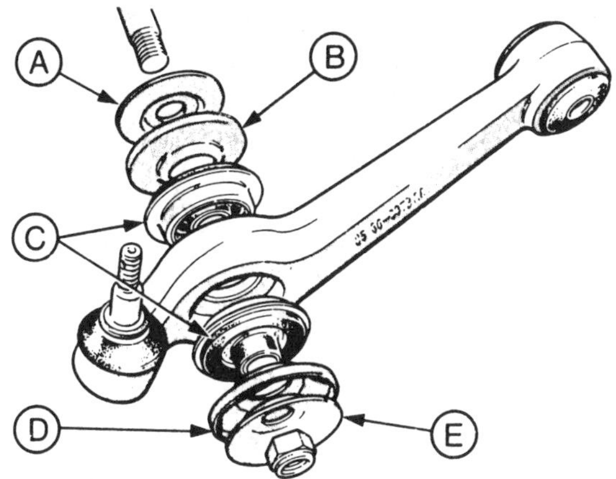

Fig 11.14 Front anti-roll bar-to-lower arm mounting (Sec 8)

A Rear (black or green) shallow dished washer
B Plastic cover (where applicable)
C Compliance bushes
D Plastic cover (where applicable)
E Front yellow or black) deep dished washer

therefore scrupulous cleanliness must be observed.

8 Using a metal tube of suitable diameter, drive the new bearing outer races fully into the hub carrier. Ensure that the races are seated correctly.

9 Pack the inner bearing races and rollers with high melting point lithium-based grease, and locate the outer bearing assembly in the hub carrier.

10 Fill the cavities between the sealing lips of the oil seal with grease, then drive it fully into the hub carrier using a block of wood or a metal tube of suitable diameter. Note that on early models the oil seal has a rubber casing, and this early type of seal should be replaced with the later type which has a metal casing. The oil seal should be renewed regardless of type, and a new seal of the correct type is normally supplied with the new wheel bearings.

11 With the drive flange mounted in a vice, as during dismantling, tap the hub carrier onto the drive flange.

12 Fit the inner bearing assembly, tapping it into place with a metal tube of suitable diameter if necessary, and fit the splined washer. Note that the bearings are self-setting on assembly, and no subsequent adjustment is required.

13 Refit the hub nut and tighten it to the specified torque.

14 Tap the dust cap into position in the hub carrier.

15 Remove the assembly from the vice, remove the roadwheel nuts, and refit the hub carrier as described in Section 6.

8 Front anti-roll bar – removal and refitting

1 To improve access, raise the front of the vehicle on ramps. Do not jack the vehicle up at this stage. Apply the handbrake.

2 Where applicable bend back the locktabs, then unscrew the two bolts securing each of the two anti-roll bar U-clamps to the vehicle underbody (photos).

3 Ensure that the handbrake is applied, jack up the front of the vehicle and support on axle stands.

4 Remove the anti-roll bar-to-lower arm securing nuts and recover the dished washers and plastic covers, where applicable (photo).

5 Unscrew and remove the nut, washer and pivot bolt securing one of the lower arms to the crossmember, and pull the end of the lower arm from the crossmember.

6 Pull the anti-roll bar from the bush in the 'free' lower arm, then slide the anti-roll bar from the remaining fixed lower arm. Recover the remaining dished washers and plastic covers (where applicable) from the ends of the anti-roll bar.

7 If necessary, the anti-roll bar compliance bushes can be renewed as described in Section 9, and the anti-roll bar U-clamp bushes can be renewed by sliding them off the ends of the bar. Note that although the U-clamp bushes are of a split design, they should not be levered open to aid fitting, and the new bushes must be slid on from the ends of the anti-roll bar. The bushes should always be renewed in pairs.

8 To refit the anti-roll bar, proceed as follows.

9 Fit the shallow dished washers (colour coded black or green) and the plastic covers (where applicable) to the ends of the anti-roll bar, then push the anti-roll bar through the bushes in the lower arms. Fit the remaining plastic covers (where applicable) and the deep dished washers (colour coded yellow or black) and loosely fit the securing nuts. Note that the convex faces of the dished washers must face the lower arm. Do not tighten the nuts fully at this stage.

10 Locate the 'free' lower arm inner pivot bush in the crossmember, and refit the pivot bolt, washer and nut. If necessary, push the outer rim of the roadwheel in order to line up the holes in the lower arm bush and

8.2A Bend back the locktabs (arrowed)...

8.2B ... unscrew the bolts and remove the anti-roll bar U-clamps

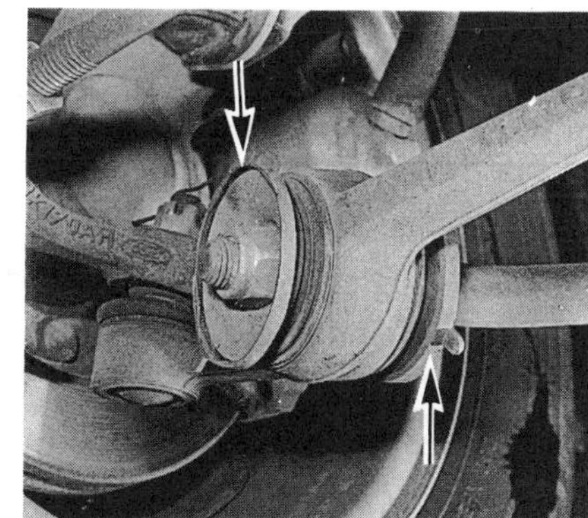

8.4 Anti-roll bar-to-lower arm mounting. Plastic covers arrowed

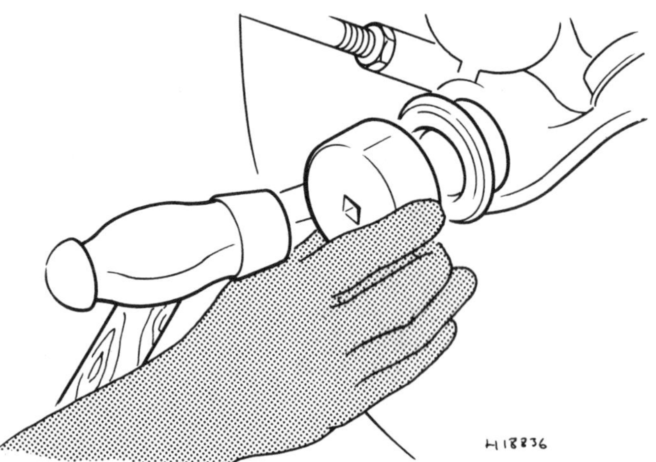

Fig 11.15 Tapping a front anti-roll bar-to-lower arm compliance bush into position (Sec 9)

the crossmember. Note that the pivot bolt head should face to the rear of the vehicle. Do not tighten the bolt at this stage.
11 Lower the vehicle so that its weight is resting on the roadwheels.
12 Refit the anti-roll bar U-clamps to the vehicle underbody. Note that various different types of clamping components have been used during production, and if any of the components are to be renewed, it is important to retain the old components for identification when ordering new parts. The same type of clamp assembly must be used on both sides of the vehicle. Tighten the bolts evenly on each clamp to the specified torque. Where applicable, secure the bolts with the locktabs.
13 Bounce the vehicle to settle the suspension, then tighten the lower arm pivot bolt, following the procedure given in Section 3, paragraph 11.
14 Tighten the anti-roll bar-to-lower arm securing nuts to the specified torque.
15 Lower the vehicle from the ramps, if not already done.

9 Front anti-roll bar-to-lower arm compliance bushes – renewal

Note: *The compliance bushes must be renewed in vehicle sets, therefore the bushes on both sides of the vehicle must be renewed at the same time. If plastic covers were not originally fitted between the dished washers and the bushes, suitable covers should be obtained for fitting during reassembly.*
1 Remove the anti-roll bar as described in Section 8, paragraphs 1 to 6 inclusive.
2 Using a thin-bladed chisel or screwdriver, carefully prise out the compliance bushes from the lower arms.
3 Tap the new bushes into place using a suitable socket or tube drift.
4 Some vehicles may have small rubber spacer washers fitted to the ends of the anti-roll bar, and these should be discarded on reassembly.
5 Refit the anti-roll bar as described in Section 8, paragraph 9 onwards.

10 Front suspension lower arm inner pivot bush – renewal

1 To improve access, raise the front of the vehicle on ramps. Apply the handbrake.
2 Unscrew and remove the nut, washer and pivot bolt securing the relevant lower arm to the crossmember.
3 Remove the anti-roll bar-to-lower arm securing nut and recover the dished washer and plastic cover (where applicable).
4 Ensure that the handbrake is applied, jack up the front of the vehicle and support on axle stands.
5 Pull the inner end of the lower arm from the crossmember.
6 The pivot bush can now be removed from the lower arm using a long bolt with nut, washers and a suitable metal tube.
7 Lubricate the new bush with soapy water, and fit with a single continuous action to avoid deformation of the bush, again using the bolt, nut, washers and tube.
8 Locate the end of the lower arm in the crossmember, and refit the pivot bolt, washer and nut. If necessary, push the outer rim of the roadwheel in order to line up the holes in the lower arm bush and the crossmember. Note that the pivot bolt head should face to the rear of the vehicle. Do not tighten the bolt at this stage.
9 Refit the plastic cover, dished washer (where applicable), and nut to the end of the anti-roll bar. Do not tighten the nut at this stage.
10 Lower the vehicle so that its weight is resting on the roadwheels, and bounce the vehicle to settle the suspension.
11 Tighten the lower arm pivot bolt, following the procedure given in Section 3, paragraph 11.
12 Tighten the anti-roll bar-to-lower arm securing nut to the specified torque.
13 Lower the vehicle from the ramps, if not already done.

11 Rear suspension and final drive unit assembly (Saloon, Hatchback and Estate models) – removal and refitting

Note: *From May 1986, revised final drive unit rear mounting bolts have been used in production. Whenever the earlier type of bolts are removed, they should be discarded and the later type fitted. The earlier bolts are coloured blue, and the later type bolts are coloured gold.*
1 Jack up the vehicle and support on axle stands. It is only strictly necessary to jack up the rear of the vehicle, but this provides only limited access. Note that the axle stands should be positioned under the side members.
2 Remove the rear section of the exhaust system (ie from the joint) with reference to Chapter 3.

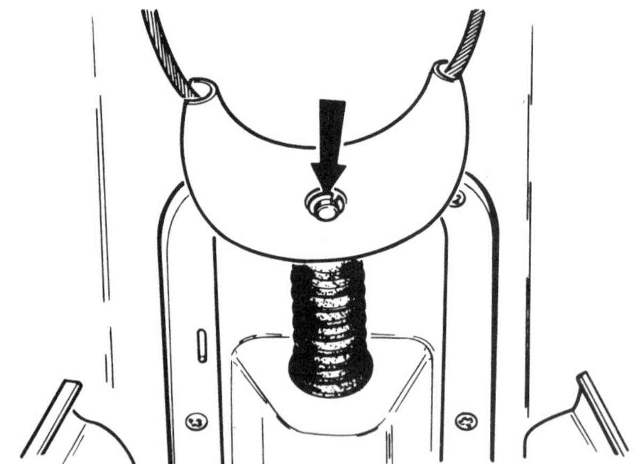

Fig 11.16 Handbrake equaliser-to-operating rod circlip and pivot pin (arrowed) (Sec 11)

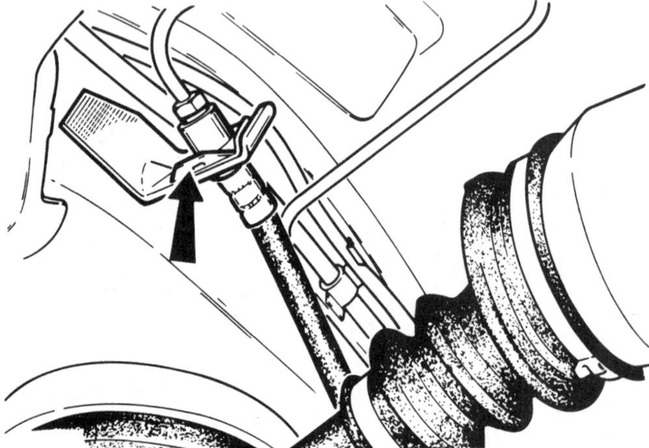

Fig 11.17 Rear underbody brake pipe bracket – U-shaped hose retaining clip arrowed (Sec 11)

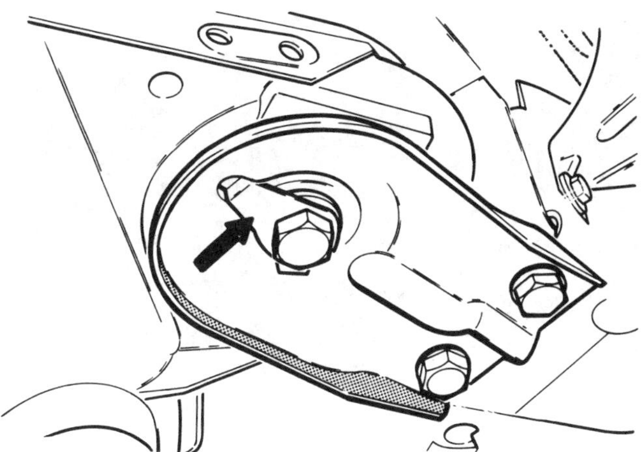

Fig 11.18 Rear suspension front guide plate – lockwasher arrowed (Sec 11)

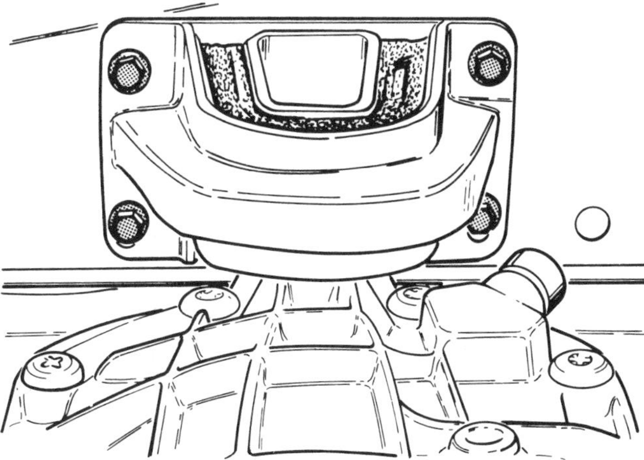

Fig 11.19 Final drive unit-to-underbody rear mounting (Sec 11)

3 Remove the propeller shaft as described in Chapter 8.
4 Disconnect the handbrake equaliser from the operating rod by removing the circlip and pivot pin. Take care not to lose the components.
5 Remove the brake cable sheaths from their brackets on the vehicle underbody.
6 Unscrew the brake pipes from the brake hoses at the brackets on the vehicle underbody. Plug the ends of the pipes and hoses to prevent leakage and dirt ingress, then detach the hoses from the brackets by removing the U-shaped retaining clips – see Fig. 11.17.
7 Where applicable, disconnect the ABS sensors, and detach the leads from the clips on the lower arms.
8 Place suitable blocks beneath the rear wheels, then lower the vehicle so that the rear coil springs are lightly loaded. Reposition the axle stands under the side members.
9 Support the final drive unit with a jack, using an interposed block of wood to spread the load.
10 Where applicable, unscrew and remove the two anti-roll bar mountings from the underbody.
11 Unscrew and remove the three bolts securing each of the front guide plates to the underbody and the suspension crossmember (see Fig. 11.18). Where applicable, bend back the lockwasher tabs on the larger bolts.
12 Unscrew and remove the four bolts securing the final drive unit rear mounting to the underbody. Note the location and number of any shims which may be fitted.
13 Working inside the rear of the vehicle, disconnect the shock absorber upper mountings. On Saloon and Hatchback models, access is gained by removing the trim covers behind the side cushions. Each cover is secured by two self-tapping screws, and the shock absorber is secured by a bolt and nut. On Estate models, fold down the rear seat backrest, fold back the floor covering and remove the front section of the luggage compartment floor, which is secured with 12 self-tapping screws. Remove the nut and washer from the shock absorber.
14 Using a jack and a wooden beam positioned beneath the longitudinal underbody side members, raise the rear of the vehicle until the rear suspension and final drive unit assembly can be withdrawn from under the vehicle.
15 If desired, the assembly can be dismantled with reference to the relevant Sections of this Chapter and Chapter 9.
16 Refitting is a reversal of removal, bearing in mind the following points.
17 Where applicable, secure the larger front guide plate bolts by bending up the lockwasher tabs.
18 Ensure that the coil springs are located correctly on their seats on the vehicle underbody.
19 When refitting the final drive unit rear mounting to the underbody, refit any shims in their original noted positions, and fit the bolts with reference to the note at the beginning of this Section.
20 Tighten all fixings to the specified torque.
21 Refit the propeller shaft with reference to Chapter 8, and refit the rear section of the exhaust system with reference to Chapter 3.
22 On completion, bleed the brakes and adjust the handbrake as described in Chapter 10, and with the vehicle level, check the final drive unit oil level as described in Chapter 9.

12 Rear suspension lower arm (Saloon, Hatchback and Estate models) – removal and refitting

Models with rear drum brakes

1 Chock the front wheels, jack up the rear of the vehicle and support on axle stands placed under the side members.
2 Remove the relevant driveshaft as described in Chapter 9.
3 Remove the handbrake cable from the clip on the lower arm.
4 Unscrew the brake pipe from the brake hose at the bracket on the lower arm. Plug the ends of the pipe and hose to prevent leakage and dirt ingress, then detach the hose from the bracket by removing the U-shaped retaining clip (photo).
5 Unscrew the brake pipe from the wheel cylinder on the brake backplate and plug the end of the pipe and the cylinder to prevent leakage and dirt ingress.
6 Unscrew the bolts securing the brake backplate to the lower arm, and tie the backplate to one side.
7 Where applicable, prise the anti-roll bar connecting strap from the lower arm.
8 Support the lower arm on a jack, and raise it slightly to place the coil spring under load.
9 Remove the shock absorber as described in Section 13.
10 Unscrew and remove the three bolts securing the front guide plate to the underbody and the suspension crossmember (photo). Where

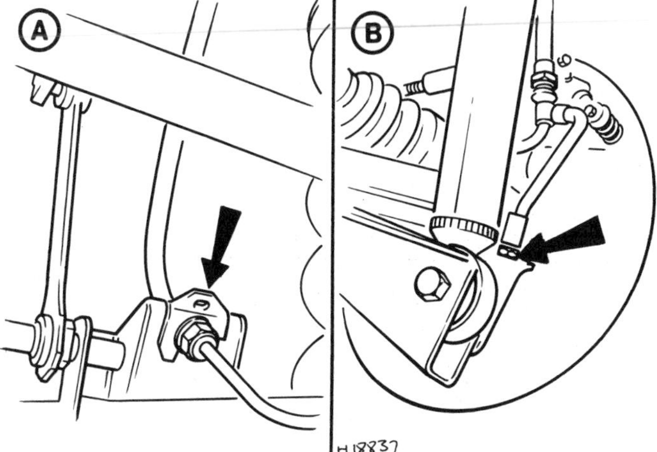

Fig 11.20 Rear suspension lower arm brake pipe brackets (arrowed) (Sec 12)

A Left-hand bracket *B Right-hand bracket*

12.4 Brake pipe bracket on lower arm. U-shaped retaining clip arrowed

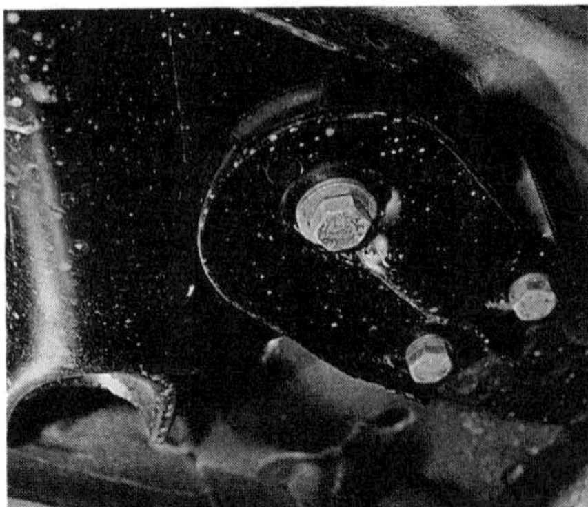
12.10 Rear suspension front guide plate

12.12 Lower arm-to-crossmember inner pivot

applicable, bend back the lockwasher tab(s) on the larger bolt.

11 Lower the lower arm, and remove the coil spring and rubber cup.

12 Note the orientation of the two lower arm-to-crossmember pivot bolts and nuts, then unscrew and remove them and withdraw the lower arm from under the vehicle (photo).

13 If the lower arm is to be renewed, unclip the brake pipe, and refit to the new arm.

14 If required, the pivot bushes may be renewed using a long bolt, nut, washers and a suitable metal tube. Lubricate the new bushes with soapy water before fitting.

15 Refitting is a reversal of removal, bearing in mind the following points.

16 Where applicable, secure the larger front guide plate bolt by bending up the lockwasher tab(s).

17 Refit the shock absorber as described in Section 13.

18 Refit the driveshaft as described in Chapter 9.

19 Before tightening the lower arm-to-crossmember pivot bolts and nuts, lower the vehicle so that its weight is resting on the roadwheels, and bounce the vehicle to settle the suspension. Ensure that the bolts are orientated as noted during removal.

20 On completion, bleed the brakes and adjust the handbrake as described in Chapter 10.

Models with rear disc brakes

Note: *A suitable puller will be required to remove the drive flange, and a new rear hub nut must be used on reassembly.*

21 With the vehicle resting on its wheels, loosen the rear hub nut. A suitable extension bar will be required, as the nut is extremely tight. Note that the left-hand nut has a left-hand thread, ie it is undone in a clockwise direction. Before loosening the nut, ensure that the handbrake is applied, and chock the relevant rear wheel.

22 Loosen the rear roadwheel nuts on the side concerned, chock the front wheels, jack up the rear of the car and support on axle stands placed under the side members.

23 Remove the rear roadwheel.

24 Remove the rear section of the exhaust system (ie from the joint) with reference to Chapter 3.

25 Unscrew the brake pipe from the brake hose at the bracket on the lower arm – see Fig. 11.20. Plug the ends of the pipe and hose to prevent leakage and dirt ingress, then detach the hose from the bracket by removing the U-shaped retaining clip.

26 Remove the handbrake cable from the clip on the lower arm.

27 Unbolt the brake caliper (with reference to Chapter 10 if necessary) and tie it to one side, taking care not to strain the brake hose.

28 Mark the position of the brake disc in relation to the hub, remove the retaining spire washer(s), and remove the disc.

29 Disconnect the driveshaft from the hub assembly by unscrewing the six securing bolts. Support the driveshaft to avoid straining the joints, or alternatively, unbolt it from the final drive unit at the inboard end and remove the driveshaft from the vehicle. At all times, avoid bending the driveshaft joints to excessive angles, and do not allow the shaft to hang down from one end.

30 Unscrew and remove the rear hub nut, and using a suitable puller, pull off the drive flange.

31 Unscrew the four bolts securing the hub carrier and splash shield to the lower arm. Remove the hub carrier and splash shield. Note that the stub axle is retained in the hub carrier.

32 Disconnect the ABS sensor, and detach the lead from the clip on the lower arm.

33 Remove the propeller shaft as described in Chapter 8.

34 Proceed as described in paragraphs 7 to 14 inclusive.

35 Refitting is a reversal of removal, bearing in mind the following points.

36 Where applicable, secure the larger front guide plate bolt by bending up the lockwasher tabs.

37 Refit the shock absorber as described in Section 13.

38 Refit the propeller shaft as described in Chapter 8.

39 When refitting the hub carrier to the lower arm, refer to the note at the beginning of Section 15.

40 When refitting the drive flange to the hub assembly, use a new hub nut, and leave tightening until the vehicle is resting on its wheels. Apply the handbrake and chock the relevant rear wheel when tightening the nut.

41 When refitting the brake disc, align the previously made marks on disc and hub.

42 Refit the rear section of the exhaust system with reference to Chapter 3.

43 Before tightening the lower arm-to-crossmember pivot bolts and nuts, lower the vehicle so that its weight is resting on the roadwheels, and bounce the vehicle to settle the suspension. Ensure that the bolts are orientated as noted during removal.

44 On completion, bleed the brakes and adjust the handbrake as described in Chapter 10.

13 Rear shock absorber – removal and refitting

Saloon and Hatchback models

1 With the weight of the vehicle resting on the roadwheels, work under the vehicle to unscrew and remove the shock absorber lower mounting bolt and nut from the relevant lower arm (photo). If desired, the rear of the vehicle can be raised on ramps to improve access.

2 Working inside the rear of the vehicle, remove the trim cover behind the side cushion. The cover is secured by two self-tapping screws (photos).

3 With an assistant supporting the shock absorber from below, unscrew and remove the upper mounting bolt and nut. Withdraw the shock absorber from under the vehicle.

4 Refitting is a reversal of removal. Tighten the mounting bolts securely.

Estate models

Note: *On models fitted with heavy duty Nivomat shock absorbers, follow the procedure given in Section 14, as the shock absorber and coil spring are an integrated unit.*

5 With the weight of the vehicle resting on the roadwheels, work under the vehicle to unscrew and remove the two shock absorber lower mounting bolts from the relevant lower arm. If desired, the rear of the vehicle can be raised on ramps to improve access.

6 Working inside the rear of the vehicle, fold down the rear seat

13.1 Rear shock absorber lower mounting – Saloon and Hatchback models

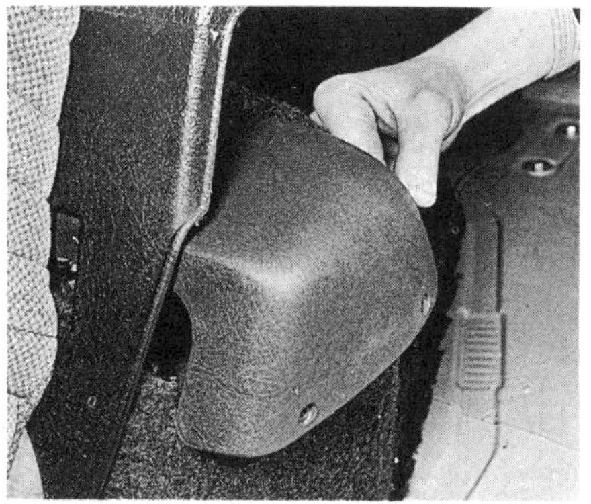

13.2A Remove the trim cover...

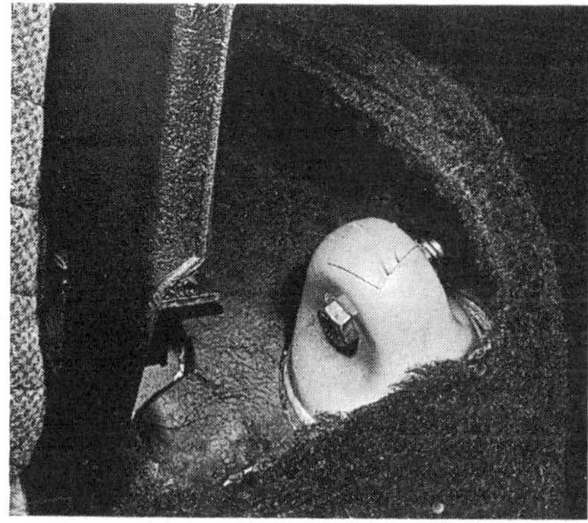

13.2B ... for access to the rear shock absorber upper mounting – Saloon and Hatchback models

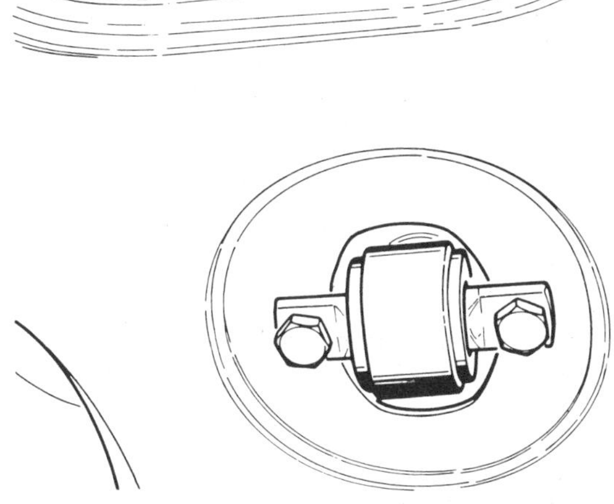

Fig 11.21 Rear shock absorber lower mounting bolts – Estate models (Sec 13)

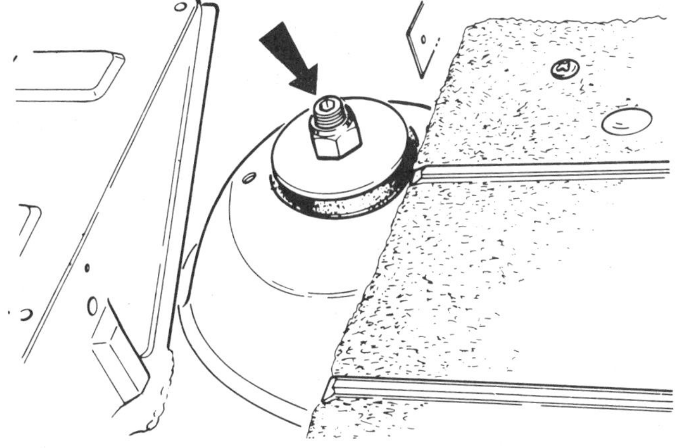

Fig 11.22 Rear shock absorber upper mounting (arrowed) – Estate models (Sec 13)

backrest, fold back the floor covering and remove the front section of the luggage compartment floor, which is secured with 12 self-tapping screws.

7 With an assistant supporting the shock absorber from below, unscrew and remove the upper mounting nut and washer. Withdraw the shock absorber from under the vehicle.

8 Refitting is a reversal of removal. Tighten the mounting bolts and nut securely.

P100 models

9 With the weight of the vehicle resting on the roadwheels, work under the vehicle to unscrew and remove the shock absorber lower mounting nut, washer, and rubber insulator. If desired, the rear of the vehicle can be raised on ramps to improve access.

10 Unscrew and remove the top mounting bolt, nut and washer from the chassis crossmember. Withdraw the shock absorber upwards.

11 Refitting is a reversal of removal. Tighten the mounting bolt and nut securely.

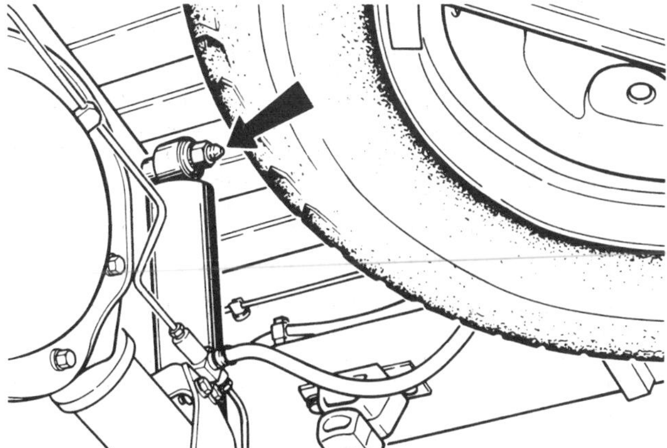

Fig 11.23 Rear shock absorber upper mounting – P100 models (Sec 13)

14 Rear coil spring (Saloon, Hatchback and Estate models) – removal and refitting

Models with rear drum brakes

1 Remove the relevant driveshaft as described in Chapter 9.

2 Unscrew the brake pipe from the brake hose at the bracket on the vehicle underbody. Plug the ends of the pipe and hose to prevent leakage and dirt ingress.

3 Where applicable, prise the anti-roll bar connecting strap from the lower arm.

4 Support the lower arm on a jack, and raise it slightly to place the coil spring under load (photo).

5 On Saloon and Hatchback models, unscrew and remove the shock absorber lower mounting bolt and nut from the lower arm.

6 On Estate models fitted with standard shock absorbers, remove the shock absorber as described in Section 13. On Estate models fitted with heavy duty Nivomat shock absorbers, disconnect the upper and lower mountings.

7 Unscrew and remove the three bolts securing the front guide plate

to the underbody and the suspension crossmember. Where applicable, bend back the lockwasher tab(s) on the larger bolt.
8 Lower the lower arm, and remove the coil spring, or coil spring/heavy duty shock absorber as applicable, and the rubber cup.
9 Refitting is a reversal of removal, bearing in mind the following points.
10 Where applicable, secure the larger front guide plate bolt by bending up the lockwasher tab(s).
11 Refit the driveshaft as described in Chapter 9.
12 On completion, bleed the brakes as described in Chapter 10.

Models with rear disc brakes

13 Chock the front wheels, jack up the rear of the vehicle and support on axle stands placed under the side members.
14 Disconnect the driveshaft from the hub assembly by unscrewing the six securing bolts. Support the driveshaft to avoid straining the joints, or alternatively, unbolt it from the final drive unit at the inboard end and remove the driveshaft from the vehicle. At all times, avoid bending the driveshaft joints to excessive angles, and do not allow the shaft to hang down from one end.
15 Proceed as described in paragraphs 2 to 8 inclusive.
16 Refitting is a reversal of removal. Where applicable, secure the larger front guide plate bolt by bending up the lockwasher tab(s), and on completion, bleed the brakes as described in Chapter 10.

15 Rear wheel bearings – renewal

Saloon, Hatchback and Estate models with rear drum brakes

Note: *There are two types of bolts used to secure the rear hub carrier to the lower arm – see Fig. 11.24. The two types of bolt must not be mixed on a vehicle, but can be changed in complete sets for the alternative type. A complete set is eight bolts, four each side. Note that the two types of bolt have different torque wrench settings. When renewing the wheel bearings, a suitable puller will be required to remove the drive flange, and a new rear hub nut must be used on reassembly.*

1 Loosen the rear hub nut with the vehicle resting on its wheels. On early models, relieve the staking before loosening the nut (photo). Later models use self-locking nuts, and it is important to note that where this type of nut is fitted, the left-hand nut has a left-hand thread, ie it is undone in a clockwise direction. Before loosening the nut, ensure that the handbrake is applied, and chock the relevant rear wheel. A suitable extension bar will be required, as the nut is extremely tight.
2 Loosen the rear roadwheel nuts on the side concerned, chock the front wheels, and jack up the rear of the vehicle and support on axle stands. Remove the rear roadwheel.
3 Remove the brake drum retaining spire washer(s) from the wheel stud(s) and remove the brake drum. Ensure that the handbrake is released before removing the brake drum, otherwise the drum will be held in place by the clamping action of the brake shoes.
4 Remove the two nylon fasteners, and remove the plastic shield from the rear of the brake backplate (photo).
5 Unscrew and remove the rear hub nut.
6 Using a suitable puller, pull the drive flange from the end of the driveshaft (photo).
7 Unscrew and remove the four bolts securing the hub carrier and brake backplate to the lower arm. Remove the hub carrier, whilst supporting the driveshaft. Support the driveshaft by placing axle stands underneath it, or by securing with string to the underbody. Note that the driveshaft joints should not be allowed to deflect through an angle exceeding 13°.
8 Refit the brake backplate with the four securing bolts to avoid straining the brake pipe.
9 With the hub carrier removed, the bearings can be renewed as follows (photo).
10 Prise the inner and outer oil seals from the hub carrier using a suitable screwdriver, and withdraw the taper roller bearings.
11 Using a soft metal drift, drive the bearing outer races from the hub carrier, taking care not to damage the inner surface of the carrier.
12 Clean the hub carrier and drive flange with paraffin, wipe dry and examine for damage and wear. Note that the components are machined to very close tolerances, and the bearings are supplied in matched pairs, therefore scrupulous cleanliness must be observed.
13 Using a metal tube of suitable diameter, drive the new bearing outer races fully into the hub carrier. Ensure that the races are seated correctly.
14 Pack the inner bearing races and rollers with high melting point lithium-based grease, and locate the outer bearing assembly in the hub carrier.
15 Fill the cavities between the sealing lips of the oil seal with grease, then drive it fully into the hub carrier using a block of wood or a metal tube of suitable diameter. Note than on early models the oil seal has a rubber casing, and this type of seal should be replaced with the later

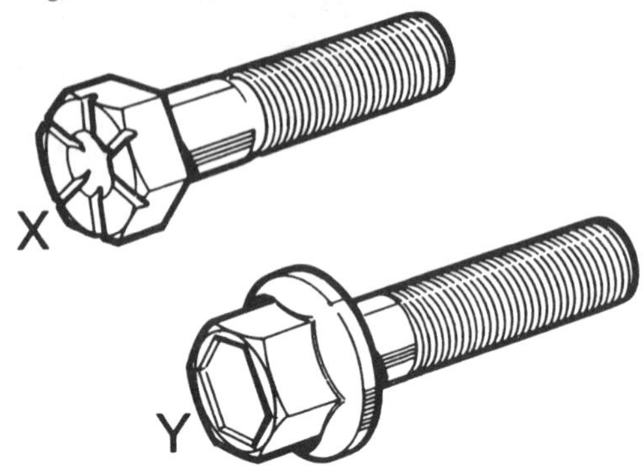

Fig 11.24 Alternative types of rear hub carrier-to-lower arm securing bolts (Sec 15)

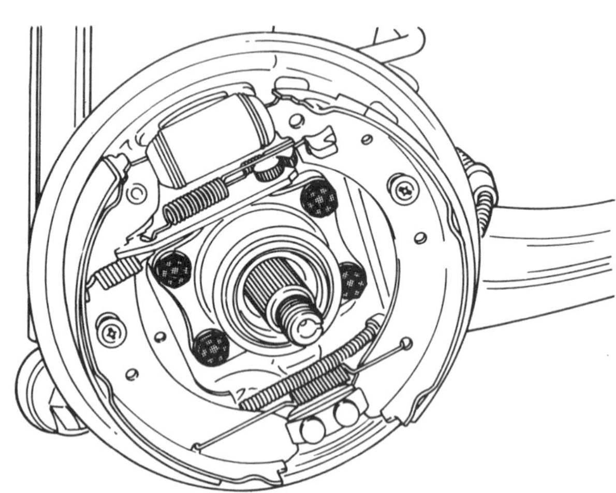

Fig 11.25 Rear hub carrier/brake backplate-to-lower arm securing bolts (Sec 15)

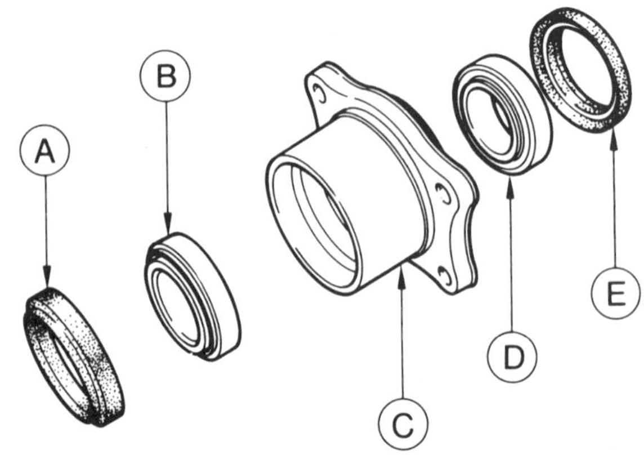

Fig 11.26 Rear hub carrier components – Saloon, Hatchback and Estate models (Sec 15)

A Outer oil seal
B Outer bearing
C Hub carrier
D Inner bearing
E Inner oil seal

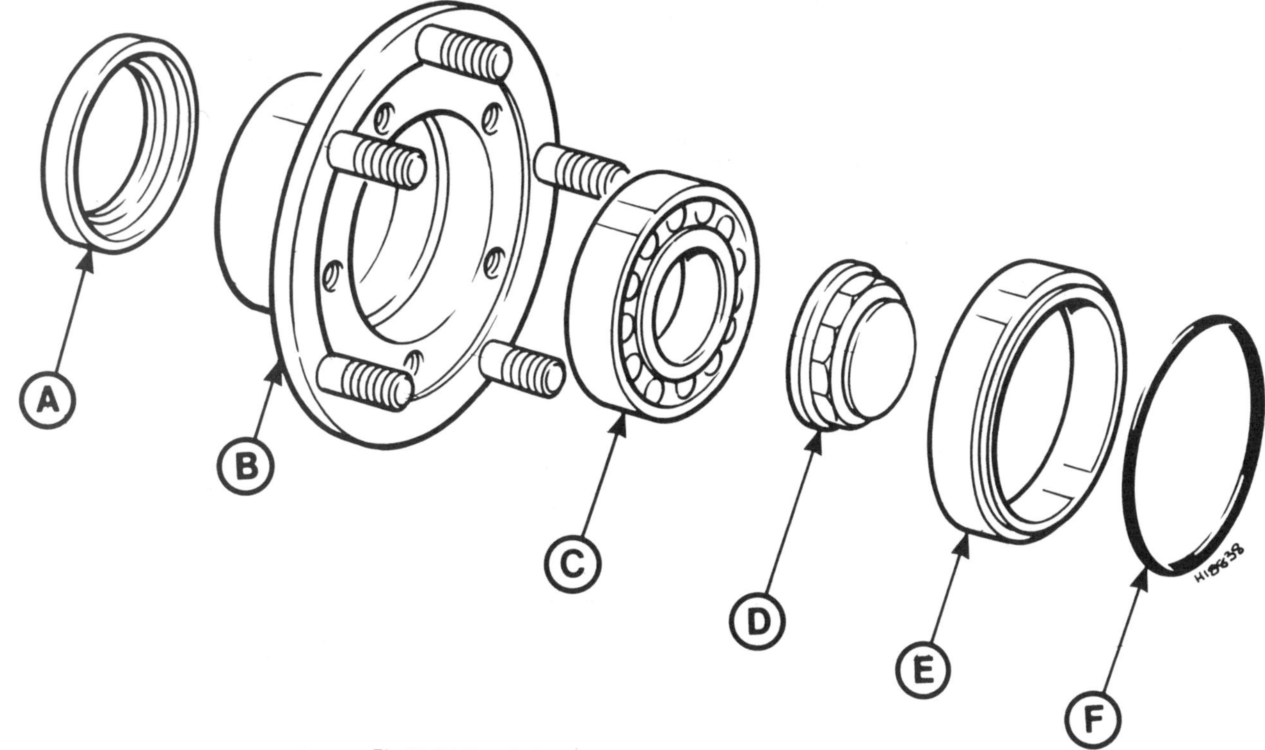

Fig 11.27 Rear hub components – P100 models (Sec 15)

A Oil seal
B Hub
C Ball-bearing
D Hub nut
E Spacer sleeve
F O-ring

14.4 Rear coil spring assembly – Saloon and Hatchback models

15.1 On early models relieve the staking (arrowed) on the rear hub nut

15.4 Remove the nylon fasteners (arrowed) to free the plastic shield from the brake backplate

15.6 Pull the drive flange from the end of the driveshaft

15.9 Hub carrier removed showing bearings and inner oil seal

type which has a metal casing. The oil seal should be renewed regardless of type, and a new oil seal of the correct type is normally supplied with the new wheel bearings.

16 Repeat the procedure given in paragraphs 14 and 15 for the outer bearing and oil seal.

17 Fit the drive flange to the hub carrier in order to centralise the bearings, then remove the securing bolts from the brake backplate, and using a soft-faced mallet, drive the drive flange/hub carrier assembly onto the end of the driveshaft.

18 Further refitting is a reversal of removal, bearing in mind the following points.

19 Refit the hub carrier/brake backplate-to-lower arm securing bolts with reference to the note at the beginning of this sub-Section.

20 Fit a new rear hub nut of the correct type, and tighten it with the vehicle resting on its roadwheels. Apply the handbrake and chock the relevant rear wheel. If a staked type nut is used, lock the nut by staking its outer ring into the groove in the driveshaft.

Saloon, Hatchback and Estate models with rear disc brakes

Note: *Refer to the note at the beginning of the previous sub-Section.*

21 Loosen the rear hub nut with the vehicle resting on its wheels. Note that the left-hand nut has a left-hand thread, ie it is undone in a clockwise direction. Before loosening the nut, ensure that the handbrake is applied, and chock the relevant rear wheel. A suitable extension bar will be required, as the nut is extremely tight.

22 Loosen the rear roadwheel nuts on the side concerned, chock the front wheels, and jack up the rear of the vehicle and support on axle stands. Remove the roadwheel and release the handbrake.

23 Unbolt the brake calliper carrier bracket (with reference to Chapter 10 if necessary) and support the calliper on an axle stand, taking care not to strain the flexible hose.

24 Mark the position of the brake disc in relation to the drive flange, remove the retaining spire washer(s), and remove the disc.

25 Unscrew and remove the rear hub nut, and using a suitable puller, pull off the drive flange.

26 Unscrew the four bolts securing the hub carrier and splash shield to the lower arm. Remove the hub carrier and splash shield, whilst supporting the driveshaft. Support the driveshaft by placing axle stands underneath it, or by securing with string to the underbody. Avoid bending the driveshaft joints to excessive angles, and do not allow the shaft to hang down from one end.

27 With the hub carrier removed, the bearings can be renewed as described in paragraphs 10 to 16 of this Section.

28 Fit the drive flange to the hub carrier in order to centralise the bearings, then using a soft-faced mallet, drive the drive flange/hub carrier assembly onto the end of the stub axle. Do not forget to fit the splash shield.

29 Further refitting is a reversal of removal, bearing in mind the following points.

30 Refit the hub carrier/splash shield-to-lower arm securing bolts with reference to the note at the beginning of the previous sub-Section.

31 When refitting the brake disc, align the previously made marks on disc and drive flange.

32 Fit a new rear hub nut of the correct type, and tighten it with the vehicle resting on its roadwheels. Apply the handbrake and chock the relevant rear wheel.

P100 models

Note: *A new rear hub nut must be used on reassembly.*

33 Remove the relevant driveshaft as described in Chapter 9.

34 Relieve the staking on the rear hub nut, and using a 50 mm socket and a suitable extension bar, unscrew the nut. Note that the nut is extremely tight.

35 Pull off the hub, and remove the O-ring and spacer sleeve from the recess in the hub.

36 Prise the oil seal from the rear of the hub using a screwdriver.

37 Using a block of wood, or a suitable metal tube inserted from the rear of the hub, tap out the ball-bearing.

38 Clean the hub with paraffin, wipe dry and examine for damage and wear.

39 Using a metal tube of suitable diameter, resting on the bearing outer race only, tap the new bearing into the hub. Ensure that the bearing is correctly seated.

40 Carefully fit a new oil seal to the rear of the hub, using a suitable metal tube.

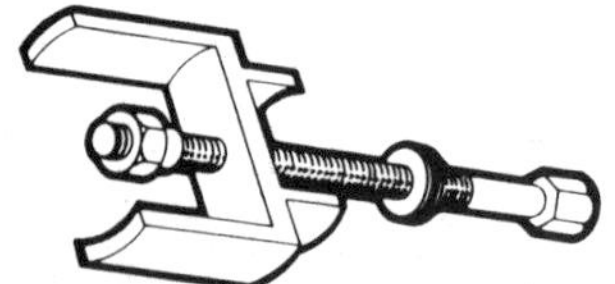

Fig 11.28 Ford special tool 15-014 for removing rear suspension front mounting rubber (Sec 16)

41 Refitting is a reversal of removal, bearing in mind the following points.

42 Fit a new rear hub nut, and stake in position after tightening to the specified torque.

43 Refit the driveshaft as described in Chapter 9.

16 Rear suspension front mounting (Saloon, Hatchback and Estate models) – renewal

1 Chock the front wheels, jack up the rear of the vehicle and support on axle stands placed under the side members.

2 Unscrew and remove the three bolts securing the relevant front guide plate to the underbody and the suspension crossmember. Where applicable, bend back the lockwasher tab(s) on the larger bolt.

3 Using a length of wood, lever the suspension crossmember downwards a few inches from the underbody, and insert the wood as a wedge.

4 Using a tool similar to the Ford special tool shown in Fig. 11.28, or a long bolt with nut, washers and a suitable metal tube, pull the mounting rubber from the crossmember.

5 Lubricate the new mounting rubber with soapy water, and use the tool described in the previous paragraph to press the rubber into the crossmember.

6 Further refitting is a reversal of removal. Where applicable, secure the larger front guide plate bolt by bending up the lockwasher tab(s).

17 Rear suspension/final drive unit rear mounting (Saloon, Hatchback and Estate models) – renewal

Note: *From May 1986, revised rear suspension/final drive unit rear mounting bolts have been used in production. Whenever the earlier type of bolts are removed, they should be discarded and the later type fitted. The earlier bolts are coloured blue, and the later type bolts are coloured gold.*

1 Chock the front wheels, jack up the rear of the vehicle and support on axle stands placed under the side members.

2 Support the final drive unit with a jack, using an interposed block of wood to spread the load.

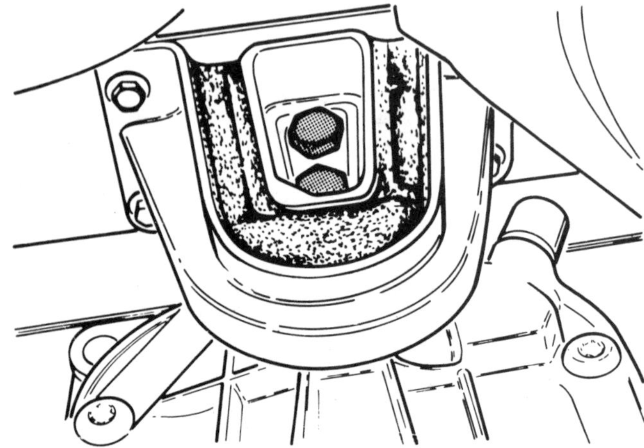

Fig 11.29 Rear suspension/final drive unit rear mounting-to-final drive unit rear cover bolts (Sec 17)

18.2 Anti-roll bar-to-lower arm connecting strap

18.3 Anti-roll bar-to-underbody securing bracket

19.7 Remove the split pin (arrowed) from the brake load apportioning valve lever

3 Unscrew and remove the four bolts securing the mounting to the underbody. Note the location and number of any shims which may be fitted.

4 Lower the final drive unit sufficiently to enable the mounting to be unbolted from the final drive unit rear cover.

5 Refitting is a reversal of removal, with reference to the note at the beginning of this Section. Refit any shims in their original noted positions, and tighten all bolts to the specified torque.

18 Rear anti-roll bar (Saloon, Hatchback and Estate models) – removal and refitting

1 Loosen the rear roadwheel nuts, chock the front wheels, jack up the rear of the vehicle and support on axle stands placed under the side members.

2 Prise off the straps which connect the anti-roll bar to the suspension lower arms (photo).

3 Unbolt the two securing brackets from the underbody, and remove the anti-roll bar (photo).

4 The connecting straps can be prised from the ends of the anti-roll bar, and the underbody mounting brackets and rubbers, which are of a split design, can be pulled off.

5 When fitting new mounting components, lubricate the rubber parts with soapy water to ease assembly.

6 Refitting is a reversal of removal. Tighten the anti-roll bar-to-underbody securing bolts to the specified torque.

19 Rear suspension and axle assembly (P100 models) – removal and refitting

Note: *All self-locking nuts and spring washers must be renewed on reassembly.*

1 Chock the front wheels, jack up the rear of the vehicle and support on axle stands placed under the side members. Note that a loaded vehicle must not be jacked under the differential casing.

2 Support the rear axle with a jack, using an interposed block of wood to spread the load.

3 Remove the propeller shaft as described in Chapter 8.

4 Remove the securing circlip and the pivot pin, and detach the handbrake equaliser from the linkage on the underbody.

5 Remove the handbrake cables from the clips on the underbody, and from the brackets on the crossmember. To remove the cables from the crossmember, remove the U-shaped retaining clips. Note that the cable adjuster is secured to the right-hand crossmember bracket. Ensure that the handbrake is released before attempting to disconnect any part of the mechanism.

6 Unscrew the brake pipe from the brake hose on the right-hand side of the chassis crossmember. Plug the ends of the pipe and hose to prevent leakage and dirt ingress, then detach the hose from the crossmember by removing the U-shaped retaining clip – see Fig. 11.30.

7 Remove the spring clip and clevis pin and disconnect the spring from the brake load apportioning valve lever on the right-hand side of the underbody (photo).

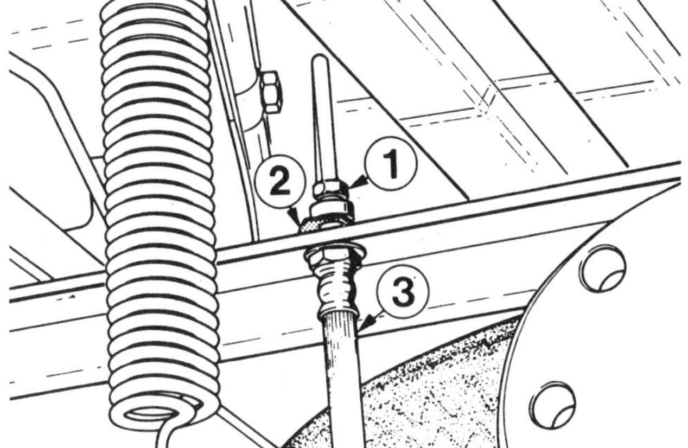

Fig 11.30 Brake pipe-to-hose connection on right-hand side of chassis crossmember – P100 models (Sec 19)

1 Brake pipe
2 U-shaped retaining clip
3 Brake hose

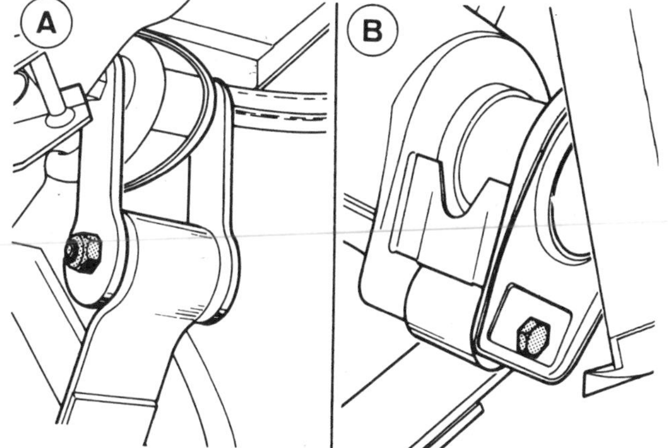

Fig 11.31 Leaf spring-to-underbody mountings – P100 models (Sec 19)

A Rear mounting shackle
B Front mounting bracket

8 Detach the exhaust system from the two rear mountings.

9 Unbolt the shock absorbers from the chassis crossmember.

10 Unbolt the leaf springs from the front brackets on the underbody.

11 Lower the rear axle.

12 Loosen the spring shackle-to-underbody bolts, then unbolt the leaf springs from the spring shackles, and remove the rear suspension and

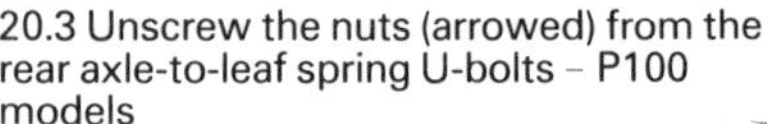

20.3 Unscrew the nuts (arrowed) from the rear axle-to-leaf spring U-bolts – P100 models

20.4 Leaf spring front bracket – P100 models

20.5 Leaf spring shackle – P100 models

axle assembly from under the vehicle, guiding the handbrake cables over the exhaust system.
13 Refitting is a reversal of removal, bearing in mind the following points.
14 Do not fully tighten the leaf spring mounting bolts or the spring shackle-to-underbody bolts until the weight of the vehicle is resting on the roadwheels.
15 Renew all self-locking nuts and spring washers.
16 Refit the propeller shaft as described in Chapter 8.
17 On completion, check the brake load apportioning valve adjustment and the handbrake adjustment, and bleed the rear brake circuit as described in Chapter 10, and check the axle oil level as described in Chapter 9.

20 Rear suspension leaf spring (P100 models) – removal and refitting

Note: *All self-locking nuts and spring washers must be renewed on reassembly.*
1 Chock the front wheels, jack up the rear of the vehicle and support on axle stands placed under the side members. Note that a loaded vehicle must not be jacked under the differential casing.
2 Support the relevant side of the rear axle with a jack, using an interposed block of wood under the axle tube to spread the load.
3 Unscrew the nuts, and remove the two U-bolts on each side of the vehicle which secure the axle to the leaf springs (photo). Note that there is no need to disconnect the shock absorber from the U-bolt counterplate.
4 Unbolt the leaf spring from the front bracket on the underbody (photo).
5 Loosen the spring shackle-to-underbody bolt, then unbolt the leaf spring from the spring shackle and remove the spring (photo).
6 Refitting is a reversal of removal, bearing in mind the following points.
7 Do not fully tighten the leaf spring mounting bolts or the spring shackle-to-underbody bolt until the weight of the vehicle is resting on its roadwheels.
8 Renew all self-locking nuts and spring washers.
9 Align the axle on the leaf spring so that the locating pin on the spring engages with the corresponding hole in the axle. Similarly ensure that the U-bolt counterplate engages with the locating pin on the leaf spring.

21 Rear suspension leaf spring shackle (P100 models) – removal and refitting

Note: *All self-locking nuts and spring washers must be renewed on reassembly.*
1 Proceed as described in Section 20, paragraphs 1 and 2.
2 Unscrew and remove the spring shackle-to-underbody bolt and the leaf spring-to-spring shackle bolt, and remove the shackle components.
3 Examine the components for wear and damage and renew as necessary.
4 Refitting is a reversal of removal, but renew all self-locking nuts and spring washers, and do not fully tighten the bolts until the weight of the vehicle is resting on its roadwheels.

22 Rear suspension leaf spring bush (P100 models) – renewal

Note: *All self-locking nuts and spring washers must be renewed on reassembly.*
1 Proceed as described in Section 20, paragraphs 1 to 3 inclusive.
2 Unbolt the relevant end of the leaf spring, and lower it to gain access to the bush. Note that if the shackle end of the spring is unbolted, the shackle-to-underbody bolt should be loosened in order to aid refitting.
3 The bush can be removed using a long bolt with nut, washers and a suitable metal tube.
4 Lubricate the new bush with soapy water and fit using the bolt, nut, washers and tube.
5 Proceed as described in Section 20, paragraphs 6 to 9 inclusive.

23 Steering wheel – removal and refitting

1 Set the front wheels in the straight-ahead position.
2 Prise the trim insert from the centre of the steering wheel, and where applicable, disconnect the horn electrical lead(s) (photos).
3 Insert the ignition key and check that the steering lock is disengaged.
4 Unscrew the retaining nut and withdraw the steering wheel from the hexagon shaped inner column (photo). If the wheel is tight on the inner column, sit in the driver's seat and tap the wheel from behind with the palms of the hands (but screw the nut back on two or three turns for safety).
5 Refitting is a reversal of removal, but check that the lug on the direction indicator cam is aligned with the cut-out in the steering wheel, and make sure that the direction indicator switch is in the neutral position. Tighten the retaining nut to the specified torque.

24 Steering wheel – centralising

1 This operation is for correcting small errors in steering wheel centralisation – up to 60°. For larger errors, remove the steering wheel and make a rough correction by repositioning the wheel on refitting.
2 Drive the vehicle in a straight line on a level surface. Note the angle by which the steering wheel deviates from the desired straight-ahead position.
3 Raise the front of the vehicle by driving it onto ramps, or with a jack and axle stands.
4 Slacken both tie-rod end locknuts. Also slacken the steering rack bellows outer clips.
5 Make alignment marks between each tie-rod end and its rod, so that the amount of rotation applied can be accurately determined.

23.2A Prise off the steering wheel trim insert...

23.2B ... and disconnect the horn electrical lead

23.4 Removing the steering wheel retaining nut

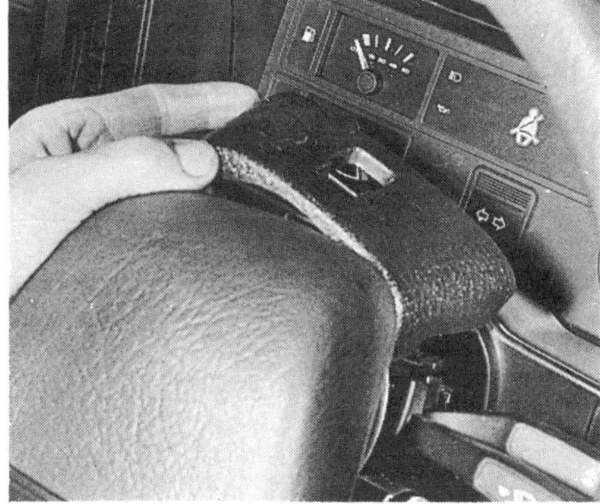
25.4A Remove the steering column upper shroud...

25.4B ... and lower shroud

6 Turn both tie-rods **in the same direction** to correct the steering wheel position. As a rough guide, 19° of tie-rod rotation will change the steering wheel position by 1°. To correct a clockwise error at the steering wheel, rotate both tie-rods anti-clockwise (when viewed from the left-hand side of the vehicle), and the reverse to correct an anti-clockwise error. Both tie-rods must be rotated by the same amount.
7 Tighten the bellows clips and the tie-rod end locknuts when adjustment is correct. Lower the vehicle.

25 Steering column – removal, overhaul and refitting

1 Set the front wheels in the straight-ahead position.
2 Disconnect the battery negative lead.

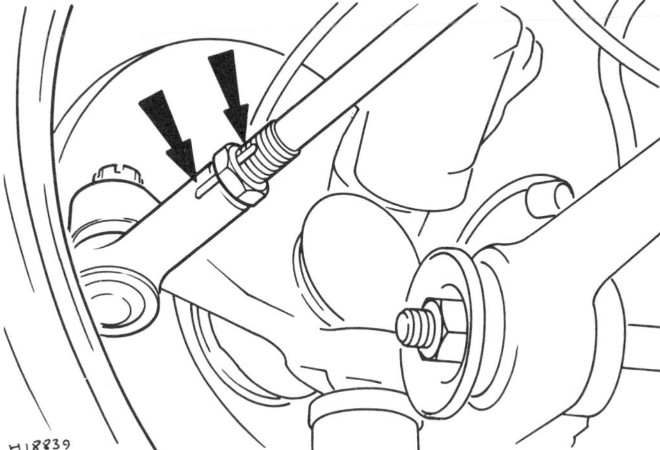

Fig 11.32 Make alignment marks (arrowed) between each tie-rod end and its rod when centralising the steering wheel (Sec 24)

3 Remove the driver's side lower facia trim panels as described in Chapter 12.
4 Remove the screws and withdraw the steering column upper and lower shrouds (photos).
5 Unscrew the two crosshead screws and withdraw the two combination switches from the column.
6 Remove the screw from the bonnet release lever and remove the lever.
7 Working in the engine compartment, unscrew the bolt securing the intermediate shaft to the inner column, swivel the clamp plate to one side, and disconnect the intermediate shaft (photos).
8 Unscrew the nuts securing the outer column to the facia.
9 Disconnect the multi-plugs and withdraw the column assembly upwards.

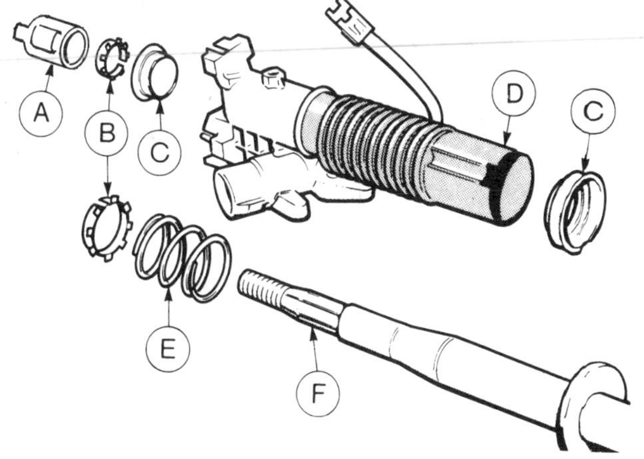

Fig 11.33 Steering column components (Sec 25)

A Direction indicator cam
B Thrust washers
C Bearings
D Outer column
E Spring
F Inner column

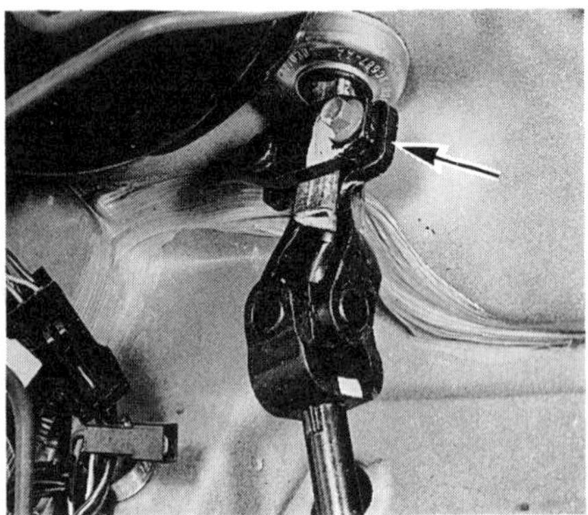
25.7A Intermediate shaft-to-inner column universal joint and clamp plate (arrowed)

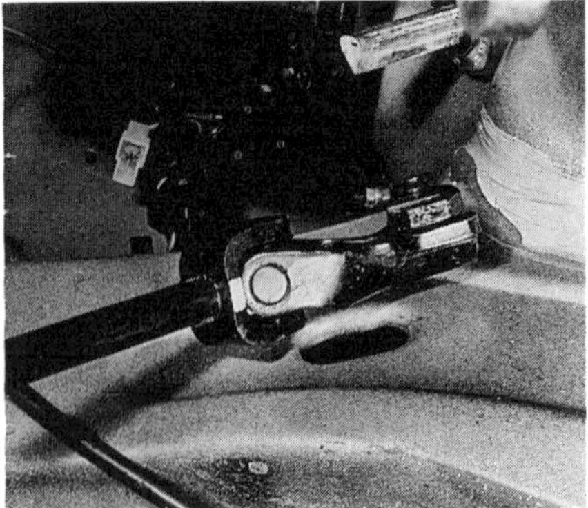
25.7B Intermediate shaft disconnected from inner column

26.3 Intermediate shaft-to-steering gear flexible coupling

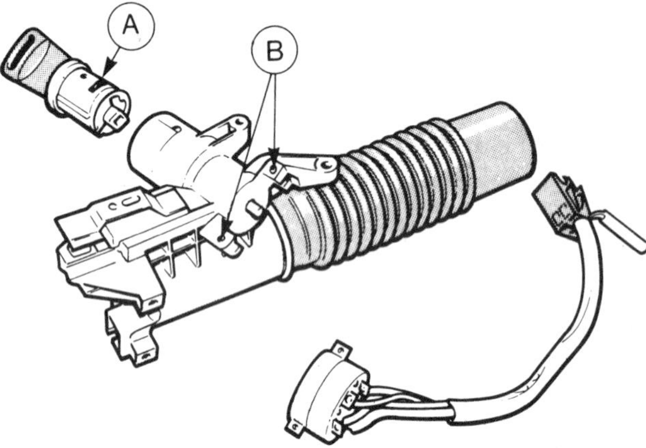

Fig 11.34 Steering lock barrel spring clip (A) and ignition switch grub screw (B) locations (Sec 25)

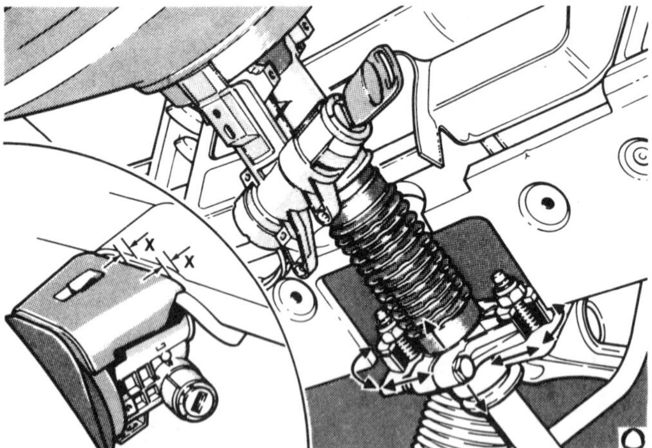

Fig 11.36 Upper column shroud-to-facia gap adjustment (Sec 25)

X = 5.0 mm (0.2 in)

10 Mount the outer column in a soft jawed vice.
11 Remove the steering wheel as described in Section 23.
12 Remove the direction indicator cam and the bearing thrustwasher.
13 Slide the inner column from the outer column, and remove the thrustwasher and spring from the inner column.
14 Lever the upper and lower bearings from the outer column.
15 Clamp the bottom of the inner column in a vice and pull off the lower nylon bush. Take care not to collapse the inner column sections, otherwise the column must be renewed.
16 If necessary, insert the ignition key and turn to position 'I', depress the spring clip with a suitable instrument and withdraw the steering lock barrel. Remove the two grub screws and withdraw the ignition switch. Note that the steering lock assembly is an integral part of the outer column and cannot be removed.

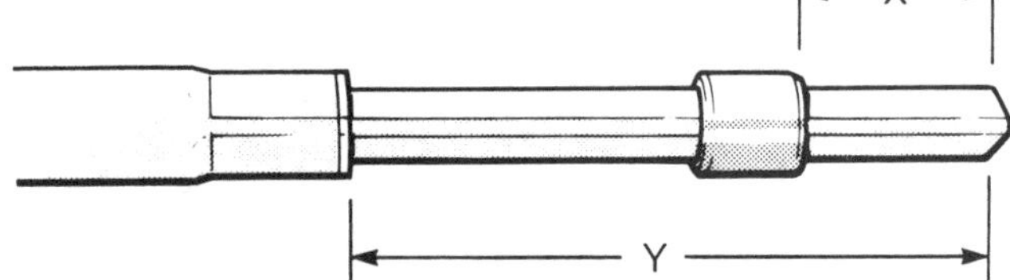

Fig 11.35 Inner column nylon bush location (Sec 25)

X = 52.0 mm (2.05 in)
Y = 186.0 to 192.0 mm (7.32 to 7.56 in)

17 Clean all the components and examine them for wear and damage. Renew them as necessary.
18 Refit the ignition switch and steering lock barrel.
19 With the triangular section of the inner column mounted in a vice, push on the nylon bush to the position shown in Fig. 11.35.
20 Lubricate the upper and lower bearings with grease, then push them into the outer column.
21 Locate the spring and thrustwasher on the inner column, then slide the inner column into the outer column.
22 Fit the upper bearing thrustwasher and the direction indicator cam.
23 Clean the hexagon section of the inner column and refit the steering wheel with reference to Section 23.
24 Check that the distance between the lower bearing in the outer column and the welded washer on the inner column is between 11.0 and 13.0 mm (0.43 and 0.51 in). If not, the column has been damaged and should be renewed.
25 Check that the bulkhead bush is serviceable and correctly fitted and renew if necessary. An incorrectly fitted bush can result in the ingress of water.
26 Refit the column assembly in the car and tighten the upper mounting nuts lightly. Loosen the mounting pinch-bolt.
27 Temporarily fit the upper column shroud and adjust the position of the steering column until there is a gap of 5.0 mm (0.2 in) between the shroud and the facia.
28 Tighten the pinch-bolt and the mounting nuts and remove the upper column shroud.
29 With the steering wheel in the straight-ahead position, reconnect the intermediate shaft and tighten the clamp plate bolt to the specified torque.
30 Refit the bonnet release lever and combination switches and reconnect the multi-plugs.
31 Refit the steering column shrouds and trim panels.
32 Reconnect the battery negative lead.

26 Steering intermediate shaft and flexible coupling – removal and refitting

1 Apply the handbrake, jack up the front of the vehicle and support on axle stands.
2 Working in the engine compartment, unscrew the bolt securing the

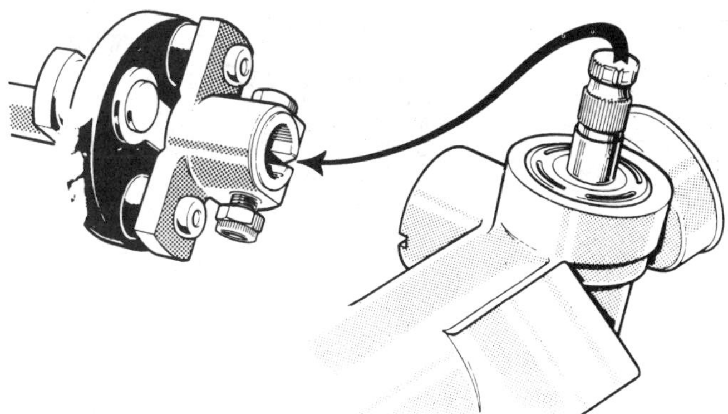

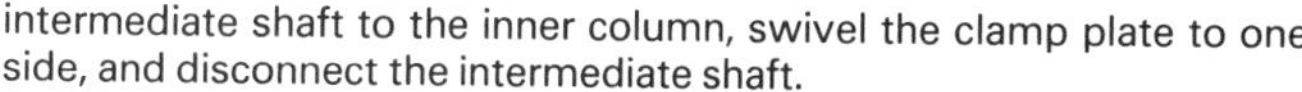

Fig 11.37 Master spline location on the steering gear pinion and intermediate shaft coupling (Sec 26)

intermediate shaft to the inner column, swivel the clamp plate to one side, and disconnect the intermediate shaft.
3 Unscrew and remove the clamp bolt securing the flexible coupling to the steering gear (photo).
4 Mark the coupling in relation to the pinion, then pull off the intermediate shaft and remove it from the vehicle. The pinion has a master spline, but making alignment marks will aid refitting.
5 Refitting is a reversal of removal, but align the marks on the coupling and pinion, and tighten all bolts to the specified torque.

27 Manual steering gear – removal and refitting

Note: *A balljoint separator tool will be required for this operation.*
1 Set the front wheels in the straight-ahead position. Ensure that the steering lock is engaged and remove the ignition key.
2 Apply the handbrake. Loosen the front roadwheel nuts, jack up the front of the vehicle and support on axle stands.
3 Remove the roadwheels. On P100 models, mark the position of the roadwheels in relation to the wheel studs.
4 Unscrew and remove the clamp bolts securing the intermediate shaft flexible coupling to the steering gear.
5 If the original steering gear is to be refitted, mark the coupling in relation to the pinion. The pinion has a master spline, but making alignment marks will aid refitting.
6 Slacken the tie-rod end locknuts.
7 Remove the split pins and unscrew the castellated nuts from the tie-rod end-to-hub carrier balljoints.
8 Using a balljoint separator tool, disconnect the tie-rod ends from the hub carriers.
9 Unscrew the two steering gear-to-front suspension crossmember securing bolts, and withdraw the steering gear from under the vehicle.
10 If required, remove the tie-rod ends as described in Section 36.
11 Refitting is a reversal of removal, bearing in mind the following points.
12 Where applicable, refit the tie-rod ends as described in Section 36.
13 If new steering gear is being fitted, the central pinion position can be ascertained by halving the number of turns required to move the rack from lock to lock.
14 Where applicable, align the marks made on the coupling and pinion.
15 When tightening the steering gear-to-front suspension crossmember bolts, the following procedure should be used. Tighten the bolts to the specified 'clamping' torque, then loosen the bolts fully. Re-tighten to the specified 'snug' torque and then further tighten the bolts through the specified angle.
16 Tighten all fixings to the specified torque, and use new split pins on the balljoint castellated nuts.
17 On P100 models, align the previously made marks on the roadwheels and wheel studs.

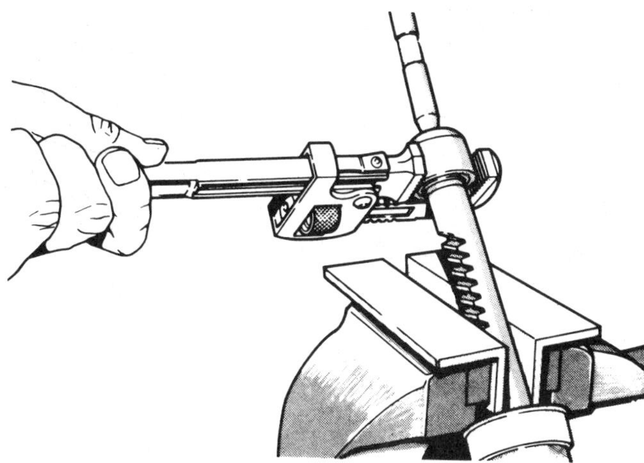

Fig 11.38 Unscrewing a tie-rod balljoint from the steering rack using a pipe wrench (Sec 28)

18 On completion, check the front wheel alignment as described in Section 37.

28 Manual steering gear – overhaul

Note: *Before overhauling the steering gear, check the availability and price of spare parts. Renewal of badly worn steering gear may prove a more economical alternative.*
1 Clean the exterior of the steering gear with paraffin and wipe dry.
2 Mount the steering gear in a soft-jawed vice, then remove and discard the clips and slide the rubber gaiters off the tie-rods.
3 Move the rack fully to the left and grip the rack in the vice. Ensure that jaw protectors are used.
4 If the original tie-rods are fitted use a pipe wrench to unscrew the balljoint from the rack and remove the tie-rod. If service replacement tie-rods are fitted use a spanner on the machined flats.
5 Remove the right-hand tie-rod in the same way.
6 Using Ford tool 13-009 or a suitable Allen key, unscrew and remove the slipper plug and remove the spring and slipper.
7 Prise out the pinion dust cover, then using Ford tool 13-009 or a locally made four segment tool, unscrew the pinion retaining nut and withdraw the pinion and bearing using a twisting action.
8 Withdraw the rack from the steering gear housing.
9 Clean all the components in paraffin and wipe dry. Examine them for wear and damage and renew them as necessary. If necessary the rack support bush in the housing can be renewed by driving it out of the housing using a suitable drift. Carefully drive the new bush into the end of the housing until it is seated as shown in Fig. 11.40. Ensure that the plastic lugs on the bush locate in the groove in the housing.
10 Lightly coat the rack with the specified semi-fluid grease and insert it into the housing.
11 Coat the pinion and bearing with grease and locate it in the housing at the same time meshing it with the rack.
12 Fit the retaining nut and tighten to the specified torque. Lock the nut by peening the housing in four places.
13 Move the rack to its central position, then fit the slipper and spring. Coat the plug with thread-locking fluid and tighten to the specified torque. Loosen the plug 60° to 70°.
14 Using a piece of string and a spring balance, check that the turning torque of the pinion is between 0.8 and 1.4 Nm (0.6 and 1.0 lbf ft). To do this accurately turn the pinion anticlockwise half a turn from its central position, and measure the torque while turning the pinion clockwise through one complete turn. Turn the pinion anticlockwise 180° back to its central position on completion.
15 If necessary, tighten or loosen the slipper plug until the turning torque is correct. Ensure that no free play exists between the rack and the slipper, then lock the plug by peening the housing at three positions

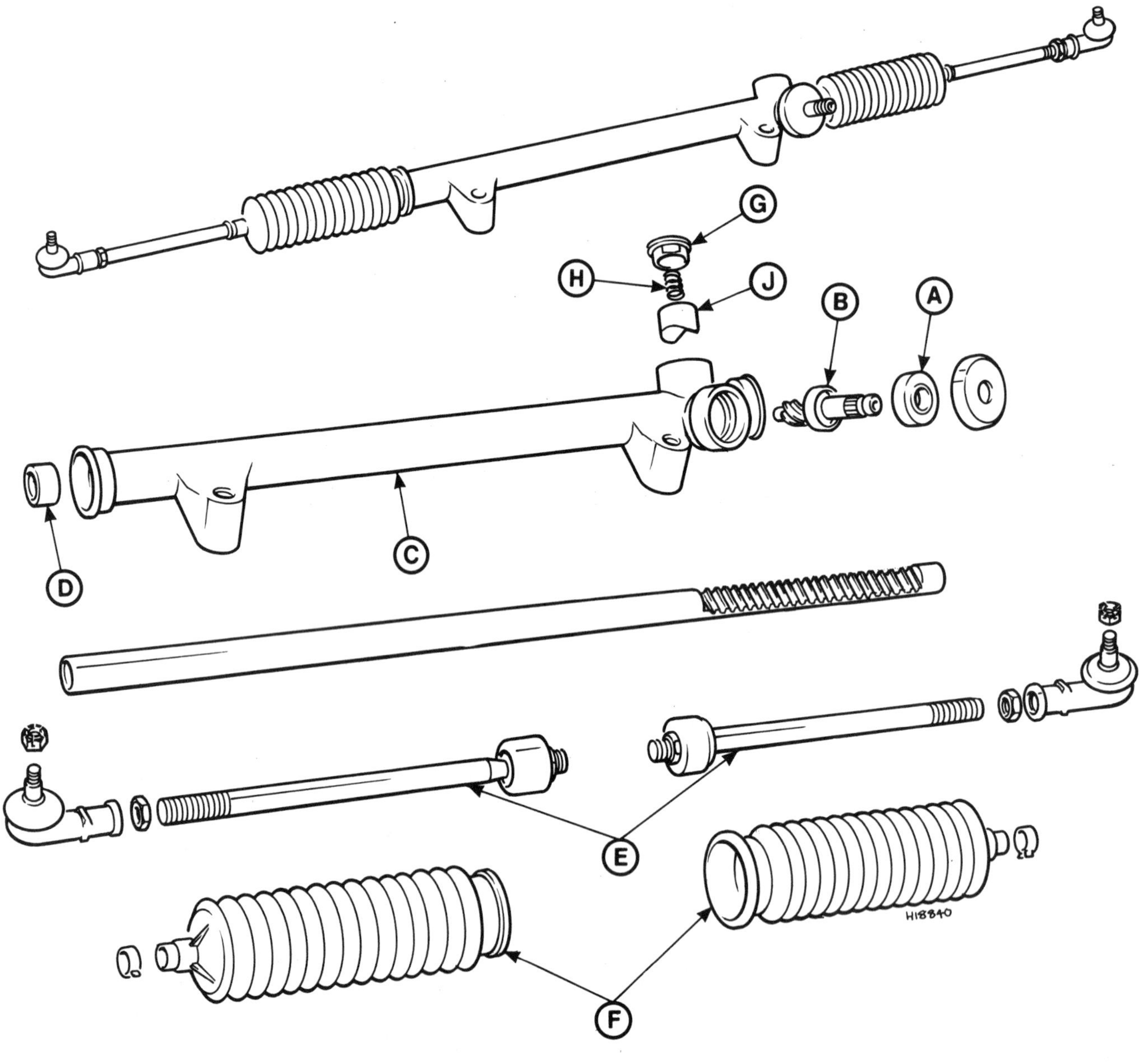

Fig 11.39 Manual steering gear components (Sec 28)

A Pinion retaining nut
B Pinion
C Steering gear housing
D Rack support bush
E Tie-rod
F Gaiter
G Slipper plug
H Spring
J Slipper

around the circumference of the plug.

16 Move the rack fully to the left and grip the rack in a soft-jawed vice as during dismantling.

17 Coat the threads of the tie-rod balljoint with Loctite 270, refit the tie-rod to the rack and tighten the balljoint to the specified torque.

18 Refit the right-hand tie-rod in the same way.

19 Refit the rubber gaiters to the steering gear housing and secure with new clips.

20 Fill the pinion dust cover with semi-fluid grease and refit over the pinion.

29 Power steering gear – removal and refitting

Note: *New power steering fluid hose O-rings will be required when refitting.*

1 The procedure is as described in Section 27 for manual steering gear with the following differences.

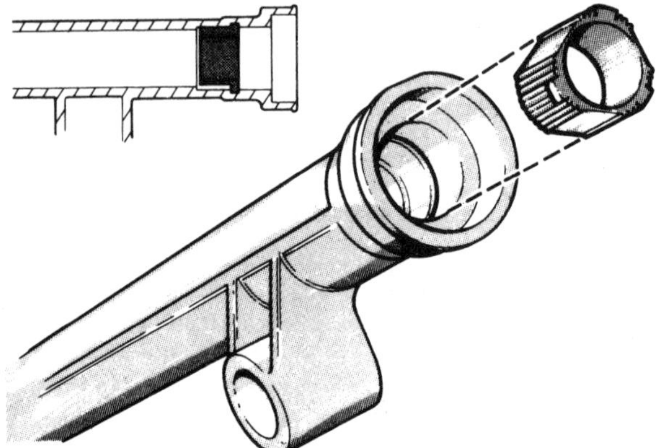

Fig 11.40 Steering rack support bush installation (Sec 28)

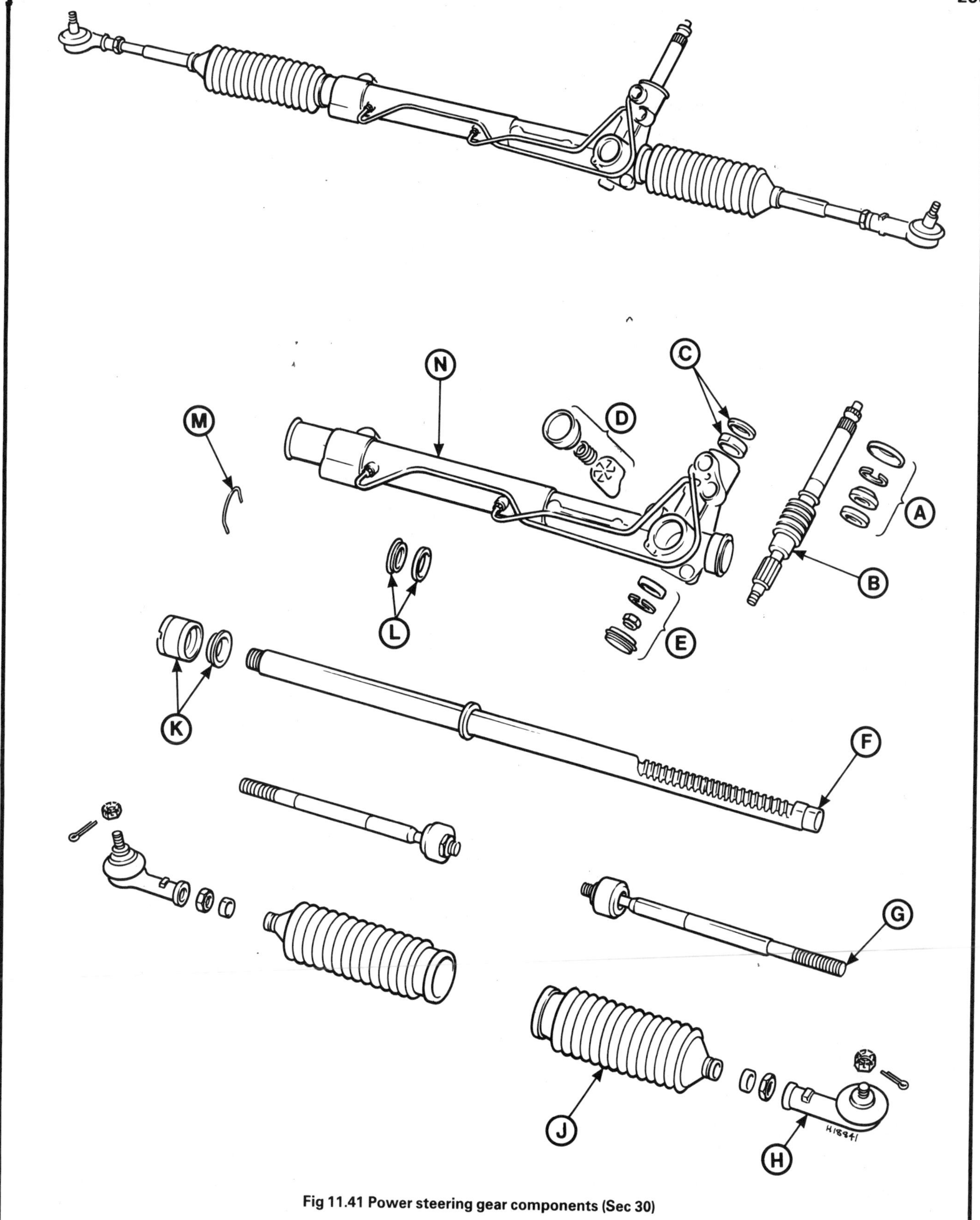

Fig 11.41 Power steering gear components (Sec 30)

A Pinion locknut assembly
B Pinion
C Pinion upper bearing and seal
D Slipper assembly
E Pinion lower bearing assembly
F Rack
G Tie-rod
H Tie-rod end
J Gaiter
K Rack support bearing and seal
L Inner rack seal and support bearing
M Rack support bearing locking wire
N Steering gear housing

2 Before removing the steering gear from the suspension crossmember, place a suitable container beneath the steering gear. Unscrew the single bolt securing the power steering fluid hoses to the pinion housing. Unscrew the hose unions and drain the power steering fluid. Plug the ends of the hoses and the steering gear apertures, or cover them with masking tape to prevent dirt ingress.
3 When refitting the fluid hoses, use new O-rings, and take care not to overtighten the unions. Note that with the unions fully tightened it is still possible to rotate and move the hoses.
4 On completion of refitting, bleed the power steering fluid circuit as described in Section 34.

30 Power steering gear - overhaul

Note: *Before overhauling the steering gear, check the availability and price of spare parts. Renewal of badly worn steering gear may prove a more economical alternative.*
1 Clean the exterior of the steering gear with paraffin and wipe dry.
2 Mount the steering gear in a soft-jawed vice, and place a suitable container under the valve body to catch expelled power steering fluid.
3 Slowly move the steering rack from lock to lock, draining the fluid from the valve body.
4 Proceed as described in Section 28, paragraphs 3 to 6 inclusive.
5 Re-position the steering gear in the vice, and centralise the rack. This can be done by halving the number of turns required to move the rack from lock to lock. Make alignment marks on the pinion and the pinion housing.
6 Prise out the plug from the pinion housing, and unscrew the pinion locknut.
7 Remove the pinion shaft dust cover, remove the circlip from the housing, and withdraw the pinion assembly using a twisting motion. Take care to prevent dirt from entering the housing.
8 Slide the seal and the bearing from the pinion shaft. Do not dismantle the valve assembly.
9 Remove the rack support bearing and seal, by rotating the bearing locking ring anticlockwise until the end of the locking wire is visible in the slot - see Fig. 11.42. Prise the end of the locking wire out of the slot and continue to rotate the locking ring until the wire is freed from the annular groove.
10 Carefully withdraw the rack from the steering gear housing. Note that the remaining power steering fluid will be released as the rack is withdrawn.
11 Remove the inner seal and support bearing from the rack.
12 Remove the pinion lower bearing circlip. Drive the bearing and seal from the pinion housing using a suitable drift.
13 If necessary, the rack support bush can be renewed as described in Section 28, paragraph 9.
14 Drive the pinion seal and plain bush from the pinion housing.
15 Clean all the components and examine them for wear and damage, renewing as necessary. Ensure that the air bypass passage is unobstructed.
16 Renew all seals and bearings as a matter of course, and renew the pinion assembly if there is any damage to the pinion or the valve sleeve.
17 When fitting PTFE seals, immerse them in boiling water for a few seconds before fitting, which will assist the seals in taking up their true shape after refitting.
18 Pack all lipped seals with grease (Calipsol SF3-131, or equivalent) before fitting.
19 Commence reassembly by fitting a new pinion seal, using Ford tool 13-010 or a suitable locally manufactured drift. Fit the plain bush using the same tool.
20 Use stiff paper or card to cover the rack teeth, and fit a new inner seal and support bearing to the rack, working from the toothed end. Seat the seal and bearing by fitting the rack to the steering gear housing.
21 Coat the rack teeth with 40 cc (1.4 fl oz) of semi-fluid grease.
22 Fit a new support bearing, seal and locking wire into the steering gear housing and over the rack. Insert the hooked end of the locking wire into the hole in the groove and drive the locking ring round clockwise until the wire is trapped. Fill the groove in the steering gear housing with grease.
23 Fit the pinion lower bearing and secure it with the circlip.
24 Fit the pinion upper bearing and seal over the pinion shaft. Centralise the rack, as described in paragraph 5, and fit the pinion, aligning the previously made marks on the pinion and housing.
25 Secure the pinion assembly by fitting the circlip in the housing. Pack the pinion shaft dust cover with grease, and locate it over the pinion shaft.
26 Fit the pinion locknut and tighten it to the specified torque. Fit a new plug over the nut.
27 Refit the slipper and spring, and fit the slipper plug after coating its threads with thread-locking fluid.
28 Tighten the slipper plug to the specified torque. Turn the pinion and move the rack from lock to lock, then centralise again.
29 Check the tightness of the slipper plug, and if necessary retighten to the specified torque.
30 Using a piece of string and a spring balance, check that the turning torque of the pinion is not less than 1.4 Nm (1.0 lbf ft).
31 Unscrew the slipper plug by 22° to 27° (approximately one-sixteenth of a turn). Check the pinion turning torque again; it must not exceed 1.7 Nm (1.3 lbf ft). The plug may be unscrewed a further 5° if necessary to achieve the correct turning torque.
32 When adjustment is correct, lock the plug by peening the housing at three points around the circumference of the plug.
33 Proceed as described in Section 28, paragraphs 16 to 20 inclusive.

31 Power steering pump - removal and refitting

Note: *New power steering fluid hose O-rings will be required when refitting.*
1 Place a suitable container under the power steering pump, unscrew the fluid hose unions, and drain the fluid. Ensure that fluid is not allowed to spill onto the alternator.

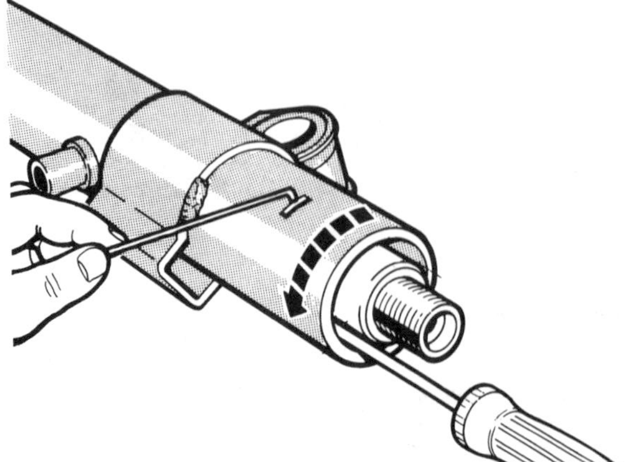

Fig 11.42 Removing the rack support bearing and seal (Sec 30)

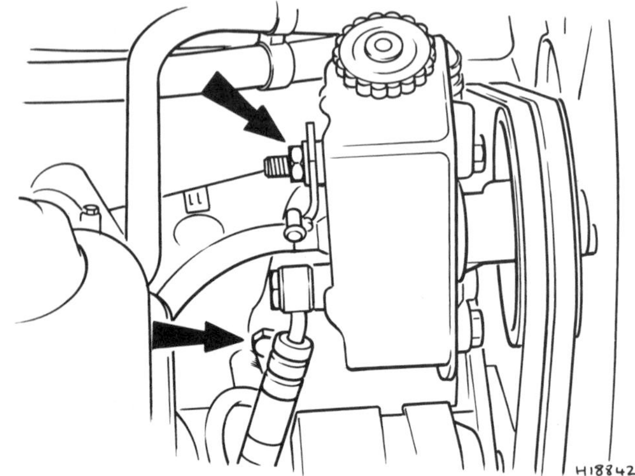

Fig 11.43 Power steering pump rear support bar bolts (arrowed) (Sec 31)

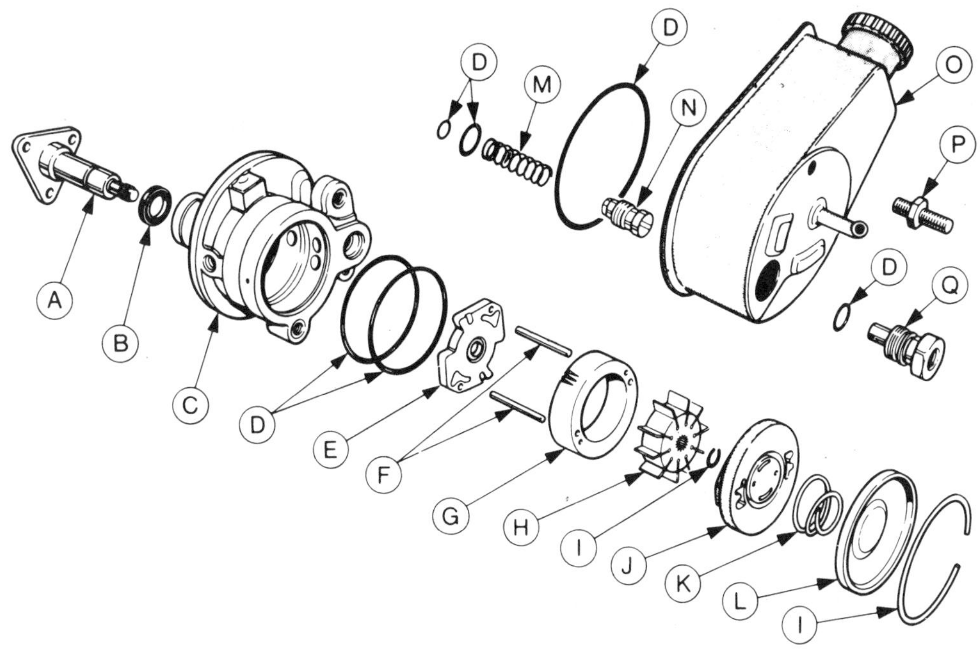

Fig 11.44 Power steering pump components (Sec 32)

A Shaft
B Seal
C Housing
D O-rings
E Thrust plate
F Dowel pins
G Pump ring
H Vanes and rotor
I Retaining rings
J Pressure plate
K Spring
L Endplate
M Flow control spring
N Flow control valve
O Reservoir
P Stud
Q Union

2 Remove the drivebelts as described in Chapter 2. Unbolt the power steering pump pulley if necessary to ease removal.
3 Unbolt the rear support bar from the pump and the engine block.
4 Unbolt the pump from its mounting bracket, and withdraw the pump from the engine.
5 Refitting is a reversal of removal, noting the following points.
6 Refit and tension the drivebelts as described in Chapter 2.
7 When refitting the fluid hoses, use new O-rings, and take care not to overtighten the unions.
8 On completion of refitting, bleed the power steering fluid circuit as described in Section 34.

32 Power steering pump – overhaul

Note: *Before overhauling the power steering pump, check the availability and price of spare parts. Renewal of a badly worn pump may prove a more economical alternative.*

1 Thoroughly clean the outside of the pump and reservoir.
2 Clamp the pump in a vice with protected jaws, shaft side downwards. **Do not** clamp on the reservoir.
3 Remove the mounting stud, the union and the O-ring from the back of the pump. Remove the reservoir from the pump housing by carefully pulling and rocking it free. Retrieve the O-rings from the housing.
4 Insert a pin punch or nail into the hole in the pump housing opposite the flow control valve. Press the punch to compress the endplate retaining ring and lever the ring out with a screwdriver.
5 Remove the endplate, spring and O-ring. If the endplate is not free, rock it gently to release it and the spring will push it up. Remove the pressure plate.
6 Take the pump out of the vice and turn it over. Remove the flow control valve and its spring.
7 Remove the circlip from the pump shaft and push out the shaft. Do not attempt to separate the pulley flange from the shaft.
8 Remove the pump ring, vanes, rotor and thrust plate. Extract the

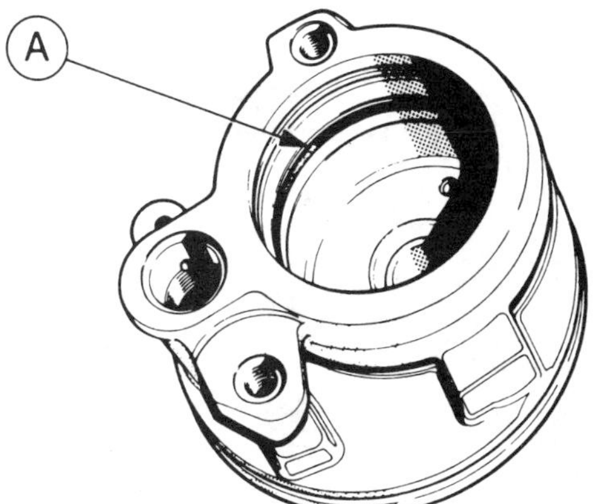

Fig 11.45 Pressure plate O-ring (A) in third groove from rear of housing (Sec 32)

Fig 11.46 Pump ring with arrow (A) uppermost (Sec 32)

pressure plate O-ring.

9 Extract the two dowel pins from the housing and remove the shaft seal, taking care not to damage the seal housing.

10 Remove the magnet and clean it, noting its location for reassembly. Keep it away from ferrous metal filings.

11 Clean all metal components in a suitable solvent and dry them. Scrupulous cleanliness must be observed from now on.

12 Fit a new pump shaft seal to the housing, using a socket or tube and a hammer to drive it home. Refit the shaft.

13 Fit a new pressure plate O-ring into the third groove from the rear of the housing – see Fig. 11.45. Lubricate the O-ring with power steering fluid.

14 Mount the housing in the vice and fit the two dowel pins.

15 Fit the thrust plate and rotor onto the shaft, with the countersunk side of the rotor facing the thrust plate. Make sure the thrust plate holes engage with the dowel pins.

16 Fit the pump ring onto the dowel pins with the arrow on the rim of the ring uppermost – see Fig. 11.46. Fit the ten vanes into the rotor slots, rounded ends outwards. Make sure the vanes slide freely.

17 Refit the circlip to the end of the pump shaft. Refit the magnet in the housing.

18 Lubricate the pressure plate with power steering fluid and fit it over the dowel pins. Make sure the spring seat is uppermost. Press the plate a little way below the O-ring to seat it.

19 Lubricate and fit the endplate O-ring in the second groove from the end. Fit the endplate spring, lubricate the endplate and press it into position so that the retaining ring can be fitted. (It may be necessary to use a G-clamp or similar device to keep the endplate depressed whilst the ring is fitted. Do not depress the plate further than necessary).

20 Fit the endplate retaining ring with its open ends away from the hole used to release it.

21 Refit the flow control valve and spring.

22 The remainder of reassembly is a reversal of the dismantling procedure. Use new O-rings and lubricate them with power steering fluid.

33 Power steering fluid hoses – removal and refitting

Note: *New fluid hose O-rings will be required when refitting.*

1 Clean around the hose unions on the steering gear. Place a suitable container beneath the steering gear, then remove the single bolt securing the hoses to the pinion housing, unscrew the hose unions and drain the power steering fluid.

2 Clean around the hose unions on the pump. Place a suitable container beneath the pump, unscrew the hose unions, and drain any remaining fluid. Ensure that no fluid is allowed to spill onto the alternator.

3 If the hoses are to be left disconnected for a long period of time, plug the ends of the hoses and the apertures in the steering gear and pump, or cover them with masking tape to prevent dirt ingress.

4 Refit in reverse order using new O-rings.

5 On completion top up the fluid and bleed the system as described in Section 34.

34 Power steering fluid circuit – bleeding

1 Unscrew the filler cap from the power steering pump reservoir and top up the fluid level to the maximum mark using the specified fluid.

2 Disconnect the low tension negative lead from the ignition coil and crank the engine several times for two second periods while slowly turning the steering wheel from lock-to-lock. Top up the fluid level if necessary and continue cranking the engine until the fluid is free of air bubbles.

3 Reconnect the coil lead and start the engine. Check the system for leaks.

4 Switch off the engine and refit the filler cap.

5 Drive the vehicle for a few miles to warm up the fluid and expel any remaining air, then stop the engine and make a final fluid level check.

35 Steering gear rubber gaiter – renewal

1 Remove the tie-rod end as described in Section 36.

2 Unscrew and remove the tie-rod end locknut from the tie-rod.

3 Remove the clips and slide the gaiter from the tie-rod and steering gear.

4 Slide the new gaiter over the tie-rod and onto the steering gear. Where applicable, make sure that the gaiter seats in the cut-outs in the tie-rod and steering gear.

5 Secure the gaiter with new clips.

6 Refit the tie-rod end locknut to the tie-rod.

7 Refit the tie-rod end as described in Section 36.

36 Tie-rod end – removal and refitting

Note: *A balljoint separator tool will be required for this operation.*

1 Loosen the relevant front roadwheel nuts, apply the handbrake, jack up the front of the vehicle and support on axle stands.

2 Remove the roadwheel. On P100 models mark the position of the roadwheel in relation to one of the wheel studs before removal.

3 Make alignment marks on the tie-rod and tie-rod end, then loosen the locknut by a quarter of a turn.

4 Extract the split pin and unscrew the castellated nut (photo).

5 Using a balljoint separator tool, release the tie-rod end from the hub carrier (photo).

6 Unscrew the tie-rod end from the tie-rod, noting the number of turns necessary to remove it.

7 Refitting is a reversal of removal, bearing in mind the following points.

8 Screw the tie-rod end onto the tie-rod the number of turns noted during removal.

9 Tighten the nuts to the specified torque, and fit a new split pin to the castellated nut.

10 On P100 models, align the previously made marks on the roadwheel and wheel stud.

36.4 Extracting the split pin from the tie-rod balljoint castellated nut

36.5 Using a balljoint separator tool to release the tie-rod end from the hub carrier

11 On completion, check and if necessary adjust the front wheel alignment as described in Section 37.

37 Front wheel alignment – checking and adjusting

1 Front wheel alignment is defined by camber, castor, steering axis inclination and toe setting. The first three factors are determined in production; only toe can be adjusted in service. Incorrect toe will cause rapid tyre wear.
2 Toe is defined as the amount by which the distance between the front wheels, measured at hub height, differs from the front edges to the rear edges. If the distance between the front edges is less than that at the rear, the wheels are said to toe-in; the opposite case is known as toe-out.
3 To measure toe, it will be necessary to obtain or make a tracking gauge. These are available in motor accessory shops, or one can be made from a length of rigid pipe or bar with some kind of threaded adjustment facility at one end. Many tyre specialists will also check toe free, or for a nominal sum.
4 Before measuring toe, check that all steering and suspension components are undamaged and that tyre pressures are correct. The vehicle must be at approximately kerb weight, with the spare wheel and jack in their normal positions and any abnormal loads removed.
5 Park the vehicle on level ground and bounce it a few times to settle the suspension.
6 Use the tracking gauge to measure the distance between the inside faces of the front wheel rims, at hub height, at the rear of the front wheels. Record this distance; call it measurement'Y' – see Fig. 11.47.
7 Push the vehicle forwards or backwards so that the wheels rotate exactly 180° (half a turn). Measure the distance between the front wheel rims again, this time at the front of the wheels. Record this distance; call it measurement 'X'.
8 Subtract measurement 'X' from measurement 'Y'. If the answer is positive it is the amount of toe-in; if negative it is the amount of toe-out. Permissible values are given in the Specifications.
9 If adjustment is necessary loosen the tie-rod end locknuts and the outer bellows clips, then rotate each tie-rod by equal amounts until the setting is correct. Hold the tie-rod ends in their horizontal position with a spanner while making the adjustment.
10 Tighten the locknuts and outer bellows clips.
11 Provided the tie-rods have been adjusted by equal amounts the steering wheel should be central when moving straight-ahead. The amount of visible thread on each tie-rod should also be equal. If necessary refer to Section 24.

38 Wheels and tyres – general care and maintenance

1 Wheels and tyres should give no real problems in use provided that a close eye is kept on them with regard to excessive wear or damage. To this end, the following points should be noted.
2 Ensure that tyre pressures are checked regularly and maintained correctly. Checking should be carried out with the tyres cold and not immediately after the vehicle has been in use. If the pressures are checked with the tyres hot, an apparently high reading will be obtained owing to heat expansion. Under no circumstances should an attempt be made to reduce the pressures to the quoted cold reading in this instance, or effective underinflation will result.
3 Underinflation will cause overheating of the tyre owing to excessive flexing of the casing, and the tread will not sit correctly on the road surface. This will cause a consequent loss of adhesion and excessive wear, not to mention the danger of sudden tyre failure due to heat build-up.
4 Overinflation will cause rapid wear of the centre part of the tyre tread coupled with reduced adhesion, harsher ride, and the danger of shock damage occurring in the tyre casing.
5 Regularly check the tyres for damage in the form of cuts or bulges, especially in the sidewalls. Remove any nails or stones embedded in the tread before they penetrate the tyre to cause deflation. If removal of a nail *does* reveal that the tyre has been punctured, refit the nail so that its point of penetration is marked. Then immediately change the wheel and have the tyre repaired by a tyre dealer. Do *not* drive on a tyre in such a condition. In many cases a puncture can be simply repaired by the use of an inner tube of the correct size and type. If in any doubt as to the possible consequences of any damage found, consult your local tyre dealer for advice.

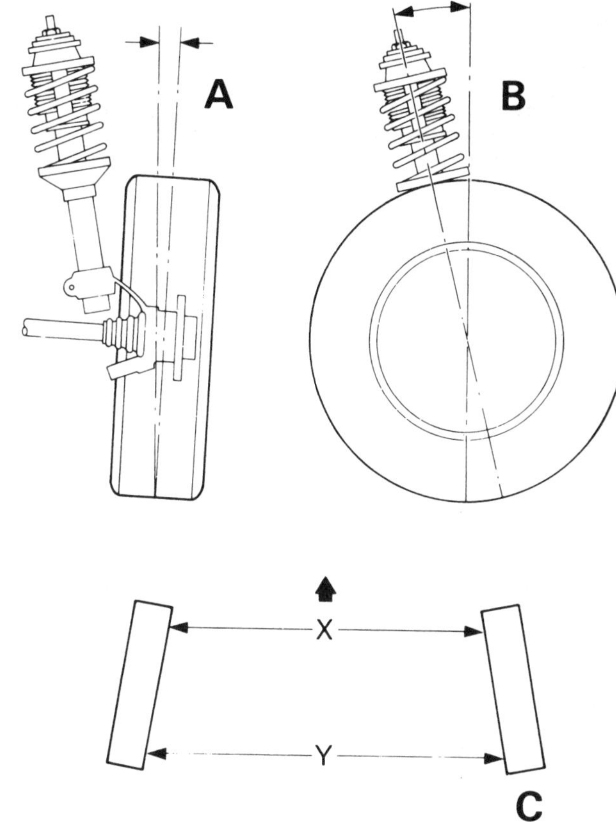

Fig 11.47 Front wheel alignment (Sec 37)

A Camber
B Castor
C Toe setting
For X and Y, see text

6 Periodically remove the wheels and clean any dirt or mud from the inside and outside surfaces. Examine the wheel rims for signs of rusting, corrosion or other damage. Light alloy wheels are easily damaged by 'kerbing' whilst parking, and similarly steel wheels may become dented or buckled. Renewal of the wheel is very often the only course of remedial action possible.
7 The balance of each wheel and tyre assembly should be maintained to avoid excessive wear, not only to the tyres but also to the steering and suspension components. Wheel imbalance is normally signified by vibration through the vehicle's bodyshell, although in many cases it is particularly noticeable through the steering wheel. Conversely, it should be noted that wear or damage in suspension or steering components may cause excessive tyre wear. Out-of-round or out-of-true tyres, damaged wheels and wheel bearing wear/maladjustment also fall into this category. Balancing will not usually cure vibration caused by such wear.
8 Wheel balancing may be carried out with the wheel either on or off the vehicle. If balanced on the vehicle, ensure that the wheel-to-hub relationship is marked in some way prior to subsequent wheel removal so that it may be refitted in its original position.
9 General tyre wear is influenced to a large degree by driving style – harsh braking and acceleration or fast cornering will all produce more rapid tyre wear. Interchanging of tyres may result in more even wear, but this should only be carried out where there is no mix of tyre types on the vehicle. However, it is worth bearing in mind that if this is completely effective, the added expense of replacing a complete set of tyres simultaneously is incurred, which may prove financially restrictive for many owners.
10 Front tyres may wear unevenly as a result of wheel misalignment. The front wheels should always be correctly aligned according to the settings specified by the vehicle manufacturer.

11 Legal restrictions apply to the mixing of tyre types on a vehicle. Basically this means that a vehicle must not have tyres of differing construction on the same axle. Although it is not recommended to mix tyre types between front axle and rear axle, the only legally permissible combination is crossply at the front and radial at the rear. When mixing radial ply tyres, textile braced radials must always go on the front axle, with steel braced radials at the rear. An obvious disadvantage of such mixing is the necessity to carry two spare tyres to avoid contravening the law in the event of a puncture.

12 In the UK, the Motor Vehicles Construction and Use Regulations apply to many aspects of tyre fitting and usage. It is suggested that a copy of these regulations is obtained from your local police if in doubt as to the current legal requirements with regard to tyre condition, minimum tread depth, etc.

39 Fault diagnosis – suspension and steering

Symptom	Reason(s)
Excessive play at steering wheel	Worn tie-rod end balljoints Worn lower suspension arm balljoints Worn intermediate shaft coupling Worn steering gear
Vehicle wanders or pulls to one side	Uneven tyre pressures Incorrect wheel alignment Worn tie-rod end balljoints Worn lower suspension arm balljoints Faulty shock absorber Accident damage
Steering heavy or stiff	Low tyre pressures Seized balljoint Seized strut top bearing Incorrect wheel alignment Steering gear damaged or lacking lubricant Power steering fault (see below)
Lack of power assistance	Fluid level low Pump drivebelt slack or broken Pump or steering gear defective
Wheel wobble and vibration	Wheel nuts loose Wheels out of balance or damaged Wheel bearings worn Worn tie-rod end balljoints Worn lower suspension arm balljoints Faulty shock absorber
Excessive tyre wear	Incorrect tyre pressures Wheels out of balance Incorrect wheel alignment Faulty shock absorbers Unsympathetic driving style

Note: *This Section is not intended as an exhaustive guide to fault diagnosis, but summarises the more common faults which may be encountered during a vehicle's life. Consult a dealer for more detailed advice.*

Chapter 12 Bodywork, trim and fittings

For modifications, and information applicable to later models, see Supplement at end of manual

Contents

Specifications

Air conditioning system

Compressor drivebelt tension ... 10.0 mm (0.4 in) deflection at the midpoint of the belt's longest run under firm thumb pressure

Torque wrench settings

	Nm	lbf ft
Front seat belt stalk-to-seat bolts	24 to 28	18 to 22
Seat belt anchor bolts	29 to 41	22 to 30
Seat belt inertia reel securing bolts	29 to 41	22 to 30
Seat mounting bolts	25 to 32	18 to 24
Cab safety grille securing bolts (P100 models)	20 to 27	15 to 20
Rear bump stop securing nuts (P100 models)	8 to 11	6 to 8
Cargo area-to-chassis bolts (P100 models)	40 to 50	29 to 37
Tailboard hinge securing screws (P100 models)	20 to 25	15 to 18
Air conditioning compressor-to-bracket bolts	65 to 75	48 to 55
Air conditioning compressor bracket-to-engine bolts:		
M10	85 to 92	63 to 68
M12	110 to 120	81 to 89
Air conditioning condenser fan assembly-to-condenser bolts:		
Models up to 1987	2 to 3	1 to 2
Models from 1987	8 to 11	6 to 8
Air conditioning condenser securing bolts (models from 1987)	27 to 33	20 to 24

1 General description

The bodyshell is of all-steel welded construction. The model range includes 4-door Saloon, 3 and 5-door Hatchback, 5-door Estate, and 2-door Pick-up body styles.

The body is of energy-absorbing monocoque construction, with a separate load-bearing rear chassis frame on P100 Pick-up models.

Corrosion protection is applied to all new vehicles, and includes zinc phosphate dipping of the body panels, and wax injection of box sections and doors.

All models have flush direct-glazed fixed glass panels, and integrated polycarbonate bumpers.

All body panels are welded, including the front wings, so it is recommended that major body damage repairs are entrusted to a dealer.

All models are fitted with a comprehensive heating and ventilation system. Warm air is provided by passing cold air over the heater matrix, through which warm engine coolant is pumped. An air conditioning system is available on certain models.

A wide range of interior equipment and trim options are available depending on model. The procedures given in this Chapter apply to original equipment fitments, and do not cover after-market products.

2 Maintenance – bodywork, underside and fittings

1 The general condition of a vehicle's bodywork is the one thing that significantly affects its value. Maintenance is easy but needs to be regular. Neglect, particularly after minor damage, can lead quickly to further deterioration and costly repair bills. It is important also to keep watch on those parts of the vehicle not immediately visible, for instance the underside, inside all the wheel arches and the lower part of the engine compartment.

2 The basic maintenance routine for the bodywork is washing – preferably with a lot of water, from a hose. This will remove all the loose solids which may have stuck to the vehicle. It is important to flush these off in such a way as to prevent grit from scratching the finish. The wheel arches and underframe need washing in the same way to remove any accumulated mud which will retain moisture and tend to encourage rust. Paradoxically enough, the best time to clean the underframe and wheel arches is in wet weather when the mud is thoroughly wet and soft. In very wet weather the underframe is usually cleaned of large accumulations automatically and this is a good time for inspection.

3 Periodically, except on vehicles with a wax-based underbody protective coating, it is a good idea to have the whole of the underframe of the vehicle steam cleaned, engine compartment included, so that a thorough inspection can be carried out to see what minor repairs and renovations are necessary. Steam cleaning is available at many garages and is necessary for removal of the accumulation of oily grime which sometimes is allowed to become thick in certain areas. If steam cleaning facilities are not available, there are one or two excellent grease solvents available, such as Holts Engine Cleaner or Holts Foambrite, which can be brush applied. The dirt can then be simply hosed off. Note that these methods should not be used on vehicles with wax-based underbody protective coating or the coating will be removed. Such vehicles should be inspected annually, preferably just prior to winter, when the underbody should be washed down and any damage to the wax coating repaired using Holts Undershield. Ideally, a completely fresh coat should be applied. It would also be worth considering the use of such wax-based protection for injection into door panels, sills, box sections, etc, as an additional safeguard against rust damage where such protection is not provided by the vehicle manufacturer.

4 After washing paintwork, wipe off with a chamois leather to give an unspotted clear finish. A coat of clear protective wax polish, like the many excellent Turtle Wax polishes, will give added protection against chemical pollutants in the air. If the paintwork sheen has dulled or oxidised, use a cleaner/polisher combination such as Turtle Extra to restore the brilliance of the shine. This requires a little effort, but such dulling is usually caused because regular washing has been neglected. Care needs to be taken with metallic paintwork, as special non-abrasive cleaner/polisher is required to avoid damage to the finish. Always check that the door and ventilator opening drain holes and pipes are completely clear so that water can be drained out (photos). Bright work should be treated in the same way as paint work. Windscreens and windows can be kept clear of the smeary film which often appears by the use of a proprietary glass cleaner, like Holts Mixra. Never use any form of wax or other body or chromium polish on glass.

5 At the intervals specified in the *'Routine maintenance'* Section at the beginning of this manual, check the operation of the door locks and check straps, and lubricate the hinges with a little oil. Also lubricate the hinges of the bonnet and boot lid or tailgate, as applicable, and the bonnet release mechanism.

3 Maintenance – upholstery and carpets

Mats and carpets should be brushed or vacuum cleaned regularly to keep them free of grit. If they are badly stained remove them from the vehicle for scrubbing or sponging and make quite sure they are dry before refitting. Seats and interior trim panels can be kept clean by wiping with a damp cloth and Turtle Wax Carisma. If they do become stained (which can be more apparent on light coloured upholstery) use a little liquid detergent and a soft nail brush to scour the grime out of the grain of the material. Do not forget to keep the headlining clean in the same way as the upholstery. When using liquid cleaners inside the vehicle do not over-wet the surfaces being cleaned. Excessive damp could get into the seams and padded interior causing stains, offensive odours or even rot. If the inside of the vehicle gets wet accidentally it is worthwhile taking some trouble to dry it out properly, particularly where carpets are involved. *Do not leave oil or electric heaters inside the vehicle for this purpose.*

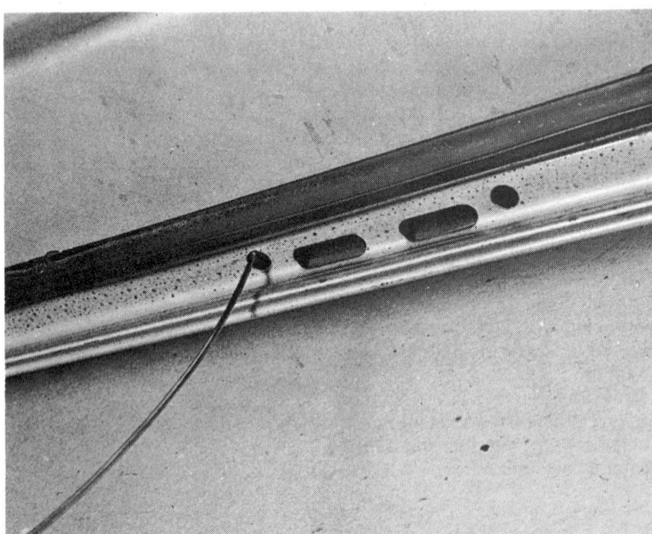

2.4A Clearing a door drain hole

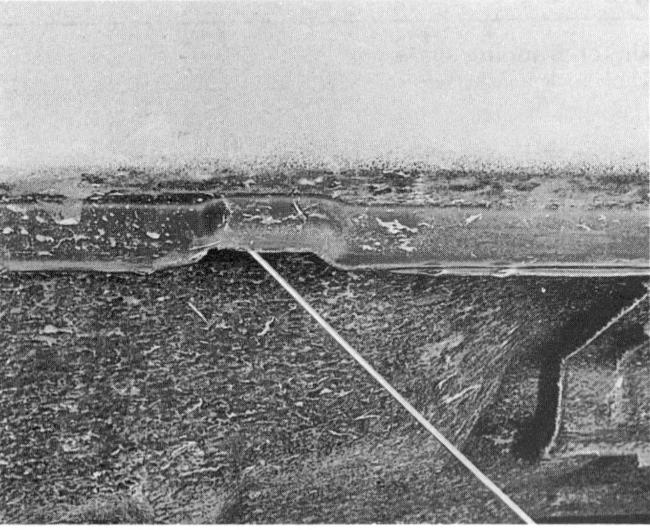

2.4B Clearing a sill drain hole

4 Minor body damage – repair

The colour bodywork repair photographic sequences between pages 32 and 33 illustrate the operations detailed in the following sub-sections.

Note: *For more detailed information about bodywork repair, the Haynes Publishing Group publish a book by Lindsay Porter called The Car Bodywork Repair Manual. This incorporates information on such aspects as rust treatment, painting and glass fibre repairs, as well as details on more ambitious repairs involving welding and panel beating.*

Repair of minor scratches in bodywork

If the scratch is very superficial, and does not penetrate to the metal of the bodywork, repair is very simple. Lightly rub the area of the scratch with a paintwork renovator like Turtle Wax New Colour Back, or a very fine cutting paste like Holts Body + Plus Rubbing Compound, to remove loose paint from the scratch and to clear the surrounding bodywork of wax polish. Rinse the area with clean water.

Apply touch-up paint, such as Holts Dupli-Color Color Touch or a paint film like Holts Autofilm, to the scratch using a fine paint brush; continue to apply fine layers of paint until the surface of the paint in the scratch is level with the surrounding paintwork. Allow the new paint at least two weeks to harden: then blend it into the surrounding paintwork by rubbing the scratch area with a paintwork renovator or a very fine cutting paste, such as Holts Body + Plus Rubbing Compound or Turtle Wax New Color Back. Finally, apply wax polish from one of the Turtle Wax range of wax polishes.

Where the scratch has penetrated right through to the metal of the bodywork, causing the metal to rust, a different repair technique is required. Remove any loose rust from the bottom of the scratch with a penknife, then apply rust inhibiting paint, such as Turtle Wax Rust Master, to prevent the formation of rust in the future. Using a rubber or nylon applicator fill the scratch with bodystopper paste, like Holts Body + Plus Knifing Putty. If required, this paste can be mixed with cellulose thinners, such as Holts Body + Plus Cellulose Thinners, to provide a very thin paste which is ideal for filling narrow scratches. Before the stopper-paste in the scratch hardens, wrap a piece of smooth cotton rag around the top of a finger. Dip the finger in cellulose thinners, such as Holts Body + Plus Cellulose Thinners; and then quickly sweep it across the surface of the stopper-paste in the scratch; this will ensure that the surface of the stopper-paste is slightly hollowed. The scratch can now be painted over as described earlier in this Section.

Repair of dents in bodywork

When deep denting of the vehicle's bodywork has taken place, the first task is to pull the dent out, until the affected bodywork almost attains its original shape. There is little point in trying to restore the original shape completely, as the metal in the damaged area will have stretched on impact and cannot be reshaped fully to its original contour. It is better to bring the level of the dent up to a point which is about $\frac{1}{8}$ in (3 mm) below the level of the surrounding bodywork. In cases where the dent is very shallow anyway, it is not worth trying to pull it out at all. If the underside of the dent is accessible, it can be hammered out gently from behind, using a mallet with a wooden or plastic head. Whilst doing this, hold a suitable block of wood firmly against the outside of the panel to absorb the impact from the hammer blows and thus prevent a large area of the bodywork from being 'belled-out'.

Should the dent be in a section of the bodywork which has a double skin or some other factor making it inaccessible from behind, a different technique is called for. Drill several small holes through the metal inside the area – particularly in the deeper section. Then screw long self-tapping screws into the holes just sufficiently for them to gain a good purchase in the metal. Now the dent can be pulled out by pulling on the protruding heads of the screws with a pair of pliers.

The next stage of the repair is the removal of the paint from the damaged area, and from an inch or so of the surrounding 'sound' bodywork. This is accomplished most easily by using a wire brush or abrasive pad on a power drill, although it can be done just as effectively by hand using sheets of abrasive paper. To complete the preparation for filling, score the surface of the bare metal with a screwdriver or the tang of a file, or alternatively, drill small holes in the affected area. This will provide a really good 'key' for the filler paste.

To complete the repair see the Section on filling and re-spraying.

Repair of rust holes or gashes in bodywork

Remove all paint from the affected area and from an inch or so of the surrounding 'sound' bodywork, using an abrasive pad or a wire brush on a power drill. If these are not available a few sheets of abrasive paper will do the job just as effectively. With the paint removed you will be able to gauge the severity of the corrosion and therefore decide whether to renew the whole panel (if this is possible) or to repair the affected area. New body panels are not as expensive as most people think and it is often quicker and more satisfactory to fit a new panel than to attempt to repair large areas of corrosion.

Remove all fittings from the affected area except those which will act as a guide to the original shape of the damaged bodywork (eg headlamp shells etc). Then, using tin snips or a hacksaw blade, remove all loose metal and any other metal badly affected by corrosion. Hammer the edges of the hole inwards in order to create a slight depression for the filler paste.

Wire brush the affected area to remove the powdery rust from the surface of the remaining metal. Paint the affected area with rust inhibiting paint like Turtle Wax Rust Master; if the back of the rusted area is accessible treat this also.

Before filling can take place it will be necessary to block the hole in some way. This can be achieved by the use of aluminium or plastic mesh, or aluminium tape.

Aluminium or plastic mesh or glass fibre matting, such as the Holts Body + Plus Glass Fibre Matting, is probably the best material to use for a large hole. Cut a piece to the approximate size and shape of the hole to be filled, then position it in the hole so that its edges are below the level of the surrounding bodywork. It can be retained in position by several blobs of filler paste around its periphery.

Aluminium tape should be used for small or very narrow holes. Pull a piece off the roll and trim it to the approximate size and shape required, then pull off the backing paper (if used) and stick the tape over the hole; it can be overlapped if the thickness of one piece is insufficient. Burnish down the edges of the tape with the handle of a screwdriver or similar, to ensure that the tape is securely attached to the metal underneath.

Bodywork repairs – filling and re-spraying

Before using this Section, see the Sections on dent, deep scratch, rust holes and gash repairs.

Many types of bodyfiller are available, but generally speaking those proprietary kits which contain a tin of filler paste and a tube of resin hardener are best for this type of repair, like Holts Body + Plus or Holts No Mix which can be used directly from the tube. A wide, flexible plastic or nylon applicator will be found invaluable for imparting a smooth and well contoured finish to the surface of the filler.

Mix up a little filler on a clean piece of card or board – measure the hardener carefully (follow the maker's instructions on the pack) otherwise the filler will set too rapidly or too slowly. Alternatively, Holts No Mix can be used straight from the tube without mixing, but daylight is required to cure it. Using the applicator apply the filler paste to the prepared area; draw the applicator across the surface of the filler to achieve the correct contour and to level the filler surface. As soon as a contour that approximates to the correct one is achieved, stop working the paste – if you carry on too long the paste will become sticky and begin to 'pick up' on the applicator. Continue to add thin layers of filler paste at twenty-minute intervals until the level of the filler is just proud of the surrounding bodywork.

Once the filler has hardened, excess can be removed using a metal plane or file. From then on, progressively finer grades of abrasive paper should be used, starting with a 40 grade production paper and finishing with 400 grade wet-and-dry paper. Always wrap the abrasive paper around a flat rubber, cork, or wooden block – otherwise the surface of the filler will not be completely flat. During the smoothing of the filler surface the wet-and-dry paper should be periodically rinsed in water. This will ensure that a very smooth finish is imparted to the filler at the final stage.

At this stage the 'dent' should be surrounded by a ring of bare metal, which in turn should be encircled by the finely 'feathered' edge of the good paintwork. Rinse the repair area with clean water, until all of the dust produced by the rubbing-down operation has gone.

Spray the whole repair area with a light coat of primer, either Holts Body + Plus Grey or Red Oxide Primer – this will show up any imperfections in the surface of the filler. Repair these imperfections with fresh filler paste or bodystopper, and once more smooth the surface with abrasive paper. If bodystopper is used, it can be mixed with cellulose thinners to form a really thin paste which is ideal for filling small holes.

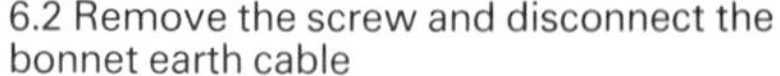

6.2 Remove the screw and disconnect the bonnet earth cable

6.4 Lifting the bonnet from the vehicle

6.9 Adjustable bonnet rubber bump stop

Repeat this spray and repair procedure until you are satisfied that the surface of the filler, and the feathered edge of the paintwork are perfect. Clean the repair area with clean water and allow to dry fully.

The repair area is now ready for final spraying. Paint spraying must be carried out in a warm, dry, windless and dust free atmosphere. This condition can be created artificially if you have access to a large indoor working area, but if you are forced to work in the open, you will have to pick your day very carefully. If you are working indoors, dousing the floor in the work area with water will help to settle the dust which would otherwise be in the atmosphere. If the repair area is confined to one body panel, mask off the surrounding panels; this will help to minimise the effects of a slight mis-match in paint colours. Bodywork fittings (eg chrome strips, door handles etc) will also need to be masked off. Use genuine masking tape and several thicknesses of newspaper for the masking operations.

Before commencing to spray, agitate the aerosol can thoroughly, then spray a test area (an old tin, or similar) until the technique is mastered. Cover the repair area with a thick coat of primer; the thickness should be built up using several thin layers of paint rather than one thick one. Using 400 grade wet-and-dry paper, rub down the surface of the primer until it is really smooth. While doing this, the work area should be thoroughly doused with water, and the wet-and-dry paper periodically rinsed in water. Allow to dry before spraying on more paint.

Spray on the top coat, using Holts Dupli-Color Autospray, again building up the thickness by using several thin layers of paint. Start spraying in the centre of the repair area and then work outwards, with a side-to-side motion, until the whole repair area and about 2 inches of the surrounding original paintwork is covered. Remove all masking material 10 to 15 minutes after spraying on the final coat of paint.

Allow the new paint at least two weeks to harden, then, using a paintwork renovator or a very fine cutting paste such as Turtle Wax New Color Back or Holts Body + Plus Rubbing Compound, blend the edges of the paint into the existing paintwork. Finally, apply wax polish.

Plastic components

With the use of more and more plastic body components by the vehicle manufacturers (eg bumpers, spoilers, and in some cases major body panels), rectification of more serious damage to such items has become a matter of either entrusting repair work to a specialist in this field, or renewing complete components. Repair of such damage by the DIY owner is not really feasible owing to the cost of the equipment and materials required for effecting such repairs. The basic technique involves making a groove along the line of the crack in the plastic using a rotary burr in a power drill. The damaged part is then welded back together by using a hot air gun to heat up and fuse a plastic filler rod into the groove. Any excess plastic is then removed and the area rubbed down to a smooth finish. It is important that a filler rod of the correct plastic is used, as body components can be made of a variety of different types (eg polycarbonate, ABS, polypropylene).

Damage of a less serious nature (abrasions, minor cracks etc) can be repaired by the DIY owner using a two-part epoxy filler repair material like Holts Body + Plus or Holts No Mix which can be used directly from the tube. Once mixed in equal proportions (or applied directly from the tube in the case of Holts No Mix),this is used in similar fashion to the bodywork filler used on metal panels. The filler is usually cured in twenty to thirty minutes, ready for sanding and painting.

If the owner is renewing a complete component himself, or if he has repaired it with epoxy filler, he will be left with the problem of finding a suitable paint for finishing which is compatible with the type of plastic used. At one time the use of a universal paint was not possible owing to the complex range of plastics encountered in body component applications. Standard paints, generally speaking, will not bond to plastic or rubber satisfactorily, but Holts Professional Spraymatch paints to match any plastic or rubber finish can be obtained from dealers. However, it is now possible to obtain a plastic body parts finishing kit which consists of a pre-primer treatment, a primer and coloured top coat. Full instructions are normally supplied with a kit, but basically the method of use is to first apply the pre-primer to the component concerned and allow it to dry for up to 30 minutes. Then the primer is applied and left to dry for about an hour before finally applying the special coloured top coat. The result is a correctly coloured component where the paint will flex with the plastic or rubber, a property that standard paint does not normally possess.

5 Major body damage – repair

Where serious damage has occurred or large areas need renewal due to neglect, it means certainly that completely new sections or panels will need welding in and this is best left to professionals. If the damage is due to impact, it will also be necessary to completely check the alignment of the bodyshell structure. Due to the principle of construction, the strength and shape of the whole car can be affected by damage to one part. In such instances the services of a Ford agent with specialist checking jigs are essential. If a body is left misaligned, it is first of all dangerous as the car will not handle properly, and secondly uneven stresses will be imposed on the steering, engine and transmission, causing abnormal wear or complete failure. Tyre wear may also be excessive.

6 Bonnet – removal and refitting

1 Support the bonnet in its open position, and place protective covers (old rags or cardboard) beneath the corners of the bonnet, and over the front wings to prevent damage to the paintwork.

2 Remove the screw and disconnect the earth strap from the rear left-hand edge of the bonnet (photo). Where applicable, disconnect the wiring from the underbonnet lamp.

3 Mark the location of the hinges on the sides of the bonnet with a soft pencil or masking tape, then loosen the four hinge bolts.

4 With the help of an assistant, remove the bolts and lift the bonnet from the vehicle (photo).

5 If required, the underbonnet insulation can be removed by prising out the two-piece plastic securing clips.

6 Refitting is a reversal of removal, bearing in mind the following points.

7 Adjust the hinges to their original marked positions before tightening the bolts.

8 On completion, check that the bonnet is central within its aperture and aligned with the surrounding bodywork. Re-adjust the hinges to give satisfactory alignment if necessary.

9 Check that the bonnet lock striker engages fully in the lock, and if

necessary adjust the position of the lock striker and/or the height of the bonnet rubber bump stops (photo).

7 Bonnet lock release cable – removal and refitting

1 Working inside the vehicle, remove the three retaining screws, and withdraw the lower steering column shroud.
2 Remove the retaining screw, and withdraw the release cable bracket from the steering column.
3 Working in the engine compartment, pull the cable sheath end fitting from its bracket, and release the cable end fitting from the lock lever (photo).
4 Release the cable from the clips in the engine compartment.
5 Pull the cable through the bulkhead into the passenger compartment, taking care not to lose the bulkhead grommet.
6 Refitting is a reversal of removal, but ensure that the grommet is correctly located in the bulkhead, and that the cable is free from sharp bends and kinks. There should be a small amount of free play at the lock end of the cable – if necessary re-route the cable to achieve this condition.
7 Note that should the release cable snap while the bonnet is shut, the bonnet may be opened as follows.
8 Apply the handbrake, jack up the front of the vehicle and support on axle stands.
9 Using an inspection lamp or torch, look up between the radiator and the radiator grille panel and locate the circular hole below the bonnet lock (photo).
10 Insert a screwdriver through the hole so that it passes to the right of the lock striker. Twist or lever the lock sliding plate to the right until the striker is released. The bonnet can now be opened.

8 Bonnet lock – removal and refitting

Models up to 1987

1 Working in the engine compartment, disconnect the cable from the bonnet lock by pulling the cable sheath end fitting from its bracket, then releasing the end fitting from the lock lever.
2 Remove the three securing screws and withdraw the lock from the front panel.
3 Refitting is a reversal of removal.

Models from 1987

4 Remove the radiator grille panel as described in Section 30.
5 Disconnect the cable from the bonnet lock by pulling the cable sheath end fitting from its bracket, then releasing the end fitting from the lock lever.
6 Detach the bracing strut from the lock by removing the screw, then remove the two securing screws and withdraw the lock from the front panel.
7 Refitting is a reversal of removal.

9 Boot lid (Saloon models) – removal and refitting

1 Open the boot lid, and place protective covers (old rags or cardboard) beneath the corners of the lid, and over the rear wings to prevent damage to the paintwork.
2 Where applicable, disconnect the wiring from the lock solenoid and 'boot lid ajar' sensor, after disconnecting the battery negative lead.
3 Release the wiring loom grommets, taking care not to lose them, then tie string to the wiring loom(s), and pull the loom(s) through the boot lid. Leave the string(s) in position in the boot lid to aid refitting of the loom(s).
4 Mark the location of the hinges on the underside of the lid using a soft pencil or masking tape, then loosen the four hinge bolts.
5 With the help of an assistant, remove the bolts and lift the boot lid from the vehicle.
6 If desired, the lock and, where applicable, the solenoid and 'boot lid ajar' sensor can be removed with reference to Section 10.
7 Refitting is a reversal of removal, bearing in mind the following points.
8 Adjust the hinges to their original marked positions before tightening the bolts.
9 On completion, check that the boot lid is central within its aperture and aligned with the surrounding bodywork. Re-adjust the hinges to give satisfactory alignment if necessary.
10 Check that the lock striker engages fully in the lock, and if necessary adjust the position of the lock striker.

10 Boot lid lock (Saloon models) – removal and refitting

1 With the boot lid raised, remove the lock barrel retaining clip.
2 Where applicable, disconnect the operating lever from the central locking solenoid/motor, then withdraw the lock barrel. Central locking

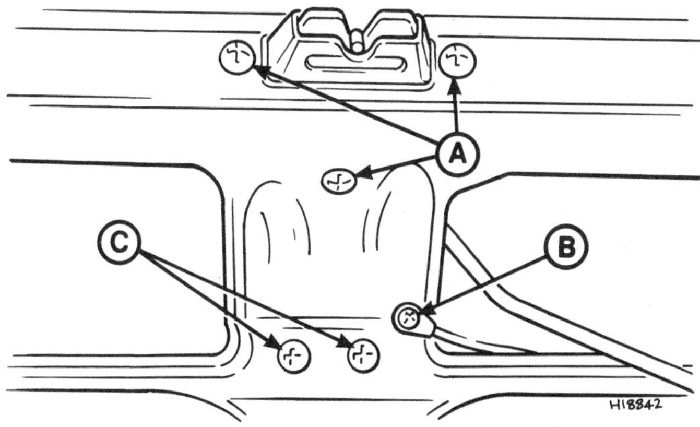

Fig 12.1 Boot lid lock – Saloon models (Sec 10)

A Lock retaining screws
B Earth lead
C Reinforcing plate screws

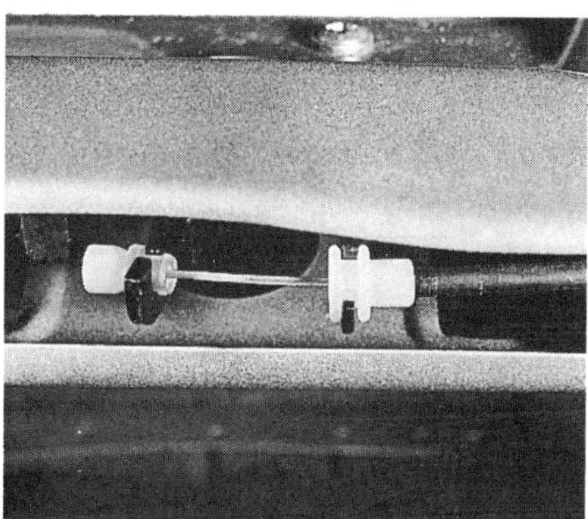
7.3 Bonnet lock release cable end fittings – models up to 1987

7.9 Access hole (arrowed) below bonnet lock

11.5 Prising out a tailgate strut retaining clip

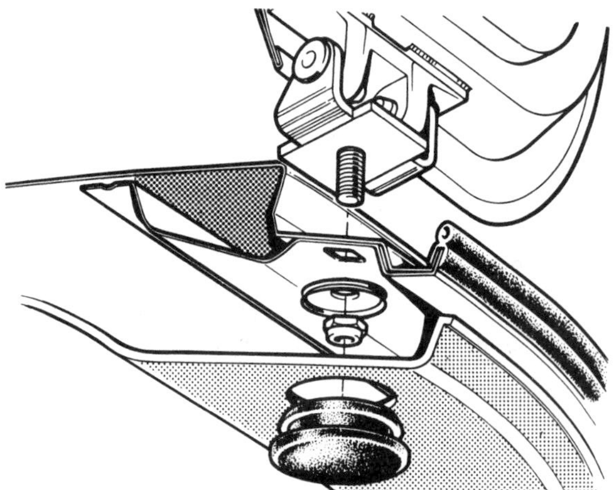

Fig 12.2 Tailgate hinge assembly – Hatchback and Estate models (Sec 11)

solenoid/motor removal and refitting is covered in Chapter 13.
3 Remove the three retaining screws from the lock assembly, if necessary loosening the reinforcing plate – see Fig. 12.1.
4 Where applicable, disconnect the battery negative lead, the earth lead from the bootlid and the 'boot lid ajar' sensor wiring plug. Removal and refitting of the 'boot lid ajar' sensor is covered in Chapter 13. Unclip the luggage compartment light switch from the lock assembly, where applicable.
5 Withdraw the lock assembly from the boot lid.
6 Commence refitting by inserting the lock assembly and loosely refitting the retaining screws.
7 Insert the lock barrel, where applicable reconnecting the operating lever to the solenoid, and refit the retaining clip.
8 Tighten the lock assembly retaining screws, and where applicable reconnect the earth lead and 'boot lid ajar' sensor wiring plug, and the battery negative lead.
9 If the reinforcing plate was loosened during removal, tighten the retaining screws.

11 Tailgate (Hatchback and Estate models) – removal and refitting

1 Disconnect the battery negative lead.
2 Open the tailgate and prise out the trim panel using a wide-bladed screwdriver.
3 Disconnect the wiring from the heated rear window, rear wash/wipe, interior light, lock solenoid and 'tailgate ajar' sensor, as applicable. Disconnect the washer fluid hose where applicable; be prepared for fluid spillage.
4 Release the wiring loom/hose grommet(s) taking care not to lose it/them, then tie string to the wiring loom(s)/hose, and pull the loom(s)/hose through the tailgate. Leave the string(s) in position in the tailgate to aid refitting of the loom(s)/hose.
5 Have an assistant support the tailgate, then disconnect the support struts by prising out the retaining clips. Do not remove the clips completely, just raise them by a maximum of 4.0 mm (0.16 in) and then pull the struts off their mountings (photo).
6 Prise out the hinge fixing covers from the headlining, unscrew the hinge nuts and washers, and with the aid of the assistant, withdraw the tailgate from the vehicle.
7 Refitting is a reversal of removal, but do not fully tighten the hinge nuts until the tailgate is positioned centrally in its aperture. If necessary, adjust the position of the lock striker so that it engages fully in the lock.

12 Tailgate lock (Hatchback and Estate models) – removal and refitting

1 Open the tailgate and prise out the trim panel using a wide-bladed screwdriver.
2 Remove the lock barrel retaining clip, and where applicable disconnect the operating lever from the central locking solenoid/motor, then withdraw the lock barrel. Central locking solenoid/motor removal and refitting is covered in Chapter 13.
3 Remove the two securing screws and detach the lock barrel support bracket from the tailgate.
4 Where applicable, disconnect the battery negative lead, the earth lead from the tailgate and the 'tailgate ajar' sensor wiring plug. Unclip the luggage compartment light switch from the lock assembly, where applicable.
5 Remove the securing screws and withdraw the lock assembly.
6 Refitting is a reversal of removal, but do not tighten the lock barrel support bracket screws until the lock barrel has been fitted.

13 Tailgate strut (Hatchback and Estate models) – removal and refitting

1 Support the tailgate in the open position using a suitable prop, or with the aid of an assistant.
2 Disconnect the strut from the tailgate by prising out the retaining clip. Do not remove the clip completely, just raise it by a maximum of 4.0 mm (0.16 in) and then pull the strut off its mounting.
3 Pull the strut from the pivot stud on the body.
4 Refitting is a reversal of removal.

Fig 12.3 Tailgate trim panel fixings – Hatchback and Estate models (Sec 12)

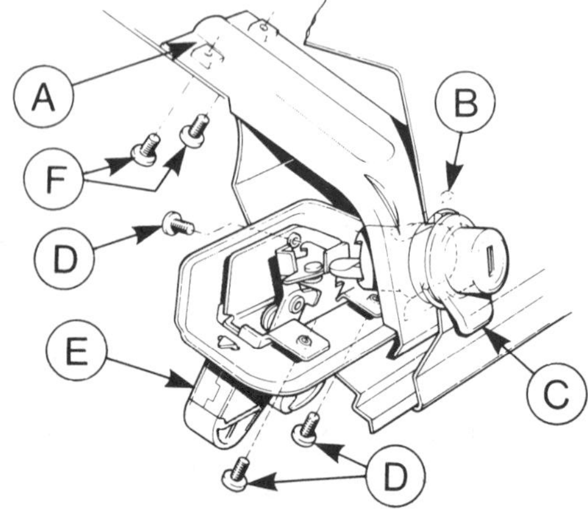

Fig 12.4 Tailgate lock assembly – Hatchback and Estate models (Sec 12)

A Lock barrel support bracket
B Lock barrel retaining clip
C Lock barrel
D Torx screws
E Lock assembly
F Screws

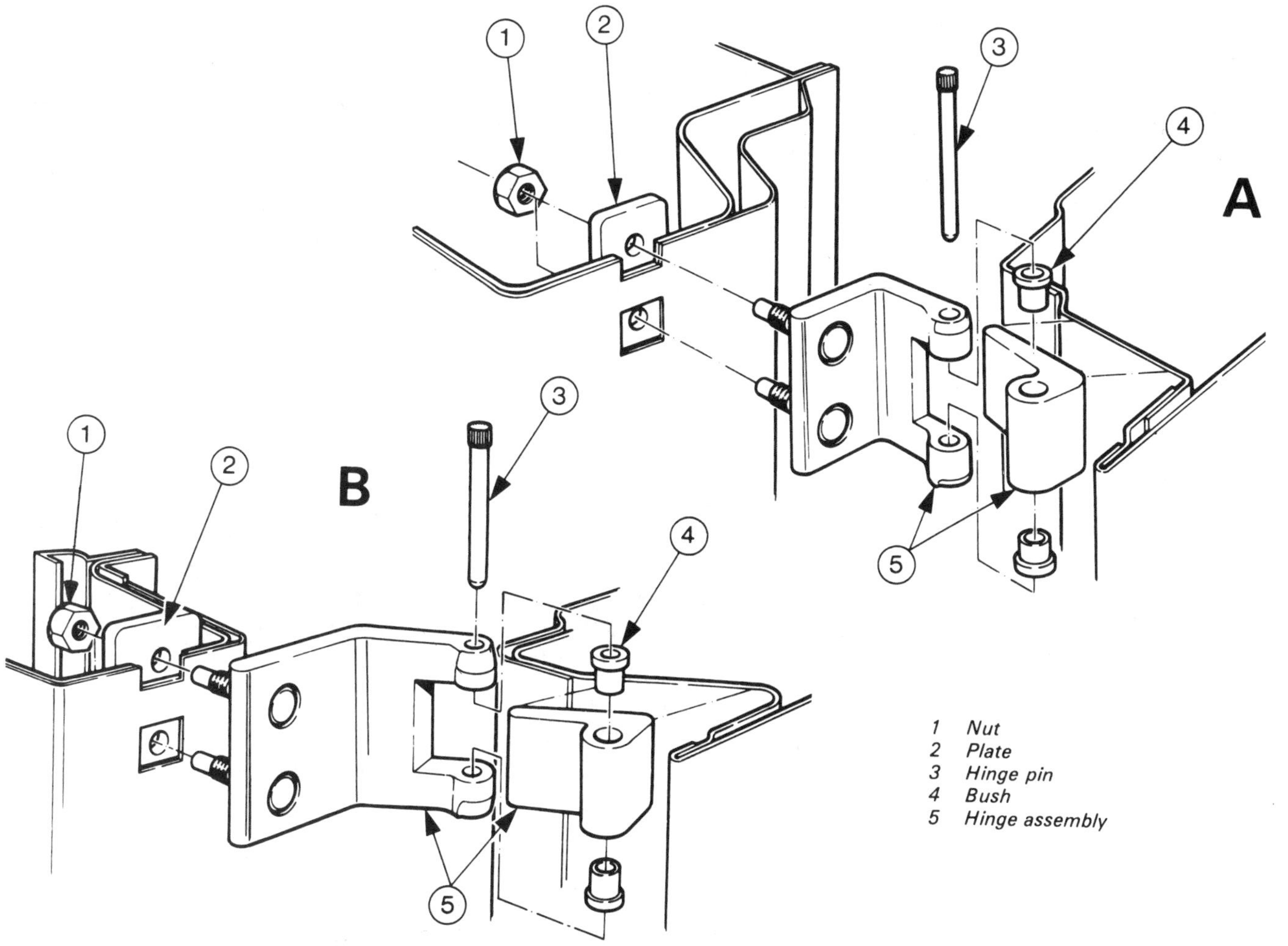

A

B

1 *Nut*
2 *Plate*
3 *Hinge pin*
4 *Bush*
5 *Hinge assembly*

Fig 12.5 Exploded view of the front door hinge (A) and rear door hinge (B) (Sec 14)

1 *Nut*
2 *Reinforcing plate*
3 *Hinge pin*
4 *Bush*
5 *Hinge assembly*

14 Door – removal and refitting

Front door

1 On models equipped with electric mirrors, electric windows, central-locking, door-mounted speakers, or 'door ajar' sensors, remove the trim panel as described in Section 15 and disconnect the wiring inside the door. Withdraw the wiring loom(s) through the grommet(s) in the front edge of the door.

2 Unscrew and remove the bolt securing the check arm to the body pillar (photo).

3 Remove the two securing screws, and withdraw the side trim panel from the footwell.

4 If working on the driver's side, remove the lower facia panels as described in Section 41, and disconnect the face level vent hose.

5 If working on the passenger side, remove the face level vent cover.

6 Support the door on blocks of wood.

7 Working through the body pillar aperture, unscrew the two securing

14.2 Remove the door check arm-to-body pillar bolt (arrowed)

15.1A Prise the cover from the window regulator handle ...

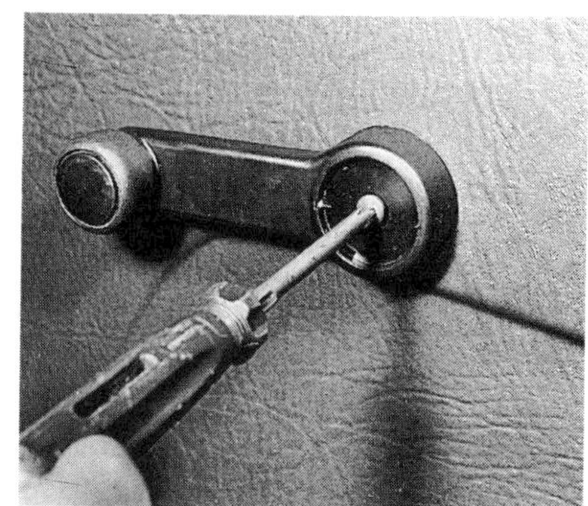

15.1B ... remove the securing screw ...

nuts and remove the reinforcing plate from the lower hinge. Repeat the procedure for the upper hinge.
8 Withdraw the door from the vehicle.
9 Refitting is a reversal of removal, but do not fully tighten the hinge bolts until the door is positioned centrally in the body aperture and aligned with the surrounding bodywork. If necessary, remove the lock striker from the body centre pillar before adjusting the door, then refit it and adjust its position so that the lock operates correctly.

Rear door

10 On models equipped with electric windows, central-locking, or 'door ajar' sensors, remove the trim panel as described in Section 15 and disconnect the wiring inside the door. Withdraw the wiring loom(s) through the grommet(s) in the front edge of the door.
11 Unscrew and remove the bolt securing the check arm to the body centre pillar.
12 Remove the centre pillar trim panel as described in Section 39.
13 Proceed as described in paragraphs 6 to 9 inclusive.

15 Door inner trim panel – removal and refitting

Front door – models up to 1987

1 On models with manually-operated windows, prise the cover from the window regulator handle, note the position of the handle with the window fully shut, then remove the securing screw and withdraw the handle and bezel (photos).
2 Remove the securing screw and withdraw the trim panel from behind the door grip (photo).
3 Remove the securing screw from the interior door handle surround, lift the handle, and withdraw the surround and grip (photos).
4 Remove the two securing screws and withdraw the door pocket (photo).
5 If working on the driver's side of models fitted with electric mirrors, first disconnect the battery negative lead, then prise the mirror switch assembly from the door trim panel and disconnect the wiring plug.
6 The trim panel can now be prised from the door. To prevent

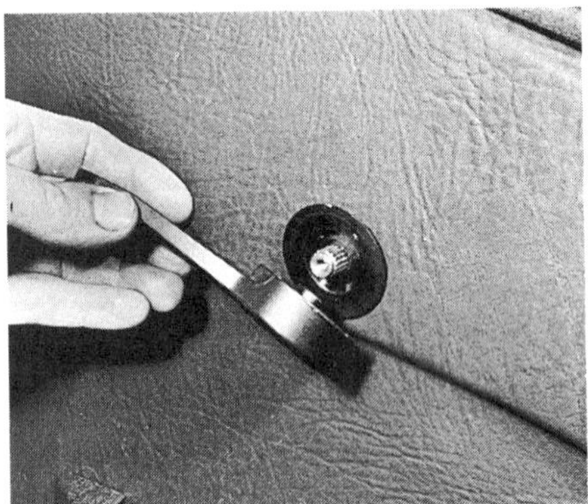
15.1C ... then withdraw the handle ...

15.1D ... and bezel

15.2 Withdraw the trim panel from behind the door grip

15.3A Remove the securing screw ...

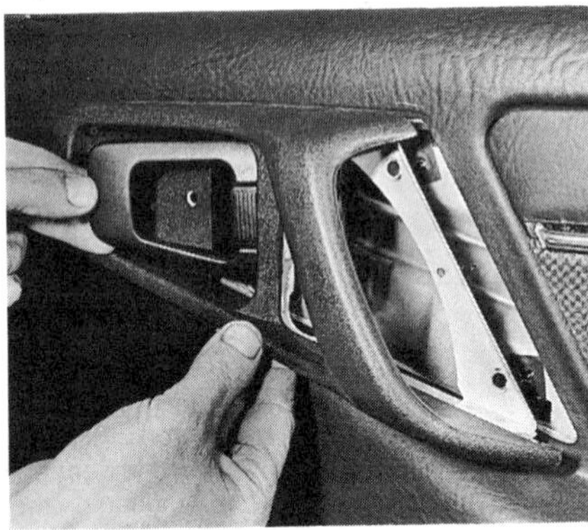
15.3B ... and withdraw the handle surround and door grip

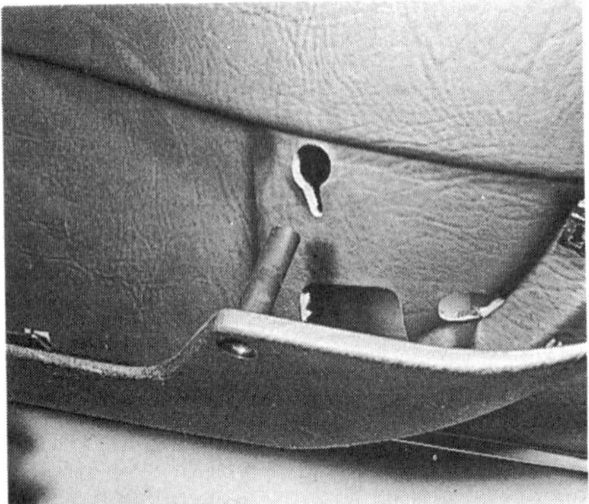
15.4 Withdraw the door pocket

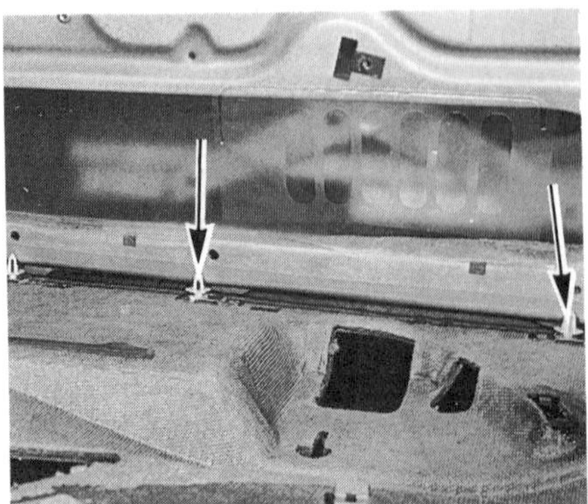
15.6 Door inner trim panel removed exposing retaining clips (arrowed)

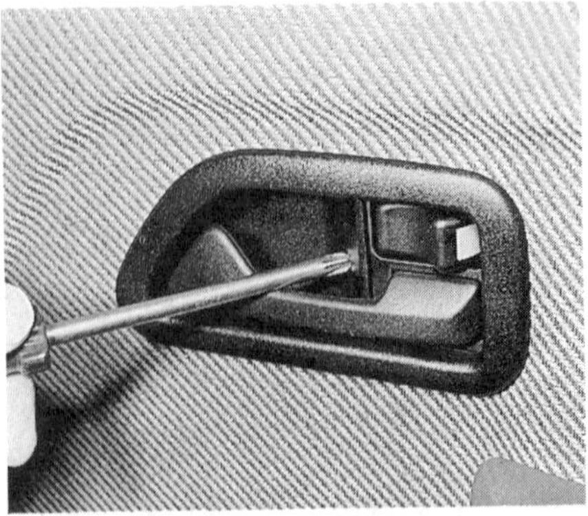
15.9 Remove the interior door handle surround securing screws

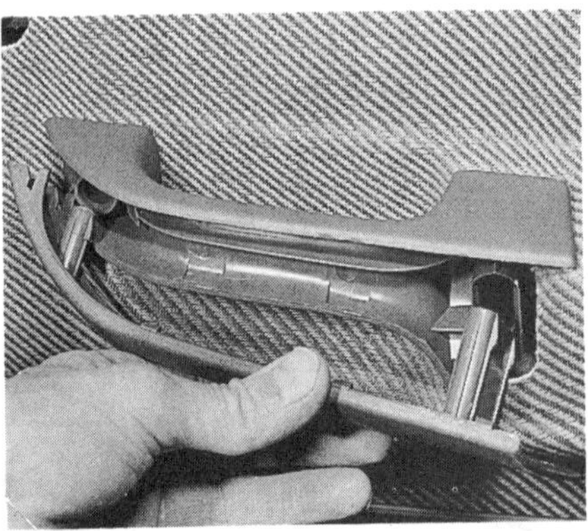
15.10A Prise out the armrest trim panel ...

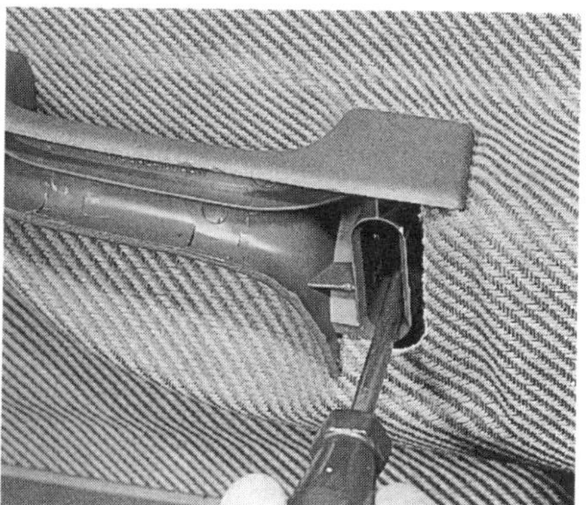
15.10B ... and remove the armrest securing screws

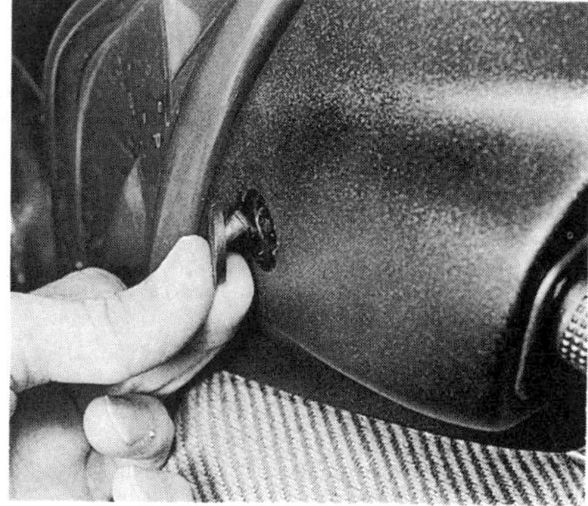
15.12A Prise the securing screw cover from the mirror control panel

15.12B Withdraw the mirror control panel

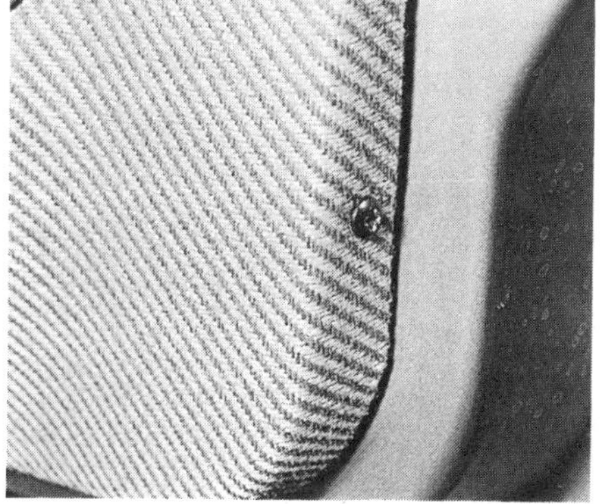
15.15A Trim panel securing screw at bottom rear edge of door

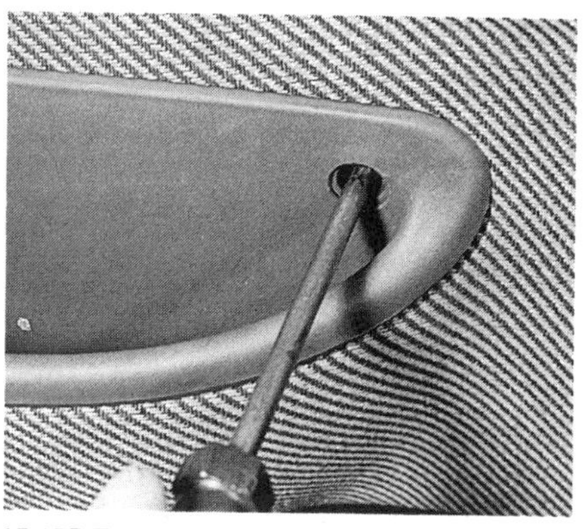
15.15B Trim panel securing screw at top edge of door pocket

15.15C Trim panel top retaining clip

damage to the panel, only prise under the retaining clips – see Fig. 12.6. It is advisable to use a forked tool similar to that shown in Fig. Fig. 12.7 to prise around the retaining clips, but failing this, use a wide-bladed screwdriver. If a clip will not release, sever it with a chisel or sharp knife, taking care not to damage the trim panel, and renew the clip on reassembly (photo).

7 Refitting is a reversal of removal, but ensure that all the retaining clips are correctly aligned before pressing them into the door, and make sure that the upper lip of the trim panel locates under the mirror trim panel.

Front door – models from 1987

8 Proceed as described in paragraph 1.

9 Remove the securing screw from the interior door handle surround, lift the handle, and withdraw the surround (photo).

10 Prise out the armrest trim panel, remove the three securing screws, and withdraw the armrest (photos).

11 On models with manually-operated mirrors, unscrew the bezel from the adjuster knob, then prise off the mirror trim panel.

12 When working on the driver's side of models with electric mirrors, prise the securing screw cover from the mirror control panel, then remove the screw and withdraw the control panel. Disconnect the wiring plug after disconnecting the battery negative lead (photos).

13 When working on the passenger side of models with electric mirrors, the mirror trim panel can simply be prised off.

14 Remove the now exposed door trim panel securing screw.

15 Remove the two trim panel securing screws from each side of the door, and the four securing screws from the door pocket, then lift the trim panel to disengage it from the top retaining clips, and withdraw the panel from the door (photos).

16 Refitting is a reversal of removal.

Rear door – models up to 1987

17 Proceed as described in paragraphs 1 to 3 inclusive.

18 On models fitted with electric windows, disconnect the battery negative lead, then prise the switch from the armrest and disconnect the wiring plug.

19 Proceed as described in paragraph 6.

20 Refitting is a reversal of removal, but ensure that all the retaining clips are correctly aligned before pressing them into the door.

Rear door – models from 1987

21 Proceed as described in paragraph 1.

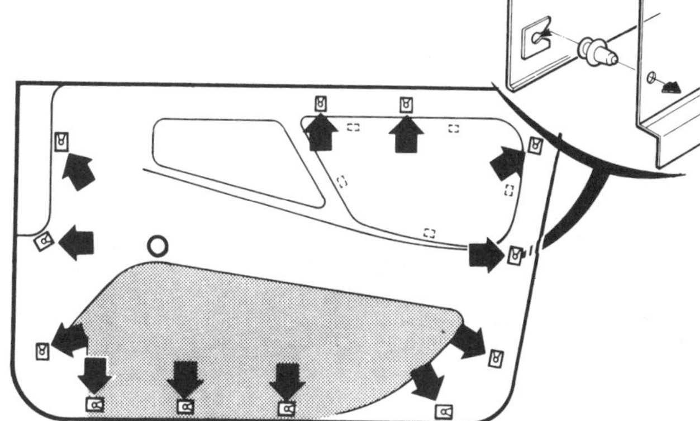
Fig 12.6 Door inner trim panel retaining clip locations (arrowed) (Sec 15)

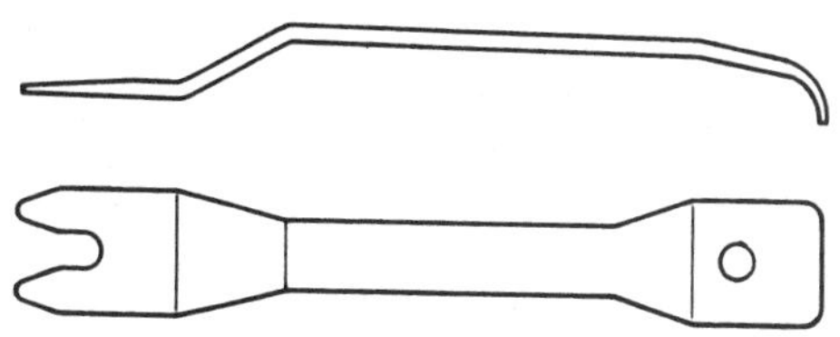
Fig 12.7 Trim panel retaining clip removal tool (Sec 15)

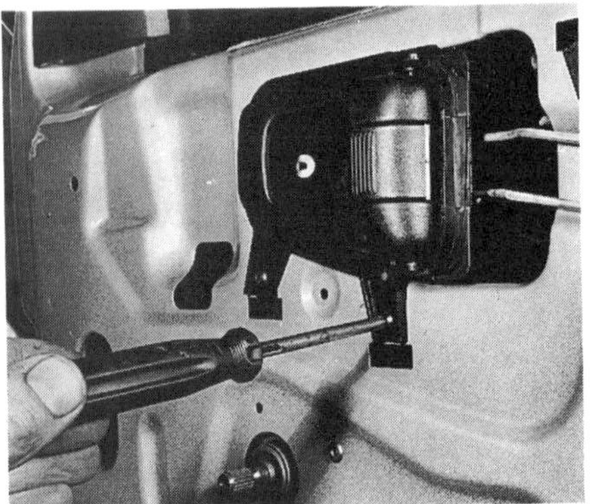

16.3A Remove the securing screws ...

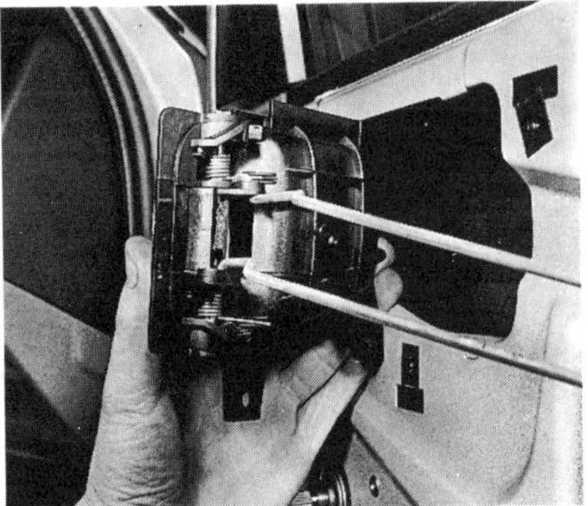

16.3B ... and slide the handle assembly from the door aperture

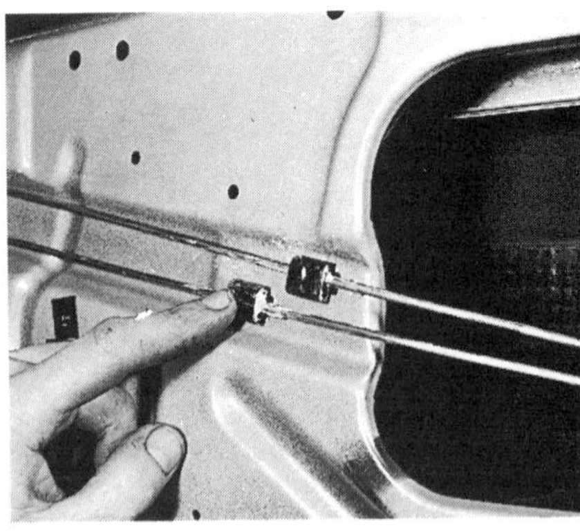

16.5 Remote control rods correctly located in their guides

22 Remove the securing screw from the interior door handle, then pull out the ashtray, and remove the two now exposed screws.
23 Lift the interior door handle, and withdraw the handle/ashtray surround.
24 Prise out the armrest trim panel, remove the three securing screws and withdraw the armrest.
25 Remove the two trim panel securing screws from each side of the door, then lift the trim panel to disengage it from the top retaining clips, and withdraw the panel from the door.
26 Refitting is a reversal of removal.

16 Door interior handle – removal and refitting

1 Remove the door inner trim panel as described in Section 15.
2 Where necessary for improved access, peel back the waterproof plastic sheet from the door.
3 Remove the two securing screws in the case of models up to 1987, or the single securing screw on models from 1987, and slide the handle assembly from the door aperture, if necessary unclipping the remote control rods from their guides (photos).
4 Disconnect the remote control rods from the handle assembly, and withdraw the handle assembly.
5 Refitting is a reversal of removal, but check that the remote control rods are correctly located in their guides (photo).

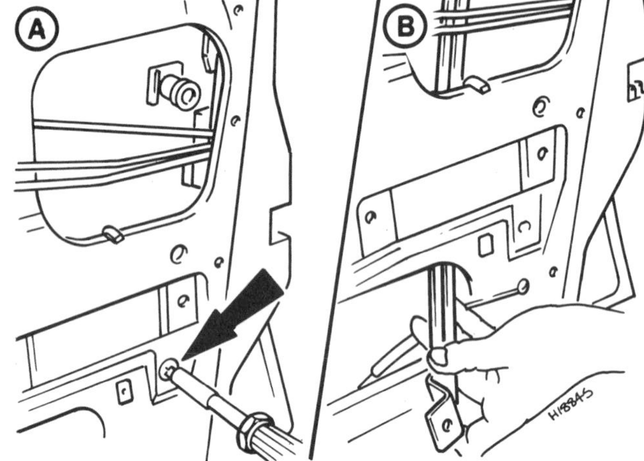

Fig 12.8 Front door window channel extension (Sec 17)

A Remove the retaining screw (arrowed)
B Withdraw the channel through the lower door aperture

17 Door exterior handle – removal and refitting

1 Remove the door inner trim panel as described in Section 15.
2 Where necessary for improved access, peel back the waterproof plastic sheet from the door.
3 If working on a front door, remove the window channel extension screw from the bottom rear corner of the door, and withdraw the channel through the lower door aperture.
4 Disconnect the handle operating rod at the lock.
5 Remove the two handle securing screws and withdraw the handle and operating rod from the door.
6 Refitting is a reversal of removal, but if working on a front door, ensure that the window channel extension is correctly located.

18 Door lock barrel – removal and refitting

1 Remove the door inner trim panel as described in Section 15.
2 Where necessary for improved access, peel back the waterproof plastic sheet from the door.
3 Remove the window channel extension screw from the bottom rear corner of the door, and withdraw the channel through the lower door aperture.
4 Working inside the door aperture, pull out the lock barrel retaining clip using pliers, then unhook the lock operating rod from the barrel, and withdraw the barrel from outside the door (photo).
5 Refitting is a reversal of removal.

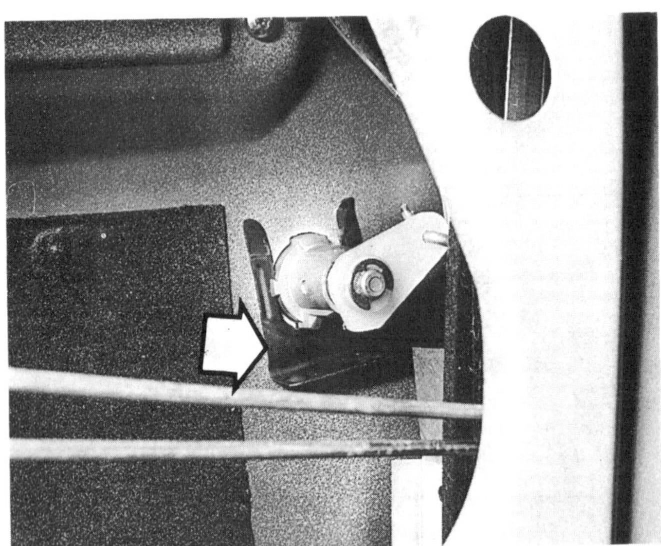

18.3 Door lock barrel location. Retaining clip arrowed

19 Door lock – removal and refitting

1 Remove the door inner trim panel as described in Section 15.
2 Where necessary for improved access, peel back the waterproof plastic sheet from the door.
3 Withdraw the window channel extension through the lower rear door aperture after removing the single securing screw if working on a front door or the two securing screws if working on a rear door.
4 Remove the three securing screws from the rear edge of the door, then reach inside the door and turn the lock to disconnect it from the control rods.
5 Where applicable, disconnect the 'door ajar' sensor wiring plug and the central locking component wiring plug(s). Central locking component removal and refitting is covered in Chapter 13.
6 Withdraw the lock from inside the door.
7 Refitting is a reversal of removal, but ensure that the window channel extension is correctly located.

20 Door check arm – removal and refitting

1 Remove the door inner trim panel as described in Section 15.
2 Unscrew and remove the bolt securing the check arm to the body pillar.
3 Unscrew and remove the two bolts securing the check arm to the door, and withdraw the check arm from inside the door. Peel back the waterproof plastic sheet where necessary for improved access.
4 Refitting is a reversal of removal.

21 Cargo area (P100 models) – removal and refitting

Note: *A suitable lifting crane and tackle will be required for this operation*
1 Disconnect the battery negative lead.
2 Remove the fuel filler cap, then drain the fuel tank as described in Chapter 3.
3 Remove the two securing screws and detach the fuel filler pipe from the cargo area.
4 Disconnect the number plate lamp and the rear lamp wiring plugs, and release the wiring from the cargo area.
5 Disconnect the earth lead from the right-hand front cargo area mounting bracket underneath the vehicle.
6 Working underneath the vehicle, remove the three Torx bolts on each side securing the cargo area to the chassis.
7 Make up a cradle to lift the cargo area from the chassis, using suitable ropes or chains attached to the tonneau tie-down points.
8 Position the crane with the lifting arm diagonally over the centre of the cargo area, and attach the cradle. Carefully lift the cargo area from the chassis. Note that the lip of the cargo area rear panel fits over the rear chassis crossmember, therefore the cargo area must be pulled rearwards as it is removed to disengage it from the crossmember.
9 Refitting is a reversal of removal, but ensure that the insulators are in place between the cargo area and the chassis. Before finally tightening the securing bolts, adjust the position of the cargo area to give an equal clearance on both sides of the vehicle between the cab rear panel and the cargo area front panel.

22 Tailboard (P100 models) – removal and refitting

1 Lower the tailboard to the horizontal position.
2 Detach the rear lamp wiring cover on one side of the vehicle by removing the two securing screws.
3 Remove the four rear lamp securing nuts, and withdraw the rear lamp assembly. Disconnect the wiring plug.
4 Raise the tailboard by approximately 20°, lift the centre pivot of one of the support arms, and when the bolt head on the tailboard is aligned with the slot in the support arm, pull the support arm clear. Repeat this procedure for the remaining support arm, and lower the tailboard to the vertical position.
5 On the side of the vehicle from which the rear lamp has been removed, remove the two screws securing the tailboard hinge to the cargo area.
6 Close the tailboard and gently lever out the hinge.
7 Pull the free end of the tailboard away from the cargo area, and

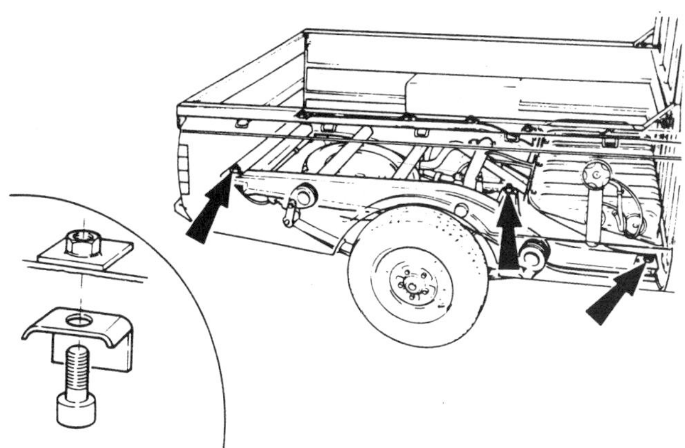

Fig 12.9 Cargo area-to-chassis Torx bolt locations (arrowed) – P100 models (one side shown for clarity) (Sec 21)

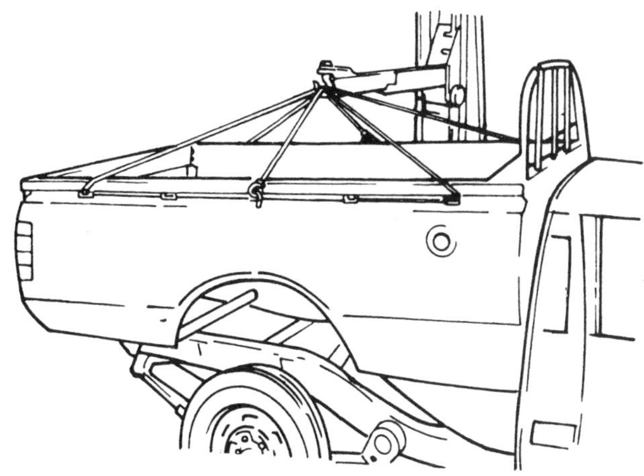

Fig 12.10 Lifting the cargo area from the chassis – P100 models (Sec 21)

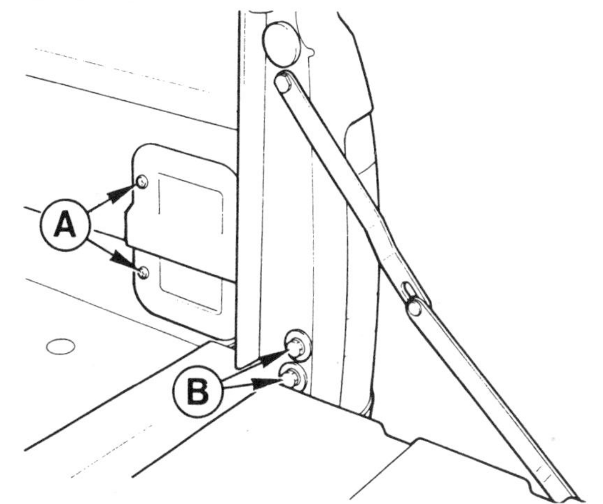

Fig 12.11 Rear lamp wiring cover screws (A) and tailboard hinge screws (B) – P100 models (Sec 22)

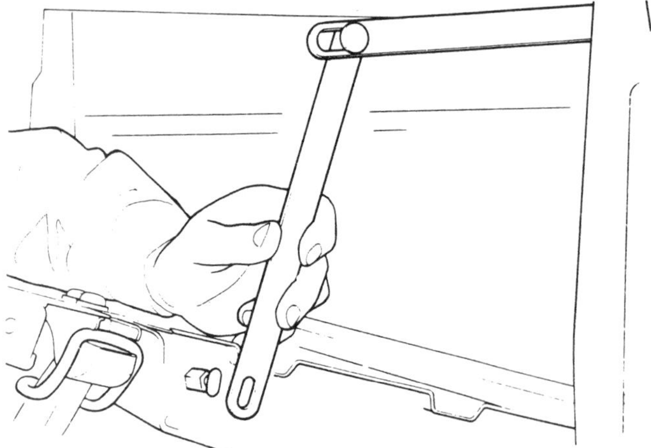

Fig 12.12 Pull the support arms clear of the tailboard – P100 models (Sec 22)

carefully prise the remaining end from its hinge. Withdraw the tailboard from the vehicle.

8 If required, the pivot bushes can be removed from the tailboard for renewal.

9 Refitting is a reversal of removal.

23 Windscreen, rear window and fixed rear quarter windows – removal and refitting

1 With the exception of the cab rear window on P100 models, all fixed glass panels are direct glazed to the body using a special adhesive. Special tools are required to remove the old glass and to fit the new glass, therefore the work is best entrusted to a dealer or replacement glass specialist.

2 The cab rear window on P100 models can be removed as follows, although it is advisable to entrust the work to a specialist.

3 Remove the six Torx bolts and nut/washer assemblies, and withdraw the safety grille from the rear of the cab.

4 Prise out one end of the trim insert from the window rubber, then pull out the remainder of the trim.

5 With the aid of an assistant, carefully push the glass and rubber into the passenger compartment.

6 Remove all traces of old sealer from the glass, rubber and cab aperture.

7 Commence refitting by pushing the window rubber into the aperture, ensuring that the trim panel and body panel engage in their respective grooves in the rubber.

8 Working from outside the cab, enter the bottom edge of the glass into the rubber, and hold the glass against the rubber while an assistant working from inside the passenger compartment pushes the rubber over the glass.

9 The trim insert must now be refitted to the rubber, preferably using a suitable windscreen trim insert tool. If no special tool is available, the trim can be refitted by prising open the rubber lips and pressing the trim into its groove, although this is likely to prove difficult and time consuming.

10 Refit the safety grille to the rear of the cab on completion.

24 Opening rear quarter window – removal and refitting

1 Remove the rear pillar interior trim panel as described in Section 39.

2 Remove the two screws securing the window catch to the body.

3 Prise the two screw covers from the hinges. Support the glass, and remove the two hinge screws, then lift out the glass.

4 If a new window is to be fitted, transfer the catch to it.

5 Refitting is a reversal of removal.

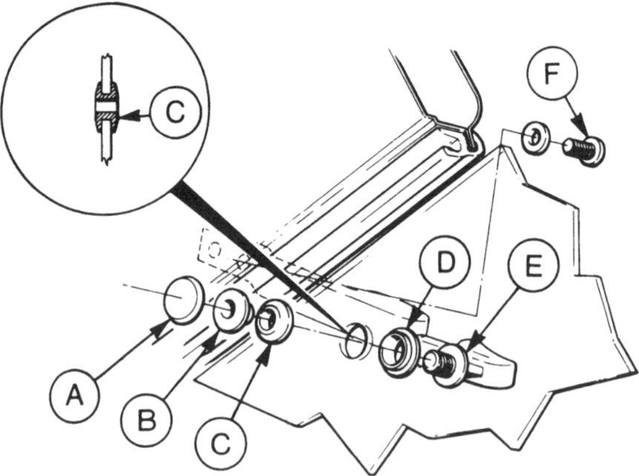

Fig 12.13 Opening rear quarter window catch (Sec 24)

A Cap
B Retainer
C Grommet
D Spacer
E Catch
F Screw (one of two)

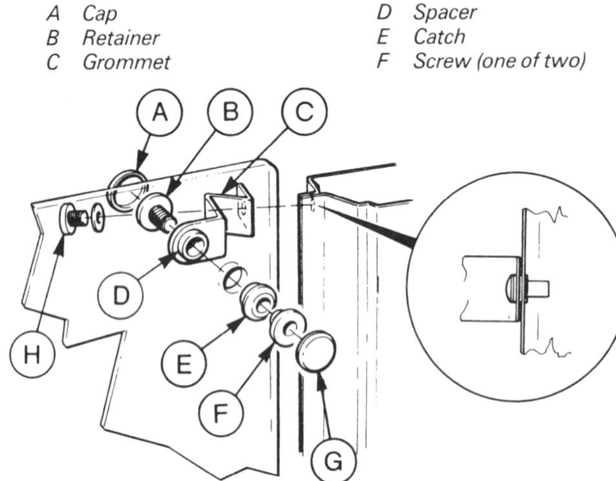

Fig 12.14 Opening rear quarter window hinge (Sec 24)

A Cap
B Screw
C Hinge
D Spacer
E Grommet
F Retainer
G Cap
H Screw

25 Door window – removal and refitting

Front door

1 Remove the door inner trim panel as described in Section 15.

2 Where necessary for improved access, peel back the waterproof plastic sheet from the door.

3 Remove the door mirror as described in Section 27.

4 Remove the window channel extension screw from the bottom rear corner of the door, and withdraw the channel through the lower door aperture.

5 Lower the window until the lower support channel is visible through the lower door aperture. Prise the regulator arms from the sockets in the support channel, then lower the window to the bottom of the door.

6 Carefully prise the weatherstrip from the rear edge of the window aperture, then tilt the window forwards and lift it outwards through the aperture – see Fig. 12.15.

7 Refitting is a reversal of removal, but position the rear window channel extension screw to allow approximately 5.0 mm (0.2 in) fore and aft movement of the window. Check to ensure that the window does not tip as it is raised, and that the regulator effort is acceptable (check that the motor is not being overloaded on models with electric windows). Adjust the channel extension screw if necessary.

Rear door

8 Proceed as described in paragraphs 1 and 2.

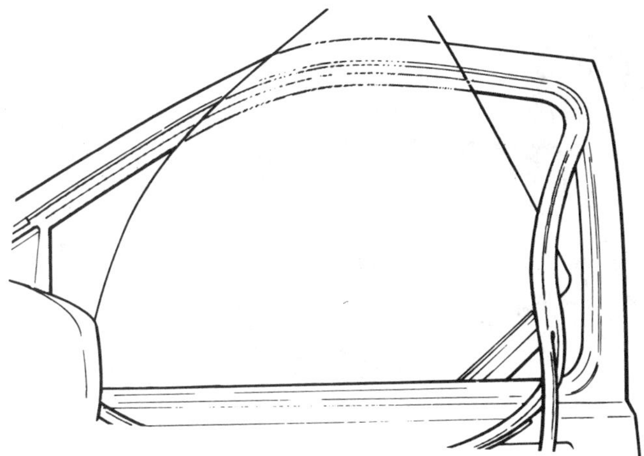

Fig 12.15 Removing a front door window (Sec 25)

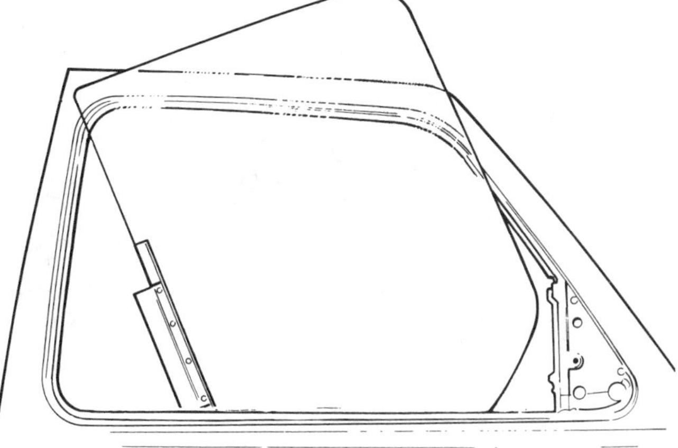

Fig 12.16 Removing a rear door window (Sec 25)

9 On Saloon and Hatchback models, prise the interior quarter trim panel from the rear of the door, then remove the now exposed screw and withdraw the exterior trim panel.
10 Remove the three window channel extension screws from the rear of the door, and withdraw the channel through the lower door aperture.
11 Lower the window until the lower support channel is visible through the lower door aperture. Prise the regulator arms from the sockets in the support channel, then lower the window to the bottom of the door.
12 Carefully prise the weatherstrip from the front edge of the window aperture, then tilt the window rearwards and lift it outwards through the aperture – see Fig. 12.16.
13 Refitting is as described in paragraph 7.

26 Door window regulator – removal and refitting

1 Remove the door inner trim panel as described in Section 15.
2 Where necessary for improved access, peel back the waterproof plastic sheet from the door.
3 Lower the window until the lower support channel is visible through the lower door aperture. Prise the regulator arms from the sockets in the support channel, then lower the window to the bottom of the door (photo).
4 Drill out the four rivets securing the regulator assembly to the inner door skin, and if working on a front door, drill out the two rivets securing the regulator guide – see Fig. 12.17.
5 On models with electric windows, disconnect the motor wiring plug after disconnecting the battery negative lead. Removal and refitting of the motor is described in Chapter 13.
6 Withdraw the regulator assembly through the lower door aperture.
7 Refitting is a reversal of removal, but fit new rivets, using a hand riveter.

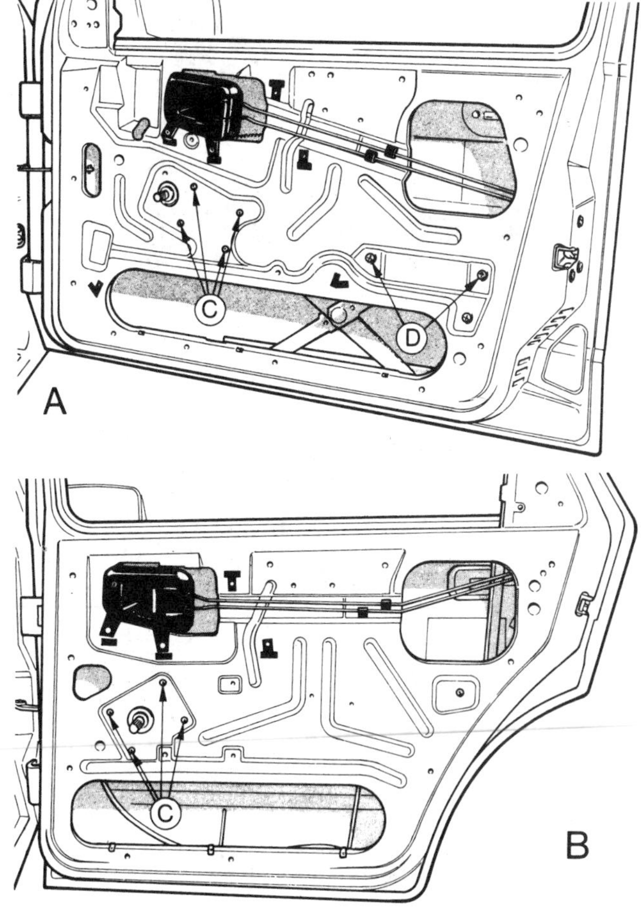

Fig 12.17 Door window regulator fixings (Sec 26)

A Front door
B Rear door
C Regulator assembly securing rivets
D Regulator guide rivets

27 Door mirror – removal and refitting

Manually-operated mirror

1 On remote-control type mirrors, unscrew the bezel from the adjuster knob (photo).
2 Prise the mirror trim panel from the door (photo).
3 Remove the three mirror securing screws, and withdraw the mirror by tilting its rear edge outwards and disengaging its front edge from under the window surround (photo). Where applicable, withdraw the mirror control cable through the door.
4 To remove the mirror glass, proceed as follows according to model.
5 On 'high specification' models with fixed (i.e. not remote control) mirrors, lever the glass assembly outwards to disengage it from the balljoint on the mirror glass mounting.
6 On 'low specification' models with fixed (i.e. not remote control) mirrors, unclip the cover, then remove the securing screw and withdraw the glass assembly.
7 On models with remote control mirrors, insert a thin screwdriver through the hole in the bottom of the mirror assembly, and whilst supporting the glass, release the locking ring – see Fig. 12.19.
8 Refitting is a reversal of removal, but ensure that the front edge of the mirror is correctly located under the window surround.

26.3 Front door window lower support channel and regulator arms

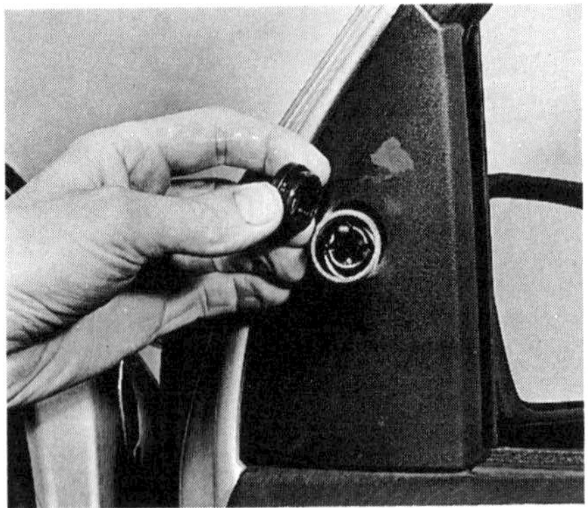
27.1 Unscrew the bezel from the adjuster knob ...

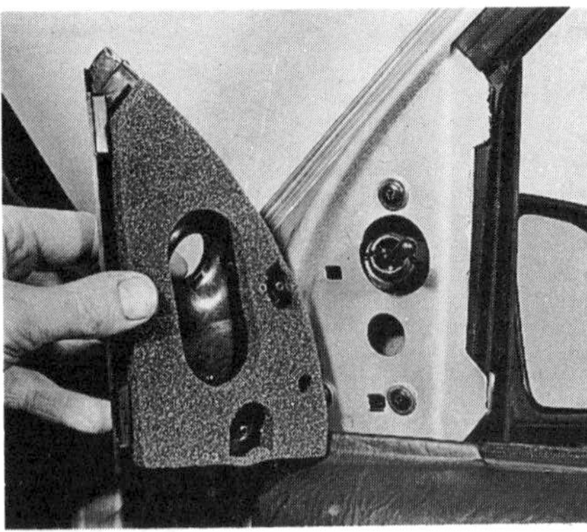
27.2 ... and prise the mirror trim panel from the door

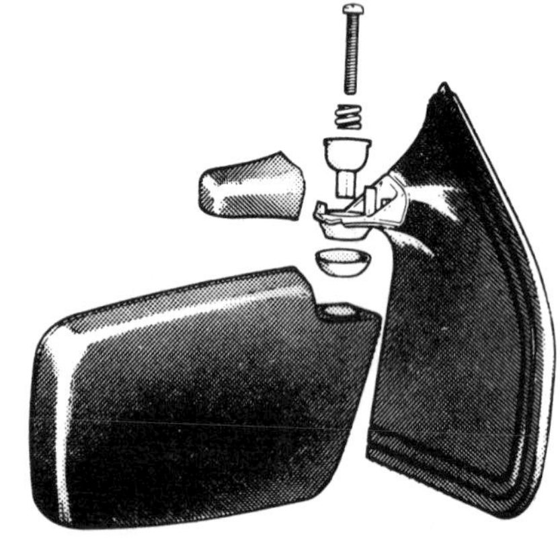
Fig 12.18 Fixed door mirror assembly (Sec 27)

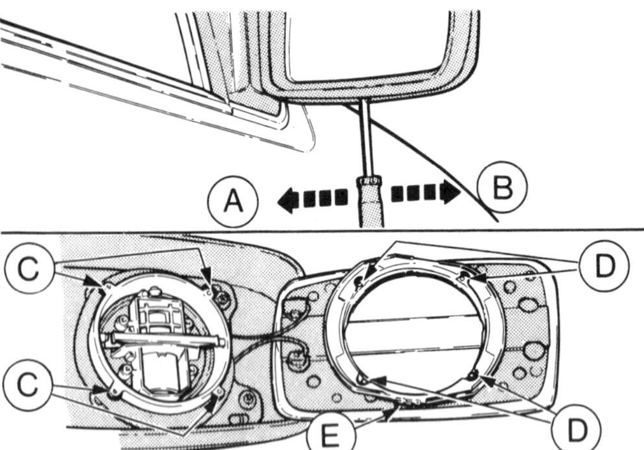

Fig 12.19 Manual remote control and electric door mirror glass removal (Sec 27)

A Locking operation
B Unlocking operation
C Locating pegs
D Locking slots
E Locking ring

Electric mirror

9 Disconnect the battery negative lead.
10 If working on the driver's side of models up to 1987, prise the mirror switch assembly from the door trim panel and disconnect the wiring plug.
11 If working on the driver's side of models from 1987, prise the securing screw cover from the mirror control panel, then remove the screw and withdraw the control panel. Disconnect the wiring plug.

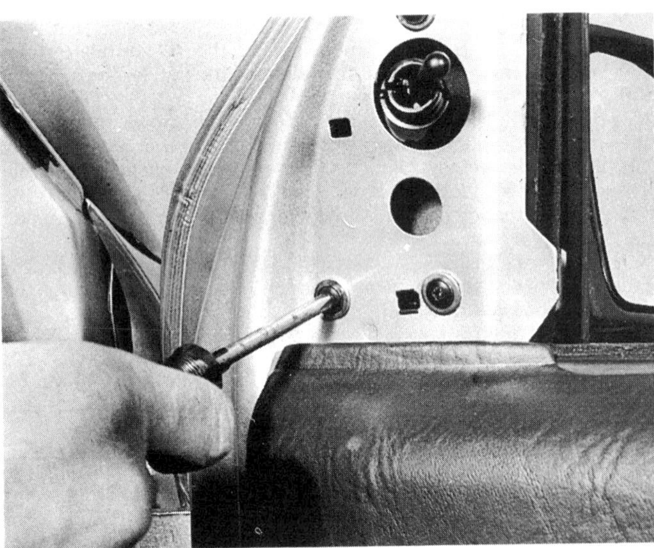
27.3 Remove the mirror securing screws

12 On models up to 1987, and when working on the passenger side of models from 1987, prise out the mirror trim panel.
13 Remove the three mirror securing screws, and withdraw the mirror by tilting its rear edge outwards and disengaging its front edge from under the window surround. Withdraw the wiring through the door.
14 To remove the mirror glass proceed as described in paragraph 7.
15 Refitting is a reversal of removal, but ensure that the front edge of the mirror is correctly located under the window surround.

28 Bumper – removal and refitting

Front bumper – models up to 1987

1 Remove the radiator grille panel as described in Section 30.
2 Disconnect the battery negative lead, then disconnect the wiring plugs from the indicators, and where applicable the foglamps.
3 Working under the front wing, release the single bumper fastener from each side of the vehicle by turning the plastic clip through 90° (quarter of a turn).
4 On Ghia models, unclip the support strap between each front wing and the bumper.
5 Unscrew the single bolt securing each bumper fixing bracket to the body front panel, then pull the bumper forwards away from the body, disengaging the retaining pegs from the clips in each wing (photo).
6 Refitting is a reversal of removal, but ensure that all fixings are correctly located and secure.

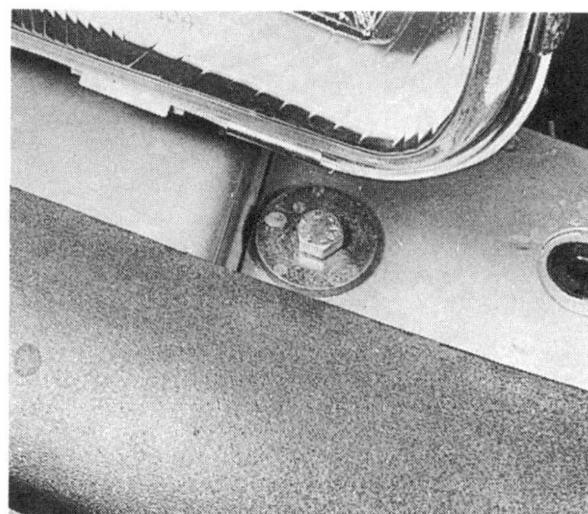
28.5 Front bumper securing bolt - models up to 1987

28.8 Front bumper securing bolt - models from 1987

28.10 Front bumper mounting spigot and socket - models from 1987

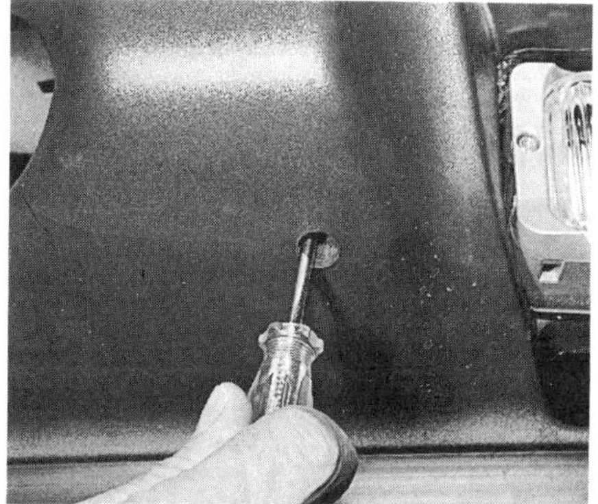
28.12A Adjusting the height of a front bumper - models from 1987

28.12B Front bumper height adjusting screw - models from 1987

28.14 Rear bumper securing bolt

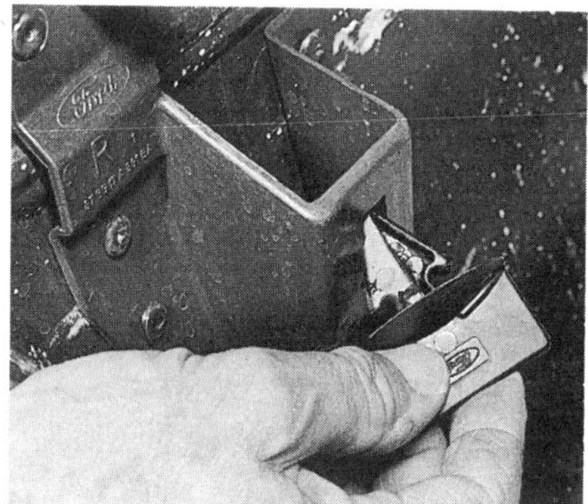
28.15 Rear bumper plastic fastener

28.16 Rear bumper removed exposing end clip on wing

28.18 Adjusting the height of a rear bumper

Front bumper - models from 1987

7 If foglamps are fitted, disconnect the battery negative lead, then disconnect the wiring plugs from the foglamps.

8 Working under the front wings, unscrew the single securing bolt from each side of the bumper (photo).

9 Release the plastic retaining screws and pull the wheel arch liners away from the ends of the bumper.

10 Pull the bumper forwards away from the body, releasing the front mounting spigots from their sockets (photo).

11 Refitting is a reversal of removal, but ensure that the reinforcing plate and O-ring are located on the right-hand mounting spigot (photos).

12 The bumper height can be adjusted by turning the adjusters located on the front mounting spigots using a suitable Torx screwdriver with a length of at least 150.0 mm (6.0 in) (photos).

Rear bumper - Saloon, Hatchback and Estate models

13 Disconnect the battery negative lead, then prise the number plate lamps from the bumper, and disconnect the wiring plugs. Withdraw the wiring through the bumper assembly.

14 Working inside the luggage compartment, unscrew the two bumper securing bolts (photo).

15 Working under the rear wings, release the single bumper fastener from each side of the vehicle by turning the plastic clip through 90° (quarter of a turn) (photo).

16 Pull the bumper rearwards away from the body, disengaging the retaining pegs from the clips in each wing (photo).

17 Refitting is a reversal of removal, but ensure that all fixings are correctly located and secure.

18 On some later models, the bumper height can be adjusted by means of the adjusters located on the mounting brackets - see paragraph 12 (photo).

Rear bump stop - P100 models

19 Working underneath the vehicle, unscrew the two securing nuts and washers from the bump stop studs, and withdraw the bump stop.

20 Refitting is a reversal of removal.

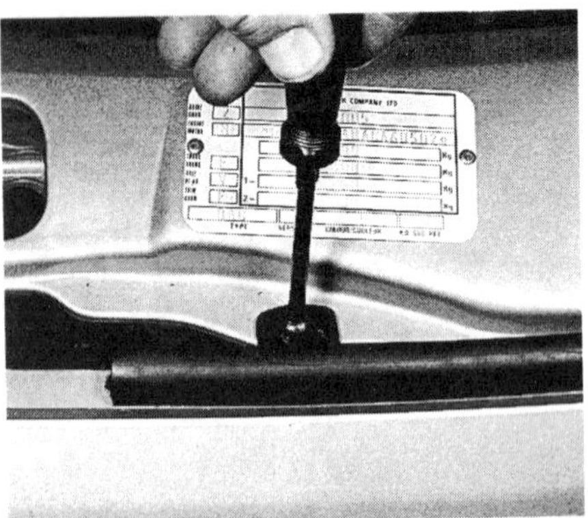
30.1 Removing a radiator grille panel securing screw - models up to 1987

30.4 Removing a radiator grille panel securing screw - models from 1987

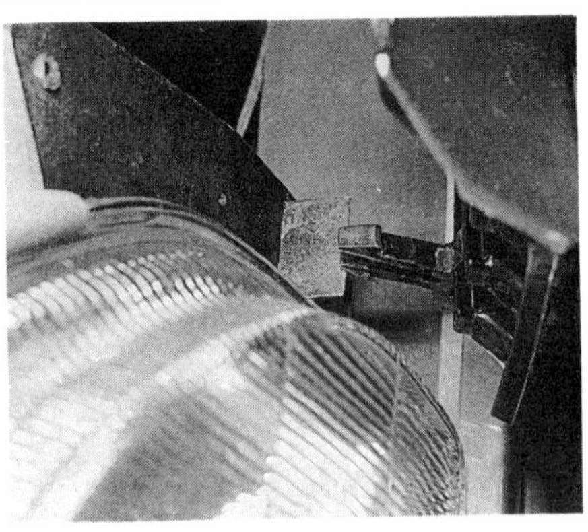
30.5A Radiator grille panel upper retaining clip - models from 1987

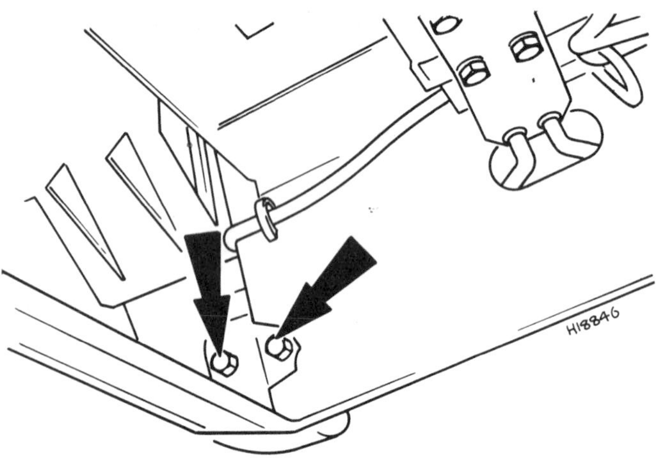

Fig 12.20 Rear bump stop securing nut locations (arrowed) - P100 models (Sec 28)

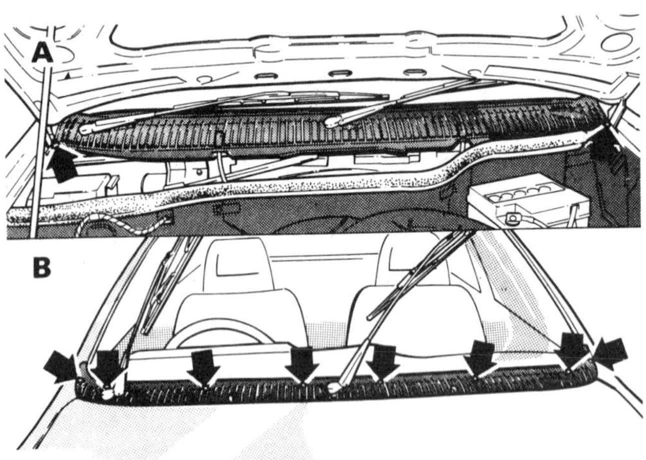

Fig 12.21 Windscreen cowl panel fixings - models up to 1987 (Sec 31)

A Securing screws located under bonnet
B Plastic securing screws

29 Bumper trim moulding - renewal

1 New bumpers are supplied without the trim moulding fitted. Special primer and adhesive tape are specified by the manufacturer to retain the moulding: it is suggested that a Ford dealer is consulted for further details.
2 A damaged moulding can be removed by simply prising it from the bumper using a screwdriver.

30 Radiator grille panel - removal and refitting

Models up to 1987

1 With the bonnet raised, remove the four grille panel securing screws from the top of the front panel (photo).
2 Lift the grille panel from its lower mounting bushes, and withdraw it from the vehicle.
3 Refitting is a reversal of removal, but ensure that the lower mounting lugs are correctly located in their bushes.

Models from 1987

4 With the bonnet raised, remove the two grille panel securing screws from the front face of the panel (photo).
5 Release the upper and lower grille retaining clips, and withdraw the grille panel from the vehicle (photos).
6 Refitting is a reversal of removal, but align the grille panel carefully before tightening the securing screws.

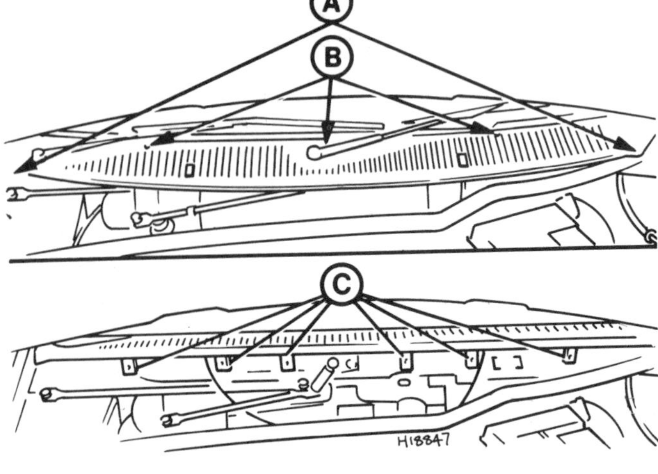

Fig 12.22 Windscreen cowl panel fixings - models from 1987 (Sec 31)

A Securing screws
B Plastic securing screws
C Front fixing clips

31 Windscreen cowl panel - removal and refitting

1 Open the bonnet and disconnect the windscreen washer hose at

30.5B Radiator grille panel lower retaining clip – models from 1987

34.2A Wheel arch liner self-tapping screw

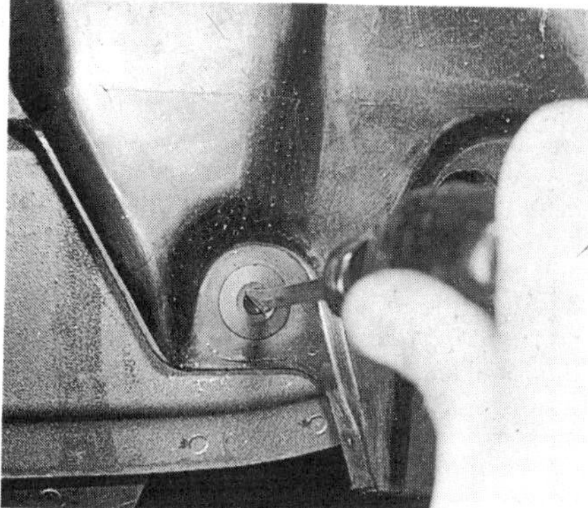

34.2B Releasing a wheel arch liner plastic clip

the T-piece connector.

2 Remove both windscreen wiper arm assemblies as described in Chapter 13.

3 Remove the single securing screw from each end of the cowl panel.

4 On models up to 1987, prise out the screw covers and remove the eight plastic screws securing the cowl panel to the body. Withdraw the panel.

5 On models from 1987, prise out the screw covers and remove the plastic securing screws. Pull the front edge of the cowl panel upwards to disengage the front fixing clips, then move the panel to the left and then to the right to disengage the hooks on the panel underside. Withdraw the panel.

6 Refitting is a reversal of removal.

32 Exterior rear pillar trim panel (Saloon models) – removal and refitting

1 Remove the interior rear pillar trim panel as described in Section 39.

2 Unscrew the three now exposed securing nuts and withdraw the exterior trim panel.

3 Refitting is a reversal of removal, but do not overtighten the securing nuts, as this may result in damage to the rubber seals.

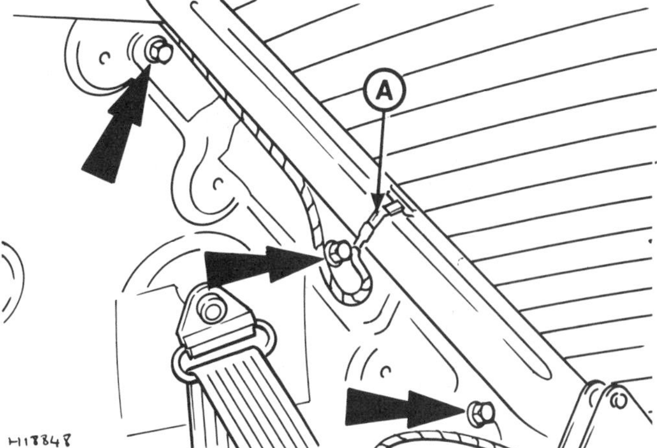

Fig 12.23 Exterior rear pillar trim panel securing nut locations (arrowed) – Saloon models (Sec 32)

A Heated rear window wiring plug

33 Cab air vent panel (P100 models) – removal and refitting

1 Remove the cab interior side trim panel as described in Section 40.

2 Working inside the cab, remove the two rubber grommets from the rear pillar, then unscrew the two now exposed nuts, and withdraw the air vent panel.

3 Refitting is a reversal of removal.

34 Wheel arch liners – removal and refitting

1 Where fitted, the wheel arch liners may be retained by self-tapping screws, plastic clips, or a combination of both.

2 To remove a liner, simply unscrew the retaining screws, or where plastic clips are fitted, release them by turning with a screwdriver (photos).

3 Refitting is a reversal of removal.

35 Fuel filler flap – removal and refitting

1 Open the filler flap and the tailgate or boot lid, as applicable.

2 Remove the fuel filler cap and then remove the screw securing the filler housing to the fuel tank neck – see Fig. 12.24.

3 Working inside the luggage compartment, depress the filler housing retaining tangs, and push the assembly out through the body panel. Recover the gasket.

4 Immerse the housing assembly in a container of hot water for approximately ten minutes, then prise the hinge cover from the housing, and using a screwdriver, prise the filler flap hinge legs out of the sockets in the housing.

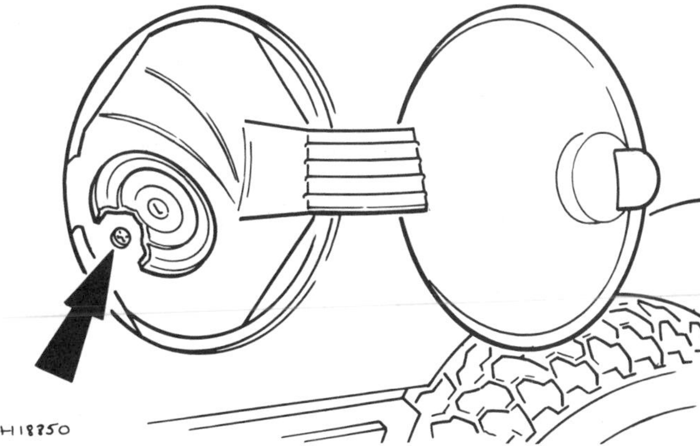

Fig 12.24 Fuel filler housing securing screw (arrowed) (Sec 35)

5 Commence refitting by warming the filler flap and housing, as during removal, then push the flap hinge legs into the housing.

6 Further refitting is a reversal of removal, ensuring that the housing gasket and retaining tangs are correctly located.

36 Inner gutter weatherstrip (Saloon, Hatchback and Estate models) – removal and refitting

1 Open both the front and rear doors to expose the relevant weatherstrip.

2 Carefully pull the weatherstrip from the base of the front pillar, taking care to release the flap which is stuck to the pillar with adhesive.

3 Pull the remainder of the weatherstrip from its flange.

4 Carefully clean the old adhesive from the base of the front pillar using methylated spirits.

5 Commence refitting by pushing the weatherstrip onto its flange at the top corner of the rear pillar, running it for approximately 200 mm (8.0 in) along the horizontal flange.

6 Align the flap on the front pillar, and apply a thin bead of rubber-based adhesive to the flap. Refit the flap to the front pillar, ensuring that it lies naturally. Should the flap not lie naturally, or start to lift, temporarily secure it in position with adhesive tape.

7 Refit the remainder of the weatherstrip, starting at the front pillar and working rearwards, then close the doors and allow the adhesive to dry for at least an hour.

37 Sunroof – removal, refitting and adjustment

Glass panel – removal and refitting

1 Open the sunblind and remove the three screws and clips shown in Fig. 12.25, then slide the lower frame rearwards into the roof.

2 Remove the six screws securing the glass panel to the sliding gear, then push the glass panel upwards and remove it from outside of the vehicle, taking care not to damage the paintwork.

3 Commence refitting by securing the glass panel to the sliding gear with the six screws.

4 Adjust the sunroof as described in paragraphs 10 and 12 to 14 inclusive, but note that there is no need to open and close the roof before checking adjustment.

5 Refit the three clips to the glass panel, then pull the lower frame forwards and secure it to the glass panel with the three screws. Tighten the screws in the order shown in Fig. 12.25.

Complete sunroof assembly – removal and refitting

6 Fully open the sliding roof panel, then remove the screw securing the roof operating handle and detach the handle.

7 Remove the four screws on each side and the two screws at the front securing the sliding roof assembly to the roof tray.

8 Lift the front rail and carefully withdraw the assembly forwards from the roof tray, taking care not to damage the paintwork.

9 Refitting is a reversal of removal, but on completion, adjust the sunroof as described in paragraph 10 onwards, and if necessary adjust the position of the roof operating handle so that with the roof in its closed position, the handle can fold into its recess.

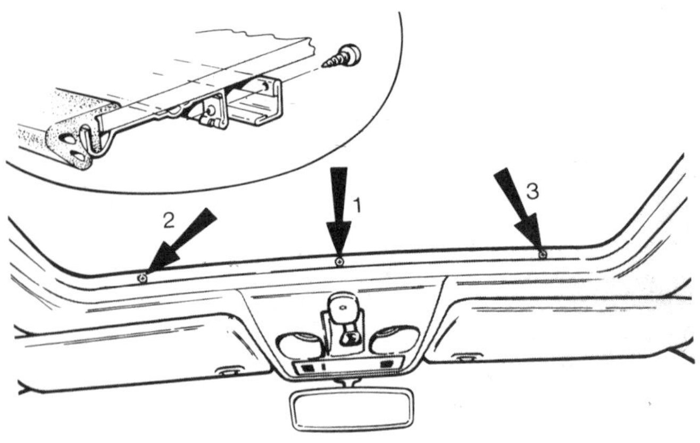

Fig 12.25 Sunroof lower frame-to-glass panel securing screws and clips (arrowed) (Sec 37)

Tighten screws in the order shown when refitting

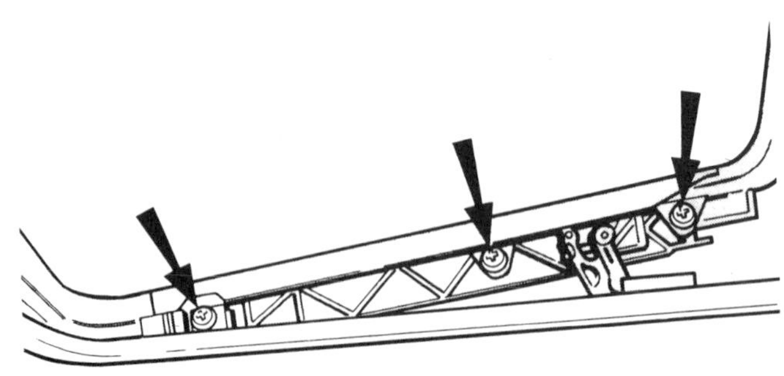

Fig 12.26 Sunroof glass panel-to-sliding gear securing screws (one side shown for clarity) (Sec 37)

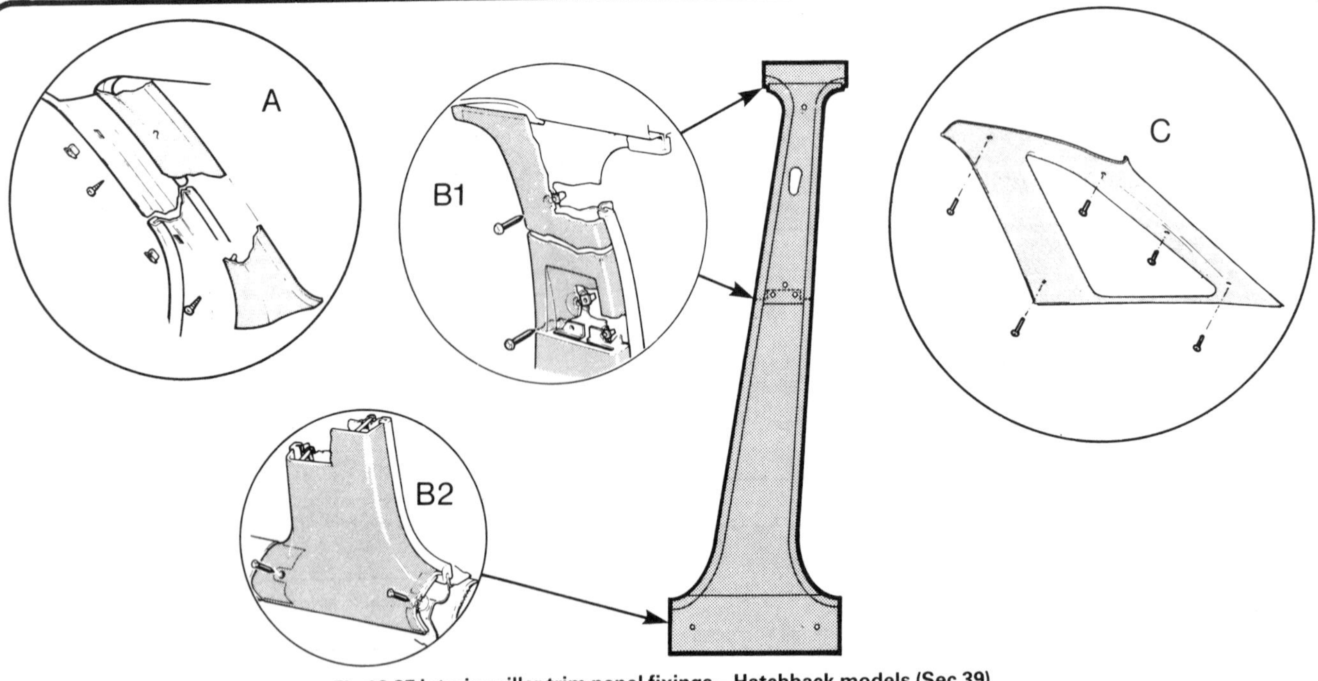

A

B1

B2

C

Fig 12.27 Interior pillar trim panel fixings – Hatchback models (Sec 39)

A Front pillar trim panel
B1 Centre pillar upper trim panel
B2 Centre pillar lower trim panel
C Rear pillar trim panel

Adjustment

10 Fully open and close the sliding roof, then check that the front edge of the glass panel is flush with, or a maximum of 2.0 mm (0.08 in) *below* the adjacent roof panel. The rear edge of the glass panel should be flush with, or a maximum of 2.0 mm (0.08 in) *above* the adjacent roof panel.
11 If adjustment is necessary, remove the three screws securing the glass panel to the lower frame – see Fig. 12.25, then slide the lower frame rearwards into the roof.
12 To adjust the front edge of the glass panel, loosen the front and centre screws securing the glass panel to the sliding gear.
13 To adjust the rear edge of the glass panel, loosen the rear and centre screws securing the glass panel to the sliding gear.
14 On completion of adjustment, tighten the glass panel-to-sliding gear securing screws.
15 Pull the lower frame forwards and secure it to the glass panel with the three screws. Tighten the screws in the order shown in Fig. 12.25.

38 Interior trim panels – general

1 The method of removal and refitting for most interior trim panels is self-explanatory. The panels are fixed in place either by screws, which may be concealed by plastic blanking plugs in some cases, or by clips on the rear of the panel.
2 When removing a panel secured by clips, prise the panel as close as possible to each clip, using a forked tool similar to that shown in Fig. 12.7 or a wide-bladed screwdriver to prevent damage to the panel.
3 Refer to the relevant Sections of this Chapter for removal and refitting details of the major trim panels.

39 Interior pillar trim panels – removal and refitting

Front pillar

1 Remove the two trim panel securing screws, and withdraw the panel.
2 Refitting is a reversal of removal.

Centre pillar

3 Where applicable, lever the seat belt height adjuster button downwards and detach the button by removing the two securing screws.
4 Unscrew the upper seat belt anchor nut, noting the fitted positions of any washers and spacers so that they can be refitted in their original positions.
5 Remove the two securing screws, and withdraw the upper trim panel.
6 Remove the two or three securing screws as applicable, and withdraw the lower trim panel, passing the seat belt webbing through the panel as it is removed.
7 Refitting is a reversal of removal.

Rear pillar – Saloon models

8 Remove the rear seat cushion as described in Section 44.
9 Unbolt the lower seat belt anchor.
10 On models with fixed rear seats, remove the backrest as described in Section 44.
11 On models with folding rear seats, remove the side cushion as described in Section 44.
12 Remove the two securing screws from the base of the pillar trim panel, then pull the trim panel from the pillar, passing the seat belt webbing through the panel as it is removed.
13 Refitting is a reversal of removal.

Rear pillar – Hatchback models

14 Remove the rear seat side cushion as described in Section 44.
15 Remove the rear parcel shelf, and where applicable unbolt the rear seat belt upper anchor and spacer.
16 On 'high specification' models, lift the seat catch release lever, push out the pin securing the link rod to the lever and disconnect the link rod.
17 Remove the securing screws from the rear parcel shelf support (nine screws on models up to 1987, eight screws from 1987 onwards), and on 'high specification' models remove the two bolts securing the rear seat catch assembly to the wheel arch, then withdraw the catch assembly. Remove the rear parcel shelf support.

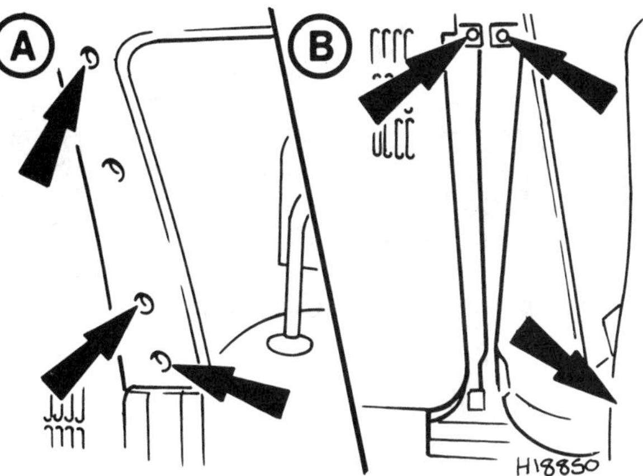

Fig 12.28 Interior rear pillar trim panel fixings (arrowed) – P100 models (Sec 39)

A Upper trim panel *B Lower trim panel*

18 Remove the five securing screws and detach the rear pillar trim panel.
19 Refitting is a reversal of removal, but where applicable check the operation of the rear seat catch on completion.

Rear pillar – P100 models

20 Remove the cover from the seat belt upper anchor, then unscrew the anchor, noting the fitted positions of any washers and spacers so that they can be refitted in their original positions.
21 Remove the three securing screws from the upper trim panel, and withdraw the panel – see Fig. 12.28(A).
22 Remove the three securing screws from the lower trim panel, then pull the panel away from the pillar and pass the seat belt webbing through the slot – see Fig. 12.28(B).
23 Withdraw the trim panel by disengaging it from the seat belt inertia reel mounting bracket.
24 Refitting is a reversal of removal.

40 Cab interior trim panels (P100 models) – removal and refitting

Side trim panel

1 Remove the rear pillar trim panel as described in Section 39.
2 Remove the side trim panel by prising out the four expander pins from the clips, then pulling out the clips and withdrawing the panel.
3 Refitting is a reversal of removal.

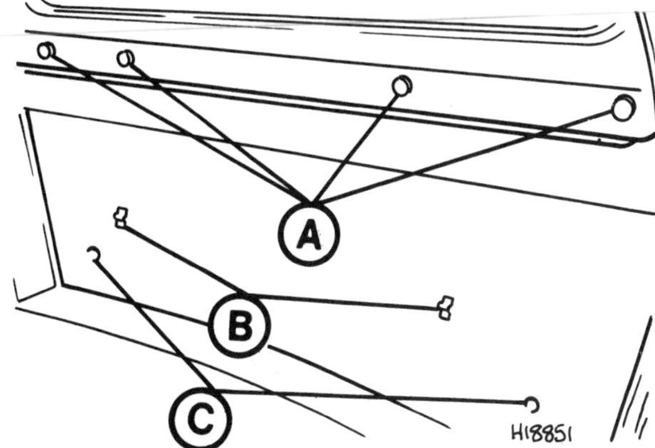

Fig 12.29 Cab interior rear panel fixings – P100 models (Sec 40)

A Upper and lower trim panel fixings
B Jack handle retaining clips
C Lower trim panel fixings

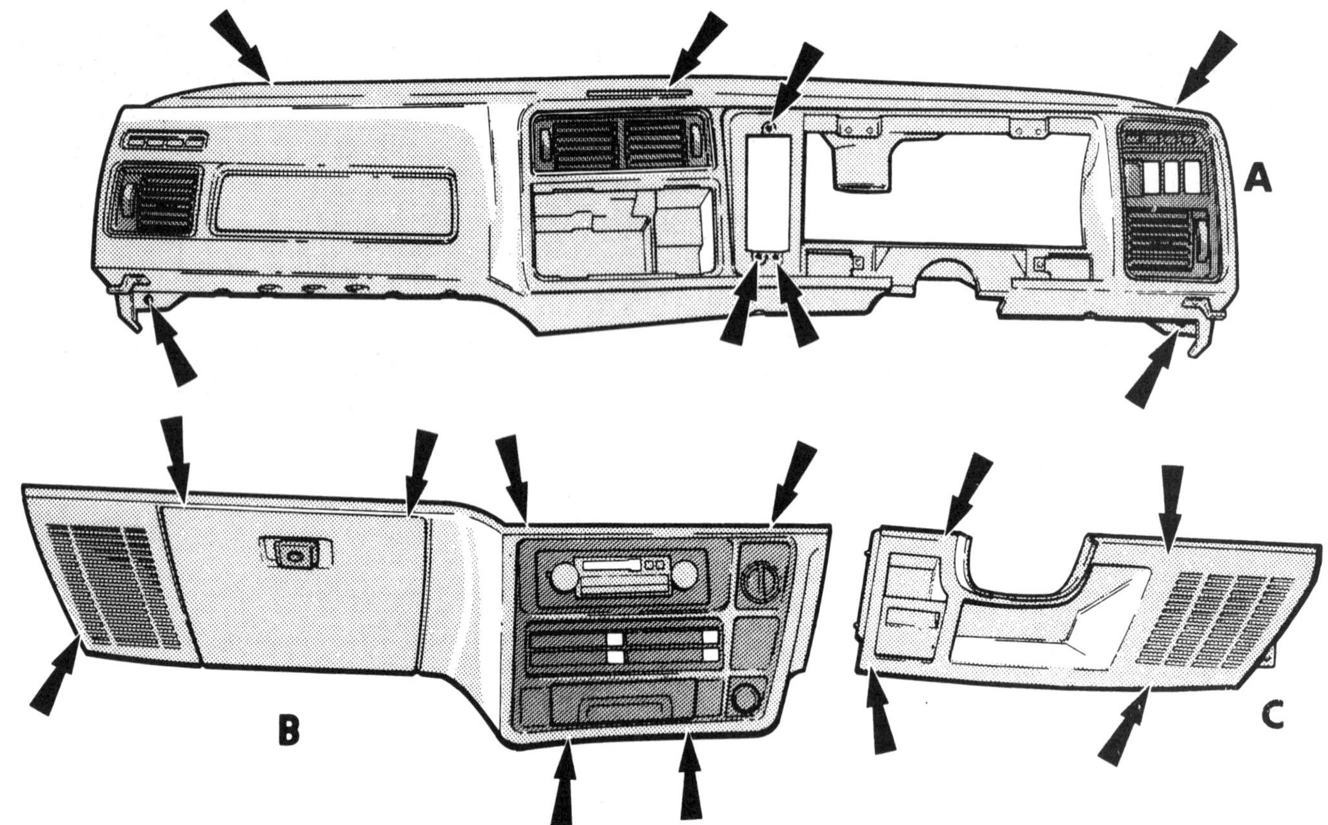

Fig 12.30 Facia panel securing screw locations (arrowed) (Sec 41)

A Upper facia panel *B Passenger side lower facia panel* *C Driver's side lower facia panel*

Upper rear trim panel

4 Remove the side trim panels from both sides of the cab as previously described in this Section.
5 Remove the cab rear window as described in Section 23.
6 Prise out the four expander pins from the trim panel clips beneath the rear window aperture, then pull out the clips.
7 Remove the blanking covers, then remove the three securing screws from the rear of the headlining.
8 Lower the rear of the headlining and remove the trim panel.
9 Refitting is a reversal of removal.

Lower rear trim panel

10 Remove the side trim panels from both sides of the cab as previously described in this Section.
11 Prise out the four expander pins from the trim panel clips beneath the rear window aperture, then pull out the clips.
12 Pull the jack handle from its two retaining clips, then remove the clips.
13 Prise out the two expander pins from the trim panel lower clips, then pull out the clips.
14 Pull the bottom edge of the trim panel away from the rear of the cab, and slide the panel out from under the upper trim panel.
15 Refitting is a reversal of removal.

41 Facia panels – removal and refitting

Note: *Refer to Fig. 12.30 for the locations of the facia panel securing screws*
1 Disconnect the battery negative lead.

Driver's side lower facia panel

2 Remove the two securing screws and withdraw the side trim panel from the right-hand side of the footwell (photo).
3 Remove the securing screws and unclip the lower and upper steering column shrouds.
4 Unclip the trim panel from the lower edge of the lower facia panel (photo).
5 Remove the four securing screws and withdraw the lower facia panel. Where applicable, disconnect the loudspeaker wiring (photo).
6 Refitting is a reversal of removal.

Passenger side lower facia panel

7 Remove the two securing screws and withdraw the side trim panel from the left-hand side of the footwell.
8 Remove the centre console as described in Section 42 to gain access to the lower facia panel securing screws.
9 Unclip the trim panel from the lower edge of the lower facia panel.
10 Unscrew the seven securing screws and withdraw the lower facia panel. Disconnect the wiring from the loudspeaker, glovebox lamp, ashtray lamp, heater switch, cigarette lighter, radio/cassette player, and loudspeaker balance control, as applicable. It is advisable to label the wiring plugs to assist refitting in the correct positions.
11 Refitting is a reversal of removal.

Upper facia panel

12 Remove the lower facia panels as described previously in this Section.
13 Remove the instrument cluster as described in Chapter 13.
14 Where applicable, remove the trip computer and 'door ajar' monitor as described in Chapter 13.
15 Remove the heater control panel as described in Section 48.
16 Prise out the front and rear foglamp, heated rear window, and heated windscreen switches and the instrument light and intermittent wiper rheostats, as applicable, from the upper facia panel, and disconnect their wiring plugs. Refer to Chapter 13 if necessary. It is advisable to label the wiring plugs to assist refitting in the correct positions.
17 Remove the five securing screws and withdraw the upper facia

41.2 Withdraw the side trim panel from the footwell

41.4 Removing a clip from the driver's side lower facia trim panel

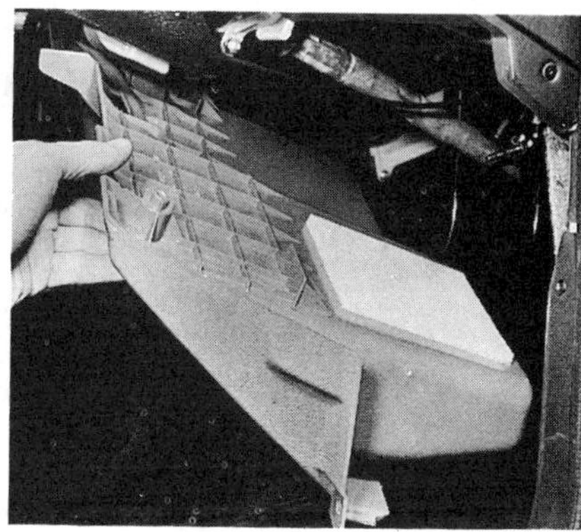
41.5 Withdrawing the driver's side lower facia panel

panel through the passenger door aperture. Disconnect the heater vent hoses, and ensure that any remaining wiring is disconnected and where applicable unclipped from the facia panel.

18 Refitting is a reversal of removal.

42 Centre console – removal and refitting

Full length console

1 Where applicable, prise the electric window switches from the front upper console panel and disconnect the wiring.

2 Remove the three securing screws from the front upper console panel, then withdraw the panel over the gear selector lever, at the same time releasing the rubber gaiter where applicable.

3 On 'high specification' models, where applicable prise the electric window switches from the rear upper console panel and disconnect the wiring. Remove the five securing screws and withdraw the rear upper console panel (photos).

4 On 'low specification' models, remove the two securing screws and release the single rear clip, then withdraw the rear upper console panel.

5 Where applicable, remove the two screws securing the lower console centre bracket to the transmission tunnel, and remove the bracket.

6 Remove the six screws securing the lower console panel, and withdraw the panel (photos).

7 Refitting is a reversal of removal.

Short console

8 Prise out the blanking plug, and remove the rear console securing screw.

9 On automatic transmission models, lift out the console tray mat and remove the front two console securing screws.

10 On manual gearbox models, prise out the blanking plugs and remove the front two console securing screws.

11 Withdraw the console over the gear selector lever, at the same time releasing the rubber gaiter where applicable.

43 Headlining – removal and refitting

Saloon, Hatchback and Estate models

1 On Saloon models, remove the rear seat back as described in Section 44.

2 Loosen the upper screws of all the pillar trim panels touching the headlining.

3 Prise off the covers and remove the screws from the passenger grab handles. Withdraw the grab handles. Similarly, prise off the blanking covers and remove the headlining securing screws from the driver's position.

4 Disconnect the battery negative lead, then prise the courtesy light(s) from the headlining or overhead console. Disconnect the wiring and remove the courtesy light(s).

5 Where applicable, remove the two securing screws and withdraw the overhead console.

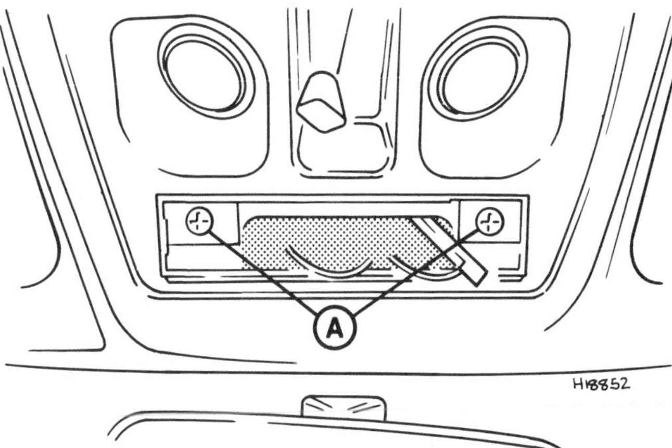

Fig 12.31 Overhead console securing screws (A) (Sec 43)

42.3A Removing a rear upper console panel front retaining screw – 'high specification' model

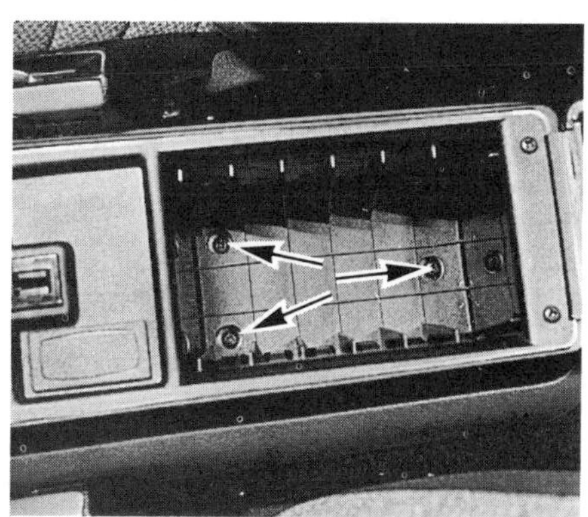
42.3B Rear upper console panel rear retaining screws (arrowed)

42.6A Removing a lower console panel front securing screw ...

42.6B ... centre securing screw ...

42.6C ... and rear securing screw

44.2 Front seat inner rear mounting

6 On models fitted with a sunroof, remove the sunroof as described in Section 37. The headlining is folded around the sunroof aperture flange and is held in place with adhesive tape and a moulding which must be removed.
7 Support the headlining, then remove the screws and withdraw the sun visors and clips. Where applicable, disconnect the wiring from the vanity mirror lamp.
8 On Estate models, remove the two plastic fasteners from the headlining between the rear door and tailgate pillars.
9 Remove the two plastic fasteners from the rear of the headlining, and withdraw the headlining through the luggage compartment.
10 Refitting is a reversal of removal.

P100 models

11 Loosen the front pillar trim panel upper securing screws.
12 Prise off the covers and remove the screws from the passenger grab handle. Withdraw the grab handle.
13 Prise off the blanking cover and remove the headlining securing screw from the driver's side.
14 Disconnect the battery negative lead, then prise the courtesy light from the headlining. Disconnect the wiring and remove the courtesy light.
15 Support the headlining, then remove the screws and withdraw the sun visors and clips.
16 Remove the blanking covers, and the three securing screws from the rear of the headlining, then withdraw the headlining through one of the door apertures.
17 Refitting is a reversal of removal.

44 Seats – removal and refitting

Front seat

1 Slide the seat fully forwards, and on seats with height adjustment unhook the tension spring from the rear crosstube. Where applicable, disconnect the wiring from the seat heating pad(s).
2 Unscrew and remove the two bolts from the inner rear seat mounting bracket and the single bolt from the outer rear seat mounting bracket (photo).
3 Slide the seat fully rearwards, then unscrew and remove the single bolt from each front seat mounting bracket. Withdraw the seat from the vehicle.
4 Refitting is a reversal of removal, but when fitting the front and rear mounting bolts, tighten the inner bolts first in each case. Where applicable locate the height adjustment tension spring between the weld pips on the crosstube.

Rear seat cushion

5 Remove the single screw from each side, securing the cushion to the heel kick panel.
6 Pull the cushion forwards and remove it from the vehicle.
7 Refitting is a reversal of removal.

Rear seat backrest (fixed rear seats)

8 Remove the seat cushion as described in paragraphs 5 and 6.
9 Remove the three now exposed Torx screws from the base of the backrest.
10 Working inside the luggage compartment, remove the three nuts securing the backrest to the body.
11 Pull the backrest forwards into the passenger compartment and remove it from the vehicle. Where applicable, feed the rear seat belt straps and buckles around the edges of the backrest.
12 Refitting is a reversal of removal.

Rear seat backrest (folding rear seats)

13 Release the catch and fold the seat backrest forwards.
14 Remove the two Torx screws from each backrest hinge.
15 Pull the backrest forwards into the passenger compartment and remove it from the vehicle. Where applicable, feed the rear seat belt straps and buckles around the edges of the backrest.
16 Refitting is a reversal of removal, but where necessary adjust the position of the seat catch striker to achieve correct operation of the catch.

Rear seat side cushion (Saloon models)

17 Working in the luggage compartment, remove the nut from the side cushion stud.
18 Working in the passenger compartment, remove the rear seat cushion as described in paragraphs 5 and 6.
19 Expose the seat backrest hinge bolt by removing the cover, then remove the bolt.
20 Pull the top of the side cushion forwards to disengage the stud from the body.
21 Straighten the metal retaining tangs at the base of the side cushion, then withdraw the cushion.
22 Refitting is a reversal of removal.

Rear seat side cushion (Hatchback and Estate models)

23 Fold down the rear seat backrest.
24 Carefully bend back the side cushion lower retaining tangs, then unhook the cushion from the upper fixing on the rear parcel shelf support (photo).
25 Refitting is a reversal of removal.

Rear seat armrest

26 Fold the rear seat backrest forwards, and remove the three armrest securing screws.
27 Remove the armrest by prising out the trim clips securing the cover material to the seat backrest.
28 Refitting is a reversal of removal.

45 Rear seat catch – removal and refitting

Saloon models

1 Working in the luggage compartment, release the seat catch by pulling the release knob, or if the cable is broken, use a screwdriver to release the catch itself.
2 Fold the backrest forwards into the passenger compartment and remove the two screws shown in Fig. 12.32.

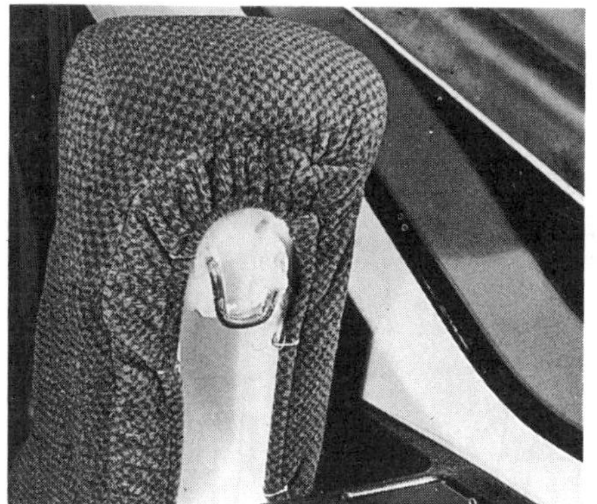
44.24 Rear seat side cushion removed exposing upper fixing hook

45.13 Rear seat catch assembly – 'high specification' Hatchback model

48.5 Control cable connection at heater (arrowed)

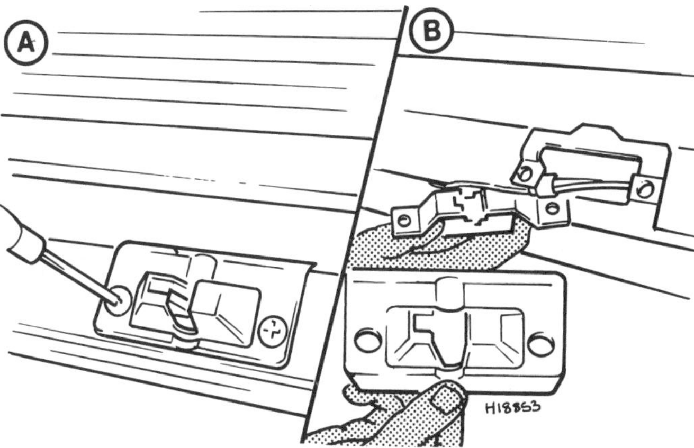

Fig 12.32 Rear seat catch fixings – Saloon models (Sec 45)

A Remove the securing screws
B Withdraw the cover and catch

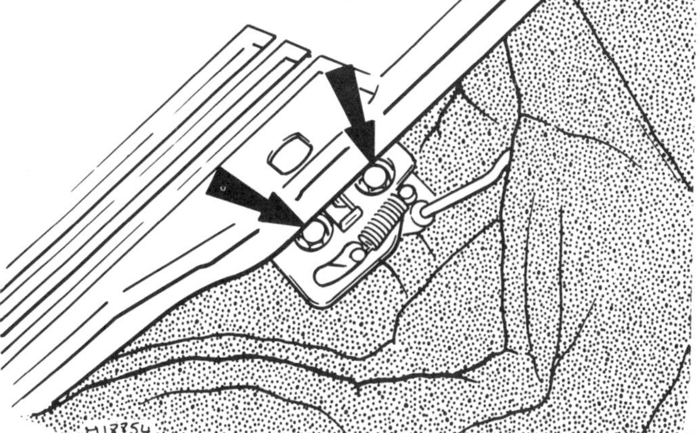

Fig 12.33 Pull back the seat cover to expose the rear seat catch securing bolts – 'low specification' Hatchback and Estate models (Sec 45)

3 Detach the cover and then remove the catch from the body.
4 Disconnect the release cable and sheath from the catch.
5 Refitting is a reversal of removal, but on completion check the catch for correct operation, and if necessary adjust the position of the striker on the seat backrest to achieve satisfactory engagement with the catch.

'Low specification' Hatchback and Estate models

6 Release the seat catch by pulling the release knob, and fold the backrest forwards into the passenger compartment.
7 Unscrew the release knob from the top of the seat backrest.
8 Carefully pull the edge of the seat cover from the flange on the seat backrest, then pull the backrest cushion away from the seat panel to gain access to the catch.
9 Remove the catch assembly by unscrewing the two securing bolts.
10 Refitting is a reversal of removal, but on completion check the catch for correct operation, and if necessary adjust the position of the striker to achieve satisfactory engagement with the catch.

'High specification' Hatchback and Estate models

11 Release the seat catch and fold the backrest forwards into the passenger compartment.
12 Remove the rear parcel shelf for improved access, then remove the screws and withdraw the cover for access to the catch.
13 Unscrew the two bolts securing the catch to the bracket on the rear wheel arch (photo).
14 Using a small screwdriver, push out the pin securing the link rod to the catch, then withdraw the catch.
15 If required, lift the release lever, push out the securing pin and remove the link rod. The lever can be removed by drilling out the two securing rivets from the parcel shelf support.
16 Refitting is a reversal of removal, but where applicable fit new rivets using a hand riveter to secure the release lever. On completion check the operation of the catch and if necessary adjust the position of the striker to achieve satisfactory engagement with the catch.

46 Front seat air cushion assembly – removal and refitting

Complete assembly – removal and refitting

1 Remove the seat as described in Section 44.
2 Straighten the seat back cover retaining tangs, and pull the cover upwards to expose the air cushion.
3 Cut through the four securing rings and remove the two screws securing the metal air tube to the side of the seat, then withdraw the assembly from the seat frame.
4 Refitting is a reversal of removal, using new cushion securing rings.

Air inflator ball – renewal

5 Remove the seat as described in Section 44.

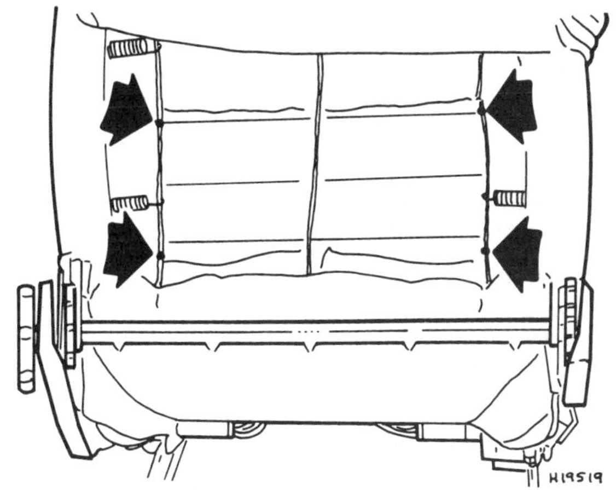

Fig 12.34 Front seat air cushion securing rings (arrowed) (Sec 46)

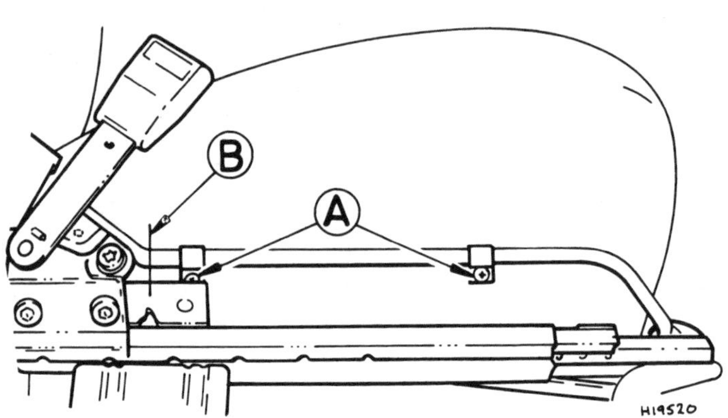

Fig 12.35 Front seat air cushion tube and inflator ball (Sec 46)

A Air tube securing screws *B Hose cutting point*

6 Remove the two screws securing the metal air tube to the side of the seat, then cut through the plastic hose as close to the end of the metal tube as possible. Discard the old tube and the inflator ball.
7 Fit a new hose clamp over the plastic hose, and warm the end of the hose in hot water until it is pliable. Push the metal tube into the plastic hose, ensuring an overlap of at least 20.0 mm (0.8 in).
8 Crimp the new clamp onto the hose to ensure an airtight seal.
9 Refit the two screws securing the tube to the side of the seat.
10 Refit the seat as described in Section 44.

47 Seat belts – removal and refitting

Front seat belt stalk

1 Remove the front seat as described in Section 44.
2 Detach the seat belt stalk from the seat by removing the two Torx screws.
3 Refitting is a reversal of removal.

Front seat belt assembly

4 Where applicable, prise out the cover from the height adjuster and detach the adjuster by removing the two screws.
5 Unscrew the seat belt upper anchor nut, noting the fitted positions of any washers and spacers so that they can be refitted in their original positions.
6 Remove the centre pillar trim panels as described in Section 39.
7 On 3-door models, remove the waist-level seat belt webbing guide, and remove the bolt securing the belt slider bar to the body. Disengage the slider bar from the heel kick panel, and slide off the belt webbing loop.
8 Unscrew the bolt securing the inertia reel unit to the centre pillar, noting the fitted positions of any washers and spacers so that they can be refitted in their original positions.
9 Refitting is a reversal of removal, taking care to install the belt without twists in the webbing, and refitting any washers and spacers in their original positions.

Rear seat belt assembly (Saloon models)

10 Remove the rear seat cushion as described in Section 44.
11 Unbolt the relevant belt anchor(s) from the floor, noting the fitted positions of any washers and spacers so that they can be refitted in their original positions. The central lap strap and buckle assemblies can be withdrawn after unbolting the anchors.
12 To remove a side belt and inertia reel assembly, proceed as follows.
13 Remove the rear pillar trim panel as described in Section 39.
14 Unscrew the upper belt anchor, noting the fitted positions of any washers and spacers so that they can be refitted in their original positions.
15 Unscrew the bolt securing the inertia reel unit to the rear pillar, again noting the positions of any washers and spacers.

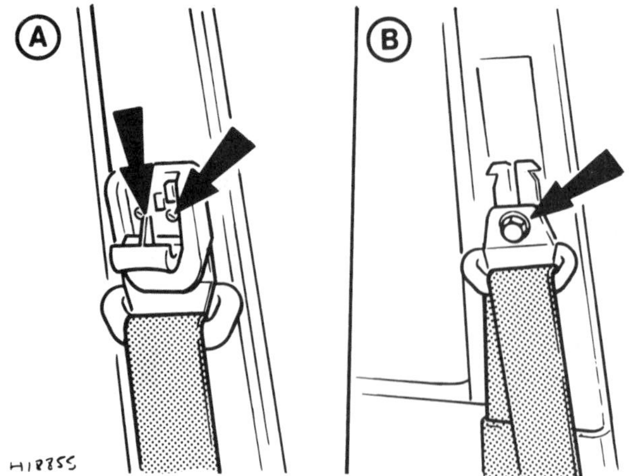

Fig 12.36 Front seat belt upper anchor fixings (Sec 47)

A Adjuster securing screws *B Anchor nut*

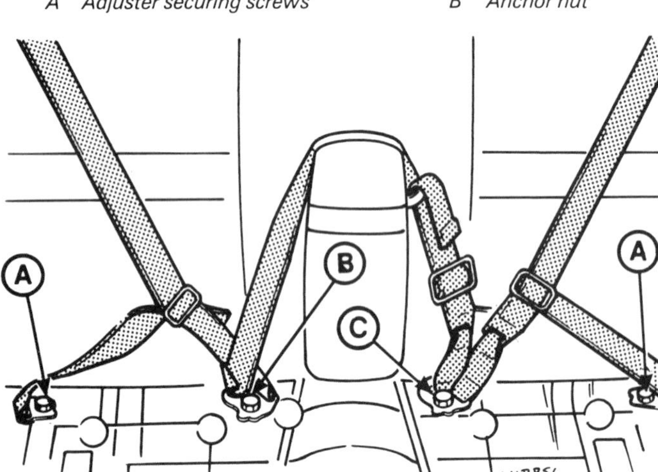

Fig 12.37 Rear seat belt lower anchors (Sec 47)

A Inertia reel belt lower anchors
B Static belt and buckle
C Twin buckle assembly

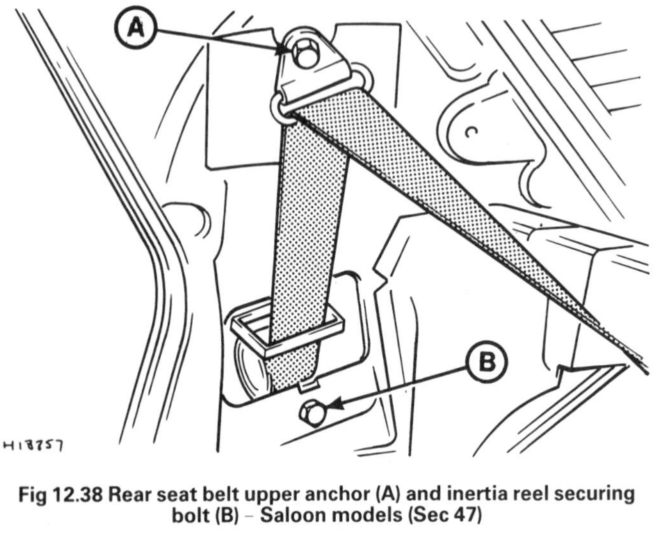

Fig 12.38 Rear seat belt upper anchor (A) and inertia reel securing bolt (B) – Saloon models (Sec 47)

16 Refitting is a reversal of removal, taking care to install the belt(s) without twists in the webbing, and refitting any washers and spacers in their original positions.

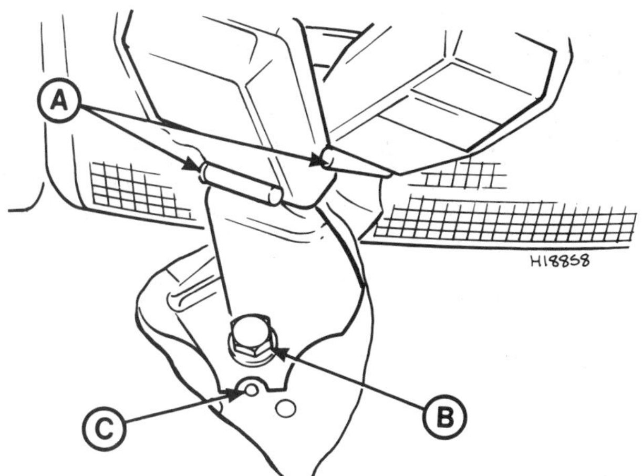

Fig 12.39 Rear seat belt twin buckle assembly lower anchor bracket – Hatchback and Estate models (Sec 47)

A Elasticated strap retaining dowels
B Anchor bolt
C Floor dimple

Rear seat belt assembly (Hatchback and Estate models)

17 Remove the rear seat cushion as described in Section 44.

18 Unbolt the relevant belt anchor(s) from the floor, noting the fitted positions of any washers and spacers so that they can be refitted in their original positions.

19 To remove the central lapstrap and buckle assemblies, disconnect the buckle(s) from the elasticated straps by withdrawing the retaining dowel(s). To prevent the strap(s) from moving into the interior of the seat, insert a length of wire through the strap loop(s).

20 To remove a side belt and inertia reel assembly, proceed as follows.

21 Unbolt the upper left anchor, noting the position of any washers and spacers, and allow the webbing to pass into the inertia reel unit.

22 On Hatchback models, pull back the inertia reel cover in the luggage compartment, and unbolt the inertia reel from the body, noting the position of any washers and spacers. Prise out the belt guide from the rear parcel shelf support, and push the guide, upper and lower anchors, and buckle plate through the aperture.

23 On Estate models, remove the luggage compartment side trim panel with reference to Section 38, then unbolt the inertia reel unit, noting the position of any washers and spacers, and withdraw the belt assembly.

24 Refitting is a reversal of removal, taking care to install the belt(s) without twists in the webbing, and refitting any washers and spacers in their original positions. Ensure that the cut-outs in the lower anchor brackets are correctly located around the raised dimples in the floor.

48 Heater controls – removal and refitting

1 Disconnect the battery negative lead.

2 Remove the securing screws and unclip the lower and upper steering column shrouds.

3 Remove the four securing screws and withdraw the instrument panel surround. Note that the bottom right-hand screw is covered by a plastic panel which must be prised out.

4 Remove the passenger side lower facia panel as described in Section 41.

5 Where necessary for improved access, detach the two vent hoses from the left-hand side of the heater, then detach the lower ends of the two control cables from the heater by removing the retaining screws (photo).

6 Unscrew the three securing screws, and remove the heater control panel by sliding it through the facia panel and withdrawing it downwards. Disconnect the wiring from the control panel illumination bulb.

7 If necessary, the bulb can be removed with its holder.

8 Refitting is a reversal of removal, bearing in mind the following points.

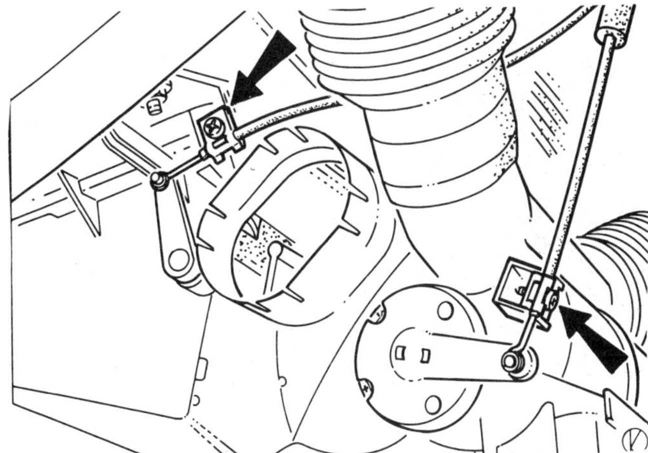

Fig 12.40 Heater control cable lower end fittings (arrowed) (Sec 48)

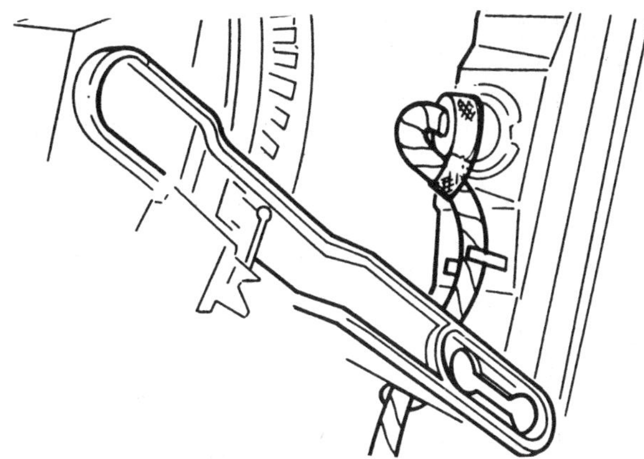

Fig 12.41 Heater control panel illumination bulb wiring loom correctly routed (Sec 48)

9 When reconnecting the wiring to the control panel illumination bulb, wrap insulating tape around the wiring loom over a length of approximately 330.0 mm (13.0 in) starting from the bulbholder. Route the loom, ensuring that it is located in the two retaining clips, bend it over and secure it to the bulbholder with insulating tape as shown in Fig. 12.41. This procedure will prevent the wiring loom from chafing against the heater control levers.

10 When reconnecting the control cables to the heater, move the control levers on the control panel to the fully up position, then attach the cables to the clips on the heater. The cable ends should project from the clips by between 0 and 4.0 mm (0 and 0.16 in). The cables are adjusted automatically by moving the control levers fully downwards. It is possible that considerable resistance may have to be overcome when moving the control levers.

49 Heater unit – removal and refitting

1 Disconnect the battery negative lead.

2 If the coolant is still hot, release the pressure in the system by slowly unscrewing the expansion tank cap. Place a thick rag over the cap to prevent scalding as the pressure is released.

3 Note the location of the two heater hoses on the engine compartment bulkhead, then disconnect and plug them (photo). Alternatively, the hoses can be secured high enough to prevent the coolant from draining.

4 To prevent unnecessary spillage of coolant when the heater unit is removed, blow into the upper heater pipe until all the coolant has been expelled through the lower pipe.

5 Remove the two securing screws and withdraw the heater pipe cover from the bulkhead. Recover the gasket (photo).

49.3 Location of heater hoses on engine compartment bulkhead

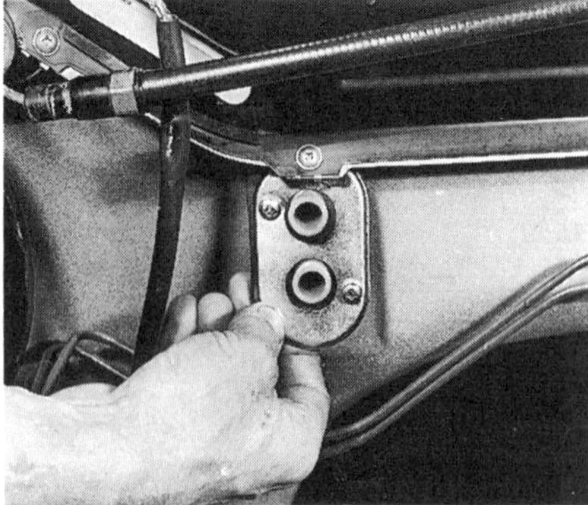
49.5 Heater pipe cover

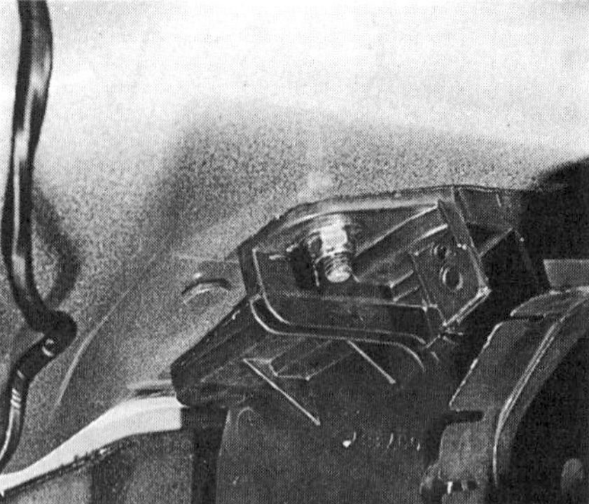
49.9A Heater mounting bolt

49.9B Withdrawing the heater

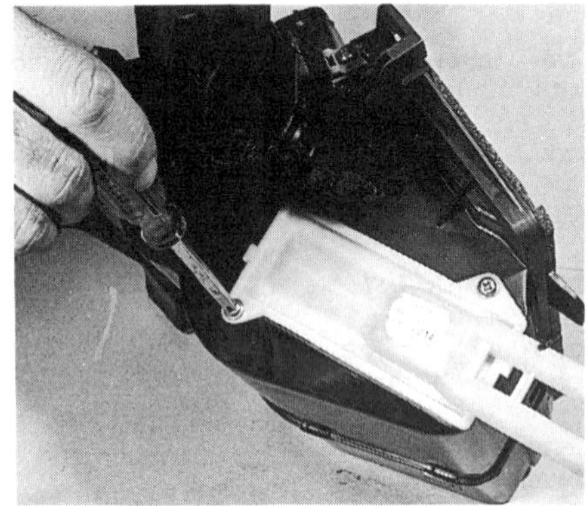
50.1A Remove the securing screws ...

50.1B ... and withdraw the heater matrix

6 Working inside the vehicle, remove the passenger side lower facia panel as described in Section 41.
7 Disconnect the ends of the two control cables from the heater by removing the two retaining screws.
8 Detach the five vent hoses from the heater.
9 Unscrew the two mounting bolts, and move the heater to the rear until the pipes are clear of the bulkhead, then withdraw the heater to the left. If necessary, remove the lower facia bracket (photos).
10 Refitting is a reversal of removal, but adjust the control cables by moving the levers on the control panel to the top and then the bottom stops. Considerable resistance may be encountered when moving the levers towards the bottom stops, which should be overcome.
11 On completion, top up the coolant level as described in Chapter 2.

50 Heater unit – overhaul

1 With the heater unit removed from the vehicle, remove the two securing screws and withdraw the heater matrix from the casing (photos).
2 Cut the heater casing gasket in line with the casing joint, then use two suitable screwdrivers to prise off the retaining clips and separate the casing halves. Withdraw the lower part of the casing to the side.
3 Remove the air flap valves, then press the control levers from the casing. Note that the 'up/down' control lever can only be removed when the marks are aligned as shown in Fig. 12.42.
4 Clean all components and hose through the matrix to remove any debris. If necessary use a chemical cleaner to clear the inner passage of the matrix. Renew the components as necessary.
5 Reassembly is a reversal of dismantling.

51 Heater motor – removal and refitting

1 Disconnect the battery negative lead.
2 Where necessary, unclip the brake servo vacuum hose for improved access.
3 On models from 1987, unclip the windscreen washer hoses and wiring from the motor cover, and secure them to the bodywork out of the way.
4 Unscrew the two securing bolts from the motor cover, pull off the rubber moulding, then withdraw the cover (photos).
5 Disconnect the wiring from the motor, and detach the earth lead from its bracket.
6 Unscrew the two motor securing nuts, and withdraw the motor assembly (photo).
7 Unclip the casing halves, then prise open the motor retaining strap using a screwdriver, or if necessary a drift.
8 Detach the wiring from the motor, then remove the motor and fan wheels from the casing.
9 Refitting is a reversal of removal.

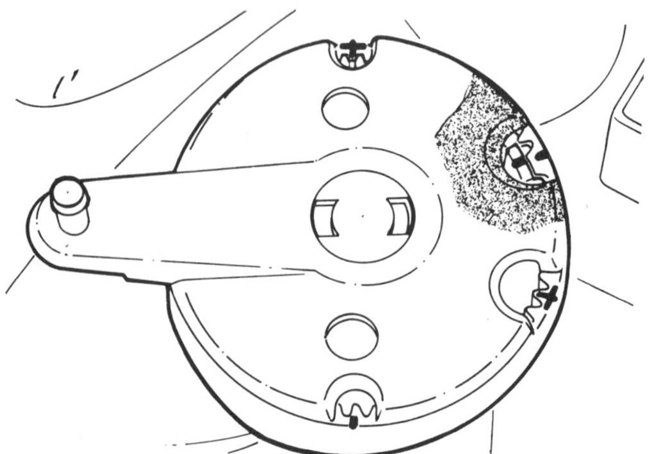
Fig 12.42 Heater 'up/down' control lever must be aligned as shown before removal (Sec 50)

Note that the cross marks are for right-hand drive vehicles

51.4A Unscrew the securing bolts ...

51.4B ... and withdraw the heater motor cover

51.6 Heater motor and wiring

52 Air conditioning system – description and precautions

Description

1 An air conditioning system is available as an optional extra on certain models. In conjunction with the heater, the system enables any reasonable air temperature to be achieved inside the vehicle; it also reduces the humidity of the incoming air, aiding demisting even when cooling is not required.

2 The refrigeration side of the air conditioning system functions in a similar way to a domestic refrigerator. A compressor, belt-driven from the crankshaft pulley, draws refrigerant in its gaseous phase from an evaporator. The compressed refrigerant passes through a condenser where it loses heat and enters its liquid phase. After passing through the dehydrator, which acts as a reservoir and filter to extract moisture from the circuit, the refrigerant returns to the evaporator where it absorbs heat from the air passing over the evaporator fins on its way to the vehicle interior. The refrigerant becomes a gas again and the cycle is repeated.

3 Various subsidiary controls and sensors protect the system against excessive temperature and pressures. Additionally, engine idle speed is increased when the system is in use to compensate for the additional load imposed by the compressor.

Precautions

4 Although the refrigerant is not itself toxic, in the presence of a naked flame (or a lighted cigarette) it forms a highly toxic gas. Liquid refrigerant spilled on the skin will cause frostbite. If refrigerant enters the eyes, rinse them with a dilute solution of boric acid and seek medical advice immediately.

5 In view of the above points, and of the need for specialised equipment for evacuating and recharging the system, any work which requires disconnection of a refrigerant line must be left to a specialist.

6 Do not allow refrigerant lines to be exposed to temperatures above 230°F (110°C), eg, during welding or paint drying operations.

7 Do not operate the air conditioning system if it is known to be short of refrigerant, or further damage may result.

53 Air conditioning system – maintenance

1 Regularly inspect the compressor drivebelt for correct tension and good condition. Tension is adjusted in the same way as for the alternator drivebelt – see Chapter 2.

2 At the intervals specified in the 'Routine maintenance' Section at

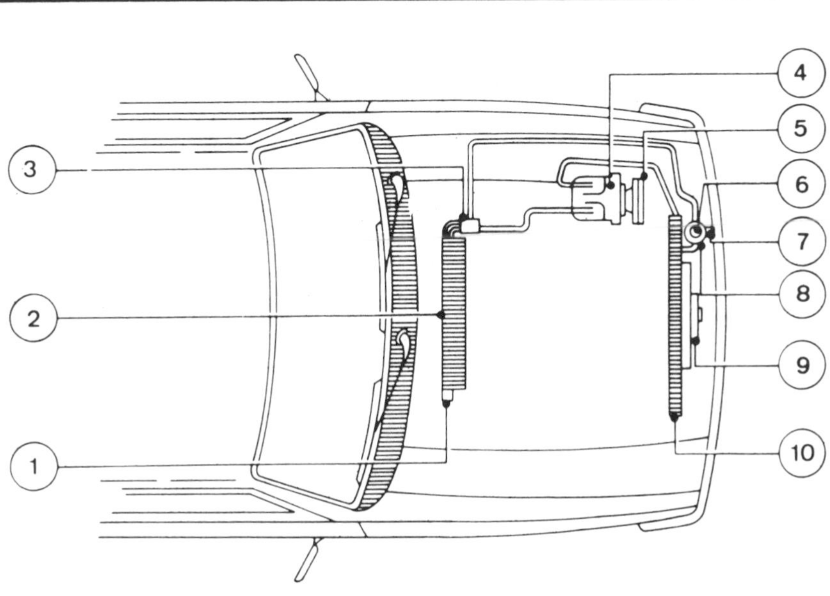

Fig 12.43 Layout of air conditioning system components (Sec 52)

1 De-ice thermostat
2 Evaporator
3 Expansion valve
4 Compressor
5 Compressor clutch
6 Pressure switch
7 Sight glass
8 Dehydrator/collector
9 Cooling fan
10 Condenser

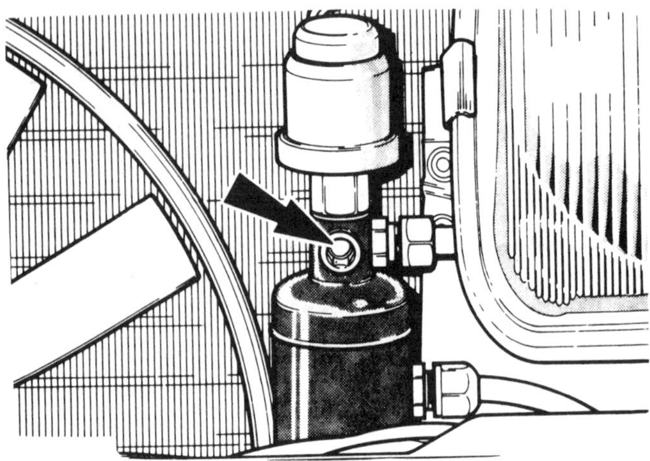
Fig 12.44 Air conditioning system refrigerant sight glass (arrowed) (Sec 53)

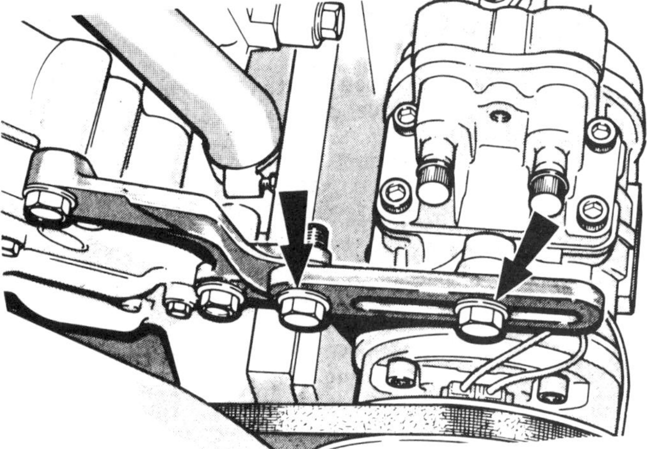
Fig 12.45 Typical air conditioning compressor mounting and pivot bolts (arrowed) (Sec 54)

the beginning of this manual, remove the radiator grille and clean any leaves, insects, etc. from the condenser coil and fins. Be very careful not to damage the condenser fins: use a soft brush, or a compressed air jet, along (not across) the fins.

3 Before refitting the grille, check the refrigerant charge as follows. The engine should be cold and the ambient temperature should be between 18 and 25°C (64 and 77°F).

4 Start the engine and allow it to idle. Observe the refrigerant sight glass and have an assistant switch on the air conditioning to fan speed III. A few bubbles should be seen in the sight glass as the system starts up, but all bubbles should disappear within 10 seconds. Persistent bubbles, or no bubbles at all, mean that the refrigerant charge is low. Switch off the system immediately if the charge is low and do not use it again until it has been recharged.

5 Operate the air conditioning system for at least 10 minutes each month, even during cold weather, to keep the seals, etc, in good condition.

6 Regularly inspect the refrigerant pipes, hoses and unions for security and good condition.

7 The air conditioning system will lose a proportion of its charge through normal seepage – typically up to 100 g (4 oz) per year – so it is as well to regard periodic recharging as a maintenance operation. Recharging should be carried out by a specialist.

54 Air conditioning system – component renewal

1 Only those items which can be renewed without discharging the system are described here. Other items must be dealt with by a Ford dealer or air conditioning specialist.

Compressor drivebelt

2 Disconnect the battery negative lead.

3 On OHC models, remove the thermo-viscous cooling fan as described in Chapter 2.

4 Slacken the compressor mounting and pivot bolts, move the compressor towards the engine and remove the old drivebelt.

5 Fit the new drivebelt, position the compressor to achieve the correct belt tension, then tighten the mounting and pivot bolts.

6 On OHC models, refit the thermo-viscous cooling fan as described in Chapter 2.

7 Reconnect the battery negative lead.

Condenser fan and motor – models up to 1987

8 Disconnect the battery negative lead, and remove the radiator grille as described in Section 30. On Ghia models, remove the front bumper as described in Section 28.

9 Disconnect the fan wiring connector at the side of the condenser.

10 Remove the three securing bolts and withdraw the fan assembly. Turn the frame to position the fan wiring on the dehydrator side to avoid damaging the wiring. Take care also not to damage the condenser fins or tube.

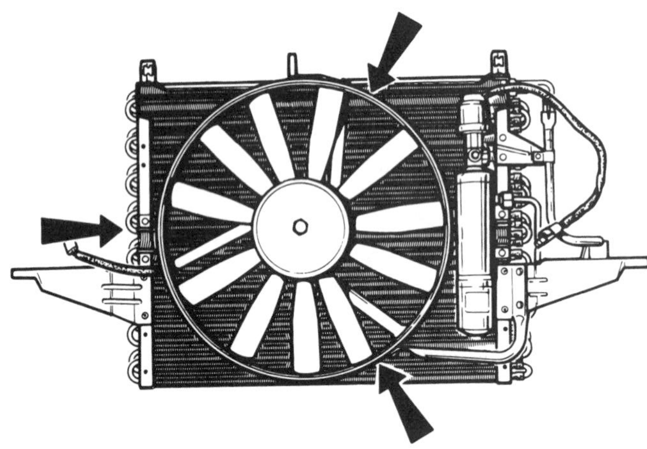
Fig 12.46 Air conditioning condenser fan assembly securing bolts (arrowed) – models up to 1987 (Sec 54)

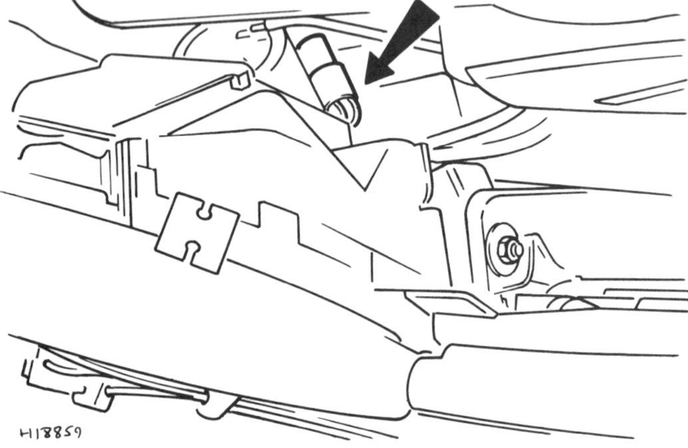

Fig 12.47 Air conditioning condenser fan wiring connector location (arrowed) – models from 1987 (Sec 54)

11 To remove the fan blades from the motor, remove the retaining nut and circlip. **The nut has a left-hand thread**, ie, it is undone in a clockwise direction.

12 With the blades removed, the motor can be unscrewed from the frame.

13 Reassemble and refit in the reverse order of dismantling and removal.

Condenser fan and motor – models from 1987

14 Disconnect the battery negative lead.
15 Remove the bonnet lock as described in Section 8.
16 Unclip the guard from the fan frame.
17 Disconnect the fan wiring connector – see Fig. 12.47.
18 Apply the handbrake, jack up the front of the vehicle and support on axle stands.
19 Unscrew the two lower condenser securing bolts and disengage the condenser from the top of the radiator by releasing the three clips.
20 Unscrew the four securing bolts and detach the fan assembly from the condenser. Withdraw the fan assembly from underneath the vehicle.
21 Proceed as described in paragraphs 11 to 13 inclusive.

De-ice thermostat

22 Disconnect and remove the battery.
23 Disconnect any vacuum hoses, windscreen washer hoses and electrical wiring as necessary, then unscrew the four securing bolts and on models up to 1987 the single nut, and remove the right-hand plenum chamber cover plate from the bulkhead.
24 Disconnect the thermostat from the evaporator casing and withdraw it. Also withdraw the thermostat probe from the casing.
25 Refitting is a reversal of removal.

Heating/air conditioning controls

26 The procedure is similar to that described in Section 48, but additionally the vacuum hoses must be disconnected from the control unit vacuum valve during removal, and reconnected when refitting.

Chapter 13 Electrical system

For modifications, and information applicable to later models, see Supplement at end of manual

Contents

Specifications

System type	12 volt, negative earth
Battery	
Charge condition:	
Poor	12.5 volts
Normal	12.6 volts
Good	12.7 volts
Alternator	
Type	Bosch, Lucas, Motorola, or Mitsubishi
Regulated output voltage at engine speed of 4000 rpm and 3 to 7 amp load	13.7 to 14.6 volts
Minimum brush length:	
All alternator types except Motorola	5.0 mm (0.20 in)
Motorola type alternators	4.0 mm (0.16 in)
Starter motor	
Type	Pre-engaged; Bosch, Cajavec, Lucas, or Nippondenso
Minimum brush length:	
All starter motor types except Bosch long frame 1.1 kW and JF, and Nippondenso	8.0 mm (0.32 in)
Bosch long frame 1.1 kW and JF, and Nippondenso type starter motors	10.0 mm (0.40 in)
Wiper Blades	Champion X-5103 (all front and Hatchback rear), Champion X-3303 (Estate rear)

Bulbs	**Fittings**	**Wattage**
Halogen headlamps	H4	60/55
Auxiliary driving lamps	H3	55
Front foglamps	H3	55
Sidelamps	Glass base	5
Direction indicator lamps	Bayonet	21
Brake/tail lamps	Bayonet	21/4
Reversing lamp(s)	Bayonet	21
Rear foglamp(s)	Bayonet	21
Rear number plate lamps	Glass base	5
Luggage compartment lamp	Bayonet	10
Underbonnet lamp	Bayonet	10
Courtesy lamp(s)	Bayonet	10
Map reading lamps	Glass base	5
Vanity mirror illumination lamp	Festoon	3
Glove compartment lamp	Glass base	3
Ashtray lamp	Glass base	1.2
Warning lamps	Glass base	1.2 or 2.5
Instrument illumination lamps	Glass base	1.2 or 2.5
Heater control illumination lamp	Glass base	1
Automatic transmission gear selector lamp	Bayonet	1.2
Clock illumination lamp	Bayonet	1.4
Cigarette lighter lamp	Glass base	1.2

Torque wrench settings	**Nm**	**lbf ft**
Alternator adjustment bolt	21 to 28	15 to 20
Alternator mounting bolts:		
With coloured patch on threads	41 to 51	30 to 38
Without coloured patch	20 to 25	15 to 18
Trip computer fuel flow sensor unit fuel pipe unions (fuel injection models)	14 to 17	10 to 13

1 General description

The electrical system is of the 12 volt negative earth type, and consists of a 12 volt battery, alternator with integral voltage regulator, starter motor and related electrical accessories, components and wiring. The battery is of the low maintenance or maintenance-free 'sealed for life' type and is charged by an alternator which is belt-driven from the crankshaft pulley. The starter motor is of the pre-engaged type, incorporating an integral solenoid. On starting the solenoid moves the drive pinion into engagement with the flywheel ring gear before the starter motor is energised. Once the engine has started, a one-way clutch prevents the motor armature being driven by the engine until the pinion disengages from the flywheel.

Further details of the electrical systems are given in the relevant Sections of this Chapter.

Caution: *Before carrying out any work on the vehicle electrical system, read through the precautions given in the 'Safety first!' Section at the beginning of this manual, and in Section 2 of this Chapter.*

2 Electrical system – precautions

It is necessary to take extra care when working on the electrical system to avoid damage to semi-conductor devices (diodes and transis-

tors), and to avoid the risk of personal injury. In addition to the precautions given in the *'Safety first!'* Section at the beginning of this manual, take note of the following points when working on the system.
1 *Always remove rings, watches, etc before working on the electrical system.* Even with the battery disconnected, capacitive discharge could occur if a component live terminal is earthed through a metal object. This could cause a shock or nasty burn.
2 *Do not reverse the battery connections.* Components such as the alternator or any other having semi-conductor circuitry could be irreparably damaged.
3 If the engine is being started using jump leads and a slave battery, connect the batteries *positive to positive* and *negative to negative.* This also applies when connecting a battery charger.
4 Never disconnect the battery terminals, or alternator multi-plug connector, when the engine is running.
5 The battery leads and alternator multi-plug must be disconnected before carrying out any electric welding on the car.
6 Never use an ohmmeter of the type incorporating a hand cranked generator for circuit or continuity testing.

3 Maintenance and inspection

1 At the intervals specified in the *Routine maintenance* Section at the beginning of this manual, carry out the following maintenance operations and checks.
2 Check the operation of all the electrical equipment, ie wipers, washers, lights, direction indicators, horn etc. Refer to the appropriate Sections of this Chapter if any components are found to be inoperative.
3 Visually check all accessible wiring connectors, harnesses and retaining clips for security, or any signs of chafing or damage. Rectify any problems encountered.
4 Check the alternator drivebelt for cracks, fraying or damage. Renew the belt if worn or, if satisfactory, check and adjust the belt tension. These procedures are covered in Chapter 2, Section 12.
5 Check the condition of the wiper blades and if they are cracked or show signs of deterioration, renew them, as described in Section 43. Check the operation of the windscreen and tailgate washers (where applicable). Adjust the nozzles using a pin, if necessary.
6 Check the battery terminals, and if there is any sign of corrosion, disconnect and clean them thoroughly. Smear the terminals and battery posts with petroleum jelly before refitting the plastic covers. If there is any corrosion on the battery tray, remove the battery, clean the deposits away and treat the affected metal with an anti-rust preparation. Repaint the tray in the original colour after treatment.
7 From 1982 Ford models have progressively been fitted with a maintenance-free battery during production. The maintenance-free battery is of 'sealed for life' cell design and does not require routine topping-up with distilled water. The only maintenance requirement with this battery type is to inspect the battery lead terminals for security and any sign of corrosion.
8 On early models equipped with a low maintenance type battery, or on later models where the battery has been replaced by one of this type from another source, the electrolyte level should be maintained just above the tops of the cells, or up to the mark on the battery case where applicable. If topping-up is necessary, add distilled water to each cell as necessary after unscrewing the cell caps or lifting up the top cover.
9 Check and if necessary top up the washer fluid reservoir and check the security of the pump wires and water pipes.
10 It is advisable to have the headlight aim adjusted using optical beam setting equipment.
11 While carrying out a road test, check the operation of all the instruments and warning lights, and the operation of the direction indicator self-cancelling mechanism.

4 Battery – testing and charging

Standard and low maintenance battery – testing

1 If the vehicle covers a small annual mileage it is worthwhile checking the specific gravity of the electrolyte every three months to determine the state of charge of the battery. Use a hydrometer to make the check and compare the results with the following table.

	Ambient temperature above 25°C (77°F)	**Ambient temperature below 25°C (77°F)**
Fully charged	1.210 to 1.230	1.270 to 1.290
70% charged	1.170 to 1.190	1.230 to 1.250
Fully discharged...	1.050 to 1.070	1.110 to 1.130

Note that the specific gravity readings assume an electrolyte temperature of 15°C (60°F); for every 10°C (18°F) below 15°C (60°F) subtract 0.007. For every 10°C (18°F) above 15°C (60°F) add 0.007.

2 If the battery condition is suspect first check the specific gravity of electrolyte in each cell. A variation of 0.040 or more between any cells indicates loss of electrolyte or deterioration of the internal plates.
3 If the specific gravity variation is 0.040 or more, the battery should be renewed. If the cell variation is satisfactory but the battery is discharged, it should be charged as described later in this Section.

Maintenance-free battery – testing

4 In cases where a 'sealed-for-life' maintenance-free battery is fitted, topping-up and testing of the electrolyte in each cell is not possible. The condition of the battery can therefore only be tested using a battery condition indicator or a voltmeter.
5 If testing the battery using a voltmeter, connect the voltmeter across the battery and compare the result with those given in the Specifications under 'charge condition'. The test is only accurate if the battery has not been subject to any kind of charge for the previous six hours. If this is not the case, switch on the headlights for 30 seconds, then wait four to five minutes before testing the battery after switching off the headlights. All other electrical components must be switched off, so check that the doors and tailgate are fully shut when making the test.
6 If the voltage reading is less than 12.2 volts, then the battery is discharged, whilst a reading of 12.2 to 12.4 volts indicates a partially discharged condition.
7 If the battery is to be charged, remove it from the vehicle (Section 5) and charge it as described later in this Section.

Standard and low maintenance battery – charging

8 Charge the battery at a rate of 3.5 to 4 amps and continue to charge the battery at this rate until no further rise in specific gravity is noted over a four hour period.
9 Alternatively, a trickle charger charging at the rate of 1.5 amps can be safely used overnight.
10 Specially rapid 'boost' charges which are claimed to restore the power of the battery in 1 to 2 hours are not recommended as they can cause serious damage to the battery plates through overheating.
11 While charging the battery, note that the temperature of the electrolyte should never exceed 37.8°C (100°F).

Maintenance-free battery – charging

12 This battery type takes considerably longer to fully recharge than the standard type, the time taken being dependent on the extent of discharge, but it can take anything up to three days.
13 A constant voltage type charger is required, to be set, when connected, to 13.9 to 14.9 volts with a charger current below 25 amps. Using this method the battery should be useable within three hours, giving a voltage reading of 12.5 volts, but this is for a partially discharged battery and, as mentioned, full charging can take considerably longer.
14 If the battery is to be charged from a fully discharged state (condition reading less than 12.2 volts) have it recharged by your Ford dealer or local automotive electrician as the charge rate is higher and constant supervision during charging is necessary.

5 Battery – removal and refitting

1 The battery is located in the engine compartment on the left-hand side of the bulkhead.

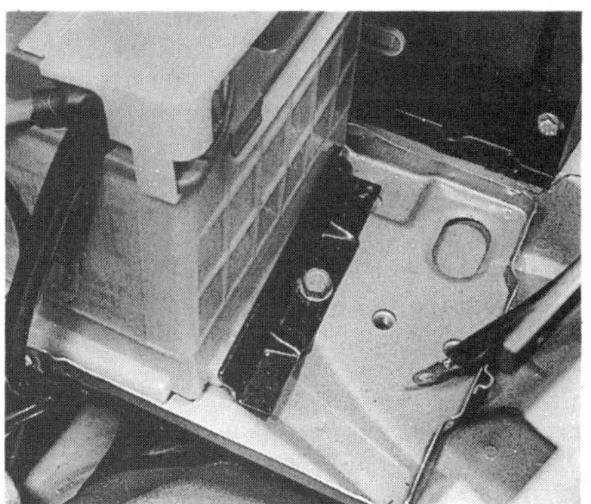

5.3 Battery securing clamp and bolt

8.2A Disconnecting the multi-plug from a Bosch type alternator

8.2B Removing the insulating cap from the main wiring terminal on a Lucas A127 type alternator (CVH model)

2 Disconnect the leads at the negative (earth) terminal by unscrewing the retaining nut and removing the bulb. Pull off the plastic cover, and disconnect the positive terminal leads in the same way.
3 Unscrew the clamp bolt sufficiently to enable the battery to be lifted from its location (photo). Keep the battery in an upright position to avoid spilling electrolyte on the bodywork.
4 Refitting is a reversal of removal, but smear petroleum jelly on the terminals when reconnecting the leads, and always connect the positive lead first and the negative lead last.

6 Alternator – description

1 One of a number of different makes of alternator may be fitted, depending on model and engine capacity. The maximum output of the alternator varies accordingly.
2 The alternator is belt-driven from the crankshaft pulley. Cooling is provided by a fan mounted outside the casing on the end of the rotor shaft. An integral voltage regulator is incorporated to control the output voltage.
3 The alternator provides a charge to the battery even at very low engine speed and basically consists of a coil-wound stator in which a rotor rotates. The rotor shaft is supported in ball-bearings, and slip rings are used to conduct current to and from the field coils through the carbon brushes.
4 The alternator generates ac (alternating current) which is rectified by an internal diode circuit to dc (direct current) for supply to the battery.

7 Alternator drivebelt(s) – checking, renewal and tensioning

Refer to Chapter 2, Section 12.

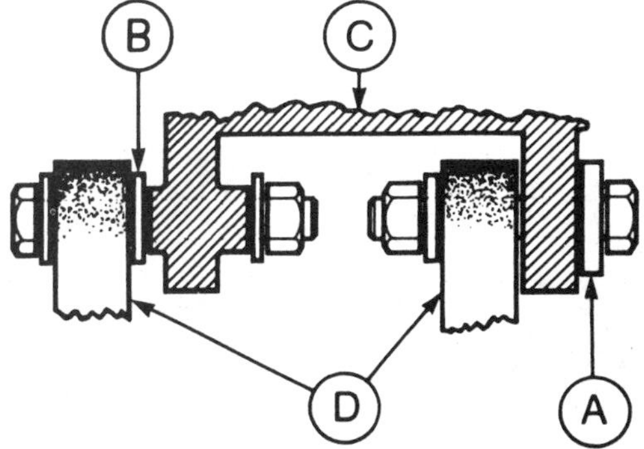

Fig 13.1 Alternator mounting bracket arrangement (Sec 8)

A Large flat washer
B Small flat washer (models up to 1985 only)
C Mounting bracket (engine)
D Mounting lugs (alternator)

8 Alternator – removal and refitting

1 Disconnect the battery leads.
2 Disconnect the multi-plug, or disconnect the wires from their terminals on the rear of the alternator, noting their locations (as applicable), then slacken the mounting and adjustment bolts and tilt the alternator towards the engine (photos).
3 Remove the drivebelt(s) from the alternator pulley(s).
4 Remove the mounting and adjustment nuts and bolts, and withdraw the alternator from the engine.
5 Refitting is a reversal of removal, noting the following points.
6 To avoid breakage of the alternator mounting bracket lugs, it is important that the following procedure is adhered to when refitting the mounting bolts.
7 Always refit the large flat washer (A in Fig. 13.1).
8 Earlier models produced before 1985 also have a small washer (B) which must be fitted between the sliding bush and the mounting bracket.
9 Ensure that the bushes and bolts are assembled as shown in Fig. 13.1, then tension the drivebelt(s) and tighten the mounting and adjustment bolts as described in Chapter 2, Section 12.

9 Alternator – fault finding and testing

Note: *To carry out the complete test procedure use only the following test equipment – a 0 to 20 volt moving coil voltmeter, a 0 to 100 amp moving coil ammeter, and a rheostat rated at 30 amps.*
1 Check that the battery is at least 70% charged by using a hydrometer as described in Section 4.
2 Check the drivebelt tension with reference to Chapter 2, Section 12.
3 Check the security of the battery leads, alternator multi-plug, and interconnecting wire.

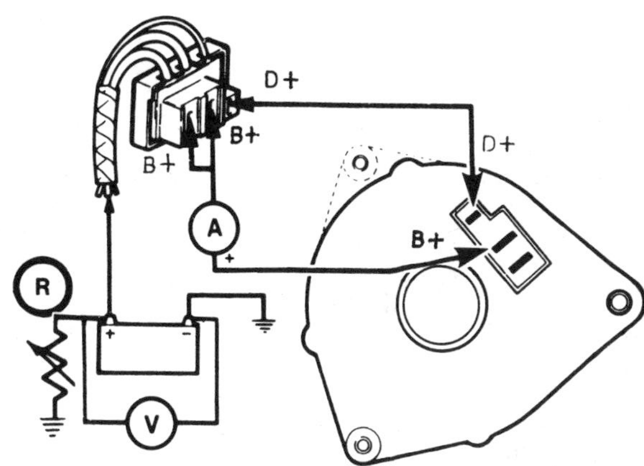

Fig 13.2 Alternator output test circuit (Sec 9)

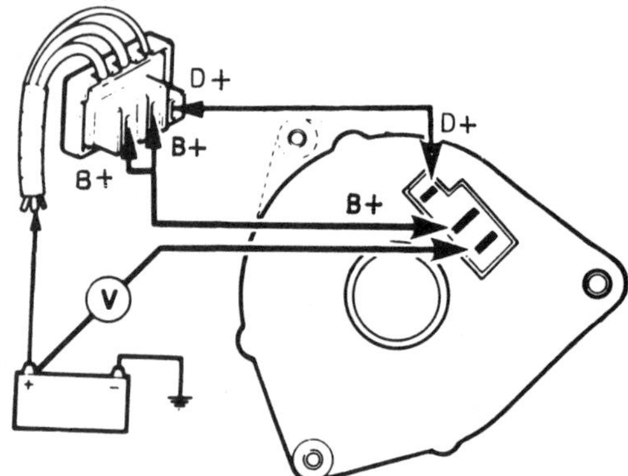

Fig 13.3 Alternator positive check circuit (Sec 9)

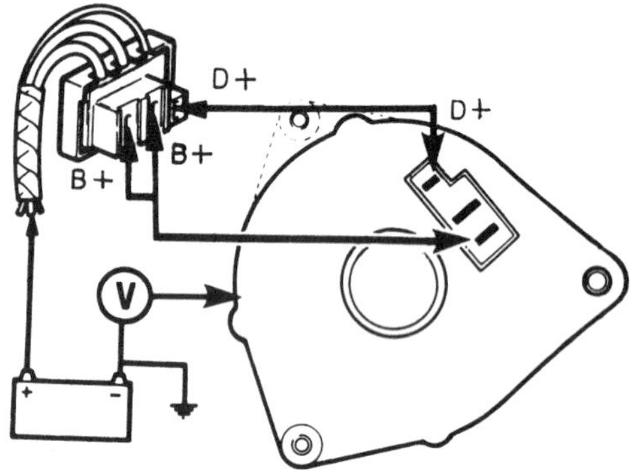

Fig 13.4 Alternator negative check circuit (Sec 9)

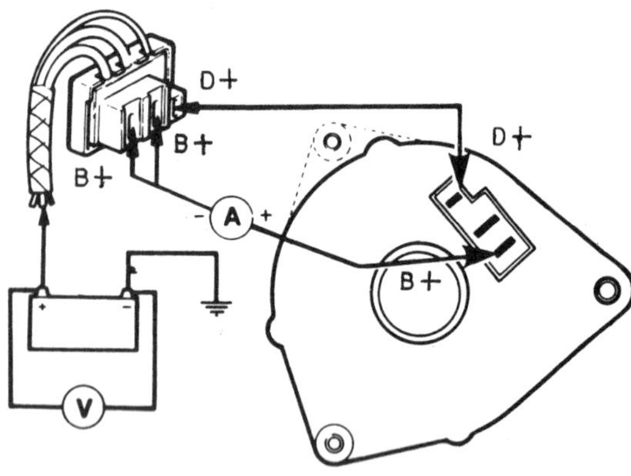

Fig 13.5 Alternator voltage regulator test circuit (Sec 9)

4 *To check the cable continuity* pull the multi-plug from the alternator and switch on the ignition, being careful not to crank the engine. Connect the voltmeter between a good earth and each of the terminals in the multi-plug in turn. If battery voltage is not indicated, there is an open circuit in the wiring which may be due to a blown ignition warning light bulb if on the small terminal.

5 *To check the alternator output* connect the voltmeter, ammeter and rheostat as shown in Fig. 13.2 Run the engine at 3000 rpm and switch on the headlamps, heater blower and, where fitted, the heated rear window. Vary the resistance to increase the current and check that the alternator rated output is reached without the voltage dropping below 13 volts.

6 *To check the positive side of the charging circuit* connect the voltmeter as shown in Fig. 13.3. Start the engine and switch on the headlamps. Run the engine at 3000 rpm and check that the indicated voltage drop does not exceed 0.5 volt. A higher reading indicates a high resistance such as a dirty connection on the positive side of the charging circuit.

7 *To check the negative side of the charging circuit* connect the voltmeter as shown in Fig. 13.4 Start the engine and switch on the headlamps. Run the engine at 3000 rpm and check that the indicated voltage drop does not exceed 0.25 volt. A higher reading indicates a high resistance such as a dirty connection on the negative side of the charging circuit.

8 *To check the alternator voltage regulator* connect the voltmeter and ammeter as shown in Fig. 13.5. Run the engine at 3000 rpm and when the ammeter records a current of 3 to 5 amps check that the voltmeter records 13.7 to 14.I5 volts. If the result is outside the limits the regulator is faulty.

10 Alternator brushes – removal, inspection and refitting

1 Remove the alternator as described in Section 8.

Bosch type alternators

2 Remove the two securing screws and withdraw the regulator/brush box assembly from the rear of the alternator (photo).

3 If the length of either brush is less than the minimum given in the Specifications, unsolder the wiring and remove the brushes and the springs (photo).

4 Wipe the slip rings clean with a fuel-moistened cloth. If the rings are very dirty use fine glasspaper to clean them, then wipe with the cloth (photo).

5 Refitting is a reversal of removal, but make sure that the brushes move freely in their holders.

Lucas A115 and A133 type alternators

6 Disconnect the wiring plug, then remove the securing screw and withdraw the interference suppression capacitor from the rear cover.

7 Extract the two securing screws and remove the alternator rear cover.

8 Make a careful note of the fitted positions of the regulator wires, then disconnect the wires from the diode pack and the brush box.

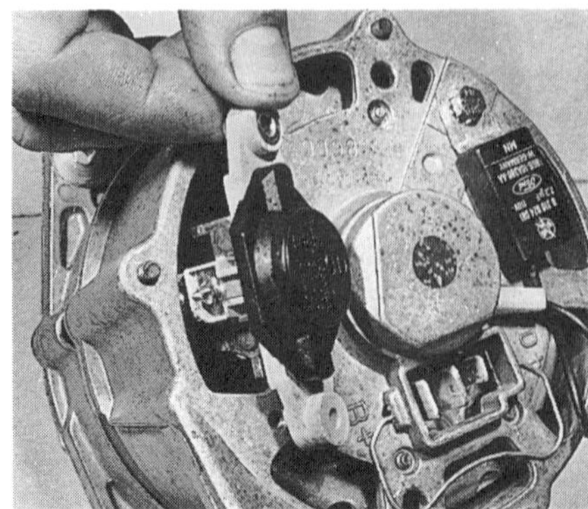
10.2 Withdrawing the regulator/brush box from a Bosch type alternator

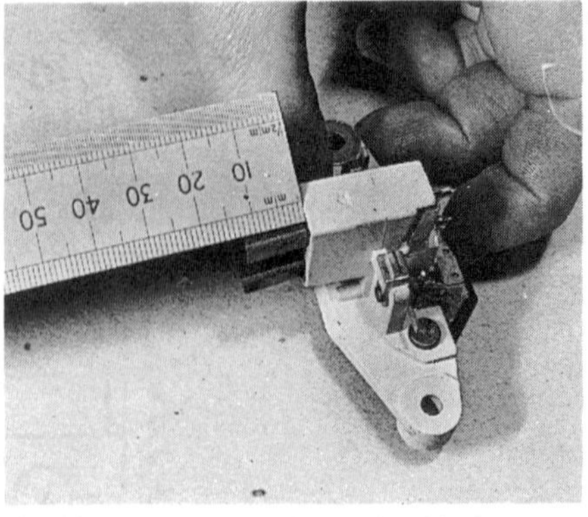
10.3 Compare the brush length with the figure given in the Specifications – Bosch type alternator

10.4 Inspect the condition of the slip rings (arrowed) – Bosch type alternator

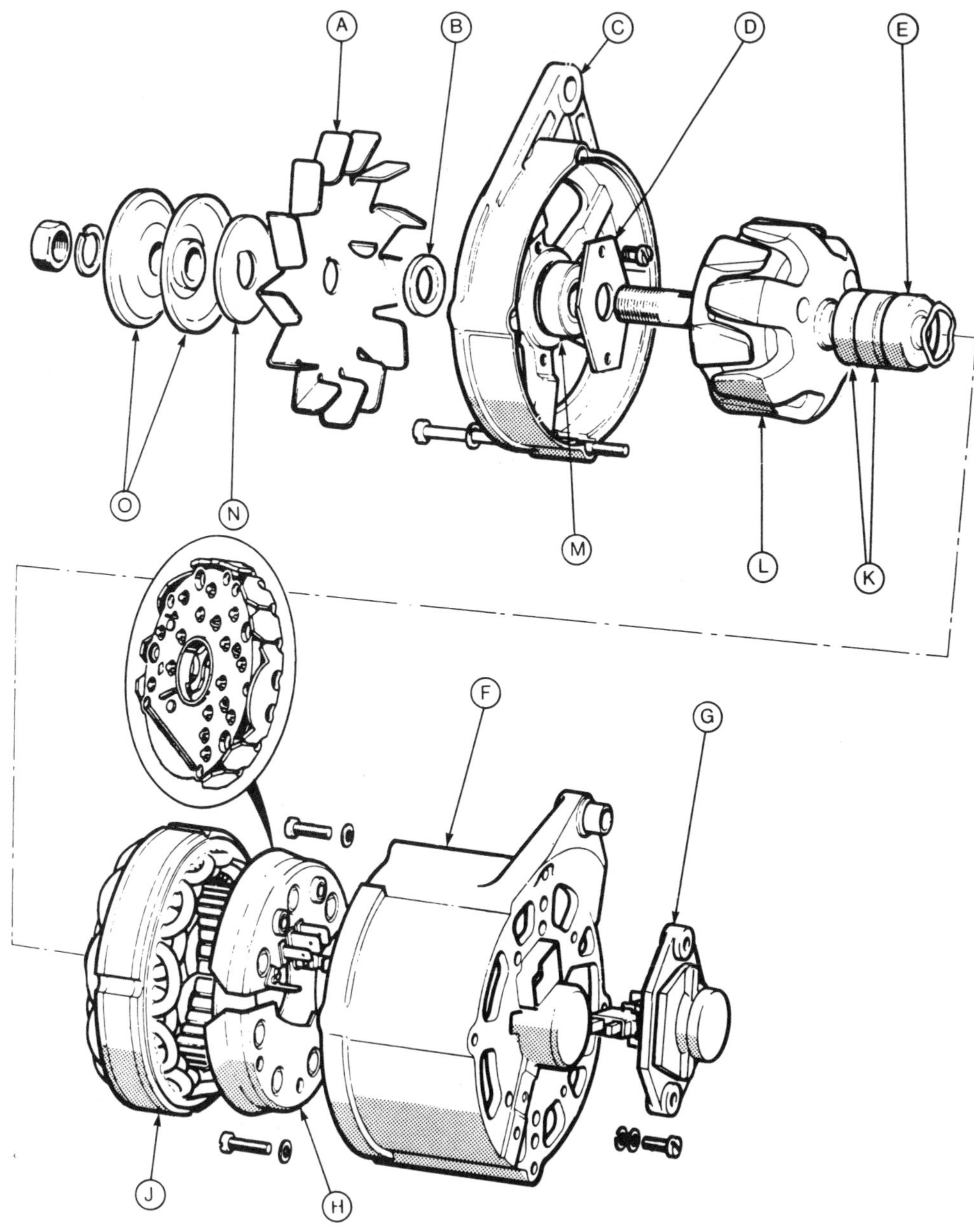

Fig 13.6 Exploded view of a Bosch type alternator (Sec 10)

A Fan
B Spacer
C Drive end housing
D Drive end bearing retaining plate
E Slip ring end bearing
F Slip ring end housing
G Brush box and regulator
H Diode pack (Inset shows alternative diode pack)
J Stator
K Slip rings
L Rotor
M Drive end bearing
N Spacer
O Pulley

9 Remove the regulator securing screws and withdraw the regulator. Note that the regulator securing screw also holds one of the brush mounting plates in position.

10 Remove the two securing screws and withdraw the brush box. Remove the securing screws and lift the brushes from the brush box.

11 If the length of either brush is less than the minimum given in the Specifications, renew both brushes.

12 Proceed as described in paragraphs 4 and 5.

Lucas A127 type alternator

13 Where applicable, for improved access remove the terminal cover from the rear of the alternator, then remove the three screws securing the regulator/brush box assembly to the rear of the alternator (photo).

14 Tip the outside edge of the assembly upwards, and withdraw it from its location. Disconnect the wiring plug and withdraw the assembly from the alternator (photo).

15 If the length of either brush is less than the minimum given in the Specifications, the complete regulator/brush box assembly must be renewed (photo).

16 Proceed as described in paragraphs 4 and 5 (photo).

Motorola type alternators

17 Remove the two securing screws and withdraw the regulator. Disconnect the regulator wires after noting their locations.

18 Remove the single securing screw (35 and 45 amp types) or two securing screws (55 and 70 amp types) and carefully withdraw the brush box.

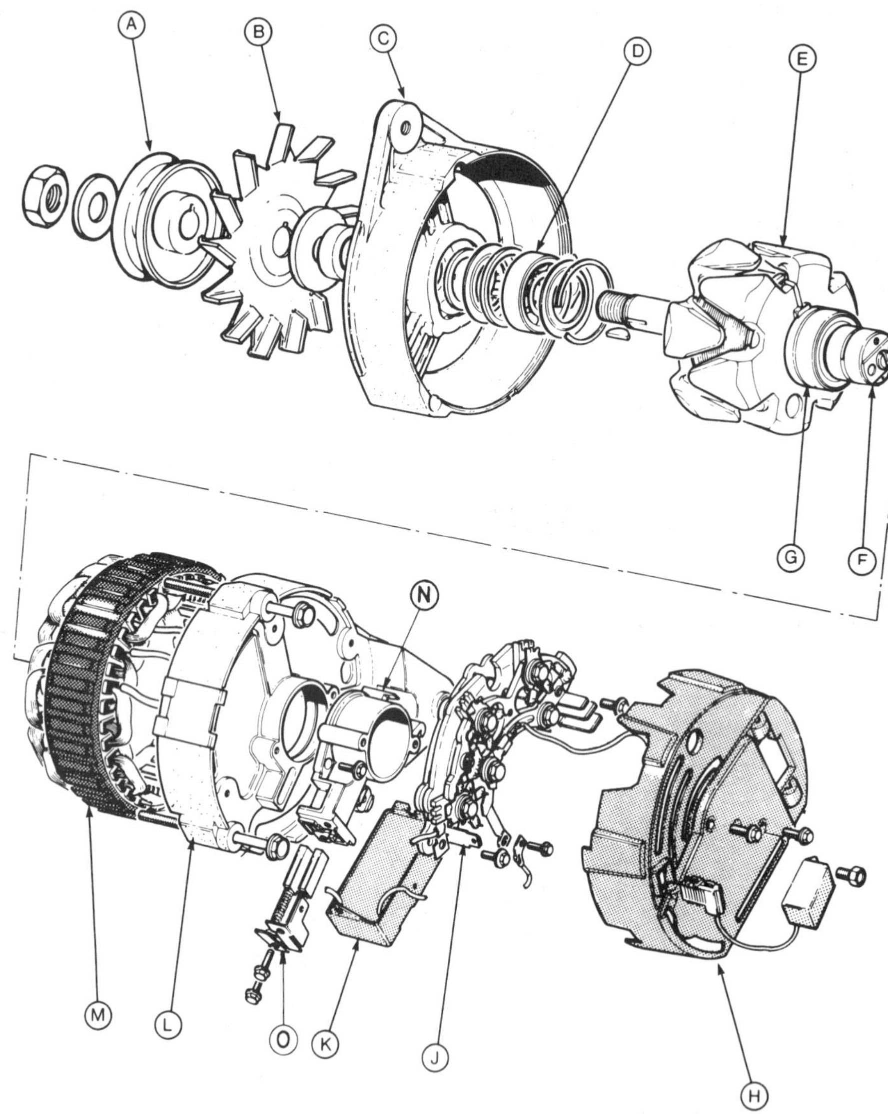

Fig 13.7 Exploded view of Lucas A115 and A133 type alternators (Sec 10)

A Pulley
B Fan
C Drive end housing
D Bearing
E Rotor
F Slip ring
G Bearing
H End cover
J Diode pack
K Regulator
L Slip ring end housing
M Stator
N Brush box
O Brushes

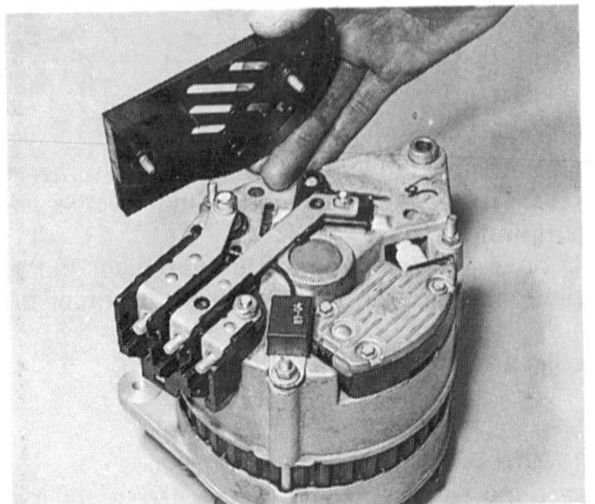

10.13 Removing the terminal cover from a Lucas A127 type alternator (CVH model). Regulator/brushbox securing screws arrowed

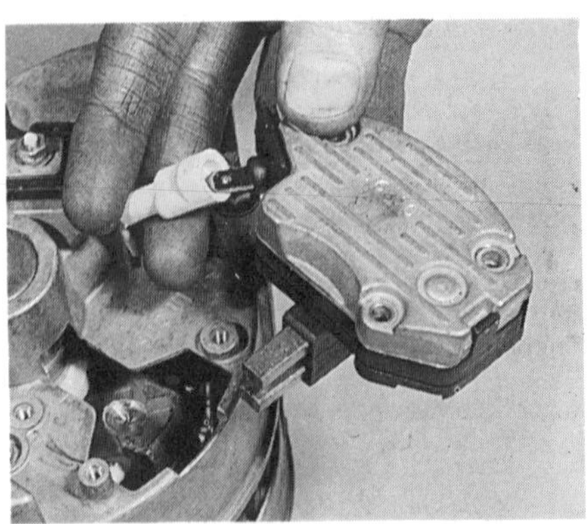

10.14 Disconnect the wiring plug and withdraw the regulator/brushbox – Lucas A127 type alternator

10.15 Compare the brush length with the figure given in the Specifications – Lucas A127 type alternator

10.16 Inspect the condition of the slip rings (arrowed) – Lucas A127 type alternator

19 If the length of either brush is less than the minimum given in the Specifications, the brush box must be renewed.
20 Proceed as described in paragraphs 4 and 5.

Mitsubishi type alternators

21 Unscrew the pulley nut. To prevent the shaft rotating, insert an Allen key in the end of the shaft.
22 Remove the spring washer, pulley, fan, spacer and dust shield.
23 Scribe an alignment mark along the length of the alternator to facilitate reassembly of the drive end housing, stator and rear housing.
24 Unscrew the through-bolts and withdraw the drive end housing from the rotor shaft.
25 Remove the seal and spacer from the rotor shaft.
26 Remove the rotor from the rear housing and the stator. This may require the application of local heat to the rear housing using a large soldering iron. Do not use a heat gun, as this may result in damage to the diodes.
27 Unscrew the four securing bolts and withdraw the diode pack/stator assembly from the rear housing.
28 Unsolder the stator leads from the diode pack terminals. Use a pair of pliers when unsoldering to act as a heat sink, otherwise damage to the diodes may occur.
29 If the length of either brush is less than the minimum given in the Specifications, the brush box must be renewed.

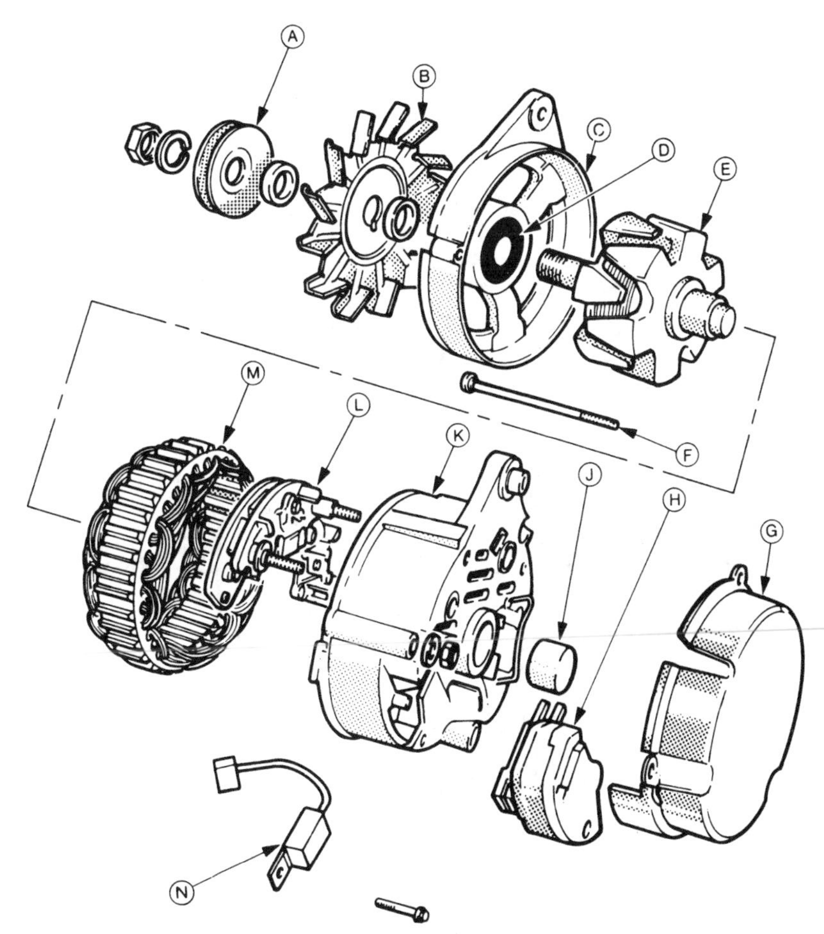

Fig 13.8 Exploded view of Lucas A127 type alternator (Sec 10)

A Pulley
B Fan
C Drive end housing
D Bearing
E Rotor
F Through-bolt
G End cover (typical)
H Voltage regulator/brush box
J Bearing
K Slip ring end housing
L Diode pack
M Stator
N Suppressor

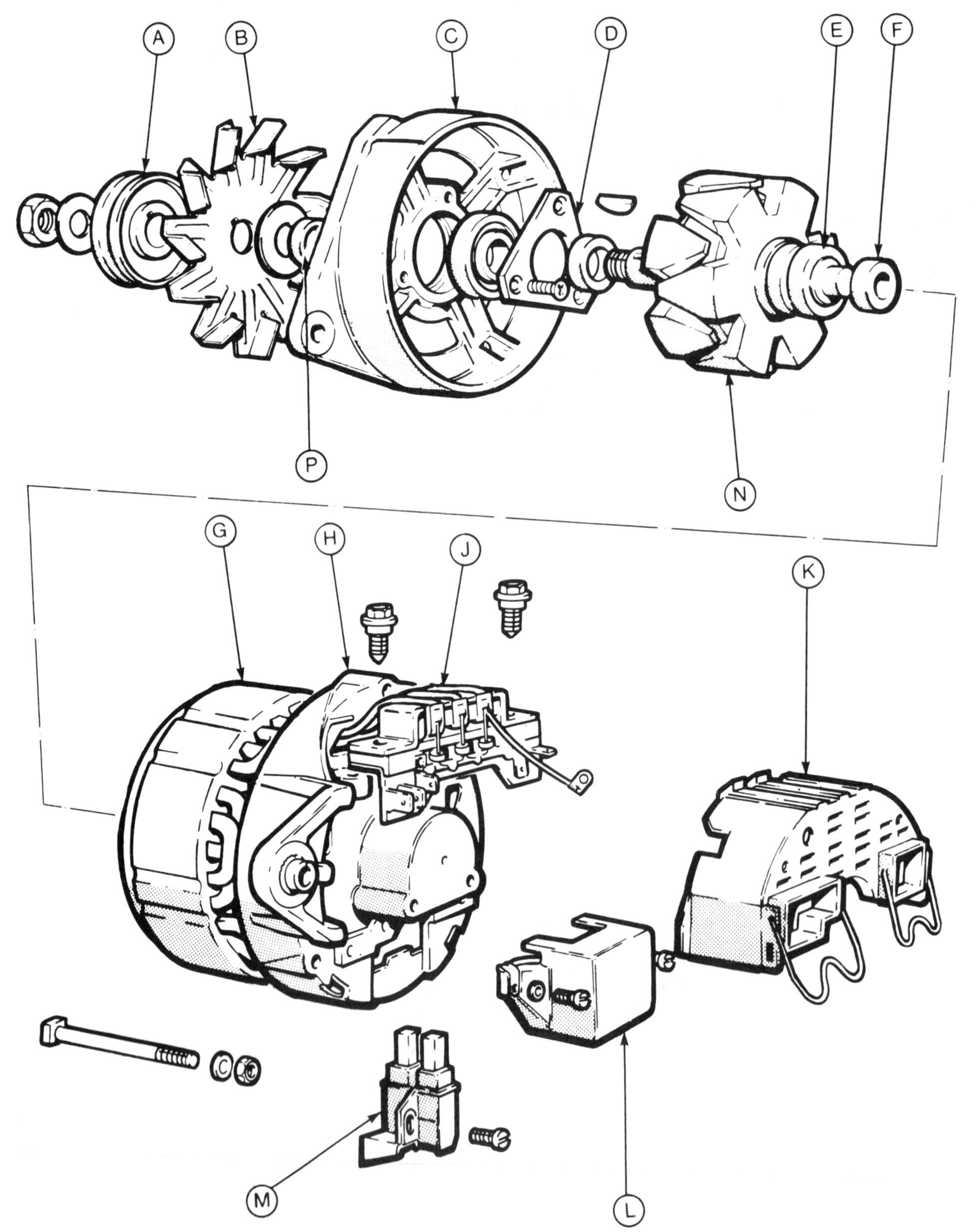

Fig 13.9 Exploded view of Motorola 35 and 45 amp alternators (Sec 10)

A Pulley
B Fan
C Drive end housing
D Drive end bearing retaining plate
E Slip ring
F Slip ring end bearing
G Stator
H Slip ring end housing
J Diode pack
K End cover
L Regulator
M Brush box
N Rotor
P Spacer

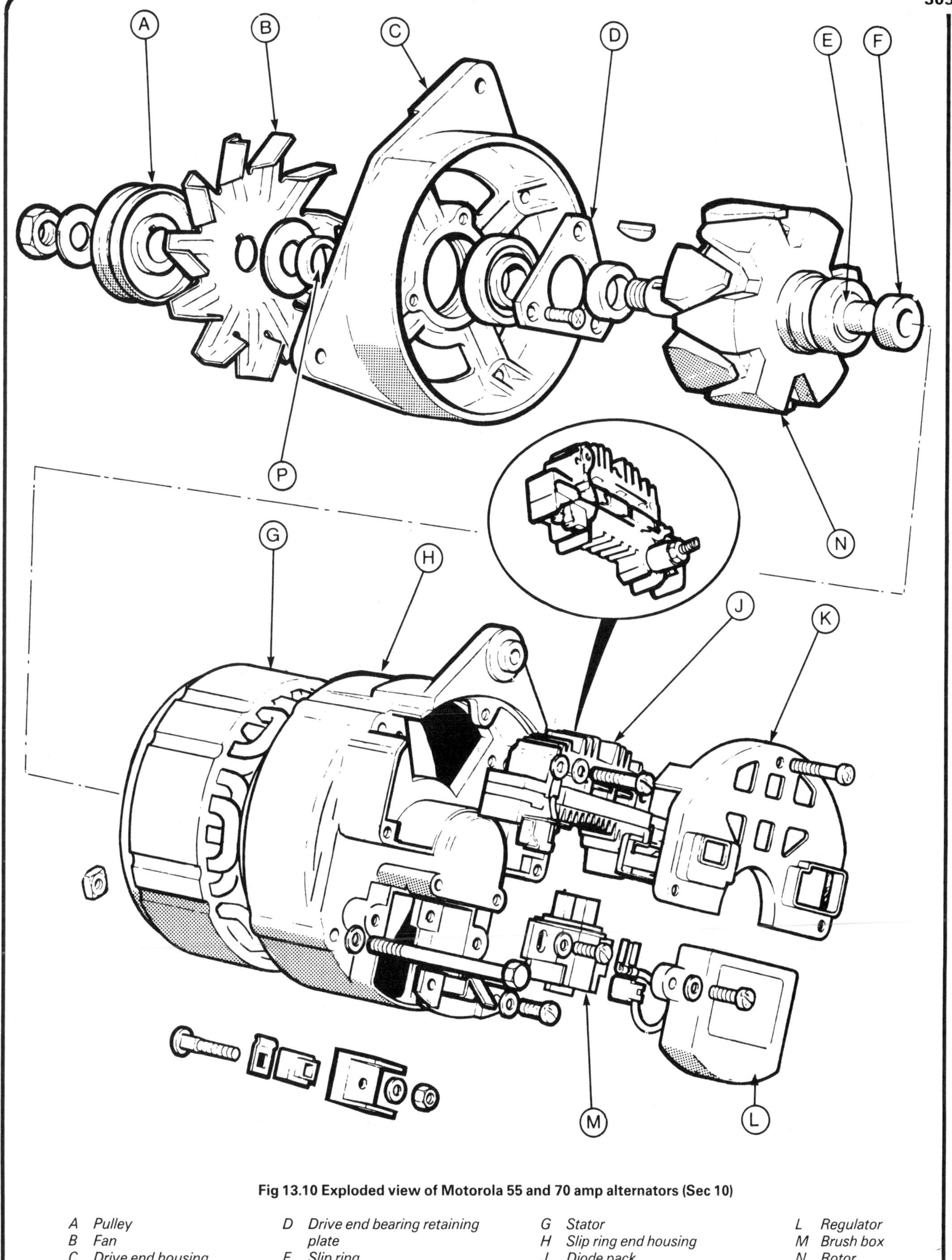

Fig 13.10 Exploded view of Motorola 55 and 70 amp alternators (Sec 10)

A Pulley
B Fan
C Drive end housing
D Drive end bearing retaining plate
E Slip ring
F Slip ring end bearing
G Stator
H Slip ring end housing
J Diode pack
K End cover
L Regulator
M Brush box
N Rotor
P Spacer

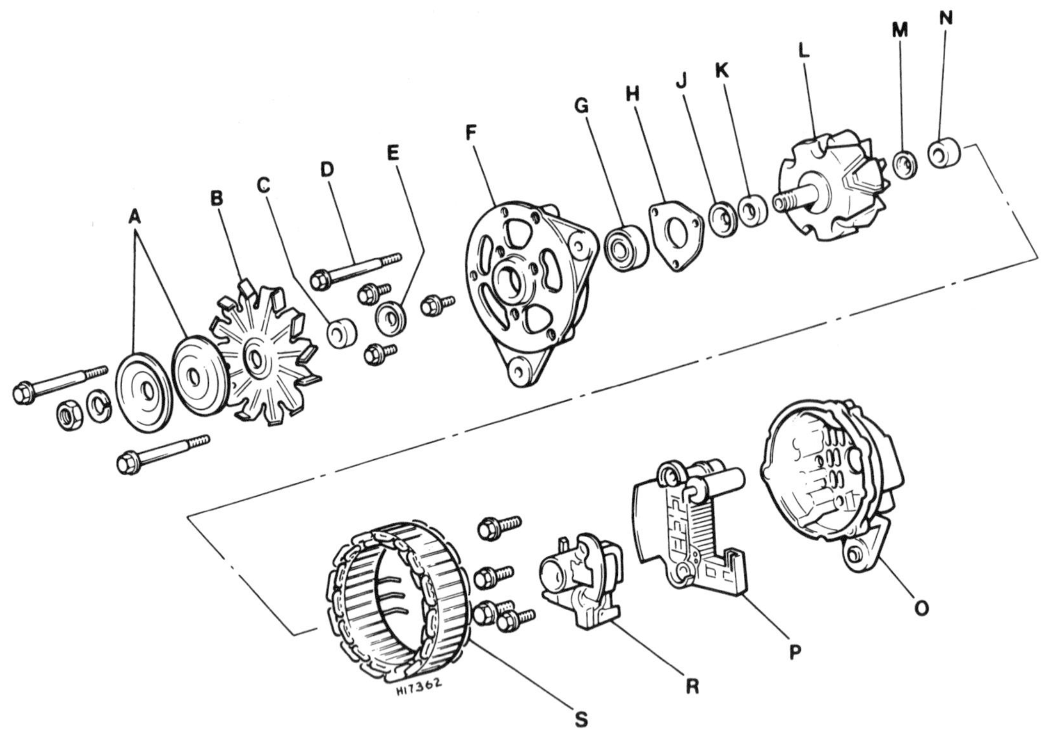

Fig 13.11 Exploded view of Mitsubishi type alternator (Sec 10)

A Pulley
B Fan
C Thick spacer
D Through-bolt
E Dust shield
F Drive end housing
G Bearing
H Bearing retainer
J Dust cap
K Thin spacer
L Rotor
M Seal
N Bearing
O Rear end housing
P Diode pack
R Brush box
S Stator

30 To renew the brush box, unsolder the connection to the diode pack, and solder the connection to the new brush box. Use a pair of pliers as a heat sink to avoid damage to the diodes.
31 Examine the surfaces of the slip rings. Clean them with a fuel-moistened cloth, or if necessary fine glasspaper and then the cloth.
32 Solder the stator leads to the diode pack terminals, again using a pair of pliers as a heat sink.

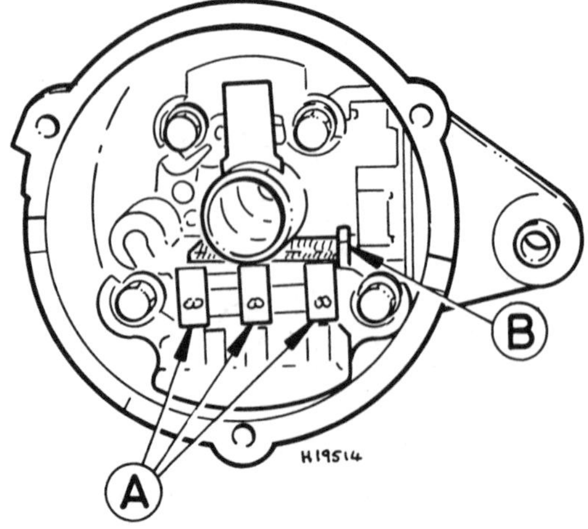

Fig 13.12 Stator-to-diode pack connections (A) and brushbox-to-diode pack terminal (B) – Mitsubishi alternator (Sec 10)

33 Refit the diode pack/stator assembly to the rear housing and tighten the securing bolts.
34 Insert a thin rod (an Allen key is ideal) through the hole in the rear housing to hold the brushes in the retracted position.
35 Fit the rotor to the rear housing and then remove the temporary rod to release the brushes.
36 Reassemble the remaining components by reversing the dismantling operations. Make sure that the scribed marks are in alignment.

11 Starter motor – testing in the vehicle

1 If the starter motor fails to operate first check the condition of the battery as described in Section 4.
2 Check the security and condition of all relevant wiring.

Solenoid check

3 Disconnect the battery negative lead and all leads from the solenoid.
4 Connect a 3 watt testlamp and a 12 volt battery between the starter terminal on the solenoid and the solenoid body as shown in Fig. 13.13. The testlamp should light. If not, there is an open circuit in the solenoid windings.
5 Now connect an 18 watt testlamp between both solenoid terminals (Fig. 13.14), then energise the solenoid with a further lead to the spade terminal. The solenoid should be heard to operate and the testlamp should light. Reconnect the solenoid wires.

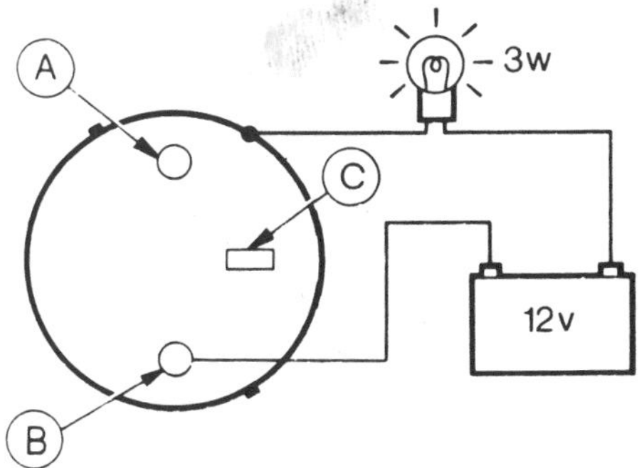

Fig 13.13 Starter motor solenoid winding test circuit (Sec 11)

A Battery terminal *C Spade terminal*
B Motor terminal

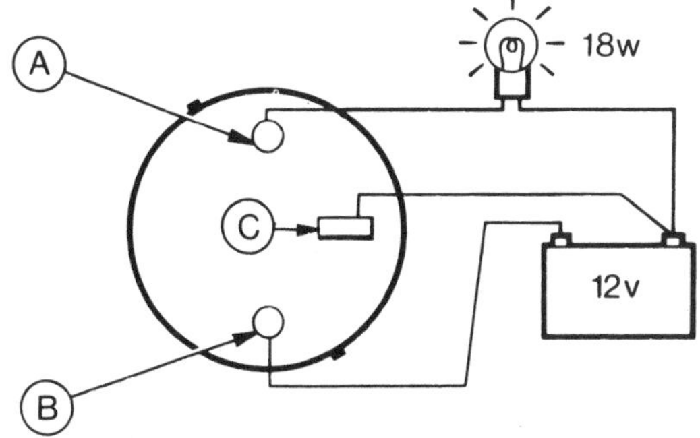

Fig 13.14 Starter motor solenoid continuity test circuit (Sec 11)

A Battery terminal *C Spade terminal*
B Motor terminal

On load voltage check

6 Connect a voltmeter across the battery terminals, then disconnect the low tension lead from the coil positive terminal and operate the starter by turning the ignition switch. Note the reading on the voltmeter which should not be less than 10.5 volts.

7 Now connect the voltmeter between the starter motor terminal on the solenoid and the starter motor body. With the coil low tension lead still disconnected operate the starter and check that the recorded voltage is not more than 1 volt lower than that noted in paragraph 6. If the voltage drop is more than 1 volt a fault exists in the wiring from the battery to the starter.

8 Connect the voltmeter between the battery positive terminal and the terminal on the starter motor. With the coil low tension lead disconnected operate the starter for two or three seconds. Battery voltage should be indicated initially, then dropping to less than 1 volt. If the reading is more than 1 volt, there is a high resistance in the wiring from the battery to the starter and the check in paragraph 9 should be made. If the reading is less than 1 volt proceed to paragraph 10.

9 Connect the voltmeter between the two main solenoid terminals and operate the starter for two or three seconds. Battery voltage should be indicated initially, then dropping to less than 0.5 volt. If the reading is more than 0.5 volt, the ignition switch and connections may be faulty.

10 Connect the voltmeter between the battery negative terminal and the starter motor body, and operate the starter for two or three seconds. A reading of less than 0.5 volt should be recorded. If the reading is more than 0.5 volt, there is a fault in the earth circuit, and the earth connections to the battery and body should be checked.

12 Starter motor – removal and refitting

1 Apply the handbrake, jack up the front of the vehicle and support on axle stands.

2 Disconnect the battery negative lead.

3 Working underneath the vehicle, unscrew the nut and disconnect the main cable from the starter solenoid (photo).

4 Disconnect the ignition switch wire from the solenoid.

5 Unscrew the three mounting bolts and withdraw the starter motor from the gearbox bellhousing (photo).

6 Refitting is a reversal of removal.

13 Starter motor (Bosch and Cajavac) – overhaul

Note: *A two-legged puller will be required to position the drive pinion thrust collar during reassembly.*

Bosch long frame and JF, and Cajavec type starter motors

1 With the starter motor removed from the vehicle and cleaned, grip the unit in a vice fitted with soft jaw protectors.

2 Remove the nut and washer securing the field winding lead to the solenoid stud and unhook the lead from the stud.

3 Remove the two securing screws, and withdraw the solenoid yoke, then unhook the solenoid armature from the actuating arm and remove the armature (photo).

4 Remove the two screws securing the commutator end housing cap, then remove the cap and rubber seal (photo).

5 Wipe any grease from the armature shaft, and remove the C-clip, or E-clip, as applicable, and shims from the end of the shaft (photos).

6 Unscrew the two nuts and remove the washers, or remove the securing screws (as applicable), then lift off the commutator end housing (photos).

7 Carefully prise the thrust retaining springs from their locations, then slide the brushes from the brush plate. Withdraw the brush plate.

8 Separate the drive end housing and armature from the yoke by tapping apart with a soft-faced hammer.

9 Remove the rubber insert from the drive end housing, then unscrew

12.3 Solenoid wiring connections on Lucas M79 type starter motor (CVH engine)

12.5 Unscrew the starter motor mounting bolts

13.3 Remove the solenoid yoke securing screws – Bosch long frame type starter motor

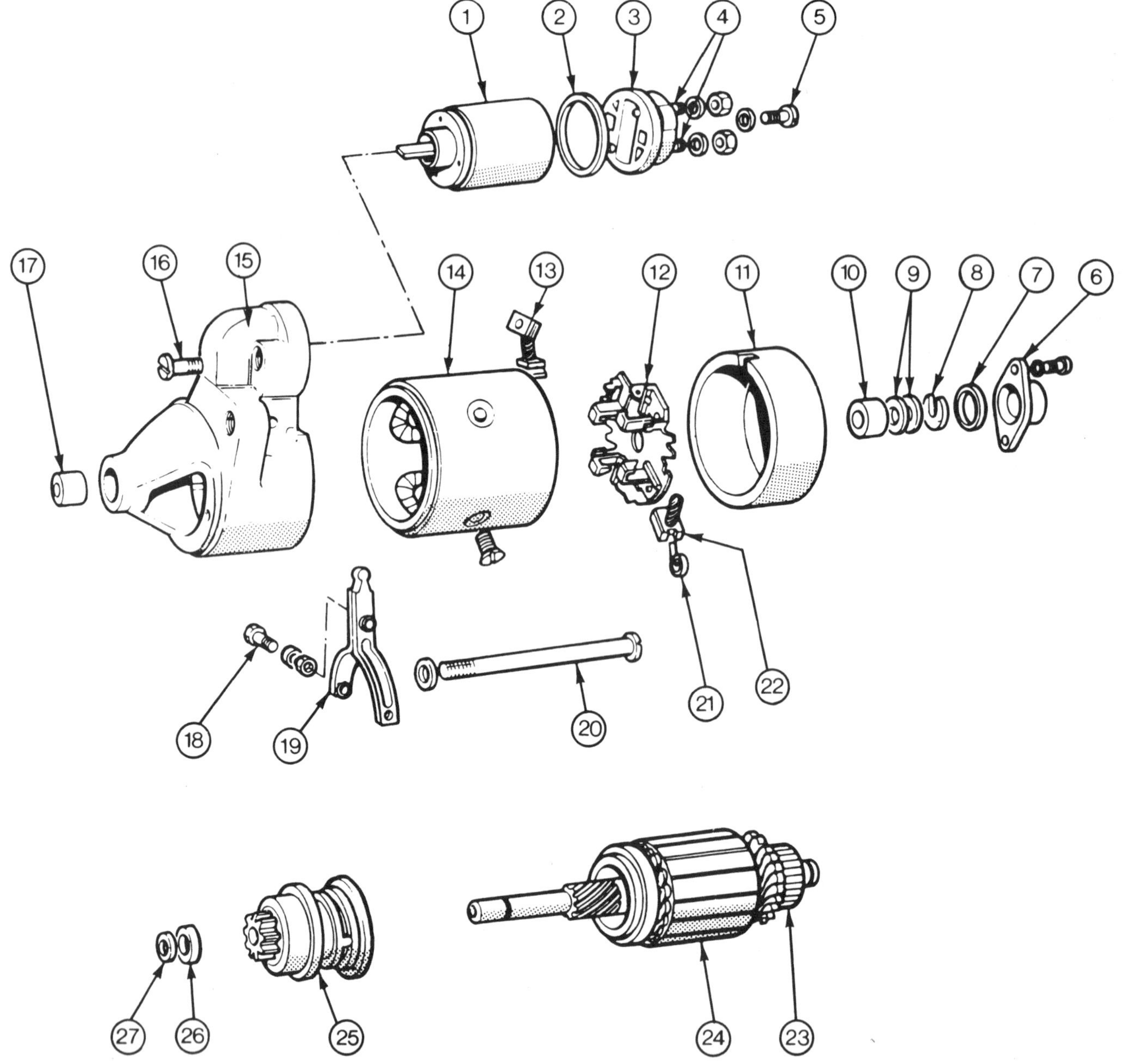

Fig 13.15 Exploded view of Bosch long frame and JF type starter motors (Sec 13)

1 *Solenoid yoke*
2 *Gasket*
3 *Switch contacts and end cover*
4 *Main terminals*
5 *Securing screw*
6 *Commutator end housing cap*
7 *Rubber seal*
8 *C-clip*
9 *Shims*
10 *Bush*
11 *Commutator end housing*
12 *Brush plate*
13 *Field winding lead*
14 *Yoke*
15 *Drive end housing*
16 *Solenoid securing screw*
17 *Bush*
18 *Pivot pin (bolt)*
19 *Actuating arm*
20 *Commutator end housing securing screws*
21 *Brush spring*
22 *Brush*
23 *Commutator*
24 *Armature*
25 *Drive pinion and clutch assembly*
26 *Thrust collar*
27 *C-clip*

the actuating arm pivot retaining nut and slide the pivot pin (bolt) from the housing.

10 Withdraw the armature assembly, complete with actuating arm, from the drive end housing (photo). Unhook the actuating arm from the drive pinion flange.

11 To remove the drive pinion from the armature shaft, drive the thrust collar down the shaft, using a suitable tube drift, to expose the C-clip. Remove the clip from its groove, and slide the thrust collar and drive pinion from the shaft. Do not grip the clutch assembly in a vice during this procedure, as damage will result (photo).

12 Examine the components and renew as necessary.

13 If the brushes have worn to less than the specified minimum, renew them as a set. To renew the brushes, cut the leads at their midpoint and make a good soldered joint when connecting the new brushes.

14 The commutator face should be clean and free from burnt spots. Where necessary burnish with fine glass paper **(not** emery) and wipe with a fuel-moistened cloth. If the commutator is in very bad condition it

13.4 Remove the commutator end housing cap securing screws – Bosch long frame type starter motor

13.5A Remove the C-clip ...

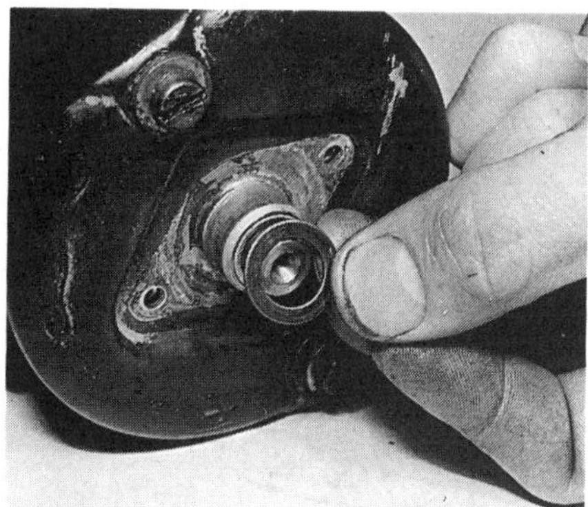
13.5B ... and shims from the end of the armature shaft – Bosch long frame type starter motor

13.6A Remove the commutator end housing securing screws – Bosch long frame type starter motor

13.6B Commutator end housing removed to expose brush plate – Bosch long frame type starter motor

13.10 Withdraw the armature assembly and actuating arm from the drive end housing – Bosch long frame type starter motor

13.11 Drive the thrust collar (A) down the armature shaft to expose the C-clip (B) – Bosch long frame type starter motor

13.14 Armature commutator face (arrowed) – Bosch long frame type starter motor

can be skimmed on a lathe provided its diameter is not reduced excessively. If recutting the insulation slots, take care not to cut into the commutator metal (photo).

15 Renew the end housing bushes which are of self-lubricating type and should have been soaked in clean engine oil for at least 20 minutes before installation. Drive out the old bushes, whilst supporting the endplate/housing, using a suitable drift.

16 Accurate checking of the armature, commutator and field coil windings and insulation requires the use of special test equipment. If the starter motor was inoperative when removed from the car and the previous checks have not highlighted the problem, then it can be assumed that there is a continuity or insulation fault and the unit should be renewed.

17 Commence reassembly by sliding the drive pinion and thrust collar onto the armature shaft. Fit the C-clip into its groove, and then use a two-legged puller to draw the thrust collar over the clip – see Fig. 13.17.

18 Refit the actuating arm to the drive pinion flange, then refit the armature assembly and actuating cam to the drive end housing.

19 Refit the actuating arm pivot pin (bolt) and secure with the retaining nut. Fit the rubber insert into the drive end housing.

20 Guide the yoke over the armature and tap onto the drive end housing.

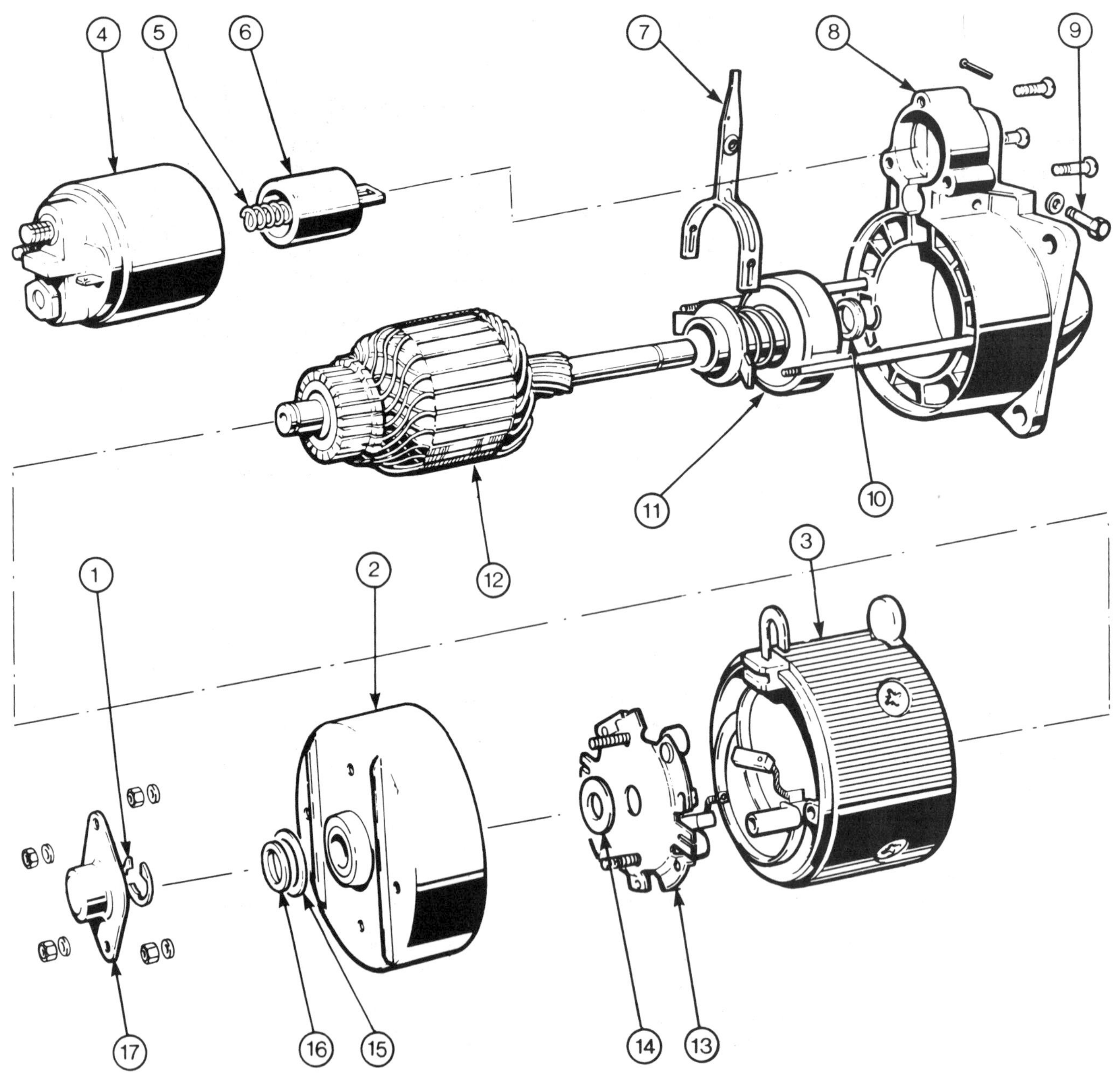

Fig 13.16 Exploded view of Cajavec type starter motor (Sec 13)

1 *E-clip*
2 *Commutator end housing*
3 *Yoke*
4 *Solenoid yoke*
5 *Solenoid return spring*
6 *Solenoid armature*
7 *Actuating arm*
8 *Drive end housing*
9 *Pivot pin (bolt) Thrust collar*
11 *Drive pinion and clutch assembly*
12 *Armature*
13 *Brush plate*
14 *Washer*
15 *Seal*
16 *Shim*
17 *Commutator end housing cap*

21 On starter motors where the commutator end housing is secured by nuts and washers, position the brush plate over the end of the armature, with the cut-outs in the brush plate aligned with the end housing securing studs.
22 On starter motors where the commutator end housing is secured by screws, position the brush plate over the end of the armature with the cut-outs in the brush plate aligned with the loops in the field windings – see Fig. 13.18. The brush plate will be positively located when the commutator end housing screws are fitted.
23 Position the brushes in their respective locations in the brush plate, and fit the brush retaining springs.
24 Guide the commutator end housing into position, at the same time sliding the rubber insulator into the cut-out in the housing. Secure the commutator end housing with the nuts and washers or screws, as applicable.
25 Slide the armature into its bearings so that the shaft protrudes as far as possible at the commutator bearing end.
26 Fit sufficient shims to the end of the armature shaft to eliminate endfloat when the C-clip or E-clip, as applicable is fitted, then fit the clip.
27 Fit the armature shaft bearing seal to the commutator end housing, then apply a little lithium-based grease to the end of the armature shaft and refit the end housing cap, securing with the two screws.
28 Apply a little lithium-based grease to the solenoid armature hook, then locate the hook over the actuating arm in the drive end housing.

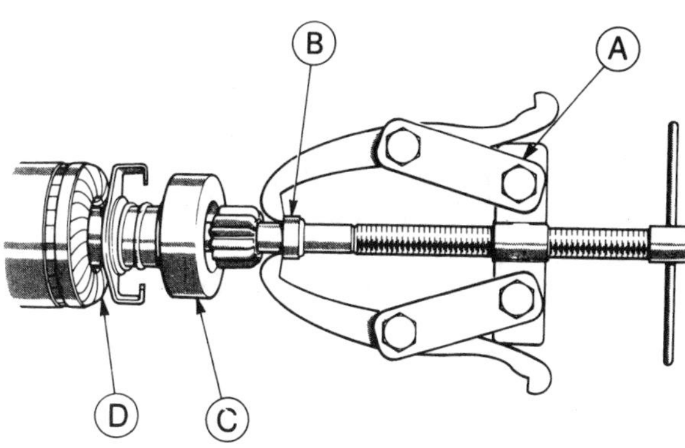

Fig 13.17 Use a two-legged puller to draw the drive pinion thrust collar over the C-clip (Secs 13 and 14)

A Two-legged puller
B Thrust collar
C Drive pinion and clutch assembly
D Armature

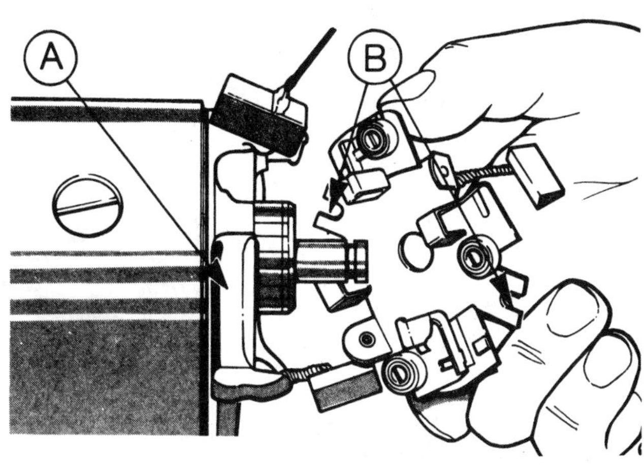

Fig 13.18 Align the cut-outs in the brush plate (B) with the loops in the field windings (A) – Bosch long frame starter motor (Sec 13)

Ensure that the solenoid armature return spring is correctly positioned, then guide the solenoid yoke over the armature. Align the yoke with the drive end housing and fit the two securing screws.
29 Reconnect the field winding lead to the solenoid stud and secure with the nut and washer.

Bosch short frame and EF type starter motors

30 The procedure is basically as described for the Bosch long frame and JF, and Cajavec starter motors, except that the brush arrangement differs, and the drive end housing and armature must be separated from the yoke before the solenoid armature can be unhooked from the actuating arm. Note that the solenoid yoke is secured by three screws.
31 To remove and refit the brush assembly, proceed as follows.
32 Release the brush holders complete with brushes by pushing the brush holders towards the commutator and unclipping them from the brush plate. Withdraw the brush plate.
33 To renew the brushes, the leads must be unsoldered from the terminals on the brush plate, and the leads of the new brushes must be soldered to the terminals.
34 To refit the brush assembly, position the brush plate over the end of the armature shaft, then assemble the brush holders, brushes and springs, ensuring that the brush holder clips are securely located. The brush plate will be positively located when the commutator end housing screws are fitted.

Bosch DM type starter motor

35 The procedure is basically as described previously for the Bosch short frame and EF type starter motors, except that a commutator end plate is fitted in place of the end housing.

Bosch DW type starter motor

36 With the starter motor removed from the vehicle and cleaned, grip the unit in a vice fitted with soft jaw protectors.
37 Remove the two securing screws and withdraw the armature shaft cover.
38 Remove the C-clip and spacer from the end of the armature shaft.
39 Unscrew the two securing screws and lift off the commutator end plate.
40 Remove the securing nut, and disconnect the wiring from the solenoid terminal.
41 Withdraw the complete yoke and armature assembly from the drive end housing.
42 Release the brushes from the brush holders, and remove the brush plate from the armature shaft.
43 Remove the armature retaining plate, and withdraw the armature from the yoke, overcoming the magnetic attraction.
44 Extract the three securing screws, and remove the solenoid yoke from the drive end housing.
45 Withdraw the complete pinion and clutch assembly from the drive end housing.
46 Unhook the solenoid armature from the actuating arm.
47 To remove the drive pinion from the armature shaft, proceed as described in paragraph 11.
48 Examine the components and renew as necessary.
49 To renew the brushes, the leads must be unsoldered from the terminals on the brush plate, and the leads of the new brushes must be soldered to the terminals.
50 Proceed as described in paragraphs 14 to 16 inclusive.
51 Commence reassembly by refitting the drive pinion to the armature shaft as described in paragraph 17.
52 Refit the pinion and clutch assembly into the drive end housing, ensuring that the ring gear carrier and rubber block are correctly located.
53 Apply a little lithium-based grease to the end of the solenoid armature and reconnect it to the actuating arm.
54 Ensure that the solenoid armature return spring is correctly positioned, then guide the solenoid yoke over the armature, and refit the three securing screws.
55 Position the brush plate over the end of the armature shaft, then assemble the brush holders, brushes and springs, ensuring that the brush holder clips are securely located.
56 Insert the armature into the yoke, making sure that the brush plate stays in place, and engage the rubber insulator with the cut-out in the yoke.
57 Refit the armature retaining plate, positioning it as shown in Fig. 13.22.
58 Refit the yoke and armature assembly to the drive end housing, aligning the sun gear with the planet gears.
59 Reconnect the wiring to the solenoid terminal, and fit the securing nut.
60 Refit the commutator end plate and secure with the two securing screws.
61 Refit the spacer and C-clip to the end of the armature shaft, then smear the end of the shaft with a little lithium-based grease.
62 Fit the armature shaft cover and secure with the two screws.

Bosch EV type starter motor

63 The procedure is basically as described previously for the Bosch DW type starter motor except that a commutator end housing is fitted in place of the end plate.

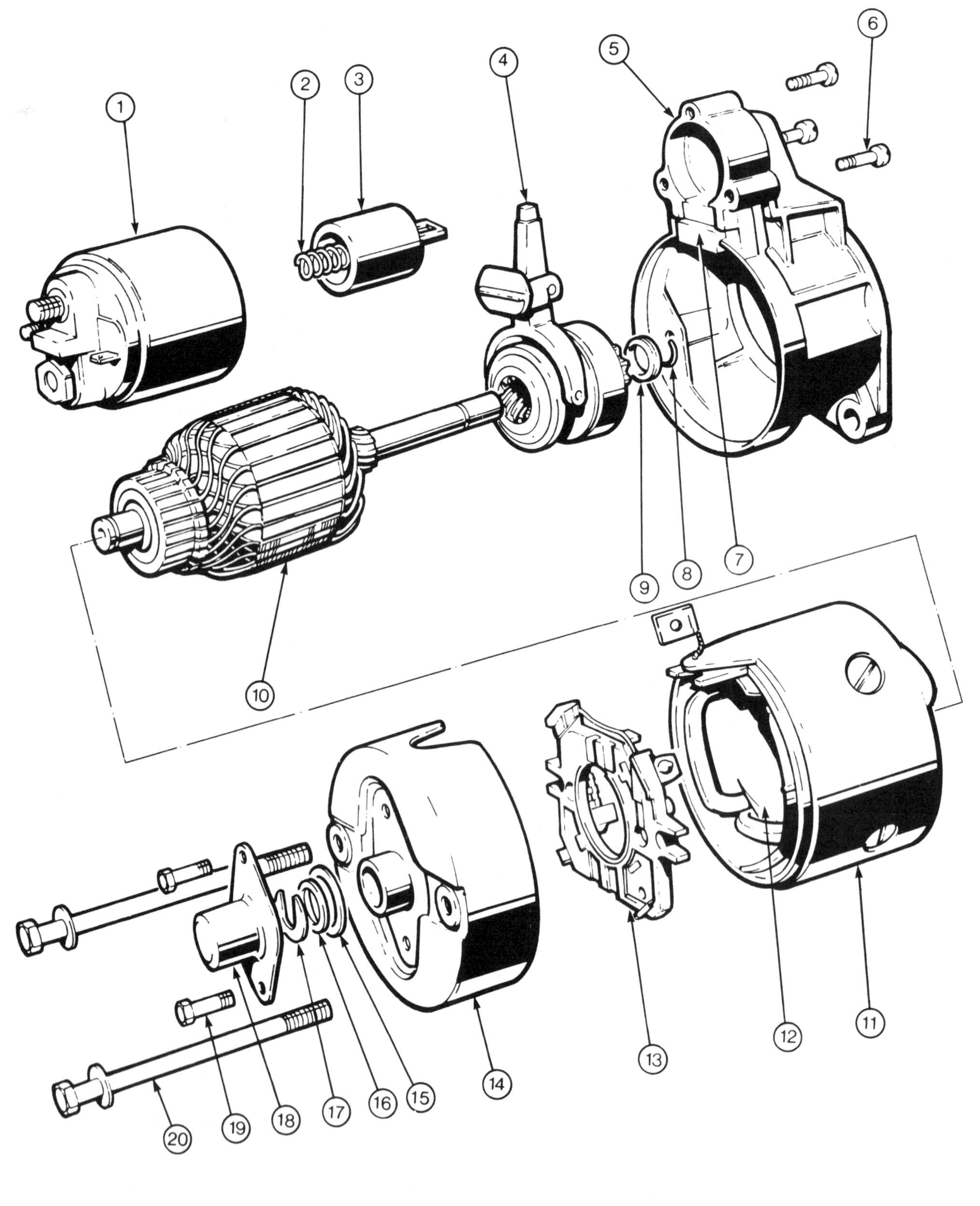

Fig 13.19 Exploded view of Bosch short frame and EF type starter motors (Sec 13)

1 *Solenoid yoke*
2 *Solenoid return spring*
3 *Solenoid armature*
4 *Actuating arm*
5 *Drive end housing*
6 *Solenoid securing screws*
7 *Rubber block*
8 *C-clip*
9 *Thrust collar*
10 *Armature*
11 *Yoke*
12 *Pole shoe*
13 *Brush plate*
14 *Commutator end housing*
15 *Seal*
16 *Shim*
17 *C-clip*
18 *Commutator end housing cap*
19 *Securing screw*
20 *Commutator end housing securing screw*

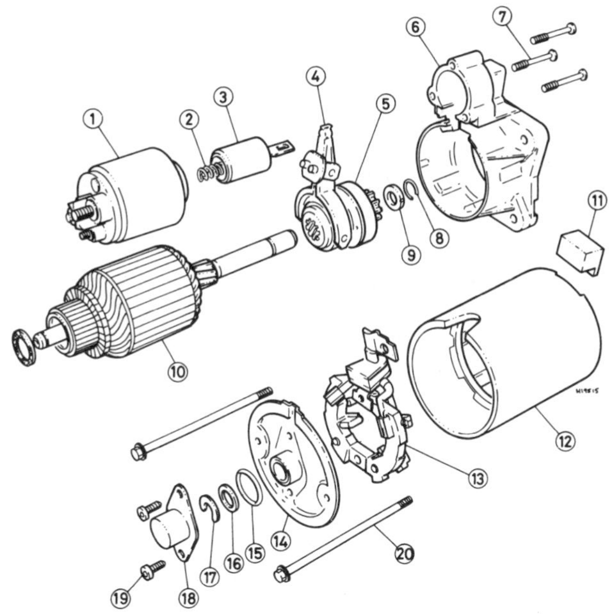

Fig 13.20 Exploded view of Bosch DM type starter motor (Sec 13)

1. *Solenoid yoke*
2. *Solenoid return spring*
3. *Solenoid armature*
4. *Actuating arm*
5. *Drive pinion and clutch assembly*
6. *Drive end housing*
7. *Solenoid securing screws*
8. *C-clip*
9. *Thrust collar*
10. *Armature*
11. *Rubber block*
12. *Yoke*
13. *Brush plate*
14. *Commutator end housing*
15. *Seal*
16. *Shim*
17. *C-clip*
18. *Commutator end housing cap*
19. *Securing screw*
20. *Commutator end housing securing screw*

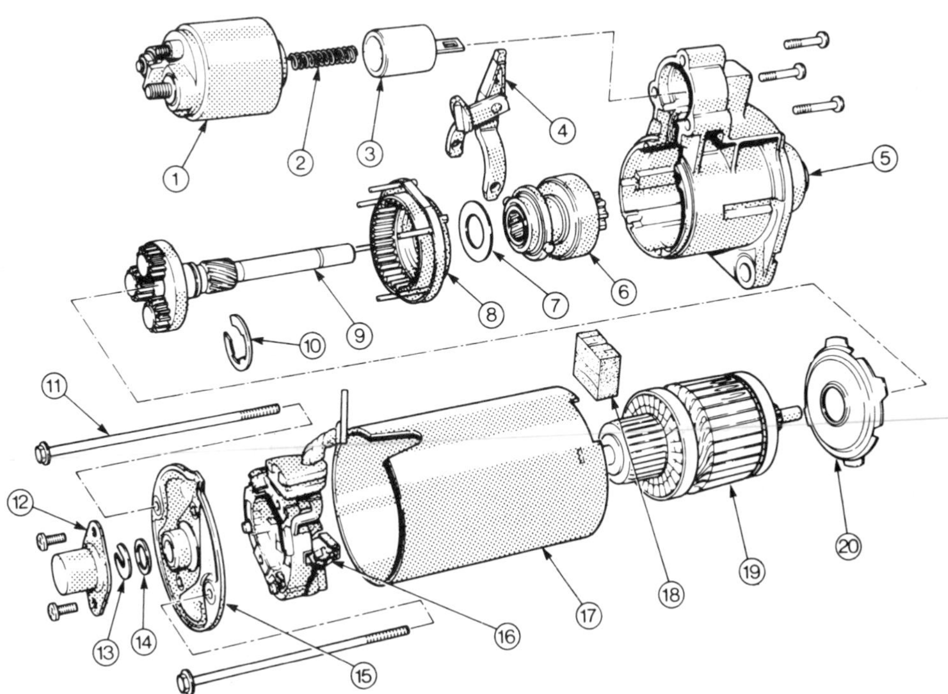

Fig 13.21 Exploded view of Bosch DW type starter motor (Sec 13)

1. *Solenoid yoke*
2. *Solenoid return spring*
3. *Solenoid armature*
4. *Actuating arm*
5. *Drive end housing*
6. *Drive pinion and clutch assembly*
7. *Spacer*
8. *Ring gear and carrier*
9. *Output shaft and planet gear assembly*
10. *Circlip*
11. *Commutator end plate securing screw*
12. *Commutator end plate cap*
13. *C-clip*
14. *Shim*
15. *Commutator end plate*
16. *Brush plate*
17. *Yoke*
18. *Rubber block*
19. *Armature*
20. *Armature retaining plate*

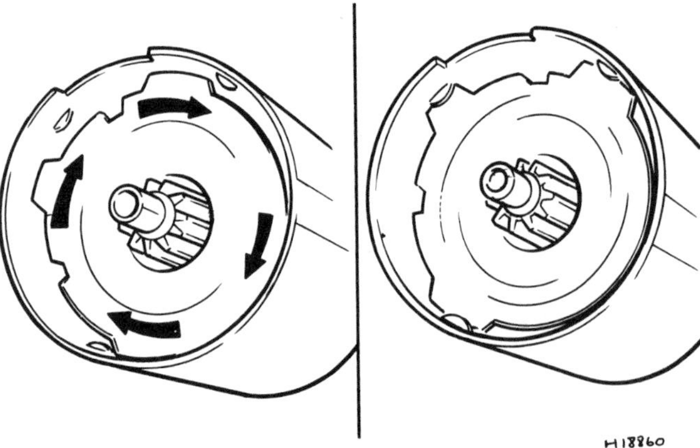

Fig 13.22 Twist armature retaining plate clockwise to position under the tangs in the yoke – Bosch DW type starter motor (Sec 13)

14 Starter motor (Lucas) – overhaul

Note: *A two-legged puller will be required to position the drive pinion thrust collar during reassembly*

5M90 type starter motor

Note: *New star clips must be obtained for the actuating arm pivot pin and the armature shaft on reassembly.*

1 With the starter motor removed from the vehicle and cleaned, grip the unit in a vice fitted with soft jaw protectors.

2 Remove the plastic cap from the end of the armature shaft, then remove the star clip from the end of the shaft, using a chisel at an angle of 45° to the shaft to distort the prongs of the clip until it can be removed (photos).

3 Unscrew the two securing nuts and remove the connector link between the solenoid and main feed terminal.

4 Unscrew the two securing nuts and withdraw the solenoid yoke and spring, then unhook the solenoid armature from the actuating arm and remove the armature (photos).

5 Remove the two drive end housing securing screws, and guide the drive end housing and armature assembly clear of the yoke (photo).

6 Withdraw the armature from the drive end housing, at the same time unhooking the actuating arm from the drive pinion.

7 Remove the rubber block and the seal from the drive end housing.

8 Drive the actuating arm pivot pin from the drive end housing using a small metal drift. The pin retaining star clip will distort under pressure, allowing removal of the pin. Remove the actuating arm.

9 To remove the drive pinion from the armature shaft, drive the thrust collar down the shaft, using a suitable tube drift, to expose the C-clip. Remove the clip from its groove, and slide the thrust collar and drive pinion from the shaft. Do not grip the clutch assembly in a vice during this procedure, as damage will result.

10 Extract the two commutator end plate securing screws, and carefully tap the end plate from the yoke. Lift the end plate clear of the yoke sufficiently to allow access to the two field brushes. Disconnect the two field brushes from the brush box to allow complete removal of the commutator end plate. Take care not to damage the gasket as the end plate is removed.

11 Remove the nut, washer and insulator from the main terminal stud on the commutator end plate, then push the stud and the second insulator through the end plate and unhook the brushes.

12 To remove the brush box, drill out the rivets securing the brush box to the end plate, then remove the brush box and gasket.

13 Proceed as described in Section 13, paragraphs 12 to 16 inclusive.

14 Commence reassembly by positioning the brush box gasket on the commutator end plate, then position the brush box on the gasket and rivet the brush box to the end plate. Use a new gasket if necessary.

15 Fit the main terminal stud and insulator to the commutator end plate, then secure the stud with the remaining insulator, washer and nut.

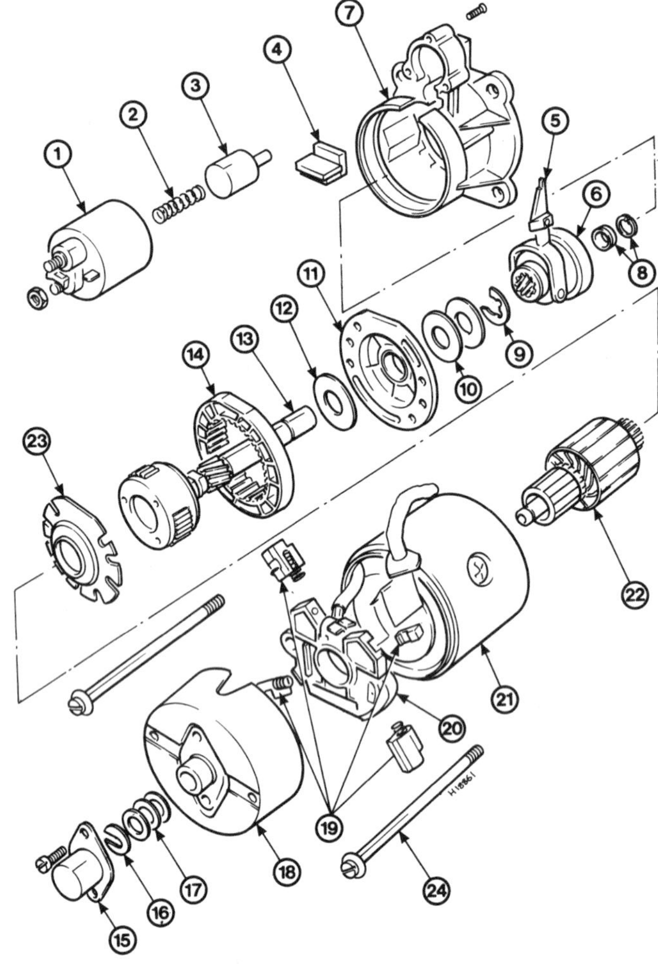

Fig 13.23 Exploded view of Bosch EV type starter motor (Sec 13)

1 *Solenoid yoke*
2 *Solenoid return spring*
3 *Solenoid armature*
4 *Rubber block*
5 *Actuating arm*
6 *Drive pinion and clutch assembly*
7 *Drive end housing*
8 *C-clip and thrust collar*
9 *Circlip*
10 *Spacers*
11 *Cover plate*
12 *Spacer*
13 *Output shaft and planet gear assembly*
14 *Ring gear*
15 *Commutator end housing cap*
16 *C-clip*
17 *Shims*
18 *Commutator end housing*
19 *Brushes*
20 *Brush plate*
21 *Yoke*
22 *Armature*
23 *Armature retaining plate*
24 *Commutator end housing securing screw*

Fit the two brushes which are attached to the terminal stud into their respective locations in the brush box.

16 Fit the two field brushes into their locations in the brush box, then position the commutator end plate on the yoke and fit the two securing screws.

17 Slide the drive pinion and thrust collar onto the armature shaft, then fit the C-clip into its groove and use a two-legged puller to draw the thrust collar over the clip – see Fig. 13.17.

14.2A Remove the plastic cap from the end of the armature shaft ...

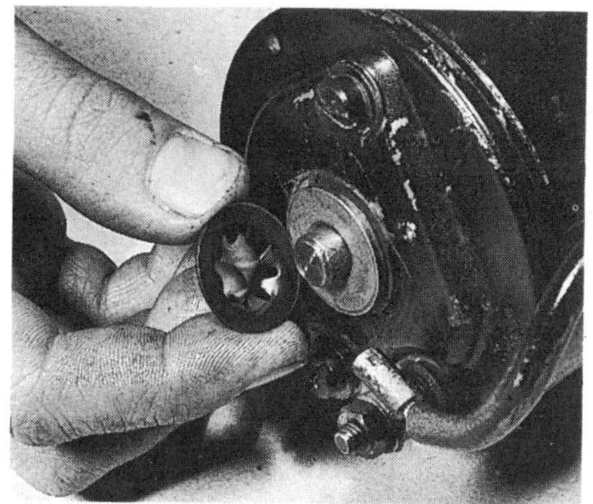
14.2B ... followed by the star clip – Lucas 5M90 type starter motor

14.4A Unscrew the solenoid yoke securing nuts ...

14.4B ... then withdraw the yoke ...

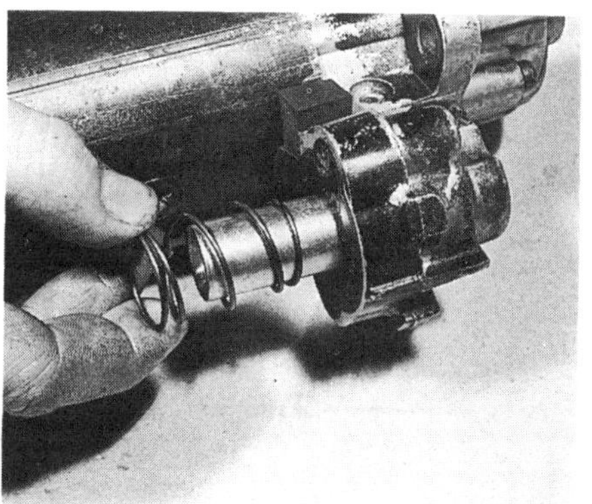
14.4C ... and spring,

14.4D ... followed by the armature – Lucas 5M90 type starter motor

14.5 Remove the drive end housing securing screws – Lucas 5M90 type starter motor

14.22 Using a soft faced hammer and socket to fit a new star clip to the end of the armature shaft – Lucas 5M90 type starter motor

18 Position the actuating arm in the drive end housing, and fit the pivot pin. Retain the pivot pin with a new star clip.
19 Refit the seal and the rubber block to the drive end housing.
20 Guide the armature into the drive end housing, at the same time engaging the actuating arm with the drive pinion.
21 Guide the armature and drive end housing into the yoke, and align the armature shaft with the commutator end plate bush. Align the notches in the yoke and the drive end housing, then secure the end housing with the two screws.
22 Fit a new star clip to the end of the armature shaft, ensuring that the clip is pressed home firmly to eliminate any endfloat in the armature (photo). Fit the plastic cap over the end of the armature shaft.
23 Reconnect the solenoid armature to the actuating arm, then refit the solenoid yoke and secure with the two nuts.
24 Refit the connector link between the solenoid and main feed terminal, and secure with the two nuts and washers.

8M90 type starter motor

25 The procedure is basically as described previously for the 5M90 type starter motor with the following differences.
26 When the armature is withdrawn from the drive end housing, the actuating arm assembly will be removed with it, along with the plastic pivot block and rubber pad. To remove the actuating arm from the drive pinion, proceed as follows.
27 Remove the C-clip from its groove and withdraw the spacer, then separate the two halves of the plastic drive collar and remove the actuating arm assembly – see Fig. 13.26.

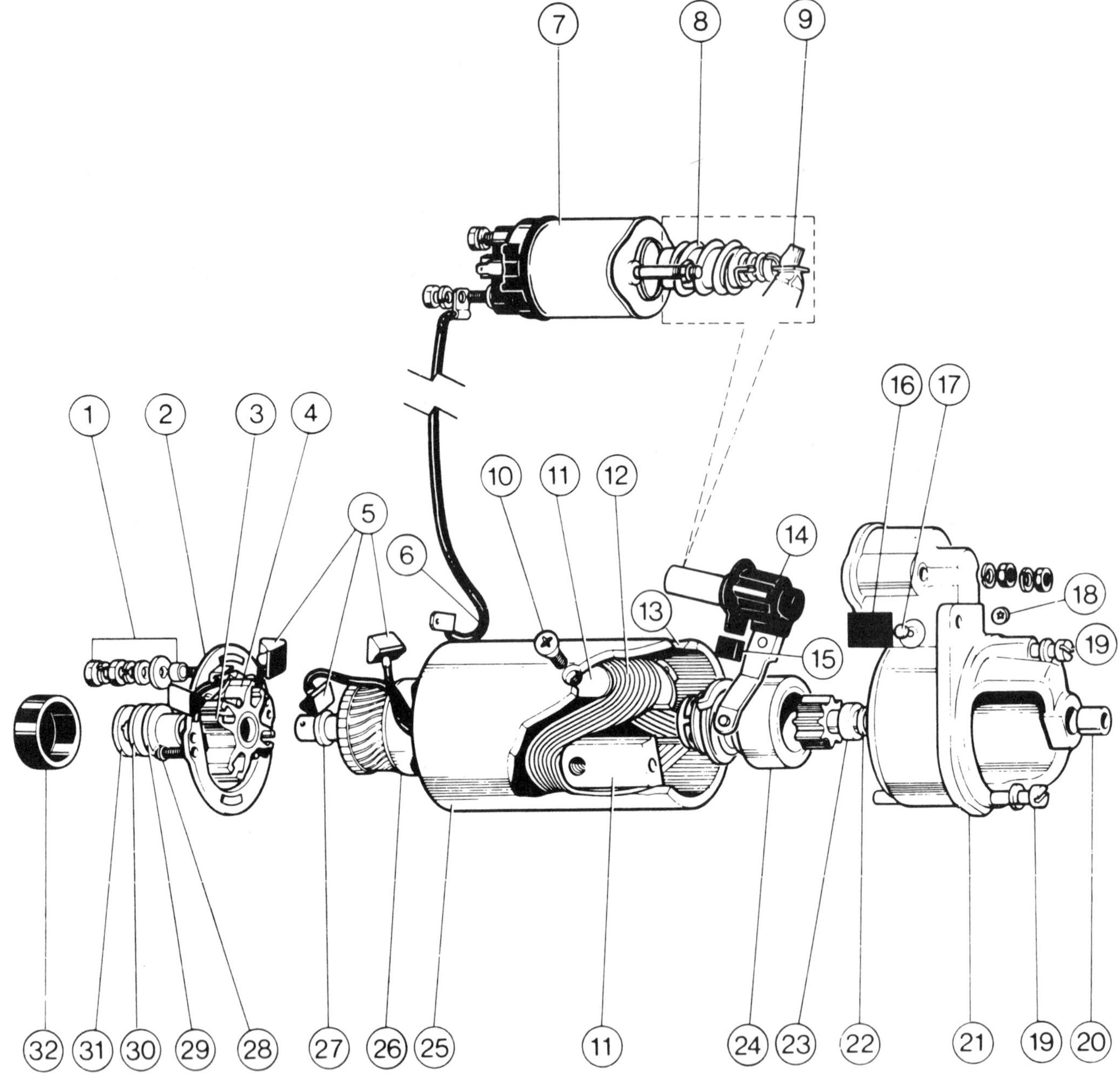

Fig 13.24 Exploded view of Lucas 5M90 type starter motor (Sec 14)

1 Main terminal nuts and washers
2 Commutator end plate
3 Brush box
4 Brush spring
5 Brushes
6 Solenoid connector link
7 Solenoid unit
8 Solenoid return spring
9 Actuating arm
10 Pole securing screw
11 Pole shoe
12 Field coils
13 Field coil earth connection
14 Rubber seal
15 Rubber block
16 Rubber seal
17 Actuating arm pivot pin
18 Star clip
19 Drive end housing securing screws
20 Bush
21 Drive end housing
22 C-clip
23 Thrust collar
24 Drive pinion and clutch assembly
25 Yoke
26 Armature
27 Thrustwasher
28 Commutator end plate securing screw
29 Bush
30 Thrustplate
31 Star clip
32 Plastic cap

28 The commutator end plate is secured by two screws, and the end plate and brush box are serviced as a complete assembly and should be renewed if required.

M79 type starter motor

29 With the starter motor removed from the vehicle and cleaned, grip the unit in a vice fitted with soft jaw protectors.

30 Unscrew the securing nut and washer and disconnect the wiring from the solenoid terminal.

31 Remove the two screws securing the commutator end housing cap and remove the cap.

32 Remove the C-clip and spacers from the end of the armature shaft.

33 Remove the two commutator end housing securing screws and withdraw the end housing.

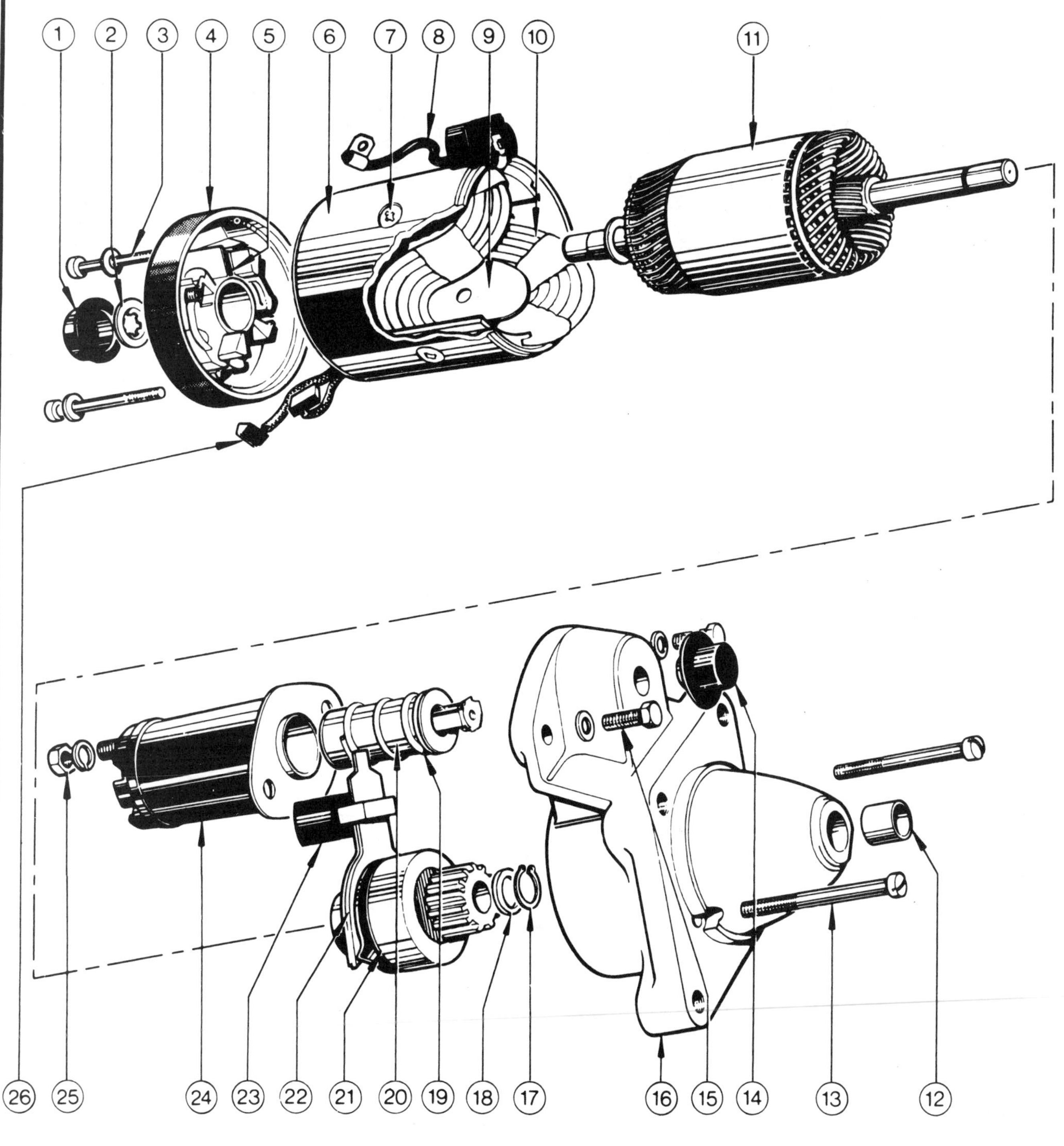

Fig 13.25 Exploded view of Lucas 8M90 type starter motor (Sec 14)

1 *Plastic cap*
2 *Star clip*
3 *Commutator end plate securing screw*
4 *Commutator end plate*
5 *Brush box*
6 *Yoke*
7 *Pole securing screw*
8 *Solenoid connector link*
9 *Pole shoe*
10 *Field coils*
11 *Armature*
12 *Bush*
13 *Drive end housing securing screw*
14 *Dust cover*
15 *Solenoid securing screw*
16 *Drive end housing*
17 *C-clip*
18 *Thrust collar*
19 *Solenoid return spring*
20 *Solenoid armature*
21 *Drive pinion and clutch assembly*
22 *Actuating arm*
23 *Actuating arm pivot*
24 *Solenoid yoke*
25 *Main terminal nut and washer*
26 *Brush*

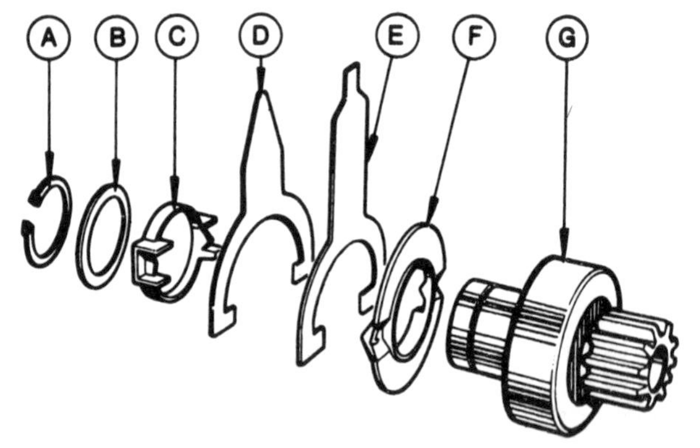

Fig 13.26 Actuating arm assembly – Lucas 8M90 type starter motor (Sec 14)

A *C-clip*
B *Spacer*
C *Drive collar half*
D *Actuating arm half*
E *Actuating arm half*
F *Drive collar half*
G *Drive pinion and clutch assembly*

Fig 13.27 Brush plate components – Lucas M79 type starter motor (Sec 14)

A *Brush plate*
B *Brush plate insulator*
C *Brush holders and springs*
D *Brushes*
E *Insulators*
F *Brush link*

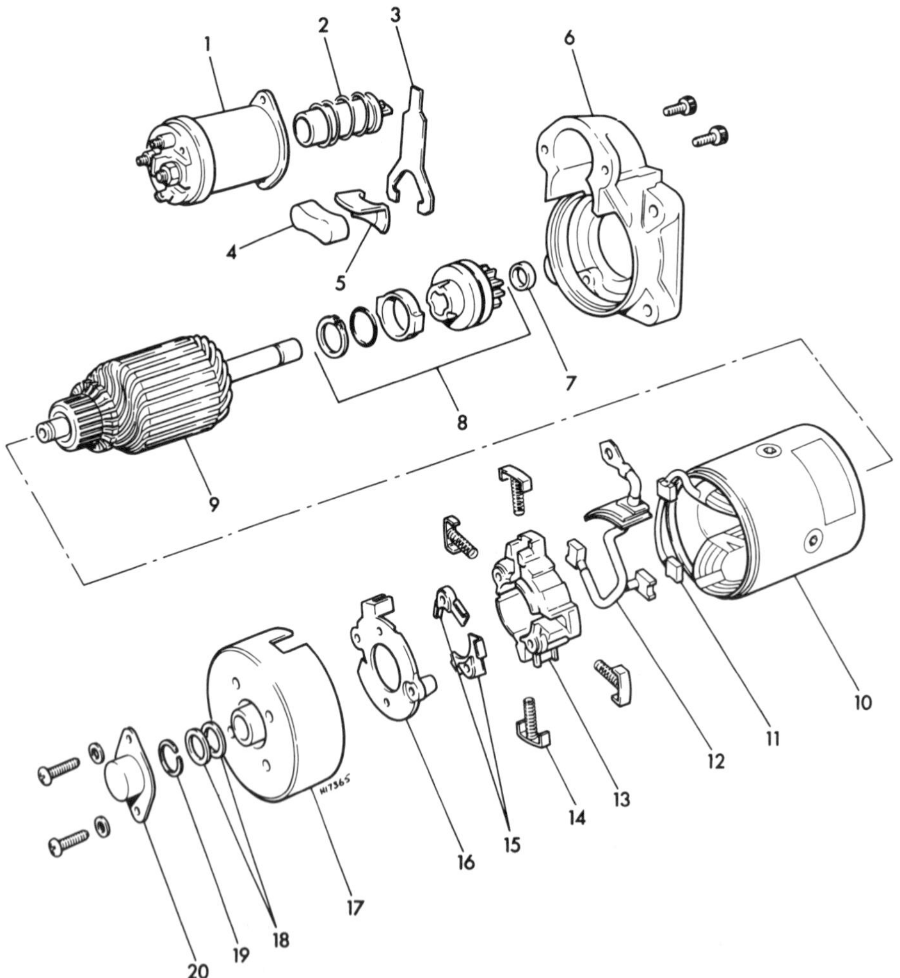

Fig 13.28 Exploded view of Lucas M79 type starter motor (Sec 14)

1 *Solenoid yoke*
2 *Solenoid armature*
3 *Actuating arm*
4 *Rubber pad*
5 *Plastic support block*
6 *Drive end housing*
7 *Thrust collar*
8 *Drive pinion and clutch assembly*
9 *Armature*
10 *Yoke*
11 *Brush*
12 *Brush link*
13 *Brush plate*
14 *Brush holder and spring*
15 *Insulators*
16 *Brush plate insulator*
17 *Commutator end housing*
18 *Shims*
19 *C-clip*
20 *Commutator end housing cap*

34 Unscrew the two securing nuts and withdraw the solenoid yoke, then unhook the solenoid armature from the actuating arm and remove the armature.
35 Remove the two drive end housing securing screws, and withdraw the end housing from the yoke and armature assembly.
36 Separate the armature from the yoke, taking care not to damage the brushes. The actuating arm will be withdrawn with the armature along with the plastic support block and rubber pad.
37 Separate the brush components from the yoke – see Fig. 13.27.
38 Remove the drive pinion from the armature shaft as described in paragraph 9.
39 To remove the actuating arm from the drive pinion, remove the retaining circlip and slide the lever and pivot assembly from the pinion.
40 Proceed as described in Section 13, paragraphs 12 to 16 inclusive.
41 Commence reassembly by refitting the actuating arm to the drive pinion and securing with the circlip.
42 Refit the drive pinion to the armature shaft as described in paragraph 17.
43 Fit the armature assembly to the yoke, and locate the actuating arm in the drive end housing, with the plastic support block and rubber pad. Note that the support block locates in the cut-out in the face of the yoke.
44 Connect the solenoid armature to the actuating arm, then refit the solenoid yoke and secure with the two nuts.
45 Align the drive end housing with the yoke and armature assembly, and fit the two securing screws.
46 Locate the brush box over the commutator, position the brushes, then fit the nylon cover over the brushes. Route the brush wiring into the locating channel, then secure the brushes in the channels with the locking clips and springs.
47 Refit the commutator end housing, locating the rubber block in the cut-out in the housing, then secure with the two screws.
48 Refit the spacers and C-clip to the end of the armature shaft, then fit the commutator end housing cap and secure with the two screws.
49 Reconnect the wiring to the solenoid terminal and fit the washer and securing nut.

15 Starter motor (Nippondenso) – overhaul

1 With the starter motor removed from the vehicle and cleaned, grip the unit in a vice fitted with soft jaw protectors.
2 Unscrew the retaining nut and washer and disconnect the wiring from the terminal on the solenoid.
3 Unscrew the two securing nuts and withdraw the solenoid yoke, then unhook the solenoid armature from the actuating arm and remove the armature.
4 Remove the two screws securing the commutator end housing cap and remove the cap.
5 Remove the C-clip from the groove in the armature shaft, and remove the spring.
6 Unscrew the two bolts and washers, and withdraw the commutator end housing.
7 Withdraw the two field brushes from the brush plate, then remove the brush plate.
8 Withdraw the armature and drive end housing from the yoke.
9 Separate the armature and actuating arm from the drive end housing, then unhook the actuating arm from the drive pinion flange.
10 Remove the drive pinion from the armature by driving the thrust collar down the shaft, using a suitable tube drift, to expose the C-clip. Remove the clip from its groove, and slide the thrust collar and drive pinion from the shaft. Do not grip the clutch assembly in a vice during this procedure, as damage will result.
11 Proceed as described in Section 13, paragraphs 12 to 16 inclusive.
12 Commence reassembly by sliding the drive pinion and thrust collar onto the armature shaft. Fit the C-clip into its groove, and then use a two-legged puller to draw the thrust collar over the clip.
13 Align the actuating arm in the drive end housing, then guide the armature into position in the end housing, at the same time locating the actuating arm over the drive pinion flange.
14 Guide the yoke over the armature, and tap the yoke up against the drive end housing.
15 Position the brush plate over the end of the armature, aligning the cut-outs in the brush plate with the loops in the field windings. The brush plate will be positively located when the commutator end housing bolts are fitted.
16 Fit the brushes to their locations in the brush plate, and retain with the springs.
17 Fit the commutator end housing and secure with the two bolts and washers.
18 Fit the spring and the C-clip to the end of the armature shaft, then smear the end of the shaft with a little lithium-based grease, and refit the commutator end housing cap, securing with the two screws.
19 Hook the solenoid armature over the actuating arm in the drive end housing, then refit the solenoid yoke and secure with the two nuts.
20 Reconnect the wiring to the solenoid terminal and fit the washer and retaining nut.

16 Fuses and relays – general

1 The main fuses and relays are located in a box in the engine compartment on the right-hand side of the bulkhead. The circuits protected are identified by symbols on the underside of the fusebox cover. On certain models, additional relays and fuses are located in various positions beneath the facia panels. If uncertain of the location of an auxiliary relay or fuse, it is suggested that a Ford dealer is consulted, as the relay and fuse locations vary substantially depending on model.
2 Always renew a fuse with one of identical rating and never renew it more than once without finding the source of the trouble (usually a short circuit). Always switch off the ignition before renewing a fuse or relay, and when renewing the wiper motor fuse keep the hands clear of the wiper linkage as it may return to the parked position. Note that the fuses are colour-coded as follows:

10A	*Red*
15A	*Blue*
20A	*Yellow*
25A	*Natural*
30A	*Green*

3 Access to the fuses and relays in the fusebox is gained by removing the loose cover and spring clip (if fitted), pulling the plastic clip and removing the cover. All fuses and relays are a push fit (photos). The

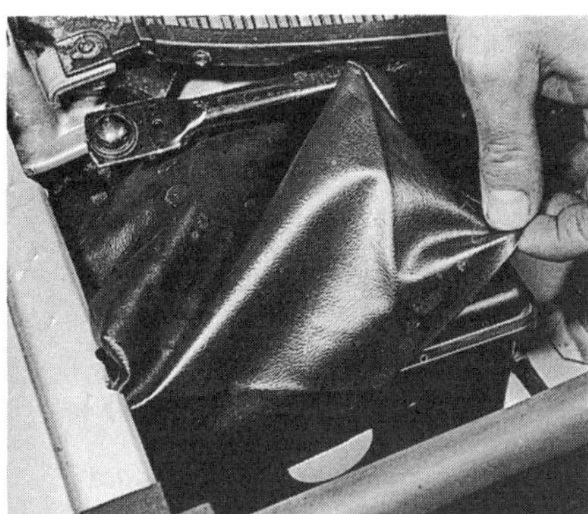
16.3A Remove the loose cover for access to the fusebox cover

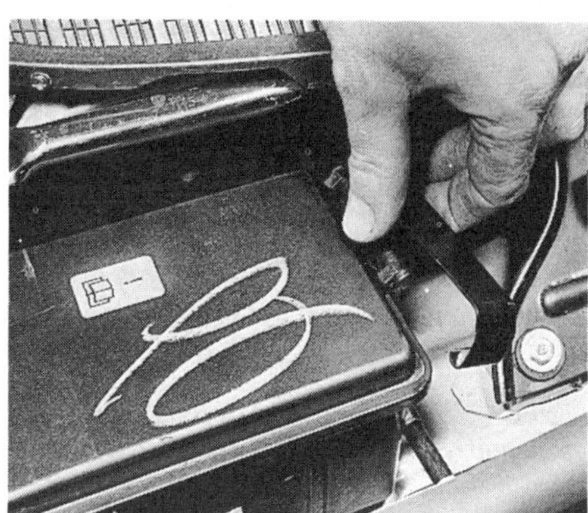
16.3B Remove the spring clip from the fusebox cover

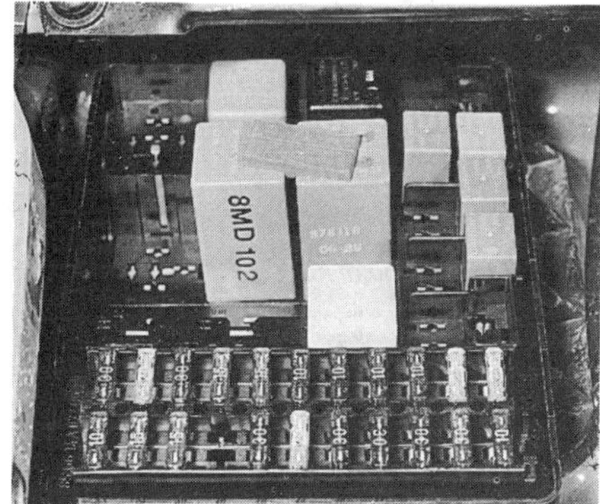

16.3C Fusebox cover removed to expose fuses and relays (1.8 CVH model shown)

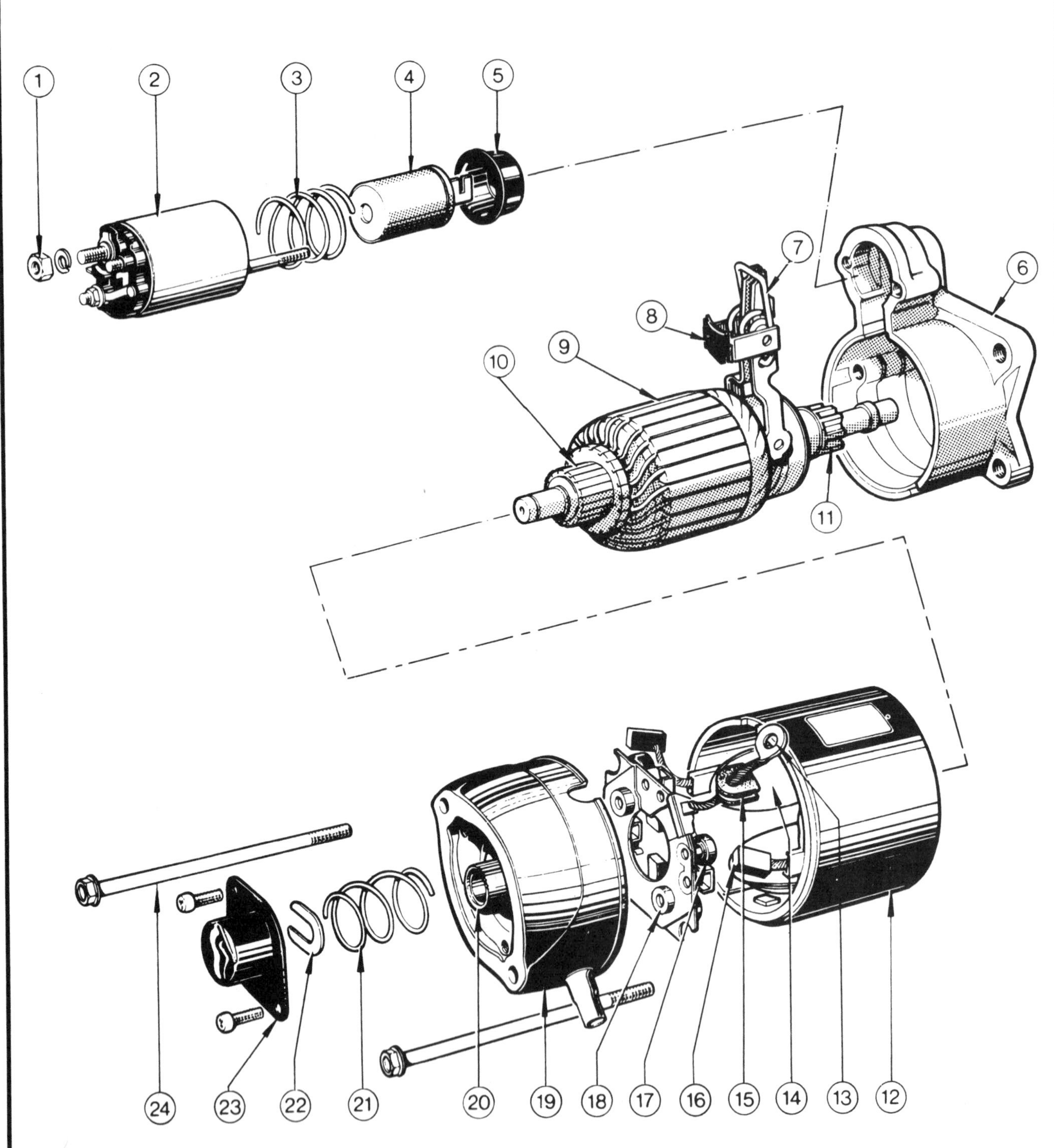

Fig 13.29 Exploded view of Nippondenso type starter motor (Sec 15)

1 *Main terminal nut and washer*
2 *Solenoid yoke*
3 *Solenoid return spring*
4 *Solenoid armature*
5 *Seal*
6 *Drive end housing*
7 *Actuating arm*
8 *Actuating arm pivot assembly*
9 *Armature*
10 *Commutator*
11 *Drive pinion and clutch assembly*
12 *Yoke*
13 *Solenoid connecting link*
14 *Pole shoe*
15 *Rubber grommet*
16 *Brush*
17 *Brush spring*
18 *Brush plate*
19 *Commutator end housing*
20 *Bush*
21 *Spring*
22 *C-clip*
23 *Commutator end housing cap*
24 *Commutator end housing securing bolt*

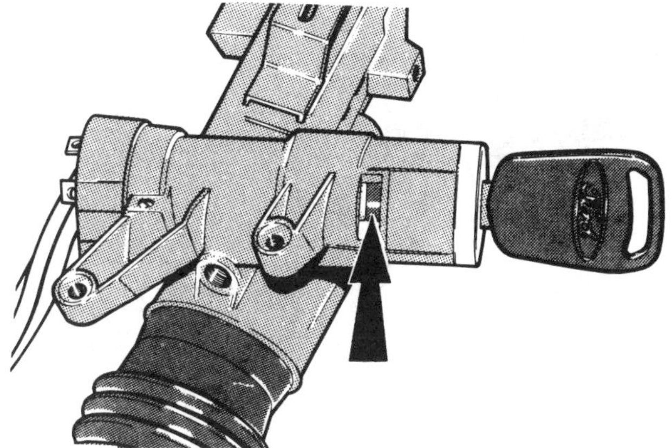

Fig 13.30 Ignition switch lock barrel spring clip location (arrowed) (Sec 17)

fuse/relay plate can be released from the fusebox for access to the wiring by carefully levering the plastic lugs around the perimeter of the plate.

4 For details of direction indicator/hazard warning flasher relay removal and refitting, refer to Section 19.

17 Ignition switch and lock barrel – removal and refitting

1 Disconnect the battery negative lead.

2 For improved access, remove the securing screws and unclip the lower and upper steering column shrouds.

3 Insert the ignition key and turn to position 'I', then, working through the access hole, depress the spring clip using a suitable tool and pull the key to withdraw the lock barrel and cylinder from the ignition switch housing. The spring clip access hole is shown in Fig. 13.30, but note that, on certain models, the spring clip must be released by inserting the tool through a small circular hole at the top of the switch housing, above the rectangular slot shown. Slight movement of the key may be necessary to allow removal of the barrel and cylinder.

4 To remove the lock barrel from the cylinder, insert the key fully into the barrel and remove the retaining circlip, taking care not to damage the circlip location, then withdraw the key approximately 5.0 mm (0.2 in) to retract the lock barrel securing lug, and withdraw the barrel from the cylinder.

5 To remove the ignition switch, disconnect the wiring plug, then remove the two grub screws and withdraw the switch.

6 Refitting is a reversal of removal, bearing in mind the following points.

7 Note that the lock barrel can only be fitted to the cylinder in one position, and check with the key fully inserted that the barrel can be turned from position 'O' to 'III' satisfactorily.

8 The open jaws of the lock barrel retaining circlip must align with the keyway register on the cylinder, and the cylinder retaining circlip must locate in the slot in the ignition switch housing.

9 On completion, check the operation of the steering lock and ignition switch in all positions.

18 Direction indicator and hazard warning flasher switch assembly – removal and refitting

1 Disconnect the battery negative lead.

2 Remove the securing screws and unclip the lower and upper steering column shrouds.

3 Remove the two securing screws and disconnect the two wiring plugs, then withdraw the switch from the steering column.

4 Refitting is a reversal of removal.

19 Direction indicator/hazard warning flasher relay – removal and refitting

1 Disconnect the battery negative lead.

2 The relay is located on a bracket above the steering column. Access is gained either by removing the driver's side lower facia panel (see Chapter 12) or the instrument panel (see Section 32).

3 Unclip the relay from the bracket, and disconnect the wiring plug (photos).

4 Refitting is a reversal of removal. Check for correct operation before refitting the facia panel or instrument panel.

20 Lighting and wash/wipe switch assembly – removal and refitting

1 The procedure is identical to that described in Section 18 for the direction indicator switch, except for the additional removal and refitting of an earth lead (photo).

21 Reversing lamp switch – removal and refitting

1 For automatic transmission models, refer to Chapter 7, Section 11. For manual gearbox models, proceed as follows.

2 Disconnect the battery negative lead.

3 Apply the handbrake, jack up the front of the vehicle and support on axle stands.

4 Working underneath the vehicle, disconnect the wiring plug, then unscrew the switch from the gearbox extension housing.

5 Refitting is a reversal of removal, but make sure that the wiring is routed clear of the exhaust system.

19.3A Direction indicator/hazard warning flasher relay location (arrowed)

19.3B Direction indicator/hazard warning flasher relay (arrowed) unclipped from mounting bracket

20.1 Lighting and wash/wipe switch assembly earth lead securing screw (arrowed)

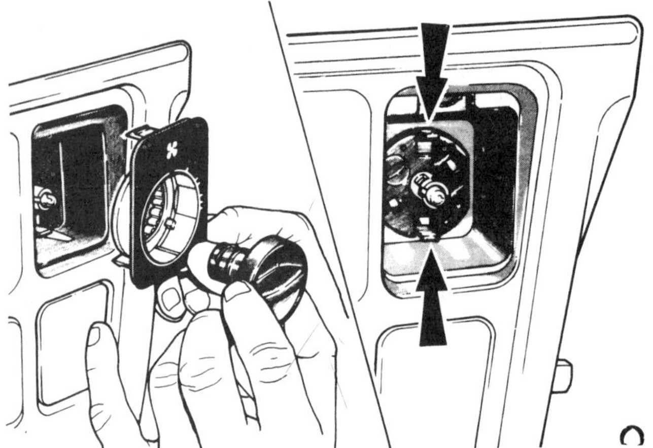

Fig 13.31 Heater blower switch removal. Switch retaining tabs arrowed (Sec 22)

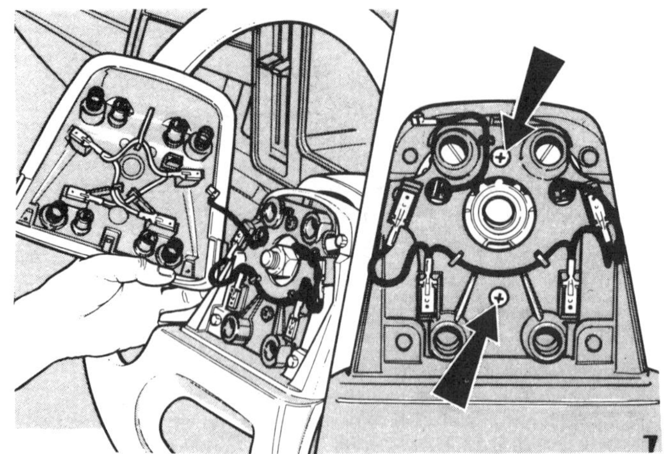

Fig 13.32 Horn switch removal – models up to 1987. Switch securing screws arrowed (Sec 24)

22 Facia panel switches – removal and refitting

1 Disconnect the battery negative lead.

Rocker switches and push button switches

2 Using a thin-bladed screwdriver, carefully prise the switch from the facia panel.
3 Disconnect the wiring plug and withdraw the switch.
4 Refitting is a reversal of removal.

Instrument panel illumination and intermittent wipe rheostats

5 Proceed as described in paragraphs 2 to 4.

Heater blower switch

6 Carefully pull off the switch knob, using pliers with padded jaws if necessary.
7 Using a thin-bladed screwdriver, prise out the switch front plate from the facia panel.
8 Squeeze the switch retaining tabs, then withdraw the switch and disconnect the wiring plug – see Fig. 13.31.
9 Refitting is a reversal of removal.

Loudspeaker balance joystick

10 Using a thin-bladed screwdriver, carefully prise the joystick front plate from the facia panel.
11 Twist the joystick assembly retaining ring anti-clockwise and remove the ring.
12 Working behind the facia panel, disconnect the wiring plug and slide out the joystick assembly.
13 Refitting is a reversal of removal, but note that the wiring plug can only be fitted in one position, and ensure that the joystick assembly locating lug engages in the corresponding hole in the facia panel.

23 Electric door mirror switch – removal and refitting

1 Disconnect the battery negative lead.

Models up to 1987

2 Using a thin-bladed screwdriver, carefully prise the switch from the door trim panel.
3 Disconnect the wiring plug and withdraw the switch (photo).
4 Refitting is a reversal of removal.

Models from 1987

5 Prise the securing screw cover from the mirror control panel, then remove the screw and withdraw the control panel.
6 Depress the switch retaining tang, then withdraw the switch from the control panel and disconnect the wiring plug.
7 Refitting is a reversal of removal.

24 Horn switch assembly (steering wheel-mounted) – removal and refitting

1 Disconnect the battery negative lead.

Switch – models up to 1987

2 Pull the trim insert from the centre of the steering wheel, and disconnect the lead from the horn push.
3 Disconnect the two leads from the horn slip ring, then remove the two securing screws and withdraw the switch assembly – see Fig. 13.32.
4 Refitting is a reversal of removal, but check the operation of the switch on completion.

Switch – models from 1987

5 Using a thin-bladed screwdriver, carefully prise the trim insert from the centre of the steering wheel. Disconnect the wire (photo).
6 Prise the steering wheel centre disc from the steering wheel, and disconnect the wire (photo).
7 Refitting is a reversal of removal.

Slip ring

8 Remove the steering wheel as described in Chapter 11.
9 On models up to 1987, remove the switch as described in paragraph 3.
10 Release the three slip ring retaining tangs and withdraw the slip ring from the steering wheel.
11 Refitting is a reversal of removal.

Slip ring contact finger

12 Remove the steering wheel as described in Chapter 11.
13 Remove the securing screws and unclip the lower and upper steering column shrouds.
14 Disconnect the contact finger wiring plug, and pull the contact finger housing from its mounting – see Fig. 13.33.
15 Refitting is a reversal of removal.

25 Courtesy lamp switch – removal and refitting

1 Disconnect the battery negative lead.
2 Open the door and remove the switch securing screw.
3 Withdraw the switch from the door pillar and pull the wiring out sufficiently to prevent it from springing back into the pillar (photo).
4 Disconnect the wiring and remove the switch.
5 Refitting is a reversal of removal.

23.3 Disconnecting the wiring plug from the electric door mirror switch – models up to 1987

24.5 Prise the trim insert from the steering wheel ...

24.6 ... followed by the centre disc – models from 1987

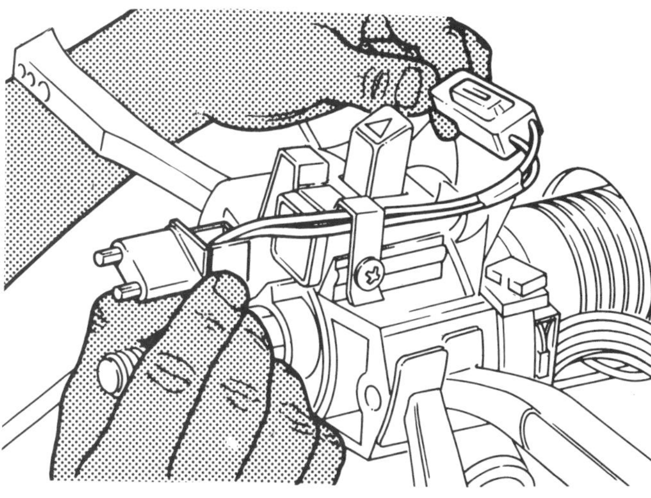
Fig 13.33 Horn switch slip ring contact finger removal (Sec 24)

5 Refitting is a reversal of removal, but ensure that the switch is refitted in its original position, as noted during removal, and test the operation of the switch on completion.

Models from 1987

6 Where applicable, unclip the tailgate/boot trim panel with reference to Chapter 12 if necessary.
7 Unclip the switch from the lock assembly, disconnect the wiring plug and remove the switch.
8 Refitting is a reversal of removal.

26 Luggage compartment lamp switch – removal and refitting

1 Disconnect the battery negative lead.

Models up to 1987

2 A level-sensitive switch is fitted to the tailgate.
3 Unclip the tailgate trim panel with reference to Chapter 12 if necessary.
4 Disconnect the wiring from the switch terminal, then remove the securing screw and withdraw the switch, noting its fitted position (photo).

27 Handbrake 'on' warning lamp switch – removal and refitting

1 Disconnect the battery negative lead.
2 Working inside the vehicle, remove the handbrake lever rubber gaiter and/or the centre console, as necessary, as described in Chapter 12.
3 Disconnect the wiring connector from the switch, then remove the two securing screws and withdraw the switch from the handbrake lever (photo).
4 Refitting is a reversal of removal.

28 Brake lamp switch – removal and refitting

1 Disconnect the battery negative lead.
2 Unclip the trim panel from the lower edge of the driver's side lower facia trim panel. If required for improved access, remove the lower facia trim panel as described in Chapter 12.
3 Disconnect the wiring from the terminal on the switch, then twist the switch anti-clockwise and remove it (photo).
4 When refitting, insert the switch into its aperture in the pedal bracket, then push the switch inwards until the switch barrel touches the pedal. *Ensure that the pedal is not moved from its stop.* Twist the

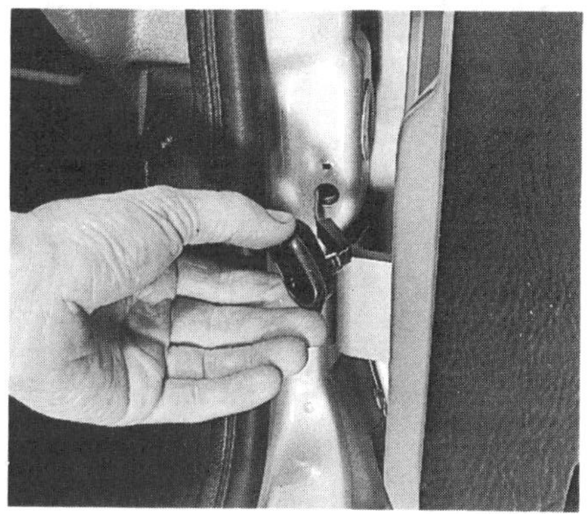
25.3 Withdrawing a courtesy lamp switch

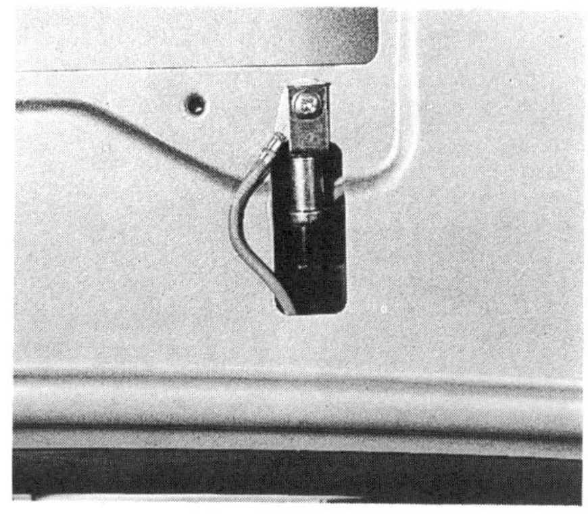
26.4 Luggage compartment lamp switch location – models up to 1987

27.3 Handbrake 'on' warning lamp switch location (arrowed)

switch clockwise to lock it in position. No further adjustment is necessary.
5 Further refitting is a reversal of removal, but check the operation of the switch on completion.

29 Oil pressure warning lamp switch – removal and refitting

1 Disconnect the battery negative lead.
2 The oil pressure warning light switch is located towards the left-hand rear of the cylinder block on OHC models, and towards the right-hand rear of the cylinder block on CVH models (photo).
3 Disconnect the wiring from the switch terminal, then unscrew and withdraw the switch. Be prepared for some oil spillage.
4 Clean the threads of the switch and its seat before refitting.
5 After refitting, run the engine and check for oil leaks around the switch, then stop the engine and check the oil level, topping-up if necessary.

30 Cigarette lighter – removal and refitting

1 Disconnect the battery negative lead.
2 Working behind the facia panel, disconnect the wiring, then push out the lighter assembly through the front of the facia panel.
3 If required, the illumination ring assembly can now be withdrawn after removing the bulbholder.
4 Refitting is a reversal of removal.

31 Clock – removal and refitting

1 Disconnect the battery negative lead.

Standard clock

2 Using a thin-bladed screwdriver, carefully prise the clock from the facia panel.
3 Disconnect the wiring plug and withdraw the clock.
4 Refitting is a reversal of removal.

Multi-function digital/analogue clock

5 Remove the single screw from the top edge of the facia panel in which the clock is housed, then withdraw the facia panel.
6 Remove the four now exposed securing screws, disconnect the wiring plug, and withdraw the clock (photo).
7 Refitting is a reversal of removal.

32 Instrument panel – removal and refitting

1 Disconnect the battery negative lead.
2 Remove the securing screws and unclip the lower and upper steering column shrouds.
3 Where applicable, remove the instrument panel illumination and intermittent wiper rheostats as described in Section 22.
4 Unclip the cover for access to the lower right-hand instrument panel surround securing screw (photos).
5 Remove the two upper and two lower securing screws, and withdraw the instrument panel surround (photo).
6 On models fitted with a trip computer, unscrew the knurled nut and disconnect the speedometer cable from the speed sender unit on the engine compartment bulkhead.
7 Detach the speedometer cable grommet from the engine compartment bulkhead.
8 Remove the two upper and two lower securing screws, and withdraw the instrument panel sufficiently to disconnect the speedometer cable and the wiring plugs. Remove the instrument panel (photos).
9 Refitting is a reversal of removal but where applicable, ensure that

28.3 Brake lamp switch location (arrowed)

29.2 Oil pressure warning lamp switch location (arrowed) – OHC engine

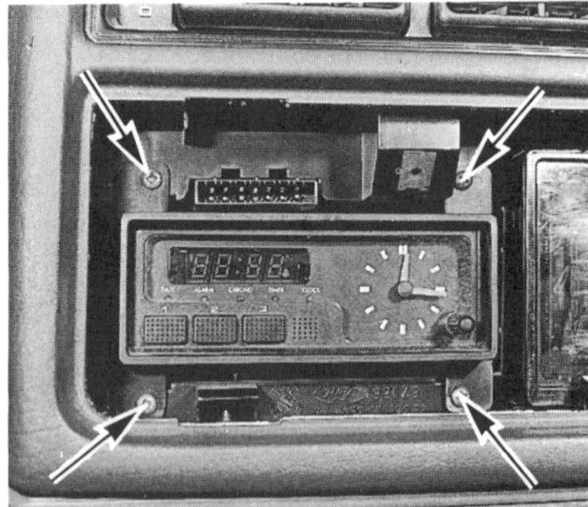
31.6 Multi-function digital/analogue clock securing screws (arrowed)

32.4A Unclip the cover ...

32.4B ... for access to the lower right-hand instrument panel surround securing screw

32.5 Removing an upper instrument panel surround securing screw

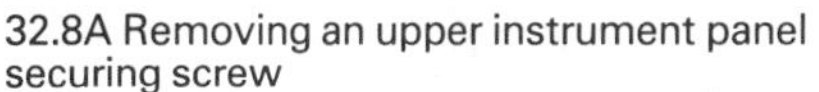

32.8A Removing an upper instrument panel securing screw

32.8B Withdraw the instrument panel ...

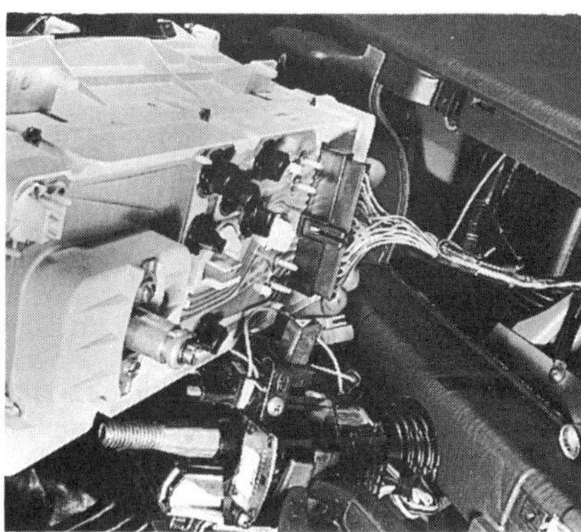

32.8C ... and disconnect the wiring plugs

the speedometer cable rubber sleeve is in place over the square inner drive on the cable connector, and not in the speedometer head.

10 On completion, pull the speedometer cable from within the engine compartment to ensure that the cable is straight between the instrument panel and the bulkhead grommet.

33 Instrument panel components – removal and refitting

1 Remove the instrument panel as described in Section 32.

Panel illumination and warning lamp bulbs

2 Twist the relevant bulbholder anti-clockwise and withdraw it from the printed circuit board on the rear of the instrument panel.

3 The bulbs may be either a push-fit in the bulbholder, or integral with the bulbholder in which case the bulb and bulbholder must be renewed as a unit (photos).

4 Refitting is a reversal of removal.

Panel lens

5 Remove the three upper and three lower securing screws and withdraw the lens from the instrument panel.

6 Refitting is a reversal of removal, but ensure that the two locating pegs on the upper corners of the instrument panel protrude through the lens, and locate the lugs on the lower edge of the lens in the cut-outs in the instrument panel.

Printed circuit board

7 Using a thin-bladed screwdriver, unclip and remove the wiring plug socket.

8 Remove all the illumination and warning lamp bulbs as described earlier in this Section.

9 Remove all the nuts and washers from the printed circuit board terminals.

10 Unclip the printed circuit board from the retainers at the back of the instrument panel, and carefully withdraw the board over the terminal pins on the gauges.

11 Refitting is a reversal of removal.

Speedometer

12 Remove the panel lens as described earlier in this Section.

13 Remove the two screws securing the speedometer to the rear of the instrument panel, taking care not to lose the two brushes. Withdraw the speedometer through the front of the instrument panel.

14 Refitting is a reversal of removal.

Tachometer

15 Remove the four or five securing screws, as applicable, and separate the two halves of the instrument panel housing.

16 Remove the three securing nuts and washers from the rear of the instrument panel housing, and withdraw the tachometer.

17 Refitting is a reversal of removal, but ensure that the tachometer engages with the locating ribs in the housing around the dial edge.

Fuel and temperature gauges – models up to 1987

18 Remove the four securing screws and separate the two halves of the instrument panel housing.

19 Remove the four securing nuts and washers from the rear of the

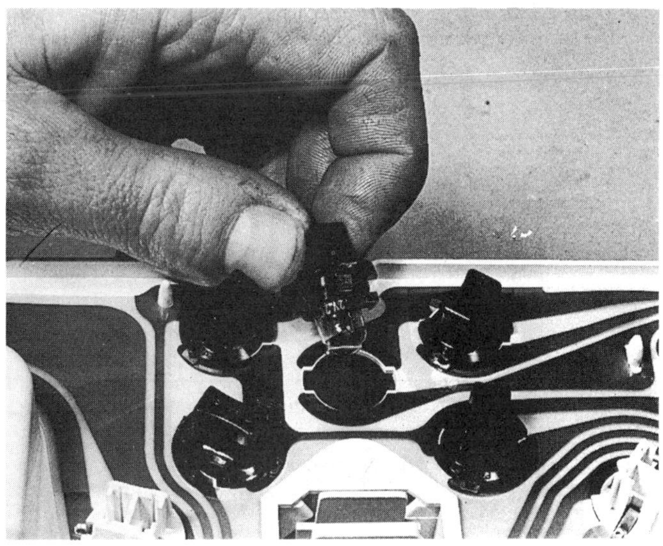

33.3A Removing an instrument panel warning lamp bulb – bulb is a push-fit in the bulbholder

33.3B Removing an instrument panel illumination bulb – bulb is integral with bulbholder

instrument panel housing, and withdraw the combined gauge assembly.
20 Refitting is a reversal of removal.

Fuel and temperature gauges – models from 1987

21 Remove the five securing screws and separate the two halves of the instrument panel housing.
22 Remove the printed circuit board as described previously in this Section.
23 On 'low specification' models, remove the two securing screws from the front of the gauge assembly, then withdraw the combined gauge assembly from the printed circuit board.
24 On 'high specification' models, simply withdraw the combined gauge assembly from the printed circuit board.
25 Refitting is a reversal of removal, but on 'high specification' models, ensure that the gauge assembly engages with the locating ribs in the housing around the gauge edge.

34 Trip computer components – removal and refitting

1 Disconnect the battery negative lead.

Computer module

2 Remove the single screw from the top edge of the facia panel in which the module is housed, then withdraw the facia panel.
3 Remove the four now exposed securing screws, disconnect the wiring plug, and carefully withdraw the module. On later models a retaining lug must be depressed before the wiring plug can be disconnected.
4 Where applicable, the mounting brackets can be removed from the module by unscrewing the securing nuts.
5 If necessary, the illumination bulb can be removed from the module by twisting the bulbholder anti-clockwise using a pair of long-nosed pliers. The bulb is a push-fit in the holder.
6 Refitting is a reversal of removal.

Speed sender unit – models up to 1987

7 The speed sender unit is located in the engine compartment on the right-hand side of the bulkhead.
8 Disconnect the wiring plug from the sender unit.
9 Unscrew the two knurled nuts from the sender unit and disconnect the two speedometer cables.
10 Remove the three securing screws and remove the bracket and sender unit.
11 Unscrew and remove the securing nut and washer, and separate the sender unit from the bracket.
12 Refitting is a reversal of removal.

Speed sender unit – models from 1987

13 Detach the wiring, hose retainers and cover panel from the bulkhead to gain access to the sender unit.
14 Proceed as described in paragraphs 7 to 9 inclusive.
15 Remove the retaining nut and washer and withdraw the sender unit.
16 Refitting is a reversal of removal.

Fuel flow sensor unit – carburettor models

17 The fuel flow sensor is located on the left-hand side of the engine compartment – see Fig. 13.34.
18 Disconnect the wiring plug from the sensor unit.
19 Refer to the *Safety first!* Section at the front of the manual, and Section 2 of Chapter 3, then disconnect the fuel pipes from the sensor unit. Note that on models up to 1987 there are three fuel pipe connections, and on models from 1987 there are two fuel pipe connections. Be prepared for fuel spillage.
20 Remove the three securing screws and withdraw the bracket and sender unit.
21 Unscrew the four nuts and separate the sender unit from the bracket.
22 Refitting is a reversal of removal, but ensure that the flow direction arrows on the fuel inlet and outlet ports are correctly orientated, and that the arrow on the rear of the unit points to the top.

Fig 13.34 Trip computer fuel flow sensor unit location – carburettor models up to 1987. Bracket retaining screws arrowed (Sec 34)

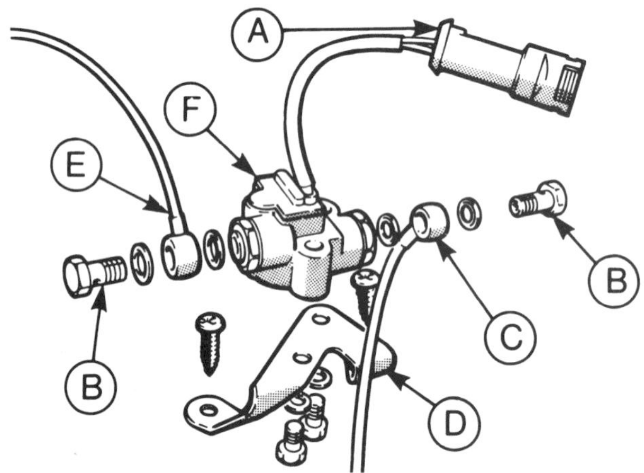

Fig 13.35 Trip computer fuel flow sensor unit – fuel injection models (Sec 34)

A Wiring plug
B Hollow bolts
C Inlet port banjo connector
D Bracket
E Outlet port banjo connector
F Sensor unit

Fuel flow sensor unit – fuel injection models

23 The sensor is located on the left-hand side of the engine compartment.
24 Disconnect the wiring plug from the sensor unit.
25 Refer to the *'Safety first!'* Section at the front of the manual, and Section 2 of Chapter 3, then unscrew the two union nuts and disconnect the fuel pipes from the sensor unit. Be prepared for fuel spillage.
26 Remove the two securing screws and withdraw the sensor unit.
27 Refitting is a reversal of removal, but ensure that the No 2 injector fuel pipe is fitted to the sensor unit outlet port marked with an arrow, and ensure that the union washers are in place – see Fig. 13.35. Tighten the fuel pipe unions to the specified torque.

35 Auxiliary warning system – description and fault diagnosis

1 Fitted to certain 'high specification' models, the auxiliary warning system (AWS) monitors the levels of fuel coolant, washer fluid and (at start-up only) engine oil. On models up to 1987, it also gives warning of brake pad wear. The five warning lights should all illuminate for a few seconds when the ignition is first switched on, then all go out. If a light remains on, the appropriate fluid level or system should be checked as

soon as possible. If a light flashes, a circuit fault is indicated and the fluid level or brake pad wear, as applicable, should be checked in the normal way.
2 On certain models the AWS also includes a graphic display unit, consisting of an outline of the car and symbols representing its doors and lamps. Warning is given to the driver of doors ajar and of running lamp bulb failure (except main beam). The brake lamp circuit is also checked; after switch-on the brake lamp symbols will remain lit until the brake pedal is first depressed. If all is well they will then extinguish.
3 The graphic display unit carries a central snowflake symbol, which will show yellow when the outside temperature falls to 4°C (39°F), and red at or below 0°C (32°F).
4 The coolant and washer fluid sensors are reed switches, operated by floating magnets. The fuel level sensor is incorporated in the gauge sender unit. The oil level sensor is built into a special dipstick.
5 Brake pad wear warning is achieved by incorporating a wire loop in the friction material of one pad on each calliper. When the loop is broken, the warning light illuminates.
6 All AWS sensors, including the 'door ajar' switches, incorporate resistors in such an arrangement that the control assembly can read the difference between open sensor contacts and an open-circuit in the wiring.
7 The AWS control unit, and (when fitted) the bulb failure monitor, are located behind the glovebox on models up to 1987.
8 On models from 1987, the control and bulb failure modules are located behind the driver's side footwell trim panel.
9 Thorough testing and fault finding should be left to a Ford dealer or other competent electrical specialist, having the necessary test equipment. Unskilled or uninformed testing may cause damage.
10 Investigation of malfunctions should begin by checking that all wiring is intact and securely connected. If checking wires or sensors for continuity, always disconnect the control unit and/or bulb failure monitor before so doing, otherwise damage may be caused.
11 Note that false oil level readings can result if the car is parked on a slope. False bulb failure warnings may occur if incorrect wattage bulbs are fitted.

36 Auxiliary warning system components – removal and refitting

1 Disconnect the battery negative lead.

Warning lamp bulbs

2 Remove the single screw from the top edge of the facia panel in which the warning lamps are housed, then withdraw the facia panel (photo).
3 Twist the relevant bulbholder through 90° to remove it from the rear of the facia panel. The bulb is integral with the bulbholder and must be renewed as a unit (photo).
4 Refitting is a reversal of removal.

Graphic display unit and bulbs

5 Remove the clock or trip computer, as applicable, as described in Sections 31 and 34 respectively.
6 Remove the display unit retaining screw and the retainer, then pull the unit forwards and disconnect the wiring plug using a thin-bladed screwdriver (photos).
7 To renew a bulb, remove the two securing screws and pull the circuit board from the back of the unit to reveal the bulbs. The bulbs are a push-fit.
8 Refitting is a reversal of removal.

Control unit and bulb failure monitor

9 Unclip the trim panel from the lower edge of the passenger side lower facia panel.
10 On models up to 1987, pull off the two clips to release the control unit/bulb failure monitor mounting bracket. Depress the retaining tab and disconnect the relevant wiring plug, then remove the two securing screws and withdraw the control unit/bulb failure monitor (photo).
11 On models from 1987, release the retaining tang and carefully slide the control unit/bulb failure monitor downwards. Depress the retaining tab and disconnect the relevant wiring plug, then withdraw the control unit/bulb failure monitor.

36.2 Remove the screw from the warning lamp facia panel

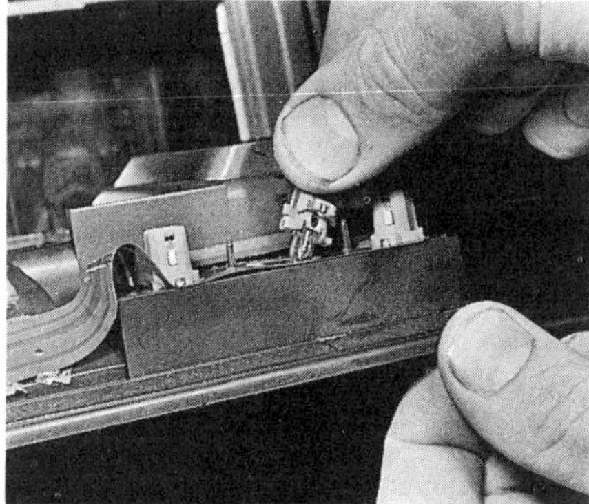
36.3 Removing an auxiliary warning lamp bulb

36.6A Removing the graphic display unit retaining screw

36.6B Disconnecting the wiring plug from the graphic display unit

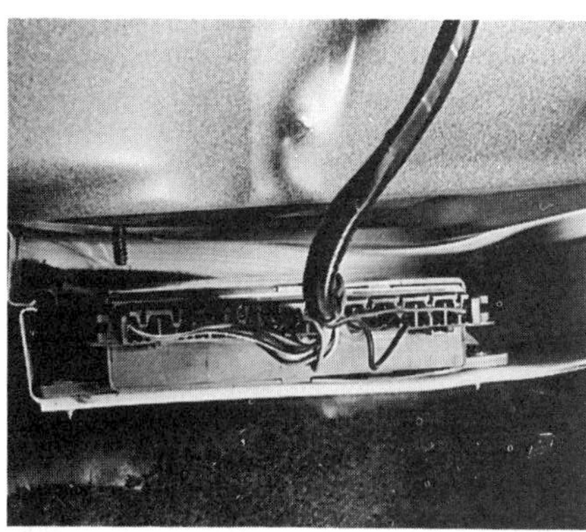
36.10 Auxiliary warning system control unit location

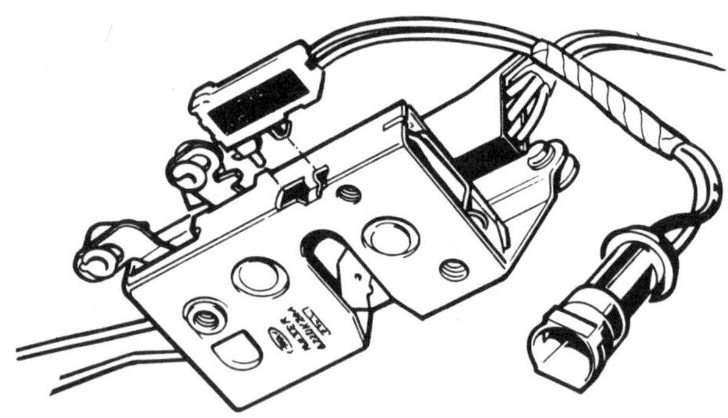

Fig 13.36 Door lock and door ajar switch (Sec 36)

12 Refitting is a reversal of removal. Note that when both a control unit and bulb failure monitor are fitted, the control unit wiring plug is coloured brown, and the bulb failure monitor wiring plug is coloured green.

Ice warning sender

13 The ice warning sender is located beneath the front panel on the right-hand side of the vehicle.
14 Where necessary, for improved access remove the horn as described in Section 41.
15 Depress the two retaining tangs, disconnect the wiring plug and withdraw the sender unit from the slot in the front panel.
16 Refitting is a reversal of removal.

Door/tailgate/boot lid ajar switches

17 Remove the relevant lock as described in Chapter 12.
18 Pull the switch from its location in the lock body, disconnect the wiring plug (if not already done) and withdraw the switch – see Fig. 13.36.
19 Refitting is a reversal of removal.

Low coolant level sensor

20 Refer to Chapter 2, Section 15.

Low washer fluid level switch

21 Syphon out the contents of the reservoir, then prise the switch from its grommet using a thin-bladed screwdriver. Disconnect the wiring plug.
22 Refitting is a reversal of removal, using a new grommet if necessary. Use a little liquid detergent as a lubricant.
23 On completion, refill the reservoir.

Low fuel level switch

24 The switch is integral with the fuel level sender unit. Details of fuel level sender unit removal and refitting are given in Chapter 3.

Low oil level switch

25 The switch is integral with the oil level dipstick. To remove, simply withdraw the dipstick from its tube and disconnect the wiring plug.
26 Refitting is a reversal of removal.

37 Courtesy lamp and luggage compartment lamp – removal and refitting

1 Disconnect the battery negative lead.
2 To remove a lamp, simply prise it from its location, using a thin-bladed screwdriver, and disconnect the wiring (photos). When working on an overhead console-mounted courtesy lamp, disconnect the wiring between the map reading lamps and the courtesy lamp before removing the courtesy lamp.
3 Refitting is a reversal of removal.

38 Map reading lamp – removal and refitting

1 Disconnect the battery negative lead.
2 Remove the courtesy lamp and disconnect the map reading lamp wires as described in Section 37.
3 Push the map reading lamp out of its location by inserting a finger through the courtesy lamp aperture.
4 Refitting is a reversal of removal.

39 Interior lamp bulbs – renewal

1 Disconnect the battery negative lead.

Courtesy lamp

2 Remove the courtesy lamp as described in Section 37.
3 Unclip the bulb from the lamp. On models fitted with an overhead console and map reading lamps, the courtesy lamp reflector must be unclipped for access to the bulb (photo).
4 Refitting is a reversal of removal.

Map reading lamp

5 Remove the map reading lamp as described in Section 38.
6 Pull the bulbholder from the rear of the lamp. The bulb is a push fit in the bulbholder (photo).
7 Refitting is a reversal of removal.

Glove compartment lamp

8 Open the glove compartment and pull the bulb from its holder.
9 Refitting is a reversal of removal.

Ashtray lamp

10 Open the ashtray and remove the tray from its housing.
11 Pull the bulbholder from the housing. The bulb is a push fit in the bulbholder.
12 Refitting is a reversal of removal.

Heater blower switch illumination lamp

13 Carefully pull off the switch knob, using pliers with padded jaws if necessary. The bulb is a bayonet fit in the end of the switch shaft.
14 Refitting is a reversal of removal.

Heater control illumination lamp

15 Refer to Chapter 12, Section 48.

Vanity mirror illumination lamp

16 Lower the sunvisor and, using a thin-bladed screwdriver, prise out the mirror and diffuser assembly. Remove the festoon bulb(s) from its/their spring contacts.
17 Refitting is a reversal of removal.

Hazard flasher switch lamp

18 Remove the securing screws and unclip the upper steering column shroud.
19 Ensure that the switch is in the 'on' position, then pull off the switch cap/bulb cover. Carefully pull the bulb from the switch using a pair of pliers with padded jaws.
20 Refitting is a reversal of removal.

Automatic transmission gear selector illumination lamp

21 Unscrew the selector lever handle from the threaded end of the lever, then remove the three securing screws and withdraw the centre console front upper panel.
22 Pull of the selector gate cover to expose the bulbholder. The bulb is a bayonet fit in the bulbholder.
23 Refitting is a reversal of removal.

Luggage compartment lamp

24 Remove the lamp by carefully prising it from its location using a thin-bladed screwdriver. Unclip and remove the bulb (photo).

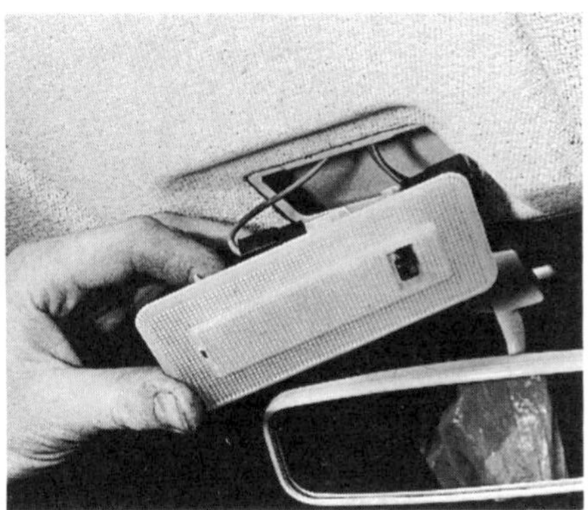
37.2A Removing a courtesy lamp

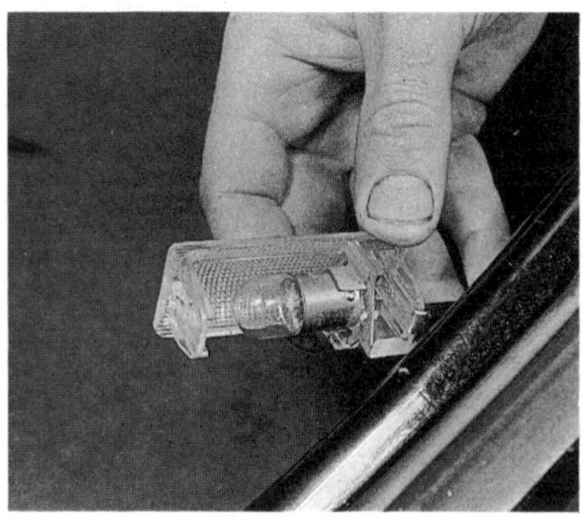
37.2B Removing a luggage compartment lamp

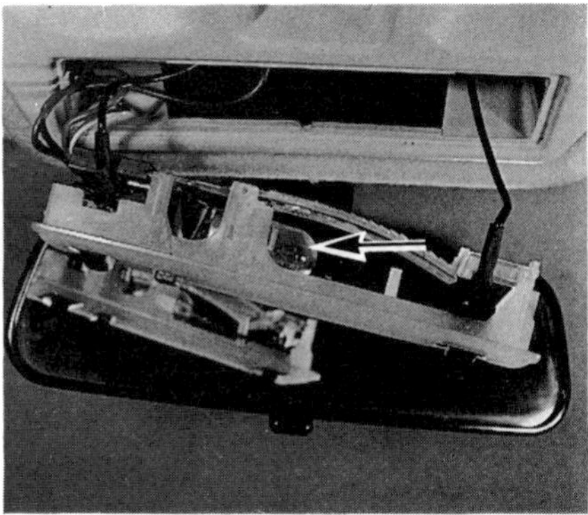
39.3 Overhead console-mounted courtesy lamp bulb (arrowed)

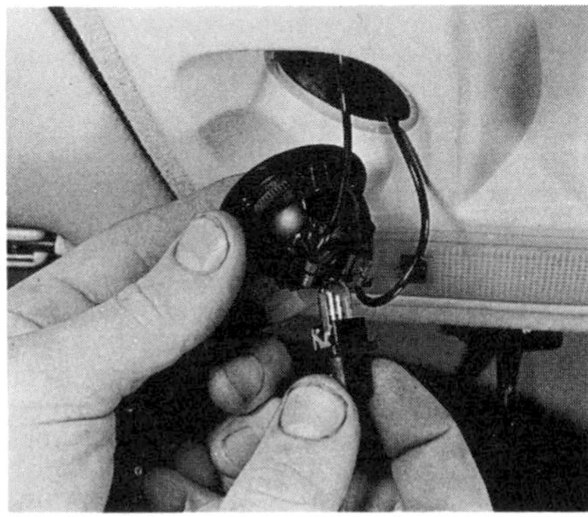
39.6 Removing a map reading lamp bulb

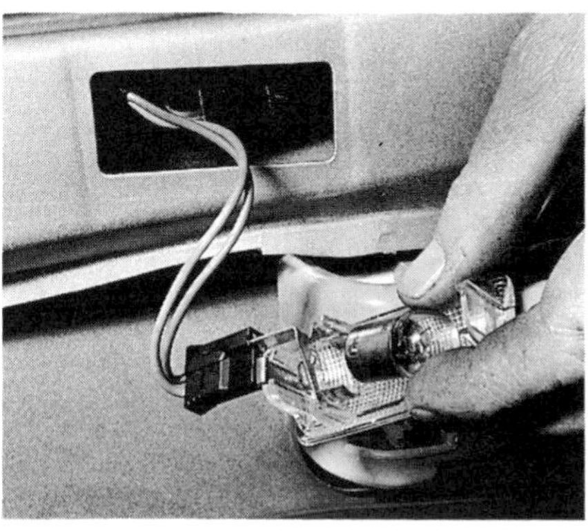
39.24 Removing a luggage compartment lamp bulb

25 Refitting is a reversal of removal.

Clock illumination lamp

26 Remove the clock as described in Section 31.
27 The bulb is a bayonet fit in the rear of the clock.
28 Refitting is a reversal of removal.

40 Underbonnet lamp - removal, refitting and bulb renewal

1 Disconnect the battery negative lead.

Removal and refitting

2 Detach the wiring connector at the left-hand bonnet hinge, and attach a length of string to the end of the wire running from the lamp.
3 If necessary, remove the underbonnet insulation by prising out the two-piece plastic securing clips, then working at the lamp, pull the wiring and the string through the bonnet panel.
4 Detach the string from the end of the wire, and remove the screw securing the lamp to the bonnet. Withdraw the lamp.
5 Commence refitting by attaching the end of the wiring to the string, and pulling the string and wiring through the bonnet panel. Further refitting is a reversal of removal.

Bulb renewal

6 Simply press and twist the bulb to remove it from the bulbholder (photo).
7 Refitting is a reversal of removal.

41 Horn - removal and refitting

1 The horn(s) is/are located in front of the radiator beneath the front panel (photo). The horn(s) may be located on either side of the vehicle depending on model.
2 Disconnect the battery negative lead.
3 Disconnect the wiring from the horn, then unscrew the securing nut and washer and withdraw the horn and bracket assembly complete.
4 Repeat the operations for the remaining horn where applicable.
5 Refitting is a reversal of removal.

42 Speedometer cable - removal and refitting

1 On models fitted with a trip computer, remove the speed sender unit as described in Section 34.
2 Remove the instrument panel as described in Section 32.
3 Pull the cable through the bulkhead into the engine compartment, and where applicable release it from the securing clips. On models fitted with a trip computer, the upper section of the cable can now be removed.
4 Apply the handbrake, jack up the front of the vehicle and support on axle stands.
5 On vehicles with a manual gearbox, extract the circlip securing the cable end to the extension housing and withdraw the cable end (photo).
6 On vehicles with automatic transmission, remove the securing screw and disconnect the cable end from the extension housing.
7 The cable can now be withdrawn from the vehicle, noting its routing so that it can be refitted in the same position.
8 Refitting is a reversal of removal, but where applicable, ensure that the speedometer cable rubber sleeve is in place over the square inner drive on the cable connector, and not in the speedometer head. Position the cable so that the coloured bands on the cable sheath line up with the bulkhead grommet and the clips in the engine compartment. Route the cable as noted during removal.
9 On completion, pull the speedometer cable from within the engine compartment to ensure that the cable is straight between the instrument panel and the bulkhead grommet.

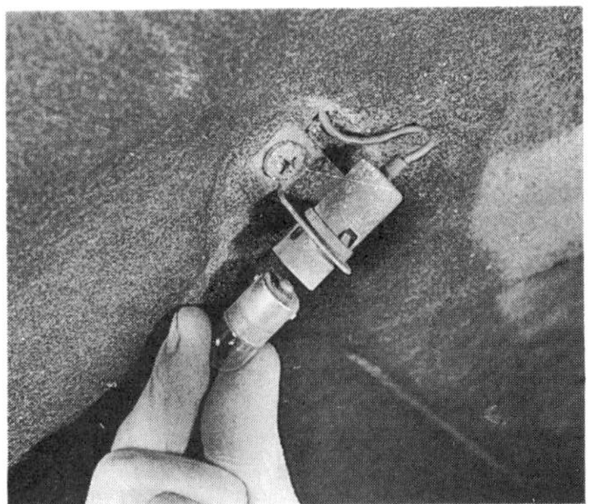

40.6 Removing an underbonnet lamp bulb

41.1 Horn location beneath front panel

42.5 Speedometer cable end fitting in manual gearbox extension housing

43 Wiper blades – renewal

1 The wiper blades should be renewed when they no longer clean the glass effectively.
2 Lift the wiper arm away from the glass.
3 With the blade at 90° to the arm, depress the spring clip and slide the blade clear of the hook, then slide the blade up off the arm (photo).
4 If necessary extract the two metal inserts and unhook the wiper rubber.
5 Fit the new rubber and blade in reverse order, making sure where necessary that the cut-outs in the metal inserts face each other.

44 Wiper arms – removal and refitting

Windscreen and rear window wipers

1 Lift the hinged covers and remove the nuts and washers securing the arms to the spindles (photo).
2 Mark the arms and spindles in relation to each other then prise off the arms using a screwdriver. Take care not to damage the paintwork.
3 Refitting is a reversal of removal.

Headlamp wipers

4 The procedure is as described in paragraphs 1 to 3, but the washer hose must be disconnected from the nozzle on the wiper arm (photo).

45 Washer nozzles – removal and refitting

Windscreen and rear window washers

1 To remove a nozzle, carefully prise it from its location using a thin-bladed screwdriver. Disconnect the washer hose and withdraw the nozzle.
2 To refit, reconnect the washer hose to the nozzle, and push the nozzle into its locating hole.
3 The nozzles can be adjusted by inserting a pin into the jet and swivelling to the required position.

Headlamp washers – washers up to 1987

4 Remove the radiator grille panel as described in Chapter 12.
5 Disconnect the washer hose from the nozzle.
6 Separate the upper and lower halves of the nozzle by prising apart with a thin-bladed screwdriver, then withdraw the nozzle halves.
7 Refitting is a reversal of removal.
8 The nozzles can be adjusted as described in paragraph 3.

Headlamp washers – models from 1987

9 Disconnect the washer hose from the nozzle on the end of the wiper arm.
10 Prise the combined wiper blade mounting and nozzle from the wiper arm using a thin-bladed screwdriver or a pair of pliers.
11 Refitting is a reversal of removal.
12 Note that the nozzles are not adjustable.

46 Windscreen wiper motor and linkage – removal and refitting

1 Disconnect the battery negative lead.
2 Remove the wiper arms as described in Section 43.
3 Remove the windscreen cowl panel as described in Chapter 12.
4 Disconnect the wiring plug from the motor.
5 Remove the seven securing screws, and withdraw the mounting bracket together with the linkage and motor (photo).
6 Unscrew the nut securing the link arm to the motor shaft, then remove the three securing bolts, and withdraw the motor from the mounting bracket.
7 Refitting is a reversal of removal.

47 Windscreen/headlamp washer pump – removal and refitting

1 Where headlamp washers are fitted, a separate pump is used. The pump(s) is/are a push-fit in the base of the washer fluid reservoir (photos). Refer to Section 48 for details of the reservoir location.
2 Disconnect the battery negative lead.
3 To remove a pump, syphon out the contents of the reservoir, then pull the pump from its grommet.
4 Disconnect the wiring plug and the washer hose.
5 Refitting is a reversal of removal, using a new grommet if necessary. Use a little liquid detergent as a lubricant.
6 On completion, refill the reservoir and check for correct operation.

Fig 13.37 Windscreen wiper motor bracket securing screws (arrowed) (Sec 46)

44.4 Removing a headlamp wiper arm

46.5 Windscreen wiper motor location – mounting bracket securing screws arrowed

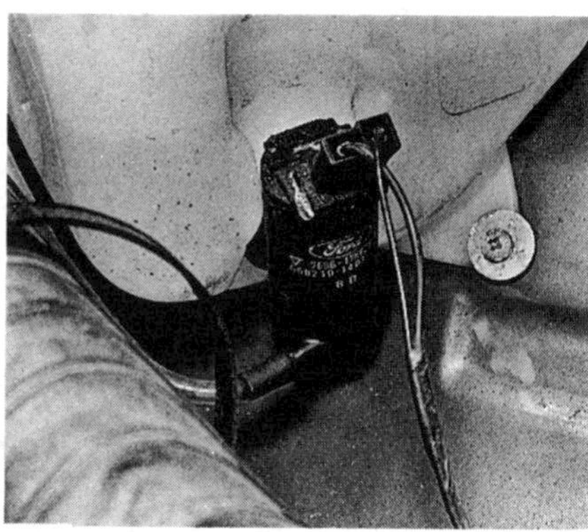
47.1A Windscreen washer pump – models up to 1987

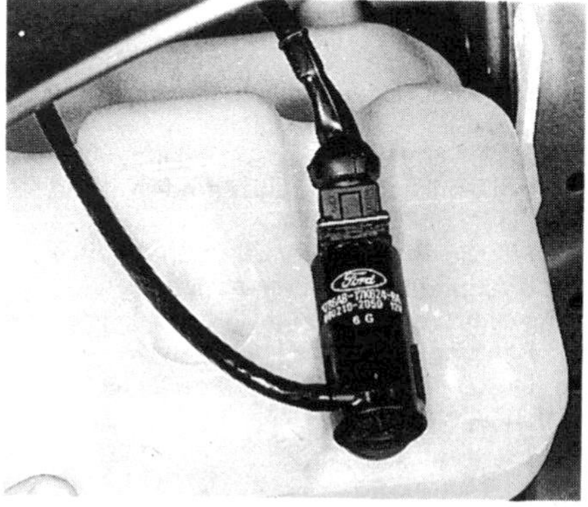
47.1B Windscreen washer pump – models from 1987

49.5 Rear window wiper motor location – mounting bracket securing bolts arrowed

48 Windscreen/headlamp washer fluid reservoir – removal and refitting

1 Where headlamp washers are fitted, a combined windscreen/headlamp washer fluid reservoir is used. On models up to 1987, the reservoir is mounted on the right-hand side of the engine compartment. On models from 1987, the reservoir is mounted under the right-hand front wing, but has a filler within the engine compartment.
2 Disconnect the battery negative lead.

Models up to 1987

3 Syphon out the contents of the reservoir, and disconnect the wiring plug(s) and washer hose(s).
4 Remove the two or three reservoir retaining screws, as applicable, then withdraw the reservoir.
5 Refitting is a reversal of removal.

Models from 1987

6 Proceed as described in paragraph 3.
7 Working under the front wing, remove the three reservoir securing screws and pull the reservoir down slightly. On vehicles fitted with front foglamps, the bumper must be removed as described in Chapter 12.
8 Withdraw the reservoir.
9 Refitting is a reversal of removal.

49 Rear window wiper motor – removal and refitting

Hatchback models

1 Disconnect the battery negative lead.
2 Remove the wiper arm as described in Section 44.
3 Open the tailgate and remove the trim panel, with reference to Chapter 12 if necessary.
4 Unscrew the earth lead and disconnect the wiring plug from the motor.
5 Remove the three securing bolts and withdraw the mounting bracket and motor from the tailgate (photo).
6 The motor can be separated from the mounting bracket by removing the three securing bolts.
7 Refitting is a reversal of removal.

Estate models

8 The procedure is as described for Hatchback models except that the washer hose must be disconnected from the motor assembly, and the mounting bracket is secured by four bolts.

50 Rear window washer pump – removal and refitting

The procedure is as described for the windscreen/headlamp washer pump in Section 47, paragraph 2 onwards.

51 Rear window washer fluid reservoir – removal and refitting

1 On models from 1987, the rear window washer circuit shares the same reservoir as the windscreen/headlamp washers. Refer to Section 48 for details.
2 On models up to 1987, the reservoir is located behind the trim panel on the left-hand side of the luggage compartment. To remove the reservoir proceed as follows.
3 Disconnect the battery negative lead.
4 Remove the trim panel with reference to Chapter 12 if necessary.
5 Operate the washers to reduce the fluid level in the reservoir.
6 Remove the reservoir filler cap, and disconnect the wiring plug and water hose.

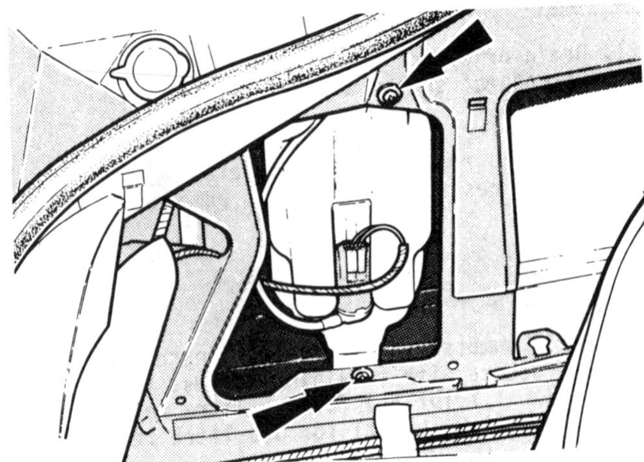

Fig 13.38 Rear window washer fluid reservoir location – Hatchback models up to 1987. Securing screws arrowed (Sec 51)

7 Remove the two securing screws and withdraw the reservoir, taking care not to spill any fluid.
8 Refitting is a reversal of removal.

52 Headlamp wiper motor – removal and refitting

Note: *On vehicles fitted with foglamps, the headlamp unit must be removed as described in Section 53 when the right-hand headlamp wiper motor is to be removed.*

1 Disconnect the battery negative lead.
2 Disconnect the washer hose from the nozzle on the end of the wiper arm, then remove the wiper arm as described in Section 44.
3 Pull the washer hose and retainer from the end of the motor shaft.
4 Remove the radiator grille panel as described in Chapter 12.
5 Where applicable, prise the trim strip from the bottom of the headlamp unit for access to the wiper motor mounting bolts (photos).
6 Remove the two mounting bolts, then working under the wheel arch, slide the wiper motor rearwards, disconnect the wiring plug and withdraw the motor.
7 Refitting is a reversal of removal, but on completion adjust the free length of the washer hose between the nozzle and the retainer on the motor shaft.

53 Headlamp unit – removal and refitting

1 Disconnect the battery negative lead.
2 Remove the radiator grille panel as described in Chapter 12.

Models up to 1987

3 Disconnect the headlamp wiring plug(s) (photo).
4 Remove the three or four headlamp securing bolts, as applicable, and the lower sliding clamp bracket bolt on the rear of the headlamp, then withdraw the headlamp (photos).
5 If required, the headlamp lens can be removed by releasing the spring clips around its edge (photo).
6 Refitting is a reversal of removal, but the headlamp securing bolts should not be tightened until the headlamp is aligned with the front grille panel.
7 On completion, check the headlamp alignment as described in Section 54.

Models from 1987

8 Disconnect the headlamp wiring plug(s) (photo).
9 Where applicable, remove the headlamp wiper motor as described in Section 52.
10 Remove the headlamp securing bolt and the two nuts, then release the anchor spring and withdraw the direction indicator lamp unit (photos).
11 Pull the headlamp forwards, then swivel it and remove it sideways.
12 If required, the headlamp lens can be removed by releasing the spring clips around its edge.
13 Refitting is a reversal of removal.
14 On completion, check the headlamp alignment as described in Section 54.

54 Headlamps – alignment

1 It is recommended that the headlamp alignment is carried out by a Ford dealer using specialist beam setting equipment. However, in an emergency the following procedure will provide an acceptable light pattern.
2 With the vehicle unladen, with a full tank of fuel, and with the tyres correctly inflated, position the vehicle approximately 10 metres (33 feet) in front of, and at right-angles to, a wall or garage door.
3 Draw a vertical line on the wall corresponding to the centre line of the car. The position of the line can be ascertained by marking the centre of the front and rear screens with crayon then viewing the wall from the rear of the car.
4 Complete the lines shown in Fig. 13.39.
5 Switch the headlamps on dipped beam and adjust them as necessary using the knobs located behind the headlamps (photo). Cover the headlamp not being checked with cloth.
6 Holts Amber Lamp is useful for temporarily changing the headlight colour to conform with the normal usage on Continental Europe.

52.5A Prise the trim strip from the bottom of the headlamp unit ...

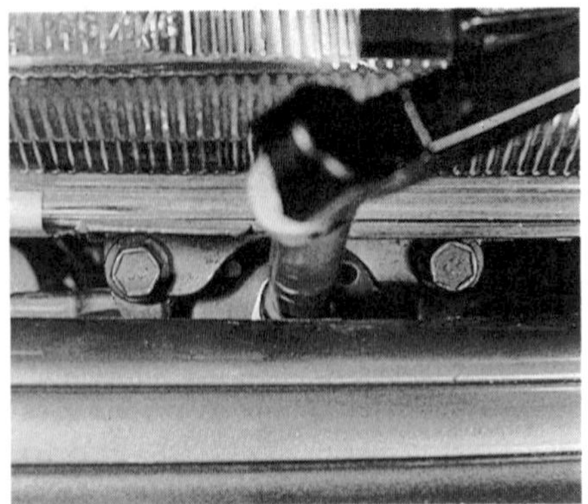

52.5B ... for access to the headlamp wiper motor mounting bolts

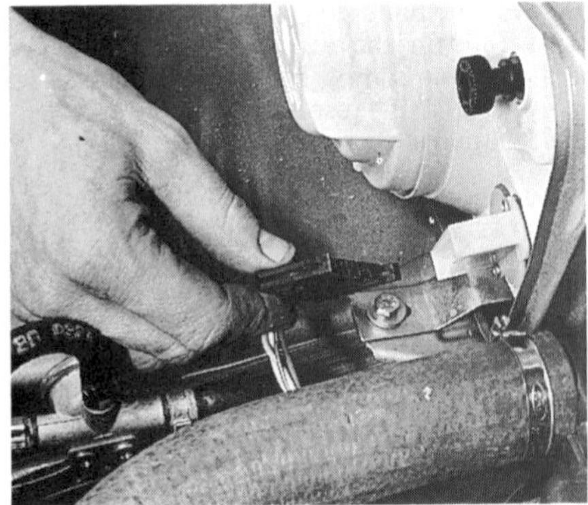

53.3 Disconnect the headlamp wiring plug – models up to 1987

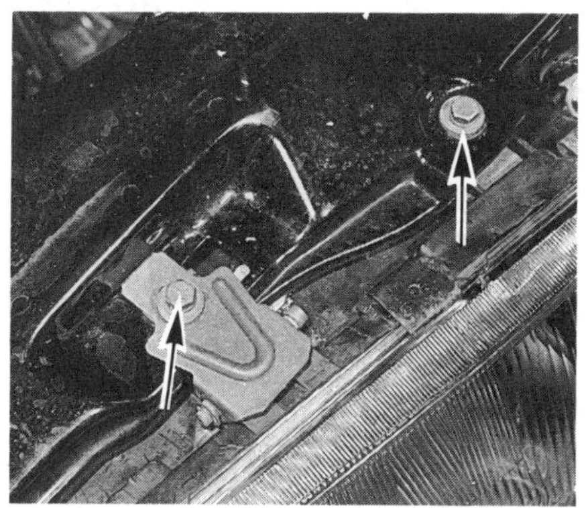
53.4A Remove the upper headlamp securing bolts (arrowed) ...

53.4B ... the rear securing bolt, ...

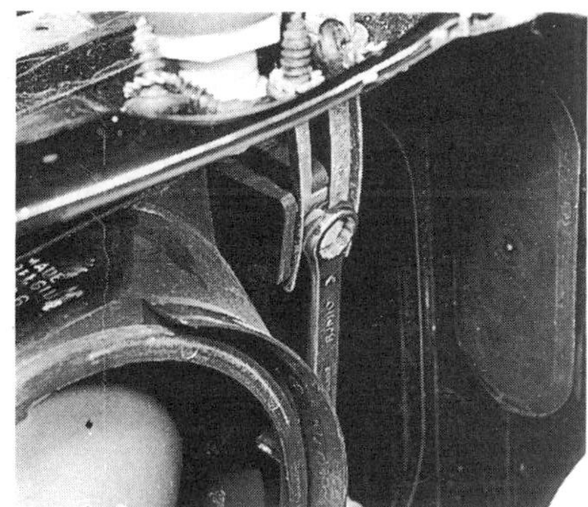
53.4C ... and the lower sliding clamp bracket bolt, ...

53.4D ... then withdraw the headlamp unit – models up to 1987

53.5 Headlamp lens spring clip

53.8 Disconnect the headlamp wiring plug – models from 1987

53.10A Remove the rear headlamp securing bolt ...

53.10B ... the upper securing nut ...

53.10C ... and the side securing nut – models from 1987

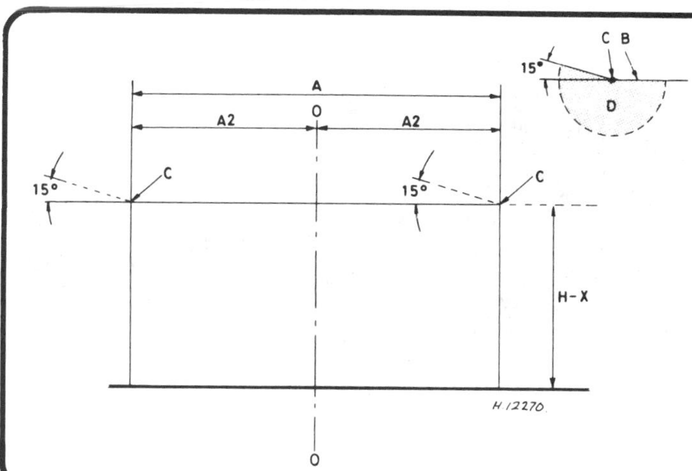

Fig 13.39 Headlamp alignment chart (Sec 54)

A Distance between headlamp centres
B Light/dark boundary
C Centre of dipped beam
D Dipped beam pattern
H Height of headlamp centre from ground
X 160.0 mm (6.3 in) for all models up to 1987
120.0 mm (4.7 in) for all models from 1987

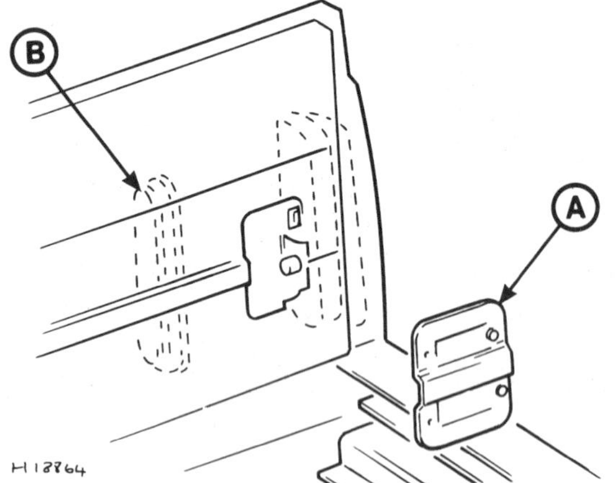

Fig 13.40 Rear lamp wiring cover (A) and rear lamp cover (B) – P100 models (Sec 55)

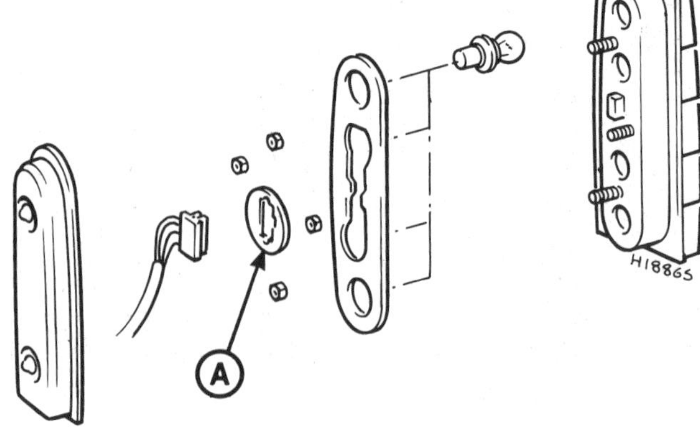

Fig 13.41 Exploded view of rear lamp assembly – P100 models (Sec 55)

A Plastic washer

55 Rear lamp unit – removal and refitting

1 Disconnect the battery negative lead.

Saloon and Hatchback models

2 Working inside the luggage compartment, press the plastic retaining tab and remove the bulbholder assembly.
3 Disconnect the wiring plug from the bulbholder.
4 Unscrew the securing nuts, and withdraw the rear lamp unit from outside the vehicle. Recover the gasket.
5 Refitting is a reversal of removal.

Estate models

6 Working inside the luggage compartment, turn the retaining tabs a quarter-turn and remove the rear side trim panel cover.
7 Push out the retaining tabs and withdraw the bulbholder.
8 Disconnect the wiring plug from the bulbholder.
9 Unscrew the four securing nuts, and withdraw the rear lamp unit from outside the vehicle. Recover the gasket.
10 Refitting is a reversal of removal.

P100 models

11 Remove the two securing screws and detach the rear lamp wiring cover from the side of the cargo area.
12 Working through the cargo area aperture, unscrew the two wing nuts and remove the rear lamp cover.
13 Disconnect the wiring plug from the back of the lamp unit.
14 Unscrew the four securing nuts and withdraw the lamp unit from outside the cargo area. Recover the gasket.
15 Refitting is a reversal of removal, but ensure that the plastic washer between the wiring plug and the lamp unit is seated correctly, and make sure that the wiring protective sheath is seated correctly in the opening in the lamp cover.

56 Front direction indicator lamp unit – removal and refitting

1 Disconnect the battery negative lead.

'Low specification' models up to 1987

2 Push the lamp unit rearwards into the bumper until the plastic retaining tang is heard to click in the locked position.
3 Withdraw the lamp unit from the front of the bumper and disconnect the wiring plug (photo).
4 Commence refitting by reconnecting the wiring plug.
5 Release the retaining tang, then refit the lamp unit to the bumper, ensuring that the pivot on the lamp unit engages with the slot in the bumper. Reconnect the battery.

'High specification' models up to 1987

6 Press the release lever at the top of the lamp unit upwards, and withdraw the unit from the bumper. Disconnect the wiring plug.
7 To refit, reconnect the wiring plug, then push the lamp unit into the bumper until it locates securely. Reconnect the battery.

All models from 1987

8 Working in the engine compartment, unhook the lamp unit anchor spring from its anchorage next to the headlamp, then withdraw the lamp unit sideways from its recess (photos). Disconnect the bulbholder by twisting it anti-clockwise.
9 Refitting is a reversal of removal, but ensure that the locating pins

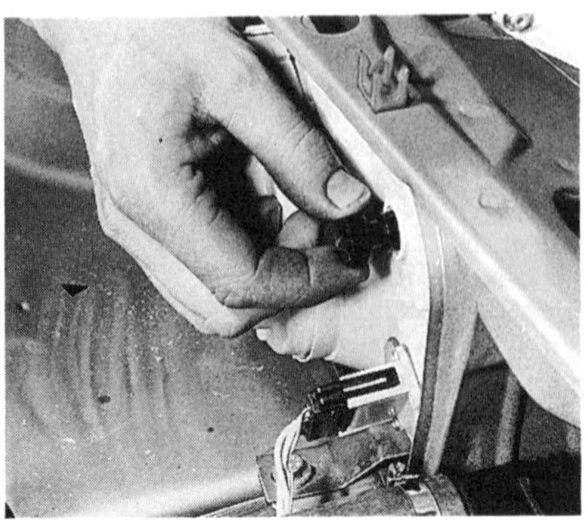

54.5 Adjusting the headlamp alignment

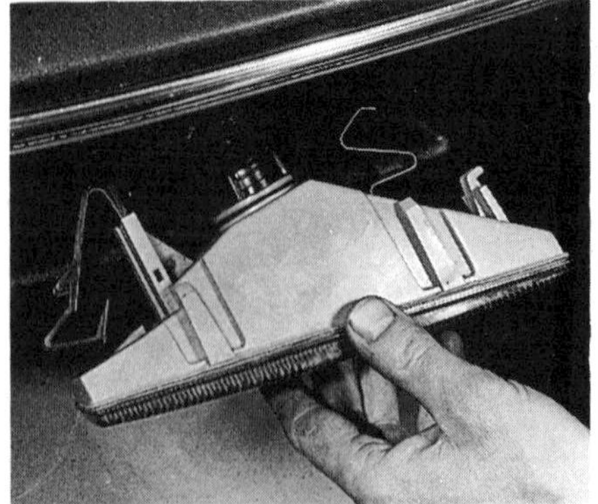

56.3 Withdrawing a front direction indicator lamp unit – 'low specification' models up to 1987

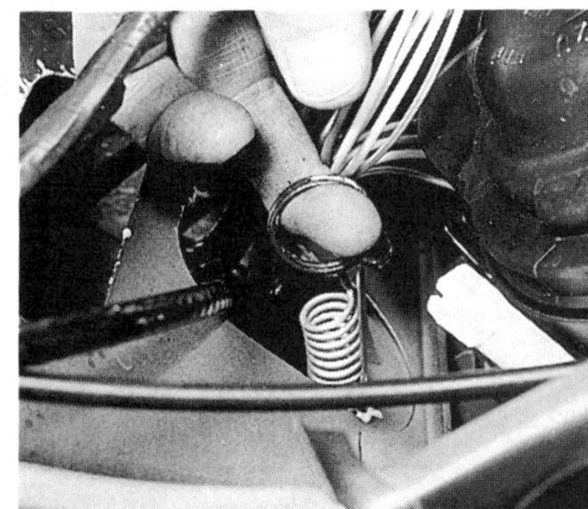

56.8A Unhook the front direction indicator lamp unit anchor spring ...

56.8B ... and withdraw the lamp unit

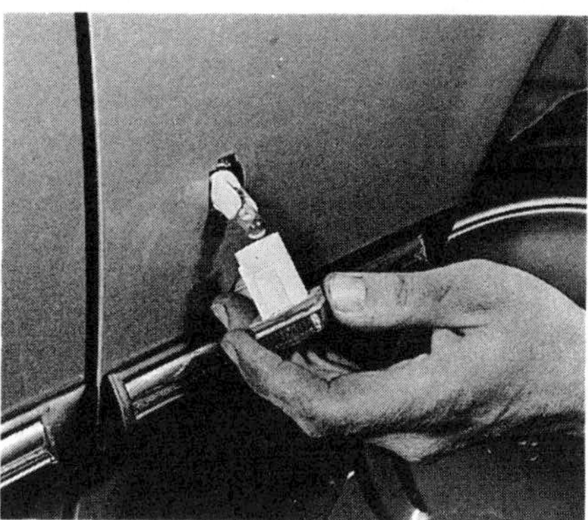

57.4 Withdrawing a front direction indicator side repeater lamp – models up to 1987

59.2 Removing a rear number plate lamp – Saloon, Hatchback and Estate models

on the lamp unit engage with the corresponding holes in the headlamp mounting panel.

57 Front direction indicator side repeater lamp – removal and refitting

1 Disconnect the battery negative lead.

Models up to 1987

2 To improve access, turn the steering onto full lock.
3 Remove the relevant wheel arch liner as described in Chapter 12.
4 Working under the wheel arch, depress the retaining tabs and withdraw the lamp through the outside of the wing (photo). Disconnect the bulbholder by twisting it anti-clockwise.
5 Refitting is a reversal of removal.

Models from 1987

6 To improve access, turn the steering onto full lock.
7 Working in the engine compartment, disconnect the wiring plug.
8 Remove the relevant wheel arch liner as described in Chapter 12.
9 Working under the wheel arch, twist the lamp clockwise and withdraw it through the outside of the wing. Feed the wiring through the holes in the wing panels.
10 Refitting is a reversal of removal.

58 Front foglamp – removal and refitting

1 Disconnect the battery negative lead.

Models up to 1987

2 Remove the relevant front direction indicator lamp unit as described in Section 56.
3 Release the retaining catch on the inside edge of the lamp, then withdraw the lamp from the bumper and disconnect the wiring plug.
4 Refitting is a reversal of removal.

Models from 1987

5 Remove the two securing screws, then withdraw the lamp forwards and disconnect the two wiring plugs.
6 Refitting is a reversal of removal, but where necessary use a new gasket between the lamp and bumper.
7 On completion, the vertical alignment of the foglamp must be adjusted using the procedure described for headlamp alignment in Section 54. For the foglamps, dimension 'X' in Fig. 13.39 should be taken as 220.0 mm (8.7 in). The adjuster screw is located on the inside edge of the lamp above the securing screw – see Fig. 13.43.

59 Rear number plate lamp – removal and refitting

1 Disconnect the battery negative lead.

Saloon, Hatchback and Estate models

2 To remove a lamp, simply prise it from the bumper using a thin-bladed screwdriver, and disconnect the wiring plug (photo).
3 Refitting is a reversal of removal.

P100 models

4 Working behind the rear crossmember, pull the wiring plug from its clip and disconnect it.
5 Pull the lamp cover from the rubber housing, then pull the rubber

Fig 13.42 Front foglamp removal – models up to 1987 (Sec 58)

A Retaining catch

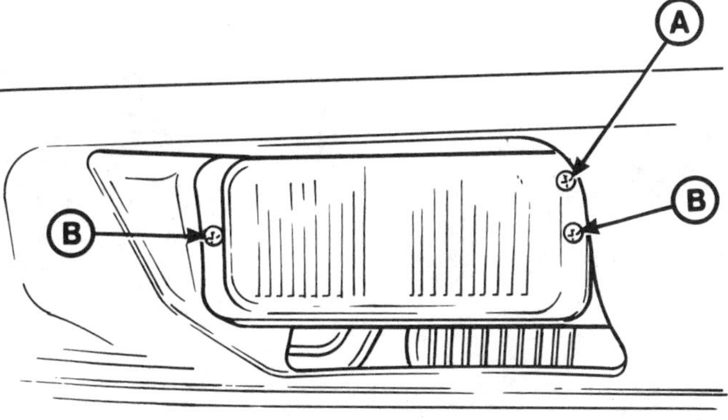

Fig 13.43 Front foglamp adjuster screw (A) and securing screws (B) – models from 1987 (Sec 58)

housing and the wiring from the crossmember.
6 Refitting is a reversal of removal.

60 Exterior lamp bulbs – renewal

Note: *The glass envelopes of the headlamp, auxiliary driving lamp and front foglamp bulbs must not be touched with the fingers. If the glass is accidentally touched, it should be washed with methylated spirits and dried with a soft cloth. Failure to observe this procedure may result in premature bulb failure.*
1 Disconnect the battery negative lead.

Headlamps

2 Working in the engine compartment, remove the headlamp rear cover by turning it anti-clockwise (photo).
3 Pull the wiring plug from the base of the bulb, then release the spring clip, grasp the bulb by its contacts and carefully withdraw it (photos). Do not touch the bulb glass.
4 Refitting is a reversal of removal, but on models up to 1987, refit the headlamp rear cover by aligning the arrow on the cover with the depression on the top of the headlamp unit and turning the cover clockwise until the arrow aligns with the lower depression. On models from 1987, the word 'OBEN' or 'TOP' on the rear cover should be exactly at the top after refitting.

Sidelamps

5 Working in the engine compartment, remove the headlamp rear cover by turning it anti-clockwise.
6 Pull the sidelamp bulbholder from its location in the headlamp reflector (photo). On 'high specification' models up to 1987 a retaining tab must be depressed before withdrawing the bulbholder. Note that the rubber sleeve should be left in position in the reflector.
7 Refitting is as described in paragraph 4.

Auxiliary driving lamps – models up to 1987

8 Twist the cover on the top of the headlamp unit anti-clockwise and remove it to expose the bulb (photo).
9 Release the bulb from the two clips, then disconnect the wiring and remove the bulb. Do not touch the bulb glass (photo).
10 Refitting is a reversal of removal.

Auxiliary driving lamps – models from 1987

11 Release the spring clip securing the cover to the rear of the headlamp unit, then remove the cover (photos).
12 Disconnect the wiring from the bulb, then release the spring clip and withdraw the bulb. Do not touch the bulb glass.
13 Refitting is a reversal of removal.

Front direction indicator lamps – models up to 1987

14 Remove the lamp as described in Section 56.
15 Twist the bulbholder anti-clockwise and withdraw it from the rear of the lamp. The bulb is a bayonet fit in the bulbholder (photo).
16 Refitting is a reversal of removal.

Front direction indicator lamps – models from 1987

17 Remove the lamp unit as described in Section 56.
18 Release the bulbholder by pressing it and turning clockwise, then withdraw the bulb from the bulbholder (photo).
19 Refitting is a reversal of removal.

Front direction indicator side repeater lamps – models up to 1987

20 To improve access, turn the steering onto full lock.
21 Remove the relevant wheel arch liner as described in Chapter 12.
22 Working under the wheel arch, twist the bulbholder anti-clockwise

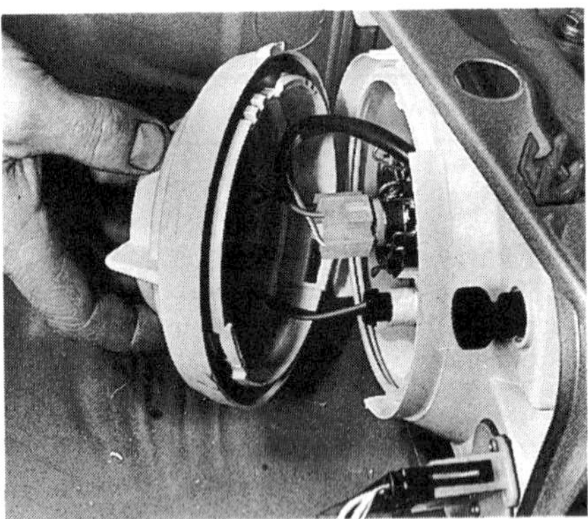

60.2 Remove the headlamp rear cover

60.3A Pull off the wiring plug ...

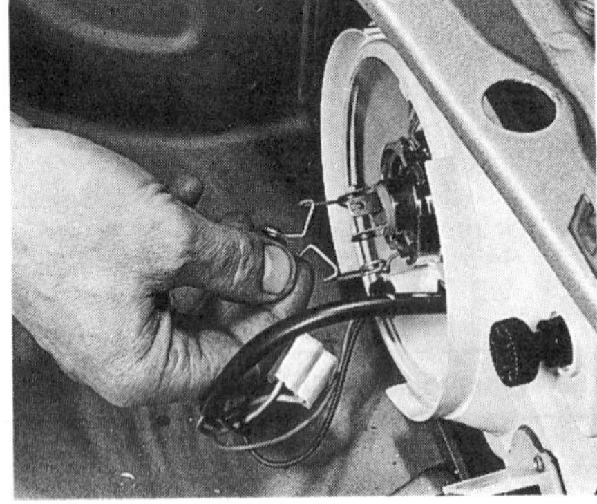

60.3B ... release the spring clip ...

60.3C ... and withdraw the headlamp bulb

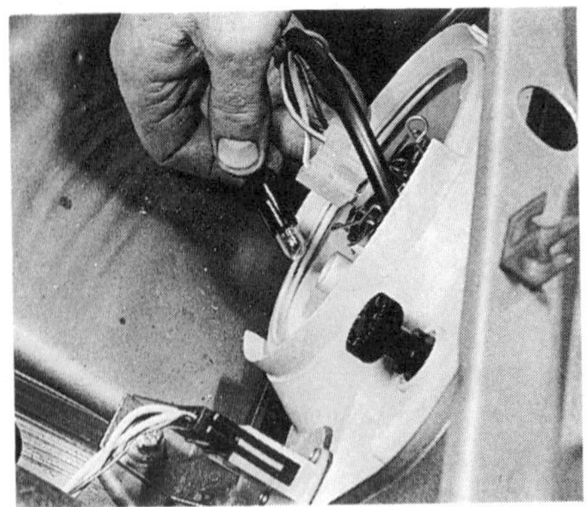

60.6 Removing a sidelamp bulbholder

60.8 Auxiliary driving lamp bulb cover – models up to 1987

60.9 Withdraw the auxiliary driving lamp bulb from the headlamp unit – models up to 1987

60.11A Auxiliary driving lamp bulb cover and spring clip – models from 1987

60.11B Auxiliary driving lamp bulb location – models from 1987

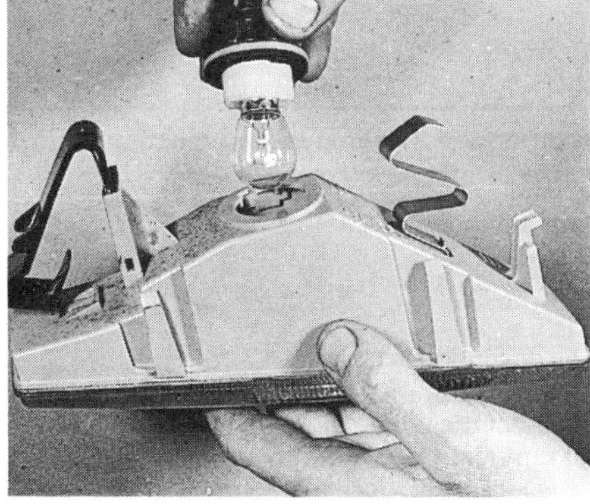
60.15 Removing a front direction indicator lamp bulb – models up to 1987

60.18 Removing a front direction indicator lamp bulb – models from 1987

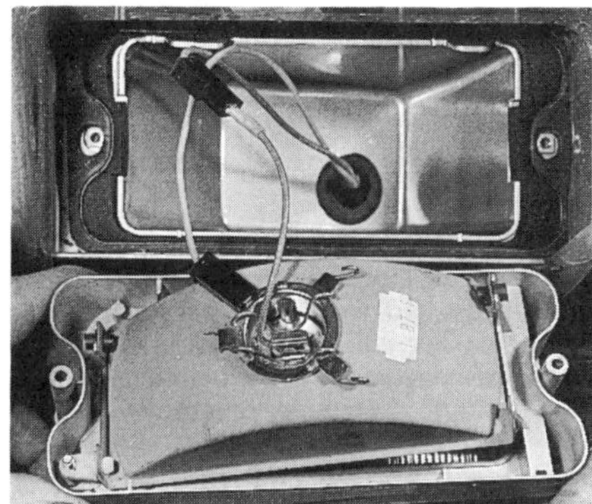
60.29 Front foglamp bulb retaining spring clip – models from 1987

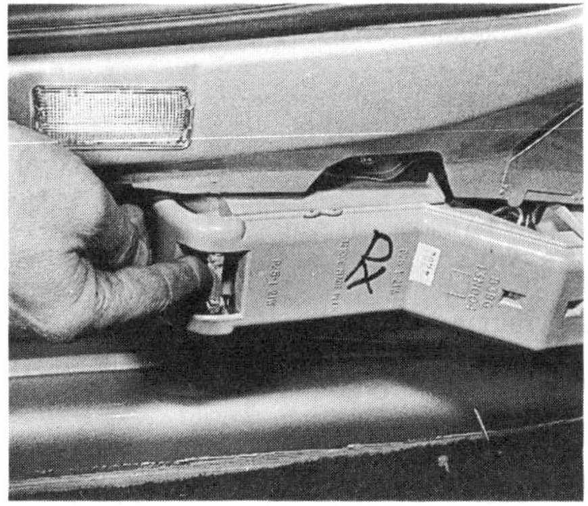
60.31A Press the plastic retaining tab ...

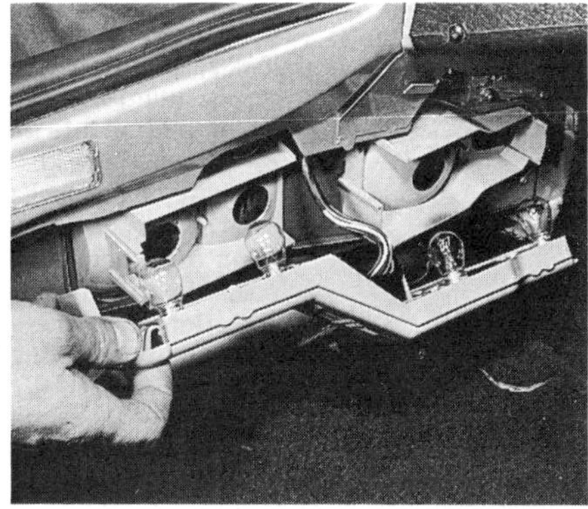
60.31B ... and remove rear lamp bulbholder assembly – Saloon and Hatchback models

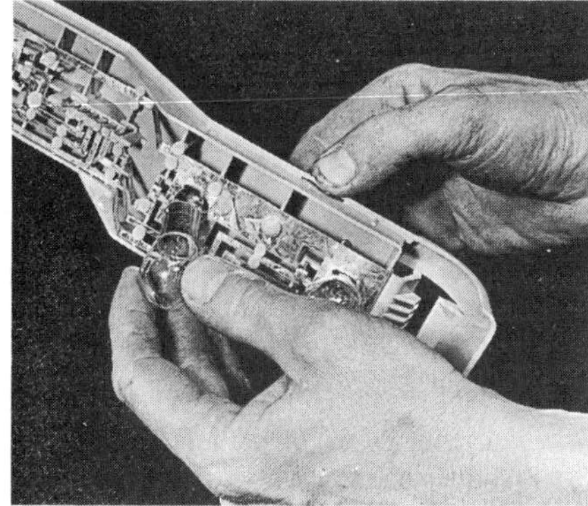
60.31C Removing a bulb from the rear lamp bulbholder – Saloon and Hatchback models

60.41 Removing a rear number plate lamp bulb – Saloon, Hatchback and Estate models

61.2 Disconnecting the wiring plug from a centre console-mounted electric window switch – models from 1987

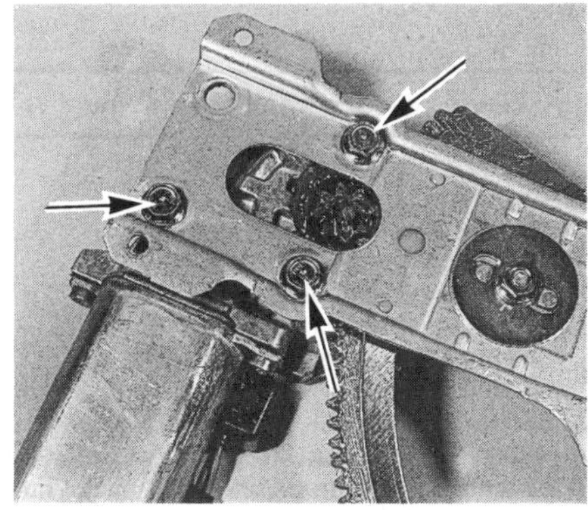
61.5 Electric window motor securing bolts (arrowed)

and withdraw it from the lamp. The bulb is a push-fit in the bulbholder.
23 Refitting is a reversal of removal.

Front direction indicator side repeater lamps – models from 1987

24 Remove the lamp as described in Section 57.
25 Twist the bulbholder anti-clockwise to remove it from the lamp. The bulb is a push-fit in the bulbholder.
26 Refitting is a reversal of removal.

Front foglamps

27 Remove the foglamp as described in Section 58.
28 On models up to 1987, remove the bulb cover from the rear of the lamp, then release the two spring clips, disconnect the wiring and withdraw the bulb. Do not touch the bulb glass.
29 On models from 1987, release the spring clip and pull the bulb from the bulbholder. Do not touch the bulb glass (photo).
30 Refitting is a reversal of removal.

Rear lamp unit – Saloon and Hatchback models

31 Working inside the luggage compartment, press the plastic retaining tab and remove the bulbholder assembly. The bulbs are a bayonet fit in the bulbholder (photos).
32 Refitting is a reversal of removal.

Rear lamp unit – Estate models

33 Working inside the luggage compartment, turn the retaining tabs a quarter-turn and remove the rear side trim panel cover.
34 Push out the retaining tabs and withdraw the bulbholder. The bulbs are a bayonet fit in the bulbholder.
35 Refitting is a reversal of removal.

Rear lamp unit – P100 models

36 Remove the two securing screws and detach the rear lamp wiring cover from the side of the cargo area.
37 Working through the cargo area aperture, unscrew the two wing nuts and remove the rear lamp cover.
38 Twist the relevant bulbholder anti-clockwise to remove it from the lamp. The bulb is a bayonet fit in the bulbholder.
39 Refitting is a reversal of removal, but ensure that the wiring protective sheath is seated correctly in the opening in the lamp cover.

Rear number plate lamp – Saloon, Hatchback and Estate models

40 Remove the lamp as described in Section 59.
41 Twist the bulbholder anti-clockwise to remove it from the lamp. The bulb is a push-fit in the bulbholder (photo).
42 Refitting is a reversal of removal.

Rear number plate lamp – P100 models

43 Pull the lamp cover from the rubber housing to expose the bulb. The bulb is a bayonet fitting in the bulbholder.
44 Refitting is a reversal of removal.

61 Electric window components – removal and refitting

1 Disconnect the battery negative lead.

Switches

2 Prise the switch from its location using a thin-bladed screwdriver, and disconnect the wiring plug (photo).
3 Refitting is a reversal of removal.

Operating motors

4 Remove the window regulator as described in Chapter 12.
5 Remove the three securing bolts, and withdraw the motor from the regulator assembly (photo).
6 Refitting is a reversal of removal, but ensure that the drive gear is correctly meshed with the regulator.

62 Central door locking components – general

Note: *If a central locking solenoid or motor is to be renewed due to jamming or overheating, the central locking relay must be renewed at the same time even if it is believed to be working correctly.*
1 On models up to 1987, the central locking system is activated by turning the key in the driver's door lock, and the locks are operated by solenoids.
2 On models from 1987, the system is activated by turning the key in either of the front door locks, and the locks are operated by electric motors.
3 Before starting work on the central locking system, unlock all the doors and the tailgate/boot. Make sure that the keys are outside the vehicle before reconnecting the battery on completion of work.
4 Various different types of central locking components have been fitted to Sierra vehicles during production, and the information given in Section 63 is all that was available at the time of writing.

63 Central door locking components – removal and refitting

1 Disconnect the battery negative lead.

Models up to 1987

Switch (driver's door lock)
2 Remove the door lock as described in Chapter 12.
3 Remove the two securing screws, then withdraw the switch from the lock assembly and disconnect the wiring plug.
4 Refitting is a reversal of removal, but ensure that the cut-out in the switch lever engages with the lock lever – see Fig. 13.44.
Solenoids (passenger and rear door locks)
5 Remove the door lock as described in Chapter 12.
6 Remove the two securing screws, then disconnect the solenoid operating rod and the wiring plug and withdraw the solenoid from the lock assembly.
7 Refitting is a reversal of removal.
Solenoid (tailgate lock)
8 Open the tailgate and remove the trim panel, with reference to Chapter 12 if necessary.
9 Disconnect the solenoid wiring plug and earth lead, and the operating rod, then remove the two securing screws and withdraw the solenoid from the tailgate.
10 Refitting is a reversal of removal.

Models from 1987

Motors (door locks)
11 Remove the door inner trim panel as described in Chapter 12.
12 Remove the retaining screws and disconnect the wiring plug and the motor operating rod, then withdraw the motor from the door.
13 Refitting is a reversal of removal.
Motor (tailgate and boot lid locks)
14 Open the tailgate/boot lid and where applicable remove the trim panel, with reference to Chapter 12 if necessary.
15 Remove the retaining screws and disconnect the wiring plug and the motor operating rod, then withdraw the motor from the tailgate/boot.
16 Refitting is a reversal of removal.

64 Seat heating pad – removal and refitting

1 Disconnect the battery negative lead.
2 Remove the seat as described in Chapter 12.
3 Remove the seat cushion trim or backrest trim as necessary.
4 Note which way round the pad is fitted, then remove the wire clips and adhesive tape which secure it to the seat. Retrieve the tie-rod and fit it to the new pad.
5 Fit the new pad with the thermostat facing the cushion foam.

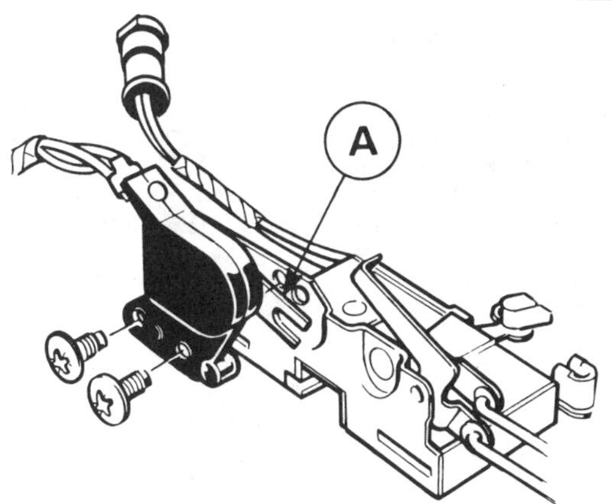

Fig 13.44 Driver's door central locking switch – models up to 1987 (Sec 63)

A Switch lever cut-out

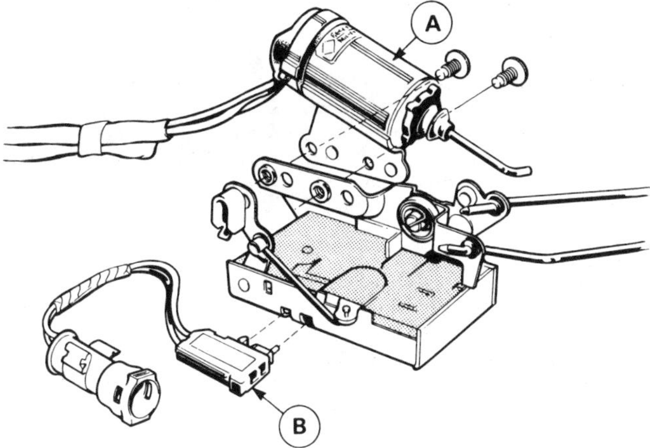

Fig 13.45 Central door locking assembly – models up to 1987 (Sec 63)

A Solenoid
B Door ajar switch (not fitted to all models)

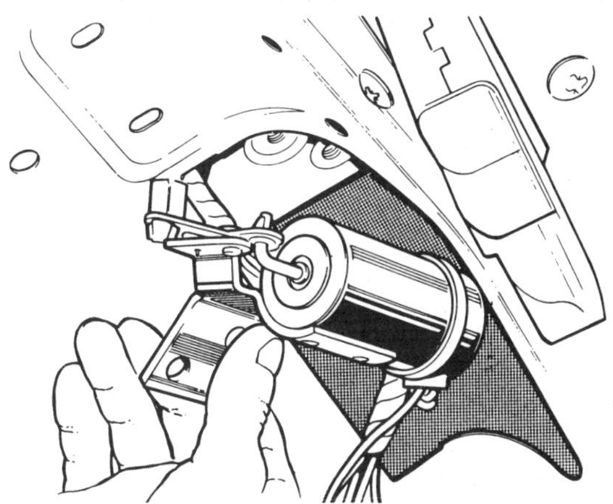

Fig 13.46 Removing a tailgate lock solenoid – Hatchback models up to 1987 (Sec 63)

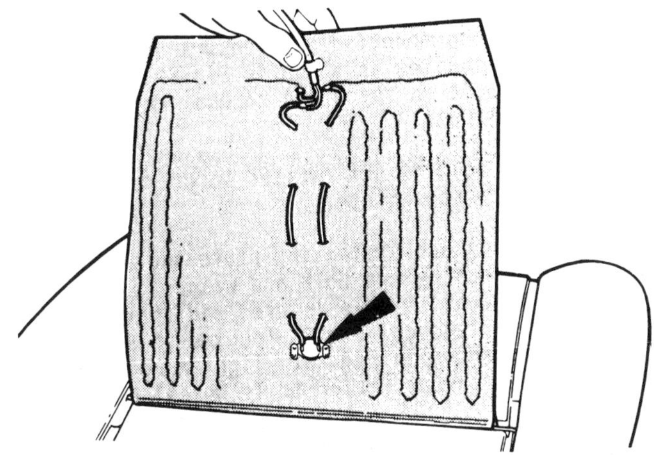

Fig 13.47 Seat heating pad (Sec 64)

Thermostat (arrowed) must face foam

Secure the pad with wire clips and tape, making sure that it is not too tight – it must be able to flex when sat on.
6 Refit the cushion or backrest trim, as applicable, being careful not to trap or kink the pad.
7 Refit the seat, reconnect the wiring and check the pads for correct operation.

65 Radio aerial (exterior-mounted) – removal and refitting

1 On models fitted with an electric aerial, disconnect the battery negative lead.

Saloon and Estate models

2 Remove the right-hand side trim panel from the luggage compartment, with reference to Chapter 12 if necessary.
3 Working outside the vehicle, unscrew the nut and remove the spacer and seal from the base of the aerial.
4 Working inside the luggage compartment, either unscrew the aerial bracket securing screw and slide the bracket from the aerial tube, or pull the base of the aerial from the rubber bush in the bracket, as applicable (photo).
5 Ensure that the aerial is fully retracted, then pull it through the hole in the bodywork into the luggage compartment (photo).
6 The aerial lead may be a push-fit in the base of the aerial, or may be secured by a knurled nut. Disconnect the aerial lead and where applicable, disconnect the wiring from the electric motor. Note that the aerial lead runs through the roof. If it is necessary to renew the lead, it may prove easier to leave the old lead in place and run a a new one under the carpet. Follow existing wiring runs where possible.
7 Refitting is a reversal of removal.

Hatchback models

8 Remove the right-hand rear seat side cushion as described in Chapter 12, Section 44.
9 Remove the rear parcel shelf.
10 On 'high specification' models, lift the seat catch release lever, push out the pin securing the link rod to the lever and disconnect the link rod.
11 Remove the securing screws from the rear parcel shelf support (nine screws on models up to 1987, eight screws from 1987 onwards). Remove the rear parcel shelf support.
12 Remove the side trim panel from the luggage compartment, with reference to Chapter 12 if necessary.
13 Proceed as described in paragraphs 3 to 7 inclusive.

P100 models

14 Pull off the plastic trim cover and unscrew the aerial securing nut.
15 Withdraw the aerial assembly, and carefully prise the base seal from the roof panel.
16 The aerial lead runs across the roof panel under the headlining, and

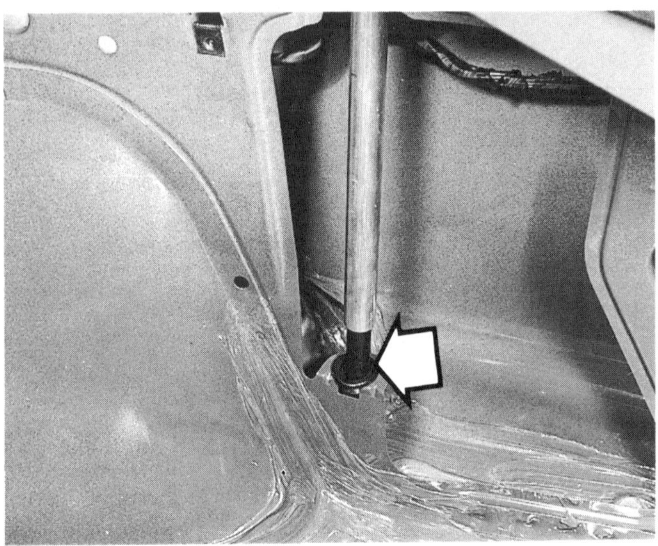

65.4 Pull the base of the aerial from the rubber bush (arrowed)

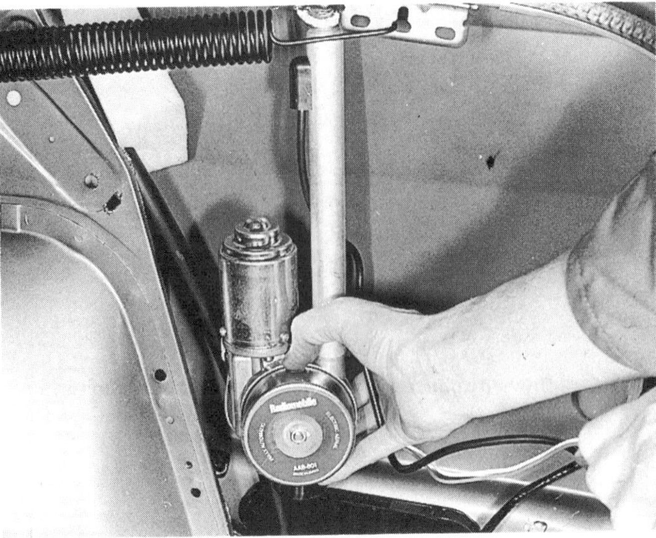

65.5 Removing an electric aerial – Saloon model

down the right-hand front pillar to the radio unit. Renewal is straightforward, but the front section of the headlining must be released for access as described in Chapter 12, and a length of string should be tied to the end of the aerial lead before removal to aid routing when refitting.
17 The aerial rod can be renewed by simply unscrewing it from the base.
18 Refitting is a reversal of removal.

66 Integral heated rear window/radio aerial amplifier – removal and refitting

1 Disconnect the battery negative lead.

Saloon models

2 Remove both rear seat side cushions as described in Chapter 12, Section 44.
3 Remove the securing screws and withdraw the rear parcel shelf.
4 Make a note of the wiring connections for use when refitting, then disconnect the wiring, remove the two securing screws, and withdraw the amplifier unit.
5 Refitting is a reversal of removal.

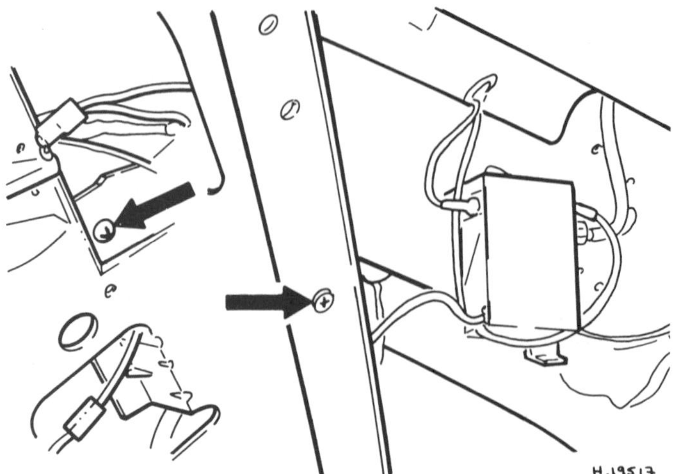

Fig 13.49 Integral heated rear window/radio aerial amplifier bracket securing screws (arrowed) – Hatchback models (Sec 66)

Hatchback models

6 Unclip the tailgate trim panel, with reference to Chapter 12 if necessary.
7 Remove the amplifier bracket securing screws, and withdraw the amplifier through the tailgate panel aperture.
8 Make a note of the wiring connections for use when refitting, then disconnect the wiring and remove the amplifier unit.
9 Refitting is a reversal of removal.

Fig 13.48 Integral heated rear window/radio aerial amplifier securing screws (arrowed) – Saloon models (Sec 66)

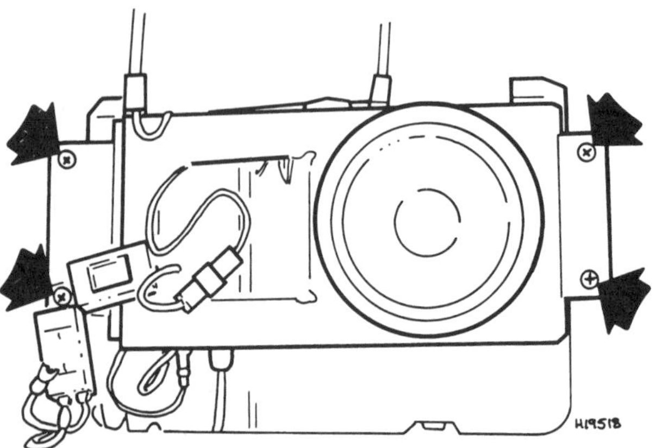

Fig 13.50 Loudspeaker/integral heated rear window/radio aerial amplifier bracket securing screws (arrowed) – Estate models (Sec 66)

Estate models

10 Unclip the tailgate trim panel, with reference to Chapter 12 if necessary.
11 Make a note of the wiring connections for use when refitting, then disconnect the wiring, remove the four securing screws, and detach the loudspeaker/amplifier bracket assembly from the tailgate.
12 Refitting is a reversal of removal.

67 Loudspeakers – removal and refitting

1 Disconnect the battery earth lead.

Upper facia panel-mounted loudspeakers

2 Prise the speaker grille from its four retaining clips in the facia using a thin-bladed screwdriver.
3 Remove the four securing screws, disconnect the wiring, and pull the loudspeaker from the facia panel.
4 Refitting is a reversal of removal.

Lower facia panel – mounted loudspeakers

5 Remove the lower facia panel as described in Chapter 12.
6 Remove the four securing screws, disconnect the wiring, and pull the loudspeaker from the facia panel.
7 Refitting is a reversal of removal.

Rear parcel shelf-mounted loudspeakers – Saloon models

8 Working in the luggage compartment, remove the single securing screw, then lift the loudspeaker into the passenger compartment and disconnect the wiring. Withdraw the loudspeaker.
9 Note that it is important not to disturb the loudspeaker mounting gasket or retainer.
10 Refitting is a reversal of removal, but ensure that the wiring does not touch the retainer, shelf, or speaker, to prevent any audible rattles.

Rear parcel shelf-mounted loudspeakers – Hatchback models

11 Working under the parcel shelf, remove the four securing screws, disconnect the wiring, and withdraw the loudspeaker.
12 Refitting is a reversal of removal.

Door-mounted loudspeakers

13 Remove the door inner trim panel as described in Chapter 12.
14 Remove the four securing screws, then withdraw the loudspeaker from the door and disconnect the wiring. Remove the loudspeaker.
15 Do not remove the loudspeaker from the moulding, as the two are a sealed assembly.
16 Refitting is a reversal of removal.

Tailgate-mounted loudspeakers – Estate models

17 Remove the tailgate trim panel with reference to Chapter 12 if necessary.
18 Remove the four securing screws, disconnect the wiring and withdraw the loudspeaker. Note that on models with an integral heated rear window/radio aerial, the aerial amplifier unit is combined with one of the loudspeaker units.
19 Refitting is a reversal of removal.

High frequency units

20 These units are used to reproduce high frequencies only, and incorporate an electronic filter network which must not be disconnected or bypassed. The units are located in the lower facia panels.
21 The removal and refitting procedure is as described for the lower facia panel-mounted loudspeakers earlier in this Section, but take care not to damage the extremely fragile speaker cones.

68 Radio/cassette player power amplifier – removal and refitting

1 Some 'high specification' models are fitted with an audio power amplifier, which is mounted as a separate unit beneath the radio/cassette unit. To remove the unit proceed as follows.
2 Disconnect the battery negative lead.
3 Remove the two screws under the top edge of the power amplifier unit.
4 Slide the unit forwards from the facia panel, until the wiring plugs can be disconnected. Disconnect the wiring plugs and remove the unit.
5 Refitting is a reversal of removal.

69 Radio/cassette player (standard fixing) – removal and refitting

1 Disconnect the battery negative lead.
2 Pull off the two control knob assemblies.
3 Release the trim panel by unscrewing the two securing nuts from the control spindles. Remove the trim panel.
4 Using a hooked instrument, pull the mounting plate securing tangs towards the centre of the radio/cassette player, then slide the unit forwards from the facia panel (photo).
5 Disconnect the wiring plugs and the aerial lead, then remove the unit.
6 Remove the plastic support bracket from the rear of the unit, and unscrew the nuts and washers from the control spindles to remove the mounting plate from the front of the unit.
7 Refitting is a reversal of removal.

69.4 Radio/cassette player securing tangs (arrowed) viewed from the rear of the unit – standard fixing

70.3 Removing a radio/cassette player using special tools – DIN fixing

70 Radio/cassette player (DIN fixing) – removal and refitting

1 An increasing number of radio/cassette players have DIN standard fixings. Two special tools, obtainable from in-car entertainment specialists, are required for removal.
2 Disconnect the battery negative lead.
3 Insert the tools into the holes in the front of the radio/cassette player and push them until they snap into place. Pull the tools outwards to release the unit (photo).
4 Pull the unit forwards and disconnect the wiring plugs and the aerial lead. Remove the unit from the facia panel.
5 To refit the radio/cassette player, reconnect the wiring and the aerial lead, then simply push the unit into its bracket until the retaining lugs snap into place.

71 Dim-dip headlamp system – general

1 Legislation in the UK introduced in April 1987 required that all vehicles registered after 1st April 1987 should be equipped with a dim-dip headlamp system.
2 The system provides the headlamps with a brightness between that of the sidelamps and the headlamps on normal dipped beam.
3 The purpose of the system is to prevent vehicles being driven on sidelamps only.
4 Full information will be given in the driver's handbook, but basically, the dim-dip lamps are in operation whenever the light switch is in the first 'ON' position and the ignition is switched on.
5 All Sierras built after 1st October 1986 are equipped with additional relays to enable the dim-dip system to be fitted.
6 For details of the relays and the dim-dip wiring circuit, refer to the wiring diagrams at the end of this Chapter.

72 Fault diagnosis – electrical system

Symptom	Reason(s)
Starter fails to turn engine	Battery discharged Battery defective internally Leads loose, or terminals corroded Loose connections at starter motor Engine earth strap loose, broken or missing Starter motor faulty or solenoid not functioning Starter motor brushes worn Commutator dirty or worn Starter motor armature faulty Field coils earthed
Starter turns engine very slowly	Battery in discharged condition Starter brushes badly worn, sticking or brush wires loose Loose wires in starter motor circuit
Starter spins but does not turn engine	Pinion or flywheel gear teeth broken or worn
Starter motor noisy or excessively rough engagement	Pinion or flywheel gear teeth broken or worn Starter motor retaining bolts loose
Battery will not hold charge for more than a few days	Battery defective, internally Electrolyte level too low or electrolyte too weak due to leakage Plate separators no longer fully effective Battery plates severely sulphated Alternator drivebelt slipping Battery terminal connections loose or corroded Alternator not charging Short-circuit causing continual battery drain Voltage regulator unit not working correctly
Ignition light fails to go out, battery runs flat in a few days	Alternator drivebelt loose and slipping or broken Alternator brushes worn, sticking, broken or dirty Alternator brush springs weak or broken Internal fault in alternator
Failure of individual electrical equipment to function correctly is dealt with under the headings listed below	
Horn	
Horn operates all the time	Horn push either earthed or stuck down Horn cable to horn push earthed
Horn fails to operate	Blown fuse Cable or cable connection loose, broken or disconnected Horn has an internal fault
Horn emits intermittent or unsatisfactory noise	Cable connections loose

Symptom	Reason(s)
Lamps	
Lamps do not come on	If engine not running, battery discharged Wire connections loose, disconnected or broken Lamp switch shorting or otherwise faulty Lamp bulb filament burnt out or bulbs broken
Lamps give very poor illumination	Lamp glasses dirty Lamps badly out of adjustment
Lamps work erratically – flashing on and off, especially over bumps	Battery terminals or earth connection loose Lamps not earthing properly Contacts in lamp switch faulty
Wipers	
Wiper motor fails to work	Blown fuse Wire connections loose, disconnected or broken Brushes badly worn Armature worn or faulty Field coils faulty
Wiper motor works very slowly and takes excessive current	Commutator dirty, greasy or burnt Armature bearings dirty or misaligned Armature badly worn or faulty
Wiper motor works slowly and takes little current	Brushes badly worn Commutator dirty, greasy or burnt Armature badly worn or faulty
Wiper motor works but wiper blades remain static	Wiper motor gearbox parts badly worn
Electrically operated windows	
Glass will only move in one direction	Defective switch
Glass slow to move	Stiff regulator or glass guide channels
Glass will not move:	
With motor running	Binding glass guide channels Faulty regulator
Motor not running	Faulty relay Blown fuse Fault in motor Broken or disconnected wire
Central door locking system	
Complete failure	Blown fuse Faulty master switch Faulty relay Broken or disconnected wire
Latch locks but will not unlock, or unlocks but will not lock	Faulty master switch Poor contact in relay multi-plug Faulty relay
One solenoid or motor will not operate	Poor circuit connections Broken wire Faulty solenoid or motor Binding bellcrank rod Binding driver's door lock button (or passenger door lock button on models from 1987) Fault in lock
Instruments	
Instrument readings increase with engine speed	Voltage stabilizer faulty
Fuel or temperature gauge gives no reading	Wiring open circuit Sender unit faulty Gauge faulty
Fuel or temperature gauge gives maximum reading all the time	Wiring short circuit Gauge faulty

Note: *This Section is not intended as an exhaustive guide to fault diagnosis, but summarises the more common faults which may be encountered during a vehicle's life. Consult a dealer for more detailed advice.*

Chapter 14 Supplement: Revisions and information on later models

Contents

1 Introduction

This Supplement contains information which is additional to, or a revision of, the information contained in the first thirteen Chapters.

The majority of the additional information contained in this Supplement refers to the 2.0 litre DOHC and 1.6 litre CVH engines, which superseded the previous 2.0 litre and 1.6 litre OHC engines in August 1989 and September 1991 respectively, and the MT75 type 5-speed manual gearbox, which was introduced with the 2.0 litre DOHC engine.

The Sections in this Supplement follow the same order as the Chapters to which they relate. The Specifications are all grouped together at the beginning for convenience, but they too follow Chapter order.

It is recommended that before any work commences, reference is made to the appropriate Section(s) of this Supplement, in order to establish any changes to procedures or specifications, before reading the main Chapter(s).

Project vehicles

The vehicles used in the preparation of this Supplement and appearing in many of the photographic sequences were a 1990 Sierra 2.0 litre GLS Hatchback model, and a 1992 1.6 litre LX Saloon model.

2 Specifications

General dimensions, weights and capacities

Dimensions

Overall width (models from 1990):*	
Saloon	1698 mm (66.9 in)
Hatchback	1694 mm (66.7 in)
Estate	1720 mm (67.8 in)
Overall height (models from 1990):	
Saloon and Hatchback	1407 mm (55.4 in)
Estate	1428 mm (56.3 in)

**Excluding rear view mirrors*

Weights

Kerb weight (models from 1990):*	
Saloon and Hatchback	1065 to 1240 kg (2343 to 2728 lbs)
Estate	1105 to 1190 kg (2431 to 2618 lbs)

**Exact kerb weights depend on models and specification*

Capacities

Engine oil:	
1.6 litre CVH engine:	
With filter	3.5 litres (6.2 pints)
Without filter	3.25 litres (5.7 pints)
2.0 litre DOHC engine:	
With filter	4.5 litres (7.9 pints)
Without filter	4.0 litres (7.0 pints)
Cooling system (including heater):	
2.0 litre DOHC engine carburettor models	7.0 litres (12.3 pints)
2.0 litre DOHC engine fuel injection models	7.3 litres (12.8 pints)
MT75 type manual gearbox	1.2 litres (2.1 pints)

1.6 litre CVH engine

General

Note: *Unless otherwise stated, the Specifications for the 1.6 litre CVH engine are as given for the 1.8 litre CVH engine in Chapter 1.*

Engine code	L6B
Bore	79.960 mm
Stroke	79.520 mm
Cubic capacity	1596 cc
Compression ratio	9.0:1
Compression pressure at starter motor speed	12.2 to 14.3 bars
Maximum continuous engine speed	6000 rpm
Maximum engine power (DIN)	59 kW at 5500 rpm
Maximum engine torque (DIN)	121 Nm at 3500 rpm

Cylinder block

Bore diameter:	
Standard class 1	79.940 to 79.950 mm
Standard class 2	79.950 to 79.960 mm
Standard class 3	79.960 to 79.970 mm
Standard class 4	79.970 to 79.980 mm
Oversize class A	80.230 to 80.240 mm
Oversize class B	80.240 to 80.250 mm
Oversize class C	80.250 to 80.260 mm

Crankshaft

Endfloat	0.09 to 0.30 mm (0.004 to 0.012 in)
Main bearing running clearance	0.011 to 0.058 mm
Main bearing journal diameter:	
Standard	57.980 to 58.000 mm
Undersize 0.25	57.730 to 57.750 mm
Undersize 0.50	57.480 mm
Undersize 0.75	57.230 to 57.250 mm
Main bearing thrustwasher thickness:	
Standard	2.301 to 2.351 mm
Oversize	2.491 to 2.541 mm
Big-end bearing running clearance	0.006 to 0.060 mm
Big-end bearing journal diameter:	
Standard	47.890 to 47.910 mm
Undersize 0.25	47.640 to 47.660 mm
Undersize 0.50	47.390 to 47.410 mm
Undersize 0.75	47.140 to 47.160 mm
Undersize 1.00	46.890 to 46.910 mm

Pistons and piston rings

Piston diameter:	
Standard class 1	79.915 to 79.925 mm
Standard class 2	79.925 to 79.935 mm
Standard class 3	79.935 to 79.945 mm
Standard class 4	79.945 to 79.955 mm
Oversize class A	80.205 to 80.215 mm
Oversize class B	80.215 to 80.225 mm
Oversize class C	80.225 to 80.235 mm
Piston ring end gap:	
Top and centre rings	0.300 to 0.500 mm (0.012 to 0.020 in)
Bottom (oil control) ring	0.250 to 0.400 mm (0.010 to 0.016 in)

Camshaft

Endfloat	0.050 to 0.150 mm (0.002 to 0.006 in)
Thrustplate thickness	4.990 to 5.010 mm (0.1966 to 0.1974 in)
Bearing journal diameter:	
Bearing No 1	44.750 mm
Bearing No 2	45.000 mm
Bearing No 3	45.250 mm
Bearing No 4	45.500 mm
Bearing No 5	45.750 mm

Valves and valve springs – general

Valve timing:	
Inlet opens	4°ATDC
Inlet closes	32°ABDC
Exhaust opens	38°BBDC
Exhaust closes	10°BTDC
Valve spring free length:	
Colour code blue/blue	47.200 mm
Colour code white/blue	45.400 mm

Inlet valves

Stem diameter:	
Standard	8.025 to 8.043 mm
Oversize 0.20	8.225 to 8.243 mm
Oversize 0.40	8.425 to 8.443 mm

Exhaust valves

Stem diameter:	
Standard	7.999 to 8.017 mm
Oversize 0.20	8.199 to 8.217 mm
Oversize 0.40	8.399 to 8.417 mm

Lubrication system

Oil type/specification	Multigrade engine oil, viscosity range SAE 10W/30 to 20W/50, to API SG/CD or better (Duckhams QXR, Hypergrade, or 10W/40 Motor Oil)
Oil capacity:	
With filter	3.5 litres (6.2 pints)
Without filter	3.25 litres (5.7 pints)
Oil pump clearances:	
Outer rotor to body	0.060 to 0.190 mm (0.002 to 0.007 in)
Inner rotor to outer rotor	0.050 to 0.180 mm (0.002 to 0.007 in)
Rotor endfloat	0.014 to 0.100 mm (0.001 to 0.004 in)

Torque wrench settings

	Nm	lbf ft
Main bearing cap bolts	90 to 100	66 to 74
Big-end bearing cap bolts	30 to 36	22 to 27
Crankshaft pulley bolt	100 to 115	74 to 85
Camshaft sprocket bolt	54 to 59	40 to 44
Flywheel bolts	82 to 92	61 to 68
Oil pump bolts	8 to 11	6 to 8
Oil pump cover bolts	8 to 12	6 to 9
Sump bolts:		
Stage 1	5 to 8	4 to 6
Stage 2	5 to 8	4 to 6
Rocker arm nuts	25 to 29	18 to 21
Cylinder head bolt:		
Stage 1	20 to 40	15 to 30
Stage 2	40 to 60	30 to 44
Stage 3	Tighten through a further 90°	Tighten through a further 90°
Stage 4	Tighten through a further 90°	Tighten through a further 90°
Camshaft cover bolts	6 to 8	4 to 6
Timing cover bolts	9 to 11	7 to 8
Timing belt tensioner bolts	16 to 20	12 to 15
Oil pick-up tube/strainer-to-oil pump bolts	8 to 12	6 to 9
Oil pick-up tube/strainer-to-cylinder block bolt	17 to 23	13 to 17
Camshaft thrustplate bolts	9 to 13	7 to 10
Crankshaft rear oil seal housing bolts	8 to 11	6 to 8

2.0 litre DOHC engine

General

Engine type	Four-cylinder, in-line, double overhead camshaft
Firing order	1-3-4-2
Engine code:	
Carburettor engine	N8A
Fuel injection engine without catalyst	N9A
Fuel injection engine with catalyst	N9C
Bore	86.00 mm
Stroke	86.00 mm
Cubic capacity	1998 cc
Compression ratio	10.3:1
Compression pressure at starter motor speed	11 to 13 bars
Maximum continuous engine speed:	
N8A engine	6050 rpm
All engines except N8A	5950 rpm
Maximum engine power (DIN):	
N8A engine	80 kW at 5600 rpm
N9A engine	92 kW at 5500 rpm
N9C engine	88 kW at 5500 rpm
Maximum engine torque:	
N8A engine	174 Nm at 3000 rpm
N9A engine	174 Nm at 2500 rpm
N9C engine	171 Nm at 2500 rpm

Cylinder block

Bore diameter:	
Standard class 1	86.000 to 86.010 mm
Standard class 2	86.010 to 86.020 mm
Oversize 0.15 class A	86.150 to 86.160 mm
Oversize 0.15 class B	86.160 to 86.170 mm
Oversize 0.5	86.500 to 86.510 mm

Crankshaft

Endfloat	0.090 to 0.300 mm (0.004 to 0.012 in)
Main bearing running clearance	0.011 to 0.048 mm
Main bearing journal diameter:	
Standard (yellow)	54.980 to 54.990 mm
Standard (red)	54.990 to 55.000 mm
Undersize 0.25 (green)	54.730 to 54.750 mm
Main bearing thrustwasher thickness:	
Standard	2.301 to 2.351 mm (0.090 to 0.093 in)
Oversize 0.38 (yellow)	2.491 to 2.541 mm (0.098 to 0.100 in)
Big-end bearing running clearance	0.006 to 0.060 mm
Big-end bearing journal diameter:	
Standard	50.890 to 50.910 mm
Undersize 0.25 (green)	50.640 to 50.660 mm

Pistons and piston rings

Piston diameter:	
Standard 1	85.970 to 85.980 mm
Standard 2	85.980 to 85.990 mm
Standard service	85.980 to 85.990 mm
Oversize 0.15	86.130 to 86.150 mm
Oversize 0.50	86.470 to 86.490 mm
Piston ring end gap:	
Top	0.300 to 0.600 mm (0.012 to 0.024 in)
Centre	0.500 to 0.800 mm (0.020 to 0.032 in)
Bottom (oil control)	0.400 to 1.500 mm (0.016 to 0.059 in)

Cylinder head

Valve guide bore	7.063 to 7.094 mm
Camshaft bearing parent bore diameter	26.000 to 26.030 mm

Camshafts

Endfloat	0.020 to 0.260 mm (0.001 to 0.010 in)

Valves and valve springs – general

Valve timing:	
Carburettor engines:	
Inlet opens	13°BTDC
Inlet closes	39°ABDC
Exhaust opens	43°BBDC
Exhaust closes	13°ATDC
Fuel injection engines:	
Inlet opens	13°BTDC
Inlet closes	51°ABDC
Exhaust opens	43°BBDC
Exhaust closes	13°ATDC
Valve spring free length:	
Inner spring	48.200 mm (1.899 in)
Outer spring	46.800 mm (1.844 in)

Inlet valves

Stem diameter:	
Standard	7.025 to 7.043 mm
Oversize 0.2	7.225 to 7.243 mm
Oversize 0.4	7.425 to 7.443 mm
Oversize 0.6	7.625 to 7.643 mm
Oversize 0.8	7.825 to 7.843 mm

Exhaust valves

Stem diameter:	
Standard	6.999 to 7.017 mm
Oversize 0.2	7.199 to 7.217 mm
Oversize 0.4	7.399 to 7.417 mm
Oversize 0.6	7.599 to 7.617 mm
Oversize 0.8	7.799 to 7.817 mm

Lubrication system

Oil type/specification	Multigrade engine oil, viscosity range SAE 10W/30 to 20W/50, to API SG/CD or better (Duckhams QXR, Hypergrade, or 10W/40 Motor Oil)
Oil capacity:	
With filter	4.5 litres (7.9 pints)
Without filter	4.0 litres (7.0 pints)
Oil filter	Champion C102

Torque wrench settings

	Nm	lbf ft
Main bearing cap bolts	90 to 104	66 to 77
Big-end bearing cap bolts:		
Stage 1	6 to 8	4 to 6
Stage 2	15 to 17	11 to 13
Stage 3	Tighten through a further 85° to 95°	Tighten through a further 85° to 95°
Crankshaft pulley bolt:		
Stage 1	45 to 58	33 to 43
Stage 2	Tighten through a further 80° to 90°	Tighten through a further 80° to 90°
Camshaft sprocket bolt	55 to 63	41 to 46
Flywheel bolts	82 to 92	61 to 68
Oil pump bolts	9 to 12	7 to 9

Torque wrench settings (continued)	**Nm**	**lbf ft**
Oil pump sprocket bolt	16 to 19	12 to 14
Oil pump chain tensioner bolt	10 to 13	7 to 10
Sump bolts and nuts	8 to 10	6 to 7
Sump studs	6 to 8	4 to 6
Sump drain plug	21 to 28	15 to 21
Sump front mounting plate	23 to 28	17 to 21
Oil baffle nuts	17 to 21	13 to 15
Oil pick-up pipe-to-cylinder block bolts	9 to 13	7 to 10
Oil pressure warning lamp switch	18 to 22	13 to 16
Cylinder head bolts:		
M11 bolts:		
Stage 1	40	30
Stage 2	55	41
Stage 3	Tighten through a further 90°	Tighten through a further 90°
Stage 4	Tighten through a further 90°	Tighten through a further 90°
M8 bolts	36 to 39	27 to 29
Camshaft cover bolts	6 to 8	4 to 6
Camshaft bearing cap nuts	22 to 26	16 to 19
Lower timing chain guide upper bolt	10 to 13	7 to 10
Lower timing chain guide lower bolt	24 to 28	18 to 21
Upper and lower timing chain cover bolts	7 to 10	5 to 7
Crankshaft rear oil seal housing bolts	8 to 11	6 to 8
Engine-to-gearbox/transmission bolts	29 to 41	21 to 30

Cooling system – 1.6 litre CVH engine

Note: *Unless otherwise stated, the Specifications for the 1.6 litre CVH engine are as given for the 1.8 litre CVH engine in Chapter 2.*

Coolant mixture

Type/specification	Soft water and antifreeze to Ford spec SDM-M97B49-A (Duckhams Universal Antifreeze and Summer Coolant)

Torque wrench settings	**Nm**	**lbf ft**
Coolant pump bolts	7 to 10	5 to 7
Thermostat housing bolts	7 to 10	5 to 7

Cooling system – 2.0 litre DOHC engine

Thermostat

Nominal temperature rating (fully open)	102°C (216°F)
Opening temperature	85 to 89°C (185 to 192°F)

Expansion tank cap

Opening pressure	1.0 to 1.4 bars (14.5 to 20.3 lbf/in)

Coolant mixture

Type/specification	Soft water and antifreeze to Ford spec SDM-M97B49-A (Duckhams Universal Antifreeze and Summer Coolant)

System capacity

Carburettor models	7.0 litres (12.3 pints)
Fuel injection models	7.3 litres (12.8 pints)

Torque wrench settings	**Nm**	**lbf ft**
Thermostat housing bolts	17 to 21	13 to 15
Water pump bolts	21 to 28	15 to 21
Water pump pulley bolts	20 to 25	15 to 18
Coolant pump/alternator drivebelt tensioner bolt	70 to 97	52 to 72

Fuel and exhaust systems – 1.6 litre CVH engine models

General

System type	Central fuel injection (CFI) controlled by EEC IV engine management system
Fuel octane rating	95 RON (premium unleaded)
Air filter element	Champion W219

Torque wrench settings	**Nm**	**lbf ft**
Inlet manifold nuts and bolts	16 to 20	12 to 15
Exhaust manifold nuts	14 to 17	10 to 13
Exhaust downpipe-to-manifold nuts	35 to 40	26 to 30
CFI unit bolts	9 to 11	7 to 8
Exhaust gas oxygen sensor	50 to 70	37 to 52
Fuel filter unions	14 to 20	10 to 15
Pulse air tube unions	29 to 35	21 to 26

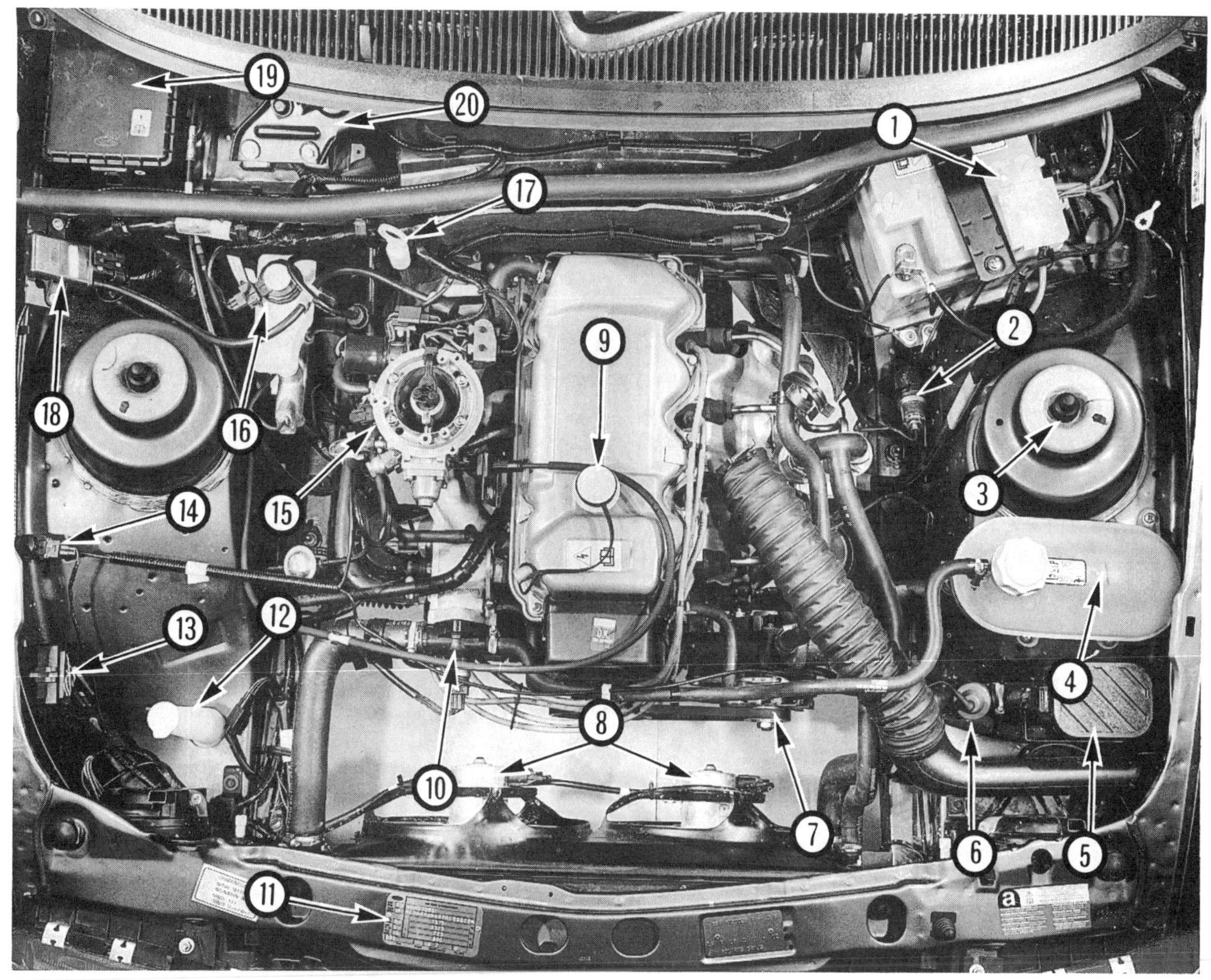

Underbonnet view of a 1992 1.6 LX model (air cleaner removed)

1 *Battery*
2 *Braking system deceleration sensitive valve*
3 *Suspension strut top*
4 *Coolant expansion tank*
5 *Pulse air filter*
6 *Vacuum-operated air valve*
7 *Alternator*
8 *Cooling fans*
9 *Oil filler cap*
10 *Thermostat housing*
11 *VIN plate*
12 *Windscreen washer reservoir*
13 *Ignition module*
14 *Pulse air control solenoid*
15 *CFI unit*
16 *Brake fluid reservoir*
17 *Engine oil level dipstick*
18 *Manifold absolute pressure (MAP) sensor*
19 *Fusebox*
20 *Windscreen wiper motor*

Underbonnet view of a 1990 2.0 GLS model

1 *Battery*
2 *Braking system deceleration sensitive valve*
3 *Ignition coil*
4 *Suspension strut top*
5 *Air cleaner*
6 *Plenum chamber*
7 *Idle speed control valve*
8 *Distributor*
9 *Oil filler cap*
10 *VIN plate*
11 *Windscreen washer reservoir*
12 *Power steering fluid reservoir*
13 *Coolant expansion tank*
14 *Manifold absolute pressure (MAP) sensor*
15 *Brake fluid reservoir*
16 *Inlet manifold*
17 *Fuel pressure regulator*
18 *Fusebox*
19 *Windscreen wiper motor*

Front underside view of a 1990 2.0 GLS model

1 *Horns*
2 *Tie-rod end*
3 *Tie-rod*
4 *Gaiter*
5 *Coolant pump*
6 *Suspension lower arm*
7 *Anti-roll bar*
8 *Starter motor*
9 *Exhaust downpipes*
10 *Crossmember*
11 *Engine sump*
12 *Oil filter*
13 *Power steering fluid pump*
14 *Windscreen washer reservoir*
15 *Cooling fans*

Fuel and exhaust systems – 2.0 litre DOHC carburettor models

General

Fuel octane rating:	
Leaded	97 RON (4-star)
Unleaded	95 RON (Premium)
Air filter element	Champion W152

Weber 2V (TLD) carburettor

Idle speed	850 ± 25 rpm	
Idle mixture (CO content)	1.0 ± 0.25%	
Fast idle speed	1800 ± 50 rpm	
Float level (with gasket)	29.0 ± 0.5 mm	
Automatic choke vacuum pull-down	5.0 ± 0.5 mm	
Throttle kicker speed (see text)	2000 ± 50 rpm	
	Primary	**Secondary**
Venturi diameter	23.0 mm	25.0 mm
Main jet	115	157
Air correction jet	175	145
Emulsion tube	F114	F3

Torque wrench settings	Nm	lbf ft
Inlet manifold nuts and bolts	20 to 24	15 to 18
Exhaust manifold nuts	21 to 25	15 to 18
Carburettor bolts	8 to 10	6 to 7

Fuel and exhaust systems – 2.0 litre DOHC fuel injection models

General

System type	Multi-point fuel injection system controlled by EEC IV engine management system
Fuel octane rating:*	
Leaded	97 RON (4-star)
Unleaded	95 RON (Premium)

Models fitted with a catalytic converter must be operated on unleaded fuel at all times.* **Do not *use leaded fuel in such models, as the catalyst will be destroyed.*

System control pressure	2.5 ± 0.2 bars
Air filter element	Champion U507
Fuel filter	Champion L204

Idle adjustments

Idle speed (not adjustable)	875 ± 50 rpm
Idle mixture (CO content) – models without catalytic converter	1.0 to 1.5%

Torque wrench settings	Nm	lbf ft
Inlet manifold nuts and bolts	20 to 24	15 to 18
Exhaust manifold nuts	21 to 25	15 to 18
Exhaust gas oxygen sensor	50 to 70	37 to 52
Throttle body bolts	9 to 11	7 to 8
Fuel rail bolts	21 to 26	15 to 19
Idle speed control valve bolts	9 to 11	7 to 8
Fuel pressure regulator bolts	9 to 12	7 to 9
Fuel filter unions	14 to 20	10 to 15

Ignition and engine management system – early 'Economy' models

Ignition timing (for replacement distributor – see Section 12)

At 800 rpm with vacuum pipe connected:	
Models using leaded fuel	16° BTDC
Models using unleaded fuel (with leaded fuel every 4th tankful)	12° BTDC

Ignition and engine management system – 1.6 litre CVH models

General

System type	Distributorless ignition system controlled by EEC IV system

Coil

Output (minimum)	37.0 kilovolts
Primary winding resistance	0.50 ± 0.05 ohm

Spark plugs

Type	Champion RC7YCC
Electrode gap	1.0 mm (0.04 in)

HT leads

Maximum resistance per lead	30 000 ohms

Torque wrench settings

	Nm	lbf ft
Air charge temperature sensor	20 to 25	15 to 18
Engine coolant temperature sensor	20 to 25	15 to 18

Ignition and engine management system – 2.0 litre DOHC carburettor models

General

System type	ESC II system

Coil

Output (minimum)	25.0 kilovolts
Primary winding resistance	0.72 to 0.88 ohm
Secondary winding resistance	4500 to 8600 ohms

Distributor

Direction of rotor arm rotation	Clockwise
Firing order	1-3-4-2 (No 1 nearest timing chain cover)

Spark plugs

Type	Champion RC7YCC or RC7YC
Electrode gap	0.8 mm (0.032 in)

HT leads

Application	Champion LS-14 (boxed set)
Maximum resistance per lead	30 000 ohms

Torque wrench settings

	Nm	lbf ft
Spark plugs	15 to 21	11 to 15
Crankshaft speed/position sensor screw	3 to 5	2 to 4

Ignition and engine management system – 2.0 litre DOHC fuel injection models

General

System type	EEC IV system

Coil

Output (minimum)	30.0 kilovolts
Primary winding resistance	0.72 to 0.88 ohm
Secondary resistance	4500 to 8600 ohms

Distributor

Direction of rotor arm rotation	Clockwise
Firing order	1-3-4-2 (No 1 nearest timing chain cover)

Spark plugs

Type	Champion RC7YCC or RC7YC
Electrode gap	0.8 mm (0.032 in)

HT leads

Application	Champion LS-14 (boxed set)
Maximum resistance per lead	30 000 ohms

Torque wrench settings

	Nm	lbf ft
Spark plugs	15 to 21	11 to 15
Air charge temperature sensor	20 to 25	15 to 18
Engine coolant temperature sensor	20 to 25	15 to 18
Fuel temperature sensor	8 to 11	6 to 8
Crankshaft speed/position sensor screw	3 to 5	2 to 4

MT75 type manual gearbox

General

Type	Five forward speeds and reverse. Synchromesh on all speeds

Ratios

1st	3.89:1
2nd	2.08:1
3rd	1.34:1
4th	1.00:1
5th	0.82:1
Reverse	3.51:1

Lubrication

Oil type/specification	Gear oil to Ford specification ESD-M2C186-A (Duckhams Uni-Matic)
Oil capacity	1.2 litres (2.1 pints)

Torque wrench settings	**Nm**	**lbf ft**
Gearbox crossmember-to-underbody bolts	30 to 40	22 to 30
Gearbox crossmember-to-gearbox bolt	52 to 71	38 to 52
Gear linkage support bracket-to-gearbox bolts	21 to 29	15 to 21
Engine-to-gearbox bolts	29 to 41	21 to 30
Oil level/filler plug	29 to 41	21 to 30
Oil drain plug	29 to 41	21 to 30

Propeller shaft – models with MT75 type gearbox

Torque wrench settings	**Nm**	**lbf ft**
Gearbox output flange studs:		
Models with GAF 30 rubber coupling	70 to 90	52 to 66
Models with GAF 41 rubber coupling	100 to 120	74 to 89
Front rubber coupling-to-vibration damper nuts	67 to 83	49 to 61

Steering

Torque wrench setting	**Nm**	**lbf ft**
Steering column adjuster through-bolt	6 to 8	4 to 6

3 Buying spare parts and vehicle identification numbers

Engine number – 1.6 litre CVH engines

On 1.6 litre CVH engines, the engine number is stamped on the front lower face of the cylinder block, on the alternator side of the timing cover.

Engine number – 2.0 litre DOHC engines

On 2.0 litre DOHC engines, the engine number is stamped on the front face of the cylinder block, below the upper timing chain cover.

4 1.6 litre CVH engine

General description

1 The 1.6 litre CVH engine was introduced in September 1991 to replace the 1.6 litre OHC engine used previously in the Sierra range. The engine is broadly similar to the 1.8 litre CVH engine described in Chapter 1, Section 41. The main differences are outlined in the following paragraphs.

2 The centre main bearing is fitted with thrustwashers to control crankshaft endfloat instead of a flanged bearing shell.

3 The hydraulic cam followers operate in a similar manner to those described for the 1.6 CVH engine in Chapter 1, Section 41, but no rollers are fitted, and the base of each cam follower is in direct contact with the cam profile.

4 A distributorless ignition system is used, and a blanking plate is therefore fitted to the cylinder head in place of the distributor drive. The fuel pump is mounted in the fuel tank.

5 The crankcase ventilation system operates in a similar manner to that described for the 1.8 CVH engine.

6 A comprehensive emissions control system is fitted, comprising Central Fuel Injection (CFI), a sophisticated engine management system, a crankcase ventilation system, a catalytic converter, and a pulse air system (to reduce exhaust gas emissions). These systems are described in more detail in Section 9 of this Chapter.

7 Unless otherwise stated in this Section, all procedures are as described for the 1.8 litre CVH engine in Chapter 1.

Major operations possible with the engine in the vehicle

8 The following operations can be carried out without removing the engine from the vehicle.

- *(a) Removal and servicing of the cylinder head*
- *(b) Removal of the camshaft after removal of the cylinder head*
- *(c) Removal of the timing belt and sprockets*
- *(d) Removal of the engine mountings*
- *(e) Removal of the clutch and flywheel*
- *(f) Removal of the crankshaft front and rear oil seals*
- *(g) Removal of the sump*
- *(h) Removal of the oil pump*
- *(i) Removal of the pistons and connecting rods*
- *(j) Removal of the big-end bearings*

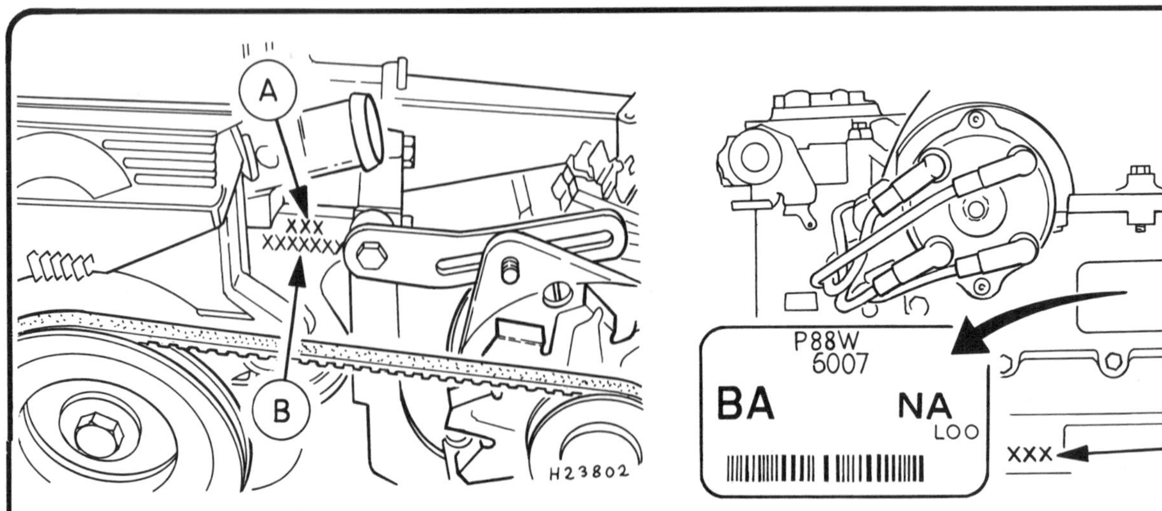

Fig. 14.1 Engine number location – 1.6 litre CVH engine (Sec 3)

A Engine code *B Engine number*

Fig. 14.2 Engine number code sticker and engine number location (A) – 2.0 litre DOHC engine (Sec 3)

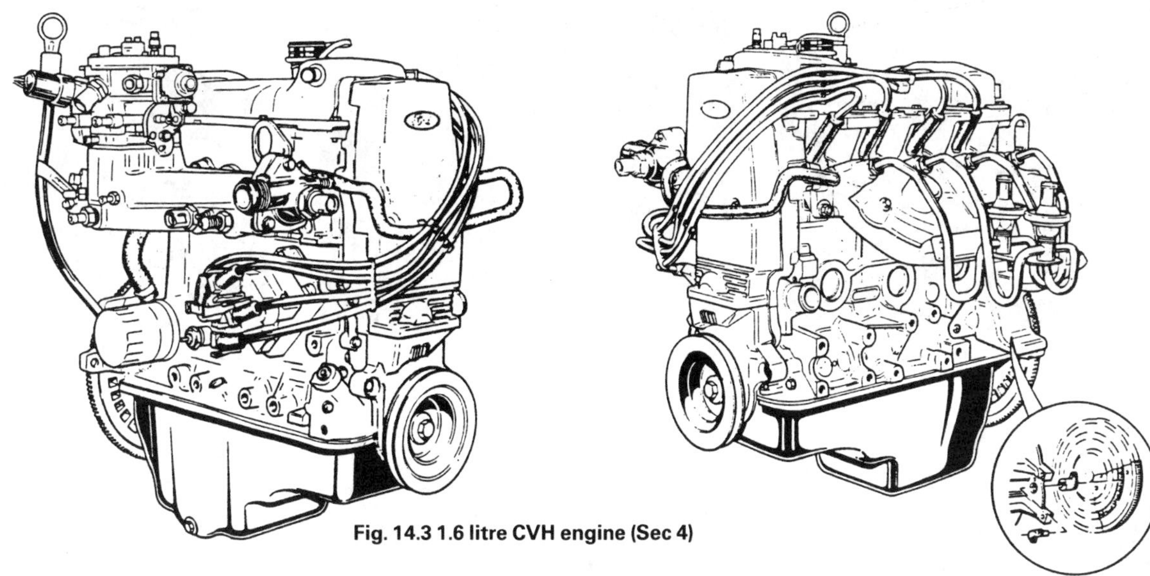

Fig. 14.3 1.6 litre CVH engine (Sec 4)

Major operations requiring engine removal

9 The following operations can only be carried out after removing the engine from the vehicle.

(a) *Removal of the crankshaft main bearings*
(b) *Removal of the crankshaft*

Engine – removal leaving manual gearbox in vehicle

Note: *A suitable hoist and lifting tackle will be required for this operation.*

10 Disconnect the battery negative lead.
11 Remove the bonnet as described in Chapter 12.
12 Remove the air cleaner with reference to Section 9 of this Chapter.
13 Disconnect the cooling fan wiring plug(s), then unscrew the retaining nuts and washers, and withdraw the fan shroud and cooling fan assembly.
14 Drain the cooling system with reference to Section 7 of this Chapter.
15 Disconnect the coolant hoses from the thermostat housing, noting their locations.
16 Disconnect the lower radiator hose from the coolant pump elbow, and disconnect the heater hose from the T-piece on the lower radiator hose.
17 Disconnect the coolant hose from the central fuel injection (CFI) unit.
18 Disconnect the brake servo vacuum hose from the inlet manifold, by carefully pressing the clip on the inlet manifold connector into the manifold using a screwdriver, and withdrawing the hose.
19 Disconnect the three vacuum hoses from the inlet manifold, noting their locations.

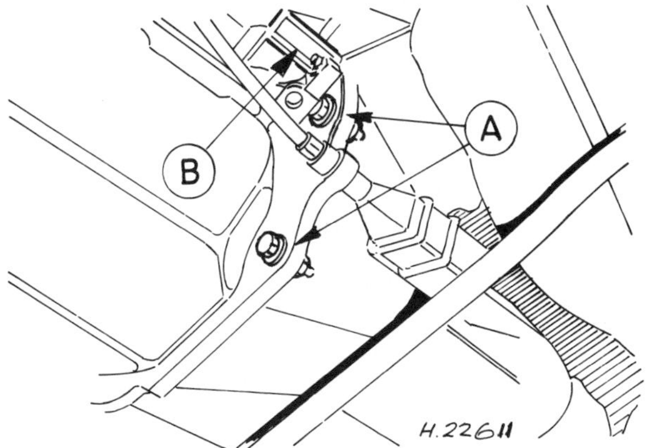

Fig. 14.4 Engine adaptor plate bolts (A) and crankshaft speed/position sensor shroud (B) – 1.6 litre CVH engine (Sec 4)

20 Disconnect the two hoses from the pulse air system check valves (photo).
21 Gradually loosen the fuel inlet pipe union on the CFI unit to relieve the pressure in the fuel system. Be prepared for fuel spray, and take adequate fire precautions. Once the pressure has reduced, disconnect the fuel inlet and return hoses. Plug the ends of the hoses to minimise petrol spillage.
22 Disconnect the throttle cable as described in Chapter 3, Section 14, if necessary.
23 Disconnect the wiring from the following components.

Alternator
Starter motor
Oil pressure warning lamp switch
Temperature gauge sender
Engine coolant temperature sensor
Intake air temperature sensor
Ignition coil
Throttle stepper motor
Throttle position sensor
Fuel injector
Cooling fan switch
Engine earth strap to battery tray

24 Unscrew and remove the top engine-to-gearbox bolts which are accessible from the engine compartment.
25 Apply the handbrake, jack up the front of the vehicle and support it on axle stands.
26 Drain the engine oil into a suitable container.
27 Remove the starter motor as described in Chapter 13.
28 Disconnect the exhaust gas oxygen sensor wiring connector, then remove the exhaust downpipe with reference to Section 9 of this Chapter.
29 Disconnect the wiring plug from the crankshaft speed/position sensor.
30 Unscrew the two nuts securing the engine mountings to the crossmember. Recover the washers.
31 Unscrew and remove the remaining engine-to-gearbox bolts, noting the location of the earth strap and any wiring brackets, and remove the two bolts from the engine adaptor plate.
32 Unscrew the securing bolt, and remove the crankshaft speed/position sensor shroud.
33 Working inside the vehicle, place a wooden block under the clutch pedal to raise it fully against its stop which will hold the automatic adjuster pawl clear of the toothed quadrant.
34 Disconnect the clutch cable from the release arm, and pass the cable through the bellhousing with reference to Chapter 5 if necessary. Note the cable routing for use when refitting.
35 Lower the vehicle to the ground, and support the gearbox with a trolley jack, using a block of wood between the jack and the gearbox to spread the load.

4.20 Pulse air system check valves (arrowed)

4.50A Upper timing cover securing bolts (arrowed)

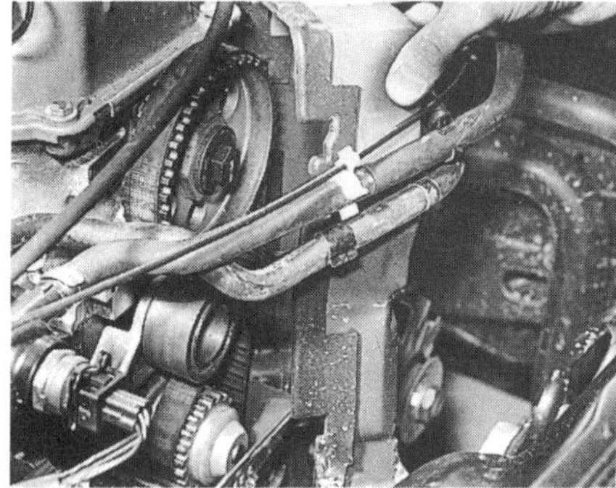
4.50B Removing the upper timing cover

4.50C Removing the lower timing cover

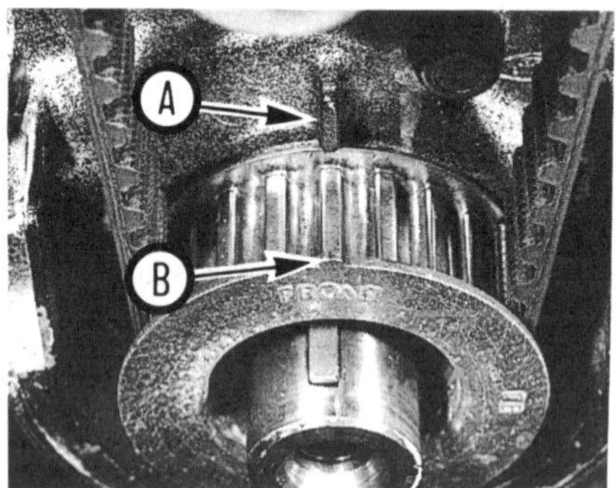

4.50D Oil pump TDC lug (A) and crankshaft sprocket lug (B)

4.60 Disconnecting the exhaust gas oxygen sensor wiring connector

36 Make a final check to ensure that all relevant wires, hoses and pipes have been disconnected to facilitate engine removal.
37 Attach a suitable hoist to the engine lifting brackets located at the front and rear of the cylinder head, and carefully take the weight of the engine. The engine should be supported horizontally; do not allow it to tilt front to rear.
38 Raise the engine until the engine mounting studs are clear of the crossmember, then pull the engine forwards to disconnect it from the gearbox. Ensure that the gearbox is adequately supported, and take care not to strain the gearbox input shaft. It may be necessary to rock the engine a little to release it from the gearbox.
39 Once clear of the gearbox, lift the engine from the vehicle, taking care not to damage the radiator fins.

Engine/manual gearbox assembly – removal and separation

Note: *A suitable hoist and lifting tackle will be required for this operation.*

40 Proceed as described in paragraphs 10 to 23 inclusive of this Section.
41 Proceed as described in Chapter 1, Section 51, paragraphs 2 to 25 inclusive, noting the following points.
42 Refer to Section 9 of this Chapter before removing the exhaust system.
43 Disconnect the wiring from the vehicle speed sensor mounted on the gearbox before removing the engine/gearbox assembly.
44 Note that the crankshaft speed/position sensor shroud (which is secured by a single bolt) must be removed before separating the engine from the gearbox.

Engine – refitting (manual gearbox in vehicle)

45 Reverse the procedure described in paragraphs 10 to 39 inclusive, noting the points made in Chapter 1, Section 53, paragraphs 2 to 10 inclusive. Refer to Section 9 of this Chapter when refitting the exhaust downpipe.

Engine/manual gearbox assembly – reconnection and refitting

46 Reverse the procedure described in paragraphs 40 to 44 inclusive, noting the points made in Chapter 1, Section 55, paragraphs 2 to 12 inclusive. Refer to Section 9 of this Chapter when refitting the exhaust system, and ensure that the vehicle speed sensor wiring plug is reconnected.

Engine dismantling – general

47 Refer to Chapter 1, Section 58, paragraphs 1 to 9 inclusive.
48 Before dismantling the main engine components, the following externally mounted ancillary components can be removed, with reference to the relevant Sections, where applicable.

Inlet manifold and CFI unit – see Section 9 of this Chapter
Exhaust manifold – see Section 9 of this Chapter
Alternator – see Chapter 13
Spark plugs and HT leads – see Section 13 of this Chapter
Ignition coil and mounting bracket – see Section 13 of this Chapter
Oil pressure warning lamp switch
Oil filter – see Chapter 1
Dipstick and tube
Engine mounting brackets
Clutch – see Chapter 5
Alternator mounting bracket
Crankshaft speed/position sensor – see Section 13 of this Chapter
Engine lifting brackets
Crankcase ventilation hose

Timing belt and sprockets – removal and refitting

Note: *Refer to the note at the beginning of Chapter 1, Section 59.*

49 If the engine is in the vehicle, carry out the following operations.

(a) *Disconnect the battery negative lead*
(b) *Remove the alternator drivebelt – see Chapter 2*
(c) *Disconnect the HT leads from the spark plugs, noting their locations, detach the bracket from the camshaft cover, and position the leads out of the way*
(d) *Move the coolant hoses from the front of the timing cover, and position them across the top of the camshaft cover out of the way*
(e) *If desired for improved access, remove the fan shroud and the cooling fan assembly, although this is not essential – see Section 7 of this Chapter*

50 Proceed as described in Chapter 1, Section 59, paragraphs 2 to 30

inclusive, noting the following differences for the 1.6 litre engine (photos).

- *(a) There is no sensor toothed disc on the crankshaft pulley*
- *(b) A two-piece timing cover is fitted, consisting of upper and lower sections, each secured by 2 bolts. No earth tag or coolant hose clip is fitted to the bolts*
- *(c) The TDC datum on the oil pump takes the form of a lug instead of a notch*
- *(d) There is no distributor rotor shaft fitted to the camshaft sprocket bolt*
- *(e) There is no timing belt backplate*

51 On completion, if the engine is in the vehicle, reverse the operations given in paragraph 49 of this Section.

Cylinder head – removal and refitting (engine in vehicle)

Note: *Refer to the note at the beginning of Chapter 1, Section 61 before proceeding.*

52 Disconnect the battery negative lead.
53 Drain the cooling system as described in Chapter 2.
54 Disconnect the expansion tank coolant hose from the thermostat housing, and the coolant bypass hose from the left-hand side of the cylinder head, then move them to one side out of the way.
55 Remove the air cleaner with reference to Section 9 of this Chapter.
56 Disconnect the HT leads from the spark plugs, identifying them for position if necessary, then unclip them from the camshaft cover and move them to one side out of the way.
57 Remove the spark plugs.
58 Disconnect the cylinder head earth lead from the battery tray.
59 The cylinder head can be removed either with or without the manifolds. If desired, the inlet manifold can be unbolted and moved to one side (after unbolting the dipstick tube), leaving the wires, hoses, pipes and cables connected, but care must be taken not to strain any of the wires, hoses or cables.
60 Disconnect the exhaust gas oxygen sensor wiring connector, then unscrew the three securing bolts and disconnect the exhaust downpipe from the manifold flange (photo). Recover the gasket.
61 If desired, remove the exhaust manifold with reference to Section 9 of this Chapter.
62 If the inlet manifold is to be removed with the cylinder head, disconnect all relevant wires, hoses, pipes and cables, otherwise unbolt the manifold and move it to one side, ensuring that it is adequately supported. Refer to Section 9 of this Chapter.
63 Proceed as described in paragraphs 73 to 76 inclusive of this Section.
64 With the cylinder head refitted, proceed as follows.
65 Refit the manifolds and/or reconnect all wires, hoses, pipes and cables as applicable, with reference to the relevant Sections.
66 Reconnect the exhaust downpipe to the manifold using a new gasket, and reconnect the exhaust gas oxygen sensor wiring connector.
67 Reconnect the earth lead to the battery tray.
68 Refit the spark plugs and reconnect the HT leads.
69 Refit the air cleaner with reference to Section 9 of this Chapter.
70 Reconnect the expansion tank hose to the thermostat housing, and the coolant bypass hose to the cylinder head.
71 Fill the cooling system as described in Chapter 2.
72 Reconnect the battery negative lead.

Cylinder head – removal and refitting (engine removed)

Note: *Refer to the note at the beginning of Chapter 1, Section 61 before proceeding.*

73 With the manifolds removed, proceed as follows.
74 Remove the timing belt as described in paragraph 50 of this Section.
75 Proceed as described in Chapter 1, Section 61, paragraphs 3 to 16 inclusive, noting the following differences for the 1.6 litre engine.

- *(a) Unscrew the cylinder head bolts in the reverse order to that shown in Fig. 14.5*
- *(b) The cylinder head gasket is identified by a single tooth on its edge, and the gasket must be fitted with the tooth nearest the oil filter end of the engine, as shown in Fig. 14.6*
- *(c) Tighten the cylinder head bolts in the order shown in Fig. 14.5, to the four stages given in the Specifications at the beginning of this Chapter*
- *(d) Ignore the reference to the studded camshaft cover bolts*

76 On completion, refit the timing belt as described in paragraph 50 of this Section.

Cylinder head – dismantling and reassembly

Refer to the note at the beginning of Chapter 1, Section 62 before proceeding.

77 With the cylinder head removed, remove the camshaft as described in paragraphs 81 to 84 inclusive of this Section.
78 Proceed as described in Chapter 1, Section 62, paragraphs 2 to 9 inclusive, but note that no dampers are fitted to the inlet valve springs on the 1.6 litre engine.
79 Refit the camshaft as described in paragraphs 89 to 96 of this Section.

Camshaft and cam followers – removal, inspection and refitting

Note: *A new camshaft oil seal and new rocker arm securing nuts should be used when refitting.*

80 Remove the cylinder head as described previously in this Section.
81 Unscrew the securing nuts and remove the rocker arm guides, rocker arms, and spacer plates, then lift out the cam followers. Keep all components in the correct order so that they can be refitted in their original locations on reassembly. It is advisable to store the cam followers upright in an oil bath until they are to be refitted. Ensure that the depth of oil is sufficient to fully cover the cam followers.

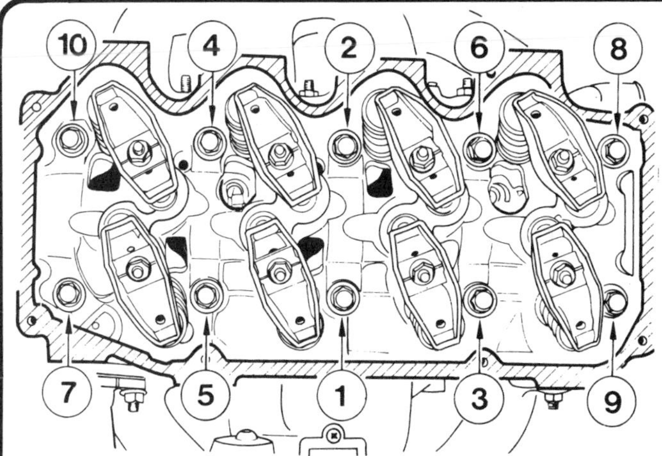

Fig. 14.5 Cylinder head bolt tightening sequence – 1.6 litre CVH engine (Sec 4)

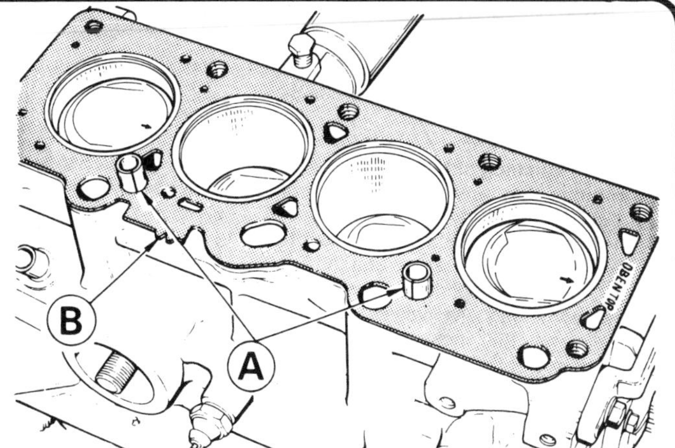

Fig. 14.6 Cylinder head gasket correctly located – 1.6 litre CVH engine (Sec 4)

A Locating bushes *B Identification teeth*

82 Prise out the camshaft oil seal, taking care not to damage the surface of the camshaft. If necessary, use self-tapping screws and a suitable pair of grips to withdraw the seal.
83 Unscrew the two securing bolts and withdraw the camshaft thrust plate from the front of the cylinder head.
84 Carefully withdraw the camshaft from the front of the cylinder head, taking care not to damage the bearings. If necessary, loosely refit the camshaft sprocket and bolt to aid removal.
85 Examine the surfaces of the camshaft journals and lobes, and the contact faces of the cam followers for wear. If wear is excessive, considerable noise would have been noticed from the top of the engine when running, and a new camshaft and followers must be fitted. It is unlikely that this level of wear will occur unless a considerable mileage has been covered. Note that the cam followers cannot be dismantled for renewal of individual components.
86 Check the camshaft bearings in the cylinder head for wear. If excessive wear is evident, it may be possible to have the head machined by a suitably equipped engineering workshop to enable a camshaft with oversize bearing journals to be fitted. The only other course of action available is renewal of the cylinder head.
87 Check the cam follower bores in the cylinder head for wear. If excessive wear is evident, the cylinder head must be renewed.
88 Check the cam follower oil ports and the oil holes in the cylinder head for obstructions.
89 Commence refitting by lubricating the camshaft, bearings and thrustplate with hypoid oil, then carefully insert the camshaft from the front of the cylinder head, taking care not to damage the bearings.
90 Locate the thrustplate in position in the cylinder head, then refit the bolts and tighten them. Note that the oil groove in the thrustplate must face the front of the engine.
91 Using a dial test indicator (if available) or feeler gauges, check that the camshaft endfloat is within the limits given in the Specifications at the beginning of this Supplement. If not, renew the thrustplate and re-check. If this does not bring the endfloat within limits, the camshaft must be renewed.
92 Smear the lip of the new camshaft oil seal with clean engine oil, then refit the seal using the camshaft sprocket bolt and a suitable tool. The tool can be improvised using a metal tube of suitable diameter and a large washer or metal disc. Draw the seal into position so that it rests on the shoulder.
93 Lubricate the cam followers with hypoid oil, then refit them to their original locations in the cylinder head.
94 Before each rocker arm is fitted and its (new) nut tightened, it is essential to ensure that the relevant cam follower is positioned at its lowest point (in contact with the cam base circle, **not** the tip of the cam lobe). Turn the camshaft (by means of the camshaft sprocket bolt if necessary) as necessary to achieve this.
95 Lubricate the tops of the cam followers, then refit the spacer plates, rocker arms and rocker arm guides to their original locations.
96 Secure the rocker arms using new nuts tightened to the specified torque, bearing in mind the point made in paragraph 94.
97 Refit the cylinder head as described earlier in this Section.

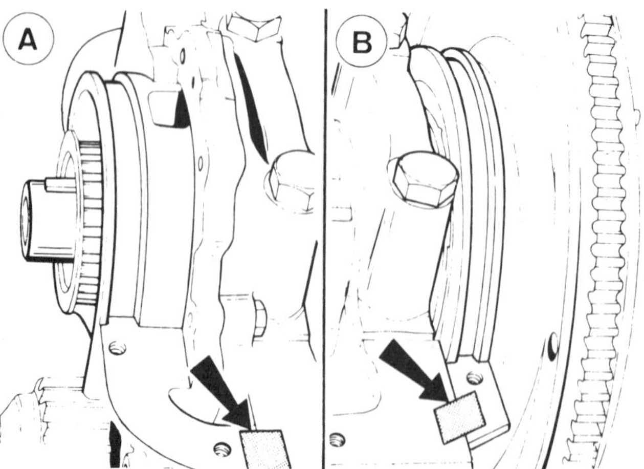

Fig. 14.7 Apply sealing compound at the points arrowed before refitting the sump – 1.6 litre CVH engine (Sec 4)

A Oil pump/cylinder block joint
B Crankshaft rear oil seal housing/cylinder block joint

Flywheel – removal, inspection and refitting

Note: *New flywheel securing bolts must be used on refitting.*

98 Refer to Chapter 1, Section 27, noting the following points.
99 If the engine is in the vehicle, refer to Section 16 of this Chapter when removing the clutch.
100 The flywheel securing bolts must be renewed when refitting, and the new bolts are supplied ready-coated with thread-locking compound.
101 The ring gear cannot be renewed independently of the flywheel. If the ring gear is badly worn or has missing teeth, a new flywheel must be fitted. Similarly, the flywheel must be renewed if the crankshaft speed/position sensor toothed disc is damaged.

Crankshaft front oil seal – renewal

102 Remove the timing belt and the crankshaft sprocket and thrustwasher as described earlier in this Section.
103 Proceed as described in Chapter 1, Section 66, paragraphs 2 to 4 inclusive.
104 Refit the thrustwasher, crankshaft sprocket and timing belt as described earlier in this Section.

Sump – removal and refitting

Note: *A new sump gasket must be used when refitting.*

105 Sump removal and refitting is easier if the engine is removed from the vehicle, however if the engine is in the vehicle, proceed as follows. If the engine has been removed from the vehicle, proceed to paragraph 108.
106 Remove the clutch with reference to Section 16 of this Chapter.
107 Drain the engine oil into a suitable container.
108 Remove the flywheel and the engine adaptor plate as described earlier in this Section.
109 Unscrew the eighteen securing bolts and withdraw the sump. If the sump is stuck, carefully tap it sideways to free it. Do not prise between the mating faces. Recover the gasket.
110 Thoroughly clean the mating faces of the cylinder block and sump.
111 Apply sealing compound to the joints between the oil pump and the cylinder block, and the crankshaft rear oil seal housing and the cylinder block, as shown in Fig. 14.7.
112 Without applying any further sealer, locate the gasket into the grooves of the oil pump and the rear oil seal housing. To hold the gasket in position, studs can be inserted temporarily in the bolt hole positions circled in Fig. 14.8. Make sure that the gasket spacing pips are seated correctly.
113 Locate the sump on the gasket, taking care not to displace the gasket, then loosely fit the securing bolts. With the sump in position, where applicable remove the studs from the bolt holes, and loosely fit the remaining securing bolts.
114 Tighten the bolts to the specified torque in the two stages given in the Specifications at the beginning of this Chapter, in the sequence shown in Fig. 14.8.

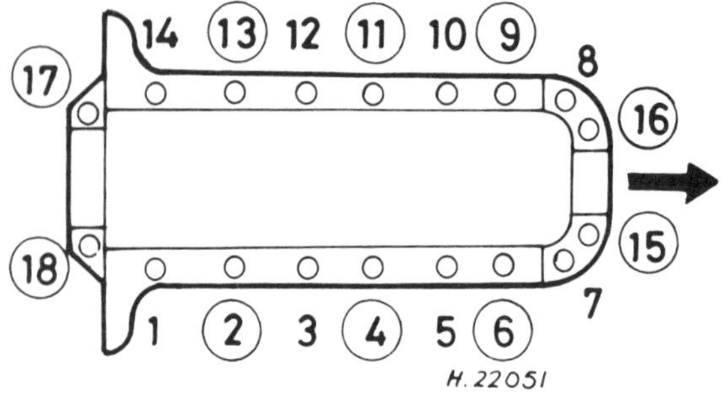

Fig. 14.8 Sump bolt tightening sequence – 1.6 litre-CVH engine (Sec 4)

Arrow indicates front of engine

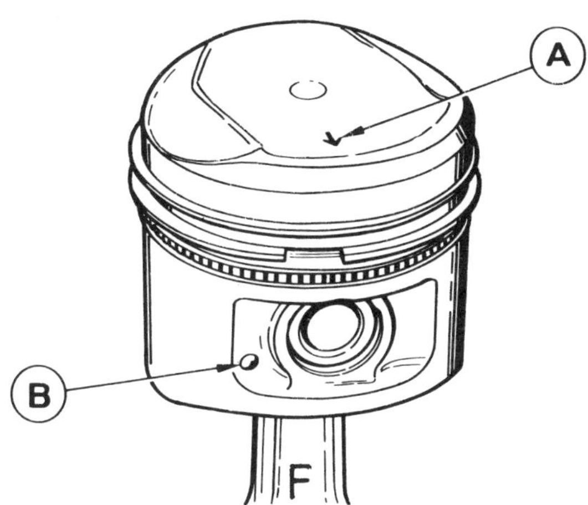

Fig. 14.9 The arrow (A) and the cast pip (B) must face the front of the engine – 1.6 litre CVH engine (Sec 4)

115 Refit the engine adaptor plate and the flywheel as described earlier in this Section.
116 If the engine is in the vehicle, refit the clutch with reference to Section 16 of this Chapter, and refill the engine with oil.

Oil pump – removal and refitting

Note: *A new oil pump gasket and a new oil pick-up tube gasket must be used on refitting.*

117 Remove the timing belt, crankshaft sprocket and thrustwasher as described earlier in this Section.
118 Remove the sump as described earlier in this Section.
119 Proceed as described in Chapter 1, Section 69, paragraphs 4 to 12 inclusive.
120 Refit the sump as described earlier in this Section.
121 Fit the crankshaft front oil seal with reference to Chapter 1, Section 66.
122 Refit the thrustwasher, crankshaft sprocket and timing belt as described earlier in this Section.

Oil pump – dismantling, inspection and reassembly

123 The procedure is as described in Chapter 1, Section 70, but refer to the Specifications at the beginning of this Chapter for the rotor clearances.

Pistons and connecting rods – removal and refitting

124 The procedure is as described in Chapter 1, Section 71, noting the following points.

(a) Remove and refit the sump and the cylinder head as described earlier in this Section
(b) When refitting a piston/connecting rod assembly, the piston must be fitted with the arrow on the piston crown and the cast pip on the piston skirt facing the front (timing belt end) of the engine – see Fig. 14.9
(c) The big-end bearing caps locate on dowels in the connecting rods, and can only be fitted in one position

Pistons and connecting rods – examination and renovation

125 Proceed as described in Chapter 1, Section 72, paragraphs 1 to 4 inclusive.
126 Before fitting the new rings to the pistons, insert them into the relevant cylinder bore and use a feeler gauge to check that the end gaps are within the limits given in the Specifications at the beginning of this Chapter. Check the end gaps with the ring at the top and the bottom of the cylinder bore.
127 Fit the oil control ring sections with the spreader ends abutted opposite the front of the piston, making sure that the ends do not overlap. The side ring gaps should be offset 120° either side of the spreader gap. Fit the tapered lower compression ring with the 'TOP' mark uppermost and the gap 120° from the spreader gap, then fit the upper compression ring with the gap 120° on the other side of the spreader gap. Note that the compression rings are coated with a molybdenum disulphide skin which must not be damaged.

Crankshaft and main bearings – removal and refitting

128 Proceed as described in Chapter 1, Section 73, noting the following points.

(a) Remove and refit the timing belt, crankshaft sprocket, and thrustwasher as described earlier in this Section
(b) Remove and refit the pistons and connecting rods with reference to paragraph 124 of this Section
(c) Remove and refit the oil pump and the pick-up tube as described earlier in this Section
(d) Note that thrustwashers are used at the centre main bearing (one each side of the bearing) instead of a thrustbearing shell to control crankshaft endfloat. Oversize thrustwashers are available to compensate for wear if necessary. The thrust washers should be fitted with the oil grooves visible
(e) The crankshaft and bearings can be examined and if necessary renovated with reference to paragraph 129 of this Section

Crankshaft and bearings – examination and renovation

129 Proceed as described in Chapter 1, Section 74, but note that if the crankshaft endfloat is more than the maximum specified amount, new thrustwashers should be fitted to the centre main bearing.

Engine reassembly – general

130 Refer to Chapter 1, Section 78, but note that if they have been removed, new rocker arm nuts will be required.

5 2.0 litre DOHC engine

General description

1 The 2.0 litre DOHC (Double Overhead Camshaft) engine was introduced in August 1989 to replace the 2.0 litre OHC engine used previously in the Sierra range. The engine is of four-cylinder, in-line type.
2 The crankshaft incorporates five main bearings. Thrustwashers are fitted to the centre main bearing in order to control crankshaft endfloat.
3 The camshafts are driven by a chain from the crankshaft, and operate the angled valves via hydraulic cam followers. One camshaft operates the inlet valves, and the other operates the exhaust valves. The operation of the cam followers is explained in Chapter 1, Section 41, but note that no rollers are fitted, and the base of each cam follower is in direct contact with the cam profile.
4 The distributor is driven directly from the front of the inlet camshaft, and the oil pump is driven by a chain from the crankshaft. An electric fuel pump is mounted in the fuel tank.
5 Lubrication is by means of a bi-rotor pump which draws oil through a strainer located inside the sump, and forces it through a full-flow filter into the engine oil galleries, from where it is distributed to the crankshaft and camshafts. The big-end bearings are supplied with oil via internal drillings in the crankshaft. The undersides of the pistons are supplied with oil from drillings in the connecting rods. The hydraulic cam followers are supplied with oil from passages in the cylinder head. The camshafts are lubricated by oil from spray tubes mounted above the camshaft bearing caps.
6 A closed crankcase ventilation system is employed, whereby piston blow-by gases are drawn from the crankcase, through a breather pipe into the inlet manifold where they are burnt with fresh air/fuel mixture.
7 Unless otherwise stated in this Section, procedures are as described for OHC engines in Chapter 1.

Maintenance and inspection

8 At the intervals specified in the *'Routine maintenance'* Section at the beginning of this manual, carry out the following tasks.
9 Check the engine oil level as described in Chapter 1, Section 2, paragraph 2.
10 Renew the engine oil and oil filter as described in Chapter 1, Section 3.
11 Inspect the engine for evidence of oil, coolant or fuel leaks, and rectify as necessary.

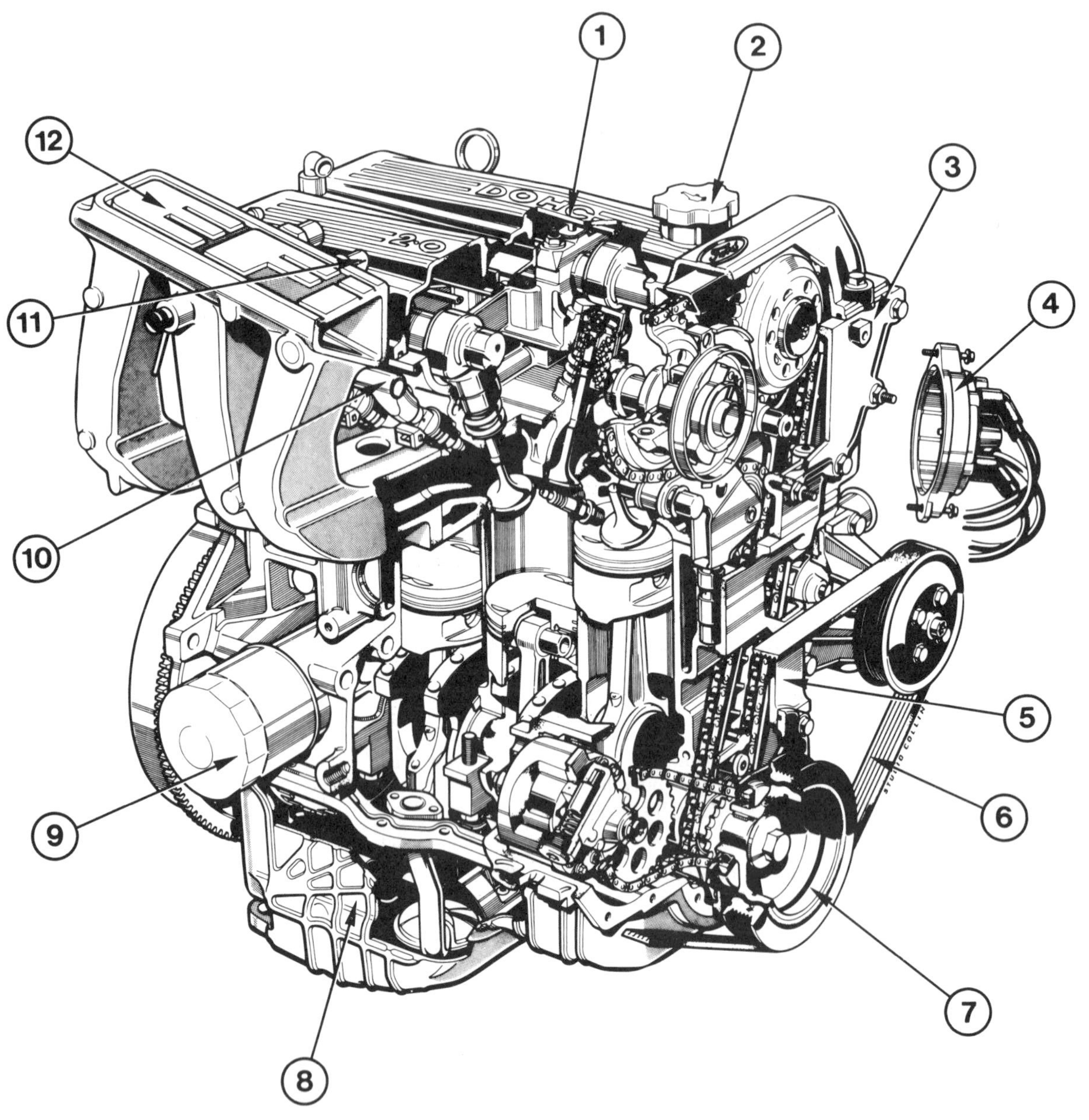

Fig. 14.10 Cutaway view of 2.0 litre DOHC fuel injection engine (Sec 5)

1 *Plastic camshaft cover*
2 *Oil filler cap*
3 *Upper timing chain cover*
4 *Distributor cap*
5 *Lower timing chain cover*
6 *Coolant pump/alternator drivebelt*
7 *Crankshaft pulley*
8 *Sump*
9 *Oil filter*
10 *Fuel rail*
11 *Crankcase ventilation connection*
12 *Inlet manifold*

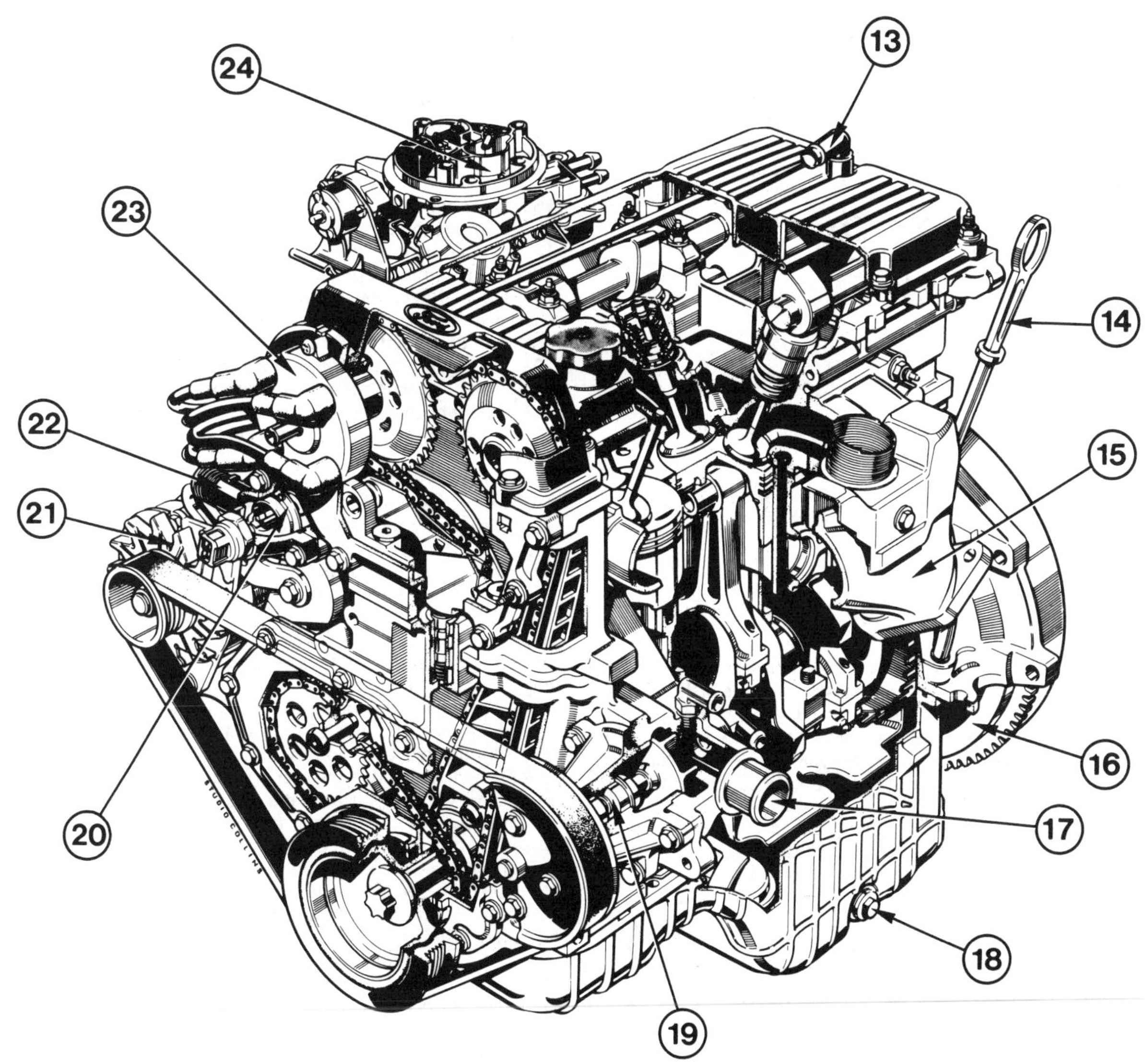

Fig. 14.11 Cutaway view of 2.0 litre DOHC carburettor engine (Sec 5)

13 Camshaft cover ventilation connection
14 Dipstick
15 Exhaust manifold
16 Flywheel
17 Coolant hose connection
18 Oil drain plug
19 Coolant pump
20 Thermostat housing
21 Alternator
22 Coolant hose connection
23 Distributor
24 Carburettor

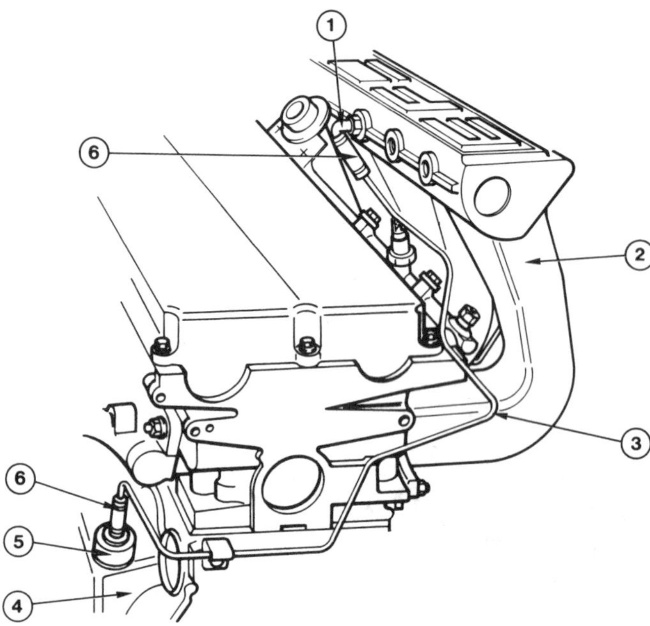

Fig. 14.12 Crankcase ventilation system – 2.0 litre DOHC fuel injection engine (Sec 5)

1	*Inlet manifold connection*	*4*	*Oil separator*
2	*Inlet manifold*	*5*	*Vent valve*
3	*Breather pipe*	*6*	*Connecting hose*

Crankcase ventilation system – description and maintenance

12 The crankcase ventilation system consists of an oil separator and vent valve fitted to the cylinder block on the left-hand side of the engine. This is connected by a pipe to the inlet manifold. The system operates according to the vacuum in the inlet manifold. Piston blow-by gases are drawn through the oil separator and the vent valve to the inlet manifold. The blow-by gases are then drawn into the engine together with the fuel/air mixture.

13 It is advisable to inspect the breather pipe and associated hoses occasionally for blockage or damage; clean or renew as necessary. A blocked breather system can cause a build-up of crankcase pressure, which in turn can cause oil leaks.

Major operations possible with the engine in the vehicle

14 The following operations can be carried out without removing the engine from the vehicle.

- *(a) Removal of the camshafts*
- *(b) Removal and servicing of the cylinder head*
- *(c) Removal of the timing chain and sprockets*
- *(d) Removal of the oil pump*
- *(e) Removal of the sump*
- *(f) Removal of the pistons and connecting rods*
- *(g) Removal of the big-end bearings*
- *(h) Removal of the engine mountings*
- *(i) Removal of the clutch and flywheel*
- *(j) Removal of the crankshaft front and rear oil seals*

Major operations requiring engine removal

15 The following operations can only be carried out after removing the engine from the vehicle.

- *(a) Removal of the crankshaft main bearings.*
- *(b) Removal of the crankshaft.*

Engine – removal leaving manual gearbox in vehicle

Note: *Refer to the warning at the end of Chapter 1, Section 9 before proceeding. A suitable hoist and lifting tackle will be required for this operation.*

16 Disconnect the battery negative lead.

17 Remove the bonnet as described in Chapter 12.

18 On carburettor models, remove the air cleaner with reference to Section 10 of this Chapter.

19 On fuel injection models, remove the air intake hose, plenum chamber, and air cleaner lid as an assembly, with reference to Section 11 of this Chapter.

20 Disconnect the breather hose from the camshaft cover, and unscrew the bolt securing the hose support bracket to the left-hand side of the cylinder head (photo).

21 Drain the cooling system with reference to Section 8 of this Chapter.

22 To provide additional working space, remove the radiator with reference to Section 8 of this Chapter.

23 Disconnect the coolant hoses from the coolant pump housing on the left-hand side of the engine.

24 Disconnect the coolant hoses from the thermostat housing.

25 Disconnect the heater coolant hose from the inlet manifold.

26 Where applicable, release the coolant hose from the bracket under the carburettor automatic choke housing.

27 On carburettor models, disconnect the vacuum pipe from the engine management module.

28 Disconnect the brake servo vacuum hose from the inlet manifold, with reference to Section 20 of this Chapter if necessary.

29 On fuel injection models, disconnect the vacuum pipes from the MAP sensor (located at the rear right-hand side of the engine compartment) and, where applicable, the air conditioning system.

30 On carburettor models, disconnect the fuel supply and return hoses at the carburettor, and plug the ends of the hoses to minimise petrol spillage. Take adequate fire precautions.

31 On fuel injection models, slowly loosen the fuel feed union at the fuel rail to relieve the pressure in the fuel system before disconnecting the union. Be prepared for petrol spillage and take adequate fire precautions. Disconnect the fuel feed hose, and disconnect the fuel return hose from the fuel pressure regulator. Plug the ends of the hoses to minimise petrol spillage.

32 Disconnect the throttle cable and move it to one side, with reference to Chapter 3, Section 14 if necessary.

33 Disconnect the HT lead from the ignition coil, and unclip it from the timing chain cover.

5.20 Removing the hose support bracket bolt from the cylinder head

5.37 Earth strap position on top engine-to-gearbox bolt (arrowed)

5.44 Removing the lower steering column clamp bolt

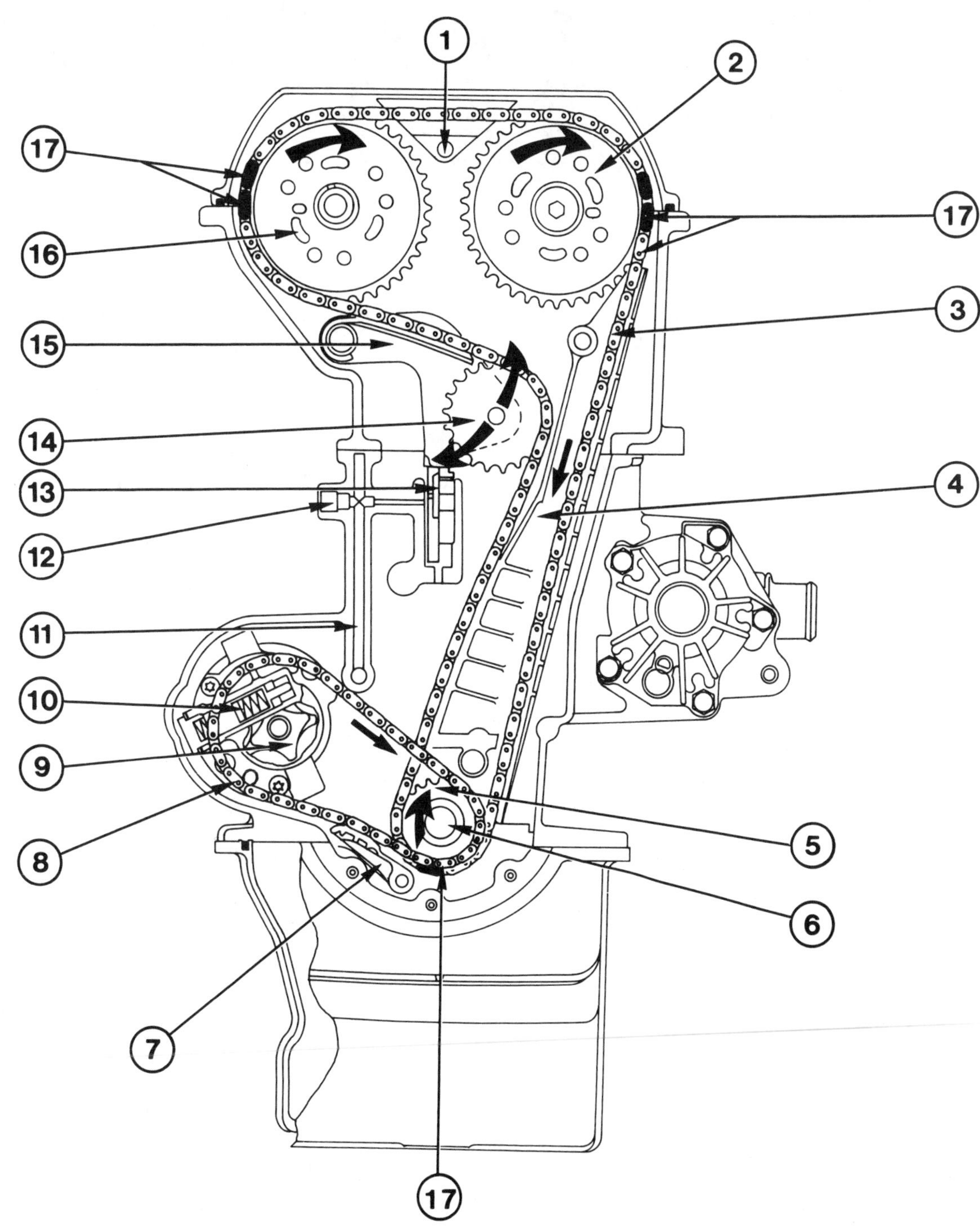

Fig. 14.13 Timing chain, oil pump drive chain and associated components – 2.0 litre DOHC engine (Sec 5)

1 *Upper timing chain guide*
2 *Exhaust camshaft sprocket*
3 *Timing chain*
4 *Lower timing chain guide*
5 *Crankshaft sprocket (double)*
6 *Crankshaft*
7 *Oil pump chain tensioner*
8 *Oil pump drive chain*
9 *Oil pump*
10 *Oil pressure relief valve*
11 *Oil passage to timing chain tensioner plunger*
12 *Plug*
13 *Timing chain tensioner plunger*
14 *Timing chain tensioner sprocket*
15 *Timing chain tensioner arm*
16 *Inlet camshaft sprocket*
17 *Copper chain links*

5.48 Engine adaptor plate bolt (arrowed)

5.51 Remove the engine mounting brackets to improve clearance

5.52 Removing a brake line securing clip from the suspension crossmember

5.53 Removing a suspension crossmember securing bolt

5.55 Lifting the engine from the vehicle

34 Disconnect the wiring from the following components as applicable, depending on model.

Alternator
Starter motor
Oil pressure warning lamp switch
Temperature gauge sender
Cooling fan switch
Anti-dieselling valve (carburettor models)
Automatic choke heater (carburettor models)
Engine coolant temperature sensor
Crankshaft speed/position sensor
Air charge temperature sensor
Throttle position sensor
Fuel temperature sensor
Fuel injectors

35 On models fitted with power steering, unbolt the power steering pump from its mounting bracket and move it clear of the engine, with reference to Section 21 of this Chapter. Note that there is no need to disconnect the fluid hoses, but make sure that the pump is adequately supported to avoid straining them.
36 On models fitted with air conditioning, unbolt the air conditioning compressor from its mounting bracket, and move it clear of the engine. **Do not** disconnect the hoses, but make sure that the compressor is adequately supported to avoid straining them.
37 Unscrew and remove the top engine-to-gearbox bolts which are accessible from the engine compartment. Note the location of the bolts, and note the positions of the earth strap and any wiring clips attached to the bolts (photo).
38 Unscrew the securing bolt, and disconnect the earth lead from the rear left-hand side of the cylinder head.
39 Unscrew the nuts securing the engine mountings to the engine mounting brackets.
40 Apply the handbrake, jack up the front of the vehicle and support it securely on axle stands.
41 Drain the engine oil into a suitable container.
42 Remove the starter motor.
43 Remove the exhaust downpipe with reference to Section 10 or 11 of this Chapter, as applicable.
44 Ensure that the steering wheel is positioned in the straight-ahead position, then remove the clamp bolt from the lower steering column clamp, swivel the plate to one side, and disconnect the lower steering column from the lower flexible coupling (photo).
45 Working inside the vehicle, place a wooden block under the clutch pedal to raise it fully against its stop, so holding the automatic adjuster pawl clear of the toothed quadrant.
46 Disconnect the clutch cable from the clutch release arm, and pass the cable through the bellhousing, with reference to Chapter 5 if necessary.
47 Support the gearbox with a trolley jack, using a block of wood between the jack and the gearbox to spread the load.
48 Unscrew and remove the remaining engine-to-gearbox bolts, and remove the bolt from the engine adaptor plate (photo). Recover any shims fitted between the sump and the gearbox when removing the lower engine-to-gearbox bolts.
49 Make a final check to ensure that all relevant wires, pipes and hoses have been disconnected to facilitate engine removal.
50 Attach a suitable hoist to the engine lifting brackets located at the front and rear of the cylinder head, and carefully take the weight of the engine.
51 To improve clearance in the engine compartment when lifting the engine, unbolt the engine mounting brackets from the cylinder block, and remove them (photo).
52 Detach the brake lines from the front suspension crossmember with reference to Chapter 10 if necessary (photo).
53 Support the crossmember with a jack (do not remove the jack from under the gearbox), then loosen the bolts securing the crossmember to the underbody. Remove the bolts from one side, and carefully lower the crossmember sufficiently to allow the sump to clear the steering rack and crossmember when pulling the engine forwards from the gearbox (photo).
54 Gently raise the engine, then pull it forwards to disconnect it from the gearbox. Ensure that the gearbox is adequately supported, and take care not to strain the gearbox input shaft. It may be necessary to rock the engine a little to release it from the gearbox.

55 Once clear of the gearbox, lift the engine from the vehicle, taking care not to damage the components in the engine compartment (photo).

Engine – removal leaving automatic transmission in vehicle

Note: *Refer to the warning at the end of Chapter 1, Section 9 before proceeding. A suitable hoist and lifting tackle will be required for this operation.*

56 Proceed as described in paragraphs 16 to 36 of this Section.
57 Unscrew and remove the top engine-to-transmission bolts which are accessible from the engine compartment. Note the location of the earth strap, vacuum pipe bracket, and transmission dipstick tube bracket, as applicable.
58 Proceed as described in paragraphs 38 to 44 of this Section.
59 Where applicable, remove the bolt securing the transmission fluid dipstick tube to the left-hand side of the cylinder block.
60 Working through the starter motor aperture, unscrew the four torque converter-to-driveplate nuts. It will be necessary to turn the crankshaft, using a suitable spanner on the crankshaft pulley bolt, in order to gain access to each bolt in turn through the aperture.
61 Support the transmission with a trolley jack, using a block of wood between the jack and the transmission to spread the load.
62 Unscrew and remove the remaining engine-to-transmission bolts, and remove the bolt from the engine adaptor plate. Recover any shims fitted between the sump and the transmission when removing the lower engine-to-transmission bolts. Where applicable, pull the blanking plug from the adaptor plate.
63 Proceed as described in paragraphs 49 to 53 of this Section.
64 Gently raise the engine, then pull the engine forwards to disconnect it from the transmission. Ensure that the torque converter is held firmly in place in the transmission housing, otherwise it could fall out resulting in fluid spillage and possible damage. It may be necessary to rock the engine a little to release it from the transmission.
65 Once clear of the transmission, lift the engine from the vehicle, taking care not to damage the components in the engine compartment.

Engine/manual gearbox assembly – removal and separation

Note: *Refer to the warning at the end of Chapter 1, Section 9 before proceeding. A suitable hoist and lifting tackle will be required for this operation.*

66 Proceed as described in paragraphs 16 to 36 of this Section.
67 Unscrew the securing bolt, and disconnect the earth lead from the rear left-hand side of the cylinder head.
68 Unscrew the nuts securing the engine mountings to the engine mounting brackets.
69 Jack up the vehicle and support it securely on axle stands. Ensure that there is enough working room beneath the vehicle.
70 To improve access, disconnect the exhaust downpipe from the manifold, and remove the exhaust system with reference to Section 10 or 11 of this Chapter, as applicable.
71 Drain the engine oil into a suitable container.
72 On models fitted with a catalytic converter, release the securing clips and withdraw the exhaust heat shield from under the vehicle for access to the propeller shaft.
73 Remove the propeller shaft as described in Section 19 of this Chapter.
74 Where applicable, bend back the locktabs, then unscrew the two bolts in each case securing the two anti-roll bar U-clamps to the vehicle underbody. Lower the anti-roll bar as far as possible.
75 Proceed as described in paragraphs 45 and 46 of this Section.
76 Support the gearbox with a trolley jack, using a block of wood between the jack and the gearbox to spread the load.
77 Unscrew the four nuts securing the gearbox crossmember to the vehicle underbody. Unscrew the central bolt securing the crossmember to the gearbox, and remove the crossmember. Note the position of the earth strap, where applicable. Recover the mounting cup, and where applicable the exhaust mounting bracket and heat shield.
78 Lower the gearbox slightly on the jack, then remove the securing circlip, and disconnect the speedometer drive cable from the gearbox.
79 Disconnect the wiring from the reversing lamp switch, and on models with fuel injection, disconnect the wiring from the vehicle speed sensor mounted in the side of the gearbox.
80 Unscrew the two securing bolts, and disconnect the gear linkage support bracket from the gearbox.
81 Using a suitable pin punch, drive out the roll-pin securing the gearchange rod to the gear linkage.
82 Attach a suitable hoist to the engine lifting brackets located at the front and rear of the cylinder head, and carefully take the weight of the engine. Arrange the lifting tackle so that the engine/gearbox assembly will assume a steep angle of approximately 40° to 45° as it is being removed.
83 To improve clearance in the engine compartment when lifting the engine, unbolt the engine mounting brackets from the cylinder block, and remove them.
84 Ensure that the steering wheel is positioned in the straight-ahead position, then remove the clamp bolt from the lower steering column clamp, swivel the plate to one side, and disconnect the lower steering column from the lower flexible coupling.
85 Detach the brake lines from the front suspension crossmember with reference to Chapter 10 if necessary.
86 Support the crossmember with a jack (do not remove the jack from under the gearbox), then loosen the bolts securing the crossmember to the underbody. Remove the crossmember securing bolts, and carefully lower the crossmember sufficiently to allow the engine sump to clear the steering rack and crossmember as the engine/gearbox assembly is removed.
87 Make a final check to ensure that all relevant wires, pipes and hoses have been disconnected to facilitate removal of the engine/gearbox assembly.
88 Raise the engine/gearbox, at the same time lowering the trolley jack which is supporting the gearbox.
89 Place a suitable rod across the vehicle underbody to support the gear linkage support bracket whilst the gearbox is removed.
90 Tilt the engine/gearbox assembly using the hoist and the trolley jack, until the assembly can be lifted from the vehicle. Take care not to damage surrounding components.
91 If the vehicle is to be moved, with the engine/gearbox assembly removed, temporarily refit the suspension crossmember and the anti-roll bar to the underbody, and reconnect the steering column to the intermediate shaft.
92 To separate the engine from the gearbox, proceed as follows.
93 Remove the starter motor.
94 Support the engine and gearbox horizontally on blocks of wood.
95 Unscrew the engine-to-gearbox bolts, noting the locations of the bolts, and the positions of the earth strap and any wiring clips attached to the bolts. Recover any shims fitted between the sump and the gearbox when removing the lower engine-to-gearbox bolts.
96 Unscrew the bolt from the engine adaptor plate.
97 Pull the engine and gearbox apart, taking care not to strain the gearbox input shaft. It may be necessary to rock the units slightly to separate them.

Engine/automatic transmission assembly – removal and separation

Note: *Refer to the warning at the end of Chapter 1, Section 9 before proceeding. A suitable hoist and lifting tackle will be required for this operation. Any suspected faults in the automatic transmission should be referred to a Ford dealer or automatic transmission specialist before removal of unit, as the specialist fault diagnosis equipment is designed to operate with the transmission in the vehicle.*

98 Proceed as described in paragraphs 16 to 36 of this Section.
99 Unscrew the securing bolt, and disconnect the earth lead from the rear left-hand side of the cylinder head.
100 Unscrew the nuts securing the engine mountings to the engine mounting brackets.
101 Jack up the vehicle and support it securely on axle stands. Ensure that there is enough working room beneath the vehicle.
102 To improve access, disconnect the exhaust downpipe from the manifold, and remove the exhaust system with reference to Section 10 or 11 of this Chapter, as applicable.
103 Drain the engine oil into a suitable container.
104 On models fitted with a catalytic converter, release the securing clips and withdraw the exhaust heat shield from under the vehicle for access to the propeller shaft.
105 Remove the propeller shaft as described in Section 19 of this Chapter.
106 Where applicable, bend back the locktabs, then unscrew the two bolts in each case securing the two anti-roll bar U-clamps to the vehicle underbody. Lower the anti-roll bar as far as possible.

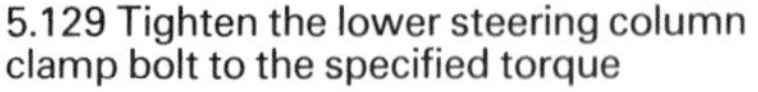

5.129 Tighten the lower steering column clamp bolt to the specified torque

5.131 Refilling the engine with oil

5.135 Tightening a suspension crossmember securing bolt

107 Support the transmission with a trolley jack, using a block of wood between the jack and the transmission to spread the load.
108 Unscrew the four bolts securing the transmission crossmember to the vehicle underbody. Unscrew the central bolt securing the cross-member to the transmission, and remove the crossmember. Note the position of the earth strap, where applicable. Recover the mounting cup, and where applicable the exhaust mounting bracket and heat shield.
109 Lower the transmission slightly on the jack.
110 Unscrew the unions and disconnect the fluid cooler pipes from the transmission. Plug the open ends of the pipes and the transmission to prevent dirt ingress and fluid leakage. Where applicable, detach the fluid cooler pipe bracket from the engine mounting bracket, and move it to one side.
111 Remove the two clips securing the selector rod, and detach the selector rod from the manual selector lever, and the selector lever on the transmission.
112 Disconnect the wiring from the starter inhibitor switch, kickdown solenoid, lock-up clutch, reversing lamp switch, and where applicable, the 3rd/4th gearchange solenoid.
113 Remove the securing screw, and disconnect the speedometer cable from the transmission extension housing. Plug the opening in the transmission to prevent dirt ingress.
114 Proceed as described in paragraphs 82 to 91 of this Section, substituting transmission for gearbox, and ignoring paragraph 89.
115 To separate the engine from the transmission, proceed as follows.
116 Remove the starter motor.
117 Support the engine and transmission horizontally on blocks of wood.
118 Working through the starter motor aperture, unscrew the four torque converter-to-driveplate nuts. It will be necessary to turn the crankshaft using a suitable spanner on the crankshaft pulley bolt in order to gain access to each nut in turn through the aperture.
119 Where applicable, remove the bolt securing the transmission fluid dipstick tube to the left-hand side of the cylinder block.
120 Unscrew the engine-to-transmission bolts, noting the locations of the bolts, and the positions of the earth strap and any wiring clips attached to the bolts. Recover any shims fitted between the sump and the transmission when removing the lower engine-to-transmission bolts.
121 Unscrew the bolt from the engine adaptor plate and, where applicable, pull the blanking plug from the adaptor plate.
122 Pull the engine and the transmission apart, ensuring that the torque converter is held firmly in place in the transmission housing, otherwise it could fall out resulting in fluid spillage and possible damage. It may be necessary to rock the units slightly to separate them.

Engine – refitting (manual gearbox in vehicle)

123 Reverse the procedure described in paragraphs 16 to 55, noting the following points.
124 Before attempting to refit the engine, check that the clutch friction disc is centralised as described in Chapter 5, Section 7.
125 Check that the clutch release arm and bearing are correctly fitted, and lightly grease the input shaft splines.
126 Check that the engine adaptor plate is correctly positioned on its locating dowels. If necessary, a cable tie can be used to temporarily secure the adaptor plate in position on the cylinder block using one of the engine-to-gearbox bolt holes.
127 If shims were fitted between the sump and the gearbox, refit them in their original locations when mating the engine to the gearbox. If the engine has been overhauled, where applicable fit the relevant shims as calculated during engine reassembly (see *'Sump – removal and refitting'* later in this Section).
128 Reconnect the clutch cable to the release arm with reference to Chapter 5, Section 3, ensuring that it is routed as noted during removal.
129 Ensure that the roadwheels and the steering wheel are in the straight-ahead position before reconnecting the lower steering column to the intermediate shaft, and tighten the clamp bolt to the specified torque (photo).
130 Refit the exhaust downpipe with reference to Section 10 or 11 of this Chapter, as applicable.
131 Fill the engine with the correct grade and quantity of oil (photo).
132 Check the throttle cable adjustment as described in Chapter 3.
133 Reconnect the coolant hoses to the coolant pump housing with reference to Section 8 of this Chapter.
134 Fill the cooling system with reference to Section 8 of this Chapter.
135 Tighten all fixings to the specified torque, where applicable (photo).

Engine – refitting (automatic transmission in vehicle)

136 Reverse the procedure in paragraphs 56 to 65 of this Section, noting the following points.
137 Check that the engine adaptor plate is correctly positioned on its locating dowels. If necessary, a cable tie can be used to temporarily secure the adaptor plate in position on the cylinder block using one of the engine-to-transmission bolt holes.
138 As the torque converter is only loosely engaged in the transmission, care must be taken to prevent the torque converter from falling out forwards. When the torque converter hub is fully engaged with the fluid pump drivegear in the transmission, distance 'A' in Fig. 7.8 (Chapter 7) must be as specified. Incorrect installation of the torque converter will result in damage to the transmission.
139 If shims were fitted between the sump and the transmission, refit them in their original locations when mating the engine to the transmission. If the engine has been overhauled, where applicable fit the relevant shims as calculated during engine reassembly (see *'Sump – removal and refitting'* later in this Section).
140 As the engine is installed, guide the torque converter studs through the holes in the driveplate. When the engine is positioned flush with the engine adaptor plate and the transmission housing, check that the torque converter is free to move axially a small amount before refitting and tightening the engine-to-transmission bolts.
141 Do not tighten the torque converter-to-driveplate nuts until the lower engine-to-transmission bolts have been fitted and tightened.
142 Ensure that the roadwheels and the steering wheel are in the straight-ahead position before reconnecting the lower steering column to the intermediate shaft.
143 Refit the exhaust downpipe with reference to Section 10 or 11 of this Chapter, as applicable.
144 Fill the engine with the correct grade and quantity of oil.
145 Check the throttle cable adjustment as described in Chapter 3.
146 Reconnect the coolant hoses to the coolant pump housing with reference to Section 8 of this Chapter.
147 Fill the cooling system with reference to Section 8 of this Chapter.
148 Tighten all fixings to the specified torque, where applicable.

Engine/manual gearbox assembly – reconnection and refitting

149 Reverse the procedure described in paragraphs 66 to 97, noting the following points.

150 Before attempting to reconnect the engine to the gearbox, check that the clutch friction disc is centralised as described in Chapter 5, Section 7.

151 Check that the clutch release arm and bearing are correctly fitted, and lightly grease the input shaft splines.

152 Check that the engine adaptor plate is correctly positioned on its locating dowels. If necessary, a cable tie can be used to temporarily secure the adaptor plate in position on the cylinder block using one of the engine-to-gearbox bolt holes.

153 If shims were fitted between the sump and the gearbox, refit them in their original locations when mating the engine to the gearbox. If the engine has been overhauled, where applicable fit the relevant shims as calculated during engine reassembly (see *'Sump – removal and refitting'* later in this Section).

154 Ensure that the roadwheels and the steering wheel are in the straight-ahead position before reconnecting the lower steering column to the intermediate shaft.

155 Reconnect the clutch cable to the release arm with reference to Chapter 5, Section 3, ensuring that it is routed as noted during removal.

156 Refit the propeller shaft as described in Section 19 of this Chapter.

157 Refit the exhaust system with reference to Section 10 or 11 of this Chapter, as applicable.

158 Fill the engine with the correct grade and quantity of oil.

159 Check the throttle cable adjustment as described in Chapter 3.

160 Reconnect the coolant hoses to the coolant pump housing with reference to Section 8 of this Chapter.

161 Fill the cooling system with reference to Section 8 of this Chapter.

162 Check and if necessary top up the gearbox oil level as described in Section 17 of this Chapter.

163 Tighten all fixings to the specified torque, where applicable.

Engine/automatic transmission assembly – reconnection and refitting

164 Reverse the procedure described in paragraphs 98 to 122 of this Section, noting the following points.

165 Check that the engine adaptor plate is correctly positioned on its locating dowels. If necessary, a cable tie can be used to temporarily secure the adaptor plate in position on the cylinder block using one of the engine-to-transmission bolt holes.

166 As the torque converter is only loosely engaged in the transmission, care must be taken to prevent the torque converter from falling out forwards. When the torque converter hub is fully engaged with the fluid pump drivegear in the transmission, distance 'A' in Fig. 7.8 (Chapter 7) must be as specified. Incorrect installation of the torque converter will result in damage to the transmission.

167 If shims were fitted between the sump and the transmission, refit them in their original locations when mating the engine to the transmission. If the engine has been overhauled, where applicable fit the relevant shims as calculated during engine reassembly (see *'Sump – removal and refitting'* later in this Section).

168 As the engine and transmission are mated together, guide the torque converter studs through the holes in the driveplate. When the engine is positioned flush with the engine adaptor plate and the transmission housing, check that the torque converter is free to move axially a small amount before refitting and tightening the engine-to-transmission bolts.

169 Do not tighten the torque converter-to-driveplate nuts until the lower engine-to-transmission bolts have been fitted and tightened.

170 Ensure that the roadwheels and the steering wheel are in the straight-ahead position before reconnecting the lower steering column to the intermediate shaft.

171 Reconnect the selector rod and adjust as described in Chapter 7, Section 7.

172 Refit the propeller shaft as described in Section 19 of this Chapter.

173 Refit the exhaust system with reference to Section 10 or 11 of this Chapter, as applicable.

174 Fill the engine with the correct grade and quantity of oil.

175 Check the throttle cable adjustment as described in Chapter 3.

176 Reconnect the coolant hoses to the coolant pump housing with reference to Section 8 of this Chapter.

177 Fill the cooling system with reference to Section 8 of this Chapter.

178 Check and if necessary top up the transmission fluid level as described in Chapter 7.

179 Tighten all fixings to the specified torque, where applicable.

Engine mountings – renewal

180 Proceed as described in Chapter 1, Section 57, but note that on certain models, it may be necessary to unbolt the engine mounting brackets from the cylinder block to allow sufficient clearance to remove the mountings.

Engine dismantling – general

181 Refer to Chapter 1, Section 19, paragraphs 1 to 8 inclusive.

182 A suitable selection of splined and Torx sockets will be required to remove many of the bolts when dismantling the engine.

183 Before dismantling the main engine components, the following externally mounted ancillary components can be removed, with reference to the relevant Chapters and the relevant Sections of this Chapter, where applicable.

Inlet manifold (and carburettor, where applicable) – see Section 10 or 11 of this Chapter, as applicable
Exhaust manifold – see Section 10 or 11 of this Chapter, as applicable.
Alternator
Coolant pump, and thermostat – see Section 8 of this Chapter
Alternator/coolant pump drivebelt tensioner – see Section 8 of this Chapter
Distributor cap, HT leads and spark plugs – see Section 14 or 15 of this Chapter, as applicable
Oil pressure warning lamp switch – see Section 23 of this Chapter
Crankshaft speed/position sensor – see Section 14 or 15 of this Chapter, as applicable
Oil filter – see Chapter 1, Section 3
Dipstick
Engine mounting brackets (if not already done)
Crankcase ventilation pipe and hoses
Clutch – see Section 16 of this Chapter
Alternator mounting bracket
Air conditioning compressor mounting bracket (where applicable)
Engine lifting brackets

Timing chain and sprockets – removal and refitting

Note: *Refer to the warning note at the end of Chapter 1, Section 9 before proceeding. A suitable puller will be required to remove the crankshaft pulley. A new crankshaft pulley bolt, a new timing chain tensioner plunger assembly, new upper and lower timing chain cover gaskets, and a new camshaft cover gasket and reinforcing sleeve sealing rings must be used on refitting.*

184 If the engine is in the car, carry out the following operations.

(a) Disconnect the battery negative lead
(b) To improve access, remove the radiator with reference to Section 8 of this Chapter. (It will be difficult to remove the crankshaft pulley with the radiator in place)
(c) On carburettor models, remove the air cleaner with reference to Section 10 of this Chapter
(d) On fuel injection models, remove the air intake hose, plenum chamber, and air cleaner lid as an assembly, with reference to Section 11 of this Chapter
(e) Disconnect the breather hose from the camshaft cover
(f) Remove the distributor cap and HT leads, and the rotor arm and housing with reference to Section 14 or 15 of this Chapter, as applicable

185 Proceed as described in paragraphs 247 to 256 inclusive of this Section.

186 Remove the alternator/coolant pump drivebelt with reference to Section 8 of this Chapter.

187 Slacken the crankshaft pulley bolt. Prevent the crankshaft from turning by engaging top gear (manual gearbox only) and having an assistant press the brake pedal hard, or by removing the starter motor and jamming the ring gear teeth with a lever.

188 Unscrew the bolt part way, and use a suitable puller to remove the crankshaft pulley. The legs of the puller must be suitably shaped to enable them to rest on the metal surfaces of the pulley. **Do not** use a puller on the rubber surface of the pulley (photos).

189 Loosen the alternator lower mounting through-bolt, then remove

5.188A Using a puller to remove the crankshaft pulley (viewed from underneath vehicle)

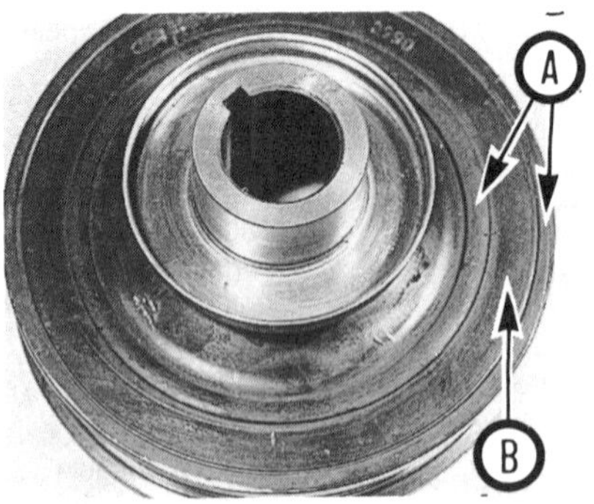

5.188B Position the legs of the puller on the metal surfaces of the pulley (A), not the rubber surface (B)

5.192 Oil pump chain tensioner securing screw (arrowed)

5.194A Lower timing chain guide upper securing bolt (arrowed)

5.194B Lower timing chain guide lower securing bolt (arrowed)

5.194C Withdrawing the lower timing chain guide

5.195 Sliding the double chain sprocket from the end of the crankshaft

5.196 Withdrawing the timing chain through the top of the timing case

5.202 Coppered link in timing chain aligned with crankshaft sprocket timing mark (arrowed)

the alternator upper mounting bolt, and swing the alternator away from the engine.

190 Unscrew the central securing bolt, and withdraw the drivebelt tensioner assembly.

191 Unscrew the eleven securing bolts, and remove the lower timing chain cover. Recover the rubber gasket.

192 Using a suitable Torx socket, unscrew the securing screw, and carefully withdraw the oil pump chain tensioner (photo).

193 Unscrew the Torx type securing bolt, and withdraw the oil pump sprocket, complete with the oil pump drive chain.

194 Unscrew the two lower timing chain guide securing bolts, noting their locations, and withdraw the timing chain guide through the top of the timing case (photos).

195 Remove the Woodruff key from the end of the crankshaft, prising it free with a screwdriver if necessary, then slide the double chain sprocket from the end of the crankshaft, and lift the chain from the sprocket (photo).

196 Withdraw the timing chain through the top of the timing case and, where applicable, remove the cable tie from the chain (photo).

197 The timing chain, sprockets and tensioner can be examined for wear and damage as described later in this Section.

198 Commence refitting as follows. Note that coppered links are provided in the timing chain to assist with refitting, but these can be difficult to see on a chain which has already been in service. If possible, position the coppered links as described during the following procedure. If the coppered links are not visible, the chain should still be refitted as described, but ignore the references to the coppered links.

199 Make sure that the slot for the Woodruff key in the end of the crankshaft is pointing vertically downwards. If necessary, temporarily refit the crankshaft pulley bolt in order to turn the crankshaft to the required position.

200 Lower the timing chain into the timing case from above, with the single coppered link at the bottom. If desired, use a cable tie to prevent the chain from dropping into the timing case, as during removal.

201 Locate the double chain sprocket loosely over the end of the crankshaft (larger sprocket nearest the crankcase), with the timing mark pointing vertically down.

202 Fit the chain over the inner, larger sprocket, aligning the coppered link in the chain with the timing mark on the sprocket (photo).

203 Coat the threads of the lower timing chain guide lower securing bolt with a suitable thread-locking compound.

204 Introduce the lower timing chain guide through the top of the

5.214 Fitting a new lower timing chain cover oil seal

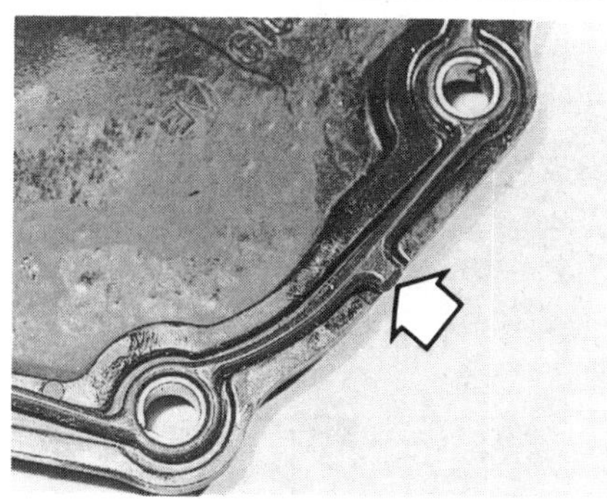
5.215 Lower timing chain cover rubber gasket in position. Ensure that lug on gasket engages with notch in cover (arrowed)

5.233 Disconnecting the heater coolant hose from the inlet manifold

timing case, manipulating the chain around the guide as necessary, then fit the chain guide lower securing bolt and tighten it finger-tight.

205 Push the double chain sprocket onto the crankshaft, engaging the notch in the sprocket with the groove in the end of the crankshaft.

206 Proceed as described in paragraphs 279 to 287 of this Section, but when fitting the chain over the camshaft sprockets, align the timing mark on each sprocket between the two corresponding coppered links in the chain.

207 Coat the threads of the lower timing chain guide upper securing bolt with a suitable thread-locking compound, then fit the bolt and tighten it finger-tight.

208 Proceed as described in paragraphs 288 to 291 of this Section.

209 Tighten the two chain guide securing bolts to the specified torque.

210 Proceed as described in paragraphs 292 to 300 of this Section.

211 Fit the oil pump drive chain around the outer crankshaft sprocket and the oil pump sprocket, then refit the oil pump sprocket, and tighten the securing bolt to the specified torque. If necessary, a screwdriver can be inserted through one of the holes in the sprocket to prevent it from turning as the securing bolt is tightened.

212 Refit the oil pump drive chain tensioner, and tighten the securing bolt to the specified torque.

213 Refit the Woodruff key to the end of the crankshaft.

214 Inspect the oil seal in the lower timing chain cover. If the oil seal is in good condition, the cover can be refitted as follows, but if the seal is damaged, or has been leaking, a new seal should be fitted to the cover. If necessary, carefully prise the old oil seal from the cover using a screwdriver, and drive in the new seal using a suitable metal tube. Make sure that the seal lip faces into the engine. Take care not to damage the timing chain cover (photo).

215 Fit the lower timing chain cover using a new rubber gasket. Note that the oil seal should be fitted dry (photo).

216 Loosely refit the timing chain cover securing bolts.

217 Refit the crankshaft pulley to the end of the crankshaft, and draw the pulley onto the crankshaft using the original securing bolt, at the same time centring the lower timing chain cover.

218 With the lower timing chain cover centralised, and the pulley fully home on the crankshaft, remove the old securing bolt, then fit a new bolt.

219 Tighten the **new** crankshaft pulley bolt to the specified torque, in the two stages given in the Specifications at the beginning of this Chapter. Prevent the crankshaft from turning as during removal.

220 Tighten the lower timing chain cover securing bolts.

221 Refit the drivebelt tensioner assembly, ensuring that the lug on the rear of the tensioner bracket engages with the corresponding hole in the cylinder block, and tighten the securing bolt.

222 Swing the alternator into position to align the upper mounting bolt hole with the corresponding hole in the drivebelt tensioner assembly, then refit the upper mounting bolt, and tighten the upper bolt and the lower through-bolt.

223 Refit the alternator/coolant pump drivebelt with reference to Section 8 of this Chapter.

224 If the engine is in the vehicle, reverse the operations described in paragraph 184.

225 Where applicable, refill the cooling system with reference to Section 8 of this Chapter.

Timing chain, sprockets and tensioner – examination and renovation

226 Examine all the teeth on the camshaft and crankshaft sprockets. If the teeth are 'hooked' in appearance, renew the sprockets.

227 Examine the chain tensioner plastic sprocket for wear. If excessive wear is evident, the complete tensioner assembly must be renewed, as the sprocket cannot be renewed independently. Note that the tensioner plunger assembly must be renewed whenever the timing chain is removed.

228 Examine the timing chain for wear. If the chain has been in operation for a considerable time, or if when held horizontally (rollers vertical) it takes on a deeply bowed appearance, renew it.

Cylinder head – removal and refitting (engine in vehicle)

Note: *Refer to the warning at the end of Chapter 1, Section 9, and the note at the beginning of the following sub-Section before proceeding. The cylinder head must not be removed when the engine is warm.*

229 Disconnect the battery negative lead.

230 On carburettor models, remove the air cleaner with reference to Section 10 of this Chapter.

231 On fuel injection models, remove the air intake hose, plenum chamber, and air cleaner lid as an assembly, with reference to Section 11 of this Chapter.

232 Drain the cooling system with reference to Section 8 of this Chapter.

233 Disconnect the heater coolant hose from the inlet manifold (photo).

234 Disconnect the breather hose from the camshaft cover, and unbolt the hose bracket from the left-hand side of the cylinder head (photo).

235 Unscrew the securing bolt and disconnect the earth lead from the left-hand rear of the cylinder head (photo).

236 Remove the distributor cap and HT leads, and the rotor arm and housing with reference to Section 14 or 15 of this Chapter, as applicable. If necessary, mark the HT leads to aid refitting.

237 The cylinder head can be removed either with or without the manifolds and fuel rail, where applicable (it is easiest to remove the head complete with the manifolds and fuel rail). If desired, the inlet manifold and the fuel rail can be unbolted and moved to one side, leaving the wires, hoses, pipes and cables connected, but care must be taken not to place any strain on them.

238 Unscrew the three securing nuts and disconnect the exhaust downpipe from the manifold. It may be necessary to jack up the front of the vehicle to gain access to the nuts (in which case apply the handbrake and support the front of the vehicle securely on axle stands). Recover the gasket.

239 If the inlet manifold and the fuel rail (where applicable) are to be removed with the cylinder head, disconnect all relevant wires, hoses, pipes and cables, otherwise, unbolt the manifold and the fuel rail, and move them to one side, ensuring that they are adequately supported. If the fuel rail is unbolted, be prepared for fuel spillage, and take adequate fire precautions. Refer to Section 14 or 15 of this Chapter, as applicable, for details.

240 Proceed as described in paragraphs 247 to 300 of this Section.

5.234 Hose bracket bolted to cylinder head (arrowed)

5.235 Disconnect the earth lead (arrowed) from the cylinder head

5.250 Removing the inlet camshaft sprocket bolt and the distributor rotor shaft

5.252A Upper timing chain guide securing lugs (arrowed)

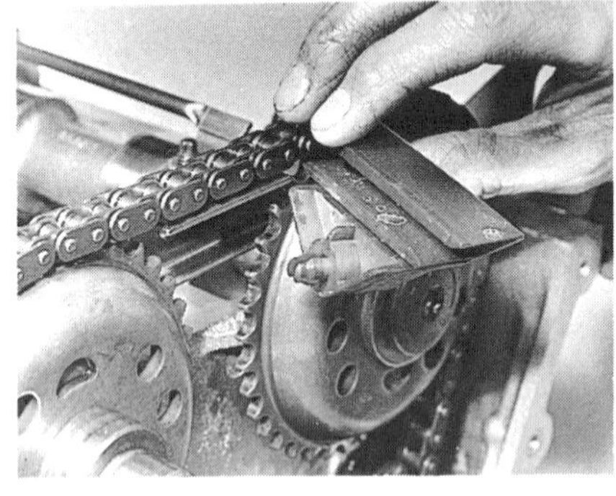

5.252B Removing the upper timing chain guide

5.254A Removing the chain tensioner arm pivot pin circlip

5.254B Withdrawing the pivot pin from the chain tensioner arm

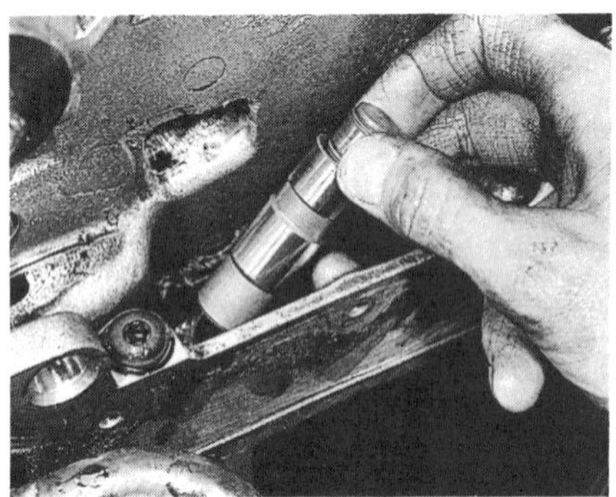

5.256 Lifting the chain tensioner plunger assembly from the cylinder head

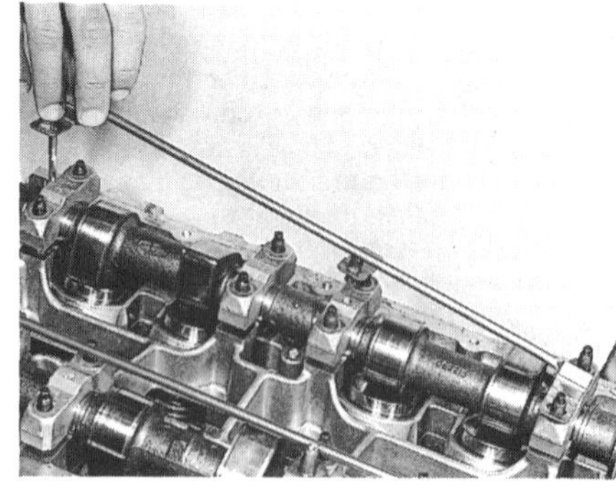

5.258 Lifting off a camshaft oil spray bar

241 With the cylinder head refitted, reverse the procedure described in paragraphs 229 to 239, noting the following points.

242 Refer to Section 14 or 15 of this Chapter when refitting the manifolds and fuel rail, as applicable.

243 Use a new gasket when reconnecting the exhaust downpipe to the manifold.

244 Ensure that the HT leads are reconnected correctly.

245 Fill the cooling system with reference to Section 8 of this Chapter.

Cylinder head – removal and refitting (engine removed)

Note: *New cylinder head bolts, a new cylinder head gasket, a new timing chain tensioner plunger assembly, a new upper timing chain cover gasket, and a new camshaft cover gasket and reinforcing sleeve sealing rings must be used on refitting. The new cylinder head bolts (both M11, and the three smaller M8 bolts) must be of the latest type with hexagonal heads.*

246 With the manifolds removed, proceed as follows.

247 Unscrew the eleven bolts and four nuts, and remove the camshaft cover. Recover the gasket.

248 Unscrew the four securing bolts and three studs, and remove the upper timing chain cover. Note the locations of the studs to aid refitting.

249 Using a spanner on the crankshaft pulley, turn the crankshaft to bring No 1 piston to the firing point. With No 1 piston at the firing point, the timing marks on the camshaft sprockets should be pointing away from each other, and should be approximately level with the top edge of the cylinder head. Timing notches are provided in the camshaft sprockets, and corresponding paint marks are provided on the outside edges of the sprockets (see Fig. 14.14).

250 Hold the inlet camshaft sprocket stationary using a tool similar to that shown in Chapter 1, Section 59, photo 59.17, then unscrew the camshaft sprocket bolt, and remove the distributor rotor shaft (photo).

251 Repeat the procedure given in paragraph 250 for the exhaust camshaft, but note that a spacer is fitted in place of the distributor rotor shaft.

252 Squeeze the upper timing chain guide securing lugs together, using pliers if necessary, and withdraw the guide from the plate at the front of the cylinder head (photos).

253 Mark the position of the timing chain in relation to the camshaft sprockets, so that the chain can be refitted in precisely its original position (ie, make alignment marks between each sprocket and a corresponding link in the chain), then slide the camshaft sprockets from the camshafts. Withdraw the sprockets and lay the timing chain over the exhaust side of the timing case, having eliminated the slack in the chain. Secure the chain using a cable tie through two of the chain links to prevent it from dropping off the crankshaft sprocket.

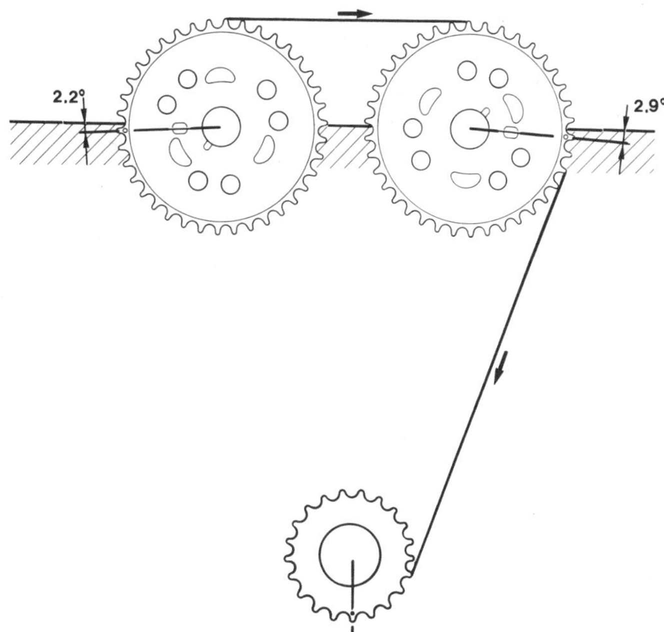

Fig. 14.14 Timing mark positions with No 1 cylinder at TDC – 2.0 litre DOHC engine (Sec 5)

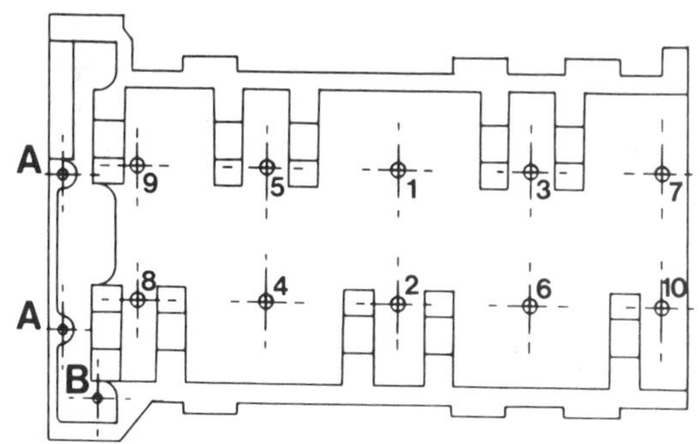

Fig. 14.15 Cylinder head bolt tightening sequence – 2.0 litre-DOHC engine (Sec 5)

A Long M8 bolts B Short M8 bolt

254 Using a suitable pair of pliers, extract the circlip from the chain tensioner arm pivot pin, taking care not to drop it into the timing case, then withdraw the pivot pin from the tensioner arm. If the pivot pin proves difficult to withdraw, an M6 bolt can be screwed into its end to facilitate removal (photos).

255 Lift the chain tensioner arm from the timing case.

256 Lift the chain tensioner plunger assembly from the cylinder head, and discard it (photo). **Warning**: *Take care when removing the plunger assembly, as there is a risk of injury if the piston flies out.*

257 Take note of the markings on the camshaft bearing caps, then progressively unscrew the bearing cap securing nuts.

258 Remove the bearing cap securing nuts, then lift off the camshaft oil spray bars, and the timing chain guide plate (photo).

259 Lift off the bearing caps, and then lift out the two camshafts (photos). Note that the inlet camshaft is normally identified by a green paint mark. If necessary, identify the camshafts so that they can be refitted in their correct positions.

260 Withdraw the cam followers from their locations in the cylinder head, keeping them in order so that they can be refitted in their original locations (photo). It is advisable to store the cam followers upright in an oil bath until they are to be refitted. Ensure that the depth of oil is sufficient to fully cover the cam followers.

261 Working at the front of the cylinder head, unscrew the three small M8 cylinder head bolts which are accessible through the timing case.

262 Working in the reverse order to that shown in Fig. 14.15, progressively loosen the remaining cylinder head bolts, and withdraw them from the cylinder head (photo).

5.259A Lifting off a camshaft bearing cap

5.259B Lifting out the exhaust camshaft

5.260 Withdrawing a cam follower

5.261 M8 cylinder head bolts (arrowed) located at front of cylinder head

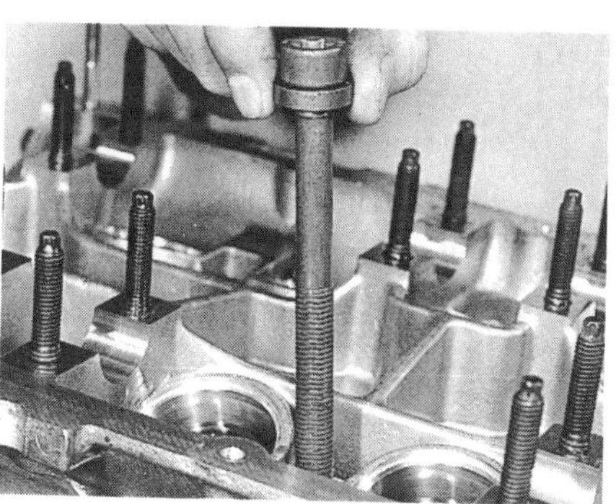

5.262 Withdrawing a cylinder head bolt

5.263 Lifting the cylinder head from the block

5.267 Fitting a new cylinder head gasket

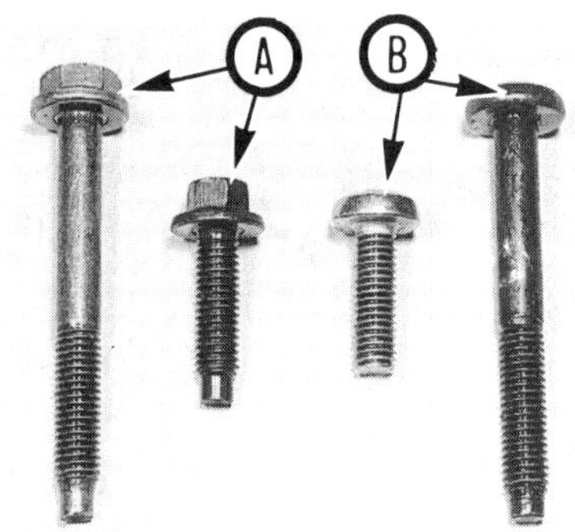

5.269 Use new cylinder head bolts with hexagonal heads (A), **not** earlier type Torx bolts (B)

5.270 Tightening a cylinder head bolt using an angle gauge

263 Lift the cylinder head from the block (photo). If the cylinder head is stuck, tap it free with a soft-faced mallet. Do not insert a lever into the joint between the cylinder head and block, as this may result in damage to the mating faces. Place the cylinder head on blocks of wood to prevent damage to the valves.
264 Recover the gasket, and the locating dowels if they are loose, noting the positions of the locating dowels.
265 Commence refitting as follows.
266 Turn the crankshaft so that No 1 piston is approximately 20.0 mm (0.8 in) before TDC. This precaution will prevent possible contact between the valves and pistons.
267 Make sure that the mating faces of the cylinder block and cylinder head are perfectly clean, then refit the locating dowels (where applicable) and locate a new gasket over the dowels. Note that the gasket can only fit in one position (photo). Do not use jointing compound.
268 Lower the cylinder head onto the gasket, making sure that the locating dowels engage.
269 Oil the threads of the **new** main cylinder head bolts, and insert them into their locations in the cylinder head. Note that the latest type cylinder head bolts with hexagonal heads should be used (photo).
270 Tighten the bolts in the order shown in Fig. 14.15 in the four stages given in the Specifications (photo).
271 Insert the three smaller M8 cylinder head bolts through the top of timing case, with reference to Fig. 14.15, and tighten them to the specified torque. Note that new bolts must be used, and that they should also be of the latest type with hexagonal heads.
272 Lubricate the cam follower bores in the cylinder head, and the cam followers themselves, then insert the cam followers into their original locations in the cylinder head.
273 Lubricate the camshaft bearing surfaces in the cylinder head and the bearing caps.
274 Lubricate the surfaces of the camshafts, then carefully lay the camshafts in their original positions in the cylinder head. Position the camshafts with the slots in their front ends pointing away from each other.
275 Refer to Fig. 14.16, and fit bearing caps L1, L3, L5, R1, R3, and R5, then lay the camshaft oil spray bars and the timing chain guide plate in position over the studs (photos).
276 Carefully tighten the bearing cap securing nuts by hand in the following stages to lower the camshafts into position.

Tighten the nuts for bearing caps L1 and R1 by half-a-turn (180°)
Tighten the nuts for bearing caps L5 and R5 by half-a-turn (180°)
Tighten the nuts for bearing caps L3 and R3 by half-a-turn (180°)

Continue to tighten the nuts in the small stages given until the bearing caps contact the cylinder head.

277 Fit bearing caps L2, L4, R2 and R4, and tap them into position on the cylinder head using light taps from a soft-faced mallet. Tighten the securing nuts evenly by hand.
278 Tighten all the bearing cap nuts to the specified torque in half-turn stages, using the following sequence.

L1 and R1
L5 and R5
L3 and R3
L2 and L4
R2 and R4

279 Fit a **new** chain tensioner plunger assembly to the housing in the cylinder head with the piston uppermost. Before fitting the new plunger assembly, refer to Fig. 14.17 and take note of the position of the piston. The assembly is normally supplied with the piston protruding slightly from the cylinder, or slightly below the top surface of the cylinder ('A'). If the new assembly is supplied with the piston partially unlatched ('B'), or fully unlatched with the latching ring visible ('C'), **it must not be used. Warning**: *Take care when installing the plunger assembly, as there is a risk of injury if the piston flies out.*

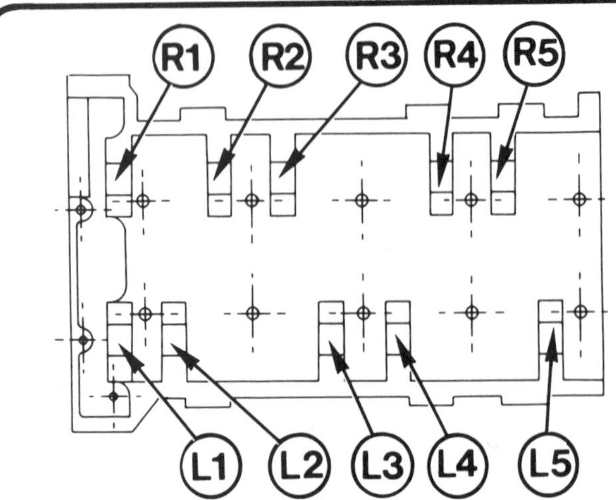

Fig. 14.16 Camshaft bearing cap tightening sequence (see text) – 2.0 litre DOHC engine (Sec 5)

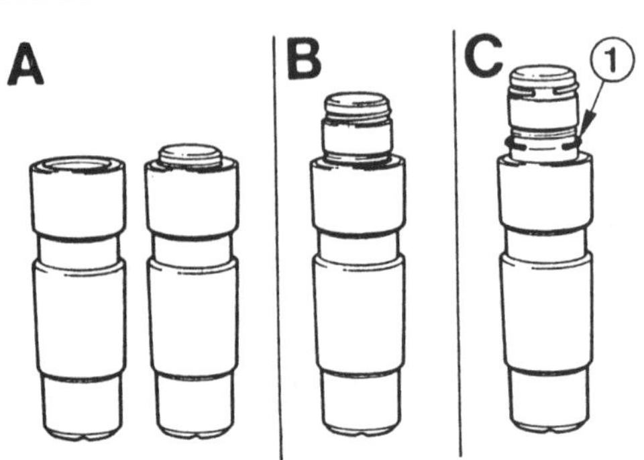

Fig. 14.17 Timing chain tensioner plunger assembly – 2.0 litre-DOHC engine (Sec 5)

A Piston retracted – plunger assembly usable
B Piston partially unlatched – discard plunger assembly
C Latching ring (1) visible – discard plunger assembly

5.275A Camshaft oil spray bars correctly fitted

5.275B Fitting the timing chain guide plate

5.283 Spacer and sprocket securing bolt fitted to end of camshaft, with camshaft in TDC position (timing marks arrowed)

280 Locate the chain tensioner arm in position, then insert the pivot pin, and secure it with the circlip. Take care not to drop the circlip into the timing case.
281 Release the cable tie securing the timing chain, and lay the chain over the exhaust camshaft sprocket, aligning the marks made previously on the chain and sprocket, so that the timing chain is taut on the exhaust side of the engine.
282 Fit the sprocket to the exhaust camshaft, with the camshaft in the TDC position (ie with the exhaust camshaft sprocket timing mark in line with the top edge of the cylinder head, pointing to the exhaust side of the engine – see paragraph 249). If necessary, use a pair of pliers on one of the unmachined sections of the camshaft to turn the camshaft to the TDC position. Take care not to damage the machined surfaces of the camshaft.
283 With the sprocket fitted, fit the spacer to the end of the camshaft, and tighten the securing bolt finger-tight (photo).
284 Lay the timing chain over the inlet camshaft sprocket, aligning the marks made previously on the chain and the sprocket.
285 Fit the sprocket to the inlet camshaft, with the camshaft in the TDC position (ie with the inlet camshaft sprocket timing mark in line with the top edge of the cylinder head, pointing to the inlet side of the engine – see paragraph 249). Again, turn the camshaft if necessary to enable the sprocket to be fitted.
286 With the sprocket fitted, fit the distributor rotor shaft to the end of the camshaft, and tighten the securing bolt finger-tight. Note that it is acceptable for the timing chain to sag slightly between the two pulleys.
287 Fit a new upper timing chain guide to the plate at the front of the cylinder head.
288 Turn the crankshaft clockwise until the inlet camshaft begins to turn.
289 If the chain tensioner plunger piston protrudes from the cylinder, unlatch the piston by pressing the chain tensioner arm down by hand.
290 If the plunger piston is below the top surface of the cylinder, a tool similar to that shown in Fig. 14.18 must be fabricated to unlatch the piston. It is suggested that 2.5 mm diameter welding rod is used to manufacture the tool. Use the tool to release the piston as follows.

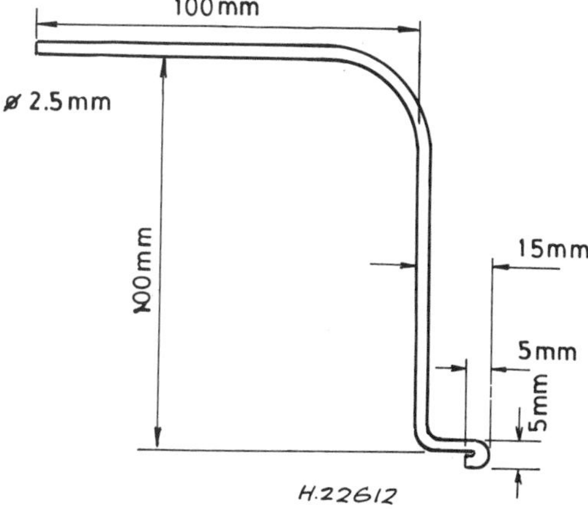

Fig. 14.18 Fabricated tool used to unlatch tensioner plunger piston – 2.0 litre DOHC engine (Sec 5)

291 Carefully lift the chain tensioner arm with a screwdriver, and insert the tool between the tensioner arm and the piston. Remove the screwdriver, and release the piston by pressing the tensioner arm down by hand. Carefully withdraw the tool once the piston has been released.
292 Tighten the camshaft sprocket securing bolts to the specified torque, holding the sprockets stationary as during removal.
293 Turn the crankshaft clockwise through two complete revolutions, and check that the timing marks on the camshaft sprockets are still aligned with the top face of the cylinder head as described in paragraph 249.
294 Turn the crankshaft clockwise through another complete revolution, and check that the timing marks on the camshaft sprockets are facing each other, directly in line with the top face of the cylinder head.
295 If the timing marks do not align as described, the timing chain has been incorrectly fitted (probably one chain link away from the correct position on one of the camshaft sprockets), and the chain should be removed from the sprockets and refitted again in the correct position as described previously.
296 Inspect the oil seal in the upper timing chain cover. If the oil seal is in good condition, the cover can be refitted as follows, but if the seal is damaged, or has been leaking, a new seal should be fitted to the cover. If necessary, carefully prise the old oil seal from the cover using a screwdriver, and drive in the new seal using a suitable metal tube. Make sure that the seal lip faces into the engine. Take care not to damage the timing chain cover.
297 Fit the upper timing chain cover using a new rubber gasket. Great care must be taken to avoid damage to the oil seal when passing the seal over the end of the inlet camshaft. Careful manipulation will be required (possibly using a thin feeler gauge) to avoid damage to the oil seal sealing lip. Note that the oil seal should be fitted dry.
298 Refit the timing chain cover securing bolts and studs in their original locations and tighten them to the specified torque (photo).
299 Remove the reinforcing sleeves from the camshaft cover, and renew the rubber sealing rings. Note that the four short reinforcing sleeves fit at the front of the cover (photo).
300 Refit the camshaft cover using a new gasket, and tighten the securing bolts and studs to the specified torque.

Cylinder head – dismantling and reassembly

Note: *A valve spring compressor will be required during this procedure. New valve stem oil seals should be used on reassembly.*

301 Proceed as described in Chapter 1, Section 62, noting the following points (photo).

- (a) *Ignore the references to removing and refitting the camshaft*
- (b) *Double valve springs are used on all the valves*
- (c) *Ignore the reference to inlet valve dampers*
- (d) *Refer to paragraph 302 of this Section if the cylinder head is to be inspected and renovated*

Cylinder head – inspection and renovation

302 Refer to Chapter 1, Section 24, noting the following points.

- (a) *Valve and valve seat cutting and regrinding can be carried out using conventional tools*
- (b) *The cylinder head cannot be resurfaced, and if the surface distortion exceeds the specified limits, the cylinder head must be renewed*

5.298 Upper timing chain cover securing stud locations (arrowed)

5.299 Fitting a camshaft cover reinforcing sleeve and sealing ring

5.301 Withdrawing the double valve springs from the cylinder head

5.313 Refitting the flywheel

5.314A Fitting a new flywheel securing bolt

5.314B Improvised tool used to hold flywheel when tightening securing bolts

Camshafts and cam followers – removal, inspection and refitting

Note: *Once the timing chain has been removed from the camshaft sprockets, do not turn the crankshaft until the timing chain has been correctly refitted – this is to prevent contact between the valves and pistons. A new timing chain tensioner plunger assembly, a new upper timing chain cover gasket, and a new camshaft cover gasket and reinforcing sleeve sealing rings must be used on refitting.*

303 If the engine is in the vehicle, carry out the following operations.

- (a) *Disconnect the battery negative lead*
- (b) *On carburettor models, remove the air cleaner with reference to Section 10 of this Chapter*
- (c) *On fuel injection models, remove the air intake hose, plenum chamber, and air cleaner lid as an assembly, with reference to Section 11 of this Chapter*
- (d) *Disconnect the breather hose from the camshaft cover*
- (e) *Remove the distributor cap and HT leads, and the rotor arm and housing with reference to Section 14 or 15 of this Chapter, as applicable. If necessary, mark the HT leads to aid refitting*

304 Proceed as described in paragraphs 247 to 260 inclusive of this Section.
305 Examine the surfaces of the camshaft journals and lobes and the contact surfaces of the cam followers for wear. If wear is excessive, considerable noise would have been noticed from the top of the engine when running, and new camshafts and followers must be fitted. It is unlikely that this level of wear will occur unless a considerable mileage has been covered. Note that the cam followers cannot be dismantled for renewal of individual components.
306 Check the camshaft bearing surfaces in the cylinder head and the bearing caps for wear. If excessive wear is evident, the only course of action available is to renew the cylinder head complete with bearing caps.
307 Check the cam follower bores in the cylinder head for wear. If excessive wear is evident, the cylinder head must be renewed.
308 Check the cam follower oil grooves and the oil ports in the cylinder head for obstructions.
309 Refit the cam followers and the camshafts as described in paragraphs 272 to 300 of this Section.
310 If the engine is in the vehicle, reverse the operations given in paragraph 303.

Flywheel/driveplate – removal, inspection and refitting

Note: *New flywheel/driveplate securing bolts must be used on refitting.*

311 Refer to Chapter 1, Section 27, noting the following points.
312 If the engine is in the car, refer to Section 16 of this Chapter when removing and refitting the clutch, where applicable.
313 There is no need to make alignment marks between the flywheel/driveplate and the end of the crankshaft, as the securing bolt holes are offset, so the flywheel/driveplate can only be fitted to the crankshaft in one position (photo).
314 The flywheel/driveplate securing bolts must be renewed when refitting, and the new bolts are supplied ready-coated with thread-locking compound (photos).
315 Check on the availability of new parts before contemplating renewal of the ring gear.

Crankshaft front oil seal – renewal

Note: *A suitable puller will be required to remove the crankshaft pulley. A new crankshaft pulley bolt, and a new lower timing chain cover gasket must be used on refitting.*

316 The crankshaft front oil seal is located in the lower timing chain cover.
317 If the engine is in the car, carry out the following operations.

- (a) *Disconnect the battery negative lead*
- (b) *To improve access, remove the radiator with reference to Section 8 of this Chapter. (It will be difficult to remove the crankshaft pulley with the radiator in place)*
- (c) *On fuel injection models, remove the air intake hose, plenum chamber, and air cleaner lid as an assembly, with reference to Section 11 of this Chapter*

318 Proceed as described in paragraphs 186 to 191 of this Section.
319 With the lower timing chain cover removed, prise the old oil seal from the cover using a screwdriver, and drive in the new seal using a suitable metal tube. Make sure that the seal lip faces into the engine. Take care not to damage the timing chain cover.

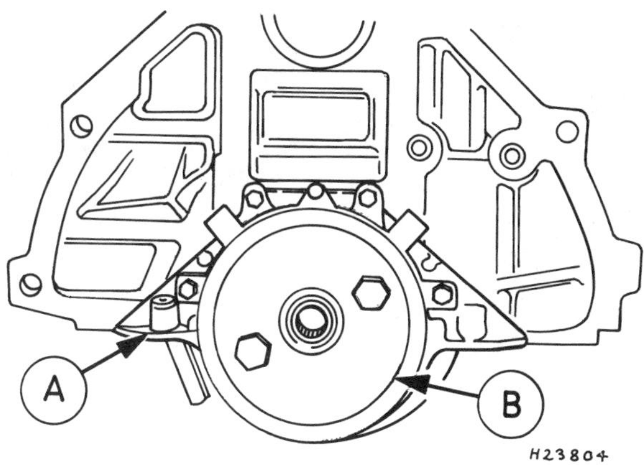

Fig. 14.19 Tool used to fit crankshaft rear oil seal – 2.0 litre-DOHC engine (Sec 5)

A Rear oil seal housing *B Special tool*

320 Refit the lower timing chain cover as described in paragraphs 215 to 223 of this Section.
321 If the engine is in the vehicle, reverse the operations given in paragraph 317.

Crankshaft rear oil seal – renewal

Note: *New flywheel/driveplate bolts must be used on refitting.*

322 Remove the flywheel/driveplate and the engine adaptor plate as described earlier in this Section.
323 Extract the seal using an oil seal removal tool if available. It may also be possible to remove the oil seal by drilling the outer face and using self-tapping screws and a pair of grips.
324 Clean the oil seal housing, then carefully wind a thin layer of tape around the edge of the crankshaft to protect the oil seal lip as the seal is installed.
325 Ideally, the new oil seal should be installed using a tool similar to that shown in Fig. 14.19. A suitable tool can be improvised using a metal tube of suitable diameter, a metal disc or flat bar, and two flywheel bolts. Draw the seal into position using the two flywheel bolts. Make sure that the seal lip faces into the engine.
326 With the oil seal installed, carefully pull the tape from the edge of the crankshaft.
327 Refit the engine adaptor plate and the flywheel/driveplate as described earlier in this Section.

Sump – removal and refitting

Note: *A new sump gasket will be required on refitting, and suitable sealing compound will be required to coat the sump and cylinder block mating faces. Shims may be required when mating the engine and gearbox/transmission – see text.*

328 Sump removal and refitting is far easier if the engine is removed from the vehicle, however if the engine is in the vehicle, proceed as follows. If the engine has been removed from the vehicle, proceed to paragraph 336.
329 Remove the clutch or automatic transmission, as applicable.
330 Remove the flywheel/driveplate and the engine adaptor plate as described earlier in this Section.
331 Drain the engine oil into a suitable container.
332 Ensure that the steering wheel is positioned in the straight-ahead position, then remove the clamp bolt from the lower steering column clamp, swivel the plate to one side, and disconnect the lower steering column from the lower flexible coupling.
333 Attach a suitable hoist to the engine lifting brackets located at the front and rear of the cylinder head, and carefully take the weight of the engine.
334 Detach the brake lines from the front suspension crossmember with reference to Chapter 10 if necessary.
335 Support the crossmember with a jack, then loosen the bolts securing the crossmember to the underbody. Remove the bolts and

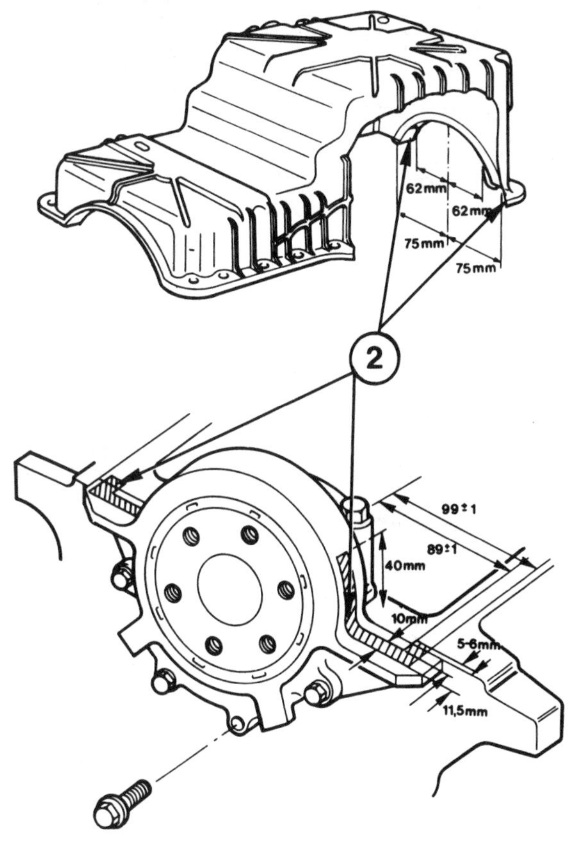

Fig. 14.20 Apply sealing compound to the sump/cylinder block mating faces at the points indicated (2) – 2.0 litre DOHC engine (Sec 5)

Dimensions are for guidance only

carefully lower the crossmember sufficiently to allow the sump to be removed.
336 If the engine has been removed, it is preferable to keep it upright until the sump has been removed to prevent sludge from entering the engine internals.
337 Unscrew the sump securing nuts and bolts, and withdraw the sump from the engine. If the sump is stuck, gently tap it sideways to free it (the sump will not move far sideways, as it locates on studs in the cylinder block). Do not prise between the mating faces of the sump and cylinder block. Recover the gasket.
338 Thoroughly clean the mating faces of the cylinder block and sump.
339 Commence refitting by locating a new gasket in the grooves in the sump.
340 Apply a suitable sealing compound to the faces of the cylinder block and sump at the points indicated in Fig. 14.20.
341 Apply suitable thread-locking compound to the sump securing studs and bolts, then locate the sump on the cylinder block and fit the securing nuts and bolts, but do not fully tighten them at this stage (photos).
342 Align the sump so that its end faces and the cylinder block are flush. To do this, use a straight-edge. If the sump cannot be positioned so that the faces of the cylinder block and sump are flush, measure the difference in height using a feeler gauge as shown (photo).
343 Tighten the sump securing nuts and bolts to the specified torque, then repeat the measurement made in paragraph 342. If the end faces of the sump and cylinder block are not flush, suitable shims must be fitted (available from a Ford dealer) between the sump and the gearbox/transmission to eliminate the clearance when mating the engine to the

5.341A Fitting the sump

5.341B Applying thread-locking compound to a sump securing bolt

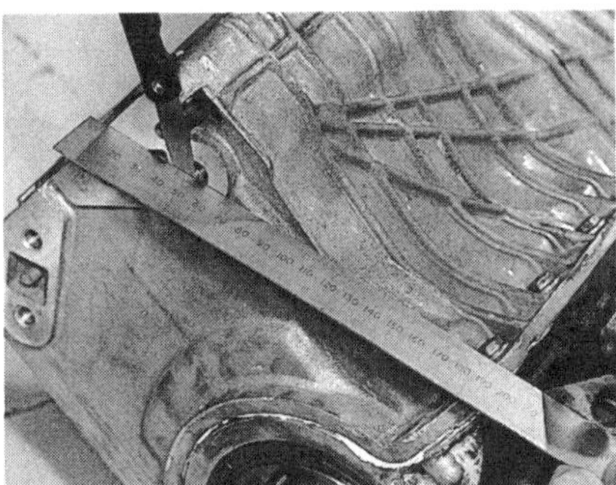
5.342 Measuring the clearance between the cylinder block and sump end faces

5.353A Oil pump securing bolts (arrowed)

5.353B Withdrawing the oil pump

5.363 Removing the oil pump cover

gearbox/transmission. Note that shims should be fitted at both sides of the sump, as required. Select suitable shims from those listed in the following table.

Clearance measured	Shims required
0 to 0.25 mm	*No shims required*
0.25 to 0.29 mm	*0.15 mm (silver)*
0.30 to 0.44 mm	*0.30 mm (light blue)*
0.45 to 0.59 mm	*0.45 mm (red)*
0.60 to 0.75 mm	*0.60 mm (black)*

344 If the engine is in the vehicle, proceed as follows.
345 Reverse the procedure described in paragraphs 329 to 335, noting the following points.
346 Ensure that the roadwheels and the steering wheel are in the straight-ahead position before reconnecting the lower steering column to the intermediate shaft.
347 Fill the engine with the correct grade and quantity of oil.
348 Refit the engine adaptor plate and the flywheel/driveplate as described earlier in this Section.
349 Refit the gearbox or automatic transmission as described in Section 17 or 18 of this Chapter, as applicable, ensuring that the required shims are fitted between the sump and the gearbox/transmission.
350 Tighten all fixings to the specified torque where applicable.

Oil pump – removal and refitting

Note: *A suitable puller will be required to remove the crankshaft pulley. A new crankshaft pulley bolt, a new lower timing chain cover gasket, and a new oil pump gasket must be used on refitting.*

351 If the engine is in the car, carry out the following operations.

- *(a) Disconnect the battery negative lead*
- *(b) To improve access, remove the radiator with reference to Section 8 of this Chapter. (It will be difficult to remove the crankshaft pulley with the radiator in place)*
- *(c) On fuel injection models, remove the air intake hose, plenum chamber, and air cleaner lid as an assembly, with reference to Section 11 of this Chapter*

352 Proceed as described in paragraphs 186 to 193 of this Section.
353 Unscrew the four securing bolts and withdraw the oil pump from the cylinder block (photos). Recover the gasket.
354 If desired, the pump can be dismantled and inspected as described later in this Section.
355 Thoroughly clean the mating faces of the pump and the cylinder block.
356 Prime the pump by injecting clean engine oil into it and turning it by hand.
357 Place a new gasket on the oil pump flange, ensuring that the gasket is correctly located so that its holes align with the oil passages in the pump.
358 Fit the oil pump, and tighten the securing bolts to the specified torque.
359 Proceed as described in paragraphs 211 to 223 of this Section.
360 If the engine is in the vehicle, reverse the operations described in paragraph 351.

Oil pump – dismantling, inspection and reassembly

361 The oil pump can be dismantled for cleaning, but if any of the components are worn, the pump must be renewed as an assembly.
362 To dismantle the pump, proceed as follows.
363 Unscrew the two securing bolts, and remove the pump cover (photo).
364 Lift the inner and outer rotors from the pump casing.
365 Unscrew the pressure relief valve plug from the pump cover, recover the washer, and withdraw the spring and plunger (photos).
366 Thoroughly clean all components in petrol or paraffin, and wipe dry using a non-fluffy rag.
367 Examine the rotors and the pump casing for signs of excessive wear on the machined surfaces. If wear is evident, the complete pump assembly must be renewed, as spare parts are not available individually.
368 Commence reassembly by lubricating the relief valve plunger. Fit the plunger and the spring, and screw the plug into place, ensuring that the washer is in place under the plug.
369 Lubricate the rotors, and fit them to the pump casing with the punch marks facing the pump cover (photo).

5.365A Unscrew the pressure relief valve plug and washer ...

5.365B ... and withdraw the spring and plunger

5.369 The punch marks (arrowed) on the oil pump rotors must face the pump cover

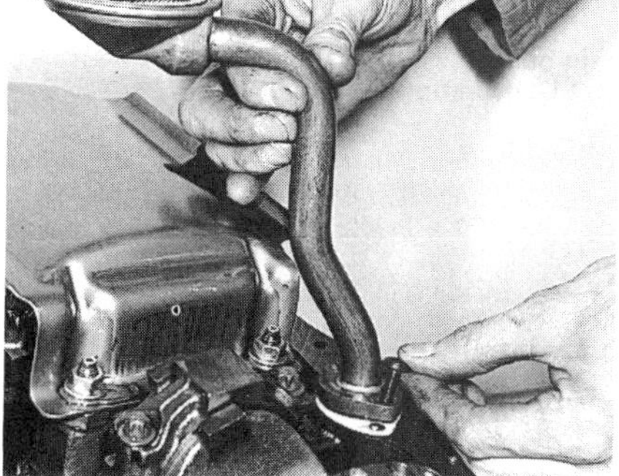

5.376 Removing the oil pick-up pipe

5.377 Withdrawing the oil baffle

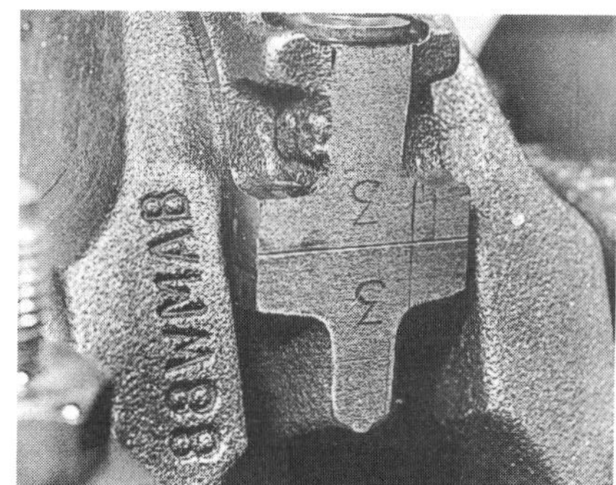

5.378 Big-end cap and connecting rod identification marks

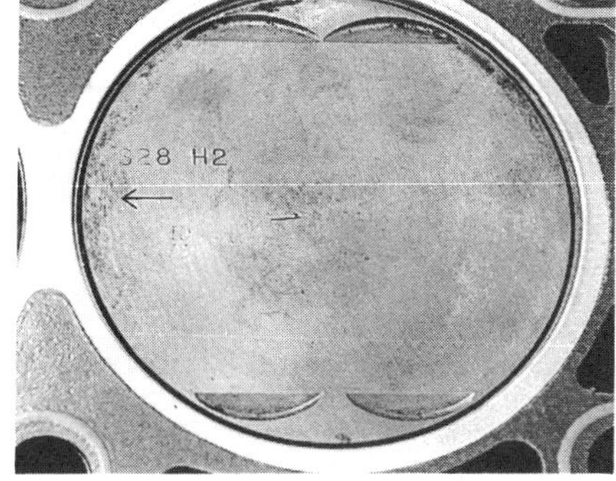

5.380 The arrow on the piston crown must point towards the front of the engine

5.388 Unscrewing a sump mounting plate securing bolt

5.389 Main bearing cap identification mark (arrowed)

370 Refit the pump cover and tighten the securing bolts.
371 Prime the pump before refitting as described in paragraph 356.

Oil pump drive chain and sprockets – examination and renovation

372 Examine all the teeth on the sprockets. If the teeth are 'hooked' in appearance, renew the sprockets.
373 Examine the chain tensioner for wear and renew it if necessary.
374 Examine the chain for wear. If it has been in operation for a considerable time, or if when held horizontally (rollers vertical) it takes on a deeply bowed appearance, renew it.

Pistons and connecting rods – removal and refitting

Note: *New connecting rod bolts and a new oil pick-up pipe gasket must be used on refitting.*

375 Remove the sump and the cylinder head as described earlier in this Section.
376 Unscrew the two securing bolts, and remove the oil pick-up pipe (photo). Recover the gasket.
377 Unscrew the four securing nuts and withdraw the oil baffle from the studs on the main bearing caps (photo).
378 Proceed as described in Chapter 1, Section 33, paragraphs 2 to 14, noting the following points (photo).
379 Take note of the orientation of the bearing shells during dismantling, and ensure that they are fitted correctly during reassembly.
380 When fitting the pistons, ensure that the arrow on the piston crown and the letter 'F' on the face of the connecting rod are pointing towards the front of the engine (photo).
381 Use new connecting rod bolts on reassembly, and before fitting, oil the threads and the contact faces of the bolts. Tighten the bolts in the three stages given in the Specifications at the beginning of this Chapter.
382 Refit the oil baffle and tighten the securing nuts.
383 Clean the mating faces of the cylinder block and the oil pick-up pipe, and refit the pick-up pipe using a new gasket.
384 Refit the cylinder head and the sump as described earlier in this Section.

Crankshaft and main bearings – removal and refitting

Note: *A new crankshaft rear oil seal and a new rear oil seal housing gasket should be used on refitting.*

385 With the engine removed from the vehicle, remove the timing chain and crankshaft sprocket, and the flywheel/driveplate as described previously in this Section.
386 Remove the pistons and connecting rods as described previously in this Section. If no work is to be done on the pistons and connecting rods, there is no need to push the pistons out of the cylinder bores.

387 Unbolt the crankshaft rear oil seal housing and remove it from the rear of the cylinder block. Recover the gasket.
388 Unscrew the two securing bolts and remove the sump mounting plate from the front of the cylinder block (photo).
389 Check the main bearing caps for identification marks, and if necessary use a centre punch to identify them (photo).
390 Before removing the crankshaft, check that the endfloat is within the specified limits by inserting a feeler gauge between the centre crankshaft web and one of the thrustwashers (the thrust washers are fitted to the crankcase, not the bearing cap). This will indicate whether or not new thrustwashers are required.
391 Unscrew the bolts and tap off the main bearing caps complete with bearing shells.
392 Lift the crankshaft from the cylinder block, and remove the rear oil seal if it is still in place on the crankshaft.
393 Extract the bearing shells, and recover the thrustwashers, keeping them identified for location.
394 The crankshaft and bearings can be examined and if necessary renovated as described later in this Section.
395 Commence refitting as follows.
396 Wipe the bearing shell locations in the crankcase, and the crankshaft journals with a soft non-fluffy rag.
397 If the old main bearing shells are to be renewed (not to do so is a false economy, unless they are virtually new) fit the five upper halves of the main bearing shells to their locations in the crankcase.
398 Fit the thrustwashers to the centre main bearing location, using a little grease to retain them if necessary. The oil grooves in the thrustwashers must face outwards (ie facing the crankshaft webs). Note that where standard thrustwashers have been fitted in production, the centre main bearing is unmarked, but if oversize (0.38 mm) thrustwashers have been fitted, the centre main bearing will carry a yellow paint mark.
399 Lubricate the crankshaft journals and the upper and lower main bearing shells with clean engine oil, then carefully lower the crankshaft into the crankcase.
400 Lubricate the crankshaft main bearing journals again, and then fit the main bearing caps in their correct locations, with the arrows on the caps pointing towards the front of the engine.
401 Fit the main bearing cap bolts, noting that the studded bolts secure bearing caps Nos 3 and 5.
402 Lightly tighten all the securing bolts, then progressively tighten all bolts to the specified torque.
403 Check that the crankshaft rotates freely. Some stiffness is to be expected with new components, but there must be no tight spots or binding.
404 Check that the crankshaft endfloat is within the specified limits by inserting a feeler gauge between the centre crankshaft web and the thrustwashers.
405 Refit the sump mounting plate to the front of the cylinder block, and tighten the securing bolts to the specified torque.
406 Carefully wind a thin layer of tape around the rear edge of the crankshaft to protect the oil seal lips as the rear oil seal is installed.
407 Refit the crankshaft rear oil seal housing, using a new gasket, and tighten the securing bolts to the specified torque.
408 Ideally, the new oil seal should be installed using a tool similar to that shown in Fig. 14.19. A suitable tool can be improvised using a metal tube of suitable diameter, a metal disc or flat bar, and two flywheel bolts. Draw the seal into position using the two flywheel bolts. Make sure that the seal lip faces into the engine.
409 With the oil seal installed, carefully pull the tape from the edge of the crankshaft.
410 Refit the pistons and connecting rods as described previously in this Section.
411 Refit the flywheel/driveplate, and the timing chain and crankshaft sprocket as described previously in this Section.

Crankshaft and bearings – examination and renovation

412 Proceed as described in Chapter 1, Section 36, noting the following.
413 Production bearing undersizes are indicated as follows.

Yellow or red paint marks on crankshaft – standard diameter main bearing journals
Green line on crankshaft front counterweight – main bearing journals 0.25 mm undersize
Green spot on counterweight – big-end bearing journals 0.25 mm undersize

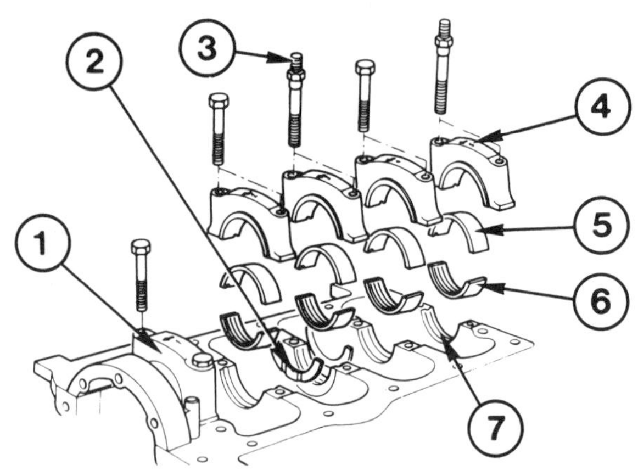

Fig. 14.21 Crankshaft main bearings and associated components – 2.0 litre DOHC engine (Sec 5)

1 Bearing cap
2 Thrustwasher
3 Stud for oil baffle
4 Identification markings
5 Bearing shell without oil groove
6 Bearing shell with oil groove
7 Bearing seat in cylinder block

Examination and renovation – general

414 Refer to Chapter 1, Section 38, but note that the connecting rod bolts should be renewed on reassembly, and when renewing the cylinder head bolts, the latest type bolts with hexagonal heads should always be used.

Engine reassembly – general

415 Proceed as described in Chapter 1, Section 39, noting the following points.
416 If they have been removed, new cylinder head bolts (both M11 and M8, of the latest type with hexagonal heads), flywheel bolts, and connecting rod bolts must be used.
417 After reassembling the main engine components, refer to paragraph 183 of this Section and refit the ancillary components listed, referring to the Sections indicated where necessary.

Initial start-up after overhaul or major repair

418 Refer to Chapter 1, Section 40, but note that when the engine is first started, a metallic tapping noise may be heard. This is due to the timing chain tensioner plunger assembly taking time to pressurize with oil, resulting in a temporarily slack chain. The noise should stop after a short time, once oil pressure has built up.

6 Cooling system – general

Coolant mixture – general

1 From 1992, the cooling system on all models is filled with a long-life coolant mixture in production (4 Year Longlife Engine Coolant/Super Plus 40). The manufacturers do not specify any renewal intervals for this later type of coolant, as it is intended to last the lifetime of the vehicle.
2 Provided any topping up is carried out with a similar coolant mixture of the correct strength, coolant renewal is unnecessary. It is advisable to renew the coolant if the vehicle has covered a particularly high mileage, or if the history of the car is uncertain, but this is up to the discretion of the individual owner.

Radiator – removal and refitting

3 On all later models, the radiator is secured to the engine compartment front panel using clips and locking pegs.
4 To remove the radiator, disconnect the relevant hoses, and if desired remove the cooling fan shroud and fan assembly with reference to Chapter 2, Section 7, then proceed as follows.
5 To release the top of the radiator, working through the cut-outs in the engine compartment front panel, remove the two radiator upper locking pegs (photo).

6.5 Removing a radiator upper locking peg

6 Working under the front of the vehicle, remove the two radiator lower mounting bolts.
7 Support the radiator from underneath, then squeeze the upper radiator locking pegs to release them from the engine compartment front panel, and lower the radiator assembly from the vehicle.
8 Refitting is a reversal of removal, with reference to Chapter 2, Section 7.

7 Cooling system – 1.6 litre CVH engine

General
1 The cooling system on 1.6 litre CVH engines is similar to that described for 1.8 litre CVH engines in Chapter 2.
2 Refer to Section 6 of this Chapter when removing the radiator.
3 All other procedures are as described in Chapter 2, although the components may differ in detail.

8 Cooling system – 2.0 litre DOHC engine

General description
1 Refer to Chapter 2, Section 1, noting the following.
2 The coolant pump is driven by the alternator drivebelt.
3 An electrically-operated cooling fan is fitted, operated by a switch in the thermostat housing.
4 The thermostat is located in a housing at the front of the inlet manifold.

Cooling system – draining
5 The procedure is similar to that described in Chapter 2, Section 3, noting the following points.

(a) A drain plug is fitted to the bottom right-hand side of the radiator
(b) No cylinder block drain plug is fitted

Cooling system – flushing
6 Proceed as described in Chapter 2, Section 4, noting the following points.
7 There is no drain plug in the cylinder block, so the engine should be flushed until water runs clear from the radiator bottom hose.
8 To reverse flush the engine, remove the thermostat and insert the hose into the inlet manifold.

Cooling system – filling
9 Refer to Chapter 2, Section 5, ignoring the reference to the bleed spigot on the thermostat housing.

Radiator – removal and refitting
10 Refer to Section 6 of this Chapter. Note that two cooling fans may be fitted on certain models.

Thermostat – removal and refitting
11 Disconnect the battery negative lead.
12 Drain the cooling system with reference to paragraph 5 of this Section.
13 On fuel injection models, for access to the thermostat housing, loosen the clips and remove the air intake tube which connects the plenum chamber to the inlet manifold.
14 Disconnect the coolant hoses from the thermostat housing (photos).
15 Disconnect the wiring plug from the cooling fan switch mounted in the thermostat housing (photo).
16 Unscrew the three securing bolts, and withdraw the thermostat housing (photo).
17 Manipulate the thermostat from the inlet manifold and recover the O-ring. If it is necessary to prise the thermostat out, take care not to damage the surface of the housing in the inlet manifold.
18 Refitting is a reversal of removal, bearing in mind the following points.
19 Ensure that the O-ring seal is correctly fitted around the edge of the thermostat.
20 When fitting the thermostat to the inlet manifold, ensure that the relief valve is located in the 12 o'clock position (photo).
21 Tighten the thermostat housing securing bolts to the specified torque.
22 Refill the cooling system with reference to Section 6 of this Chapter.

Coolant pump – removal and refitting
Note: *A new O-ring seal must be used on refitting.*

23 Disconnect the battery negative lead.
24 On fuel injection models, for access to the coolant pump, remove the air intake hose, plenum chamber, and air cleaner lid as an assembly, with reference to Section 11 of this Chapter.

8.14A Disconnect the coolant hoses ...

8.14B ... from the thermostat housing

8.15 Disconnect the cooling fan switch wiring plug

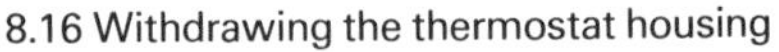
8.16 Withdrawing the thermostat housing

8.20 Thermostat relief valve (arrowed) should be located in the 12 o'clock position

8.28 Withdrawing the coolant pump from the cylinder block (engine removed)

25 Drain the cooling system with reference to paragraph 5 of this Section.

26 Remove the coolant pump/alternator drivebelt as described later in this Section.

27 If the pump pulley is to be removed, it is easiest to do this with the pump in position as follows. Prevent the pulley from rotating using a strap wrench (which can be improvised using an old drivebelt and a large socket and wrench), and unscrew the four pulley securing bolts. Withdraw the pulley.

28 Position a suitable container beneath the coolant pump to catch the coolant which will be released as the pump is removed, then unscrew the five securing bolts and withdraw the pump from the housing in the cylinder block (photo). Recover the O-ring seal.

29 Before refitting, clean the mating faces of the coolant pump and the cylinder block.

30 Refitting is a reversal of removal, bearing in mind the following points.

31 Use a new O-ring seal (photo).

32 Tighten the coolant pump securing bolts, and where applicable the pump pulley securing bolts to the specified torque.

33 On completion, refill the cooling system with reference to Section 6 of this Chapter.

Coolant pump housing hose connections – modification

34 On models up to May 1990, the coolant hoses were connected to the coolant pump housing as shown in Fig. 14.22.

35 On models from May 1990, the heater hose (A) and the expansion tank hose (B) connections were swapped over.

36 If the hoses are disconnected on earlier models, such as during engine removal, they should be reconnected as on later models, ie connect the heater hose to connection 'B' and connect the expansion tank hose to connection 'A' – see Fig. 14.22. This will prevent the possibility of noises from the heater matrix due to air in the system.

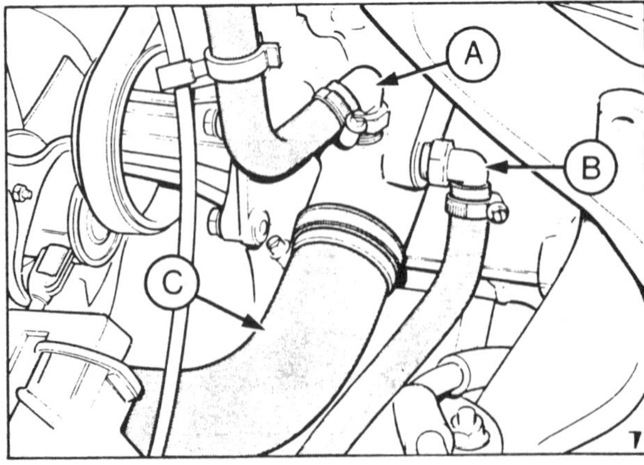

Fig. 14.22 Coolant pump housing hose connections – 2.0 litre-DOHC engine (Sec 8)

A Heater hose connection – up to May 1990
B Expansion tank hose connection – up to May 1990
C Bottom radiator hose

Coolant pump/alternator drivebelt – checking, renewal and tensioning

37 Three different types of drivebelt arrangement are used depending on model. On models without power steering, the drivebelt is tensioned by moving the alternator. On models with power steering, the power steering pump is also driven by the coolant pump/alternator drivebelt, and an automatic belt tensioner is fitted. On models with air conditioning, the drivebelt drives the alternator, coolant pump, power steering pump, and air conditioning compressor, and an automatic belt tensioner is fitted.

38 At the intervals specified in *'Routine maintenance'* at the beginning of this manual, the condition of the drivebelt should be checked, and on models without power steering, the tension should be checked and if necessary adjusted.

39 Check the full length of the drivebelt for cracks or deterioration. It will be necessary to turn the engine in order to check the portion of the belt in contact with the pulleys. If a drivebelt is unserviceable, renew it as follows.

40 On models without power steering, loosen the alternator mounting and adjustment bolts, and pivot the alternator towards the cylinder block. Slip the drivebelt from the pulleys.

41 On models with power steering, the automatic tensioner can be released using a 17 mm socket and a wrench on the boss in the centre of the pulley. Lever the tensioner assembly clockwise, and slide the belt from the pulleys, then slowly release the tensioner.

42 To fit a new belt on models without power steering, slide the belt over the pulleys, then lever the alternator away from the cylinder block until the specified belt tension is achieved. Lever the alternator using a plastic or wooden lever at the pulley end to prevent damage. It is helpful to partially tighten the adjustment link bolt before tensioning the drivebelt. When the correct tension is achieved, tighten all the bolts.

43 To fit a new belt on models without power steering, lever the tensioner clockwise as during removal, then slide the belt over the pulleys, and slowly release the tensioner.

Coolant pump/alternator drivebelt tensioner (models with power steering) – removal and refitting

44 Remove the coolant pump/alternator drivebelt as described in the previous sub-Section.

45 Loosen the alternator lower mounting through-bolt, then remove the alternator upper mounting bolt, and swing the alternator away from the engine.

46 Unscrew the central securing bolt, and withdraw the drivebelt tensioner assembly (photo).

47 Commence refitting by positioning the tensioner on the cylinder block, ensuring that the lug on the rear of the tensioner bracket engages with the corresponding hole in the cylinder block. Tighten the securing bolt.

48 Swing the alternator into position to align the upper mounting bolt hole with the corresponding hole in the drivebelt tensioner assembly, then refit the upper mounting bolt, and tighten the upper bolt and the lower through-bolt.

49 Fit the drivebelt using a reversal of the removal procedure, and release the tensioner to tension the drivebelt.

50 Observe the tensioner indicator, which should be central in its slot – see Fig. 14.26.

8.31 Coolant pump O-ring (arrowed)

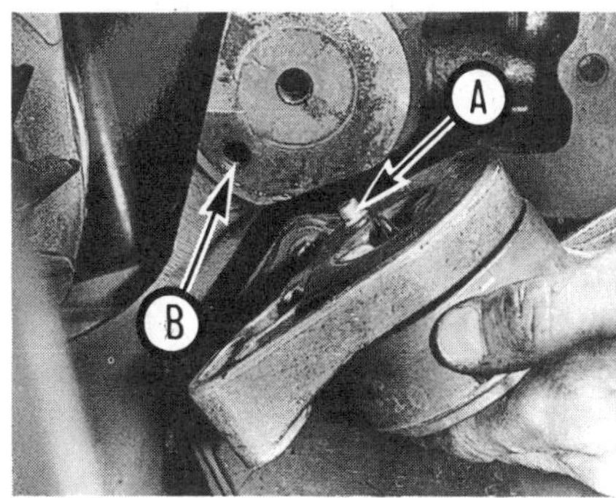

8.46 Withdrawing the coolant pump/alternator drivebelt tensioner assembly. Note lug (A) on tensioner which engages with hole (B) in mounting bracket

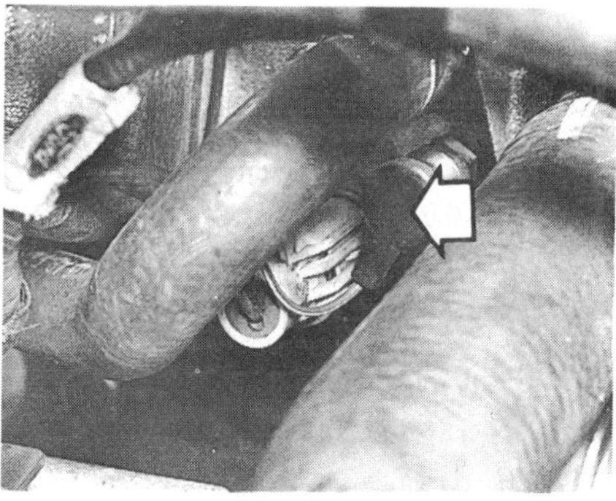
8.60 Temperature gauge sender location (arrowed)

Electric cooling fan – removal and refitting

51 Disconnect the battery negative lead.

52 To provide additional clearance when removing the cooling fan shroud assembly (which is removed from below the vehicle), apply the handbrake, then jack up the front of the vehicle and support it securely on axle stands.

53 Disconnect the wiring plug(s) from the motor(s), and where applicable, unclip the wiring from the fan shroud.

54 Unclip the expansion tank hose from the fan shroud.

55 Unscrew the two nuts securing the fan shroud to the top of the radiator, then tilt the top of the shroud away from the radiator, and lift the shroud to release the lower securing clips. Withdraw the assembly from below the vehicle.

56 To remove the fan blades, prise the securing clip from the end of the motor shaft.

57 The motor can be separated from the fan shroud by unscrewing

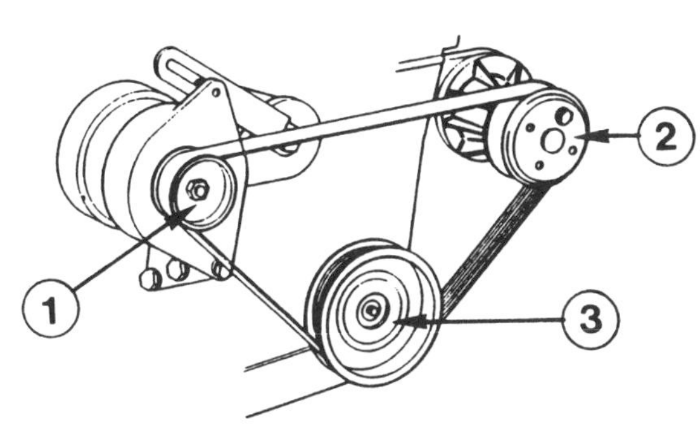

Fig. 14.23 Coolant pump/alternator drivebelt arrangement – 2.0 litre DOHC models without power steering (Sec 8)

1 Alternator
2 Coolant pump
3 Crankshaft pulley

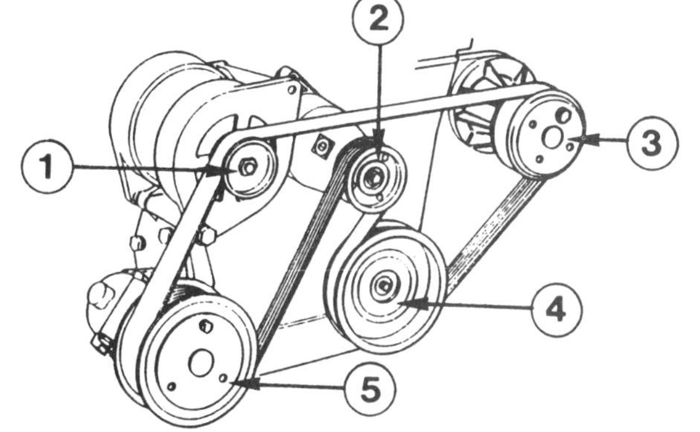

Fig. 14.24 Coolant pump/alternator drivebelt arrangement – 2.0 litre DOHC models with power steering (Sec 8)

1 Alternator
2 Automatic belt tensioner
3 Coolant pump
4 Crankshaft pulley
5 Power steering pump

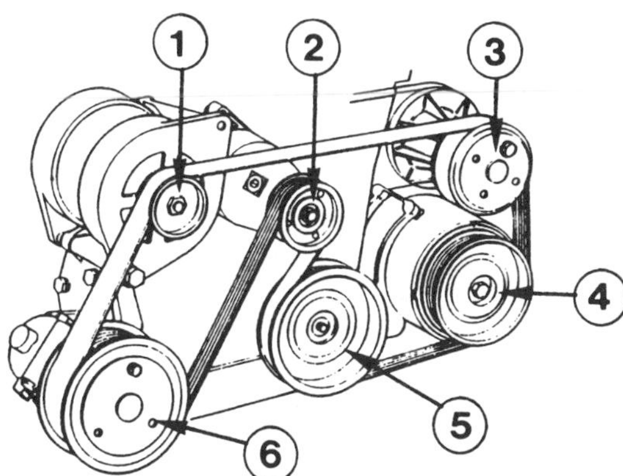

Fig. 14.25 Coolant pump/alternator drivebelt arrangement – 2.0 litre DOHC models with power steering and air conditioning (Sec 8)

1 Alternator
2 Automatic belt tensioner
3 Coolant pump
4 Air conditioning compressor
5 Crankshaft pulley
6 Power steering pump

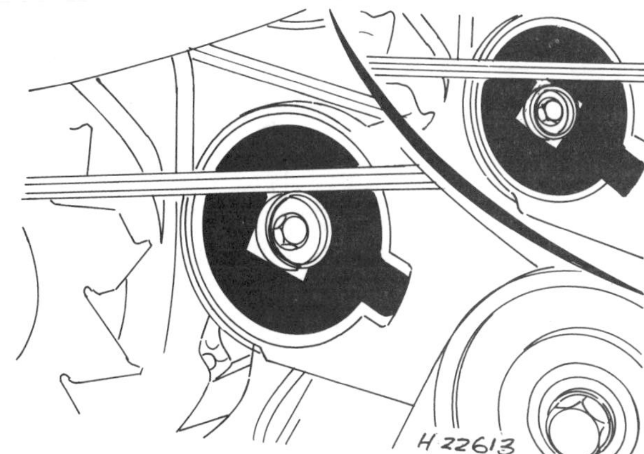

Fig. 14.26 Alternator/coolant pump drivebelt tensioner indicator position – 2.0 litre DOHC engine (Sec 8)

Inset shows tensioner at maximum adjustment

the three securing nuts and bolts.

58 Note that two cooling fans may be fitted, depending on model. Both fans are secured to the shroud in the same manner.

59 Refitting is a reversal of removal, but when fitting the fan blades, ensure that the drive dog on the motor shaft engages with the slot in the rear of the fan blades.

Temperature gauge sender – removal and refitting

60 The temperature gauge sender is located at the front of the inlet manifold (photo).

61 Removal and refitting is as described in Chapter 2, Section 16.

Cooling fan switch – removal and refitting

62 The cooling fan switch is located in the end of the thermostat housing.

63 Removal and refitting of the switch is as described for the temperature gauge sender in Chapter 2, Section 16.

9 Fuel injection system – 1.6 litre CVH models

General description

Note: *Following disconnection of the battery, the information stored in the EEC IV module memory will be erased. After reconnecting the battery, the engine should be allowed to idle for three minutes. Once the engine has reached normal operating temperature, the idle speed should be increased to 1200 rpm and maintained for approximately 2 minutes which will allow the module to 're-learn' the optimum idle values. It may be necessary to drive the vehicle in order for the module to 're-learn' the*

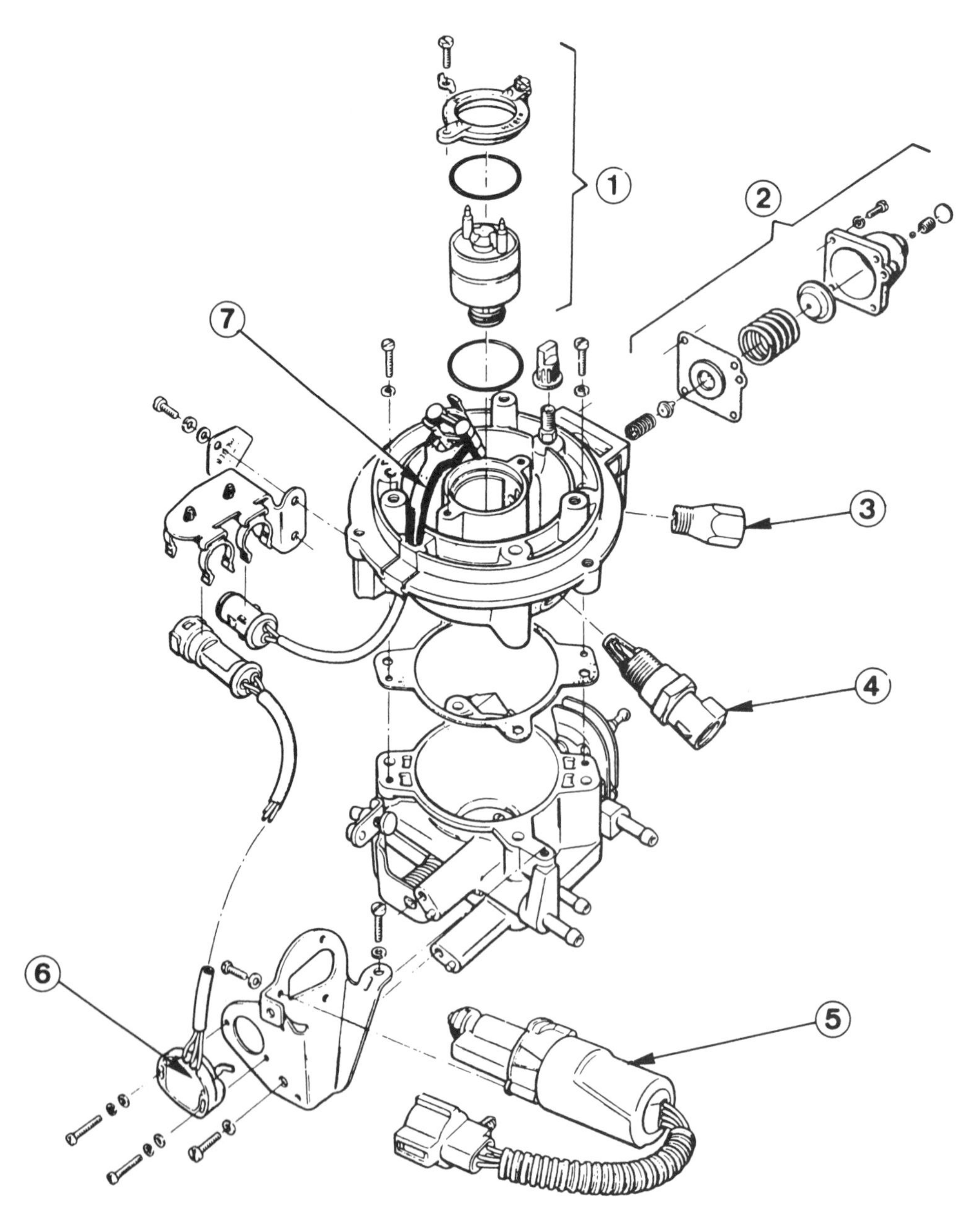

Fig. 14.27 Exploded view of Central Fuel Injection (CFI) unit – 1.6 litre CVH engine (Sec 9)

1 Fuel injector assembly
2 Fuel pressure regulator components
3 Fuel inlet connector
4 Air charge temperature (ACT) sensor
5 Throttle valve control motor
6 Throttle position sensor
7 Fuel injector wiring

values under load. The module should complete its learning process after approximately 5 miles (8 kilometres) of varied driving.

1 The fuel injection system is under the overall control of the EEC IV engine management system (see Section 13 of this Chapter), which also controls the ignition timing.
2 Fuel is supplied from the rear-mounted fuel tank by an electric fuel pump which is integral with the fuel level sender unit mounted inside the fuel tank. Fuel passes via a fuel filter to the Central Fuel Injection (CFI) unit. A fuel pressure regulator, mounted on the CFI unit maintains a constant fuel pressure to the fuel injector. Excess fuel is returned from the regulator to the tank.
3 The CFI unit, resembling a carburettor, houses the throttle valve, throttle valve control motor, throttle position sensor, air charge temperature sensor, fuel injector, and pressure regulator.
4 The duration of the electrical pulse supplied to the fuel injector determines the quantity of fuel injected, and pulse duration is computed by the EEC IV module on the basis of information received from the various sensors. The fuel injector receives a pulse twice per crankshaft revolution under normal operating conditions, and once per crankshaft revolution under engine idle conditions. A ballast resistor is used in the fuel injector control circuit.
5 Inducted air passes through the air cleaner into the CFI unit. The volume of air entering the engine is calculated by the EEC IV module from information supplied by various sensors. These sensors include the air charge temperature sensor and throttle position sensor, mounted in the CFI unit; a crankshaft speed/position sensor which supplies information on engine speed; and a manifold absolute pressure sensor which measures the pressure of the air entering the engine.
6 Additional sensors inform the EEC IV module of engine coolant temperature, and vehicle speed (from a gearbox-mounted sensor).
7 An exhaust gas oxygen (HEGO) sensor enables the EEC IV module to control the fuel/air mixture to suit the operating parameters of the catalytic converter, and no manual mixture adjustment is possible.
8 Idle speed is controlled by a throttle valve control motor which controls the position of the throttle valve under conditions of idling, deceleration/part throttle, and engine start-up and shut-down.
9 A pulse air system is fitted to reduce the exhaust gas emissions during engine warm-up. The system is controlled by a vacuum-operated valve, which is operated by the EEC IV module via a solenoid. The system introduces air into the exhaust manifold to increase the exhaust gas temperature, which oxidises more of the pollutants, and brings the catalyst up to working temperature more quickly. The system operates until the catalyst reaches operating temperature, when the control solenoid shuts off the system.
10 On certain models, an evaporative emission control system may be fitted. This prevents the release of fuel vapour into the atmosphere. With the ignition switched off, vapours from the fuel tank are fed to a carbon canister where they are absorbed. When the engine is started, the EEC IV module opens a purge solenoid valve, and the fuel vapours are fed into the inlet manifold and mixed with fresh air. This cleans the carbon filter. A blow-back valve prevents intake air being forced back into the fuel tank.
11 A fuel pump inertia switch is fitted. This switch breaks the electrical circuit to the fuel pump in the event of an accident or similar impact, cutting off the fuel supply to the engine.
12 A 'limited operation strategy' (LOS) means that the vehicle is still driveable, albeit at reduced power and efficiency, in the event of a failure in the EEC IV module or its sensors.

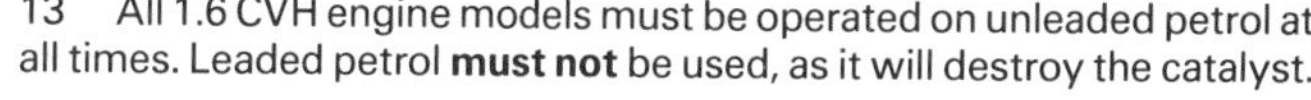

13 All 1.6 CVH engine models must be operated on unleaded petrol at all times. Leaded petrol **must not** be used, as it will destroy the catalyst.

Maintenance and inspection

14 Refer to Chapter 3, Section 3, noting the following points.
15 No adjustment of idle speed or mixture is possible.
16 Additionally, renew the fuel filter at the specified intervals, and the pulse air filter element at the specified intervals.

Air cleaner – removal and refitting

17 Refer to Chapter 3, Section 5, but note that there is no need to disconnect the battery negative lead, and ignore the references to the vacuum pipe and the air charge temperature sensor.

Fuel filter – renewal

Note: *Refer to Chapter 3, Section 47 before proceeding.*

18 Proceed as described in Chapter 3, Section 51, noting the following points.
19 The fuel filter is located under the rear of the vehicle, above the right-hand driveshaft (photo). For access to the filter, chock the front wheels, then jack up the rear of the vehicle and support it on axle stands.
20 To remove the filter, the mounting bracket must first be removed from the floor after unscrewing the securing bolt. The filter can then be removed from the bracket after unscrewing the clamp bolt.

Fuel pump – testing

Note: *Refer to Chapter 3, Section 2 before proceeding.*

21 Refer to Chapter 3, Section 53, noting the following points.
22 Ignore the reference to the fuel flow damper.
23 Note that the inertia cut-off switch is located in the spare wheel well on all models (photo).

Fuel pump/fuel level sender unit – removal and refitting

Note: *Refer to Chapter 3, Section 2 before proceeding.*

24 Remove the fuel tank as described in Chapter 3, Section 11.
25 Unscrew the fuel pump/fuel level sender unit by engaging two crossed screwdrivers in the slots on either side of the unit mounting flange. Recover the seal.
26 Refitting is a reversal of removal, but fit a new seal, and refit the fuel tank as described in Chapter 3, Section 11.

Fuel system – depressurising

Note: *The fuel system will remain pressurised after the engine is switched off. Refer to Chapter 3, Section 47 before proceeding.*

27 Disconnect the battery negative lead.
28 Remove the air cleaner assembly as described earlier in this Section.
29 Position a suitable container or a sufficient quantity of absorbent cloth beneath the fuel inlet connection on the CFI unit.
30 Use an open-ended spanner on the flats of the inlet union screwed into the CFI unit to prevent it from turning while the inlet pipe union is loosened (photo). Allow all pressure/fuel seepage to dissipate before fully unscrewing the union if it is to be disconnected, or tightened if another part of the system is to be worked on.
31 The system will remain depressurised until the fuel pump is primed prior to starting the engine. Remove the container or cloth, as applicable, on completion.

9.19 Fuel filter location (arrowed) under rear of vehicle

9.23 Fuel pump inertia cut-off switch location (arrowed) under spare wheel

9.30 CFI unit fuel inlet union (arrowed)

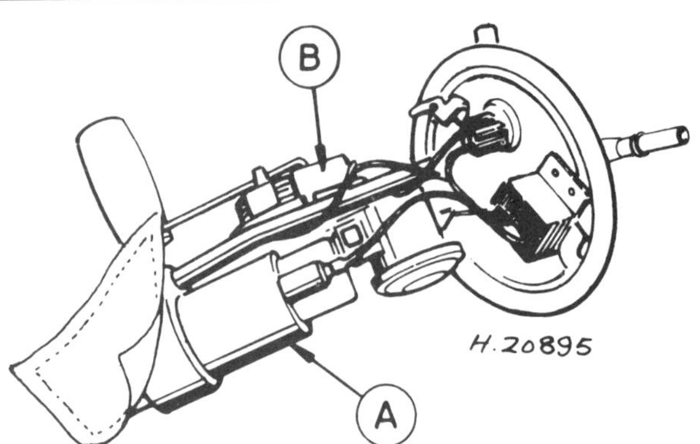

Fig. 14.28 Combined fuel pump/fuel level sender unit – 1.6 litre CVH models (Sec 9)

A Fuel pump *B Fuel level sender unit*

CFI unit – removal and refitting

Note: *Refer to Chapter 3, Section 2 before proceeding. A new gasket must be used on refitting.*

32 Disconnect the battery negative lead.
33 Remove the air cleaner assembly as described earlier in this Section.
34 Depressurise the fuel system as described previously in this Section, and disconnect the fuel inlet pipe from the CFI unit.
35 Disconnect the fuel return pipe from the CFI unit. Be prepared for fuel spillage.
36 Disconnect the throttle cable from the linkage on the CFI unit with reference to Chapter 3, Section 14 if necessary.
37 Either partially drain the cooling system with reference to Section 8 of this Chapter, or clamp the coolant hoses as close as possible to the CFI unit to minimise coolant loss, then disconnect the hoses from the unit.
38 Disconnect the air charge temperature sensor, throttle position sensor, and throttle valve control motor wiring plugs.
39 Disconnect the vacuum pipe from the CFI unit.
40 Unscrew the four securing bolts, and lift the CFI unit from the inlet manifold (photo). Recover the gasket.
41 Refitting is a reversal of removal, bearing in mind the following points.
42 Ensure that all mating faces are clean, and use a new gasket.
43 Top up the cooling system with reference to Section 8 of this Chapter.
44 On completion, turn the ignition on and off five times to pressurise the system, and check for fuel leaks.

Fuel pressure regulator – removal and refitting

Note: *Refer to Chapter 3, Section 2 before proceeding. On completion of refitting, the fuel system pressure should be checked by a Ford dealer at the earliest opportunity.*

45 Remove the CFI unit as described previously in this Section.
46 Remove the four screws securing the regulator housing to the CFI unit, then carefully lift off the housing and recover the ball, cup, large spring, diaphragm, valve, and small spring, noting the position and orientation of all components (see Fig. 14.27). **Do not** attempt to prise the plug from the regulator housing, or adjust the Allen screw (if no plug is fitted); this will alter the fuel system pressure.
47 Examine all components and renew any defective items as necessary.
48 Commence reassembly by supporting the CFI unit on its side so that the regulator components can be fitted from above.
49 Fit the small spring, valve, diaphragm (ensuring that it locates correctly), large spring, and the spring cup.
50 Carefully place the ball into position on the spring cup, and ensure that it locates correctly.
51 Refit the regulator housing, taking great care to avoid disturbing the ball, and once correctly in position, tighten the screws evenly to avoid distorting the diaphragm.
52 Refit the CFI unit as described previously in this Section.
53 On completion, the fuel system pressure should be checked by a Ford dealer at the earliest opportunity.

Fuel injector – removal and refitting

Note: *Refer to Chapter 3, Section 2 before proceeding. New fuel injector seals must be used on refitting.*

54 Disconnect the battery negative lead.
55 Remove the air cleaner as described previously in this Section.
56 Depressurise the fuel system as described previously in this Section.

9.40 CFI unit securing bolts (arrowed)

9.57 Disconnecting the fuel injector wiring plug

9.58A Removing an injector retaining collar securing bolt and locktab

9.58B Removing the injector retaining collar

9.59 Withdrawing the fuel injector

9.60 Removing the seal from the injector retaining collar

9.64 Fuel injector ballast resistor location (arrowed)

9.74 Throttle valve control motor (A) and wiring plug (B)

57 Release the securing lugs and disconnect the fuel injector wiring plug (photo).
58 Bend back the injector retaining collar securing bolt locktabs, then unscrew the bolts. Remove the injector retaining collar (photos).
59 Withdraw the injector from the CFI unit, noting its orientation, then withdraw the injector seals (photo).
60 Remove the seal from the injector retaining collar (photo).
61 Refitting is a reversal of removal, bearing in mind the following points.
62 Use new injector seals and lubricate them with clean engine oil before fitting.
63 Ensure that the locating peg on the injector is correctly positioned – see Fig. 14.29.

Fuel injector ballast resistor – removal and refitting

64 The ballast resistor is located on the right-hand side of the engine compartment (photo).
65 Disconnect the battery negative lead.
66 Disconnect the ballast resistor wiring connector, then remove the securing screw, and withdraw the ballast resistor from the body panel.
67 Refitting is a reversal of removal.

Throttle position sensor – removal and refitting

68 Disconnect the battery negative lead.
69 Unclip and disconnect the sensor wiring connector, pulling on the plug, not on the wiring.
70 Remove the two securing screws, and withdraw the sensor from the throttle valve shaft.
71 Refitting is a reversal of removal, but ensure that the sensor actuating arm locates correctly on the throttle valve spindle.

Throttle valve control motor – removal and refitting

Note: *On completion of refitting, the idle speed should be checked by a Ford dealer at the earliest opportunity.*

72 Disconnect the battery negative lead.
73 Remove the air cleaner assembly as described previously in this Section.
74 Disconnect the wiring connectors from the throttle valve control motor, and the throttle position sensor, pulling on the plugs, not on the wiring (photo).
75 Remove the three screws securing the motor and the throttle position sensor assembly mounting bracket to the CFI unit, and withdraw the assembly.
76 Remove the three motor securing screws, and withdraw the motor from the bracket.
77 Refitting is a reversal of removal, bearing in mind the following points.
78 Ensure that the throttle position sensor actuating arm locates correctly on the throttle valve spindle, and that the mounting bracket aligns with its locating pegs.
79 On completion, the idle speed should be checked by a Ford dealer at the earliest opportunity.

Exhaust gas oxygen (HEGO) sensor – removal and refitting

Note: *A new sealing ring should be used on refitting.*

80 Ensure that the engine and the exhaust system are cold.
81 Disconnect the battery negative lead.
82 Apply the handbrake, then jack up the front of the vehicle, and support it securely on axle stands.
83 Disconnect the sensor wiring plug halves by releasing the locktabs and pulling on the plug halves, not the wiring.
84 Slide the heat shield from the sensor (photo).
85 Unscrew the sensor from the exhaust downpipe, and recover the sealing ring. **Do not** touch the tip of the sensor if it is to be refitted.
86 Commence refitting by ensuring that the sensor threads and the corresponding threads in the downpipe are clean.
87 Refit the sensor using a new sealing ring, and tighten it to the specified torque.
88 Further refitting is a reversal of removal, but on completion start the engine, and check for leaks around the sensor sealing ring.

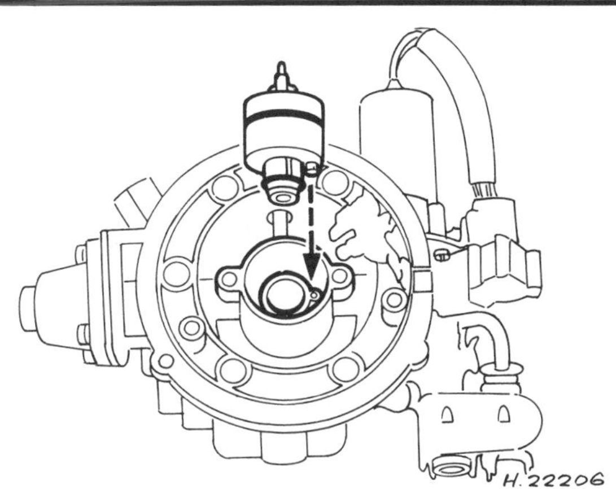

Fig. 14.29 Align locating peg on injector with slot in CFI unit when refitting (Sec 9)

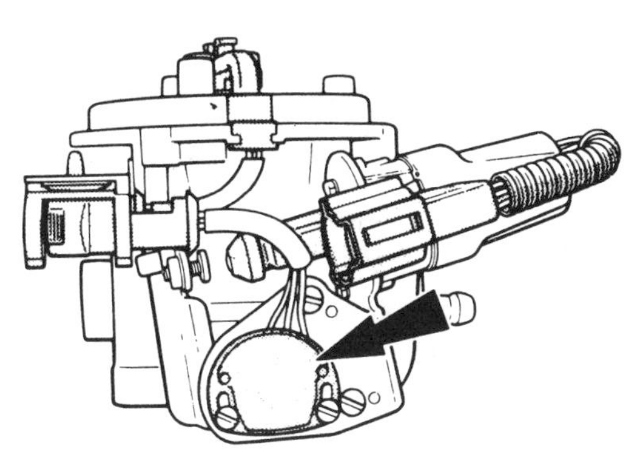

Fig. 14.30 Throttle position sensor location (arrowed) on side of CFI unit (Sec 9)

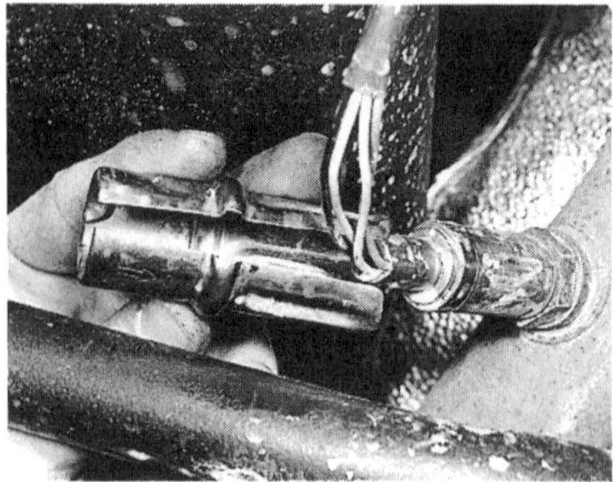
9.84 Sliding the heat shield from the exhaust gas oxygen sensor

9.90 Withdrawing the pulse air filter element and gauze

9.92 Vacuum-operated air valve (arrowed)

9.96 Pulse air delivery check valves (arrowed)

9.98 Unscrewing a pulse air delivery tube union

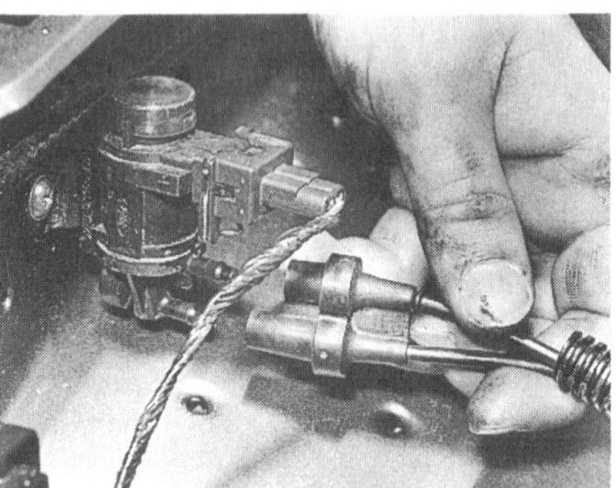
9.102 Disconnecting the vacuum pipe connector from the pulse air control solenoid

Pulse air filter element – renewal

89 The pulse air filter is located at the front left-hand side of the engine compartment.

90 To renew the filter element, simply unclip the filter cover, then lift out the metal gauze, and withdraw the filter element (photo).

91 Refitting is a reversal of removal. Ensure that the holes in the gauze and the filter element are positioned on the engine side of the filter housing.

Vacuum-operated air valve (pulse air system) – removal and refitting

92 The valve is mounted at the end of the pulse air filter housing (photo).

93 Disconnect the vacuum hose from the top of the valve, then loosen the hose clips at either end of the valve, and remove the valve. Note the orientation of the arrow on the valve body, which denotes the direction of flow.

94 Refitting is a reversal of removal, ensuring that the arrow on the valve body is orientated as noted before removal.

Pulse air delivery tubing – removal and refitting

95 Remove the air cleaner assembly as described previously in this Section.

96 Loosen the hose clips, and disconnect the air hoses from the check valves next to the exhaust manifold (photo).

97 Remove the two bolts securing the check valve bracket to the exhaust manifold.

98 Unscrew the unions securing the air tubes to the manifold, then carefully withdraw the tubing assembly, taking care not to distort the tubes (photo).

99 Refitting is a reversal of removal.

Pulse air control solenoid – removal and refitting

100 The solenoid is located at the right-hand side of the engine compartment.

101 Disconnect the battery negative lead.

102 Disconnect the vacuum pipe connector from the solenoid (photo).

103 Disconnect the solenoid wiring plug, pulling on the plug, not the wiring.

104 Unscrew the securing screw, and withdraw the solenoid from the body panel.

105 Refitting is a reversal of removal, ensuring that the locating lug is correctly positioned, and noting that the vacuum pipes will only fit in one position.

Carbon canister – removal and refitting

106 The carbon canister (where fitted) is located on the right-hand side of the engine compartment.

107 Disconnect the battery negative lead.

108 Pull the plastic pipe from the canister (the connector is a push-fit in the canister).

109 Unscrew the securing bolt and lift the canister from its location.

110 Refitting is a reversal of removal.

Carbon canister purge solenoid – removal and refitting

111 The purge solenoid is located to the rear of the carbon canister, on the right-hand side of the engine compartment.

112 Disconnect the battery negative lead.

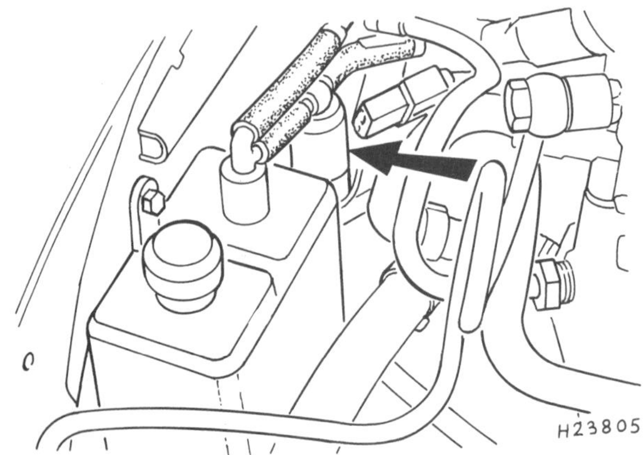

Fig. 14.31 Carbon canister purge solenoid location (arrowed) – 1.6 litre CVH models (Sec 9)

113 Disconnect the solenoid wiring plug halves by releasing the locktabs and pulling on the plug halves, not the wiring.
114 Note the locations of the two solenoid pipes, and the orientation of the solenoid to assist with refitting.
115 Disconnect the two pipes from the solenoid, and withdraw the solenoid from its location.
116 Refitting is a reversal of removal, ensuring that the solenoid pipes are correctly reconnected, and that the solenoid is correctly orientated as noted before removal.

Inlet manifold – removal and refitting

Note: *Refer to Chapter 3, Section 2 before proceeding. A new manifold gasket must be used on refitting.*

117 Proceed as described in paragraphs 32 to 36 inclusive of this Section.
118 Partially drain the cooling system with reference to Section 7 of this Chapter.
119 Disconnect the coolant hoses from the thermostat housing and the CFI unit.
120 Disconnect the vacuum and breather hoses from the inlet manifold and the CFI unit, noting their locations. Refer to Section 20 of this Chapter when disconnecting the brake servo vacuum hose.
121 Disconnect the wiring from the following components.

Air charge temperature sensor
Throttle position sensor
Throttle valve control motor
Engine coolant temperature sensor
Cooling fan switch
Temperature gauge sender

122 Unbolt the dipstick tube from the inlet manifold, and withdraw the dipstick and dipstick tube from the cylinder block.
123 Make a final check to ensure that all relevant wires, hoses and pipes have been disconnected to facilitate removal of the manifold.
124 Unscrew the six securing nuts and the single bolt securing the inlet manifold to the cylinder head, then lift the manifold from the cylinder head and recover the gasket.
125 If desired, the CFI unit can be removed from the inlet manifold as described earlier in this Section.
126 If necessary, the thermostat and housing can be removed from the manifold with reference to Chapter 2.
127 Refitting is a reversal of removal, bearing in mind the following points.
128 Ensure that all mating faces are clean and renew all gaskets.
129 Tighten the manifold nuts and bolt progressively to the specified torque.
130 Make sure that all wires, hoses and pipes are correctly reconnected as noted before removal.
131 Top up the cooling system with reference to Section 6 of this Chapter.
132 On completion, turn the ignition on and off five times to pressurise the system, and check for fuel leaks.

Exhaust manifold – removal and refitting

Note: *A new manifold gasket and downpipe gaskets must be used on refitting.*

133 Disconnect the battery negative lead.
134 Remove the air cleaner as described earlier in this Section, and pull the hot air pick-up pipe from the exhaust manifold hot air shroud.
135 Remove the pulse air delivery tubing as described earlier in this Section.
136 Remove the securing bolts, and withdraw the hot air shroud from the manifold.
137 Disconnect the exhaust gas oxygen sensor wiring plug, then unscrew the securing nuts, and disconnect the exhaust downpipe from the manifold. Recover the gasket. Support the exhaust downpipe from underneath the vehicle (eg with an axle stand) to avoid placing unnecessary strain on the exhaust system.
138 Unscrew the securing nuts, and lift the manifold from the cylinder head. Recover the gasket.
139 Refitting is a reversal of removal, bearing in mind the following points.
140 Ensure that all mating faces are clean, and renew all gaskets.
141 Tighten the manifold securing nuts progressively to the specified torque, and similarly tighten the exhaust downpipe securing nuts.

Exhaust system – checking, removal and refitting

142 Refer to Chapter 3, Section 44, noting the following points.
143 Flanged joints incorporating gaskets may be used to join exhaust sections on certain models. Where applicable, renew the gaskets on refitting.
144 On models fitted with a catalytic converter, disconnect the battery negative lead and disconnect the exhaust gas oxygen (HEGO) sensor wiring plug before removing the downpipe.

10 Carburettor fuel system – 2.0 litre DOHC models

General description

1 The basic layout of the system is similar to that described in Chapter 3, Section 1, noting the following points.

(a) *The system uses an electric fuel pump, which is combined with the fuel level sender unit mounted in the fuel tank*
(b) *No fuel pressure regulator or vapour separator is fitted*
(c) *A Weber 2V TLD carburettor is used, which is described in more detail later in this Section*
(d) *All engines can be operated on 95 RON unleaded petrol without any adjustment. Leaded petrol (97 RON) can be used if desired, with no adverse effects*

Air cleaner – removal and refitting

2 Proceed as described in Chapter 3, Section 5, but note that the camshaft cover breather hose must be disconnected before the air cleaner can be removed.

Air cleaner intake air temperature control – description and testing

3 Refer to the information given for OHC models in Chapter 3, Section 6.

Fuel pump – testing

4 The procedure is as described for 1.6 litre CVH models in Section 9 of this Chapter.

Fuel pump/fuel level sender unit – removal and refitting

5 The procedure is as described for 1.6 litre CVH models in Section 9 of this Chapter.

Carburettor (Weber 2V TLD) – description

6 The Weber 2V TLD carburettor is similar to the Weber 2V type carburettor described in Chapter 3, Section 22, noting the following.
7 The secondary throttle valve is vacuum-operated.
8 An anti-dieselling (anti-run-on) valve is fitted.
9 An electrically-heated automatic choke is fitted, with vacuum and mechanical pull-down systems.
10 A throttle kicker is fitted, to damp the action of the throttle valve as it closes, and to reduce exhaust gas emissions. The throttle kicker is vacuum-operated by vacuum from the inlet manifold or throttle housing. When the throttle is opened, the vacuum operates the throttle kicker, which lifts the throttle valve above its normal idle position. When the throttle is released, the damper slows the closing of the throttle valve. This reduces the amount of partially burnt air/fuel mixture entering the engine as the throttle is closed, thus reducing exhaust gas emissions.

Carburettor (Weber 2V TLD) – removal and refitting

Note: *Refer to Chapter 3, Section 2 before proceeding. A new gasket must be used when refitting the carburettor. A tachometer and an exhaust gas analyser will be required to check the idle speed and mixture on completion.*

11 Disconnect the battery negative lead.
12 Remove the air cleaner as described in Chapter 3, Section 5.
13 Disconnect the wiring from the anti-dieselling (anti-run-on) valve.
14 Disconnect the wiring from the automatic choke heater.
15 Disconnect the fuel supply and return hoses, noting their locations to aid refitting. Plug the ends of the hoses to minimise petrol spillage.
16 Disconnect the link arm from the throttle linkage.
17 Disconnect the vacuum pipe.
18 Release the coolant hose from the bracket under the automatic choke housing.

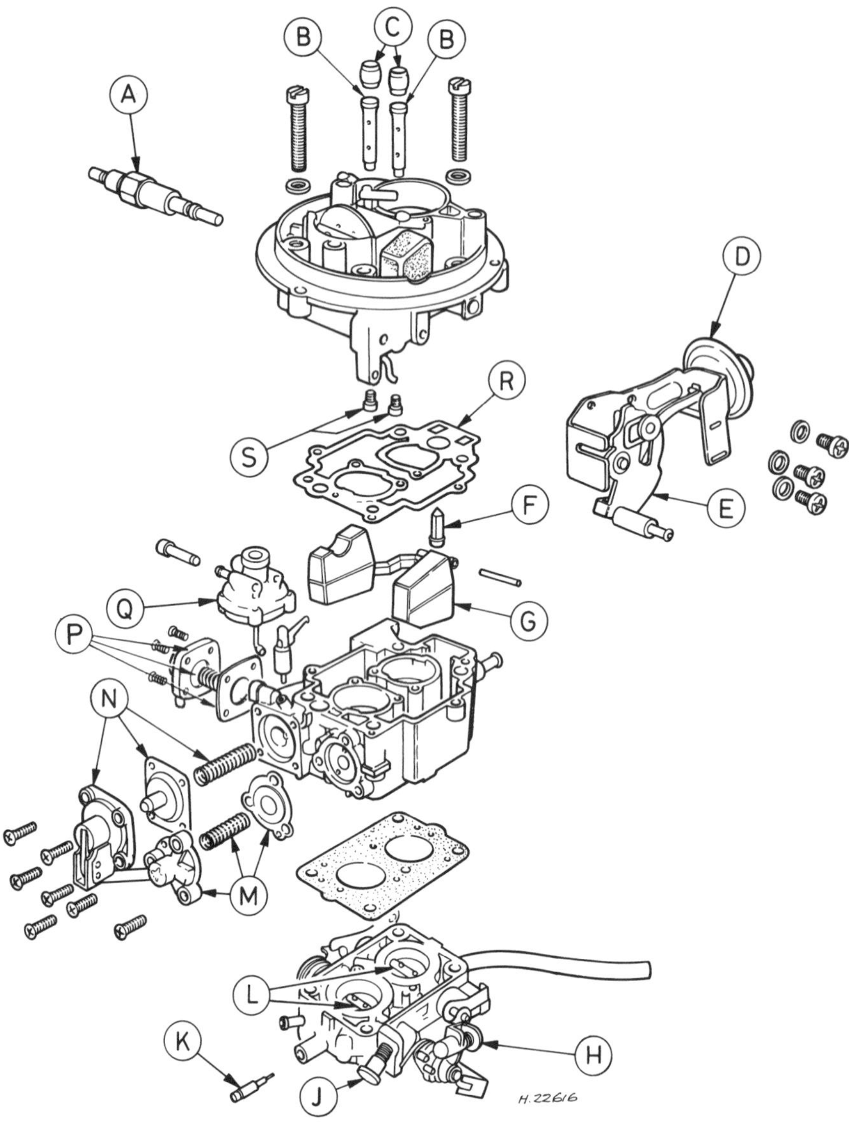

Fig. 14.32 Exploded view of Weber 2V TLD type carburettor (Sec 10)

A Anti-dieselling valve
B Emulsion tubes
C Air correction jets
D Choke pull-down diaphragm assembly
E Choke linkage
F Needle valve
G Float
H Fast idle adjustment screw
J Idle speed adjustment screw
K Idle mixture adjustment screw
L Throttle valves
M Power valve assembly
N Accelerator pump assembly
P Low vacuum enrichment device
Q Throttle kicker
R Gasket
S Main jets

Fig. 14.33 Throttle kicker assembly – Weber 2V TLD type carburettor (Sec 10)

1 Fuel inlet
2 Choke plate
3 Accelerator pump cover
4 Throttle kicker pivot lever
5 Plastic cover
6 Throttle kicker
7 Secondary throttle valve vacuum diaphragm

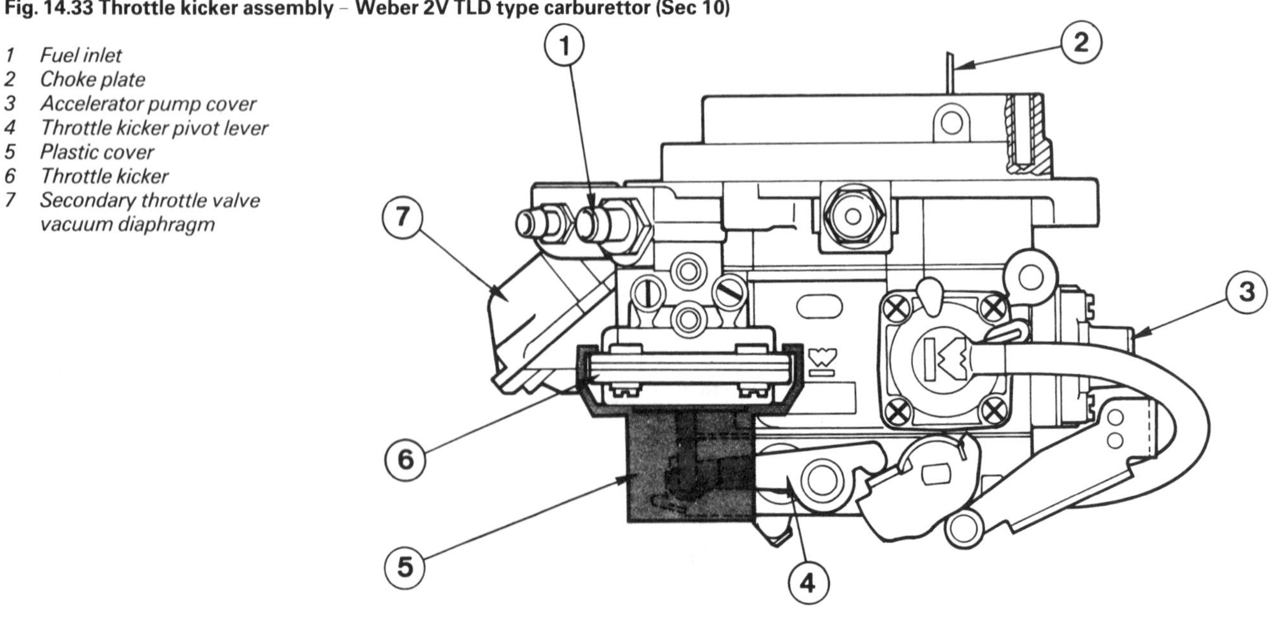

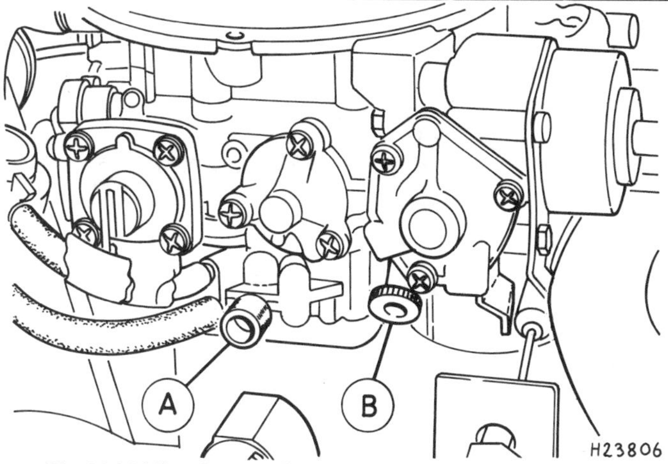

Fig. 14.34 Idle mixture adjustment screw (A) and idle speed adjustment screw (B) – Weber 2V TLD type carburettor (Sec 10)

19 Unscrew the four Torx screws, and lift the carburettor from the inlet manifold. Recover the gasket.
20 Refitting is a reversal of removal, bearing in mind the following points.
21 Ensure that the mating faces of the inlet manifold and the carburettor are clean, and use a new gasket.
22 Ensure that all hoses, pipes and wiring are correctly routed, and free from restrictions. If any of the hoses were originally secured with crimped type clips, discard these and use new worm drive clips on refitting.
23 Make sure that the coolant hose is correctly positioned in the bracket under the automatic choke housing.
24 On completion, check and if necessary adjust the idle speed and mixture as described later in this Section.

Carburettor (Weber 2V TLD) – idle speed and mixture adjustment

25 Proceed as described in Chapter 3, Section 17, noting the following points.
26 Ensure that the vacuum pipe and the camshaft cover breather hose are securely connected to the air cleaner, and are free from restrictions.
27 When warming up the engine, run the engine until the cooling fan cuts in.
28 If adjustment of the mixture (CO content) is required, the air cleaner must be removed for access to the adjustment screw as follows.
29 Remove the air cleaner and prise the tamperproof seal from the mixture screw.
30 Loosely refit the air cleaner, ensuring that the vacuum pipe and the camshaft cover breather hose are securely connected and free from restrictions (there is no need to secure the air cleaner in position).
31 On completion, fit a new tamperproof seal to the mixture screw (the service replacement plug is coloured blue), and refit the air cleaner assembly.

Needle valve and float (Weber 2V TLD carburettor) – removal, refitting and adjustment

Note: *Refer to Chapter 3, Section 2 before proceeding. A new carburettor top cover gasket must be used on reassembly, and if the needle valve housing is removed, a new washer must be used. A tachometer and an exhaust gas analyser will be required to check the idle speed and mixture on completion.*

Removal and refitting

32 Disconnect the battery negative lead.
33 Remove the air cleaner with reference to Chapter 3, Section 5.
34 Thoroughly clean all external dirt from the carburettor.
35 Disconnect the fuel supply and return hoses from the carburettor, noting their locations to aid refitting, and plug their ends to minimise petrol spillage.
36 Disconnect the wiring from the automatic choke.
37 Disconnect the wiring from the anti-dieselling (anti-run-on) valve.

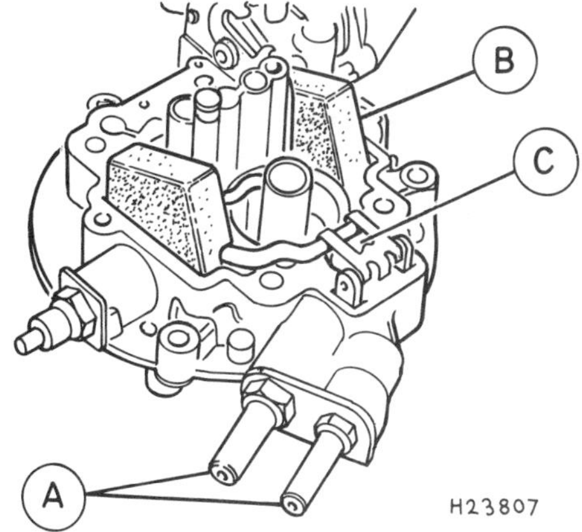

Fig. 14.35 Float and needle valve locations in carburettor top cover – Weber 2V TLD type carburettor (Sec 10)

A Fuel hose connections
B Float
C Needle valve

38 Remove the four Torx screws securing the carburettor to the inlet manifold.
39 Remove the two securing screws, and lift off the carburettor top cover, leaving the carburettor main body in place on the inlet manifold.
40 Slide the float retaining pin from the carburettor top cover, tapping it gently if necessary, then lift out the float and needle valve.
41 If desired, the needle valve housing can be unscrewed from the top cover. Recover the washer.
42 Inspect the components for damage, and renew as necessary. Check the needle valve for wear, and check the float assembly for leaks by shaking it to see if it contains petrol.
43 Clean the mating faces of the carburettor main body and the top cover.
44 Refitting is a reversal of removal, bearing in mind the following points.
45 Use a new washer when refitting the needle valve housing.
46 When refitting the float and needle valve, ensure that the tag on the float locates under the spring clip on the needle valve.
47 Before refitting the carburettor top cover, check and if necessary adjust the float level as described in paragraphs 51 to 55. Check the float and needle valve for full and free movement.
48 If the fuel hoses were originally secured with crimped clips, discard these and use new worm drive clips on refitting.
49 When refitting the air cleaner, ensure that the vacuum pipe and the camshaft cover breather hose are securely connected and free from restrictions.
50 On completion, check and if necessary adjust the idle speed and mixture as described earlier in this Section.

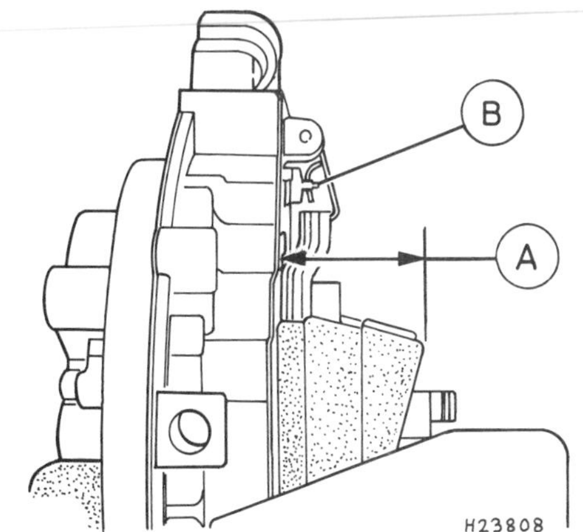

Fig. 14.36 Float level adjustment – Weber 2V TLD type carburettor (Sec 10)

A Check dimension
B Adjustment tag

Adjustment

51 With the carburettor top cover removed as described previously, proceed as follows.

52 Fit a new gasket to the top cover, then hold the carburettor top cover in a vertical position, with the needle valve uppermost and shut.

53 Measure the distance between the top cover gasket and the bottom of the float – see Fig. 14.36.

54 If the distance is not as specified, adjust by bending the tag on the float assembly.

55 Refit the carburettor top cover by reversing the removal operations, with reference to paragraphs 48 to 50, using a new gasket.

Secondary throttle valve vacuum diaphragm (Weber 2V TLD carburettor) – renewal

Note: *Refer to Chapter 3, Section 2 before proceeding.*

56 Proceed as described in Chapter 3, Section 26, noting the following.

57 To disconnect the diaphragm operating rod from the throttle linkage, pull the lower section of the rod downwards, and twist the end of the rod from its socket.

58 When refitting the diaphragm, make sure that the vacuum hole in the housing is aligned with the corresponding holes in the diaphragm and the cover.

Power valve diaphragm (Weber 2V TLD carburettor) – renewal

Note: *Refer to Chapter 3, Section 2 before proceeding.*

59 Proceed as described in Chapter 3, Section 27, paragraphs 1 to 9 inclusive.

Low vacuum enrichment diaphragm (Weber 2V TLD carburettor) – renewal

Note: *Refer to Chapter 3, Section 2 before proceeding.*

60 Proceed as described in Chapter 3, Section 28.

Accelerator pump diaphragm (Weber 2V TLD carburettor) – renewal

Note: *Refer to Chapter 3, Section 2 before proceeding.*

61 Proceed as described for the power valve in Chapter 3, Section 27, paragraphs 1 to 9, but note the following.

62 The accelerator pump cover is secured by four screws.

63 The diaphragm return spring is fitted between the pump housing and the diaphragm, not between the diaphragm and the cover.

64 When removing the return spring, the supply valve should come out on the end of the spring, complete with the O-ring seal. Check the valve and the O-ring for damage, and renew them if necessary. When refitting, ensure that the O-ring seal is correctly fitted to the end of the valve.

Automatic choke unit (Weber 2V TLD carburettor) – removal, overhaul, refitting and adjustment

Note: *Refer to Chapter 3, Section 2 before proceeding. A tachometer and an exhaust gas analyser will be required to check the idle speed and mixture on completion.*

Removal, overhaul and refitting

65 Remove the carburettor top cover as described in paragraphs 32 to 39 of this Section, then proceed as described in Chapter 3, Section 30, paragraph 7 onwards, ignoring the reference to the bi-metal housing clamp ring. Refer to the following paragraphs before checking the vacuum pull-down.

Vacuum pull-down adjustment

66 Proceed as described in Chapter 3, Section 30, paragraphs 23 to 29, noting the following.

67 Ignore the reference to the bi-metal housing clamp ring when removing and refitting the bi-metal housing.

68 Fit a new plug to the pull-down diaphragm cover on completion of adjustment.

69 Refer to the Specifications at the beginning of this Chapter for the correct pull-down clearance.

Fast idle speed adjustment

70 Proceed as described in Chapter 3, Section 30, paragraphs 37 to 44, noting the following.

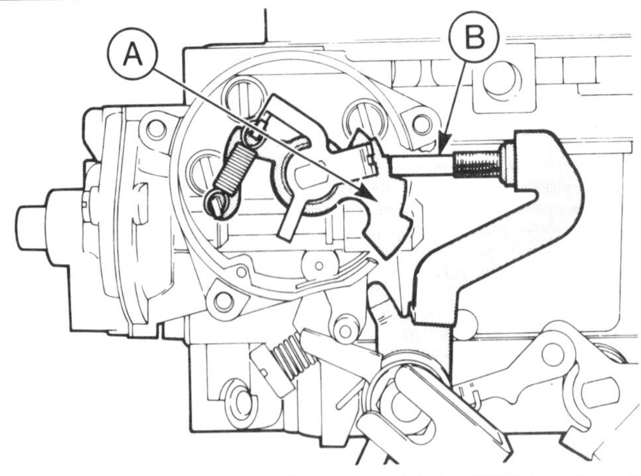

Fig. 14.37 Fast idle speed adjustment – Weber 2V TLD carburettor (Sec 10)

A Fast idle cam *B Adjustment screw positioned on middle step of cam*

71 The fast idle adjustment screw should be positioned on the third (middle) step of the fast idle cam – see Fig. 14.37.

72 Refer to the Specifications at the beginning of this Chapter for the correct fast idle speed.

Throttle kicker (Weber 2V TLD carburettor) – removal, refitting and adjustment

Removal and refitting

73 Disconnect the battery negative lead.

74 Remove the air cleaner assembly with reference to Chapter 3, Section 5.

75 Disconnect the throttle kicker vacuum hose.

76 Withdraw the plastic shield from the throttle kicker.

77 Remove the two securing screws, then disconnect the operating rod from the throttle linkage, and withdraw the assembly from the carburettor.

78 The assembly can be dismantled by removing the four securing screws and lifting off the diaphragm cover. Recover the spring.

79 Carefully withdraw the diaphragm and the operating rod assembly from the housing. Examine the condition of the diaphragm, and renew it if necessary.

80 Clean the mating faces of the housing and the diaphragm cover.

81 Commence reassembly by inserting the diaphragm and operating rod assembly into the housing.

82 Refit the spring, and the cover, ensuring that the spring is correctly located, and tighten the securing screws progressively to avoid distorting the diaphragm.

83 Further refitting is a reversal of removal, but before refitting the plastic shield, check the throttle kicker adjustment as described in the following paragraphs.

Adjustment

84 Warm the engine up to normal operating temperature, and check the idle speed and mixture settings as described earlier in this Section.

85 Remove the air cleaner assembly.

86 Withdraw the plastic shield from the throttle kicker, if not already done.

87 Disconnect the throttle kicker vacuum hose, and connect the throttle kicker directly to the inlet manifold using a suitable length of tubing.

88 Start the engine and note the engine speed (rpm). The engine speed should increase above the normal idle speed, and should be as given in the Specifications.

89 If the engine speed is not as specified, remove the tamperproof plug from the top of the throttle kicker housing, and turn the adjustment screw to give the specified speed.

90 On completion of adjustment, fit a new tamperproof cap.

91 Disconnect the tubing from the inlet manifold, and reconnect the throttle kicker vacuum hose.

92 Refit the plastic shield and the air cleaner.

Inlet manifold – removal and refitting

Note: *A new manifold gasket must be used on refitting.*

Note: *Refer to Chapter 3, Section 2 before proceeding. A new inlet manifold gasket must be used on refitting, and if the carburettor is removed, a new carburettor-to-inlet manifold gasket will be required.*

93 Disconnect the battery negative lead.
94 Partially drain the cooling system with reference to Section 8 of this Chapter.
95 Remove the air cleaner as described earlier in this Section.
96 Disconnect the coolant hoses from the thermostat housing and the inlet manifold, noting their locations to assist with refitting.
97 Disconnect the fuel supply and return hoses from the carburettor. Plug their ends to minimise petrol spillage.
98 Release the coolant hose from the bracket under the automatic choke housing.
99 Disconnect the HT leads from the spark plugs, and move them to one side.
100 Disconnect all relevant wiring and vacuum pipes from the carburettor, thermostat housing and inlet manifold, noting the locations as an aid to refitting. Refer to Section 20 of this Chapter when disconnecting the brake servo vacuum hose.
101 Disconnect the crankcase breather hose from the inlet manifold.
102 Disconnect the throttle cable from the throttle linkage with reference to Chapter 3, Section 14 if necessary.
103 Make a final check to ensure that all relevant wires, pipes and hoses have been disconnected to facilitate removal of the manifold.
104 Unscrew the ten bolts and two nuts securing the manifold to the cylinder head.
105 Lift the manifold clear of the cylinder head and recover the gasket.
106 Recover the two plastic spark plug spacers from the recesses in the cylinder head.
107 If desired, the carburettor can be removed from the manifold by unscrewing the securing screws. Refer to the carburettor removal and refitting procedure given earlier in this Section if necessary.
108 Refitting is a reversal of removal, bearing in mind the following points.
109 Ensure that all mating faces are clean.
110 Ensure that the spark plug spacers are in position in the cylinder head recesses before refitting the manifold.
111 Renew all gaskets.
112 Tighten all manifold securing nuts and bolts progressively to the specified torque.
113 Make sure that all hoses, pipes and wires are securely reconnected in their original positions.
114 On completion, refill the cooling system with reference to Section 8 of this Chapter, check the adjustment of the throttle cable as described in Chapter 3, Section 14, then check, and if necessary adjust, the idle speed and mixture as described earlier in this Section.

Exhaust manifold – removal and refitting

Note: *A new manifold gasket and downpipe gaskets must be used on refitting.*

115 Proceed as described in Chapter 3, Section 43, noting the following points (photos).
116 Remove the air cleaner as described earlier in this Section.
117 The manifold hot air shroud is secured by a single bolt.
118 Ignore the references to the spark plug HT leads and the engine lifting brackets.

Exhaust system – checking, removal and refitting

119 Refer to Chapter 3, Section 44, noting that flanged joints incorporating gaskets may be used to join exhaust sections on certain models. Where applicable, renew the gaskets on refitting.

11 Fuel injection system – 2.0 litre DOHC models

General description

1 The fuel injection system is under the overall control of the EEC IV engine management system (see Section 15 of this Chapter), which also controls the ignition timing.
2 Fuel is supplied from the rear-mounted fuel tank by an electric fuel pump which is integral with the fuel level sender unit mounted inside the fuel tank. Fuel passes via a fuel filter and a pressure regulator to the fuel rail. The fuel rail acts as a reservoir for the four fuel injectors, which inject fuel into the cylinder inlet tracts, upstream of the inlet valves. The fuel injectors are operated in pairs by electrical pulses supplied by the EEC IV module, and fuel is injected by one pair of injectors every half-revolution of the crankshaft. The duration of each electrical pulse determines the quantity of fuel injected, and pulse duration is computed by the EEC IV module on the basis of information received from the various sensors.
3 Inducted air passes through the air cleaner, and through a plenum chamber before passing on to the cylinder inlet tracts via the throttle valve and inlet manifold. The volume of air entering the engine is calculated by the EEC IV module from information supplied by various sensors. These sensors include an air charge temperature sensor mounted in the inlet manifold, which measures the temperature of the air entering the engine; a manifold absolute pressure sensor which measures the pressure of the air entering the engine; a throttle position sensor; and a crankshaft speed/position sensor which supplies information on engine speed.
4 Additional sensors inform the EEC IV module of fuel temperature, engine coolant temperature, and vehicle speed (from a gearbox-mounted sensor).
5 Idle speed is controlled by a variable orifice solenoid valve which regulates the amount of air bypassing the throttle valve. The valve is

10.115A Exhaust manifold gaskets in position on cylinder head

10.115B Fitting the exhaust manifold

11.20 Air intake tube securing nut (arrowed)

11.22 Lifting out the air cleaner element

11.29 Fuel rail fuel feed union (arrowed)

controlled by the EEC IV module; there is no provision for direct adjustment of the idle speed.

6 On models without a catalytic converter, idle mixture adjustment is by means of a potentiometer connected directly to the EEC IV module. On models fitted with a catalytic converter, an exhaust gas oxygen (HEGO) sensor enables the EEC IV module to control the fuel/air mixture to suit the operating parameters of the catalytic converter, and no manual mixture adjustment is possible.

7 On models equipped with a catalytic converter, an evaporative emission control system is fitted. This prevents the release of fuel vapour into the atmosphere. With the ignition switched off, vapours from the fuel tank are fed to a carbon canister where they are absorbed. When the engine is started, the EEC IV module opens a purge solenoid valve, and the fuel vapours are fed into the inlet manifold and mixed with fresh air. This cleans the carbon filter. A blow-back valve prevents intake air being forced back into the fuel tank.

8 A fuel pump inertia switch is fitted. This switch breaks the electrical circuit to the fuel pump in the event of an accident or similar impact, cutting off the fuel supply to the engine.

9 A 'limited operation strategy' (LOS) means that the vehicle is still driveable, albeit at reduced power and efficiency, in the event of a failure in the EEC IV module or its sensors.

10 All models can be operated on unleaded petrol without the need for any adjustments. Note that models fitted with a catalytic converter must only be operated on unleaded petrol, and leaded petrol **must not** be used.

Maintenance and inspection

11 Refer to Chapter 3, Section 3, noting the following points.

12 No adjustment of idle speed is possible.

13 There is no requirement to check the idle mixture, and on models fitted with a catalytic converter, the idle mixture cannot be adjusted.

14 Refer to paragraphs 17 to 24 of this Section when renewing the air cleaner element.

15 Ignore the reference to the air cleaner intake air temperature control.

16 Additionally, renew the fuel filter at the specified intervals.

Air cleaner element – renewal

17 Disconnect the battery negative lead.

18 Disconnect the wiring plug from the idle speed control valve at the front of the plenum chamber.

19 Loosen the clamp, and detach the air intake hose from the air intake tubing.

20 Unscrew the securing nut, and release the air intake tube from the bracket on the engine compartment front panel (photo).

21 Release the air cleaner lid securing clips, then lift away the air intake tube, plenum chamber and air cleaner lid as an assembly, disconnecting the breather hose from the air intake tube.

22 Lift out the air cleaner element, then wipe the inside of the air cleaner lid and casing clean (photo).

23 Fit the new element with the sealing lip uppermost.

24 Further refitting is a reversal of removal.

Air cleaner – removal and refitting

25 Proceed as described in paragraphs 17 to 22 of this Section.

26 Proceed as described in Chapter 3, Section 50, paragraphs 2 to 5 inclusive.

Fuel filter – renewal

27 The procedure is as described for 1.6 litre CVH models in Section 9 of this Chapter.

Fuel pressure regulator – removal and refitting

Note: *Refer to Chapter 3, Section 47 before proceeding. A new pressure regulator seal will be required on refitting.*

28 Disconnect the battery negative lead.

29 Slowly loosen the fuel rail fuel feed union to relieve the pressure in the system (photo). Be prepared for fuel spillage, and take adequate fire precautions.

30 Disconnect the fuel return hose from the pressure regulator (photo). Again, be prepared for fuel spillage.

31 Disconnect the vacuum pipe from the top of the pressure regulator.

32 Unscrew the two securing bolts, and withdraw the regulator from the fuel rail. Recover the seal.

33 Fit a new seal to the regulator, and lubricate with clean engine oil.

34 Fit both the securing bolts to the regulator, then position the regulator on the fuel rail, and tighten the securing bolts.

35 Further refitting is a reversal of removal, but if the fuel return line was originally secured with a crimped type clip, discard this and use a new worm drive clip.

36 On completion, check the fuel line connections for leaks, pressurising the system by switching the ignition on and off several times.

Fuel pump – testing

37 The procedure is as described for 1.6 litre CVH models in Section 9 of this Chapter.

Fuel pump/fuel level sender unit – removal and refitting

38 The procedure is as described for 1.6 litre CVH models in Section 9 of this Chapter.

Idle speed and mixture – adjustment

Note: *Refer to Chapter 3, Section 47 before proceeding. Before carrying out any adjustments ensure that the ignition timing and spark plug gaps are as specified. To carry out the adjustments an accurate tachometer and an exhaust gas analyser (CO meter) will be required.*

39 Idle speed is controlled by the EEC IV module, and manual adjustment is not possible, although the 'base' idle speed can be adjusted by a Ford dealer using special equipment.

40 On models with a catalytic converter, the mixture is controlled by the EEC IV module, and no manual adjustment is possible.

41 On models without a catalytic converter, the idle mixture can be adjusted as follows.

42 Run the engine until it is at normal operating temperature.

43 Stop the engine and connect a tachometer and an exhaust gas analyser in accordance with the manufacturer's instructions.

44 Start the engine and run it at 3000 rpm for 15 seconds, ensuring that all electrical loads (headlamps, heater blower, etc) are switched off, then allow the engine to idle, and check the CO content. Note that the reading will initially rise, then fall and finally stabilise.

45 If adjustment is necessary, remove the cover from the mixture adjustment potentiometer (located at the rear right-hand side of the engine compartment, behind the MAP sensor), and turn the screw to give the specified CO content (photos).

11.30 Disconnecting the fuel return hose (arrowed) from the pressure regulator

11.45A Remove the cover from the mixture adjustment potentiometer ...

11.45B ... to enable mixture adjustment

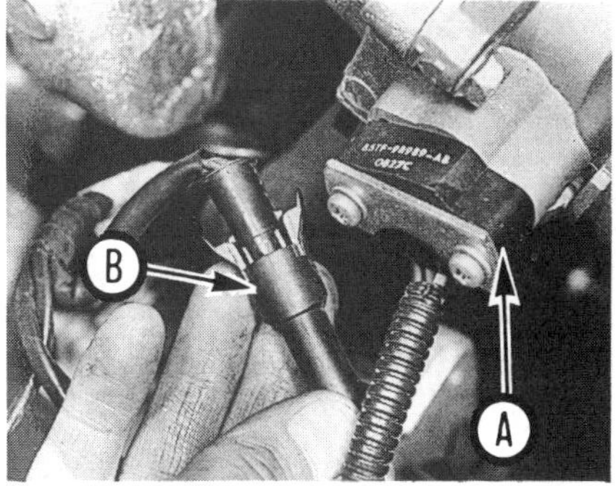

11.54 Throttle position sensor (A) and wiring plug (B)

11.62 Withdrawing the idle speed control valve and gasket

11.69 Disconnecting the fuel feed hose from the fuel rail

46 If adjustment does not produce a change in reading, the potentiometer may be at the extreme of its adjustment range. To centralise the potentiometer, turn the adjustment screw 20 turns clockwise followed by 10 turns anti-clockwise, then repeat the adjustment procedure.
47 Checking and adjustment should be completed within 30 seconds of the meter readings stabilising. If this has not been possible, run the engine at 3000 rpm for 15 seconds, then allow the engine to idle. Re-check the CO content and carry out further adjustments if necessary.
48 On completion of adjustment, stop the engine and disconnect the tachometer and the exhaust gas analyser. Refit the cover to the adjustment screw.

Mixture adjustment potentiometer – removal and refitting

49 The potentiometer is located at the rear right-hand side of the engine compartment, behind the MAP sensor.
50 Disconnect the battery negative lead.
51 Remove the securing screw, then withdraw the potentiometer and disconnect the wiring plug.
52 Refitting is a reversal of removal.

Throttle position sensor – removal and refitting

53 Disconnect the battery negative lead.
54 Free the throttle position sensor wiring plug from the retaining clip located on the underside of the throttle body. Disconnect the wiring plug halves by releasing the locktabs and pulling on the plug halves, not the wiring (photo).
55 Unscrew the two sensor securing screws, and withdraw the sensor from the throttle shaft.
56 Refitting is a reversal of removal, noting that the sensor fits with the wiring at the bottom, and ensuring that the sensor actuating arm engages correctly with the throttle spindle.

Idle speed control valve – removal and refitting

Note: *A new gasket should be used on refitting.*

57 Disconnect the battery negative lead.
58 Loosen the securing clip, and disconnect the air intake hose from the throttle body.
59 Unscrew the securing nut, and release the air intake tube from the bracket on the engine compartment front panel.
60 Disconnect the wiring plug from the idle speed control valve.
61 Release the air cleaner lid securing clips, then remove the air intake tube, plenum chamber, and air cleaner lid as an assembly, disconnecting the breather hose from the air intake tube.
62 Unscrew the two securing bolts, and withdraw the valve from the air intake tube. Recover the gasket (photo).
63 Clean the valve and air intake tube mating faces before refitting, taking care not to allow dirt to enter the air intake tube.
64 Refitting is a reversal of removal, using a new gasket.
65 On completion, start the engine and check that the idle speed is stable – if not, check for air leaks around the valve. Switch on all available electrical loads and check that the idle speed is maintained – if not, suspect a faulty valve.

Fuel injectors – removal and refitting

Note: *Refer to Chapter 3, Section 47 before proceeding. New fuel injector seals should be used on refitting.*

66 Disconnect the battery negative lead.
67 If desired, to improve access, disconnect the wiring from the intake air temperature sensor in the inlet manifold. Similarly, the throttle cable can be moved to one side by disconnecting the cable from the throttle linkage with reference to Chapter 3, Section 14, and the spark plug HT leads can be disconnected and moved to one side, noting their locations and routing to aid refitting.
68 Slowly loosen the fuel rail fuel feed union to relieve the pressure in the system. Be prepared for fuel spillage, and take adequate fire precautions.
69 Disconnect the fuel feed hose from the fuel rail (photo).
70 Disconnect the fuel return hose from the fuel pressure regulator. Again, be prepared for fuel spillage.
71 Disconnect the vacuum pipe from the top of the fuel pressure regulator.
72 Disconnect the wiring plugs from the fuel temperature sensor and the fuel injectors, noting their locations to assist with refitting.
73 Unscrew the two securing bolts, and withdraw the fuel rail.
74 Lift the fuel injectors from their locations in the cylinder head (photo).

11.74 Lifting a fuel injector from the cylinder head

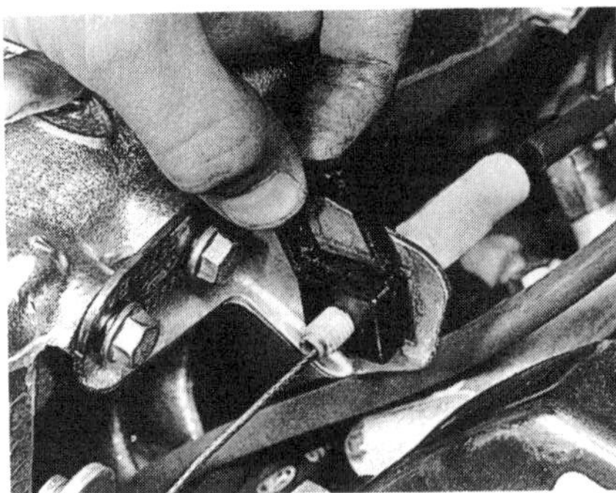
11.104A Disconnect the throttle cable from the securing bracket ...

11.104B ... and the throttle linkage

11.110 Four of the inlet manifold securing bolts

11.111 Removing a spark plug spacer from the cylinder head recess

75 Overhaul of the fuel injectors is not possible, as no spares are available. If faulty, an injector must be renewed.
76 Commence refitting by fitting new seals to both ends of each fuel injector. It is advisable to fit new seals to all the injectors, even if only one has been removed. Lubricate the seals with clean engine oil.
77 Further refitting is a reversal of removal, ensuring that all hoses, pipes and wiring plugs are correctly connected.
78 On completion, where applicable, check and if necessary adjust the idle mixture as described earlier in this Section.

Throttle body – removal and refitting

Note: *A new gasket should be used on refitting.*

79 Disconnect the battery negative lead.
80 Free the throttle position sensor wiring plug from the retaining clip located on the underside of the throttle body. Disconnect the wiring plug halves by releasing the locktabs and pulling on the plug halves, not the wiring.
81 Disconnect the throttle cable from the throttle linkage, with reference to Chapter 3, Section 14 if necessary.
82 Loosen the securing clip, and disconnect the air intake hose from the throttle body.
83 Unscrew the four securing bolts and withdraw the throttle body from the inlet manifold. Recover the gasket.
84 Refitting is a reversal of removal, bearing in mind the following points.
85 Ensure that the mating faces of the throttle body and the inlet manifold are clean, and fit a new gasket.
86 On completion, adjust the throttle cable with reference to Chapter 3, Section 14, and where applicable, check and if necessary adjust the idle mixture as described earlier in this Section.

Exhaust gas oxygen (HEGO) sensor (models with catalytic converter) – removal and refitting

87 The procedure is as described for 1.6 CVH models in Section 9 of this Chapter.

Carbon canister (models with catalytic converter) – removal and refitting

88 Where fitted, the carbon canister is located on the right-hand side of the engine compartment, underneath the coolant expansion tank.
89 Disconnect the battery negative lead.
90 Pull the plastic pipe from the canister (the connector is a push-fit in the canister).
91 Unscrew the securing bolt and lift the canister from its location.
92 Refitting is a reversal of removal.

Carbon canister purge solenoid (models with catalytic converter) – removal and refitting

93 The purge solenoid is located next to the carbon canister on the right-hand side of the engine compartment.
94 Disconnect the battery negative lead.
95 Disconnect the solenoid wiring plug halves by releasing the lock-tabs and pulling on the plug halves, not the wiring.
96 Note the locations of the two solenoid pipes, and the orientation of the solenoid to assist with refitting.

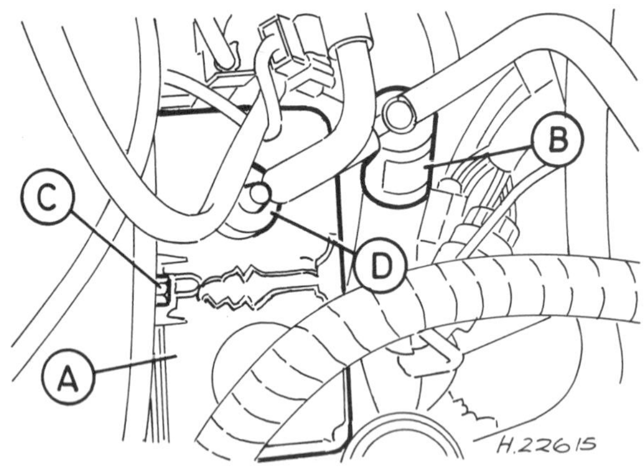

Fig. 14.38 Carbon canister and purge solenoid locations – 2.0 litre DOHC model (Sec 11)

A Carbon canister
B Purge solenoid
C Canister retaining bolt
D Pipe

97 Disconnect the two pipes from the solenoid, and withdraw the solenoid from its location.
98 Refitting is a reversal of removal, ensuring that the solenoid pipes are correctly reconnected, and that the solenoid is correctly orientated as noted before removal.

Inlet manifold – removal and refitting

Note: *Refer to Chapter 3, Section 47 before proceeding. New manifold gaskets and new fuel injector seals must be used on refitting.*

99 Disconnect the battery negative lead.
100 Partially drain the cooling system with reference to Section 8 of this Chapter.
101 Disconnect the coolant hoses from the thermostat housing and the inlet manifold.
102 Disconnect the air intake hose from the front of the inlet manifold.
103 Disconnect the breather hoses and the vacuum hoses from the inlet manifold, referring to Section 20 of this Chapter when disconnecting the brake servo vacuum hose.
104 Disconnect the throttle cable from the throttle linkage with reference to Chapter 3, Section 14 if necessary (photos).
105 Disconnect the HT leads from the spark plugs, noting their locations to aid refitting, and move them to one side.
106 Disconnect the wiring from the cooling fan switch, the engine coolant temperature sensor, and the temperature gauge sender.
107 Release the throttle position sensor wiring connector from the clip under the throttle body, and separate the two halves of the connector.
108 Remove the fuel injectors as described previously in this Section.
109 Check that all relevant wiring, hoses and pipes have been disconnected to facilitate removal of the manifold.
110 Unscrew the ten bolts and two nuts securing the inlet manifold to the cylinder head, and carefully withdraw the manifold (photo). Recover the gasket.
111 Recover the two plastic spark plug spacers from the recesses in the cylinder head (photo).
112 If desired, the manifold can be dismantled with reference to the relevant paragraphs of this Chapter.
113 Refitting is a reversal of removal, bearing in mind the following points.
114 Ensure that the spark plug spacers are in position in the cylinder head recesses before refitting the manifold.
115 Renew all gaskets.
116 Tighten all manifold securing nuts and bolts progressively to the specified torque.
117 Refit the fuel injectors as described previously in this Section.
118 Make sure that all hoses, pipes and wires are securely reconnected in their original positions.
119 On completion, refill the cooling system with reference to Section 8 of this Chapter, check the adjustment of the throttle cable as described in Chapter 3, Section 14, and check and if necessary adjust the idle speed and mixture as described earlier in this Section.

Exhaust manifold – removal and refitting

Note: *A new manifold gasket must be used on refitting.*

120 Disconnect the battery negative lead.
121 Disconnect the wiring plug from the idle speed control valve at the front of the plenum chamber.
122 Loosen the clamp, and detach the air intake hose from the air intake tubing.
123 Unscrew the securing nut, and release the air intake tube from the bracket on the engine compartment front panel.
124 Release the air cleaner lid securing clips, then lift away the air intake tube, plenum chamber and air cleaner lid as an assembly, disconnecting the breather hose from the air intake tube.
125 On models fitted with a catalytic converter, disconnect the exhaust gas oxygen sensor wiring plug.
126 Unscrew the securing nuts and disconnect the exhaust downpipe from the manifold. Recover the gasket. Support the exhaust downpipe from underneath the vehicle (eg with an axle stand) to avoid placing unnecessary strain on the exhaust system.
127 Unscrew the six securing nuts, and lift the manifold from the cylinder head. Recover the gasket.
128 Refitting is a reversal of removal, bearing in mind the following points.
129 Ensure that all mating faces are clean, and use a new gasket.
130 Tighten the manifold securing nuts and the downpipe securing nuts progressively to the specified torque (where given).

Exhaust system – checking, removal and refitting

131 Refer to the information given for the 1.6 litre CVH engine in Section 9 of this Chapter.

12 Ignition and engine management system – early 'Economy' models

Modified components

1 The original type distributor and ignition module for these early models (built between 1982 and 1984) are no longer available.
2 If renewal of either component is necessary, alternative components (available from a Ford dealer) must be fitted as described in the following paragraphs.

Distributor – renewal

Note: *Refer to Chapter 4, Section 2 before proceeding. A timing light will be required to check the ignition timing after fitting the new distributor.*

3 Turn the crankshaft to bring No 1 cylinder to the firing point, with the 16° BTDC mark on the crankshaft pulley aligned with the pointer on the crankshaft front oil seal housing, as described in Chapter 4, Section 9.
4 Fit the new distributor to the engine as described in Chapter 4, Section 9, then proceed as follows.
5 Cut the original distributor wiring plug from the wiring loom. Make the cut close to the connector.
6 Strip back 10 mm of insulation from each of the wires on the wiring loom and the adaptor loom supplied with the new distributor.
7 Solder the adaptor loom wires to the corresponding identically coloured wires in the main loom.
8 Carefully insulate each individual soldered joint using insulating tape, then apply tape to cover the join between the looms.
9 Fit the new distributor cap (and screening can, where applicable), and connect the HT leads.
10 Connect the adaptor loom to the distributor.
11 Start the engine, and adjust the ignition timing to the specified value (see 'Specifications' at the beginning of this Chapter), as described in Chapter 4, Section 10, noting that the vacuum pipe must be left connected.

ESC module – renewal

Note: *Refer to Chapter 4, Section 2 before proceeding.*

12 Remove the module complete with its securing bracket, as described in Chapter 4, Section 12.
13 Fit the new module, slightly behind the old module position, on the flat vertical surface of the body panel, and secure with the two screws supplied. Note that the module must be mounted against the flat area of the body panel to prevent distortion of the module, and to ensure good heat transfer from the module to the body.
14 Reconnect the module vacuum pipe.
15 Connect the adaptor loom supplied with the new module between the module and the old module's wiring plug.
16 Where applicable, refit the coil to its original location.

13 Ignition and engine management system – 1.6 litre CVH models

General description

1 A development of the EEC IV (Electronic Engine Control IV) engine management system is used to control both the ignition and fuel injection systems.
2 A fully electronic Distributorless Ignition System (DIS) is fitted to 1.6 litre CVH models. The mechanical distribution of high tension voltage (by a rotating distributor) is replaced by 'static' solid state electronic components.
3 The system selects the most appropriate ignition advance setting for the prevailing engine operating conditions from a three-dimensional map of values stored in the EEC IV control module memory. The module selects the appropriate advance value according to information sup-

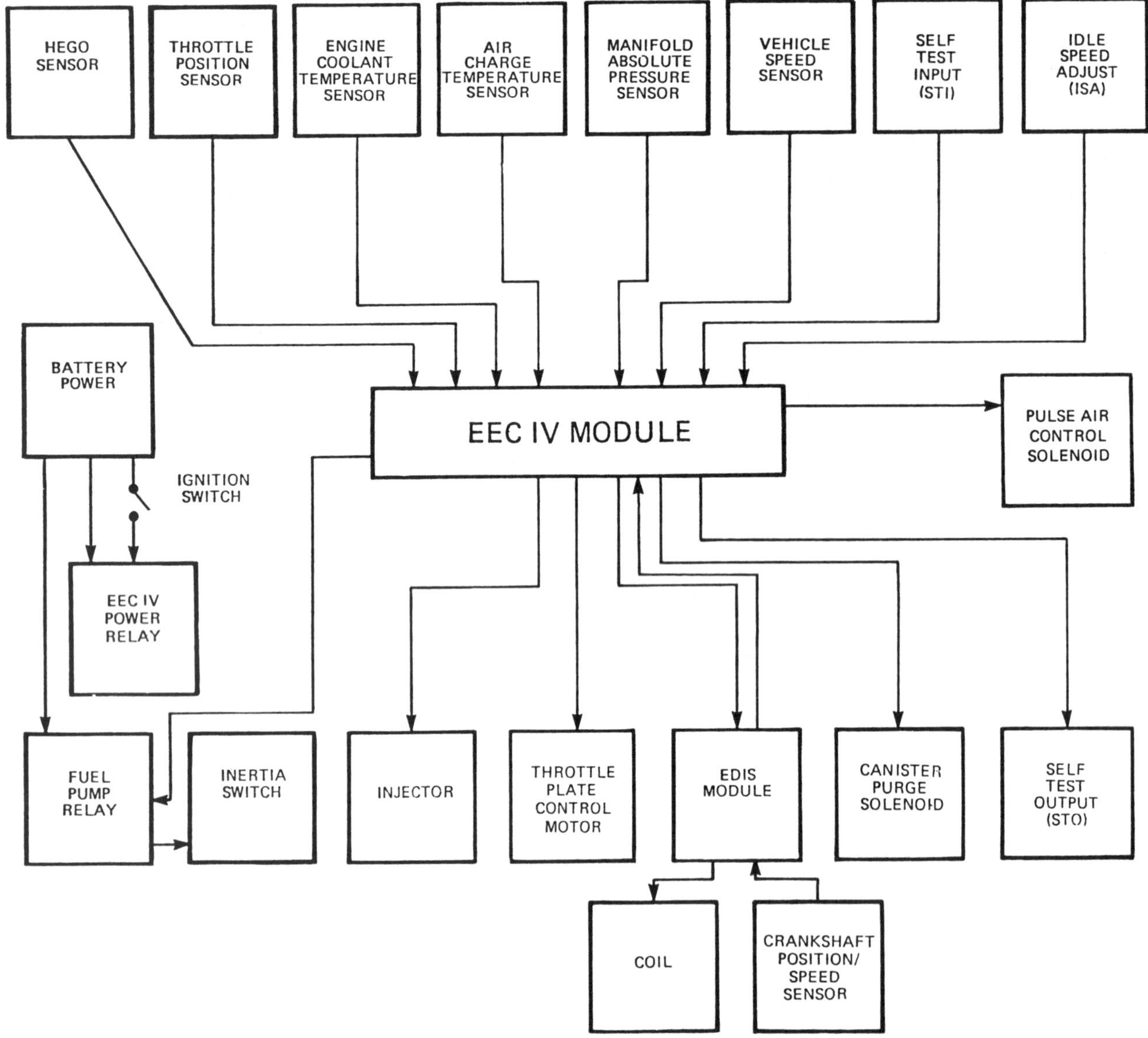

Fig. 14.39 Schematic diagram of EEC IV system operation for 1.6 litre CVH models (Sec 13)

plied on engine load, speed, and operating temperature from various sensors.

4 The EEC IV module receives information from a crankshaft speed/position sensor (similar to that described for the ESC Hybrid system in Chapter 4, Section 1, except that the sensor is activated by a toothed disc on the flywheel), a throttle position sensor, an engine coolant temperature sensor, an air charge temperature sensor, a manifold absolute pressure (MAP) sensor, a vehicle speed sensor (mounted on the gearbox), and an exhaust gas oxygen sensor.

5 The module provides outputs to control the fuel pump, fuel injector, throttle valve control motor, pulse air control solenoid, carbon canister purge solenoid (where applicable), and the ignition system.

6 Using the inputs from the various sensors, the EEC IV module computes the optimum ignition advance and fuel injector pulse duration to suit the prevailing engine conditions. A 'limited operation strategy' (LOS) means that the vehicle is still driveable, albeit at reduced power and efficiency, in the event of a failure in the module or one of its sensors.

7 Further details of the fuel injection system components are given in Section 9.

Spark plugs and HT leads – inspection and renewal

Note: *Refer to Chapter 4, Section 2 before proceeding.*

8 Proceed as described in Chapter 4, Section 4, but ignore the references to the distributor cap (the HT leads are connected directly to the coil), and refer to the Specifications at the beginning of this Chapter for the correct spark plug type and gap.

Coil – description and testing

9 The coil is located towards the front right-hand side of the cylinder block (photo).

10 The coil has two primary and two secondary windings.

11 One secondary winding supplies current to numbers 1 and 4 cylinders simultaneously, while the other supplies current to numbers 2 and 3 cylinders. Whenever either of the coils is energised, two sparks are generated. For example, one spark is produced in No 1 cylinder on its compression stroke, while the other is produced in No 4 cylinder on its exhaust stroke. The spark in No 4 cylinder is 'wasted' and has no detrimental effect on engine performance.

12 Testing of the coil should be entrusted to a Ford dealer or a suitable specialist.

Coil – removal and refitting

Note: *Refer to Chapter 4, Section 2 before proceeding.*

13 Disconnect the battery negative lead.

14 Remove the two securing screws, and withdraw the plastic ignition module shroud.

13.9 Ignition coil (A) and suppressor (B) viewed from underneath vehicle with cover removed

13.15A Disconnecting the ignition coil wiring plug ...

13.15B ... and the suppressor wiring plug

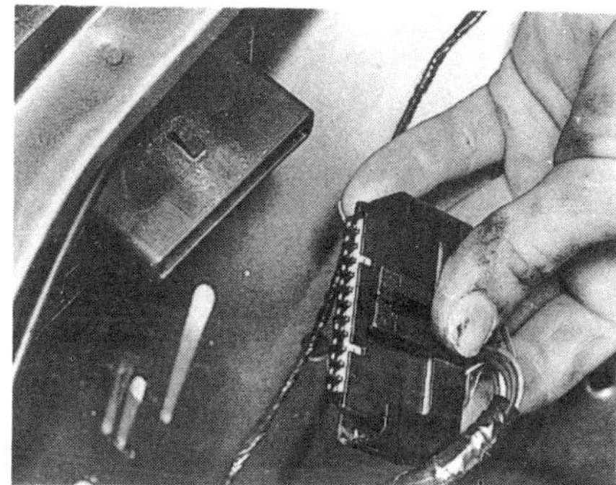
13.22 Disconnecting the ignition module wiring plug

13.28 Engine management module withdrawn from its mounting bracket

15 Disconnect the ignition coil wiring plug and the suppressor wiring plug, pulling on the plugs, not on the wiring (photos).
16 Release the securing lugs, and disconnect the HT leads from the coil, noting their locations to aid refitting.
17 Remove the four Torx screws, and withdraw the coil from the cylinder block.
18 Refitting is a reversal of removal, but ensure that the HT leads are correctly reconnected. The HT lead terminals on the coil are numbered to avoid confusion.

Ignition timing – adjustment

19 The ignition timing is controlled by the EEC IV module, and no adjustment is possible.

Electronic modules – removal and refitting

Note: *Refer to Chapter 4, Section 2 before proceeding.*

Ignition module

20 The ignition module is located at the front right-hand side of the engine compartment.
21 Disconnect the battery negative lead.
22 Release the securing lug and pull the wiring plug from the module. Pull on the plug, not on the wiring (photo).
23 Remove the two securing screws, and withdraw the module from the body panel.
24 Refitting is a reversal of removal.

Engine management module

25 The module is located in the passenger compartment, behind the glovebox.
26 Disconnect the battery negative lead.
27 Open the glovebox, and carefully pull it from its retaining clips.
28 Unclip and withdraw the module from its retaining bracket (photo).
29 The wiring plug is secured by a screw which is integral with the plug. Disconnect the wiring plug and withdraw the module.
30 Refitting is a reversal of removal, noting that the wiring plug will only fit in one position.

Crankshaft speed/position sensor – removal and refitting

31 The sensor is located at the left-hand rear of the cylinder block, above the starter motor (photo).
32 Disconnect the battery negative lead.
33 Remove the securing screw, and withdraw the sensor shroud.
34 Disconnect the sensor wiring plug.
35 Remove the Torx securing screw, and withdraw the sensor.
36 Refitting is a reversal of removal.

Engine coolant temperature sensor – removal and refitting

37 The sensor is located in the side of the inlet manifold.
38 Disconnect the battery negative lead.
39 Partially drain the cooling system with reference to Section 7 of this Chapter.

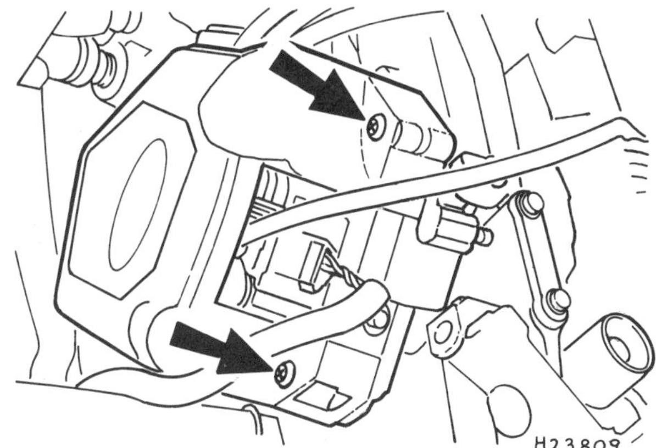

Fig. 14.40 Ignition module shroud securing screws (arrowed) – 1.6 litre CVH models (Sec 13)

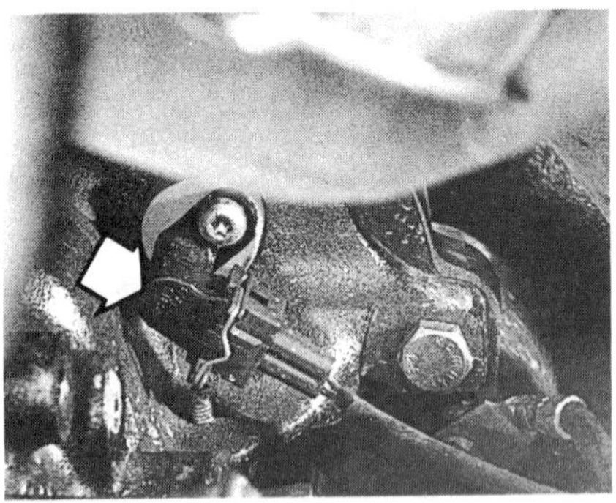

13.31 Crankshaft speed/position sensor (arrowed) viewed from front of engine with shroud removed

13.40 Disconnecting the engine coolant temperature sensor wiring plug

13.43 Air charge temperature sensor location (arrowed)

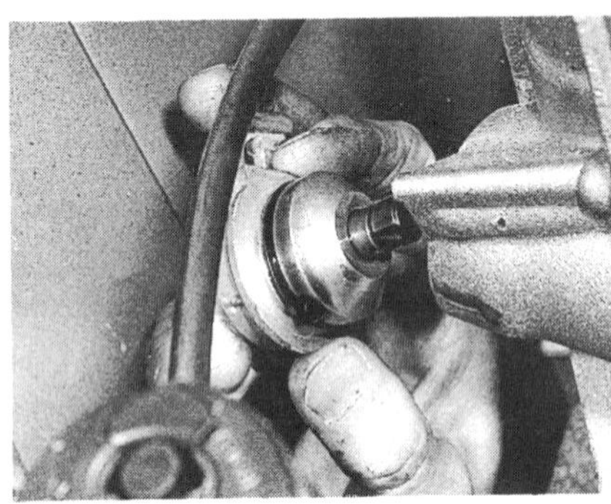

13.53 Withdrawing the vehicle speed sensor from the gearbox casing

13.56 Manifold absolute pressure (MAP) sensor location

40 Disconnect the sensor wiring plug by pulling on the plug, not the wiring (photo).
41 Unscrew the sensor from the inlet manifold and remove it.
42 Refitting is a reversal of removal, but refill the cooling system with reference to Section 7 of this Chapter.

Air charge temperature sensor – removal and refitting

43 The sensor is located in the side of the CFI unit (photo).
44 Disconnect the battery negative lead.
45 Disconnect the sensor wiring plug by pulling on the plug, not the wiring.
46 Unscrew the sensor from the CFI unit and remove it.
47 Refitting is a reversal of removal, but coat the threads of the sensor with suitable sealant before fitting.

Vehicle speed sensor – removal and refitting

48 The sensor is located in the left-hand side of the gearbox/transmission.
49 Disconnect the battery negative lead.
50 Jack up the vehicle and support it securely on axle stands.
51 Detach the sensor wiring connector from its bracket, and separate the two halves of the connector.
52 Unscrew the securing bolt, and withdraw the wiring connector bracket, noting its orientation.
53 Withdraw the sensor from the gearbox/transmission casing (photo).
54 Before refitting the sensor, examine the O-ring, and renew if damaged or worn.
55 Refitting is a reversal of removal, ensuring that the wiring connector bracket is correctly located.

Manifold absolute pressure (MAP) sensor – removal and refitting

56 The sensor is located at the rear right-hand side of the engine compartment (photo).
57 Disconnect the battery negative lead.
58 Remove the two screws securing the sensor to the body panel, and carefully withdraw the sensor, taking care not to strain the wiring.
59 Disconnect the wiring plug from the sensor, pulling on the plug not the wiring, then disconnect the vacuum hose and remove the sensor.
60 Refitting is a reversal of removal.

14 Ignition and engine management system – 2.0 litre DOHC carburettor models

General description

1 The basic operating principles of the ignition system are as described in Chapter 4, Section 1.
2 A development of the ESC II (Electronic Spark Control II) system is used to control the operation of the engine.
3 The ESC II module receives information from a crankshaft speed/position sensor (similar to that described for the ESC Hybrid system in Chapter 4, Section 1, except that the sensor is activated by a toothed disc on the rear of the crankshaft, inside the cylinder block), and an engine coolant temperature sensor.
4 The ignition advance is a function of the ESC II module, and is controlled by vacuum. The module is connected to the carburettor by a vacuum pipe, and a transducer in the module translates the vacuum signal into an electrical voltage. From the vacuum signal, the module determines engine load; engine speed and temperature are determined from the crankshaft speed/position sensor and the engine coolant temperature sensor. The module has a range of spark advance settings stored in its memory, and a suitable setting is selected for the relevant engine speed, load and temperature. The degree of advance can thus be constantly varied to suit the prevailing engine speed and load conditions.

Spark plugs and HT leads – inspection and renewal

Note: *Refer to Chapter 4, Section 2 before proceeding.*

5 Proceed as described in Chapter 4, Section 4, noting the following points.

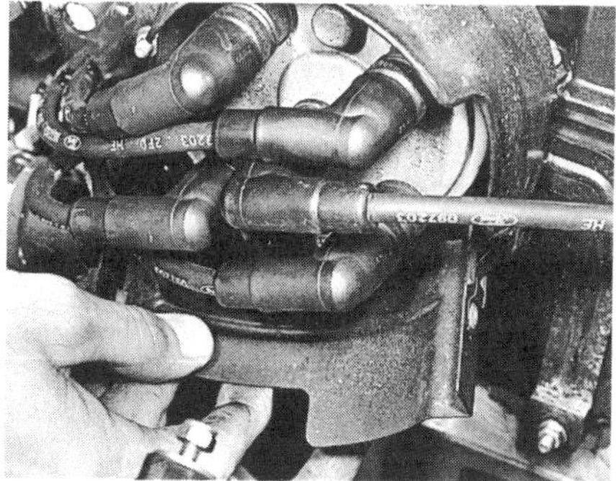
14.11A Unclipping the lower section ...

14.11B ... and the upper section of the distributor shield

14.14 Removing the distributor cap and rotor arm

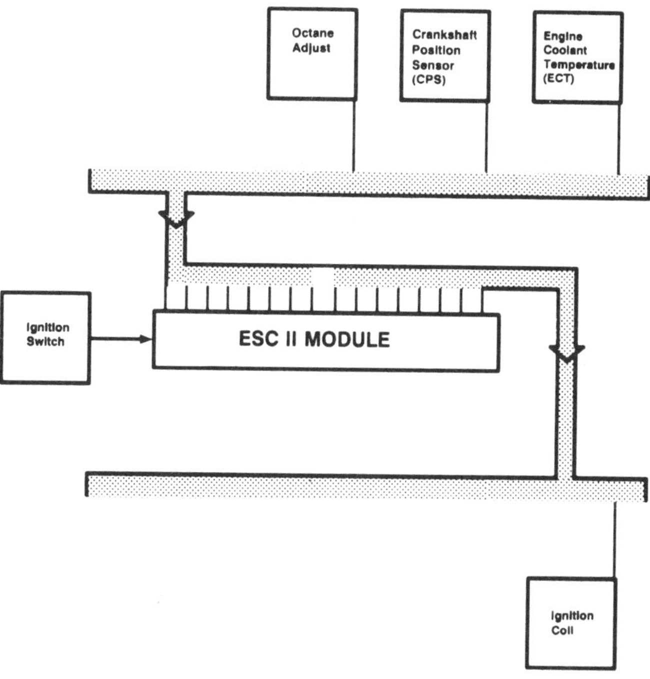

Fig. 14.41 Schematic diagram of ESC II system operation for 2.0 litre DOHC carburettor models (Sec 14)

6 Refer to the Specifications at the beginning of this Chapter for the correct spark plug type and gap.
7 When refitting the spark plugs, coat their threads with suitable anti-seize compound, taking care not to contaminate the electrodes, then refit the plugs and tighten them to the specified torque.

Coil – description and testing

Note: *Refer to Chapter 4, Section 2 before proceeding.*

8 The coil is located on the left-hand side of the engine compartment, and is secured by a metal strap.
9 To test the coil, refer to Chapter 4, Section 5. Refer to the Specifications at the beginning of this Chapter for the coil primary and secondary winding resistances.

Distributor cap and rotor arm – removal and refitting

Note: *Refer to Chapter 4, Section 2 before proceeding.*

10 Disconnect the battery negative lead.
11 Unclip the lower section of the distributor shield from the upper section, then unscrew the two securing nuts, and withdraw the upper section of the shield from the studs on the upper timing chain cover (photos).
12 If necessary, identify each HT lead for position, so that the leads can be refitted to their correct cylinders, then disconnect the leads from the spark plugs by pulling on the connectors, not the leads. Similarly, disconnect the HT lead from the coil, and release it from the clip on the timing chain cover.
13 Using a suitable Torx key or socket, unscrew the two distributor cap securing screws, then lift off the cap.
14 The rotor arm is a push-fit on the end of the rotor shaft (photo).
15 If desired, the rotor housing can be pulled from the timing chain cover.
16 Refitting is a reversal of removal, ensuring that the rotor arm is pushed fully home on the rotor shaft. Make sure that the HT leads are fitted to their correct cylinders. Note that the rotor arm will only fit in one position.

Ignition timing – adjustment

17 The ignition timing is controlled by the ESC II module, and no adjustment is possible.

ESC II module – removal and refitting

Note: *Refer to Chapter 4, Section 2 before proceeding.*

18 The module is located on the left-hand side of the engine compartment.
19 Disconnect the battery negative lead.
20 Disconnect the vacuum pipe from the module.
21 Depress the locking tab, and disconnect the wiring plug from the module.
22 Remove the two securing screws, and withdraw the module from the body panel.
23 Refitting is a reversal of removal.

14.28 Removing the crankshaft speed/position sensor (engine removed)

Crankshaft speed/position sensor – removal and refitting

24 The sensor is located at the right-hand rear of the cylinder block, behind the oil filter.

25 Disconnect the battery negative lead.

26 Access is most easily obtained from underneath the vehicle. To improve access, apply the handbrake, then jack up the front of the vehicle and support it securely on axle stands.

27 Disconnect the wiring plug from the sensor.

28 Remove the securing screw and withdraw the sensor from its location in the cylinder block (photo).

29 Before refitting the sensor, examine the O-ring and renew if damaged or worn.

30 Refitting is a reversal of removal, noting the torque setting for the sensor screw.

Engine coolant temperature sensor – removal and refitting

31 The sensor is located in the side of the inlet manifold. The removal and refitting procedure is as described for 1.6 litre CVH models in Section 13 of this Chapter.

15 Ignition and engine management system – 2.0 litre DOHC fuel injection models

General description

1 The basic operating principles of the ignition system are as described in Chapter 4, Section 1.

2 A development of the EEC IV (Electronic Engine Control IV) engine management system is used to control both the ignition and fuel injection systems.

3 The EEC IV module receives information from a crankshaft speed/position sensor (similar to that described for the ESC Hybrid system in Chapter 4, Section 1, except that the sensor is activated by a

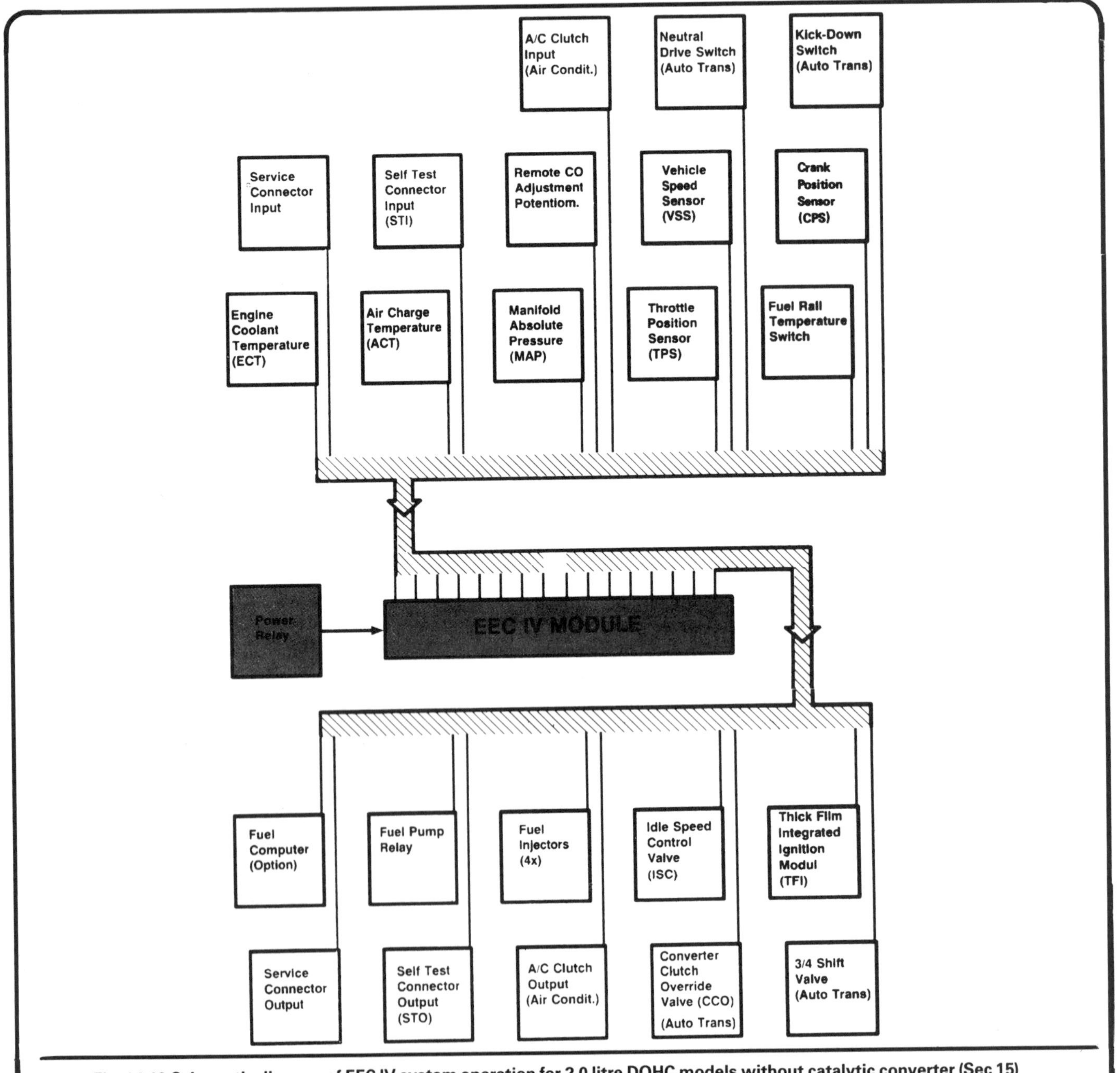

Fig. 14.42 Schematic diagram of EEC IV system operation for 2.0 litre DOHC models without catalytic converter (Sec 15)

toothed disc on the rear of the crankshaft, inside the cylinder block), a throttle position sensor, an engine coolant temperature sensor, a fuel temperature sensor, an air charge temperature sensor, a manifold absolute pressure (MAP) sensor, and a vehicle speed sensor (mounted on the gearbox). Additionally, on models with a catalytic converter, an additional input is supplied to the EEC IV module from an exhaust gas oxygen (HEGO) sensor. On models with automatic transmission, additional sensors are fitted to the transmission to inform the EEC IV module when the transmission is in neutral, and when the kickdown is being operated.

4 The module provides outputs to control the fuel pump, fuel injectors, idle speed, ignition system and automatic transmission (see Section 18). Additionally, on models with air conditioning, the EEC IV module disengages the air conditioning compressor clutch when starting the engine, and when the engine is suddenly accelerated. On models fitted with a catalytic converter, the EEC IV module also controls the carbon canister purge solenoid valve (see Section 11).

5 Using the inputs from the various sensors, the EEC IV module computes the optimum ignition advance, and fuel injector pulse duration to suit the prevailing engine conditions. A 'limited operation strategy' (LOS) means that the vehicle is still driveable, albeit at reduced power and efficiency, in the event of a failure in the module or one of its sensors.

6 Further details of the fuel injection system components are given in Section 11.

Spark plugs and HT leads – inspection and renewal

Note: *Refer to Chapter 4, Section 2 before proceeding.*

7 Proceed as described in Chapter 4, Section 4, noting the following points (photo).

8 Refer to the Specifications at the beginning of this Chapter for the correct spark plug type and gap.

9 When refitting the spark plugs, coat their threads with suitable anti-seize compound, taking care not to contaminate the electrodes, then refit the plugs and tighten them to the specified torque.

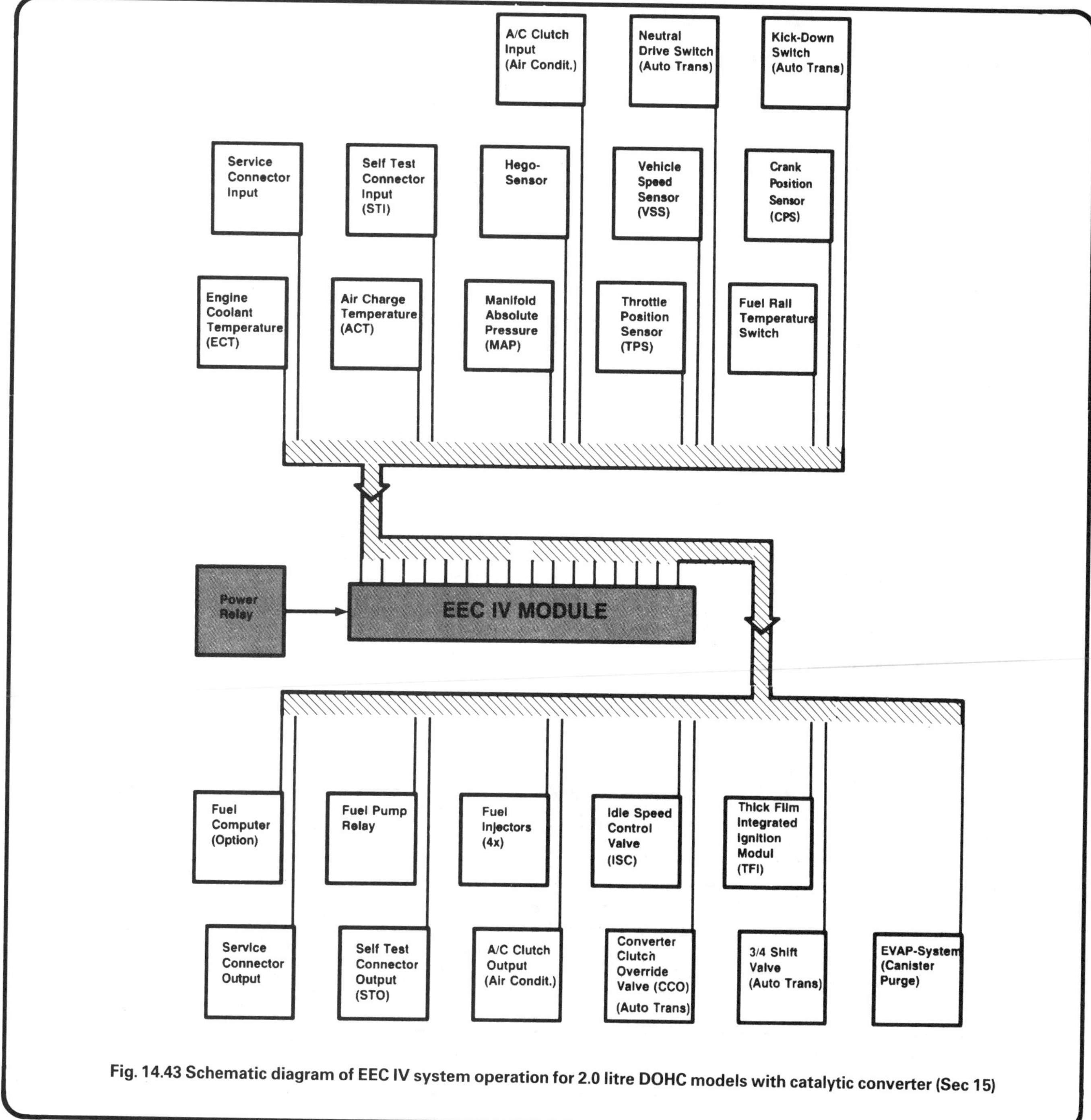

Fig. 14.43 Schematic diagram of EEC IV system operation for 2.0 litre DOHC models with catalytic converter (Sec 15)

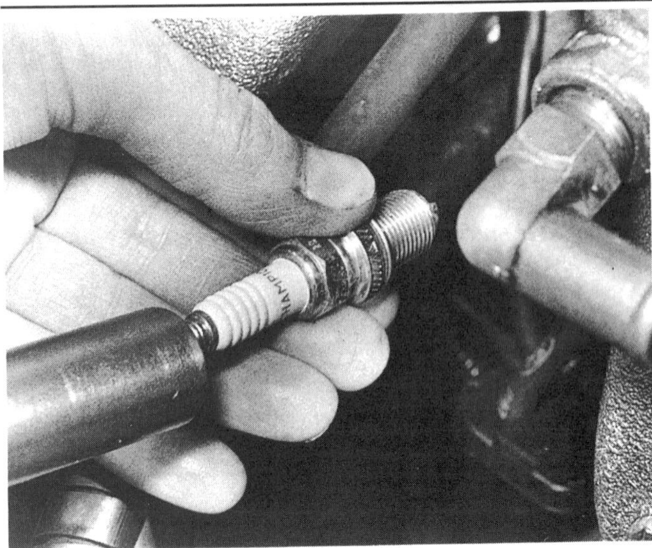

15.7 Removing a spark plug

Coil – description and testing

Note: *Refer to Chapter 4, Section 2 before proceeding.*

10 The coil is located on the left-hand side of the engine compartment, and is secured by a metal strap (photo).

11 To test the coil, refer to Chapter 4, Section 5. Refer to the Specifications at the beginning of this Chapter for the coil primary and secondary winding resistances.

Coil – removal and refitting

Note: *Refer to Chapter 4, Section 2 before proceeding.*

12 Refer to Chapter 4, Section 6, but note that the coil/ignition module heat shield must be removed for access to the coil securing bolts. The heat shield is secured by two screws. Note that on certain models, an earthing lead and/or a suppressor may be secured by one of the coil securing bolts (photo).

Distributor cap and rotor arm – removal and refitting

13 The procedure is as described for carburettor models in Section 14 of this Chapter.

Ignition timing – adjustment

14 The ignition timing is controlled by the EEC IV module, and no adjustment is possible.

Electronic modules – removal and refitting

Note: *Refer to Chapter 4, Section 2 before proceeding.*

Ignition module

15 The ignition module is located on the left-hand side of the engine compartment, beneath the coil (photo).

16 Disconnect the battery negative lead.

17 Remove the two securing screws, and withdraw the coil/ignition module heat shield.

18 Release the locking lug and disconnect the ignition module wiring plug. Pull on the plug, not on the wiring.

19 Remove the two securing screws, and withdraw the module from the body panel.

20 Refitting is a reversal of removal, ensuring that the underside of the module and the corresponding area of the body panel are clean.

Engine management module – models up to 1990

21 Refer to Chapter 4, Section 12, paragraph 15 onwards.

Engine management module – models from 1990

22 Refer to the procedure given for 1.6 litre CVH models in Section 13 of this Chapter.

Crankshaft speed/position sensor – removal and refitting

23 The procedure is as described for carburettor models in Section 14 of this Chapter.

Engine coolant temperature sensor – removal and refitting

24 The sensor is located in the side of the inlet manifold, behind the throttle body. The removal and refitting procedure is as described for 1.6 litre CVH models in Section 13 of this Chapter.

Air charge temperature sensor – removal and refitting

25 The sensor is located in the upper section of the inlet manifold.

26 Disconnect the battery negative lead.

27 Disconnect the sensor wiring plug by pulling on the plug, not the wiring (photo).

28 Unscrew the sensor from the inlet manifold and remove it.

29 Refitting is a reversal of removal, noting the torque setting for the sensor.

Fuel temperature sensor – removal and refitting

30 The sensor is located in the top of the fuel rail.

31 Disconnect the battery negative lead, and to improve access, disconnect the wiring plug from the air charge temperature sensor (in the inlet manifold). Disconnect the sensor wiring plug by pulling on the plug, not the wiring.

32 Disconnect the fuel temperature sensor wiring plug, again pulling on the plug (photo).

33 Unscrew the sensor from the fuel rail and remove it.

34 Refitting is a reversal of removal, noting the torque setting for the sensor.

Vehicle speed sensor – removal and refitting

35 The sensor is located in the left-hand side of the gearbox/transmission. The removal and refitting procedure is as described for 1.6 litre CVH models in Section 13 of this Chapter.

Manifold absolute pressure (MAP) sensor – removal and refitting

36 The sensor is located on the right-hand side of the engine compartment. Removal and refitting is as described for 1.6 litre CVH models in Section 13 of this Chapter (photo).

15.10 Ignition coil viewed with heat shield removed

15.12 Suppressor secured by one of the coil securing bolts

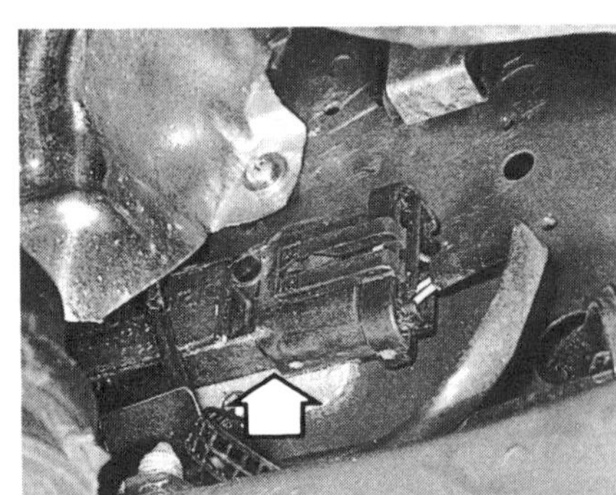

15.15 Ignition module location (arrowed)

15.27 Disconnecting the air charge temperature sensor wiring plug

15.32 Disconnecting the fuel temperature sensor wiring plug

15.36 Manifold absolute pressure (MAP) sensor location

16 Clutch

'Low-lift' clutch components – 1.6, 1.8 and 2.0 litre OHC models

1 Modified clutch components are available to reduce the pedal pressure required to operate the clutch. Some later models may have been fitted with these components in production.

2 Overhaul procedures are unaffected, but 'Low-lift' components are not interchangeable with standard clutch components. The clutch driven plate and pressure plate are stamped 'Low-lift' for identification.

Clutch release bearing – models with MT75 type gearbox

3 On models fitted with an MT75 type gearbox, the clutch release bearing may be secured to the arm using a circlip instead of spring clips. Otherwise, all procedures are as described in Chapter 5.

17 MT75 type manual gearbox

General description

1 The MT75 type gearbox is of five-speed type, and is fitted to 2.0 litre DOHC models.

2 The gearbox design is completely new, and owes nothing to the previous types used in the Sierra range. The MT75 gearbox is lighter, more compact, and more reliable than its predecessors.

3 The gearbox casing consists of front and rear housings manufactured from aluminium alloy, and as the 5th gear components are accommodated in the main casing, there is no need for an extension housing.

4 The floor-mounted gear lever operates the selector shaft via an external rod which protrudes from the front of the gearbox casing.

5 Production of the MT75 gearbox is heavily automated, and ease of production was a prime design consideration. As a result, many special

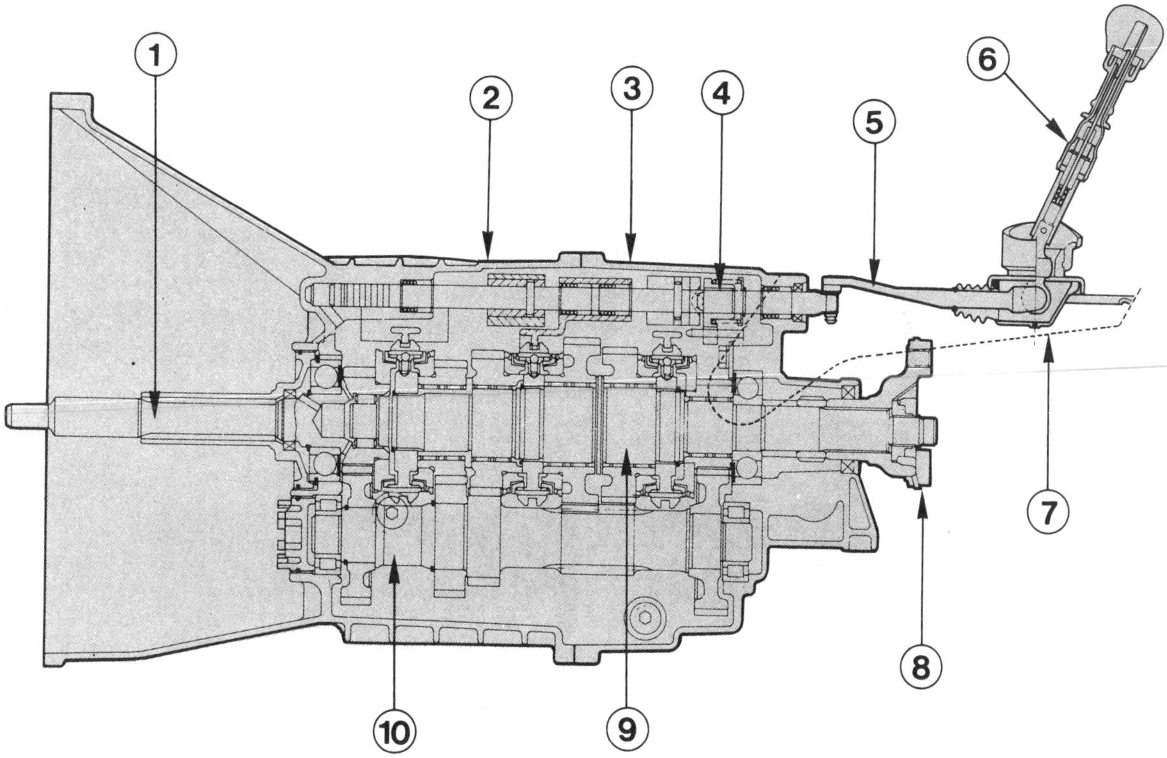

Fig. 14.44 Sectional view of MT75 type manual gearbox (Sec 17)

1 Input shaft
2 Front housing
3 Rear housing
4 Gear selector shaft (internal)
5 Gear selector rod (external)
6 Gear lever
7 Gear linkage support bracket
8 Output flange
9 Mainshaft
10 Countershaft

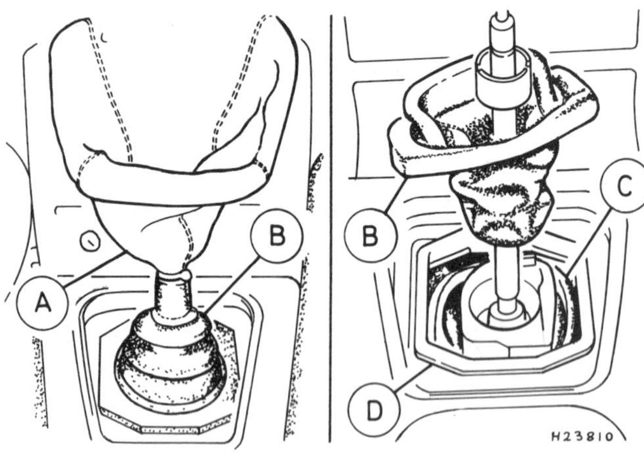

Fig. 14.45 Gear lever gaiters – MT75 type gearbox (Sec 17)

A *Outer gaiter*
B *Inner gaiter*
C *Noise damping pad*
D *Retaining frame*

tools are required to overhaul the gearbox, and these tools cannot readily be improvised by the home mechanic. Overhaul of the MT75 type gearbox is considered beyond the scope of the DIY enthusiast, therefore the coverage provided is restricted to removal and refitting of the gearbox and gear selector linkage, and maintenance tasks.

6 Overhaul of the gearbox should be entrusted to a Ford dealer, who will have access to the specialist tools and knowledge required.

Maintenance and inspection

7 Proceed as described in Chapter 6, Section 2, noting that the oil level should be 0 to 5.0 mm (0 to 0.2 in) below the lower edge of the filler/level hole (photo). Ignore the reference to oil seal renewal.

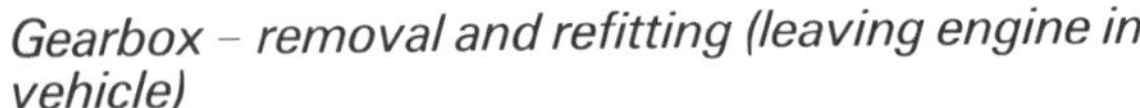

Gearbox – removal and refitting (leaving engine in vehicle)

8 Removal of the engine and gearbox as an assembly is described in Section 5 of this Chapter.

9 Disconnect the battery negative lead.

10 Unscrew and remove the top engine-to-gearbox bolts which are accessible from the engine compartment. Note the location of the bolts, and note the positions of the earth strap and any wiring clips attached to the bolts.

11 Jack up the vehicle and support it on axle stands.

12 To improve access, disconnect the exhaust downpipe from the manifold and remove the exhaust system as described in Section 10 or 11 of this Chapter, as applicable.

13 On models fitted with a catalytic converter, release the securing clips and withdraw the exhaust heat shield from under the vehicle for access to the propeller shaft.

14 Remove the propeller shaft with reference to Section 19 of this Chapter.

15 Where applicable, bend back the locktabs, then unscrew the two bolts securing each of the two anti-roll bar U-clamps to the vehicle underbody. Lower the anti-roll bar as far as possible.

16 Disconnect the wiring from the starter motor, and remove the starter motor with reference to Chapter 13 if necessary.

17 Support the gearbox with a trolley jack, and an interposed block of wood to spread the load.

18 Unscrew the four nuts securing the gearbox crossmember to the vehicle underbody. Unscrew the central bolt securing the crossmember to the gearbox, and remove the crossmember. Note the position of the earth strap, where applicable. Recover the mounting cup, and where applicable the exhaust mounting bracket and heat shield (photo).

19 Lower the gearbox slightly on the jack, then remove the securing circlip and disconnect the speedometer drive cable from the gearbox (photo).

20 Disconnect the wiring from the reversing lamp switch, and on models with fuel injection, disconnect the wiring from the vehicle speed sensor mounted in the side of the gearbox (photo).

21 Unscrew the two securing bolts, and disconnect the gear linkage support bracket from the gearbox (photo).

17.7 Gearbox oil filler/level plug (arrowed)

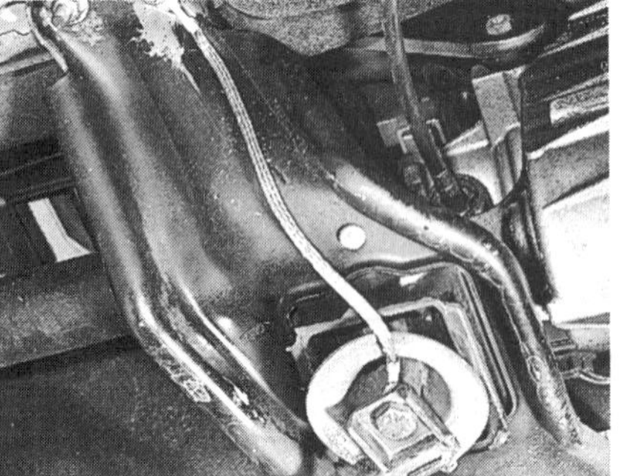

17.18 Gearbox crossmember and earth strap

17.19 Speedometer drive cable connection at gearbox

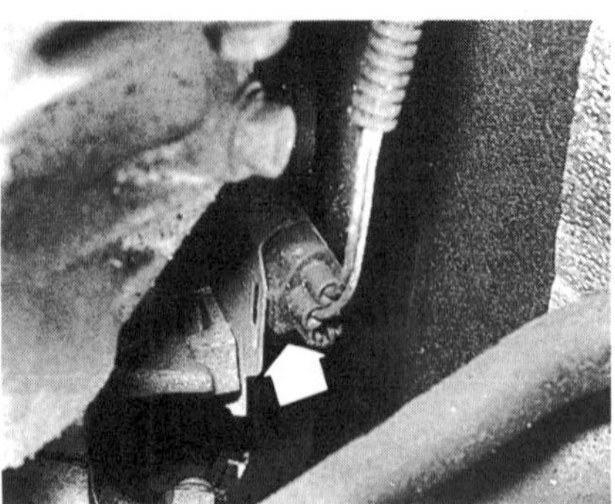

17.20 Vehicle speed sensor wiring plug and bracket (arrowed) – fuel injection model

17.21 Gear linkage support bracket securing bolt (arrowed)

22 Using a suitable pin punch, drive out the roll-pin securing the gearchange rod to the gear linkage.
23 Place a suitable rod across the vehicle underbody to support the gear linkage support bracket whilst the gearbox is removed.
24 Working inside the vehicle, place a wooden block under the clutch pedal to raise it fully against its stop, so holding the automatic adjuster pawl clear of the toothed quadrant.
25 Disconnect the clutch cable from the clutch release arm, and pass the cable through the bellhousing, with reference to Chapter 5 if necessary. Take note of the routing of the cable to aid refitting.
26 Unscrew and remove the remaining engine-to-gearbox bolts, and remove the bolt from the engine adaptor plate. Recover any shims fitted between the sump and the gearbox when removing the lower engine-to-gearbox bolts.
27 With the aid of an assistant, lift the gearbox from the engine, using the trolley jack to take the weight. Do not allow the weight of the gearbox to hang on the input shaft. It may be necessary to rock the gearbox a little to release it from the engine.
28 With the gearbox removed, temporarily reconnect the anti-roll bar to the underbody if the vehicle is to be moved.
29 Refitting is a reversal of removal, taking note of the following points.
30 Before attempting to refit the gearbox, check that the clutch friction disc is centralised as described in Chapter 5, Section 7.
31 Check that the clutch release arm and bearing are correctly fitted, and lightly grease the input shaft splines.
32 Check that the engine adaptor plate is correctly positioned on its dowels. If necessary, a cable tie can be used to temporarily secure the adaptor plate in position on the cylinder block using one of the engine-to-gearbox bolt holes.
33 If shims were fitted between the sump and the gearbox, refit them in their original locations when mating the engine to the gearbox. If the engine has been overhauled, where applicable fit the relevant shims as calculated during engine reassembly (see Section 5 *'Sump – removal and refitting'*).
34 Reconnect the clutch cable to the release arm with reference to Chapter 5, Section 3, ensuring that it is routed as noted during removal.
35 Refit the propeller shaft with reference to Section 19 of this Chapter.
36 Refit the exhaust system with reference to Section 10 or 11 of this Chapter, as applicable.
37 Tighten all fixings to the specified torque, where applicable.
38 On completion, check the gearbox oil level, and top up if necessary.

Gear linkage – removal and refitting

39 Working inside the vehicle, unclip the knob from the gear lever by pressing it sideways. Do not turn the gear lever knob.
40 Where applicable, detach the tray from the centre console.
41 Release the gear lever outer gaiter from the centre console/tray, then turn it inside out and pull it up the gear lever.
42 Detach the gear lever inner gaiter, together with the retaining frame, from the centre console.
43 Proceed as described in paragraphs 11 to 25 of this Section, ignoring paragraph 23.
44 Manipulate the rubber gaiter from the gear linkage support bracket for access to the base of the gear lever.
45 Remove the circlip and the pivot pin, then disconnect the gear shift rod from the base of the gear lever. Withdraw the gear shift rod.
46 Remove the circlip securing the base of the gear lever to the gear linkage support bracket, and withdraw the gear lever assembly through the floor from inside the vehicle, and the gear linkage support bracket from under the vehicle.
47 The gear lever assembly cannot be dismantled, and must be renewed as a unit if faulty.
48 Refitting is a reversal of removal, bearing in mind the following points.
49 Reconnect the clutch cable to the release arm with reference to Chapter 5, Section 3, ensuring that it is routed as noted during removal.
50 Refit the propeller shaft with reference to Section 19 of this Chapter.
51 Refit the exhaust system with reference to Section 10 or 11 of this Chapter, as applicable.
52 Tighten all fixings to the specified torque, where applicable.

18 A4LD type automatic transmission

General description – 2.0 litre DOHC models

1 An A4LD type automatic transmission with partial electronic control is fitted to 2.0 litre DOHC models. Some early models may be fitted with a conventionally controlled transmission as described in Chapter 7. The transmission with partial electronic control can be identified by looking at the lock-up clutch solenoid wiring plug, which has three wires instead of the previous two.
2 The later type transmission behaves in exactly the same way as the earlier type for gearchanges up and down between 1st and 2nd and 2nd and 3rd gears, but the changes up from 3rd to 4th, and down from 4th to 3rd, and the torque converter lock-up clutch are controlled by the EEC IV engine management module (see Section 14 or 15 of this Chapter, as applicable). This provides more accurate control of the transmission according to the prevailing engine operating conditions.
3 The procedures described in Chapter 7 are unaffected.

Kick-down solenoid – modification

4 On models from late 1989, a modified kick-down solenoid with a shorter operating cable is fitted.
5 The removal, refitting and adjustment procedures are as described in Chapter 7, Section 5, but note that the clearance between the kickdown lever and its stop should be between 0.5 and 1.0 mm (0.02 to 0.04 in).

Transmission (2.0 litre DOHC models) – removal and refitting (leaving engine in vehicle)

6 Removal of the engine and automatic transmission as an assembly is described in Section 5 of this Chapter.
7 To remove the transmission separately, refer to the procedure in Chapter 7, Section 4, noting the following points.
8 Ignore the references to the kickdown cable, and on models fitted with a transmission having partial electronic control, ignore the references to the vacuum pipe.
9 Remove and refit the exhaust system with reference to Section 10 or 11 of this Chapter, as applicable.
10 Remove and refit the propeller shaft with reference to Section 19 of this Chapter.

19 Propeller shaft – models with MT75 type gearbox

General description

1 A modified propeller shaft is used in conjunction with the MT75 type gearbox.
2 Instead of the splined spigot on the end of the propeller shaft which fits into the gearbox on earlier models described in Chapter 8, a vibration damper is fitted between the front end of the propeller shaft and the output flange on the gearbox.

Propeller shaft – removal and refitting

Note: *New nuts must be used to secure the propeller shaft to the gearbox on refitting.*

3 The removal and refitting procedure is as described in Chapter 8, Section 3, but note that on models fitted with a catalytic converter, the exhaust heat shield must be removed from the underbody for access to the propeller shaft. Also note that instead of pulling the propeller shaft from the rear of the gearbox, carry out the following procedure.
4 Counterhold the gearbox output flange studs using a suitable socket, ensuring that the studs cannot turn in the output flange, and unscrew the three nuts securing the propeller shaft rubber coupling to the vibration damper.
5 The propeller shaft can now be disconnected from the gearbox.
6 Two types of rubber coupling may be fitted to the propeller shaft, and both carry identifying marks – either 'GAF 30' or 'GAF 41'.
7 When reconnecting the propeller shaft to the gearbox, proceed as follows according to the type of rubber coupling used.

GAF 30 coupling

8 Check that the studs are seated securely in the gearbox output

Fig. 14.46 Exhaust heat shield fixings (arrowed) – 2.0 litre DOHC models with catalytic converter (Sec 19)

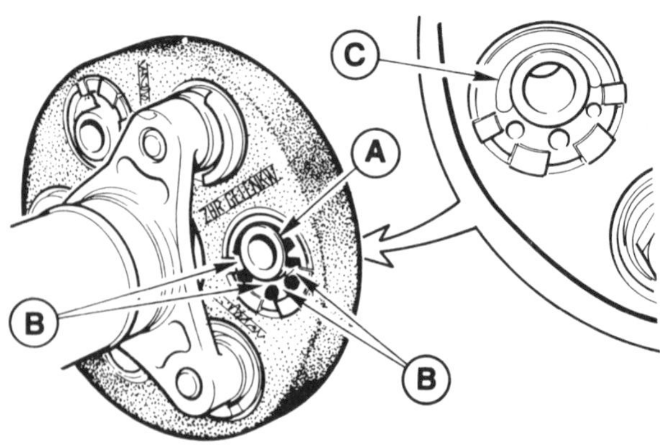

Fig. 14.47 GAF 30 type propeller shaft rubber coupling (Sec 19)

A Metal bush
B Rubber 'spokes'
C Rubber skin (front side only)

flange by applying a torque of 80 Nm (59 lbf ft) to the stud heads using a torque wrench. If a stud turns, it must be removed and refitted as follows.
9 Clean the stud threads at the gearbox flange end.
10 Apply two drops of thread-locking fluid to the threads at 180° to one another.
11 Insert the stud and tighten it to a torque of 80 Nm (59 lbf ft). The stud must be fitted and tightened within 5 minutes of applying the thread-locking fluid.
12 Allow the thread-locking fluid to harden for 30 minutes, then reconnect the propeller shaft to the gearbox.
13 Before reconnecting the propeller shaft to the gearbox, the washers on both sides of the coupling must be greased, and the condition of the rubber coupling must be checked as follows.
14 Examine the rubber 'spokes' for cracks – see Fig. 14.47. If cracks are visible, the complete propeller shaft and coupling assembly must be renewed with one of the later GAF 41 type (the propeller shaft is balanced with the rubber coupling as an assembly, and therefore the coupling **must not** be removed from the propeller shaft). Cracks in the rubber skin (area 'C' in Fig. 14.47) are insignificant.
15 Secure the propeller shaft rubber coupling to the vibration damper using new nuts.
16 Further refitting is a reversal of removal.

GAF 41 coupling

17 Check that the studs are seated securely in the gearbox output flange by applying a torque of 110 Nm (81 lbf ft) to the stud heads using a torque wrench. If a stud turns, it must be renewed, and the new stud must be tightened to a torque of 110 Nm (81 lbf ft). Note that only studs with hexagonal collars must be used (Torx type studs must not be used).
18 Secure the propeller shaft rubber coupling to the vibration damper using new nuts.
19 Further refitting is a reversal of removal.

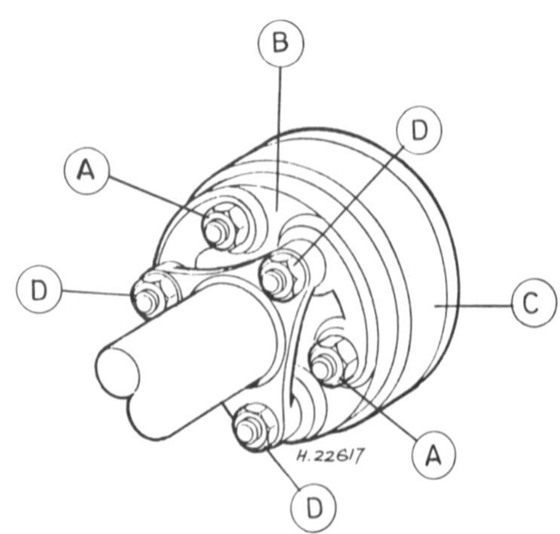

Fig. 14.48 GAF 41 type propeller shaft rubber coupling (Sec 19)

A Coupling-to-vibration damper nuts
B GAF 41 type coupling
C Vibration damper
D Propeller shaft-to-coupling nuts

Propeller shaft front rubber coupling – renewal

20 The rubber coupling cannot be renewed on models fitted with an MT75 gearbox, as it is balanced as an assembly with the propeller shaft at the factory.
21 The rubber coupling is not available as a spare part, and if worn or damaged, the complete propeller shaft must be renewed. If the propeller shaft is renewed, always fit the latest GAF 41 type (see earlier in this Section) as a replacement.

Propeller shaft vibration damper – removal and refitting

Note: *New nuts must be used to secure the propeller shaft to the gearbox on refitting, and on models fitted with a GAF 41 type rubber coupling, new studs must be used to secure the vibration damper to the gearbox output flange.*

22 The propeller shaft vibration damper is attached to the gearbox output flange.
23 Two alternative types of vibration damper may be used, depending on whether a GAF 30 or GAF 41 type rubber coupling is used (see earlier in this Section).
24 To remove the vibration damper, detach the propeller shaft rubber coupling from the damper as described earlier in this Section, then unscrew and remove the studs securing the damper to the gearbox output flange.
25 For models fitted with a GAF 30 type rubber coupling, proceed as described in paragraphs 9 to 16 of this Section.
26 On models fitted with a GAF 41 type rubber coupling, new studs must be used to secure the vibration damper to the gearbox output flange, and new nuts must be used to secure the rubber coupling to the vibration damper. Further refitting is a reversal of removal, ensuring that all fixings are tightened to the specified torque.

20 Braking system

Front disc pads (later models) – inspection and renewal

1 On some later models, slightly revised front brake components are used. A new type of retaining clip is used to secure the pads in the calliper and the calliper body is modified accordingly. Also, plastic covers are fitted to the calliper guide bolts (photos).
2 Procedures are unchanged from those given in Chapter 10

Brake servo vacuum hose – modification

3 From mid-1989, a new type of brake servo vacuum hose-to-inlet manifold connector has been used in production. The connector com-

20.1A Later type front disc pad retaining clip

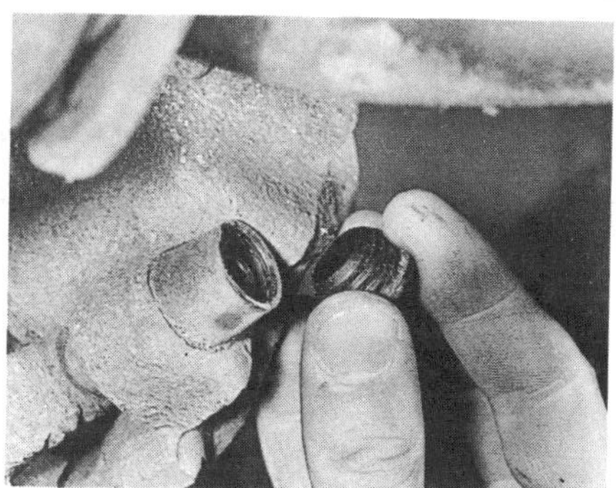
20.1B Removing a calliper guide bolt cover

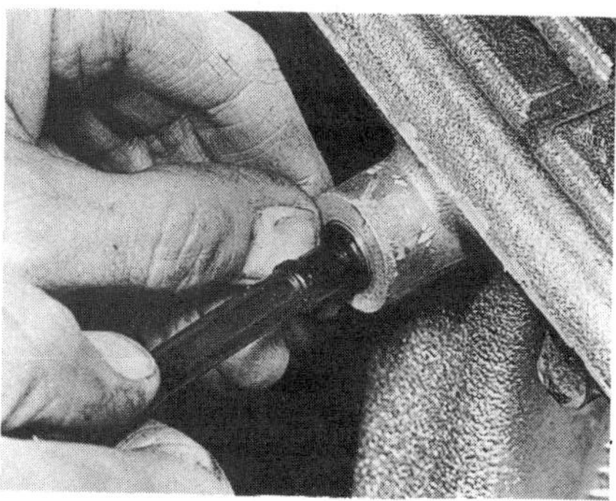
20.4 Disconnecting a later type brake servo vacuum hose

prises three parts; a collet which locks the hose in position, an O-ring, and a brass insert which is pressed into the inlet manifold.
4 To disconnect the hose from the inlet manifold, applying light even pressure, push and hold the flange of the collet against the manifold. While holding the collet forward, gently pull the hose from the collet (photo). Take care not to pull at an angle or use excessive force, as this can cause the collet to snatch and lock the hose.
5 To reconnect the hose, push the hose into the collet until the swage on the hose is hard against the collet flange. Pull gently on the hose to check that it is locked by the collet.

Load apportioning valve (P100 models from mid-April 1989) – adjustment

6 The procedure is as described in Chapter 10, Section 27, but note that dimension 'X' in Fig. 10.35 has been revised to 92.0 mm (3.6 in) with the vehicle unladen at normal kerb weight.

21 Steering

Adjustable steering column – removal, overhaul and refitting

Note: *A new adjuster locknut and washer must be used on reassembly.*

1 The procedure is as described in Chapter 11, Section 25, but to dismantle the adjuster assembly, proceed as follows.
2 Remove the locknut and washer securing the adjuster through-bolt.
3 Remove the through-bolt, adjuster handle, locking plates, sliders and washers, then unclip the spring assembly.
4 Reassemble the components as follows.
5 Refit the spring to the adjuster assembly bracket.
6 Align the washers, sliders and locking plates, ensuring that the handle locking plate is fitted so that the cut-out and Ford logo are positioned as shown in Fig. 14.50.
7 Coat the through-bolt threads with a suitable thread-locking compound, then refit the through-bolt and the adjuster handle, ensuring that all components are engaged.
8 Position the handle in the locked position, and secure the through-bolt with a new locknut and washer.

Power steering pump (2.0 litre DOHC models) – removal and refitting

9 The pump is mounted on a bracket on the front right-hand side of the cylinder block.
10 Place a suitable container under the pump, unscrew the fluid pipe unions, and drain the fluid.
11 Remove the drivebelt with reference to Section 8 of this Chapter.
12 Prevent the pulley from rotating using a strap wrench (which can be improvised using an old drivebelt and a large socket and wrench), and unscrew the three pulley securing bolts (photo). Withdraw the pulley.
13 Unscrew the three pump securing bolts from the front of the pump bracket, and the single bolt from the rear of the bracket, and withdraw the pump (photos).
14 Refitting is a reversal of removal, bearing in mind the following points.
15 Reconnect the fluid unions using new O-rings.
16 On completion, bleed the power steering fluid circuit as described in Chapter 11, Section 34 (photo).

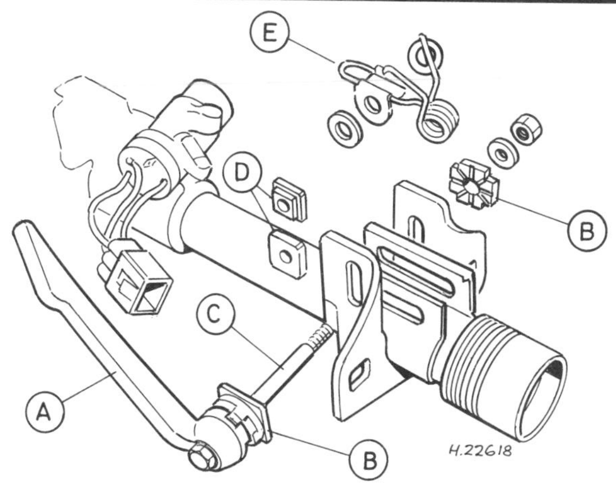

Fig. 14.49 Adjustable steering column assembly (Sec 21)

A Adjuster handle
B Locking plates
C Through-bolt
D Sliders
E Spring

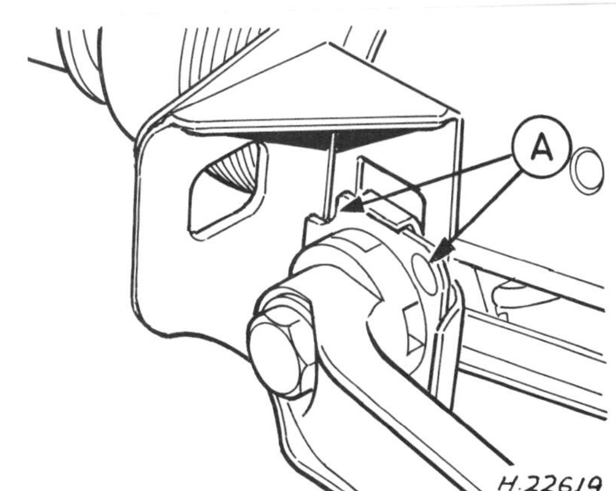

Fig. 14.50 Cut-out and logo (A) must be positioned as shown when reassembling adjustable steering column (Sec 21)

21.12 Unbolt the power steering pump pulley ...

21.13A ... for access to the front pump securing bolts (arrowed)

21.13B Power steering pump rear securing bolt

21.16 Topping up the power steering fluid level

22 Bodywork and fittings

Tailgate (Hatchback models up to 1990) – renewal

1 On models with an integral heated rear window/radio aerial, note that the radio aerial lead is routed through different openings in the rear bodywork and the tailgate from 1990.

2 If a new, later specification tailgate is to be fitted to an earlier vehicle, a new opening must be made in the bodywork for the aerial lead.

3 Ideally, this work should be carried out by a Ford dealer, who will have the necessary template available to ensure that the opening is positioned accurately.

Rear doors (Estate models) – renewal

4 The door internal components have been modified on later models. If a new, later specification rear door is to be fitted to an earlier vehicle, the door panels must be modified as follows to enable refitting of the original components.

5 Remove all the serviceable components and fasteners from the original door.

6 Working on the new door, use a small round file to elongate the door interior handle mounting hole ('A' in Fig. 14.51) vertically downwards so that it will align with the mounting hole in the handle/ashtray bezel. Refit the original retaining clip.

7 The earlier type of trim fasteners (located at 'B' in Fig. 14.51) are no longer used and must be replaced with the latest type of fasteners, available from a Ford dealer.

Door lock (from 1990) – removal and refitting

Note: *Do not bend or stretch the cable during removal and refitting, as the operation of the lock will be impaired.*

8 From 1990, cable-operated door locks have been fitted to all Sierra models. To remove the later type of lock, proceed as follows.

9 Remove the door inner trim panel as described in Chapter 12, Section 15.

10 Where necessary for improved access, peel back the waterproof plastic sheet from the door.

11 Remove the securing screw, and withdraw the window channel extension through the door's lower aperture.

12 Disconnect the door outer handle and the lock barrel (front doors) operating rods at the lock assembly.

13 Disconnect the battery negative lead, and disconnect the door lock motor and the alarm system wiring plugs (where applicable).

14 Remove the screw securing the door interior handle to the door panel.

15 Remove the three lock securing screws from the rear edge of the door, then withdraw the lock assembly complete with the operating cable and the door interior handle.

16 To disconnect the cable from the lock, proceed as follows.

17 Carefully prise the cover plate from the lock, using a screwdriver.

18 Using a suitable pair of pliers, carefully remove the outer cable from the groove in the lock assembly casing.

19 Extend the inner cable until the flats on the plastic end piece align with the guide, then withdraw the cable.

20 Commence reassembly and refitting as follows.

21 Align the flats on the inner cable end piece with the cable guide, and refit the inner cable.

22 Using a suitable pair of pliers, carefully refit the outer cable to the groove in the lock assembly casing.

23 Refit the lock cover plate.

24 Insert the lock, cable and interior handle into the door, and refit the three lock securing screws.

25 Push the interior handle assembly towards the lock to adjust the cable, and when adjustment is correct, refit and tighten the interior handle securing screw.

26 Further refitting is a reversal of removal, ensuring that the window channel extension is correctly located.

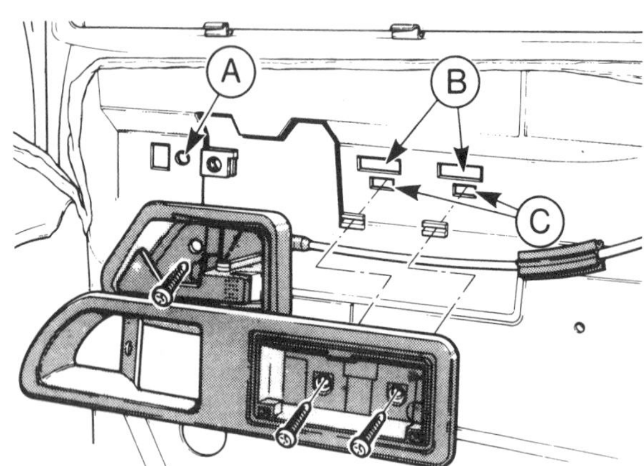

Fig. 14.51 Later type rear door – Estate models (Sec 22)

A Internal handle mounting hole
B Earlier type trim fasteners
C Revised ashtray/handle mounting holes

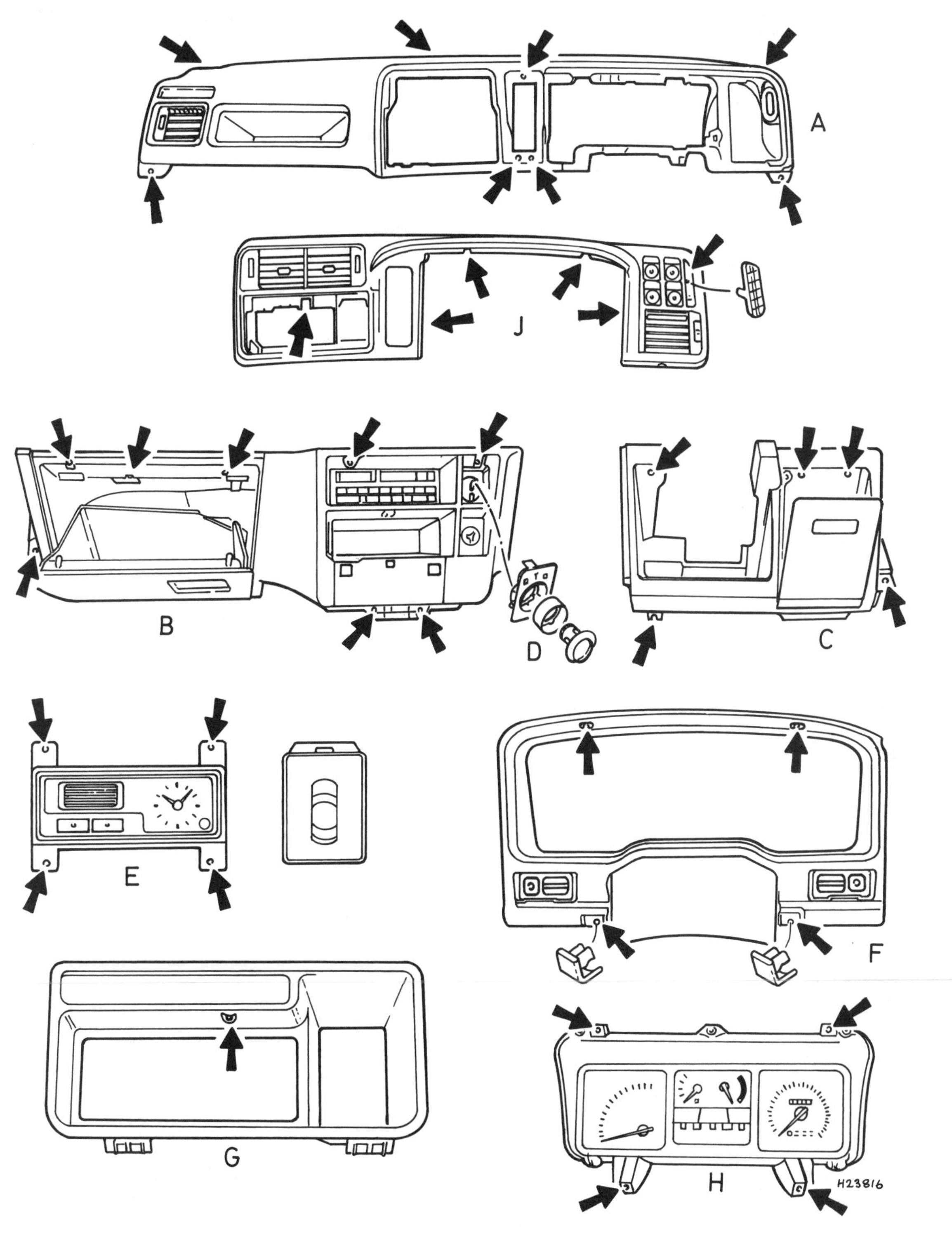

Fig. 14.57 Facia components and securing screw locations (arrowed) – models from 1992 (Sec 22)

pper facia panel
senger's side lower facia l
's side lower facia panel
D *Heater fan control cover and bezel*
E *Clock/auxiliary warning system display*
F *Instrument panel surround and screw covers*
G *Clock/auxiliary warning system display surround*
H *Instrument cluster*
J *Instrument cluster surround*

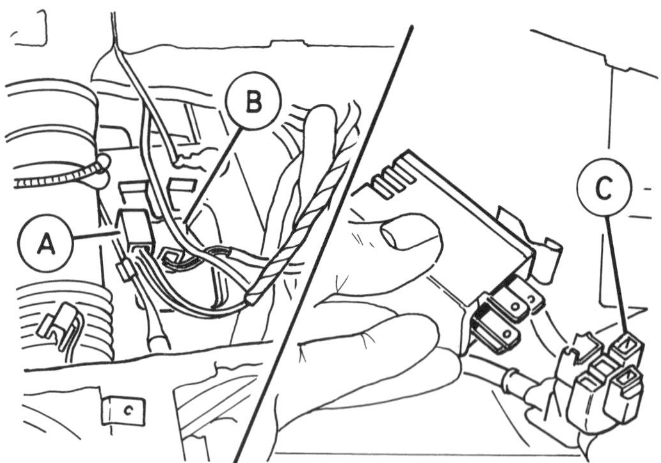

Fig. 14.58 'Lights on' warning module location (Sec 23)

A 'Lights on' warning module
B Direction indicator relay
C 'Lights on' warning module wiring plug

Fig. 14.59 Electric sunroof relay (A) and motor securing bolts (B) (Sec 23)

23 Electrical system

Alternator (2.0 litre DOHC engine) – removal and refitting

1 The procedure is as described in Chapter 13, Section 8, noting the following points.

(a) *Remove and refit the drivebelt with reference to Section 8 of this Chapter*
(b) *Ignore the reference to Fig. 13.1, as a through-bolt is used instead of the bolts shown*

Electric sunroof switch – removal and refitting

2 Disconnect the battery negative lead.
3 Using a thin-bladed screwdriver, carefully prise the switch from the overhead console.
4 Disconnect the wiring plug and remove the switch.
5 Refitting is a reversal of removal.

Oil pressure warning lamp switch (2.0 litre DOHC models) – removal and refitting

6 Proceed as described in Chapter 13, Section 29, noting that the switch is located on the right-hand side of the cylinder block, between the core plugs.

Instrument panel (from 1992) – removal and refitting

7 The procedure is as described in Chapter 13, Section 32, but note that both instrument panel surround lower securing screws are located beneath plastic covers (photo).
8 The steering column shrouds are secured by six screws, five through the lower shroud, and one through the upper shroud.

Tachometer (from 1990) – removal and refitting

9 The procedure is as described in Chapter 13, Section 33, but before the tachometer can be withdrawn from the instrument panel housing, the printed circuit board must be carefully pulled from the tachometer terminals. Ensure that the printed circuit board is pushed fully home when refitting.

'Lights on' warning module – removal and refitting

10 Remove the instrument panel as described earlier in this Section or in Chapter 13, Section 32.
11 Unclip the direction indicator relay from the steering column support bracket.
12 Unclip the 'lights on' warning module from the steering column support bracket, disconnect the wiring plug and remove the module.
13 Refitting is a reversal of removal.

Electric sunroof relay – removal and refitting

14 Remove the overhead console as described in Section 22 of this

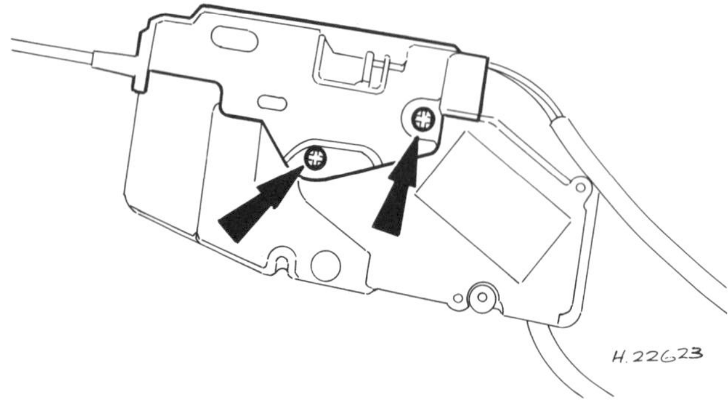

Fig. 14.60 Front door central locking motor securing screws (arrowed) – models from 1990 (Sec 23)

Chapter.
15 Unclip the relay from the motor assembly, and disconnect the wiring plug.
16 Refitting is a reversal of removal.

Electric sunroof motor – removal and refitting

17 Remove the overhead console as described in Section 22 of this Chapter.
18 Disconnect the motor wiring plug.
19 Unscrew the three securing bolts, and withdraw the motor assembly from the roof.
20 Refitting is a reversal of removal, but ensure that the drive gear is aligned with the roof operating mechanism.

Central door locking motors (from 1990) – removal and refitting

21 On models from 1990, the door locking motors are incorporated in the door lock units.
22 To remove a motor, remove the door lock as described in Section 22 of this Chapter.
23 Remove the two securing screws, and detach the motor from the lock assembly.
24 Refitting is a reversal of removal, ensuring that the motor o ing rod engages with the lock lever.

Anti-theft alarm – general description

25 From 1990, certain models are fitted with an anti-the
26 The alarm system consists of a control module m the driver's side facia; trip switches fitted to the doors,

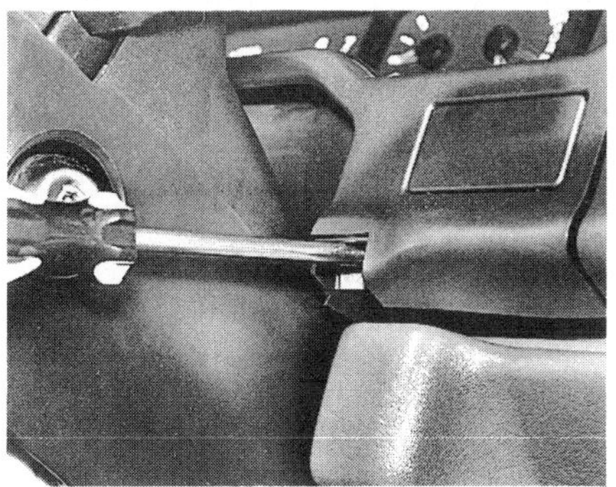
23.7 Removing an instrument panel surround lower securing screw (cover removed)

23.26 Bulkhead insulation pulled back to expose alarm horn

23.30 Removing the anti-theft alarm control module

and bonnet; activating switches fitted to the front door locks; an additional horn mounted at the bulkhead next to the battery; and an indicator light mounted on the top of the facia (photo).

27 The alarm system has a self-diagnosis function, which allows a Ford dealer to carry out fault diagnosis using suitable specialist equipment. In the event of a problem with the alarm system, it is advisable not to tamper with the components until appropriate fault diagnosis has been carried out.

Anti-theft alarm control module – removal and refitting

28 Disconnect the battery negative lead.

29 Release the carpet trim panel from under the driver's side facia.

30 Reach up behind the facia and locate the control module, then release the plastic retaining clips using a screwdriver, and lower the module (photo).

31 Disconnect the wiring plug and withdraw the module.

32 Refitting is a reversal of removal.

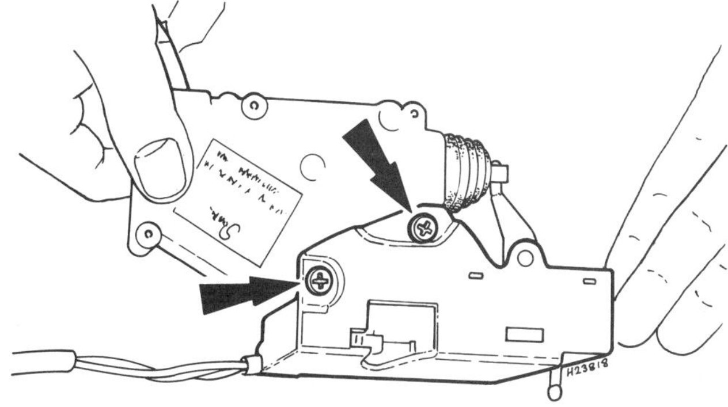

Fig. 14.61 Rear door central locking motor securing screws (arrowed) – models from 1990 (Sec 23)

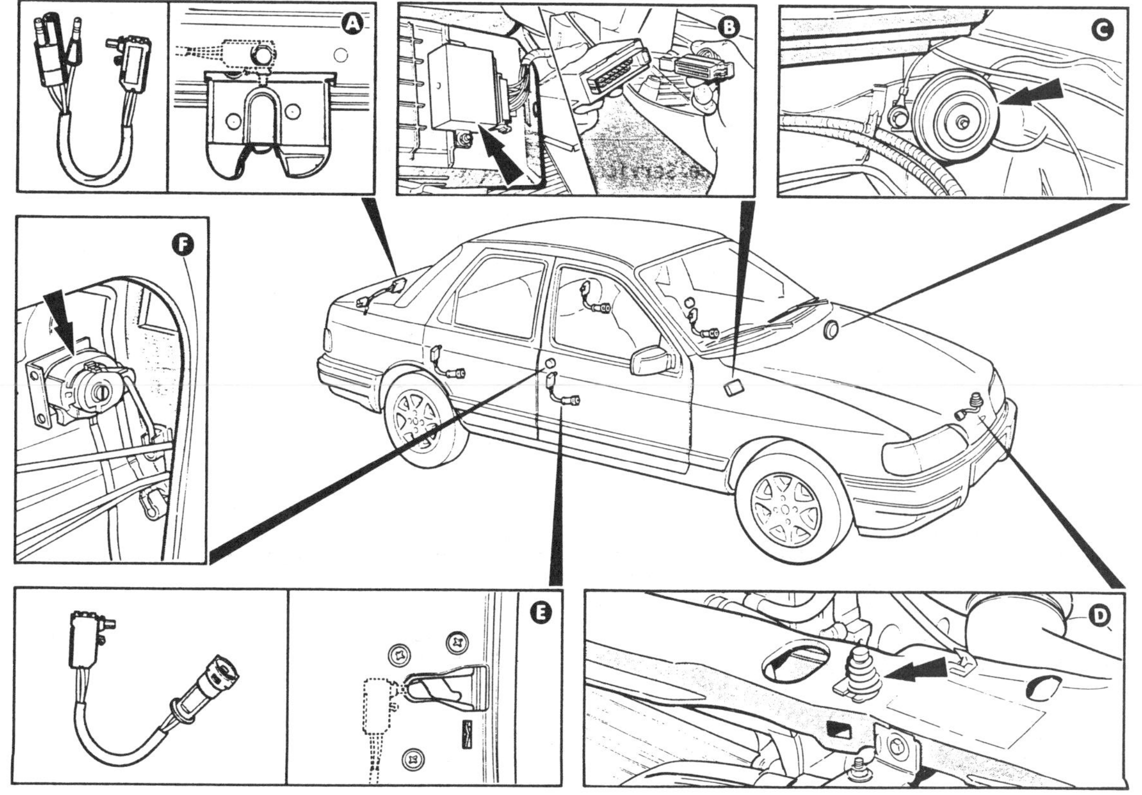

Fig. 14.62 Anti-theft alarm system components (Sec 23)

A Tailgate/boot lid switch
B Control module
C Horn
D Bonnet switch
E Door switch
F Activating switch

NOTES:

1. All diagrams are divided into numbered circuits depending upon their function e.g Diagram 2 : Exterior lighting all models.
2. Some components may appear on more than one diagram so their positions are given in coded form in the key below e.g. 2/A1 denotes a component on diagram 2 grid location A1.
3. Feed wires are coloured red (black when switched) and originate from diagram 1. All other diagrams feed from fuse connections or common feeds.
4. Earth wires on all diagrams are coloured brown.
5. The tables below show where common feeds and common earths interconnect between diagrams.
6. Not all items are fitted to all models.
7. Brackets show how the circuit may be connected in more than one way.

COMMON EARTH POINT	DIAGRAM/ GRID REF.
G1004	2/C1
	4/B1
	4/B5
	4a/B1
G1005	1/A8
	2/C8
	4/B4
	4/B8
	4a/B8
G1007	1/K1
	2/E2
	2a/E2
	3/F2
	3a/F3
	4/K2
	4a/C2
G1009	1/F1
	3/E3
G1010	1/M5
	2/M6
	3a/M5
	4a/M6
G1014	3/L7
	3a/L6

FUSE	RATING	CIRCUIT
1	30A	Electric Windows
2	30A	Heated Rear Window, Heated Mirrors
3	10A	Wiper
4	30A	Heater Blower, Rear Wiper Motor, W/Screen Washer
5	30A	Headlamp Washer
6	15A	Horn - Steering Wheel Switch
7	15A	Driving Lamps
8	10A	Clock, Wiper Intermit., Warning Lamps
9	15A	Flasher, Stop Lamp, Reversing Lamp
10	15A	Front Fog Lamp
11	30A	Door Locking, Tailgate Release
12	25A	Interior Lights, Clock, Cigar Lighter
13	10A	Hazard, Horn - Multifunction Lever
14	10A	LH High Beam
15	10A	RH High Beam
16	10A	LH Low Beam, Rear Fog Lamp
17	10A	RH Low Beam
18	10A	LH Side, Licence, Engine Lamp
19	10A	RH Side, Glove Box, Switch Illumination
20		Free
21	1A	Fuel Computer
22	20A	Fuel Injection

Wire Colours

B	Blue	Rs	Pink
Bk	Black	S	Grey
Bn	Brown	V	Violet
Gn	Green	W	White
R	Red	Y	Yellow

COMMON FEED	DESCRIPTION	DIAGRAM/ GRID REF.
S1021	COMMON IGNITION FEED	1/L1
		2/H3
		3/J2
		4a/H2
S1022	COMMON BATTERY FEED	1/J2
		2/H2

ITEM	DESCRIPTION	DIAGRAM/ GRID REF.
1	Alternator	1/A3
2	Ashtray Illumination	2a/G5
3	Auto. Trans. Inhibitor Switch	1/G4
		2/E5
4	Auto. Trans. Relay	1/H2
5	Auto. Trans. Relay (Only 2.0 OHC With Elec. Aerial, From 1985)	1/H2
6	Auto. Trans. Selector Illumination	2a/J4
7	Auxiliary Warning Module (Low Series)	4/J4
8	Auxiliary Warning Module (High Series)	4/H7
		4a/G5
9	Battery	1/G7
10	Brake Pad Sender LH	4/D4
		4/D8
11	Brake Pad Sender RH	4/D1
		4/D5
12	Bulb Failure Module	4a/H6
13	Carburettor Stepper Motor	1/C7
14	Central Locking Actuator LH Front	3a/G8
15	Central Locking Actuator LH Rear	3a/L8
16	Central Locking Actuator RH Rear	3a/L1
17	Central Locking Actuator Tailgate	3a/M5
18	Central Locking Relay	3a/H6
19	Central Locking Switch	3a/H1
20	Cigar Lighter Front	2a/F5
21	Cigar Lighter Rear	2a/K5
22	Clock	2a/F6
23	Coolant Temp. Sensor	1/B4
		1/B7
		1/F5
24	Dip Beam Relay (From 1985)	2/C5
25	Distributor	1/D1
		1/D3
		1/D5
		1/E7

Notes, tables, wire colours and key to wiring diagrams. Models up to 1987

ITEM	DESCRIPTION	DIAGRAM/ GRID REF.
26	Door Ajar Sender LH Front	4a/F8
27	Door Ajar Sender LH Rear	4a/K8
28	Door Ajar Sender RH Front	4a/F1
29	Door Ajar Sender RH Rear	4a/K1
30	Driving Lamp Relay	2/C4
31	Econolight Switch (Amber)	1/G8
32	Econolight Switch (Red)	1/H8
33	Electric Choke	1/F4
34	Electric Door Mirror	3a/E1
		3a/E8
35	Electric Mirror Control Switch	3a/F2
36	Electric Window Control Switch Front	3a/H4
37	Electric Window Control Switch Rear	3a/K1
		3a/K8
38	Electric Window Motor LH Front	3a/F8
39	Electric Window Motor LH Rear	3a/J8
40	Electric Window Motor RH Front	3a/F1
41	Electric Window Motor RH Rear	3a/J1
42	Electronic Ignition Module	1/C1
43	Engine Comp. Lamp/Switch	2a/D5
44	ESC 1 Ignition Module	1/C2
45	ESC 2 Ignition Module	1/B5
		1/C8
46	Flasher Lamp LH	2/A8
47	Flasher Lamp LH Side Marker	2/E8
48	Flasher Lamp RH	2/A1
49	Flasher Lamp RH Side Marker	2/E1
50	Flasher Relay	2/H5
51	Foglamp Front	2/A2
		2/A7
52	Foglamp Relay	2/C5
53	Foglamp Switch Front	2/H2
54	Foglamp Switch Rear	2/H3
55	Footwell Illumination	2a/D2
		2a/D7
56	Fuel Computer	4a/G5
57	Fuel Flow Sensor	4a/C7
58	Fuel Sender	1/M6
		4/L3
		4/L7
		4a/L5
59	Fuel Shut Off Valve	1/F4
60	Glove Box Lamp/Switch	2a/E7
61	Graphic Display Module	4a/H5
62	Handbrake Warning Switch	1/L6
63	Headlamp Unit LH	2/A6
		4a/A6
64	Headlamp Unit RH	2/A3
		4a/A3
65	Headlamp Washer Pump	3/C3
66	Headlamp Washer Relay	3/D4
67	Heated Rear Window	3/L5
		3a/L5
68	Heated Rear Window Relay	3/C3
69	Heated Rear Window Relay (Auto. Off)	3a/B3
70	Heated Rear Window Switch	3/H3
71	Heated Rear Window Switch (Auto. Off)	3a/H2
72	Heater Blower Illumination	2a/E5
73	Heater Blower Motor	3/G6
74	Heater Blower Switch	3/G5
75	Horn	3/A7
		3a/A7
76	Horn Relay	3a/C4
77	Horn Switch	3a/J3
78	Ice Warning Sender	4a/A4
79	Ignition Coil	1/C1
		1/C2
		1/C5
		1/D7
80	Ignition Relay	1/G2

ITEM	DESCRIPTION	DIAGRAM/ GRID REF.
81	Ignition Switch	1/M1
82	Instrument Cluster	1/M3
		2/F4
		2a/E3
		4a/H3
83	Instrument Illumination Control	2a/F3
		4a/J4
84	Interior Lamp Delay Relay	2a/B3
85	Interior Lamp Door Switch LH Front	2a/E8
86	Interior Lamp Door Switch LH Rear	2a/J8
87	Interior Lamp Door Switch RH Front	2a/E1
88	Interior Lamp Door Switch RH Rear	2a/J1
89	Interior Lamp/Switch Front	2a/H4
90	Interior Lamp/Switch Rear	2a/K4
91	Licence Plate Lamp	2/M3
		2/M6
		4a/M3
		4a/M6
92	Light Cluster LH Rear	2/M8
		4a/M8
93	Light Cluster RH Rear	2/M1
		4a/M1
94	Light/Wiper Switch	2/J3
		3/J3
		4a/K3
95	Low Brake Fluid Sender	1/F2
96	Low Coolant Sender	4/D2
		4/D6
97	Low Oil Sender	4/E3
		4/E7
98	Low Washer Fluid Sender	4/C2
		4/C6
99	Luggage Comp. Lamp/Switch	2a/M4
100	Manifold Heater (1.8/2.0 OHC Only From 1985)	1/F5
101	Manifold Heater Relay (1.8/2.0 OHC Only From 1985)	1/J7
102	Multifunction Switch	2/J4
		3/J5
103	Oil Pressure Switch	1/F7
104	Power Hold Relay	1/J6
105	Reversing Lamp Switch	2/D5
106	Seat Belt Warning Relay	2a/B5
		4/E2
		4/E6
107	Spark Plugs	1/E1
		1/E3
		1/E5
		1/F7
108	Speed Sensor	4a/E2
109	Starter Motor	1/G5
110	Stop Lamp Switch	2/F4
		4a/E4
111	Tailgate Ajar Sender	4a/M4
112	Tailgate Release Actuator	3a/M4
113	Tailgate Release Relay	1/J5
		3a/C5
114	Tailgate Release Switch	3a/K5
115	Vanity Mirror Illumination	2a/G7
116	Warning Lamp Cluster	4/K2
		4/K7
117	Wash/Wipe Switch Rear	3/H3
118	Washer Pump Front	3/B3
119	Washer Pump Rear	3/L8
120	Wiper Intermittent Relay Front	3/B5
121	Wiper Intermittent Relay Rear	3/C4
122	Wiper Intermittent Speed Control	3/H4
123	Wiper Motor Front	3/E3
124	Wiper Motor Rear	3/M6

Key to wiring diagrams continued. Models up to 1987

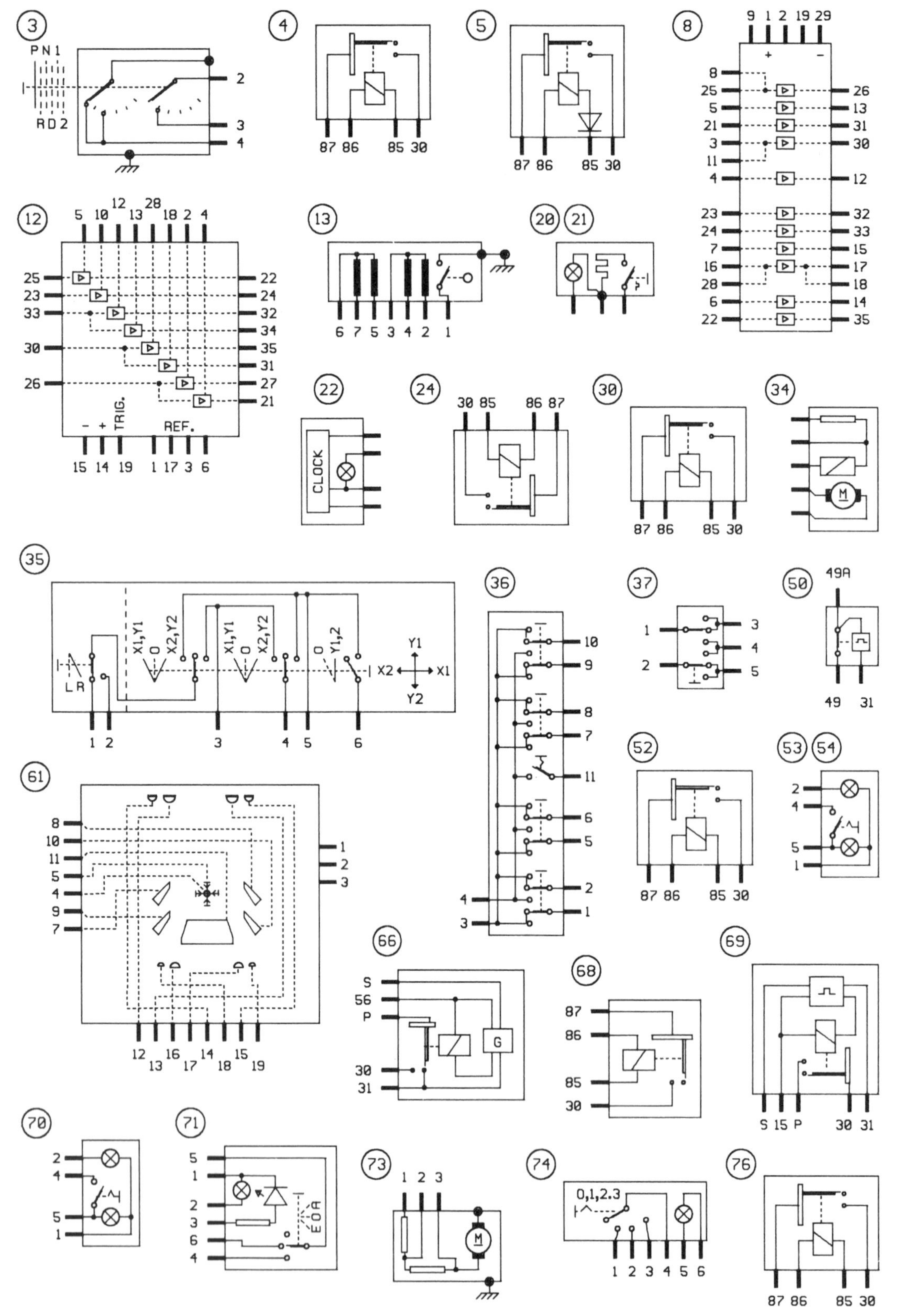

Internal connection details. Models up to 1987

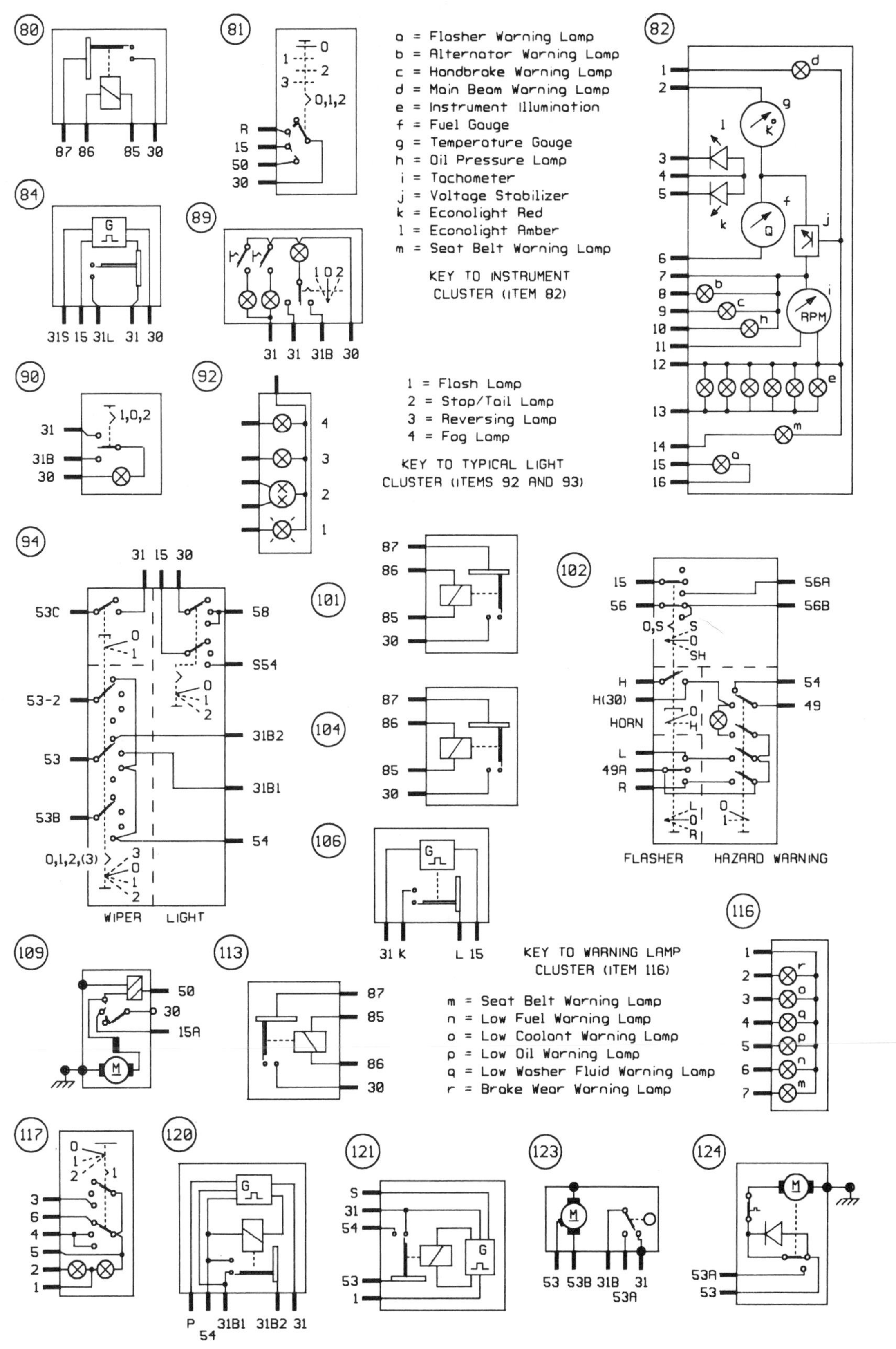

Internal connection details continued. Models up to 1987

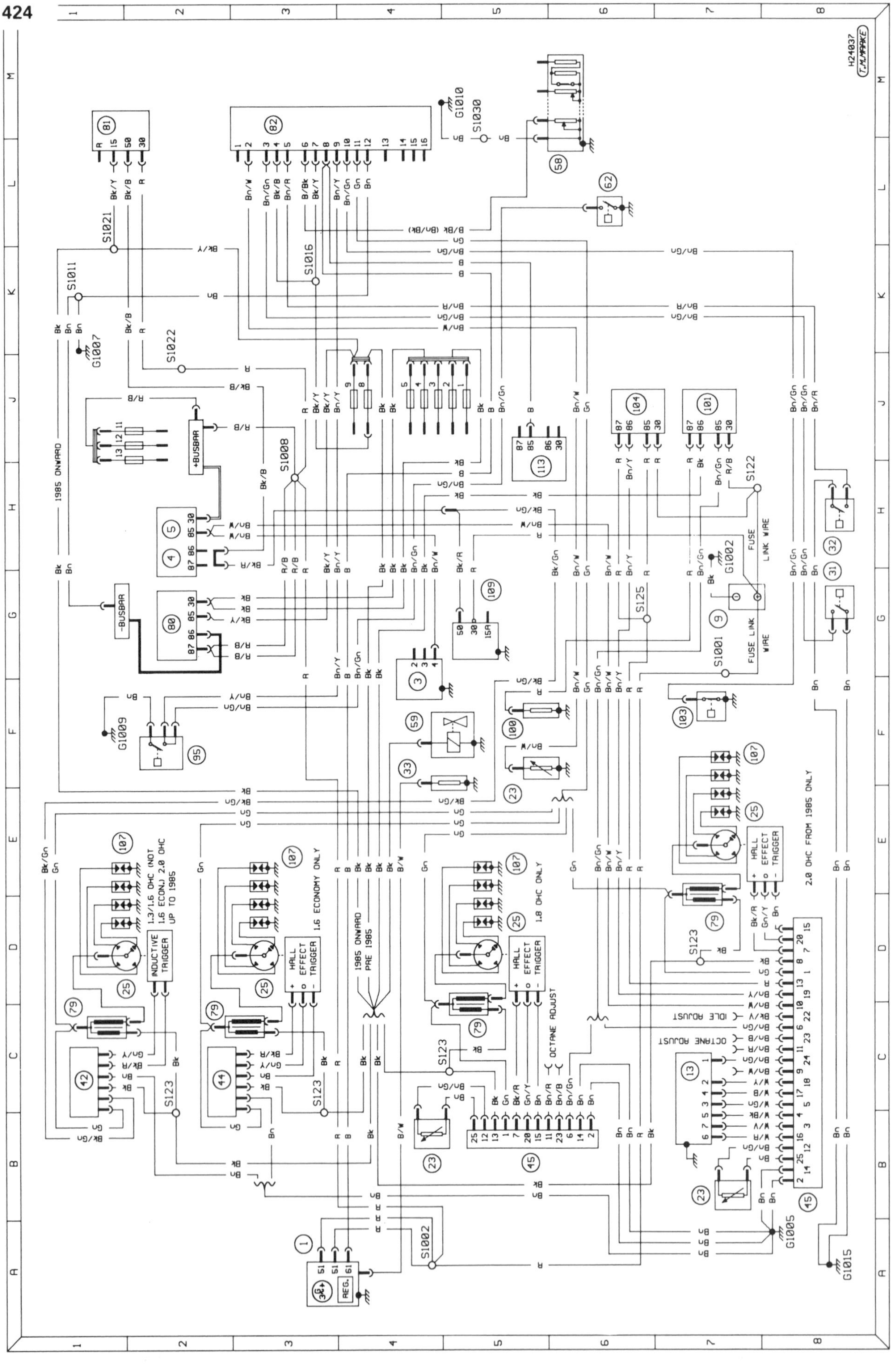

INDUCTIVE TRIGGER
1.3/1.6 OHC (NOT 1.6 ECON.) 2.0 OHC UP TO 1985

HALL EFFECT TRIGGER
1.6 ECONOMY ONLY

1985 ONWARD
PRE 1985

HALL EFFECT TRIGGER
1.8 OHC ONLY

OCTANE ADJUST
IDLE ADJUST

HALL EFFECT TRIGGER
2.0 OHC FROM 1985 ONLY

-BUSBAR
+BUSBAR

FUSE LINK WIRE

H24037
T.M.MARKE

Diagram 1. Starting, charging and ignition (except fuel injection). Models up to 1987

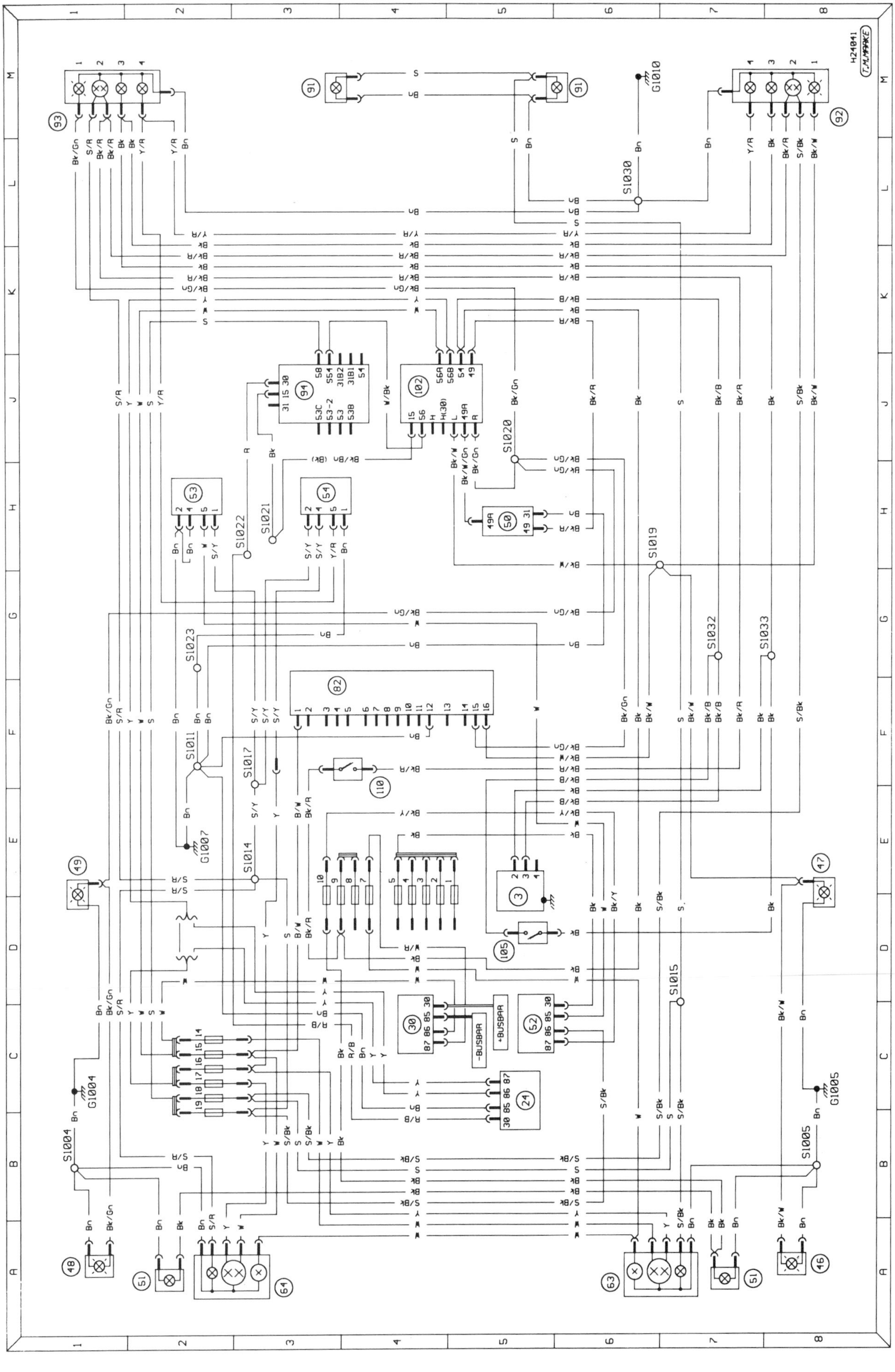

Diagram 2. Exterior lighting. Models up to 1987

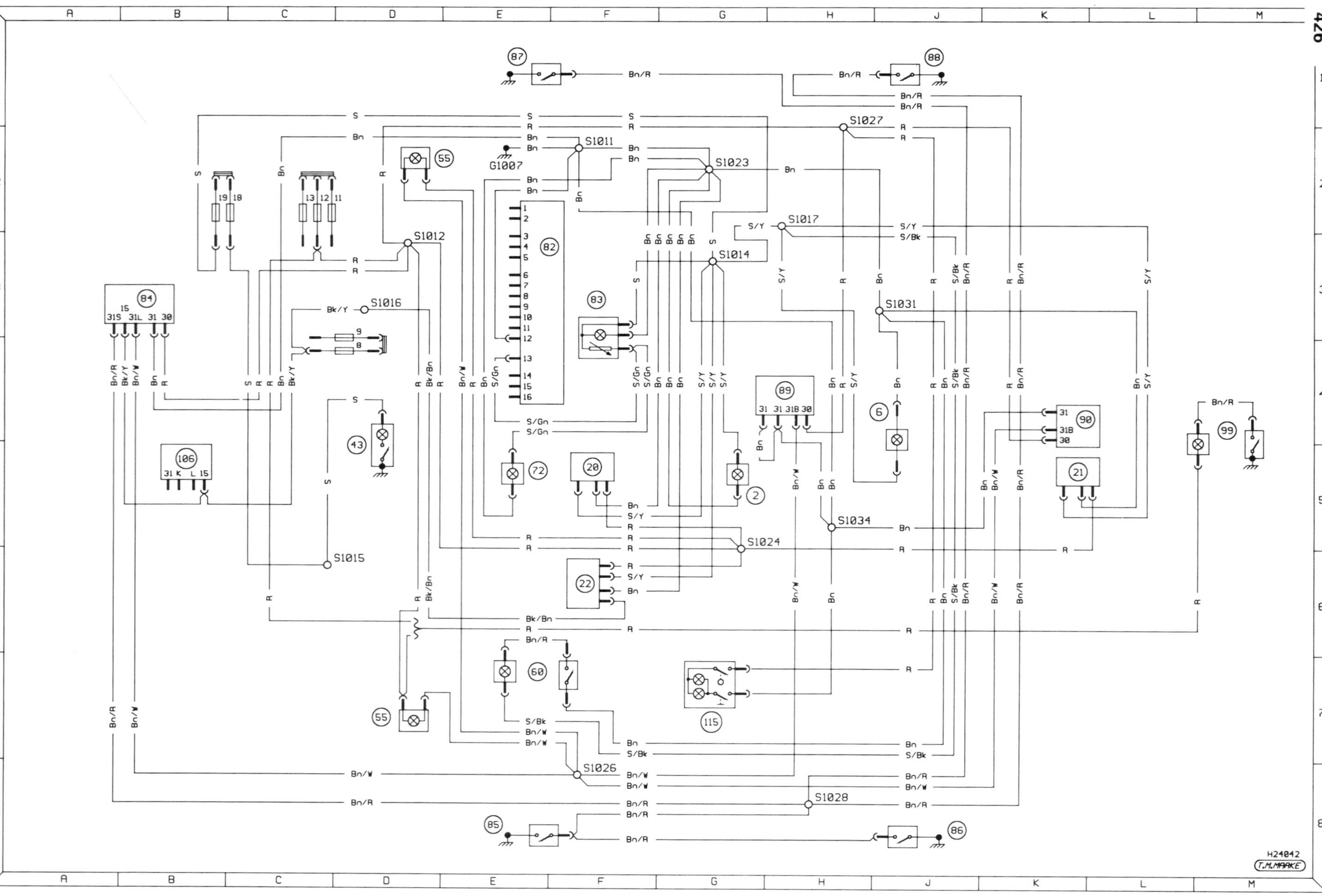

Diagram 2a. Interior lighting. Models up to 1987

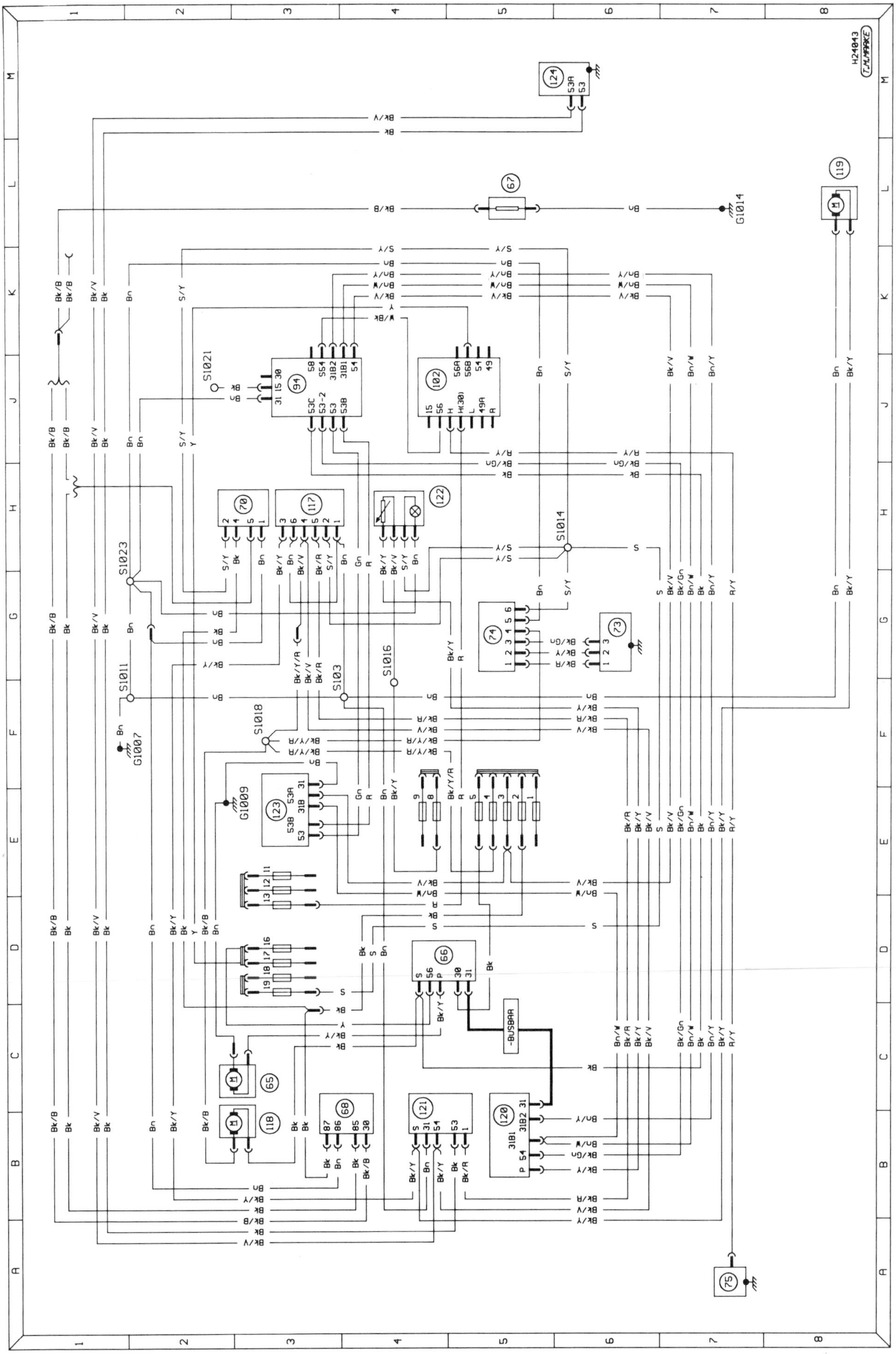

Diagram 3. Ancillary circuits (low series). Models up to 1987

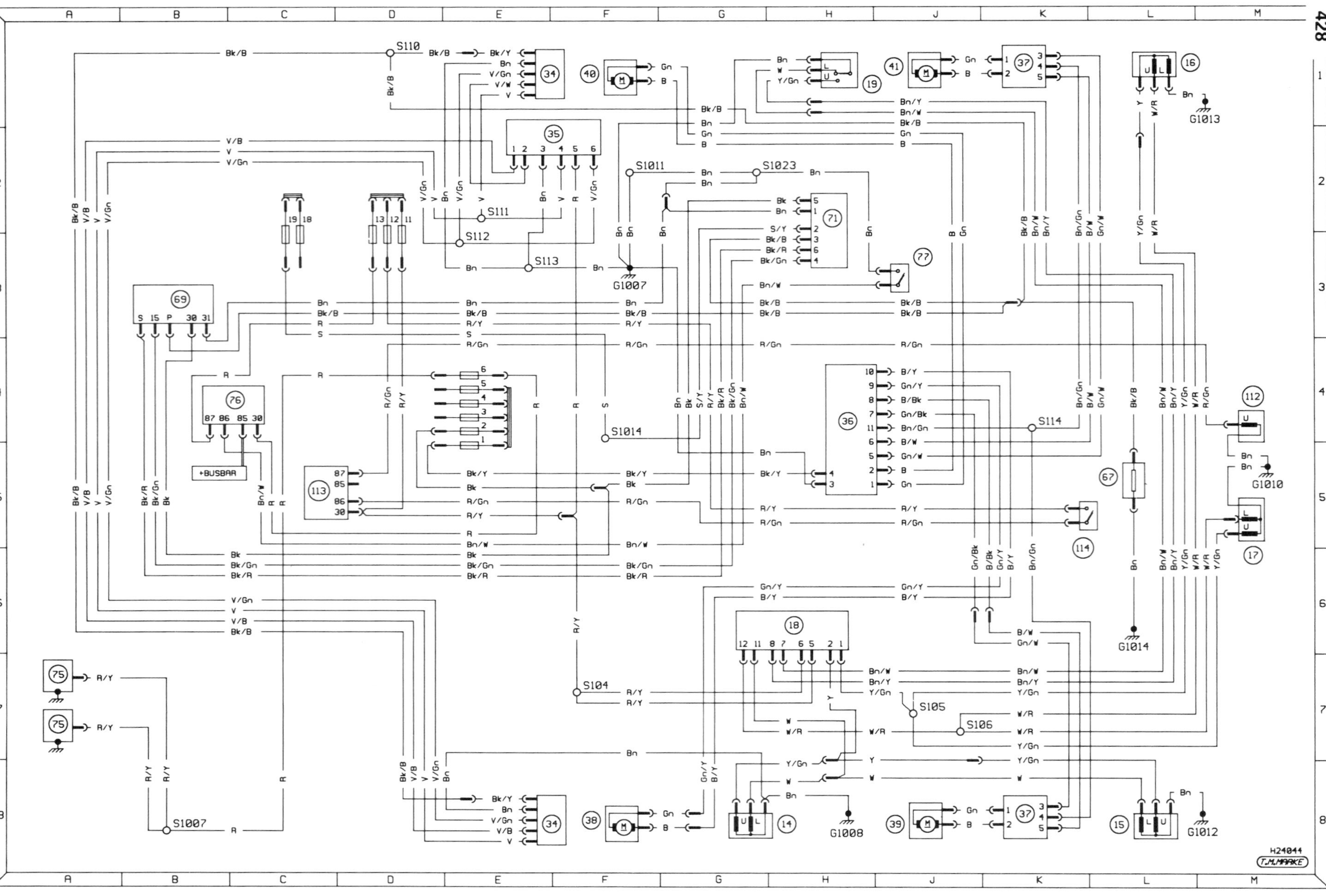

Diagram 3a. Additional ancillary circuits (high series only). Models up to 1987

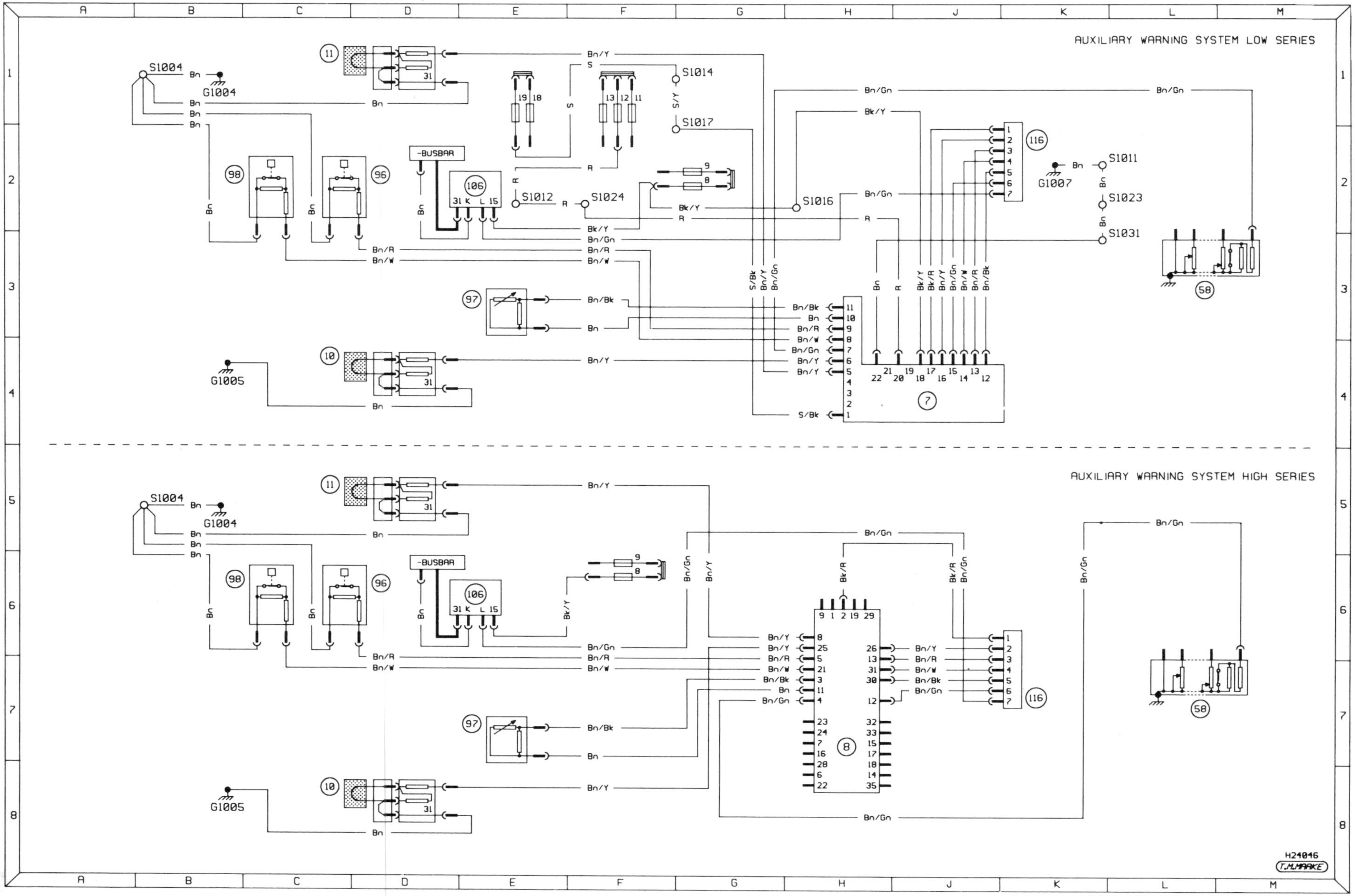

AUXILIARY WARNING SYSTEM LOW SERIES

AUXILIARY WARNING SYSTEM HIGH SERIES

H24046

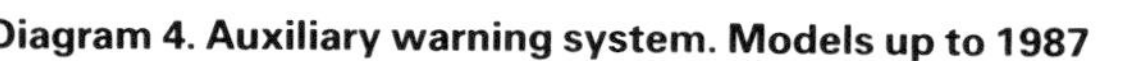

Diagram 4. Auxiliary warning system. Models up to 1987

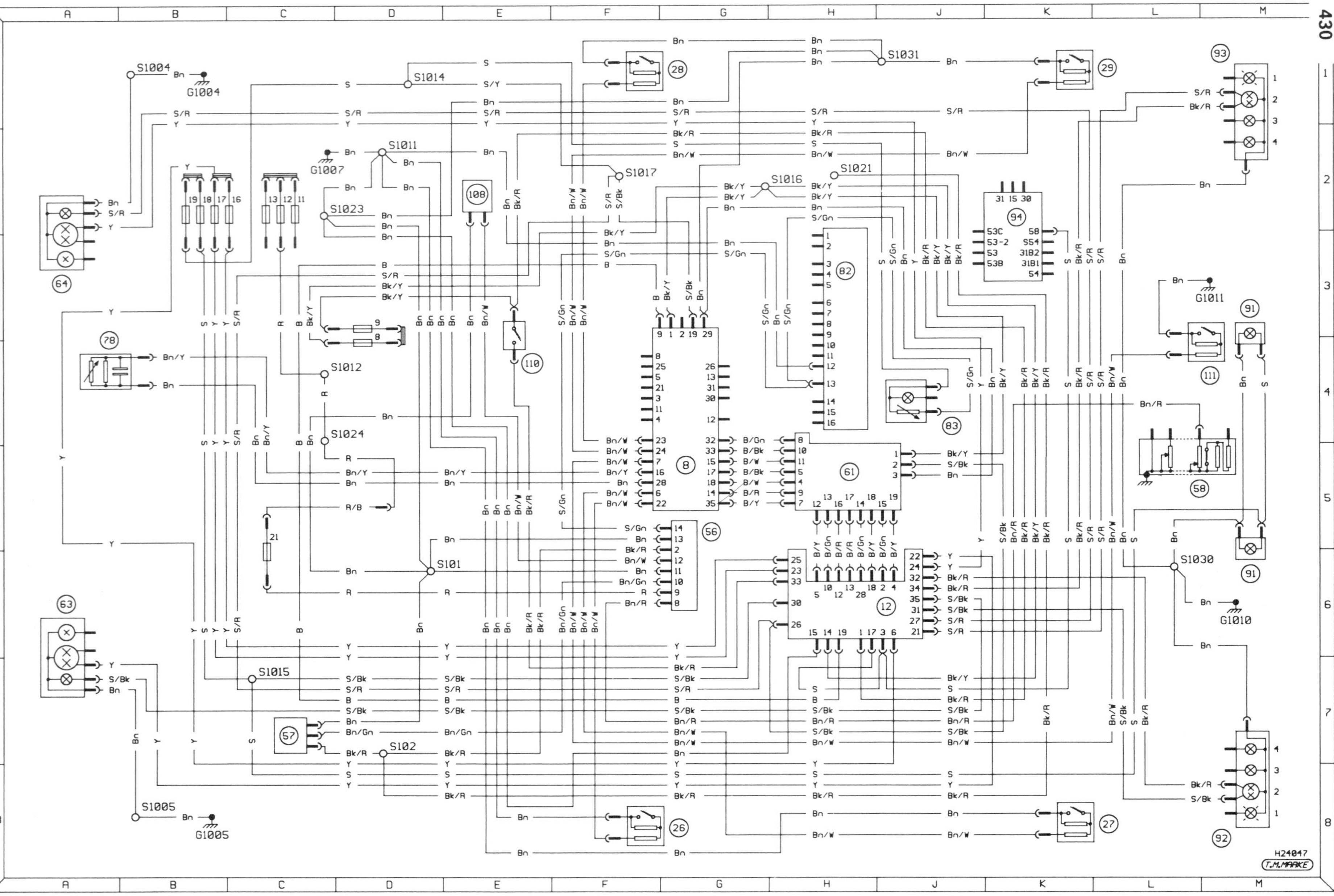

Diagram 4a. Graphic display system and fuel computer. Models up to 1987

NOTES:

1. All diagrams are divided into numbered circuits depending upon their function e.g Diagram 2 : Exterior lighting all models.
2. Some components may appear on more than one diagram so their positions are given in coded form in the key below e.g. 2/A1 denotes a component on diagram 2 grid location A1.
3. FEED WIRES ARE COLOURED RED (BLACK WHEN SWITCHED) AND ORIGINATE FROM DIAGRAM 1. ALL OTHER DIAGRAMS FEED FROM FUSE CONNECTIONS OR COMMON FEEDS (SEE BELOW).
4. Earth wires on all diagrams are coloured brown.
5. The tables below show where common feeds and common earths interconnect between diagrams.
6. Not all items are fitted to all models.
7. Brackets show how the circuit may be connected in more than one way.

FUSE	RATING	CIRCUIT
1	20A	LH Main Beam, LH Driving Lamp
2	20A	RH Main Beam, RH Driving Lamp
3	10A	LH Dip Beam
4	10A	RH Dip Beam
5	10A	LH Side Lamp
6	10A	RH Side Lamp
7	15A	Instrument Illum., Licence Plate Lamp
8	15A	Radio (From 1989 Only)
9	30A	Headlamp Wash
10	20A	Interior Lamps, Clock, Door Locking, Mirrors
11		Free
12	10A	Hazard Warning Lamps
13	30A	Cigar Lighter
14	30A	Horn
15	30A	Wiper Motors, Washer Pump
16	30A	Heated Rear Window, Heated Mirrors
17	20A	Front Fog Lamps, Dim/Dip
18	30A	Heater Blower
19		Free
20	15A	Flashers, Reversing Lamps
21	15A	Stop Lamps
22	10A	Control Circuits
23	30A	Fuel Pump
24	20A	Power Windows
30	20A	Anti-lock Brake
31	30A	Anti-lock Brake Pump
36	1A	Fuel Computer

COMMON FEED	DESCRIPTION	DIAGRAM/ GRID REF.
S1002	COMMON BATTERY FEED . . .	1/F4, 2/H6, 3c/F6
S1004	COMMON BATTERY FEED . . .	1/J2, 1a/K6, 2/J3, 2a/J3, 2b/H2, 3/K3, 3a/J3, 3c/K6, 3d/H2, 4/J2
S1012	COMMON IGNITION FEED . . .	1/H2, 1a/C3, 1a/C4, 1a/F4, 1a/J2, 2/F4, 3b/H2, 4/E3
S1042	COMMON CRANKING FEED . . .	1/J1, 1a/C1, 3b/H3

WIRE COLOURS

B	Blue
Bk	Black
Bn	Brown
Gn	Green
R	Red
Rs	Pink
S	Grey
V	Violet
W	White
Y	Yellow

COMMON EARTH POINT	DIAGRAM/ GRID REF.
G1002	1/F8, 1a/L8, 3/D7, 3b/E8, 4/F8
G1003	1/B8, 1a/A3, 1a/D8, 2/B8, 2a/B8, 3a/B8, 3b/B8, 3c/B8, 4/B8
G1004	2/B1, 2a/B1, 3a/B1, 3c/B1, 3d/B1
G1005	1/E1, 2/E2, 2a/E2, 2b/E1, 3/F2, 3a/E2, 3c/E1, 3d/E1
G1006	1a/M7, 3/F8, 3a/F8, 3b/F8, 3d/E7
G1007	1a/F6, 4/B4
G1009	2/L7, 2a/L7, 3c/L7
G1010	2b/M3, 3/M3, 3d/M3
G1011	1/J1, 2/G1, 2a/G1, 2b/H1, 3/K1, 3a/G2, 3c/H1, 3d/G1
G1013	1/J8, 2/F7, 2a/F8, 3c/J7, 3d/K7, 4/H8
G1014	1/C1, 2/C2, 2a/C1, 2b/B1, 3c/D2, 3d/C2
G1016	3c/G8, 3d/F7, 4/F8

KEY TO SYMBOLS

PLUG-IN CONNECTOR

EARTH

BULB

DIODE

FUSE

S1012 SOLDERED JOINT

Notes, tables, wire colours and key to symbols on wiring diagrams. Models from 1987 to May 1989

ITEM	DESCRIPTION	DIAGRAM/ GRID REF.
1	ABS Hydraulic Control Unit	3b/D2
2	ABS Hydraulic Motor Relay M6	3b/L6
3	ABS Main Relay M7	3b/K6
4	ABS Module	3b/J6
5	ABS Relay VII (PRE 1989)	3b/G3
6	ABS Warning Indicator	3b/L3
7	Air Flow Sensor	4/B6
8	Air Temp. Sensor	1a/B8
9	Alternator	1/A3, 1a/A4, 3/A3
10	Amplifier/Graphic Equalizer	5/C7, 5/J2
11	Antenna Module	3/L5, 5/E2, 5/E4, 5/F7, 5/L7, 5/M2, 5/M5
12	Ashtray Illumination	2b/H6
13	Auto. Gear Actuator	1/D7
14	Auto. Trans. Inhibitor Switch	1/D4, 2a/B5
15	Auto. Trans. Relay XII	1/G2
16	Auto. Trans. Selector Illumination	2b/J5
17	Auxiliary Warning Module	3c/H6, 3d/H6
18	Battery	1/E8, 1a/L8, 3/C8, 3b/D8, 4/E8
19	Bulb Failure Module	3c/H2, 3d/G2
20	Carburettor Stepper Motor	1a/G7
21	Cargo Space Lamp	2b/M5
22	Cargo Space Lamp Switch	2b/M3
23	Central Locking Motor LH Front	3a/G8
24	Central Locking Motor LH Rear	3a/M8
25	Central Locking Motor RH Front	3a/G1
26	Central Locking Motor RH Rear	3a/M1
27	Central Locking Motor Tailgate	3a/M4
28	Cigar Lighter	2b/G5
29	Clock	2b/G6
30	Coolant Temp. Sensor	1/C5
31	Cooling Fan Motor	1a/A7
32	Cooling Fan Switch	1a/C8
33	Crank Position Sensor	1a/C7
34	Dim/Dip Relay II	2/G4
35	Dim/Dip Relay B	2/G5
36	Dimmer Switch	2/L3
37	Dip Beam Relay F	2/F5
38	Distributor	1a/C2, 1a/D5, 1a/H2, 1a/J7, 4/B5
39	Door Ajar Sender LH Front	3d/F8
40	Door Ajar Sender LH Rear	3d/L8
41	Door Ajar Sender RH Front	3d/F1
42	Door Ajar Sender RH Rear	3d/L1
43	Door Ajar Sender Tailgate	3d/M4
44	EEC IV Module	4/J6
45	Electric Choke	1a/A6, 1a/C3, 1a/F2, 1a/F5
46	Electric Door Mirror	3/E1, 3/E8,
47	Electric Mirror Control Switch	3/F2
48	Electric Window Control Switch Front	3a/J4
49	Electric Window Control Switch Rear	3a/K1, 3a/K8
50	Electric Window Motor LH Front	3a/F8
51	Electric Window Motor LH Rear	3a/J8
52	Electric Window Motor RH Front	3a/F1
53	Electric Window Motor RH Rear	3a/J1
54	Electronic Ignition Module	1a/B2
55	Engine Management Relay D	1a/A5, 1a/K5, 4/H2
56	Engine Management Relay M2	1a/K5
57	Engine Management Relay XI	1a/D6, 1a/K2, 1a/G5, 4/G1
58	Engine Temp. Sensor	1a/B7, 1a/F1, 1a/F7, 4/C5
59	ESC 2 Ignition Module	1a/F8
60	Fader Control (4 Way)	5/C4, 5/J4
61	Flasher/Hazard Switch	2a/K4
62	Flasher Lamp LH	2a/A8
63	Flasher Lamp LH Side Marker	2a/E8
64	Flasher Lamp RH	2a/A1
65	Flasher Lamp RH Side Marker	2a/E1
66	Flasher Relay L1	2a/K5
67	Foglamp Front	2a/A2, 2a/A7
68	Foglamp Relay H	2a/E4
69	Foglamp Switch Front	2a/J1
70	Foglamp Switch Rear	2a/J2
71	Fuel Computer	3d/K5
72	Fuel Flow Sensor	3d/C7
73	Fuel Injectors	4/E4
74	Fuel Pump	4/M4
75	Fuel Sender	1/L4, 3d/L5
76	Fuel Shut Off Valve	1a/C3, 1a/J3
77	Glove Box Lamp/Switch	2b/F7
78	Graphic Display Module	3c/H5, 3d/G5
79	Handbrake Warning Switch	1/K5
80	Headlamp Unit LH	2/A6, 3c/A6
81	Headlamp Unit RH	2/A3, 3c/A3
82	Headlamp Washer Pump	3a/C1
83	Headlamp Washer Relay III	2/H2, 3a/F2, 3c/F3
84	Headlamp Wiper Motor	3a/A2, 3a/A6
85	Heated Rear Window	3/M5
86	Heated Rear Window Relay E (PRE 1989)	3/E4
87	Heated Rear Window Timer Relay IV	3/F4
88	Heated Rear Window Switch (PRE 1989)	3/J2
89	Heated Rear Window Switch (POST 1989)	3/K2
90	Heated Windscreen	3/F6
91	Heated Windscreen Relay L3	3/J4
92	Heated Windscreen Switch	3/J3
93	Heated Windscreen Timer Relay L2	3/K4
94	Heater Blower Illumination	2b/F5
95	Heater Blower Motor	3/G6
96	Heater Blower Switch	3/G5
97	High Beam Relay X	2/F4
98	Horn	3/A6, 3/A7

Key to wiring diagrams. Models from 1987 to May 1989

ITEM	DESCRIPTION	DIAGRAM/ GRID REF.
99	Horn Relay C	3/F4
100	Horn Switch	3/L4
101	Hybrid Ignition Module	1a/B7, 1a/F2
102	Ice Warning Sender	3d/A4
103	Idle Speed Valve	4/D5
104	Ignition Coil	1a/C2, 1a/C5, 1a/G2, 1a/H6, 4/C5
105	Ignition Relay I	1/H4
106	Ignition Switch	1/K1, 3b/L2, 5/C1, 5/D3, 5/F7, 5/K7, 5/L4, 5/M2
107	Inertia Switch	4/M3
108	Instrument Cluster	1/K3, 1a/M3, 2/J4, 2a/J3, 2b/F2, 3b/K3, 4/K3
109	Instrument Illumination Control	2b/G2, 3c/J2, 3d/J2
110	Interior Lamp Delay Relay VI	2b/E2
111	Interior Lamp Door Switch LH Front	2b/E8
112	Interior Lamp Door Switch LH Rear	2b/J8
113	Interior Lamp Door Switch RH Front	2b/E1
114	Interior Lamp Door Switch RH Rear	2b/J1
115	Interior Lamp/Switch Front (High Series)	2b/J3
116	Interior Lamp/Switch Front (Low Series)	2b/J3
117	Interior Lamp/Switch Rear	2b/K3
118	Kickdown Actuator	1/D6
119	Kickdown Relay VIII	1/H2
120	Kickdown Switch	1/J4
121	Licence Plate Lamp	2/M3, 2/M6
122	Light Cluster LH Rear	2/M8, 2a/M8, 3c/M8
123	Light Cluster RH Rear	2/M1, 2a/M1, 3c/M1
124	Light Switch	2/L3, 2a/K3, 2b/J2, 3/L3, 3a/J3, 3c/K4, 3d/J3
125	Link (Fitted When Manual Trans.)	1/F2
126	Low Brake Fluid Sender	1/C3, 3b/E3
127	Low Washer Fluid Sender	3d/C1
128	Luggage Comp. Lamp	2b/L5
129	Luggage Comp. Lamp Switch	2b/M4
130	Manifold Heater	1a/J1, 1a/F6
131	Manifold Temp. Switch	1a/E2
132	Oil Pressure Switch	1/B6
133	Radio Unit	5/C2, 5/D5, 5/E8, 5/K3, 5/K6, 5/K8
134	Reversing Lamp Switch	2a/D5
135	Spark Plugs	1a/D2, 1a/D5, 1a/J2, 1a/K7, 4/A5
136	Speaker LH Door	5/C8, 5/D8, 5/J3, 5/J6
137	Speaker LH Front	5/A2, 5/A5, 5/A8, 5/G3, 5/G6, 5/H8
138	Speaker LH Rear	5/F5, 5/F8, 5/M3, 5/M6
139	Speaker RH Door	5/C3, 5/D6, 5/J1, 5/J4
140	Speaker RH Front	5/A1, 5/A3, 5/A6, 5/G1, 5/G4, 5/H6
141	Speaker RH Rear	5/F3, 5/F6, 5/M1, 5/M4
142	Speed Sensor	3d/E4
143	Starter Motor	1/D5
144	Stop Lamp Switch	2a/H3, 3b/J3, 3c/F5
145	Suppressor	1a/J5, 1a/K4, 3/C4, 4/E4
146	TFI Module	4/C8
147	Throttle Position Sensor	4/C4
148	Trailer Flasher Indicator	2a/H5
149	Vacuum Switch	1/G6
150	Vacuum Valve (From 1988)	1a/A6
151	Warning Lamp Cluster	3d/K6
152	Windscreen Washer Pump	3a/C1
153	Wiper Intermittent Relay V	3a/E3
154	Wiper Intermittent Speed Control	3a/G4
155	Wiper Motor Front	3a/E4
156	Wiper Motor Rear	3a/M6
157	Wiper Switch	3a/H3
158	Wheel Sensor LH Front	3b/B8
159	Wheel Sensor LH Rear	3b/L8
160	Wheel Sensor RH Front	3b/B1
161	Wheel Sensor RH Rear	3b/L1

Key to wiring diagrams continued. Models from 1987 to May 1989

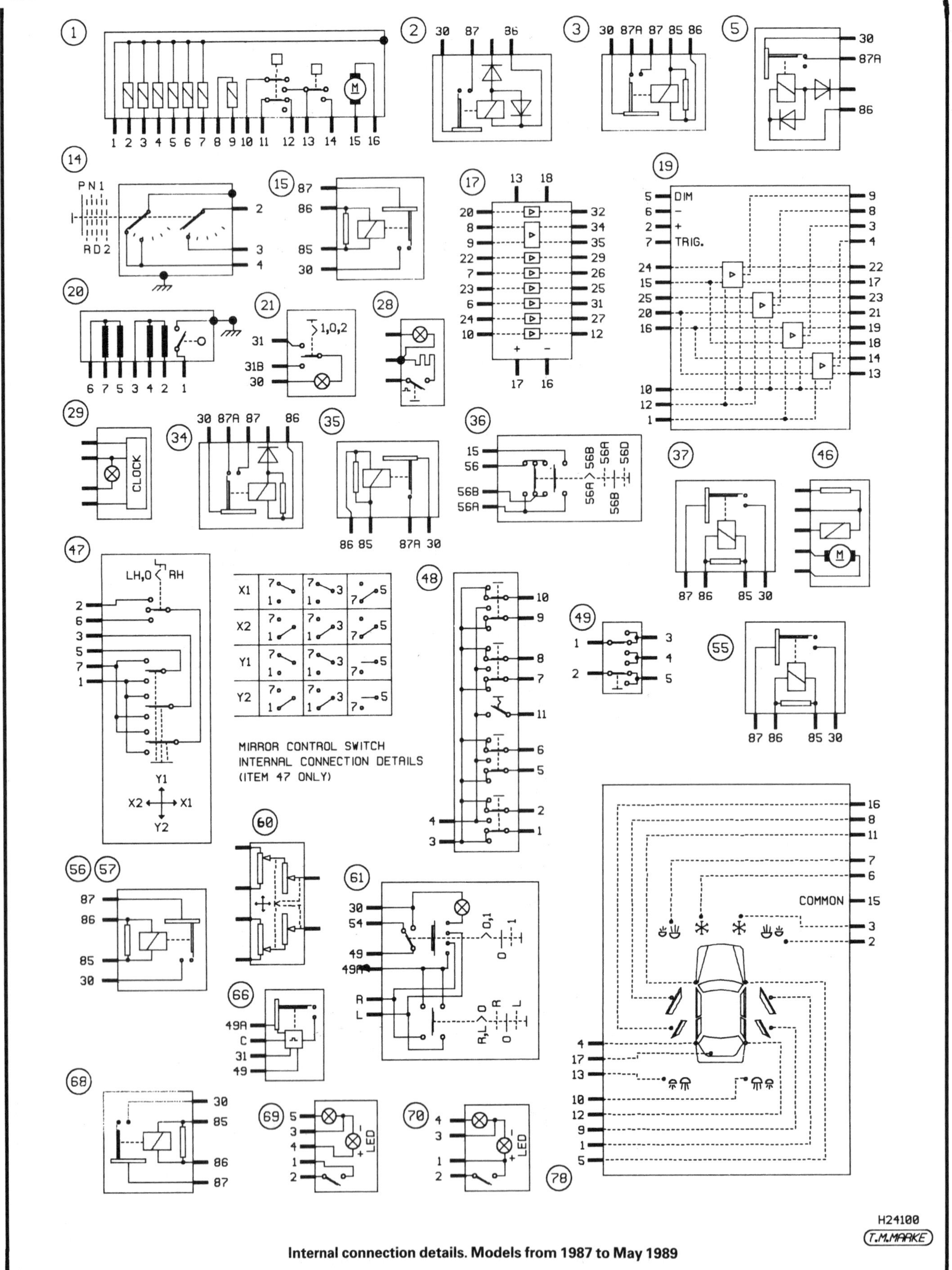

Internal connection details. Models from 1987 to May 1989

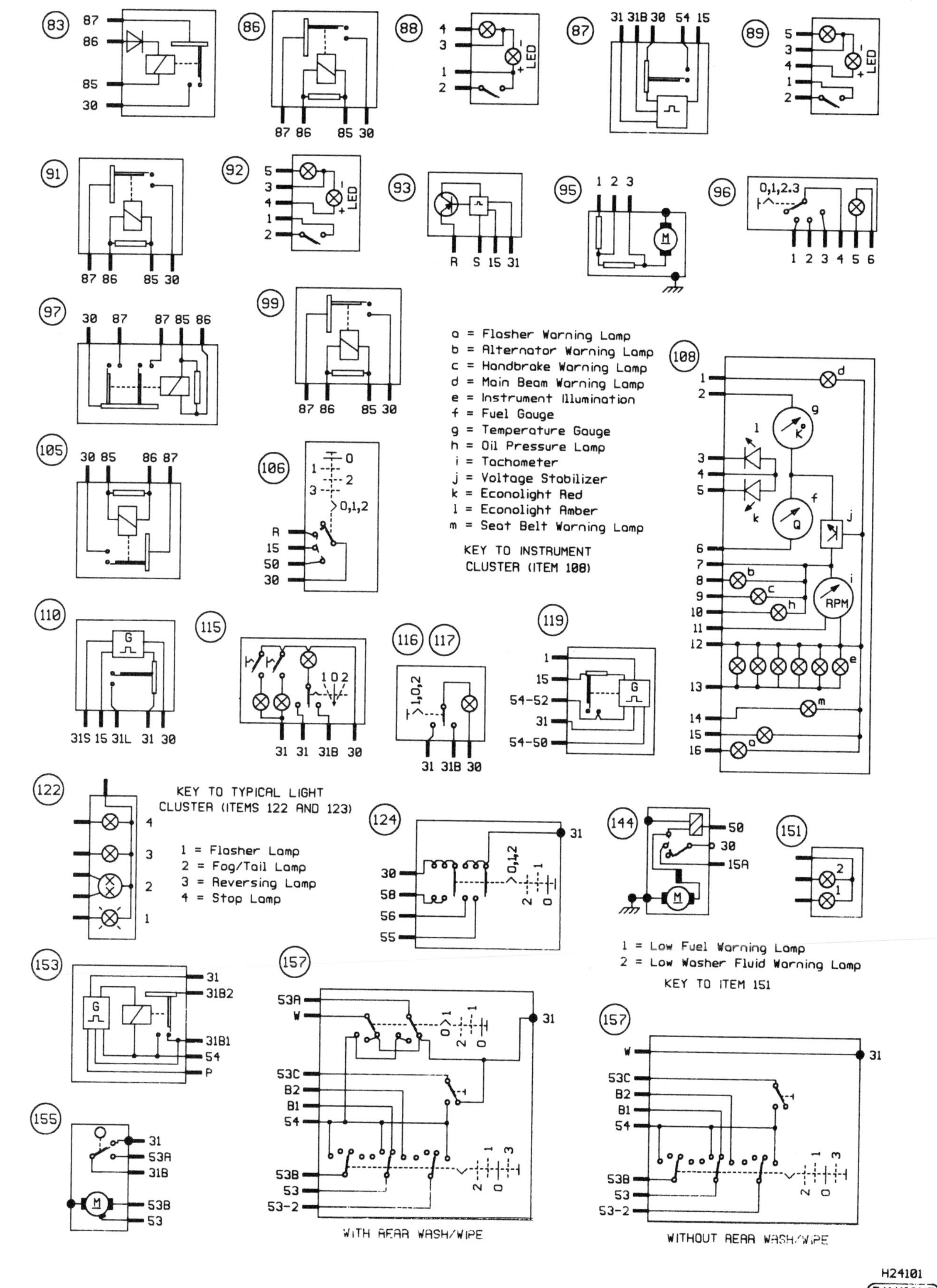

Internal connection details continued. Models from 1987 to May 1989

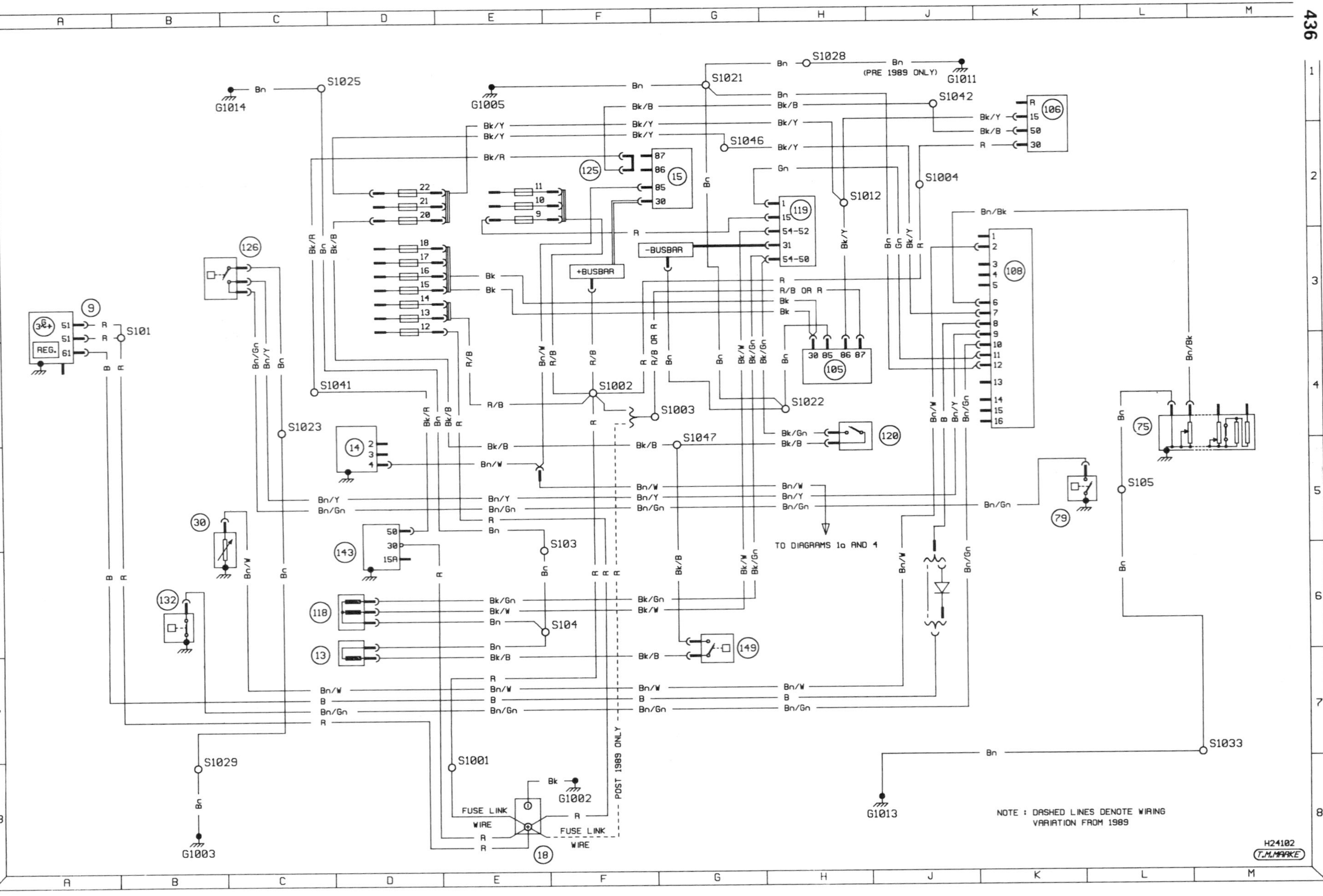

Diagram 1. Starting, charging and warning lamps. Models from 1987 to May 1989

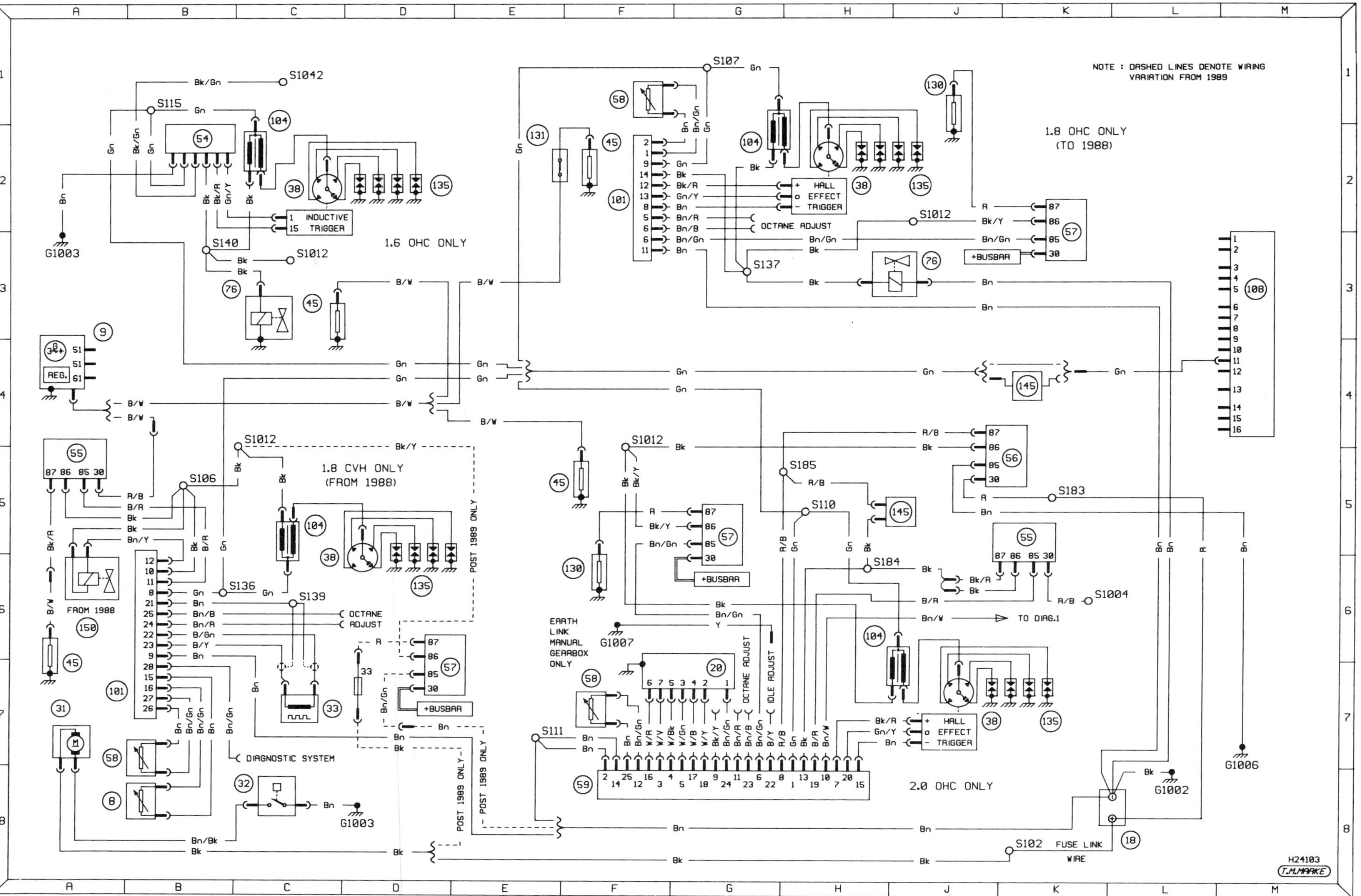

Diagram 1a. Ignition variations. Carburettor models from 1987 to May 1989

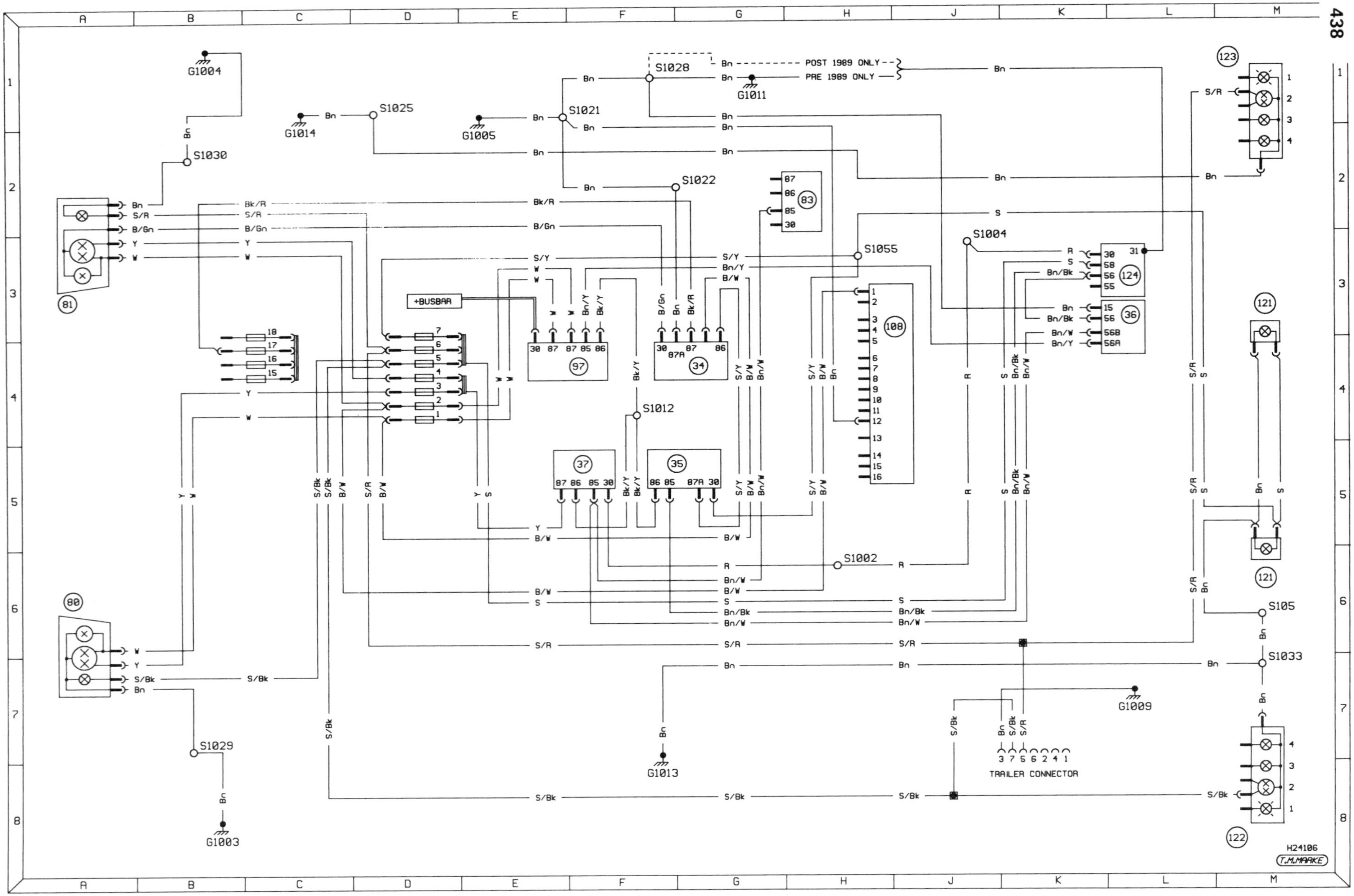

Diagram 2. Exterior lighting – head/sidelamps. Models from 1987 to May 1989

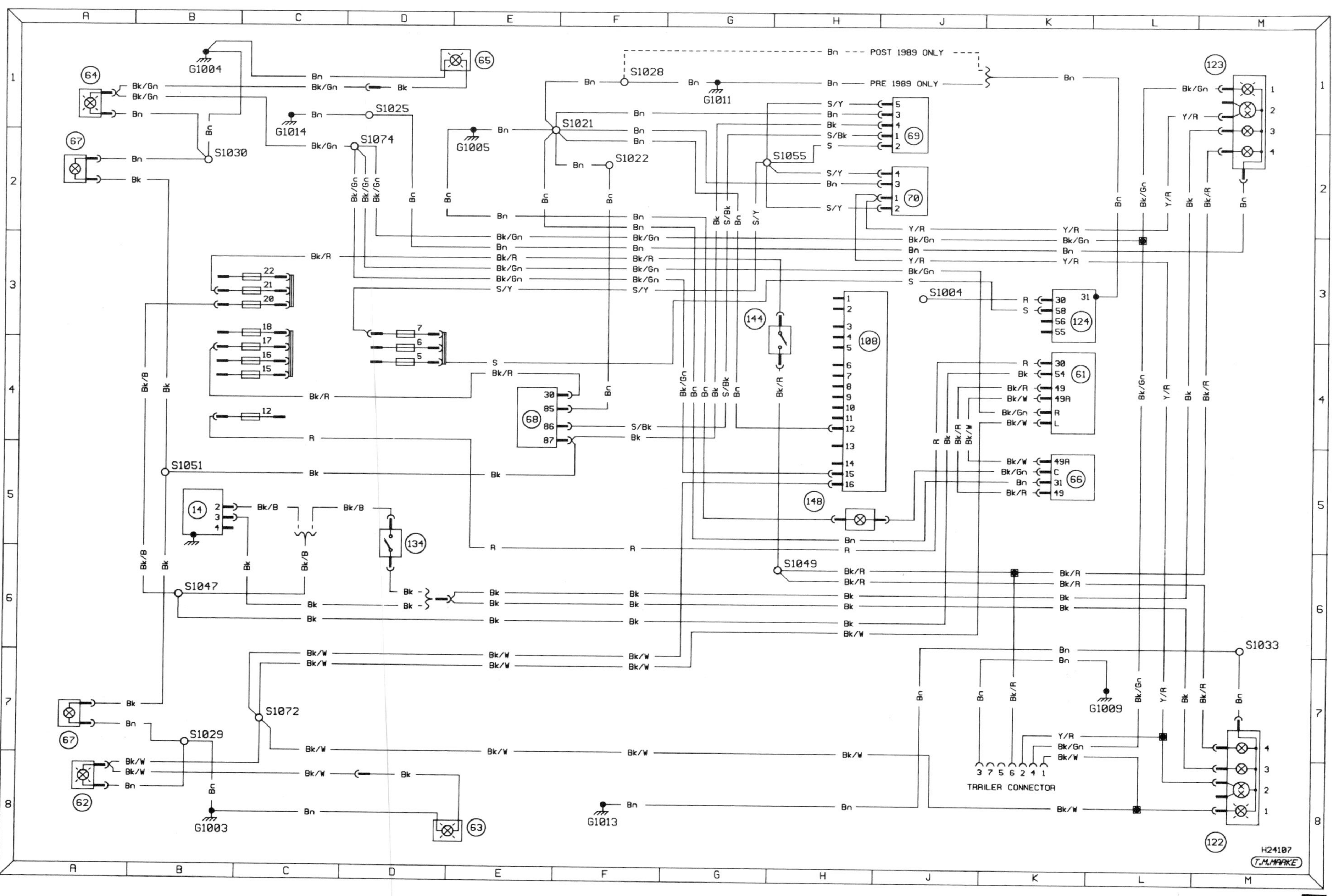

Diagram 2a. Exterior lighting – signal warning lamps. Models from 1987 to May 1989

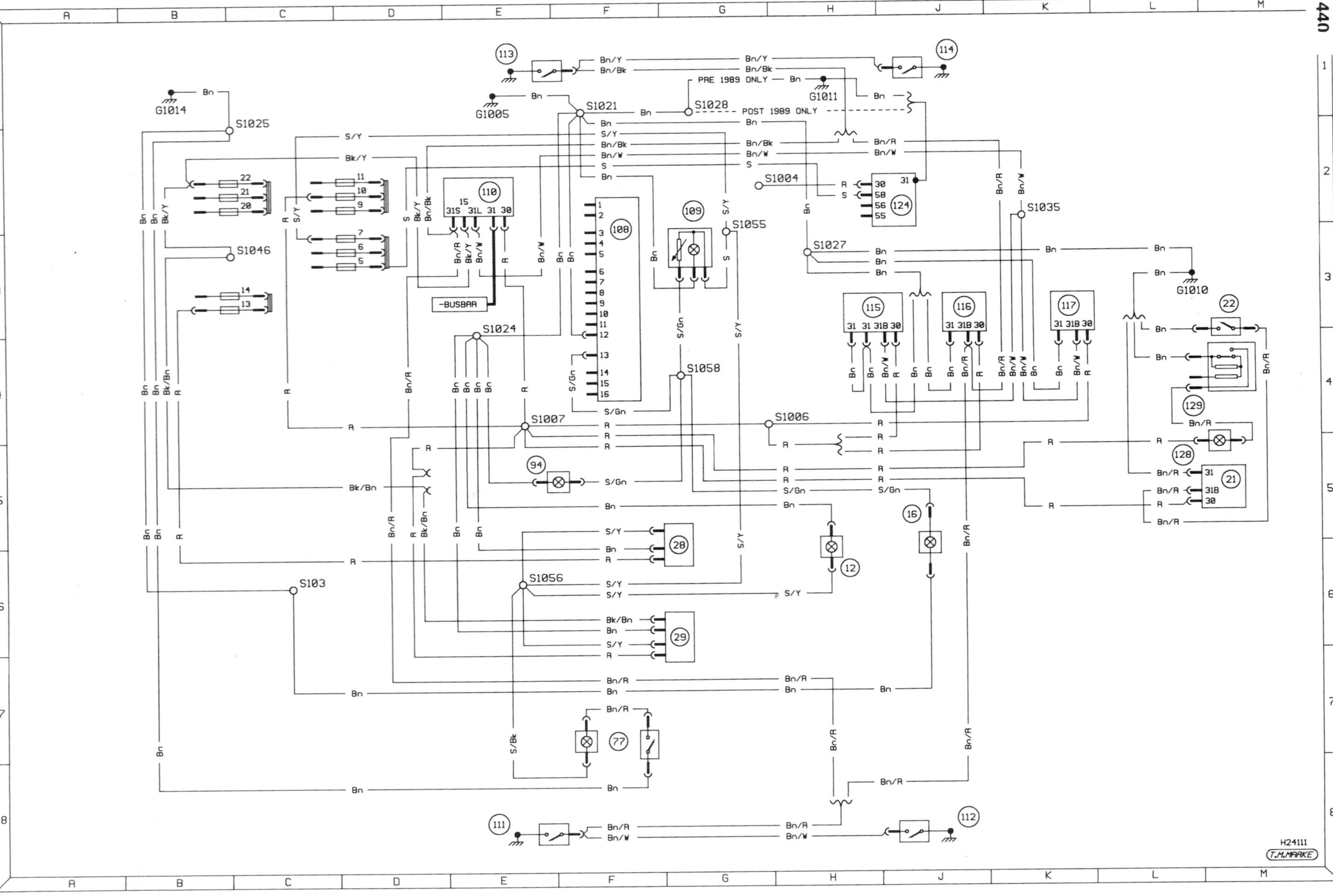

Diagram 2b. Interior lighting. Models from 1987 to May 1989

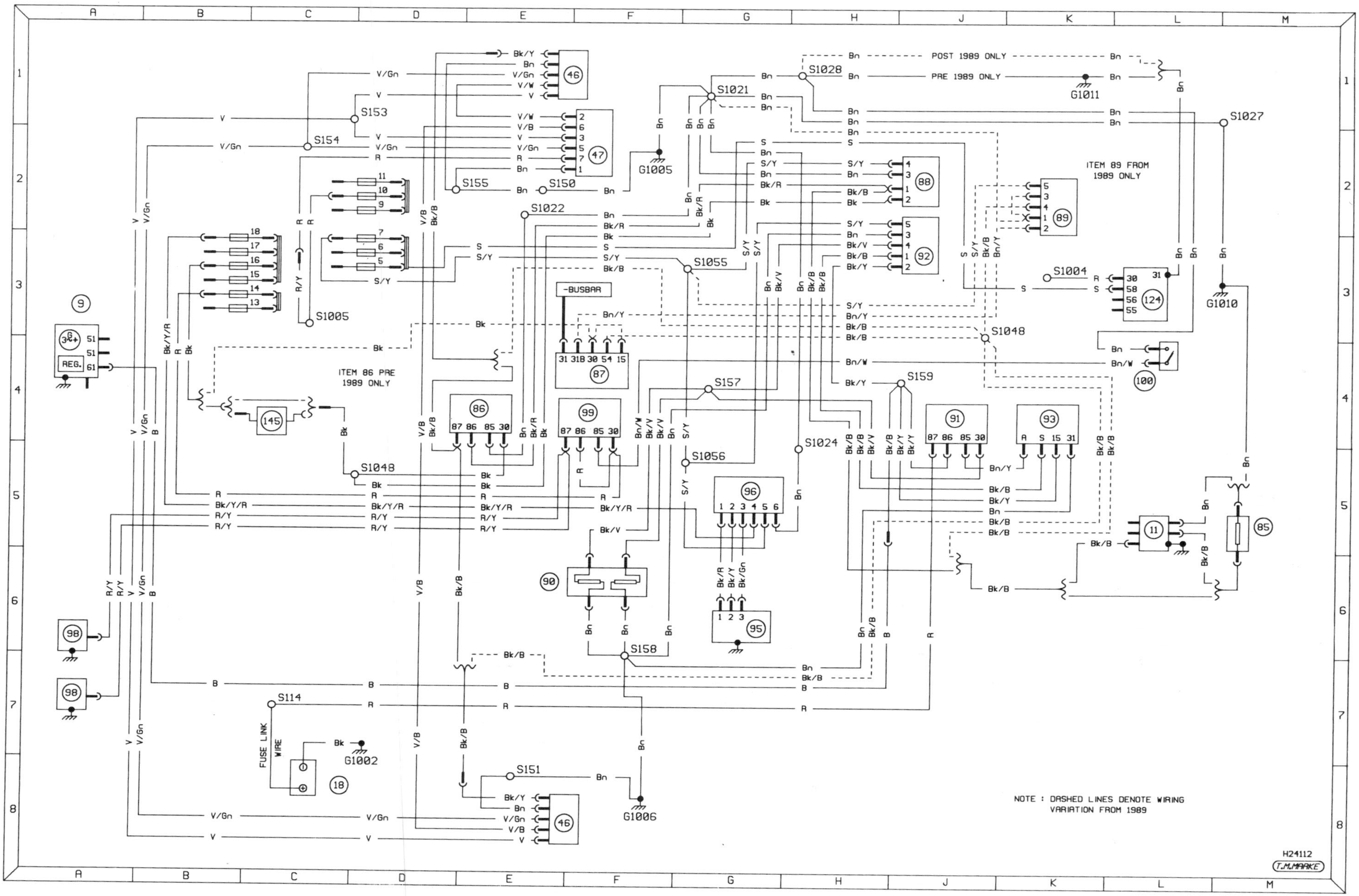

Diagram 3. Ancillary circuits – horn, heater blower, heated mirrors and screens. Models from 1987 to May 1989

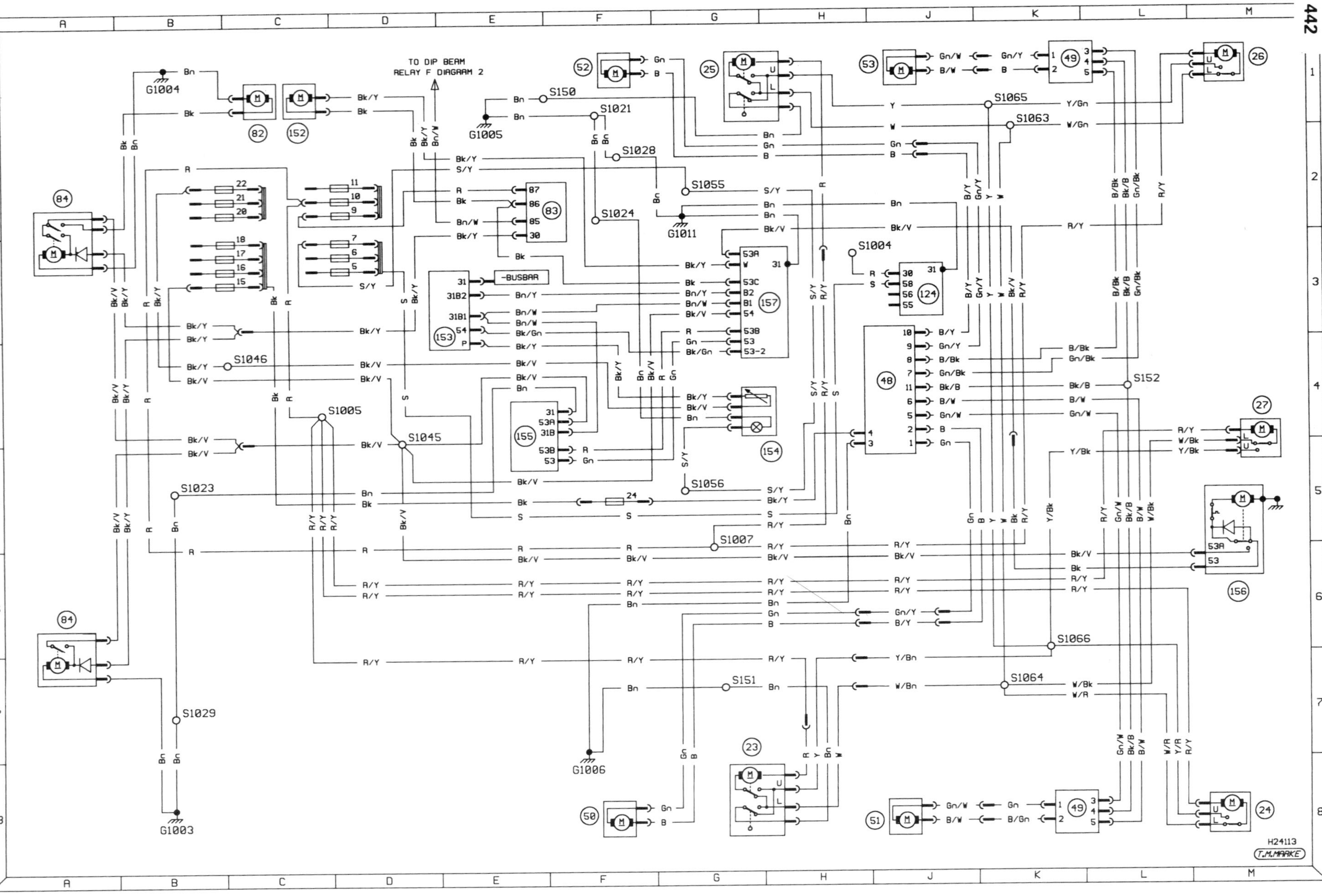

Diagram 3a. Ancillary circuits – wash/wipe, central locking and electric windows. Models from 1987 to May 1989

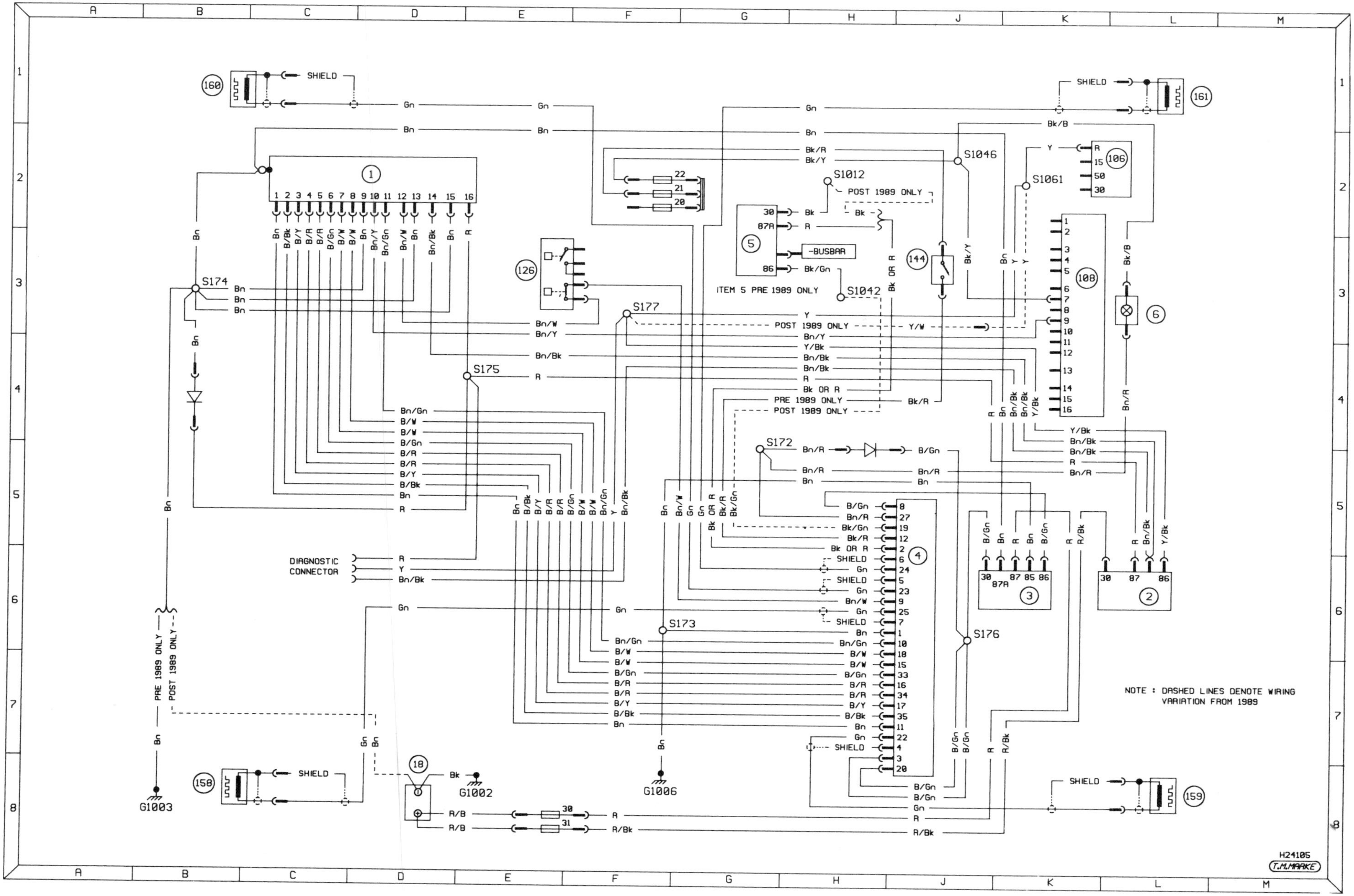

NOTE : DASHED LINES DENOTE WIRING VARIATION FROM 1989

Diagram 3b. Anti-lock braking system. Models from 1987 to May 1989

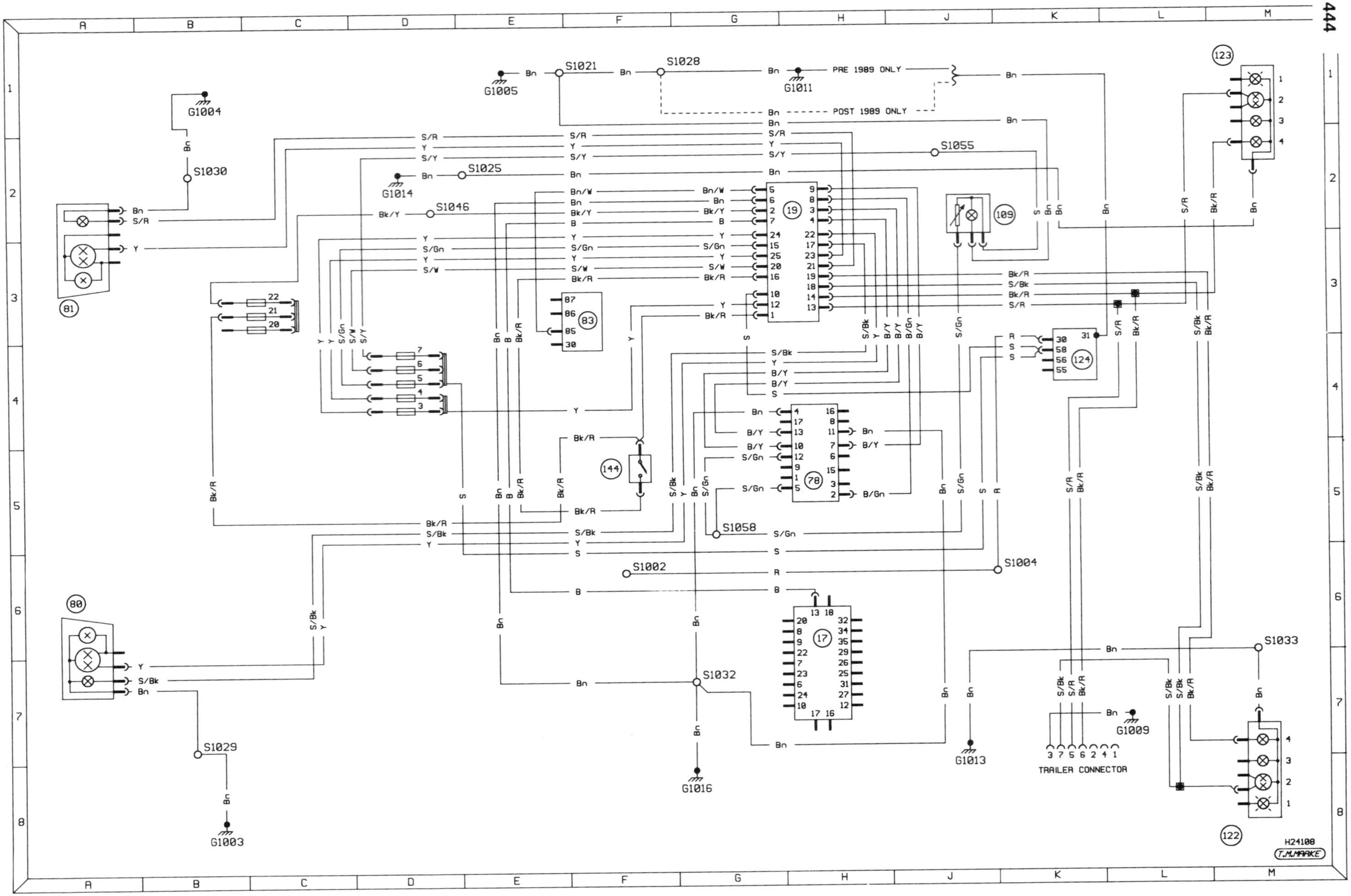

Diagram 3c. Graphic display system – bulb failure. Models from 1987 to May 1989

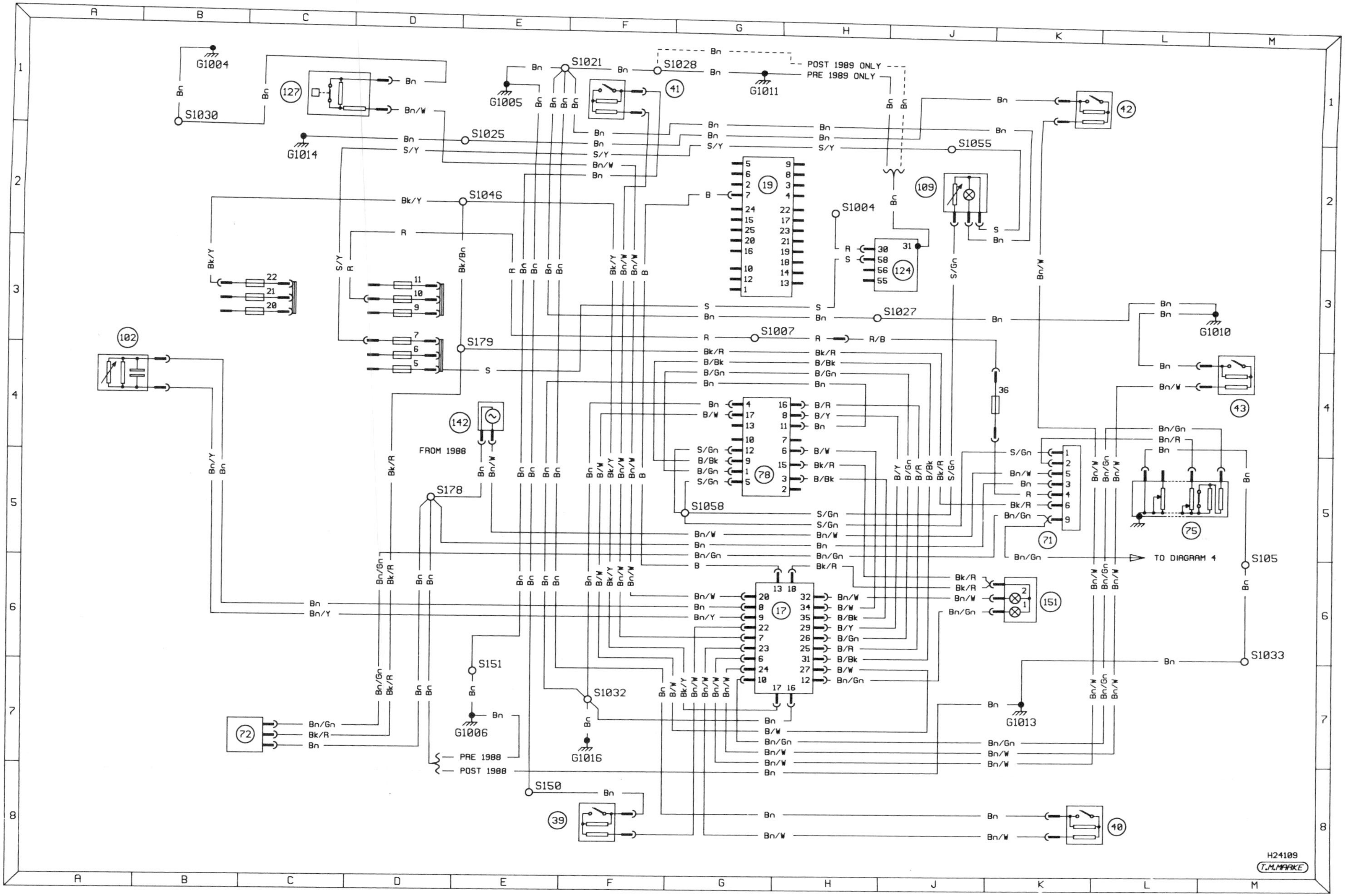

Diagram 3d. Graphic display system – auxiliary warning, door ajar and fuel computer. Models from 1987 to May 1989

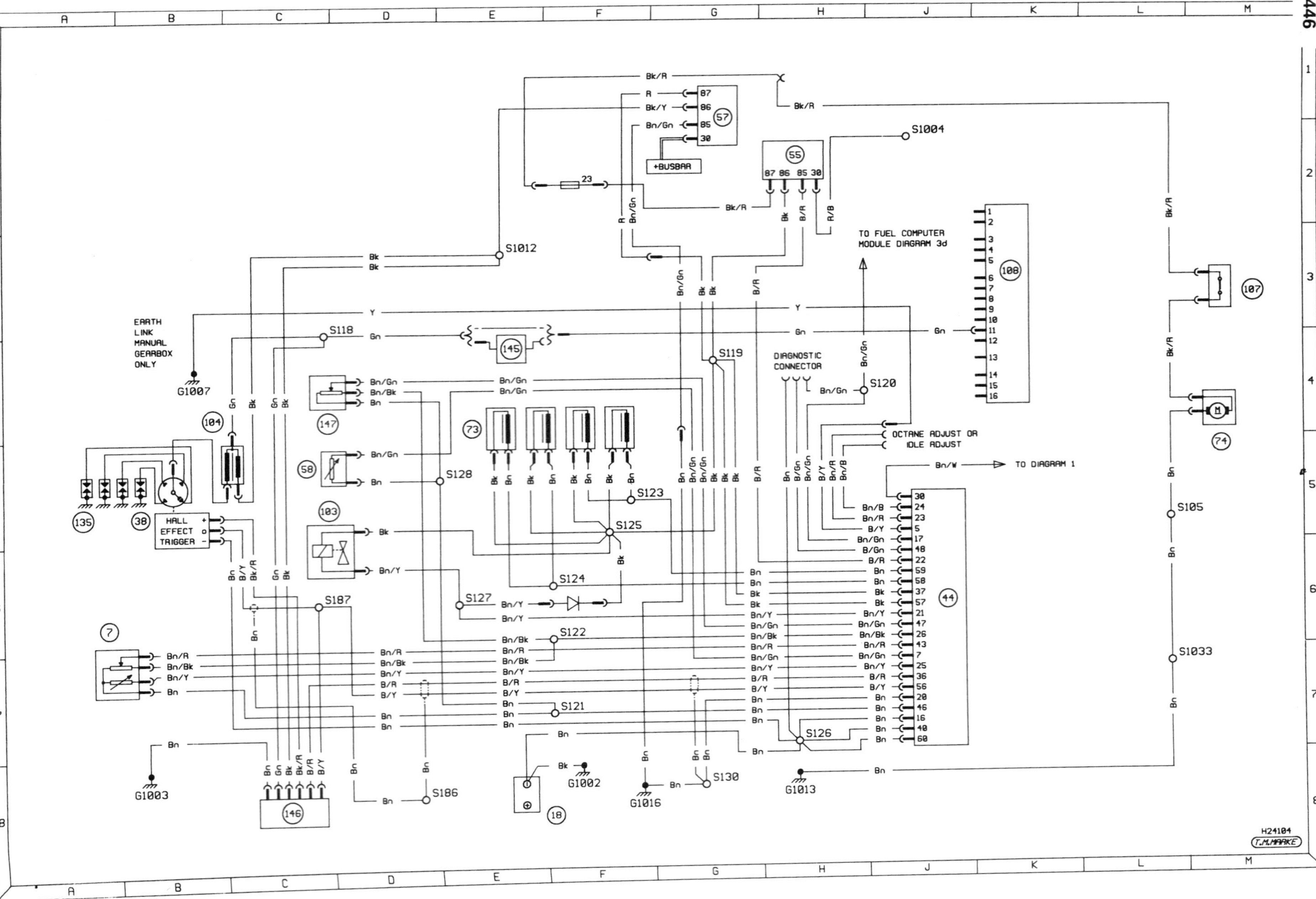

Diagram 4. 2.0 EFi fuel injection and ignition. Models from 1987 to May 1989

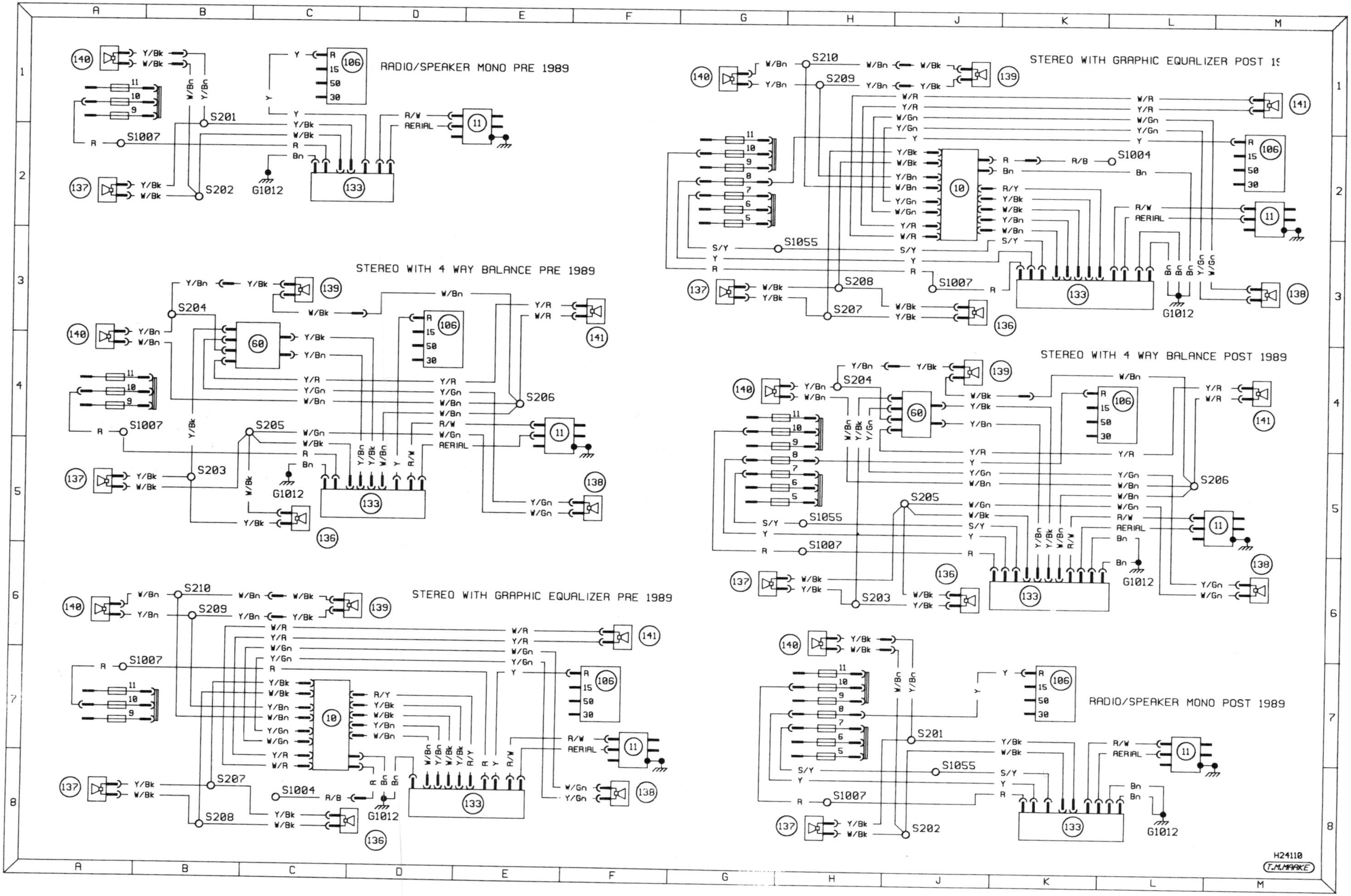

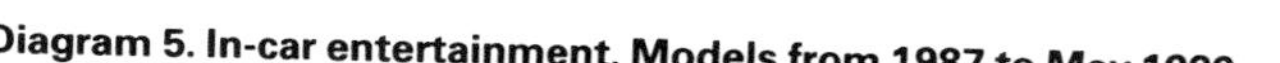

RADIO/SPEAKER MONO PRE 1989

STEREO WITH GRAPHIC EQUALIZER POST 1989

STEREO WITH 4 WAY BALANCE PRE 1989

STEREO WITH 4 WAY BALANCE POST 1989

STEREO WITH GRAPHIC EQUALIZER PRE 1989

RADIO/SPEAKER MONO POST 1989

H24110

T.M.MARKE

Diagram 5. In-car entertainment. Models from 1987 to May 1989

NOTES:

1. All diagrams are divided into numbered circuits depending on function e.g. Diagram 2: Exterior lighting.
2. Items are arranged in relation to a plan view of the vehicle.
3. Items may appear on more than one diagram so are found using a grid reference e.g. 2/A1 denotes an item on diagram 2 grid location A1.
4. Complex items appear on the diagrams as blocks and are expanded on the internal connections page.
5. Feed wires are coloured red (black when switched) and all earth wires are coloured brown.
6. Brackets show how the circuit may be connected in more than one way.
7. Not all items are fitted to all models.

WIRE COLOURS

B	Blue
Bk	Black
Bn	Brown
Gn	Green
R	Red
Rs	Pink
S	Grey
V	Violet
W	White
Y	Yellow

FUSE	RATING	CIRCUIT
1	15A	LH Main Beam, LH Driving Lamp
2	15A	RH Main Beam, RH Driving Lamp
3	7.5A	LH Dip Beam
4	7.5A	RH Dip Beam
5	5A	LH Sidelamp
6	5A	RH Sidelamp
7	15A	Instrument Illum., Numberplate Lamp
8	15A	Radio
9	15A	Headlamp Wash
10	7.5A	Interior Lamps, Clock, Door Locking, Mirrors
12	10A	Hazard Warning Lamps, Anti-theft, Door Locking
13	20A	Cigar Lighter, Radio Amplifier
14	10A	Horn
15	15A	Wiper Motors, Washer Pump
16	20A	Heated Rear Window, Heated Mirrors
17	15A	Front Foglamps, Dim/Dip
18	25A	Heater Blower
20	10A	Direction Indicators, Reversing Lamps
21	7.5A	Stop Lamps
22	4A	Control Circuits
23	20A	Fuel Pump
24	30A	Power Windows
30	20A	Anti-lock Brake
31	30A	Anti-lock Brake Pump 1
32	15A	Lambda Sensor
33	30A	Cooling Fan
34	30A	Anti-lock Brake Pump 2
35	1A	EEC V Module
37	1A	Fuel Computer

KEY TO SYMBOLS

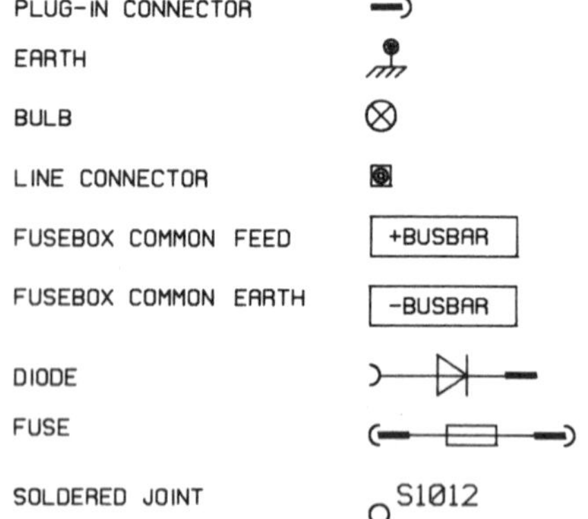

Notes, tables, wire colours and key to symbols on wiring diagrams. Models from 1990 onwards

H24300
T.M.MARKE

ITEM	DESCRIPTION	DIAGRAM/ GRID REF.
1	ABS Hydraulic Control Unit	3b/C2
2	ABS Main Relay M12	3b/H6
3	ABS Module	3b/G6
4	ABS Pump Relay M13	3b/J6
5	ABS Pump Relay M14	3b/K6
6	ABS Warning Indicator	3b/L3
7	Air Temp. Sensor	1a/G1, 4/B6, 4a/C5
8	Alternator	1/A3, 1a/A4, 3/A3
9	Amplifier (Audio)	5/K6
10	Amplifier/Graphic Equalizer	5/K2
11	Antenna Module	3/L5, 5/C1, 5/C5, 5/K2, 5/K6
12	Anti-theft Module	5a/D2
13	Anti-theft Switch	5a/H2, 5a/H7
14	Ashtray Illumination	2b/H6
15	Auto. Gear Actuator	1/D7
16	Auto. Trans. Inhibitor Switch	1/D4, 2a/B6
17	Auto. Trans. Relay XII	1/F2
18	Auto. Trans. Selector Illumination	2b/J6
19	Auxiliary Warning Module	3c/H6, 3d/G6
20	Ballast Resistor	4/D2, 4a/G8
21	Battery	1/F8, 1a/H8, 2/F7, 2a/G8, 2b/C8, 3/C8, 3a/D8, 3b/D8, 3c/E8, 3d/D8, 4/F8, 4a/F8, 5/D8, 5a/D8
22	Bonnet Switch	5a/A4
23	Bulb Failure Module	3c/H3, 3d/G2
24	Canister Purge Solenoid	4/D3
25	Cargo Space Lamp (Estate Only)	2b/M5, 5a/L6
26	Cargo Space Lamp Switch (Estate Only)	2b/M4, 5a/M3
27	CD Player	5/J5
28	Central Locking Motor LH Front	3a/H8, 5a/H8
29	Central Locking Motor LH Rear	3a/M8, 5a/L8
30	Central Locking Motor RH Front	3a/H1, 5a/H1
31	Central Locking Motor RH Rear	3a/M1, 5a/L1
32	Central Locking Motor Tailgate	3a/M5
33	Cigar Lighter	2b/F6
34	Clock	2b/F7
35	CO Adjuster Potentiometer	4a/C6
36	Coolant Temp. Gauge Sender Unit	1/C6
37	Cooling Fan Motor	1/A5
38	Cooling Fan Relay	1/J6
39	Cooling Fan Switch	1/B5
40	Crank Position Sensor	1a/C6, 1a/H1, 4/D5, 4a/E3
41	Dim/Dip Relay II	2/G3

ITEM	DESCRIPTION	DIAGRAM/ GRID REF.
42	Dim/Dip Relay B	2/F5
43	Dip Beam Relay F	2/E5
44	Dimmer Switch	2/L3
45	Direction Indicator Flasher Relay	2a/K5
46	Direction Indicator/Hazard Switch	2a/K4
47	Direction Indicator Lamp LH	2a/A8
48	Direction Indicator Lamp RH	2a/A1
49	Direction Indicator Side Repeater LH	2a/D8
50	Direction Indicator Side Repeater RH	2a/D1
51	Distributor	1a/C2, 1a/D6, 1a/J2, 4a/B5
52	Door Ajar/Lamp Switch LH Front	3d/F8, 5a/F8
53	Door Ajar/Lamp Switch LH Rear	3d/L8, 5a/K8
54	Door Ajar/Lamp Switch RH Front	3d/F1, 5a/F1
55	Door Ajar/Lamp Switch RH Rear	3d/L1, 5a/K1
56	Door Ajar/Lamp Switch Tailgate (Sapphire & Hatchback Only)	2b/M4, 3d/M4, 5a/L4
57	E.D.I.S. Module	4/E4
58	EEC IV Module	4/K6, 4a/K6
59	Electric Choke	1a/A6, 1a/C3, 1a/E3
60	Electric Door Mirror	3/F1, 3/F8
61	Electric Mirror Control Switch	3/F2
62	Electric Window Control Switch Front	3a/J4
63	Electric Window Control Switch Rear	3a/K1, 3a/K8
64	Electric Window Motor LH Front	3a/F8
65	Electric Window Motor LH Rear	3a/J8
66	Electric Window Motor RH Front	3a/F1
67	Electric Window Motor RH Rear	3a/J1
68	Electronic Ignition Module	1a/B1, 4a/B8
69	Engine Management Relay D	1a/E1, 4/J1, 4a/H1
70	Engine Management Relay XI	4/H1, 4a/G1
71	Engine Temp. Sensor	1a/B6, 1a/G1, 4/B6, 4a/C4
72	ESC 2 Ignition Module	1a/B6
73	Foglamp Front	2a/A2, 2a/A7
74	Foglamp Relay H	2a/E5
75	Foglamp Switch Front	2a/J1
76	Foglamp Switch Rear	2a/J2
77	Fuel Computer	3d/K5
78	Fuel Gauge Sender Unit	1/L4, 3d/L5
79	Fuel Injectors	4/B4, 4a/F4
80	Fuel Pump	1a/F8, 4/M4, 4a/M4
81	Fuel Pump Relay	1a/D7
82	Fuel Rail Temp. Switch	4a/J4
83	Fuel Shut Off Solenoid	1a/B3, 1a/C8
84	Glove Box Lamp/Switch	2b/E7
85	Graphic Display Module	3c/H5, 3d/G5
86	Graphic Equalizer	5/H5
87	Handbrake Warning Switch	1/K5
88	Headlamp Unit LH	2/A6, 3c/A6

H24301

T.M.MARKE

Key to wiring diagrams. Models from 1990 onwards

ITEM	DESCRIPTION	DIAGRAM/ GRID REF.
89	Headlamp Unit RH	2/A3, 3c/A3
90	Headlamp Washer Pump	3a/C1
91	Headlamp Washer Relay III	3a/F2
92	Headlamp Wiper Motor	3a/A2, 3a/A7
93	Heated Rear Window	3/M5
94	Heated Rear Window Timer Relay IV	3/C5
95	Heated Rear Window Switch	3/J3
96	Heated Washer Jet	3/A1, 3/A8
97	Heated Windscreen	3/F5
98	Heated Windscreen Relay L3	3/J5
99	Heated Windscreen Switch	3/J2
100	Heated Windscreen Timer Relay L2	3/K5
101	Heater Blower Illumination	2b/E4
102	Heater Blower Motor	3/G6
103	Heater Blower Switch	3/G5
104	Heater End Switch	3/F6
105	High Beam Relay X	2/F4
106	Horn	3/A7, 5a/A6
107	Horn Relay C	3/C6
108	Horn Switch	3/L4
109	Hybrid Ignition Module	1a/F3
110	Ice Warning Sender	3d/A4
111	Idle Speed Solenoid	4a/C5
112	Ignition Coil	1a/C1, 1a/D6, 1a/H2, 4/C5, 4a/B4
113	Ignition Relay I	2/G5, 2a/F4, 3/D5, 3a/E5
114	Ignition Switch	1/K1, 1a/M1, 2/K2, 2a/K1, 2b/G2, 3/L2, 3a/K2, 3b/K2, 3c/L2, 3d/K2, 4/L1, 4a/L1, 5/M1
115	Inertia Switch	1a/E8, 4/M3, 4a/M3
116	Instrument Cluster	1/K3, 1a/M3, 2/J3, 2a/H4, 2b/F2, 3b/L3, 4/L3, 4a/K3
117	Instrument Illumination Control	2b/G3, 3c/J2, 3d/J2
118	Intake Air Valve	4/B8
119	Interior Lamp Delay Relay VI	2b/D2
120	Interior Lamp Door Switch LH Front	2b/E8
121	Interior Lamp Door Switch LH Rear	2b/J8
122	Interior Lamp Door Switch RH Front	2b/E1
123	Interior Lamp Door Switch RH Rear	2b/J1
124	Interior Lamp/Switch Front (High Series)	2b/J3
125	Interior Lamp/Switch Front (Low Series)	2b/J3
126	Interior Lamp/Switch Rear	2b/K3
127	Kickdown Actuator	1/D6
128	Kickdown Relay VIII	1/H3
129	Kickdown Switch	1/H4
130	Lambda Sensor	4/D7, 4a/B6
131	Lamp Cluster LH Rear	2/M8, 2a/M8, 3c/M8
132	Lamp Cluster RH Rear	2/M1, 2a/M1, 3c/M1
133	Lamp Switch	2/L3, 2a/K3, 2b/G3, 3/L3, 3a/K3, 3c/K4, 3d/H3, 5/M3
134	Lamps On Warning Module	2b/G7
135	Link (Fitted When Manual Trans.)	1/F2
136	Low Brake Fluid Sender Unit	1/C3, 3b/D2
137	Low Washer Fluid Sender Unit	3d/C1
138	Luggage Comp. Lamp (Sapphire/Hatchback)	2b/M5, 5a/L5
139	MAP Sensor	4/G4, 4a/J4
140	Number Plate Lamp	2/M3, 2/M6
141	Oil Pressure Switch	1/B7
142	Power Delay Relay M5	4/K5
143	Radio Unit	5/C3, 5/C7, 5/H2, 5/H8
144	Reversing Lamp Switch	2a/D6
145	Spark Plugs	1a/D2, 1a/E6, 1a/J2, 4/C4, 4a/A5
146	Speaker LH Door	5/B3, 5/B7, 5/J3, 5/K8
147	Speaker LH Rear	5/D7, 5/L3, 5/L8
148	Speaker RH Door	5/B1, 5/B5, 5/J1, 5/K5
149	Speaker RH Rear	5/D5, 5/L1, 5/L5
150	Speed Sensor	1/H7
151	Starter Motor	1/C6
152	Stop Lamp Switch	1/J4, 2a/H4, 3c/F5
153	Suppressor	1a/K5, 4/B5, 4a/E3
154	Throttle Control Motor	4/B5
155	Throttle Position Sensor	4/B7, 4a/C4
156	Trailer Flasher Indicator	2a/H5
157	Vacuum Valve	1a/H3
158	Warning Lamp Cluster	3d/K6
159	Washer Pump Front/Rear Screen	3a/C1
160	Wiper Intermittent Relay V Front	3a/E4
161	Wiper Intermittent Relay IX Rear	3a/E2
162	Wiper Intermittent Speed Control	3a/H5
163	Wiper Motor Front	3a/F5
164	Wiper Motor Rear	3a/M6
165	Wiper Switch	3a/H4
166	Wheel Sensor LH Front	3b/B8
167	Wheel Sensor LH Rear	3b/M8
168	Wheel Sensor RH Front	3b/B1
169	Wheel Sensor RH Rear	3b/M1

H24302
T.M.MARKE

Key to wiring diagrams continued. Models from 1990 onwards

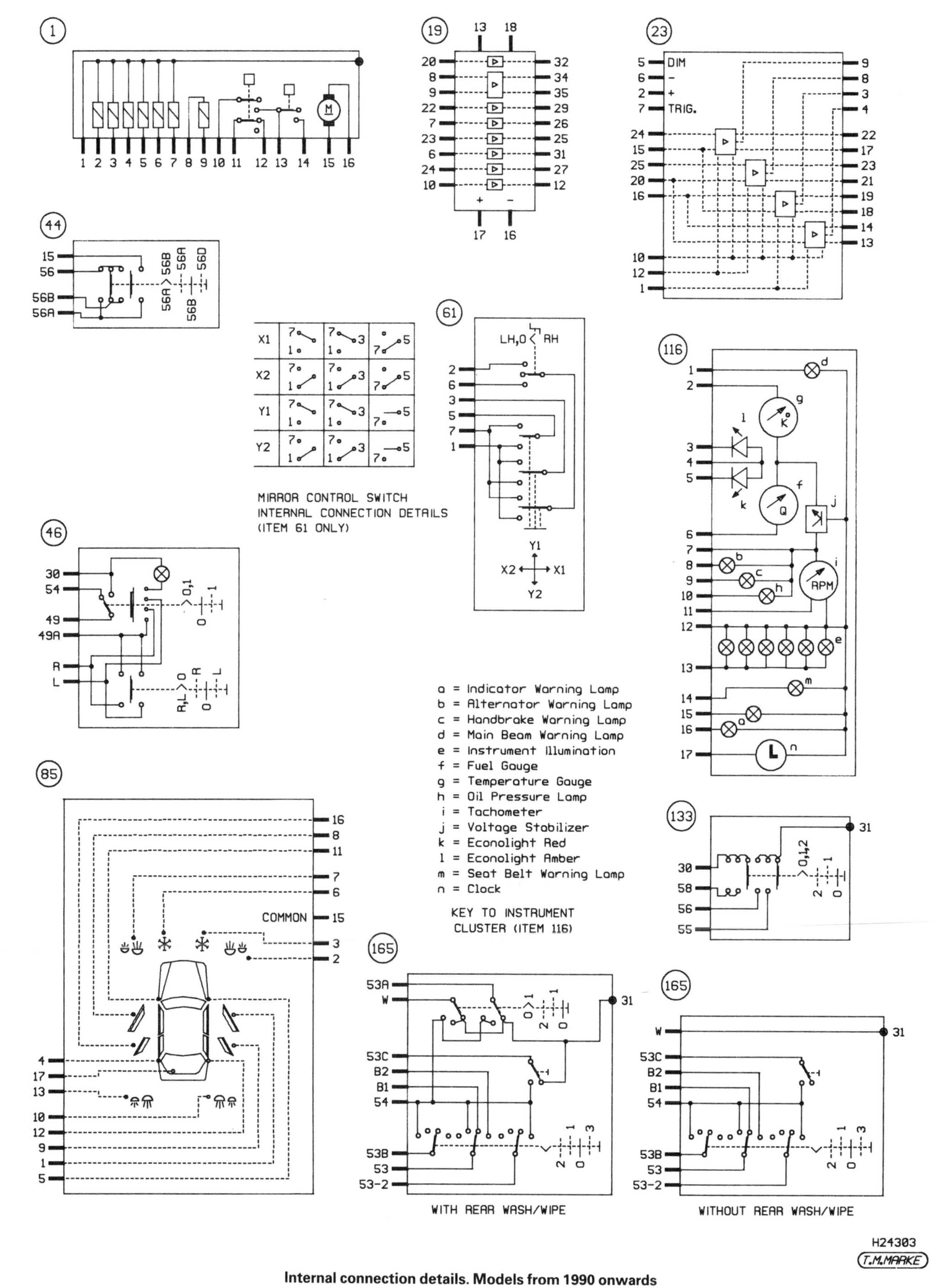

Internal connection details. Models from 1990 onwards

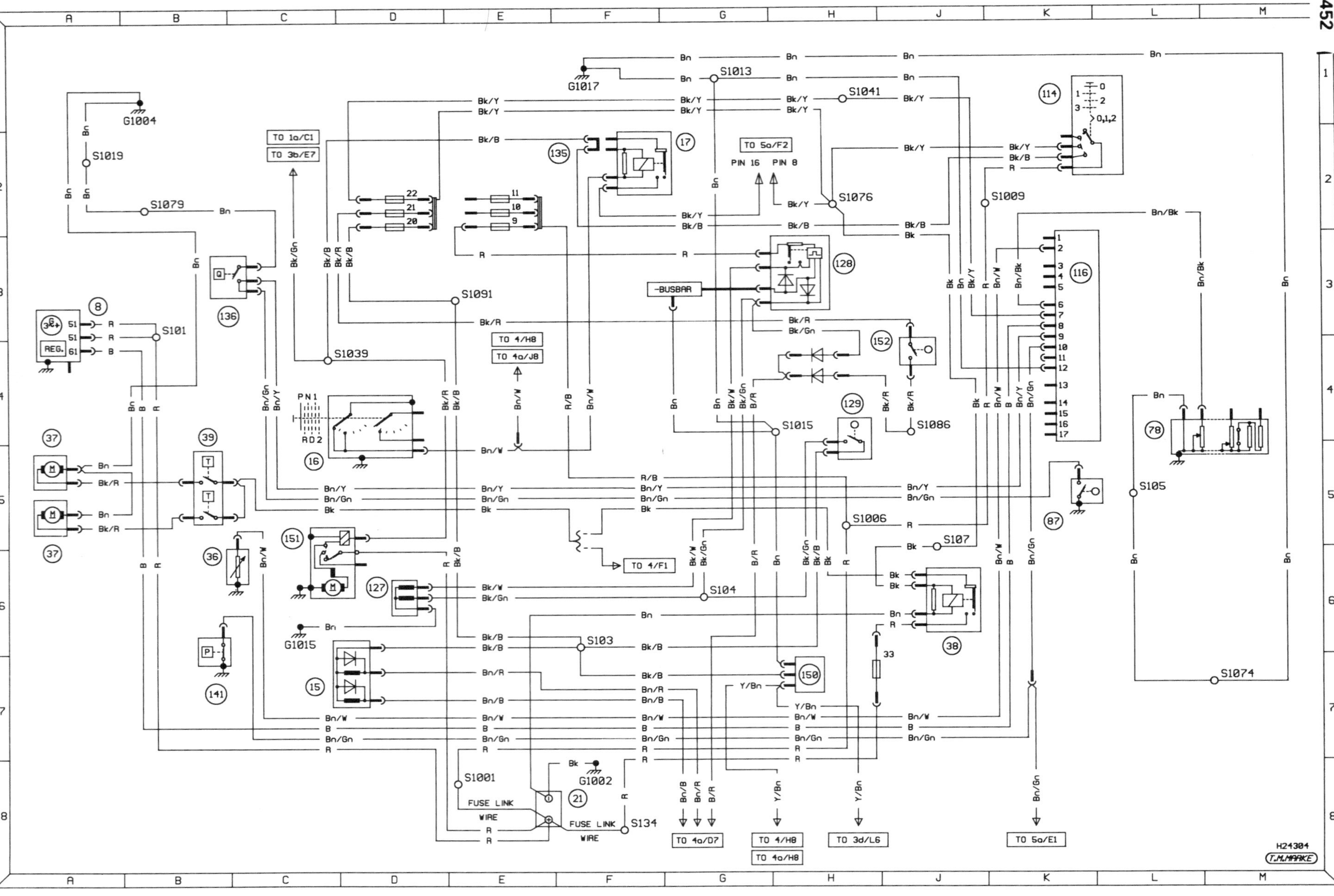

Diagram 1. Starting, charging, automatic transmission and warning lamps. Models from 1990 onwards

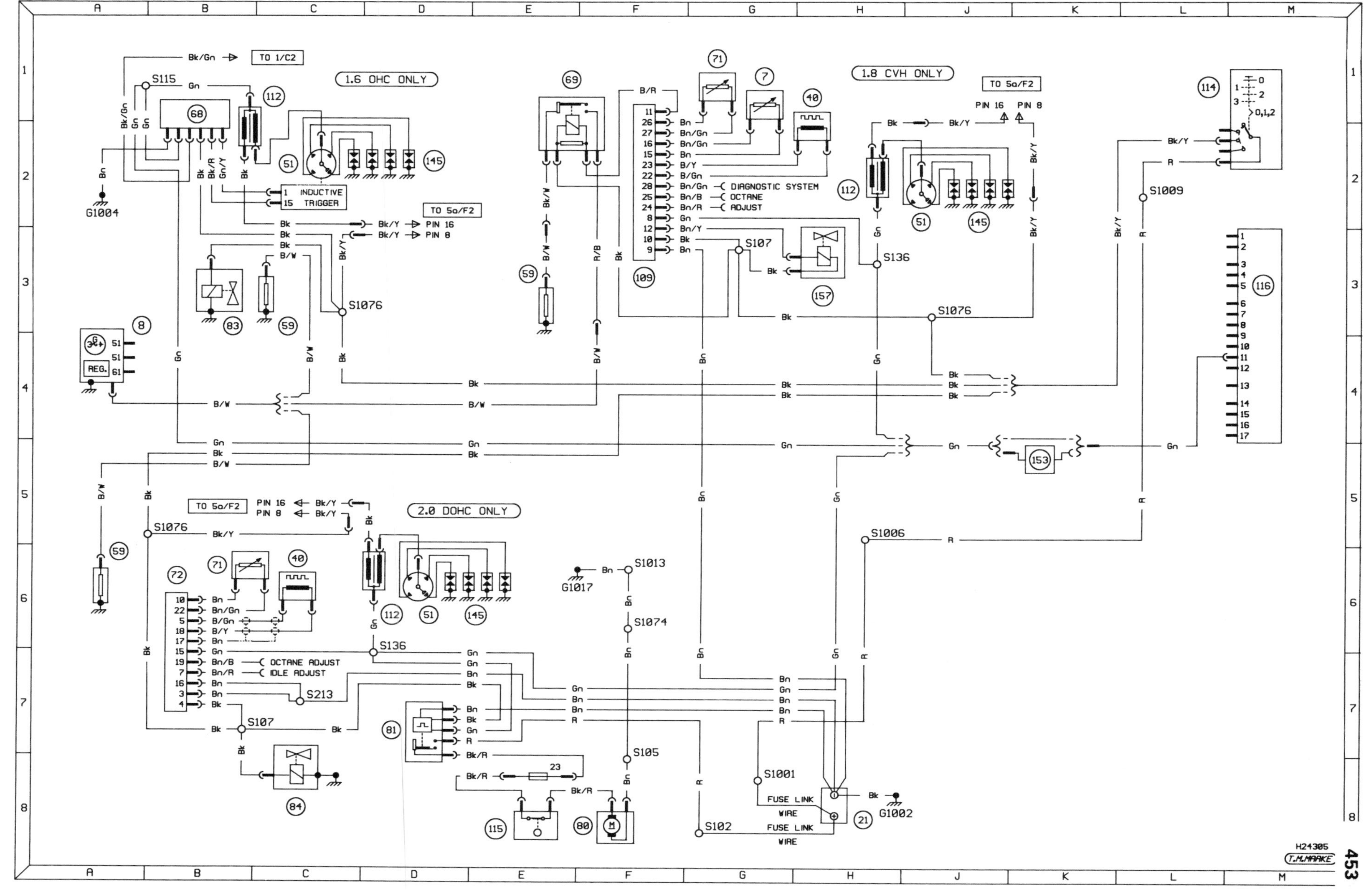

1.6 OHC ONLY
1.8 CVH ONLY
2.0 DOHC ONLY
TO 1/C2
TO 5a/F2
PIN 16
PIN 8
INDUCTIVE TRIGGER
DIAGNOSTIC SYSTEM
OCTANE
ADJUST
OCTANE ADJUST
IDLE ADJUST
REG.
FUSE LINK WIRE
FUSE LINK WIRE
H24305
T.M.MARKE

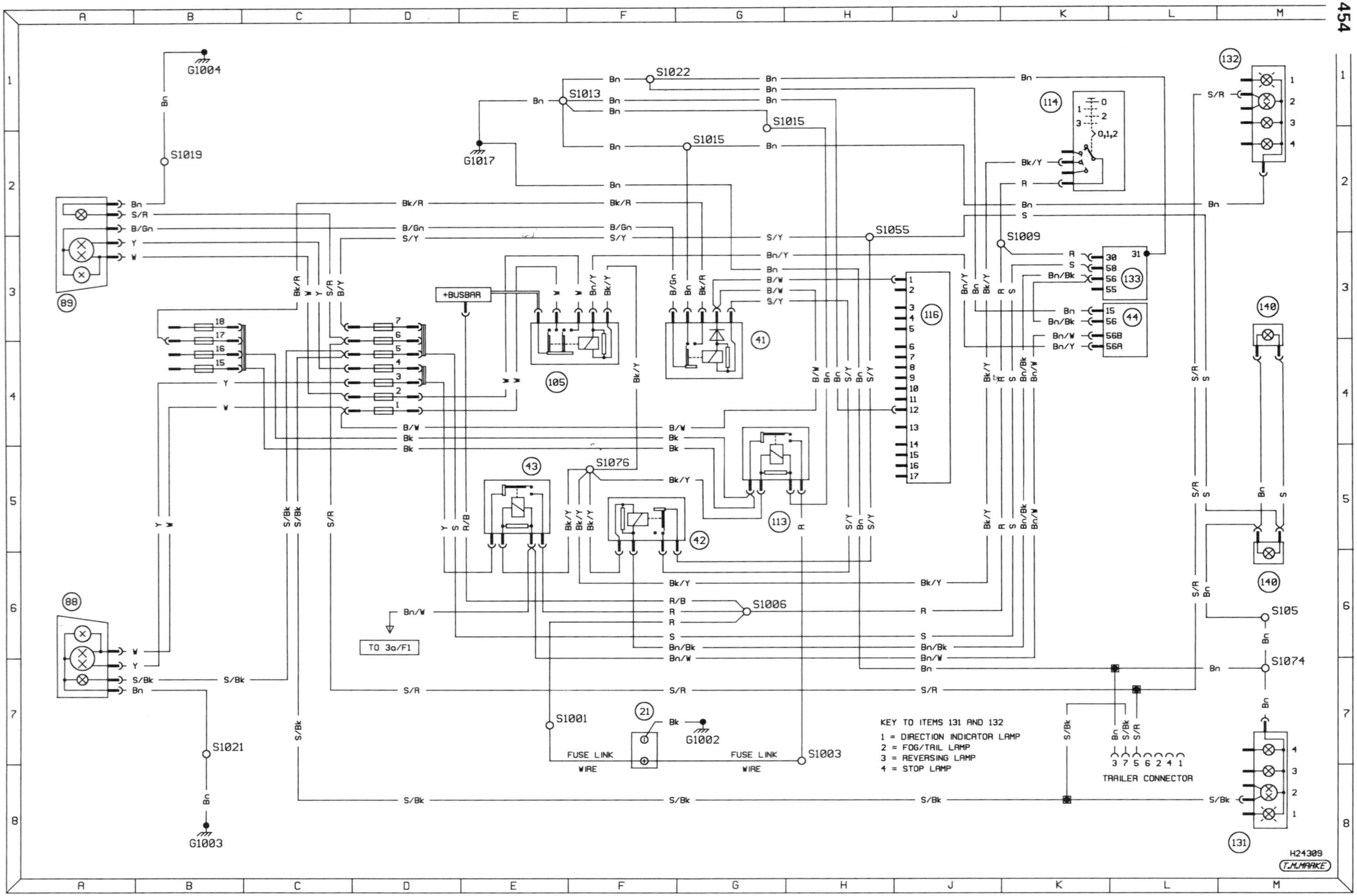
KEY TO ITEMS 131 AND 132
1 = DIRECTION INDICATOR LAMP
2 = FOG/TAIL LAMP
3 = REVERSING LAMP
4 = STOP LAMP
TRAILER CONNECTOR
3 7 5 6 2 4 1
FUSE LINK WIRE
FUSE LINK WIRE
+BUSBAR
TO 3a/F1
G1004
G1017
G1003
G1002
S1019
S1013
S1022
S1015
S1055
S1009
S1076
S1006
S1001
S1003
S1021
S105
S1074
H24309
T.M.MARKE

Diagram 2. Exterior lighting – head/side lamps. Models from 1990 onwards

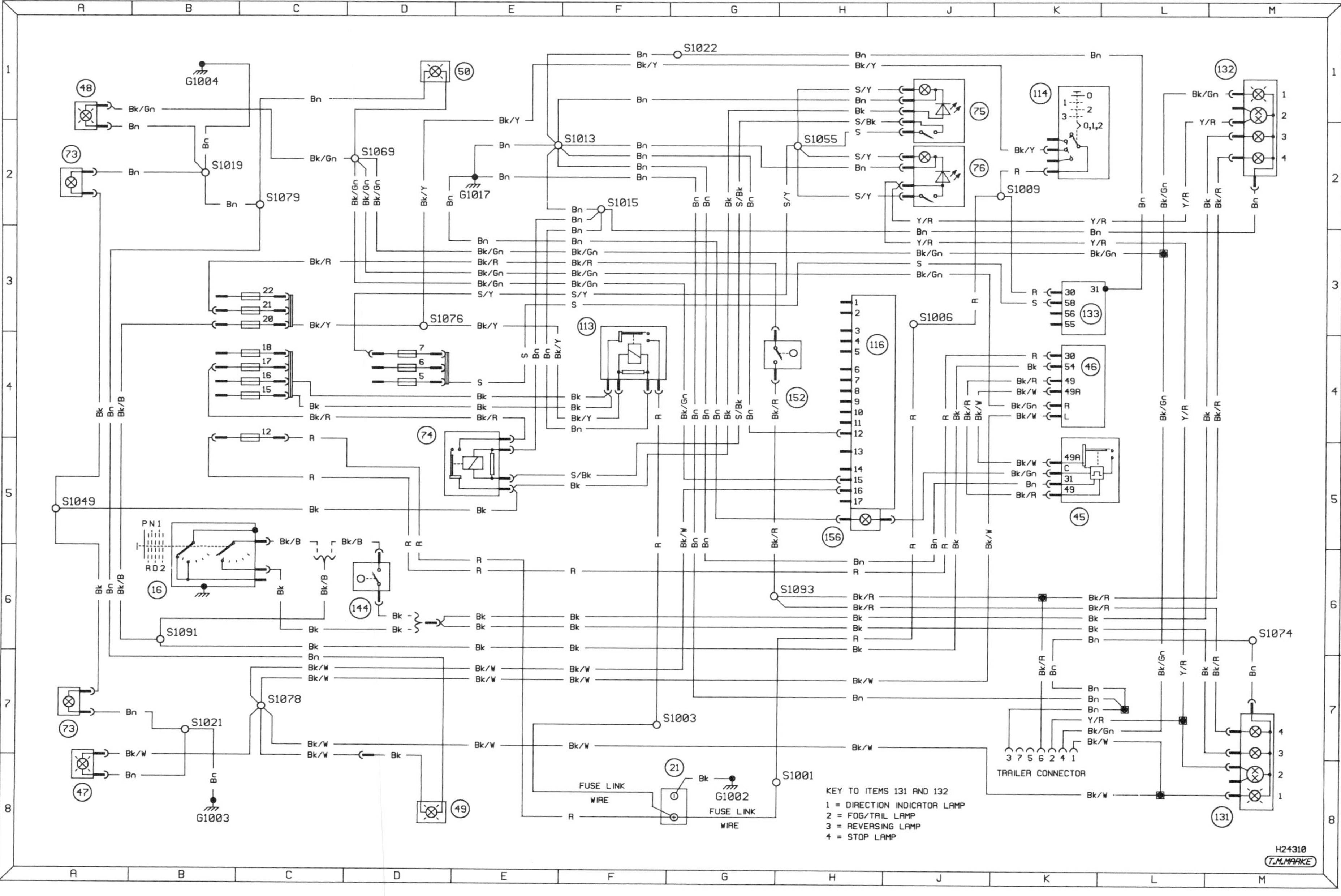

Diagram 2a. Exterior lighting – signal warning lamps. Models from 1990 onwards

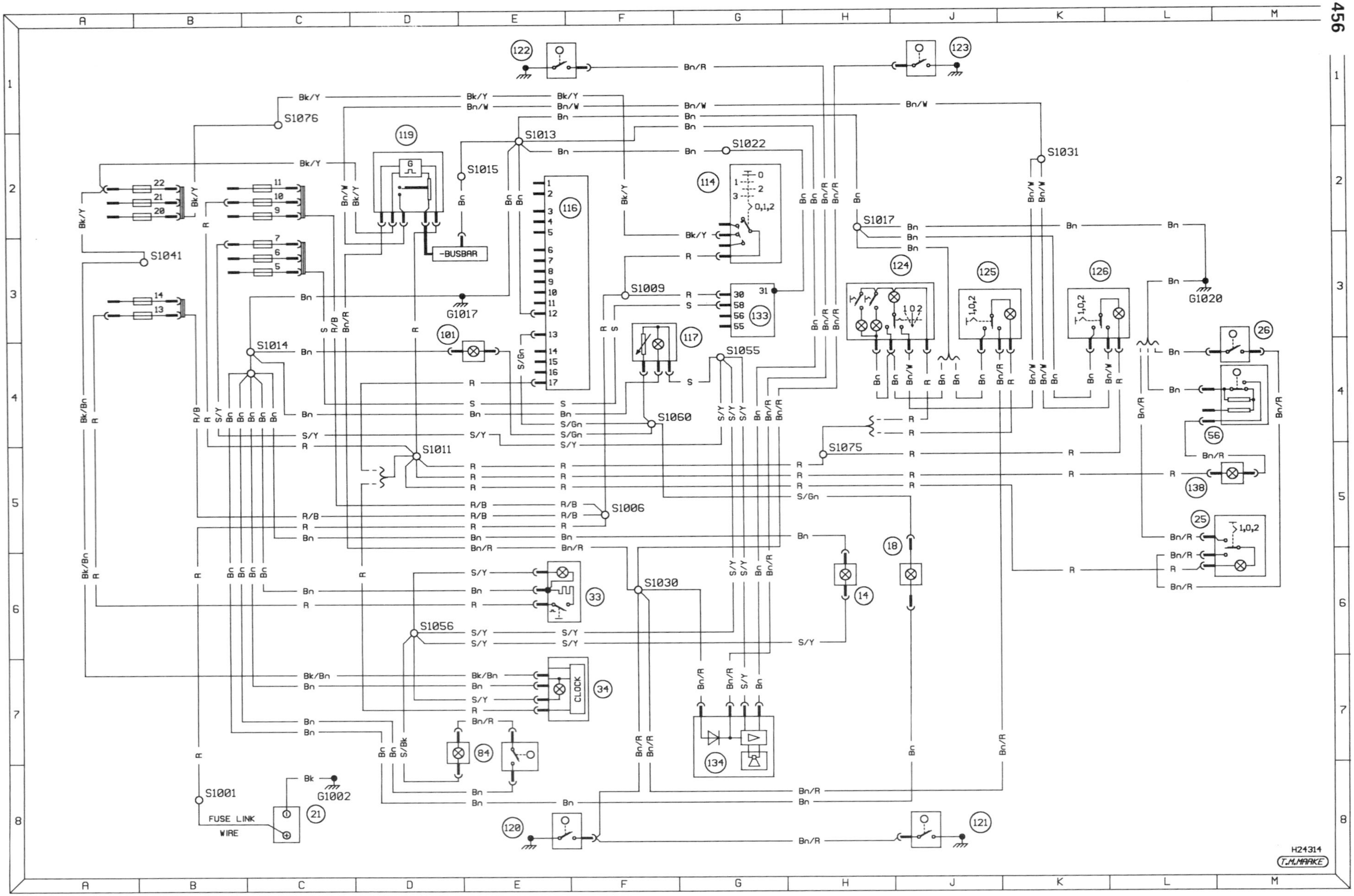

Diagram 2b. Interior lighting. Models from 1990 onwards

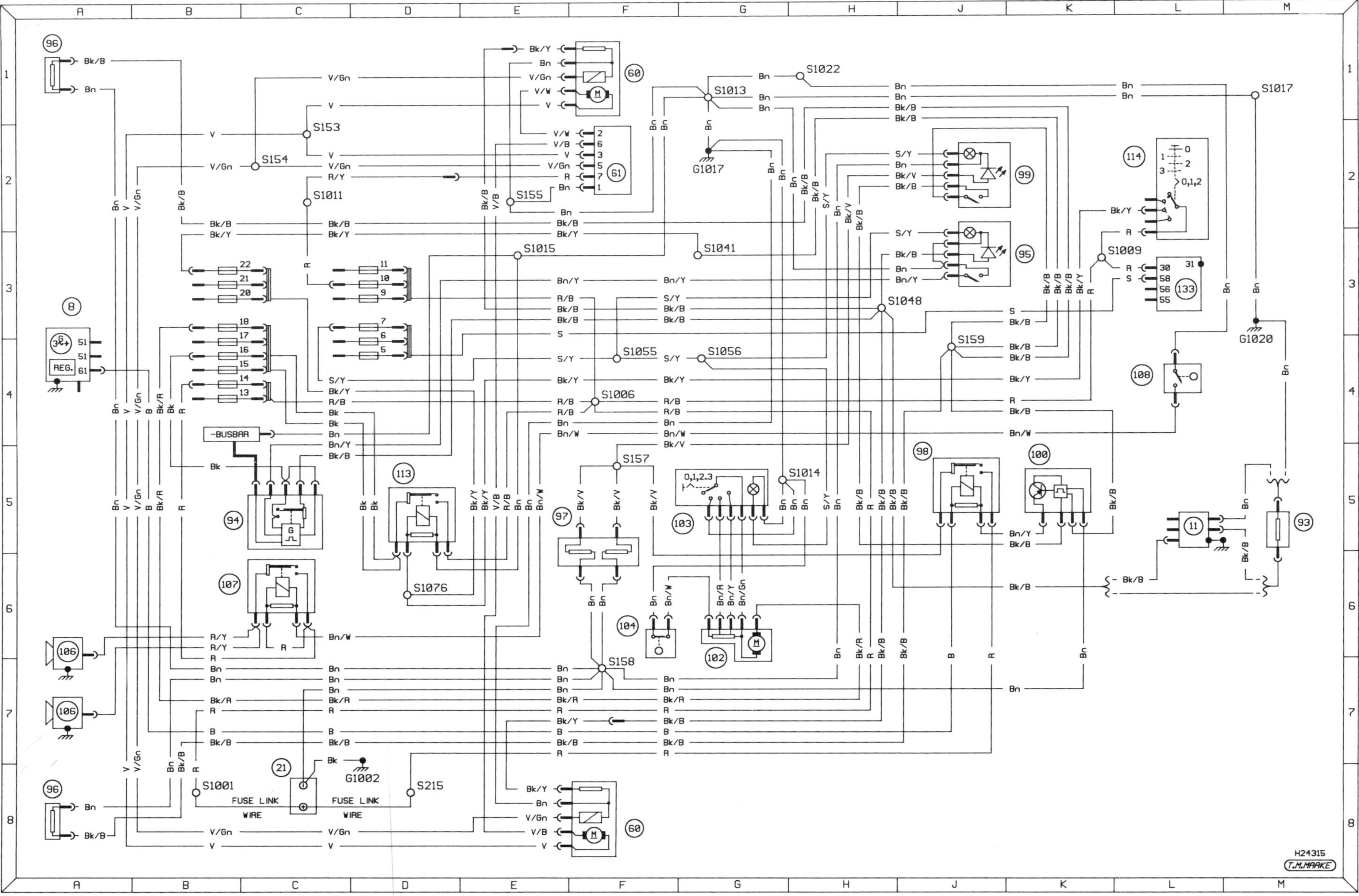

Diagram 3. Ancillary circuits – horn, heater blower, heated mirrors and screens. Models from 1990 onwards

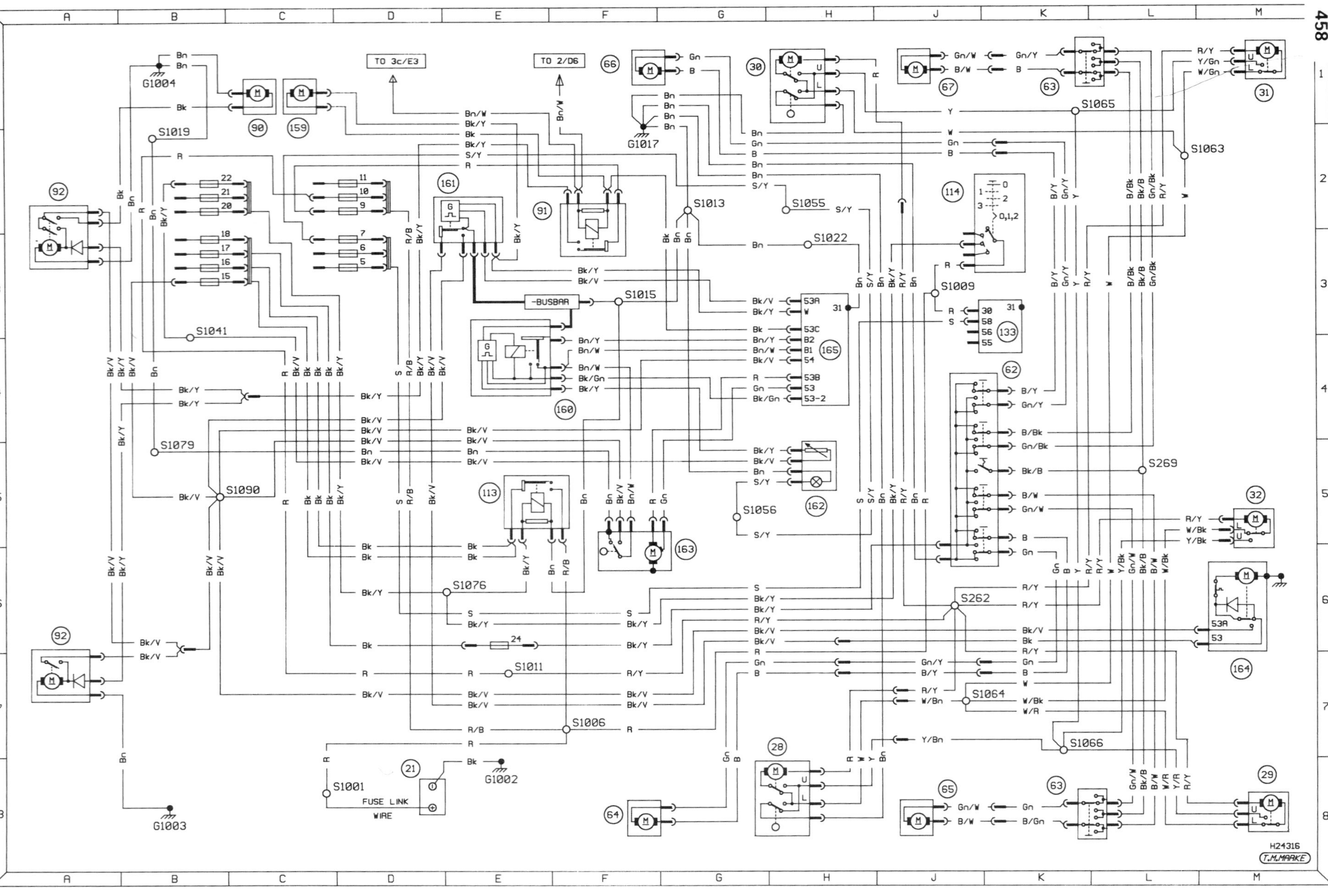

Diagram 3a. Ancillary circuits – wash/wipe, central locking and electric windows. Models from 1990 onwards

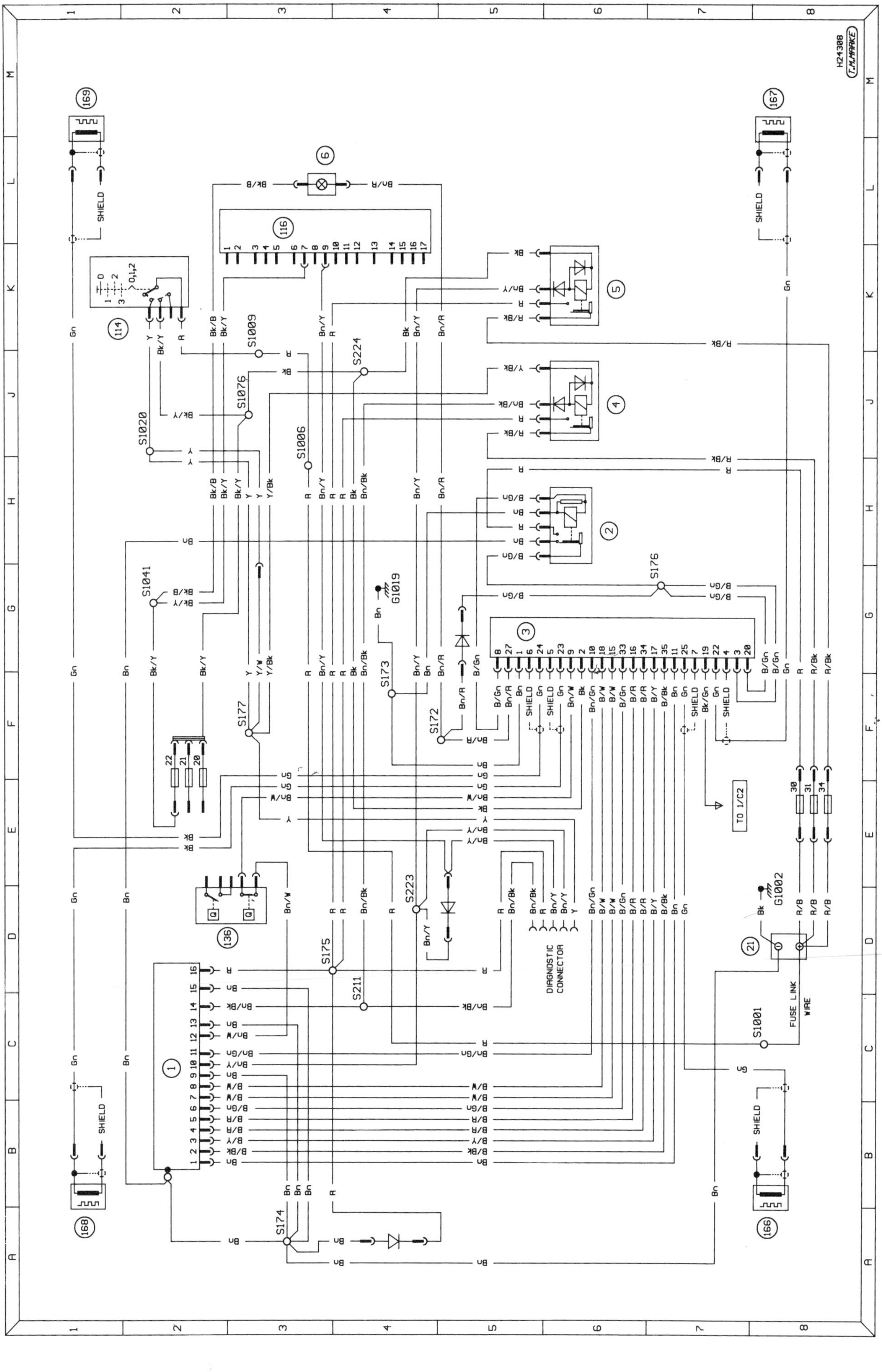

Diagram 3b. Anti-lock braking system. Models from 1990 onwards

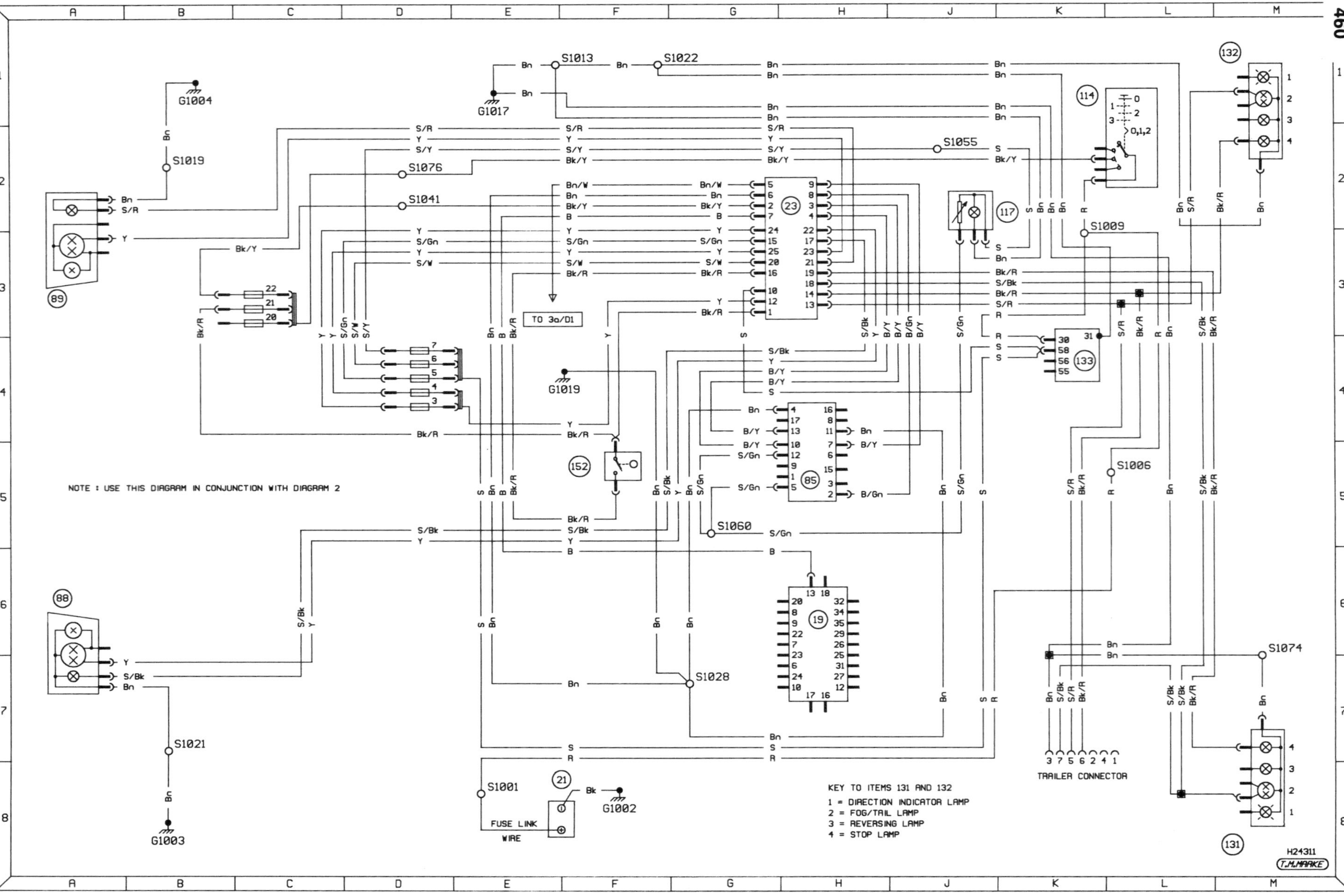

Diagram 3c. Graphic display system – bulb failure. Models from 1990 onwards

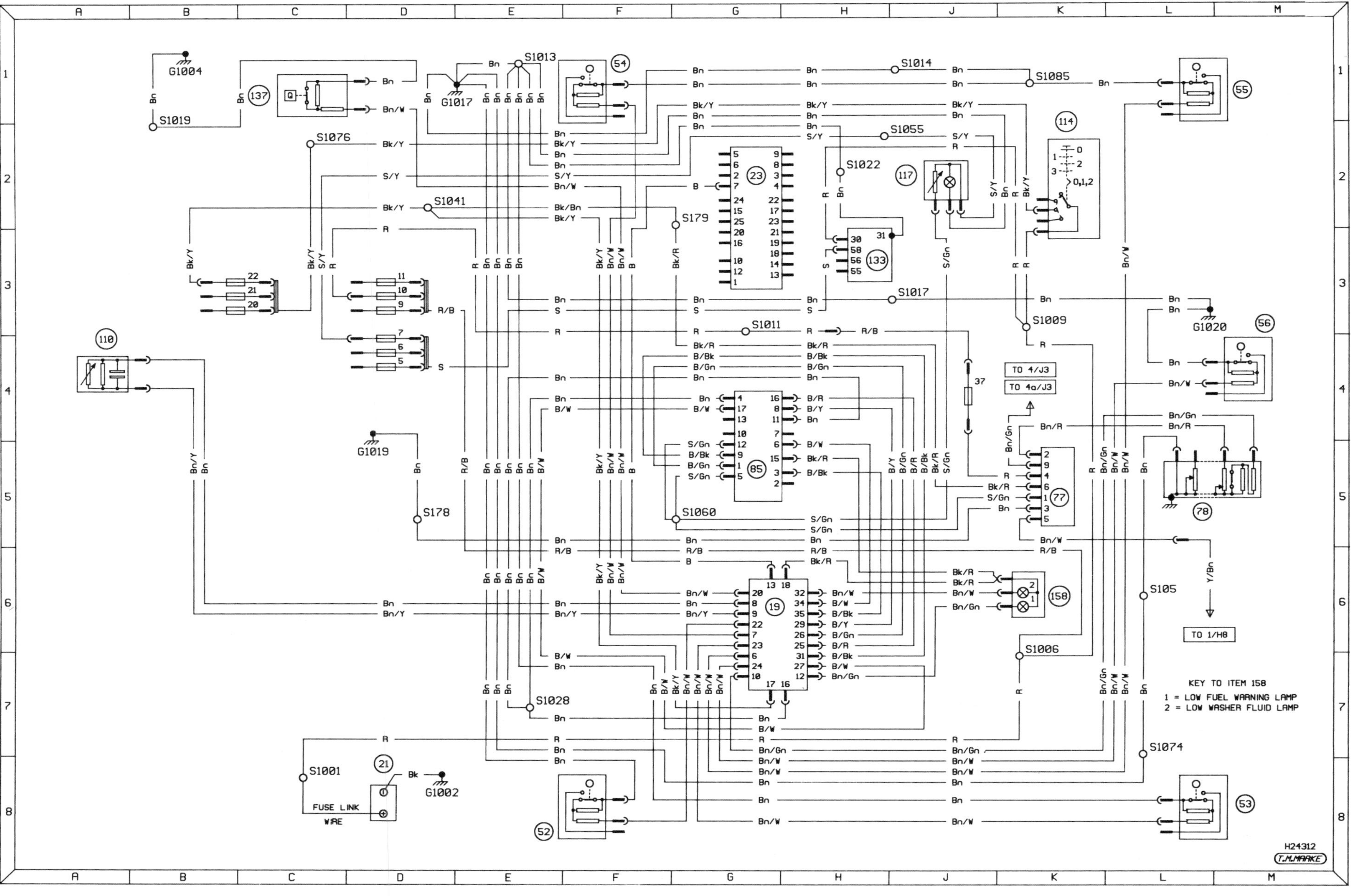

Diagram 3d. Graphic display system – auxiliary warning, door ajar and fuel computer. Models from 1990 onwards

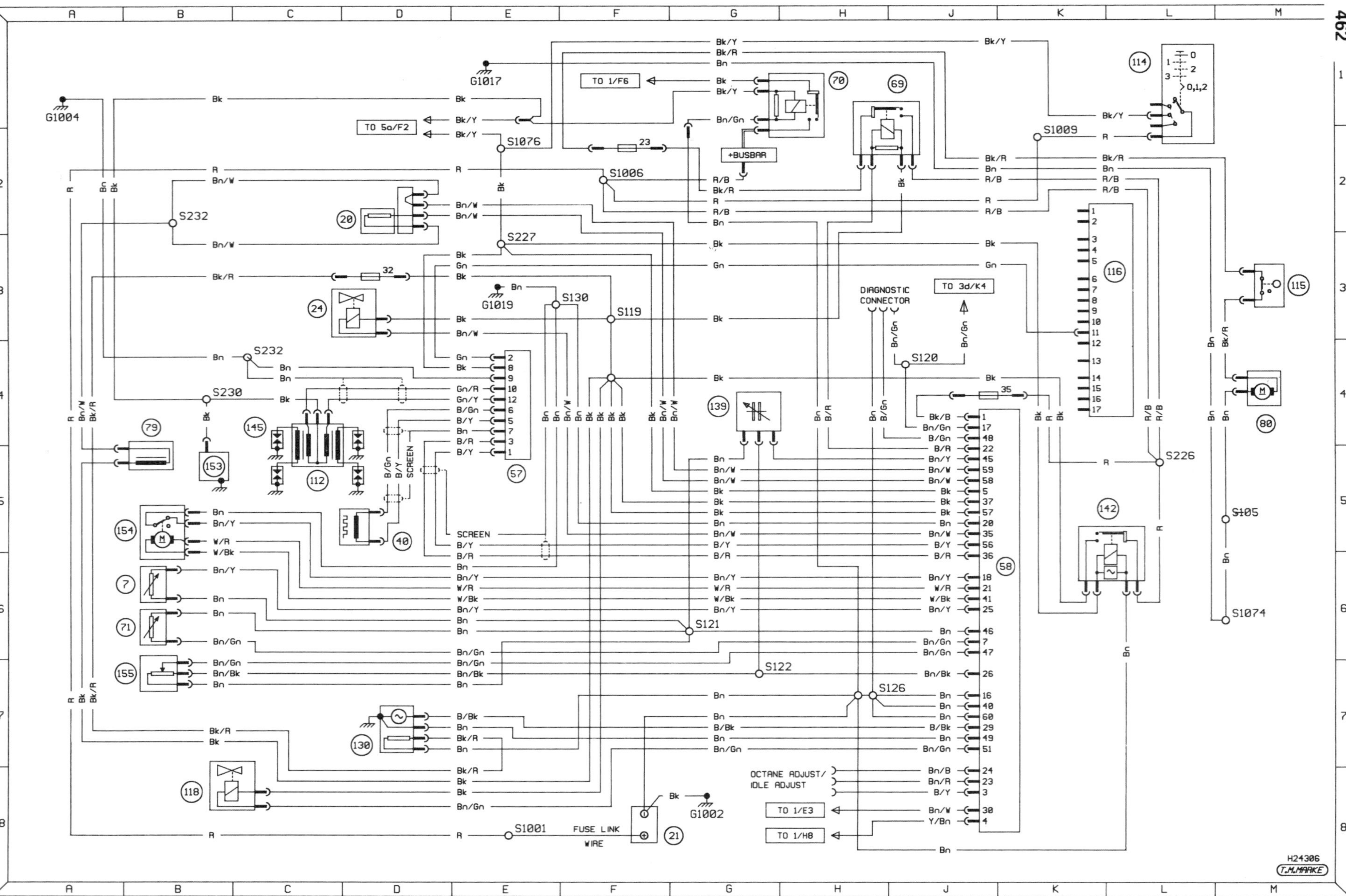

Diagram 4. 1.6 CVH engine CFI fuel injection and ignition systems. Models from 1990 onwards

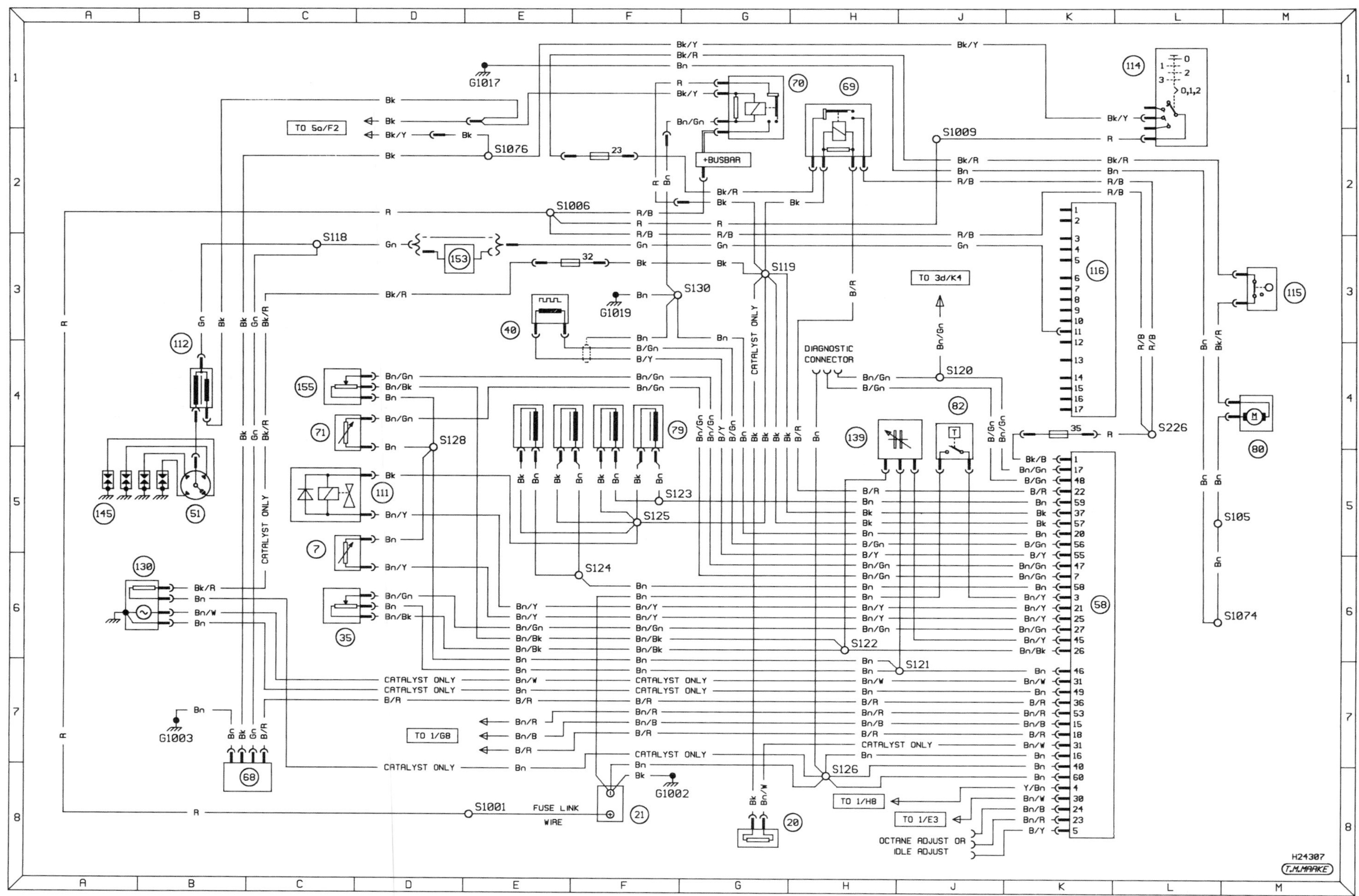

Diagram 4a. 2.0 litre DOHC engine EFI fuel injection and ignition systems. Models from 1990 onwards

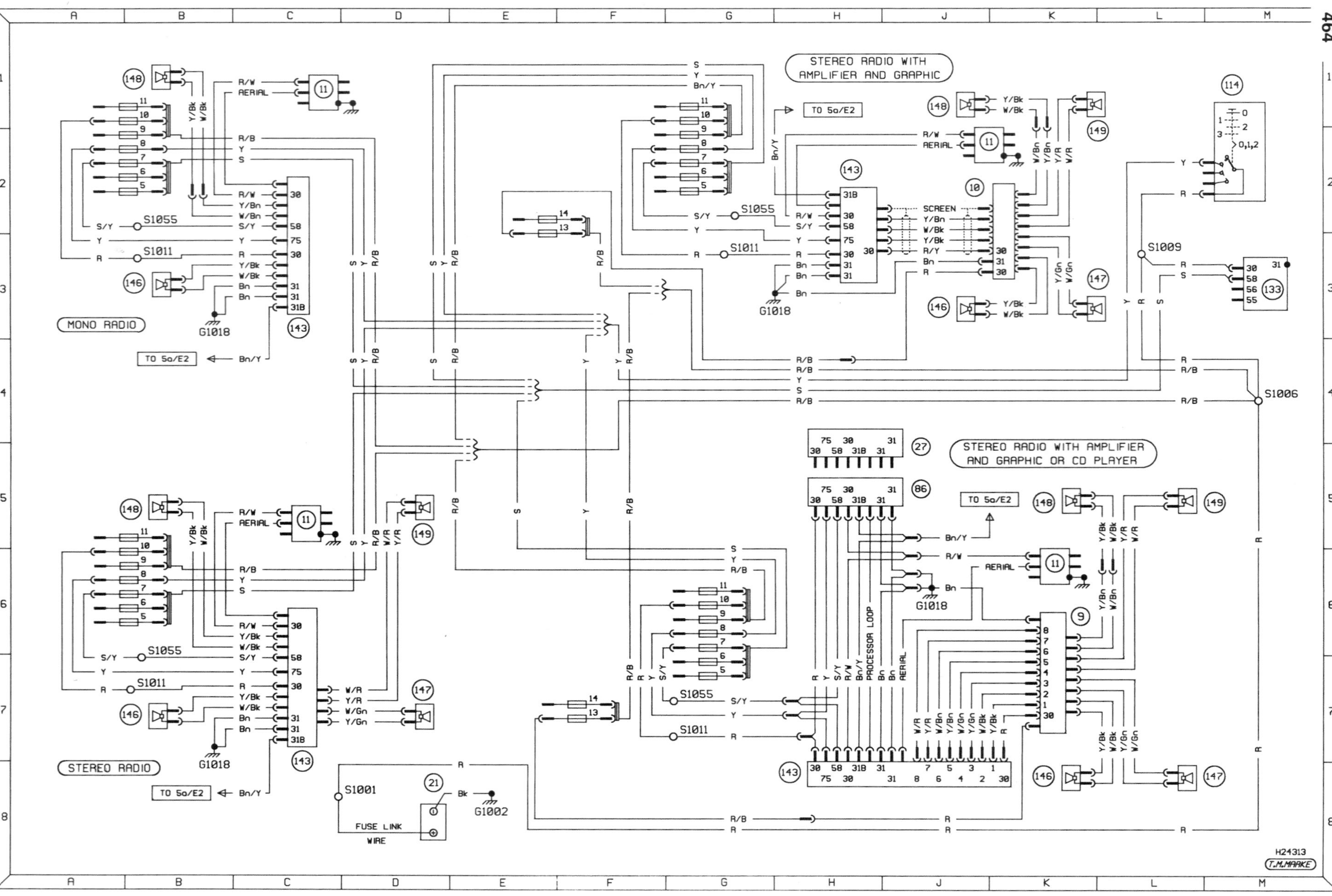

Diagram 5. In-car entertainment. Models from 1990 onwards

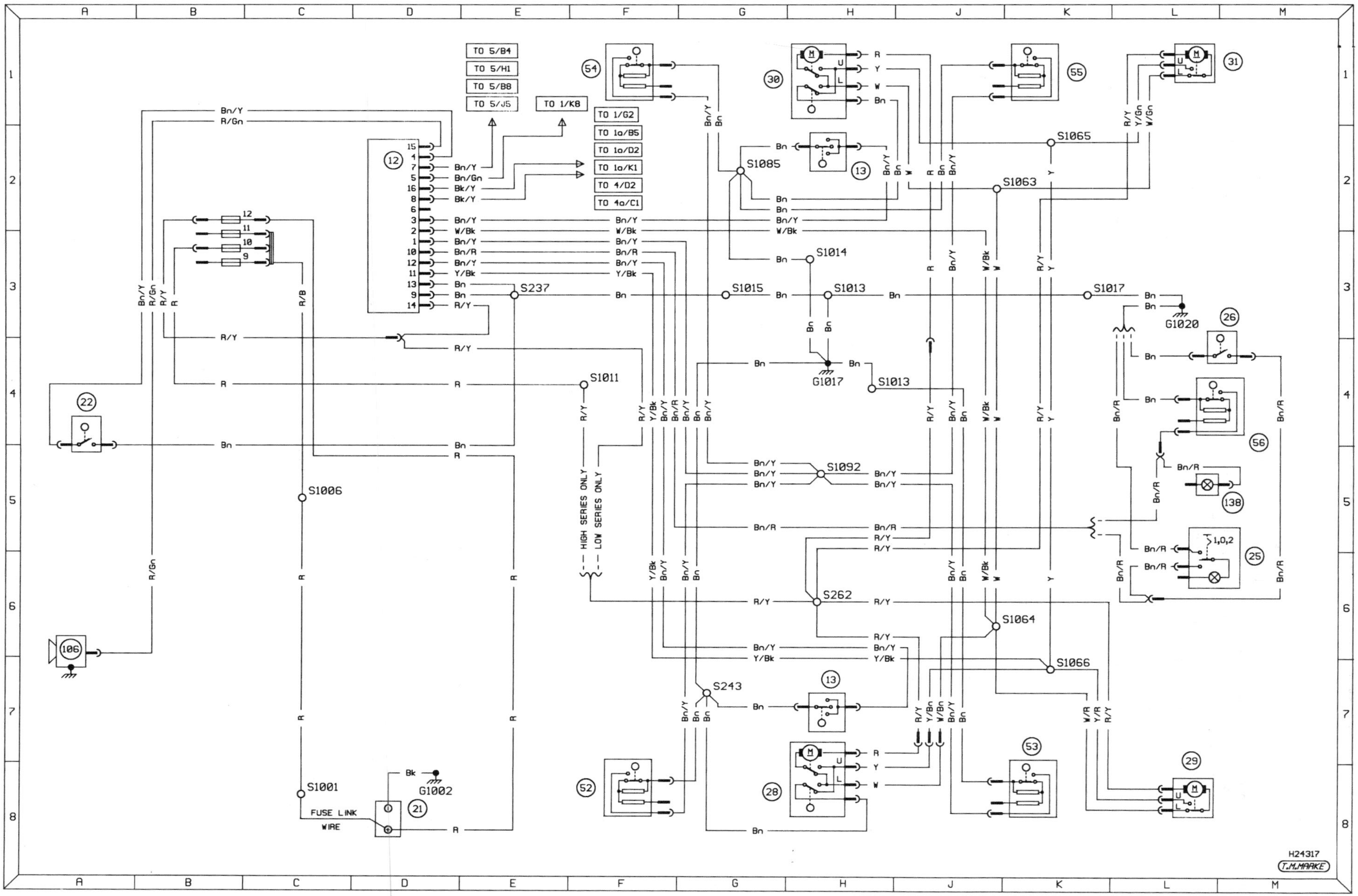

Diagram 5a. Anti-theft alarm. Models from 1990 onwards

NOTES:

1. All diagrams are divided into numbered circuits depending upon their function e.g Diagram 2 : Exterior lighting all models.
2. Some components may appear on more than one diagram so their positions are given in coded form in the key below e.g. 2/A1 denotes a component on diagram 2 grid location A1.
3. Feed wires are coloured red (black when switched) and originate from diagram 1. All other diagrams feed from fuse connections or common feeds.
4. Earth wires on all diagrams are coloured brown.
5. The tables below show where common feeds and common earths interconnect between diagrams.
6. Not all items are fitted to all models.
7. Brackets show how the circuit may be connected in more than one way.

Wire Colours

B	Blue	Rs	Pink
Bk	Black	S	Grey
Bn	Brown	V	Violet
Gn	Green	W	White
R	Red	Y	Yellow

FUSE	RATING	CIRCUIT
1	20A	LH Main Beam, Dim/Dip
2	20A	RH Main Beam
3	10A	LH Dip Beam
4	10A	RH Dip Beam
5	10A	LH Side Lamps
6	10A	RH Side Lamps
7	10A	Instrument Illumination
8	10A	Rear Fog Lamps
9		Free
10	20A	Interior Lamps, Clock
11		Free
12	10A	Hazard Warning Lamps
13	30A	Cigar Lighter
14	30A	Horn
15	30A	Wiper Motor, Washer Pump
16		Free
17	20A	Dim/Dip
18	30A	Heater Blower
19		Free
20	15A	Flasher, Reversing Lamps
21	15A	Stop Lamps
22	10A	Clock, Brake Indicator
23		Free
24		Free

ITEM	DESCRIPTION	DIAGRAM/ GRID REF.
1	Alternator	1/A3
2	Battery	1/E8
		2/F8
		3/D8
3	Cigar Lighter	3/G5
4	Clock	1/H5
5	Coolant Temp. Sensor	1/C6
6	Dim/Dip Relay II	2/G4
7	Dim/Dip Relay B	2/G5
8	Dimmer Switch	2/L3
9	Dip Beam Relay F	2/F5
10	Distributor	1/D5
11	Electronic Ignition Module	1/C5
12	Flasher/Hazard Switch	2/L4
13	Flasher Lamp LH	2/A8
14	Flasher Lamp LH Side Marker	2/E8
15	Flasher Lamp RH	2/A1
16	Flasher Lamp RH Side Marker	2/E1
17	Flasher Relay 1	2/K5
18	Foglamp Switch Rear	2/J2
19	Fuel Sender	1/L4
20	Fuel Shut Off Valve	1/D6
21	Handbrake Warning Switch	1/K5
22	Headlamp Unit LH	2/A6
23	Headlamp Unit RH	2/A3
24	Heater Blower Illumination	3/E6
25	Heater Blower Motor	3/F6
26	Heater Blower Switch	3/F5
27	High Beam Relay X	2/F4
28	Horn	3/A6
29	Horn Relay C	3/E4
30	Horn Switch	3/J4
31	Ignition Coil	1/D5
32	Ignition Relay I	1/H4
33	Ignition Switch	1/K2
		3/L1
34	Instrument Cluster	1/K3
		2/H3
		3/H3
35	Interior Lamp Door Switch LH Front	3/H8
36	Interior Lamp Door Switch RH Front	3/H1
37	Interior Lamp/Switch	3/K4
38	Licence Plate Lamp	2/M4
		2/M5
39	Light Cluster LH Rear	2/M8
40	Light Cluster RH Rear	2/M1
41	Light Switch	2/L3
		3/K3
42	Low Brake Fluid Switch	1/C3
43	Oil Pressure Switch	1/B6
44	Radio Unit	3/J6
45	Reversing Lamp Switch	2/B6
46	Spark Plugs	1/E5
47	Speaker LH Door	3/M8
48	Speaker RH Door	3/M1
49	Starter Motor	1/E6
50	Stop Lamp Switch	2/H4
51	Windscreen Washer Pump	3/C1
52	Wiper Intermittent Relay V	3/E2
53	Wiper Motor Front	3/F4
54	Wiper Switch	3/K2

COMMON EARTH POINT	DIAGRAM/ GRID REF.
G1002	1/F8
	2/F8
	3/D8
G1005	1/F1
	2/E2
	3/E3
G1006	1/J8
	2/H8
	3/G8

COMMON FEED	DESCRIPTION	DIAGRAM/ GRID REF.
S1003	COMMON BATTERY FEED	1/G2
		2/H5
S1004	COMMON BATTERY FEED	1/J2
		2/J3
		3/J3
S1012	COMMON IGNITION FEED	1/H1
		2/F4

Notes, tables, wire colours and key to wiring diagrams. P100 models from 1988 onwards

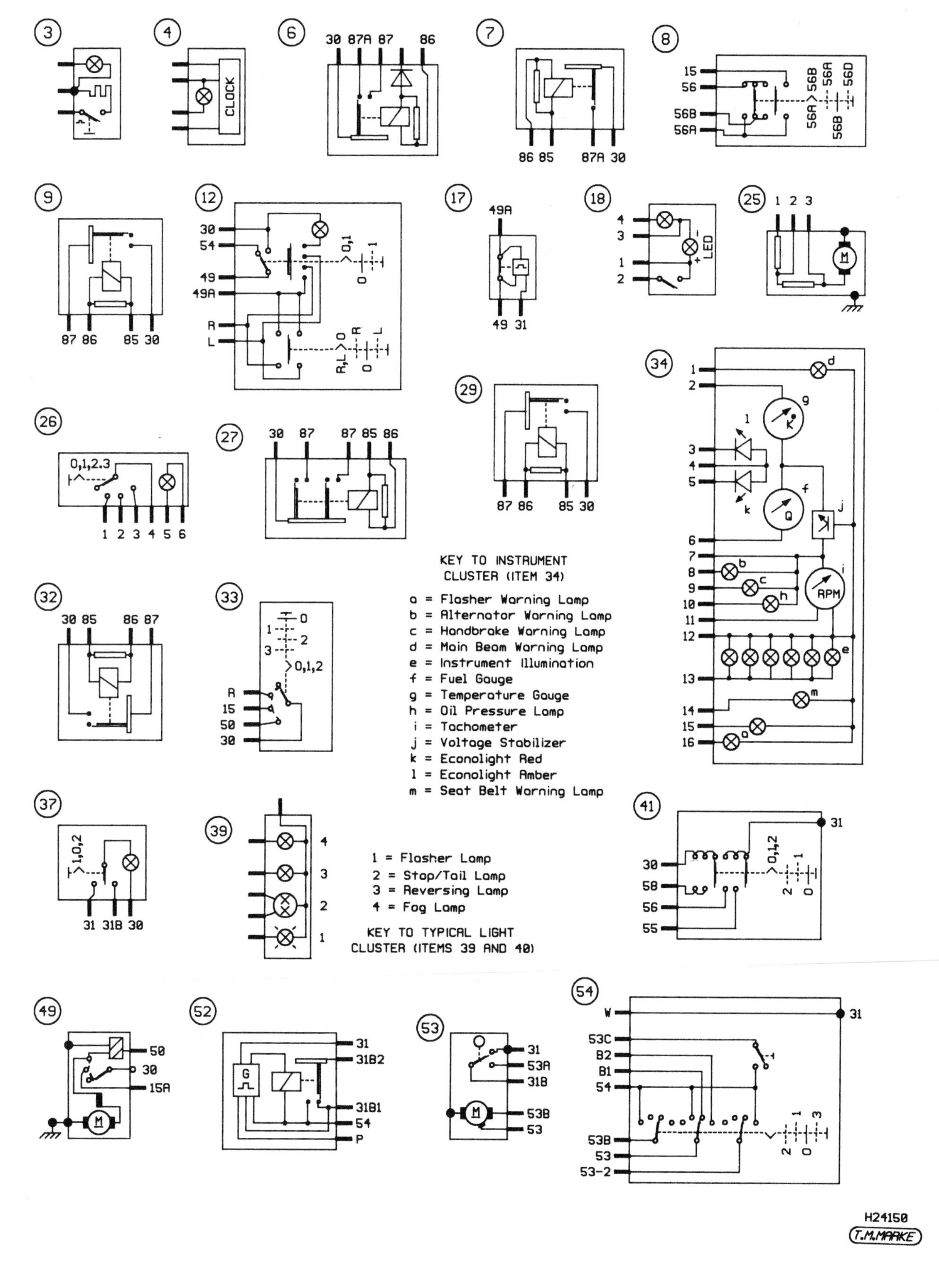

Internal connection details. P100 models from 1988 onwards

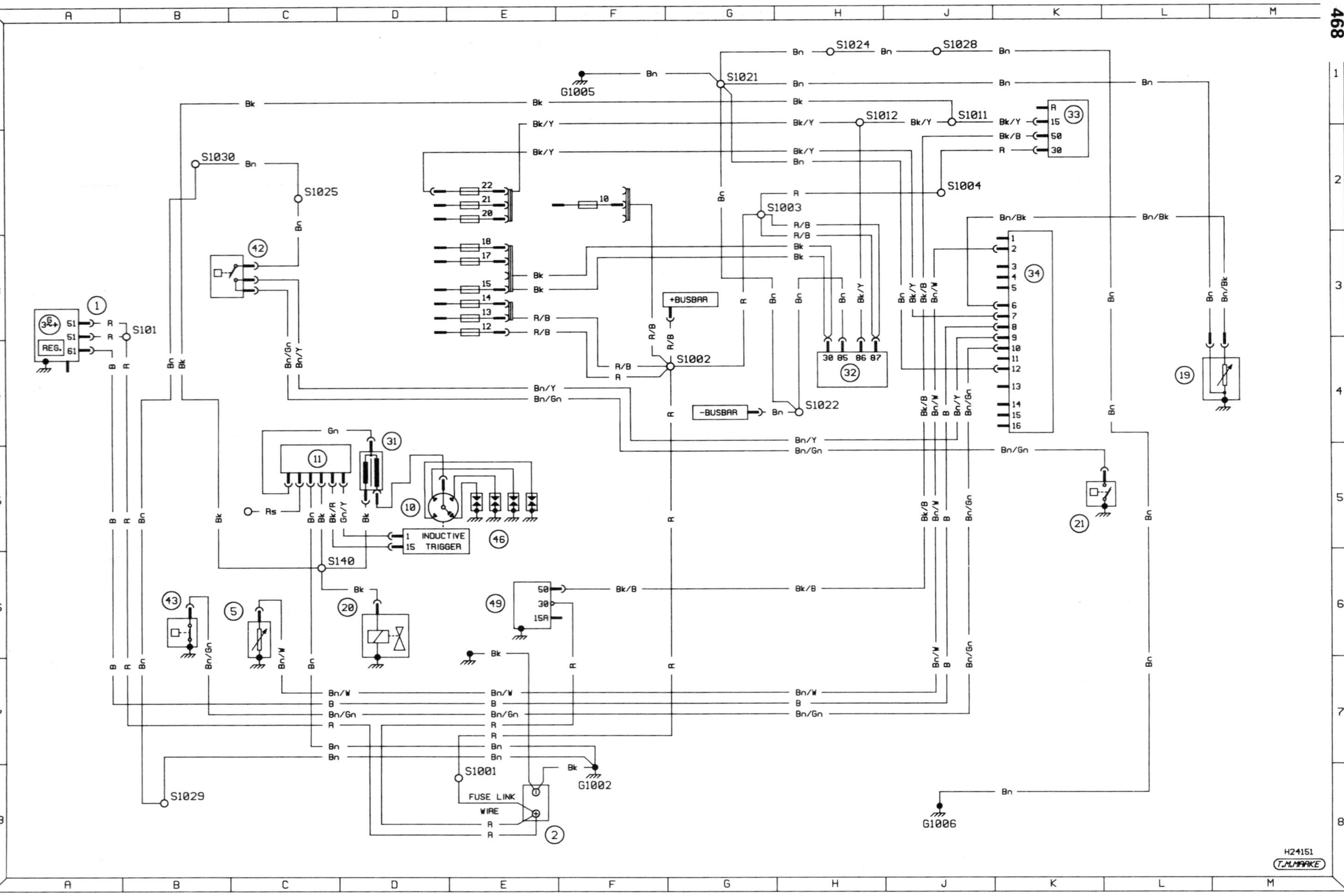

Diagram 1. Starting, charging and ignition. P100 models from 1988 onwards

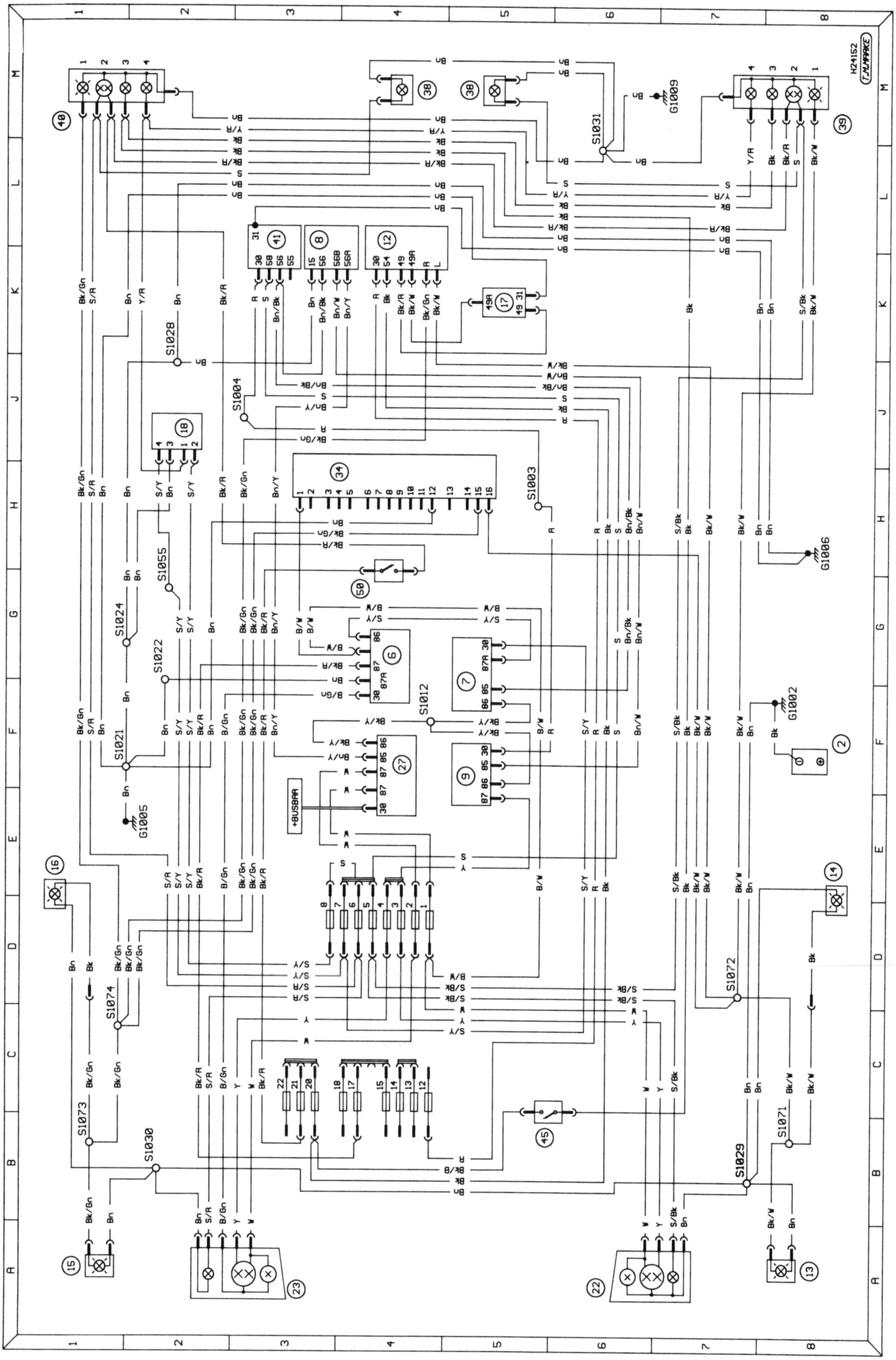

Diagram 2. Exterior lighting. P100 models from 1988 onwards

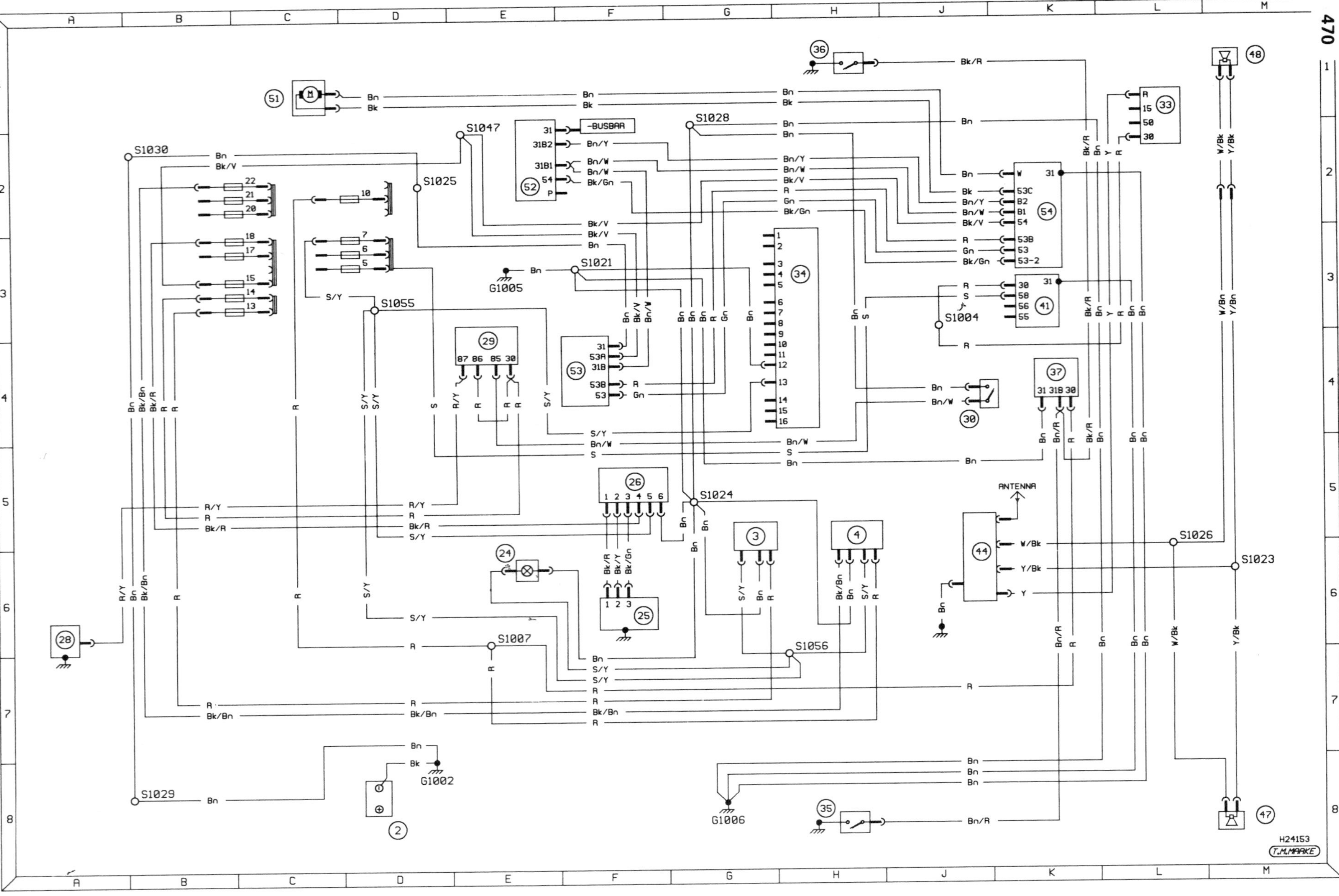

Diagram 3. Ancillary circuits and interior lighting. P100 models from 1988 onwards

Index

G

H

I

J

K

L

M

N

O

P

U

V

W